On the Historicity of Jesus

On the Historicity of Jesus

Why We Might Have Reason for Doubt

Richard Carrier

Sheffield Phoenix Press
2014

Published by Sheffield Phoenix Press
Department of Biblical Studies, University of Sheffield
45 Victoria Street, Sheffield S3 7QB

www.sheffieldphoenix.com

A CIP catalogue record for this book
is available from the British Library

Typeset by the HK Scriptorium
Printed by Lightning Source

ISBN 978-1-909697-35-5 (hbk)
ISBN 978-1-909697-49-2 (pbk)

CONTENTS

List of Tables and Figures

Figures

Tables

Preface

This book is the second of two volumes examining a daring question: whether there is a case to be made that Jesus never really existed as a historical person. The alternative is that the Jesus we know originated as a mythical character, in tales symbolically narrating the salvific acts of a divine being who never walked the earth (and probably never existed at all). Later, this myth was mistaken for history (or deliberately repackaged that way), and then embellished over time. Though I shall argue it's likely this alternative is true and that Jesus did not in fact exist, I cannot assume it has been conclusively proved here. In fact, it may yet be proved false in future work, using the very methods I employ (which were proposed and defended in my previous volume, *Proving History: Bayes's Theorem and the Quest for the Historical Jesus*).

Hence the point of this book is not to end the debate but to demonstrate that scholars need to take this hypothesis more seriously before dismissing it out of hand, and that they need much better arguments against it than they've heretofore deployed. A better refutation is needed, and a better theory of historicity, which, actually, credibly explains *all* the oddities in the evidence. If this book inspires nothing else, I'll be happy if it's that. But this book may do more. It might inspire more experts to agree with the possibility at least that Jesus Christ was born in myth, not history. And their continuing examination of the case may yet result in a growing consensus against the grain of current assumptions.

Either outcome would satisfy me. For my biases are such as to make no difference what the result should be. I only want the truth to be settled. Nevertheless, all historians have biases, and only sound methods will prevent those from too greatly affecting our essential results. No progress in historical knowledge, in fact no historical knowledge at all, would be possible without such methods. Hence my previous volume developed a formal historical method for approaching this (or any other) debate, which will produce as objectively credible a conclusion as any honest historian can reach. One need merely plug all the evidence into that method to get a result. However, because this volume can't address every single item of evidence (it merely addresses the best evidence there is), its conclusion may yet be brought down, even with its own method, simply by introducing something it omits. If so, I welcome it.

Though I already discussed my biases and background, and the origin of this project, in the preface to *Proving History*, for the reader's convenience I shall repeat that here. I am a marginally renowned atheist, known across America and many other corners of the world as an avid defender of a naturalist worldview and a dedicated opponent of the abuse of history in the service of supernaturalist creeds. I am a historian by training and trade (I received my PhD in ancient history from Columbia University) and a philosopher by experience and practice (I have published peer-reviewed articles in the field and am most widely known for my book on the subject, *Sense and Goodness without God: A Defense of Metaphysical Naturalism*).

I have always assumed without worry that Jesus was just a guy, another merely human founder of an entirely natural religion (whatever embellishments to his cult and story may have followed). I'd be content if I were merely reassured of that fact. For the evidence, even at its best, supports no more startling conclusion. So, I have no vested interest in proving Jesus didn't exist. It makes no difference to me if he did. I suspect he might not have, but then that's a question that requires a rigorous and thorough examination of the evidence before it can be confidently declared. Most secular scholars agree—even when they believe Jesus existed, they do not *need* to believe that. Believers, by contrast, and their apologists in the scholarly community, cannot say the same. For them, if Jesus didn't exist, then their entire worldview topples. The things they believe in (and *need* to believe in) more than anything else in the world will then be under dire threat. It would be hard to expect them ever to overcome this bias, which makes bias a greater problem for them than for me. They *need* Jesus to be real, but I don't need Jesus to be a myth.

Most atheists agree. And yet so much dubious argument has appeared on both sides of this debate (including argument of such a technical and erudite character that laymen can't decide whom to trust) that a considerable number of atheists approached me with a request to evaluate the arguments on both sides and tell them whose side has the greater merit or whether we can even decide between them on the scanty evidence we have. That's how my involvement in this matter began, resulting in my mostly (but not solely) positive review of Earl Doherty's *The Jesus Puzzle*. My continued work on the question has now culminated in over forty philanthropists (some of them Christians) donating a collective total of $20,000 for Atheists United, a major American educational charity, to support my research and writing of a series of books, in the hopes of giving both laymen *and* experts a serious evaluation of the evidence they can use to decide who is more probably right.

The first step in that process was to assess the methods so far employed on the subject and replace them if faulty. I accomplished that in the previous volume, in which I demonstrated that the most recent method of using 'historicity criteria' in the study of Jesus has been either logically invalid or factually incorrect, and that only arguments structured according to Bayes's Theorem have any chance of being valid and sound. Here I apply that method to the evidence for Jesus and show what results.

Though this is a work of careful scholarship, the nature of its aims and funding necessitate a style that is approachable to both experts and laymen. By the requirements of my grant, I am writing as much for my benefactors as my fellow scholars. But there is a more fundamental reason for my frequent use of contractions, slang, verbs in the first person, and other supposed taboos: it's how I believe historians should speak and write. Historians have an obligation to reach wider audiences with a style more attractive and intelligible to ordinary people. And they can do so without sacrificing rigor or accuracy. Indeed, more so than any other science, history can be written in ordinary language without excessive reliance on specialized vocabulary (though we do need some), and without need of any stuffy protocols of language that don't serve a legitimate purpose. As long as what we write is grammatically correct, accurate and clear, and conforms to spoken English, it should satisfy all the aims of history: to educate and inform and advance the field of knowledge. This very book, just like the last, has been written to exemplify and hopefully prove that point.

The support I received for this work has been very generous. As before, I must thank Atheists United for all their aid and assistance, and all those individual donors who gave so much, and for little in return but an honest report. No one (not even Atheists United, who provided me with the financial grant in aid, nor any donor to that fund) was given any power to edit or censor the content of this work or to compel any particular result. They all gave me complete academic freedom. That also means I alone am responsible for everything I write. Atheists United wanted to see what I came up with, and trusted me to do good work on the strength of my reputation and qualifications, but they do not necessarily agree with or endorse anything I say or argue. The same follows for any individual donors.

More particular thanks are in order for them, who made this work possible. Benefactors came not only from all over the United States but from all over the world—from Australia and Hong Kong to Norway and the Netherlands, even Poland and France. Not all wanted to be thanked by name, but of those who did (or didn't object), my greatest gratitude goes to the most generous contributors: Jeremy A. Christian, Paul Doland, Dr Evan Fales, Brian Flemming, Scott and Kate Jensen, Fab Lischka, and most generous of all, Michelle Rhea and Maciek Kolodziejczyk. Next in line are those who also gave very generously, including Aaron Adair, John and Susan Baker, Robert A. Bosak Jr, Jon Cortelyou, Valerie Mills Daly, Brian Dewhirst, Karim Ghantous, Frank O. Glomset, Paul Hatchman, Jim Lippard, Ryan Miller, Dr Edwin Neumann, Lillian Paynter, Benjamin Schuldt, Vern

Sheppard, Chris Stoffel, James Tracy, Stuart Turner, Keith Werner, Jonathan Whitmore, Dr Alexander D. Young, Frank Zindler and Demian Zoer. But I am grateful even for the small donors, whose gifts collectively added up to quite a lot, including the generosity of David F. Browning, David Empey, Landon Hedrick, Gordon McCormick and many others.

This book would never have been written without all their support. Many even provided valuable advice toward improving it. It is very rewarding to present this book, as I did the last, to those who respect and enjoy my work enough to keep me employed just to educate themselves and the public about what many consider an obscure issue, and above all, who have patiently waited so long for the payoff. Special thanks also go to David Fitzgerald (author of *The Mormons* and *Nailed: Ten Christian Myths That Show Jesus Never Existed at All*) for his help, advice and friendship. And to Earl Doherty (author of *The Jesus Puzzle* and *Jesus: Neither God nor Man*) and Evan Fales (who may one day come out with *Reading Sacred Texts: An Anthropological Approach to the Gospel of St. Matthew*), for their particular assistance and perspective. I don't always agree with them, but their often-brilliant work did influence me, even if not always in the direction they may have hoped.

1

The Problem

> There is a widespread view that it is futile to go back and dig up old foundations, to go back over matters that were established long ago. Why not accept the sound results of a century's worth of good scholarship and get on instead with building on those pillars of scholarly wisdom?[1]

1. *Isn't This Just Bunk?*

In 1999 I wrote an exposé for *Skeptical Inquirer* on a then-recent FOX documentary about ancient Egypt.[2] I had never been interested in the crazy theories going around about the pyramids, but when a major television network started presenting them as credible news, and with suspect tactics at that, it offended me as a historian. So I investigated the claims in the documentary, contacting some who were interviewed for it, and wrote on what I found. The show's editors had quoted interviews out of context, conflated credible with ridiculous claims, mixed serious scholars with lay theorists as if there were no difference in their credibility, made several claims that were highly dubious if not outright false (while rarely presenting any criticism, and then only a token), and sometimes even misrepresented (or didn't honestly reveal) to those being interviewed what the actual intent of the documentary was and how their interviews would be used. Some of those interviewed were rightly outraged at what FOX had done.

Thanks to that article, however, I had sealed my fate. Ever since, I've been the target of countless emails from kooks some call 'pyramidiots', people who passionately advocate bizarre and often (let's be honest) stupid theories about the pyramids. They were built in 20,000 BCE. Their builders

1. Mark Goodacre, *The Case against Q: Studies in Markan Priority and the Synoptic Problem* (Harrisburg, PA: Trinity Press, 2002), p. 6. He is, of course, speaking rhetorically.

2. Richard Carrier, 'Flash! Fox News Reports That Aliens May Have Built the Pyramids of Egypt!', *Skeptical Inquirer* 23 (September–October 1999), pp. 46-50 (see www.csicop.org/si/9909/fox.html).

must have used lasers and levitation rays. Psychics have predicted archaeological discoveries in them. Their configuration proves the existence of extraterrestrial civilizations, or the preternatural wisdom of the ancients, or the existence of God and the Intelligent Design of the universe. And so on. They typically have some thousand-page treatise they want me to read that, they insist, proves their new outlandish claim, and if I don't read it, I'm participating in 'the conspiracy' to suppress their research.

Yet I will never live long enough to examine and fact-check all the theories, books and papers these people have tried to send me, even if I made it my single purpose in life to try. So I don't waste even a minute on any of them. I dismiss them all out of hand. Their emails and treatises go right in the trash. I will, however, send them one email in reply, with a simple rule: get even one of their novel claims published in a peer-reviewed journal specializing in Egyptology or archaeology, or in a book published by a respected academic or peer-reviewed press, and then I'll read it. They will insist they can't, because of some conspiracy by 'the establishment' to prevent acceptance of any such paper (either for some ordinary or paranoid reason, it differs with each one). But as a professional in the field, I know, first-hand, that's just bunk. If you really have the evidence and can prove it, the scholarly community will usually publish it. Our conversation ends.

This isn't the only subject on which I get this kind of crank email. It was just for a time the most pronounced and continuous—and silly, since I'm not an Egyptologist and have no interest in the field. I only published on the subject as a journalist, and that only once, long ago. But I've published more widely on numerous other subjects and built a reputation as a skeptic and expert in various other areas, which inevitably attract similar people, from creationists to UFOlogists and everything in between. My response is always the same. After all, I have no choice. If I can't examine every pyramidiot scheme in a lifetime, I certainly can't examine every nutty scheme in hundreds of other fields besides. Hence my rule: unless they get something published *properly*, I'm not warranted in spending any time on it. That's the way it has to be.

So when I was approached by people claiming Jesus didn't exist, I simply assumed this was more of the same. Since I'm an expert in ancient history, and particularly in historical methods and the origins of Christianity, it at least made more sense why advocates of *that* crazy idea would start sending me things. But more than that happened. A growing number of skeptics, not just advocates, started approaching me and asking about these claims. They said the arguments sounded pretty convincing, and they hadn't seen any credible debunking of them, yet weren't qualified themselves to know if they were being duped by sloppy or dishonest scholarship. I responded to these sincere inquiries with the same general reply: the non-existence of Jesus is simply not plausible, as arguments from silence in the matter aren't valid, nor could they ever be sufficient to challenge what is, after all, the near-universal consensus of well-qualified experts. I would briefly explain why, but then more questions would come. Occasionally I would point out what was wrong with this or that ridiculous claim, either factually or methodologically. There is certainly plenty of nonsense going around from deniers of Jesus' historicity, so it's never hard to find something too silly to credit. But eventually enough people in the atheist and skeptical community, people whose judgment I trusted, were asking me to at least read *The Jesus Puzzle* by Earl Doherty and report on its merits (published by Canadian Humanist Press in 2000, with a sequel, *Jesus: Neither God Nor Man*, published in 2009). He wasn't the only or the first author to argue the point, but everyone agreed he was the one who made the most convincing case.

Normally, as with all crank claims, I wouldn't acquiesce, but instead insist that Doherty get at least one peer-reviewed paper published before I'd bother. He had, in the *Journal of Higher Criticism,* but as that journal has the specific agenda of publishing essentially those kinds of argument, an appearance there wasn't an entirely convincing reason to pay more attention. But once the number of requests from respectable people reached a tipping point, I decided I'd give his book a go, hoping that would be the end of it, and I would at least get a good article out of it, which I could then direct everyone to once and for all. I resolved to essentially 'peer review' his book, the way I would any paper submitted to a journal.

But the result surprised me. I found his book well-researched, competently argued, devoid of any of the ridiculous claims I'd heard from other historicity deniers, and more convincing than I'd thought possible. In my critical review I pointed out the merits *and* flaws of his book (including the sorts of things I would insist upon as a peer reviewer before accepting it for academic publication), but on balance the merits were greater.[3] He had a good case. I wasn't entirely convinced. But I *was* convinced the subject deserved more research. And so my journey began.

2. *The Debate Today*

Jesus Christ is the standard appellation for the man who either founded or inspired the Christian religion. There were many men named Jesus back then. In fact it was among the most common of names (the name is actually Joshua; 'Jesus' is just a different way to spell it now: see Chapter 6, §3). Adding 'Christ' thus designates the particular Jesus who, one way or

3. Richard Carrier, 'Did Jesus Exist? Earl Doherty and the Argument to Ahistoricity', *The Secular Web* (2002) at www.infidels.org/library/modern/richard_carrier/jesuspuzzle.html.

another, intentionally or not, got the whole movement called 'Christianity' started, a religion that worshipped this Jesus as 'the Christ' (which simply means 'Anointed', the very thing meant by 'Messiah'). Hence the Jesus we're concerned with here is Jesus Christ, as now understood.

Many scholars believe that 'Christ' is a name or label attached to Jesus after his death, beginning a pattern of increasing legendary development upon a humbler story of some real man named Jesus. But not all scholars agree. In fact, there is no identifiable consensus about who or what Jesus was, or when or why he acquired the moniker of Christ. And while all these scholars debate (or even ignore) one another in all this, for over a hundred years now some scholars (and not just cranks) have argued there was no Jesus Christ in any real sense at all. They maintain the Christian religion began with the idea of a *mythical* man, not a historical one. The 'historical' Jesus, on their account, was *entirely* a legendary development, eclipsing the original myth and leaving us with the mistaken impression that there must have been a real Jesus who was later known as Christ.

For this book I'll dub those who maintain there was a real 'Jesus' of some relevant sort *historicists*, and those who argue this Jesus was mythical, *mythicists*. Though there have been many valid criticisms of mythicists, many of the same objections apply to historicists as well (who have often made just as many mistakes of fact and method), and if we allow *historicism* to become respectable by limiting its claims to what can be reasonably proved, leaving aside all speculation and conjecture and error as simply that and nothing more, we should give *mythicism* the same opportunity. Yet in practice there is no consensus even among historicists as to what is historical about Jesus and what not, and what is instead legendary or mythical or merely erroneous.[4] Indeed, these unresolved disagreements extend to almost every significant question about Jesus. Nevertheless, most scholars agree *some* elements of the things said about Jesus *aren't* historically true, and many even conclude *most* are. Mythicists just continue going in the same direction other scholars have already been heading. But do they go too far?

In *Jesus Outside the New Testament*, Robert Van Voorst lists seven general counter-arguments against mythicism, and this constitutes a typical summary of the case usually made against it.[5] But that case is rather weak. Van Voorst says mythicists tend to overstate the strength of their arguments from silence. Yet, as I'll show in coming chapters, those arguments don't

4. I document this lack of consensus in Richard Carrier, *Proving History: Bayes's Theorem and the Quest for the Historical Jesus* (Amherst, NY: Prometheus Books, 2012), pp. 11-14.

5. Robert Van Voorst, *Jesus Outside the New Testament* (Grand Rapids, MI: Eerdmans: 2000), pp. 13-16.

have to be overstated to be compelling. Van Voorst says mythicists tend to date all the Gospels unreasonably late (after 100 CE). Yet mythicism doesn't require this—and even mainstream scholars are starting to agree some of the Gospels might indeed be that late. Van Voorst says mythicists overstate the implications of the widely acknowledged mythic elements, legendary developments and contradictions in the Gospels. Yet he acknowledges these elements exist, which can still support a mythicist theory without being overstated. Van Voorst says mythicists tend to be far too skeptical of the authenticity of the earliest non-biblical (and even many biblical) passages about Jesus. Yet mythicism does not require such excessive skepticism—and some of it is not excessive.

Van Voorst also objects that mythicists often have an anti-Christian agenda, which is certainly true, but that is not relevant to the merit of their work. He further objects that no ancient critic of Christianity challenged the historical reality of Jesus. But that's not quite true (as even Van Voorst admits in a footnote—and as I'll show later, he misses yet more examples: see Chapter 8, §§6 and 12), and it's impertinent anyway, since we have no criticisms of Christianity of *any* sort until well into the second century, far too late for such critics to know the real truth of the matter, especially if Christians themselves had forgotten (or weren't telling).[6] Hence if the idea of a historical Jesus was already developing in the latter half of the first century, then Van Voorst's own objection to overstating an argument from silence turns against him, for we cannot argue from the silence of documents we don't have, and we don't have any first-century documents from critics of Christianity. Hence we cannot know what such critics were saying—because no one tells us.[7]

Finally, Van Voorst says mythicists 'have failed to advance other, credible hypotheses to account for the birth of Christianity and the fashioning of a historical Christ' and, as a result, 'biblical scholars and classical his-

6. For Van Voorst's admitted exception: *Jesus Outside the New Testament*, p. 15 n. 35.

7. Some will claim Mt. 28.11-15 is the one exception, but that's still a Christian source that can't be usefully dated or traced to anyone who actually knew the facts of the matter (rather than was merely gainsaying a gospel they heard), even if it was based on fact, and it isn't: it is in fact a Christian fabrication (it only makes sense in the context of Matthew's unique story, which is obviously fictional, and is a response to Mark's story, which is probably just as fictional) and thus cannot actually be linked to any real critics of Christianity (much less critics who would be in any position to know there was no Jesus). See Chapter 8 (§12), Chapter 10 (§§4 and 5) and Carrier, *Proving History*, pp. 199-204, updating Richard Carrier, 'The Plausibility of Theft', in *The Empty Tomb: Jesus Beyond the Grave* (ed. Robert Price and Jeffery Lowder; Amherst, NY: Prometheus Books, 2005), pp. 349-68 (358-59).

torians now regard [mythicism] as effectively refuted'.[8] Yet that conclusion depends on the merits of his use of the word 'credible'. Most mythicists in fact *start* by constructing hypotheses for the origin and development of Christianity and *then* argue that the evidence fits their scenario better than any other. Whether these efforts are 'credible' remains to be determined. For it is not demonstrated by anything Van Voorst argues, and whether it is demonstrated by anything anyone else argues we can only begin to ask after reading the present book—or other more recent books, since Van Voorst wrote before he could examine the superior work of more recent mythicists such as Earl Doherty or Thomas Thompson or Thomas Brodie, and no one of Van Voorst's calibre has yet addressed their arguments properly either.[9]

In other words, the case against mythicism (at least as represented by Van Voorst) consists of arguing that there are flaws (mostly flaws of exaggeration) in the scholarship of mythicists, yet without demonstrating that any of those flaws are actually relevant. That scholars err does not automatically disqualify the rest of their work or their conclusions. And the fact that exaggerated premises are unwarranted does not entail that the same conclusion cannot be reached from more moderate premises instead. Thus his every argument is a *non sequitur.* Only one of Van Voorst's arguments bears on the actual evidence rather than its abuse, and that argument isn't logically valid, either—for his argument from silence stands refuted by his own reasoning.

Yet that doesn't mean mythicism is vindicated. It's still a fallacy to declare a conclusion true merely because arguments against it are fallacious. Just because Van Voorst identifies no valid objection to mythicism

8. Van Voorst, *Jesus Outside the New Testament*, p. 16.

9. Bart Ehrman, in *Did Jesus Exist? The Historical Argument for Jesus of Nazareth* (San Francisco, CA: HarperOne, 2012), attempted to provide one, but is essentially a careless and poorly researched popular market book and not a proper scholarly critique. You can review my demonstrations of this on my blog: a summary (with links to my more detailed discussions) is available in Richard Carrier, 'Ehrman on Historicity Recap', *Richard Carrier Blogs* (July 24, 2012) at freethoughtblogs.com/carrier/archives/1794 (for a complete list of my blog entries on Ehrman's work see freethoughtblogs.com/carrier/archives/category/bart-ehrman). For a published summary (with expanded evidence) see Richard Carrier, 'How Not to Argue for Historicity', in *Bart Ehrman and the Quest of the Historical Jesus of Nazareth: An Evaluation of Ehrman's* Did Jesus Exist? (ed. Frank Zindler and Robert Price; Cranford, NJ: American Atheist Press, 2013), pp. 15-62. Maurice Casey has just published his own defense of historicity, *Jesus: Evidence and Argument or Mythicist Myths?* (Edinburgh: T. & T. Clark, 2014), too late to be addressed in this volume; but for a critical review see Richard Carrier, 'Critical Review of Maurice Casey's Defense of the Historicity of Jesus', *Richard Carrier Blogs* (March 3, 2014) at http://freethoughtblogs.com/carrier/archives/4282.

does not mean mythicism has merit. After all, it might be possible to expand or qualify his objections into a successful refutation (and Van Voorst cites various scholars who have attempted this, and in many other respects his section on this topic remains required reading). But that has to actually be done before anyone can claim it has been. And merely refuting one theory (such as Doherty's) won't suffice at that, any more than refuting a single conception of a historical Jesus is sufficient to refute *all* conceptions of a historical Jesus.

Therefore, it's necessary to test a minimal theory of historicity (such that if even *that* theory isn't true, then none are) against a minimal theory of myth (such that if *that* theory isn't true, then no other is likely to be). And this test must be logically valid, and give the best possible opportunity to either theory, before whatever conclusion we reach can be considered fair.

3. *Myth versus History*

As I demonstrated in the first chapter of *Proving History*, many contradictory theories of a historical Jesus are defended today. Some joke that there are as many theories of Jesus as there are scholars to propose them. Each different conception of the historical Jesus and his relationship to the origins of the Christian religion will here be called a *theory of historicity*. Such a theory aims to explain all extant evidence by proposing that certain things are true of the historical Jesus and his influence *and* that certain things are *not* true (or not known to be true) of the historical Jesus and his influence.

The latter cannot be separated from the former. For proposing to explain any evidence as a *later* development in the church entails that that evidence was *not* caused by anything Jesus said or did (or had said or done to him). In practice, of course, an honest historian has to admit she often doesn't know how some particular development in the evidence came about, and thus doesn't know whether it's in any way causally linked to a historical Jesus or not. But even then she will be saying, in effect, that the probabilities are roughly equal either way, which *still* entails taking a particular position as to what's possible or likely. Anyone who examines the literature of the present generation of scholars will find that, indeed, by this standard there are almost as many theories of historicity as there are experts to pronounce them, and there is no apparent consensus as to whose theory is more probably correct, nor any indication of such a consensus developing any time soon.

But just as there are countless theories of historicity, there are also countless *Jesus myth theories*. Indeed, just as with historicism, there are almost as many Jesus myth theories as there are experts to pronounce them. And the range of these theories is truly marvelous, from the more ridiculous ('the bulk of the New Testament is a hoax perpetrated by the Roman Senatorial elite') to the less ridiculous ('the original Jesus stories were a clever political metaphor against the ruling elite'), to the least ridiculous (which I shall explore here), that 'the earliest Christians preached a celestial being named Jesus Christ, then later this godlike figure was fictionally placed in a historical setting just as other gods were, and the original concept eventually forgotten, dismissed, or suppressed'. I think most scholars, once informed of the underlying facts, would agree only the latter has any plausibility (if there is any plausibility to be had), so any Jesus myth theory that entails rejecting even *that* is probably a theory of no likelihood worth considering. I'll have more to say about this (and what the minimal theory of historicity must be to compete against it) in the next two chapters.

But even then, whatever theory is proposed, it is often immediately weighed down with an enormous array of elaborations, which are often significantly less defensible than the core theory alone would have been. Yet one should never propose more than is necessary to explain the evidence. The more complex a theory has to be, the less likely it is to be true. Hence I'll assume for convenience that what I just suggested is the *most* plausible theory is the *only* plausible theory, and attempt to explain and present it as simply as possible with no unnecessary elaborations. For if even *that* theory cannot be shown to be more credible than historicity, it's unlikely any other theory will succeed where it failed. However, I do allow that I can be proven wrong about that, on this matter as in anything else, if someone or presents evidence presently unknown to me that adequately supports some other theory. And in *Proving History* I laid out a sound method by which that could be done. The same method I will use here.

4. *Mythicists versus Historicists*

Though many mythicists may seem as crazy as their theories, the proposal of mythicism itself is not crazy. A model example is King Arthur. Like Jesus, many detailed historical narratives and biographical facts about this 'great king' are on record (along with a widespread belief that, like Jesus, he will one day return). Yet after considerable inquiry it seems almost certain no such man ever existed. Michael Wood provides a good survey of how myths like this arise and why, and how the Arthur legend incorporates old stories and elements from various cultures and times, and persons (both real and fictional), which were all co-opted and incorporated into Arthur's story, including elements from British, Scottish, Welsh and French traditions, and from both Christian and Celtic pagan religions. King Arthur was essentially created by assembling pieces from numerous facts and myths, into a new unified—and unifying—myth that had great cultural resonance, persisting even to this day.[10] This myth essentially became historicized by a culture-wide application of an affective fallacy: the more powerfully a story affects a people, emotionally and morally, the more it is believed to be real. Eventually the truth of what the story symbolized was confused with the truth of the story itself.

There is nothing crazy or bizarre about that. Mainstream historians are entirely comfortable with King Arthur being a mythical hero historicized, by some such process, even if they debate the exact details or confess the details can't be known. Of course, the King Arthur legend developed over centuries. But centuries are not required, as I'll show in Chapter 6. One prominent example studied of late is the rapid historicization of the mythical Ned Ludd. As the supposed founder of the Luddite movement, Ned Ludd had many contradictory traditions arise about him, quite rapidly—in fact, within forty years of his alleged techno-sabotage in 1779, an event that historians have failed to find any evidence of. Nor have they discovered any evidence of the man at all, despite a vastly better survival of books and records than is enjoyed for any period of antiquity (we even have daily newspapers). And yet already by 1810 he was a revered hero and imagined founder of a movement of anti-technocrats (known as the Luddites), and all manner of stories were circulating about him, letters were forged in his name, and eventually biographical novels about him written. Though Ned Ludd's non-existence cannot be *decisively* proved, this is true of almost any myth. But in this case, the evidence for the man being a myth seems as compelling as it could ever be expected to be.[11] Yet, again, mainstream historians are not shocked by this. The notion that Ned Ludd is a myth is not considered crazy.

The King Arthur legend sold a particular product: a unified England. Anyone who believed dearly in that goal was likely to believe dearly in King Arthur. The message and the story were eventually regarded as one and the same, the symbolism so powerful and passions so high that to deny the one was to deny the other. Likewise, the Ned Ludd myth fueled a protest movement by providing a hero and a mission to rally behind, again with the aim of generating unity. In fact, there were many separate movements that co-opted the Ned Ludd story each in their own way, and a unified story about him only evolved later. The same thing happened in Melanesian

10. Michael Wood, *In Search of Myths and Heroes: Exploring Four Epic Legends of the World* (Berkeley, CA: University of California Press, 2005), pp. 206-60.

11. See Kevin Binfield (ed.), *Writings of the Luddites* (Baltimore, MD: Johns Hopkins University Press, 2004), though Binfield remains agnostic. A.J. Droge has compared Ludd's case to Jesus in 'Jesus and Ned Lud[d]: What's in a Name?', *CAESAR: A Journal for the Critical Study of Religion and Human Values* 3 (2009), pp. 23-25, with a useful bibliography on the subject.

Cargo Cults, which still revere completely mythical heroes who were nevertheless quite rapidly placed in history and believed to be real (most famously 'Tom Navy' and 'John Frum'), again within mere decades of their supposed appearance, and again serving the aim of creating unity and a moral authority to commend (see sources and discussion in Chapter 5, Element 29). Much the same could be claimed of Christianity, with different movements co-opting the Jesus story to promote their own ideals, and a unified church arising only later.

The aim would always be the same: to promote unity within the movement and (it would be hoped) society by promoting a popular myth to rally behind and believe in. And often success at that depended on selling the myth as true. As with King Arthur or Ned Ludd, so with Jesus Christ: to deny the historicity of these men or their stories would quickly become tantamount to denying the unifying message their stories were crafted and employed to sell. Promoting their historicity also made it easier to effect moral reform, by attaching the authority for that reform to a historical person. Because a 'made-up man' was not generally considered capable of having any moral authority at all.

Even in biblical studies there is nothing new or crazy about this idea. The patriarchs are safely assumed now to be nonhistorical, and thus entirely mythical. This is no longer considered radical or fringe, but is in fact the most widespread mainstream view among scholars (see sources and discussion in Chapter 5, Element 44). Thus Moses is now regarded as fictional, yet like Jesus he performed miracles, had a whole family and huge numbers of followers, gave speeches and had travels, and dictated laws. No mainstream historian today believes the book of Deuteronomy was even written in the same century as Moses, much less by Moses, or that it preserves anything Moses actually said or did—yet it purports to do so, at extraordinary length and in remarkable detail. No real historian today would accept as valid an argument like 'Moses *had* to have existed, because so many sayings and teachings were attributed to him!' And yet if this argument is invalid for Moses, it's invalid for Jesus.

Similarly, it's now the mainstream view that the book of Daniel was written in the second century BCE and is a complete fiction, representing the elaborate adventures and speeches of the sixth-century prophet Daniel as if they were a fact (see sources and discussion in Chapter 4, Element 7). Historians doubt even the existence of Daniel. But even if he existed, historians are certain the book of Daniel does not contain anything he authentically said or did. Rather, this Daniel, and everything he is supposed to have said and done, was invented to create a historical authority for a new vision of society, to inspire a new unity and a new moral order against the immoral rule of dominating foreigners. We must accept that the same is at least possible for Jesus.

So the idea that Jesus was originally mythical, like King Arthur or Ned Ludd or Moses or Daniel, is not *inherently* crazy. It could only be called crazy if the evidence for a historical Jesus were substantially more impressive than the evidence for the historicity of the likes of King Arthur or Ned Ludd (or Moses or Daniel). Whether that's the case is what the present book will examine. But an increasing number of mainstream scholars are starting to at least reconsider the question. A conference sponsored by the Center for Inquiry's Committee for the Scientific Examination of Religion in Amherst, New York, in December of 2008 gathered numerous reputable historians to begin debating how much we could even claim to know about the historical Jesus—and most agreed the answer was very little, or even nothing. In fact a growing number of mainstream experts are expressing doubt that much of anything can be reliably known about the historical Jesus, as I showed in the first chapter of *Proving History*. And as I'll show in Chapter 3 here, more are coming to the side of doubt.

Nevertheless, this book won't defend any particular mythicist, whether the experts I name in Chapter 3 or the many amateurs who've published their own cases. In my observation, the mythicist case has often been mired in or mixed up with poor, questionable or obsolete scholarship, therefore giving the impression that it isn't worth looking at, because in such a state it doesn't look either strong or valid. Until mainstream scholars start seriously examining their arguments in proper detail, and only dismissing the bad, instead of the good along with the bad, they won't even know if the case *is* strong or valid. But the fault here largely falls on the mythicists, who have failed to police the bad scholarship among their ranks with appropriate criticism, have failed to develop or employ any clear methodology in defense of their own conclusions, and have failed to distinguish the core of their argument from the excesses of speculation they pile upon it.

But this chief failing of the mythicists is much the same as the chief failing of the historicists. It's inordinately easy to make any theory fit the facts, or to make the facts fit any theory. Consequently, as I demonstrated in the first chapter of *Proving History*, historicists defend dozens of completely contradictory theories of the historical Jesus, and yet all are accepted as plausible by mainstream academia, even though such acceptance should be a scandal. A field that generates dozens of contradictory conclusions about the same subject is clearly bereft of anything like a reliable method. But the very same flaw befalls the mythicists, whose community is likewise plagued by dozens of completely contradictory theories of the Jesus myth. If such a state is a scandal for historicity (and it should be), it is equally a scandal for mythicism. The passionate certainty with which *every* historicist and mythicist defends their own theory of the evidence is far out of proportion to what the evidence could ever support. All the more so, since logic entails that, even at most, only one of them can be right, and therefore almost all of them must be wrong—in fact, it's entirely possible *all* of them are wrong.

The first conclusion this should impress upon you is that even if you are convinced (perhaps by this very book) that Jesus probably didn't exist, you should *not* then simply trust that any additional claims supporting that conclusion are true or sound. There is a lot of bad scholarship on this subject, which advances claims with far more confidence than is at all warranted, or rests on assumptions that are anything but established, or relies of facts that simply aren't true. In short, if you are a layperson in this matter, exercise extreme caution when reading or listening to myth advocates. What I discuss here, throughout this book, about proper methodology should always be applied to them. But for the very same reasons, if you are an expert, don't let the existence of bad scholarship defending this same conclusion lead you to believe that good scholarship could never get the same result.

The second conclusion all this should impress upon you is that even if you are *not* convinced that Jesus probably didn't exist, you should *not* then simply trust that historicity has been well defended. Historicists have a lot of work to do before they can claim to have their house in order. Their sins are many. They have far too quickly assumed that various fundamental conclusions in the field are settled, which in fact are not, such as the dating of New Testament documents (as I'll discuss in Chapter 7). They have routinely overstated what the evidence can actually prove, conflating conjectures with demonstrable facts almost as often as mythicists do, and they lack anything like a coherent methodology (both of which I extensively demonstrated in *Proving History*). They have also frequently ignored, denied or somehow remained ignorant of key facts. I've met many historians of Jesus who didn't know many of the things I will survey in this book, almost none of which should be controversial anymore. They also tend to dismiss criticism far too quickly, without addressing it or even paying attention to it. And they often simply mishandle the evidence, such as assuming the Gospels are historical narratives rather than symbolic myths (despite conclusive evidence of the latter, as I'll prove in Chapter 10), or overlooking what is obviously missing from the book of Acts which we should expect to be there if Jesus existed (as I'll show in Chapter 9), or vastly overplaying the value of the extrabiblical evidence (as I'll demonstrate in Chapter 8), or overestimating how much they can honestly explain away.

But all that still does not entail the mythicists are right, any more than the similar failings of the mythicists entail they are wrong. It only entails that historicists are wrong to simply dismiss all the challenges posed by mythicists—because the historicists still have a great deal of work to do that, so far, they are only pretending has been done. But since both houses are in a mess, *both* have a great deal of work to do. Admitting this is the first step toward progress.

5. *The Aim of This Book*

This book will advance the debate in two respects. It will survey the most relevant evidence for and against the historicity of Jesus, and it will do so with the fewest unnecessary assumptions, testing the simplest theories of historicity and myth against one another.

But one thing this book is *not* is a comprehensive survey of all evidence, theories and arguments of mythicists and historicists alike. Though one can begin to explore the history of this debate, and the many different theories of both sides, by following some of the references throughout this book (in Chapters 2 and 3 especially), my aim is not to attack or defend any particular scholar or work, but rather to construct the most defensible version of each position (which in either case will be a simpler and less ambitious theory than any heretofore defended), and test their relative merits against the most pertinent evidence.

But since this book intends only to begin, not end, a proper debate, I hope to see it carefully critiqued by experts in the field. I want to see a scholarly and constructive debate develop that will advance the entire discussion, resolving matters of methodology if nothing else (such a debate should already have begun over the release of *Proving History*), but hopefully also making a clear, objectively defensible case either for or against the historicity of Jesus, one that all reasonable experts can agree is sound. In his own excellent book on the origins of Christian myth traditions, Burton Mack provides a list of scholars and their recent diverse work that needs to be synthesized and applied to reconstructing the origins of Christianity, which provides a major example of the kind of work that really does need to be done.[12] Like Mack, throughout this book I will cite many scholars whose work also needs to be synthesized and applied to the same result. Above all, historians need to apply serious energy to resolving the issues of dating and authorship surveyed in Chapter 7.

Since the theories I will compare here are the minimal ones, the simplest possible theories that I think have any chance of explaining the evidence, many on both sides of the debate will want to do one better and defend more elaborate theories of historicity or mythicism. But if mythicists want to expand on my minimal theory at all (or, conversely, if historicists want

12. Burton Mack, *The Christian Myth: Origins, Logic, and Legacy* (New York: Continuum, 2006), pp. 76-78 (although his entire book is in effect a call for further work to be done, and thus well worth reading).

to defend any more elaborate theory of historicity than I present), I ask that they do so responsibly, with sound methodology, according to the standards set out in *Proving History*. Even if you reject those methods, you must replace them with methods more defensible. So you have to defend those alternative methods, which means you must demonstrate that they are in fact a more defensible means of getting at the truth (in other words, that they will produce reliable results that we can all trust). And above all, to advance beyond the present work, mythicists need to be as restrained in their claims and as rigorous in their dependence on evidence as they expect historicists to be—and vice versa.

Finally, however, one last remark is needed on mistaking Christian apologetics for objective (or even mainstream) scholarship (a point I'll briefly revisit in the next chapter). It will not be the aim of this book to debunk apologetic reconstructions of the historical Jesus or the origins of Christianity. I take only secular scholarship seriously—which doesn't mean secular *scholars* (since a great deal of secular scholarship is produced by the devout), but rather scholars who rely on secular methods and principles of scholarship (a good example being the late Raymond Brown). Because apologetics differs from scholarship. Apologists ignore methodological distinctions between the possible and the probable in order to maintain the defensibility of a religious dogma. But that isn't how objective scholars behave. If it is realistically possible that Jesus didn't exist, then it is no longer possible to argue that we *know* he existed. We can only argue that he may have existed, or probably did. This would not be an unusual result in the field of history. But on this specific subject it presents a threat to traditional religion, a threat recognized by Christian apologists, who will disregard facts and logic in opposing it if they have to.

This threat to religion is also recognized by many mythicists who do indeed have an agenda against Christianity—some perhaps spiteful, though most simply out of ire against apologists whom they perceive as having lied to them and manipulated the evidence in defense of completely untenable theories of historicity. Some mythicists thus conflate what apologists argue (a triumphalist theory of the historical Jesus) with what is far more defensible (a far more mundane theory of the historical Jesus), and in justified outrage against the former, unjustifiably attack *all* historicity, even the most defensible kind. This approach must be discarded, as must also the apologetical kind. Neither should be accepted as legitimate. Both are driven by agendas to exclude credible and objective methods and claims.

6. *Summary of Remaining Chapters*

The argument of this book can be summarized as follows. A Bayesian argument requires attending to the question of applicable background knowledge, constructing therefrom a prior probability for all competing hypotheses, and then evaluating the consequent probabilities (the likelihoods) of all the evidence on each hypothesis. In accordance with this method, I must formally define the hypotheses to be compared: that of historicity (in Chapter 2) and that of myth (in Chapter 3). In each case I will define the simplest possible theory, which shall thus encompass all other more complex theories that have any claim to plausibility.

Then I must set out all the applicable background knowledge that will affect our estimates of prior and consequent probability for these hypotheses, first from the established history of Christianity and its origins (Chapter 4), and then everything else pertaining to its historical context and comparable phenomena in other contexts (Chapter 5). This is unfortunately necessary, I have found, because even the most erudite scholars in the field are unaware of most of it. Yet the origins and development of Christianity can *only* be understood in light of it.

With all that background work done, then I must determine the relative prior probabilities of each hypothesis, by ascertaining the clearest and most applicable reference class for which we have sufficient data (Chapter 6). Then I must determine the consequent probability of all the evidence on each hypothesis, which I will do by breaking the evidence down into categories and treating each separately but cumulatively, after first attending to questions of dating and authorship (Chapter 7). The four categories I develop will then each receive a chapter, in the order of latest to earliest: the extrabiblical evidence, both secular and non-canonical (Chapter 8); the canonical Acts (Chapter 9); the canonical Gospels (Chapter 10); and finally the canonical Epistles (Chapter 11). I will then tie everything together and argue for a conclusion (Chapter 12).

Readers who want to cut to the chase may wish to skip Chapters 4 through 9, and instead read on from here to the end of Chapter 3 and then jump directly to Chapters 10 through 12, then go back to read Chapters 4 through 9 if you want to see the relevance of that material to the rest. Otherwise, if you want to build up to the conclusion in logical order, being made aware first of all the evidence that relates to the rest of the book, you should read all the chapters in their given order.

7. *Applying Bayes's Theorem*

I explained all the mechanics and technicalities of applying Bayes's Theorem (or BT) to historical questions in *Proving History,* where I also answered every typical objection to this notion. Here I will only summarize the key points that will come up often in the present volume.

To know whether any theory is the most probably true, you must compare it with all other viable theories (no theory can be defended in isolation).

To effect such a comparison you must establish four premises: (1) the prior probability that the theory you are testing is true, (2) the converse of which is the prior probability that some other theory is true instead, and then (3) the consequent probability that we would have all the evidence we actually have if your theory is true, and (4) the consequent probability that we would have all that same evidence if some other theory is true instead. From these four premises a conclusion follows with logical necessity, which is simply the probability that your theory is true.

To ascertain these probabilities with the kind of vague, problematic and incomplete data typically encountered in historical inquiry, you must estimate all four probabilities as being as far against your most preferred theory as you can honestly and reasonably believe them to be. And you must present sufficient reasons and evidence for this conclusion in each case. This will produce a conclusion *a fortiori*, which you can assert with as high a confidence level as could ever be obtained on the available data—because any adjustment of your estimates toward what they truly are will then only make your conclusion even more certain. That way, since each premise consists of as unfavorable a probability as is reasonably defensible, you will know with logical certainty (if you have accounted for all the available evidence and done so correctly) that the probability your theory is true will be the probability you calculate *or higher* (and often much higher). Conversely, you can be certain it is that probability *or lower* if you instead input estimates as far *in favor* of your theory as you can honestly believe.

That conclusion only follows, of course, given all the knowledge and evidence available to you at the time. Hence newly uncovered evidence can change your conclusion—which possibility is already accounted for by stating your conclusion as a *probability*. For example, if your conclusion is that your hypothesis *h* is true to a probability of 95%, and then some new evidence effectively proves *h* false, that possibility was already accounted for by your original allowance of a 5% chance *h* was false even before the new evidence appeared. And of course even that new conclusion that *h* is false will be stated as a probability—that could be overturned again if yet more evidence arises.

8. *Elements and Axioms*

Essential to a successful use of BT in historical analysis is a transparency of assumptions and inferences. First of all, I shall rely on the twelve rules and twelve axioms of historical method that I laid out in the second chapter of *Proving History*. Here, I shall also state my assumed background knowledge (in Chapters 2 through 7), which shall often consist of numbered elements, each being a particular claim to fact that requires an empirical defense (plus a set of basic definitions of terms I will frequently use), but once thus defended will be employed as an assumption of fact for the remainder of the book. This will allow my critics to more easily identify all of my assumptions for examination and challenge.

Finally, the present work should be regarded as superseding all my prior work. Since my research for this book changed many of the views and conclusions I voiced in various places and publications before this, wherever contradictions may result with anything I have previously said or written, what I say in this book should be taken as my current opinion on the matter, and any previous claims or arguments of mine now contradicted should be regarded as revised or abandoned.

That said, I first must turn to defining the two hypotheses that will be subjected to the following inquiry: the basic historicity hypothesis and the basic myth hypothesis.

2

The Hypothesis of Historicity

1. *Myth from History*

It's quite common for historical persons to become surrounded by a vast quantity of myth and legend, and very rapidly, too, especially when they become the object of religious veneration. Thus, the fact that this has happened never in itself argues that the person in question didn't exist. One relatively recent example is the elevation of the Ethiopian emperor Haile Selassie to the status of a god . . . by people he never asked this favor from and even repeatedly begged to stop. His deification (and continued worship to this day) is the foundation of the modern Rastafarian faith, which claims hundreds of thousands of adherents worldwide. It's telling that we know he professed to his death his own Christian faith and his continual despair at the fact that he had been elevated into a revered divinity so quickly—despite his protests (and one would think if your own god protested your worshiping him, you'd listen—and yet here we are). Myths and legends about him quickly grew—even within his own lifetime, and all the more rapidly in the two decades after his death in 1975. And yet none had any basis in fact. At all. Yet still they remain the central affirmations of a living faith.

The parallel with Jesus ought to be cautionary: if this could happen to Selassie, it could even more easily have happened to Jesus, there being no universal education or literacy, or even media per se in the ancient world.[1] Perhaps Jesus himself continually begged his followers not to worship him. Yet they did anyway. We wouldn't know, because unlike Selassie, the only records we have of Jesus are written by his devoted worshipers. So perhaps everything told about Jesus is just as made up as everything now told about Selassie. Yet it's told anyway. And not just told, but believed completely by

1. On the differences between antiquity and modernity and the significance of this for legendary growth see Richard Carrier, *Not the Impossible Faith: Why Christianity Didn't Need a Miracle to Succeed* (Raleigh, NC: Lulu.com, 2009), pp. 161-218 (also 329-68, 385-405).

every adherent of the faith, even in the face of overwhelming evidence to the contrary.

But not merely the cautionary, but the factual parallels are numerous, too. Edmund Standing summarizes this point elegantly:

Looking at the status of Haile Selassie in the Rastafari religion we find the following: (1) The coming to earth of a messianic figure who was prophesied in the Old Testament; (2) a birth accompanied by miracles; (3) a child with immense divinely given wisdom who possessed miraculous powers; (4) a messiah whose actions were prefigured in Old Testament writings; (5) a man who could perform miracles and in whose presence miracles occurred; (6) a man who was worshiped and held to be divine by thousands who had not even met him; (7) a man who was the incarnation of God and who continues to live on despite evidence of his death; (8) a man who is prayed to and communicated with by his followers; (9) a savior who will one day return to gather up a chosen people who will live under his rule in a kingdom of God. Despite the facts related to the *actual* historical figure of Selassie, as we see, Rastafarians have built an extensive religious mythology around him, and even did so within his lifetime.

> Imagine if, at some point in the future . . . the vast bulk of the historical record was lost . . . [and] that the only records of Selassie's existence that had survived were the devotional accounts of Rastafarians. [Then . . .] the only story historians would have to work with would be made up of layers of mythology. The story of Selassie, a man who arose in a time in which Ethiopians were excitedly awaiting the coming of a Messiah, would be filled with references to the fulfillment of Old Testament prophecies, stories of miracles, tales of God walking the earth, and the denial of the reality of the Messiah's death. They would read that Selassie is still alive and that part of the proof of this is that followers can 'communicate in spirit' with him. As a result of this, surely there would be some who would adopt a 'mythicist' position with regard to the historical Selassie.[2]

And yet, of course, if they did, they would be wrong. Because there really *was* a Selassie. He just wasn't anything even remotely like the 'narratives' his worshipers wrote and told about him. In the scenario Standing imagines, the truth about the 'historical' Selassie would have been completely lost. Fragments of the truth would remain in the surviving devotional texts of his worshipers, but without any independent sources to check them against, we would have no way to know which details were historical and which mythical. We are hardly in any better position with respect to Jesus, for whom all direct sources (if ever there were any) have been completely lost, and all we have are the devotional claims and

2. From Edmund Standing, 'Against Mythicism: A Case for the Plausibility of a Historical Jesus', *Think* 9 (Spring 2010), pp. 13-27.

tales of his fanatical worshipers. This means reconstructing the historical Jesus may simply be impossible.[3] But that in no way means there was no historical Jesus.

There are significant differences, however, that break down Standing's analogy. First are the letters of Paul, which actually precede the Gospels by decades and are the nearest evidence we have to the original Jesus (if such there was), yet these letters only know a cosmic man and contain no real history of him at all (as I will demonstrate in Chapter 11). Second are the methods of the Gospels' construction, which are so thoroughly mytho-symbolic that their composition actually argues against their containing any true historical data at all (a point I will examine in Chapter 10). And finally, Standing's assumption that we can expect independent records to have vanished in the case of Jesus is actually not quite as likely as he thinks. If Jesus was as famous as Selassie, it would be strange to hear nothing about him—almost as strange as it would be in Selassie's case now (as I'll explain in Chapter 8).

To avoid this oddity we must conclude that the real Jesus was a virtual nobody. But there are still problems with the evidence that suggest he wasn't even that (as I'll explain in Chapters 8, 9 and 10). Nevertheless, Standing's methodological proposals are sound: only if the differences I allege are actually there will the comparison fail. Otherwise, it's perfectly possible that a real Jesus underlies all the extant myths about him. Just as is the case for Haile Selassie. It's happened before in Christian tradition, both to real, and to fictional persons (as I suspect any survey of the plethora of saints worshiped in late antiquity and the Middle Ages would discover).[4] So which was it for Jesus?

3. As I demonstrated in Chapter 5 of *Proving History*, all attempts to do this so far have failed to maintain any logical validity; and as I also show in Chapter 1 there, every scholar who has seriously examined the methodologies involved agrees with me on that.

4. For discussion of different kinds of 'myth-making' phenomena that quickly envelop historical characters in Christian tradition (whether they were ever real or not) see Bart Ehrman, *Peter, Paul, and Mary Magdalene: The Followers of Jesus in History and Legend* (New York: Oxford University Press, 2006); Rose Jeffries Peebles, *The Legend of Longinus in Ecclesiastical Tradition and in English Literature, and its Connection with the Grail* (Baltimore, MD: J.H. Furst Company, 1911); Thomas Hahn, 'Judas: The Medieval Oedipus', *Comparative Literature* 32 (Summer 1980), pp. 225-37; and Paul Franklin Baum, 'The Mediæval Legend of Judas Iscariot', *Proceedings of the Modern Language Association of America* 31 (1916), pp. 481-632; and Dennis MacDonald, 'A Conjectural Emendation of 1 Cor 15.31-32: Or the Case of the Misplaced Lion Fight', *Harvard Theological Review* 73 (January–April 1980), pp. 265-76.

2. *The Basic Problem*

The historicity of Jesus Christ is currently the default consensus. Several respectable books have defended the thesis against detractors.[5] But they all suffer from two fatal flaws: by soundly debunking weak versions of mythicism, they fallaciously conclude strong ones needn't even be examined; and they defend the historicity of Jesus by defending the historicity of particular claims about Jesus using the very methods I and others have proven to be logically invalid across the board.[6] By using invalid methods to establish their premises, they thereby arrive at an invalid conclusion, which they then use to invalidly reject alternative theories. This is not the way to defend the historicity of Jesus.

A greater gaffe in defense of Jesus' historicity is to make claims that are conspicuously *opposite* the truth of the matter, as when E.P. Sanders boasts that 'the sources for Jesus are better . . . than those that deal with Alexander [the Great]'.[7] A more suicidal remark for his case could hardly be imagined. Unlike Jesus, we have over half a dozen relatively objective historians discussing the history of Alexander the Great (most notably Diodorus, Dionysius, Rufus, Trogus, Plutarch and more). These are not romances or propagandists, least of all fanatical worshipers, or anyone concerned about dogma, but disinterested historical writers employing some of the recognized skills of critical analysis of their day on a wide body of sources they

5. Most importantly, R.T. France, *The Evidence for Jesus* (Downers Grove, IL: InterVarsity Press, 1986); and Gerd Theissen and Annette Merz, *The Historical Jesus: A Comprehensive Guide* (Minneapolis, MN: Fortress Press, 1996), in which pp. 90-118 tackle objections directly (but no more correctly than Van Voorst in *Jesus Outside the New Testament*: see my discussion of the latter in Chapter 1, §2). France's work has been somewhat updated in F.F. Bruce and E. Güting, *Ausserbiblische Zeugnisse über Jesus und das frühe Christentum: einschliesslich des apokryphen Judasevangeliums* (Basel: Brunnen Verlag, 2007). On Bart Ehrman's poor treatment of the subject in *Did Jesus Exist?*, and now Maurice Casey's, see note in Chapter 1 (§2).

6. See in particular Chapters 1 and 5 of *Proving History*; my conclusions are corroborated in Chris Keith and Anthony LeDonne (eds.), *Jesus, History and the Demise of Authenticity* (New York: T. & T. Clark, 2012); Dale Allison, 'The Historians' Jesus and the Church', in *Seeking the Identity of Jesus: A Pilgrimage* (ed. Beverly Roberts Gaventa and Richard Hays; Grand Rapids, MI: William B. Eerdmans, 2008), pp. 79-95; Hector Avalos, *The End of Biblical Studies* (Amherst, NY: Prometheus Books, 2007), pp. 185-217; Gerd Theissen and Dagmar Winter, *The Quest for the Plausible Jesus: The Question of Criteria* (Louisville, KY: John Knox Press, 2002); Stanley Porter, *The Criteria for Authenticity in Historical-Jesus Research: Previous Discussion and New Proposals* (Sheffield: Sheffield Academic Press, 2000); and so on.

7. E.P. Sanders, *The Historical Figure of Jesus* (London: Penguin Press, 1993), p. 3.

had available that we do not. Which doesn't mean we trust everything they say, but we still cannot name even *one* such person for Jesus, and 'none' is not 'more' than half a dozen.

Lest one complain that these historians wrote 'too late', this is actually of minor significance because, unlike Jesus, they still had contemporary and eyewitness sources to work from. In fact, our best historian of Alexander is Arrian, who though he wrote five hundred years later, nevertheless employed an explicit method of using only three eyewitness sources (two of them actual generals of Alexander who wrote accounts of their adventures with him). He names and identifies these sources, explains how he used them to generate a more reliable account, and discusses their relative merits. That alone is *quite a great deal more* than we have for Jesus, for whom we have not a single named eyewitness source in any of the accounts of him, much less a discussion of how those sources were used or what their relative merits were. Not even for the anonymous witness claimed to have been used by the authors of the Gospel of John, which claim isn't even credible to begin with (that source is almost certainly fabricated, as I'll show in Chapter 10, §7), but in any case we're not told who he was, why we should trust him or what all exactly derives from him.

And that's not all. We have mentions of Alexander the Great and details about him in *several contemporary or eyewitness sources still extant*, including the speeches of Isocrates and Demosthenes and Aeschines and Hyperides and Dinarchus, the poetry of Theocritus, the scientific works of Theophrastus and the plays of Menander. We have not a single contemporary mention of Jesus—apart from, at best, the letters of Paul, who never even knew him, and says next to nothing about him (as a historical man), or the dubious letters of certain alleged disciples (and I say alleged because apart from known forgeries, none ever say they were his *disciples*), and (again apart from those forgeries) none ever distinctly place Jesus in history (see Chapters 7 and 11). The eyewitness and contemporary attestation for Alexander is thus vastly better than we have for Jesus, not the other way around. And that's even if we count only extant texts—if we count extant *quotations* of lost texts in *other* extant texts, we have literally hundreds of quotations of contemporaries and eyewitnesses that survive in later works attesting to Alexander and his history. We have not even one such for Jesus (e.g. even Paul never once *quotes* anyone he identifies as an eyewitness or contemporary source for any of his information on Jesus).

And even that is not all. For Alexander we have contemporary inscriptions and coins, sculpture (originals or copies of originals done from life), as well as other archaeological verifications of historical claims about him. For example, we can verify the claim that Alexander attached Tyre to the mainland with rubble from Ushu—because that rubble is still there and dates to his time; the city of Alexandria named for him dates from his lifetime as expected; archaeology confirms Alexander invaded Bactria; etc. We also have archaeological confirmation of many of his battles and acts, including the exact time and day of his death—because contemporary records of these exist in the recovered clay tablet archives of Persian court astrologers. None of this is even remotely analogous to Jesus, for whom we have absolutely zero archaeological corroboration (e.g. none of the tombs alleged to be his have been verified as such), much less (as we have for Alexander) actual archaeological attestation (in the form of coins, inscriptions and statues—claims to the contrary are generally bogus, as I'll discuss in Chapter 7, §2).[8]

It's ridiculous to claim the source situation is *better* for Jesus than for Alexander the Great (or indeed any comparably famous person of antiquity). The exact *reverse* is the case, by many orders of magnitude. This is not the way to defend the historicity of Jesus.[9]

We still can't make the opposite inference from this, though, because obviously Alexander the Great was far more famous and influential in his lifetime than Jesus, even by the most grandiose reports in the Gospels—and their claims in that regard are surely hugely exaggerated as it is (they

8. On all these points see discussion and sources referenced throughout Krzysztof Nawotka, *Alexander the Great* (Newcastle upon Tyne: Cambridge Scholars, 2010); Waldemar Heckel and Lawrence Tritle, *Alexander the Great: A New History* (Malden, MA: Wiley-Blackwell, 2009); and Joseph Roisman (ed.), *Brill's Companion to Alexander the Great* (Leiden: Brill, 2003); with: Georges Le Rider, *Alexander the Great: Coinage, Finances, and Policy* (Philadelphia, PA: American Philosophical Society, 2007); Carmen Arnold-Biucchi, *Alexander's Coins and Alexander's Image* (Cambridge, MA: Harvard University Art Museums, 2006); Frank Holt, *Alexander the Great and Bactria: The Formation of a Greek Frontier in Central Asia* (Leiden: Brill, 1988); A.B. Bosworth, *From Arrian to Alexander: Studies in Historical Interpretation* (New York: Oxford University Press, 1988); and A.J. Heisserer, *Alexander the Great and the Greeks: The Epigraphic Evidence* (Norman, OK: University of Oklahoma Press, 1980). On the Babylonian archives: Bert VanderSpek, 'Darius III, Alexander the Great and Babylonian Scholarship', *Achaemenid History*, Vol. XIII (Leiden: Nederlands Instituut voor het Nabije Oosten, 2003), pp. 289-346; Bert VanderSpek, 'The Astronomical Diaries as a Source for Achaemenid and Seleucid History', *Bibliotheca Orientalis* 50 (1993), pp. 91-101; Leo Depuydt, 'The Time of Death of Alexander the Great: 11 June 323 BC, ca. 4:00-5:00 PM', *Die Welt des Orients* 28 (1997), pp. 117-35.

9. A similar argument, even more ridiculous, is that we have more evidence for Jesus than we have for Emperor Tiberius (who would have been Jesus' most famous contemporary). This is thoroughly refuted (fruitfully revealing the same points as I made for Alexander) by historian Matthew Ferguson in 'Ten Reasons to Reject the Apologetic 10/42 Source Slogan', *AdversusApologetica* (October 14, 2012) at http://adversusapologetica.wordpress.com/2012/10/14/ten-reasons-to-reject-the-apologetic-1042-source-slogan. That argument appears to have originated in Christian apologetics: see Gary Habermas and Mike Licona, *The Case for the Resurrection of Jesus* (Grand Rapids, MI: Kregel Publications, 2004), p. 233.

certainly must be, or else we have a problem, as I'll explain in Chapter 8). Thus, that we have vastly more evidence for Alexander in no way argues Jesus didn't exist. It only argues that Jesus was many orders of magnitude less significant in his contemporary historical impact. It entails he was a relative nobody. But plenty of relative nobodies nevertheless existed. And yet *that* point does not permit the inference that he *did* exist, either. Possibly is not probably.

Another wrong way to argue the case for a historical Jesus is to simply make things up. We find, for example, Bruce Chilton declaring, in a standard reference in the field no less, that 'Jesus is acknowledged as a figure of history' now more than ever due to 'the unearthing of new information' consisting of 'both literary documentation and archaeological evidence'. Yet not even a single item of that new evidence pertains to the historical Jesus—it consists solely of background evidence, such as the Dead Sea Scrolls, almost none of it mentioning or attesting to Jesus (or even, in fact, early Christianity), while the rest consists only of obviously late fictions about him (like the *Gospel of Judas*). So Chilton's remark is disingenuous at best, and deceitful at worst (as he does not tell his readers what I just did, thus leaving the uninformed reader to think we've discovered new sources mentioning or attesting to Jesus). That is certainly not the way to defend the historicity of Jesus.

Even worse, Chilton then invents an elaborate biography for Jesus involving miraculous knowledge of his private personal and intellectual development, and events and choices in his life, based on nothing but a naive acceptance of uncorroborated claims made in the Gospels, combined with gratuitous assumptions of what 'must' have been the case.[10] Thus he asserts as if it were a known fact that Jesus was 'marginalized' in Nazareth during his youth because he was an illegitimate child, that on childhood trips to Jerusalem Jesus emotionally experienced 'an excited sense of the vastness of the Israel he was a part of', that 'he ran away from his family' in a fit of religious passion, that after becoming a 'disciple' of John the Baptist 'he learned this master's *kabbalah*, the mystical practice of ascent to the divine Throne', which became 'a guiding force for the rest of his life', and sundry other speculations declared as facts, including: Jesus fled to Syria to avoid the clutches of Herod Antipas; Jesus seized the temple with a private army ('with a large crowd and in force'); and Jesus experienced a temptation 'in the wilderness' near 'Caesarea Philippi' at the end of his ministry in which he was tempted to raise an armed rebellion against Rome. This last is par-

10. Bruce Chilton, 'Historical Jesus', in *Dictionary of Biblical Criticism and Interpretation* (ed. Stanley Porter; New York: Routledge, 2007), pp. 159-62 (161). That this is an official entry on the topic of 'the historical Jesus' is a good example of what's wrong with Jesus studies today.

ticularly strange, as Chilton seems confused between the transfiguration, which in the Gospels takes place near Caesarea Philippi (and late in Jesus' ministry) but involved no temptation, and the Temptation, which in the Gospels takes place in a diametrically opposite time and place—and in neither case is there any mention of raising an armed rebellion against Rome.

This is almost the shoddiest method of doing history conceivable. Yet Chilton insists 'a historical picture of Jesus . . . involves the literary inference of what he must have taught and done to have generated that movement and its literature'. But such an 'inference' as he draws is not history. It's historical fiction. History concerns not what scholars subjectively think 'must' have happened, but what the evidence allows us all to claim actually *did* happen. It should not surprise historians that there are so many who are ready to doubt the historicity of Jesus, when they see a historical Jesus being defended as speciously as this, even by *bona fide* experts, in official reference books no less. This only makes the case for (or assumption of) historicity look *delusional*, not well established. So this is not the way to defend the historicity of Jesus either.

What's particularly damning about this example is that it's so myopically foolish. As Helmut Koester observes (ironically in a book edited by Bruce Chilton), 'the vast variety of interpretations of the historical Jesus that the current quest has proposed is bewildering', which ought to humble Chilton into seriously doubting his account can be correct, when every expert similarly situated is just as confident in a completely different account.[11] Indeed, the diversity and disagreement among *bona fide* experts on every detail of Chilton's 'reconstruction' of Jesus are broad and profound. *That* is what an entry on the 'historical Jesus' should say. It's shocking to see the same tendentious presumption, and substitution of speculation for fact, among historicists as historicists claim to find in mythicists. Historicists have a huge plank to remove from their own eye before they can complain of the splinter in anyone else's. They need to get their own house in order, and scold the likes of Chilton every bit as fervently as they scold mythicists who succumb to the same presumptions and fallacies. His entry should never have passed peer review—at least without requiring an explicit declaration that it's all tendentious speculation with which almost all scholars would substantially disagree.

Indeed, a common failure in the historicist community is a lack of a cautionary sense of irony. Among the many Jesuses imagined and defended by

11. Helmut Koester, 'The Historical Jesus and the Historical Situation of the Quest: An Epilogue', in *Studying the Historical Jesus: Evaluation of the State of Current Research* (ed. Bruce Chilton and Craig Evans; Leiden: Brill, 1994), pp. 535-45 (544). I summarize the diversity and disagreement Koester observes (and the scores of other experts who have observed exactly the same thing) in Chapter 1 of *Proving History*.

historians, currently the most popular is the view that Jesus was an apocalyptic prophet (a detail notably nowhere to be found in Chilton's account). But judging by the book of Daniel, Daniel was an apocalyptic prophet, too, yet we know that book is complete fiction. Thus, finding evidence that the character of Jesus depicted in the Gospels was an apocalyptic prophet is no more a guarantee of his historicity than it is of Daniel's. Which is to say, no guarantee at all. When we know many of Jesus' apocalyptic predictions were learned from (perhaps even faked) hallucinations of a bizarre and monstrous Jesus-double in heaven (written up as the book of Revelation), the idea that he 'must' have been historical in order to have issued apocalyptic prophecies simply goes out the window. He didn't even have to be historical to dictate whole letters (Rev. 1.10–3.22), or issue pithy sayings (Rev. 14.13; 19.9; and 21.5). So why are we to assume the Gospels are any more historical than the book of Daniel—which is substantially similar, being a collection of sayings and narratives, involving miracles and interactions with historical persons? Why are we to assume that the sayings attributed to Jesus in the Gospels didn't come from the very same origin as the sayings attributed to Jesus in the book of Revelation? Yes, we cannot presume they did. But neither can we simply presume they didn't. A case has to be made. And that case has to be logically valid and sound.

Ultimately, the basic problem is as stated by Rudolf Bultmann in 1941: 'the Jesus Christ who is God's Son, a preexistent divine being, is at the same time a certain historical person, Jesus of Nazareth', the teasing apart of which makes for a complicated task.[12] This is the basic problem of historicity: we have no source (none whatsoever) on the latter Jesus. We only have the former. From which we must 'extract' the latter by some device. Which has resulted in two general categories of theory: those that hold that the equation between them is true (Jesus of Nazareth really is the preexistent son of God), whose advocates I call the ***triumphalists***, and those that hold that this cosmic Jesus was a legendary development, from the mere man (Jesus of Nazareth) to the more fabulous myth (that the same Jesus is also the Preexistent son of God), whose advocates I call the ***reductivists***. Mythicists, of course, seek to explain the same fact (of the equation of these two persons) by reversing the order of causation, proposing there was a legendary development from the original myth (of a preexistent son of God) to the more earthly man (Jesus of Nazareth). But in either case, whether for the mythicist or the reductivist, the fundamental question is, 'How did that happen?'

How each reductivist answers that question is what becomes his or her theory of historicity. And as long as any such theory is true, mythicism is

12. Schubert Ogden (ed.), *New Testament and Mythology and Other Basic Writings by Rudolf Bultmann* (Philadelphia, PA: Fortress Press, 1984), p. 32.

false. Likewise, how each mythicist answers that question is what becomes his or her theory of myth. And as long as any such theory is true, *historicism* is false. So how do we test the one against the other?

3. *Hypothesis Formation and Prior Probability*

As we saw in Chilton's case, and can see in the case of any other scholar claiming to know things about the historical Jesus, many theories of historicity are too speculative, some even more so than theories of myth, and most are as much as or nearly so. That so many historians defend theories that 'could' be true, but for which not enough evidence survives to really know, exposes a serious methodological problem in the field, which I discussed and demonstrated in *Proving History.* There I (and other scholars I cite) find dozens of contradictory Jesuses proposed. They can't all be true. And that means odds are none are. That there are so many theories like this is a testament to how easy it is to construct a theory that looks seductively tantalizing and explains all the evidence. Which means the ease of constructing such a theory counts *against* any such theory being true, not in favor of it. Because the prior probability that any such theory is correct must necessarily be very small—until we can reliably eliminate all competing theories.

To quantify the point, if scholars of equal competence defend from the same exact evidence ten different Jesuses, the *initial* odds that any one of them is correct can be no better than 1 in 10 (and almost certainly worse than that, since it's entirely possible *none* of those Jesuses is correct). This is because a prior probability is the probability we must assign *before* looking at specific evidence for and against each theory. What happens when we do look at that evidence is accounted for in the consequent probabilities (the probability that we would have the evidence we do if that particular theory were true, in contrast to what that probability would be if some other theory were true). But before we do that, all we have are the competing proposals of roughly equally competent observers from the same body of evidence.

That means it's not wise to defend the historicity of Jesus by defending a *particular* theory of historicity. It makes far more sense to class together several (or hopefully all or nearly all) theories of historicity by claims they make in common. For example, if all ten contradictory theories of historicity all make the same claim (e.g. that a man named Jesus who was later called Christ was crucified under Pontius Pilate), then the prior probability of 'historicity' per se would not be 1 in 10 but nearly 100%—if, that is, the prior probability of mythicism, and other theories of historicity, were nearly zero. Because the full 100% (the full probability-space) must be apportioned among all logically possible theories. But that means even if the prior probability of myth were as high as, say, 25%, we would still have in this case a prior probability of historicity of 75% (because 100% – 25% = 75%), as long as we stick with that minimum historical claim about Jesus. Otherwise, for each of the ten competing theories of historicity, unless we can demonstrate otherwise, the prior probability of any one of them being true is *at best* a paltry 7.5% (1/10th of the full 75%), far *less* than the 25% prior probability for myth (though again, only in this hypothetical scenario). If we classed 3 of the 10 theories together (by, let's say, the claim that Jesus was an apocalyptic prophet) and insisted on defending only that, then (all else being equal) we'd still have a prior probability of only maybe 25% (1/3rd of the whole 75%), which leaves us with *equal* odds against myth. So it may be better to drop unnecessary claims like that (no matter how well evidenced they may be) and focus only on what all or most theories of historicity assert in common. Because that will stand the best chance of showing the inadequacy of mythicism (if such can be done).

But trade-offs may be necessary. A simpler theory will always have a higher prior probability, but will be less successful at explaining problematic evidence. To explain such evidence (to make that evidence highly probable on your theory) you often have to add elements to the theory. For example, as I discuss in *Proving History*, all the ancient accounts we have of how and why Jesus came to be crucified are historically unintelligible.[13] Thus, the hypothesis 'there was a man named Jesus, who was later called Christ, who was crucified under Pontius Pilate', does not make this evidence very probable at all. Such a fact, had it occurred, would sooner have produced much more intelligible accounts of the how and why of it. Indeed, it should have produced apologetic accounts of those facts in the very Epistles, yet nary a word on this is to be found there (as I'll show in Chapter 11). Thus, historicists need to 'dress up' their theory with a whole series of elaborations, 'assumptions' that serve to explain these oddities in the evidence, making them probable again. And these *are* assumptions—since such details are not present in the sources. Indeed, that's precisely the problem these assumptions are meant to solve. And as I discuss extensively in *Proving History*, this procedure of adding *ad hoc* assumptions to a theory is *not* illegitimate. It simply has to be accounted for correctly when combining and dividing probabilities.

There are two ways this procedure can go.[14] If you have no evidence whatsoever that an assumption you are adding is true (that is, *independently* of the oddity you are inventing it to explain), but also no evidence it's false, then you must halve the prior probability. I explain the mathematical reason for this in *Proving History*, but in short if there is no evidence for or

13. Carrier, *Proving History*, pp. 139-41.
14. Carrier, *Proving History*, pp. 80-81.

against a claim, then its probability is 50%, which means the probability-space shared by all theories, those *with* this assumption and those without it, is half occupied by theories with this assumption and half occupied with theories without it. So if our total prior were 75%, the prior probability of a theory *with* this added assumption being true can only be 37.5% (half of 75%). Which is unlikely to permit the new assumption to make any improvement in the final probability (and thus such assumptions are often not worth adding). On the other hand, if you have *evidence* that an assumption you are adding is true (again, *independently* of the oddity you are inventing it to explain), then you're in a better situation. For example, if given certain background evidence (such as regarding the way early Christians can be independently established to have behaved, or regarding the documented psychology of religious fanatics in general) an assumption is already highly probable, then *that* probability is substituted for the halving of probability just discussed.

For instance, if it can be independently proven that early Christians interpreted the Old Testament (OT) allegorically 90% of the time in a given context, then a theory that depends on their doing so in a specific case (assuming nothing in that case argues for or against this otherwise) will share 90% of the probability-space with theories that exclude this assumption—not 50%. Hence in the hypothetical scenario at hand, such a theory would have a prior probability of 67.5% (9/10ths of 75%). Or if this subordinate probability were as near to 100% as makes all odds (like the assumption that Christians were human beings essentially biologically the same as other human beings), then the prior probability would effectively just be the full 75%. Conversely, implausible fringe theories, which depend on assumptions that are extremely improbable to begin with, are of such low prior probability that they don't even show up in the math (also for reasons I explain in *Proving History*).

This is in effect the role that background knowledge plays in determining probabilities: things that are established as basically certain can safely be assumed without lowering your prior probabilities. Of course this works the other way around, too. If an assumption you propose is actually demonstrably *improbable*, then you actually lower your theory's prior probability by *less* than half. That's why implausible additions to a theory meant only to rescue that theory from failing to fit the evidence can never logically succeed at that—because they will always lower the prior probability more than they will increase the consequent probability, and thus they will actually *lower* the posterior probability (the actual probability that your theory is true), instead of raising it as such an addition was supposed to do. In other words, such desperate theories simply become increasingly improbable, and thus unbelievable.

Accordingly, all triumphalist theories can be shown to have vanishingly small prior probabilities. They also happen to do a poor job of explaining the evidence.[15] Hence, none are worth any objective historian's consideration. Perhaps such a hypothesis can still be rationally maintained on evidence *other* than the historical, but that is of no relevance to historians, who are tasked with determining only what the historical evidence supports. And that will be the only question asked here. That leaves reductivist and mythicist hypotheses.

In *Proving History* I demonstrated that we can parcel out the entire prior probability-space to just four classes of hypothesis altogether:

1. h = 'Jesus was a historical person mythicized'
2. $\neg h$ = 'Jesus was a mythical person historicized'
3. h_0 = 'Jesus was a historical person not mythicized' (triumphal)
4. $\neg h_0$ = 'Jesus was a mythical person not historicized' (postmodern)

As I argued there, the latter two classes of hypothesis, even collectively, consume a vanishingly small piece of the prior-probability-space (certainly less than a one in a million share).[16] They can therefore be ignored. That leaves us with bare historicism and bare mythicism. However, both must be more developed than this, not only to make our job easier by ruling out all implausible variations of them, but also to leave us with hypotheses that make more substantial predictions. This will give us in each case a minimal theory, one that does not entail any ambitious or questionable claims (thus keeping its prior probability relatively high), but still leaves us with a theory substantial enough to test (thus keeping its consequent probability relatively high as well).

The minimal Jesus myth theory I will develop in the next chapter. Here I will develop the minimal theory of historicity. It's important to take note of this step. For it must be made to avoid a common error on both sides of the debate, that of conflating plausible with implausible theories. In general we have those two theories of historicity, the reductive theory (Jesus was an ordinary but obscure guy who inspired a religious movement and copious legends about him) and the triumphalist theory (the Gospels are totally or almost totally true). Either side of the historicity debate will at times engage in a fallacy here, citing evidence supporting the reductive theory in defense of the triumphalist theory (as if that were valid), or citing the absurdity of the triumphalist theory as if this refuted the reductive theory (as if *that*

15. As I show, e.g., in Richard Carrier, 'Christianity's Success Was Not Incredible', in *The End of Christianity* (ed. John Loftus; Amherst, NY: Prometheus Books, 2011), pp. 53-74, 372-75.

16. Carrier, *Proving History*, pp. 204-205.

were valid). The same error occurs the other way around: citing evidence against a hyperbolic theory of myth as refuting a reasonable one, or *defending* a hyperbolic theory by citing evidence in support of a reasonable one. Both procedures are again invalid.

4. *The Minimal Theory of Historicity*

There were thousands of men named Jesus in Judea in any given generation, so obviously countless historical men of that name 'existed' in a trivial sense. It's even statistically certain that several men of that name were crucified by Romans, even by Pontius Pilate. It's also statistically likely that several men named Jesus participated in the early Christian movement. If 1 in 26 Jewish men of that time were named Jesus (as the data indicates is close to likely),[17] and a hundred men were crucified in Judea in any given year (a number that is arguably unreasonably low), we can be certain Pilate alone (governing ten years) crucified dozens of men named Jesus (unless, of course, crucifixion was actually rare). And if the first Christian congregation consisted of merely two dozen people, probably at least one of those original Christians was named Jesus. Indeed, if we were to believe Acts and accept there were at the cult's origin 120 followers of Jesus (Acts 1.15), we could be certain there were four or five Jesuses among them.

But none of these men would be Jesus Christ, the man whose existence we are trying to locate. Conversely, it's very easy to show that the man depicted in the Gospels didn't exist, not only because they each present quite different men of rather different characters (the Synoptic Jesus is simply nothing like the Johanine Jesus), but also because the Jesus of the Gospels doesn't behave like a real person at all, nor rarely do any of the people around him in the narrative, nor does much of what he does correspond to things that really happen (as if walking on water were to be believed; or that he could transmute water to wine, but never saw fit to transmute lead to gold for the benefit of the poor), oddities I'll take more note of in Chapter 10. But showing that the Gospel Jesus didn't exist does not show Jesus Christ didn't exist, because it could still be the case that the real Jesus Christ is the one who *inspired* these unrealistic narratives about him, and that some actual facts about him really are hidden in there somewhere (even if we can never find out which facts those are). We also can't pick some specific details (like that he employed himself as a faith healer and exorcist), then refute them, and then declare he didn't exist, because some Jesus Christ might still remain without those specific things being true of him.

17. Richard Bauckham, *Jesus and the Eyewitnesses: The Gospels as Eyewitness Testimony* (Grand Rapids, MI: William B. Eerdmans, 2006), p. 85.

For example, there are twelve 'facts' about the historical Jesus that are widely regarded as 'almost' indisputable:

> (1) Jesus was baptized by John the Baptist, (2) he was a Galilean who preached and healed, (3) he called disciples and spoke of twelve of them, (4) he confined his activity to Israel, (5) he engaged in a controversy about the Temple, (6) he was crucified outside Jerusalem by the Roman authorities, (7) his followers continued as an identifiable movement after his death, and (8) some Jews persecuted some members of this new movement . . . [and (9)] Jesus was probably viewed as a prophet by the populace, [10] he often spoke of the kingdom of God, [11] he criticized the ruling priests as part of his Temple controversy, and [12] he was crucified as 'king of the Jews' by the Romans.[18]

But this is not a minimal Jesus, since taking some of these facts away would not result in any scholar concluding that Jesus did not exist. Indeed, many scholars already conclude some of these *aren't* true facts about Jesus, yet they still maintain Jesus existed, just as a different kind of fellow than this portrait maintains. Indeed, apart from (7) and (8), which could be true even of a mythical Jesus, every single one of these elements has no support whatever *except* in the Gospels (and later Christian literature based on them)—and if the Gospels can't be trusted on any facts (and I'll show in Chapter 10 they can't), then they can't be trusted in these. We should doubt them all.

Indeed, in Chapter 5 of *Proving History* I demonstrated several of these 'indisputable' facts to be very doubtful indeed, and showed how the usual scholarly arguments in defense of all of them are logically invalid. They are all the more questionable given that many (if not all) of them should have been remarked upon in the (authentic) Epistles, but are bizarrely and entirely absent there. No mention is even made there of his having appointed disciples (a problem I'll explore in Chapter 11). At most we could perhaps get some indirect support for (though nothing like a proof of) item (10) from the Epistles (that Jesus spoke of the kingdom of God), but even that runs into the problem of where it came from—a real Jesus, or a hallucinated one (the problem of Revelation once again), or a fabricated one (like the book of Daniel). This is very much a problem, because the Epistles themselves (apart from those we know are forgeries) do not mention any source *but* revelation (and claims teased out of the Old Testament), if they ever mention any sources at all for any of the information they convey by or about Jesus (again as I'll show in Chapter 11).

That leaves only (7) and (8) as having any credible evidence behind them (both directly from the Epistles, and from the whole history of the cult generally), and yet (8) isn't really a fact about Jesus at all, and (7) can just

18. Porter, *Criteria for Authenticity*, p. 111 (esp. n. 28).

as well support a hallucinated celestial Jesus as a historical earthly one. From the Epistles we might be able to get back (6) and (10) only by reducing them to the much less ambitious 'he was crucified (most likely in Roman occupied Judea)' and 'he preached something controversial', both of which we might loosely infer from statements made in the Epistles. But even that would be a stretch, given the ambiguity of what is actually said there. At the very least, he was certainly said to have been killed by the powers that be and hung on a stake. By whom and when then wouldn't matter so much, nor would it matter whether it was actually he or some of his followers who preached whatever it was that inspired his subsequent deification.

But notice that now we don't even require what is considered essential in many church creeds. For instance, it is not necessary that Jesus was crucified under Pontius Pilate. Maybe he was. But even if we proved he wasn't, that *still* does not vindicate mythicism. Because the 'real' Jesus may have been executed by Herod Antipas (as the *Gospel of Peter* in fact claims), or by Roman authorities in an earlier or later decade than Pilate (as some early Christians really did think). Some scholars even argue for an earlier century (and they have some real evidence to cite). I'll say more about these possibilities in Chapter 8 (§1). My point at present is that even if we proved the founder of Christianity was executed by Herod *the Great* (not even by Romans, much less Pilate, and a whole forty years before the Gospels claim), as long as his name or nickname (whether assigned before or after his death) really was Jesus and his execution is the very thing spoken of as leading him to the status of the divine Christ venerated in the Epistles, I think it would be fair to say Jesus existed, that his historicity is established and the mythicists are then simply wrong. I would say this even if Jesus was never really executed but only believed to have been. Because even then it's still the same historical man being spoken of and worshiped.[19]

19. Thus we get no advantage from an even more ambitious list than Porter's, of 'fifteen minimal facts' developed earlier by E.P. Sanders, as summarized in Mark Strauss, *Four Portraits, One Jesus: An Introduction to Jesus and the Gospels* (Grand Rapids, MI: Zondervan, 2007), p. 372:

> (1) Jesus was born about 4 BC near the time of the death of Herod the Great; (2) he spent his childhood and early adult years in Nazareth, a Galilean village; (3) he was baptized by John the Baptist; (4) he called disciples; (5) he taught in the towns, villages, and countryside (but apparently not in the cities) of Galilee; (6) he preached 'the kingdom of God'; (7) about the year 30 he went to Jerusalem for Passover; (8) he created a disturbance in the temple area; (9) he had a final meal with the disciples; (10) he was arrested and interrogated by Jewish authorities, specifically the high priest; (11) he was executed on the orders of the Roman prefect, Pontius Pilate; (12) his disciples at first fled; (13) they saw him (in what sense is not certain) after his death; (14) as a consequence, they believed he would return to found the

This gets us down to just three minimal facts on which historicity rests:

1. An actual man at some point named Jesus acquired followers in life who continued as an identifiable movement after his death.
2. This is the same Jesus who was claimed by some of his followers to have been executed by the Jewish or Roman authorities.
3. This is the same Jesus some of whose followers soon began worshiping as a living god (or demigod).

That all three propositions are true shall be my minimal theory of historicity. As occasion warrants I might add features on to test the merits of more complex theories, but unless I explicitly say otherwise, the above is the theory I shall be testing against the minimal Jesus myth theory. Because if any one of those premises is false, it can fairly be said there was no historical Jesus in any pertinent sense. And at least one of them must be false for any Jesus myth theory to be true.

One thing that will become clear in the course of this book is that this minimal theory is unsustainable. Which means the only chance historicity

> kingdom; (15) they formed a community to await his return and sought to win others to faith in him as God's Messiah.

As with Porter's list, none of these facts are attested anywhere outside the Gospels and literature derivative thereof (and what is here added is even more dubious than what Porter included), except (6), which is Porter's (10), and (13) through (15), which expand on Porter's (7), but these are not facts about Jesus per se, but about his subsequent followers, which could be just as true of an ahistorical, mystically perceived Jesus, so their being true would not in itself support historicity. Strauss also mentions a smaller list (*Four Portraits*, pp. 356-57):

> [According to many scholars] what can be known about Jesus can be summarized in a few short statements: [1] he came from Nazareth; [2] he was baptized by John; [3] he preached and told parables about the coming of the kingdom of God; [4] he viewed this kingdom as coming in the near future and (perhaps) as already present in some sense; [5] he performed, or was believed to have performed, exorcisms and healings; [6] he gathered a group of Disciples around him; [7] he associated with outcasts and sinners; [8] he challenged the Jewish leaders of his day; [9] he was arrested and charged with blasphemy and sedition; and [10] he was crucified by the Romans.

Here again nothing is attested outside the Gospels and Gospel-dependent literature (as I explain in Chapter 8), except (3) and (4) insofar as this is just Porter's (10). And none of these is a *sine qua non* for a historical Jesus. Indeed for any one of them we can easily find scholars who doubt or deny it (and several certainly are not well founded: for instance, see my discussion of (1), (2) and (5) in Chapter 5 of *Proving History*).

will have of being more likely than a minimal mythicism is if a theory of historicity is developed that is sufficiently elaborate to overcome minimal mythicism in overall consequent probability. But as mentioned earlier, such elaboration necessarily lowers historicity's prior probability, indeed far below that of myth—unless such elaborations can be shown to be necessarily the case or very probably the case, independently of the evidence they are invented to explain.

Nothing like that has been done. Hence anyone who will wish to continue denying the claim that Jesus never really existed will have to advance the field of Jesus studies with a theory of historicity that not only somehow maintains a high enough prior probability to have any chance of being true, but also successfully explains all the evidence, including a lot of evidence that is not so easy to explain (surveyed in Chapters 8 through 11). If such a theory can be successfully developed, I welcome it. But until one is, as the second half of this volume will show, the historicity of Jesus does not appear to have the merit it is presumed to.

Before this can be demonstrated, however, I must define the minimal Jesus myth theory that presents any challenge to historicity. And to that we now turn.

3

The Hypothesis of Myth

1. *From Inanna to Christ*

There survives a strange early Christian text hardly anyone knows about called the *Ascension of Isaiah*. Like the book of Daniel, it is a forgery, purporting to derive somehow from the ancient prophet Isaiah, recounting his mystical ascent into the heavens, where he saw and learned in advance the secret things of the Christian gospel. The original version of this text doesn't survive. We have later redactions, complete with a kind of 'pocket' gospel tacked in. Though extant manuscripts date from the fifth to the twelfth century, all the evidence we have for this text and within it indicates it was originally composed sometime in the first or second century CE.[1] The earliest version in fact was probably composed around the very

1. The final redaction of this appears to unite two separate texts (the 'Martyrdom of Isaiah' and the actual 'Ascension of Isaiah'), the latter being the text of which I am speaking here, which consists of chaps. 6–11 of the united whole. For this I have excerpted and adapted the translation provided in Willis Barnstone, *The Other Bible* (San Francisco, CA: Harper Collins, 1984), pp. 517-31. For scholarly analysis see Jonathan Knight, *The Ascension of Isaiah* (Sheffield: Sheffield Academic Press, 1995), and *Disciples of the Beloved One: The Christology, Social Setting and Theological Context of the Ascension of Isaiah* (Sheffield: Sheffield Academic Press, 1996), with additional collation, translation and commentary in Corpus christianorum: series apocryphorum, 7 and 8 (1995). However, contrary to the assumptions of Knight, there is no way the 'Martyrdom' was originally a part of the 'Ascension': even though the former came to comprise chaps. 1–5 of the now-combined text, it ends with Isaiah's death and refers 'back' to the 'Ascension' tale as if it had been written before it (in *Ascension of Isaiah* 3); then suddenly a completely new story begins in chap. 6, with a new introduction, and no mention or awareness of the preceding material (much less that Isaiah had just died in the previous chapter). Knight's only arguments for unity are that the unified text is more elaborate (yet that could be from subsequent embellishment, exactly as happened to the epistles of Ignatius, or simply because the Latin translation was briefer) and he can explain why the 'pocket gospel' was deleted (in the Latin and Slavonic) by supposing an anti-Docetic motive (but he has no actual evidence of either that motive or that the material was deleted rather than added). The one argument is

same time as the earliest canonical Gospels were being written.[2] It thus includes some very early Christian belief, almost as early as anything in the New Testament.

In this text, Isaiah goes into a trance before all the king's court and says he was taken up into the heavens, where at each stage he sees and hears particular things, and the angel lifting him up tells him various secrets. I have here removed all the extraneous material (a lot of which is repetitive) and quote just the features of the story I want to draw attention to:

The Vision That Isaiah ben Amoz Saw

> [6.1] In the twentieth year of the reign of Hezekiah, king of Judah, Isaiah the son of Amoz came to Hezekiah. . . . [6.10] And there while Isaiah was speaking by the Holy Spirit in the hearing of all . . . he saw a vision. [6.13] And the angel who was sent to make him behold that vision came neither from the firmament, nor from the angels of glory of this world, but from the seventh heaven. . . . [6.15] And the vision which the holy Isaiah saw was not from this world but from the world which is hidden from the flesh. [6.16] And after Isaiah had seen this vision, he narrated it to Hezekiah, and to Josab his son and to the other prophets who had come, [7.1] . . . saying:
>
> [7.2] I saw a sublime angel . . . [7.3] and he took hold of me . . . [7.9] and we **ascended to the firmament**, I and he, and there I saw Sammael [*i.e., Satan*] and his hosts, and a great struggle was taking place there, and the angels of Satan were envious of one another. [7.10] And as it is above, so is it also on the earth, for the likeness of that which is in the

logically invalid, and the other is a speculation and not an argument—but it is also illogical: an anti-Docetist would have fixed the account, not deleted the whole thing, and in fact what the pocket gospel is replaced with in the manuscripts lacking it is even more Docetic than what was removed. All the other evidence is against Knight (see following notes, and even his own observations in *Disciples*, 68-69).

2. That the 'Ascension' text cannot date later than the early second century is evidenced by the fact that the text of the 'Martyrdom' assumes the legend of 'Nero's return' is still an imagined threat (in *Asc. Is*. 4, so that must have been written within decades of his death), and is unaware of any other emperor having persecuted Christians, two facts that place it nearer the same time as the book of Revelation (with which it has a lot else in common besides that: see Chapter 7, §3), and since the 'Martyrdom' refers back to the 'Ascension' (see previous note), the latter must have been written even earlier. See Knight, *Ascension*, pp. 9-10; *Disciples*, pp. 33-34 and 205-208; and F. Crawford Burkitt, *Jewish and Christian Apocalypses* (London: H. Milford, 1914), p. 46. Knight's argument that the 'Martyrdom' seems aware of the pocket gospel in the 'Ascension' (*Asc. Is*. 3.13-18 parallels 11.2-22) would at best only confirm that the interpolation of that pocket gospel occurred sometime in between (or was actually produced by the author of the 'Martyrdom').

firmament is also on the earth. . . . [7.13] And after this the angel brought me up above the firmament, into the first heaven. . . . [*and so on repetitively all the way to the sixth heaven, seeing ever more glorious beings at each level*] . . . [8.18] and all the angels [*in the sixth heaven*] cried out to the primal Father, and his Beloved the Christ, and the Holy Spirit, all with one voice. . . .

[8.25] And the angel who conducted me saw what I was thinking and said, 'If you rejoice already in this light of the sixth heaven, how much more will you rejoice when in the seventh heaven you see that light where God and his Beloved are . . . who in your world will be called 'Son'. [8.26] Not yet is he revealed, who **shall enter this corrupted world**, nor the garments, thrones, and crowns which are laid up for the righteous, those who believe in that Lord who **shall one day descend in your form**.'

[9.1] And he conveyed me into the air of the seventh heaven . . . [9.5] And the angel said unto me, 'He who gave permission for you to be here is your Lord, God, the Lord Christ, who will be called 'Jesus' on earth, but his name you cannot hear until you have ascended out of your body. . . . [9.12] And this Beloved will descend in the form in which you will soon see him descend—that is to say, in the last days, the Lord, who will be called Christ, will descend into the world. [9.13] . . . And after he has descended and **become like you** in appearance, **they** will **think** that he is **flesh** and **a man**. [9.14] And **the god of that world** will stretch forth his hand against the Son, and **they** will lay hands on him and crucify him on a tree, without knowing who he is. [9.15] So his descent, as you will see, is hidden from the heavens so that it remains unperceived who he is. [9.16] And when he has made spoil of the angel of death, he will arise on the third day and will remain in that world five hundred and forty-five days [*i.e., one and a half years*]. [9.17] And then many of the righteous will ascend with him.' . . .

[9.26] And then the angel said to me, 'Here are prepared heavenly garments that many from that world receive, if they believe in the words of that one who, as I have told you, shall be named, and if they observe those words and trust them, and **believe** in his cross'. . . .

[9.27] And I saw someone standing by, whose glory surpassed that of all . . . [9.29] and all the angels drew near and worshipped him and gave praise. . . . [9.31] Then the angel who conducted me said to me, 'Worship this one', and I did. [9.32] And the angel said unto me, 'This is the Lord of All Glory whom you have seen'. . . .

[10.7] And I heard the words of the Most High, the Father of my Lord, as he spoke to my Lord Christ who shall be called Jesus, [10.8] 'Go and descend through all the heavens, **descend to the firmament and to that world**, even to the angel in the realm of the dead, but to Hell you shall not go. [10.9] And you shall become like the form of all who are in the five heavens. [10.10] And with carefulness you shall **resemble the form of the angels of the firmament and the angels also who are in the realm of the dead**. [10.11] And none of **the angels of this world** shall know that you, along with me, are the Lord of the seven heavens and of their angels. [10.12] And they will not know that you are mine until **with the voice of Heaven** I have summoned **their** angels and their lights, and my mighty voice is made to resound to the sixth heaven, that you may judge and destroy the prince and his angels and the gods of this world, and the world which is ruled by them. [10.13] For they have denied me and said, "We are alone, and there is none beside us". [10.14] And afterwards **you will ascend from the angels of death to your place, and this time you will *not* be transformed** in each heaven, but in glory you will ascend and sit on My right hand. [10.15] And **the princes and powers of this world** will worship you.' . . .

[10.17] Then I saw that my Lord went forth from the seventh heaven to the sixth heaven [*the angel then tells Isaiah to watch how Jesus transforms as he descends*] . . . [10.19] And when the angels who are in the sixth heaven saw him they praised and extolled him, for he had not yet been transformed into the form of the angels there. . . . [10.20] But then I saw how he descended into the fifth heaven, and there took the appearance of the angels there, and they did *not* praise him, for his appearance was like theirs. . . . [*and likewise the fourth heaven; and the third heaven, where he now must also give a password to the doorkeepers to enter through the gate of that heaven; and likewise the second heaven; and then the first*] . . . [10.29] And then he descended **into the firmament where the prince of this world dwells**, and he gave the password . . . and **his form was like theirs**, and they did not praise him there, but struggled with one another in envy, for there the power of evil rules, and the envying of trivial things. [10.30] And I beheld, when **he descended to the angels of the air** and **he was like one of them**. [10.31] Then he gave no password, for they were plundering and doing violence to one another.

[11.1] After this, I beheld, and the angel who talked with me and conducted me said unto me, 'Understand, Isaiah, son of Amoz, because for this purpose have I been sent from God'. . . .

At this point several paragraphs have been inserted summarizing a lost non-canonical Gospel bearing some similarities with the New Testament Gospels, with a birth to Joseph and a virgin Mary, and a great deal else. That 'pocket gospel' is overly elaborate and completely unlike the rest of the text, either in style or content (e.g. evincing an oddly sudden zeal for specific details), and it does not correspond at all to what (in chaps. 9 and 10) Isaiah was told he would later see (in chaps. 10 and 11). This pocket gospel is also missing from several manuscripts—in fact, it is missing from all manuscripts that lack chaps. 1–5 as well, thus signifying an earlier state of the text.[3] With that pocket gospel removed, the text continues:

3. Both Latin (L2) and Slavonic (S) manuscripts not only omit the 'Martyrdom' (and thus only know of a text of *Asc, Is.* that begins at chap. 6) but also omit 11.3-22, the whole pocket gospel (see Corpus christianorum: series apocryphorum, 7 [*Ascensio*

> [11.23] And then I saw him and **he was in the firmament** but he had not changed to their form, and all the angels of the firmament and Satan saw him, and they worshipped him. [11.24] And great sorrow was occasioned there, while they said, 'How did our Lord descend in our midst, and we perceived not the glory which was upon him?' . . . [*And this Lord continues ascending thus through the first five heavens, and then the sixth*] [11.32] And I saw how he ascended into the seventh heaven, and all the righteous and all the angels praised Him. And then I saw how he sat down on the right hand of God. . . . [11.37] Both the end of this world [11.38] and all of this vision will be consummated in the last generations.
>
> [11.39] And then Isaiah made him swear that he would not tell this to the people of Israel, nor permit any man to write down these words. [11.40] 'As far as you understand from the king what is said in the prophets, so far shall you read and that's all'.

That Isaiah refused to allow this prophecy to be written down begs the question of how the reader is supposed to have come upon a text of it. But I'll set that aside.

Key to understanding this text is the evidence that it's been tampered with. Even apart from the manuscript evidence confirming this, the text itself confirms it. In the first part we're told that high above in the firmament of this world there are copies of all the things on earth, and there the 'rulers of this world' fight over who will control the earth below. As I'll demonstrate in Chapter 5 (Elements 34-38) this was a popular belief, and one accepted by Paul and the author of the anonymous Epistle to the Hebrews, both in the New Testament. And with this in mind God commands his Son (here a preexistent divine being called Lord Christ, and soon to be dubbed Lord Jesus Christ) to descend 'to the firmament and to that world, even to the angel in the realm of the dead' (10.8) and to take 'the form of the angels of the firmament and the angels also who are in the realm of the dead' (10.10) so 'none of the angels of this world shall know' who he is (10.11), and thus (Isaiah's guiding angel explains) 'they will think that he is flesh and a man' (9.13, a line not present in all versions, see below), in a 'form' like Isaiah's (8.26, likewise not present in all versions), and then 'the god of that world will stretch forth his hand against the Son, and they will lay hands on him and crucify him on a tree, without knowing who he is' (9.14). And then 'he will arise on the third day and will remain in that world' for one and a half years (9.16)—thus fulfilling the predictions of Daniel (see Chapter 4, Element 7), although in no way conforming to any account in the New Testament (even in Acts 1.3 Jesus sticks around after his resur-

Isaiae], pp. 231 and 315), replacing it with a new version of 11.2 (which I will discuss shortly).

rection barely more than a month).[4] Indeed, that Jesus hung around after his resurrection for a whole year and a half would have sounded patently absurd even then, begging the question: what is really being said here?

Notice that up to this point in the story nothing is ever said about Jesus visiting earth or being killed by Jews or Romans—or conducting a ministry for that matter (of any sort at all).[5] The 'they' who will think he is a man and not know who he is and kill him are only ever said to be Satan and his angels. No other subject is mentioned for that pronoun, nor is any other implied. God clearly intends Jesus to do nothing more than go to the firmament, and for no other reason than to be killed by Satan and his sky demons, then rise from the dead and conduct affairs there for over a year (doing what, it's not said), and then ascend to heaven. In other words, instead of conducting a ministry on earth, Jesus is commanded to go straight to the firmament and die, and rise from the dead, and then remain where he had died for a year and a half (9.16; cf. 10.12-14; although the duration is omitted from some versions), and then ascend to the heavens. The 'tree' on which he is crucified (9.14) is thus implied to be one of the 'copies' of trees that we're told are in the firmament (7.10).[6] Certainly no mention is made here of this happening in or anywhere near Jerusalem.

Likewise, it's only said 'none of the angels of this world shall know' who he is (10.11), not 'none of the Jews' or 'none of the authorities in Israel' or any such thing (which is essentially just what Paul himself says in 1 Cor. 2.6-10). The text also does not identify any further stage of descending from the firmament to earth before entering the realm of the dead (not even in chap. 11—the redactors made no effort to connect their later insertion of a completely out-of-place 'gospel' narrative to the sequential 'descent-by-stages' storyline of the previous chapters). In 10.30 it's implied Jesus descends to a lower part of the firmament (where he finds he needs no password to get in), but he is still then among 'the angels of the air'. He goes no further. Back in 10.8 it was said he shall descend 'even to the angel in the realm of the dead' (though specifically *not* to Hell), but as we'll see in Chapter 5 (e.g. in Plutarch's account in *On the Face That Appears in the Orb of the Moon*), many theologians of this period regarded the 'realm of

4. Irenaeus, *Against All Heresies* 1.3.2 reports that Christians who claimed the Gospels were allegories for celestial events also claimed Jesus continued speaking to his disciples for a year-and-a-half after his resurrection, which must mean that Jesus continued appearing in revelations for that span of time.

5. My perspective on this document has been inspired by the analysis in Earl Doherty, *Jesus: Neither God nor Man (The Case for a Mythical Jesus)* (Ottawa: Age of Reason, 2009), pp. 119-26, which is well worth reading, even if I don't always concur with it.

6. Although to be more precise it is the things on earth that are the 'copies' of their 'truer' versions in the heavens (Element 38).

the dead' to be up in the sky, not in an underworld (see Chapter 5: Element 37), and there is no indication here that anything else was meant.

In fact, of his killers God specifically says, '*they* will not know that you are mine until *with the voice of Heaven* I have summoned *their* angels and their lights, and my mighty voice is made to resound to the sixth heaven' (10.12), in other words the truth will be revealed to Christ's murderers by God's resounding voice that will be heard across all the seven levels of heaven, which of course is not what happens in the New Testament Gospels (no divine voice is heard across the world revealing Jesus's true identity, least of all to those who killed him), yet here 'they' become aware of who he is almost right away (11.23). What can only be meant here are the demons and demon princes who kill him in the firmament (as 11.23 says), since they are the only ones who can be expected to hear this voice, along with 'their angels and lights', their subordinates (since men don't have 'angels and lights' under them to summon). Nor did the killers of Jesus ever 'know' Jesus was a divine being, yet here we are told they did: once God told them. This cannot mean the Jews and Romans. It can only mean Satan and his angelic princes. Therefore, 10.12 clearly says *those* are his killers, not the humans interpolated into the story in chap. 11. At any rate, before the final chapter, no one else but these demons is ever mentioned as being at all involved in this event, and no mention is ever made of Jesus going anywhere else but to the firmament to die.

Only in the final chapter is the story suddenly changed and elaborated with all manner of details that are never even a component of God's original orders (as described in chap. 10), nor in the angel's account of God's plan to Isaiah (in chap. 9), nor even plausibly concordant with them—both in terms of plot *and* literary style, 11.2-22 clearly do not derive from the same author as the rest of chaps. 6 through 11 (as many experts conclude). That this is confirmed in manuscript evidence only makes it all the more conclusive. This eleventh chapter thus appears to have been redacted to 'include' a complete earthly 'gospel' story, as if it were what was being referred to in chaps. 9 and 10, when that hardly makes sense—the two accounts don't fit each other at all.

In line with this, two other key phrases also appear to have been interpolated: 'they will think that he is flesh and a man' (9.13) and he shall 'descend in your form' (8.26) are both missing from the Latin version. Although the Latin text is frequently abbreviated, that is unlikely to explain the coincidental omission of these specific phrases, the *only* statements outside the pocket gospel that refer to Jesus becoming like a man. Nevertheless, those statements would still be compatible with a celestial event (as human sorcerers could fly into the air and be met with there, and earliest Christian belief certainly held that Jesus had assumed the form of a man), so we needn't rule them out.

But if we conclude that the original text of the *Ascension of Isaiah* did not include most of the material currently found in chap. 11, but that the original text ended instead in a manner consistent with what is said in chaps. 9 and 10 (and indeed the repetitive nature of the text up to that point entails we should expect the conclusion to conform closely and repetitively to what chaps. 9 and 10 say will happen), then we should first look to the manuscripts that omit this pocket gospel to see if there are any clues to what originally was there. This is what we see (translating from the Latin text):

> [11.1] After this, the angel said to me, 'Understand, Isaiah, son of Amoz, because for this purpose have I been sent from God, that everything be revealed to you. For before you no one ever saw, nor after you will anyone be able to see, what you have seen and heard'. [11.2] **And I saw one like a son of man, dwelling among men, and in the world, and they did not know him.** [11.23] And I saw him **ascend into the firmament** but he did not change himself into another form, and all **the angels above the firmament** saw him, and they worshipped him.

This new version of 11.2 describes a kind of earthly sojourn, but in an absurdly brief fashion. This actually looks like a rewrite of the Jewish scripture of Bar. 3.38, where God himself was 'seen on earth and conversed with men', which would sooner suggest a revelatory experience was going to be described. Hence it's notable how this *Ascension* text transforms Baruch: it does not have Jesus *converse* with men or *seen* by men, but has him only *among* men yet *completely unknown to them. Ascension Isaiah* 11.2 also rewrites Dan. 7.13, saying that what Isaiah saw was 'one like a son of man', the one who in Daniel appears among the clouds and will receive an eternal kingdom over the whole universe (Dan. 7.14).

But there is still something missing—and it's not the gospel that was later inserted. I suspect this version of 11.2 is closer to the original, but that it was followed by a more detailed explanation of what this meant and what happened (all as anticipated in chaps. 9 and 10). That is now missing. Instead, in this version of the text, Jesus descends to the firmament (10.29), then to the lower air (10.30), and then is suddenly in 'the world among men' (11.2), where he at last takes the form of a man, but no one knows him there. He then suddenly rises into the firmament in 11.23, in his original form, and is only *then* seen—by angels. Notably missing is what happened in between. Where is his execution, for example? Something has been removed. Not only are we missing the original story (of Satan and his angels killing him, as we're told to expect in 9.14), but we also expect to hear an account of 'God's resounding voice' across the heavens, since Isaiah had heard he would see that, too (10.12), likewise an account of 'many of the righteous' ascending with Jesus (9.17; or in the Latin, being sent by Jesus) and Jesus hanging around for over a year (9.16, although this detail seems to have been abbreviated out of the Latin). Notably, *none of these things are in the pocket gospel that was later inserted either.* So that clearly was not what was removed from the original.[7] What had to have been in the original is the *original* gospel foretold in chaps. 9 and 10. But that is not what is in any manuscript of the *Ascension of Isaiah* in chaps. 10 and 11 now. Whatever was originally in the text at this point is lost to history (though possibly not entirely: see Chapter 8, §6).

Further evidence lies in the fact that in this version of the text (which is the same in the Latin and in the Slavonic), it is the angels 'above' the firmament who first see Jesus in 11.23-24, with no mention of the angels in the firmament—whereas all other manuscripts have Satan and his angels see him in the firmament (as we should expect). That has to be a mistranslation, since 'above the firmament' defines the 'first heaven', yet even in this text the angels in the first heaven will worship him in 11.25-26, so the text as written is confusing two different orders of angels. This also does not correspond to what God says Isaiah will see (in 10.11-15 and 10.29-31). And of course it makes no sense to skip over Satan and his angels at this point, as if suddenly they didn't exist (when we're told in 10.11 to expect a description of *their* surprise at this point).

It would appear the redactor who produced this version of the text was trying to erase an account of Satan's reaction, and likewise that of the warring angels of the air and the firmament. He has likewise removed the account of God's celestial voice summoning the stars, and what Jesus did in the year and a half (or whatever period) *before* he ascended and was recognized (as we were told to expect in 10.12-15). Also deleted is any mention of the men Jesus was supposed to bring with him (9.17; or in the Latin, his 'sending' of 'heralds' throughout the earth). Undeniably, a lot has been removed—probably because it could not be gelled with the historicizing account embraced by later Christians who were preserving this text. A Jesus who is killed by Satan in the sky and then only appears to men in revelations (as the citation of Bar. 3.38 implies was going to happen) had to be erased. One redactor just deleted it and tinkered a little with the then-adjoining verses (the text that appears in the Latin and the Slavonic), while another just replaced it with a more desirable and orthodox gospel (which is the text that appears everywhere else).

Given widespread evidence of Christian fabricating and tampering with texts, this should not be surprising (see Chapter 4, Element 44; and Chapter 7, §7). But even if we imagine that the prior probability of *either* version of the eleventh chapter of the *Ascension of Isaiah* being authentic is as low as one in a thousand (an *a fortiori* rate of interpolation in Christian texts: see note in Chapter 11, §8), the evidence is so overwhelmingly improbable

7. Even Knight agrees something from 'the lost Greek original' is missing from all extant manuscripts at this point (*Disciples*, p. 69).

on the assumption of authenticity (a million to one at best) that we can be certain what we have in that chapter now is not what was in the original. The original text cannot have been either (a) the elaborate pocket gospel, which fails to correspond with the preceding material in too many ways to be even remotely likely, or (b) the version that lacks that (but has in its place a completely different 11.2 and a revised 11.23), which not only flubs the sequence of events (by deleting Jesus' expected glorious appearance to the angels of the firmament), and is implausibly brief (given the verbosity of the rest of the text), but also fails to contain any of the events that previous chapters told us would be recounted here.[8]

Whether you share that conclusion or not, what is undeniable is that this text provides all the elements of a plausible *theory*: the narrative goes out of its way to explain that the firmament contains copies of everything on earth (which implies this fact is relevant to the subsequent narrative somehow, just as we shall see the same remark is in Hebrews: see Chapter 11, §5); it indisputably places Satan and his demons, the only 'princes and authorities and rulers and powers' of which it speaks, in outer space (yet still 'in this world', distinctly below the first heaven, and thus in the recognized realm of flesh and corruption: see Element 35); and for two whole chapters it belabors *exclusively* and at length the role and actions of these (and only these) 'powers' in the crucifixion of Jesus on an unidentified 'tree'. If we didn't have Chapter 11 (and certainly if this were also the only document describing Christian belief), we would conclude nothing else but that this Jesus Christ was being described as a preexistent divine being descending below the moon to be killed by sky demons in outer space. Because it then says nothing else.

We have even more reason than that to be suspicious here. For the initial story told of Jesus in the *Ascension of Isaiah* sounds a lot like a story of another descending-and-ascending, dying-and-rising god, originating over a thousand years before the Christian era. In the *Descent of Inanna,* we are given a similarly repetitious account of a goddess (Inanna, variously otherwise known as Ishtar or Astarte), the very 'Queen of Heaven' (and daughter of God), who descends 'from the great above'. Thus 'abandoning

8. The defects of the inserted gospel are even greater than the defects of the version that fails to mention what we expect (and which not only fails to explain what happens after 11.2 but flubs 11.23), and thus the one is even less probable on a theory of authenticity than the other. Yet in either case the likelihood of having the text in the given state we have, if what we have is an unaltered text, is in my opinion no better than a million to one against. With a prior probability of a thousand to one the other way, that gets us odds of a thousand to one *in favor* of my conclusion—that the text in both traditions is missing what it originally contained. Using the odds form of Bayes's Theorem (see Chapter 12, §1): $P(\text{MISSING}|e)/P(\neg\text{MISSING}|e) = 1/1000 \times 1{,}000{,}000/1 = 1000/1$.

heaven' she descends from outer space all the way past earth into the realm of the dead below it, fully intending to be killed there and then resurrected three days later. Just like in the *Ascension of Isaiah*, the narrative relates her plans in advance to ensure this, and then relates how it happens exactly to plan. And like the 'Jesus' figure in the the *Ascension of Isaiah*, Inanna is crucified (nailed up), and notably not on earth, but in a non-earthly realm (the sub-world, in accordance with Sumerian lore of the time), and not by people, but by demons—and their godly overlords, who happen to be the gods of death, yet another coincidence with the *Ascension* (and like the narrative that ends up in the Gospels, Inanna is *also* humiliated and condemned to death in a kind of kangaroo court). Most importantly, just as Jesus must descend through seven levels of heaven, shedding layers of his glory at each stage and thereby humbling his appearance (which the *Ascension of Isaiah* repeatedly equates with garments), so Inanna descends through seven levels of the underworld, shedding layers of her regalia at each stage and thereby being humbled in her appearance—until at last she is naked (the most mortal and vulnerable state of all), and that's when she is killed.

This is an extremely unlikely coincidence, particularly given the highly repetitious nature of both texts. It cannot be believed that the author of the *Ascension* just 'by coincidence' ended up telling almost the very same story, right down to its characteristic repetitions, seven-stage descent and disrobing, crucifixion by demons, and resurrection. Inanna, like Jesus, was also God's child, and like the *Ascension*, in the *Descent* her plans are explained before being described. There are many differences in these two tales, certainly. For instance Inanna escapes the realm of the dead by trading places with her (apparently haughty) husband, Tammuz, who is dragged into hell by its demons. But the skeletal structure of the story in the *Ascension* clearly derives from this pre-Christian religion—whether by circuitous route or not. We know the Jews were long familiar with this sacred story of Inanna's descent. Jeremiah 7.18 and 44.15-26 complain of the prevalence of Inanna-cult among Palestinian Jews, even in the heart of Jerusalem itself, and Ezek. 8.14 explicitly mentions women in Jerusalem weeping for the fate of Tammuz (which would be his dragging into hell at the behest of the resurrected Inanna), which ceremony is also known to have preceded a rejoicing at his *own* resurrection.[9] Clearly the tale has

9. That Tammuz himself was also believed to have been resurrected is attested by Origen, *Selecta in Ezechielem*, in J.-P. Migne, Patrologiae cursus completus: series graeca 13.800; see also *Apostolic Constitutions* 5.12 and further discussion and sources in Carrier, *Not the Impossible Faith*, pp. 17-18 (with n. 1, p. 45). Possibly this cult of Inanna and Tammuz was an early form of the seasonal exchange of dying-and-rising known for other pairs of gods, such as Castor and Pollux. See Element 31 in Chapter 5.

instead been co-opted and 'improved' by folding into it particularly Jewish and more 'modern' religious notions. For instance, Jesus acts at the behest of the God Most High to ultimately overthrow Satan, and the descent is accomplished through levels of Heaven rather than levels of Hell. But that the story was changed to suit new and different sensibilities and purposes is precisely how religious syncretism works.

Insufficient evidence survives to ascertain whether this is the route from which Christianity *itself* derived, but with this text the evidence is undeniable that Christianity had merged its own myth with this pre-Christian dying-and-rising god concept very early and very thoroughly. Because the *Ascension of Isaiah* itself is unmistakably influenced by, and in outline derived from, the Inanna descent myth, whether directly or indirectly. And yet that myth already contains two elements supposedly distinctive of Jesus Christ as a dying-and-rising god: the humiliation, trial and crucifixion of the worshiped divinity, and the resurrection in three days. And this is definitely what happens in their respective stories. After she is stripped naked and judgment is pronounced against her, Inanna is 'turned into a corpse' and 'the corpse was hung from a nail' and 'after three days and three nights' her assistants ask for her corpse and resurrect her, and 'Inanna arose' according to her plan, because she knew her father 'will surely bring me back to life', exactly as transpires.[10] Indeed, there is a third parallel. Inanna's resurrection is secured by a ritual involving the divine 'food of life' and the divine 'water of life'. The Eucharist is only a few steps away. If all those elements are removed from Christianity, it's hard to think what could possibly remain that makes Jesus' historicity at all likely. If the Jesus of the Gospels *wasn't* humiliated, tried and crucified, if he *didn't* originate the Eucharist (which is just another resurrection-securing ritual of food and drink), then the depth of mythmaking that very rapidly surrounded him is truly extreme—and if it can be that extreme, why would we balk at the idea that the rest is myth, too?

In one of the earliest Christian texts we have, the apostle Paul says God's plan of Christ's death-defeating sacrifice was a 'secret' kept 'hidden' (1 Cor. 2.7) and only recently known by 'revelation' (1 Cor. 2.10), such that 'none of the rulers of this world knew; for had they known it, they would not have crucified the Lord of Glory' (1 Cor. 2.8). This looks like a direct paraphrase of an early version of the *Ascension of Isaiah*, wherein Jesus is

10. Translation and background: Samuel Noah Kramer, *History Begins at Sumer: Thirty-Nine Firsts in Man's Recorded History* (Philadelphia, PA: University of Pennsylvania Press, 3rd rev. edn, 1981), pp. 154-67 (quoted excerpts from p. 162, lines 1-3; p. 160, line 3; and p. 163, lines 10-12 and 15-22). See also Pirjo Lapinkivi, *The Neo-Assyrian Myth of Ištar's Descent and Resurrection* (Helsinki: Neo-Assyrian Text Corpus Project, 2010).

also the 'Lord of Glory', his descent and divine plan is also 'hidden' and the 'rulers of this world' are indeed the ones who crucify him, in ignorance of that hidden plan (see the *Ascension of Isaiah* 9.15; 9.32; 10.12, 15). It even has an angel predict his resurrection on the third day (9.16), and the Latin/ Slavonic contains a verse (in 11.34) that Paul actually cites as scripture, in the very same place (1 Cor. 2.9).[11]

So is Paul here referring to the demonic execution of Jesus in outer space? That would certainly explain why he would say this cannot have been seen by anyone, but is known only by revelation (1 Cor. 2.9-10; cf. Rom. 16.25-26). That this makes particular sense—in fact, more sense than what's usually assumed—is what I shall argue in Chapter 11. Here my aim is not to argue that this theory is true, but to explain what this theory is.

2. *The Basic Problem*

There is a large array of books and scholars who have advanced various Jesus myth theories over the last two centuries. A historicist might complain that there are too many different theories advanced, but that would only be the pot calling the kettle black. As discussed in the previous chapter (and in Chapter 1 of *Proving History*), there are 'too many different theories' of historicity as well, and if those are taken seriously, the fact that mythicism finds the same diversity of disagreement can be no objection to it any more than it would be a valid objection to historicity. We must agree that most theories of historicity are false (since only one of the hundreds defended can actually be correct), yet historicity might still be true. So, too, mythicism.

I won't explore the many flawed or ridiculous Jesus myth theories that have gone around or still circulate. I will only mention here the most credible defenses of mythicism, ranked in order of the extent to which they hold to the 'rules' and 'axioms' I summarized in Chapter 2 of *Proving History*. At the top of that list is Earl Doherty's *The Jesus Puzzle: Did Christianity Begin with a Mythical Christ?* and *Jesus: Neither God nor Man (The Case for a Mythical Jesus)*, complete with an extensive Website in support of both (jesuspuzzle.humanists.net). I recommend a reader start with the

11. This same scriptural quotation (verbatim or nearly) appeared in other apocalypses as well, yet (as in the *Asc. Is.*) not as a citation of scripture but simply what an angel says (see Corpus christianorum: series apocryphorum 8 [*Ascensio Isaiae*], pp. 590-92). Paul thus is not only using a lost Apocalypse for his information about Jesus in 1 Corinthians 2 (and thus for his crucifixion), but he assumes his fellow Christians are intimately familiar with that Apocalypse as well, and revered it as scripture (see Element 9 in Chapter 4). We can rightly wonder what relationship that Apocalypse had to the *Ascension of Isaiah*. May it have been an earlier redaction of it?

first of these, and treat the other as an appendix to it. Meanwhile the most prestigious support for myth, coming from renowned doctors of biblical studies, are Thomas Thompson's *The Messiah Myth: The Near Eastern Roots of Jesus and David,* and Thomas Brodie's *Beyond the Quest for the Historical Jesus: A Memoir of a Discovery.* Whether some very insignificant Jesus might still lay at the origin of Christianity is a question Thompson considers unanswerable, but he still argues that the Gospels are fiction top to bottom, leaving nothing left that we can consider a 'historical' Jesus. Arthur Droge, professor of early Christianity at the University of California, San Diego, and Kurt Noll, associate professor of religion at Brandon University, agree with that agnostic assessment.[12] Brodie only takes this to its natural conclusion, that originally there was no Jesus at all. So Doherty is not alone.

Another PhD in the field making the case is Robert Price, with a whole series of books on the matter, from *Deconstructing Jesus* and *The Incredible Shrinking Son of Man* to *Jesus Is Dead* and *The Case against the Case for Christ*, and most recently (and most valuably) *The Christ-Myth Theory and its Problems*. Price's efforts have been more controversial and are often more debatable, but nevertheless much of what he says has enough merit to at least consider, even if you reject it in the end. Among the controversies he has created is his tendency to advance and defend multiple contradictory accounts of the evidence, although that's in many ways more honest than what historicists do, since Price fully acknowledges the evidence is insufficient to confirm only one theory, and therefore many compete for viability. And in effect this is what historicists tacitly assume in accepting, even if themselves rejecting, the many contradictory theories of their colleagues without scandal.

Before this new vanguard of scholars arose, the most famous recent defender of the Jesus myth was George Wells, with over half a dozen books spanning forty years, from *Did Jesus Exist?* in 1975 to *Cutting Jesus Down to Size* in 2009. His approach has evolved into essentially the position of Thompson, that there may yet be a historical Jesus behind it all but there simply isn't sufficient evidence to know, as everything claiming to be about him is fiction. I place Wells near the bottom of my list of worthies because his competence in ancient history is not overly strong, and thus, although he has a lot of sound points to make, some of his premises and conclusions become untenable in light of background facts unknown to him. Before

12. A.J. Droge, 'Jesus and Ned Lud[d]: What's in a Name?', *CAESAR: A Journal for the Critical Study of Religion and Human Values* 3 (2009), pp. 23-25; Kurt Noll, 'Investigating Earliest Christianity without Jesus', in *'Is This Not the Carpenter?' The Question of the Historicity of the Figure of Jesus* (ed. Thomas Thompson and Thomas Verenna; Sheffield: Equinox 2012), pp. 233-66.

Wells, the very best *outdated* defense of the Jesus myth concept is Arthur Drews's *The Christ Myth*, published in 1910, which despite its flaws still has many sound points to make that are as true today as they were then. I could name other advocates now and in the past who may have worthwhile things to say in the matter, but as they often fall below acceptable bars of reliability or scholarly qualifications they cannot contribute as much toward changing the scholarly consensus at this point.

As with the historicists, I do not believe any one of the scholars I've named is 'right', but that the truth lies somewhere among them all. Just as one would not read, say, Robert Eisenman's *James the Brother of Jesus: The Key to Unlocking the Secrets of Early Christianity and the Dead Sea Scrolls* and conclude 'this is erudite and interesting, but complete bollocks, therefore Jesus didn't exist', so one should not read any particular mythicist and likewise conclude 'this is erudite and interesting, but complete bollocks, therefore Jesus *did* exist'. We all accept that every historicist is probably wrong about something, possibly quite a lot of things (they must be—as they all disagree), but we do not then conclude *historicity* is bunk. We conclude the truth lies somewhere among them all. We should approach mythicism the same way.

Historicists will usually agree that once we trim away everything that's wrong or too speculative or inadequately demonstrated, we'll have *something* that can be reliably affirmed about the historical Jesus (even if it's literally nothing more than that he existed). And if this is how we behave in reaction to the contradictions and errors among historicists (and we must—as otherwise only a complete agnosticism about the historical Jesus would logically remain), we are obligated to behave the same in reaction to the contradictions and errors among mythicists. As for historicists, so for them: once we trim away everything that's wrong or too speculative or inadequately demonstrated, we may yet have something that can be reliably affirmed about the historical Jesus (even if only that he didn't exist—or that we can't reliably know he did).

The same point can be expanded beyond the mainstream. For there are as many *absurd* theories of historicity as there are absurd Jesus myth theories. That Jesus toured India, or flew to North America, or exchanged letters with King Abgar, or convinced King Agrippa to back him on state currency as the Messiah, or that Jesus fathered a royal dynasty with Mary and then his kin had to dodge imperial attempts to eliminate their bloodline, or that he staged all his miracles, including faking his death and resurrection simply to set himself up as King of the Jews (which plan then failed), or that the canonical Gospels are literally and entirely true down to the smallest detail are all theories of historicity that I must honestly say are extraordinarily untenable. Yet all have been advanced and defended by scholars somewhere at some time—the last of these especially, which even today has whole colleges pledged to defending it. So finding equally absurd theories among the mythicists is no more a strike against mythicism as the above theories are against historicity. We simply set them aside as not worth even considering, leaving only the tenable theories to entertain. As for historicity, so for myth.

To avoid the monstrous task of a complete fact-check of every mythicist book I've listed (which books I consider to be advancing tenable theories—just not necessarily the correct ones), I will take the obvious shortcut. I won't bother defending *any* of the elaborations or specific but unnecessary claims of any author. I will instead construct the most minimal, plausible Jesus myth theory and see how it holds up. As with the minimal theory of historicity (defined in the previous chapter), there may yet be much else we can show to be true, but before we can proceed down that path we must first settle the basic question of whether we ought to be interpreting the evidence with the assumption that a historical Jesus existed, or that he did not. Hence I'll pit minimal historicity against minimal mythicism and see which has the greater merit in the final analysis. Other scholars can then build on that conclusion. Which is what should have been done in the first place. Indeed, I see this as one of the greatest methodological mistakes of mythicists: instead of *first* convincing the establishment of the basic merits of their interpretational framework and *then* recruiting the scholarly community in developing further conclusions therefrom, they immediately launch with elaborate conclusions about everything, making their theory all too easy to straw-man into the dustbin.

And that's essentially what has happened. In Chapter 1 I already discussed Van Voorst, who in a few pages directly rebuts mythicism (though really just Drews and Wells), and cited Theissen and Merz, who summarize a lengthier case against many generic mythicist claims, but only the weakest premises, and they never directly interact with any specific mythicist thesis. Other examples of recent criticism likewise touch only on some aspects of mythicism, and often inaccurately.[13] And yet these are the only scholarly attempts to refute mythicism worth reading, with the exception of several very outdated but still noteworthy works, which reveal (in their

13. For example, see the quasi debate between Robert Price and a gamut of historicists in *The Historical Jesus: Five Views* (ed. James Beilby and Paul Rhodes Eddy; Downers Grove, IL: IVP Academic, 2009), esp. pp. 55-103, 133-37, 178-82, 226-32, 282-87, and the very limited exchange between G.A. Wells ('The Historicity of Jesus') and Morton Smith ('The Historical Jesus') in *Jesus in History and Myth* (ed. R. Joseph Hoffmann and Gerald Larue; Buffalo, NY: Prometheus Books, 1986), pp. 25-54. For Bart Ehrman's and Maurice Casey's recent attempts at joining the debate, see note in Chapter 1 (§2).

very efforts to rebut it) how popular was the idea, even among some experts of the time, that Jesus was a myth.[14]

All are examples of the inadequacy of scholarly responses even from the earliest days of the controversy. In fact, the assumption that mythicism has been 'refuted' rests entirely on a series of fallacious rebuttals merely assumed to have been decisive. Shirley Jackson Case, for instance, soundly rebuts only *certain* mythicist arguments. That Case (and everyone afterward) concluded mythicism *itself* had thus been soundly rebutted is simply incorrect (see Chapter 11, §11). Early mythicism of the sort Case documents was launched from many sound intuitions that remain forceful, but was often flawed and naive, and certainly methodologically unsound, as is a lot of myth advocacy still today (and all the early-twentieth-century critics remain quite right about that).

Accordingly, we need to wipe the slate clean and start over, using a humbler, more informed and more methodologically sound approach. Only if *that* effort then fails (without being made into a straw man all over again) can it be concluded that mythicism *tout court* has been refuted. And then we can get on with the study of the historical Jesus.

3. *The Minimal Jesus Myth Theory*

Despite countless variations (including a still-rampant obsession with indemonstrable 'astrological' theories of Gospel interpretation that you won't find much sympathy for here), the basic thesis of every competent mythicist, then and now, has always been that Jesus was originally a god, just like any other god (properly speaking, a demigod in pagan terms; an archangel in Jewish terms; in either sense, a deity),[15] who was later historicized, just as countless other gods were, and that the Gospel of Mark (or Mark's source) originated the Christian myth familiar to us by build-

14. John E. Remsberg, *The Christ: A Critical Review and Analysis of his Existence* (Amherst, NY: Prometheus Books, 1994 [orig., 1909]); Thomas James Thorburn, *The Mythical Interpretation of the Gospels: Critical Studies in the Historic Narratives* (New York: Scribner, 1916); Maurice Goguel, *Jesus the Nazarene: Myth or History?* (New York: D. Appleton, 1926); and most importantly Shirley Jackson Case, *The Historicity of Jesus: A Criticism of the Contention That Jesus Never Lived; A Statement of the Evidence for his Existence; An Estimate of his Relation to Christianity* (Chicago: University of Chicago Press, 2d edn, 1928). There is also an important discussion of mythicism in the special second edition of Schweitzer's *Quest of the Historical Jesus*, which was for a long time available only in German (since 1913), and only recently in English as Albert Schweitzer, *The Quest of the Historical Jesus* (tr. John Bowden; (London: SCM Press, 2000).

15. On the Jewish use of angelology and demonology to speak of what pagans regarded as gods (and what even we today would call gods), see my discussion in Chapter 4 (§3) and Element 11.

ing up an edifying and symbolically meaningful tale for Jesus, drawing on passages from the Old Testament and popular literature, coupled with elements of revelation and pious inspiration. The manner in which Osiris came to be historicized, moving from being just a cosmic god to being given a whole narrative biography set in Egypt during a specific historical period, complete with collections of wisdom sayings he supposedly uttered, is still an apt model, if not by any means an exact one. Which is to say, it establishes a proof of concept. It is in essence what all mythicists are saying happened to Jesus.

Distilling all of this down to its most basic principles we get the following set of propositions:

1. At the origin of Christianity, Jesus Christ was thought to be a celestial deity much like any other.
2. Like many other celestial deities, this Jesus 'communicated' with his subjects only through dreams, visions and other forms of divine inspiration (such as prophecy, past and present).
3. Like some other celestial deities, this Jesus was originally believed to have endured an ordeal of incarnation, death, burial and resurrection in a supernatural realm.
4. As for many other celestial deities, an allegorical story of this same Jesus was then composed and told within the sacred community, which placed him on earth, in history, as a divine man, with an earthly family, companions, and enemies, complete with deeds and sayings, and an earthly depiction of his ordeals.
5. Subsequent communities of worshipers believed (or at least taught) that this invented sacred story was real (and either not allegorical or only 'additionally' allegorical).

That all five propositions are true shall be my minimal Jesus myth theory. As occasion warrants I might add features on to test the merits of more complex theories, but unless I explicitly say otherwise, the above is the theory I shall be testing against the minimal theory of historicity. Because if any one of the first four premises is false, it can fairly be said Jesus did not begin his life in myth (he just ended up there), and at least one of those premises must be false for 'Jesus was a real historical man' to be a relevantly true statement. The fifth premise, however, is uncontroversially a given, being already compatible with historicity, and well enough confirmed in the evidence as to not be in doubt.

Unlike the minimal theory of historicity, however, what I have just said is not strictly entailed. If 'Jesus Christ began as a celestial deity' is false, it could still be that he began as a political fiction, for example (as some scholars have indeed argued—the best examples being R.G. Price and

Gary Courtney).[16] But as will become clear in following chapters (especially Chapter 11), such a premise has a much lower prior probability (and thus is already at a huge disadvantage over Premise 1 even before we start examining the evidence), and a very low consequent probability (though it suits the Gospels well, it just isn't possible to explain the evidence in the Epistles this way, and the origin of Christianity itself becomes very hard to explain as well). Although I leave open the possibility it may yet be vindicated, I'm sure it's very unlikely to be, and accordingly I will assume its prior probability is too small even to show up in our math. This decision can be reversed only by a sound and valid demonstration that we must assign it a higher prior or consequent, but that I leave to anyone who thinks it's possible. In the meantime, what we have left is Premise 1, such that if *that* is less probable than minimal historicity, then I would be convinced historicity should be affirmed (particularly as the 'political fiction' theory already fits historicity and thus is not really a challenge to it—indeed that's often the very kind of fiction that gets written about historical persons).

This same conclusion follows for Premise 2, which could also be false and mythicism still be true, but only on the alternative hypothesis that everything said about (and said to have been said by) Jesus was an outright and deliberate fabrication (or the product of such a deranged reading of scripture as to beg every question of why the movement would even have found followers), which again has a very low prior probability (certainly much lower by far than Premise 2), and a very low consequent probability (given, again, all the evidence in the Epistles, as well as the background knowledge to be surveyed in Chapters 4 and 5). Of course, by Premise 2 I do not mean to assert that this celestial Christ really *did* communicate with people by such supernatural means, only that this is what the original Christian founders sincerely believed was happening—or at the very least *claimed* was happening.[17] Likewise, I am not here saying there *wasn't* a lot that was deliberately (and thus deceitfully) made up about what Jesus said and did. As most mainstream scholars would agree, a lot certainly was. But that *all* of it would be is what I deem too improbable to credit.

Premises 3 and 4 could similarly be denied and mythicism still be true, so long as we posited that the founders of Christianity hallucinated the entire life and fate of an earthly Christ, or outright lied about it ever having

16. R.G. Price, *Jesus: A Very Jewish Myth* (n.p.: RationalEvolution.net, 2007); and R.G. Price, *The Gospel of Mark as Reaction and Allegory* (n.p.: RationalEvolution.net, 2007); Gary Courtney, *Et Tu, Judas? Then Fall Jesus!* 2nd ed. (Lincoln, NE: iUniverse, 2004).

17. On how fine the line really was between the two see Carrier, *Not the Impossible Faith*, pp. 281-85 (and sources there cited). See also Richard Carrier, 'Why the Resurrection Is Unbelievable', in *Christian Delusion: Why Faith Fails* (ed. John Loftus; Amherst, NY: Prometheus Books, 2010), pp. 291-315 (300-301, 305-307).

occurred.[18] But again, either possibility has an extremely low prior probability, and though it may command a high consequent probability (since lies and hallucinations often look exactly the same as the truth—that's in fact why they are ever believed in the first place), I suspect it would entail a lower consequent probability than Premises 3 and 4, or at best none better. Perhaps such a theory can still claim a higher consequent probability than historicity, but I doubt that, and in any case that's someone else's business to prove. More to the point, even if such a theory were sustained, I suspect it would still end up with a lower posterior probability than would result from Premises 3 and 4, so the merits of such a theory would be moot. It would still be false, and the theory here defended true instead. In any case, it's the extremely small prior probability of these 'alternatives' that matters for the moment, because that means they take up so little of the prior-probability-space that we can safely ignore them.

Finally, Premise 5 is already an effective certainty, as it is true *even if historicity is true*, and is so well verified in background evidence that its prior probability is as near to 100% as makes all odds. So the possibility of its being false will not be an issue. Since Premise 5 is certainly true, and the prior probability of any of Premises 1 through 4 being false *and* historicity still not being true is vanishingly small (certainly less than a tenth of one percent by any reasonable estimate), if I assign ¬*h* to be the theory defined by Premises 1 through 5, I can safely assume that *h* entails historicity (given my minimal definition of historicity as a hypothesis in Chapter 2) and that these exhaust all relevant possibilities, and therefore I have a proper binary test, *h* and ¬*h*, just two hypotheses to compare against each other, such that if one is false, the other is true.

Certainly, when framed like this, technically ¬*h* (non-historicity) must also include all Jesus myth theories *not* defined by Premises 1 through 5 (that is, all theories of the evidence for Jesus that entail historicity is false *and* at least one of Premises 1 through 5 is false), but since their prior probability (even collectively) is surely less than a tenth of one percent (as I just reasoned), and their posterior probability not sufficiently high to make enough of a difference (especially in relation to minimal historicity), these theories share such a small portion of the probability-space occupied by ¬*h* that they can simply be ignored.[19] In other words, if ¬*h* (as I have minimally defined it) is false, it's simply the case that historicity is probably true.

With both the hypotheses of historicity and myth duly defined, now we must turn to a survey of the essential background knowledge governing their comparison.

18. The only alternatives to it taking place in a 'supernatural realm'. But the latter could have been imagined to be in outer space *or* on earth and still conform to minimal mythicism as I have defined it: see note in Chapter 11 (§8).

19. On this methodological point see Carrier, *Proving History*, pp. 70-71, 86, 205.

4

Background Knowledge (Christianity)

1. *A Romulan Tale*

In Plutarch's biography of Romulus, the founder of Rome, we are told he was the son of god, born of a virgin; an attempt is made to kill him as a baby, and he is saved, and raised by a poor family, becoming a lowly shepherd; then as a man he becomes beloved by the people, hailed as king, and killed by the conniving elite; then he rises from the dead, appears to a friend to tell the good news to his people, and ascends to heaven to rule from on high. Just like Jesus.

Plutarch also tells us about annual public ceremonies that were still being performed, which celebrated the day Romulus ascended to heaven. The sacred story told at this event went basically as follows: at the end of his life, amid rumors he was murdered by a conspiracy of the Senate (just as Jesus was 'murdered' by a conspiracy of the Jews—in fact by the Sanhedrin, the Jewish equivalent of the Senate), the sun went dark (just as it did when Jesus died), and Romulus's body vanished (just as Jesus' did). The people wanted to search for him but the Senate told them not to, 'for he had risen to join the gods' (much as a mysterious young man tells the women in Mark's Gospel). Most went away happy, hoping for good things from their new god, but 'some doubted' (just as all later Gospels say of Jesus: Mt. 28.17; Lk. 24.11; Jn 20.24-25; even Mk 16.8 implies this). Soon after, Proculus, a close friend of Romulus, reported that he met Romulus 'on the road' between Rome and a nearby town and asked him, 'Why have you abandoned us?', to which Romulus replied that he had been a god all along but had come down to earth and become incarnate to establish a great kingdom, and now had to return to his home in heaven (pretty much as happens to Cleopas in Lk. 24.13-32; see Chapter 10, §6). Then Romulus told his friend to tell the Romans that if they are virtuous they will have all worldly power.[1]

1. Luke converts this glorious appearance tale into a hidden god narrative (a reversal that befits how Christianity was also inverting the message of Romulus:

Plutarch tells us that the annual Roman ceremony of the Romulan ascent involved a recitation of the names of those who fled his vanishing in fear, and the acting out of their fear and flight in public, a scene suspiciously paralleling the pre-redacted ending of Mark's Gospel (at 16.8).[2] Which would make sense of his otherwise bizarre ending—we are then to assume what followed his story is just what followed the story he is emulating: an appearance of the Lord, delivering the gospel, which is then proclaimed to the people (the very thing Mark tells us to anticipate: 14.28 and 16.7). In fact, Livy's account, just like Mark's, emphasizes that 'fear and bereavement' kept the people 'silent for a long time', and only later did they proclaim Romulus 'God, Son of God, King, and Father', thus matching Mark's 'they said nothing to anyone', yet obviously assuming that somehow word got out.

It certainly seems as if Mark is fashioning Jesus into the new Romulus, with a new, superior message, establishing a new, superior kingdom. This Romulan tale looks a lot like a skeletal model for the passion narrative: a great man, founder of a great kingdom, despite coming from lowly origins and of suspect parentage, is actually an incarnated son of god, but dies as a result of a conspiracy of the ruling council, then a darkness covers the land at his death and his body vanishes, at which those who followed him flee in fear (just like the Gospel women, Mk 16.8; and men, Mk 14.50-52), and like them, too, we look for his body but are told he is not here, he has risen; and some doubt, but then the risen god 'appears' to select followers to deliver his gospel.[3]

promising, at least in the meantime, a hidden spiritual kingdom rather than a visible earthly one: 2 Cor. 4.18; Rom. 14.17), but otherwise the details are essentially the same (in fact, the similarities are even more numerous than proposed here, as I'll show in Chapter 10, §6; and in Element 47). See also Richard Carrier, 'The Spiritual Body of Christ and the Legend of the Empty Tomb', in *Empty Tomb* (ed. Price and Lowder), pp. 105-232 (180-84, 191).

2. Mark also happens to be one of the recited names of those who fled the vanishing of Romulus—as is a cognate of Luke ('they shout out many local names, like Marcus, Lucius, and Gaius', Plutarch, *Romulus* 29.2). These were very common names, however; and Lukas was a contraction of Lucanus, not Lucius (though the names are related). So the fact that Mark and Luke are the two Gospels that most conspicuously emulate the story of Romulus is perhaps just a coincidence.

3. This tale is widely attested as pre-Christian: in *Romulus* 27-28, Plutarch, though writing c. 80–120 CE, is certainly recording a long-established Roman tale and custom, and his sources are unmistakably pre-Christian: Cicero, *Laws* 1.3, *Republic* 2.10; Livy, *From the Founding of the City* 1.16.2-8 (1.3–1.16 relating the whole story of Romulus); Ovid, *Fasti* 2.491-512 and *Metamorphoses* 14.805-51; and Dionysius of Halicarnassus, *Roman Antiquities* 2.63.3 (1.71–2.65 relating the whole story of Romulus); see also a later reference: Cassius Dio, *Roman History* 56.46.2. The story's antiquity was acknowledged even by Christians: Tertullian, *Apology* 21.

There are many differences in the two stories, surely. But the similarities are too numerous to be a coincidence—and the differences are likely deliberate. For instance, Romulus's material kingdom favoring the mighty is transformed into a spiritual one favoring the humble. It certainly looks like the Christian passion narrative is an intentional transvaluation of the Roman Empire's ceremony of their own founding savior's incarnation, death and resurrection (see Element 47). Other elements have been added to the Gospels—the story heavily Judaized, and many other symbols and motifs pulled in to transform it—and the narrative has been modified, in structure and content, to suit the Christians' own moral and spiritual agenda. But the basic structure is not original.

There were, in fact, numerous pre-Christian savior gods who became incarnate and underwent sufferings or trials, even deaths and resurrections.[4] None of them actually existed. Neither did Romulus. Yet all were placed in history, and often given detailed biographies. Just like Plutarch's.

2. *Background Knowledge*

We cannot claim to understand the Christian religion and its documents if we ignore such background knowledge as this. We cannot estimate what was likely or typical unless we know everything relevant we can know about the context of the time, including comparative evidence, from religions and movements of that time and place and religions and movements throughout history.

Knowing the background of the Romulus myths and rituals drastically changes what we will consider possible or likely in the case of Jesus, and yet that's just one single item. Think how much difference will be made by knowing a *hundred* such items. We also cannot arrive at accurate judgments if we ignore all the data we actually have from Christianity's earliest documents, yet many scholars ignore a surprising amount of that data when formulating theories and estimates of likelihood. We can't do that. We need to attend to as complete and secure a body of background knowledge as possible so we can correctly condition all our probability estimates on it as Bayes's Theorem requires.[5]

4. Most certainly Osiris, Zalmoxis, Dionysus, Inanna, and others: see Carrier, *Not the Impossible Faith*, pp. 17-19, 85-113 (more will be said on this point here and in following chapters: Elements 14, 31, and 46-48).

5. We also have to take into account how much we *don't* know about antiquity (because assuming we know everything is itself a fallacy that undermines many theories and estimates); see Carrier, *Proving History*, pp. 129-34, and Carrier, 'Spiritual Body', in *Empty Tomb* (ed. Price and Lowder), pp. 180-82.

Background knowledge should consist of facts beyond reasonable dispute. Some of these facts are theoretical, but are so well established from the facts available that we can treat them as tantamount to established facts. Most of this body of material is not specific to Christianity (e.g. the laws of physics), and most that is specific to Christianity is (or ought to be) already well known by experts in Jesus studies. Which is why experts are more qualified to judge theories in ancient history: a thorough knowledge of the evidence and contextual background is necessary to make credible estimates of likelihood (I've already said enough about this in Chapter 2 of *Proving History*). But no one can be an expert in everything. And evaluating claims about Jesus requires understanding the modern science of hallucination and psychosomatic illness, as well as the established findings of modern sociology, psychology and cultural anthropology. But even some of the historical material is surprisingly not known to many experts. I have selected the most important of those elements to present here, which will play a significant part in evaluating the remaining evidence in following chapters. In fact, everything here to follow is what any theory of the origins of Christianity must fit and take into account. For what follows is true regardless of whether Jesus existed as a historical person or not. Hence even a *historical* Jesus can only be understood in this context.

As I explained in *Proving History*, in science, usually background knowledge (or *b*) includes *all* previous data while evidence (or *e*) is limited to new data (from a single experiment or study). History only occasionally gets new data. What historians are keen to know is not just whether new data changes what we should believe, but more often what a particular body of evidence warrants believing. And historians examine both questions in terms of causal explanation: determining what happened (the events of history) is a function of determining what caused the evidence we now have, and determining *why* that happened requires determining what caused the events thus discerned (I provided all the logical demonstrations and explanations of these points in *Proving History*). Thus what goes in *e* is ordinarily what historians believe stands in need of a causal explanation ('How did that evidence come about?'). Everything else goes in *b*. Data can be moved between these two sets however you desire as long as you are consistent (e.g. what you put in *e* stays in *e* throughout a single equation). That this demarcation is arbitrary makes no difference to the method, since the mathematics must work out the same (if it doesn't, you've made a mistake somewhere). Thus some of what follows could be moved from *b* to *e* if you so desired, but doing so can make no difference to the final outcome.

3. *Elemental Definitions*

I must first define some terms I will frequently use. Other terms I define as I present them, including a few already in Chapter 1, presenting each word in bold where it is defined. These definitions are not intended to be normative. So there is no sense in arguing whether my definitions are 'right' or 'wrong'. They merely specify what I mean when I use those terms, regardless of what anyone else might mean, or what any dictionaries say, or any other conventions. As long as you treat my definitions as nothing more than explanations of what I mean, confusion will be forestalled.

I shall use **god** to mean any celestial being with supernatural power, and **God** to mean a supreme creator deity. Though by this definition angels and demons are indeed gods, I'll sometimes (but not always) use **angel** or **archangel** to refer to 'gods' that are believed to be acting as messengers or servants of God and **demon** to refer to 'gods' who are believed to be acting in opposition to God (the terminology was already this fluid even among early Christians: e.g. 2 Cor. 4.4; 1 Cor. 8.5; Gal. 4.8-9), although I will also on occasion use 'demon' more neutrally in the context of pagan belief (in which there were both good and evil demons, all of whom gods).[6] I shall mean by **Jesus Christ** the name given by the earliest known Christians to a man who was believed to have historically existed (whether on earth or only in heaven—or both) and to have in some sense originated the Christian religion (for the meaning of his name see Chapter 6, §2). I shall mean by **Christianity** (and all cognate terms) any cult venerating this Jesus Christ as a divine being. And by **cult**, of course, I do not mean the pejorative but the standard anthropological term for any community of worship distinguished by a system of religious rituals and doctrines.

I shall mean by **messiah** (the Hebrew word of which 'Christ' is a translation) any man in fact, myth, or prophecy who is (a) anointed by the Hebrew God to (b) play a part in God's plan to liberate his Chosen People from their oppressors and (c) restore or institute God's true religion. This means 'anointed' in any sense then understood (literally, figuratively, cosmically or symbolically), 'liberate' in any sense then claimed (physically or spiritually), 'oppressors' in any sense then identified (whoever or whatever they may be) and 'religion' in the fullest sense (cult, mores, sacred knowledge, and the resulting social order)—and I specify only 'play a part', not necessarily bring to fruition. All Jewish kings and high priests were, of course, 'messiahs' in the basic sense of being anointed to represent God. But here I shall mean a messiah conforming to (a) through (c). Yet I do not assume

6. For more on the terminology of celestial beings see Elements 11, 36 and 37.

there must be only *one* messiah of that kind. Neither did the Jews (see scholarship cited in Elements 3 and 4).[7]

I've seen some scholars question or deny that the Jews had any prior notion of a messiah before the advent of Christianity. But such a denial is accomplished only by proposing an implausibly hyper-specific definition of 'messiah', then showing no such thing was previously imagined, and concluding 'the Jews had no prior notion of a messiah'. This is a textbook fallacy of equivocation: start with a term defined one way, then end with the same term defined in a completely different way, often without noticing a switch has been made. To avoid this, I shall stick to my minimal definition, since I am certain anyone meeting criteria (a), (b) and (c) would have been regarded by at least some ancient Jews or Judaizers as a messiah. I attach no other baggage to the term—no particular eschatology or scheme of liberation. Jews of antiquity were clearly quite flexible in all such details, as everyone agrees (see Element 2).

I shall mean by **crucifixion** (and 'being crucified' and all other cognate terms and phrases) as *any* hanging up of the living or dead as a punishment, regardless of the exact details of how. The shape of the cross or fixture, the position of the body, whether the victim is killed first or hung while alive and left to die, even the manner of hanging, whether nailing or lashing, or whether to a rock or tree or stake or doorway or anything else, all of that can (and certainly did) vary, and yet the act still constitutes crucifixion if (a) a body is hanged by anything other than a noose around the neck and (b) this hanging is a punishment. Even the ancient terminology was no more specific than that (in fact it was less so), hence I see no valid reason ours should be.[8] For example, the Bible described one method of execution as to 'hang in the sun' (in the Septuagint, literally, *exēliazō* = *ex hēliou*, 'out in the sun', or *apenanti tou hēliou*, 'against the sun'), which implies the intent was for the hanged to die from exposure (Num. 25.4 and 2 Sam. 21.6, 9, 13). That is essentially a form of crucifixion, however it was effected. Likewise, when Joshua hung on trees the king of Ai and the kings of the Amorites (Josh. 8.29 and 10.26-27), and when the Law of Moses calls for the executed to be hanged on trees or planks (*xulon* in the Greek) even when already dead (Deut. 21.22-23), or when Haman and his sons are hung on a giant pole (*xulon* again in Greek translations of Est. 5.14; 7.9-10; and 8.7, these are all forms of crucifixion. Many scholars of Jewish antiquity agree.[9]

7. Matthew Novenson, *Christ among the Messiahs: Christ Language in Paul and Messiah Language in Ancient Judaism* (Oxford: Oxford University Press, 2012).

8. This and what follows have already been thoroughly demonstrated in Gunnar Samuelsson, *Crucifixion in Antiquity: An Inquiry into the Background of the New Testament Terminology of Crucifixion* (Tübingen: Mohr Siebeck, 2011).

9. See Richard Carrier, 'The Burial of Jesus in Light of Jewish Law', in *Empty Tomb*

In using the term 'crucifixion' this way I do not mean to rule out finer distinctions for those who want to make them. Someone else, for example, may want to restrict the term to an actual means of killing, thus including only those hung up alive to die, rather than the hanging of corpses. But since I see no contradiction in the idea of crucifying a corpse (and the ancient terminology does not exclude it), I think such a restriction is too fastidious. Since there was no standard practice of crucifixion even among the Romans (we can't be sure if everyone they crucified was nailed or merely tied up or even impaled, or exactly where or how or to what), if we are too particular we will anachronistically exceed the ideas and vocabulary of the period. The Greek word for crucify (*stauroō*) literally means 'staked' or 'palisaded', and frequently meant not just crucified but also impaled, or even setting up spiked walls around a fort. Hence 'to stake (*stauroō*) someone on a pole (*xulon*)' is what happens in the early Greek translation of Est. 7.9 using the exact same verb used of the crucifixion of Jesus in the New Testament, as well as the exact same word for 'post' or 'tree' used in the Septuagint text of the old Torah Law (that passage in Deuteronomy), which is *also* the same word used for the cross and crucifixion of Jesus in the New Testament. Thus, as the ambiguity existed then, I preserve it myself.

I shall mean by **resurrection** (and all similar terms) any restoration of life to the dead (whether permanent or not), though I shall distinguish when the term is used literally or figuratively. Merely the survival or ascension of an already-immortal soul does not count as a 'restoration' in this sense and thus is not a resurrection, but abandoning the corpse altogether and rising to life in a completely new body *does* count and thus *is* a resurrection. As with the term 'messiah', I've seen recent attempts to claim that pagans had no notion of resurrection, again by producing a hyper-specific definition of one particular kind of resurrection, proving they didn't have or accept it, then concluding they had no notion of resurrection at all. But such specificity did not exist in ancient vocabulary. Many different Jewish and Christian sects believed in many different kinds of resurrection, and all were called 'resurrection'.[10] And there were yet more kinds of resurrection imagined among the pagans, and considerable overlap between their ideas and those of the Jews and Christians.[11] I shall thus avoid any fallacy of anachronistic precision by using all words for 'resurrection' to mean just what they meant

(ed. Price and Lowder), pp. 369-92 (esp. pp. 375-79); with D.J. Halperin, 'Crucifixion, the Nahum Pesher and the Rabbinic Penalty of Crucifixion', *Journal of Jewish Studies* 32 (1981), pp. 32-46; and J.A. Fitzmyer, 'Crucifixion in Ancient Palestine, Qumran Literature, and the New Testament', *Catholic Biblical Quarterly* 40 (1978), pp. 493-513.

10. Carrier, 'Spiritual Body', in *Empty Tomb* (ed. Price and Lowder), esp. pp. 107-13, 126, 137-38.

11. Carrier, *Not the Impossible Faith*, pp. 85-127.

to *everyone* in antiquity, whether pagan, Jew, or Christian: rising from a state of death to be alive again. Nothing more.

I shall mean by **outer space** everything above the atmosphere as presently known. In ancient understanding this included (a) everything in or under the 'firmament' (also known as the *aēr* or 'sublunar sphere') extending above the highest visible clouds all the way to the orbit of the moon, *and* (b) all the heavens beyond (also then known as the 'ether' or 'ethereal realm'). The notion that any of this region may have been a vacuum did exist at the time, but only as a controversial theory rejected by most religious cosmologists, and only embraced typically by atomists and others generally hostile to the supernatural. Most people of the time thought the *aēr* extended all the way to the moon (while everything beyond that was filled with a breathable 'ether'), when in fact (as we now know) the real atmosphere extends only a minuscule fraction of that distance.

So when they spoke of beings and events 'in the air', they were often speaking of what *we* mean by outer space. This is even more obvious when they spoke of beings and events in the spheres of heaven above the moon. Accordingly, if an ancient author was speaking of what we call outer space, I will say 'outer space'. This does not mean I attribute to them a modern knowledge of the extraterrestrial vacuum. It only means they were thinking of realms beyond the terrestrial domains of mountains, clouds, and birds. For it was already common knowledge among the educated of the time that the moon's distance from the earth was hundreds of thousands of miles (see Element 34). So when they used terms that we often translate as 'air', they were often not referring to what we mean by 'the air' today but a far more vast and frightening realm of fantastic possibilities, which many thought was trafficked by gods and filled with strange animals or spirits (see Elements 36-38).

I shall use **gospel** for the general idea of the 'good news' or 'salvific message' that any group of Christians (or other savior cult) may have preached (and which may have varied in content from group to group), and **Gospel** for the actual written books of that title or genre (which attempted to convey 'a gospel' in some fashion or other). In accordance with growing convention, I shall also use **Septuagint** or the abbreviation LXX to mean, in fact, the translation of the OT into Greek made by the Jewish scholar Theodotion in the second century (whereas previous to Christianity was the similar but not always identical **Old Greek** translation, which is no longer completely extant); and I'll use **NT** and **OT** for New Testament and Old Testament, respectively. I shall also use **church** to mean any Christian congregation (regardless of sect or state of organization) and **the church** as a stand-in for the whole Christian movement (in all its diversity), and **Church** to mean any major regional Christian institution (or all of them collectively) that had the political power to force compliance and suppress heresy among its own adherents. By this definition the Coptic, Eastern Orthodox, and Catholic Churches became the most prominent and powerful Churches, but Churches in this sense didn't likely exist anywhere until the second century at the earliest. Before that 'the church' only consisted of diverse and loosely affiliated 'churches'.

I shall use **orthodox** or **orthodoxy** to refer to all the churches, literature, and institutions (and their ideologies and interpretations) that eventually evolved over the course of the fourth century CE into the politically victorious sects that we now call Churches or the Church. I shall use **heretical** (and all related terms) for all other churches. Though no church of those later periods much resembled any churches of the first and second centuries (as most scholars agree, Christian ideology, institutions and beliefs had by then changed considerably), the consolidated sects that would later call their view 'orthodoxy' (and all others 'heresy') did each evolve from one particular lineage of the era (albeit with continual cross-fertilization with other Christian sects and pagan cults), and then kept or altered documents from that era that supported that, and destroyed or abandoned documents that did not, creating a selection bias in the preservation of literature that bears a particular (albeit anachronistic and often inconsistent) sectarian stamp (see Elements 20-21 and 44).

So when I speak of an orthodox sect in the first two centuries, I do not mean the sect that was closer or more faithful to the originating traditions of the religion. I believe all sects deviated from the original religion and innovated freely and in equal measure, and the victorious Churches of the early Middle Ages looked nothing at all like the original faith of Peter or even Paul. Rather, I mean the sects that evolved into those later Churches, bearing the closest ancestral relationship to them, in ideology and institutional continuity. Thus, I am not endorsing any Church's claim to 'orthodoxy' ('right doctrine'), nor am I using terms like 'heretical' pejoratively, but rather acknowledging that a small handful of Churches (such as the Orthodox, Coptic, and Catholic) gained dominance in certain regions and then called themselves 'orthodox'. None of these Churches sprang out of nowhere, but all evolved from earlier sects that bear a closer resemblance to them than other sects did, and their selection, modification and endorsement of documents reflects what *they* chose to call 'orthodoxy'. Hence, for convenience, so shall I.

Finally, my publisher requires me to employ BCE ('Before the Common Era') and CE ('Common Era') in lieu of of BC ('Before Christ') and AD ('Anno Domini' = 'In the Year of the Lord'), even though in my own opinion the original notation is more familiar and there is no good reason to change it.[12]

12. For my editorial on this subject see Richard Carrier, 'B.C.A.D.C.E.B.C.E', *Richard Carrier Blogs* (January 16, 2012), at http://freethoughtblogs.com/carrier/

4. *Elemental Background Knowledge*

To make my assumptions more transparent, I will survey the often less-well-known background knowledge I shall be relying on in later chapters, and break it down into units or 'elements' that can be tested or debated individually. When elements agree with the near-universal consensus of contemporary scholarship I won't exhaust any effort to survey the evidence but merely present them as given. I do not assume such elements are beyond any possibility of debate, only that the evidence is such that the burden must be on anyone who would deny them. The remaining elements I will demonstrate to be true with an adequate citation of evidence and scholarship, only because I keep encountering experts who deny them or don't know of them (even when a majority of experts already agree with me).[13] More elements will be enumerated in the next chapter (and we must add to all these the background facts already presented in the three chapters before and the six chapters after).

As I explained in Chapter 1, some readers might prefer to skip the rest of this and the next chapter, and only return to them later. Alternatively, you may be content to read only the first paragraph of every element—continuing only if you disagree with what is asserted there or want to see why I conclude it's true (otherwise moving on to the next numbered element). Crucially, none of these elements assume or entail historicity is true or false, they are all compatible with both. They simply must all be taken into account when evaluating either.

5. *Elements of Christian Origin*

Element 1: The earliest form of Christianity definitely known to us originated as a Jewish sect in the region of Syria-Palestine in the early first century CE. Some historians would challenge this, but their theories have yet to

archives/166.

13. In every case, the argument I develop for each element could be reproduced in formal Bayesian terms, but to keep things simple I present them in colloquial terms. As background knowledge, the procedure for each would be to assign a neutral prior probability (which for each simple binary true/false statement is 0.5) and then ask how probable the total body of human knowledge is on h (that the claim is true) and how probable it is on $\neg h$ (that the claim is false), especially the evidence specifically enumerated here (the evidence most directly determinative of h or $\neg h$), and then stating the posterior probability that results, which in some cases is 'maybe' (meaning: more than merely possible, but still not certain) and in others is 'certainly' (meaning: not absolutely certain, but certain to a very high probability), or some degree in between. I have carefully worded my claims in each element to reflect this.

survive peer review or persuade anything near a consensus agreement among experts. Rather than prove it true here, I will simply state it as a given fact of our background knowledge, to be revised only if it is clearly disproved.

Element 2: When Christianity began, Judaism was highly sectarian and diverse. There was no 'normative' set of Jewish beliefs, but a countless array of different Jewish belief systems vying for popularity. We know of at least ten competing sects, possibly more than thirty, and there could easily have been more. But we know very little about them, except that they differed from one another (sometimes radically) on various political, theological, metaphysical, moral and other issues. In fact the evidence we do have establishes that, contrary to common assumption, innovation and syncretism (even with non-Judaic theologies) was actually typical of early-first-century Judaism, even in Palestine, and thus Christianity looks much less like an aberration and more like just another innovating, syncretistic Jewish cult.[14] Further support for this point is provided in Elements 30 and 33. No argument, therefore, can proceed from an assumption of any universally normative Judaism.

Element 3: (a) When Christianity began, many Jews had long been expecting a messiah: a divinely chosen leader or savior anointed (literally or figuratively 'christened', hence a 'Christ') to help usher in God's supernatural kingdom, usually (but not always) by subjugating or destroying the enemies of the Jews and establishing an eternal paradise (see previous definition in §3, and following discussion in Elements 4 and 5). (b) We

14. For a summary of the evidence and sources collectively establishing this element see Carrier, 'Spiritual Body', in *Empty Tomb* (ed. Price and Lowder), pp. 107-13, with support in James Charlesworth and Petr Pokorný (eds.), *Jesus Research: An International Perspective* (Grand Rapids, MI: Eerdmans, 2009), pp. 58-59. Indeed, there, primarily only Palestinian sects are considered; when considering Judaism of the Diaspora, Jewish sects and views diverge even more: see Erich Gruen, *Diaspora: Jews amidst Greeks and Romans* (Cambridge, MA: Harvard University Press, 2002); and Erich Gruen, *Heritage and Hellenism: The Reinvention of Jewish Tradition* (Berkeley, CA: University of California Press, 1998); J. Andrew Overman and Robert MacLennan (eds.), *Diaspora Jews and Judaism* (Atlanta, GA: Scholars Press, 1992); with Margaret Williams, *The Jews among the Greeks and Romans: A Diasporan Sourcebook* (Baltimore, MD: Johns Hopkins University Press, 1998). But even in Palestine, diversity and Hellenization was a common reality: see Morton Smith, 'Palestinian Judaism in the First Century', in *Israel: Its Role in Civilization* (ed. Moshe Davis; New York: Seminary Israel Institute of the Jewish Theological Seminary of America, 1956), pp. 67-81; Alan Segal, 'Jesus and First-Century Judaism', in *Jesus at 2000* (ed. Marcus Borg; Boulder, CO: Westview Press, 1997), pp. 55-72; and James Charlesworth *et al.* (eds.), *Qumran-Messianism: Studies on the Messianic Expectations in the Dead Sea Scrolls* (Tübingen: Mohr Siebeck, 1998), pp. 25-27.

can reasonably infer that if those 'enemies' were ever considered to be invisible demons (rather than the actual Roman legions, for example) the way would have been open to imagine a messianic victory over Israel's enemies that could only be perceived spiritually (see Element 28). Otherwise the messiah was typically expected to achieve a transparent military victory. Sometimes (as in the Enochic literature) it was both. (c) That Jewish expectations of some kind of messiah in the early Roman Empire were widespread, influential, and very diverse (and thus incapable of being fixed to any single view) has been well established by experts on ancient messianism.[15]

Element 4: (a) Palestine in the early first century CE was experiencing a rash of messianism. There was an evident clamoring of sects and individuals to announce they had found the messiah. (b) It is therefore no oddity or accident that this is exactly when Christianity arose. It was yet another messiah cult in the midst of a fad for just such cults. (c) That it among them would alone survive and spread can therefore be the product of natural selection: so many variations of the same theme were being tried, odds are one of them would by chance be successful, hitting all the right notes and dodging all the right bullets. The lucky winner in that contest just happened to be Christianity.[16]

This element is often denied, or its basis not well understood, so I will pause to establish it before moving on. 'Messiah', 'Son of Man', 'the Righteous One', and 'the Elect [or Chosen] One' were all popular titles for the expected messiah used by several groups in early-first-century Judaism, as attested, for instance, in the Book of the Parables of Enoch, a Jewish

15. Stanley Porter (ed.), *The Messiah in the Old and New Testaments* (Grand Rapids, MI: William B. Eerdmans, 2007); Markus Bockmuehl and James Carleton Paget (eds.), *Redemption and Resistance: The Messianic Hopes of Jews and Christians in Antiquity* (New York: T. & T. Clark, 2007); Magnus Zetterholm (ed.), *The Messiah in Early Judaism and Christianity* (Minneapolis: Fortress Press, 2007); Charlesworth *et al.* (eds.), *Qumran-Messianism*; Craig Evans and Peter Flint (eds.), *Eschatology, Messianism, and the Dead Sea Scrolls* (Grand Rapids, MI: William B. Eerdmans, 1997); James Charlesworth (ed.), *The Messiah: Developments in Earliest Judaism and Christianity* (Minneapolis, MN: Fortress Press, 1992); Jacob Neusner, *Messiah in Context: Israel's History and Destiny in Formative Judaism* (Philadelphia, PA: Fortress Press, 1984); and Jacob Neusner *et al.* (eds.), *Judaisms and their Messiahs at the Turn of the Christian Era* (New York: Cambridge University Press, 1987). See also C.A. Evans, 'Messianism', in *Dictionary of New Testament Background* (ed. Craig Evans and Stanley Porter; Downers Grove, IL: InterVarsity Press, 2000), pp. 698-707.

16. On this being the case see Richard Carrier, 'Christianity's Success Was Not Incredible', in *The End of Christianity* (ed. John Loftus; Amherst, NY: Prometheus Books, 2011), pp. 53-74, 372-75, along with Carrier, *Not the Impossible Faith.*

text composed before 70 CE.[17] The Dead Sea Scrolls attest to one or several such cults around that same time. Indeed, messianic apocalypticism was intense at Qumran, where the keepers of the scrolls were already expecting the imminent end of the world, and attempting different calculations from the timetable provided in the book of Daniel (see Element 7) to predict when the first messiah would come—and many of their calculations came up 'soon'. The early first century CE was in their prediction window.[18] And many of their texts were used by other cults of the time. A copy of the so-called Damascus Document, for instance, turns up a thousand years later in a stash of Jewish texts at Cairo Geniza.[19]

Even the early-first-century Jewish philosopher Philo of Alexandria wrote an apocalyptic text sharing and adapting the messianic expectations of his generation.[20] The Gospels likewise assume (or, depending on how much you trust them, report) that 'messiah fever' was so rampant in Judea then that countless people were expecting Elijah to be walking among them, some even believed that Jesus, or John the Baptist, was that very man, risen from the dead, which many Jews believed presaged the imminent coming of a messiah and the ensuing end of the present world order (which many believed had become corrupted beyond human repair), because this had been predicted in Mal. 4.5-6, the very last passage of the traditional OT.[21]

The only surviving historian of early-first-century Palestine confirms this picture. Josephus records the rise and popularity of several false messiahs in the same general period as Christianity was getting started. He does not explicitly call them messiahs—he probably wanted to avoid reminding his Gentile audience that this was the product of Jewish ideology, and instead claimed it was the product of fringe criminals and ruffians (he likewise catalogues various other rebel bandits and demagogues as well). But the descriptions he provides belie the truth of the matter. As David Rhoads

17. See M. Black, 'The Messianism of the Parables of Enoch: Their Date and Contribution to Christological Origins', in *The Messiah* (ed. Charlesworth), pp. 145-68; J.C. VanderKam, 'Righteous One, Messiah, Chosen One, and Son of Man in 1 Enoch 37–71', in *The Messiah* (ed. Charlesworth), pp. 169-91; and in Neusner *et al.*, *Judaisms and their Messiahs*. In the NT Jesus is of course 'the Messiah' (Christ), but is also called 'the Chosen One' (Mt. 12.18; Lk. 9.35; 23.35), 'the Righteous One' (Lk. 23.47; Acts 3.14; 7.52; 22.14; 1 Jn 2.1; Rev. 16.5) and 'The Son of Man' (countless instances, e.g., Mt. 12.30; Mk 14.41; Lk. 22.48; Acts 7.56; Jn 1.51; etc.), among a great many other epithets, both familiar and strange.

18. See John Collins, 'The Expectation of the End in the Dead Sea Scrolls', in *Eschatology* (ed. Evans and Flint), pp. 74-90 (esp. 76-79, 83).

19. See Lawrence Schiffman and James VanderKam (eds.), *Encyclopedia of the Dead Sea Scrolls* (Oxford: Oxford University Press, 2000), I, pp. 166-70.

20. Philo, *On Rewards and Punishments* 79-172 (esp. § 95).

21. See Mk 9.9-13; 8.27-28; 6.14-16; Mt. 17.10-13; 16.13-14; Lk. 9.18-19; 9.7-9.

put it, 'Josephus tends to avoid messianism when he relates the history of the first century'; in fact he deliberately 'suppressed the religious motivations of the revolutionaries by ascribing [to them] evil and dishonorable intentions' instead. But their messianic basis remains unmistakable. Scholarly analysis confirms this.[22] Josephus recounts at least four messianic figures of the early first century, and documents how enormously popular they were, compelling the Romans to mass military action to suppress them.[23]

'The Samaritan' gathered followers and said he would reveal the lost relics of the true Samaritan temple on Mount Gerizim—an act with obvious messianic meaning (the Samaritans believing themselves to be the true Jews; this is alluded to even in Jn 4.20-26, which attests the Samaritans *also* expected an imminent messiah). The original Jewish congregation led by Joshua had stood at God's command 'upon Mount Gerizim to bless the people' after crossing the Jordan (Deut. 27.12), which is to say, when Joshua (the original Jesus—the names are identical: see Chapter 6, §3) crossed the Jordan on the day the nation of Israel was conceptually begun. Thus, the original Joshua inaugurated the nation of Israel by crossing the Jordan and congregating at Gerizim; and since the last messiah (the new Joshua) was to reconstitute Israel, he, too, could expect to begin the task by a blessing on Mount Gerizim.

'Theudas' gathered followers and said he would part the Jordan—another act with obvious messianic meaning: Joshua (the original Jesus) had also miraculously parted the Jordan upon beginning his conquest of Israel (Joshua 3), so this was another obvious symbolic starting point for the *re*-conquest of Israel. Similarly, the Christian Jesus (again, 'Joshua')

22. See D. Mendels, 'Pseudo-Philo's *Biblical Antiquities*, the 'Fourth Philosophy', and the Political Messianism of the First Century CE', in *The Messiah* (ed. Charlesworth), pp. 261-75 (quote from Rhoads: p. 261 n. 4); which is thoroughly supported by Craig Evans, 'Josephus on John the Baptist and Other Jewish Prophets of Deliverance', in *The Historical Jesus in Context* (ed. Amy-Jill Levine, Dale Allison, Jr and John Dominic Crossan; Princeton, NJ: Princeton University Press, 2006), pp. 55-63, which contains all the relevant references in Josephus.

23. Which may have been a key to Christianity's success: by avoiding mass territorial action (and focusing instead on spiritual combat), they avoided armed conflict and thus survived, by gaining more converts over a wider area than were lost to sporadic persecutions. See Carrier, *Not the Impossible Faith*, pp. 219-45, with pp. 147-60, 259-96. This may even have been a lesson learned from observing the fate of other movements. But natural selection alone would determine it: agitative cults would be wiped out, leaving more pacifist cults to dominate the market (then it became simply a competition among products for sale). A non-existent messiah (whose lordship and victory were known only spiritually and thus never a worldly militaristic threat) would thus have an enormous competitive advantage at these earliest stages (see Elements 23-28).

is depicted as beginning his messianic career by symbolically parting (or passing through) the Jordan, in the form of his baptism.

'The Egyptian' (possibly a Jewish cult leader from Alexandria) also gathered followers and preached from the Mount of Olives (just as Jesus Christ does in the Gospels), claiming he would topple the walls of Jerusalem—an obvious allusion to the miraculous felling of the walls of Jericho, another deed of the first Jesus (the biblical Joshua), in fact in the first battle that followed his crossing of the Jordan, making this another symbol of beginning the conquest of Israel. Preaching from the Mount of Olives could also imply messianic pretensions—as it was commonly believed a messiah would stand there in the last days (Zech. 14.1-9). Thus, the Egyptian was preaching another metaphor for the *re*-conquest of Israel, again the very task only the Christ was expected to accomplish. Indeed, as Craig Evans argues, even the very name 'Egyptian' evokes the out-of-Egypt path of the original Joshua (hence 'Jesus').

Another (unnamed) 'impostor' mentioned by Josephus ('impostor' being obvious code for 'false messiah'—who else would he be pretending to be?) gathered followers and promised them salvation if they followed him into the wilderness—an obvious reference to Moses, and, as Craig Evans shows, this 'impostor' created symbolic allusions to the temptation narrative in Exodus, promising rest in the wilderness and deliverance from evil. So just as those who tempted God in the wilderness lost their God-promised rest, those who ritually reversed this behavior could expect to see the restoration of God's promise.[24] The messianic intentions are evident here.

This means all four of these messiahs, as reported by Josephus, were equating themselves with Jesus (Joshua) and making veiled claims to be the Christ (messiah). In other words, here we have in Josephus four Jesus Christs. Ours simply makes five. The Gospel character of Jesus thus fits right into the trend documented by Josephus.[25]

24. Evans, 'Josephus on John the Baptist', whose analysis is corroborated by Rebecca Gray, *Prophetic Figures in Late Second Temple Jewish Palestine: The Evidence from Josephus* (New York: Oxford University Press, 1993). See Exod. 17.1-7; Num. 20.1-13; and Ps. 95.7b-11, a passage that Evans notes is cited and commented on in the NT as well (in Heb. 3.7–4.13). The temptation narrative in the Gospels bears the same connection (see Chapter 10, §4).

25. We should at least consider the possibility that all these stories are fiction (the fact that all emulate Joshua but each, conveniently, in a different way could suggest literary or parabolic fabrication), but if so, this story-cluster can have only two origins: the Jewish public (i.e., oral lore picked up by Josephus) or Josephus himself (or some other Jewish author he is using as a source, most likely in this case Justus of Tiberias, or some lost Jewish apocryphon). In the one case we still have confirmation of the same messianic fad (in this case creating popular tales and rumors of messiahs), and in the other case we have an improbability (that a single Jewish author invented a messianic

Even 'John the Baptist' (at least as depicted in the Gospels) was a messianic figure (e.g. Jn 1.20; Lk. 3.15), or otherwise telling everyone the messiah would arrive in his lifetime (Mt. 3.1-12; Mk 1.1-8; Lk. 3.1-20; Jn 1.15-28). And he was enormously popular (the Gospels and Acts claim so, and Josephus confirms it), thus further exemplifying the trend of the time. This messianic Baptist cult may even have influenced or spawned Christianity itself (see Element 33). The cult of Simon Magus might likewise have been promoting its own messiah. Acts certainly depicts Simon Magus as a messianic pretender (Acts 8.9-11), again with enormous popularity, just like the others in Josephus. The historicity of this Simon has been questioned, but the historicity of his worship as a divine being has not.[26] If the biblical account of him reflects the truth (of the historical man or the celestial demigod he once was) he would be another example confirming the same trend.

Even skeptical scholars agree there were many pretenders who:

> [D]o not simply announce the will of God but (a) lead actions of deliverance (b) involving 'revolutionary changes' (c) in accord with God's 'design' and (d) corresponding to one of the great historical formative acts of deliverance led by Moses or Joshua.[27]

fever with remarkable coincidence precisely when the messianic cult of Christianity arose and messianic cults were composing the texts stashed at Qumran, yet this same author doesn't position Christianity among them or mention the cults of Qumran, and is even too coy to identify the fad he thus invented as messianic). The most probable fabrication hypothesis is that Josephus (or Justus of Tiberias?) took actual rebel movements and mapped onto them this 'new Joshua' motif himself, yet that would mean the idea of inventing miracle-working, popular-movement-style 'Jesus Christs' readily occurred to him. The improbability of this coinciding (in time and concept) with an 'actual' Jesus Christ (which the author completely fails to connect with them by the same motifs) would then argue in favor of our Jesus Christ being as fabricated as these. But note also how most of them *also* die at the hands of the Romans. If they were historical, then these figures might have even been *trying* to get themselves killed, so as to fulfill the prophecy of Dan. 9.26 and thereby usher in the end of the world as promised in Daniel 12. God had promised that the Jews would rule the universe (Zech. 14), but their sins kept forestalling his promise (Jer. 29; Dan. 9), which would also create a motive for would-be messiahs to perform atonement acts, which could include substitutionary self-sacrifice (see Element 43), out of increasing desperation (Elements 23-26). Christianity almost becomes predictable in this context.

26. See Stephen Haar, *Simon Magus: The First Gnostic?* (New York: Walter de Gruyter, 2003), pp. 11-15; challenging this Simon's historicity is Gerd Lüdemann, *Untersuchungen zur simonianischen Gnosis* (Göttingen: Vandenhoeck & Ruprecht, 1975).

27. R.A. Horsley, '"Messianic" Figures and Movements in First-Century Palestine', in *The Messiah* (ed. Charlesworth), pp. 276-95 (282). Horsley still insists these are not messianic movements, but that assertion depends on an implausibly specific definition of 'messiah' (or an excessively irrational denial of obvious inferences): see my discussion of definitions (§3). Similarly in Sean Freyne, 'The Herodian Period', in

There were other messianic pretenders *after* the first Jewish War as well. But already across the whole generation before that war numerous self-proclaimed 'messiahs' were gathering followers and making claims of miraculous powers and the coming end of the world-order at this very time, and we have no reason to assume Josephus has given us accounts of them all, only the most famous or a representative sample. Notably, again, all whom he recorded accounts of were pretending to be a new Jesus ('Joshua'). Jesus would thus be symbolically recognized as a messianic name (see Chapter 6, §3; and Element 6). And all of them reenact Exodus-like events. Even John the Baptist is exploiting Exodus symbolism by baptizing in the Jordan: the waterway crossed from death to life (from the slavery of Egypt to the paradise of the Holy Land—by way of 'the wilderness' in between), using in his own case a baptismal re-birthing ceremony. In everyone's view the messiah was to free the Jews from slavery. The Exodus narrative was an obvious and popular model for that. Hence the fact that the Exodus is often a key motif in the NT suggests similar thinking.

It is reasonable to infer that once the literal, militaristic versions of this idea had been seen to fail (or indeed to be impossible, given the unstoppable might of the legions), it would not be unthinkable to adapt the same idea to being freed from the slavery not of the Romans or the corrupt Jewish elite, but the slavery of invisible demons (and death itself) instead. Anyone who took that step would essentially end up with a movement like Christianity (see Elements 23-28). For the 'gospel' of Jesus was already seen as the symbolic Exodus ritual and narrative for every Christian's escape from exactly that kind of spiritual slavery (e.g. Romans 7–8; 1 Corinthians 10). The only question is whether this Jesus was a real messianic pretender just like all these others, part of an established widespread trend (into which he would fit very well), who also failed just as they did, being killed by the authorities just as they were, but whose surviving followers merely came up with a successful way to repackage and sell his ideas, turning him into a *spiritually* victorious messiah, after his superficially material defeat—or whether Jesus was a spiritually conceived messiah right from the beginning.[28]

Redemption and Resistance (ed. Bockmuehl and Paget), pp. 29-43: like Horsley, Freyne is only skeptical in respect to an over-restrictive definition of 'messiah'; whereas given my definition, his evidence completely confirms my conclusion. The same can be said of Martin Goodman, 'Messianism and Politics in the Land of Israel, 66-135 C.E.', in *Redemption and Resistance* (ed. Bockmuehl and Paget), pp. 149-57.

28. If Jesus did exist, his followers may have repackaged the dead Jesus into a spiritual one consciously or not—that is, by merely *claiming* to have been visited by his risen spirit *or* by their subconscious minds constructing that experience for them (see Element 15).

Regardless, all the evidence is clear enough on the general fact of the matter: the first century had exploded with messianic fervor, to the point that it's not at all surprising one of these countless new messianic cults would become more successful than the rest (the others being wiped out or not adopting the right mix of popular attributes), even standing a fair chance of becoming a world religion (as any successful cult has a shot at doing). And Christianity is exactly such a messianic cult (as later elements establish), arising exactly when such cults were popular, and in the very same place.

Element 5: Even before Christianity arose, some Jews expected one of their messiahs heralding the end times would actually be killed, rather than be immediately victorious, and this would mark the key point of a timetable guaranteeing the end of the world soon thereafter. Such a concept was therefore not a Christian novelty wholly against the grain of Jewish thinking, but already exactly what some Jews were thinking—or could easily have thought. This is the most controversial element in our background knowledge, many scholars being so intent on denying it. So I must discuss the evidence at some length, although I shall do this more thoroughly elsewhere.[29]

First, the Talmud provides us with a proof of concept at the very least (and actual confirmation at the very most). It explicitly says the suffering servant who dies in Isaiah 53 is the messiah (and that this messiah will endure great suffering before his death).[30] The Talmud likewise has a dying-and-rising 'Christ son of Joseph' ideology in it, even saying (quoting Zech. 12.10) that this messiah will be 'pierced' to death.[31] Modern scholars are too quick to dismiss this text as late (dating as it does from the fourth to sixth century), since the doctrine it describes is unlikely to be. For only when Jews had no idea what Christians would do with this connection would they themselves have promoted it. There is no plausible way later Jews would invent interpretations of their scripture that supported and vindicated Christians. They would not invent a Christ with a father named Joseph who dies and is resurrected (as the Talmud does indeed describe). They would not proclaim Isaiah 53 to be about this messiah and admit that

29. Richard Carrier, 'Did Any Pre-Christian Jews Expect a Dying-and-Rising Messiah?' [in review]; see also Carrier, *Not the Impossible Faith*, pp. 34-49 (with a correction: p. 34 arguably misreads Isa. 49.7 [cf. p. 49 n. 30]; as had already been suggested on p. 37). Essentially the same conclusion is argued by rabbinical scholar Daniel Boyarin, *The Jewish Gospels: The Story of the Jewish Christ* (New York: New Press, 2012), pp. 129-56.

30. *b. Sanhedrin* 98b and 93b.

31. *b. Sukkah* 52a-b.

Isaiah had there predicted this messiah would die and be resurrected. That was the very biblical passage Christians were using to prove their case. Moreover, the presentation of this ideology in the Talmud makes no mention of Christianity and gives no evidence of being any kind of polemic or response to it. So we have evidence here of a Jewish belief that possibly predates Christian evangelizing, even if that evidence survives only in later sources.

The alternative is to assume a rather unbelievable coincidence: that Christians and Jews, completely independently of each other, just happened at some point to see Isaiah 53 as messianic and from that same passage preach an ideology of a messiah with a father named Joseph (literally or symbolically), who endures great suffering, dies and is resurrected (all in accord with the savior depicted in Isaiah 53, as by then understood). Such an amazing coincidence is simply improbable. But a causal connection is not: if this was a pre-Christian ideology that influenced (and thus caused) *both* the Christian *and* the Jewish ideologies, then we have only one element to explain (the rise of this idea once, being adapted in different ways), instead of having to believe the same idea arose twice, purely coincidentally. Two improbable events by definition are many times less likely than one.[32] That means the invented-once theory is many times more likely than the invented-twice one. Conversely, if we choose instead to fall on this sword of improbability and insist, against all likelihood, that yes, the same ideas arose twice independently of each other within Judaism, then this entails the idea was very easy for Jews to arrive at (since rabbinical Jews, independently of Christians, clearly arrived at it), which then entails it was not an improbable development in the first place. And thus neither will it

32. We might have evidence of a strand of that prior tradition in the early-first-century Targum of Jonathan ben Uzziel on Isaiah 53 (a kind of paraphrastic commentary in Aramaic; Jonathan ben Uzziel was traditionally a student of Hillel, who died c. 10 CE, and a contemporary of Shammai, who died c. 30 CE), which explicitly identifies the suffering servant there as the Christ—but otherwise transforms the narrative to suppress or downplay the element of his dying. But anyone who read this Targum, and then the original Hebrew (or Greek), could put two and two together: 'this servant is the messiah' plus 'this servant dies and is buried and then exalted' = 'the messiah dies and is buried and then exalted', the very doctrine we see in the Talmud, which just happens to be the same doctrine adopted by Christians. This Targum was multiply tampered with over the years, however (see Bruce Chilton, *The Glory of Israel: The Theology and Provenience of the Isaiah Targum* [Sheffield: JSOT Press, 1982], e.g., p. 94), so nothing conclusive can be decided by it (even though, again, it is unlikely Jews would change the Targum to make Isaiah 53 messianic *after* Christianity started using Isaiah 53 to support their cause), although Jintae Kim makes a case for the reading being early in 'Targum Isaiah 53 and the New Testament Concept of Atonement', *Journal of Greco-Roman Christianity and Judaism* 5 (2008), pp. 81-98.

have been improbable for Christians (or their sectarian predecessors among the Jews), any more than it was for Talmudic Jews. Clearly dying messiahs were not anathema. Rabbinical Jews could be just as comfortable with the idea as Christians were (more on this point in Chapter 12, §4).

This dying-messiah doctrine is not only found in the Talmud but is more considerably spelled out in the seventh-century *Apocalypse of Zerubbabel* (*Sefer Zerubbabel*), which likewise prophesies that there will be two messiahs, a Messiah ben David and a Messiah ben Joseph, and that the latter messiah (the Son of Joseph) would come first and be killed by an evil tyrant named Armilus (whom some scholars conjecture is a Hebraicism for Romulus, i.e., Rome). But all would not be lost, because the second messiah (the Son of David) would soon appear and resurrect him, and the end of the world would soon follow.[33]

Quite simply, if anyone were to merge these two messiahs into a single person (the Son of Joseph and the Son of David, one who dies and rises and one who returns to bring victory), we would have Christianity: a messiah fathered by a Joseph who is killed by an evil power and is then resurrected and anointed 'the Son of David', destined to return triumphant. It is far more likely that Christians united two figures already imagined in earlier Jewish apocalyptic thought than that rabbinical Jews took a novel messiah from the heretical sect of Christianity and elaborately split it into two messiahs, with otherwise all the same attributes (and then make no mention of how this responds to Christianity or why they would even do that).[34]

33. See translation in John Reeves, *Trajectories in Near Eastern Apocalyptic: A Postrabbinic Jewish Apocalypse Reader* (Atlanta, GA: Society of Biblical Literature, 2005), pp. 40-66, where the Messiah ben Joseph appears (p. 57), is killed (pp. 59-60), then resurrected (pp. 60-61) by the Messiah ben David, after which the apocalypse follows. The narrative in this text was adapted to contemporary political circumstances of the later Middle Ages, but it is clear from the Talmud that the outline of it long predated that period, and thus long predates this redaction of it.

34. The Dead Sea Scrolls also speak of two messiahs, one 'Messiah of Aaron', who would be the 'true high priest', and a 'Messiah of Israel', who would be a kingly warlord figure. See Evans and Flint (eds.), *Eschatology*, pp. 5-6; and Peter Flint, 'Jesus and the Dead Sea Scrolls', in *Historical Jesus in Context* (ed. Levine, Allison and Crossan), pp. 110-31; and Florentino García Martínez and Eibert J.C. Tigchelaar (eds.), *Qumranica minora*, Vol. II (Boston: Brill, 2007), pp. 13-32. But it's debated whether these are actually two messiahs, or what kind of messiahs they are: see L.D. Hurst, 'Did Qumran Expect Two Messiahs?', *Bulletin for Biblical Research* 9 (1999), pp. 157-80 (although note that his conclusion is reversed when we adopt my definition of messiah rather than his). It's also debated whether one of the Qumran fragments says one of these messiahs 'will be pierced' and killed, or whether he will pierce and kill someone else, and I consider that question presently unresolvable (the manuscript is too damaged to tell). See Helmut Koester, 'The Historical Jesus and the Historical Situation of the Quest: An Epilogue', in *Studying the Historical Jesus: Evaluation*

But the Talmud and the *Apocalypse of Zerubbabel* are not our only evidence of a pre-Christian dying-messiah theme. The book of Daniel (written well before the rise of Christianity) explicitly says a messiah will die shortly before the end of the world (Dan. 9.2; 9.24-27; cf. 12.1-13). This is already conclusive. Given my definition of 'messiah' (in §3), Christianity looks exactly like an adaptation of the same eschatological dying-messiah motif in Daniel. And the Wisdom of Solomon, an important scripture to the first Christians, presents a son of God who is despised, killed, resurrected and crowned as a king in heaven (cf. 2.12-22; 5.1-23), a narrative that could easily have been taken by some as referring to the messiah—and even if not, it certainly established a heroic model that one could adapt into a dying messiah already within pre-Christian Judaism, which would thus already be intelligible to Jews. This Wisdom of Solomon archetype could even have been associated with the despised-and-dying servant of Isaiah 53, as they sound quite similar (innocent righteous men humiliated and killed by the wicked, but exalted and made triumphant). Isaiah 53 was already understood to contain an atonement–martyrdom framework applicable to dying heroes generally.[35] And the whole concept of a suffering, martyred hero was an established Jewish archetype (see Element 43).

But of the more specific notion of a dying messiah, we also have other pre-Christian evidence in the form of a Dead Sea Scroll designated 11Q13, the Melchizedek Scroll.[36] This is an apocalyptic pesher, a document attempting to discover hidden messages in the scriptures by finding secret links

of the State of Current Research (ed. Bruce Chilton and Craig Evans; Leiden: Brill, 1994), pp. 535-45; and Craig Evans, 'The Recently Published Dead Sea Scrolls and the Historical Jesus', in *Studying the Historical Jesus* (ed. Chilton and Evans), pp. 547-65 (553-54); and the debate between Hershel Shanks, 'The "Pierced Messiah" Text—An Interpretation Evaporates', *Biblical Archaeology Review* 18 (July/August 1992), pp. 80-82; and James Tabor, '4Q285: A Pierced or Piercing Messiah?—The Verdict Is Still Out', *Biblical Archaeology Review* 18 (November/December 1992), pp. 58-59; as well as the discussion and scholarship cited in Martin Abegg, 'Messianic Hope and 4Q285: A Reassessment', *Journal of Biblical Literature* 113 (Spring 1994), pp. 81-91.

35. Jarvis Williams, *Maccabean Martyr Traditions in Paul's Theology of Atonement: Did Martyr Theology Shape Paul's Conception of Jesus's Death?* (Eugene, OR: Wipf & Stock, 2010), pp. 53-63, 72-84.

36. 11Q13 = 11QMelch ii.18-20. For the scroll's text, translation and notes, see Alex Jassen, *Mediating the Divine: Prophecy and Revelation in the Dead Sea Scrolls and Second Temple Judaism* (Leiden: Brill, 2007), pp. 90-95; John Sietze Bergsma, *The Jubilee from Leviticus to Qumran: A History of Interpretation* (Leiden: Brill, 2007), pp. 277-91, with Géza Vermès, *The Complete Dead Sea Scrolls in English* (New York: Penguin Press, 7th edn, 2011), pp. 532-33; and Christian Metzenthin, *Jesaja-Auslegung in Qumran* (Zurich: TVZ, 2010), pp. 314-23; see also Abegg, 'Messianic Hope and 4Q285', pp. 89-90; and Lara Guglielmo, '11Q13, Malchî Sedek, Co-Reference, and Restoration of 2 18', *Henoch* 33 (2011), pp. 61-72, with a somewhat weak rebuttal by

among disparate and previously unrelated verses (see Elements 8 and 16), which together communicate God's plan, most commonly (and certainly in this case) his plans for the coming messiah, the defeat of evil and the end of the world. There are many such pesherim at Qumran. But this one tells us about the 'messenger' of Isaiah 52–53 who is linked in Isaiah with a 'servant' who will die to atone for everyone's sins (presaging God's final victory), which (as we have already seen) later Jews definitely regarded as the messiah. At Qumran, 11Q13 appears to say that this messenger is the same man as the 'messiah' of Daniel 9, who dies around the same time an end to sin is said to be accomplished (again presaging God's final victory), and that the day on which this happens will be a great and final Day of Atonement, absolving the sins of all the elect, after which (11Q13 goes on to say) God and his savior will overthrow all demonic forces. And all this will proceed according to the timetable in Daniel 9. Thus, 11Q13 appears to predict that a messiah will die and that this will mark the final days before which God's agent(s) will defeat Belial (Satan) and atone for the sins of the elect.

Not all scholars have recognized this in 11Q13 or conceded it. Though I find no sound basis for rejecting it, I'll endeavor to prove it elsewhere.[37] Regardless of how one chooses to understand the text of 11Q13, we still have Dan. 9.24-27, which is already unmistakably clear in predicting that a messiah will die shortly before the end of the world, when all sins will be forgiven; and Isaiah 53 is unmistakably clear in declaring that all sins will be forgiven by the death of God's servant, whom the Talmud identifies as the messiah. So there is no reasonable basis for denying that some pre-Christian Jews would have expected at least one dying messiah, and some could well have expected his death to be an essential atoning death, just as the Christians believed of Jesus (Element 10).

Even apart from 11Q13 there is evidence the Dead Sea community may have already been thinking this, since one of their manuscripts of Isaiah explicitly says the suffering servant figure in Isaiah 53 shall be 'anointed' by God and then 'pierced through for our transgressions'.[38] Contrary to

Darrell Bock, 'Is That All There Is? A Response to Lara Guglielmo's 11Q13, Malchî Sedek, Co-Reference, and Restoration of 2 18', *Henoch* 33 (2011), pp. 73-76.

37. In Carrier, 'Did Any Pre-Christian Jews Expect a Dying-and-Rising Messiah?'

38. For this and the following points see the discussion of the pre-Christian interpretation of Isaiah 53 in Martin Hengel, 'The Effective History of Isaiah 53 in the Pre-Christian Period', in *The Suffering Servant: Isaiah 53 in Jewish and Christian Sources* (ed. Bernd Janowski and Peter Stuhlmacher; Grand Rapids, MI: William B. Eerdmans, 2004), pp. 75-146; see pp. 103-105 on the divergent text of 1QIsa[a], where the suffering servant figure of Isaiah 52–53 is 'pierced' rather than 'bruised' in Isa. 53.10 and correspondingly in Isa. 53.5 he is 'pierced through for our transgressions' rather than merely 'wounded' for them; likewise in that same scroll, Isa. 52.14 has God declare of him that he shall have 'anointed his appearance beyond that of any

modern rhetoric, there is no actual evidence that Jews would have rejected such a notion (as I explain in Chapter 12, §4). Neither was such a thing incompatible with expectations of a victorious messiah, since God's righteous were always expected to be resurrected, which included the messiah, and accordingly the earliest Christians expected their dying messiah to soon return victorious, even imagining his resurrection had already occurred to signal the end was nigh, being in fact 'the firstfruits' of the apocalyptic resurrection of the whole world (1 Cor. 15.20-23) and signaling his messianic victory over the powers of darkness (Element 37).

This should not surprise us. Even the original forgers of Daniel 9 were already imagining something along these lines. Modern scholars are generally agreed that its authors were saying that the then-high-priest Onias III was a Messiah (a Christ), and his death would presage a universal atonement, after which would come the end of the world—effected by the coming of the angel Michael.[39] That's already just one or two tweaks away from the Christian gospel. One of those tweaks would be simply equating the messiah who dies with the savior who returns to complete God's plan (in other words, once again, combining the two figures into one): the second of which in Daniel is, again, the archangel Michael, called 'the great prince' in Dan. 12.1, whom a later interpreter could easily read as being the same 'prince' of Dan. 9.26-27 (the words are not identical but have a corresponding meaning), because the events of Dan. 12.9-12 are the same events, yet are assumed to follow the event of Michael's 'rising' in 12.1 (which in the LXX employs exactly the same word used of Jesus' resurrection in Mk 9.31 and 10.34). So it could appear Michael was meant to be the 'prince' in Dan. 9.26-27. Because in Dan. 12.9-12 Michael is the one doing the things the 'prince' does in Dan. 9.26-27.

That this Michael is 'the resurrected messiah' would thus have been an easy inference for a later interpreter to make, in which event 9.25-26 could easily be read as being not about a Christ *and* a Prince but a Princely

man, and his form beyond that of the sons of man', which Hengel considers allusive to the anointing of high priests in Lev. 21.10 and 16.32, which would make this figure a messiah in the broadest sense—therefore anyone who saw this figure's atoning death as *eschatological* would also regard him as a messiah in the narrower sense that I have defined (in §3).

39. As explained in Daniel 12; Michael is not there called a messiah, but plays the role of what many Jews expected of the final messiah. Both Michael and Melchizedek were regarded as God's celestial high priest in Jewish writings generally, thus they would have commonly been equated: Joseph Fitzmyer, 'Further Light on Melchizedek from Qumran Cave 11', in *Essays on the Semitic Background of the New Testament* (London: Geoffrey Chapman, 1971), pp. 245-67 (254-55). This would further link these figures to the pre-Christian Jewish theology of God's Logos and celestial firstborn son, also named Jesus (Element 40).

Christ, all one and the same person, who dies (9.26) and then rises from the dead (9.26-27 and 12.1). The Christian gospel is thus already right there in Daniel, the more so if Daniel 9 had been linked with Isaiah 52–53, which is exactly what 11Q13 appears to do. But even without such a connection being made, the notion that a Christ was expected to die to presage the end of the world *is already clearly intended* in Daniel, even by its original authors' intent, and would have been understood in the same way by subsequent readers of Daniel. The notion of a dying messiah was therefore already mainstream, well before Christianity arose. That this messiah did not correspond to any specific definition of any specific kind of messiah is not relevant, since we know the Jews had many diverse notions of a messiah, and frequently innovated.

Once the idea was out there, there would be no getting that cat back into the bag. In Daniel's originally intended case, the end of the world did not come (in fact everything after the death of its intended messiah did not occur as the forgers' prophecy predicted), so later Jews had only two options: either reject Daniel as a false prophecy (and we know the Jews who initiated Christianity had *not* done that) or conclude 'Daniel' wasn't talking about Onias III but some other messiah *in the future* (necessitating attempts to reinterpret the 490-year timetable in Dan. 9.24 to figure out what time in history Daniel was actually talking about), which is clearly what many Jews did—the author of 11Q13 in particular. In other words, the authors of Daniel were plainly saying, and by many were read as saying, that the last Christ *was to die*—shortly before the final end when God's chosen agent (in Daniel, the archangel Michael; in 11Q13, Melchizedek) would descend from heaven, defeat the forces of evil once and for all, and resurrect the dead. This means many Jews were *expecting* a dying messiah, as a sign the end was nigh.

I believe the force of all these arguments is strong, and resistance to them can only at this point be blindly dogmatic. But even if scholars remain obstinate against an established *fact* of a pre-Christian dying-christology, in the face of the same evidence they can no longer insist upon its *implausibility*. Because even if you are uncertain of the fact of it, this same evidence still conclusively proves that the proposition 'Christianity arose from a sect of Jews that came to expect a dying messiah' is a *plausible hypothesis*, even if we can't prove such a sect existed, because (a) we know there were many diverse sects of Jews with many diverse notions against the leading orthodoxy, and we know nothing about most of them (Element 2); therefore (b) an argument from silence to the conclusion 'no such sect existed' cannot be sustained;[40] whereas (c) the scriptural inspiration and logic for such an idea is

40. On the facts and logic of this point, and other scholars making it, see Carrier, *Proving History*, pp. 129-34 (with pp. 117-19).

easily discerned (so easy, in fact, that Talmudic Jews also discerned it)—and if it's easy for us, it would have been easy for at least someone to have noticed it during centuries of hundreds of Jewish scholars and sectarians scrambling to look for God's secret messages in scripture (Element 8). That later Talmudic Jews hit upon essentially the same conclusions verifies the point.

This means that in logical terms, 'Christianity arose from a sect of Jews that came to expect a dying messiah' is a plausible hypothesis that we can then test against the evidence. Because there is no evidence against that hypothesis or its plausibility. So if it explains the evidence better than alternatives, then it is more probably true than alternatives (and as a hypothesis it's already more likely than, e.g., 'Christians only started believing this because Jesus actually rose from the dead'). We therefore do not require direct evidence of 'there was a sect of Jews that came to expect a dying messiah'. Because if all other evidence is better explained by that proposition, then that other evidence *is* evidence for that proposition. Such indirect inference is routine in historical argument. That Henry assassinated William II is a hypothesis, which we can argue for from whether it better explains the evidence of what subsequently happened, without requiring a confession by Henry or an eyewitness to the deed.[41]

Since we lack evidence detailing the beliefs of dozens of Jewish sects, and no evidence at all naming (much less describing in detail) which sect Christianity grew out of (e.g. what sect Peter was most enamored with or devoted to before he joined or launched the movement; or, on a historicist thesis, what sect or sects Jesus originally came from or was educated in; or even what sects Paul was influenced by, if any before the Christian sect, that led him to abandon the Pharisee sect). So we know it's very likely we *won't* have evidence of such a thing as that the sect Christianity grew out of was already expecting a dying messiah.[42] Thus, whether it was or not is either unknowable (in which case it can't be denied as a possibility nor even declared an improbability) or can be inferred from evidence we do have: such as that the crucifixion of the Christian messiah was always said to have been discovered in scripture (1 Cor. 15.3-4 and Rom. 16.25-26), combined with all the evidence we have surveyed here, from the book of Daniel, the Talmud, the *Sefer Zerubbabel*, and the Melchizedek Scroll.

I believe this amounts to ample evidence that at least some pre-Christian Jews were expecting a dying messiah to presage the end of the world; and even should anyone reject that conclusion, it still cannot be denied that the *hypothesis* (that some pre-Christian Jews were expecting a dying messiah to presage the end of the world) is at least plausible enough to take

41. See discussion of this example in Carrier, *Proving History*, pp. 273-75.

42. That this eliminates the strength of any argument from silence, see previous note.

seriously, given all that same evidence. Its prior probability simply cannot be established as low, and from the evidence here surveyed, it looks more likely to be high.

Element 6: The suffering-and-dying servant of Isaiah 52–53 and the messiah of Daniel 9 (which, per the previous element, may already have been seen by some Jews as the same person) have numerous logical connections with a man in Zechariah 3 and 6 named 'Jesus Rising' who is confronted by Satan in God's abode in heaven and there crowned king, given all of God's authority, holds the office of high priest, and will build up 'God's house' (which is how Christians described their church).[43]

In the Septuagint text, Zechariah is commanded in a vision to place the crown of kingship upon 'Jesus' (Zech. 6.11) and to say immediately upon doing so that 'Jehovah declares' that this Jesus is 'the man named "Rising" and he shall rise up from his place below and he shall build the House of the Lord'. The key noun is *anatolē,* which is often translated 'East' because it refers to where the sun rises (hence 'East'), but such a translation obscures the fact that the actual word used is the noun 'rising' or 'rise' (as in 'sunrise'), which was not always used in reference to a compass point, and whose real connotations are more obvious when translated literally. In fact by immediately using the cognate verb 'to rise up' (*anatelei*, and that explicitly 'from his place below') it's clear the Septuagint translator understood the word to mean 'rise' (and Philo echoes the same pun in his interpretation, and thus also understood: see Element 40). We know Zechariah meant this in some way to be Jesus ben Jehozadak, the legendary first high priest of the second temple (as I'll discuss shortly). But by implying this event may have occurred in heaven, interpreters could think differently. And we know some did (Element 40).

If this 'Jesus Rising' were connected to the dying servant who atones for all sins in Isaiah (and perhaps also with Daniel or 11Q13), it would be easy to read out of this almost the entire core Christian gospel. Connecting the two figures in just that way would be natural to do: this same 'Jesus' who is named 'Rising' (or, in both places, 'Branch' in the extant Hebrew, as in 'Davidic heir', or so both contexts imply) appears earlier in Zechariah 3, where 'Jesus' is also implied to be the one called 'Rising' (in 3.8). Both are also called 'Jesus the high priest' throughout Zechariah 3 and 6, hence clearly the same person. And there he is *also* called God's 'servant'. And it is said that through him (in some unspecified way) all sin in the world

43. God's house is, of course, God's temple, which is what Christians sometimes called their church (each member was God's temple, but also collectively they were each a part of a single body and thus *collectively* God's temple): 1 Cor. 3.16-17; 6.16-20; 10.17; 12.12-27; 2 Cor. 6.16; Rom. 12.4-5. See Element 18.

will be cleansed 'in a single day' (Zech. 3.9). Both concepts converge with Isaiah 52–53, which is also about God's 'servant', whose *death* cleanses the world's sins (Isa. 52.13 and 53.11), which of course would thus happen in a single day (as alluded in Isa. 52.6). And as we saw earlier, Jews may have been linking this dying 'servant' to the dying 'Christ' killed in Daniel 9 (in 11Q13), whose death is *also* said to correspond closely with a conclusive 'end of sin' in the world (Dan. 9.24-26), and both figures (in Daniel and 11Q13) were linked to an expected 'atonement in a single day' after a period of 490 years, whose starting point one needed only to discover in order to predict the end of the world (see Element 5).

These dots are so easily connected, and with such convincing force for anyone enamored of the thought process generating the Jewish pesherim as a literary genre, that it would be astonishing if *no* Jews had thought of this. Not ever, by anyone, in the whole of their fevered composition of pesherim? (See Element 8.) That seems quite improbable. Nevertheless, I am not here declaring Christianity was born from making this connection, only that it is certainly plausible to *hypothesize* it was.[44] I will provide further evidence for that being the case in Element 40, where Christian and Jewish theology also coincide at exactly this point, but here I am concerned only with the existence of the *scriptural* coincidences, which definitely predated Christianity in public documents used as sacred scripture by all Jews, and thus by all would-be founders of Christianity.

As I mentioned, an 'exoteric' reading of Zechariah 3 and 6 would conclude the author originally meant the first high priest of the second temple, Jesus ben Jehozadak (Zech. 6.11; cf. Hag. 1.1), who somehow came into an audience with God, in a coronation ceremony (one would presume in heaven, as it is in audience with God and his angels and attended by Satan) granting him supreme supernatural power over the universe (Zech. 3.7). But such a scene hardly seems descriptive of any living person, and would more readily be 'esoterically' read as being about a *celestial* being named Jesus (as in fact we know it was, Philo of Alexandria having made exactly this inference: see Element 40), who was given by God supreme authority over the universe in defiance of Satan (Zech. 3.1-2). As it happens, the name Jehozadak means in Hebrew 'Jehovah the Righteous', so one could also read this as 'Jesus, the son of Jehovah the Righteous', and thereby conclude this is really 'Jesus, the son of God'.

This is notable considering the evidence we have of a preexistent son of God named Jesus in pre-Christian Jewish theology, connected with this

44. That Zechariah 3 was a seminal scripture in the founding of Christianity has been argued before: see Daniel Stökl ben Ezra, *The Impact of Yom Kippur on Early Christianity: The Day of Atonement from Second Temple Judaism to the Fifth Century* (Tübingen: Mohr Siebeck, 2003), pp. 194-97.

very passage (discussed in Element 40). The fact that in his coronation scene his dirty rags are replaced with magnificent raiment in heaven (Zech. 3.3-5) could also have been read as a resurrection metaphor, such a change of garments being a common metaphor for that at the time.[45] But even without that assumption, if this Jesus had ever been connected in previous (but now lost) pesherim with the dying Christ figure in Isaiah and Daniel (by linking them all through Zech. 3.8-9), then we would have a man who dies and is then named Rising and said to 'rise' (just like Michael the Prince in Daniel) in order to be given all power and authority (which would imply a resurrection more than sufficiently to almost any Jew of the day) and who somehow conclusively atones for all sins in a single day.

The significance of this is that if such a connection had been made, the connector would have before him, in a simple pesher of Jewish scripture, a celestial being named Jesus Christ Rising, a high priest of God, in opposition to Satan, who is wrongly executed even though innocent, and dies to atone for all sins, is buried and subsequently 'raised', exalted to the highest station in heaven, appointed king with supreme heavenly power by God, and who will then build God's house (the church). That sounds exactly like Christianity. And all from connecting just three passages in the OT that already have distinctive overlapping similarities. Such a coincidence cannot be ignored; it must be included in our background knowledge. Would Christians *really* have been that lucky, that all this connected so obviously? Or are we seeing here where the whole idea of the Christian gospel came from in the first place?

Element 7: (a) The pre-Christian book of Daniel was a key messianic text, laying out what would happen and when, partly inspiring much of the very messianic ferver of the age, which by the most obvious (but not originally intended) interpretation predicted the messiah's arrival in the early first century, even (by some calculations) the very year of 30 CE. (b) This text was popularly known and widely influential, and was known and regarded as scripture by the early Christians.

This fact is already attested by the many copies and commentaries on Daniel recovered from Qumran,[46] but it's evident also in the fact that the

45. See Carrier, 'Spiritual Body', in *Empty Tomb* (ed. Price and Lowder), pp. 114-15, 132-47, 157, 212 (n. 166). The heavenly ascent narrative known to Ignatius, Irenaeus and Justin Martyr (see Chapter 8, §6) may have alluded to this passage in Zechariah, if this is what is intended by mentioning the lowly state of Jesus' attire when he enters God's heavenly court in Justin Martyr, *Dialogue with Trypho* 36.

46. On the numerous copies of Daniel among the Dead Sea Scrolls, including fragments of commentaries on it, see Peter Flint, 'The Daniel Tradition at Qumran', in *Eschatology* (ed. Evans and Flint), pp. 41-60, and F.F. Bruce, 'The Book of Daniel

Jewish War itself may have been partly a product of it. As at Qumran, the key inspiring text was the messianic timetable described in the book of Daniel (in Dan. 9.23-27). By various calculations this could be shown to predict, by the very Word of God, that the messiah would come sometime in the early first century CE. Several examples of these calculations survive in early Christian literature, the clearest appearing in Julius Africanus in the third century.[47] The date there calculated is precisely 30 CE; hence it was expected on this calculation (which was simple and straightforward enough that anyone could easily have come up with the same result well before the rise of Christianity) that a messiah would arise and be killed in that year (as we saw Daniel had 'predicted' in 9.26: see Element 5), which is an obvious basis for setting the gospel story precisely then (I'll revisit this point later on here and in Chapter 8), or else a basis for believing that, of all messianic claimants, 'our' Jesus Christ was the one for real.

For all of this to be coincidence is unlikely. Different calendars and calculations might have given slightly different years, but every *straightforward* calculation falls around the same period. And the Christian calculation was the most obvious, and therefore the most likely to have been arrived at before the fact. This kind of messianic math was very possibly the cause of the whole explosion of messianic claims and expectations in that very century (Element 4). Josephus even implies that this prophecy caused the Jewish War—certain Jewish factions being so convinced by it that they were certain God's messiah would descend to defeat the Romans. Which didn't happen, of course, resulting in their crushing defeat. But messianic fever remained so great it had thus led to a suicidal war. Arguably only a belief in a supernaturally backed messianic event could have mobilized armies among the Jews. Several other historians near to the event confirm it was indeed this belief that inspired that revolt.[48]

and the Qumran Community', in *Neotestamentica et semitica: Studies in Honour of Matthew Black* (ed. E. Earle Ellis and Max Wilcox; Edinburgh: T. & T. Clark, 1969), pp. 221-35.

47. Julius Africanus, in his lost *History of the World*, which excerpt survives in the collection of George Syncellus, *Excerpts of Chronography* 18.2. Other examples of this kind of calculation survive in Tertullian, *Answer to the Jews* 8, and Clement of Alexandria, *Miscellanies* 1.21.(125-26).

48. Josephus, *Jewish War* 6.312-16; verified in Suetonius, *Life of Vespasian* 4.5, and Tacitus, *Histories* 5.13.2. Josephus's discussion does not here identify Daniel by title but he does elsewhere (in Josephus, *Jewish Antiquities* 10.276), and here he clearly intends no other text given his description (of two rulers who would come, and the presence of an actual timetable, two features not found together in any other passage of the Bible). Josephus himself correctly interprets the Danielic prophecy to have been regarding the Maccabees (Josephus, *Jewish Antiquities* 12.321-22), yet *also*

If Daniel was behind much or all of the first-century craze for messiahs, it could have inspired Christianity as well (with or without a historical Jesus), Christianity being just another messianic cult like all the others. And we can verify this at least as far as the Gospels. Mark quotes a passage from the Danielic timetable (Mk 13.14), and Matthew provides the attribution (Mt. 24.15). Thus the earliest texts that place Jesus's death in Palestine around 30 CE were clearly aware of the very prophetic text placing a messiah's appearance and death around 30 CE. And that's a fact, whatever we decide to make of it. (Personally, I think if Jesus just 'happened' to die in 30 CE, then that would be a rather convenient coincidence; whereas if the year of the crucifixion was fudged or fabricated to match the prophecy, even for a historical death, then no lucky coincidence is required. It is therefore the more probable hypothesis.)

The irony in all of this is that Daniel 9 was an attempt to fix a failed prophecy in Jeremiah (Dan. 9.2, responding to Jer. 25.11-12), yet this 'fix' also failed, prompting later Jews to try and salvage this double failure by 'reinterpreting' *Daniel* this time and thus doing to Daniel what Daniel had unsuccessfully attempted to do to Jeremiah. Christianity was the most successful result. Of course, then the Christians had to spoil it by creating their own prophesy that the end of the world would come within the lifetimes of those hearing the good news. Which prophesy also failed.[49] It would be comical if it wasn't sad. But the cognitive dissonance caused by those earlier failures would explain the eventual success of a 'reinterpretation' that couldn't be falsified: a messiah who triumphs in heaven, and reveals this fact from heaven, in secret, to a select few.

This is essentially Christianity in a nutshell (whether Jesus existed or not). The need to innovate an ironclad solution to the failure of God's scripture (in Jeremiah, as patched up by Daniel) would certainly inspire both creativity to that end and its passionate acceptance—and with a 'spiritual' solution there could be no evidence against it (even in principle) and thus no more cognitive dissonance over it (see Element 28). The only thing left to cope with was the continuing failure of Christian prophets to get straight

acknowledges (in 10.276) that it was about the Roman sack of Jerusalem, imagining the prophecy as having been twice fulfilled.

49. And this cycle of predicting the end, followed by failure, then revising of the prediction, has continued ever since. See John Loftus, 'At Best Jesus Was a Failed Apocalyptic Prophet', in *Christian Delusion* (ed. Loftus), pp. 316-43. That Christians taught that Jesus had predicted the imminent end is undeniable: Heb. 1.10–2.5; 10.36-37; 1 Cor. 1.28; 6.13; 7.29-31; 1 Thess. 4.15; 2 Pet. 3.5-13; 1 Jn 2.15-18; and of course Mark 13 and Matthew 24. On the continuing cycle of failure after that, see Bernard McGinn *et al.*, *The Continuum History of Apocalypticism* (New York: Continuum, 2003); and Jonathan Kirsch, *A History of the End of the World* (San Francisco, CA: Harper, 2006).

when the world would end, but history proves that has never been a difficulty. A heavenly victory simply made it easier. 'Yes, the world didn't end today as we thought, but at least we're still saved'. That's the mantra Christians have sustained the faith with for two thousand years.

But it all began with Jeremiah—and the book of Daniel. Experts agree Daniel was forged in the second century in part to 'explain' the death of the high priest Onias III in 171 BCE, who was at the time believed to be the (or a) messiah (he is most likely the 'Christ' who is killed in Dan. 9.26), and to support the subsequent (and otherwise technically illegitimate) Maccabean regime by 'predicting' God's defeat of their opponent, Antiochus IV, in 164 BCE and then the coming end of the world (which didn't happen—in fact, much of what Daniel predicts after Chapter 9 didn't go to plan, providing a clue as to when it was written).[50] This *original* meaning required a particular method of calculating years according to the timetable, using overlapping rather than sequential periods, the only way to get Jeremiah's numbers to fit actual history up to Onias's death (and thereby 'predict' this messiah would die in 171 BCE). Obviously that was more awkward than simply counting sequentially. So subsequent reinterpreters, certain the 'inspired' Daniel could not have made a mistake, summed these years sequentially (the more obvious way), and chose different starting points (whatever could count as a 'word concerning the restoration of Jerusalem'), which (depending on what calendar you use) gets various dates for the messiah's death in the early first century CE.

The Christian religion could thus in a sense be explained as an attempt to explain away Daniel's failed prediction of a divinely supported military victory for Israel over its Gentile oppressors (which continually didn't happen), by imagining (unlike Daniel) a 'spiritual' kingdom instead of an actual one, and repeatedly postponing the actual one to an ever-receding future. Among the Dead Sea Scrolls, for example, in what's called 'The Son of God' text (4Q246), we have a redaction of Daniel in which it is predicted that one day a great and righteous man will be born and be called the son of God and rule an eternal kingdom. Though here it was still imagined as a kingdom achieved by conquest, followed by an eternal reign of peace, it's an easy thing to explain the failure of this to happen time and again by relocating that conquest into the spiritual realm (see Elements 23 through 28). And that's exactly what the Christians did: they imagined a righteous man was born and was called the son of God and now rules an eternal kingdom—a kingdom that no one can see. And they imagined this hap-

50. A good discussion of all of this is provided for Daniel 9 in André Lacocque, *The Book of Daniel* (Atlanta, GA: John Knox Press, 1979); but any professional commentary on Daniel 9 will make the same point, for example John Collins, *Daniel: A Commentary* (Minneapolis, MN: Fortress Press, 1993).

pened exactly when Daniel appears to have predicted it would. And they imagined it followed the death of their Christ exactly as Daniel had said it would. And their own Gospels cite this passage in Daniel as confirmation. So the book of Daniel was clearly a seminal text in the development of Christianity, influencing the core of the gospel itself, including belief in the crucifixion and its prophetic importance. This is all the case whether Jesus existed or not, so this does not answer whether he did; it only entails he didn't have to.

Element 8: (a) Many messianic sects among the Jews were searching the scriptures for secret messages from God about the coming messiah, in both the Hebrew Bible *and* the Septuagint (and beyond: see Element 9). The Christians were thus not engaging in novel activity when they did the same. (b) Since countless Jews were already doing this, and had been for a century or more, we must conclude the Jews who would become the first Christians had already been doing it long before they became Christians (since it would be extremely bizarre if they weren't). Thus it is incorrect to assume Christians only started doing this after the fact; for we know they and their sectarian predecessors were already doing it before the fact.

Indeed this was a fad of the time, evident throughout the Dead Sea Scrolls and the Talmuds and Jewish literature elsewhere. The whole pesher genre is devoted to this activity.[51] The Dead Sea pesher possibly linking the dying messiah of Daniel to the dying servant of Isaiah is an example (Element 5). Everyone was feverishly searching the scriptures to find secret messages about the messiah and God's eventual plan for the Jews, and often finding these messages in the weirdest places. Indeed the Christians took it to a level of veritable lunacy (the book of *Hermas*, e.g., would peg anyone who wrote it today as all but insane), and the authors of the Dead Sea Scrolls seem not too far from it themselves.

Many doctrines originated from this search, each community's search finding something different. Any pattern would be considered inspired—due to the routine fallacy of assuming a consistent pattern is too much a coincidence to be there by chance (when in fact many coincidentally con-

51. On the genre of the pesherim and how they constructed hidden meanings from past scriptures, see Shani Tzoref, 'Qumran Pesharim and the Pentateuch: Explicit Citation, Overt Typologies, and Implicit Interpretive Traditions', *Dead Sea Discoveries* 16 (2009), pp. 190-220 (with scholarship cited therein); and Bruce Chilton, 'Commenting on the Old Testament (with Particular Reference to the Pesharim, Philo and the Mekilta', in *It Is Written—Scripture Citing Scripture: Essays in Honour of Barnabas Lindars, SSF* (ed. Barnabas Lindars, D.A. Carson and H.G.M. Williamson; New York: Cambridge University Press, 1988), pp. 122-40. The practice is praised in Philo, *On the Contemplative Life* 3.28-29.

sistent patterns will be there by chance, owing to the vast size and complexity of the scriptures and the inherent ambiguity and multivalent meaning of words). Hence countless different sectarian 'discoveries' were possible, each colored by the moral, political, theological, or other assumptions and expectations brought to the text. And it is because of this that countless different sects and interpretations of God's plan arose, with Christianity among them.[52] In fact, so many Jews were engaged in looking for these kinds of hidden meanings, for so long, that we can be nearly certain that all the most obvious patterns would inevitably have been discovered.

Element 9: What in the early first century were considered the inspired scriptures of God consisted of a larger network of texts than are now collected in the OT, including texts outside the canon and texts that no longer exist and also variants of texts that do exist (even canonical texts) but which often said different things then than extant versions now do. In other words, anyone trying to construct their picture of the messiah from hidden messages in the 'Bible' (per the previous element) would have been using texts and variants not in any current Bible today, and Christianity can be understood only in light of this fact.

Jewish authorities did not establish a canon until the second century CE, so no actual 'Old Testament' existed at the dawn of Christianity, just a sea of scriptures, from which different sects selected their own collections. The earliest Christians clearly held in their sacred collection books no longer in the Bible, including the Wisdom of Solomon and the *Book of Enoch* (which show their influence throughout the NT), and others. Codex Sinaiticus, for example, one of the earliest surviving Christian Bibles, includes in its OT 'canon' 2 Esdras, Tobit, Judith, 1 Maccabees, *4 Maccabees, Wisdom of Solomon,* and Sirach (otherwise known as the 'Book of the All-Virtuous Wisdom of Jesus ben Sira'). These and other texts influenced everything the earliest Christians said or believed about Jesus. Jude 14, for example, explicitly cites *Enoch* as scripture, and Jude 9 quotes another scripture

52. In addition to the evidence already surveyed (such as for the use of Daniel), see also Alison Salvesen, 'Messianism in Ancient Bible Translations in Greek and Latin', in *Redemption and Resistance* (ed. Bockmuehl and Paget), pp. 245-61; Joachim Schaper, *Eschatology in the Greek Psalter* (Tübingen: J.C.B. Mohr [Paul Siebeck], 1995), esp. pp. 93-94, 101-107; and the other works cited in previous notes on ancient messianism. For Christian examples, see Craig Evans and James Sanders (eds.), *Early Christian Interpretation of the Scriptures of Israel: Investigations and Proposals* (Sheffield: Sheffield Academic Press, 1997); G.K. Beale and D.A. Carson (eds.), *Commentary on the New Testament Use of the Old Testament* (Grand Rapids, MI: Baker Academic, 2007); the latter also discusses other Jewish interpretations of the same messianic passages (thus confirming Christianity's creative use of the Bible to this end was part of a wider trend and not itself novel).

now lost (which has been tentatively identified as the *Revelation of Moses*). *Enoch* was also a part of the scriptures collected at Qumran (e.g. 4Q204), along with many other books found in Codex Sinaiticus, and others known from nowhere else. Other texts they may have used include the *Apocalypse of Moses*, or any of the lost Danielic or Ezekiel literature we have pieces of from Qumran, where we have found fragments of many scriptures that have not survived anywhere else.[53]

Another important scripture of the period was the apocryphal *Psalms of Solomon*, which established many of the standard beliefs about the messiah, including his roles as king, judge, and shepherd, his designation as 'Son of David' (even though one would presume that that could not be meant literally, David having been dead for many centuries: although see Chapter 11, §9), as well as his assuming the title of Christ and Lord ('Lord Messiah').[54] Many other connections between the *Psalms of Solomon* and Christianity are evident, including the messiah's freedom from sin (17.36) and empowerment by the Holy Spirit (17.37). Though the *Psalms* describe this messiah in the manner of a military conqueror (e.g. 17.21-26), it is still somewhat circumspect, saying 'he shall destroy the godless nations *with the word of his mouth*' (17.24, 17.35-36) and that he will use no weapons or armies (17.33). It also says God will 'raise him up for the house of Israel to educate him' (17.42), which could easily inspire proto-Christian thinking: for 'raise him up' (*anastēsai auton*) is identical in wording to 'resurrect him', and can even be read as saying God will resurrect this messiah *to educate Israel*. I am not arguing here that Christians got this idea of a spiritual dying-and-rising messiah from this scripture, only that we have to take seriously the possibility that they in part did, because this text was widely regarded as scripture at the time, and Jews everywhere were searching their scriptures for hidden meanings just like this.

Since, like all Jews, proto-Christians would have been searching this scripture (and others) for secret messages about the messiah, anyone who interpreted this chapter in light of Dan. 9.26, for instance, could easily derive the core Christian gospel therefrom, yet again (see Elements 6 and 17). It's certainly not improbable to see in the *Psalms of Solomon* a prediction of a metaphorically victorious messiah, who uses no armies or weapons but conquers solely through the power of his words (in other words, his teachings), especially for Jews who were convinced that scriptures like this were not to be taken at what they appeared to say, but as concealing their

53. For example, 4Q385-391 contain lost writings of Ezekiel and Jeremiah; fragments of lost writings of Daniel are discussed in Bruce, 'Book of Daniel and the Qumran Community', pp. 223-25.

54. See discussion in Joseph L. Trafton, 'The Psalms of Solomon', in *Historical Jesus in Context* (ed. Levine, Allison and Crossan), pp. 256-65.

true meaning, as a great many Jews of that time thought (Element 8). And if you were already convinced the last Christ must die as Daniel predicted (Elements 5 and 7), a verse seeming to say he will be resurrected is available here as well.

There were also evidently several scriptures early Christians were using that we don't have and don't even know the titles of. Clement of Rome, for example, quotes as scripture texts we know nothing about, and yet which clearly influenced earliest Christianity.[55] But not only did now-lost scriptures and non-canonical scriptures influence early Christianity, but so did canonical scriptures that said different things than the versions we now have. Early Christians even claimed the Jews had erased passages from the scriptures that predicted things about the Christ. In reality, the Christians probably just had textual variants and interpolated passages in their manuscripts—which can only have predated Christianity (and thus were Jewish in origin) unless they were forged by Christians to 'create' prophetic verification of their religion. For example, Paul quotes a now-lost variant reading of Isaiah in Rom. 9.33 (see Chapter 11, §8). Likewise, Irenaeus reports that in Jeremiah there was a passage saying, 'and the Lord, the Holy One of Israel, remembered his dead, which aforetime fell asleep in the dust of the earth, and he went down unto them, to bring the tidings of his salvation, to deliver them'. No such passage exists in Jeremiah now, and it's hard to think where it could have been. But Irenaeus is fully confident it was there.[56] This and several other passages Christians insisted had been removed by the Jews from *their* copies of 'the Bible', but were clearly present in the copies of 'the Bible' the Christians were relying on. Earlier, Justin Martyr had documented a whole slew of such passages, now missing from extant Bibles but which he was sure existed in his.[57] Origen later commented on this sort of thing being commonplace.[58] We can even see examples in the first epistle of Clement (see Chapter 8, §5). How many other examples were there that we don't have a surviving reference to?

Likewise, Christians often trusted the Septuagint over the Hebrew text of the Bible. The infamous case of the 'virgin' birth prediction is well known.[59] But Irenaeus also says Ps. 119.120 says, 'nail my flesh out of fear',

55. See Chapter 8 (§5). There may have been many texts like that: see, e.g., Matthias Henze (ed.), *Hazon Gabriel: New Readings of the Gabriel Revelation* (Atlanta, GA: Society of Biblical Literature, 2011).

56. Irenaeus, *Demonstration of the Apostolic Preaching* 78.

57. Justin Martyr, *Dialogue with Trypho* 71-73.

58. Origen, *Letter to Africanus* 2-9.

59. See Tim Callahan, *Bible Prophecy: Failure or Fulfillment?* (Altadena, CA: Millennium Press, 1997), pp. 115-16; and Raymond Brown, *The Birth of the Messiah: A Commentary on the Infancy Narratives in the Gospels of Matthew and Luke* (Garden City, NY: Doubleday, 1993), §5 B3.

and therefore predicts the crucifixion, which is true only in the Greek; the Hebrew says, 'my flesh trembles from fear of you', which is certainly the original reading. The Greek translation Irenaeus used literally reads, 'nail my flesh from fear of you, as I am afraid of your judgments', which makes no sense really, yet differs from the perfectly sensible Hebrew by only a single word. Nevertheless, Christians trusted this erroneous variant, and based their religious beliefs thereon.[60] Irenaeus likewise says his copy of the Psalms said, 'spare my soul from the sword, fasten my flesh with nails, for the assemblies of the wicked have risen up against me', which in fact is an entirely different verse than appears in either the Hebrew *or* the Greek that we now have. He was thus using a different version of the Bible than survives today in any form at all. And Irenaeus is not an aberration here. Exactly the same thing is said in the *Epistle of Barnabas,* which was once a part of some early Christian Bibles.[61]

We know these kinds of deviant manuscripts were all over the place even before Christianity began. Greek versions of the scriptures were found (and thus evidently used and studied) among the Dead Sea Scrolls in Palestine, so Greek-based interpretations could easily pre-date Christianity. Even a Hebrew copy of Isaiah at Qumran, for example, replaces the word 'bruised' with the word 'pierced' in both Isa. 53.5 and 53.10. That's the very passage we previously discussed as predicting the messiah's death when connected with Dan. 9.25-26, and here now we see this variant *also* linking Isaiah 53 with Psalms 22, a connection the Christians *also* made, as we see in Mark's construction of the crucifixion narrative (see Chapter 10, §4). Thus it can't always have been Christians doctoring texts to conform to the crucifixion—for here we have a variant text that could readily evoke an expected crucifixion for the atoning servant of Isaiah 53 long before there even were Christians.[62]

Thus Christians were not relying on the biblical texts we have. They had different versions to work from, as well as books now no longer in the Bible at all. Which means whenever a Christian text claims there was (or

60. Irenaeus, *Demonstration of the Apostolic Preaching* 79.

61. *Epistle of Barnabas* 5. This is in the Codex Sinaiticus, one of the oldest Bibles in the world (transcribed in the early fourth century CE), and the epistle itself was probably written in the early second century CE and thus half a century at least before the time of Irenaeus (see note in Chapter 8, §6).

62. Again, the Qumran version of Isaiah (1QIsa[a]) says 'he was wounded for our transgressions, he was *pierced* for our iniquities . . . it pleased Jehovah to *pierce* him . . . to make his life an offering for sin' (which in effect means the same thing in English as 'he was *nailed up* for our iniquities . . . it pleased Jehovah to *nail him him up*'). For examples of other variant readings of otherwise-known scriptures found at Qumran, see John Collins and Craig Evans (eds.), *Christian Beginnings and the Dead Sea Scrolls* (Grand Rapids, MI: Baker Academic, 2006), p. 10.

indeed even quotes) a scripture that we can't find in the Bible (e.g. Jn 7.38; Lk. 24.46-47; Mt. 2.23; Mk 9.12; even 1 Cor. 2:9), we should presume they were looking at a textual variant we no longer have (and thus the scripture *was* there, and probably there before Christianity, at least in some of the manuscripts available to them), or were citing a book *other* than any now in the OT (such as any of those mentioned earlier, although there were also others we no longer even know about). Likewise, Christians didn't always say they were citing or deriving an idea from scripture, yet we can identify where they got it from ourselves, which means there must also have been many more cases where they *also* derived a text or idea from a *variant* scripture now lost to us or no longer in the canon, *without* telling us that is what they were doing.[63]

Element 10: Christianity began as a Jewish messianic cult preaching a spiritually victorious messiah. This means that (a) sometime in the early first century at least one of the many diverse sects of Jews came to believe and preach that (b) a certain Jesus was an eschatological Christ, (c) despite his having been crucified and buried by the powers that be (whether temporal or supernatural), (d) because (or so they preached: 1 Cor. 15.3-8 and Gal. 1.11-12) he had afterward appeared to certain favored people and convinced them he was this Christ and (e) had to die in atonement for all sins but (f) had risen from the dead to sit at the right hand of God in order to begin the work (through the sect he was thus founding) of preparing for God's kingdom until (g) the time when this Christ would descend from heaven to complete his mission of destroying God's enemies, resurrecting the dead, and establishing an eternal paradise (e.g. Romans 8; 1 Cor. 10.11 and 15.23-26; 1 Thess. 4.14-17). (h) At this time Jesus was already believed to be a preexistent being (1 Cor. 8.6; 10.1-4; Phil. 2.6-8; and Rom. 8.3; see also Element 40), but (i) was not believed to be identical to God, but to be his appointed emissary and subordinate, not God himself but given God's authority, being God's 'son' in the same sense as angels and kings traditionally were (see my discussion of the resulting linguistic ambiguity in §3).

None of this should be controversial.[64] Some scholars might challenge the notion that the earliest Jesus cult regarded the death of Jesus to be

63. On this and many other of the points made here see Magne Sæbø (ed.), *Hebrew Bible, Old Testament: The History of its Interpretation. Volume I: From the Beginnings to the Middle Ages (until 1300). Part 1: Antiquity* (Göttingen: Vandenhoeck & Ruprecht, 1996), esp. Oskar Skarsaune, 'The Question of Old Testament Canon and Text in the Early Greek Church', pp. 443-50, which documents many more examples.

64. This is all undeniably explicit in later texts such as Heb. 1.1-4 and Col. 1.12-20 (and elsewhere, e.g., Heb. 2.10, which echoes 1 Cor. 8.6), but I shall proceed to demonstrate these claims are already in the earliest letters of Paul and even pre-

an atonement sacrifice, but the fact of the matter is our earliest Christian documents widely attest this was a standard, fundamental, and pervasive Christian belief, and affords no evidence of any prior version of Christianity (1 Cor. 15.3; Rom. 3.23-26; 5.6-11; 2 Cor. 5.18-19). This is particularly clear in Galatians 1–2, where Paul emphatically insists 'preaching another gospel' is enough to condemn anyone as cursed and shunned (Gal. 1.6-9), but that his gospel was in accord with that of the 'pillars' Peter, James and John (Gal. 2.6-10), whom he implies are the founders of Christianity (he certainly here treats them as the ultimate authorities whose blessing any Christian apostle required; and he again confirms their primacy in 1 Cor. 15.3-8, although the reliability of the text on this point has been questioned: see note in Chapter 11, §2). Since the 'pillars' and their 'gospel' were thus not condemned as 'anathema' by Paul, they cannot possibly have been preaching anything so radically different from him as a Jesus who hadn't atoned for anyone's sins (much less a Jesus who hadn't been crucified!).

Any challenge to this conclusion cannot be a disagreement as to the *evidence*, but only in respect to *theory*, that is, one might propose the *theory* that there was a previous version of the religion upon which Paul innovated the atoning death, and then test that theory against the evidence. I just here predict it won't test well. Hence I am rejecting it. The only dispute evident throughout Galatians 2 is over the matter of the observance of the specific strictures of the Jewish law, the doing away of which very clearly was an innovation of Paul (see Element 20). But that was only an *interpretation* of the gospel, not the gospel itself (e.g. this abolition of the Law is nowhere stated in Paul's matching declaration of the gospel that was revealed to him in 1 Cor. 15.3-8 or anywhere else), therefore an agreement could be reached without either side declaring the other anathema (Gal. 2.6-10).

Some scholars might also challenge the assumption that apocalyptic hopes were innate to Christianity from the beginning. But this really can no longer be doubted. The Epistles are rife with no other view (again, see Romans 8; 1 Cor. 10.11; 15.23-26; 1 Thess. 4.14-17), and they long predate the Synoptic Gospels. The Synoptic Gospels are rife with no other view (as everyone agrees), and they long predate the Gospels of John and (almost certainly) Thomas, and only *there* do we first see the replacement of an

Pauline creeds. On the related 'high Christology' debate see Andrew Chester, 'High Christology—Whence, When and Why?', *Early Christianity* 2 (2011), pp. 22-50; his results corroborate mine, and are further supported by the evidence I adduce for Elements 36 and 40-42. See also Jonathan Knight, *Disciples of the Beloved One: The Christology, Social Setting and Theological Context of the Ascension of Isaiah* (Sheffield: Sheffield Academic Press, 1996), pp. 135-39 and 296-303.

actual apocalypse with a metaphorical one that had already transpired.[65] Thus the idea of an immanent 'invisible kingdom' replacing the imminent *physical* kingdom that was previously expected to arrive (but disturbingly hadn't) was a later development in Christianity and not a founding belief.[66] Far more foundational was the belief that the resurrection of Jesus had been the *firstfruits* (and therefore a positive sign) of the general apocalyptic resurrection very soon to come (1 Cor. 15.20-24).[67]

And finally, some (though mostly fundamentalist Christians) might challenge the claim that at this stage Christians did not regard Jesus as identical to God.[68] But this is undeniably clear. Jesus is the *power* of God and the *wisdom* of God, but not himself God (1 Cor. 1.24), only the image of God (literally, 'God's icon', 2 Cor. 4.4; though compare 1 Cor. 11.7, where the same is said of ordinary men, but there only through their unity with Christ); he was *made* by God (1 Cor. 1.30). He sits *at the right hand* of God and *pleads with* God on our behalf (Rom. 8.34). All things were made *by* God, but *through* the agency of Christ (1 Cor. 8.4-6). Christ is given the *form* of a god, but refuses to seize that opportunity to make himself *equal* to God, but submits to incarnation and death instead, for which obedience God *grants* him supreme authority (Phil. 2.5-11). And Christ will in the

65. 'The kingdom of the Father is already spread upon the earth and men do not see it', *Gos. Thom.* 113, which is compatible with the Synoptic idea of a spiritual kingdom soon to be followed by a physical one (brought on clouds of glory) but still conspicuous for lacking any such notion here; the Gospel of John is full of similar sentiments (which likewise erases from the story all the mentions of a coming apocalypse, as are found throughout the Synoptic Gospels and the Epistles).

66. This is well enough argued in Bart Ehrman, *Jesus: Apocalyptic Prophet of the New Millennium* (New York: Oxford University Press, 1999). That the *Gospel of Thomas* is far more certainly a late text (of the early to mid-second century), see the thorough discussions of Nicholas Perrin, *Thomas and Tatian: The Relationship between the Gospel of Thomas and the Diatessaron* (Leiden: Brill, 2002); and Klyne R. Snodgrass, 'The Gospel of Thomas: A Secondary Gospel', in *The Historical Jesus: Critical Concepts in Religious Studies*, Vol. IV: *Lives of Jesus and Jesus outside the Bible* (ed. Craig Evans; New York: Routledge, 2004); and now Mark Goodacre, *Thomas and the Gospels: The Case for Thomas's Familiarity with the Synoptics* (Grand Rapids, MI: William B. Eerdmans, 2012). I find attempts to argue the contrary too weak to rest any conclusion on; and they still cannot reliably date *Gos. Thom.* even if correct.

67. See Carrier, 'Why the Resurrection Is Unbelievable', in *Christian Delusion* (ed. Loftus), pp. 291-315 (306).

68. Some scholars challenge the *converse* claim, that Jesus was thought from the start to be a preexistent being of any sort. Chester, 'High Christology', demonstrates the implausibility of the claim that Christianity began without a notion of Jesus being a preexistent being. There is simply no evidence to support that conjecture, and all the evidence we do have indicates otherwise (e.g. 1 Cor. 8.6 and Phil. 2.5-11, which are corroborated by the implications of Rom. 8.3).

end deliver the kingdom *to* God, who only gave Christ the authority to rule and wage war on God's behalf; and in the end Christ will give that authority *back* to God (1 Cor. 15.24-28). Thus in our earliest sources Jesus was always distinguished as a different entity from God, and as his subordinate.[69] Even in Colossians he is the *image* of God, not God himself; in fact, he is 'the firstborn of all creation' (and thus a created being), and 'God dwelled *within* him', in the same sense as was imagined for Jewish prophets, priests and kings (Col. 1.15-19). Thus in Rom. 1.4 (and all of Hebrews 1) Jesus is only *appointed* the 'Son of God'. This was precisely how the phrase 'Son of God' and the concepts of divine 'incarnation' and 'indwell-

69. Rom. 1.7-8; 2.6; 5.1, 11; 6.11, 23; 7.25; 8.39; 10.9; 15.6, 30; 16.27, etc.; 1 Cor. 1.3-4; 6.11; 15.57, etc.; 2 Cor. 1.2-3; 11.31; 13.14, etc.; Gal. 1.1; 1.3, etc.; Phil. 1.2, 11; 3.3, 14; 4.19, etc.; 1 Thess. 1.1; 3.11-13; 4.14; 5.9, etc.; and so on. In contrast to all this evidence, Rom. 9.5 is often cited as saying Jesus was identical to God (it would then be the only passage in Paul that ever says this), but many early Christians punctuated the text differently, and accordingly modern translations disagree on the meaning, some holding that it was meant to distinguish a spontaneous praise of God with a statement about Jesus coming in the flesh. See A.W. Wainwright, 'The Confession "Jesus is God" in the New Testament', *Scottish Journal of Theology* 10 (1957), pp. 278-82; W.L. Lorimer, 'Romans IX. 3-5', *New Testament Studies* 13 (1967), pp. 385-86; and Bruce Metzger, 'The Punctuation of Rom. 9:5', in *Christ and the Spirit in the New Testament* (ed. B. Lindars and S. Smalley; Cambridge: Cambridge University Press, 1973), pp. 95-112. From the other passages in Paul it is clear he did not believe Jesus was 'the' God over all, so at most he can only have meant here 'a' god (a subordinate god, in the henotheistic sense: see Element 11; notably, in accord with this, the passage does not say Christ is necessarily *ho theos*, 'the God', but just *theos*, '[a] god'). But I think it's far more likely (on the evidence of the whole Pauline corpus) that the text has become corrupted. In Rom. 1.25 Paul says something almost identical, that the Creator is 'blessed forever. Amen' (*eulogētos eis tous aiōnas amēn*, word-for-word identical to the conclusion of Rom. 9.5), and in 2 Cor. 11.31 Paul says God is the 'father' of Christ and therefore 'the one who is blessed forever' (*ho ōn eulogētos eis tous aiōnas*), which is very similar to the phrase in Rom. 9.5; likewise in 2 Cor. 1.3 Paul says God is 'blessed' because he is the *father* of Christ, not because he *is* the Christ. It is far more likely that Rom. 9.5 originally repeated this sentiment than that it said something radically new that outright contradicts it. I would thus expect that the phrase *ho patēr* originally appeared before the *ho ōn* in Rom. 9.5, which would create an apt parallel with the preceding 'whose are the fathers' in the same line, in which case Paul wrote 'my brethren are the Israelites . . . whose are the fathers [i.e., the patriarchs] and out of whom is Christ in the flesh, whose father is the blessed God over all. Amen'. Indeed, Christ's divine paternity is otherwise conspicuous for its absence in this sentence, which (in light of the other identical 'blessing' passages in Paul) strongly indicates that it was originally present here. For additional bibliographies on this problem see Douglas Moo, *The Epistle to the Romans* (Grand Rapids, MI: William B. Eerdmans, 1996), pp. 565-68, and Robert Jewett, *Romans: A Commentary* (Minneapolis, MN: Fortress Press, 2007), pp. 566-69 (although neither Moo nor Jewett consider the reconstruction of the text I just proposed, nor the evidence I advanced for it).

ing' were then understood by the Jews.[70] This was therefore not a radical idea but entirely in accord with popular Jewish theology. This would still make Jesus *a* god by my terminology (and in common pagan parlance), but not in the usual vocabulary of Jews (who would sooner call such a divine being an archangel or celestial 'lord').

6. *Elements of Christian Religion*

Element 11: The earliest definitely known form of Christianity was a Judeo-Hellenistic mystery religion. This is also beyond any reasonable doubt, yet frequently denied in the field of Jesus research, often with a suspiciously intense passion. So I shall here survey a case for it.[71]

To say Christianity was a mystery religion is not to say that Christianity is *exactly like* any other mystery religion, any more than *any* mystery religion was 'exactly like' any other. Often when scholars deny that Christianity was a mystery religion, they really mean it wasn't just one of the already-existing mystery religions superficially overhauled with Jewish concepts. Christianity wasn't 'Osiris Cult 2.0'. Which is certainly true. But that's all that anyone's evidence can prove. If instead we define a mystery religion as any Hellenistic cult in which individual salvation was procured by a ritual initiation into a set of 'mysteries', the knowledge of which and participation in which were key to ensuring a blessed eternal life, then Christianity was demonstrably a mystery religion beyond any doubt.

If we then expand that definition to include a set of specific features held in common by *all* other mystery religions of the early Roman era, then Christianity becomes even more demonstrably a mystery religion, so much

70. See my discussion in Carrier, *Not the Impossible Faith*, pp. 247-57; and Carrier, *Proving History*, pp. 145-49; and more extensively, Adela Yarbro Collins and John Collins (eds.), *King and Messiah as Son of God: Divine, Human, and Angelic Messianic Figures in Biblical and Related Literature* (Grand Rapids, MI: Eerdmans, 2008); and Charles Gieschen, *Angelomorphic Christology: Antecedents and Early Evidence* (Boston: Brill, 1998). See also Craig Evans, 'The Recently Published Dead Sea Scrolls and the Historical Jesus', in *Studying the Historical Jesus: Evaluations of the State of Current Research* (ed. Bruce Chilton and Craig Evans; Leiden: Brill, 1994), pp. 563-65; and Margaret Barker, *The Great High Priest: The Temple Roots of Christian Liturgy* (New York: T. & T. Clark, 2003), pp. 60-62, 210-12. On pagan equivalents (from which one can see Jesus was assigned all the royal titles associated with Greco-Roman kings and emperors), see Erwin Goodenough, 'The Political Philosophy of Hellenistic Kingship', *Yale Classical Studies* 1 (1928), pp. 55-102.

71. See also Marvin Meyer (ed.), *The Ancient Mysteries: A Sourcebook of Sacred Texts* (Philadelphia, PA: University of Pennsylvania Press, 1987), pp. 225-27 (with bibliography pro and con) and pp. 252-54; with Jaime Alvarez, *Romanising Oriental Gods: Myth, Salvation and Ethics in the Cults of Cybele, Isis and Mithras* (Leiden: Brill, 2008), pp. 396-97, 420-21, etc.

so, in fact, that it's impossible to deny it was deliberately constructed as such. Even the earliest discernible form of Christianity emulates numerous cultic features and concepts that were so unique to the Hellenistic mystery cults that it is statistically beyond any reasonable possibility that they all found their way into Christianity by mere coincidence. They formed a coherent, logical and repeatedly replicated system of ideas in every other mystery cult. It would be irrational to conclude the same wasn't so of Christianity. Christianity cannot be understood apart from this fact. And any theory of historicity that fails to account for it cannot be credible.[72]

That Christianity taught eternal salvation for the individual cannot be denied. That it taught that this salvation was procured by initiation rituals (such as undergoing baptism and partaking of the Eucharist) cannot be denied. And that these rituals involved an induction into a set of 'mysteries', the knowledge of which and participation in which were key to ensuring a blessed eternal life, is explicitly stated throughout the authentic epistles of Paul—and nearly everywhere else in the NT. In Paul's letters essential Christian doctrines are routinely called *mysteries*.[73] The NT evinces other common vocabulary of mystery cult, used with the same peculiar connotations, not just *mystērion* (divine secret), but *teleios* (mature [as higher ranking initiates]), *nēpios* (immature [as lower ranking initiates]), *skēnē* (body [as discardable and unneeded for salvation]), *epoptēs* (witness [to the mysteries]), etc.[74]

72. The oft-cited article to the contrary by Bruce Metzger, 'Considerations of the Methodology in the Study of the Mystery Religions and Early Christianity', *Harvard Theological Review* 48 (January 1955), pp. 1-20, is so profoundly inept in its analysis that it must be rejected. The argument 'it was different from *x*, therefore it wasn't influenced by *x*' (which describes more than half the arguments Metzger deploys) is fallacious to the point of ridiculous: this, as well as nearly every other argument Metzger constructs, would rule out *every* mystery religion as being a mystery religion (e.g. the argument, on p. 11, that certain terms are not found in Paul's letters: that is true of most mystery religions, by Metzger's own admission, pp. 6-7), which of course is so absurd a conclusion as to refute his entire case. His remaining arguments (e.g. that Jews never syncretized their religion with surrounding religions) are simply false, or irrelevant to explaining the *origins* of Christianity (like the fact that Christianity underwent even more syncretism in later centuries). The same mistakes uniformly plague the analysis of Devon Wiens, 'Mystery Concepts in Primitive Christianity and in its Environment', *Aufstieg und Niedergang der römischen Welt* II.23.2 (New York: W. de Guyter, 1980), pp. 1248-84.

73. Collectively in the plural in 1 Cor. 4.1 and 13.2 (and 14.2); individually in the singular in Rom. 11.25-26; 16.25-26; 1 Cor. 2.7; 15.51 (and 1 Cor. 2.1 in some mss.; replaced with the more contextually inappropriate *martyrion* in others). Pseudo-Paulines use the same terminology: Eph. 1.9; 3.3-4, 9; 5.32; 6.19; Col. 1.26, 27; 2.2; 4.3; 2 Thess. 2.5-10 (cf., e.g., Rev. 17.5-7); 1 Tim. 3.9, 16.

74. See Rom. 16.25-26; 1 Cor. 2-3; 2 Cor. 5; Eph. 3.1-10; Col. 1.26-28; 2 Pet. 1.16; Mk 4.11-12; etc.

In fact, 'in the Pauline epistles we have more than isolated terms and ideas of the type in question. In certain contexts, as, e.g., 1 Corinthians [2.1–3.2], we light upon *groups* of conceptions which have associations with the Mystery-Religions. This cannot be accidental.'[75] This concept framework is found in other places as well (e.g. 2 Cor. 5; 1 Cor. 4.1; Heb. 5.11-14, etc.). This does not require Christianity to have used these concepts *identically* to any other mystery cult, any more than any other cult did. It only entails some influence and employment of mystery-cult themes, and that Christianity was constructed in a fashion similar to those cults, even while, like each of them, it remained distinct, with each borrowed element altered by receiving an appropriate Jewish twist.[76] We should thus concur with Jaime Alvarez, who proposes what he calls a 'commensality' approach of 'complex transfers' among mystery cults, Christianity included, such that instead of Christianity being a direct reworking of a specific preceding mystery cult (which it is not), we should see it as the reworking of a Jewish cult from a 'common trough of current ideas', including those collectively shared among the mystery cults of its day, transforming them in the process.[77] And yet even transformed, certain fundamental elements remain in common.

All mystery religions centered on a central savior deity (literally called the *sōtēr*, 'the savior', which is essentially the meaning of the word 'Jesus', as explained in Chapter 6, §3), always a son of god (or occasionally a daughter of god), who underwent some sort of suffering (enduring some sort of trial or ordeal) by which they procured salvation for all who participate in their cult (their deed of torment having given them dominion over death). These deaths or trials were literally called a 'passion' (*patheōn*, lit. 'sufferings'), exactly as in Christianity.[78] Sometimes this 'passion' was an

75. Harry Angus Alexander Kennedy, *St. Paul and the Mystery-Religions* (London: Hodder & Stoughton, 1913), p. 121 (on mystery religion vocabulary: pp. 115-98). Despite being out of date, Kennedy's study remains correct in many respects, as verified and reinforced in Hugo Rahner, *Greek Myths and Christian Mystery* (New York: Harper & Row, 1963), and by the scholarship cited in coming notes. I should also note that Samuel Angus, *The Mystery-Religions and Christianity: A Study in the Religious Background of Early Christianity* (London: J. Murray, 1925) is also obsolete, but still contains a lot of useful data, and like Kennedy, some of his arguments have been confirmed and are now mainstream (though others have been refuted and are now regarded as quaint). By contrast, though often cited, Joscelyn Godwin, *Mystery Religions in the Ancient World* (New York: Harper & Row, 1981) is only to be used with caution, being occasionally under-sourced or overstating the facts. Far better references are to follow.

76. Alvarez, *Romanising Oriental Gods*, pp. 396-97.

77. Alvarez, *Romanising Oriental Gods*, pp. 420-21.

78. For Christianity: Heb. 2.10; 9.26; Phil. 3.10; 2 Cor. 1.5; Mk 8.31; etc. For other mystery cults see, e.g., Herodotus, *Histories* 2.171.1 (on the mysteries of Osiris);

actual death and resurrection (Osiris); sometimes it was some kind of terrible labor defeating the forces of death (Mithras), or variations thereof. All mystery religions had an initiation ritual in which the congregant symbolically reenacts what the god endured (like Christian baptism: Rom. 6.3-4; Col. 2.12), thus sharing in the salvation the god had achieved (Gal. 3.27; 1 Cor. 12.13), and all involve a ritual meal that unites initiated members in communion with one another and their god (1 Cor. 11.23-28). All of these features are fundamental to Christianity, yet equally fundamental to all the mystery cults that were extremely popular in the very era that Christianity arose.[79] The coincidence of all of these features together lining up this way is simply too improbable to propose as just an accident.

Plutarch, *On Isis and Osiris* (= *Moralia*) 17.357f, 20.358f (on Osiris and others); Euripides, *Bacchae* 492, 500, 786, 801, 1377 (on the Bacchic mysteries).

79. Kennedy, *St. Paul and the Mystery-Religions*, pp. 229-55 (baptism as a universal ritual in the mystery cults), pp. 256-79 (sacred meals). Recent scholarship confirms the basic picture. On the Bacchic and Eleusinian mysteries: Radcliffe Edmonds III, *Myths of the Underworld Journey: Plato, Aristophanes, and the 'Orphic' Gold Tablets* (Cambridge: Cambridge University Press, 2004); Martin Nilsson, *The Dionysiac Mysteries of the Hellenistic and Roman Age* (Lund: Gleerup, 1957); M.L. West, *The Orphic Poems* (New York: Oxford University Press, 1983), pp. 1-38; for some practices and terminology: Richard Seaford, 'Dionysiac Drama and the Dionysiac Mysteries', *The Classical Quarterly* 31 (1981), pp. 252-75. On the Mithraic mysteries: Manfred Clauss, *The Roman Cult of Mithras: The God and his Mysteries* (New York: Routledge, 2000), cf. esp. pp. 14-15 (with 174 n. 30) and 108-13 on the features it shares with other mystery cults (including the ritual of symbolically emulating the god's labors to achieve personal salvation in the hereafter, and the ritual of sharing a sacred meal with other initiates); see also Marvin Meyer, 'The Mithras Liturgy', in *The Historical Jesus in Context* (ed. Levine, Allison and Crossan), pp. 179-92; Gary Lease, 'Mithraism and Christianity: Borrowings and Transformations', *Aufstieg und Niedergang der römischen Welt* II.23.2 (New York: W. de Gruyter, 1980), pp. 1306-32 (1309 for the generic features Christianity shares with all mystery cults; the specific influence of Mithraism on early Christianity is unlikely, however—they instead arose around the same time, in a parallel phenomenon of creating mystery cults from major ethnic cults, Persian in the one case, Jewish in the other—they are therefore separate instances of the same phenomenon); Roger Beck, *Beck on Mithraism* (Burlington, VT: Ashgate, 2004); and Roger Beck, *The Religion of the Mithras Cult in the Roman Empire: Mysteries of the Unconquered Sun* (New York: Oxford University Press, 2006), the latter works correcting or superseding David Ulansey's *The Origins of the Mithraic Mysteries* (New York: Oxford University Press, 1989); see also Richard Gordon, *Image and Value in the Graeco-Roman World: Studies in Mithraism and Religious Art* (Brookfield, VT: Ashgate, 1996). On Isis–Osiris cult: Malcolm Drew Donalson, *The Cult of Isis in the Roman Empire: Isis Invicta* (Lewiston, NY: E. Mellen Press, 2003); Sarolta Takacs, *Isis and Sarapis in the Roman World* (Leiden: Brill, 1995); Reinhold Merkelbach, *Isis Regina, Zeus Sarapis: Die griechisch-ägyptische Religion nach den Quellen dargestellt* (Stuttgart: B.G. Teubner, 1995); Sharon Kelly Heyob, *The Cult of Isis among Women in the Graeco-Roman World* (Leiden: Brill, 1975); and Robert

Notably all the mystery religions were products of the same sort of cultural syncretism. The Eleusinian mysteries were a syncretism of Levantine and Hellenistic elements; the mysteries of Attis and Cybele were a syncretism of Phrygian and Hellenistic elements; the mysteries of Jupiter Dolichenus were a syncretism of Anatolian and Hellenistic elements; Mithraism was a syncretism of Persian and Hellenistic elements; the mysteries of Isis and Osiris were a syncretism of Egyptian and Hellenistic elements. Christianity is simply a continuation of the same trend: a syncretism of Jewish and Hellenistic elements. Each of these cults is unique and different from all the others in nearly every detail—but it's the general features they all share in common that reflect the overall fad that produced them in the first place, the very features that made them popular and successful within Greco-Roman culture.

Unfortunately we know very much less about these other cults than Christianity, because Christians chose not to preserve any of their sacred literature—sometimes deliberately destroying it, as we might infer from the fate of books 2 and 3 of Hippolytus's *Refutation of All Heresies* (in which, according to what he says at the end of book 1, he exposed all the secrets of the mystery religions, yet these chapters were mysteriously removed and remain lost to this day). But our ignorance is also due to the fact that much of what the mystery cults taught was kept secret, being so sacred that only initiates sworn to secrecy would be told the true content of the mysteries of each cult (the same was true of Christianity: see Element

Wild, *Water in the Cultic Worship of Isis and Sarapis* (Leiden: Brill, 1981). On the Samothracian mysteries: Susan Guettel Cole, *Theoi Megaloi: The Cult of the Great Gods at Samothrace* (Leiden: Brill, 1984), which surveys evidence of baptisms (31-33), passion plays (48), ritual meals (36-37) and a duo of resurrected gods (1-7). On the mysteries of Attis and Cybele: Lynn Roller, *In Search of God the Mother: The Cult of Anatolian Cybele* (Berkeley, CA: University of California Press, 1999); Giulia Sfameni Gasparro, *Soteriology and Mystic Aspects in the Cult of Cybele and Attis* (Leiden: Brill, 1985); and Maria Grazia Lancellotti, *Attis, between Myth and History: King, Priest, and God* (Leiden: Brill, 2002). Note that all of the above literature confirms moral teachings were linked to every mystery cult (a fact still often denied). The Thracian deity Zalmoxis was also anciently believed to have died and risen from the dead, procuring salvation for all who share in his cult (including a ritual eating and drinking), as attested by Herodotus in the fifth century BCE, which also suggests an early mystery cult: cf. Herodotus, *Histories* 4.94-96; Plato, *Charmides* 156d; and discussion and sources in Carrier, *Not the Impossible Faith*, pp. 86, 100-105; and Mircea Eliade, *Zalmoxis the Vanishing God: Comparative Studies in the Religions and Folklore of Dacia and Eastern Europe* (Chicago: University of Chicago Press, 1972). On the Sumerian dying-and-rising gods Innana and Tammuz (Astarte and Adonis) and others like them see Element 31. There were probably many other mystery cults that we know nothing or next to nothing about: see Origen, *Against Celsus* 6.22 and Michael Cosmopoulos (ed.), *Greek Mysteries: The Archaeology and Ritual of Ancient Greek Secret Cults* (New York: Routledge, 2003).

13).[80] But enough evidence survives to reconstruct all the common features I've mentioned, and more.

There is one notable exception, the *Golden Ass* of Apuleius (also known as the *Metamorphoses*), which is a kind of Acts for the Isis cult (recorded in the fashion of a novel, thus in a sense disguising its sacred nature), which medieval Christians preserved intact. This tells us many things about the religion, including its initiation ritual: the initiation, Apuleius tells us, resembles a 'voluntary death' (*instar voluntariae mortis*), after which one is 'reborn' (*renatus*). After you were baptized into the cult (literally, with an ablution of water), the day of initiation became a new 'birthday' and the priest who initiated you became your new father. As Apuleius describes it, 'I approached the border of death, and once the threshold of Proserpina [Lady Death] was crossed, I was conveyed through all the elements, and came back' to life (all of which he again calls a 'rebirth').[81] Christianity's initiation ritual also involved a baptism, and was conceptually identical: you symbolically underwent death and resurrection, and are thereby 'reborn' with a new 'father' (in this case, God—see Element 12—although, just like in the Isis cult, in earliest Christianity the one who initiated you could also be called your father: 1 Cor. 4.15).

Mithras cult also involved an initiatory baptism.[82] As did the Eleusinian cult, which even practiced substitutionary baptism on behalf of the dead

80. That there nevertheless were 'gospels' in other mystery cults recounting their myths and teachings is certain, as they are referred to in extant texts: for example, for Isis–Osiris cult, Apuleius, *Metamorphoses* 11.22-23 (cf. 11.28-30) mentions such sacred writings, as does Plutarch, *On Isis and Osiris* (= *Moralia*) 80.383e (there called *hiera grammata*, 'sacred writings') also 5.351f, 352b; the Egyptian Manetho had allegedly written that cult's Holy Bible (*Hiera biblos*) sometime before the end of the third century BCE (notably the very time the Hebrew 'Holy Bible' was supposedly being translated into Greek); cf. J. Gwyn Griffiths, *Plutarch's De Iside et Osiride* (Cardiff: University of Wales Press, 1970), p. 80. The Dionysiac mysteries also appear to have had a set of gospels no longer extant: Nilsson, *The Dionysiac Mysteries*, pp. 116-18, 133; West, *Orphic Poems*, pp. 25-29. Similarly, recovered paraphernalia of the Mithras cult include the equivalent of 'graphic novels' (painted or carved in stone) recounting the narrative of the Mithras gospel. No text survives to tell us what stories the scenes illustrate, but there clearly must have been such a text. The *tauroctony* or 'bull-slaying' is only the most climactic scene, abundantly represented, but there was a whole sequence of 'story cells', including a miraculous nativity, Mithras dragging the bull to a cave, life springing from its blood, Mithras eating of its flesh, his ascension or exaltation, and various scenes featuring Mithras and the Supreme God (probably Sol Invictus, 'The Invincible Sun').

81. Apuleius, *Metamorphoses* 11.21-25; 11.16.

82. Tertullian, *On Baptism* 5. Per Beskow, in 'Tertullian on Mithras', in *Studies in Mithraism: Papers Associated with the Mithraic Panel Organized on the Occasion of the XVIth Congress of the International Association for the History of Religions, Rome*

(to bring salvation to those who hadn't yet been baptized in life), centuries before Christians adopted the same practice, as evident already in the earliest known churches (1 Cor. 15.29), which is yet another unlikely coincidence.[83] In many if not all the mystery cults, these baptisms effected salvation in part by washing away sins, exactly the same function claimed of Christian baptism.[84] Which is another unlikely coincidence (although predating Christianity, Judaism did not have this element until after contact with Hellenism; before that, only blood sacrifice could remove sin).

In Apuleius's account of the Isis cult, initiation was also 'consummated' with a 'sacred meal' on 'the third day' of the completed rites, implying the meal fully united him to his savior god or goddess and his fellow initiates, the very thing accomplished by the Eucharist within Christianity. And just as for Christians, by undergoing these rites the Isis initiate procured eternal life for himself in the hereafter. In other words, personal salvation. There appears to have been a similar sacred meal securing eternal life in the mysteries of Mithras.[85] Thus, for all these reasons, Christianity is certainly in essentials a Hellenistic mystery religion, differing from others only in its

1990 (ed. John Hinnells; Rome: L'Erma di Bretschneider, 1994), pp. 51-60, argues that the Mithraic 'baptism' was only an anointing of the forehead, but that is not a relevant difference. How a baptism was performed would naturally be highly variable from cult to cult (just as it is from sect to sect in Christianity today).

83. See Hans Conzelmann, *1 Corinthians: A Commentary on the First Epistle to the Corinthians* (Philadelphia, PA: Fortress Press, 1975), pp. 275-76; with Plato, *Republic* 364e-365a. For evidence that Bacchic and Attis cults also regarded their baptisms as 'rebirthing' ceremonies, see Peter Kingsley, *Ancient Philosophy, Mystery, and Magic: Empedocles and Pythagorean Tradition* (New York: Oxford University Press, 1995), p. 264-69; that a Dionysian (i.e., Bacchic) ritual washed away sins (inherited over many generations): Kingsley, *Ancient Philosophy*, p. 261 n. 37 (cf. Plato, *Phaedrus* 244d-245a and 265b), the ritual in question most likely the baptism (per the evidence in Conzelmann). That baptism was conceived as part of a 'rebirthing' ceremony in Mithras cult as well: Hans Dieter Betz, *The 'Mithras Liturgy': Text, Translation, and Commentary* (Tübingen: Mohr Siebeck, 2003), p. 51 (lines 505-11).

84. That Jesus through one's baptism awarded liberation from sins (Rom. 6.20-23; Col. 1.13-14) just like Bacchus does in his mystery cult (see previous note), and apparently as baptisms do in the mystery cults generally, see Tertullian, *Prescription against Heretics* 40 and *On Baptism* 4-5. In the Osiris cult (as evinced in the *Book of the Dead* and elsewhere), it was your sins that weighed your soul down in the afterlife, dooming you to a bad outcome (your soul, in the form of your heart, being weighed on a scale against a feather: if your soul is heavier, it is devoured by a monster; lighter, you move on to eternal life); so the fact that baptismal rebirth into communion with Osiris freed you from this outcome entails that this cult, too, held some equivalent concept of washing away or forgiving sins through baptism. See W.B. Ober, 'Weighing the Heart against the Feather of Truth', *Bulletin of the New York Academy of Medicine* 55 (July–August 1979), pp. 636-51.

85. Justin, *Apology* 1.66; Tertullian, *Prescription against Heretics* 40.

Jewish details and framework, just as Mithraism differs from all others in its Persian details and framework, and Isis–Osiris cult differs from all others in its Egyptian details and framework, and so on.

Christianity also conforms to four universal trends distinctive of the Hellenistic mystery religions, and is therefore unmistakably a product of these same cultural trends:

1. *syncretism* of a local or national system of religious ideas with distinctly Hellenistic ideas (and the ideas of other nations and localities whose diffusion was facilitated by Hellenism);
2. a *monotheistic trend*, with every mystery religion evolving from polytheism (many competing gods) to henotheism (one supreme god reigning over subordinate deities), marking a trajectory toward monotheism (only one god);
3. a shift to *individualism*, placing the religious focus on the eternal salvation of the individual rather than the welfare of the community as a whole;
4. and *cosmopolitanism*, with membership being open and spanning all environments, provinces, races, and social classes (and often genders).

That all four features were universal to all the known mystery religions has been abundantly demonstrated in current scholarship, as has the enormous popularity of these new religions, and the rise of these features and their popularity centuries before Christianity. Christianity fits exactly within this trend and in that respect looks exactly like every other mystery religion developed during this period—indeed, it is a relative latecomer. It is thus an expected phenomenon of its time and evinces an unmistakable transformation of the very different Jewish religion into something more palatably identical to popular pagan religious movements arising from every *other* 'foreign' culture under the Roman Empire.[86] To understand this we must take a closer look at each element in turn.

(1) *Syncretism* is the creative merging of religious ideas, borrowing and adapting elements from several religions to create something new. This trend is evident in all the mystery religions,[87] as well as Christianity. This trend indeed parallels the rise of eclecticism in science and philosophy (the merging of different philosophical ideas into a new superior whole, rather

86. See Petra Pakkanen, *Interpreting Early Hellenistic Religion: A Study Based on the Mystery Cult of Demeter and the Cult of Isis* (Helsinki: Suomen Ateenan-Instituutin Saatio, 1996); in which see esp. pp. 65-83 for a survey of various pagan mystery religions and their identifiable features. See also Marvin Meyer (ed.), *The Ancient Mysteries: A Sourcebook of Sacred Texts* (Philadelphia, PA: University of Pennsylvania Press, 1987); and Alvarez, *Romanising Oriental Gods.*

87. See Pakkanen, *Interpreting Early Hellenistic Religion*, pp. 85-100, 129-35.

than dogmatically adhering to one school of thought), and is thus representative of the entire cultural matrix of the time (which, of course, never ceased: later Christians adopted pagan holidays, such as Christmas, and absorbed pagan gods, in both fact and concept, in the guise of a cult of saints, and a great deal else besides).[88] We'll see more evidence of how this syncretism produced Christianity as we go along. But in general, this so routinely occurred, it would be improbable for Christianity to not also have been a product of it (I answer the usual objections to this in Elements 30-38, but of course it must be noted that syncretists themselves never claim they are borrowing; they always portray what they borrowed as a natural development of their native cult—so hostility to borrowing would produce no barrier to actually doing it).

(2) Christianity's *monotheism* was also not original. Indeed, it was entirely parallel to the henotheism already popularly promoted by the mystery cults.[89] Within those cults is a clear trend toward a focus on one supreme god and the demotion of other gods to the status of either minions (becoming the equivalent of angels and demons) or 'aspects' of the one God, thus folding numerous gods into one, each being thought a different guise of the same god. This trend is already evident in Herodotus, and thus began even before the Hellenistic period. Christian rhetoric hardly conceals the fact that it is identically henotheistic, with not just the one God (to whom was later assimilated and originally subordinated the additional gods of the Lord Christ and the Holy Spirit), but many other subordinate gods, including a 'god of this world' (i.e., Satan: 2 Cor. 4.4) and a panoply of angels (divine 'messengers') and demons (literally, *daimones* or *daimonia*,

88. On eclecticism in science and philosophy: Richard Carrier, 'Christianity Was Not Responsible for Modern Science', in *Christian Delusion* (ed. Loftus), pp. 396-419 (405-406; with p. 416 n. 26). On Christmas (both its date and rituals) being originally pagan: Francis James and Miriam Hill (eds.), *Joy to the World: Two Thousand Years of Christmas* (Portland, OR: Four Courts, 2000). On the cult of saints being a syncretization (not a direct adoption) of pagan polytheism: Peter Brown, *Cult of the Saints: Its Rise and Function in Latin Christianity* (Chicago: University of Chicago Press, 1981), with James Howard-Johnston and Paul Antony Hayward (eds.), *The Cult of Saints in Late Antiquity and the Middle Ages: Essays on the Contribution of Peter Brown* (New York: Oxford University Press, 1999); and that there remained also a definite Jewish background to this process of syncretism in creating the Christian cult of saints: William Horbury, 'The Cult of Christ and the Cult of the Saints', *New Testament Studies* 44 (1998), pp. 444-69.

89. See Pakkanen, *Interpreting Early Hellenistic Religion*, pp. 100-109, 136; Hendrik Simon Versnel, *Ter Unus: Isis, Dionysos, Hermes: Three Studies in Henotheism* (Leiden: Brill, 1990); and for subsequent development of this trend: Polymnia Athanassiadi and Michael Frede (eds.), *Pagan Monotheism in Late Antiquity* (New York: Oxford University Press, 1999).

'divinities') possessed of all the same roles, attributes, and powers of pagan gods (see my definitions in §3). That they were not called gods is merely semantics, a rather transparent attempt to deploy doublespeak to conceal what was really a syncretism of Jewish monotheism and pagan polytheism, producing a system of theology that was conceptually identical to pagan henotheism, differing only in the superficial use of words—which difference was *itself* a product of that syncretism, it being the Jewish contribution; the multiplication of divinities being the pagan one.[90]

This had already been occurring within Judaism before the rise of Christianity, which merely continued the process to its logical conclusion.[91] Thus when Paul says,

> We know an idol is nothing in the cosmos, and that there is no God except the one, for although there are ones called gods, either in heaven or on earth (as there are indeed many gods and many lords), yet for us there is the one God, the Father (from whom all things come, and we come to him) and the one Lord, Jesus Christ (through whom all things come, and we come through him) (1 Cor. 8.4-6).

Here we have a plain declaration of henotheism: yes, there are many gods, but we *worship* only two of them, and the second of them we only worship as a subordinate of the other (and thus call that subordinate divinity not 'God' himself but by one of that God's titles, Lord). Spoken like a true henotheist. The only thing unique about it is its restrictions on worship (and a corresponding use of titles)—which derives from Judaism. The rest is pagan.

(3) The third trend was the rise of religious *individualism*.[92] Under the Hellenistic mystery cults, religion became a personal individual *choice* to join or not to join (in contrast with old-style paganism in which a public cult was simply maintained regardless of whether anyone participated or believed); and the motivation to participate became an *individual* reward (personal salvation) rather than a communal reward (such as successful crops and, thereby, the survival of the community). Thus the mystery religions co-opted what had once been agricultural deities (whose dying and rising or descent

90. See Larry Hurtado, 'Monotheism, Principal Angels, and Christology', in *The Oxford Handbook of the Dead Sea Scrolls* (ed. Timothy Lim and John Collins; Oxford: Oxford University Press, 2010), pp. 546-64; and the scholarship on Judeo-Christian 'principalities and powers' (see Element 37).

91. See, e.g., Margaret Barker, *The Great Angel: A Study of Israel's Second God* (Louisville, KY: Westminster/John Knox Press, 1992); Larry Hurtado, *One God, One Lord: Early Christian Devotion and Ancient Jewish Monotheism* (Philadelphia: Fortress Press, 1988); and Alan Segal, *Two Powers in Heaven: Early Rabbinic Reports about Christianity and Gnosticism* (Leiden: Brill, 1977).

92. Pakkanen, *Interpreting Early Hellenistic Religion*, pp. 109-21, 130, 136-37.

and ascent originally corresponded to the seasonal fertility of the earth) and reinterpreted their narratives as metaphors for personal salvation (each individual literally sharing in the demigod's dying and rising or descent and ascent, with eternal life as the end product, rather than continued agricultural fertility in the here and now). So the fact that Christianity *also* turned what was originally a communal aim (the resurrection and salvation *of Israel as a whole*) into an individualistic one (the resurrection and salvation *of individual Christians*, hence of only those who individually chose to join the faith—and indeed creating a cultic model for this in the *individual resurrection of Jesus*) is entirely parallel with what the mystery religions were doing, and thus again fully reflective of the same cultural trend.

(4) Finally, *cosmopolitanism* was part of the same trend. Each mystery religion explicitly created a new group identity transcending all traditional borders and distinctions. Members of the cult became universal brothers and sisters regardless of their actual family ties or geographical, national, or social origins. Mystery cults were thus no longer restricted to a single city, state, or race, or even social status, but spread everywhere and accepted everyone (whether slave or free, rich or poor, citizen or foreigner; in most cases even male or female), thereby uniting all classes, races, and peoples in a new common humanity.[93] So when Paul writes that 'for in one spirit were we all baptized into one body, whether Jews or Greeks, whether bond or free' and thus we are all brothers (1 Cor. 12.12-13; cf. also Gal. 3.26-29; Rom. 12.4-5; and 1 Cor. 10.17; 12.12-25) he is echoing an ideology that had already been popularized by the Hellenistic mystery religions. Indeed he is here pulling Christianity even more into the orbit of this trend, by doing away with the requirement of initiates to first become Jews through circumcision and other rites (Rom. 10.4-9; Philippians 3; Galatians 2, 5, 6).

This reflected a parallel trend in the rise of associations, guilds, burial clubs and fraternities that also allowed people to explore new group identities.[94] This included the development of 'fictive kinship language', in which members of a religious cult or fraternity would call one another 'brother' and 'sister' (and sometimes elders of the group 'fathers' and 'mothers'), exactly as Christians did.[95] This was a common practice in mystery cults, too, so again to see it in earliest Christianity is more evidence of it being part of the same trend. In all these cults and fraternities, key to maintaining

93. Pakkanen, *Interpreting Early Hellenistic Religion*, pp. 121-28, 130, 137.

94. Pakkanen, *Interpreting Early Hellenistic Religion*, pp. 48-49, 52-54.

95. John Kloppenborg, 'Associations in the Ancient World', in *Historical Jesus in Context* (ed. Levine, Allison and Crossan), pp. 323-38 (esp. 329). That Christians called one another 'brothers' is evident throughout the Epistles (e.g. 1 Cor. 7.12; 15.6, 31; see Element 12). Paul considers himself the 'father' of those he converted (1 Cor. 4.15; cf. also Phlm. 10), just as was the practice in Isis cult.

this fictive kinship was the sharing of sacred meals dedicated to their patron god (in which bread, wine and fish were the most common components).[96] Indeed, we know these groups set up rules to keep them reverent, and from degenerating into disrespectful partying or other bad behavior, exactly as Paul seeks to accomplish for the Christian equivalent (in 1 Cor. 11.20-34).[97] Likewise in the mystery cults, sharing in the Lord's meal or baptism or other ritual often united members in a common family by adoption as the sons of their supreme God, thereby making them immortal demigods in the afterlife, like their Savior Lord,[98] which is essentially the view Christians held of their own salvation, as they gained in every respect the glorious, immortal, invincible bodies otherwise only gods enjoyed (1 Cor. 15.35-54; 2 Corinthians 5), and similarly achieved this through adoption as the sons of their supreme God (see next element).

It is therefore undeniable that Christianity was a Judeo-Hellenistic mystery religion, exactly conforming to the trends in religious development that befell nearly every other national culture within the Roman Empire, from the Egyptians to the Persians. Christianity was simply the result of this trend finally befalling the Jews. There may well have been precedents for this already, if Josephus is to be believed in his report that the Essene sect of the Jews conducted itself like a mystery religion, complete with four levels of initiation, including a baptism at the first of them, a communal meal, and swearing to keep the secret of their mysteries even under pain of death (and, of course, a belief in their personal salvation through resurrection).[99] There is also evidence of such mysteries within other varieties of pre-Christian Judaism, which were kept secret from the public.[100] We

96. See J. Gwyn Griffiths, *The Isis-Book: Metamorphoses, Book XI* (Leiden: Brill, 1975), pp. 318-19; and following note.

97. Evidence of the same rule-making for other cult's sacred meals: Kloppenborg, 'Associations', pp. 335-36.

98. Edmonds, *Myths of the Underworld Journey*, pp. 82-108, 198-201. See also Jean-Pierre Vernant, 'Mortals and Immortals: The Body of the Divine', *Mortals and Immortals: Collected Essays* (Princeton, NJ: Princeton University Press, 1991), pp. 27-49.

99. Josephus, *Jewish War* 2.137-42 and 2.150-53.

100. Explicitly stated in the Qumran text 'Hymns of the Just', esp. in 1.1; 3.5; 3.8-12; 4.1; 11.34-36; 13.8-12, 28; 14.21; 15.1-2; 16.22; 18.3; 19.15; 20.9; 21.1-2; 22.13-14; see Robert M. Price, *The Pre-Nicene New Testament: Fifty-Four Formative Texts* (Salt Lake City, UT: Signature Books, 2006), pp. 887-928. See also James Scott, 'Throne-Chariot Mysticism in Qumran and in Paul', in *Eschatology, Messianism, and the Dead Sea Scrolls* (ed. Craig Evans and Peter Flint: Grand Rapids, MI: William B. Eerdmans, 1997), pp. 101-19 (esp. 105-106); and Margaret Barker, *The Great High Priest: The Temple Roots of Christian Liturgy* (New York: T. & T. Clark, 2003), pp. 1-33 and *On Earth as It Is in Heaven: Temple Symbolism in the New Testament* (New York: T. & T. Clark, 1995), pp. 59-60.

just know too little about any of these precedents to know how much they may have led to or influenced Christianity.

Element 12: From as early as we can ascertain, Christians believed they became 'brothers' of the Lord Jesus Christ through baptism (Rom. 6.3-10), which symbolized their death to the world and rebirth as the 'adopted sons of God', hence they became the brothers of the Lord, *the* son of God.[101] Thus Jesus was only 'the firstborn among many brethren' (Rom. 8.29).

Element 13: Like all mystery cults, Christianity had secret doctrines that initiates were sworn never to reveal, and that would be talked about and written about publicly only in symbols, myths and allegories to disguise their true meaning (see Element 14).[102]

Clement of Alexandria, though writing in the early third century, explains:

> Now it is not wished that all things should be exposed indiscriminately to all and sundry, nor should the benefits of wisdom be communicated to those who have not even in a dream been purified in soul (for it is not allowed to hand to every chance comer what has been procured with such laborious efforts); nor are the mysteries of the Word to be expounded to the profane.[103] . . . Those who instituted the mysteries, being philosophers, buried their doctrines in myths, so as not to be obvious to all. Did they not then, by veiling human opinions, prevent the ignorant from handling them? And was it not more beneficial for the holy and blessed contemplation of realities, that they be concealed?[104] . . . So these [secrets] we shall find indicated by symbols under the veil of allegory.[105]

This feature of all the mystery religions of antiquity is well known,[106] but here Clement is saying this was a good practice, even a necessary practice,

101. There are numerous passages that confirm this: Rom. 8.15-29; 9.26; Gal. 3.26-29; 4.4-7; and Heb. 2.10-18; Eph. 1.5; 1 Jn 5.1-4 (and likewise 1 Jn 2.28–3.10; 4.8; 5.18-20); with Rom. 6.3-10; Col. 2.12. See also Irenaeus, *Demonstration of the Apostolic Preaching* 3 and 8; with Carrier, 'Spiritual Body', in *Empty Tomb* (ed. Price and Lowder), pp. 142-47. The notion could easily be derived from *Ps. Sol.* 17.27.

102. See Guy Stroumsa, *Hidden Wisdom: Esoteric Traditions and the Roots of Christian Mysticism* (Leiden: Brill, 1996).

103. Clement of Alexandria, *Miscellanies* 5.9 (§57.2-3).

104. Clement of Alexandria, *Miscellanies* 5.9 (§58.4-5).

105. Clement of Alexandria, *Miscellanies* 5.9 (§58.6).

106. As Philo of Alexandria put it, as quoted in John of Damascus, *Parallels* 533c, 'It is not lawful to speak of the sacred mysteries to the uninitiated'. See Thomas Harrison, *Divinity and History: The Religion of Herodotus* (New York: Clarendon Press, 2000), pp. 182-89, especially with regard, e.g., to Herodotus, *Histories* 2.170-71; Euripides, *Bacchae* 20-54, 470-74; and Plutarch, *The Obsolescence of Oracles* 14.417b-

and that Christianity likewise adheres to it. Earlier Clement had outright said there is a secret understanding of the gospel that he is forbidden to tell his readers.[107] But here he goes on to explain:

> For the prophet says, 'Who shall understand the Lord's parable but the wise and understanding, and he that loves his Lord?' It is but for few to comprehend these things. For, they say, it is not out of envy that the Lord passed on in a certain Gospel, 'My mystery is for me, and for the sons of my house'.[108]

Clement further explains that the Epistles confirm this same division, of some teachings reserved only for insiders; and then even within the church there was another special set of knowledge and teachings reserved only for 'mature' believers (*teleioi*, 'the perfected'), who were distinguished from lower-ranking initiates called 'children' (*nēpioi*, 'babes', the newly baptized being newly born). These were well-recognized code words in the mystery cults, which meant the same thing there as they clearly do for Clement here: 'babes' were Christians not yet inducted into the higher mysteries, while the 'mature' had been, and thus knew teachings that other Christians did not. But Clement also indicates in the above quotes that there were also teachings that 'babes' were privy to that non-Christians (the 'profane') were not to be told.

Obviously the only way any of this could have been maintained is if initiates at each level were sworn to secrecy, and as we know this was the case in all other mystery cults, and Christianity was likewise a mystery cult (see Element 12), we can be certain this was the case there, too. Thus, when Clement quotes Rom. 16.25-26, which says 'the mystery' of Christianity was a secret hidden within scripture but now revealed and taught 'to all nations for the obedience of faith', Clement says this means 'that is, to those from "all nations" who are believers', and not, in fact, indiscriminately to everyone. Clement then adds, 'But even only to a few of *them* [meaning, Christian believers] is shown what those things are which are contained in the mystery'.[109] Clement says this was rightly so, as Plato himself had said, when discussing God in a letter (sent on a tablet), 'We must speak in enigmas, so that, should this tablet come by any mischance on its leaves either by sea or land, he who reads may remain ignorant'.[110]

Clement then says:

c; and *On Isis and Osiris* 9.354c–11.355d; 58.374e; 78.382e-f. See also Clauss, *Roman Cult of Mithras*, p. 14.

107. Clement of Alexandria, *Miscellanies* 1.12.

108. Clement of Alexandria, *Miscellanies* 5.10 (§63.6-7).

109. Clement of Alexandria, *Miscellanies* 5.10 (§64.6).

110. Clement of Alexandria, *Miscellanies* 5.10 (§65.1-2).

> Akin to this is what the holy apostle Paul says, preserving the prophetic and truly ancient secret (from which the teachings that were good were derived by the Greeks): 'But we do speak wisdom among the mature [*teleioi*]—not the wisdom of this world, or of the princes of this world, who will be done away with, but we speak the wisdom of God, hidden in a mystery' [1 Cor. 2.6-7]. Then proceeding, he thus inculcates the caution against the divulging of his words to the multitude in the following terms: 'But I, brethren, could not speak to you as spiritual men, but as carnal men, as babes [*nēpioi*] in Christ. I have fed you with milk, not with solid food: for you could not receive it; even now you can't receive it. For you are still carnal men' [1 Cor. 3.1-3]. If, then, 'the milk' is said by the apostle to belong to the babes, and 'solid food' to be the food of the mature, then 'milk' will be understood to be catechetical instruction—the first food, as it were, of the soul—and 'solid food' is beholding the highest mysteries.[111]

That last phrase, 'beholding the highest mysteries', is in Greek *epoptikē theōria*, terminology very specific to mystery cult. This is corroborated by others. Origen explains there were different ranks of initiation, with secrets in the church withheld until each rank was achieved, and the lowest rank were the babes, fed only milk.[112]

It's evident that their reading of Paul is correct. Paul very clearly does say that there is some teaching he can't impart to his Corinthian readers because they are not of sufficient rank in the church, and he very clearly uses the particular terminology of mystery cult, distinguishing initiates (newborn babes) from the *teleioi*, those who presumably have 'completed' all the mysteries. He says the truth (the 'wisdom' that is not of men or angels) that the *teleioi* are taught is a secret and 'hidden in a mystery', and thus he explains he can't tell them what it is. One has to have a more mature spiritual understanding first (1 Corinthians 2, throughout which the 'us' and 'we' he is referring to must be the apostles and *teleioi*, not the whole congregation), because without that the truth will seem ridiculous to them (*mōria*) and they won't be able to understand it (1 Cor. 2.14–3.3). That is how he says the advanced teachings would seem even to baptized initiates, just as the *introductory* teachings seem ridiculous to *outsiders* but can still be understood by the babes in Christ (1 Cor. 1.17-31; 3.18-19).

111. Clement of Alexandria, *Miscellanies* 5.10 (§65.4–66.2); but all of 5.4-11 illustrates the point.

112. Origen, *Against Celsus* 3.51-61. See also Hippolytus, *Apostolic Tradition* 15-21, who describes the process of ascending from outsider to insider (first initiation), then from babe to mature (second initiation) as typically taking years to complete (and his manual does not even cover the teaching of the mature, nor ascending into the priesthood for that matter, which would by then have been yet another stage).

The mysteries the beginners are taught, Paul says, are 'nothing other than Jesus Christ and him crucified' (1 Cor. 2.2), the most basic gospel (outlined in 1 Cor. 15.3-5). But there is also a special 'wisdom', he says, that was taught to advanced members (the *teleioi*), which Paul sees as the root of the problem he is addressing at Corinth: because those he is speaking to have not yet been initiated into the highest mysteries, they are splitting into factions (e.g. some declaring themselves for Paul, some for Apollos: 1 Cor. 3.3-4), not being aware of that 'higher' teaching that (Paul is assuming) would sort them out and resolve their dispute. Indeed, Paul implies that Apollos imparted to them some new mysteries that weren't among those taught them by Paul, and Paul explains Apollos was only building on what Paul taught (1 Cor. 3.5-24), suggesting that Paul is saying their different teachings don't *really* contradict each other, but rather that Apollos was imparting a second tier of deeper understanding (the mystery cults generally had more than two levels of mysteries to enter; so Christianity may have, too: see below). Hence, he says, 'this is how one should regard us [i.e., the apostles], as servants of Christ and stewards of the mysteries of God' (1 Cor. 4.1). Paul elsewhere mentions there being many mysteries (which together constituted complete 'knowledge') and implies only the most advanced knew them all (1 Cor. 13.2). Thus, Paul assumes throughout 1 Corinthians 8 that Christians with certain secret knowledge can partake of pagan-sacrificed meat but that this might mislead Christians not yet privy to that knowledge, and therefore higher-ranking Christians should not encourage this by setting a bad example (thus he develops the compromise in 1 Corinthians 10), all of which entails there were levels of teaching kept hidden from lower ranks of Christians.[113]

We see something similar in the Dead Sea Scrolls, one of which mentions secrets held by insiders of differing rank, using the same distinctions between 'babes' and 'adults' and 'milk' versus 'meat'.[114] All of this is confirmed for Christianity in the book of Hebrews, which also speaks of 'milk' and 'solid food' and the distinction between those in the church who are not ready to receive the latter, who again are called 'babes', and those who are able to receive it, because of their more advanced spiritual training, who are again called the 'mature' (Heb. 5.11–6.3). It likewise speaks of more

113. Note that Paul also at one point uses a technical term from the mystery cults that meant induction into the mysteries: *mueō*, whose principal meaning was 'initiate into the mysteries', which Paul uses in Phil. 4.12, but metaphorically, and in too ambiguous a way to be certain if his metaphor was to Christian mysteries or pagan mysteries (the former, I think, is more likely, but unprovable from this datum alone).

114. Qumran 'Hymns of the Just' 4 (with 13.8-12, 28; 16.22; 'babes' and 'adults' and 'milk' and 'meat' distinction in 14.21 and 21.1-2). See Price, *Pre-Nicene*, pp. 887-928.

basic principles of Christ (the 'first principles'), which are enumerated as 'repentance from dead works; faith toward God; the doctrine of baptisms; and of laying on of hands; and of resurrection of the dead; and of eternal judgment'. This is evidently the litany of what would be imparted by the 'initial' mysteries, or possibly several ranks of mysteries (since there is more to this list than Paul said one's first initiation began with), and this is all distinguished from the final mysteries, by which one is 'perfected', which this author implies is contained in what follows (in Hebrews 6 through 13).

It's worth noting that these hints of there being more than just two levels of initiation (first becoming newborn babes, then becoming perfected) accords with other mystery cults, which typically had three or four levels. In the second century, the letters of Ignatius also suggest there were multiple levels, when he says he can't tell the Trallians some of the Christian mysteries because they are still 'babes' and thus not able to receive the secrets he is hinting at (which from context seem to be something about the nature of Satan, his role in attacking the church, and its connection with esoteric knowledge about the heavenly realms and the names of various angels and celestial powers), but that there are still other teachings even he has not received yet (which he knows will involve more knowledge of the structure of heaven and some sort of detailed angelology).[115] That entails at least three levels of initiation were known to him and his fellow congregants. This may have been the case in Paul's time as well.

Clement himself describes four levels of initiation in the church of his own day, consisting of 'faith' (*pistis*), 'knowledge' (*gnōsis*), 'love' (*agapē*) and 'inheritance' (*klēronomia*).[116] One ascends through these stages to achieve immortality:

> Which takes place whenever one is held up by the Lord through faith, then through knowledge, then through love, and then ascends along with him to where the God and watcher of our faith and love resides. Whence at last it is that knowledge is passed down to those fit and selected for it, because immense preparation and previous training is necessary in order to hear what is said, and to live a life of restraint, and to advance intelligently to the fullness of righteousness that is according to the law. It leads us to the endless and perfect end, teaching us beforehand the future life that we shall lead, according to God, and with gods. . . .
>
> After which redemption, the reward and the honors are assigned to those who have become perfect [lit. 'to those who have become *teleioi*'], when they will be done with purification, and ceased from all service (though it be holy service, and among saints). Then they become pure in

115. Ignatius, *Epistle to the Trallians* 5.

116. Clement of Alexandria, *Miscellanies* 7.10 (§55.7–56.1). See Robin Lane Fox, *Pagans and Christians* (New York: Alfred A. Knopf, 1987), pp. 316-17, 733 (n. 11).

> heart, next to the Lord, where they await their return to eternal contemplation. Then they are called by the appellation of 'gods', being destined to sit on thrones with the other gods that have been first put in their places by the Savior.[117]

Clement's previous designation of that final rank as the 'inheritance', and then here describing it as reaching the status of 'god', placed 'next to the Lord', destined to sit on a throne in heaven and eternally contemplate reality, might be an important clue to what it meant to be a *teleios*, a Christian admitted to the highest mysteries: full inheritance as God's son, something more than by mere adoption, but complete equivalence to God's firstborn. This could be the underlying idea when Paul says those in the church of his own rank 'have the mind of Christ' and thus can properly judge all things because they have full knowledge of all the mysteries (1 Cor. 2.16). Paul elsewhere hints at a secret doctrine in 2 Cor. 12.3, where he says a man he knows (most scholars believe he is speaking of himself) experienced a spiritual ascent 'into the third heaven' where he heard teachings he was forbidden to tell (thus again evincing a secret mystery teaching), a notion of ascent that accords with Clement's description of the highest mysteries in Christianity.[118]

Whether either of those last points is correct or not, Paul clearly references secret doctrines kept from the public, plus more secret doctrines kept even from most Christians and reserved instead for those who were 'mature'. Clement fully confirms this.[119] As does Origen, Ignatius and

117. Clement of Alexandria, *Miscellanies* 7.10 (§56.1-7); the whole of 7.10 describes these levels and the knowledge requisite to ascend each. It need not be assumed that Clement is saying that lower ranking church members were not saved, since Clement and every other Christian, from Paul onward, declares that baptism (into 'faith') was sufficient; rather, those inducted but not yet fully ascended would still get eternal life, because they could ascend the remaining ranks in heaven (e.g. Origen, *On the First Principles* 2.11.4-7, which is in accord with Origen, *Against Celsus* 1.9-10).

118. See James Tabor, *Things Unutterable: Paul's Ascent to Paradise in its Greco-Roman, Judaic, and Early Christian Contexts* (Lanham, MD: University Press of America, 1986), p. 122.

119. Though we do not have conclusive evidence that Clement's four-stage system was already in place under Paul, I believe it is not unreasonable to suspect that it was, or something approaching it. That is not necessary to my point (since we do have conclusive evidence of at least two stages in Paul's time and that's sufficient to establish this element as fact), but the existence from the very start of the system Clement describes should be seriously considered. Not only because such systems might already have been employed in earlier Jewish sects (and thus simply been adapted to the new gospel), but also because this is how religions develop: their originators elaborate systems and hierarchies within a matter of years, not centuries. Hence I should not have to respond to the objection that developed systems and hierarchies within Christianity didn't arise for another century. That assumption has always been implausible on its face. Any

Hebrews. This evidence is only supported further by the more general point that this was a standard feature of all mystery cults, and Christianity clearly was one (as shown in Element 11), so we should expect it shared this feature as well, especially as even pre-Christian Judaism had similar traditions of secret doctrines.[120]

Element 14: Mystery cults spoke of their beliefs in public through myths and allegory, which symbolized a more secret doctrine that was usually rooted in a more esoteric astral or metaphysical theology. Therefore, as itself a mystery religion with secret doctrines, Christianity would have done the same.

The most explicit discussion of this fact can be found in Plutarch's book on the myths and teachings of the mystery cult of Isis and Osiris, which he wrote and dedicated to a priestess of that cult, Clea.[121] Plutarch says the highest aim of any religion is to learn the truth behind its stories and rituals, the truth about the gods. And part of that consisted in realizing that the stories and narratives of the gods were only allegories for higher truths:

> Clea, whenever you hear the mythical stories told by the Egyptians about their gods—of their wanderings, dismemberments, and many experiences like these—you must remember what I said earlier and not think that any of these things is being said to have actually happened like that or to have actually come to pass.[122]

He then goes on to summarize what is essentially the 'gospel' of Isis and Osiris, a typical mythic narrative of events transpiring on earth leading

community that organizes and expands over three continents (as Paul's letters show Christianity already had) will rapidly need a clear hierarchy and organization within a matter of years. To assume that no one thought of this or saw any need for it for a whole century (much less three) is absurd. Likewise, since Paul reveals there were already at least two levels of initiation in the cult, there is no reason to assume there were not more. If there were already two, there could just as easily have been four (as Josephus attests the Essenes already had). Paul's letters just never had an occasion to discuss the details of this.

120. For further support of this last point see the analysis of Margaret Barker, 'The Secret Tradition', *Journal of Higher Criticism* 2 (Spring 1995), pp. 31-67; and Margaret Barker, 'The Temple Roots of the Christian Liturgy', in *Christian Origins: Worship, Belief and Society* (ed. Kieran O'Mahony; Sheffield: Sheffield Academic Press, 2003), pp. 29-51. On secrets and initiations in Judaism see previous notes.

121. Plutarch, *On Isis and Osiris* 1.351c and 351f (this Clea was also the dedicatee of his book on *The Bravery of Women* 1.242e-f). Another discourse on this topic was delivered by Maximus of Tyre, in his fourth oration, 'Poetry and Philosophy on the Gods' (sometime in the second century), which also explicitly links allegorical mythmaking to mystery cult practice.

122. Plutarch, *On Isis and Osiris* 11.355b.

to Osiris's death and resurrection.[123] He then closes by repeating the point that Clea knows better than to really believe these stories, that 'in fact, you yourself detest' those who take them literally, and that she (like all true believers) sees them as 'but window dressing' that points us to something else more profound.[124]

Plutarch then goes on to survey what this underlying truth might actually be. He first brings up the theory of Euhemerus that all such tales are the mythification of past kings into current gods, but then he rejects this as impious and absurd.[125] Instead, 'better', he says, is the theory that these earthly tales are of the 'sufferings' (*pathēmata*) not of gods or men, but of 'great divinities' (*daimonōn megalōn*, 'great demons' in Christian vernacular), divine beings with incarnate bodies capable of suffering and corruption. This, he says, was just as in other mystery cults (he alludes definitely to those of Dionysus and Demeter, meaning the Bacchic and Eleusinian mysteries, of which Clea was also a participant), where there are also 'mythical stories' told of the wanderings and sufferings of those gods, but 'all is concealed behind mystic sacraments and initiations, not spoken or shown to the multitude', thereby preserving the truth. Plutarch says the stories of Isis and Osiris 'have the same explanation'.[126] Hence it's important to note that Paul also speaks of 'the sufferings' (*pathēmata*) of Christ, just as Plutarch says 'the sufferings' of other savior gods were spoken of in other mystery cults.[127] As Plutarch explains, the true story is that Isis and Osiris are celestial gods engaged in a war in outer space between good and evil demons.[128] The tales that relate their adventures on earth are just an allegory for this higher reality, which is actually going on in heaven (see Element 37).

Plutarch also explores another explanation, in which a god's narrative myth is reduced to purely naturalistic and mystical allegories, and thus not about actual beings at all—but he indicates this is not the view he shares.[129] He prefers the demonological theory, and accepts the other more thoroughgoing allegorization as only a supplemental explanation at best, concluding that 'individually these theorists are wrong, but collectively they are right' because all the things they describe are a *part* of the gods in question, not

123. Plutarch, *On Isis and Osiris* 12.355d–19.358e.

124. Plutarch, *On Isis and Osiris* 20.358e-359a.

125. Plutarch, *On Isis and Osiris* 21.359c–24.360d.

126. Plutarch, *On Isis and Osiris* 25.360d-f.

127. 2 Cor. 1.5 and Phil. 3.10. Likewise 1 Pet. 1.11; 4.13; 5.1 (on which see Chapters 7 and 11).

128. Plutarch, *On Isis and Osiris* 26.361b–27.361e.

129. Plutarch, *On Isis and Osiris* 32.363d–46.369e; 49.371a–80.384c.

identical to those gods.[130] He says these demigods control all the things their myths are said to allegorize; in fact, those who think the gods simply *are* these natural forces and mystical truths he denounces as atheists or idolators.[131] Thus, Plutarch continually returns to and defends the demonological theory (in which cosmic good and evil beings, and their struggles and battles, lie behind it all) as being 'the wisest' view (just as Paul calls the secret teachings of Christianity the *real* wisdom, a wisdom not of this world, in 1 Corinthians 2).[132] Plutarch cannot, of course, come out and tell us what the initiates to the Isiac mysteries are actually told. If he knew he would have been sworn to secrecy, and in any event would not offend Clea by exposing them to the public. But we can read between the lines: he would of course prefer of all explanations the one actually in accord with what the highest ranking initiates like Clea were taught. Thus we can infer it accorded most closely with his demonological theory. And as he says all other mystery religions have 'similar explanations', we can infer this was the common trend among them all.

It was common in fact to see all sacred literature (even revered poetry about the gods) as allegorical, not meant literally, such that one had to 'lift the veil' through interpretation to reveal the true meaning of a text, much as Paul says Christians must approach the OT (2 Cor. 3.12–4.6). Though Paul could imagine actual historical events being arranged to convey the allegory (1 Cor. 10.1-11) it's obvious (as with Plutarch) that this would not always be a necessary understanding, even among Christians. For instance, Paul clearly does not regard the historicity of the tale of Sarah and Hagar to be relevant to his allegorical understanding of it, which he assumes his Christian congregations will readily accept (Gal. 4.22-31: see Chapter 11, §9). And anyone who welcomed the *reading* of sacred stories as allegory would welcome the *writing* of sacred stories as allegory. Obviously, since Paul believed the OT was so written and endorsed as such by God.

The same had already occurred among the pagans. Homer, for example, came to be increasingly read (even from as early as the time of Plato) as allegorically representing deeper cosmic truths through his superficial narratives of the gods, and as such Homer was treated as divinely inspired scripture.[133] The Jews had already caught the same bug and were treating

130. Plutarch, *On Isis and Osiris* 45.369a-d.

131. Plutarch, *On Isis and Osiris* 64.376f–67.378a (see also 70.379b–71.379e).

132. Plutarch, *On Isis and Osiris* 46.369d.

133. See Robert Lamberton, *Homer the Theologian: Neoplatonist Allegorical Reading and the Growth of the Epic Tradition* (Berkeley, CA: University of California Press, 1986). For broader analysis of this whole trend among pagans see J. Gwyn Griffiths, *Plutarch's De Iside et Osiride* (Cardiff: University of Wales Press, 1970), pp. 100-101 and 419-20, and Luc Brisson, *How Philosophers Saved Myths: Allegorical*

their scriptures the same way before Christianity arrived on the scene. And as Paul attests, Christians adopted the same practice. All simply embraced the same way of reading divine secrets out of sacred texts. The Jewish theologian Philo, for example, a contemporary of Paul, interprets the tale of Lot's wife turning into a pillar of salt as an allegory for spurning a teacher's instruction and locking one's gaze instead on what one knew before.[134] Thus such a story did not have to be historical to be 'true'.

Not all myths and interpretations had merit. Philo could simultaneously denounce 'cleverly devised fables' while himself interpreting a biblical text as symbolic allegory and calling that the 'real truth'. It depended, he argues, on whether one saw correctly, being in the right state of mind as one read: 'as many as are able to contemplate the facts related' in the stories of the Bible while they are 'in their incorporeal and unclothed state, living rather in the soul than in the body', will see that the true meaning lies in the allegory, not 'what are contained in the plain words of the scriptures'.[135] Philo thus says the tales of Eve and the Serpent 'are not mere fabulous inventions, in which poets and sophists delight, but are rather types shadowing forth some allegorical truth, according to some mystical explanation', and thus the story is symbolic.[136] He regards Abraham's father, Terah, as nonhistorical, merely an allegory, in contrast to Socrates, 'who really existed', and he likewise deems Sarah and Hagar as not real people but just allegorical symbols (just as Paul apparently did).[137] Accordingly, Philo composed entire books about how to read the scriptures allegorically, and frequently relies on this procedure for understanding what the scriptures 'really' meant.[138]

If Philo respects *reading* sacred stories that way, he would have to respect *composing* them that way. Indeed, as historical events never in fact work out so neatly as an allegory requires, even if someone believed an allegorical story 'had' to also be superficially true (though it is clear Paul

Interpretation and Classical Mythology (trans. Catherine Tihanyi; Chicago: University of Chicago Press, 2004); for pagans, Jews, and Christians see Annewies van den Hoek, 'Allegorical Interpretation', in *Dictionary of Biblical Criticism and Interpretation* (ed. Stanley Porter; New York: Routledge, 2007), pp. 9-12; and Jean Pépin, *Mythe et allégorie: les origines grecques et les contestations judéo-chrétiennes* (Paris: Études Augustiniennes, 1976). See also Chilton, 'Commenting on the Old Testament'.

134. Philo, *On Flight and Discovery* 22.121-22.

135. Philo, *On Abraham* 41.236 and 41.243. See also Philo, *On the Descendants of Cain* 7 and *On Abraham* 98-102.

136. Philo, *On the Creation* 55.157.

137. Philo, *On Dreams* 1.58 and *On Mating with the Preliminary Studies* 6-7.

138. We have three of his books *On Allegorical Interpretation*; for other examples of his reliance on the procedure, see *On the Change of Names* 28.152, *On Dreams* 1.27.172, etc. See Jean Pépin (ed.), *La tradition de l'allégorie de Philon d'Alexandrie à Dante: Études historiques* (Paris: Études Augustiniennes, 1987).

and Philo didn't), an allegorical tale would still have to be invented and then *passed off* as superficially true. And as Plutarch explained for the mystery religions, this same thing would also be done to conceal the true meaning from the public. He describes the result of this as the multitude 'superstitiously' believing the stories are true, while initiates like Clea and himself knew better. For instance:

> There is a doctrine which modern priests hint at to satisfy their conscience, but only in veiled terms and with caution: namely that the god Osiris rules and reigns over the dead, being none other than he whom the Greeks call Hades or Pluto. The truth of this statement is misunderstood and confuses the masses, who suppose that the sacred and the holy one, who is in truth Osiris, lives in the earth and under the earth, where are concealed the bodies of those who appear to have reached their end. He is actually very far removed from the earth [i.e., in outer space], being undefiled, unspotted, and uncorrupted by any being which is subject to decay and death.[139]

In fact, Plutarch believes, the souls of the dead ascend into outer space, where Osiris will preside over them as their heavenly king.[140] This much Plutarch can reveal. The more sacred details he omits.

What the priests were doing by speaking this way was not deemed lying. For instance, Philo says Moses (whom Philo, like many Jews, believed wrote the Torah) tells no fable when he says 'there were giants on the earth in those days' (Gen. 6.4), but meant only allegorically that there were men of heavenly wisdom. Philo then says Moses would never tell a fable, because he only tells the truth, so, just like Plutarch, anyone who takes that statement about giants literally Philo compares to idolaters and men deceived.[141] Thus, for Philo 'the truth' is the allegorical meaning of the text, not its literal meaning. We have to appreciate the significance of this. For us, even as Philo explains it, 'Moses' told a lie, plainly saying what is not true, that giants once walked the earth. But for Philo, as long as this statement has a higher symbolic meaning that is true, Moses isn't lying. Those who don't have the holy spirit of wisdom and understanding will only *think* he's lying—or believe the literal meaning and thus believe what is false. Take note of this. Because people who think this way will both read *and write* books differently than we expect.[142]

139. Plutarch, *On Isis and Osiris* 78.382e.

140. Plutarch, *On Isis and Osiris* 78.382f-383a (and see Elements 31 and 34-38).

141. Philo, *On the Giants* 58-60. See also Philo, *On Providence* 2.40-41 (translated and discussed in Lamberton, *Homer the Theologian*, pp. 49-51).

142. For discussion of this point see Peter Struck, *Birth of the Symbol: Ancient Readers and the Limits of their Texts* (Princeton, NJ: Princeton University Press, 2004); Bruce Malina, *The Social Gospel of Jesus: The Kingdom of God in Mediterranean*

The gospel story found in Mark, for example, could have begun as a set of mythic models for common Christian rituals and realities such as baptism and the Eucharist and facing persecution and martyrdom and performing miracles of healing, exorcism and prophecy. If that were so (and we'll see how likely it is in Chapter 10), then we would have to conclude it also establishes a model for initiation into the secret teachings of the Christian mysteries (in Mk 4.11-12):

> And [Jesus Christ] said unto [his closest followers], 'Unto *you* is given the *mystery* of the kingdom of God: but to *outsiders*, everything is given in parables, so that seeing they may see, but not know; and hearing they may hear, but not comprehend; lest they should turn and be forgiven.'

Within the narrative Jesus is speaking of his parables (paraphrasing, or quoting a lost variant of, Isa. 6.9-10). But insiders might have been taught that the narrative *itself* is constructed the same way, and thus the notion that Jesus is speaking only of his parables is what *outsiders* are meant to think. Indeed, that the Gospel actually *tells* the secrets behind his parables suggests the real secrets lie elsewhere in the text, as otherwise they were here being revealed, which defeated the purpose of concealing them in the first place. We'll see evidence of all this in Chapter 10. But here I mean only to establish its plausibility.

In his early-third-century rebuttal to the pagan critic Celsus (who wrote in the late second century), the Christian teacher Origen says an allegorical understanding of sacred writings is common to pagans, Jews *and* Christians, and that in fact Christians frequently understand the scriptures allegorically, including their own Gospels. 'The historical parts' of the Bible, Origen declares, 'were written with an allegorical purpose, being most skillfully adapted not only for the multitude of the simpler believers, but also for the few who are willing or even able to investigate matters intelligently'. Indeed, he says, 'what other inference can be drawn than that they were composed so as to be understood allegorically in their chief sig-

Perspective (New York: Routledge, 2000); and Bruce Malina, *The New Jerusalem in the Revelation of John: The City as Symbol of Life with God* (Collegeville, MN: Liturgical Press, 2000), with Bruce Malina and John Pilch, *Social Science Commentary on the Book of Revelation* (Minneapolis, MN: Fortress Press, 2000). See also John Dominic Crossan, *The Power of Parable: How Fiction by Jesus became Fiction about Jesus* (New York: HarperOne, 2012); Thomas Thompson, *The Messiah Myth: The Near Eastern Roots of Jesus and David* (New York: Basic Books, 2005); Thomas Brodie, *The Birthing of the New Testament: The Intertextual Development of the New Testament Writings* (Sheffield: Sheffield Phoenix Press, 2004); and Randel Helms, *Gospel Fictions* (Amherst, NY: Prometheus Books, 1988).

nification?'[143] Those who approach the text literally, he says, have 'a veil of ignorance' upon them and thus 'read but do not understand the figurative meaning', whereas this veil 'is taken away by the gift of God' from those who have achieved sufficient philosophical perfection.[144] Origen thus echoes what is said by Paul in 2 Corinthians 3, that readers of the Bible have a veil over their hearts which prevents them from understanding its true meaning—which, Paul makes clear, is the *allegorical* meaning. Origen even says that the Jewish and Christian narratives are better because they have been designed to be more morally edifying than the licentious fables of the pagans. Thus 'our narratives keep expressly in view the multitude of simpler believers', just as Plato had commanded be done, as Origen says, by purging all immoral tales from the poets and crafting only acceptable myths in their place (a leading theme of Plato's *Republic*).

Origen is clear in meaning that the Gospels were likewise allegorically constructed and not to be taken literally as Celsus was doing.[145] Origen cannot mean all the stories were 'also' literally true, as Celsus was arguing that they are in that case absurd, and Origen is responding by saying they are not absurd because they have a sublime *allegorical* meaning. But that only cancels their absurdity if they are *not* also literally true. At most, some of them may be true, while for the others their literal meaning only had use in edifying the 'simpler' believers in the way Plato had meant: false tales told in order to trick the masses into doing the right thing. Origen cites Plato's very argument to that effect in his own defense, so he clearly meant the Bible (the NT included) served the same role. Elsewhere he is explicit: when it comes to the actual meaning of what the Gospels say, 'mature' believers are taught one thing, but 'simpler' believers are taught another, and in result, he says, many passages in the Gospels are *literally* false and only *allegorically* true; as Origen put it, 'the spiritual truth was often preserved, as one might say, in a material falsehood'.[146] And indeed, from extensive analyses of his writings, Joseph Trigg and Gunnar Hällström have each found that Origen did indeed believe it was better for the

143. Origen, *Against Celsus* 4.48-49 (see also 1.42). Origen is not alone. The pagan critic Porphyry observed that all Christians and Jews treated their text this way, and Eusebius concurs: Eusebius, *History of the Church* 6.19.4 (quoting Porphyry, *Against the Christians* 3).

144. Origen, *Against Celsus* 4.50. See also Justin Martyr, *Dialogue with Trypho* 90.

145. Origen, *Against Celsus* 4.51-52. Thus, Origen asks that Celsus 'seek the help of one who is capable of initiating him into the actual meaning of the narratives' before judging their veracity: Origen, *Against Celsus* 6.23; that is, he asks that Celsus become a Christian, as then he will be taught these secrets.

146. Origen, *Commentary on the Gospel according to John* 1.9-11 and 10.2-6.

'simpleton' to believe literally in what the Bible says even when that literal meaning isn't true.[147]

This reasoning is most explicitly endorsed by Eusebius (in the early fourth century), who argues that it was necessary to lie like this for the cause of Christianity, and that the Bible thus contained many such lies—Eusebius even claims Plato got this edifying idea *from* the Bible. In fact, Eusebius's entire treatise on God's *Preparation for the Gospel* argues that every good idea the Greeks had actually came from Moses. And among those 'good ideas' Eusebius includes the following, under the heading 'that it is necessary sometimes to use falsehood as a medicine for those who need' it:

> [As was said by the Athenian in Plato's *Laws*] 'And even the lawmaker who is of little use. . .if he dared lie to young men for a good reason, then can't he lie? For falsehood is something even more useful than [the truth], and sometimes even more able to bring it about that everyone willingly keeps to all justice.' [Then is said by Clinias] 'Truth is beautiful, stranger, and steadfast. But to persuade people of it is not easy.' You would find many things of this sort being used even in the Hebrew scriptures, such as concerning God being jealous or falling asleep or getting angry or being subject to some other human passions, for the benefit of those who need such an approach.[148]

To understand what Eusebius means, it is important to know how the Platonic dialogue he quotes continues:

> Athenian: Be it so; yet it proved easy to persuade men of the Sidonian fairy-tale, incredible though it was, and of numberless others.
> Clinias: What tales?
> Athenian: The tale of the teeth that were sown, and how armed men sprang out of them. Here, indeed, the lawgiver has a notable example of how one can, if he tries, persuade the souls of the young of anything, so that the only question he has to consider in his inventing is what would do most good to the State, if it were believed; and then he must devise all possible means to ensure that the whole of the community constantly, so long as they live, use exactly the same language, so far as possible, about these matters, alike in their songs, their tales, and their discourses. If you, however, think otherwise, I have no objection to your arguing in the opposite sense.

147. Joseph Trigg, 'Divine Deception and the Truthfulness of Scripture', in *Origen of Alexandria: His World and his Legacy* (ed. Charles Kannengiesser and William Peterson; Notre Dame, IN: University of Notre Dame Press, 1988), pp. 147-64; Gunnar Hällström, *Fides simpliciorum according to Origen of Alexandria* (Helsinki: Societas Scientiarum Fennica, 1984).

148. Eusebius, *Preparation for the Gospel* 12.31. The passage he quotes is Plato, *Laws* 663e. Note that the section heading could possibly be by a later editor, though I doubt it, and it accurately describes the argument Eusebius makes nevertheless.

Clinias: Neither of us, I think, could possibly argue against your view.[149]

Plato had already had the Athenian argue that justice is the only real road to happiness, and therefore by this argument people can be persuaded to be good. But he then addresses the possibility that the truth will not suffice, or that justice is not in fact the only real road to happiness, by arguing that lying is acceptable, and in fact *even more effective* in bringing about what is desired—that the people will be good—and thus teachers should employ lies for the benefit of the community.

The added significance here is the distinction being made between the 'young' as the targets of this manipulation: here we have the conceptual parallel to the 'babes' in Christ who need 'milk' because they are not yet ready to receive the *real* food (the true teaching) of the Christian religion (see Element 13). This is the very point Plato makes, saying that one thing is to be told to 'the mature' of understanding, and another thing told to 'children' (including adolescents, but metaphorically he means anyone philosophically immature), and from the latter the real truth will be kept, such that, he says, only after an initiation into the appropriate mysteries can they receive it.[150] The second-century pagan orator Maximus of Tyre attests the same concept, even evoking the 'milk' metaphor.[151] Eusebius agrees, as did Origen. This same attitude could thus have been ingrained within the church from its very inception.

As we saw before (in Element 13), in the early third century Clement of Alexandria also referred approvingly to the letters of Plato in which he makes the same argument, that the common people aren't prepared to understand the truth and thus must be told a superficial lie to conceal it from them, and that it would be concealed within riddles and myths only symbolizing or pointing to the truth.[152] Centuries later Augustine would condemn this widely held principle (that 'it is expedient to deceive the people in matters of religion', a view he suggests was also endorsed by the Roman scholar Varro in the early first century BCE), yet at the same time still defends allegorical readings of the Bible when the literal meaning clearly could not be true (as when, e.g., it contradicted established science,

149. Plato, *Laws* 663e-664b. See also Plato, *Republic* 2.414-17.

150. Plato, *Republic* 2.378a-e.

151. Maximus of Tyre, *Orations* 4.3.

152. Plato, *Letters* 2.312d; 2.314a-14c. See Julius Elias, *Plato's Defense of Poetry* (Albany, NY: State University of New York Press, 1984); Radcliffe Edmonds III, *Myths of the Underworld Journey: Plato, Aristophanes, and the 'Orphic' Gold Tablets* (New York: Cambridge University Press, 2004), pp. 161-71 (in context, pp. 159-220); Kathryn Morgan, *Myth and Philosophy from the Presocratics to Plato* (New York: Cambridge University Press, 2000).

a specific problem Augustine was apologetically addressing).[153] Today we call that hypocrisy. At any rate, even Augustine, for all his protests, only confirms that the view was entrenched and widely embraced—even by himself.

Origen gives us the most candid discussion of this doctrine within the church: 'Each person understands the Scriptures according to his capacity. One takes the sense from them more superficially, as if from the surface of a spring. Another draws up more deeply as from a well.'[154] Though Origen thinks literal interpretations can be 'helpful' for edifying the 'simple' believer, they are not the actual truth, which can sometimes even be exactly the opposite. Sometimes Paul himself, Origen says, 'wanted to conceal the forbidden meaning of a passage as something not appropriate for simple folk or for the common hearing of those who are led only by faith to what is better', and yet, 'so we would not mishear his words, he was then compelled' to give clues to the real meaning of what he said, so that we would know 'there was something forbidden and secret in that passage'. As for example, when Paul says, 'Behold, I tell you a mystery' about the nature of the resurrection, Origen says, 'this is his way of introducing things deeper and more secret which are appropriately kept hidden from the multitude'. Origen concludes, 'as is even written in Tobit, "It is good to keep the king's mystery a secret", but respectable and fitting "to honorably reveal the works of God" to the multitude with what is *conveniently* true'.[155] Thus, there is a gospel for the simpleton (the 'babes' in Christ) and a gospel for 'grown ups', and Origen explains that the latter is concealed from the 'simpleton' because it might turn him away from the faith and thus away from salvation, while only a few people of sufficient maturity are really fit to understand the truth.[156] Clement of Alexandria makes the same argument, using Paul's own language of 'carnal' vs. 'spiritual' understanding of the Gospel text.[157]

It is in this context that we might better understand Paul's claim that the gospel preached in public appeared to be 'foolishness' to outsiders, a 'stumbling block' to their understanding (1 Cor. 1.18-25; see Chapter 12, §4), but was not such to those who understood its secret meaning—the gospel *not* preached in public, but only to insiders (1 Cor. 2.4–3.3). This was quite the same in other mystery cults: when in his own mythic narrative Dionysus speaks in riddles and is called foolish, he responds, 'One will seem to be

153. Augustine, *City of God* 4.27 vs. Augustine, *Confessions* 5.14. See also Augustine, *On Lying* 7 and 24-26.

154. Origen, *Homilies on Jeremiah* 18.4.2.

155. Origen, *Against Celsus* 5.19 (see also 5.14-16).

156. Origen, *Against Celsus* 1.9-10 and 3.45-46.

157. Clement of Alexandria, *Who Is the Rich Man That Shall Be Saved* 5.

foolish if he speaks wisely to an ignorant man'.[158] Paul is in effect saying the same thing. So, too Origen. Thus it is plausible that, like other mystery cults, Christianity also came to be packaged with a set of earthly tales of its savior that were not meant to be taken literally, except by outsiders—and insiders of insufficient rank, who were variously called even by their own leaders 'babes' or 'simpletons'.

Element 15: Christianity began as a charismatic cult in which many of its leaders and members displayed evidence of schizotypal personalities. They naturally and regularly hallucinated (seeing visions and hearing voices), often believed their dreams were divine communications, achieved trance states, practiced glossolalia, and were (or so we're told) highly susceptible to psychosomatic illnesses (like 'possession' and hysterical blindness, muteness and paralysis).[159] These phenomena have been extensively documented in modern charismatic cults within numerous religious traditions, and their underlying sociology, anthropology and psychology are reasonably well understood (in addition to what follows, see also Element 29).

For example, we know the first Christians regularly practiced glossolalia. Acts 2 mythologizes this phenomenon, depicting the first Christians 'speaking in tongues' in the middle of Jerusalem as if this actually meant miraculously speaking foreign languages fluently that they were never taught, when in fact we know 'speaking in tongues' actually meant (as it does now) babbling in random syllables, which no one could really understand except special interpreters who were 'inspired' by the holy spirit to miraculously understand and translate for their congregation. We know this because Paul tells us so (in 1 Corinthians 14; in fact the phenomenon is addressed throughout 1 Corinthians 12–14). Thus Acts has taken this real phenomenon and exaggerated it into a legendary power. But we know from Paul it operated differently. And in fact, the phenomenon Paul describes is known across the world, in countless cultures and religious traditions,

158. Euripides, *Bacchae* 479-480.

159. I will discuss the other phenomena shortly, but the phenomenon of psychosomatic illness and its cultural framing is discussed in Edward Shorter, *From Paralysis to Fatigue: A History of Psychosomatic Illness in the Modern Era* (New York: Maxwell Macmillan International, 1992), and in the *Journal of Psychosomatic Research* (e.g. J. Stone *et al.*, 'Conversion Disorder: Current Problems and Potential Solutions for DSM-5', *Journal of Psychosomatic Research* 71 [2011], pp. 369-76). For its connection to hallucinators and 'possession' phenomena in modern cults, see Horst Figge, 'Spirit Possession and Healing Cult among the Brasilian Umbanda', *Psychotherapy and Psychosomatics* 25 (1975), pp. 246-50; and E.D. Wittkower, 'Spirit Possession in Haitian Vodun Ceremonies', *Acta psychotherapeutica et psychosomatica* 12 (1964), pp. 72-80.

and has been extensively studied.[160] When we see in antiquity a phenomenon we've documented scientifically as commonly occurring in various cultures, it's far more likely to be the same phenomenon than something entirely new yet coincidentally identical. We must therefore conclude the first Christians had some social and anthropological similarities to other cults that practice glossolalia.

Acts represents this as a recurring practice in the church: Acts 10.46; 19.6 (confirmed in Mk 16.17); and in 1 Cor. 14.18, Paul himself says he spoke in tongues more than anyone, and throughout that chapter makes clear it was so commonly happening to others in his churches that he had to set up rules to govern it. And as for glossolalia, so for the other phenomena Paul reports as regularly practiced by the first Christians. The most important of which for our purposes was hallucination (visual and auditory). Humans are actually biologically predisposed to hallucinate. The neurophysiology of hallucination is built-in and thus must have evolved for some useful function (or as a side-effect of something else that did). Studies of shamanism and the cultural role of prophets and holy men have found evidence that hallucinators were often given positions of religious authority across the world, possibly even as far back as prehistoric times.[161] The propensity to hallucinate

160. Felecitas Goodman, *Speaking in Tongues: A Cross-Cultural Study in Glossolalia* (Chicago: University of Chicago Press, 1972); Watson Mills, *Speaking in Tongues: A Guide to Research on Glossolalia* (Grand Rapids, MI: William B. Eerdmans, 1986); Gerald Hovenden, *Speaking in Tongues: The New Testament Evidence in Context* (London: Sheffield Academic, 2002). On this and the other 'signatory' behaviors of the original cult (including visions and hearing voices) see Gordon Fee, *The First Epistle to the Corinthians* (Grand Rapids, MI: Eerdmans, 1987), pp. 590-99, 652-713; and Ronald Kydd, *Charismatic Gifts in the Early Church* (Peabody, MA: Hendrickson Publishers, 1984). For a good and accessible summary of the scientific literature on glossolalia see Scott Semenyna and Rodney Schmalz, 'Glossolalia Meets Glosso-Psychology: Why Speaking in Tongues Persists in Charismatic Christian and Pentecostal Gatherings', *Skeptic* 17 (2012), pp. 40-43.

161. See Miranda Aldhouse-Green and Stephen Aldhouse-Green, *The Quest for the Shaman: Shape-Shifters, Sorcerers and Spirit-Healers of Ancient Europe* (London: Thames & Hudson, 2005); and I.M. Lewis, *Ecstatic Religion: A Study of Shamanism and Spirit Possession* (New York: Routledge, 1989). For Mediterranean antiquity see Peter Green, *Alexander to Actium: The Historical Evolution of the Hellenistic Age* (Berkeley, CA: University of California Press, 1990), pp. 408-13, 594-95; Robin Lane Fox, 'Seeing the Gods', in *Pagans and Christians* (New York: Alfred A. Knopf, 1987), pp. 102-67; E.R. Dodds, 'Dream-Pattern and Culture-Pattern', in *The Greeks and the Irrational* (Berkeley, CA: University of California Press, 1951), pp. 102-34 (with more on prophetic trances and ecstasies in 'The Blessings of Madness', pp. 64-101). Crucial context is also provided by A.D. Nock, *Conversion: The Old and the New in Religion from Alexander the Great to Augustine of Hippo* (Baltimore, MD: Johns Hopkins University Press, 1933). On the role of dreams as authoritative communications

is molded by cultural context (people hallucinate frequently in cultures that promote and accept it, but suppress their capacity to hallucinate in cultures that denigrate and reject it), but also exists on a biological spectrum, from almost no capacity to a crippling capacity—and everything in between.[162]

Schizophrenia results when your biological propensity to hallucinate is ramped up to such an extreme that it interferes with your ability to function. This is how most mental disorders originate. For example, a natural and necessary brain function that prompts us to remember whether we have completed a necessary task (and to clean and organize things, and to build mental lists of what we have to do or have already done, and so on), when overactive leads to a disability called OCD (obsessive-compulsive disorder). Depression is likewise an extreme and hasty activation of otherwise normal emotions. Thus many functions appear in populations along a spectrum. In the case of behaviors such as organizing, cleaning, double-checking, some people have weak motivators (people who routinely forget things and don't care about being disorganized); most have normal motivators of varying degree (from carefree to fastidious), and some have strong motivators (and those people we say have OCD). Likewise with hallucination: some people have no capacity for it, some have a normal capacity for it in varying degrees (further modulated by their culture), and some have an overriding capacity for it (and become disabled by schizophrenia). Those in the middle are called 'normals' or 'neurotypicals'.

from the gods: John Hanson, 'Dreams and Visions in the Graeco-Roman World and Early Christianity', *Aufstieg und Niedergang der römischen Welt* II 23 (New York: W. de Gruyter, 1980), pp. 1395-1427 and William Harris, *Dreams and Experience in Classical Antiquity* (Cambridge, MA: Harvard University Press, 2009).

162. The role of hallucination in world religion is discussed from both a historical and scientific perspective in John Horgan, *Rational Mysticism: Dispatches from the Border between Science and Spirituality* (Boston: Houghton Mifflin, 2003); Robert Buckman, *Can We Be Good without God? Biology, Behavior, and the Need to Believe* (Amherst, NY: Prometheus Books, 2002); Eugene D'Aquili and Andrew Newberg, *Why God Won't Go Away: Brain Science and the Biology of Belief* (New York: Ballantine, 2001); and Eugene D'Aquili and Andrew Newberg, *The Mystical Mind: Probing the Biology of Religious Experience* (Minneapolis, MN: Fortress Press, 1999); Pascal Boyer, *Religion Explained: The Evolutionary Origins of Religious Thought* (New York: Basic Books, 2001); and Joseph Giovannoli, *The Biology of Belief: How our Biology Biases our Beliefs and Perceptions* (Rosetta Press, 2000). See also: William James, *The Varieties of Religious Experience: A Study in Human Nature* (London: Longmans, Green, 1902), with Charles Taylor, *Varieties of Religion Today: William James Revisited* (Cambridge, MA: Harvard University Press, 2002); and Ernst Arbman, *Ecstasy, or Religious Trance, in the Experience of the Ecstatics and from the Psychological Point of View* (3 vols.; Stockholm: Bokförlaget 1963-70). For surveys of the modern science of hallucination generally, see later note (e.g. Sacks, etc.).

Normals can hallucinate when exposed to triggers. The most common of which is sleep paralysis (where normals hallucinate at the threshold between being asleep and awake); but the most familiar are pharmaceuticals (many drugs induce hallucination, including several that were not only available in antiquity but known in antiquity), while the most culturally transmitted are trance behaviors.[163] Extreme fatigue, heat, illness, fasting, grief and sleep or sensory deprivation ('incubation') can all induce hallucination in normals. And by the time of Christianity, cultural practices had long developed to intentionally trigger hallucination, including fasting and sensory or sleep deprivation, but more typically rhythmic prayer or chanting or the use of music or dance to induce an ecstatic state (Paul alludes to singing and prayer as likely trance-inducing behaviors in his congregations in 1 Cor. 14.12-15; see also Acts 16.25; Eph. 5.19; and Col. 3.16; which might suggest also dance, as in other cultures whirling or spinning are known triggers). Fasting (i.e., starving) is also attested within the church.[164] But with increasing experience, a normal can hallucinate more easily, with minimal use of triggers, depending on their biological propensity.[165] Such trance-inducing behaviors had already become a standard feature of Jewish religion by the time Christianity began.[166]

163. On sleep paralysis and hallucination (from which many UFO abduction claims originate, for example), see Bruce Bower, 'Night of the Crusher: The Waking Nightmare of Sleep Paralysis Propels People into a Spirit World', *Science News* 168 (July 9, 2005), pp. 27-29; and A. Mavromatis, *Hypnagogia: The Unique State of Consciousness between Wakefulness and Sleep* (London: Routledge, 1987). For my own experience with this phenomenon see Carrier, 'Spiritual Body', in *Empty Tomb* (ed. Price and Lowder), pp. 184-88. I assume the reader is already well enough familiar with the ability of natural chemicals to induce hallucination as well (from cannabis and hemp to ergot and mushrooms), but for that and other causes see Oliver Sacks, *Hallucinations* (New York: Alfred A. Knopf, 2012).

164. Mt. 9.15; Mk 2.18-20; Lk. 5.33-35 (also, e.g., 2.37; 18.12); Acts 13.2-3; 14.23; 27.21-23; 1 Cor. 7.5; 2 Cor. 6.5; 11.27. On early Christian visionary tradition and its possible link to rituals of fasting see Andrew Lincoln, 'The "Philosophy" Opposed in the Letter [to the Colossians]', in *The New Interpreter's Bible: New Testament Survey* (ed. Fred Craddock; Nashville, TN: Abingdon Press, 2005), pp. 242-47.

165. For my own experience with this see Richard Carrier, *Sense and Goodness without God: A Defense of Metaphysical Naturalism* (Bloomington, IN: AuthorHouse, 2005), pp. 11-14.

166. See Alan Segal, 'Religiously-Interpreted States of Consciousness: Prophecy, Self-Consciousness, and Life After Death', *Life after Death: A History of the Afterlife in the Religions of the West* (New York: Doubleday, 2004), pp. 322-50; and Alan Segal, 'Heavenly Ascent in Hellenistic Judaism, Early Christianity and their Environment', *Aufstieg und Niedergang der römischen Welt* II.23.2 (New York: W. de Gruyter, 1980), pp. 1333-94; and James Tabor, *Things Unutterable: Paul's Ascent to Paradise in its*

In fact, normals with a high propensity for hallucination have been identified as *schizotypal*, meaning they hallucinate nearly as easily as schizophrenics do but are not so prone to it as to be disabled. A schizotypal is 'a relatively well-adjusted person who is functional despite, and in some cases even because of, his or her anomalous perceptual experiences'.[167] Hallucination in schizotypals in fact has been shown to reduce their anxiety and thus has a positive personal function. In modern cultures a prevalent hostile attitude toward hallucinatory behavior still often drives schizotypals to become loners (because they are characterized as weirdos or insane and there is no recognized place for them), but in cultures that embrace hallucinators we see the opposite. For example, where we find cults that socially integrate schizotypals or even elevate them to positions of leadership, we find that schizotypals begin to congregate and socialize.[168] In fact,

Greco-Roman, Judaic, and Early Christian Contexts (Lanham, MD: University Press of America, 1986).

167. Gordon Claridge and Charles McCreery, 'A Study of Hallucination in Normal Subjects', *Personality and Individual Differences* 2 (November 1996), pp. 739-47; see also Gordon Claridge, 'Schizotypy and Schizophrenia', in *Schizophrenia: The Major Issues* (ed. Paul Bebbington and Peter McGuffin; London: Heinemann Professional, 1988), pp. 187-200; Gordon Claridge (ed.), *Schizotypy: Implications for Illness and Health* (New York: Oxford University Press, 1997); and: L.C. Johns *et al.*, 'Prevalence and Correlates of Self-Reported Psychotic Symptoms in the British Population', *British Journal of Psychiatry* 185 (2004), pp. 298-305; and Maurice M. Ohayon, 'Prevalence of Hallucinations and their Pathological Associations in the General Population', *Psychiatry Research* 97 (December 27, 2000), pp. 153-64; Charles McCreery and Gordon Claridge, 'Healthy Schizotypy: The Case of Out-of-the-Body Experiences', *Personality and Individual Differences* 32 (January 5, 2002), pp. 141-54; C.A. Ross, S. Joshi and R. Currie, 'Dissociative Experiences in the General Population', *American Journal of Psychiatry* 147 (1990), pp. 1547-52; Richard Bentall, Gordon Claridge and Peter Slade, 'The Multi-Dimensional Nature of Schizotypal Traits: A Factor Analytic Study with Normal Subjects', *British Journal of Clinical Psychology* 28 (1989), pp. 363-75; T.B. Posey and M.E. Losch, 'Auditory Hallucinations of Hearing Voices in 375 Normal Subjects', *Imagination, Cognition and Personality* 3 (1983), pp. 99-113. See also Arbman, *Ecstasy*.

168. See S. Day and E. Peters, 'The Incidence of Schizotypy in New Religious Movements', *Personality and Individual Differences* 27 (July 1999), pp. 55-67; Mike Jackson and K.W.M. Fulford, 'Spiritual Experience and Psychopathology', *Philosophy, Psychiatry, and Psychology* 4 (1997), pp. 41-65 (with discussion, same issue, pp. 66-90); Roland Littlewood, 'From Elsewhere: Prophetic Visions and Dreams among the People of the Earth', *Dreaming* 14 (June–September 2004), pp. 94-106; Felicitas Goodman, Jeanette Henney and Esther Pressel, *Trance, Healing, and Hallucination* (New York: Wiley, 1974). On culture making the difference between isolation vs. integration of schizotypals: Richard Castillo, 'Trance, Functional Psychosis, and Culture', *Psychiatry* 66 (Spring 2003), pp. 9-21. On schizotypals gaining leadership roles in contemporary cults see Figge, 'Spirit Possession', and Wittkower, 'Spirit

culture determines how easily and frequently even normals will hallucinate, as well as how accepted and revered schizotypals will be.[169] Modern 'first world' cultures are actually profoundly atypical among world cultures in stigmatizing and suppressing hallucinatory tendencies.[170] As scientific observers have concluded, 'the folk theory of visions and voices adopted by a culture may be important in determining whether a hallucination is viewed as veridical or as evidence of insanity', which in turn greatly affects the commonality and acceptance of hallucination within a population.[171]

Accordingly, in antiquity, where schizotypals would routinely be regarded as prophets and holy men (and not seen as insane, as they are in modern cultures), we can expect schizotypals will actually gravitate into religious cults that socially integrate them or even grant them influence and status. The availability of niches of strong social support for schizotypals would explain why in antiquity there were few reported cases of psychosis (and why hallucination was not regarded as a major index of insanity except when wholly crippling or conjoined with fever), and why miracles and visions (not just Christian and Jewish, but pagan as well) were so frequently reported and widely believed to be genuine. Obviously schizotypals would prefer the company of people who take them seriously. As a result, they will tend to be found in religious movements that did not originate within the governing elite (where Greek ideals of scientific rationalism largely prevailed). In fact, we should expect the leaders and originators of revela-

Possession', with Alexander Moreira-Almeida, Francisco Lotufo Neto and Bruce Greyson, 'Dissociative and Psychotic Experiences in Brazilian Spiritist Mediums', *Psychotherapy and Psychosomatics* 76 (2007), pp. 57-58.

169. See Bruce Bower's excellent summary article on all of this in 'Visions for All', *Science News* 181 (April 7, 2012), pp. 22-25, which summarizes the state of the latest research on normal hallucination in religious communities, especially in light of its recent examination by Tanya Luhrmann in *When God Talks Back* (New York: Alfred A. Knopf, 2012). See also Ethan Watters, *Crazy Like Us: The Globalization of the American Psyche* (New York: Free Press, 2010), for evidence of the fact that many 'mental illnesses' are socially constructed, and often what is 'insane' in one culture is welcomed as 'normal' in another, often without detriment.

170. See my discussion in Carrier, 'Spiritual Body', in *Empty Tomb* (ed. Price and Lowder), pp. 184-88. This is also discussed in Goodman, Henney and Pressel, *Trance, Healing, and Hallucination.*

171. Peter Slade and Richard Bentall, *Sensory Deception: A Scientific Analysis of Hallucination* (Baltimore, MD: Johns Hopkins University Press, 1988), pp. 69-108 (80). See also Leonard Zusne and Warren Jones, *Anomalistic Psychology: A Study of Extraordinary Phenomena of Behavior and Experience* (Hillsdale, NJ: Erlbaum Associates, 1982); Fred Johnson, *The Anatomy of Hallucinations* (Chicago: Nelson-Hall, 1978); and the recent popular summary of the science of hallucination in Sacks, *Hallucinations.*

tory movements such as Christianity to have commonly been schizotypal.[172] After all, where else would we find them?

And yet even non-schizotypals can become regular trance hallucinators within cults and cultures that encourage and develop their capacities in this regard. Even in hostile cultures (like our own), normals find themselves hallucinating with remarkable frequency, particularly within the context of religious assumptions and expectations (Christians hallucinate Christ; Buddhists hallucinate Buddha), and psychological priming (UFO enthusiasts hallucinate encounters with aliens; the bereaved hallucinate encounters with the recently deceased).[173] In cultures that encouraged, rewarded and facilitated this phenomenon, normals would be even more prone to hallucinate, and their hallucinations would even more closely conform to priming, anchoring, suggestion and cultural framing.[174] I have elsewhere

172. For example, schizotypals appear to have held positions of respect or authority in both Bacchic and Jewish fringe sects of the time: Joan Taylor, *Jewish Women Philosophers of First-Century Alexandria: Philo's 'Therapeutae' Reconsidered* (New York: Oxford University Press, 2003), pp. 339-40 (which becomes especially poignant in light of the work of Evan Fales on St. Teresa: see later note). See also Harry Angus Alexander Kennedy, *St Paul and the Mystery-Religions* (London: Hodder & Stoughton, 1913), pp. 31-67, and scholarship cited in a previous note (e.g. E.R. Dodds, etc.).

173. Phillip Wiebe, *Visions of Jesus: Direct Encounters from the New Testament to Today* (New York: Oxford University Press, 1997); John Cornwell, *The Hiding Places of God: A Personal Journey into the World of Religious Visions, Holy Objects, and Miracles* (New York: Warner Books, 1991); C. Green and C. McCreery, *Apparitions* (London: Hamish Hamilton, 1975); Katharine Holden and Christopher French, 'Alien Abduction Experiences: Some Cues from Neuropsychology and Neuropsychiatry', *Cognitive Neuropsychiatry* 7 (2002), pp. 163-78; W.D. Rees, 'The Hallucinations of Widowhood', *British Medical Journal* 4 (1971), pp. 37-41; Vaughan Bell, 'Ghost Stories: Visits from the Deceased', *Scientific American Online* (December 2, 2008), http://www.scientificamerican.com/article.cfm?id=ghost-stories-visits-from-the-deceased. See also Nicholas Spanosa, Cheryl Burgessa and Melissa Faith Burgessa, 'Past-Life Identities, UFO Abductions, and Satanic Ritual Abuse: The Social Construction of Memories', *International Journal of Clinical and Experimental Hypnosis* 42 (1994), pp. 433-46.

174. As one can learn from reference works in psychology: priming is where recent exposure (even subconsciously) to ideas, words, images and other perceptual context will influence what is hallucinated; anchoring is when someone focuses on particular concepts (such as a set of expectations or things they were told) and then all subsequent memories and perceptions are anchored to that focus (hallucinations can thus become structured by and around that anchor); suggestion is where something a respected friend or leader *says* you remember or experience becomes in fact what you remember or experience (and people are highly susceptible to suggestion when in a trance state); and cultural framing is the obvious effect of one's upbringing and background knowledge and expectations structuring what one hallucinates (e.g. in antiquity people routinely hallucinated journeying up through seven levels of heaven, because culturally that's how everyone believed the cosmos was organized). Cultural framing

discussed the anthropology of prophets and how their deepest, most reverent plans or desires will manifest in their visions, as will solutions to cognitive dissonance. In fact, there I also discuss how the esteem in which hallucinators were held could easily inspire motivated leaders to *pretend* to be schizotypal.[175] This is ironic, as in our culture we would expect people to pretend *not* to be schizotypal, as being such is stigmatized rather than esteemed. But this only illustrates how very different ancient culture was from our own, a fact we must take into account when explaining the origins of Christianity. At any rate, this anthropological fact entails the first apostles may have only *pretended* to have visions and spirit communications, although we lack the kind of data we would need to distinguish pretense from reality in their case.[176]

Among the ways that social pressures and constructs can mold collective hallucination and limit hallucinatory content, social hierarchy and hazard is a major factor relevant to cults like Christianity.[177] If acceptance in

does not prevent innovative ideas from appearing in hallucinations, not only because of the other factors that can be overriding (priming, anchoring and suggestion), but also because hallucinations can be highly desire-driven: to resolve certain anxieties or cognitive dissonance, or to express certain creative thoughts, revisions to the status quo can even be what someone wants most to hallucinate, and so they will (e.g. if ever it became socially or politically important that there be only four heavens, a percipient might hallucinate that and report it as confirmation that previous beliefs had been wrong, or were even the cause of social problems the percipient wants most to solve). For some of the conditions under which hallucination is facilitated and guided, and its susceptibility to suggestion and cultural framing, in both normals and schizotypals, see Alfred Heilbrun Jr, 'Hallucinations', in *Symptoms of Schizophrenia* (ed. Charles Costello; New York: John Wiley & Sons, 1993), pp. 56-91.

175. See Carrier, *Not the Impossible Faith*, pp. 259-96, and 'Burial of Jesus', in *Empty Tomb* (ed. Price and Lowder), pp. 387-88 (and notes there on p. 392).

176. But for an anthropologically informed defense of that possibility, see Evan Fales, 'The Road to Damascus', *Faith and Philosophy* 22 (2005), pp. 442-59, supported by the referenced discussions in the preceding note, and by Evan Fales, 'Scientific Explanations of Mystical Experiences, Part I: The Case of St. Teresa', *Religious Studies* 32 (1996), pp. 143-63; and Evan Fales, 'Scientific Explanations of Mystical Experiences, Part II: The Challenge to Theism', *Religious Studies* 32 (1996), pp. 297-313; and Evan Fales, 'Can Science Explain Mysticism?', *Religious Studies* 35 (1999), pp. 213-27. Note that Fales believes pretense might not even be required, that persons can convince themselves that they have seen or heard what they claim, or that their own inner thoughts and feelings can legitimately be described in terms of seeing and hearing more substantive things than mere thoughts and feelings. Sometimes no distinction was made between dreams and waking visions (e.g. compare the Greek text of Longus, *Daphnis and Chloe* 2.8.4 with 1 Cor. 15.5-8). See William Harris, *Dreams and Experience in Classical Antiquity* (Cambridge, MA: Harvard University Press, 2009).

177. The following points derive from the analyses of Goodman, Henney and Pressel, *Trance, Healing, and Hallucination* (on Shaker and other modern cults)

a group requires shared experience and affirmation of shared beliefs and perceptions, people will be inclined to hallucinate what the group expects (or even *claim* to have done so, when in fact they didn't).[178] Thus 'mass hallucination' occurs in various cults not in the sense that everyone objectively hallucinates exactly the same thing, but in the sense that everyone subjectively hallucinates what they *believe* is the same thing. And that can occur when a whole congregation simultaneously engages trance-induc-

and other studies of hallucination in social and religious contexts. See also Carrier, 'Spiritual Body', in *Empty Tomb* (ed. Price and Lowder), pp. 194-95.

178. It's much more difficult to scientifically study pretenders, but we know enough in psychology to confirm that people do engage in conforming behaviors, arguably far more often than hallucinatory behaviors, so this will also have been a factor in early Christianity, no less than in any other cult in history. This means actual hallucination is often not even necessary. Many members of a cult will claim to have seen or heard things, when in fact they didn't, and *pretend* to go along, because (a) they want to belong (and this is the only way to fulfill their desire to fit in), or they need the benefits the community provides (such as food, shelter, love, companionship), or (for reasons of dysphoria or dissonance outside the cult) they *want* to believe its claims are true because they are ultimately comforting (such as giving their lives hope or meaning that they did not previously have), or they want the power and influence that being a revered spiritual leader affords them (if they can be adequately convincing and also effective at winning support). These psychological motivations can be quite powerful, and have certainly been documented to compel people to engage in conforming behavior in other contexts, so it can surely happen in this context as well. These members will pick up all the social cues and simply agree with everyone, to both fit in and convince themselves, which if sustained can even alter their memory so that they honestly believe they saw or heard things they didn't (or else they will delusionally refuse to acknowledge, even to themselves, that they didn't).

On these and other psychological features of cults see Christopher Partridge (ed.), *UFO Religions* (New York: Routledge, 2003); Marc Galanter, *Cults: Faith, Healing, and Coercion* (New York: Oxford University Press, 1989); and Marc Galanter, 'Cults and Charismatic Group Psychology', in *Religion and the Clinical Practice of Psychology* (ed. Edward Shafranske; Washington, DC: American Psychological Association, 1996), pp. 269-96; Philip Zimbardo and Robert Vallone (eds.), *Persuasion, Coercion, Indoctrination and Mind Control* (Lexington, MA: Glenn Custom, 1983); Leon Festinger, Henry Riecken and Stanley Schachter, *When Prophecy Fails: A Social and Psychological Study of a Modern Group That Predicted the Destruction of the World* (Minneapolis, MN: University of Minnesota Press, 1956); also relevant are the more general analyses of the psychology of belief: Robert Cialdini, *Influence: The Psychology of Persuasion* (New York: William Morrow, 1993); Richard Petty and John Cacioppo, *Attitudes and Persuasion: Classic and Contemporary Approaches* (Dubuque, IA: William C. Brown, 1981); and Muzafer Sherif and Carl Hovland, *Social Judgment: Assimilation and Contrast Effects in Communication and Attitude Change* (New Haven, CT: Yale University Press, 1961). On the relevant memory science (and how we can change and fabricate our own memories through suggestion, habituation and wishful thinking), see scholarship cited in Carrier, *Proving History*, p. 322 n. 104.

ing triggers and a common experience is sought—perhaps at the behest of a charismatic leader anchoring everyone to the same experience through the power of suggestion. They don't check every detail, because if they report the same things in rough outline, then the differences (if any are even reported) will be overlooked (as a result of our innate tendency toward verification bias) or even adopted by others through memory contamination, such that experiences are remembered as even more similar the more they are discussed. This contamination can occur even during the process of hallucination, as what one member, especially an anchoring leader, says then influences others to have the same experience. These effects will manifest when hallucinating subjects are pressured or socialized to conform to the group (or desire to so conform) and when what one 'experiences' in trance states is regarded as a major test of such belonging, as was the case in earliest Christianity.[179]

This role of social pressure can also set constraints based on social hierarchy. In modern Shaker cults, for example, if in your visions and hallucinations of heavenly beings you claim Jesus Christ appeared to you, this is understood as claiming apostolic election—you are claiming God is choosing you for leadership status within the church. If the existing leadership hierarchy or even members of the congregation do not agree with this appointment, whether out of disapproval or envy (or simple practicality: not everyone can be in charge), they would accuse the person of lying or having been misled by a false or deceiving spirit (a tactic we know the earliest Christians employed).[180] If enough members and leaders backed this play, the person would either have to recant, be exorcised or expelled.

The mere knowledge that this can happen (plus the understanding of the hardships and responsibilities that attend even successfully becoming an apostle) thus suppresses hallucinations of Jesus. Members will consistently hallucinate other beings instead (or only ever report having done so), simply to avoid conflict or denunciation (or to avoid a missionary or leadership role altogether). We should expect this same social phenomenon in the original church, which is why only apostles 'saw the Lord', as that is what it was to *be* an apostle: to be one whom the Lord chose to reveal himself (1 Cor. 9.1; 15.5-8; Gal. 1.11-12; note how Gal. 1.8 indicates that revelations from lesser divinities couldn't make one an apostle). This also explains why their number was limited. The Lord might still communicate to lower ranking members through intermediaries (angels and benevolent spirits), but you dare not claim to have 'seen the Lord' unless you were ready to fight (and

179. So 1 John 4; Gal. 1.6-12; 1 Thess. 5.19-24; 2 Cor. 13 and 10.3-6; 1 Timothy 6; 2 Thess. 2.11; 1 Tim. 4.1 and 2 Tim. 3.5.

180. For evidence of Christians 'thought-policing' themselves in just this way: Carrier, *Not the Impossible Faith*, pp. 385-406.

were likely to win) the ensuing socio-political battle for acceptance as an apostle (a status Paul had to labor greatly to achieve for himself, as revealed in Galatians 1–2).

All of this provides considerable background support to what several scholars have already argued: that the origin of Christianity can be attributed to hallucinations (actual or pretended) of the risen Jesus. The prior probability of this conclusion is already extremely high, given the background evidence just surveyed; and the consequent probabilities strongly favor it as well, given the evidence we can find in the NT.[181] Christian fundamentalists are really the only ones who do not accept this as basically an established fact by now. But it is important to acknowledge the broader point as well, that Christian leaders, and many congregants, were either schizotypal or normal trance-induced hallucinators (or pretended to be), and they routinely engaged in hearing voices and seeing visions from heaven (or pretended to), and moreover regarded anything their subconscious mind hit upon during an ecstatic state as an inspired communication through the holy spirit.[182]

There are many reasons not to trust Acts as a faithful record of much that went on in the early church (as I'll show in Chapters 7 and 9), but it may contain hints and reflections of historical reality, as in the case of speaking in tongues: a real phenomenon widely practiced in the church, but in Acts so mythologized that at best only the skeletal core of the story can be trusted, not any of the details. Just as in this case, we also have confirmation in Paul that Christian leaders and congregants regularly hallucinated visions and voices; so when we find similar reports in Acts we can expect this reflects, and thus confirms, the same underlying reality, such that some

181. See Jack Kent, *The Psychological Origins of the Resurrection Myth* (London: Open Gate, 1999); James Crossley, 'Against the Historical Plausibility of the Empty Tomb Story and the Bodily Resurrection of Jesus', *Journal for the Study of the Historical Jesus* 3 (June 2005), pp. 171-86; Michael Goulder, 'The Baseless Fabric of a Vision', in *Resurrection Reconsidered* (ed. Gavin D'Costa; Oxford: Oneworld Publications, 1996), pp. 48-61; and Michael Goulder, 'The Explanatory Power of Conversion Visions', in *Jesus' Resurrection: Fact or Figment: A Debate between William Lane Craig and Gerd Lüdemann* (ed. Paul Copan and Ronald Tacelli; Downers Grove, IL: InterVarsity Press, 2000), pp. 86-103. For an argument supporting this conclusion from the overall nature of how Christianity began and developed see Carrier, 'Christianity's Success Was Not Incredible', in *End of Christianity* (ed. Loftus); and from the evidence for the 'resurrection' specifically: Carrier, 'Why the Resurrection Is Unbelievable', in *Christian Delusion* (ed. Loftus).

182. On the belief that one's intuition can have the authority of the Holy Spirit (a belief held by many Jews and Christians) see Jn 14.26; Wis. 9.13-18; Dan. 2.19-22; and Exodus 31; see Philo, *On the Giants* 19-27, for an attempt at supplying an underlying theory.

of these reports might derive from the skeletal core of a true story, and even those that don't (but are instead wholly fabricated to suit the author's purpose) still likely reflect a phenomenon *in general* that was familiar to the author and his Christian readers.

Thus, in Acts 2, we see the entire church hallucinating floating tongues of fire and then babbling in tongues in a mass ecstatic trance. In Acts 7, in the middle of the Sanhedrin court, Stephen hallucinates Jesus floating up in the sky, but no one else there sees it. In Acts 9, Paul hallucinates a booming voice and a beaming light from heaven (and suffers hysterical blindness as a result); and Ananias hallucinates an entire conversation with God. In Acts 10, Cornelius hallucinates a conversation with an angel, and Peter falls into a trance and hallucinates an entire cosmic dinner scene in the sky. In Acts 16, Paul hallucinates a revelation of a man who tells him where to travel (this story probably drawing in one way or another on Paul's own mention of receiving such a revelation in Gal. 2.2). In Acts 27, Paul hallucinates a conversation with an angel. Many Christians receive spirit communications ('prophesy'), as indicated in Acts 19.6 and 21.9-10—and Acts 2.17, which quotes Joel 2.28-31 as being fulfilled in the church: 'I will pour out my Spirit upon all flesh, and your sons and your daughters shall prophesy, and your young men shall see visions, and your old men shall dream dreams'.

Paul confirms this general picture first-hand. In Gal. 1.11-12, Paul says he learned the gospel only from a hallucinated encounter with Jesus (a 'revelation') whom he experienced 'within' himself (Gal. 1.16). He confirms this in Rom. 16.25-26, where Paul says, 'My gospel and the preaching of Jesus Christ is according to a revelation'.[183] The other apostles received their information from revelations as well. 'Unto us', Paul says (meaning the apostles), 'God revealed [the secrets of the gospel] through the Spirit' (1 Cor. 2.10). And in 1 Cor. 15.1-8 Paul says, 'the gospel I preached' (which in Galatians and Romans he confirms came only by revelation) is the same gospel Peter and the others preached (this is the whole gist of Galatians 1 and 2: see discussion in Chapter 11), who also experienced special isolated visions of the Christ just like Paul's, which again was the qualifying requirement to be an apostle (1 Cor. 9.1: 'Am I not an apostle? Have I not seen Jesus our Lord?'). In Gal. 2.2, Paul mentions having another revelation that gave him instructions on where he should go and what he should do, as if there were nothing remarkable about this, indicating he had revelations often, and his congregants accepted this as normal.

Likewise, in Rom. 12.6, Paul says Christians in all congregations 'have gifts differing according to the grace that was given to us; if it be proph-

183. On the authenticity of this passage, see following note.

ecy, let us prophesy according to the proportion of our faith' (and Paul indicates that these prophets were communicating with spirits, which were under the prophet's control: 1 Cor. 14.19-32). Thus, in 1 Cor. 11.4-5, Paul sets rules for 'every man praying or prophesying' in the churches and 'every woman praying or prophesying', and in 1 Corinthians 14, Paul sets rules to prevent a problem arising in the church of so many people describing their hallucinations and spirit communications and speaking in tongues that they were talking over one another (on hallucinations in particular: 1 Cor. 14.26, 30).

In 1 Cor. 12.10, Paul elaborates on the gifts the holy spirit had given members of the church, and they include 'to some, prophecy; to others, the discerning of spirits; to another the power of speaking in tongues; and to another the interpretation of those tongues'. In 1 Cor. 12.28, Paul ranks the members of the church in order of authority: 'God has set some in the church, *first* apostles, *secondly* prophets, *thirdly* teachers, then those with powers [he most likely means exorcists], then charismatic healers, then aids, administrators, and speakers in tongues', indicating a whole gamut of behaviors in the church that make original Christianity even more similar to modern cults engaged in the same (see also Eph. 1.17; 3.2-5; 4.11; and Hebrews 2). The ability to 'discern spirits' meant an intuitive (they would say 'inspired') judgment of whether a spirit communicating with a member is of God or the Devil, which further confirms the frequency of auditory hallucinations (and the readiness with which 'intuition' was interpreted as divinely inspired). We see this in 1 Thess. 5.20, where Paul says they should not shun prophesying in the church but *test* the spirits that communicate with them (see also 1 Jn 4.1–5.13, e.g., 'do not believe every spirit that communicates with you').[184]

In 2 Corinthians 12, Paul says he and others have many glorious 'visions and revelations of the Lord', and among these he includes hallucinated trips to heaven where the hallucinator hears and sees strange things, much like the entire book of Revelation, which is a veritable acid trip, an extended hallucination of the bizarrest kind, an example of the kind of thing going on all the time in the early churches (even despite the fact that that particular example is probably wholly fabricated). Paul then goes on to relate in that same chapter a whole two-way conversation he had with God, demonstrating that he not only heard voices but conversed with them; he also says he experiences an 'abundance of revelations' (2 Cor. 12.7). And in 1 Cor. 14.6, Paul says 'what use am I to you, unless I speak to you by way of a revela-

184. I discuss this reliance on inspired thoughts, visions and spirit communications in forming beliefs in the early church in Carrier, *Not the Impossible Faith*, pp. 385-406. See also Hanson, 'Dreams and Visions', pp. 1421-25.

tion, or knowledge [*gnōsis*, meaning spiritual knowledge], or prophesying, or teaching?' which entails hallucination was both respected *and* expected of him; it was also desired and sought after in the church among all the congregants (1 Cor. 14.1, 'earnestly desire these spiritual gifts', and 1 Cor. 14.12, 'you are eager for them').

Similarly, the fact that Christians regarded as inspired scripture such books as Daniel, which depict authoritative information coming from God through both visions and dreams, entails that Christians believed authoritative information came from God through visions and dreams (otherwise they would not deem such books as honest or reliable, much less scripture). They could therefore see their own visions and dreams as communications from God, too. Thus, even if books such as Revelation are fabricated, as symbolic discourses on the times, they still represent themselves as genuine hallucinatory experiences. As Rev. 1.1-2 says, the whole book describes:

> the revelation of Jesus Christ, which God provided to show to his servants what must soon take place, and he made it known by sending his angel to his servant John, who bore witness to the word of God and to the testimony of Jesus Christ, even to all that he saw.

Which means even as a fabrication this book still demonstrates the esteem with which even the wildest hallucinatory experiences were held, which were believed so fervently to be genuine experiences that an author could gain authority for what he was writing by claiming to have hallucinated it. This is a radically different cultural context than we live in now.

As we'll see in the next chapter (Element 29), earliest Christianity can be characterized as a revitalization movement. It is thus notable that 'trance behavior', including the regular mission-oriented hallucination among leaders and members, 'looms large in the descriptive data of most of the revitalization movements known from the historical and the ethnographic record', which movements also frequently practice glossolalia, prophesy, 'faith healing', possession and exorcism.[185] Earliest Christianity thus perfectly aligns with known anthropological models, and can only be understood in that context.

Element 16: The earliest Christians claimed they knew at least some (if not all) facts and teachings of Jesus from revelation and scripture (rather than from witnesses), and they regarded these as *more reliable sources* than word-of-mouth (only many generations later did Christian views on this point noticeably change). As Paul says in Rom. 16.25-26:

185. Goodman, Henney and Pressel, *Trance, Healing, and Hallucination*, p. 351.

> My gospel and the preaching of Jesus Christ [is] according to the revelation of the mystery which was kept secret for long ages, but now is made visible through the prophetic scriptures and is made known to all nations, according to the command of the eternal God, for the obedience of faith.[186]

And in Galatians 1 he swears up and down, repeatedly, that he did not learn the gospel from oral tradition, but revelation alone, thus illustrating the order of values: he and his congregations respected revelations far more than human traditions (see Chapter 11, §§2 and 6).[187]

That some teachings and sayings of the Lord came by revelation, not from a living Jesus, has been noted before.[188] The entire book of Revelation establishes this happened: not only in that book do new teachings come from a (supposedly) hallucinated Jesus, but this imaginary Jesus even dictates entire letters (Rev. 1.17–3.22). Paul's belief that Jesus preached that we can abandon the Torah law and still be saved likewise came to him by revelation (as Galatians 1–2 establishes: see Elements 19 and 20). Paul even credits his knowledge of the inauguration of the Eucharist meal (what Jesus said and did on that occasion) as coming to him directly 'from the Lord', which means the content of 1 Cor. 11.23-27 was learned in a vision (see Chapter 11, §7). Otherwise he would cite his *actual* authority (whoever it was who told him of this), and not 'the Lord', since otherwise it's obvious the words to follow come from the Lord, so that would not have to be stated *unless* to indicate that that's where Paul learned of them (as he says: '*I* received this from the Lord', not someone else). Paul likewise says in Rom. 16.25-26 that Jesus' *kērygma*, the 'message he preached', came by revelation. In Rom. 8.2, Paul says 'Jesus Christ will reveal these things to you, that I speak truly. He is the mouth altogether free from falsehood, by which the Father has truly spoken', which confirms that people often received communications from Jesus via revelation (even if indirectly: i.e., through intuited feelings attributed to the holy spirit, or visions or prophetic messages communicated through angels or subordinate spirits), and no one thought this was unusual or inferior to any other source. To the contrary, Paul's argument in Galatians 1 entails Christians had the opposite

186. I am, of course, presuming the authenticity of this passage (as I shall continue to do): see Chapter 7 (§7). It may be of the Pauline school rather than by Paul himself (since much the same is said in Eph. 3). But as such it would still represent the thinking of Pauline Christianity. Its sentiments are well enough corroborated elsewhere in Paul's writings (see Element 15).

187. I further demonstrate this aspect of early Christian 'faith-based' epistemology in Carrier, *Not the Impossible Faith*, pp. 281-85 and 385-406 (with support in pp. 329-68).

188. See, e.g., D.E. Aune, 'Christian Prophecy and the Messianic Status of Jesus', in *The Messiah* (ed. Charlesworth), pp. 404-22.

view: that information derived by revelation was more authoritative and trustworthy than any human tradition (again, see Chapter 11, §§2 and 6).

Thus, Paul frequently rests on the authority of things Jesus said, and yet in 2 Cor. 13.3 he says 'you desire proof that Christ is speaking in me' (per Gal. 1.16) which entails he received at least some of these teachings of Jesus through revelation—and some among his congregations dared question if he really had or if they were really coming from Jesus, rather than a false spirit. Confirming this is the fact that in 1 Cor. 14.37, Paul says his rules of order for the commotion in the church (of a mass of people talking over and interrupting one another announcing revelations, prophesying, speaking in tongues, and interpreting them: see Element 15) are 'a command of the Lord' (in contrast to occasions where he says he has no command of the Lord to cite: e.g. 1 Cor. 7.25). But it is very improbable that a living Jesus would have foreseen the complex discipline problem going on in Paul's churches, so as to have pronounced rules for it (long before the problem ever existed or even could have existed), and it is clear no one at Corinth had heard of these rules before; because they were newly created to deal with the occasion—yet, Paul says, they should obey them, because 'the Lord commands it'. Paul was therefore still receiving teachings from the celestial Jesus.

And of course anything Jesus taught after his 'resurrection' (and indeed the very fact of his resurrection) came to the earliest Christians by revelation. This is confirmed by 1 Cor. 15.1-8, where the 'gospel' that Paul 'received' and 'preached' came by revelation, not a transmitted human tradition, and that the risen Jesus only 'appeared' in visions to everyone just as to himself. The first point is confirmed by identical wording: 'I would have you know, brethren, **that the gospel I preached** . . . I did not **receive** it from a man, nor was I taught it, but it came through a revelation of Jesus Christ' (Gal. 1.11-12), which corresponds to, 'I would have you know, brethren, **that the gospel I preached** . . . I delivered to you in the first place what I also **received**' (1 Cor. 15.1, 3). No other conclusion is possible: the facts following this declaration are the very facts he claims to have learned only by revelation (even if on different occasions), and those facts are 'that, according to the scriptures, Christ died for our sins, and that he was buried, and that, according to the scriptures, he rose again on the third day, and that he appeared' to various apostles at various times (1 Cor. 15.4-8). I'll discuss this further in Chapter 11 (§§2 and 4).

Paul always assumes there was no difference between the Lord's appearance to him and the Lord's appearances to others (Paul makes no distinction in 1 Cor. 9.1, where 'seeing the Lord' makes you an apostle, with no special status being imagined for those who saw the Lord in any way other than he did), and he never has to make any apology for it being otherwise (he simply assumes everyone accepts that his authority is equal to any other apostle's: see Chapter 11, §2). And this conforms to natural probability (i.e., it is vastly more likely that these appearances were hallucinated, in reality or pretense, than that anyone actually rose from the dead). Above all, the sequence of appearances in 1 Cor. 15.5-8 entails singular, isolated events that lasted only briefly. Clearly Jesus was not hanging around during it all. He appeared only momentarily, to one or another apostle or group, and then others had to await another event to see him. This is explicit when Paul says Jesus appeared 'at the same time' only *once* to a large number of brethren, but not on any other of the occasions listed. This fits hallucinatory encounters, not a leader alive again rallying his followers.

All of the above confirms that some Christians could claim to know some teachings by and things about Jesus by revelation. But second to this, some facts about and teachings and sayings from the Lord were known by finding them 'hidden' in scripture. Again, Paul said that 'my gospel and *the preaching* of Jesus Christ' does not just come from revelations but is also 'now made visible through the prophetic scriptures' (Rom. 16.25-26). Accordingly, Paul says we must resort to the scriptures to 'teach us' things about Jesus (Rom. 15.3-4), and that we should not 'go beyond' the scriptures in our claims about Jesus (1 Cor. 4.6). In Rom. 1.1-6, Paul says 'the gospel' of Jesus was written 'beforehand through the prophets in the holy scriptures'. And thus, of course, it is outright stated in Jn 20.9 that 'they knew not the scripture, that he must rise from the dead' and in Lk. 24.25-27 and 24.44-47, where Jesus declares that 'everything written about me in the law of Moses and the prophets and the psalms must be fulfilled' such that when you understand the scriptures properly you will see 'it is written that the Christ should suffer and on the third day rise from the dead, and that repentance and forgiveness of sins should be preached in his name to all nations' (essentially what Paul himself means in Gal. 3.1).

Such statements suggest that when Paul says in 1 Cor. 15.3-4 that 'according to the scriptures' Jesus died for our sins, was buried and rose on the third day, he might not mean these things happened *in accordance* with prophecy, but that in fact the scriptures *are where we learn of them*. The same exact phrase 'according to *x*' is how sources were cited in antiquity (e.g. 'according to Herodotus, the Greeks defeated the Persians'). Thus Paul appears to be saying what Jesus is made to say in Luke, that these facts are learned about Jesus from the scriptures, and that extracting that information from the scriptures requires proper divine inspiration (Lk. 24.45). Thus Rom. 16.25-26 could be saying that a hallucinated Jesus taught Paul (and other apostles) exactly what the risen Jesus teaches them in Luke 24: that certain facts about him can be found in the scriptures, and how to find them.

I do not claim to have proved that point here, but only to have established its plausibility, from all the remaining evidence (likewise in the next element). Fully confirming that plausibility is the fact that pre-Christian Jews were already doing this. They, too, were finding 'hidden messages' in the scriptures and thereby learning 'facts' about their present reality and God's plans and deeds.[189] The entire pesher genre was devoted to that very thing (see Element 8; and for an example, Element 5). If Jews were already doing this in droves before Christianity, and then Christians suddenly appeared preaching that they, too, had found 'secret messages' in the Bible, we must conclude they may well have been getting their information *from* the Bible, in the very same way other Jews were. In other words, we cannot declare this to be too improbable to propose. Because there is sufficient background evidence to lend it credence. Likewise claiming revelation as a source of information. That is clear from the book of Revelation, for example, but again from Jewish precedent, where revelation was a routine source of information about earthly and heavenly beings and events and God's plan for them. Like the *Ascension of Isaiah* discussed in Chapter 3 (§1), and the book of Daniel, and the Enochic literature (which the earliest Christians regarded as scripture).

The precedent is thus well established. A living, earthly Jesus was simply *not* the only available source for receiving sayings and teachings from and about him.

Element 17: The fundamental features of the gospel story of Jesus can be read out of the Jewish scriptures. The influence of the OT on the NT has been much written on,[190] but here I mean to say that this fact, in conjunction with the evidence of previous elements (e.g. the pre-Christian pesher literature, Christian claims to have found hidden information in the scriptures, etc.), makes it plausible to ask whether the gospel was actually discovered and learned *from* the scriptures, rather than the scriptures being consulted after the fact as a merely defensive reinforcement for key claims Christians were making supposedly on other grounds. For this point it's enough to illustrate how easy it would have been to do this, even beyond what was already shown in Element 6.[191]

189. Aune, 'Christian Prophecy'.

190. For example, G.K. Beale and D.A. Carson (eds.), *Commentary on the New Testament Use of the Old Testament* (Grand Rapids, MI: Apollos, 2007); Craig Evans (ed.), *From Prophecy to Testament: The Function of the Old Testament in the New* (Peabody, MA: Hendrickson Publishers, 2004); Steve Moyise (ed.), *The Old Testament in the New Testament* (Sheffield: Sheffield Academic Press, 2000); John Court (ed.), *New Testament Writers and the Old Testament: An Introduction* (London: SPCK, 2002); Stanley Porter (ed.), *Hearing the Old Testament in the New Testament* (Grand Rapids, MI: William B. Eerdmans, 2006).

191. See also Earl Doherty, *Jesus: Neither God nor Man (The Case for a Mythical Jesus)* (Ottawa: Age of Reason, 2009), pp. 83-96.

As I've already noted, the Wisdom of Solomon declares that the wicked will 'condemn to a shameful death' the holiest man of God (which in the first century would entail a crucifixion, in contrast to an honorable death like decapitation), because they are 'blinded by their wickedness' and 'do not know the secret purposes of God' (Wis. 2.20-22; compare 1 Cor. 2.7-9); this righteous man they kill will be the 'son of god' (Wis. 2.18), who criticizes the current religious order and promotes strange teachings (Wis. 2.12-16); those who kill him will scorn and reject him, and mock him during his torture and execution, saying surely God will come to rescue him (which, to an interpreter looking for hidden connections, links this text with the same man in Ps. 22.7-8, which Psalm is heavily drawn upon to construct the crucifixion scene in Mark 15: see Chapter 10, §4); and this righteous man will be killed but then restored to life and exalted by God to stand again and judge those who killed him (Wisdom 5).

Earlier I demonstrated the links some Jews had likely made between the 'messiah' killed in Daniel 9 and the 'righteous servant' killed in Isaiah 52–53 (Element 5). The 'righteous man and son of God' killed in Wisdom of Solomon (who is, like the innocent righteous man killed in Isaiah, scorned and rejected of men, executed, and then exalted by God) could easily have been linked to the same network of passages and thus believed to have been prophetical of the same messiah, which then (as just noted above) ties into that network also Psalm 22, which gives us the three-day cycle: first Psalm 22, execution and mockery (v. 16 even implying crucifixion specifically, especially in variants known at Qumran); then Psalm 23, burial and sojourn among the dead (the funeral psalm); and then Psalm 24, ascension and exaltation 'on the first day of the week', where the very same unusual phrasing found in Mk 16.1 is found in Ps. 24.1 in the LXX (thus Mark is clearly quoting, and therefore alluding to, that Psalm), which altogether gives us the entire gospel spelled out by Paul in 1 Cor. 15.3-4.[192]

Tying all of this in to Isaiah is what gives us the strongest evidence of this: the particular, and peculiar, concept of this messiah dying 'for our sins' (which notion is only reinforced by linking this to Dan. 9.24, which would then imply the same thing). The relevant material in Isaiah describes an itinerant preacher whose beautiful feet walk the land 'bringing the gospel' and 'announcing salvation' (Isa. 52.7). This preacher God 'will reveal' to all nations, but possibly only through an elect few (52.10, using *apokalypsei*, the term for revelation; that he is revealed only to an elect few, and then *reported* to others, is implied in 53.1; just as Clement appears to have thought of Jesus: see Chapter 8, §5). This preacher is 'God's servant' ('God's *child*'

192. See *Proving History*, pp. 131-34 and 139-41, and Carrier, 'Spiritual Body', in *Empty Tomb* (ed. Price and Lowder), pp. 158-61.

in the Septuagint) who will 'deal wisely and be exalted and raised up very high' (52.13) even though he will be 'despised, and rejected of men, a man of sorrows, and acquainted with grief' (53.3). In fact, 'he has borne our griefs and carried our sorrows' (in the Septuagint 'he bears our sins and suffers for us') and though we thought he was being punished by God (53.4), in fact 'he was wounded for our sins, he was bruised for our iniquities' or even *pierced* for our iniquities in some pre-Christian manuscripts (see note in Element 9). Indeed, 'with his stripes we are healed' (53.5) because 'the Lord gave him up for our sins' (53.6; the word is *paradidōmi* in the Septuagint, identical to the word often translated as 'he was betrayed' in 1 Cor. 11.23, even though referring to exactly the same event, his being delivered up to die for our sins; and likewise this is the same word used for that event throughout the Gospels: see Chapter 11, §7). Explicitly, he is killed even though innocent, and killed specifically 'because of the sins' of God's people (53.8-9), for God 'shall make his life an offering for sin' (53.10) because he 'bears their sins' (53.11). And this servant will then be exalted by God and his days prolonged (and also in reward he shall be shown the light of understanding, receive an inheritance, and divide all spoils with the mighty) 'because he poured out his life unto death, and was numbered with the transgressors, yet bore the sin of many, and made intercession for the transgressors' (53.11-12) That a later second temple Jew would readily take to mean *he would be resurrected* (as the only obvious way you can die yet be rewarded for this death with a prolonging of your days, and receiving wisdom and inheritance and spoils, is to be made alive again). All just from Isaiah 52–53. Connecting this to the nearly identical figure described in the Wisdom of Solomon would only make this all the more obvious, likewise the figures in Psalms 22 and Daniel 9 and 12 (as well as Zechariah 3 and 6).

All of this is not itself a proof that Christians *did* find every key element of their gospel by scouring scripture for secret messages, producing their gospel like a pesher (with assistance from 'revelations' and ecstatic 'inspiration'). But the evidence above is sufficient to establish that they *could* have. The usual claim, of course, is that Christians sought out Isaiah 53 *after the fact* (and all scholars agree it was a key text employed by Christians as a prophecy of their Christ), and not as inspiration (i.e., finding the passage first, and then concocting a savior to match). But we don't really know it was the one and not the other (see Element 16). Prior to any specific evidence either way, the one is as likely as the other. The ease with which we can produce the Christian gospel solely by constructing a messianic pesher out of the OT scriptures (and other scriptures the Christians used) is therefore something we must include in our background knowledge.

Element 18: Jesus Christ was regarded as having fulfilled (and thereby replacing) by his death the two greatest annual sacrifices in the Jewish religion, Passover and Yom Kippur (see Element 10), and thereby had replaced the temple as a relevant religious institution (see Element 28).

Passover celebrated the Jews' rescue from death, which began their exodus from Egypt to the Promised Land (Exodus 12). The angel of death 'passed over' their houses, sparing their lives, on account of the blood of the sacrificed lamb (or goat: 12.5) smeared across their door frame (sides and crossbeam), whose flesh they also ate in communal household meals (12.7-13, 22-23). The Passover sacrifice was killed and eaten 'in the night' (12.6, 8), just as the Eucharist was (1 Cor. 11.23-26), and many commentators have noted the similarities between them (see Chapter 11, §7). Yom Kippur cleansed the whole congregation of Israel of all its sins for one year, and so this sacrifice had to be repeated every year to maintain its salutary effect (Lev. 16), and in between various lesser sacrifices had to be performed for specific sins committed since the last general atonement. That atonement sacrifice, procuring a general forgiveness of sins, was called the Day of Atonement (Lev. 23.27). Two goats were chosen and lots were cast (Lev. 16.7-10), choosing one to 'carry the sins' of Israel and be driven into the wilderness (16.8-10, 21-22), while the other was killed and its blood sprinkled on the altar to atone for Israel's sins (16.15-16, 30-34).

Paul declared that 'Christ is our Passover sacrifice' (1 Cor. 5.7) and therefore God will 'pass over' our sins (Rom. 3.25; see also evidence in Element 43), while at the same time preaching that Christ was the definitive atonement sacrifice (and therefore the definitive Yom Kippur).[193] Hebrews 9 lays this out in detail (see Chapter 11, §5). Although Paul is not its author and its date is disputed (see Chapter 7, §3), nevertheless, Paul clearly taught this, too, frequently saying Jesus' death atoned for all sins once and for all (1 Cor. 15.3; Gal. 1.4; 3.13; 2 Cor. 5.18-19; Rom. 3.24-26; 5.6-11), which was the function of the Yom Kippur sacrifice (except that that had to be repeated every year, whereas Christ's was final, for reasons explained in Hebrews). Thus the earliest gospel combined the two major Jewish rituals of salvation: from death (as the angel 'passed over' the households protected by the lamb's blood) and from all other wages of sin (the annual cleansing of Israel's sins by the ritual of the goats at Yom

193. 1 Corinthians 5 implies the Lord's Supper *is* the Passover, which would mean the role of 'remembrance' in 1 Cor. 11.23-26 is intended to reflect the same role of remembrance in Exod. 12.14, and therefore 1 Cor. 11.23-26 *also* confirms that Christ's death was understood as a Passover sacrifice (the body of both sacrifices was eaten to procure salvation from death, and both involve a ritual use of the blood from the same body being eaten: see Chapter 11, §7). And of course the Gospels unanimously link the two.

Kippur), thereby connecting atonement with salvation and eternal life. (Further reason why the death of Jesus was connected with Passover and not just Yom Kippur is provided in Element 43, which shall more directly survey the Jewish background.)

Per Element 10, the earliest known Christian 'gospel' preached that Jesus' death had atoned for all sins and procured salvation for all adherents. Christians therefore had no need for the Jewish temple or any of its rituals, which existed for the purpose of maintaining a conduit to God and cleansing Jews of their sins (e.g. Lev. 4 and 16). Christians now had their own conduit to God (Jesus Christ 'in us') and were permanently cleansed of all sins (by Jesus' death) and therefore had no need of priests to act as intermediary. Accordingly, as the Epistles make clear, priests had no more role to play in Christian worship, communion with God, or salvation.

Therefore, a distinguishing element of the earliest Christian sect of Judaism was that Christians themselves are now the temples of god (Gal. 6.14-17) and thus God dwells *in them* (1 Cor. 3.16; 6.19; 2 Cor. 6.16). Likewise Eph. 2.19-22 and 3.16-19 and 1 Peter 2 (e.g. 'like living stones be yourselves built into a spiritual house, to be a holy priesthood, to offer spiritual sacrifices acceptable to God through Jesus Christ', 1 Pet. 2.5). In the words of the earlier redaction of the letter of Ignatius to the Ephesians (15.3), 'Let us do all things as those who have Him dwelling in us, that we may be His temples, and He may be in us as our God, which indeed He is, and will manifest Himself before our faces'. And as Clement of Alexandria would later put it, 'This is in reality righteousness: not to desire other things, but to wholly be the consecrated temple of the Lord.'[194] Indeed, the Eucharist meal would have brought God into oneself by actually consuming (symbolically) the body of his appointed Lord, in whom God's spirit resided (just compare 1 Cor. 11.23-27 with 10.16-22).

Because God now dwelled in each *person*, then he did not dwell only in the holy of holies as mainstream Judaism held. And if all one's sins were thereby cleansed, there was no need of further rituals or sacrifices. There was therefore no need of priests or the temple. Replacing not just Yom Kippur but also Passover, the two great temple sacrificial rituals, was essential to accomplish that end (see Element 43), and had the obvious connotation of not just procuring forgiveness of sins (the role of Yom Kippur) but procuring salvation from death (the role of Passover). Which two facts completed the Christian system of salvation.

194. Clement of Alexandria, *Miscellanies* 4.25. This was a logical progression in ancient cultic thinking, from an occasional to a permanent state of holiness (see Carrier, *Not the Impossible Faith*, p. 137), and from a proximate to a direct communion with God: see Carrier, 'Spiritual Body', in *Empty Tomb* (ed. Price and Lowder), pp. 145-47.

7. *Elements of Christian Development*

Element 19: The apostle Paul is the earliest known Christian writer, yet he did not know a living Jesus but was converted by revelation some time after Jesus is said to have died, and did not begin writing anything we know of until many years after his conversion (Galatians, e.g., was written about seventeen years after: 1.18; 2.1).

Element 20: (a) The earliest known Christians proselytized Gentiles but required them to convert to Judaism. (b) Paul is the first known Christian to discard that requirement (having received a special revelation instructing him to), and he had to fight the earliest known leaders of the cult for acceptance of that radical idea. (c) But some books in the NT are from the sect that did not adopt this innovation but remained thoroughly Jewish (most obviously Matthew, the letters of John and James, and Revelation).

Most scholars concede this. The primary evidence is Galatians 1–2, and supporting that is the fact that in his extended defense of this novelty in Romans, Paul is unable to cite the authority of a historical Jesus even once (see, e.g., Rom. 14.14).[195] This entails that if Jesus lived, then he never taught anything other than a Jewish religion for Jews, and countenanced admitting only those Gentiles who first became Jews through circumcision and adherence to Torah law (such as Jewish dietary requirements and Sabbath observance, although possibly all rituals pertaining to the temple had been replaced by the cult paid to Christ: e.g. see 1 Jn 2.3-4 vs. 5.16), as such a procedure for converting Gentiles was already in accordance with Torah law (Exod. 12.48).

Element 21: (a) Paul and other NT authors attest that there were many rival Christian sects and factions teaching different gospels throughout the first century. In fact, evidence of such divisions and disagreements date as far

195. See Alan Segal, 'Conversion and Messianism: Outline for a New Approach', in *The Messiah* (ed. Charlesworth), pp. 296-340; W.D. Davies, 'The Jewish Sources of Matthew's Messianism', in *The Messiah* (ed. Charlesworth), pp. 494-511; David Sim, *The Gospel of Matthew and Christian Judaism: The History and Social Setting of the Matthean Community* (Edinburgh: T. & T. Clark, 1998); and my discussion of this same point in Carrier, *Proving History*, pp. 170-72. The Pseudo-Pauline letters of Ephesians (3.3-12) and Colossians (1.24-29) also report that Paul originated this innovation. The original sect survived for a few centuries but never significantly grew; for example, Epiphanius, in *Panarion* 29, discusses a sect called 'the Nazoreans', which we know to have been the original name for the Christians (Acts 24.5; Jerome, *Letters* 112.13), 'who confess that Christ Jesus is Son of God, but all of whose customs are in accordance with the [Torah] Law' (on these Christians see Chapter 8, §1).

back as extant records go. Yet we know very little about these other versions of Christianity (and in some cases nothing at all). And (b) of these only a few amalgamated sects survived the process of competition to remain in the Middle Ages, and those sects controlled nearly all choices as to what texts to preserve into the present, and which texts to ignore or abandon; and for the former, they also had complete custody of those texts for over a thousand years of hand-copying and editing.[196]

Of course Paul mentions factions sometimes advocating one apostle's teaching over another, and argues Christians should accommodate them all and not make divisions. Paul names himself, Apollos and Cephas [Peter] (1 Cor. 1.12; 3.4-22), although supposedly Paul and Apollos regarded themselves as teaching roughly the same thing (1 Cor. 4.6; 16.12), and Paul and Peter came to a somewhat uneasy détente, with Peter accepting Paul's innovative Torah-free gospel and Paul accepting Peter's continuing adherence to a Torah-observant gospel (Galatians 2). But Paul also frequently refers to gospels of Jesus Christ so alien to his own that they must be declared anathema and shunned (Gal. 1.6-10; 2 Cor. 11.4-15; Rom. 16.17-18) and many other NT texts likewise allude to various early Christian sects being condemned (but almost never described).[197]

We therefore cannot simply assume surviving texts report what was normative for the original or earliest sects of Christianity. There is a great deal we just don't know, and we have to factor that ignorance into our reasoning, as many scholars have pointed out.[198] The epistles written during the first generation of Christians (from the 30s to the 60s CE) reveal a highly fragmented church already from the earliest recorded time, rife with fabricated new gospels and teachings effectively beyond the control of any central authority. And if this much divergence had already occurred in Paul's generation, the amount of divergence in later generations would have been even greater. There is no guarantee that all the beliefs originally touted by Paul, for example, would even be those to survive the ensuing competition among rival factions. We already know (per Element 20) that the teachings

196. This last point hardly needs defense, but does require qualification: there are comparatively few exceptions of texts (1) preserved by Jews and Muslims, but none of those *both* date prior to the fourth century *and* pertain (in any direct sense) to the origins and development of Christianity; and (2) recovered archaeologically (e.g. in papyri, inscriptions, coins), but *almost* none of those pertain (in any direct sense) to the origins and development of Christianity, while those that do are extremely few, extremely sparse in content, and late (mid-second century at the earliest, and most much later).

197. For example, Heb. 13.8-9; 2 Thess. 2.2-15; 1 Tim. 1.3-7; 4.1-16; 2 Tim. 3.5; Tit. 3.9; 1 Jn 2.18-26 and 4.1; 2 John 7; 3 John 9-10; Jude 3-4, 8-16; 2 Pet. 1.15-21; 3.16; Rev. 2.2, 6, 14, 15, 20; Acts 20.29-30; Mk 13.22; Mt. 7.15-23; 24.11, 24; etc.

198. See my discussion of this problem in Carrier, *Proving History*, pp. 129-34.

of the original apostles did not survive that competition (Jewish Christianity stagnated and died out, and we have almost no texts from it). And we know the teachings of even 'orthodox' Christianity in the second century deviated considerably from the simpler faith taught by Paul (for whom there was no trinity, e.g., nor was Jesus identical to God; and a great deal else besides). And yet the 'orthodox' Christianity of that century was no more likely to be closer to original Christianity than any of the countless other sects its adherents deemed 'heretical', and we can easily see how incredibly diverse and bizarre *they* were.[199] (See my definitions in §3.)

Thus, if Christian sectarian divergence was already considerable in the early first century, and very considerable in the following century, we must assume it was somewhere in between in the late first century, which entails there must have been quite a lot of practically unknown divergence and development in that period, far more even than indicated in the letters of Paul for the generation preceding it.

Element 22: (a) We have no credible or explicit record of what happened within the Christian movement between 64 and 95 CE (or possibly even as late as 110 CE). And (b) unlike almost any other cult we might consider for comparison, we know the leadership of the Christian church had been catastrophically decimated by the beginning of that period.

Given that Acts is not a paragon of reliability (see Chapter 9) one might doubt whether we even have a reliable record of what went on *before* 64 (the 'authentic' letters of Paul [see Chapter 7, §3] would then be all we really had, and they all date generally to a single late decade, that of the 50s). Likewise, the evidence of ecclesial events for the whole three or four decades after 95 is not what one would characterize as robust, either. Indeed, the fact that 1 Clement was written in 95 is really a traditional date and not actually secured by any trustworthy evidence; in fact, I am fairly certain it was written in the 60s (see Chapter 7, §6, and Chapter 8, §5). But even if we set all that aside and look on what we have with as rosy a view as we can stomach, then we can *still* say that nothing we have says *anything* about what happened between 64 (the year of the Neronian persecutions as reported in Tacitus and Suetonius) and 95 (the year that *1 Clement* was 'traditionally' written). This is effectively a dark age in the early church, a thirty-year black box in which we can't reconstruct what happened. In fact

199. See, e.g., David Brakke, *The Gnostics: Myth, Ritual, and Diversity in Early Christianity* (Cambridge, MA: Harvard University Press, 2010); and Marvin Meyer, *The Gnostic Discoveries: The Impact of the Nag Hammadi Library* (San Francisco, CA: HarperSanFrancisco, 2005). A lot of this weirdness was already catalogued by the early third century: Tertullian, *Prescription against Heretics*; Irenaeus, *Against Heresies*; Hippolytus, *Refutation of All Heresies*.

we can barely reconstruct what happened in the ten years either side of that, which makes for fifty years (half a century) of largely untracked development within the movement. Back then, that was an average human lifetime.

Even texts that may have been written in that thirty-year zone (like perhaps some of the Gospels) do not discuss any developments or events in that period. The only record of events in the church that has any chance of being other than fictional comes centuries later (since wildly implausible hagiographies and legends in the interim are hardly credible: see, e.g., discussion in Chapter 8 of Papias and Hegesippus, §§7 and 8). And that is only the succession of bishops recorded in Eusebius, which is devoid of any historical information but the names and offices. Such succession lists are typically untrustworthy anyway, as gaps in succession lists (such as for philosophical schools) were always intolerable and thus would be filled by fabrication if necessary, and Eusebius exhibits a reliance on unreliable sources for his list (e.g. Hegesippus), which only confirms our suspicions.[200]

In contrast, in the sources we have *before* Eusebius tried to smooth things over, we see much less certainty about what happened. For example, the inconsistent lists of apostles scattered across the four Gospels demonstrates that 'by the time the gospels were composed, which disciples belonged to the twelve was no longer known', and thus fundamental facts about the cult's own history and leadership had been lost already in the course of the first century.[201] This was surely the one detail that should have been easily and consistently remembered for generations, unless some major disruption in the cult's traditions had occurred. Instead, already by the second half of the first century the leadership council of 'the twelve' (if such there was) no longer existed and left no identifiable heirs, and no one could even remember who all was on it, or even what had happened to them. Indeed, for most of them there are no historical accounts at all, beyond very late and obviously fabricated legends, and for the rest, the accounts we have (such as in Acts) either assume or establish their early deaths, or don't seem aware of what happened to them at all (see Chapters 8 and 9).

By contrast, we have a lot of scattered information about the people, events and schisms within Christianity in the middle and later decades of the second century—but near total silence for the thirty to fifty years of the latter first to early second century. Acts presents us with a 'history' of the church movement from its origins in the 30s to around 60 or 62 CE (although still omitting a great deal; e.g. it says almost nothing about Egyptian or North African Christianity, or Christianity east of the Empire,

200. Eusebius, *History of the Church* 3.

201. Robert Funk, 'Do the Gospels Contain Eyewitness Reports?', in *Finding the Historical Jesus: Rules of Evidence* (ed. Bernard Brandon Scott; Santa Rosa, CA: Polebridge, 2008), pp. 31-39 (38).

or even Christianity in Italy and points west; it tells us little about the rival factions of Christianity, such as that of Apollos; etc.). But oddly nothing else like this was ever again produced for over two centuries—unless, of course, Acts is as bogus as the many apocryphal 'Acts' generated in the second century (see Element 44; and Chapter 7, §5), and if that's the case, then we don't really even have the history of the church to the year 62. Because apart from Acts we have only the letters of Paul, all produced during the *end* of that same period (the last authentic letter of Paul is unlikely to date much later than where Acts ends).

The only thing we next hear is that the Neronian persecution wiped out Christianity at Rome, possibly after Rome burned in 64 CE.[202] Although no Christian ever recorded any information about this event; it is known (even to medieval Christian writers) only through Tacitus, which suggests either the story is a fiction or that the event produced a rather complete destruction of all Christian witnesses at Rome.[203] And then the Jewish War between 66 and 70 CE wiped out Christianity at Jerusalem, home of the original church (Gal. 1.18; 2.1).[204] Again, no Christian record of what happened to any Christians or their churches in Judea during this event was ever made (at least none known to us), suggesting again a rather thorough eradication. A decade or two before that (most likely around 47 CE), a famine had also ravaged the Middle East, the main proving grounds of Christian evangelism at the time, which would also have considerably reduced the normal life expectancy of the church membership, especially its leaders, insofar as leadership always tended to be elderly.[205] Though it's possible some of the

202. Tacitus, *Annals* 15.44 (which claims perhaps hundreds were captured and confessed to arson and executed). Although that might have suffered interpolation (see following note), Suetonius, *Nero* 16.2, corroborates a Neronian purge of Christianity—unless that, too, is an interpolation, although by the second century, Christians certainly believed Nero had purged the Christian *leadership* at Rome (in apocryphal Christian legend, Nero executed Peter and Paul and their peers at Rome, as told in the *Acts of Peter* and the *Acts of Paul*). We have no conclusive evidence of any Christians surviving this.

203. Of course, if this event never happened (and I suspect it didn't: see Chapter 8, §10), then we are even more in the dark about the fate and progress of Christianity at Rome.

204. Josephus, *Jewish War* 6.420-34 and book 7 relates the destruction of Jerusalem and its inhabitants.

205. Acts 11.27-30; Josephus, *Jewish Antiquities* 20.50-53; it may have lasted several years and affected even the food supply of the city of Rome: Suetonius, *Life of Claudius* 18; Dio Cassius, *Roman History* 60.11.1-5. On Christianity's slow growth in this period (vs. exaggerated numbers in Christian propaganda) see Carrier, *Not the Impossible Faith*, pp. 407-48. There were probably of course additional persecution events (in this early period mostly led by Jewish authorities) that we should also add as factors increasing mortality beyond the average. Although we mustn't exaggerate that

leadership escaped all these events, we actually have no evidence any did. From 60 to 95 all (authentic) letter writing within the church ceases for the whole thirty years (a chilling sign), and no one writing after that period (Clement of Rome? See Chapter 8, §5) indicates that anyone survived those events. Certainly neither Peter nor Paul nor any other apostle from their time is known to have survived beyond the year 70.

There are some claims to be found that the disciple John survived into the second century, but Eusebius reveals this to be mistaken, as *that* John was often being confused with a different and later John.[206] The odds are already hundreds or even thousands to one against anyone having lived from the early 30s CE into the reign of Trajan (c. 100 CE), as was being claimed of John (and that only in unreliable sources many generations later). In fact, life expectancy in the ancient world was already short, even in times of plenty, much less when a massive war, persecution and famine are added to further cull numbers.[207]

Even in the best of times, no more than one in three people made it to 55 or above. Yet if anyone started in the apostolate at, for example, age 15 in the year 30, they would be 55 in the year 70. And it is far more likely the first apostles were in their 20s or 30s, not teenagers, which would make them around 65 or 75 in the year 70. Teenagers would have incredible difficulty earning the respect or deference of those in their 20s or 30s, much less of elder folk, and therefore would be ineffective as evangelists. So it is very unlikely the first apostles were of teen age. Indeed, such a thing would be so remarkable it could not have failed to have been remarked upon in the sources we have. Yet only one in five *teenagers* would reach age 65, and barely one in twenty would make it to age 75—and that's *without* wars, famines and persecutions reducing their survival rate. Factor those in, and we can expect none of the original 'twelve' (if 1 Cor. 15.5 is to be trusted) will have made it much beyond the year 75 (to which age the chances of a 25 year-old surviving are one in eight in *normal* conditions). Combine these

factor: see Candida Moss, *The Myth of Persecution: How Early Christians Invented a Story of Martyrdom* (New York: HarperOne, 2013).

206. Read Eusebius, *History of the Church* 3.23 in light of his more critical observations at 3.39.

207. On this and following statistical remarks I follow the data provided in T.G. Parkin, *Demography and Roman Society* (Baltimore, MD: Johns Hopkins University Press, 1992), p. 144. You can see some calculations for survival odds at http://www.richardcarrier.info/lifetbl.html ('Estimated Life Expectancy in the Ancient World'). If John was around 15 when he was made an apostle, he would be around 85 by the year 100, which has a probability of survival less than 1 in 200; if John was 25 at the start, then he would be 95 by year 100, which would have odds of thousands to one against; the odds only decline exponentially from there. And again, this is without factoring in the war, famine and persecutions.

prior expectations with the lack of any reliable evidence of anyone so surviving, and the silence of evidence against it (such as the complete absence of letters or writings from, to, or about these or any other leaders composed in that period), and we must conclude that in all probability all the original leaders were by then dead.

The significance of all this is that in that period (from 64 to 95 CE) we have no clear idea who was in charge or which churches they controlled or what schisms developed or what disputes arose or how they were resolved, or even whether they *were* resolved. We cannot know if the secret oral knowledge known to Paul and reserved for 'mature' members of the church was accurately or devotedly passed on—or if it was, to whom, or in what ways it was altered. And we cannot identify anyone who was in a position to prevent the development of novel interpretations and beliefs—even when Peter and Paul were still alive, the Epistles reveal their inability to prevent such schismatic developments (Element 21), so control of dogma must have been even less efficacious when no clear authority remained. And with no clear authority in control for thirty years—an entire generation—there is no limit to what can happen to an institution and its teachings, especially one built (at least in substantial part) on myths and secrets, two things that are the easiest to change (hence see Chapter 6, §7).

5

Background Knowledge (Context)

The previous chapter surveyed the background knowledge directly relating to the Christian religion (origins, beliefs and development) that we must take into account when evaluating any hypothesis regarding the historical existence of Jesus. This chapter will survey the most important background knowledge regarding the context in which Christianity began (political, religious and literary), as well as its most pertinent scientific and historical analogs.

1. *Elements of Political Context*

The origin of Christianity makes sense only within the peculiar political context that produced it, and in light of analogous movements throughout history.[1]

Element 23: The Romans annexed Judea to the imperial province of Syria in 6 CE, bringing the center of the Holy Land under direct control of the Roman government, ending Jewish sovereignty over Jerusalem and the temple of the Most High God, along with most of the Holy Land that had been promised by God to the Jews.[2]

In fact, God had promised that the Jews would not only rule their own land, city and temple, but subjugate all peoples and rule the whole world as the chosen people of God (Zech. 14.9-18; Psalm 2), which was also a common feature of messianic belief (Elements 3 and 4), one timetable for which

1. See, in general, Richard Ascough, 'Historical Approaches', in *Dictionary of Biblical Criticism and Interpretation* (ed. Stanley Porter; New York: Routledge, 2007), pp. 157-59; with Stephen Hunt, 'Anthropology and Interpretation', in *Dictionary* (ed. Porter), pp. 12-14, and Stephen Hunt, 'Socio-Scientific Approaches', in *Dictionary* (ed. Porter), pp. 337-40.

2. Jewish sovereignty was briefly returned to Herod Agrippa I by Emperor Claudius between 41 and 44 CE. But between 6 and 36 CE there was no evident prospect of this happening, and even when it did, it was so short lived as to be inconsequential.

predicted this outcome was imminent (Element 7). The Roman annexation contradicted all of this, which would have inevitably produced cognitive dissonance between what Jews expected (the fulfillment of God's promise) and what happened (the Jews lost their sovereignty and became a subject people). The result was a permanent state of violent tension between the Roman occupation and Jewish rebellion that concluded in three devastating wars (against Nero in 66–70 CE, against Trajan in 115–117 and against Hadrian in 132–136) and countless smaller rebellions (beginning with Judas the Galilean in 6 CE), all of which the Jews consistently lost.

Element 24: (a) Owing to their vastly greater resources (in materials, money and manpower) and superior technical ability (in the training, equipping and supplying of their armies) the Romans were effectively invincible and could never be expelled from Judea by force or diplomacy. (b) This fact was so empirically evident and publicly tested and demonstrated on such a wide scale that it had to have been evident to at least some Jews, even while many either didn't see it, denied it even when seen, or imagined celestial aid would redress the imbalance.

In other words, the traditional messianic hope (of a conclusive military victory over all of Israel's neighbors) was a doomed hope, and that would have been obvious *to at least some Jews*. History would of course decisively prove this, as messianic movements were either wiped out quickly (Element 4) or led to the utter defeat and destruction of Jerusalem and the entire Jewish polity (already in the Neronian War of the 60s; even more so in the subsequent wars under Trajan and Hadrian: Element 23). This had happened before, most infamously to both Carthage and Corinth in the same year (146 BCE), which any educated observer would know about. In fact, up to the time Christianity began, Roman victory was always the outcome, without exception, for every nation that ever stood against any concerted Roman conquest and occupation.

For example, even the infamous defeat of Varus by the Germans in 9 CE was decisively redressed by Germanicus only a few years later, illustrating the futility even of a *victory* against the Romans. This was a phenomenon so consistently repeated that it had already become a popular joke by the time of Christ, which is called even still a 'Pyrrhic victory', from the legend, widely circulated in antiquity, that in the third century BCE the Greek upstart Pyrrhus had won his victories against the Romans at such cost that he declared 'one more victory and I'm done for' (or words to that effect), which prophecy was fulfilled in short order. After centuries of history repeating itself like this without fail, only a fool would bank on a future rebellion against the Romans having any other outcome. And though fools were always to be found, not all men are fools.

It would therefore be extremely improbable if *no* early-first-century Jews could foresee this (even if most, evidently, did not). Predicting this outcome would have been all the easier for anyone aware of recent analogous events, from the fates of Carthage and Corinth to the early Jewish rebellions described by Josephus, which were so quickly and easily suppressed that the reality must have become apparent to some. It would have been a simple matter to put two and two together: Roman military might plus Jewish military messianism equals the inevitable destruction of the Jews.

Element 25: The corruption and moral decay of the Jewish civil and temple elite (regardless of to what extent it was actual or merely perceived) was a widespread target of condemnation and often a cause of factionalizing among Jewish sects. This is evident throughout the narrative of Josephus regarding the causes and outcomes of the Jewish War, as well as in the literature recovered at Qumran (e.g. 4Q500), and in much of the apocryphal, apocalyptic and pseudepigraphical literature produced or popularized by first-century Jews.[3] It is also a persistent theme in the Christian Gospels, which in that context do not seem aberrant in this respect but in fact typical.[4]

Element 26: For many Jews in the early first century (in accord with the previous element) the Jewish elite became the scapegoats for God's failed promises (in accord with Elements 23 and 24): the reason God withheld their fulfillment (and instead allowed the Romans to rule) was imagined to be the Jewish elite's failure to keep God's commandments and govern justly (already a common theme throughout the OT, e.g., Jeremiah 23 and 25, the latter being the very prophecy whose 'mystery' is decoded in Daniel to produce the timetable that was now indicating the messiah would arrive in the early first century: Element 7). God would come through only when all sin had ended and been atoned for (Dan. 9.5-24).

The Dead Sea Scrolls, for example, repeatedly denounce the Jewish civil and temple elite as responsible for the evil that has befallen the land, in terms similar to those found in the Christian Gospels. And since the sins of the Jews are what kept God from holding back his promised judgment (as

3. See, e.g., George Nickelsburg, '*First* and *Second Enoch*: A Cry against Oppression and the Promise of Deliverance', in *The Historical Jesus in Context* (ed. Amy-Jill Levine, Dale C. Allison Jr and John Dominic Crossan; Princeton, NJ: Princeton University Press, 2006), pp. 87-109.

4. See, e.g., Jonathan Klawans, 'Moral and Ritual Purity', in *The Historical Jesus in Context* (ed. Levine, Allison and Crossan), pp. 266-84 (which corroborates some of the following elements as well).

explained in Jeremiah 23 and 25, and Daniel 9), any plan that would cancel those sins would be seen as removing that obstacle and thus ushering in God's promise. The fact that Daniel and Isaiah both connect the death of a messiah or savior with a final cancellation of Israel's sins (see Elements 4 to 7) thus would have made those texts of primary interest to any apocalyptic Jew. A messiah's atoning death (Elements 5, 10 and 18) therefore would have an obvious *apocalyptic* significance and function. The end of the world (and a fulfillment of God's promises) could not occur without something like it, and scripture was practically handing it to them (Element 17).

Element 27: (a) The temple at Jerusalem was the central focus of most Jewish messianic hopes (as, for the Samaritans, was Mount Gerizim), which entailed that as long as the 'corrupt' Jewish elite controlled it, God would continue Israel's 'punishment' (in accord with Elements 25 and 26); and as long as the Romans remained in power, they would maintain the corrupt Jewish elite's control of the temple. Accordingly, (b) Jewish religious violence often aimed at seizing physical control of the temple and its personnel.[5]

Element 28. A spiritual solution to the physical conundrum of the Jews would have been a natural and easy thing to conceive at the time. Those Jews who believed they could physically retake control of the temple naturally pinned their hopes on military messianism (as exemplified by the Zealots and the Sicarii, and everyone who led actual rebellions against Rome, from Judas the Galilean to Bar Kochba). But if any Jews had realized that such a reconquest was impossible (as some must, in accord with Element 24) but still sought a means to escape their cognitive dissonance (in accord with Element 23) without denying the evident facts or abandoning deep-seated religious beliefs (and it is reasonable to assume at least some Jews did seek such means without going to such ends), then for them only one solution remained: to deny the physical importance of the temple at Jerusalem itself.

5. See R.G. Hamerton-Kelly, 'Sacred Violence and the Messiah: The Markan Passion Narrative as a Redefinition of Messianology', in *The Messiah: Developments in Earliest Judaism and Christianity* (ed. James Charlesworth; Minneapolis, MN: Fortress Press, 1992), pp. 461-93; and Margaret Barker, *The Great High Priest: The Temple Roots of Christian Liturgy* (New York: T. & T. Clark, 2003). Although I don't agree with Barker's every theory, such as that Jesus was an actual high priest (since he could more easily have been a Platonic ideal of one, as Hebrews 9 implies: see Chapter 11, §5), she collects considerable evidence of interest on the subject of the temple's importance and Christianity's solution to the problem it posed.

That would require replacing it, and not with another temple (as that would only recreate the same problem all over again and thus not in fact solve it, as was evident in the fate of the Samaritan messianic uprising at Gerizim: Element 7), but with something intangible, which neither the Romans nor the corrupt Jewish elite could control (as the intangible cannot be seized or occupied), and which required neither money nor material power to bring about or maintain (the two factors perceived to have corrupted the original temple cult—and to always favor the Romans, who alone had boundless quantities of both), and whose ruler was himself incapable of corruption (and there was only one who was truly incapable of corruption: God).

This does not entail that anyone *did* think this, only that it would have been an easy and natural progression of thought from problem to solution, and therefore not implausible. It fits the political and religious context and our understanding of human nature and ingenuity. Therefore, if any religious innovator had proposed that God had arranged a supreme sacrifice capable of cleansing all sins once and for all (such as, e.g., through the ritual atoning sacrifice of his firstborn son: Element 10), and further arranged that God's spirit would, as a result, dwell forever within each individual who pledged himself to him (and thus no longer dwell, or dwell only, within the temple at Jerusalem: Element 18), then his message would resonate among many Jews as an ingenious and attractive solution to the problem of Jewish elite corruption and Roman invincibility (Elements 23-26), by eliminating the relevance of the temple to messianic hopes, and thus eliminating the basis for any doomed military conflict with Rome, and further eliminating the problem of the corrupt Jewish elite by simply disinheriting them from God's kingdom and removing them as middlemen between the people and their God—all without requiring the deployment of any physical or military resources. One simply had to declare that it had been done. God's will. Sorted.

The basic Christian gospel—imagining that the death of a messiah had conclusively atoned for all sins (as the OT could already be understood to say, per Elements 5, 6, and 17), and that by joining with him (through adoption by baptism, in accord with Element 12; and through symbolic consumption of his body and blood, in accord with Element 18) God would dwell in us (instead of the temple)—would thus be recognized by many Jews as an ingenious and attractive idea.[6] Especially since the end result

6. It should not have to be stated, but the objection that no Jew would countenance the drinking of blood is of no relevance to the *symbolic* drinking of blood; symbolic cannibalism is not really cannibalism. By analogy, Christian baptism was a symbolic death (e.g. Rom. 6.4 and Col. 2.12), and yet no Jews objected to it on the grounds that it was murder.

would be that instead of taking orders from the Jewish elite, we would have as our sovereign no fallible men but Christ himself, God's appointed Lord, directly speaking to his subjects from the right hand of God in heaven (by spirit and angelic communication, and secret messages planted in scripture, in accord with Elements 8 and 15).[7] Thus the problem of elite corruption is seemingly removed without requiring violence or money or diplomacy or military victory. God has his victory; and all cognitive dissonance is resolved.

The only sacred space this doctrine required one to physically control was one's own body, a notion already popularized by philosophical sects such as the Stoics, who taught that nothing external can conquer a man who in his wisdom remains internally free. Not death, nor imprisonment, nor torture represented any victory over him. This was therefore a battle one could always win, even against the 'invincible' Romans. One merely had to believe it, to *feel* it was true, that God now lived in you. No other evidence was required. Thus it should not surprise us that Christianity converted all the military imagery of popular messianism into spiritual metaphor, to represent what we would now call a *culture* war.[8] This aligns perfectly with the notion of a spiritual transfer of authority to the people, negating the relevance of the temple and the Jewish elite, while retaining the most fundamental requirements of being Jewish (namely, faith and obedience to the commandments of God; though even that would later be done away with, per Element 20).

The relevance of this observation is that the earliest Christian gospel makes far more sense as a product of its political context than it does when completely divorced from that context, and in consequence, theories of historicity that ignore that fact are unlikely to have any objective merit. The centrality of the temple was a continual problem for the Jews. A physical location requiring political control entailed military domination. So long as the Romans had the latter, the Jews would never have the former. The Zealots took the logical option of attempting to remove the Romans and restore Jewish control. But the Christians took the only other available option: removing the temple from their entire soteriological (or 'salvation') scheme.[9]

7. The need of an immortal, incorruptible 'high priest' to replace the existing priestly class is expressed in Heb. 7.25-27 and Hebrews 9 (see Chapter 11, §5).

8. See my discussion in Carrier, *Not the Impossible Faith*, pp. 225-30 (to which can be added such examples as Ignatius, *To Polycarp* 6, and the logic behind Wis. 5.17-22, which clearly influenced 1 Thess. 5.8-9 and Eph. 6.12-17).

9. Many elements of this are supported by Mark Strauss, *Four Portraits, One Jesus: An Introduction to Jesus and the Gospels* (Grand Rapids, MI: Zondervan, 2007), pp. 366, 368-70, 376; Marcus Borg, *Jesus: Uncovering the Life, Teachings, and*

Christians could then just await God's wrath to come from heaven (in accord with Element 10), while in the meantime, God's promise could be delivered unto the kingdom they had *spiritually* created (Rom. 14.17-18; 1 Cor. 4.19-20), first in an anticipatory way (in the moral and 'supernatural' success of the Christian community), and then in the most final way (in the apocalypse itself: e.g. 1 Cor. 15.24, 50; 6.9-10; Gal. 5.19-25; 1 Thess. 4.10-5.15). That the Christians and the Zealots both may have come from the same sectarian background, and pursued collectively the only two possible solutions to the problem facing the Jews at the time, reveals Christianity to be more akin to something inevitable than something surprising.[10]

Element 29: Further supporting the previous element is the fact that what are now called 'Cargo Cults' are the modern movements most culturally and socially similar to earliest Christianity, so much so that Christianity is best understood in light of them. For not only are their attributes remarkably similar, but so are the socio-political situations that created them; and it is this distinct parallel of both cause and effect that makes the comparison illuminating. In the words of I.C. Jarvie:

> One of the most remarkable things about apocalyptic millenarian movements [like the Cargo Cults] is that, despite the fact that they crop up at all periods of history, in all parts of the world, and in all sorts of different social set-ups, we can find remarkable similarities between them.[11]

Indeed.

Relevance of a Religious Revolutionary (San Francisco, CA: HarperSanFrancisco, 2006), pp. 225-60; and Bruce Malina, *The Social Gospel of Jesus: The Kingdom of God in Mediterranean Perspective* (Minneapolis, MN: Fortress Press, 2001); and Bruce Malina, *The New Testament World: Insights from Cultural Anthropology* (Atlanta, GA: John Knox Press, 3rd edn, 2001), as well as his *Social Science Commentary* series on the NT—although caution in employing Malina is warranted, as he over-simplifies a great deal, but as long as you allow for unstated complexities and exceptions at every point, most of what he argues can be validly applied to the origins of Christianity, and corroborates the analysis given here.

10. D. Mendels, 'Pseudo-Philo's *Biblical Antiquities*, the "Fourth Philosophy", and the Political Messianism of the First Century C.E.', in *The Messiah* (ed. Charlesworth), pp. 261-75, argues the authors of the *Biblical Antiquities* rewrote and expanded various OT stories in order to communicate values contrary to those of the Zealots regarding the solution to Judea's social problems, illustrating that Christians weren't the only ones looking for an alternative. That Christians and Zealots might both stem (at least in significant part) from the same sect (the Essenes, who were in turn regarded as deriving their views from the Samaritans), see Carrier, 'Spiritual Body', in *Empty Tomb* (ed. Price and Lowder), pp. 109, 200 n. 23, 201 nn. 26-28, 31, and Element 33 below.

11. I.C. Jarvie, *The Revolution in Anthropology* (London: Routledge & K. Paul, 1964), p. 50.

These cults rocked numerous small Melanesian island nations in the early twentieth century, producing a variety of savior religions often surrounding mythical (but fully historicized) messiahs, from John Frum to Tom Navy, men who never really existed but were believed to have been real persons who visited the islands and would return messianically one day with ships or planes full of marvelous 'cargo', including the resurrected dead of the island peoples. Some of these cults did worship real people, yet who had nothing to do with founding the cult and are quite perplexed at having been deified (like Prince Philip, the current husband, 'royal consort', of the Queen of England, who is worshiped as the savior deity in one of these cults). Notably, in no case was the savior god, despite being conceived from the start as a historical person, ever an actual founder of any of these religions, yet they are always portrayed as such in their sacred stories, issuing teachings and prophecies and establishing 'their' church.

The earliest documented of these uprisings was the Vailala Madness in the Territory of Papua.[12] But all subsequent cults had similar features: they are all charismatic apocalyptic cults (in this case arising in Melanesia), characterized by glossolalia and mass hysteria, prophesying, receiving secret communications from God (who thus provided instructions on forming the religion and its teachings), and experiencing powerful and convincing visions (thus cargo cults were schizotypal cults: Element 15). In fact, in several documented cases things that were seen in visions or merely prophesied were later believed to have historically happened, within just fifteen years (some such ideas originating in 1919 became fully historicized beliefs by 1934), demonstrating rapid legendary development.[13] Cargo cults were also characterized by radical reform (abandoning old traditional cult and instituting a new), apocalyptic expectations (preaching a coming end of the world in which all injustices would be redressed, the dead raised, and the

12. Peter Worsley, *The Trumpet Shall Sound: A Study of 'Cargo' Cults in Melanesia* (London: MacGibbon & Kee, 2nd edn, 1968), treats the entire Cargo Cult phenomenon (see pp. 75-92 for the 'Vailala Madness'). For a more first-hand account of that: F.E. Williams, 'The Vailala Madness in Retrospect', in *Essays Presented to C.G. Seligman* (ed. E.E. Evans-Pritchard *et al.*; London: Kegan Paul, Trench, Trubner, 1934), pp. 369-79. On other Cargo Cults see G.W. Trompf, *Cargo Cults and Millenarian Movements: Transoceanic Comparisons of New Religious Movements* (New York: Mouton de Gruyter, 1990); Peter Lawrence, *Road Belong Cargo: A Study of the Cargo Movement in the Southern Madang District, New Guinea* (Manchester: Manchester University Press, 1964); Kenelm Burridge, *Mambu: A Study of Melanesian Cargo Movements and their Ideological Background* (New York: Harper & Row, 1960). Wikipedia maintains an informative page on the cargo cults, both individually and collectively: http://en.wikipedia.org/wiki/Cargo_cult. There are also some relevant similarities in modern UFO cults: Christopher Partridge (ed.), *UFO Religions* (New York: Routledge, 2003).

13. Worsley, *The Trumpet Shall Sound*, pp. 90-91.

faithful rewarded), and a strong moral dimension—as well as new diversions of charity from which the movement's leaders benefitted, similar to what the letters of Paul show happened in early Christianity.[14]

Peter Worsley's study of cargo cults (and related millenarian movements such as the Native American 'Ghost Dance' movement of the late nineteenth century) found that they arise in one of three conditions—though sometimes more than one condition is present, and notably all three were present at the origin of Christianity:

1. First in racially and culturally fragmented societies; 'the main effect of the millenarian cult is to overcome these divisions and to weld previously hostile and separate groups together into a new unity' against the ruling power; and 'the social necessity which produces this drive towards integration is the subjection of all the separate units to a common authority', like a foreign imperial power (and, of course, the local elite who support it, who are then seen as in collusion with it).[15] Christianity, too, arose in a racially and culturally fragmented society under the thumb of a foreign power. The first Christians sought to resolve this tension by recruiting Gentiles to become Jews, but very soon Paul saw (consciously or not) that Christianity had to relax that requirement to achieve its goal of unity, making this an almost inevitable development, since the need of it would have been all but obvious, while the alternative was certain to fail, as in fact it did.[16]

2. And 'the second major type of society in which millenarian cults develop is the agrarian, and especially feudal, state' where 'the cults arise among the lower orders—peasants and urban plebeians—in opposition to the official régimes', because 'due to the material conditions of their lives, they lack any organization which could give practical expression to their common interests, and they do not see their common interests except in times of social crisis', so they must then create such an organization.[17] Christianity likewise originated in an agrarian society, with an effectively feudal structure (with powerful landholders controling economic and political institutions and exploiting a peasantry), and among the lower orders, in a condition of growing social crisis (see Elements 22-25 and Element 4), where no political organization for expressing their concerns was made available, thus necessitating that they create one. This would explain Christianity's rapid organization into 'churches' with a hierarchy and rules of

14. See J. Duncan M. Derrett, 'Financial Aspects of the Resurrection', in *Empty Tomb* (ed. Price and Lowder), pp. 393-409.

15. Worsley, *The Trumpet Shall Sound*, p. 228.

16. See Element 20. That Paul's variant would inevitably prevail over the original one by making this unifying goal easier to achieve is a fact I discuss in Carrier, *Not the Impossible Faith*, pp. 51-52.

17. Worsley, *The Trumpet Shall Sound*, pp. 228-29.

order (1 Cor. 11–14 and 6; cf. Rom. 16.1; 1 Cor. 1.2; 12.28; 16.19; etc.), and its steady move toward control of orthodoxy through an increasingly organized political system independent of the imperial government. This same pattern is observed in other cases: most millenarian movements begin with a 'terrific release of emotional energy' and 'the overthrow or reversal of the present social order' and 'the promise of heaven on earth—soon', but this revolutionary aspect has a brief life; if the movement survives, it does so only by becoming an institutionalized expression of a more distant future promise, with more muted emotional energy, and more socially conservative.[18] Just as happened to Christianity.

3. And 'there is a third type of social situation in which activist millenarian ideas are likely to flourish', which is 'when a society with differentiated political institutions is fighting for its existence by quite secular military–political means, but is meeting with defeat after defeat', such that 'when the political structure of a society is smashed by war or other means, or fails to answer the needs of a people who wish to carry on the struggle, then a prophetic, often millenarian, leadership is likely to emerge'.[19] In other words, when 'the military solution' to oppression and social disfunction so consistently fails and is so obviously unlikely to succeed, social pressures produce apocalyptic, non-militarized grassroots movements instead, which arise from a retooling of the dominant native religion. Apocalypticism (both its eager expectation and its florid description through revelation and pronouncement) becomes a way to passively voice discontent with the ruling powers and re-envision a better society, proclaiming that God himself will bring it upon us soon—rather than taking up arms to bring it about directly, a solution already seen to be incapable of success; and since it 'must' happen, as God would not abandon his people, God must be waiting in the wings.

This so appositely describes the situation and solution of early Christianity (Elements 22-25) that it is again a conspicuous match. So the sociological situation that spawned Christianity had *all three* conditions for generating millenarian cults exactly like Christianity. In fact, these are now recognized as the common conditions giving rise to all martyrdom movements, from Islamic to Buddhist to pagan, Jewish, and Christian: a subject people, in relative poverty, powerless, effectively dominated by a foreign people (either directly or through collusion with an unresponsive local elite) who are racially and culturally different from themselves, and whose economic and military capability is so awesome it cannot be overcome.[20]

18. Jarvie, *The Revolution*, pp. 51, 72.

19. Worsley, *The Trumpet Shall Sound*, p. 230.

20. See my discussion of this fact, and the relevant scholarship confirming it, in Carrier, *Not the Impossible Faith*, pp. 219-45.

Anthropology thus teaches us that Christianity is exactly the sort of thing one would expect to arise in those conditions.[21] And we should also expect it to take on the characteristics typical of those conditions: it would arise from an oppressed natives' religion (Judaism) in a time of escalating, unresolvable crisis (as in early-first-century Palestine), and it would prominently adopt matryrdom, apocalypticism, a program of social-moral reform and its own internal political organization separate from the established political and religious institutions. It will also syncretically merge (per Element 11) its local faith with useful or admired elements of the cultural and religious ideas of their oppressors in order to 'co-opt' them and produce a 'greater' religion than either the failed local cult or the illegitimate alien cult—as all these other millenarian movements did.[22] When the conditions are added that strongly support schizotypal cult behavior (Element 15), the features thereof will be integrated as well (as happened with the Cargo Cults).[23] And when the further condition is added of a rising popularity of syncretic unification movements such as the Hellenistic mystery religions (Element 11), we could again have described what Christianity would look like without ever having heard of it. Can that really be a coincidence?

21. Essentially the same conclusion is reached by James Crossley, *Why Christianity Happened: A Sociohistorical Account of Christian Origins (26–50 CE)* (Louisville, KY: Westminster John Knox Press, 2006).

22. Cargo Cults integrated elements of Christianity and otherwise secular but 'Western' cultural objects and ideas (Jarvie, *The Revolution*, pp. 64-66); even modern apocalyptic Islamic extremism integrates Western (often fascist) political philosophy, tactics and technologies, as well as mythologies (e.g. conspiracy theories), to become something new. This is always claimed to be a 'return' to the 'true' faith, in defiance of historical fact. Thus, what is actually new could always be sold as old: see Carrier, *Not the Impossible Faith*, pp. 129-34. Notably, the availability of guns and explosives has made it seem like military victory is still possible (because immediate engagements produce terrorizing results that seem to vindicate the perpetrators' righteousness) and therefore Islamic extremists remain militarized. I suspect if it were not for those technologies, they would have become demilitarized, like early Christianity, the Cargo Cults and other millenarian movements in the same mold, except where it has actually succeeded (e.g. Iran).

23. In connection with this fact, I discuss how this element caused such movements to be led by prophets rather than 'politicians' (or philosophers) in Carrier, *Not the Impossible Faith*, pp. 259-96. I would add a final necessary causal ingredient, that of a cultural framework in which such movements make sense (such as has been provided by Middle Eastern cultures, Jewish and pagan, since long before the rise of Christianity, and long since: Element 10, and the remaining elements in this chapter). By contrast, e.g., Tibet has no comparable cultural framework, and thus (to my knowledge) has not developed a millenarian movement of this Western type (but martyrdom movements of a different kind), despite otherwise being locked in nearly the same socio-political conditions.

2. *Elements of Religious and Philosophical Context*

Element 30: Early-first-century Judea was at the nexus of countless influences, not only from dozens of innovating and interacting Jewish sects (Elements 2 and 33), but also pagan religions and philosophies (Elements 31 and 32). The influence of the latter is sometimes denied, but cannot be, not only because pagans lived, traveled, and traded all throughout Judea (with significant populations in cities throughout the Holy Land, from the pagan quarters of Caesarea, Gaza, Ptolemais, Tiberias and Sepphoris to the ten cities of the Decapolis and major port cities such as Tyre and Ashkelon, and likewise in Samaria, which was right in the center of the Holy Land, with ongoing interactions with the surrounding districts through pilgrimage and trade),[24] but even more so because Jerusalem, and all Judea, was frequented

24. See Zeev Safrai, 'The Gentile Cities of Judea: Between the Hasmonean Occupation and the Roman Liberation', in *Studies in Historical Geography and Biblical Historiography* (ed. Zecharia Kallai, Gershon Galil and Moshe Weinfeld; Leiden: E.J. Brill, 2000), pp. 63-90; Louis Feldman, *Judaism and Hellenism Reconsidered* (Leiden: Brill, 2006); Jonas Greenfield, 'The Languages of Palestine, 200 BCE–200 C.E.', in *Al Kanfei Yonah: Collected Studies of Jonas C. Greenfield on Semitic Philology*, Vol. I (ed. Shalom Paul, Michael Stone and Avital Pinnick; Leiden: Brill, 2001), pp. 376-87; D. Flusser, 'Paganism in Palestine', in *The Jewish People in the First Century*, Vol. II (ed. Shemuel Safrai and Menahem Stern; Assen: Van Gorcum, 1974–76), pp. 1065-1100, and (in the same volume) G. Mussies, 'Greek in Palestine and the Diaspora', pp. 1040-64; Martin Hengel, *Judaism and Hellenism: Studies in their Encounter in Palestine during the Early Hellenistic Period* (Philadelphia, PA: Fortress Press, 1974); Morton Smith, *Palestinian Parties and Politics That Shaped the Old Testament* (New York: Columbia University Press, 1971); and Morton Smith, 'Palestinian Judaism in the First Century', in *Israel: Its Role in Civilization* (ed. Moshe Davis; New York: Harper, 1956), pp. 67-81.

Even Mark Chancey, in *The Myth of a Gentile Galilee* (Cambridge: Cambridge University Press, 2002), confirms there were plenty of Gentiles in Galilee as well (predominately in its cities and cities adjacent), just not 'as many' as some scholars have claimed (note, e.g., his discussion of pagans in Samaria, pp. 153-55, and his overall conclusion, pp. 155-82). But influence only requires a presence, not a huge one. Contact is contact. Likewise, see discussion of the Gentile presence in Judea before and after the Hasmoneans (and one must remember that influences that had already been integrated with various sects of Judaism *before* the Hasmoneans would have remained *after* them) in Jack Pastor, *Land and Economy in Ancient Palestine* (New York: Routledge, 1997).

Ironically, attempts to deny this also confirm it: in the Christian apologetic treatise by Paul Eddy and Gregory Boyd, *The Jesus Legend: A Case for the Historical Reliability of the Synoptic Jesus Tradition* (Grand Rapids, MI: Baker Academic, 2007), pp. 101-32 extensively documents and thus concedes the vast presence of foreign influences throughout the whole of Palestine; the authors then try to insist that all Jews in Palestine were completely resistant to all these influences in almost every respect,

by millions of pilgrims from the diaspora every year, many (such as Philo of Alexandria) thoroughly Hellenized, who brought with them ideas and teachings from the foreign communities they came from. Acts 2.5-11 and 6.9 are thus reflecting the reality, and that in Jerusalem itself.

These latter ideas would have infiltrated Palestinian society in two ways. Some would arrive by simple report: pagans and Jewish pilgrims retelling what they heard and knew and what they thought about it; and likewise bringing books with them, to loan, sell or read aloud; it would also be incredible to think that *none* of the cities in Palestine had public libraries, which were otherwise a standard feature of major cities of the time, and surely a feature of every city with a large Gentile presence, such as Caesarea or Tyre.[25] But others would arrive through prior syncretism: diaspora Jews combined pagan religious and philosophical ideas with their own Jewish faith (as Philo of Alexandria did—and just as what were then 'mainstream' Palestinian Jews had done before when they adopted notions of hell and resurrection, and the Devil as a supernatural enemy of God, all from their pagan Zoroastrian overlords centuries before), and then came to Judea and promulgated their new ideas as *Jewish* ideas rather than pagan.[26] Paul himself is an example: a diaspora Jew, from either Tarsus (Acts 9.11; 21.39; 22.3) or Damascus (Gal. 2.17; 2 Cor. 11.26), whose own version of Christianity, ultimately accepted even by the founders (the 'pillars' of Gal. 2), was laden with ideas from pagan philosophy, literature and mystery cult.[27]

which is an absurd notion, and a conclusion they completely fail to prove (the fallacies of argument from ignorance and false generalization are rife throughout, especially in repeatedly leaping from premises about 'most' to conclusions about 'all', and in mistaking opinions for facts).

25. See Konstantinos Staikos, *The History of the Library in Western Civilization*, Vols. I and II (Athens: Kotinos Publications, 2004). I will discuss Greco-Roman libraries as standard urban features in Richard Carrier, *Science Education in the Early Roman Empire* (in review).

26. On the previous Jewish syncretism with Zoroastrianism see Carrier, *Not the Impossible Faith*, pp. 85-99. On other examples of ongoing Jewish syncretism: Lars Hartman, *'Into the Name of the Lord Jesus': Baptism in the Early Church* (Edinburgh: T. & T. Clark, 1997), pp. 3-8; M.L. West, *The Orphic Poems* (New York: Oxford University Press, 1983), pp. 33-35; and Carl Holladay, *Fragments from Hellenistic Jewish Authors,* Volume IV: *Orphica* (Atlanta, GA: Scholars Press, 1996); Stanley Rosenbaum, *Understanding Biblical Israel: A Reexamination of the Origins of Monotheism* (Macon, GA: Mercer University Press, 2002); and Mark Smith, *The Origins of Biblical Monotheism: Israel's Polytheistic Background and the Ugaritic Texts* (New York: Oxford University Press, 2001).

27. On the influence of pagan mystery religion see Element 10; on the influence of pagan philosophy see Element 32. Note that early Christian (as also Jewish) art was also highly syncretistic, adopting pagan and Jewish motifs as Christian symbols, or merging

Two common objections to this conclusion are (1) that the ideas exhibiting influence (as in Philo or Paul) are in many ways *different* from their ideological sources, and (2) we do not have direct archaeological confirmation of the presence of such ideas (e.g. in the form of pagan books or references to same). But neither objection is logically valid, because (1) syncretism always changes the adopted ideas by plucking them out of their original system and combining them with other ideas, and therefore differences are *expected*, and thus cannot argue against the existence of influence, and (2) almost nothing survives from ancient Palestine that would be relevant to determining what 'wasn't' there in the first century (certainly in terms of books, much less in terms of orally transmitted texts and cultural knowledge), therefore this is simply *not* a valid argument from silence.[28] In contrast, the evidence of transmission vectors heavily transiting and residing in Palestine (as surveyed above) is conclusive, and to suggest that all those transmission vectors were there year in and year out for centuries and not transmitting anything is to argue against all human probability.

Likewise, though someone like Philo or Paul could light upon one idea or two that was only accidentally similar to pagan counterparts, it is massively improbable that they could do this dozens of times over. Such a

pagan, Jewish and Christian motifs into new hybrid symbols: Thomas Mathews, *The Clash of Gods: A Reinterpretation of Early Christian Art* (Princeton, NJ: Princeton University Press, 1993); Fred Albertson, 'An Isiac Model for the Raising of Lazarus in Early Christian Art', *Jahrbuch für Antike und Christentum* 38 (1995), pp. 123-32; Robin Margaret Jensen, *Understanding Early Christian Art* (New York: Routledge, 2000). On syncretism in Jewish art: Joseph Gutmann, *Ancient Synagogues* (Chico, CA: Scholars Press, 1981); Othmar Keel and Christoph Uehlinger, *Gods, Goddesses, and Images of God in Ancient Israel* (trans. Allan Mahnke; Minneapolis, MN: Fortress Press, 1996); Leonard Rutgers (ed.), *What Athens Has to Do with Jerusalem: Essays on Classical, Jewish, and Early Christian Art and Archaeology in Honor of Gideon Foerster* (Leuven: Peeters, 2002); Steven Fine, *Art and Judaism in the Greco-Roman World: Toward a New Jewish Archaeology* (Cambridge: Cambridge University Press, 2005).

28. On the requirements of a valid argument from silence see Carrier, *Proving History*, pp. 117-19. The premise is also dubious, since we actually do have archaeological evidence of pagan influence on Second Temple Judaism in the Dead Sea Scrolls. See, e.g., Matthew Goff, 'Gilgamesh the Giant: The Qumran *Book of Giants*' Appropriation of Gilgamesh Motifs', *Dead Sea Discoveries* 16.2 (2009), pp. 221-53; and John J. Collins, *Daniel: A Commentary* (Minneapolis, MN: Fortress Press, 1993), pp. 395-97, where clear pagan influences on the book of Enoch are identified—and yet nearly a dozen manuscripts of Enoch were recovered from Qumran: Jozef Milik (ed.), *The Books of Enoch: Aramaic Fragments of Qumran Cave 4* (Oxford: Clarendon Press, 1976). And Enoch was a seminal text in the origin of Christianity.

coincidence has only one plausible explanation: influence.[29] Moreover, as both wrote in excellent Greek—as did the authors of several of the books found at Qumran, and numerous persons in Palestine transcribing (and thus also evidently reading) Greek inscriptions and grave markers—and Greek could then only be learned in pagan-style schools based on pagan models of pagan literary classics and commentary (which would undeniably transmit pagan religious and philosophical knowledge)—to suggest there was *no* transmission of pagan knowledge and ideas there is to suggest the absurd.[30]

29. Some people have a hard time grasping the fact that parallels can entail influence even when many differences remain. One of my readers suggested I make this point with *West Side Story*: it's 'nothing' like *Romeo and Juliet*, taking place in twentieth-century America, with Latin gangs fighting Anglo gangs, who fight with fists and knives and not swords, and they aren't families, just gangs, and no one is named Romeo or Juliet—yet to claim *West Side Story* was not influenced by *Romeo and Juliet* would be absurd: it's a deliberate emulation! This is the case with all acts of mythmaking and syncretism: the variants of a theme will obviously differ in countless ways, but the parallels that remain are too specific and numerous to exist by coincidence. Direct emulation and borrowing are simply by far the most likely hypothesis in such a case (see Carrier, *Proving History*, pp. 192-204).

30. On the inevitably pagan nature of all Greek education in antiquity (and the failure of any group, Jews and Christians included, to develop any sanitized alternative), see Raffaella Cribiore, *Gymnastics of the Mind: Greek Education in Hellenistic and Roman Egypt* (Princeton, NJ: Princeton University Press, 2001), with Harry Gamble, *Books and Readers in the Early Church: A History of Early Christian Texts* (New Haven, CT: Yale University Press, 1995), pp. 6-7; Gerard Ellspermann, *The Attitude of the Early Christian Latin Writers toward Pagan Literature and Learning* (Washington, DC: Catholic University of America Press, 1949), pp. 1-3; Hénri Marrou, *A History of Education in Antiquity* (New York: Sheed & Ward, 3rd edn, 1956), pp. 314-29; Yun Lee Too (ed.), *Education in Greek and Roman Antiquity* (Boston: Brill, 2001), pp. 405-32; see also my discussion in Chapter 9 of my forthcoming *Science Education in the Early Roman Empire*.

Though very conservative Jews (who should not be conflated with *all* Palestinian Jews) distinguished learning Greek from studying Greek philosophy (*b. Sotah* 49b; see E.A. Judge, 'The Reaction against Classical Education in the New Testament', *Journal of Christian Education* 77 (1983), pp. 7-14 [9]), *some* philosophy and religion *inevitably* were taught when studying under an ordinary grammarian (who used pagan books to instruct by and gave commentary and glosses on their content, such as a passage's meaning and significance); thus, avoiding the philosophy schools could not have prevented exposure to philosophy. And not all Palestinian Jews were archconservatives anyway. Even at Qumran we have undeniable evidence of advanced Greek writing and education: see Matthew Richey, 'The Use of Greek at Qumran: Manuscript and Epigraphic Evidence for a Marginalized Language', *Dead Sea Discoveries* 19 (2012), pp. 177-97. Considerably more evidence of this has been recovered from Masada and Jericho (180).

Finally, one might concede the knowledge existed but that 'the Jews' would never adopt ideas from foreign cultures and religions. That is a dubious premise (history does not support it), but even if granted, what conservative or elite Jews would do can have no bearing on what desperate, radical or fringe Jewish sects would do. And Christianity did not originate within conservative or elite Judaism but from the radical fringes, as a protest movement against conservative elite Judaism, and thus represents the very kind of heresy conservatives were always combating (Element 2). By the very fact of their being heretical, any innovations such an embattled sect might resort to in order to 'reform' the Judaism of their day would not be confined to what conservative Jews would allow. In fact, anthropological precedent tells us syncretism in that case is actually *likely* (Element 29). And ultimately, such adaptations, even if *we* can see their pagan roots, would always have been marketed as Jewish, not pagan (exactly as happened to Jewish adaptations from Zoroastrianism).

Element 31: Incarnate sons (or daughters) of a god who died and then rose from their deaths to become living gods granting salvation to their worshipers were a common and peculiar feature of pagan religion when Christianity arose, so much so that influence from paganism is the only plausible explanation for how a Jewish sect such as Christianity came to adopt the idea (again, Element 11). For example, you won't find this trend in ancient China. No such gods are found there. If Christianity had begun in China, its claims would indeed have been unique and astonishing. Yet in its actual Greco-Roman context it was neither unique nor astonishing. Thus it cannot be a coincidence that Christianity arose with an idea matching a ubiquitous pagan type unique to the very time and place it was born. Any theory of historicity, to be plausible, must take this into account.[31]

In the middle of the second century, Justin Martyr wrote the following:

> When we say that the Logos, who is the firstborn of God, Jesus Christ our teacher, was produced without sexual union, and was crucified and died, and rose again, and ascended to heaven, we propound nothing new or different from what you believe regarding those whom you call Sons of God. [In fact] . . . if anybody objects that [our god] was crucified, this is in common with the sons of Zeus (as you call them) who suffered, as previously listed. Since their fatal sufferings are all narrated as not similar but different, so his unique passion should not seem to be any worse—

31. For this and other aspects of Christianity that only make sense as localized cultural diffusion, see Carrier, 'Christianity's Success Was Not Incredible', in *End of Christianity* (ed. Loftus). For the entire background of pagan resurrected gods and heroes—not all of whom were paid cult as savior gods, but still refuting any notion that 'resurrection' was a novel or foreign concept in pagan culture, see Carrier, *Not the Impossible Faith*, pp. 85-127.

indeed I will show, as I have undertaken, and as the argument proceeds, that he was better; for Jesus is thus shown to be better by his actions.[32]

Thus even Christians acknowledged the ubiquity of the dying-and-rising son-of-god theme in their surrounding pagan culture, and recognized it as a common theme even when every story differed in details from every other (on that being how syncretism works, see again Element 11).[33]

The dying-and-rising son (sometimes daughter) of god 'mytheme' originated in the ancient Near East over a thousand years before Christianity and was spread across the Mediterranean principally by the Phoenicians (Canaanites) from their base at Tyre (and after that by the Carthaginians, the most successful Phoenician cultural diffusers in the early Greco-Roman period), and then fostered and modified by numerous native and Greco-Roman cults that adopted it. The earliest documented examples are the cult of Inanna and Dumuzi (also known as Ishtar and Tammuz), the cult of Baal and Anat, and the cult of Marduk (also known as Bel or Baal, which basically meant 'the Lord'), all of whose resurrection stories are told in Sumerian, Ugaritic and Assyrian tablets (respectively) long predating the advent of Christianity.[34] That in pre-Christian belief Inanna was indeed killed and her corpse resurrected I already demonstrated in Chapter 3 (§1), providing the most indisputable example.

These cults then influenced the development of others in the Greco-Roman era, including the cult of a resurrected Adonis. Although too few pre-Christian texts about this specific Adonis cult survive to reconstruct its liturgy, in the third century the Christian scholar Origen says in his *Comments on Ezekiel* that Tammuz is still worshiped in his day under the name Adonis, and as such 'certain rites of initiation are conducted' for him, 'first, that they weep for him, since he has died; second, that they rejoice for

32. Justin Martyr, *Apology* 1.21, 22.

33. See, for another example, Tertullian, *Prescription against Heretics* 40.

34. Previous attempts to deny that these were dying-and-rising gods have been thoroughly refuted by Tryggve Mettinger in *The Riddle of Resurrection: 'Dying and Rising Gods' in the Ancient Near East* (Stockholm: Almqvist & Wiksell International, 2001); and Tryggve Mettinger, 'The Dying and Rising God: The Peregrinations of a Mytheme', in *Ethnicity in Ancient Mesopotamia* (ed. W.H. van Soldt; Leiden: Nederlands Instituut voor het Nabije Oosten, 2005), pp. 198-210. For Inanna specifically (and likely Tammuz as well), see Carrier, *Not the Impossible Faith*, pp. 17-20; and Pirjo Lapinkivi, *The Neo-Assyrian Myth of Ištar's Descent and Resurrection* (Helsinki: Neo-Assyrian Text Corpus Project, 2010). For Baal specifically, see M.S. Smith, *The Ugaritic Baal Cycle*, Vol. I (Leiden: E.J. Brill, 1994); and M.S. Smith and W. Pitard, *The Ugaritic Baal Cycle*, Vol. II (Leiden: E.J. Brill, 2009). For Marduk specifically, see Tikva Frymer-Kensky, 'The Tribulations of Marduk: The So-Called "Marduk Ordeal Text"', *Journal of the American Oriental Society* 103 (January–March 1983), pp. 131-41, but only in light of the further analysis and evidence in Mettinger.

him because he has risen from the dead' [*apo nekrōn anastanti*], by way of explaining the reference in Ezekiel to women 'weeping for Tammuz' at the gates of Jerusalem (Ezek. 8.14), which Ezekiel was denouncing as pagan.[35] We know that refers to the resurrection story of Inanna, which we have on clay tablets long predating Christianity, and there is evidence of a corresponding resurrection story for Tammuz—already widely known in Jerusalem long before Christianity, as Ezekiel was attesting.[36]

It is far more likely the resurrection of this Adonis (in the cult to which Origen refers; not all Adonis cults were necessarily the same) had been celebrated long before Christianity began than that it would be a recent innovation. Surely Origen would know if it were and make obvious sport of the fact; it would likewise be incredible that even at this early stage major pagan cults would fundamentally change their entire religion in emulation of Christianity, which was a little known, wholly uninfluential cult that was rarely liked.[37] And indeed Lucian directly attests to there being a resurrection myth for the Syrian Adonis half a century before Origen, and it's clear Lucian is relating an ancient ceremony of its celebration, not some recent novelty.[38] So it is far more likely a resurrected Adonis cult was not new. The more so as we can confirm several other examples of

35. Zechariah 12.11 also mentions 'the mourning of Hadad-Rimmon in the valley of Megiddo', this being a known epithet of the Ugaritic Baal at the time, who became the resurrected savior god of the Greco-Roman-era mystery cult of Jupiter Dolichenus.

36. It has long been suspected that the complete cycle traded resurrections between Inanna and Dumuzi (as Origen's comment implies), and recent discoveries have supported this conclusion: see Benjamin Foster, 'Descent of Ishtar to the Netherworld', in *Before the Muses: An Anthology of Akkadian Literature* (Bethesda, MD: CDL Press, 3rd edn, 2005), pp. 498-505, where recovered fragments imply a period of rejoicing after mourning the death of Dumuzi (Tammuz), which would indicate he, too, recovered from his death. A similar cycle of mourning and rejoicing over the death and 'revival' of the god Attis would develop later (see later note).

37. Contrary to claims that Christianity was booming in its first two centuries, it was in fact an extremely small fringe cult until the later third century: I survey the evidence and scholarship on this point in Carrier, *Not the Impossible Faith*, pp. 407-47, to which can now be added the analysis of Adam Schor, 'Conversion by the Numbers: Benefits and Pitfalls of Quantitative Modeling in the Study of Early Christian Growth', *Journal of Religious History* 33 (December 2009), pp. 472-98 (and note that Schor's models even presume the incredibly implausible starting point of one thousand Christians in 40 CE, and yet still don't get a significantly different result).

38. Lucian, *On the Syrian Goddess* 6 (written c. 160 CE), which records, like Origen, that national ceremonies of mourning for his death are followed the next day by celebrations of his returning to life and ascending into outer space. For pre-Christian evidence of this same Adonis cult see Stephanie Lynn Budin, *The Myth of Sacred Prostitution in Antiquity* (New York: Cambridge University Press, 2008), pp. 94-99.

clearly pre-Christian dying-and-rising gods well known across the Roman Empire: the savior cult of the resurrected Zalmoxis (of Thracian origin) is clearly attested in Herodotus centuries before Christianity; the imperial cult of the resurrected Romulus is likewise attested in several pre-Christian authors (see Chapter 4, §1); and the Egyptian savior cult of the resurrected Osiris is likewise undeniably ancient.[39]

Well before Christianity, inscriptions among the Egyptian pyramids had long declared of Osiris (usually in the voice of his sister-wife Isis):

> I have come to thee . . . that I may revivify thee, that I may assemble for thee thy bones, that I may collect for thee thy flesh, that I may assemble for thee thy dismembered limbs . . . raise thyself up, king, Osiris; thou livest![40]
>
> Raise thyself up; shake off thy dust; remove the dirt which is on thy face; loose thy bandages.[41]

39. For Romulus and Osiris, see Chapter 4 (§1 and Element 11, respectively); for the antiquity of Osiris as a dying-and-rising savior god, see Bojana Mojsov, *Osiris: Death and Afterlife of a God* (Oxford: Blackwell, 2005), pp. 38-53 and S.G.F. Brandon, *The Savior God: Comparative Studies in the Concept of Salvation* (Westport, CT: Greenwood Press, 1963), pp. 17-36 (with an introductory discussion of the role of Isis on pp. 1-16); this is undeniably confirmed in pre-Christian texts: see following notes. For Zalmoxis, see Herodotus, *Histories* 4.94-96, with Carrier, *Not the Impossible Faith*, pp. 86-87, 100-105. For many other examples of resurrected gods and heroes in pagan tradition see Carrier, *Not the Impossible Faith*, pp. 85-90. Dionysus (aka Bacchus) was likewise killed (torn apart) and resurrected ('born again' from a piece of his corpse), but as a baby: Justin Martyr, *Apology* 1.69; Plutarch, *On Isis and Osiris* (= *Moralia*) 35.364f; Diodorus Siculus, *Library of History* 5.75.4; see also Richard Seaford, 'Dionysiac Drama and the Dionysiac Mysteries', *Classical Quarterly* 31 (1981), pp. 252-75 (260-68); and M.L. West, *The Orphic Poems* (Oxford University Press, 1983), pp. 140-43, 161-63. There is no evidence that Mithras was a 'resurrected' savior (his 'passion' procuring salvation probably involved some other ordeal than his death; for discussion and scholarship on Mithraism see Chapter 4, Element 11; although some form of resurrection belief was involved in the cult: Tertullian, in *Prescription against Heretics* 40, mentions 'an image of a resurrection' being featured in it). It is difficult to reconstruct the belief system of early Attis cult. The evidence is either scattered or late; and from what we do have, it seems his ordeal might have been the periodic return to life of an eternally preserved corpse, which would be an example of a variant of the same mytheme, but one too far removed from the norm to make an ideal example: see Giulia Sfameni Gasparro, *Soteriology and Mystic Aspects in the Cult of Cybele and Attis* (Leiden: E.J. Brill, 1985), pp. 26-63; and Maria Grazia Lancellotti, *Attis, between Myth and History: King, Priest, and God* (Leiden: Brill, 2002), pp. 142-64.

40. *Pyramid Texts* 1684a-1685a and 1700 (= Utterance 606; cf. also Utterance 670). Translation (here and following) from Samuel Mercer, *The Pyramid Texts* (London: Longmans, Green, 1952).

41. *Pyramid Texts* 1363a-b (= Utterance 553).

> Osiris, collect thy bones; arrange thy limbs; shake off thy dust; untie thy bandages; the tomb is open for thee; the double doors of the coffin are undone for thee; the double doors of heaven are open for thee . . . thy soul is in thy body. . .raise thyself up![42]

It is absurd to insist there is no parallel in concept here to what would later be claimed for Jesus. Jesus is clearly very much like Osiris: both die and both get raised in improved bodies and both end up living as lords in heaven (not on earth).

As surveyed for Element 14, Plutarch is explicit about the cosmic version of the Osiris myth: he says Osiris *actually* incarnates and *actually* dies (albeit in outer space; but he dies, too, as Plutarch admits, also in the myth that places his death on earth at a single time in history) and is *actually* restored to life in a new supernatural body (just as Jesus was, as Paul thoroughly explains in 1 Cor. 15).[43] Plutarch has this event repeated only annually (as was also likely the case for Ishtar and Tammuz), but that's not a relevant difference, since syncretism with Jewish apocalypticism fully explains the replacement of a cyclical with a one-time resurrection (in fact the peculiarly Jewish logic of that modification is fully explained in Hebrews 9; see Element 43, and Chapter 11, §5). Similarly, the resurrections of Romulus and Zalmoxis were and remained singular events in history (and likewise, in public myth, that of Dionysus), demonstrating the flexibility of the mytheme in just this respect. I already discussed the example of Romulus in Chapter 4 (§1).

Speaking of the entire genre of incarnated dying-and-rising gods, Plutarch writes:

> Now we hear the theologians affirming and reciting, sometimes in verse and sometimes in prose, that God is deathless and eternal in his nature, but due to some predestined design and reason, he undergoes transformations of his person, and at one time enkindles his nature into fire and makes it entirely like everything else, and at another time he undergoes all sorts of changes in his forms and his passions and powers, even as the universe does today, but he is still called by the best known of his names. The more enlightened, however, concealing from the masses this transformation into fire, call him Apollo because of his solitary state, and

42. *Pyramid Texts* 207b-209a and 2010b-2011a (= Utterance 676).

43. Plutarch uses cognates of *anabiōsis* ('return to life') and *paliggenesis* ('born again') in *On Isis and Osiris* (= *Moralia*) 35.364f, which are undeniably clear in their meaning (other tales as well, Plutarch says, agree with 'what is said of the dismemberments, returns to life and rebirths of Osiris'). On Paul's view of the resurrection of Jesus, as being in a different body than was buried, see Carrier, 'Spiritual Body', in *Empty Tomb* (ed. Price and Lowder), pp. 105-55 (see in particular 1 Cor. 15.35-38 in conjunction with 2 Cor. 5.1-4).

> Phoebus because of his purity and stainlessness. And as for his turning into winds and water, earth and stars, and into the generations of plants and animals, and his adoption of such guises, they speak in a deceptive way of what he suffers in his transformation as a tearing apart, as it were, and a dismemberment. . . . They give him the names of Dionysus, Zagreus, Nyctelius, and Isodaetes, and they narrate deaths and vanishings, followed by returns to life and resurrections—riddles and myths quite in keeping with his transformations.[44]

Thus Plutarch attests to there being many historical narratives of pagan gods becoming incarnate and dying, their corpses vanishing, and rising from the dead, which are meant to allegorize what is really going on, which (as he implies here and explains elsewhere) is more cosmic in nature (see Element 14). But the myths were still there, and everywhere known.[45] The public ubiquity of dying-and-rising god myths, always the divine sons or daughters of a supreme god, and often being worshiped as personal saviors, is therefore beyond dispute, and could not have failed to play a major role in the origins of Christianity—otherwise we must posit an extremely improbable coincidence.

Element 32: By whatever route, popular philosophy (especially Cynicism, and to some extent Stoicism and Platonism and perhaps Aristotelianism) influenced Christian teachings.[46]

44. Plutarch, *On the E at Delphi* (= *Moralia*) 9.388f-389a.

45. The component of vanishing corpses as a mytho-type for translation to heaven is demonstrated to have been a commonplace in pagan literature of the time in Richard C. Miller, 'Mark's Empty Tomb and Other Translation Fables in Classical Antiquity', *Journal of Biblical Literature* 129 (2010), pp. 759-76. He shows this theme was so distinctive of pagan tradition (as opposed to Jewish literature) that it is unlikely to have come from anywhere else. That translation to heaven was almost *always* understood by pagans to be bodily (typically by the assumption of a new, indestructible, divine body) see Carrier, 'Spiritual Body', in *Empty Tomb* (ed. Price and Lowder), pp. 110-13, 137-39, 212 nn. 169-70, particularly in regard to Philo, who often uses words such as 'incorporeal' to refer to what he actually means are physical bodies of astral material.

46. Popular philosophy's influence on Paul: Stephen Finlan, *The Apostle Paul and the Pauline Tradition* (Collegeville, MN: Liturgical Press, 2008), pp. 26-28; and Troels Engberg-Pedersen, *Cosmology and Self in the Apostle Paul: The Material Spirit* (Oxford: Oxford University Press, 2010), along with the debate between Engberg-Pedersen, John Levison and John Barclay in the *Journal for the Study of the New Testament* 33 (2011), pp. 406-43, which collectively only confirms the influence of pagan philosophies, debating only to what extent Paul modified their ideas by combining them with Jewish ones (to create something new and different, the very definition of syncretism).

The influence of Cynicism has been particularly argued and debated in recent scholarship.[47] But most of this debate talks past the point. It is not necessary to suppose that Q (discussed in Chapter 7, §4, and Chapter 10, §6) or any of the sayings of Jesus *directly* emulate Cynic sources (although that is a hypothesis deserving consideration). Rather, there could have also been influence from Cynics and Cynic philosophy on the Jewish sects that later influenced or grew into Christianity (possibly even just orally through itinerant Cynic preachers, but still also possibly by written sources). And it is this influence that cannot reasonably be denied. Even apart from whether or not such concepts and teachings originated with a historical Jesus, there are undeniably Cynic elements in the Gospels. These could be simple borrowings from Cynic teachings circulating everywhere, by adopting those that were attractive and merging them with Jewish moral values similarly selected from those commonly available, to produce a more ideal hybrid. Much of this may already have preceded Christianity, through other Jewish sects, and some of it may have come together as the Christian movement formed, and some possibly introduced after.

By the nature of syncretism, again, the differences (the Cynic ideals that were 'not' adopted, or were modified, or even rejected and replaced with contrary Jewish ideals) do not argue *against* adoptions and adaptations. Just as their many differences from other Jewish sects did not mean the Christians were not influenced by Judaism, so also their differences with the Cynics did not mean they were not influenced by Cynics. As in religion,

47. Francis Gerald Downing, *Cynics and Christian Origins* (Edinburgh: T. & T. Clark, 1992); and Francis Gerald Downing, *Cynics, Paul and the Pauline Churches* (London: Routledge, 1998); and L.E. Vaage, 'Jewish Scripture, Q and the Historical Jesus: A Cynic Way with the Word?', in *The Sayings Source Q and the Historical Jesus* (ed. A. Lindemann; Leuven: University Press, 2001), pp. 479-95; all in light of, e.g., Strauss, *Four Portraits, One Jesus*, pp. 366-68; and William Arnal, *The Symbolic Jesus: Historical Scholarship, Judaism and the Construction of Contemporary Identity* (London: Equinox, 2005), pp. 17-25 (who makes the quite correct point that being influenced by Cynicism does not make someone a Cynic, much less non-Jewish, and therefore most criticisms of the Cynic-influence hypothesis are based on fallacious black-and-white thinking that has no place in serious scholarship); see also William Arnal, *Jesus and the Village Scribes: Galilean Conflicts and the Setting of Q* (Minneapolis, MN: Fortress Press, 2001), pp. 52-59 (whose criticism is not against there having been Cynic *influence*, but against certain implausible theories that have been built on this premise). On Cynicism in general: William Desmond, *Cynics* (Berkeley, CA: University of California Press, 2008); and William Desmond, *The Greek Praise of Poverty: Origins of Ancient Cynicism* (Notre Dame, IN: University of Notre Dame Press, 2006). On what 'Cynic influence' looked like in other movements, useful for finding and understanding the same influence within Christianity and Judaism: James Francis, *Subversive Virtue: Asceticism and Authority in the Second-Century Pagan World* (University Park, PA: Pennsylvania State University Press, 1995).

so in philosophy: eclecticism, the combining and melding of philosophies and the picking and choosing of ideas and ideals to produce unique combinations more or less favoring yet still differing from one sect or other, was the norm (Elements 2, 11 and 30). The first-century Stoic philosopher Musonius Rufus, for example, shows clear signs of having been influenced by Cynicism, and in result taught things very similar to Jesus, concerning, for example, charity, pacifism, forgiveness and brotherly love. And if that can be so for him, it can be so for Jesus, or anyone in the Christian tradition after him, or the Jewish tradition before him.[48] And so, too, any other popular philosophy of the age.

Element 33: In addition to its pagan influences, Christianity was also (obviously) influenced by several Jewish sects (see, in general, Elements 1-5), and can be understood only in this context, too. This means the role must be considered not just of the OT and many other Jewish scriptures then revered (see Elements 6-9), but of specific Jewish sects and their distinctive ideologies and innovations, many of which we do not in fact know much or anything about (such as the so-called Galilean sect, whose particular beliefs, apart from being somehow opposed to the Pharisees, are otherwise unknown).[49]

Christianity is a syncretism of pagan and Jewish salvation ideology, and as such differs from each precisely in what it borrows from the other. Therefore both must be understood, or at least be 'on our theoretical radar'. Even considering what is known, influences have been detected from the Pharisees (especially the liberal branch associated with the pre-Christian R. Hillel), the Essenes (and/or the sect[s] represented at Qumran), and certainly the Baptists—the pre-Christian Jewish sect led (if not founded) by John the Baptist around the assumed time of Christianity's birth—and possibly the Therapeutae (or whatever sectarian influence they and Christian-

48. For translations of the extant lectures of Rufus see Cora Lutz, *Musonius Rufus: The Roman Socrates* (New Haven, CT: Yale University Press, 1947); and Cynthia Ann Kent King, *Musonius Rufus: Lectures and Sayings* (Charleston, SC: Createspace, 2011). For some of the similarities (and differences) between Rufus and Jesus see Richard Carrier, 'On Musonius Rufus: A Brief Essay', at *The Secular Web* (1999), http://www.infidels.org/library/modern/richard_carrier/musonius.html. His teachings on charity, pacifism, forgiveness, and brotherly love are surveyed in *Discourses* 10, 14 and 19, and exemplified in stories told about him by others (collected in Lutz).

49. On this general problem of ignorance, see Carrier, *Proving History*, pp. 129-34. For sources on the Galilean sect: Carrier, 'Spiritual Body', in *Empty Tomb* (ed. Price and Lowder), pp. 109, 200-201 n. 24.

ity share in common), or even the Samaritans.[50] The more these influences are examined, the less original Christianity appears.

50. Connections with the Pharisees: Harvey Falk, *Jesus the Pharisee* (New York: Paulist Press, 1985); Hyam Maccoby, *Jesus the Pharisee* (London: SCM Press, 2003). Connections with the Essenes and/or Qumran sect (which are far too numerous to be coincidental): James Charlesworth (ed.), *Jesus and the Dead Sea Scrolls* (New York: Doubleday, 1992); Joseph Fitzmyer, *The Dead Sea Scrolls and Christian Origins* (Grand Rapids, MI: William B. Eerdmans, 2000); C.D. Elledge, *The Bible and the Dead Sea Scrolls* (Atlanta, GA: Society of Biblical Literature, 2005); James Charlesworth (ed.), *The Bible and the Dead Sea Scrolls*, Vol. III [= *The Scrolls and Christian Origins*] (Waco, TX: Baylor University Press, 2006).

Note that the association of the Dead Sea Scrolls with a community at Qumran has been questioned (and with it the conclusion that they all derive from a single sect) but the scrolls appear coherent enough that they likely derive from the same sect even if stashed there by refugees and not by inhabitants of Qumran (on the ongoing controversy see wikipedia: http://en.wikipedia.org/wiki/Qumran). Likewise the similarities between the Qumran sect and what is independently known of the Essene sect have been questioned, but we know there were at least six and possibly nine different sects of Essenes (and therefore no such thing as a 'normative' Essene sect), and the similarities at Qumran are sufficient to adduce a high probability that the sect represented at Qumran was either Essene or heavily influenced by Essenes: on both points see sources and scholarship cited in Carrier, 'Spiritual Body', in *Empty Tomb* (ed. Price and Lowder), pp. 109, 200-201 nn. 23, 25, 27.

The Therapeutae sect also bore similarities to both Christians and Essenes: Carrier, 'Spiritual Body', pp. 109, 200 n. 22; with Joan Taylor, *Jewish Women Philosophers of First-Century Alexandria: Philo's 'Therapeutae' Reconsidered* (Oxford: Oxford University Press, 2003), esp. pp. 31-32. And as the Essenes were then regarded as a sect of the Samaritans (Carrier, 'Spiritual Body', pp. 200-201 nn. 23, 27, and 28), we might also find connections between Samaritanism and Christianity: see R.T. Anderson, 'Samaritan Literature', in *Dictionary of New Testament Background* (ed. Craig Evans and Stanley Porter; Downers Grove, IL: InterVarsity Press, 2000), pp. 1052-56; and in the same volume, H.G.M. Williamson and C.A. Evans, 'Samaritans', pp. 1056-61. On the Baptist cult (also known as the Hemerobaptists) see sources and scholarship cited in Carrier, 'Spiritual Body', pp. 108, 199 n. 18; and Joan Taylor, *The Immerser: John the Baptist within Second Temple Judaism* (Grand Rapids, MI: William B. Eerdmans, 1997); on this sect's possible connections with Christianity: Clare Rothschild, *Baptist Traditions and Q* (Tübingen: Mohr Siebeck, 2005); and Lars Hartman, *'Into the Name of the Lord Jesus': Baptism in the Early Church* (Edinburgh: T. & T. Clark, 1997), pp. 9-35. On possible links between Essenes, Zealots and Christianity: S.G.F. Brandon, *Jesus and the Zealots* (New York: Scribner, 1967); and now Reza Aslan, *Zealot: The Life and Times of Jesus of Nazareth* (New York: Random House, 2013).

On the myriad links claimed between Christianity and Judaism in general (and some sects in particular) see John Meier, *A Marginal Jew: Rethinking the Historical Jesus* (4 vols.; New York: Doubleday, 1991-2009); Geza Vermés, *Jesus the Jew* (London: Collins, 1973); Geza Vermés, *The Religion of Jesus the Jew* (Minneapolis, MN: Fortress Press, 1993), and Geza Vermés, *Jesus in his Jewish Context* (Minneapolis, MN: Fortress Press, 2003); Bruce Chilton, *Rabbi Jesus* (New York: Doubleday, 2000);

The beatitudes, for example, are barely more than a redaction of pre-Christian beatitude literature recovered from Qumran.[51] And the collection at Qumran by no means represents all the literature that would have been available to the first Christians. Indeed even what was there survives now only in scraps and fragments—in other words, we barely have a fraction *of what was at Qumran*. Think of all the new ideas, scriptures, concepts, interpretations, variants, genres and precedents we have discovered just in these fragments, and then realize what must be the number of other ideas, scriptures, concepts, interpretations, variants, genres and precedents there were in those times that we have *not* discovered (hence Element 9). This makes it impossible to argue that anything now thought peculiar to Christianity did *not* derive from some preexisting Jewish precedent (in one of the well-known sects, or one of the lesser-known), which has simply become lost in the scarce transmission of evidence from the past (hence Element 2).

It must also be considered that Jewish sectarianism was often not associated with formal institutions or control hierarchies and would therefore have been extremely fluid. For example, a sect of Essenes could adopt many of the teachings of the Pharisee Hillel and then go on to see itself as the genuine expression of the Baptists, and thereby look like all three sects. Which would make classification challenging, but ultimately unnecessary, since it really doesn't matter whether we identified it as an Essene sect or a Pharisee sect or a Baptist sect—no matter what we chose to call it, it would still be a hybrid of them all, and we would still need to attend to how it was influenced by each. As I've mentioned, this kind of eclecticism was a cultural fad of the time, characterizing philosophical schools as well as the sciences (Element 11); so it would be natural to see it anywhere experimentation and innovation were especially rampant, and this was certainly the case in first-century Judaism (Element 2).

E.P. Sanders, *Jesus and Judaism* (Philadelphia, PA: Fortress Press, 1985); Donald Hagner, *The Jewish Reclamation of Jesus: An Analysis and Critique of Modern Jewish Study of Jesus* (Grand Rapids, MI: Academie Books, 1984); and James Charlesworth (ed.), *Jesus' Jewishness: Exploring the Place of Jesus within Early Judaism* (New York: Crossroad, 1991).

51. See, e.g., the analysis of 4Q525 and others in Craig Evans, 'The Recently Published Dead Sea Scrolls and the Historical Jesus', in *Studying the Historical Jesus: Evaluations of the State of Current Research* (ed. Bruce Chilton and Craig Evans; Leiden: Brill, 1994), pp. 559-61; and in Craig Evans, 'Jesus and the Dead Sea Scrolls from Qumran Cave 4', in *Eschatology, Messianism, and the Dead Sea Scrolls* (ed. Craig Evans and Peter Flint; Grand Rapids, MI: William B. Eerdmans, 1997), pp. 91-100. For other examples see Peter Flint, 'Jesus and the Dead Sea Scrolls', in *Historical Jesus in Context* (ed. Levine, Allison and Crossan), pp. 110-31.

Element 34: Popular cosmology at the dawn of the Common Era in the Middle East held that the universe was geocentric and spherical and divided into many layers (see Chapter 3, §1), with the first layer of 'heaven' often called the 'firmament' (being the foundation holding up all the others) and consisting of all the air between the earth and the moon (or sometimes the same term only meant the topmost part of this: the sphere traveled by the moon). This expanse was known even then to extend hundreds of thousands of miles (see discussion in Chapter 4, §3).[52] Above that were several more levels of heaven, the number varying depending on the scheme adopted, but the most commonplace view was that there were seven in all, one for each major celestial body: the region from the moon to Mercury being the first, then on to Venus, the Sun, Mars, Jupiter, Saturn (not always in that order), and finally the sphere of the stars (astronomers tended to regard the stars as distant suns; theologians tended to favor the theory that the stars comprised a single layer of lights at the top of heaven).

This view was particularly popular with Jewish theologians, and readily accepted by the earliest Christians.[53] This model had already been read out of scripture even before the explosion of scientific discoveries that began in the classical period (the sixth and fifth centuries BCE) and took off in the Hellenistic (the fourth through second centuries BCE). As Genesis said, 'In the beginning God created the heavens and the earth', and 'the earth was without form and void, and darkness was upon the face of the deep, and the Spirit of God was moving over the face of the waters'; then God creates and separates light and darkness, producing the first evening and day, and then 'God said, "Let there be a firmament in the midst of the waters, and let it separate the waters above from the waters below"', and so it was done, 'and God called the firmament Heaven', and that was the second day. Then 'God said, "Let the waters under the heavens be gathered together into one place, and let the dry land appear." And it was so. God called the dry land Earth, and the waters that were gathered together he called Seas' (Gen. 1.1-10).

52. That the distance to the moon had to be in the hundreds of thousands of miles was argued (then famously) by Aristarchus and later proved by the (equally famous) astronomers Hipparchus and Posidonius over a century before the dawn of Christianity (as reported in, e.g., Cleomedes, *On the Heavens* 1.7; 2.1; and 2.3; and Pliny the Elder, *Natural History* 2.21.85). On this kind of knowledge being routine among the well-educated of the time, see my future books *Science Education in the Early Roman Empire* and *The Scientist in the Early Roman Empire*.

53. See James Tabor, *Things Unutterable: Paul's Ascent to Paradise in its Greco-Roman, Judaic, and Early Christian Contexts* (Lanham, MD: University Press of America, 1986), pp. 63-68, 116-21.

In this account God does not create *ex nihilo*. There were primordial waters, and a formless and empty earth.[54] God began creation by separating the primordial waters, which he did by forming a solid dome (in later cosmology, a sphere) called the 'firmament', *raqia* in Hebrew, or *stereōma* in Greek (a 'solid body', often the foundation or framework of a building).[55] In this account, the firmament is called heaven, but it's clear what is meant is the *floor* or *basement* of heaven, heaven itself being the 'waters above' the firmament. The rest is the world below, including the earth and its seas. In Gen. 1.20 birds are allowed to fly above the earth, but *kata to stereōma tou ouranou*, 'across the firmament of heaven'; so the 'firmament' was not just the roof of the first heaven but the whole sky holding up the heavens, the place where birds fly. The term could thus refer to the region of the air, or its ceiling, depending on the context.

At the time Genesis was written, it was thought all the stars and planets and sun and moon were located on the same level, and thus Genesis says God attached them all to the firmament (1.14-17), so there would be the atmosphere up to the firmament (the place of clouds and air), the firmament itself (with all its stars and sun and moon), then the heavens above (the place of the celestial waters), effectively a three-level system. But by the time Christianity began, astronomy had been well established and its basic findings more widely known, and thus it was known that the moon is on one level, the sun on another, the planets on yet other levels, and the stars beyond (as Paul was aware: 1 Cor. 15.41), which is what expanded the levels imagined for heaven to at least seven.

The structure of heaven is debated in the Talmud.[56] But the general opinion resolved there is that there are either two heavens (the firmament and the 'heaven of heavens' above it) or seven heavens, which were interpreted in different ways. In one scheme, the first heaven is just the sky (or the lower part thereof); the second is the firmament separating that sky from the other heavens and containing all the stellar objects (such as moon, sun, and stars); the third is where millstones grind heavenly grain into manna; the fourth contains 'the heavenly Jerusalem and the Temple and the Altar', where the archangel Michael ('the great Prince') pays cult to God; the fifth

54. Genesis 1.1 ('In the beginning God created the Heavens and the Earth') is a summary heading of what's about to be described, not the first action God took, as is clear from the fact that God does not name the Heavens until he separates it *out* of the primordial waters (in Gen. 1.2-8), and God does not name the Earth until he makes it appear (in Gen. 1.9-10) out of material already present (Gen. 1.2). See following note.

55. On the cosmology of Genesis and its cultural background see Edward Babinski, 'The Cosmology of the Bible', in *Christian Delusion* (ed. Loftus), pp. 109-47 (119-33 for the biblical account).

56. *b. Ḥagigah* 12b.

is where the angelic host resides; the sixth contains warehouses of hail and snow and rain; and the seventh is where reside the souls of the righteous dead and the souls of those yet to be born, as well as a magic water that resurrects the dead.

So says the Talmud. But the actual contents of each heaven could vary from account to account. *1 Enoch* and *2 Enoch* both incorporate a seven-level heaven in their accounts; as did the *Ascension of Isaiah* (as we saw in Chapter 3, §1), where again there are seven heavens, and the firmament is beneath them (holding them up), consisting of all the air above the earth and its ceiling (7.9-13; 10.27-31), and the distance between the earth and the top of this firmament is vast (7.28). Likewise among the Dead Sea Scrolls, the 'Songs of the Sabbath Sacrifice' (4Q400-407 and 11Q17) also describe seven ascending levels of heaven, with different temples and thrones and angels in each.[57] Similarly, the first-century *Testament of Levi* (the third book of the *Testaments of the Twelve Patriarchs*) gives a different account of the seven heavens and what's in them. Yet that's just another example of a great many narratives that can be found in early Christian and Jewish literature.

So this notion of seven heavens, with the heavenly firmament at the bottom separating the earth from the higher heavens, had certainly become a fundamental Christian doctrine.[58] It was clearly a component of Christian belief even from earliest times. Paul assumes Jesus will descend 'from heaven' (*ouranos*) and then snatch us up 'into the clouds' (*nephelai*) to meet him in the 'air' (*aēr*, meaning the terrestrial part of the atmosphere, i.e., the firmament); thus he distinguishes heavens above from air below (1 Thess. 4.16-17). And Paul mentions (without assuming anyone would challenge him or even think twice about it) that he knows a man (probably himself) who traveled up to 'the third heaven' (2 Cor. 12.2-4), where he says the garden of Eden was located (a common belief in Jewish cosmology of the time: Element 38).

Element 35: Popular cosmology of the time also held that the sub-heaven, the firmament, was a region of corruption and change and decay, while the heavens above were pure, incorruptible and changeless. This view was most widely popularized by Aristotle and then by philosophers after him who adopted it, though many did not, and it remained a debated topic in science well into the Roman era. Nevertheless, it was such a good fit for

57. See Daniel Stökl ben Ezra, *The Impact of Yom Kippur on Early Christianity: The Day of Atonement from Second Temple Judaism to the Fifth Century* (Tübingen: Mohr Siebeck, 2003), p. 85.

58. For example, Clement of Alexandria, *Miscellanies* 4.25 and 7.10 (§57.5); Origen, *On the First Principles* 2.11.6-7; Irenaeus, *Demonstration of the Apostolic Preaching* 9.

religious beliefs of the time that theologians clung to Aristotle's original scheme.[59]

This was especially popular among those who favored Platonism in their construction of the universe. For example, Plutarch confidently asserts that 'this terrestrial universe', or the *perigeios* ['the stuff around the earth'], 'and the moon along with it is irregular and variable and ever changing', whereas 'this is not true' of the rest of the universe (the regions above the moon).[60] The same view of things is affirmed by the famous pre-Christian author Cicero, Paul's predecessor, and by the Jewish theologian Philo, Paul's contemporary.[61] It is repeated or assumed in countless cases across pagan, Jewish and Christian literature of the period.

Paul clearly embraced this view himself, and assumed his Christian congregations did as well. For example, in 1 Cor. 15.40-50, Paul divides the world into the region of decay (the 'terrestrial' world, the *epigeia*, the 'earthly' places, meaning 'on or above the earth') and the region of indecay (the 'celestial' world, the *epourania*, the 'heavenly' places, meaning 'in the heavens'), which distinction is also reflected in 2 Cor. 5.1-5. This is the same division of worlds that Plato, Philo and Plutarch described. As Philo attests, this notion had already been assimilated in pre-Christian Jewish thought.[62]

Element 36: Because of this division between the perfect unchanging heavens and the corrupted sublunar world, most religious cosmologies required intercessory beings, who bridge the gap between those worlds, so God need not descend and mingle with corruption. This concept can already be seen in the cosmology of Plato.[63] It only became increasingly popular thereafter. Thus, Plutarch tells us that there are 'holy demons [*daimones*], guardians of men' which 'interpret and serve, being intermediary between gods and men, since they send up above the prayers and requests of men, and take back down to us revelations and gifts of blessings', and thus act as interme-

59. Aristotle, *On the Heavens* 1.2 (see also 1.3.270b) and *Meteorology* 1.2–1.3; etc. Plato had already voiced something like it before Aristotle turned it into a more intelligible theory (e.g. Plato, *Phaedrus* 246d-247d).

60. Plutarch, *On Isis and Osiris* 45.369c-d and 48.370f–49.371c. The same is assumed throughout his astrophysical treatise *On the Face That Appears in the Orb of the Moon*.

61. Cicero, *On the Republic* 6.17; Philo, *On the Life of Moses* 2.118-27; and Philo, *On the Creation of the World* 36.

62. Besides the evidence in elements to follow (36 through 39), see Margaret Barker, *The Great High Priest: The Temple Roots of Christian Liturgy* (New York: T. & T. Clark, 2003), pp. 207-10.

63. Plato, *Symposium* 202e-203a.

diaries, intercessory beings, between men and gods.[64] Plutarch also says, 'it is not the gods . . . but demons [*daimones*], the ministers of the gods, who are in charge of oracles' in temples, because the gods themselves are too lofty to descend and deal with men.[65]

This view had become fully assimilated by many sects in Judaism.[66] Thus, in the *Ascension of Isaiah* (see Chapter 3, §1), we also hear of mediator beings who had to travel up and down through the heavens to carry gifts and communications between men and God, even needing passwords to 'open' the gates from one heaven to the next. The very same concept was taught in Mithraism.[67] The Jewish theologian Philo provides the obvious explanation: God does not condescend to lower himself to the sublunar world, so he sends angels and intermediaries to help and communicate with mankind, and it is these beings who deliver revelations and commandments, and the most important of these intermediary beings was the 'divine Logos' (see Element 40; see also my discussion of the equivalence of angels and mediary gods in Chapter 4, §3; and in Element 11).[68]

Thus, as Origen says of Jacob's dream in Gen. 28.12, 'a divine vision was presented to the view of our prophet Jacob—a ladder stretching to heaven, and the angels of God ascending and descending upon it, and the Lord supported upon its top', which he says tells us there are indeed many heavens and beings that travel between God and man.[69] This is the same view reflected in Jn 1.51, 'And he said to him, "Truly, truly, I say to you, you shall see the heaven opened, and the angels of God ascending and descending upon the Son of man"'. The same notion is represented again in the fact that it is the Holy Spirit that descends at Jesus' baptism (Mk 1.10), while God does not deign to descend himself, but only shouts from his station above (Mk 1.11). Jesus was clearly regarded as one of those beings. Romans 8.34; 1 Jn 2.1; and Heb. 7.25 all establish that Jesus' role was to advocate on our behalf in the presence of God, one of the common roles of an intermediary deity; in 1 Thess. 4.16 Jesus (not God himself) 'descends' from heaven to collect us; in Heb. 4.14 (with 8.1-5 and 9.11-24) we're told Jesus 'passed

64. Plutarch, *On Isis and Osiris* 25.360d-27.361e (especially 25.360d-e and 26.361b-c)

65. Plutarch, *On the Obsolescence of Oracles* 16.418e.

66. See Jonathan Knight, *Disciples of the Beloved One: The Christology, Social Setting and Theological Context of the Ascension of Isaiah* (Sheffield: Sheffield Academic Press, 1996), pp. 91-127.

67. See Marvin Meyer, 'The Mithras Liturgy', in *The Historical Jesus in Context* (ed. Amy-Jill Levine, Dale Allison Jr and John Dominic Crossan; Princeton, NJ: Princeton University Press, 2006), pp. 184-85.

68. Philo, *On Dreams* 1.68-71. This is also the consistent thesis of Philo's treatise *On the Giants*.

69. Origen, *Against Celsus* 6.21.

through the heavens' for us, descending to effect his death and ascending to accomplish its effects, which is also affirmed in Eph. 4.8-10. For similar reasons Mithras was called the 'Mediator' (*mesitēs*).[70] Accordingly, Jesus was also called the 'Mediator' (*mesitēs*).[71]

Irenaeus further explains Jesus' role as a mediator deity:

> The baptism of our resurrection proceeds through these three points: God the Father, bestowing on us resurrection through His Son, by the Holy Spirit. For as many as carry the Spirit of God are led to the Logos, that is to the Son; and the Son then brings them to the Father; and the Father then causes them to possess incorruption. Without the Spirit it is not possible to behold the Logos of God, nor without the Son can any draw near to the Father—for the knowledge of the Father is the Son, and the knowledge of the Son of God is through the Holy Spirit; and, according to the good pleasure of the Father, the Son ministers and dispenses the Spirit to whomsoever the Father wills and in whatever way He wills.[72]

This was not out of line with Jewish theology of the time, which had many similar notions of mediator beings negotiating between earth and heaven and God and man.[73] In the *Ascension of Isaiah*, for example, a mediator being (an angel) must descend to carry Isaiah through the many heavens and back again, and another mediator being, Jesus, must descend and reascend to accomplish his tasks on God's behalf.

As Paul regarded Jesus to have been a preexistent being who humbled himself, died and then was exalted 'very high' (Phil. 2.6-8), he clearly understood Jesus in the same sense as the intermediary beings common throughout Jewish and pagan theology. It was *through* Jesus that God accomplished all things, even creation itself (1 Cor. 8.6), and now our present salvation (see again Element 10). Jesus is thus the intermediary agent of God's will from above. And this was a common concept in both pagan and Jewish religious thought.

70. Plutarch, *On Isis and Osiris* 46.369e.

71. 1 Timothy 2.5 ('there is one God, and one Mediator between God and men, himself man, Christ Jesus'); Heb. 8.6 ('But now has [Christ] obtained a more excellent ministry, given that he is also the Mediator of a better covenant, which hath been enacted upon better promises'); 9.15 (Christ 'is the Mediator of a new covenant'); 12.24 ('and to Jesus the Mediator of a new covenant'). The 'Mediator' mentioned in Gal. 3.19-20 might also mean Jesus (if the unspoken assumption, or perhaps secret teaching being hinted at, is that Jesus was secretly the Lord who communicated the first law to Moses), but in any event that passage entails belief in mediator beings generally.

72. Irenaeus, *Demonstration of the Apostolic Preaching* 7.

73. Alex Jassen, *Mediating the Divine: Prophecy and Revelation in the Dead Sea Scrolls and Second Temple Judaism* (Boston: Brill, 2007); and Loren Stuckenbruck, *Angel Veneration and Christology* (Tübingen: J.C.B. Mohr, 1995).

Element 37: The lowest heaven, the firmament, the region of corruption and change, was popularly thought to be teeming with invisible spirits (*pneumata* or *psychai*) and demons (*daimones* or *daimonia*), throughout the whole space, who control the elements and powers of the universe there, meddle in the affairs of man, and do battle with one another. In pagan conception some of these demons were evil and some were good, and the good demons were often intermediary deities (per the previous element). In Jewish conception all the demons were evil, defying the will of God; and they did the bidding of fallen angels who also set up residence in the firmament, who were once intermediary deities serving God but who were cast down and took up residence in the lower realm. And the leader of these fallen angels was Satan, also known by many other names (e.g. the Devil, Belial, Beelzebul, Lucifer, Sammael, or just the Adversary, the literal meaning of the word Satan).

Satan had once been God's servant but was often at odds with him (e.g. Job 1.6–2.7; Zech. 3.1-2; 1 Chron. 21.1). Then in the intertestamental literature, under influence from Zoroastrianism, which also had an Adversary, who represented evil and darkness and waged war against the God of good and light, Jewish theology began to convert their Adversary into the same role. Stories were then developed of a time when Satan rebelled and was cast down from heaven by God, trapped in the lower realm, where he then set up dominion. Many of these stories stemmed from associating the Serpent with Satan and then interpreting the Genesis story of the Serpent's fall (Gen. 3.1-19) as the story of Satan's fall. For example, Wis. 2.24 says, 'it was by the envy of the Devil that death came into the world', a reference to the Genesis tale (in which it is by the wiles of the 'Serpent' that death comes into the world). Christians adopted this view (Heb. 2.14). This led to 'reinterpreting' Satan's role in stories such as that of Job, which in cosmic history occurred *after* Satan's fall.[74]

Many angels were cast down along with Satan, who then took sexual liberties with the first human women (the progeny of Adam and Eve), and one of the products of these unions were the demons (malevolent spirits), a notion arising from the interpretation of a curious story told in Gen. 6.1-8. These demons and fallen angels then brought abundant evil into the world, requiring God to drown everyone in the great flood. A version of this story is told in *1 Enoch* and *2 Enoch*, for example, and another in the book of *Jubilees*, and different versions appear in various other places (e.g. it is assumed in Philo's treatise *On the Giants* that the angels mating with human women in the Genesis tale are demonic beings, and we likewise hear of the same in Irenaeus, *Demonstration of the Apostolic Preaching* 18). But

74. See, e.g., Michael Stone, 'The Fall of Satan and Adam's Penance: Three Notes on the "Books of Adam and Eve"', *Journal of Theological Studies* 44 (April 1993), pp. 143-56.

the flood only destroyed all flesh, not the demons or fallen angels. Thus, the firmament still came to be dominated by countless demons, invisible malevolent spirits, who were ruled in turn by the fallen angels, who had set up their own thrones, dominions and principalities in the firmament in mockery of the heavenly thrones, dominions and principalities occupied by obedient angels appointed by God (as, e.g., those arrayed in the fourth heaven according to the *Testament of Levi*). And these 'demonic' angels were ruled in turn by Satan, the 'prince [*archōn*] of demons' (Mk 3.22; Mt. 12.24; and Lk. 11.15).[75]

As we hear in the books of Enoch:

> One from the order of the archangels deviated, together with the division that was under his authority. He thought up the impossible idea that he might place his throne higher than the clouds which are above the earth, and that he might become equal to my power. And I hurled him out from the height, together with his angels. And he was flying around in the air, ceaselessly, above the abyss.

And so, likewise, the division of angels under his command who rebelled with him (*2 Enoch* 29.4-5).[76]

This demonological view of the universe was fundamental to Christianity's understanding of why the world needed Christ's sacrifice and how that event functions soteriologically. Everything that was wrong with the world was due to these demonic beings and their influence and power in the

75. Evidence of this pre-Christian Jewish demonology is surveyed extensively in Dale Basil Martin, 'When Did Angels Become Demons?', *Journal of Biblical Literature* 129 (2010), pp. 657-77; Martin may be a little over-fastidious in his treatment of the vocabulary (I believe the language and concepts were more fluid than he assumes), but that won't matter for our purposes, since in English we can define 'demon' to mean any of these dark powers without distinction (see Chapter 4, §3), unless greater precision is, for whatever reason, both possible and necessary. At any rate, that this demonology of fallen angels and their progeny was a doctrine prevalent in the Dead Sea Scrolls is demonstrated in J.A. Sanders, 'Dissenting Deities and Philippians 2.1-11', *Journal of Biblical Literature* 88 (September 1969), pp. 279-90. For additional evidence and discussion of this intertestamental development see Archie Wright, *The Origin of Evil Spirits: The Reception of Genesis 6:1-4 in Early Jewish Literature* (Tübingen: Mohr Siebeck, 2nd edn, 2013), and George Nickelsburg, 'The Experience of Demons (and Angels) in 1 Enoch, Jubilees, and the Book of Tobit', *PSCO Minutes* [Philadelphia Seminar on Christian Origins] (March 10, 1988), http://ccat.sas.upenn.edu/psco/year25/8803a.shtml.

76. This is an example of reading Satan's fall out of Isa. 14.12-15, which speaks of 'Lucifer' trying to set up his abode in heaven and being cast down by God. This is probably the verse being referenced in Lk. 10.18 (implying Jesus was present when that happened). Tertullian, *Against Marcion* 2.10, also read the vision regarding the king of Tyre in Ezek. 28.11-19 as being in fact about Satan and his fall from the Garden. See also Origen, *On the First Principles* 1.5.5 and *Against Celsus* 6.44.

sublunar realm, separating man from God (particularly by infecting and corrupting the Jewish and pagan elite, among whom were the very priests charged with mediating between man and God).[77] So these forces had to be magically defeated, and God had to be reconnected with men directly through a new backchannel that bypassed all demonic and angelic power and influence.

These were not novel ideas. The pagan world was awash with similar thinking. It was commonly thought that 'the whole air [*aēr*] is full of [invisible] souls which are called demons [*daimones*] and [some of these are] heroes', that is demigods, and these are the beings that send men dreams and revelations (i.e., intermediary beings: see Element 36).[78] Thus, for example, Plutarch tells us that Isis and Osiris were originally 'great demons' [*daimones*], which he explains are neither gods nor men but something in between, being divine *but also incarnate*, which come in varying degrees of good and evil. As a result, 'there are great and strong beings in the atmosphere' [the *periechōn*, 'the surrounding (air)'] that are evil and delight in blasphemies and other perversions of religion and are the cause of all manner of bad things that happen from the forces of nature, but there are also 'holy demons, guardians of men' which serve men and gods as intermediaries.[79] And these beings, though usually immortal, are capable of suffering and dying (because of their dual nature).[80] Accordingly, for their heroic service (enduring suffering and trials), Plutarch says, 'Isis and Osiris were transformed through their virtue from "good demons" into "gods", just as later Hercules and Dionysus were', and now they have supreme power over all domains, above and below. But to renew and maintain his control over the universe, periodically Osiris descends into the firmament, where he acquires a body that is then killed (in a struggle with the demons there), and with the assistance of Isis he is resurrected and reascends to heaven in his immortal divine body (see again Elements 11 and 31).[81]

In the popular cosmology of the educated, which was more informed by the sciences of the time, the realm of the dead was also transferred from an 'underworld' (which made less sense now that it was known that the earth is a sphere) to the 'firmament'. Plutarch, for example, explains that 'Hades' is actually the region between the earth and the moon, which

77. See my analysis in Carrier, *Not the Impossible Faith*, pp. 148-54.

78. Diogenes Laertius, *Lives of Eminent Philosophers* 8.32 (8.30 for the invisibility of these souls and of the *aithēr*, 'ether', above the firmament).

79. Plutarch, *On Isis and Osiris* 25.360d–27.361e (especially 25.360d-e and 26.361b-c). On some demons being good and others evil, see also Plutarch, *On the Obsolescence of Oracles* 16.418e and 17.419a.

80. Plutarch, *On the Obsolescence of Oracles* 17.419b-e and 19.420a-b.

81. Plutarch, *On Isis and Osiris* 27.361e and 30.362e.

is filled with all manner of souls and spirits, including the souls of the dead, which ascend as high as their virtue allows—sins being imagined as weighing souls down (as in Egyptian mythology, discussed in Element 11); while virtuous souls, accordingly, were so light that they float all the way to the top; some even live on the moon (like a cosmic Isle of the Blessed).[82] The heavy souls, meanwhile, weighed down by their sins, become (in this scheme) evil demons.[83] This is why the sublunar realm was peopled with demons. Evil beings could not even ascend as high as the moon, much less to realms above.[84]

Jewish demonology was structured similarly, but was more faithful to the original Zoroastrian picture of a cosmos at war between sons of light and sons of darkness, with a supreme evil deity (Satan) in charge of the latter. As we saw in chapter 3 (§1), the *Ascension of Isaiah* 7.9-10 says Isaiah was carried up by an angel and together they 'ascended to the firmament' where they saw Satan and his hosts 'and a great struggle was taking place there, and the angels of Satan were envious of one another'. And likewise 10.29-31 says, 'the firmament' is 'where the prince of this world dwells' along with countless demons, which he calls 'the angels of the air', which all 'struggle with one another in envy . . . plundering and doing violence to one another'.

Another version of this pre-Christian Jewish demonology is articulated by Philo:

> Those beings, whom other philosophers call demons, Moses usually calls angels. And they are souls hovering in the air. And let no one suppose that what is here stated is a fable, for it is necessarily true that the universe must be filled with living things in all its parts, since every one of its primary and elementary portions contains its appropriate animals and such as are consistent with its nature—the earth containing terrestrial animals, the sea and the rivers containing aquatic animals, and the fire such as are born in the fire (but it is said, that such as these last are found chiefly in Macedonia), and then also the heaven containing the stars: for

82. Plutarch, *On the Face That Appears in the Orb of the Moon* 27.942f and 27.943c. For further evidence of the widespread nature of this view and its origins see Plutarch, *Moralia, Volume XII* (trans. Harold Cherniss and William Helmbold; Loeb Classical Library; Cambridge, MA: Harvard University Press, 1957), pp. 195-96 (note *d*) and 201 (note *c*).

83. Plutarch, *On the Face That Appears in the Orb of the Moon* 29.944a–30.944e; see also *Moralia, Volume XII* (1957), pp. 211 (note *f*) and 212 (note *b*).

84. On Plutarch's demonology and its ultimate origins in Zoroastrian demonology (which was the same source from which Jewish demonology developed) see J. Gwyn Griffiths, *Plutarch's De Iside et Osiride* (Cardiff: University of Wales Press, 1970), pp. 18-33, 56, 383-87 (Griffiths traces it to the syncretism of Xenocrates, a pupil of Plato and Aristotle and eventual head of Plato's Academy).

> there are entire souls pervading the universe, being unadulterated and divine.... It is therefore necessary that the air also should be full of living beings. And these beings are invisible to us, inasmuch as the air itself is not visible to mortal sight. But it does not follow, because our sight is incapable of perceiving the forms of souls, that for that reason there are no souls in the air. But it follows of necessity that they must be perceived by the mind, in order that like may be seen by like....
>
> Some of these souls have descended into bodies, and others have not thought it worthwhile to approach any one of the portions of the earth, and these, when hallowed and surrounded by the ministrations of the Father, the Creator has been accustomed to employ as hand-maidens and servants in the administration of mortal affairs. But those having descended into the [lower world] as into a river, at one time are carried away and swallowed up by the voracity of a most violent whirlpool, and at another time, striving with all their power to resist its impetuosity, they at first swim on the top of it, and afterwards fly back to the place from which they started....
>
> If, therefore, you consider that souls, and demons, and angels are things differing not only in name, but also in reality, you will then be able to discard that most heavy burden, superstition. But as men in general speak of good and evil demons, and in like manner of good and evil souls, so also do they speak of angels, looking upon some as worthy of a good appellation, and calling them ambassadors of man to God, and of God to man, and sacred and holy on account of this blameless and most excellent office. But others, again, you will not err if you look upon as unholy and unworthy of any address.[85]

Thus we have a scheme of intermediary beings (per Element 36) and invisible creatures of varying kinds, in which some have become corrupted by their interaction with the world below, becoming unholy angels, or demons, or evil spirits.

It is in the context of all the above that Christianity in general, and passages in the NT in particular, must be understood. As Paul says:

> The things which the Gentiles sacrifice, they sacrifice to demons [*daimonia*], and not to God. And I would rather you not have communion with demons. You cannot drink the cup of the Lord, and the cup of demons. You cannot partake of the table of the Lord, and of the table of demons (1 Cor. 10.20-21).

For Paul, these demons were real beings meddling in the world and corrupting and misleading mankind. Those called 'gods' and 'lords' and worshiped as such by the pagans were all in fact evil demons (1 Cor. 8.5). This notion was pervasive in early Christianity. For example, 'some shall fall away from the faith, giving heed to seducing spirits [*pneumata*] and the teachings of demons [*daimonia*]' (1 Tim. 4.1), and those who 'believe God

85. Philo, *On the Giants* 6-16.

is One do well; for the demons [*daimonia*] also believe, and shudder' (Jas 2.19). Thus we are told we must shun the 'wisdom that is not a wisdom that comes down from above, but is earthly, sensual, demonic' (Jas 3.15), where the term for 'demonic', *daimoniōdēs* ('of demons') is chosen precisely because it is assumed that demons reside in the realm of the earthly, and not in the realm 'above' it from where true wisdom descends.

In Rom. 8.38, we also hear that Christians are opposed by and must overcome 'angels' [*aggeloi*] and 'principalities' [*archai*] and 'powers' [*dunameis*], which does not mean temporal human powers (those threats he already enumerated in v. 35), not only because 'angels' clearly are no such thing, but also because human powers are not typically described in these terms. There was no such office in the Roman Empire as a 'principality' (*archē*), and the term was at that time rarely used in that way; and 'powers' for Paul typically meant supernatural powers, powers *over the universe*, not political power (e.g. 1 Cor. 12.28-29; 2 Cor. 2.12; Gal. 3.5). We also know these terms were widely used in Jewish apocrypha to refer to the demonic powers holding the sublunar world in thrall.[86] These terms were also used for God's authorities as well (e.g. Col. 1.16; Eph. 1.20-21). Thus, 'principalities' meant angels assigned certain domains by God, or fallen angels assigned certain domains by Satan (or having seized those domains, by one device or another; for the world of the fallen was not as orderly and obedi-

86. See G.H.C. MacGregor, 'Principalities and Powers: The Cosmic Background of Paul's Thought', *New Testament Studies* 1 (1954), pp. 17-28; Bo Reicke, 'The Law and This World according to Paul', *Journal of Biblical Literature* 70 (1951), pp. 259-76. Though this interpretation was opposed by Wesley Carr, *Angels and Principalities: The Background, Meaning, and Development of the Pauline Phrase* hai archai kai hai exousiai (New York: Cambridge University Press, 1981), he is pretty much alone, and could only reach his conclusions by engaging in specious argumentation that ignores the rest of Jewish and Christian literature and relies on assuming all passages arguing against him are conveniently 'interpolations'. Accordingly, his methods and analysis were thoroughly refuted by Walter Wink, *Naming the Powers: The Language of Power in the New Testament* (Philadelphia, PA: Fortress Press, 1984). The current view is best represented by Wink and by George H. van Kooten, *Cosmic Christology in Paul and the Pauline School: Colossians and Ephesians in the Context of Graeco-Roman Cosmology, with a New Synopsis of the Greek Texts* (Tübingen: Mohr Siebeck, 2003), pp. 95-103. See also Alan Segal, 'Ruler of This World: Attitudes about Mediator Figures and the Importance of Sociology for Self-Definition', in *Jewish and Christian Self-Definition*, Vol. II, *Aspects of Judaism in the Graeco-Roman Period* (ed. E.P. Sanders; Philadelphia, PA: Fortress Press, 1981), pp. 245-68, 403-13; and Alan Segal, *Two Powers in Heaven: Early Rabbinic Reports about Christianity and Gnosticism* (Leiden: Brill, 1977). Also of interest is Clinton Arnold, *Powers of Darkness: Principalities and Powers in Paul's Letters* (Downers Grove, IL: InterVarsity Press, 1992). Although Arnold and Wink are true believers (they think demons are real), their scholarship remains apt.

ent). Many other angels were then subordinate to those princes. 'Powers' then meant spirits with control over the forces of the universe, which could again mean holy spirits (or simply *the* Holy Spirit), which were the 'powers' by which Christians effected miracles (most commonly, power over demons, to expel them from their abodes), or unclean spirits, demons, who similarly could effect miracles, also having seized power over aspects of the sublunar world (or been assigned such power by fallen angelic princes).

As Plutarch explains (see Element 14), in the common demonological worldview, the 'elements' and powers of the universe were not identical to the demons (the 'divinities') named after them, but the demons were the cosmic beings *in control of* those elements and powers—unlike what the 'scientists' say, which (Plutarch explains) is that these personifications are mere allegorical fictions, and all that really exist are the mindless elements and forces of nature (a view too atheistic for Plutarch). Anyone who accepted a demonological theory (as Plutarch did) was by definition rejecting that scientific worldview. The Christians were most definitely demonologists. Thus, when Paul says Jesus must destroy 'every principality' [*archē*] and 'every authority' [*exousia*] and 'power' [*dunamis*], the most important of which is Death itself [*Thanatos*], he does not mean human government officials but the demonic powers that were in a state of rebellion against God, and thus were Christ's 'enemies' (1 Cor. 15.24-28).[87] This for the same reason as in Romans, but all the more so as Paul elsewhere says all human authorities are God's ministers, and thus *not* his enemies (Rom. 13.1-7), so he clearly cannot mean human authorities here (see Chapter 11, §8).

The only term used to describe these 'enemies' that Paul ever uses to refer to human authorities is the generic 'authority' [*exousia*]. Otherwise when he speaks of human leaders he uses *archōn*, 'principal', as in 'first in rank', not *archē*, 'principality', and he never speaks of them as 'powers'. In Rom. 13.1-7, for example, Paul is certainly speaking of human authorities, which he says Christians should always obey. The terms he uses here are *exousiai hyperechousai*, 'those holding higher authority', and *archontes*, 'principals' (or 'princes'), and he says none would have authority [*exousia*] if God had not put them there—in fact, he says, they should be regarded as the ministers of God, and so opposing 'the authorities' is tantamount to opposing God. But we know the same terms could also be used to refer to the demonic kingdom. It simply depended on context. Likewise, since angels could be assigned 'authority', just as human officials could (e.g. 1 Pet. 3.22), again which kind of 'authority' you meant depended on context.

87. So, e.g., Irenaeus, *Demonstration of the Apostolic Preaching* 85 and 96. A similar line-up appears in 1 Pet. 3.22, where Jesus is put in charge of a celestial array of 'angels [*aggeloi*], authorities [*exousiai*], and powers [*dunameis*]'.

The same follows for *archōn*, 'principal, prince, headman'. This is evident in Eph. 2.2, which was forged in Paul's name but clearly by someone of his sect, and relatively early in the development of the church. There we have the statement that before baptism each Christian 'once walked according to the fashion [*aiōn*] of this world [*kosmos houtos*], according to the prince [*archōn*] of the domain [*exousia*] of the air [*aēr*], the spirit [*pneuma*] who is now working in the sons of disobedience'. Here, just as 'authority' is clearly being used of a supernatural dominion and not a human office, so also the word *archōn* is used to refer to a celestial being, Satan. Thus it, too, could be used of nonhuman authorities without need of explanation. And here we also have a clear expression of common Judeo-Christian demonology: Satan rules over the firmament, the entire 'domain of the air', which was considered 'this world' (as opposed to the other, heavenly world above).

We should understand the same when Paul speaks of 'this world' as that which 'we ought not conform ourselves to' (Rom. 12.2), which is soon to 'pass away' (1 Cor. 7.31), and from which comes a 'wisdom' that is 'folly to God' (1 Cor. 3.19), and in which sinners live (1 Cor. 5.9-11). We can be certain of this, because Paul himself said that this part of the universe was under the dominion of Satan, whom he calls 'the god of this world', who, Paul says, is actively blinding mankind so they can't see the divine light radiating from Jesus (2 Cor. 4.4).[88] Paul frequently references Satan as their principal enemy, who presently ruled all flesh but whom God would one day destroy.[89] Satan likewise has his own angels, which he sends down to torment us (2 Cor. 12.7).

This was always how Christians understood Paul. As Origen explains, when Paul uses these terms in such contexts, he means demonic powers. For there are 'spirits of wickedness, or malignant spirits, or unclean demons' who have made themselves into 'principalities' and 'powers' and 'rulers of the darkness of the world'.[90] The *Acts of John* (v. 98) likewise says that among 'the devils and Satan' and their violent deeds plaguing us there are 'powers [*dunameis*], authorities [*exousiai*], principalities [*archai*]', and

88. Paul could also mean 'the god of this age', the word *aiōn* meaning 'era', but often indicating the temporal realm; but since Paul certainly does not mean Satan ruled over the heavens, he clearly is referring to the sublunar domain (which would be dissolved in the end); Ignatius, *Ephesians* 17 and 19; *Magnesians* 1; *Trallians* 4; and *Romans* 7 also call Satan 'the prince of this world' (combining the language of Ephesians and 2 Corinthians). The same term is used for Satan in Jn 12.31; 14.30; and 16.11.

89. Rom. 16.20; 1 Cor. 5.5; 7.5; 2 Cor. 2.11; 11.13-15; 1 Thess. 2.18. See also 2 Thess. 2.3-10; Eph. 4.27; 6.11; 1 Tim. 1.20; 3.6-7; 5.15; 2 Tim. 2.26; Jas 4.7; 1 Pet. 5.8; 1 Jn 3.10, 5.19; Jude 9; and of course this is the standard doctrine throughout the Gospels and Revelation.

90. Origen, *On the First Principles* 1.8.4.

'demons' [*daimones*] (presumably without special powers or dominion), as well as 'feats [*energeiai*], boasts [*apeilai*], and spirits [*thumoi*]', which terms probably all refer to different kinds of spirits (miracle-working spirits, boastful or threatening spirits—and angry spirits, the *thumos* being typically regarded as the seat of anger). And in the Christian expansion of the *Ascension of Isaiah* we hear again of 'the prince of this world, and of his angels, authorities and powers' (1.4) and that 'Beliar, the angel of lawlessness, is the ruler of this world' (2.4), and 'Beliar the great ruler, the king of this world, will descend, having ruled the world since it came into being; indeed, he will descend from his firmament in the likeness of a man' to kill and persecute (4.2), along with other 'princes and powers of that world' (10.15).[91]

Accordingly, we read in Eph. 6.11-12 that we need the 'armor of God' to resist the 'wiles of the Devil', because 'we wrestle *not* against flesh and blood, but against principalities [*archai*], against authorities [*exousiai*], against the rulers [*kosmokratores*] of the darkness of this [world], against spiritual wickedness in the heavenly places [*epourania*]'. Likewise, Eph. 3.10 says the success of the church will demonstrate the wisdom of God 'to the principalities [*archai*] and powers [*dunameis*] in the heavenly places'. Here, in both passages, these terms are certainly referring to demonic princes and authorities, not human ones. Another forgery in the name of Paul, but again from the same sect and period, says Christ has 'cast off the principalities [*archai*] and authorities [*exousiai*] and made a public example of them, freely triumphing over them' (Col. 2.15), again using this terminology for demonic agents.[92]

In Gal. 4.3-9, we also hear of 'elements of the cosmos' [*stoicheia tou kosmou*] enslaving people (before baptism freed them), and these 'cosmic elements' we're told are 'in their nature not gods', because they are 'poor

91. Note that (as I've abundantly shown) at this point in history Satan and his demons were thought to live in the sky (hence in outer space); the notion of either inhabiting (and ruling) a subterranean hell would not arise for many more centuries; that notion began originally as a doctrine about their ultimate fate *after* Jesus returns (e.g. Rev. 20), which later became conflated with a separate tradition that God's *own* angels (not demons) will carry out future punishments in a subterranean hell (e.g. *Apocalypse of Peter*).

92. The word *apekduomai*, 'take off from oneself', is frequently translated here as 'despoil, disarm' in modern Bibles, but that actually makes little sense. In normal use, that word would mean 'take off *for* oneself', which would have to mean he *took* the principalities and powers *for himself*, but this sentence is about the beings, not their offices, so that translation cannot be correct; it confuses what is actually being said here. This word *usually* refers to undressing oneself (e.g. Col. 3.9), and thus is surely meant here to say that Christ freed himself from their power (casting off their authority over him).

and weak', yet some people want to turn back and be their slaves again even after knowing the true god. It is generally agreed that Paul does not mean here mindless elements but elemental spirits, those who, as Plutarch explained, control and rule over the elements and whom philosophers mistakenly think are mere allegories for the elements, but as Plutarch insists, are actually the demons in control of those elements.[93] This is fairly clear from Paul's language, since one does not become a 'slave' of mindless natural elements or consider them 'gods', nor does one say they are 'not gods by nature' merely because they are poor and weak—rather than, say, because they are in fact mindless forces.

So likewise we can understand Col. 2.8-10, where we are warned not to be deceived or live according to the 'elements of the cosmos' [*stoicheia tou kosmou*] but to live instead 'according to Christ'. Again, the elemental spirits are here understood to be the beings opposed to Christ, who *deceive* us (and thereby deceived men into promoting 'philosophies' and 'traditions' that are not according to Christ), because Christ alone 'is the head of all principality [*archē*] and authority [*exousia*]'. Deception, after all, is the particular activity of Satan and his hosts (e.g. 2 Cor. 11.3, 14; Gal. 1.8-9), who tempt us thereby to sin (e.g. 1 Cor. 7.5; 2 Cor. 2.11). That Colossians associates subservience to the 'elements of the cosmos' (2.8, 20) with the 'worship of angels' and the receiving of visions (2.18) verifies the point.[94]

Learning all of this was once a component of the secret teaching given to Christians of varying ranks (Element 13).[95] It's unlikely that Paul came to be completely reinterpreted by all later Christians. We have seen enough evidence that Paul does in fact mean supernatural powers and princes when he speaks thereof, inhabiting and traversing the firmament, and all later Christian interpreters understood him to mean that. It was clearly a fundamental component of Christian teaching in all documents post-dating Paul. And from the preponderance of evidence here, we should conclude it was certainly a fundamental component of Christian teaching in Paul—and therefore in the original Christian church as a whole, as he clearly felt it required no defense or explanation in his correspondence.

93. See Reicke, 'The Law and This World according to Paul'. See *Testament of Solomon* 34 for a later example of demons referring to themselves as 'elements' (we would now say 'elementals').

94. See the analysis of Andrew Lincoln, 'The "Philosophy" Opposed in the Letter [to the Colossians]', in *The New Interpreter's Bible: New Testament Survey* (ed. Fred Craddock; Nashville, TN: Abingdon Press, 2005), pp. 242-47.

95. For example, Ignatius, *Trallians* 5; *Smyrnaeans* 6; and the Syriac *Ephesians* 3.9. And in Origen's introductory textbook for new initiates, although by his time much of the doctrine seems to have been lost (as he professes not to know certain things that were clearly known to Paul and his congregations): Origen, *On the First Principles* 1.5.2.

Element 38: (a) In this same popular cosmology, the heavens, including the firmament, were not empty expanses but filled with all manner of things, including palaces and gardens, and it was possible to be buried there. (b) In this worldview everything on earth was thought to be a mere imperfect copy of their truer forms in heaven, which were not abstract Platonic forms but actual physical objects in outer space.

This cosmological view is explicit in Hebrews:

> According to the law almost everything is cleansed by blood, and apart from the shedding of blood there is no forgiveness. So it was necessary that the copies of the things in the heavens should be cleansed with these [i.e., with Jewish blood rites]; but the heavenly things themselves with better sacrifices than these. For Christ entered not into a holy place made with hands built to look like the true one, but into heaven itself, now to appear before the face of God on our behalf (9.22-24).

Here we have multiple heavens (plural) in which reside the *true* versions of everything (including the temple itself), and of which the things on earth are only imperfect copies. The celestial temple is 'not made with hands' because it was made by God, just like our celestial bodies will be (2 Cor. 5.1). We see this already in the Dead Sea Scrolls, where the 'Songs of the Sabbath Sacrifice' (4Q400-407 and 11Q17) describe seven ascending levels of heaven, several of which have more perfect 'copies' of the temple and the holy of holies (the inner chamber of the temple), and in yet higher ones 'angels offer pure and perfect sacrifices'. There are even versions of earthly things in the firmament, as we learn in the *Ascension of Isaiah* 7.10, which says, 'as it is above, so is it also on the earth, for the likeness of that which is in the firmament is also on the earth'. Although *those* things would not be the perfect models, which resided only in the perfect heavens above, but half-corrupt imitations, in between the models above and their earthly copies below.[96]

Thus, Heb. 12.21-22 says that when Moses ascended the mountain to receive the commandments he beheld the true 'Mount Zion and the city of the living God, the *heavenly* Jerusalem' inhabited by 'innumerable angels in festal gathering' and 'the assembly of the firstborn who are enrolled in heaven' and 'the spirits of just men made perfect' (the *teleioi*, the same term used for higher ranking Christians: Element 10) and, of course, God. And God told Moses to make everything in the earthly temple according to the pattern of the true version he saw in heaven (Exod. 25.40). Thus Heb. 8.5 says the earthly priests 'serve a copy and a shadow of the heav-

96. For examples of other objects and structures in the heavens (roads, houses, pens, scrolls, chariots) see, again, Babinski, 'Cosmology', in *Christian Delusion* (ed. Loftus) along with Jaco Gericke, 'Can God Exist if Yahweh Doesn't?', in *End of Christianity* (ed. Loftus), pp. 131-54 (esp. pp. 144-49).

enly sanctuary, for when Moses was about to erect the tabernacle, he was instructed by God, saying, "See that you make everything according to the example that was shown to you on the mountain"'. It is therefore in this context that we must understand sayings such as 'whatever you bind on earth shall be bound in heaven, and whatever you loose on earth shall be loosed in heaven' (Mt. 16.19; again in 18.18). This is a reference to everything having its (superior) double in heaven.

We know Paul shared this view. In 2 Cor. 12.2-4, he says a man (possibly Paul himself) 'was taken as far up as the third heaven', where 'Paradise' (*paradeisos*) was located. The notion that Paradise (meaning the Garden of Eden) was located in the third heaven is also explained in the apocryphal *Revelation of Moses*, and likewise assumed in *2 Enoch,* and is a part of the same cosmological tradition.[97] As Irenaeus says, Paradise was 'a place better than this world, excelling in air, beauty, light, food, plants, fruit, water, and all other necessaries of life'.[98] In other words, the perfect versions of all these things, of which their counterparts in the earthly realm were but poor imitations. The OT describes only one singular 'Paradise' (the same word used by Paul, according to the Septuagint text of Gen. 2.8–3.24) and that was 'in Eden', and in that Paradise God specially made its own trees and plants and a river and angelic beings, all in its own soil, and also versions of every animal. Many later texts of the Bible use the same word to refer generically to gardens, but these would be examples of imperfect attempts to copy the *original* Garden.

This worldview is also described by Philo, who explains that the air extends from the earth to the moon, and the earth, air, and water all move, mix, and change below the moon, while above all that are the unchanging heavens (see again Element 35), where reside the true models and forms of all things, including the true animals, of which all things below the moon are just imperfect copies. He further explains that the elements below the moon are the perceptible ones, the rest are invisible to the senses, but are seen with the eye of the mind.[99] And these perfect versions in heaven are *themselves* copies of the even-more-perfect *ideas* of them in the mind of God. Because God made perfect invisible copies of everything in heaven first (including a perfect invisible earth, and a perfect invisible star of which all other stars are copies, and so on), which were themselves copies of their

97. *Revelation of Moses* 37.4-5; 40.1-2. This text is otherwise known as the Greek edition of the *Life of Adam and Eve*, an early-first-century Jewish document, possibly translating an even earlier account in Hebrew or Aramaic. See also *2 En.* 8.1–9.1 [redaction A and B] and 42.3 [redaction A].

98. Irenaeus, *Demonstration of the Apostolic Preaching* 11.

99. Philo, *On the Life of Moses* 2.118-27.

even-truer forms in the mind of God; *then* God made the material (and thus inferior) copies of all these things, the versions that we know and see.[100]

For example, Philo says, 'from the model of the cosmos, perceptible only by the intellect, the Creator made an incorporeal heaven, and an invisible earth, and the form of air and of empty space', and the latter 'he called the abyss, for empty space is very deep and yawning with immense width', and 'then he created the incorporeal substance of water and of air' and then from 'a model of the sun, perceptible only to the intellect' God then made 'a star above the heavens, the source of those stars which are perceptible by the external senses', a 'universal light', of which our sun is but a copy.[101]

The true copies that were first created can only be seen by the mind, in fact only a pure and reverent mind. Philo goes on to explain that the true heaven is incorporeal, but the visible heaven is corporeal and called the firmament. Thus the firmament itself is a copy of the heavens above it. A mind that is separated from the body can rise on wings into the 'air' (the region subject to chaos and change) and then to the 'higher' firmament, and then to the heavenly bodies (moon, sun and stars), then to the true incorporeal heavens above, where the *true* versions of all things can be seen; and of these heavens there are many levels, at the top of which is the Great King.[102] There were even two Adams, the perfect celestial Adam, and the copy of him, the Adam made of earth who fathered mankind (see Element 39). So 'the incorporeal world was already completed, having its seat in the divine Logos' (see Element 40), 'and the world perceptible by the external senses was made on the model of it'; and the first part of that 'was the heaven that is more correctly called "the firmament", because it is corporeal'.[103] The idea of all this goes at least as far back as Plato,[104] but by Philo's time it had become more sophisticated, with at least three levels of creation: the perfect ideas in God's mind, then perfect quasi-physical celestial forms of those ideas, then earthly copies thereof.

This meant there were things in heaven. The *Testament of Abraham*, for example, says Abraham was shown structures in heaven, including gates and roads and thrones and halls and tables and linens and books with ink and quill and so on, as well as an (apparently) resurrected Adam and Abel observing and judging the souls of the dead. And in fact the *Revelation of Moses* says Adam was buried in Paradise, literally up in outer space, in the

100. Philo, *On the Creation of the World* 29-31, 36, 70-71.
101. Philo, *On the Creation of the World* 29, 31.
102. Philo, *On the Creation of the World* 70-71.
103. Philo, *On the Creation of the World* 36.
104. Plato, *Phaedrus* 246d-247d.

third heaven, complete with celestial linen and oils.[105] Thus human corpses could be buried in the heavens. Because there was obviously soil up in Paradise—in fact, not only is all manner of celestial vegetation planted in it, but when Adam is buried in it, he is buried in the same place from which God took the clay of which Adam was made. In many other Jewish apocrypha there are accounts of all manner of solid structures in all other levels of heaven, too, so tombs and graves obviously can exist there as well. Thus, according to the *Revelation of Moses*, Adam is cast down from Paradise, residing on earth below for the remainder of his life; but in death his body is carried back up to the heavens for burial. Abel is likewise buried there, and later so is Eve, and many others among the righteous dead.[106] This also means the original Tree of Life is in outer space (being in the very Paradise which is located in the third heaven), just as the true Temple and Altar of God are in outer space.

Element 39: (a) In this cosmology there were also two Adams: one perfect celestial version, of which the earthly version (who fathered the human race) is just a copy. And (b) the first Christians appear to have connected their Jesus Christ to that original celestial Adam.

In Philo's scheme, the first Adam was an invisible perfect man, having no gender and being immortal and imperishable, and this is what explains there being two creation accounts in Genesis (Gen. 1-2.3 vs. Gen. 2.4-25): the first related to the creation of the true man, and the second related to the creation of his mortal copy.[107] Although Philo thinks a lot of the creation account is allegorical (for him there was no Paradise and no Serpent, for example),[108] it is clear other Jewish theologians disagreed with him (as we've seen ample evidence of: see Elements 37 and 28). And as we saw, even Philo clearly imagines a real cosmos with a real heavens with perfect versions of things, of which the things below are imperfect copies—and the things in the heavens can be seen only by higher, spiritual senses (the pure intellect), unlike ordinary 'material' things that are seen by our 'external' (material) senses.

In response to the question of why God put the 'material' Adam in Paradise but didn't do the same for the perfect heavenly Adam, Philo answers that 'some persons have said, when they imagined that Paradise

105. *Revelation of Moses* 32–41 (esp. 32.4, 37–40); see also Tabor, *Things Unutterable*, p. 116. Obviously the canonical NT book of Revelation likewise depicts heaven as full of places, structures and objects.

106. *Revelation of Moses* 21.6.

107. Philo, *On the Creation of the World* 134-36.

108. Philo, *On the Creation of the World* 153-65.

was a garden, that because the man who was created was endowed with senses, therefore he naturally and properly proceeded into a sensible place', whereas 'the other man, who is made after God's own image, being appreciable only by the intellect, and invisible, had all the *incorporeal* species for his share'; but Philo thinks rather that *all* this Paradise stuff is allegorical and not literally meant.[109] However, it's clear that Philo was dissenting from a view other Jews held, and the view of those others was that there were two Paradises, the material one and the heavenly one, or possibly more than two, many levels or 'emanations', from the perfect Paradise on high, to the more material Paradise in the third heaven, to the many gardens on earth, which are all copies of those.

Of the two Adams, Philo also says, 'there are two kinds of men, the one made according to the image of God, the other fashioned out of the earth', because 'the image of God is the mold for all other things, and every imitation aims at this, of which it is an imitation'.[110] And, therefore, 'the races of men are twofold: for one is the heavenly man, and the other the earthly man' and 'the heavenly man, as being born in the image of God, has no participation in any corruptible or earthlike essence', whereas 'the earthly man is made of loose material . . . a lump of clay'.[111]

This doctrine obviously predates Philo, and Philo has simply made his own modifications to it, because the same tradition was also shared by Paul and thus evidently influenced the earliest Christian theology.[112] Philo's language of 'the heavenly man' and 'the earthly man', 'the first man' and 'the second man', and the idea of there being two Adams, is paralleled in (but adapted differently by) Paul.[113] We see this, for example, in 1 Cor. 15.45-49 (to be read with 15.21-24). Philo says the heavenly man is imperishable and immortal and the earthly man is 'by nature' mortal and perishable, exactly in agreement with Paul. Both also call the earthly Adam the 'first man'. Paul then calls Jesus the 'last Adam', but describes him in terms identical to Philo's 'second' man (who in order of creation was really the first).[114] Notably, Philo's 'celestial' Adam can be seen only by the eye of the intellect, just as Origen says the body of the resurrected Jesus was invisible to the exter-

109. Philo, *Questions and Answers on Genesis* 1.8.

110. Philo, *Allegorical Interpretation* 2.4-5.

111. Philo, *Allegorical Interpretation* 1.31.

112. See Stephen Hultgren, 'The Origin of Paul's Doctrine of the Two Adams in 1 Corinthians 15.45-49', *Journal for the Study of the New Testament* 25 (2003), pp. 343-70 (note that even Hultgren misses some of the evidence I include here); and Stefan Nordgaard, 'Paul's Appropriation of Philo's Theory of "Two Men" in 1 Corinthians 15.45-49', *New Testament Studies* 57 (2011), pp. 348-65.

113. See Carrier, 'Spiritual Body', in *Empty Tomb* (ed. Price and Lowder), pp. 110-50.

114. Hultgren, 'The Origin of Paul's Doctrine', pp. 344-46, 350.

nal senses and could be seen only with spiritual vision.[115] Origen also says that this invisible resurrection body was the original 'mold' for the body of flesh that Jesus had previously worn, and thus his fleshly body was only an earthly copy of his true, original (and final) body. Paul describes similar notions in 2 Corinthians 5, where it appears our true bodies (of which our present bodies are copies) already await us in heaven.

We have already seen that Paul's Jesus was a preexistent celestial being (Element 10). And here we see that this idea of a preexistent heavenly man predates even Christianity. So when Paul describes Jesus as the 'man of heaven', he likely has in mind the same cosmic being. As Philo explains, the perfect celestial man created in Gen. 1.27 is the actual 'image' of God (and the earthly Adam is just a *copy* of that image), and this sounds exactly like Jesus, who was *also* the 'image' of God (of whom *the Christians themselves* are copies: Rom. 8.29; 1 Cor. 15.49; 2 Cor. 3.18; thus qualifying 1 Cor. 11.7). Paul flat out says Christ 'is the image of God' (2 Cor. 4.4); and another Pauline author says Christ 'is the image of the invisible God' and 'the firstborn of all creation' (Col. 1.15), which explicitly connects Paul's Christ with Philo's primordial Adam, the celestial one, who was in fact the firstborn of all creation. We must conclude Paul agreed, since he clearly understood Jesus to be the first created being: as it is *through* Jesus that God created everything else (1 Cor. 8.6), and Paul explicitly calls Jesus God's firstborn (in Rom. 8.29).

So even if Paul is identifying this preexistent being with a historical person, he is clearly *adding* onto that person the identity of a celestial being already conceived by Jews before Christianity began. One might even suggest that the simpler explanation is that Paul is talking about the same celestial man, and adding onto *that* other ontological identities (like 'messiah'), rather than starting with a historical man and equating him with a preexistent heavenly being. But we cannot conclude on this evidence alone as to which hypothesis is the more likely. What distinguishes Christianity's talk of the 'two Adams' from Philo's talk of the 'two Adams', apart from Philo's own Platonizing tendencies, is that Christianity claimed a special fate for the celestial Adam (he descended from the heavens to die and rise from the dead), and placed it as a historical event—presumably a recent historical event, portending that the 'end was nigh' (since Christ's resurrection was imagined by Paul to be the 'firstfruits' of the general eschatological resurrection: 1 Cor. 15.20). But apart from that, the Christians appear to have been working from the same core Jewish doctrine that there was a perfect celestial Adam, firstborn of all creation, and (somehow) that man turned out to be Jesus.

115. Origen, *Against Celsus* 2.64-67.

Element 40: In fact, the Christian idea of a preexistent spiritual son of God called the Logos, who was God's true high priest in heaven, was also not a novel idea but already held by some pre-Christian Jews; and this preexistent spiritual son of God had already been explicitly connected with a celestial Jesus figure in the OT (discussed in Element 6), and therefore some Jews already believed there was a supernatural son of God named Jesus—because Paul's contemporary Philo interprets the messianic prophecy of Zech. 6.12 in just such a way.[116] This is the prophecy about a high priest crowned king in heaven named 'Jesus Rising', God's 'servant', who will 'rise' from below and be given godly authority and somehow be involved in cleansing the world of sin.

As discussed in Element 6, in Zechariah 6 we have a man named Jesus being crowned king, 'rising' from his place below, and building up God's house, which is a feasible description of our Jesus; and this same Jesus appearing in Zechariah 6 also appears in Zechariah 3, where he is given supreme authority over God's domain (just as our Jesus was), and somehow ends all sins in a single day (just as our Jesus does), and this same Jesus is in both passages called a high priest (as was our Jesus). Discussing this Jesus figure in Zechariah, Philo argues:

> 'Behold, the man named Rising!' is a very novel appellation indeed, if you consider it as spoken of a man who is compounded of body and soul. But if you look upon it as applied to that incorporeal being who is none other than the divine image, you will then agree that the name of 'Rising' has been given to him with great felicity. For the Father of the Universe has caused him to rise up as the eldest son, whom, in another passage, he calls the firstborn. And he who is thus born, imitates the ways of his father.[117]

In the same book, Philo says that even if no one is 'worthy to be called a Son of God', we should still 'labor earnestly to be adorned according to his firstborn Logos, the eldest of his angels, the ruling archangel of many names'.[118] Elsewhere Philo adds that 'there are two Temples of God, and one is this cosmos, wherein the High Priest is his Firstborn Son, the divine Logos' (whom Philo elsewhere identifies as the primordial 'image of God').[119]

116. Philo, *On the Confusion of Tongues* 62-63.

117. Philo, *On the Confusion of Tongues* 63.

118. Philo, *On the Confusion of Tongues* 146-47.

119. Philo, *On Dreams* 1.215; see also Philo, *On the Giants* 52. That the 'divine Logos' is the 'image of God' is also explicitly declared in Philo, *On the Creation* 31 as well as in Philo, *On the Confusion of Tongues* 62, 97 and 147; *On Dreams* 1.239; 2.45; *The Special Laws* 1.81; *On Flight and Finding* 101. That this is an intermediary being (per Element 36), see Philo, *Who Is the Heir of Things Divine?* 205-206. For more sources on this Jewish doctrine of the 'Logos' as a divine being, which Christianity

And Philo also says this 'divine Logos' is the being whom God used 'as an instrument' to create the universe, and the one whom God appointed the Lord over all creation.[120] We know Jesus was also called the firstborn of God, the Logos, and God's high priest in the heavens, and the one through whom all things were made, and who was appointed Lord of the universe, and was the true image of God; and Christians were also called upon to try and emulate him and adorn themselves like him, just as Philo is calling us to do.[121] This is far too improbable to be a coincidence. Philo and Christianity must have this notion from a common tradition preceding both.[122]

Of course, our Jesus is only explicitly called 'the Logos' in Jn 1.1, a very late document (see Chapter 7, §4). But he is recognized by Paul as the 'firstborn' son of God (Rom. 8.29), and the 'image of God' (2 Cor. 4.4), through whom God created all things (1 Cor. 8.6), and therefore a preexistent being (evident also in Phil. 2.6-8 and 1 Cor. 10.1-4).[123] It's likely Paul

simply co-opted, see Daniel Boyarin's commentary in Amy-Jill Levine and Marc Zvi Brettler (eds.), *The Jewish Annotated New Testament* (Oxford: Oxford University Press, 2011), pp. 546-49.

120. The one through whom the universe was created: Philo, *On Allegorical Interpretation* 3.96 and *The Special Laws* 1.81. That over all the universe 'God put in charge his own true Logos, his firstborn Son, who is to take charge of his sacred flock, like the prefect of a great king', see Philo, *On Agriculture* 50-52. Curiously, Philo immediately goes on to say that we can know this is true because 'it is written, 'Behold, I am he and I will send my messenger [lit. "my angel"] into your presence, who shall guard you on the road', which is a partial quotation of Exod. 23.20 (concluding 'and bring you to the place which I have prepared'), which happens to be the very scripture with which Mark begins his Gospel: 'The beginning of the Gospel of Jesus Christ, the Son of God: as it is written in the prophets: "Behold, I send My messenger into your presence, who shall prepare the road for you"' (Mk 1.2), which Mark alters at the end to mean John the Baptist, but the original scripture clearly indicates (just as Philo understood it to) that the messenger (lit. 'angel') is the one who will *protect* us and *bring* us to salvation (and, according to Philo, that was the 'firstborn son of God', the Logos), not the one who will 'prepare' the way for him. I can only speculate, but must wonder: is it possible that in the *original* text (whatever may have been Mark's source), the Gospel began with this verse referring to *Jesus* (and thus quoting Exodus correctly), and that this was altered by Mark so as to fit John the Baptist into the story (where evidently he had not been before)? Unfortunately we cannot know for sure.

121. That we ought to imitate Christ: 1 Cor. 11.1; Rom. 8.29; 1 Cor. 15.49; 2 Cor. 3.18.

122. See Hultgren, 'Origin of Paul's Doctrine', pp. 350-54.

123. See Sean McDonough, *Christ as Creator: Origins of a New Testament Doctrine* (New York: Oxford University Press, 2009). McDonough provides a considerable survey of relevant background knowledge establishing the very early development of the Christian doctrine of Christ as the agent of Creation (which is only corroborated by the evidence I survey here and in Element 10), although I believe his analysis of the Gospels has things the wrong way around (e.g. Mark was not inspired to believe Jesus

just never had occasion to use the title of 'Logos' to describe Jesus (just as Philo doesn't trouble himself to mention it every time he speaks of the same being). Because otherwise these certainly appear to be the same man. Just because this one connection is first explicitly stated in the Gospel of John does not mean its authors introduced it. Likewise, in Hebrews Jesus is not only the firstborn son of God, but also God's high priest in the heavens and again the image of God, the supreme of all angels, a preexistent being through whom God created all things (Hebrews 1 and 8), all just like Philo's celestial Jesus.[124] And Col. 1.12-20 says *its* Jesus is the firstborn of all creation, the image of God, through whom God created all things, too. So it cannot be a coincidence that Philo says his 'Logos', 'the firstborn son of God', God's incorporeal high priest in outer space, is also none other than 'the image of God', and God's agent of creation, again connecting this 'Logos' creature to Paul's Christ, who is also the 'image' of God and God's 'firstborn son' and also a preexistent being of the highest rank—since Paul says it is Christ, and no other being, through whom God created all things.

This also suggests Philo is saying this firstborn Logos is in fact the true Adam (as discussed in Element 39), which is corroborated by Philo's explanation elsewhere that the earthly Adam was made in the image of the *second* Adam in heaven, the divine Logos, who was in turn the image of God; and we know (from the previous element) that this celestial man who was the image of God and of whom the earthly man is a copy is indeed that first-created Adam.[125] Likewise, Philo calls this high priest and divine Logos 'the man for real' of whom the earthly priests are but a copy, again connecting this divine being with the 'true Adam' in outer space.[126] This also explains why this firstborn celestial son is called the Logos (meaning 'Reason'). In every passage where Philo explains that the first-created Adam is the 'image' of God, he further explains that this is because the image of God is not the human body but the intellect—hence 'reason' is the image of God. Therefore it would be obvious that any incorporeal being created as the true 'image' of God would be called (indeed would *be*) Reason, and therefore the Logos. We cannot therefore see this as a late development in Christology, but as in fact already a pre-Christian feature of Jewish theology. If it was known to Philo, it had to have been known to Paul.

is the Creator by any actual historical reports; rather, Mark is inventing narratives that cast Jesus in the role of Creator: see, e.g., on how this would have originated the idea that he was a carpenter or the son of a carpenter, in Chapter 10, §4).

124. Jesus is God's 'eternal high priest' in later Christian thought as well (e.g. Polycarp, *Philippians* 12).

125. Philo, *Questions and Answers on Genesis* 2.62.

126. Philo, *On Dreams* 1.215 (*ho pros alētheian anthrōpos*).

Jesus therefore must have been known as the Logos even in Paul's time. It's clear in Paul that the first Christians regarded Jesus to be the preexistent 'image of God' through whom God created all things (2 Cor. 4.4; 1 Cor. 8.6); and that can only ever have been understood to be the Logos, not only as the Reason which was and necessarily had to be the 'image' of God (unlike the human body, which obviously could not), but also as the Word (the second meaning of Logos) by which God created all things (Gen. 1.3, 6, 9, 11, 14, 20, 24, 26). Even on these considerations the probability that Paul would understand Jesus in any other way is vanishingly small. But the fact that Paul also understood Jesus to be the firstborn son of God *as well as* the preexistent image of God only further lines this creature up with Philo's Logos, who is similarly identified. It is even further in support of this conclusion that pagan theology had a similar concept—the savior god Osiris was also called the Logos and the one through whom all was created and governed—thus demonstrating the notion was ubiquitous (and might even have been a common element of mystery religion).[127]

I have heard doubts whether Philo (or his source) was aware of the whole sentence he quotes from Zechariah and thus of the name 'Jesus' being in it. But such doubts are unwarranted. Nearly the whole sentence in Zechariah, in the Greek translation quoted by Philo, reads:

> You shall make crowns, and set them upon the head of Jesus the son of Jehovah the Righteous, the high priest, and say to him, 'Thus says the almighty Lord, **"Behold, the man whose name is Rising [*anatolē*]"** and he shall rise up [*anatelei*] from his place below and shall build the house of the Lord, and receive power, and sit and rule upon his throne' (Zech. 6.11-13).

The whole sentence (of which Philo quotes only the part here in bold thus identifies the man spoken of as both God's *son* and *high priest*, and in the very same sentence names him Jesus. This creates a series of coincidences far too improbable to imagine on any other conclusion than that Philo and Paul were talking about the same figure: Jesus the Son of Jehovah the Righteous, the image of God, God's agent of creation, God's high priest and firstborn son (see Elements 6 and 10).

Paul identifies his Jesus with all the same attributes (except the detail of his being high priest, which we find in Hebrews), which is a very unlikely coincidence: two cosmic men named Jesus assigned all the same unusual attributes; and two of those attributes (sonship and high

127. Plutarch, *On Isis and Osiris* 54.373b; 67.377f (Osiris is also called 'the first' and 'the lord', 2.351f-352a). The idea of a divine 'Logos' was a widespread cross-cultural theological meme in antiquity: see Glenn Chesnut, 'The Ruler and the Logos in Neopythagorean, Middle Platonic, and Late Stoic Political Philosophy', *Aufstieg und Niedergang der römischen Welt* II.16.2 (New York: W. de Gruyter, 1978), pp. 1310-32.

priesthood) are stated in the same sentence in Zechariah that Philo quotes from, a quote about a man Philo himself then links to Philo's own notion of God's firstborn *son* and *high priest*, another improbable coincidence—unless Philo (or his source) was well aware of the rest of the sentence and taking it into account in his interpretation. Philo even makes use of the same pun (between the noun and verb forms of *anatolē*) in his (or his source's) interpretation that the sentence in Zechariah plays on. Indeed, it ought to be absurd to suggest that Philo, a very erudite biblical scholar, had never read Zechariah and thus didn't know the remaining content of this passage, or where the line even came from. Thus we can safely conclude Philo (or his source) was aware of the fact that this cosmic firstborn son was named Jesus. Because denying that (no matter by what excuse) requires asserting a series of improbable coincidences, whereas affirming it does not.

There is another significance to all this. Philo says of the earthly high priest that he wears 'an emblem of that Logos which holds together and regulates the universe, for it is necessary that [the earthly high priest] who is consecrated to the Father of the Universe should have as his paraclete His son, the most perfect in virtue, to procure forgiveness of sins'.[128] Notably the Gospel of John, which explicitly calls Christ the Logos, also calls the Holy Spirit the 'paraclete' whom Christ will send (Jn 14.6, 26; 15.26; 16.7). The word *paraklētos* most commonly meant a 'legal advocate', and so in the epistle 1 John we're told that 'if any man sin, we have an Advocate with the Father, Jesus Christ the righteous' (1 Jn 2.1), this time calling Christ himself a paraclete, and also connecting him to the 'Father' of the Universe and with supreme virtue and with his role in 'procuring' forgiveness of sins (Paul also calls Jesus our 'advocate' in Rom. 8.34, but using a different word).

From Philo we can see that there is nothing novel about any of this. Philo's remarks prove that some Jews already believed that God had a firstborn son in heaven, a preexistent being through whom God created the universe, the very image of God, the supreme of all beings next to God, whose name could already be identified as Jesus (per Philo's explanation of Zechariah 6), and who advocates on our behalf to procure forgiveness of sins, and that all earthly priests were but a copy of him. Not only is this

128. Philo, *On the Life of Moses* 2.134-35. In *On the Life of Moses* 2.99, Philo also says God has two 'powers', the one that is called God (the Creator), and the one that is called Lord (the king and judge); it's reasonable to see how God could assign the second power to a subordinate (Jesus), thereby making him Lord. There are numerous passages in Paul that would confirm this theological model, but it's not important to the present discussion.

clearly the same deity as Jesus in Christian documents such as the canonical book of Hebrews (see Chapter 11, §5),[129] but it is clearly the same deity worshiped by Paul and all Christians he had any communication with. It is therefore, so far as we can tell, the same deity Christianity began with. Any theory of the origins of Christianity must take this into account.

Element 41: (a) The 'Son of Man' (an apocalyptic title Jesus is given in the Gospels) was another being foreseen in the visions of Enoch to be a preexistent celestial superman whom God will one day put in charge of the universe, overthrowing all demonic power, and in a text that we know the first Christians used as scripture (*1 Enoch*).[130] (b) According to that scripture, this 'Son of Man' will in the appointed day reveal divine secrets to mankind, when also his *name* will be revealed; and it is implied that he may be the Christ (Jesus likewise was regarded as holding the divine secrets and revealing them).[131] (c) But his identity has been kept secret so evildoers will not know him when the time comes (just like Jesus).[132] (d) Yet he already sounds in many respects like the same being as the primordial Adam (Element 39) and Logos (Element 40). The fact that at Qumran he was already

129. As Hugh Anderson concludes for the book of Hebrews, its 'author shared the same thought world as Philo, and that he drew on the same Greek rhetorical and philosophical sources for much of his vocabulary and many of his ideas is irrefutable': Hugh Anderson, 'The Jewish Antecedents of the Christology in Hebrews', in *The Messiah: Developments in Earliest Judaism and Christianity* (ed. James Charlesworth; Minneapolis, MN: Fortress Press, 1992), pp. 512-35 (518).

130. *1 Enoch* 39, 45-46, 48-49, 51-53, 55, 61-62, 69, 71. See Carrier, *Proving History*, pp. 150-51; and for detailed inquiry into the apocalyptic Son of Man concept and its Jewish origins see (and compare): Maurice Casey, 'Son of Man', in *The Historical Jesus in Recent Research* (ed. James Dunn and Scot McKnight; Winona Lake, IN: Eisenbrauns, 2005), pp. 315-24; Thomas Kazen, 'The Coming of the Son of Man Revisited', *Journal for the Study of the Historical Jesus* 5 (June 2007), pp. 155-74; Mogens Müller, *The Expression 'Son of Man' and the Development of Christology: A History of Interpretation* (Oakville, CT: Equinox, 2008); Larry Hurtado and Paul Owen (eds.), *Who Is This Son of Man? The Latest Scholarship on a Puzzling Expression of the Historical Jesus* (New York: T. & T. Clark, 2011); Leslie Walck, *The Son of Man in the Parables of Enoch and in Matthew* (London: T. & T. Clark, 2011). See also John Gager, 'The Gospels and Jesus: Some Doubts about Method', *Journal of Religion* 54 (July 1974), pp. 244-72 (264-66); Edwin Broadhead, 'Reconfiguring Jesus: The Son of Man in Markan Perspective', in *Biblical Interpretation in Early Christian Gospels. Vol. 1, The Gospel of Mark* (ed. Thomas R. Hatina; New York: T. & T. Clark, 2006), pp. 18-30; and Daniel Boyarin, *The Jewish Gospels: The Story of the Jewish Christ* (New York: The New Press, 2012).

131. *1 Enoch* 46; 48.5-6, 11; 68.38. Jesus: Ignatius, *Philadelphians* 9; Col. 2.2-3. See also Rom. 16.25-26; 1 Cor. 2.7-10 and 4.1; Eph. 1.3-10 and 3.1-5; Col. 1.26-27.

132. *1 Enoch* 61.10-18. Jesus: Phil. 2.5-11 (cf. 1 Cor. 2.7-9).

fully equated with Melchizedek (see following element) only confirms all these figures were at times thought to be the same.[133]

Element 42: There is a parallel tradition of a perfect and eternal celestial high priest named Melchizedek, which means in Hebrew 'Righteous King'. We have already seen that a celestial Jesus was already called Righteous and King by some pre-Christian Jews. And a connection between the Christ and the Melchizedek figure was probably made before Christianity, as the very Dead Sea scroll that appears to link the dying Christ of Daniel 9 to the dying servant of Isaiah 52–53 is specifically a pesher on this Melchizedek figure, and by the most obvious interpretation it states that its dying Christ (the Anointed in the Spirit) *is* Melchizedek. (See Elements 40 and 41, with Elements 5 and 6.)

Unfortunately this scroll is so badly damaged we can't be certain if the Christ spoken of there (the one who was probably imagined as dying to atone for the sins of the elect: see Element 5) is meant only to be someone who prepares the way for Melchizedek or is said to be Melchizedek, who would then come and judge all creation.[134] Scholars are divided on that. I'm fairly certain that they are the same figure, but making the case for that involves too lengthy an argument for too uncertain a conclusion for my present purposes. Either way, in 11Q13 Melchizedek is certainly a savior figure, a divine being of some kind, who lives in outer space, presumably visits earth in some capacity, and defeats Satan and his angels. He is also somehow involved in 'liberating the captives' and forgiving the sins of the elect through some special (and final) Day of Atonement.

What else do we hear about this mysterious Melchizedek figure? Philo tells us 'God made Melchizedek, the King of Peace', into 'his own high priest', referring to Gen. 14.18, where the mysterious Melchizedek, 'king of Salem' (which means 'King of Peace'), is also a 'priest of the Most High God', and appears and brings to Abram 'bread and wine' and blesses

133. J. Harold Ellens, 'The Dead Sea Scrolls and the Son of Man: An Assessment of 11Q13', *Henoch* 33 (2011), pp. 77-87.

134. 11QMelchizedek (11Q13); for text, translation and notes see John Sietze Bergsma, *The Jubilee from Leviticus to Qumran: A History of Interpretation* (Boston: Brill, 2007), pp. 277-91; and Alex Jassen, *Mediating the Divine: Prophecy and Revelation in the Dead Sea Scrolls and Second Temple Judaism* (Boston: Brill, 2007), pp. 90-95; on the debate over whether Melchizedek is the Christ in this passage, see Lara Guglielmo, '11Q13, Malchî Sedek, Co-Reference, and Restoration of 2 18', *Henoch* 33 (2011), pp. 62, as well as Jassen, p. 93 n. 31; and Bergsma, p. 289; Guglielmo and Bergsma make far more convincing arguments. See also Florentino García Martínez and Eibert J.C. Tigchelaar (eds.), *Qumranica minora*, Vol. II (Boston: Brill, 2007), pp. 18-20 and 98-108 (esp. pp. 100-102, with the note in Element 5 on the two-messiah tradition at Qumran).

him.[135] We never hear about this Melchizedek otherwise, neither before this nor after (apart from one mysterious reference implying he was an eternal priest in Ps. 110.4), which inspired esoteric speculation in the Jewish apocrypha about who he might be, and how there could have been a priest of Jehovah before there were even Jews (Abram does not get circumcised nor christened 'Abraham' nor even begin to father the Jewish people until Genesis 17). The general theme of most speculations and traditions was that Melchizedek must have been a supernatural being who, as the ultimate high priest (serving in heaven for all eternity), was in some fashion the ultimate agent of atonement.[136] For example, in *2 Enoch,* Melchizedek is 'miraculously born before the flood and would come again at the end of time', and the Melchizedek pesher says that when he does come he will cancel all sins in a single day, and possibly do so by his death (or through the death of some other Christ).[137]

Of course, in Jewish understanding, all kings (e.g. 1 Sam. 15.17) *and* all high priests were Christs (Lev. 4.5, 16; 6.22), thus, being both, Melchizedek would be understood as a Christ, and thus passages about 'the' Christ could easily be connected to him in the pesherim, particularly once he evolved into a salvific, apocalyptic figure, as he clearly had become by the time of the Dead Sea Scrolls. Once you see him as having the attributes of *the* Christ, the fact that he was already *a* Christ would automatically warrant linking him to messianic passages in the scriptures, and this is exactly what the scribes at Qumran appear to be doing. And the Christians seem to have done so as well. Crispin Fletcher-Louis, for example, argues that there is evidence in the Gospel of Mark indicating that 'Jesus' thought he was the high priest Melchizedek.[138] Yet we could just as easily use all his same evidence to argue that Mark is *depicting* Jesus as such, in his characteristically veiled way.

However, unlike 11Q13, the book of Hebrews argues that Jesus is Melchizedek's *replacement.* In this account we're told Melchizedek 'is first, by translation of his name, King of Righteousness, and then he is also King

135. Philo, *Allegorical Interpretation* 3.79-89; §82 seems to imply that Melchizedek is the Logos (particularly in light of 80-81 before it) but not explicitly enough to be certain. See also Clement of Alexandria, *Miscellanies* 4.25; and Josephus, *Jewish Antiquities* 1.180.

136. Stökl ben Ezra, *Impact of Yom Kippur*, pp. 90-92.

137. Charles Gieschen, 'The Different Functions of a Similar Melchizedek Tradition in 2 Enoch and the Epistle to the Hebrews', in *Early Christian Interpretation of the Scriptures of Israel: Investigations and Proposals* (ed. Craig Evans and James Sanders; Sheffield: Sheffield Academic Press, 1997), pp. 364-79 (378-79).

138. Crispin Fletcher-Louis, 'Jesus as the High Priestly Messiah: Part 1' and 'Part 2', *Journal for the Study of the Historical Jesus* 4 (2006), pp. 155-75 and 5 (2007), pp. 157-79.

of Salem, that is, King of Peace', just as Philo said, but more importantly, 'he is without father or mother or genealogy, and has neither beginning of days nor end of life, but being like the Son of God, he continues a priest forever'.[139] The author then goes on to explain that Melchizedek was the eternal high priest of the *old* covenant, and Jesus is the eternal high priest of the *new* covenant. Thus we're told that 'when another priest arises in the likeness of Melchizedek, one who has become a priest not according to a legal requirement concerning bodily descent but by the power of an indestructible life' (7.15-16) then 'a former commandment is set aside because of its weakness and uselessness (for the law made nothing perfect)' and 'a better hope is introduced' in its place, which, unlike other priestly appointments, came about by a divine oath, as (we're reminded) scripture has said, 'The Lord has sworn and will not change his mind, "Thou art a priest forever"' (Heb. 7.18-22; 5.6), quoting Ps. 110.4 ('The Lord has sworn and will not change his mind, "Thou art a priest forever, after the order of Melchizedek"').

We have already seen that an eternal high priest in the heavens was also known as the Logos, named Jesus, the firstborn son of God, and God's agent of creation (see Element 40). And our Jesus seems to do all the things that Melchizedek does in 11Q13. So they seem to be the same creature. That contradicts the notion of Jesus replacing him. There cannot be two high priests in the celestial temple, so if Melchizedek 'continues a priest forever' and never dies, how can he have been replaced? Where did he go? Perhaps there were esoteric answers to those questions at one point. We might note that Melchizedek is not called the *high* priest forever, just a *priest* forever. Perhaps, then, his replacement was only a demotion, becoming Jesus' subordinate in the celestial temple hierarchy.

The most we can make out is that Hebrews says we needed a new eternal high priest in the heavens, even though we had one already, because a switch at the helm was needed in order to inaugurate a new covenant. So to accomplish that, all the roles and properties assigned to Melchizedek were transferred to Jesus, one way or another. However, existing tradition already declared Jesus, the eternal firstborn son of God, high priest. So the sect that became Christianity must have adopted a doctrine whereby that appointment hadn't happened yet, but was something yet to happen. Before that, the Logos was the agent of creation but otherwise without assignment, waiting for the day God could bring his secret plan to fruition. In the

139. Hebrews 7.1-3 (in its full context: 7.1–9.28). Earlier in Hebrews (Heb. 5–6) the authors explain that what they mean by connecting Jesus to Melchizedek involves matters crossing too much into secret teachings that the letter's recipients might not be ready to hear; it's possible this latter part of the letter constitutes that advanced teaching (which only those of sufficient rank would proceed to), unless something else even more esoteric was being hinted at there.

meantime, Melchizedek held the post of celestial high priest. Otherwise we would have to suppose Hebrews is concealing a secret doctrine that Jesus actually *was* Melchizedek and was either hiding under that name until his resurrection or was then renamed 'Jesus' and given new powers (see Chapter 11, §4). Only one or the other can explain what Hebrews says, given what we know of prior Jewish Melchizedek tradition.

Element 43: (a) Voluntary human sacrifice was widely regarded (by both pagans and Jews) as the most powerful salvation and atonement magic available. (b) Accordingly, any sacred story involving a voluntary human sacrifice would be readily understood and fit perfectly within both Jewish and pagan worldviews of the time.

Of course, Jews and pagans both embraced a value for martyrdom as a morally praiseworthy end of a just man.[140] The most beloved martyr in pagan imagination was Socrates, unjustly executed by the state on a false charge of challenging state religion (but in reality, for preaching wisdom that would lead to the salvation of the community as well as individual souls); and he voluntarily went to his death, to *prove* he was a just man. Judaism also had a tradition of beloved martyrs well before Christians, and pagans had their own martyr tradition as well.[141] The *Acts of the Pagan Martyrs* (or *Acts of the Alexandrians*), for example, is a collection of pagan martyrologies dating from the early Roman Empire. Thus, self-sacrifice was not a shameful end but a heroic one that could inspire admiration and emulation, and execution by the state was often the cause of death for these beloved heroes. And in accord with this, the 'suffering righteous man', even to the extent of being humiliated and executed though innocent, was also a beloved hero-type in Jewish literature and imagination.[142] Many pagans held a similar view (see Element 46). All of which is important, because that which was regarded as heroic would never be regarded as embarrassing.

Even more importantly, 'substitutionary sacrifice' was also a well-known religious concept within both pagan and Jewish theology. The idea of a hero standing in for his nation or people (and thus 'substituting' for it or them) and voluntarily exchanging his death for their salvation (*he dies so*

140. See Carrier, *Not the Impossible Faith*, pp. 24-34, 221-31, 240-45 and following note.

141. Robert Doran, 'Narratives of Noble Death', in *The Historical Jesus in Context* (ed. Levine, Allison and Crossan), pp. 385-99, esp. 389-92 (Jewish martyrs) and 392-99 (pagan martyrs); and Jarvis Williams, *Maccabean Martyr Traditions in Paul's Theology of Atonement: Did Martyr Theology Shape Paul's Conception of Jesus's Death?* (Eugene, OR: Wipf & Stock, 2010), pp. 27-63.

142. See Carrier, *Proving History*, pp. 131-34, 141.

they may live) was a common motif in Greco-Roman culture.[143] A prominent example in Roman patriotic history was the legendary general Publius Decius Mus, who fulfilled a formal religious ritual in Roman culture called the *devotio*, in which a hero is anointed to sacrifice himself in a battle in exchange for the victory of his army (and hence, in consequence, the victory, liberty and survival of the Roman people collectively), which is basically what Jesus does (or was understood to have done).[144] Decius gave his life 'as though sent from heaven as an expiatory offering for all the wrath of the gods, who would avert the disaster from his own troops and take it to the enemy'.[145] Ancient Greek myth had its equivalent: Codrus, King of Athens, voluntarily gave his life to ensure the salvation of his people in fulfillment of a prophecy that if he gave his life, they would be saved; and 'so the Athenians, by the power of a leader offering himself to death for the salvation of the fatherland, were freed from war'.[146] The Jews embraced the same value system—the Maccabean literature, for example, includes a tale of the seven martyrs who, by giving their lives, save the land, literally atoning for the sins of Israel, and thus becoming a 'ransom for the sin of our nation'.[147] In fact, Jewish use of human sacrifice as atonement magic appears several times in the OT.[148]

143. Several examples are documented in Doran, 'Narratives of Noble Death', pp. 385-99 (387-88 on Decius); and Walter Burkert, *Structure and History in Greek Mythology and Ritual* (Berkeley, CA: University of California Press, 1979), pp. 59-77 (and its connection with animal sacrifice: pp. 54-55).

144. Hendrik Simon Versnel, 'Two Types of Roman *devotio*', *Mnemosyne* 29 (1976), pp. 365-410; and Hendrik Simon Versnel, 'Self-Sacrifice, Compensation and the Anonymous Gods', in *Le sacrifice dans l'antiquité* (ed. Jean Pierre Vernant *et al.*; Geneva: Fondation Hardt, 1980), pp. 135-94.

145. Doran, 'Narratives of Noble Death', p. 388; Livy, *From the Foundation of the City* 8.9–8.10.

146. Doran, 'Narratives of Noble Death', p. 387; Justin Trogus, *Epitome of Pompeius Trogus* 2.6.16-21. There were apparently many other examples then widely known: see Stökl ben Ezra, *Impact of Yom Kippur*, pp. 171-73; and Jennifer K. Berenson Maclean, 'Barabbas, the Scapegoat Ritual, and the Development of the Passion Narrative', *Harvard Theological Review* 100 (July 2007), pp. 309-34 (esp. 313-16).

147. 4 Maccabees 17.20-22; see Stökl ben Ezra, *Impact of Yom Kippur*, pp. 115-17; Burton Mack, 'The Christ and Jewish Wisdom', in *The Messiah: Developments in Earliest Judaism and Christianity* (ed. James Charlesworth; Minneapolis, MN: Fortress Press, 1992), pp. 192-221 (206); and Jintae Kim, 'The Concept of Atonement in the Fourth Servant Song in the LXX', *Journal of Greco-Roman Christianity and Judaism* 8 (2011–2012), pp. 21-33; and Jintae Kim, 'The Concept of Atonement in Early Rabbinic Thought and the New Testament Writings', *Journal of Greco-Roman Christianity and Judaism* 2 (2001–2005), pp. 117-45. That this thinking had influenced the development of early Christianity is argued in Jarvis Williams, *Maccabean Martyr Traditions*.

148. King David resorted to human sacrifice, crucifying the sons of Saul at the

In this system of understanding, the more awful and shameful the manner of death, the more heroic and powerful it was. This thinking dates at least as far back as Plato, who confronts the logic of the nihilist Glaucon in relating the legend of Gyges, who upon acquiring a ring of invisibility was able to do anything without detection and thus seized supreme power by murder and other sins. And so, Glaucon argued, no one is really just; they only wish to *seem* just, because that's all that is useful. Glaucon then argues that the only way to know if a man is truly just is to take everything away from him and treat him completely as an unjust man, despised by everyone, and punished to the utmost, including torments and, finally, crucifixion (the Jewish model for the very same notion appears in the book of Job). If a man, after all this, remains just to the end, only then will we know he was a just man—although Glaucon argues that such a man would by the end conclude justice was something not worth all that he suffered, and therefore one ought to be *un*-just, and, like Gyges, merely conceal one's crimes.

The answer then made to Glaucon is that the gods will always know, and therefore the just will have their reward. That this misses his point is not addressed in the dialog, illustrating that sometimes theoretical analysis in antiquity was not always very sophisticated. And in the same way, in the final analysis Jesus' sacrifice on the cross was not awesome at all but trivial, as he knew all along he would be resurrected and glorified (and thus he was not in fact sacrificing anything); so the fact that Christians never noticed this flaw in their logic should thus not surprise us, as Plato never noticed it either. They were as philosophically naive as he was, and remained so for nearly two thousand years. So we cannot object to this argument by claiming they would have noticed its flaw; because they didn't.

To fully understand the point, Glaucon's argument should be read in full:

> The just man would be a simple and noble man, who . . . does not wish to *seem* but actually *be* good. So we must deprive him of the seeming. For if he is going to be thought just he will have honors and gifts because of that esteem. We cannot be sure in that case whether he is just for justice's sake or for the sake of the gifts and honors. So we must strip him bare

beginning of the harvest, to appease the Lord and atone for the sins of Israel in order to persuade Jehovah to end a famine (and it worked: 2 Sam. 21.1-14; it might not be a coincidence that the 'seven sons' here slain correspond to the 'seven sons' slain in 4 Maccabees; notably in 2 Samuel the atonement sacrifice occurs the day after Passover, exactly when Jesus is killed; that being the day when the barley harvest begins, the first of the harvests: Deut. 16.9-10; Lev. 23.11). A plague had similarly been lifted by Aaron and Moses by performing a human sacrifice to appease Jehovah (spearing an interracial couple and crucifying apostate leaders: Num. 25.1-8), an act which again atoned for the sins of Israel (Num. 25.13). On human sacrifice in the OT and ancient Israelite religion generally see *End of Christianity* (ed. Loftus), pp. 146-47, 186-88; *Christian Delusion* (ed. Loftus), pp. 226-27.

> of everything but justice and make his state the opposite of his imagined counterpart. Though doing no wrong, he must have the repute of the greatest injustice, so that he may be put to the test as regards justice, by not softening because of this ill repute and the consequences thereof. But let him hold on his course unchangeable even unto death, seeming all his life to be unjust though being just, that so, both men [i.e., this man, and another who gets to merely *seem* just] having reached the limit, the one of injustice, the other of justice, we may pass judgement which of the two is the happier. . . . What they will say is this: that such being his disposition, the just man will have to endure the lash, the rack, chains, the branding-iron in his eyes, and finally, after every extremity of suffering, he will be crucified, and so will learn his lesson that not to *be* but to *seem* just is what we ought to desire.[149]

This, of course, is the opposite logic embraced by the Christians; it's the kind of 'human wisdom', the wisdom of clever words, that Paul vehemently denounces. So we can expect someone of his disposition to flip Glaucon's argument upside down: if a man remained just all the way to that horrible end, all the way to the cross, and *still* he deemed that outcome best, then Glaucon's nihilistic reasoning would be refuted, and by his very own premises. And then Glaucon's intellectual opponents would be 'vindicated', as this just man is rewarded after death by God, being exalted to the highest.

This completely explains the moral logic of the Christian creed that Paul repeats to the Philippians (see Chapter 11, §4): in perfect accord with the lesson Plato was teaching in his dialogue (which lesson later became a stock element of Stoic philosophy), Jesus is given the opportunity to seize all power ('equality with god'), just like Gyges, but *unlike* Gyges, Jesus rejected it (Phil. 2.6), and took the other path: he became nothing, a slave to the elements, a mortal, accepting humiliation (*tapeinoō*) and death, 'even death on a cross' (Phil. 2.7-8; see also Gal. 3.13), and 'therefore God highly exalted him' (Phil. 2.9). This is Plato's moral philosophy in a nutshell: this is a stock example of the just and wise man known throughout pagan philosophy—not always *accepted*, but known; and among those yearning most for morality and justice, it was not just known but admired and praised. It was therefore not a radical idea. In fact, it is simply a merging of a popular philosophical idea (the just man enduring the cross) with a popular religious idea (the suffering savior god). It was already the standard trope in all the mystery religions that it was by suffering some ordeal (often death) that the god procured salvation for his adherents (Element 31). And as we saw earlier, legendary kings and generals and martyrs readily volunteered to fulfill that role, too. And they were valorized for it.

149. Plato, *Republic* 2.361b-362a.

In Jewish religion, the sacrificial narrative of Abraham and Isaac was a primary model: the firstborn son being sacrificed, but a substitute is made available instead, explaining why *animals* and not *people* are sacrificed to god. Thus 'almost all the law codes in the Pentateuch include a law concerning sacrifice or redemption of the first-born of humans and animals'.[150] In this matrix of reasoning, Jesus' crucifixion and atoning death was a natural extension of both Jewish and pagan traditions of human sacrifice, of 'beloved sons' in particular, to procure salvation for the nation or kin group.[151] Jesus' sacrifice, in fact, is *based* on the Isaac story, which had already been rabbinically linked with Passover. In legend both events occur on the same day, and the Isaac narrative is explicitly represented as the original Passover in texts such as *Jubilees* 17–18.[152] Thus, in Galatians 3 and 4, Paul links Jesus with both Isaac and the Passover lamb.[153] And we know that Paul (and later Christians) explicitly linked Christ's death with the Passover sacrifice (see Element 18).

Both narratives involve substitutionary sacrifice, but the Jesus sacrifice reverses the Isaac sacrifice. In the Isaac story, in place of the singular sacrifice of Abraham's beloved firstborn son, animals must be slain every year in perpetuity. The one equals the other. Logically, therefore, a singular sacrifice of God's beloved firstborn son would be a sufficient substitute for all animal sacrifices in perpetuity. Therefore, if you wanted to be rid of those animal sacrifices (in other words, if you wanted to be rid of the otherwise divinely ordained temple cult and all the corrupt political and economic

150. Karin Finsterbusch, 'The First-Born between Sacrifice and Redemption in the Hebrew Bible', in *Human Sacrifice in Jewish and Christian Tradition* (ed. Karin Finsterbusch, Armin Lange and K.F. Diethard Römheld; Leiden: Brill, 2007), pp. 87-108 (87); see, e.g., Deut. 15.19-22 and 14.22; Num. 18.16; Exod. 13; 22.29-30; etc. The underlying religious logic of sacrificing people or animals manifested a primitive concept of 'redirected vengeance' to expiate divine anger: see René Girard, *Violence and the Sacred* (trans. Patrick Gregory; Baltimore, MD: Johns Hopkins University Press, 1977); and Yitzhaq Feder, *Blood Expiation in Hittite and Biblical Ritual: Origins, Context, and Meaning* (Atlanta, GA: Society of Biblical Literature, 2011).

151. Jon Levenson, *The Death and Resurrection of the Beloved Son: The Transformation of Child Sacrifice in Judaism and Christianity* (New Haven, CT: Yale University Press, 1993).

152. Levenson, *Death and Resurrection*, pp. 176-77 (with much more evidence throughout pp. 173-99).

153. Levenson, *Death and Resurrection*, pp. 210-19. The connections with the Isaac narrative are more obvious (e.g. Gal. 3.16; 4.28, etc.); the connections with the Passover narrative appear by allusion in Paul's slavery and freedom metaphor (vs. turning back to the material world: cf. Exod. 16.1-3; Num. 14.1-4), in Gal. 4.3, 8-9; in the contrast made between Sinai and Jerusalem (Gal. 4.25-26); and being saved because you are 'known' by God (Gal. 4.9), just as the Israelites are 'known' by the Lord and thus passed over (Exod. 12.11-14, 23).

powers that controlled it, as many Jews did: Element 28), logic would compel you to look for a singular human sacrifice to accomplish that, and it would have to be the most powerful sacrifice imaginable, which to any Jew would be the sacrifice of God's firstborn son, which we've already seen some Jews already believed existed (Element 40) and was already named Jesus (Element 6). The problem of the temple cult that the Jews faced therefore entailed a solution that is essentially the core teaching of Christianity. It would therefore not be a wholly radical step for any Jew to propose that solution, but in fact entirely in accord with much Jewish thinking at the time.[154]

3. *Elements of Literary Context*

Element 44: In Jewish and pagan antiquity, in matters of religious persuasion, fabricating stories was the norm, not the exception, even in the production of narratives purporting to be true. In fact, the persuasive power of representing a story as true was precisely why fabricated stories were often represented as true. We therefore must approach all ancient religious literature from an assumption of doubt, and must work to confirm any given story or account as true, not the other way around. Because prior probability *always* favors fabrication in that genre.

That this is true becomes obvious the moment all ancient religious literature is examined together as a complete set: the number of fictional treatises posing as factual in that set is vast; the number of honest factual narratives is comparatively few. This is already provable from Christian literature alone. But first I will focus on Jewish and pagan literature—in other words, everything *besides* Christian literature—in order to establish the literary context in which Christian literature must be understood. Then I will show how Christian literature fits exactly the same trend.

First, the Jewish apocrypha: even the Maccabean literature contains a lot that is dubious and is hardly trusted as more than historical fiction; but collections like the Enochic literature are obvious wholesale fabrication.[155] The book of Tobit, the *Ascension of Isaiah*, the *Revelation of Moses*

154. Similarly, 'if Jesus is the true Isaac, and the Church is the body of Jesus' (as Paul argues in, e.g., Rom. 12.4-5; 1 Cor. 12.27, etc.), then 'it follows . . . that the Church . . . must see itself in the role of Isaac, that is, as the promised son of the freeborn woman' in Galatians 4 (Levenson, *Death and Resurrection*, pp. 212, 217). Jesus therefore *is* the lamb substituted for Isaac, thereby sparing Isaac, in other words the church. Thus the salvation logic of earliest Christianity made perfect sense within the Jewish worldview no matter which way one looked at it.

155. The fictionality of the Enochic literature is self-evident. On the Maccabean literature as historical fiction: Sara Raup Johnson, *Historical Fictions and Hellenistic Jewish Identity: Third Maccabees in its Cultural Context* (Berkeley, CA: University

(and countless other Revelation texts—the Jews invented a vast library of apocalyptic literature), *Joseph and Aseneth*, the *Testimonies of the Twelve Patriarchs*, the haggadic midrashim (such as, but not only, the *Midrash Rabbah*)—are *all* fiction posing as fact. And that's pretty much the whole of Jewish faith literature.[156] It's long been known that most of the OT is fiction (Exodus, Job, Ruth) or forgery (Daniel, Deutero-Isaiah, Deutero-Zechariah).[157] Indeed, it's not like any non-fundamentalist scholar thinks the Elijah–Elisha narrative in the Kings literature is more than minutely factual at best, as if anyone actually had reliable *sources* for any of it.[158] Likewise Philo's biographies of biblical characters (e.g. *Life of Moses*; *On Joseph*; etc.), or stories added (or perhaps even invented) by Josephus about

of California Press, 2004); in fact, Johnson concludes, not only is 'the historical truth of the events' recorded in 3 Maccabees 'simply irrelevant' to its author, except insofar as to make his story seem true (p. 218), but the 'juxtaposition of history and fiction, combining historical verisimilitude with a remarkable disregard for historical accuracy, [is] characteristic of a wide variety of Jewish Hellenistic texts' (p. 217).

156. See, e.g., Esther Chazon, Michael Stone and Avital Pinnick (eds.), *Pseudepigraphic Perspectives: The Apocrypha and Pseudepigrapha in Light of the Dead Sea Scrolls* (Leiden: Brill, 1999); the Sheffield Academic Press series Guides to Apocrypha and Pseudepigrapha (1995–); David Aune, *The New Testament in its Literary Environment* (Philadelphia, PA: Westminster Press, 1987); James Charlesworth (ed.), *The Old Testament Pseudepigrapha* (2 vols.; Garden City, NY: Doubleday, 1983–1985); George Wesley Buchanan, *Jewish Documents of Deliverance from the Fall of Jerusalem to the Death of Nahmanides* (Dillsboro, NC: Western North Carolina Press, 1978); and so on. See also Craig Evans (ed.), *The Interpretation of Scripture in Early Judaism and Christianity: Studies in Language and Tradition* (Sheffield: Sheffield Academic Press, 2000); and Lawrence Wills (ed.), *Ancient Jewish Novels: An Anthology* (New York: Oxford University Press, 2002).

157. See, e.g., Israel Finkelstein and Neil Silberman, *The Bible Unearthed: Archaeology's New Vision of Ancient Israel and the Origin of its Sacred Texts* (New York: Free Press, 2001); and Israel Finkelstein and Amihai Mazar, *The Quest for the Historical Israel: Debating Archaeology and the History of Early Israel* (Atlanta, GA: Society of Biblical Literature, 2007); Thomas Thompson, *The Mythic Past: Biblical Archaeology and the Myth of Israel* (New York: Basic Books, 1999); Thomas Thompson, *Early History of the Israelite People: From the Written and Archaeological Sources* (New York: Brill, 1992); and Thomas Thompson, *The Historicity of the Patriarchal Narratives: The Quest for the Historical Abraham* (New York: W. de Gruyter, 1974); William Dever, *What Did the Biblical Writers Know, and When Did They Know It? What Archaeology Can Tell Us about the Reality of Ancient Israel* (Grand Rapids, MI: William B. Eerdmans, 2001); Hector Avalos, *The End of Biblical Studies* (Amherst, NY: Prometheus, 2007). See also *The New Interpreter's Bible: Old Testament Survey* (Nashville, TN: Abingdon Press, 2006).

158. In fact most of it is probably complete fabrication, stories added century after century as new points needed to be made: see Susanne Otto, 'The Composition of the Elijah–Elisha Stories and the Deuteronomistic History', *Journal for the Study of the Old Testament* 27 (June 2003), pp. 487-508.

them (in the *Jewish Antiquities*). One of the most astonishing examples is the first-century collection called the *Biblical Antiquities*, once attributed to Philo, but whose actual authors are unknown. This is basically a whole second Bible, in which often minor characters in the OT are picked out and given embellished background stories and adventures, none of which based on a lick of fact.[159] This is essentially identical to what Philo and Josephus do for the more famous figures; and so, too the haggadic midrashim—from the *Midrash Rabbah* to the often wild legends scattered throughout the Talmud, not just about biblical characters, but about rabbis as well, only some of which are likely to be true.[160] It's all of the same piece: this is what Jewish faith literature looked like. Fake stories, passed off as fact. That was the *norm*.[161]

This was equally true of pagan faith literature (already partly explored in Element 14). Of course the so-called novels were all religious narratives (and they do not actually say they are fiction), as were all the tragedies dramatizing mythology, and even some comedies poking fun at religion; yet all these texts were fiction. The entire corpus of mythology (stories of gods, heroes and sages) and paradoxography (collections of incredible tales) in antiquity was certainly not based in fact (hardly at all). Yet these were the standard modes of writing faith literature in pagan cultures. In Hebrew culture the standard model for the same thing was the historical narrative: Exodus, Daniel, Ruth, Job, the Elijah–Elisha narrative in 1 and 2 Kings—this was what Jewish 'mythology' looked like, which is why it is fallacious to assume all mythology looks the way Greeks and Romans wrote it, since every culture has its own way of composing its myths. But myths they are. And the models can even change over time. As pagan literature came to revere the historical narrative as well, the trend of representing mythology

159. Frederick Murphy, *Pseudo-Philo: Rewriting the Bible* (New York: Oxford University Press, 1993). There are interesting parallels between this work and the canonical book of Acts, the case for which is unfortunately still only accessible in German: Eckart Reinmuth, *Pseudo-Philo und Lukas: Studien zum Liber Antiquitatum Biblicarum und seiner Bedeutung für die Interpretation des lukanischen Doppelwerks* (Tübingen: Mohr, 1994).

160. See, e.g., Alan Avery-Peck, 'The Galilean Charismatic and Rabbinic Piety: The Holy Man in the Talmudic Literature', in *The Historical Jesus in Context* (ed. Levine, Allison and Crossan), pp. 149-65.

161. See, e.g., Jo-Ann Brant, Charles Hedrick and Chris Shea (eds.), *Ancient Fiction: The Matrix of Early Christian and Jewish Narrative* (Atlanta, GA: Society of Biblical Literature, 2005); A.J. Droge, '"The Lying Pen of the Scribes": Of Holy Books and Pious Frauds', *Method and Theory in the Study of Religion* 15 (2003), pp. 117-47; and Bruce Metzger, 'Literary Forgeries and Canonical Pseudepigrapha', in *New Testament Studies: Philological, Versional, and Patristic* (Leiden: Brill, 1980), pp. 1-22.

in poetry and drama began to decline and in its place arose a new trend of representing mythology in prose history and biography, which looked exactly like actual history and biography, yet was complete fabrication (see my discussion of 'myth' as a quasi genre in Chapter 10, §2).

A classic example of this trend is seen in the phenomenon of euhemerization (Element 45). Thus, 'lives' of nonhistorical demigods were written, as if they actually existed and could be placed in history, and one could argue about which stories about them were true and which false, even though in fact they never existed at all (and so *all* the stories about them were false). A good example of this is Plutarch's biography of Romulus: this was a Roman adoption of a Greek demigod who later was associated with some of the founding legends of the Roman people (his Greek origins by then completely forgotten: Element 47). Yet Plutarch saw fit to write a straightforward historical biography about him, in which he ponders what stories are true and what false, and includes this alongside biographies of actual persons such as Alexander the Great or Julius Caesar, written in exactly the same style. In the same fashion, historians like Livy or Dionysius would include mythological figures in their otherwise straightforward histories as if they actually existed. In fact, representing myth as fact became so popular, a trend arose of 'inventing' sources to cite as one's authorities, thus completing the representation that myths were actual histories. This is how myth began to look under the Roman Empire. When we collect all of this pagan faith literature together, we see exactly the same outcome: almost all of it is fabricated, yet passed off as true. This was the *norm*.[162]

Even outside of faith literature, standards and practices were not as we would wish them to be. What were represented as sober histories were not consistently honest or reliable. A good story often trumped any interest in what actually happened.[163] And speeches and sayings were routinely

162. On all of the above see Alan Cameron, *Greek Mythography in the Roman World* (New York: Oxford University Press, 2004); and Justin Meggitt, 'Popular Mythology in the Early Empire and the Multiplicity of Jesus Traditions', in *Sources of the Jesus Tradition: Separating History from Myth* (ed. R. Joseph Hoffmann; Amherst, NY: Prometheus, 2010), pp. 55-80.

163. Even the ancients themselves knew this, and complained about it constantly; and modern historians have long known it and articulated the point extensively. See, e.g., my analysis in Carrier, *Not the Impossible Faith*, pp. 161-81; and Carrier, 'Why the Resurrection Is Unbelievable', in *Christian Delusion* (ed. Loftus), pp. 291-96; and the surveys in Charles Fornara, *The Nature of History in Ancient Greece and Rome* (Berkeley, CA: University of California Press, 1983); Colin Hemer, 'Ancient Historiography', in *The Book of Acts in the Setting of Hellenistic History* (Tübingen: J.C.B. Mohr, 1989), pp. 63-100; Averil Cameron (ed.), *History as Text: The Writing of Ancient History* (Chapel Hill, NC: University of North Carolina Press, 1990); Michael Grant, *Greek and Roman Historians: Information and Misinformation* (New York:

invented for historical figures (and obviously for nonhistorical figures as well), based on the reasoning that 'it's what they must have said'.[164] Or, of course, what an author *wants* them to have said. Much of the development in the Gospel tradition exemplifies this; but it's evident also in the Jewish apocrypha, and even the later Jewish canon: Deuteronomy was not written by Moses nor were the words in it spoken by either him or God; and Daniel is likewise a total fabrication (Element 7). Pagans, not embracing the same concept of authoritative 'scripture', had less pressing need to 'attribute' sayings to authorities in this way, although they did so. This is almost certainly the case for the many collections of sayings attributed to particular 'sages' in Diogenes Laertius's *Lives of Eminent Philosophers* (in the first half of Book I), but it is most clearly exemplified in the practice of forgery: attempting to give authority to a system of statements by attributing them to a respected philosopher (such as Aristotle) or scientist (such as Galen).[165] Letters were similarly forged often enough to become their own genre.[166] As were fake histories and documents of all kinds.[167] So when Christians started doing the same, they were taking up a venerable tradition.

Finally, the most startling example of this problem is that the standard method of constructing biographies of revered men was intrinsically fab-

Routledge, 1995); John Marincola, *Authority and Tradition in Ancient Historiography* (New York: Cambridge University Press, 1997).

164. See in particular (besides the scholarship in the previous note) F.W. Wallbank, 'Speeches in Greek Historians', in *Selected Papers: Studies in Greek and Roman History and Historiography* (New York: Cambridge University Press, 1985), pp. 242-61; A.B. Bosworth, *From Arrian to Alexander: Studies in Historical Interpretation* (Oxford: Oxford University Press, 1988), pp. 94-134; Ronald R. Newell, 'The Forms and Historical Value of Josephus' Suicide Accounts', in *Josephus, the Bible, and History* (ed. Louis Feldman and Gohei Hata; Leiden: Brill, 1989), pp. 278-94; Conrad Gempf, 'Public Speaking and Published Accounts', in *The Book of Acts in its First Century Setting: I: Ancient Literary Setting* (ed. Bruce Winter and Andrew D. Clarke; Grand Rapids, MI: Eerdmans, 1993), pp. 259-303. See also Fornara, *Nature of History*, pp. 142-68; Hemer, *Book of Acts*, pp. 63-100; Grant, *Greek and Roman Historians*, pp. 44-53; etc.

165. This phenomenon as a whole is surveyed well in Bart Ehrman, *Forged* (New York: HarperOne, 2011), and *Forgery and Counterforgery: The Use of Literary Deceit in Early Christian Polemics* (New York: Oxford University Press, 2014). For the pagan context in particular, see pp. 13-42; the rest surveys countless examples in early Christian history.

166. C.D.N. Costa, *Greek Fictional Letters* (New York: Oxford University Press, 2001); Patricia Rosenmeyer, *Ancient Epistolary Fictions: The Letter in Greek Literature* (New York: Cambridge University Press, 2001).

167. See, e.g., Erich Gruen, 'Fact and Fiction: Jewish Legends in a Hellenistic Context', in *Hellenistic Constructs: Essays in Culture, History, and Historiography* (ed. Paul Cartledge, Peter Garnsey and Erich Gruen; Berkeley, CA: University of California Press, 1997), pp. 72-88.

ricatory. A great deal of ancient biography, even of real people, was constructed of myth and fiction, frequently telescoping things a person *said* (or wrote) into entire fake stories about things they *did* (or that were done to them), even in the most incredible ways. This has been shown for the ancient biographies of historical poets and philosophers, whose entire biographies are almost wholly made up, based loosely on their *writings*, rather than any kind of biographical sources. For example, Euripides' marital troubles were invented based on things different characters say about marriage in his plays, and not on anything that had anything to do with the actual Euripides or sources about his life. Most biographies of philosophers and poets in antiquity were of this type: inventions passed off as facts.[168] And in the case of non-existent persons (like Romulus or Moses), this was again the *norm*. They would get complete biographies, with origins and deaths and adventures and quips and teachings and family and friends, including siblings with names, a home town, the whole shebang. All invented. There was nothing exceptional or unusual about this at all. This is what *typically* happened. It therefore cannot be regarded as improbable.

Thus we must heed, and can now understand the serious force, of the words of James Crossley on this matter:

> People could in fact create stories grounded in lives of figures who may have been deemed historical actors who really did live, breathe and die (e.g., [*Jubilees*], [*Genesis Apocryphon*], [*Joseph and Aseneth*], Midrashic and haggadic literature, etc.), yet such stories could hardly be said to give genuine historical insight as to what really happened millennia ago when Moses was supposed to receive the Law, when Abram went down to Egypt, or when Joseph wed Aseneth (etc.), if indeed these events did happen. To give another particularly relevant example, the traditions surrounding the book of Esther are chaotic, going off in all kinds of directions and are frequently contradictory. These are not assimilated into one Jewish theology and the inconsistencies are not the reason they are

168. Mary Lefkowitz, *The Lives of the Greek Poets* (Baltimore, MD: Johns Hopkins University Press, 1981); and Mary Lefkowitz, 'Biographical Mythology', in *Antike Mythen: Medien, Transformationen und Konstruktionen* (ed. Ueli Dill; New York: Walter de Gruyter, 2009), pp. 516-31; Janet Fairweather, 'Fiction in the Biographies of Ancient Writers', *Ancient Society* 5 (1974), pp. 231-75; and Janet Fairweather, 'Traditional Narrative, Inference, and Truth in the Lives of the Greek Poets', *Papers of the Liverpool Latin Seminar* 4 (1983), pp. 315-69; Barbara Graziosi, *Inventing Homer: The Early Reception of Epic* (New York: Cambridge University Press, 2002); Ava Chitwood, *Death by Philosophy: The Biographical Tradition in the Life and Death of the Archaic Philosophers Empedocles, Heraclitus, and Democritus* (Ann Arbor, MI: University of Michigan Press, 2004). See also Bruno Gentili and Giovanni Cerri, *History and Biography in Ancient Thought* (Amsterdam: J.C. Gieben, 1988). This fact is conceded all too briefly by Richard Burridge, *What Are the Gospels? A Comparison with Graeco-Roman Biography* (New York: Cambridge University Press, 1992), pp. 138-39.

> assumed to be historically inaccurate. But historically inaccurate they are and it is hardly going too far to assume something similar was happening in the Gospel traditions, a point that should not have to be made. Moreover these Jewish stories continued to have a powerful emotive effect and needed to be defended in the light of different contexts.

Thus, Crossley concedes, people often invented these things because they needed to believe them (or needed others to believe them), and therefore *had* to represent them as factual.[169] This is obvious in 'the expanded Jewish stories of, for example, Moses, Abraham, Joseph, Elijah and numerous rabbis'. In some cases the reasons for fabrication are unclear, seeming only to make great heroes seem greater, or to tell stories through them that then carried more telling weight, or simply because it sounded right. But many examples 'which cannot be historically accurate, rewrite stories of figures in the past to justify a belief in the present'. Indeed, that was a routine practice. Hence, 'it follows that it is perfectly possible for the Gospel writers to do the same'. They are certainly in the same boat, because often 'historically inaccurate storytelling was done for fairly recent figures', too. 'Stories of rabbis are one example', and another 'is the rapid emergence of miraculous and legendary traditions surrounding pagan figures, such as Alexander or Augustus, even within their own life times'.

Thus, Crossley concludes:

> It [should] seem blindingly obvious that people invent stories and the sifting of fact from fiction or fiction from fact has been one of the most notable features in the history of critical biblical scholarship. . . . [So] if we are going to take Christianity seriously in its Jewish and pagan contexts then we must expect the Gospel writers to make up stories just as Jews and pagans did. Historically speaking it is extremely unlikely that the Christians behind the Gospel traditions were immune to this standard practice.[170]

He is entirely correct. In fact, our conclusion must be even stronger than this: for when we look at all faith literature together, most of it *by far* was fabricated to a great extent, and most was fabricated *in its entirety.* This leaves us with a *very* high prior probability that Christian literature will be the same.

And we can confirm this to be the case. If we exclude devotional and analytical literature (e.g. apologies, commentaries, instructionals, hymnals) and only focus on 'primary source documents' about earliest Christi-

169. On why passing myths off as facts always conferred a rhetorical advantage and thus would almost always inevitably occur and win out, see Chapter 8 (§12).

170. James Crossley, 'Against the Historical Plausibility of the Empty Tomb Story and the Bodily Resurrection of Jesus', *Journal for the Study of the Historical Jesus* 3 (June 2005), pp. 171-86 (178-82).

anity, we find that *most* Christian faith literature in its first three centuries is fabricated—indeed, most *by far*. We'll see some examples in Chapter 8. But the most obvious category is the Christian apocrypha and pseudepigrapha: hundreds of forged documents, from faked letters of Paul to Seneca, to faked letters of Clement of Rome (and by that I mean beyond *1 Clement,* if that is even authentic), more faked letters from Peter and Paul than are even in the NT (e.g. *3 Corinthians*, *3 and 4 Peter*, etc.; for the fact that there are already forged letters in the NT, see Chapter 7, §3), even faked letters from Jesus (several in Revelation already; another, from Jesus to Abgar, is reproduced in Eusebius), and fabricated Gospels and Acts and Apocalypses far outnumbering the canonical ones, as well as countless legends and tales passed off as fact (in the commentaries of Papias and Hegesippus, e.g.: see Chapter 8, §§7 and 8), and countless other fictions (the *Epistle of Barnabas,* e.g.; or the *Decree of Tiberius,* cited as authoritative proof that Emperor Tiberius converted to Christianity).[171]

There were in fact over forty different Gospels written, of which even fundamentalists agree only the canonical four are in any way authentic (while most mainstream scholars entertain the possibility that only one or two of those are, at best), plus over half a dozen different Acts.[172] Exam-

171. Many examples are collected, discussed or listed in Bart Ehrman, *Lost Scriptures: Books That Did Not Make It into the New Testament* (New York: Oxford University Press, 2003); and Bart Ehrman, *Lost Christianities: The Battles for Scripture and the Faiths We Never Knew* (New York: Oxford University Press, 2005); Price, *Pre-Nicene New Testament* (e.g. pp. 841-49 [3 and 4 Peter], pp. 885-86 [Letter of Jesus to Abgar], pp. 1141-44 [3 Corinthians]); John Loftus, *Why I Became an Atheist: A Former Preacher Rejects Christianity* (Amherst, NY: Prometheus Books, 2008), pp. 167-76; David Trobisch, 'Who Published the Christian Bible?', *CSER Review* 2.1 (2007), pp. 29-30; and, most extensively, F. Lapham, *Introduction to the New Testament Apocrypha* (London: T. & T. Clark International, 2003); Wilhelm Schneemelcher and R. McL. Wilson (eds.), *New Testament Apocrypha*, Vols. I and II (Louisville, KY: Westminster/John Knox Press, 1991); and James H. Charlesworth (ed.), *The New Testament Apocrypha and Pseudepigrapha: A Guide to Publications with Excursuses on Apocalypses* (Chicago: American Theological Library Association, 1987). For the 'Decree of Tiberius' see Tertullian, *Apology* 5. The *Shepherd of Hermas*, which along with *Barnabas* was once in the orthodox Christian canon, was also likely forged or redacted over time (Price, *Pre-Nicene New Testament*, pp. 1001-89).

172. Christopher Tuckett, 'Forty Other Gospels', in *The Written Gospel* (ed. Markus Bockmuehl and Donald Hagner; Cambridge: Cambridge University Press, 2005), pp. 238-53; Charles Hedrick, 'The 34 Gospels: Diversity and Division among the Earliest Christians', *Bible Review* 18 (June 2002), pp. 20-31, 46-47; Helmut Koester, 'Apocryphal and Canonical Gospels', *Harvard Theological Review* 73 (January–April 1980), pp. 105-30. None of these lists are complete. See, e.g., Rodolphe Kasser *et al.*, *The Gospel of Judas: From Codex Tchacos* (Washington, DC: National Geographic, 2006); R. Blackhirst, 'Barnabas and the Gospels: Was There an Early *Gospel of*

ples of this fabricatory activity in early Christian faith literature are vast in quantity.[173] This was clearly the norm, not the exception. Most of what Christians wrote were lies. We therefore should approach everything they wrote with distrust. (See also Chapter 7, §7; and Chapter 8, §§3 and 4.)

Element 45: A popular version of this phenomenon in ancient faith literature was the practice of euhemerization: the taking of a cosmic god and placing him at a definite point in history as an actual person who was later deified. We already noted Plutarch's criticism of the trend (which he frowns upon, but in so doing concedes its popularity) in Element 14.[174]

Euhemerus was a Greek writer of the early third century BCE, who wrote a book called *The Sacred Scriptures* in which he depicted an imaginary scholar discovering that Zeus and Uranus were once actual kings. In the process Euhemerus invents a history for these 'god kings', even though we know there is no plausible case to be made that either Zeus or Uranus was ever a real person. Yet the idea caught on; biographies and histories of non-existent people proliferated, and ancient literature flowered with attempts to assign mythic heroes and gods to real historical periods and places.[175] Even before that there were attempts to develop a 'historical' Hercules to justify territorial disputes in the Peloponnesus, and afterwards the origin of Rome was explained by appealing to an eponymous godman named 'Romulus'. And many other uses were found for the procedure, as we saw for inventing King Arthur, Ned Ludd, Abraham, Moses, and other national heroes I explored in Chapter 1 (§4). There was nothing at all unusual about doing this.

Element 46: Ancient literature also proliferated a variety of model 'hero' narratives, some of which the Gospel Jesus conforms to as well, and one of these hero-types was widely revered among pagans: the pre-Christian

Barnabas?', *Journal of Higher Criticism* 7 (Spring 2000), pp. 1-22. Among the 'other' Acts are the Acts of Peter, Acts of Philip, Acts of John, Acts of Paul, Acts of Thomas, Acts of Pilate and the Acts of Andrew. Note that if we are to presume that four out of forty Gospels were authentic, then the prior probability that any specific Gospel is authentic will be only one in ten at best. For any given Acts, those chances are one in eight. In other words, probably not.

173. Besides the countless examples referenced in the sources in the previous note, see, in general, D.A. Carson, 'Pseudonymity and Pseudepigraphy', in *Dictionary of New Testament Background* (ed. Evans and Porter), pp. 857-64.

174. See, again, Plutarch, *On Isis and Osiris* 22.359e–24.360c and 29.362c.

175. See Jacob Stern, 'Heraclitus the Paradoxographer: *Peri Apistōn*, "On Unbelievable Tales"', *Transactions of the American Philological Association* 133 (Spring 2003), pp. 51-97 (who treats the entire genre as well as the specific work in the title).

narratives of the life and death of Socrates and Aesop. These match those of Jesus in the following respects:

1. They all came from a humble background (Socrates was the son of a stonemason; Aesop was a slave).
2. Yet all were exalted as a moral hero and an exemplary man, who was in the right, and whose teachings one ought to follow.
3. And that despite all of them having opposed and denounced the established religious authorities and having challenged the received wisdom of their people.
4. All attacked the sin and greed of the religious and political elite.
5. All attended the parties of sinners and ate and drank with them.
6. Yet all consistently denounced sinners, and sought to reform them.
7. All taught with questions, parables and paradoxes.
8. All taught to love truth, despise money and have compassion on others.
9. All taught that they wanted to save everyone's soul.
10. All were despised by some and beloved by others for their teachings.
11. All were publicly mocked in some way.
12. All were renowned to be physically ugly or deformed.[176]
13. All were executed by the state for blasphemy, a crime they did not commit.
14. All were *actually* executed for speaking against the sin and greed of the authorities.
15. All voluntarily went to their deaths, despite all having had the power to escape.
16. All prophesied God's wrath would befall their killers; and all were right.
17. All were subsequently revered as martyrs.
18. And all at the outset had been given a gift of the spirit from God.[177]

The fact that this was a recognized and *widely revered* hero narrative puts the lie to any claim that Christians were in any way radical in conforming their Jesus to it. In fact, even if Jesus existed, we still must worry about how

176. That this was believed about Jesus: Justin Martyr, *Dialogue with Trypho* 88; Tertullian, *On the Flesh of Christ* 9; Clement of Alexandria, *The Instructor* 3.1; Origen, *Against Celsus* 6.75; cf. Isa. 52.14; 53.2-3. For Aesop: Lawrence Wills, 'The Aesop Tradition', in *Historical Jesus in Context* (ed. Levine, Allison and Crossan), pp. 222-37 (223); for Socrates: Kenneth Lapin, 'Picturing Socrates', in *A Companion to Socrates* (ed. Sara Ahbel-Rappe and Rachana Kamtekar; Oxford: Blackwell, 2006), pp. 110-55.

177. Aesop was given a spirit that gave him a supernatural power of speaking; Socrates was given a spirit that spoke to him and counseled him toward wisdom; and Jesus, of course, was given the Holy Spirit.

much of his narrative is being forced into this model for that very reason, and therefore still not historically true.

We can add to all this that 'Socrates, like Jesus, turned the other cheek and forgave the enemies who had caused his death'.[178] We can likewise add that Aesop and Jesus were both itinerant preachers in a peripheral region who ended up in a central holy city and were both plotted against and executed by its priests (Delphi for Aesop; Jerusalem for Jesus). Likewise, for Aesop a 'gospel' was written about his birth, life, teachings and death, and many different redactions were then made of it, just as happened for Jesus.

We've also noted already the connections between the Gospel Jesus and the Cynics (Element 32). It is therefore significant that Socrates was the spiritual founder of the Cynics, Diogenes the Cynic having been the student of one of Socrates' pupils, Antisthenes, and Cynicism remaining more faithful to the original teachings of Socrates than any other subsequent sect (including Platonism), and Diogenes in fact believing this was the case.[179] And Aesop fulfilled in his life and death many of the values espoused by Socrates and the Cynics. It is therefore not likely an accident that a Jewish religion espousing values well in tune with the Cynics would revere as their founding hero someone who corresponds exactly to the Aesop–Socratic dying-hero type that was also promoted and revered by the Cynics.

Socrates we can be certain was a historical person (see Chapter 8, §2). But Aesop is not likely to have been.[180] There is no strong evidence that Aesop ever actually lived (he is supposed to have flourished in the seventh

178. Emily Wilson, *The Death of Socrates* (Cambridge, MA: Harvard University Press, 2007), p. 141. Discussing the parallels between Jesus and Socrates: Paul Gooch, *Reflections on Jesus and Socrates: Word and Silence* (New Haven, CT: Yale University Press, 1996), pp. 12-16; James Hankins, 'Socrates in the Italian Renaissance', in *A Companion to Socrates* (ed. Sara Ahbel-Rappe and Rachana Kamtekar; Oxford: Blackwell, 2006), pp. 337-52 (348); and Wilson, *Death of Socrates*, pp. 141-69.

179. Socrates' links to Cynicism: Susan Prince, 'Socrates, Antisthenes, and the Cynics', in *Companion to Socrates* (ed. Ahbel-Rappe and Kamtekar), pp. 75-92; and Luis Navia, *Socrates: A Life Examined* (Amherst, NY: Prometheus Books, 2007).

180. B.E. Perry, *Studies in the Text History of the Life and Fables of Aesop* (Haverford, PA: American Philological Association, 1936). See the earliest redaction of the *Life of Aesop* 1-19 for Aesop's nativity story, and *Life of Aesop* 91-142 for his passion story (concluding in his death). See also Anton Wiechers, *Aesop in Delphi* (Meisenheim: A. Hain, 1961); B.E. Perry, 'Demetrius of Phalerum and the Aesopic Fables', *Transactions and Proceedings of the American Philological Association* 93 (1962), pp. 287-346; Leslie Kurke, 'Aesop and the Contestation of Delphic Authority', in *The Cultures within Ancient Greek Culture: Contact, Conflict, Collaboration* (ed. Carol Dougherty and Leslie Kurke; New York: Cambridge University Press, 2003), pp. 77-100; Wills, 'The Aesop Tradition'; and David Watson, 'The Life of Aesop and the Gospel of Mark: Two Ancient Approaches to Elite Values', *Journal of Biblical Literature* 129 (2010), pp. 699-716.

century BCE), much less wrote the fables attributed to him.[181] But even if either is true, the biographies written about him are still unlikely to have any basis in fact, and no historian today believes they are. Aesop was more likely invented to place a name to a growing collection of fables passed down from numerous oral sources. Historical facts were then invented about him, and then detailed biographies were written, in some respects similar to the Gospels. If that's what happened, then Aesop would be an example of a mythical person who 'became' the historical author of a collection of parables he didn't in fact write (which are often similar in moral and symbolic purpose to the parables of Jesus), and then about whom fictional biographies were written, which were then passed off as fact. It's easy to see how this could happen for Aesop. So in principle the same could have happened for Jesus.

Element 47: Another model hero narrative, which pagans also revered and to which the Gospel Jesus also conforms, is the apotheosis, or 'ascension to godhood' tale, and of these the one to which the Gospels (and Acts) most conform is that of the Roman national hero Romulus. I discussed this already in Chapter 4 (§1), and the points made there should be considered a component of the element here.

The more general point is that this narrative concept of a 'translation to heaven' for a hero (often but not always a divine son of god) was very commonplace, and always centered around a peculiar fable about the disappearance of their body. All these fables were different from one another, and therefore those differences are irrelevant to the point: all still shared the same core features (see my discussion of how syncretism works in Element 11). And when it comes to the Romulus fable in particular, the evidence is unmistakable that Christianity conformed itself to it relatively quickly—even if all these attributes were accumulated over time and not all at once.

Romulus, of course, did not exist. He was invented, along with legends about him (largely put together from previous Greek and Etruscan mythol-

181. All references to him are centuries late and based on legendary assumptions that stem from his later faith narrative, not contemporary documents or witnesses. See previous note for scholarship on the evidence for Aesop and what can be said regarding his historicity. The best case for his historicity is attempted in Nikoletta Kanavou, 'Personal Names in the *Vita Aesopi* (*Vita G* or *Perriana*)', *Classical Quarterly* 56 (May 2006), pp. 208-19, but even she is uncertain of the strength of her case, and she overlooks the fact that her only real argument, that Aesop was a common Thracian slave name (pp. 218-19), could in fact be how the mythic name was assigned to previously anonymous fables: a common slave-type was drawn up, assigned a common slave-name, assigned to the fables, and then a biography built up around the figure thus created.

ogy), much later in Roman history than he is supposed to have lived.[182] His name was eponymous (essentially an early form of the word 'Roman'), and his story was meant to exemplify ideal Roman aspirations and values, using a model similar to Greek tragedy, in which the hero sins in various ways but comes to self-understanding and achieves peace by the time of his death. He otherwise exhibits in his deeds the 'exemplary qualities' of Rome as a social entity, held up as a model for Roman leaders to emulate, such as ending 'the cycle of violence' initiated by his sin and pride by religiously expiating the sin of past national crimes in order to bring about a lasting peace.[183] His successor, Numa, then exemplified the role of the ideal, sinless king, a religious man and performer of miracles whose tomb was found empty after his death, demonstrating that he, too, like his predecessor Romulus, rose from the dead and ascended to heaven.[184]

The idea of the 'translation to heaven' of the body of a divine king was therefore adaptable and flexible, every myth being in various ways different but in certain core respects the same. But the Gospels conform to the Romulus model most specifically.[185] There are twenty parallels, although not every story contained every one. In some cases that may simply be the result of selection or abbreviation in the sources we have (and therefore the silence of one source does not entail the element did not then exist or was not known to that author); and in some cases elements might have been deliberately removed (or even reversed) by an author who wanted to promote a different message (see discussion in Chapter 10, §2, of how mythmaking operated in antiquity). For example, the 'radiant resurrection body' (probably the earlier version of Christian appearance narratives) was later

182. Gary Forsythe, *A Critical History of Early Rome* (Berkeley, CA: University of California Press, 2005), pp. 93-102; Robin Hard and H.J. Rose, *The Routledge Handbook of Greek Mythology* (New York: Routledge, 2004), pp. 600-602; Timothy Wiseman, *The Myths of Rome* (Exeter: University of Exeter Press, 2004), pp. 138-48; Dylan Saylor, 'Dirty Linen, Fabrication, and the Authorities of Livy and Augustus', *Transactions of the American Philological Association* 136 (Autumn 2006), pp. 329-88.

183. Rex Stem, 'The Exemplary Lessons of Livy's Romulus', *Transactions of the American Philological Association* 137.2 (Autumn 2007), pp. 435-71.

184. Hans Dieter Betz, 'Plutarch's Life of Numa: Some Observations on Graeco-Roman "Messianism"', in *Redemption and Resistance: The Messianic Hopes of Jews and Christians in Antiquity* (ed. Markus Bockmuehl and James Carleton Paget; New York: T. & T. Clark, 2007), pp. 44-62.

185. See the extensive treatment of this point (and discussion of all the heroes who match the type) in Richard Miller, 'Mark's Empty Tomb and Other Translation Fables in Classical Antiquity', *Journal of Biblical Literature* 129 (2010), pp. 759-76. In the following I have adapted his table of parallels from pp. 772-73, but changing their order.

transformed into a 'hidden-god narrative' (another common trope both in paganism and Judaism) as suited any given author.[186]

But when taken altogether the Romulus and Jesus death-and-resurrection narratives contain all of the following parallels:

1. The hero is the son of God.
2. His death is accompanied by prodigies.
3. The land is covered in darkness.
4. The hero's corpse goes missing.
5. The hero receives a new immortal body, superior to the one he had.
6. His resurrection body has on occasion a bright and shining appearance.
7. After his resurrection he meets with a follower on a road from the city.
8. A speech is given from a summit or high place prior to ascending.
9. An inspired message of resurrection or 'translation to heaven' is delivered to a witness.
10. There is a 'great commission' (an instruction to future followers).
11. The hero physically ascends to heaven in his new divine body.
12. He is taken up into a cloud.
13. There is an explicit role given to eyewitness testimony (even naming the witnesses).
14. Witnesses are frightened by his appearance and/or disappearance.
15. Some witnesses flee.
16. Claims are made of 'dubious alternative accounts' (*which claims were obviously fabricated for Romulus, there never having been a true account to begin with*).
17. All of this occurs outside of a nearby (but central) city.
18. His followers are initially in sorrow over the hero's death.
19. But his post-resurrection story leads to eventual belief, homage and rejoicing.
20. The hero is deified and cult subsequently paid to him (in the same manner as a god).

Romulus, of course, was also unjustly killed by the authorities (and came from a humble background, beginning his career as an orphan and a shepherd, a nobody from the hill country), and thus also overlaps the Aesop–Socratic type (see Element 46), and it's easy to see that by combining the two, we end up with pretty much the Christian Gospel in outline (especially when we appropriately Judaize the result: Elements 3-7, 17-20, and 39-43). Some of the parallels could be coincidental (e.g. resurrected bodies being associated with radiance was itself a common trope, both within Judaism

186. See first note in Chapter 4, §1, and my discussion in Carrier, 'Spiritual Body', in *Empty Tomb* (ed. Price and Lowder), pp. 182-84 (with pp. 154, 190-93).

and paganism), but for *all of them* to be coincidental is extremely improbable.[187] The Christian conception of Jesus' death and resurrection appears to have been significantly influenced by the Roman conception of Romulus's death and resurrection.

187. A mathematical objection is sometimes raised here using the Lincoln–Kennedy coincidences as a counter-example (see the analysis at Snopes.com: http://www.snopes.com/history/american/lincoln-kennedy.asp). The reasoning being that clearly there is no causal relation in that case, therefore large lists of coincidences can occur by chance (an example of the multiple comparisons fallacy). However, this is an invalid analogy for two reasons: first, the coincidences in the Lincoln–Kennedy case are all trivial and meaningless and most have no conceptual connection with each other (moreover, some are actually false; the number of 'true' coincidences is only fifteen); second, the amount of available data on Lincoln and Kennedy is vast compared to that on Romulus and Jesus or any other ancient person, mythical or historical (due to the enormous disparity in survival of sources and documents from the two periods). Combine those two conditions and the likelihood of a long list of parallels occurring purely by chance is high (since no rules govern which parallels 'count' and there are so many data points, so the frequency of random parallels is high). But when *neither* condition obtains, the frequency is *not* high. In the Romulus–Jesus case, the probability is extremely low that the filter destroying almost all data about them would just 'by coincidence' preserve twenty meaningful and substantial parallels conceptually connected to each of their death-and-resurrection accounts. The Lincoln–Kennedy coincidences, e.g., are often highly likely to occur between any two people (millions of people have the same number of letters in their name, for example); whereas the Romulus–Jesus parallels are not (how many people are hailed son of god? How many have the world covered by a supernatural darkness at their deaths? How many have their corpses conspicuously vanish? How many visit their friends on the road from their city in a resurrected body to commission them to spread their gospel? Etc.). Thus, even with a large database, twenty such parallels would be unlikely; it is only the more so with so small a database. Most of the Lincoln–Kennedy coincidences have, again, no conceptual connection to each other (what has the year of a man's birth to do with the nature of his death?); but the Romulus–Jesus parallels do (all relate to describing the narratives of their deaths, and the religious aftermath directly connected thereto). Thus, the ability to find connected data points unconstrained by any parameters does not obtain in the latter case, greatly reducing the probability of even trivial parallels, much less substantial ones (e.g. if I get to count any coincidences between two people, I can always find some; but if I am required to find only coincidences pertaining to the accounts of their death, not so much—except insofar as I am counting things that are frequently true of deaths in general, but none of the Romulus–Jesus parallels are such). When we get to the next element (Element 48), the probability of coincidence as explanation plummets (as to get many parallels between any two people is one thing, but to find them across a dozen people is wholly another), and yet in that instance the fact that that probability is extremely low won't even matter (as I'll explain in Chapter 6). On the matter of discerning meaningful coincidences generally, see discussion in Carrier, *Proving History*, pp. 192-204.

Even if we discounted that for any reason, the Romulus parallels definitely establish that all these components were already part of a recognized hero-type, and are therefore not surprising or unusual or unexpected. The story of Jesus would have looked familiar, not only in the same way all translation stories looked familiar even when different in many and profound ways, but also in the very specific way that among all such tales it looked the most like the story of Romulus, which was publicly acted out in passion plays every year. And this was the national founding hero of the Roman Empire. What better god's tale to emulate or co-opt?

Element 48: Finally, the most ubiquitous model 'hero' narrative, which pagans also revered and to which the Gospel Jesus also conforms, is the fable of the 'divine king', what I call the Rank–Raglan hero-type, based on the two scholars who discovered and described it, Otto Rank and Lord Raglan.[188] This is a hero-type found repeated across at least fifteen known mythic heroes (including Jesus)—*if* we count only those who *clearly* meet *more than half* of the designated parallels (which means twelve or more matches out of twenty-two elements), which requirement eliminates many historical persons, such as Alexander the Great or Caesar Augustus, who accumulated many elements of this hero-type in the tales told of them, yet not that many.

The twenty-two features distinctive of this hero-type are:

1. The hero's mother is a virgin.
2. His father is a king or the heir of a king.
3. The circumstances of his conception are unusual.
4. He is reputed to be the son of a god.
5. An attempt is made to kill him when he is a baby.
6. To escape which he is spirited away from those trying to kill him.
7. He is reared in a foreign country by one or more foster parents.
8. We are told nothing of his childhood.
9. On reaching manhood he returns to his future kingdom.
10. He is crowned, hailed or becomes king.
11. He reigns uneventfully (i.e., without wars or national catastrophes).
12. He prescribes laws.
13. He then loses favor with the gods or his subjects.
14. He is driven from the throne or city.
15. He meets with a mysterious death.
16. He dies atop a hill or high place.

188. Alan Segal (ed.), *In Quest of the Hero* (Princeton, NJ: Princeton University Press, 1990).

17. His children, if any, do not succeed him.
18. His body turns up missing.
19. Yet he still has one or more holy sepulchers (in fact or fiction).
20. Before taking a throne or a wife, he battles and defeats a great adversary (such as a king, giant, dragon or wild beast).

and

21. His parents are related to each other.
22. He marries a queen or princess related to his predecessor.

Many of the heroes who fulfill this type also either (a) performed miracles (in life or as a deity after death) or were (b) preexistent beings who became incarnated as men or (c) subsequently worshiped as savior gods, any one of which honestly should be counted as a twenty-third attribute.[189] Of these qualifying features, Jesus shares all three. Likewise, many who fit this hero type 'fulfilled prophecy', and although that was commonly the case for heroes generally (far beyond the specific hero-type described here), it is another feature Jesus shares in common with them, and which honestly should be counted as a twenty-fourth attribute.[190] But I shall work from the traditional twenty-two.

The fifteen people who score more than half of those twenty-two features, in order of how many they score (from most to least) is as follows:[191]

189. See, e.g., Charles Talbert, *What Is a Gospel? The Genre of the Canonical Gospels* (Philadelphia, PA: Fortress Press, 1977). Unquestionable miracle workers on the following list are Moses, Jesus, Theseus (who returned from the dead to fight supernaturally in wartime), Dionysus, Hercules (apart from his own supernatural feats in life, as a deity he answered prayers), Zeus, Osiris and Asclepius (the latter three were celebrated miracle-bringing gods), which already is more than half the list (eight in all). Others on the Rank–Raglan list may also have miracle legends associated with them.

190. I thank Loren Petrich and Aaron Adair for pointing this out and providing research confirming it. Those who share this element would include (besides obviously Jesus): Moses (Exod. 1.8-10, 22, and Josephus, *Antiquities of the Jews* 2.205-208); Oedipus (Sophocles, *Oedipus the King* 705-25, 785-99, 849-59); Perseus (Apollodorus, *The Library* 2.4.1-4); Romulus (Livy, *From the Founding of the City* 1.3-1.5); Theseus (David Kovacs, 'And Baby Makes Three: Aegeus' Wife as Mother-to-Be of Theseus in Euripides' Medea', *Classical Philology* 103 [July 2008], pp. 298-304); Jason (Apollonius of Rhodes, *Argonautica* 1.5); Pelops ('Pelops' and 'Hippodamia', *Oxford Classical Dictionary* [ed. Simon Hornblower and Antony Spawforth; Oxford: Oxford University Press, 3rd edn, 1995], pp. 1134, 711); and Hercules (Marco Fantuzzi and Richard Hunter, *Tradition and Innovation in Hellenistic Poetry* [New York: Cambridge University Press, 2004], pp. 125, 205-207). Which is again more than half the list (nine in all). It is entirely possible others on the Rank–Raglan list also met this criterion.

191. These scores are taken from Segal (ed.), *Quest*, pp. 138-44; except the scoring for Osiris is my own, based on the information in Plutarch's *On Isis and Osiris*; and I have reduced some scores based on my own examination of the evidence (applying the

1. Oedipus (21)
2. Moses (20)
3. Jesus (20)
4. Theseus (19)
5. Dionysus (19)
6. Romulus (18)
7. Perseus (17)
8. Hercules (17)
9. Zeus (15)
10. Bellerophon (14)
11. Jason (14)
12. Osiris (14)
13. Pelops (13)
14. Asclepius (12)
15. Joseph [i.e., the son of Jacob] (12)

This is a useful discovery, because with so many matching persons it doesn't matter what the probability is of scoring more than half on the Rank–Raglan scale by chance coincidence. Because even if it can happen often by chance coincidence, then the percentage of persons who score that high should match the ratio of real persons to mythical persons. In other words, if a real person can have the same elements associated with him, and in particular so many elements (and for this purpose it doesn't matter whether they actually occurred), then there should be many real persons on the list—as surely there are far more real persons than mythical ones. The number of real persons in the course of antiquity must number in the hundreds of millions, whereas the number of mythical persons invented over that same course of time will be in the thousands at most. Certainly, by any calculation the latter could not possibly outnumber the former—and even if they were equally numerous, then half the names on the list should be actual persons. But this is not the case. No known historical persons are on the list.[192] *Only* mythical people ever got fitted to this hero-type.[193] *Yet*

criteria must be reasonably rigorous to be meaningful: see earlier note on the Lincoln–Kennedy case).

192. For Moses and Joseph, see references in earlier note. The others hardly need a reference. They've been recognized as mythical throughout the last century of classical scholarship. Any inquiry into their origins ends the same: they began as deities long before they were translated into men and placed into history (e.g. Hercules, Dionysus, Osiris) or they began as heroic characters in absurdist supernatural dramas that have no plausible claim to historicity (e.g. Jason, Perseus, Bellerophon).

193. Alexander the Great and Mithradates of Pontus are the only historical figures who come close: Alexander scoring items 2-4, 9-10, 12, 16-17 and 22, for only 10 points; Mithradates, items 1-2, 10, 12-14, 16-17, 20 and 22, for likewise 10. They

every single one of them was regarded as a historical person and placed in history in narratives written about them.

Therefore, whether fitting more than half the Rank–Raglan criteria was always a product of chance coincidence or the product of causal influence, either way we can still conclude that it would be *very unusual* for any historical person to fit more than half the Rank–Raglan criteria—because if it were *not* unusual, then many historical persons would have done so. But not even one did. We might not know the cause of this fact, but a fact it is nonetheless, and a fact we can make use of (as I will in §3 of the next chapter).

Jesus scores twenty out of twenty-two, according to Matthew's Gospel (and whether these attributes were original or lately appended to his legend won't matter, as I'll explain in §4 of the next chapter; but note that even in Mark's Gospel, Jesus scores a 14, and even that would place him well above the bottom of the list). The first nineteen hardly require defense (e.g. his father is the heir of King David; he is seized by the authorities, abandoned by his followers, and driven from Jerusalem to his execution; strange things happen at his death, and the death itself is a strangely sudden expiration; he dies atop the hill named Golgotha; etc.).[194] The remaining

can only be grossly overscored by an inappropriately loose assignment of criteria. One might propose Alexander rates 13, e.g., by scoring items 13, 15, and 18 but (a) Alexander only dealt with occasionally disobedient troops, assassins and rebellions by conquered peoples and he was never in any significant way 'abandoned' by the gods or the Macedonians; (b) his cause of death was disputed, not mysterious (and it involved nothing supernatural); (c) his body didn't vanish, but was taken to Egypt by his general Ptolemy where it remained to be viewed for centuries. In the same respect, contra Adrienne Mayor (*The Poison King: The Life and Legend of Mithradates, Rome's Deadliest Enemy* [Princeton, NJ: Princeton University Press, 2010], pp. 371-76), stories of attempts to assassinate Mithradates during his childhood and teen years do not correspond to attempting to kill him 'as a baby', and at once disqualify him from the criterion 'we are told nothing of his childhood'. He was also not explicitly identified as the son of a god; there is no actual evidence his parents were related; a comet corresponding with his conception and birth does not relate to *how he was conceived*; he was not actually spirited away as a baby or raised in a foreign land (but merely traveled his own land incognito as a teen); having never left his kingdom as a child, he can't have 'returned' to it; wars during his reign disqualify him from 'reigns uneventfully', and do *not* correlate with battling a single great foe before ascending his throne; there was nothing actually mysterious or supernatural about his death; his body never vanishes; and not having vanished, his body can't 'yet still have' a tomb (it is just simply entombed).

194. Note that crucifixion was supposed to take days to kill; thus Jesus' rapid death is itself mysterious: even Pilate is surprised by it (Mk 15.44), and the centurion amazed by it (Mt. 27.54). It also is accompanied by an abundance of prodigies, establishing it as mysterious and supernaturally potent.

hit (number 20) may not be as obvious, but he scores it: just as Oedipus confronts and defeats the riddling Sphinx, Jesus confronts and defeats the temptations of the Devil (also known as the Adversary, and as a Serpent or Dragon, and 'Prince of the World'), in both cases before going to claim their kingdom (of course, even in earliest Christian tradition Satan is the power whom Jesus most decisively defeats so as to effect the salvation of the faithful ever after).[195]

The only two elements Jesus does not score are the last I've listed: we cannot establish (21) that his parents were originally imagined as related or (22) that he ever married (much less the daughter of his predecessor). However, the peculiar absence of that last element practically advertises the fact that he does merit that element *allegorically*: from the earliest time Jesus was imagined to have taken the 'church' as his bride, which was indeed understood to be the 'daughter' of his predecessor (the nation of Israel).[196] So in all honesty we could assign him that element as well. But as it is not 'literal' I will leave his score at twenty.[197] Nevertheless, even then he is nearly the highest scoring person in history, next only to Oedipus; and if we granted that last element, he would be tied even with him for highest score.

Jesus might even have outranked Oedipus. A later tradition held that indeed his parents were relatives, and it is possible that had been a tradition from very early on that just wasn't recorded in our Gospels.[198] However, by

195. For Satan as adversary, serpent, and prince of the world, see Element 37; For Satan as dragon: Rev. 12.9; 20.2; Satan as devouring beast: 1 Pet. 5.8; as prince or ruler, and metaphor of 'doing battle' with Satan': Eph. 2.2; 6.11-12. Satan has a 'kingdom' (which would make him a king): Lk. 4.5-6; 11.18. Jesus 'doing battle' with Satan: 'and he was there in the wilderness forty days, tempted by Satan, and was with the wild beasts, and the angels ministered unto him' (Mk 1.13) is expanded into a more elaborate spiritual battle in Mt. 4.1-11 and Lk. 4.1-13; Satan has power over death, and 'death' is the last enemy Jesus will defeat: Heb. 2.14; 1 Cor. 15.25-26; 15.54-57.

196. 2 Cor. 2.2; Eph. 5.22-25; Mk 2.19-20; Mt. 9.15; 25.1-13 (also perhaps 22.1-10); Lk. 5.34-35; Jn 3.27-30; Rev. 19.7-9 and 21.2; and perhaps also implied in Rom. 7.1-6 and Rev. 22.17. Origen explained this concept at length: see R.P. Lawson, *Origen: The Song of Songs, Commentary and Homilies* (Ancient Christian Writers, 26; London: Longmans, Green, 1957).

197. Attempts to deny this always devolve into specious apologetics. For example, in Richard Horsley, *The Liberation of Christmas: The Infancy Narratives in Social Context* (New York: Crossroad, 1989), pp. 162-72 (163), it is claimed Jesus can't be considered a 'king' because 'Jesus explicitly refuses to become a king' (no citation is given for that assertion), ignoring Mt. 2.2; 21.5; 25.34; 27.11, 29, 37, 42. This is simply denialism. Horsley's other rejections of the Raglan criteria are similarly baseless. And yet even he concedes Matthew's nativity account corresponds to the Rank hero type (166-72).

198. The *Protevangelion of James* explicitly says Mary is, like Joseph, a descendant of David (§ 10.1).

the time we hear of this detail, Jesus was being transformed into a different character. For example, Infancy Gospels were then being written about him, introducing narratives of his childhood. If we scored on attributes all the way into the late second century, this would remove one element ('we hear nothing of his childhood'), and add another ('his parents were related to each other'), keeping his score the same.[199] However, since the Infancy Gospels clearly are discordant with the early mythology of Jesus and are an entirely new phenomenon, whereas the possibility of his parents being related might actually have been imagined much earlier,[200] he might have scored the full twenty-two points, making him a better fit for the Rank–Raglan hero-type than any other man in history. And even without these assumptions, he still ranks among the highest. That is a stunning fact, which must be considered, and accounted for.

4. *Conclusion*

The point of this and the previous chapter has been to summarize all the facts we must take into account, as being in our total background knowledge, when assigning all probabilities going forward. In my experience, a great deal of what has been surveyed up to this point remains unknown even to many experts in the study of Jesus. This is why I took the trouble to survey so much. Because all of it must be taken into account by *anyone* who wishes to reconstruct the historical Jesus or the origins of Christianity. It is equally crucial to understanding how to evaluate and interpret the evidence for or against the historicity of Jesus—and how to estimate the prior probability of either. And to that question I now turn.

199. It is sometimes suggested that Luke's introduction of Jesus after his twelfth year counts as a narrative from his childhood (Lk. 2.40-42). But that is most likely intended to be the eve of his bar mitzvah (or its ancient equivalent), which would have occurred upon his thirteenth birthday (the end of his twelfth year), and thus is actually a story about introducing him as a man. See Ivan Marcus, *The Jewish Life Cycle: Rites of Passage from Biblical to Modern Times* (Seattle, WA: University of Washington Press, 2004), pp. 84-105. But counting this as a story of his childhood anyway would still only reduce his score from 20 to 19.

200. Luke has Mary connected by family to a priest and a daughter of Aaron (Lk. 1.5, 36; with Num. 18.1-7), and includes two men named Levi in the ancestry of Joseph (Lk. 3.24, 29), which could imply both were descendants of Levi and therefore relatives.

6

The Prior Probability

1. *Heroes Who Never Existed*

In 1945 Betty Crocker was rated in a national survey as the second most admired woman in America, and to this day a street is named after her in Golden Valley, Minnesota, where she still lives. Her father was William Crocker, a successful corporate executive in the food industry, and she started her career answering letters on cooking questions for her father's company, then acquired her own national radio show where she delivered cooking advice for twenty-four years. Later she had her own television show, while making appearances on other TV shows and in TV commercials to promote her products. I've seen actual video tapes of her cooking and speaking, and her picture still adorns various General Mills baking products. She has also published several cookbooks, and now has her own Website. All that is 100 percent true. And yet she doesn't exist. She was never born, never lived, never spoke, never appeared on TV, and never wrote a word. Others simply wrote or appeared in her name. Welcome to the world of the mythical corporate mascot.[1]

If we were examining the question of whether a corporate mascot existed, what would we initially suspect? Would we assign that a high prior probability? Probably not. And rightly. What might the ratio be of modern corporate mascots who are historical vs. pseudohistorical? *Not* counting, of course, impossible beings like talking animals and cartoon heroes, whose ahistoricity is automatically assumed even without investigation, based on prior probabilities alone. After all, the prior probability that a talking tiger really exists and shills for breakfast cereal is sufficiently small that we don't bother investigating the evidence; we simply assume Tony the Tiger doesn't exist. But what about Betty Crocker, Aunt Jemima, Ronald McDonald? We

1. Susan Marks, *Finding Betty Crocker: The Secret Life of America's First Lady of Food* (New York: Simon & Schuster, 2005). For a similar analogy see Diane Roberts, *The Myth of Aunt Jemima: Representations of Race and Region* (New York: Routledge, 1994).

are usually familiar enough with the practice of modern corporations not to assume a heavily marketed corporate spokesperson really exists. Some do. But most don't.

And because of this, some of us have to actually check before being *certain* there really was a Colonel Sanders, and even those of us who don't need to, already knew—so even we didn't just *assume*. And we wouldn't. We know better. The mere fact of being a corporate mascot is in and of itself enough to warrant a somewhat lower prior probability of their historicity, though not so low that it requires much evidence to overcome it. Just one look on Wikipedia and I'm convinced Colonel Sanders existed. But where would we be if all our records and documents were destroyed, and a whole generation gone by (much less ten of them), and all that remained were some random scraps attesting to the details of Betty Crocker as I listed above? We would then think it certain she really existed, even though she didn't. Now what if there was a fanatical cult of Betty Crocker worshipers who didn't preserve any documents calling her existence into question (because they alone decided what documents to collect and save and what to ignore and let rot), and instead they wrote and preserved elaborate biographies about her, giving her a whole family and a captivating life story, interweaving her 'sayings' throughout (based on her 'newspaper column' and 'television appearances'), even depicting her performing wondrous miracles before crowds of thousands? Could this happen? Yes. In those conditions, it would be surprisingly easy. Is there any way we could find out the truth? In most cases, probably not. And yes, that should worry you.[2]

There were no corporate mascots in antiquity, of course. But a close equivalent were *religious* mascots: the demigods, the most popular 'front men' for the Supreme Beings (Elements 31 and 36). Betty Crocker was created in a unique environment of modern business marketing—unlike, say, ancient savior gods. But the similarity is that the created person and their fictional biography symbolize and communicate a message the company wants to sell, and the fictional spokesperson becomes a reliable way to sell the product attached to and advocated by them. And if we see that a religion's products are certain moral and social structures and reforms (and the cosmological and metaphysical foundations they rest upon), then an analogy holds. Whether he was historical or not, the 'Jesus of worship' was also 'created' in a unique environment of ancient *religious* marketing, to promote a social agenda (the product being 'sold'), and just as Betty Crocker's ahistoricity makes sense against a background of similar fabrications for similar ends (like Aunt Jemima, Uncle Ben, or Ronald McDonald), so Jesus' ahistoricity makes sense against a background of similar fabrica-

2. Although for the converse example of Haile Selassie, see chapter 2 (§1).

tions for similar ends (like Romulus, Dionysus, or Theseus). Exactly as for King Arthur, Ned Ludd, Moses, or Daniel (as I explained in Chapter 1, §4): people seek to create unity by creating a historical founder and then rallying around his sayings and deeds.

Their actual existence was not a requirement, and indeed was often a detriment (since it's much easier to make up things about a person who never existed than about one who actually did: see §7). But *belief* in their existence was a requirement (for their story to have real authoritative impact). Yet this could be procured by simply creating evidence. Outside of fundamentalism, few scholars believe the resurrection account in John 20 has any basis in fact; to the contrary, its every detail was obviously invented 'so that you would believe Jesus is the Christ' (Jn 20.31). If that could be done to create belief in the *event* it describes, it could be done to create belief in the *man*. The purpose is the same. And anyone willing to tell the one lie will be just as willing to tell the other. The more so if the liar himself has already been fooled into believing these things, and thus thinks he is merely reinforcing a belief that surely 'must' be true (so, e.g., if Jesus 'must' have existed, he 'must' have been born somewhere, and 'must' have had a family, who 'must' have had names; and so on it goes). Yet not even that would be necessary, since one always had to feed converts milk before they could handle the meat (Element 13). Sometimes you just have to get people to believe something in order to save them. You just have to get them to go along with the program, which 'surely' is really best for them in the end.

Religion at the time was, after all, a real, heartfelt, and very profitable business. In fact, the need to promote a brand was more important to religious institutions and communities precisely *because* they believed their mascots were real. Accordingly, completely mythical persons ended up with their own historical narratives, such as Plutarch's biographies of Romulus and Theseus, mixed in among biographies of real leaders and generals, without any distinction. Fabricating biographies and biographical data for non-existent people was a common fad of the time (Elements 44 and 45). School children in antiquity would have to memorize the genealogy and family relations of Ajax; even though Ajax never existed and thus had no genealogy or family relations.[3] And as I noted in Chapter 1 (§4), everything we know about the prophet Daniel, from what he did to what he said, to his basic life story, comes from a book that was wholly fabricated; so even if he existed, the 'Daniel' of Daniel is a complete fiction. This book even got expanded over time, adding even more fabricated tales, like Bel and the Dragon. That's what religious believers do with their heroes: make things up.

3. For this general phenomenon see Raffaella Cribiore, *Gymnastics of the Mind* (Princeton, NJ: Princeton University Press, 2001), pp. 198-99.

So how do we tell the difference? How do we determine whether the Gospels are like the book of Daniel or the life of Romulus . . . or an account of a real person based on some real facts instead? Looking at the *evidence* is part of the required task, and that we will do in coming chapters. But step one is determining the most defensible prior probability in the matter, just like figuring the prior probability that either Ronald McDonald or Colonel Sanders is real, before checking any facts in the matter. Drawing on the concluding hypotheses of Chapters 2 and 3, what's the prior probability that Jesus was a euhemerized mythical hero rather than a mythologized historical man?

2. *Determining Prior Probability*

We could ask what the prior probability is that *any* person about whom stories are told is historical or not. And certainly, if we picked anyone out of a hat who was claimed to be historical, the odds would be respectably high that they *are* historical. Because usually that's the case; made-up people are comparatively less common. However, we must always apply the *rule of greater knowledge*: if we know more about the person we are inquiring about, enough to know that he belongs to a narrower reference class than 'just anyone' claimed to be historical, then we must take that knowledge into account.[4] The information that we use to identify the narrowest reference class for which we have usable frequency data is information we must then move from *e* into *b* (from *evidence* into *background knowledge*), and therefore we cannot bring it up again when asking about consequent probabilities later. But as long as we obey that rule, the outcome will remain logically valid, and that's all we need.

All of this I have already explained in Chapters 3, 4 and 6 of *Proving History*. So I won't revisit the logical point. What matters at present is that we *know* Jesus belongs to the Rank–Raglan hero class (Element 48), and we have good frequency data for that class (at least 'good' by the standards of ancient history), and there is no narrower class for which we can say the same; therefore we must take that knowledge into account when assigning a prior probability of historicity to Jesus. And if we do that, then any of the details we are using to place him in that class have thereby been 'used up' to generate a prior probability, and they cannot affect any further probabilities going forward. So we might see some of them again in Chapter 10 (by way of example), but when we assign consequent probabilities there, we will be taking other elements of the Gospels into account.

In a sound Bayesian formula, prior probability is based on the general expectations produced by our background knowledge, as distinct from what

4. See Carrier, *Proving History*, p. 233.

we consider the evidence that needs to be explained by our hypothesis. This is the way historians divide those two sets of information, which can differ from what scientists typically do, but the result is the same.[5] We do not have to explain how or why Jesus became a Rank–Raglan hero in order to see that he did (whatever the reason and however it happened); so the resulting correlation data can be used without presuming anything about how that correlation came about. And that means we can put that specific data (the Rank–Raglan-assigning data) in our background knowledge and see what it gets as an expected frequency: how often are people in that class historical vs. ahistorical? Because, given the fact that Jesus belongs to that class, the prior probability that Jesus is historical has to be the same as the prior probability that *anyone* we draw at random from that class is historical. This is a logically necessary fact.

Just as 'the prior probability that Jesus was raised from the dead by a supernatural agency is the same as the prior probability that a supernatural agency raised Romulus from the dead, or Asclepius [etc.]', so, too, the prior probability that Jesus is historical is the same as the prior probability that Romulus is historical, or Moses or Hercules or anyone else in the same class.[6] Again, as with the resurrection claim, the *evidence* in the case of Jesus can be much stronger than for any of the others; but that is accounted for with the consequent probabilities. Here we're only talking about the *prior* probability. We'll get to the evidence later. The prior probability is not the *posterior* probability, and only the latter is the probability that Jesus existed. But we have to start somewhere, and this is the best starting point, because here the frequency data are sufficiently clear and there is no narrower reference class we can say the same for.

It won't really matter what you start with to determine prior probability, however, because whatever you *don't* use for that will become a part of *e* (the evidence) anyway, which you will then have to deal with later, and when you do you will get the same mathematical result regardless.[7] I will demonstrate that for this case later in this chapter. But for now, we have a clear-cut reference class to draw a prior from. And so our analysis can begin.

3. *Using the Rank–Raglan Reference Class*

The name 'Jesus Christ' literally means 'Savior Messiah', which actually just means 'Anointed Savior'. The author of the Gospel of Matthew

5. See Chapter 4 (§4); with Carrier, *Proving History*, p. 301 (n. 10), and 'background knowledge vs. evidence', p. 333.

6. Carrier, *Proving History*, pp. 242-45.

7. Carrier, *Proving History*, pp. 239-42.

was well aware of this, and even made a point of it.[8] Jesus is an English derivation from the Greek spelling of the Hebrew name Joshua (*Yeshua*), which means 'Yahweh saves'. Christ is from the Greek *christos,* meaning 'anointed', which in Hebrew is *māšîaḥ*, 'messiah'.

That should make us suspicious from the start. Isn't his name abnormally convenient? The 'Christ' part was assigned by those who believed he was the messiah, and thus not accidental. But what are the odds that his birth name would be 'Savior', and then he would be hailed as the Savior? Are historical men who are worshiped as savior gods usually so conveniently named? No, not usually. Are mythical men who are worshiped as savior gods usually so conveniently named? Surely more often than historical men are.[9] Obviously it's more likely that a mythical godman would be conveniently named than that a historical one would be. Indeed, I would expect the ratio must surely exceed 2 to 1. That is, for every deified man who is conveniently named, there are surely at least two mythical godmen with convenient names. And that even looks too generous to me—the actual ratio must surely be higher than 2 to 1. So if we settle on 2 to 1, any adjustment of the odds toward what they truly are will only make the historicity of Jesus *less* probable. And that would leave us with a prior probability of 33% that Jesus was historical, and 67% that he was not.

This remains the conclusion even if we start with a neutral prior of 50% (by assuming no historical facts in our background knowledge at all), and then start our analysis by introducing the fact of Jesus being a conveniently named deity, and all the background data pertaining to that, and work each item of evidence in individually, using the posterior probability from each as the prior probability in the next.[10] To show what I mean, I will pick numbers at random just to illustrate how it won't matter in the end what those numbers are. First, we would find the reference class of all men, which would be divided between all mythical and all historical men. Suppose there were 5,000 historical men and 1,000 mythical men (obviously these are huge undercounts, but again, I just made these numbers up; as we'll see in a moment, it won't matter very much in the end what they actually are). The prior probability of being mythical would then be 1,000 / 6,000 (one thousand divided by the sum of that same one thousand and the other

8. Mt. 1.20-21.

9. Analogously, the mythical Abraham is conveniently named ('father of many') in Gen. 17.5 (and his original name, Abram, 'exalted father', is no less convenient), similarly anticipating what he would become *in the future*, which doesn't tend to happen in the real world.

10. For this method, see Carrier, *Proving History*, p. 168, and 'iteration, method of', p. 337.

five thousand) which equals 1/6, or about 17%; and the prior probability of being historical would be 5,000 / 6,000, which equals 5/6, or about 83%.

We would then add the evidence that Jesus was a godman (a man worshiped as divine). Suppose 1 in 4 mythical men are godmen and 1 in 2 historical men are godmen (that's absurd, of course, and makes Jesus even more likely to be historical, when surely it would be the other way around, but I'm going with this just to make my point that these numbers don't matter). The probability that Jesus would be a godman, given that he was a mythical man, would then be 1/4; and the probability given that he was a historical man would be 1/2. The posterior probability that Jesus was historical would then be 240/264 (which reduces to 60/66), or about 91%.[11]

We could then use that as our updated prior probability that Jesus is historical, and add the next item of evidence: that Jesus was conveniently named. In the imaginary scenario so far there are 250 mythical godmen (1/4 x 1,000) and 2,500 historical godmen (1/2 x 5,000); if 10 mythical godmen are conveniently named, and twice as many mythical godmen are conveniently named as historical godmen are, then there are 5 historical godmen who are conveniently named. The probability, therefore, that Jesus would be conveniently named, given that he was a mythical godman, would be 10/250, which is 1/25; and the probability given that he was a historical godman would be 5/2500, which is 1/500. The posterior probability that Jesus was historical would then be 1/3, or the same 33% we started with—back when we just skipped all this and went straight to the reference class 'all conveniently named godmen', in which 1/3 were historical and 2/3 not (because, we concluded, at least twice as many mythical godmen must have convenient names than historical godmen do).[12] Change the ratio however you please, and the same reasoning will follow. So there is no getting around the fact that if the ratio of conveniently named mythical godmen to conveniently named historical godmen is 2 to 1 or greater, then the prior probability that Jesus is historical is 33% or less.

But this is a hypothetical reference class ('all conveniently named godmen'). We don't have any clear or statistically solid data about the frequency of historical to nonhistorical persons in that class; I merely guessed (albeit reasonably, based on our total background knowledge that coincidences are rarer in actual fact than in human invention) that the ratio of mythical persons to historical persons in that class is 2 to 1 or greater, and therefore

11. (5/6) x (1/2) / [(5/6) x (1/2)] + [(1/6) x (1/4)] = (5/12) / (5/12) + (1/24) = (10/24) / (10/24) + (1/24) = (10/24) / (11/24) = (240/264) = 0.9091 (rounding to the fourth decimal place).

12. (240/264) x (1/500) / [(240/264) x (1/500)] + [(24/264) x (1/25)] = (240/132,000) / (240/132,000) + (24/6600) = (240/132,000) / (240/132,000) + (480/132,000) = (240/132,000) / (720/132,000) = (1/550) / (3/550) = (550/1650) = 1/3.

the prior probability that a person in that class is historical is 1 in 3 or less. One might still question my intuitions here. Are coincidences of name *really* rarer in actual fact than in human invention? And even if rarer, how much rarer? And so on. In reality I don't think these challenges are at all plausible. The fact is, it's simply less likely that a historical man would be conveniently named Savior and then become a savior, than that a mythical man created to be a savior would be conveniently named Savior.

Even if we tried to work the question from the probability of any Jew actually being named Jesus (which is roughly 1 in 26),[13] in comparison to the probability of any savior god being named Savior (among that god's many names, and Jesus also had many names, from Christ to Lord to Emmanuel), we'd end up even worse off. Because probably most savior gods were called Savior (*sōtēr* in Greek), I'd say that ratio is closer to 1 in 2, and that is over *ten times* more likely than 1 in 26, not just two times more likely as we were suggesting before. But again, we don't have clear or reliable data to build this result from; we'd just be working again from plausible but still hypothetical datasets. We could even avoid these conclusions altogether by retreating to the hypothesis that 'Jesus', like Christ, was never his real name but a name assigned to him (even if by himself) and thus not a coincidence after all, but intentional. We can easily imagine this having happened to any of the 'Jesus Christs' surveyed in Josephus (Element 4), none of whom were named Jesus (so far as we know), but all of whom were casting themselves in the role of Jesus (i.e., Joshua). And there are other things one could argue. So either way, I think this approach is shaky.

Not so for the Rank–Raglan reference class. That works just like a 'corporate mascot' reference class would today. Counting as the Rank–Raglan reference class all heroes who score above half the total criteria, we have fourteen members (besides Jesus, who makes fifteen); we can ascertain that those are the only members (or at least, there are no other known *historical* persons who are members; and adding mythical persons would only make the ensuing argument stronger, by reducing the prior probability that any member of the class was historical); and we can conclude with reasonable certainty that none of those fourteen members were ever historical persons—all of them are mythical. That means a historical Jesus is literally unique among all Rank–Raglan heroes. So to assume he was the sole exception in human history would be a rather extraordinary claim. But

13. For a handy table of name frequencies among ancient Jews see Richard Bauckham, *Jesus and the Eyewitnesses: The Gospels as Eyewitness Testimony* (Grand Rapids, MI: William B. Eerdmans, 2006), pp. 85-88 (counts for male names are against a total of 2,625, so divide any number in the first column by that to get the overall name frequency; the numbers given are still rough estimates, being generated from disparate sources, but they are close enough for our purposes).

since we cannot *assume* Jesus is nonhistorical, the probability that he is must be based on the law of succession from the uniform experience of the other fourteen persons in the same class, which is (s+1)/(n+2) = (0+1)/(14+2) = 1/16 = 0.0625, or barely 6%.[14] That would be my lower bound for the prior probability that Jesus existed.

Of course, fundamentalists would refuse to accept that Moses and Joseph are mythical (two of the fourteen in that class); but that they are not historical is accepted by almost all secular experts in biblical antiquities and even most religious experts (Jewish and Christian), and is pretty hard to deny on the evidence we have (Element 44). Nevertheless, because I want to produce a prior probability as far against myth as I can reasonably believe it to be, so as to produce an argument *a fortiori* to my eventual conclusion, I will 'grant' the fundamentalists their unwarranted assumption, even against our background evidence, and count Moses and Joseph as historical persons.[15] Since it would be special pleading to assume that only Jewish heroes are 'special' that way, we should balance the scales and say that up to two of the pagans on the list may be historical as well (I am fairly certain that's not true, but again, I'm arguing *a fortiori*; and since only the count matters, it doesn't matter who the two are). That gives us 4 historical persons out of 14, which means the 15th member has a prior probability of being historical of (s+1)/(n+2) = (4+1)/(14+2) = 5/16 = 0.3125, or around 31%. I'll be additionally generous and just bump that up to an even 33% (1 in 3), the same probability I came up with from the coincidence of Jesus Christ's name. I cannot reasonably believe the prior probability is any higher than that, nor do I think anyone else can reasonably believe that. And so that is my upper bound, which I will use as the prior probability that Jesus existed as a historical person from here on out.

Again, even if we started from a neutral prior of 50% and walked our way through 'all persons claimed to be historical' to 'all persons who became Rank–Raglan heroes', we'd end up again with that same probability of 1 in 3. For example, if again there were 5,000 historical persons and 1,000 mythical persons, the prior probability of being historical would be 5/6; and of not being historical, 1/6. But if there are 10 mythical men in the Rank–Raglan class and 5 historical men (the four we are granting, plus one

14. See 'Laplace's Rule of Succession', in Carrier, *Proving History*, p. 337. The variable *s* equals the number of confirmed cases of what we are looking for in the set of decided cases (in this case, zero, as none of the fourteen known cases are known to be historical), and the variable *n* equals the total number of cases in that set (regardless of whether any are historical there are fourteen known Rank–Raglan heroes), prior to adding the one not yet decided (Jesus).

15. On this method of argument see Carrier, *Proving History*, pp. 85-88, and '*a fortiori*, method of', p. 333.

more, who may or may not be Jesus), then the probability of being in that class given that someone was historical would be 5/5000, which is 1/1000; and the probability given that they were mythical would be 10/1000, which is 1/100. This gives us a final probability of 1/3, hence 33%.[16] No matter how you chew on it, no matter what numbers you put in, with these ratios you always end up with the same prior probability that Jesus was an actual historical man: just 33% at best.

4. *The Causal Objection*

Doesn't this presuppose that Jesus began as a Rank–Raglan hero? No. Even if his story was rebuilt so that he would only belong to that class later (for example, if Matthew was the first ever to do that), it makes no difference. Regardless of how anyone came to be a Rank–Raglan hero, it still almost never happened to a historical person (in fact, so far as we can actually tell, it *never* happened to a historical person, ever). Many of the heroes in that class may well have also begun very differently and only been molded into the Rank–Raglan hero type later. Thus, being conformed to it later has no bearing on the probability of this happening. The probability of this happening to a historical person, based on all the evidence of past precedent that we have, is still practically zero. Even at our most generous it can be no better than 6%. Unless we reject the data we have and *suppose* that there were more historical persons in that class than the evidence suggests. But even when we do that, it goes beyond reason to estimate the number of such persons at any more than 1/3 of those in the class (and even *that* is beyond reason in my opinion). Which entails a *maximum* 33% prior probability that any member of that class was historical.

We can imagine two possibilities: (1) the elements added to Matthew were already around from the beginning (and were perhaps even known to Mark, who chose not to use them so he could sell a different theology) or (2) they were invented later (perhaps by Matthew himself, and thus not known to Mark, even if some were invented by Jesus himself during his own lifetime). Option (2) would entail that the legend of Jesus was fabricated and hero-typed very early and very rapidly (decisively refuting any claim that this couldn't have happened: see §7), while option (1) would entail Jesus himself was probably fabricated, being hero-typed from the very start. Certainly, if Jesus *started* as a Rank–Raglan hero, the probability that he was a historical man who just 'happened' to match every point on the scale is extremely small. Clearly, the overwhelming odds in that case

16. (5/6) x (1/1000) / [(5/6) x (1/1000)] + [(1/6) x (1/100)] = (5/6000) / (5/6000) + (1/600) = (1/1200) / (5/6000) + (10/6000) = (1/1200) / (15/6000) = (1/1200) / (1/400) = (400/1200) = 1/3.

would favor his being fabricated out of whole cloth (since getting away with claiming such wild fabrications so soon after a *real* man's death, when the less glamorous truth would be known to too many witnesses, would be even more difficult). So we cannot object to the assigned prior of 33% by proposing (1). If anything, (1) would entail a much *lower* prior probability that he was historical, much nearer to zero in fact. We should in that case adopt the lower bound of 6%.

So anyone who wants to resist this conclusion has only one option: (2) that Jesus was *remade* in the image of a Rank–Raglan hero later on, and was never such originally. But you cannot embrace (2) without also embracing the general principle that massive, rapid legendary development is possible, and not only that, but you must also accept the specific conclusion that it undeniably occurred in the case of Jesus (so this completely eliminates any recourse to the last objection examined in this chapter, in §7: that rapid legendary development is improbable). Given the evidence of how often that kind of massive and rapid legendary development happened to historical persons, versus how often it happened to *non*-historical persons, we must surely conclude it happens to the latter far more often; and when it happens in such a way as to generate a Rank–Raglan hero, it appears *never* to have happened to historical persons. But it perhaps could; that's at least more likely to happen then than in condition (1). So we should perhaps in that case adopt the upper bound of 33%. That percentage simply represents the highest possible frequency with which that ever happened to historical persons (relative to those in the same class who weren't historical).

5. *The Alternative Class Objection*

What if we decided instead to use the 'Jesus Christs' surveyed by Josephus as a reference class? Wouldn't that give us a different prior, one more supportive of historicity? There were four of them, and all (we might presume) were historical (it raises an interesting question if they were not, but I will set that aside). The prior probability that Jesus was historical could then be imagined to be (4+1)/(4+2) = 5/6, or 83%. But how many of those men are also in the Rank–Raglan hero class? None, so far as we know (and thus we cannot assume any were or ever came to be). We can therefore all but rule this option out. The probability of a Rank–Raglan hero also belonging to the Josephan Christ class is low (as we have no instances of it happening on record), whereas Jesus *definitely* belongs to the Rank–Raglan hero class. The rule of greater knowledge thus requires us to derive our prior from the latter. The former can't override it. The Rank–Raglan class is also a larger class with more data points in it, thus it affords us better evidence to estimate frequencies from. When we combine both facts (that 'historical' Josephan Christs tend not to be Rank–Raglan heroes; and we have a lot better evidence for Rank–Raglan heroes), we cannot warrant using the Josephan class over the Rank–Raglan class.

But it really wouldn't matter anyway. Even if we used the Josephan Christ class, the fact that Jesus is *also* in the Rank–Raglan class would still have to be accounted for, and that would go into the remaining evidence. As shown earlier, even if we did use the 83% probability as our starting prior, once we introduced the Rank–Raglan evidence we would end up with a new prior of 33% all over again. Remember, before, we imagined 5,000 historical persons per total of 6,000 persons to get an 83% initial prior. Suppose we have similar numbers for Josephan Christs, five of them historical for every one that is mythical, which would produce the same probability (and this is just what we are assuming when we derive an 83% probability of being historical from the four instances of historicity in Josephus). We *still* know that twice as many Rank–Raglan members are not historical as are, so we will *still* have numbers in ratio to each other like 10 mythical members to 5 historical members, and this ratio will still hold, so far as we know, for all Josephan Christs. Therefore, being a Josephan Christ will make no difference. We will still end up with a 33% prior probability that a member of both classes (Josephan Christs and Rank–Raglan heroes) will be historical. That prior would be much higher for someone who was a Josephan Christ but *not* a Rank–Raglan hero, but Jesus is not such a person. Instead, for someone who is both, for all we know, they are as likely to be historical as any Rank–Raglan hero. Therefore, that is the reference class we should start with. Because there is no avoiding the consequences of its contents anyway.

The same will follow for any other 'alternative' reference class proposed. So no objection can be made from the prospect of alternative reference classes. The fact that Jesus is a Rank–Raglan hero simply always has the same mathematical consequence, no matter what you try to replace it with. Only if we had different data than we do, or much more data, could we come to any different conclusion than that.

6. *The Complexity Objection*

The 'minimal myth' hypothesis developed in Chapter 3 is not simply 'Jesus began as a mythical person'. It has five separate components, and as such could possibly have a much lower prior than nonhistoricity does generally. This is because adding elements to a theory always reduces its prior.[17] For example, if the prior probability of 'myth' is 67% but the prior probability of a 'celestial deity' is only twice that of a 'political fiction' (see Chapter 3, §3), and these were the only viable kinds of 'myth', then the prior probability

17. See Carrier, *Proving History*, pp. 80-81, and 'gerrymandering', p. 336.

of the hypothesis I will be testing against historicity will be only 45% (vs. 22% for 'political fiction'), and not the full 67% (67% being the converse of the 33% prior probability of historicity). Each additional element could reduce it further. This would not entail historicity is more likely to prevail, since it would remain the case that it's twice as likely that *some* myth theory is true than that any theory of historicity is (unless the evidence we then examine alters those odds, of course).[18] But having to account for both theories of myth would make our analysis more complicated.

In Chapter 3, however, I already argue why the effect of conjoining all five elements is so minimal that we can mathematically ignore it. Because even in conjunction they still occupy nearly all the probability-space reserved for 'myth', so we can treat that theory as equivalent to 'nonhistoricity' altogether. First, the 'celestial deity' element is, on background evidence alone,[19] at least hundreds of times more likely than any alternative account of the mythical origin of belief in Jesus. Anyone who believes

18. See Carrier, 'Plausibility of Theft', in *Empty Tomb* (ed. Price and Lowder), p. 368 n. 38; although the point made there I explain more clearly in the last part of the first section of Richard Carrier, 'Stephen Davis Gets It Wrong' (2006) at http://www.richardcarrier.info/Carrier--ReplyToDavis.html, which I here quote:

> In his critique of Martin, Davis suggests that even if 'the probability of the falsity of [a hypothesis] H is .6', i.e. 60%, it would still be rational to believe H if each of the only four other possibilities has a mere .15 or 15% probability of being true. This is unsound reasoning. In the scenario he describes, there would be a 60% chance that some one of the other explanations is true (which he labels A, B, C and D), so it would not be rational to believe H. What would be rational is to conclude that you don't know which explanation is true. For example, if Alexander [the Great] died and the only options available were all natural causes except H, which was 'murder', then there would be a 60% chance that Alexander died of natural causes, and therefore it would not be rational to believe he was murdered. Though it would make sense in a gambling scenario to bet on H, that would only be the case if you had to bet, or could afford to lose. But history is not gambling. If you get to bet your life on A, B, C, D, or H, or not bet anything at all, in Davis' scenario the rational choice would be to refrain from betting, since no matter which bet you placed, the odds would always favor your death. In such a case it would never be rational to say 'I believe H will be a winning bet' even if it's the best bet on the table. . . . As far as sound historical argument goes, it would never be rational to say 'I believe H is true' when you know H more probably than not is false.

This conclusion is all the more so if we have the option to bet on either H or 'A, B, C, or D' as a unit. As then rejecting H would even be the best bet.

19. For example, the precedents of mystery religions (Element 13); schizotypal cults (Element 15); and Jewish pre-Christian belief in a celestial Son of God named Jesus (Elements 6 and 40); and so on.

otherwise will have to demonstrate an alternative differential in prior probability, and until that happens I will stick with my estimate. Even just two-hundredths of 67% is a mere 0.33% (a mere third of a percent), too little to make any visible difference to the math (since I will always round up to the nearest whole percentage point; and 33.33% minus 0.33% is still 33%). And recall that we are very much *under*-estimating the prior probability of myth, and the amount by which we are underestimating it is many whole percentage points, more than enough to wash out any fraction of a percent. So we needn't concern ourselves with fractions of a percent at this stage.[20]

The same follows for all the other elements, only with even greater force. The evidence we have and all our background knowledge (e.g. Elements 15, 16 and 29) render the hallucinatory (and/or pseudo-hallucinatory) origin of Christianity vastly more likely than any non-hallucinatory origin, within the context of all mythic origins (i.e., among all theories of *myth*, those that *don't* posit a hallucinatory origin, feigned or actual, are extremely unlikely on prior considerations alone; this may be different among theories of historicity, but here the question is how to divide up the probability space for *myth*). Similarly, any theory of myth that requires a vastly greater *scale* of lying and/or hallucination than the theory I am positing will for that very reason be vastly less probable than it. Finally, that subsequent Christians believed Jesus was historical is an established fact in our background knowledge, and therefore the probability that it is false is virtually zero; and therefore it consumes effectively all the probability-space reserved for myth. In other words, any theory of myth that denied this would have an absurdly low prior. It therefore can be ignored as well.

In result, alternative theories of myth all collectively (even when summed together) have a prior probability less than a percentage point and therefore can be ignored (unless the evidence *very* strongly and clearly supported one of them, but if it did, it would already have become the mainstream view by now). That leaves the remainder of the probability-space (the whole 67%) occupied by the minimal theory I outline in Chapter 3, which I will test against historicity for the remainder of this book.

7. *Rapid Legendary Development*

That leaves one common objection: if Jesus was a celestial deity already euhemerized by the time the Gospels were written, then that supposedly suggests an extraordinarily rapid pace of legendary development, which must surely be very improbable. But this is not a valid objection, for three decisive reasons.

20. On washing out insignificant priors, see Carrier, *Proving History*, pp. 85-88.

First, a deity can easily be euhemerized from day one. It does not require any time lag at all. Especially if that deity is euhemerized to create an exoteric allegory for both the public and new initiates, whose esoteric meaning is explained only to more advanced members (Elements 13 and 14). Although the deities and heroes in the Rank–Raglan class were either euhemerized centuries after they were first worshiped as deities (like Osiris), or at the moment of their invention they were placed centuries in the past (like Jason), this was not because either was necessary for the process to work. Rather, it was because euhemerization had not become popular until centuries after these gods had become popular (in the case of preexistent deities), or because a cultural trend had already been established of placing all heroes in the same imagined Age of Heroes (around the assumed time of the Trojan War), as if nothing exciting ever happened in any other century of history (or, in the case of Romulus, because legend required that he be placed in the already-traditional century of Rome's founding—so he would have been placed there no matter when his tale was created). We can therefore draw no conclusions about what was *possible* simply from what early Greeks and Romans *chose to do*.

Second, we have ample background evidence that such rapid legendary development is possible and indeed common, therefore its being improbable is not a conclusion derived from our background knowledge but a conclusion firmly against it.[21] We saw this already in the case of Haile Selassie

21. For more discussion and examples of rapid legendary development see Carrier, 'Why the Resurrection Is Unbelievable', in *Christian Delusion* (ed. Loftus), pp. 291-96; 'Spiritual Body', in *Empty Tomb* (ed. Price and Lowder), pp. 168-82; Carrier, 'Plausibility of Theft', in *Empty Tomb* (ed. Price and Lowder), pp. 355-59; and Richard Carrier, *Sense and Goodness without God: A Defense of Metaphysical Naturalism* (Bloomington, IN: AuthorHouse, 2005), pp. 227-41; as well as Kris Komarnitsky, *Doubting Jesus' Resurrection: What Happened in the Black Box?* (Drapper, UT: Stone Arrow Books, 2nd edn, 2014); Matt McCormick, 'The Salem Witch Trials and the Evidence for the Resurrection', in *End of Christianity* (ed. Loftus), pp. 195-218; Chris Hallquist, *UFOs, Ghosts, and a Rising God: Debunking the Resurrection of Jesus* (Cincinnati, OH: Reasonable Press, 2008), pp. 68-87; Robert Price, 'Is There a Place for Historical Criticism?', *Religious Studies* 27 (1991), pp. 371-88; and Robert Price, 'Jesus: Myth and Method', in *Christian Delusion* (ed. Loftus), pp. 273-90. Another good example of vast and rapid legendary development is the weaving of fabulous tales about St Genevieve within a mere ten years of her death: see Jo Ann McNamara and John Halborg, *Sainted Women of the Dark Ages* (Durham, NC: Duke University Press, 1992), pp. 17-37 (cf. 'Text A', §§19-20, 23, 32-34, 36, 39, 44-47, 50-51). Also relevant to this conclusion is the fact that in antiquity 'fact checking' was not commonly valued and rarely possible: see Carrier, *Not the Impossible Faith*, pp. 161-218, 329-68, 385-406 (with Carrier, *Sense and Goodness*, pp. 246-47). This would greatly increase the rate and scale of legendary development possible compared to modern times. And yet even in modern times that rate can be high (as the cases of Roswell and Selassie prove).

in Chapter 2 (§1). Even the Roswell myth evolved from tinfoil in the desert to a whole flying saucer with autopsied alien bodies recovered from it, all in just forty years. And that was in one of the most modern and educated societies in history, with mass media and even extensive debunking in print.[22] And yet, as I noted for Haile Selassie, if we had only the writings of Roswell believers, and none mentioning what any early critics said (the exact situation we are in for Jesus), we would be none the wiser.

In fact, it's actually far easier to invent stories about a non-existent person than about one who recently lived. Because then there are no witnesses to gainsay or correct you, and no living traditions to compete with (assuming either made any difference at all). And yet, as we've seen, Jesus underwent *vast* legendary development *very* rapidly, becoming a Rank–Raglan hero, complete with absurd mythical biographical elements (e.g. the nativity tales, the confrontation with the Devil in the wilderness, the supernatural global darkness at his death), within the space of only a few decades.[23] Either this happening to a historical person is therefore highly probable (and therefore 'rapid legendary development' cannot be regarded as improbable), or it didn't happen to a historical person (and therefore this 'rapid legendary development' argues *against* Jesus having existed, rather than the other way around). Either way, no valid objection remains.

Third, the corollary claim that Christians would have had institutions in place to reverently preserve the truth and thus prevent any legendary embellishment or invention is not only contrary to fact (all the evidence we have argues against, and none for, the existence of any such institutions within early Christianity, and the ubiquitous divergences and contradictions among the Gospels alone prove no such institution was operating), but also moot. Such an institution, had it existed, would just as readily preserve a fabrication. The issue is not whether a tradition was preserved reverently (although the many contradictory Gospels prove it was not), but whether the tradition being 'reverently preserved' was based on fact or an allegorical fiction in the first place.[24] The fact that divergent Gospels were prolifer-

22. See Philip J. Klass, *The Real Roswell Crashed Saucer Coverup* (Amherst, NY: Prometheus Books, 1997); and Karl T. Pflock, *Roswell: Inconvenient Facts and the Will to Believe* (Amherst, NY: Prometheus Books, 2001).

23. On the specific example of the sun being darkened over the whole earth (already in Mark) as proof of rapid legendary development and the absence of any eyewitness check on same, see Carrier, *Proving History*, pp. 41-45, and 'eyewitness check', p. 336. On the additional example (in Matthew) of a massively embellished empty tomb narrative (including a public mass resurrection of countless holy men in Jerusalem), see Carrier, 'Why the Resurrection Is Unbelievable', in *Christian Delusion* (ed. Loftus), pp. 294-96.

24. On how this crucial distinction is generally ignored by defenders of oral tradition, and how oral tradition actually still changes over time (and quite rapidly) in deliberate, history-eclipsing ways even in the presence of preserving institutions, see

ating beyond anyone's control already in Paul's lifetime (Element 21), and that reliance on secret traditions and allegorical storybuilding would have prevented nearly any check on the development of new traditions (Elements 13 and 14), and that there were tremendous disruptions in Christianity's leadership and literary activity in its earliest period and the Gospels appear around the very time the original founders would most likely have been dead (Element 22), effectively refutes any argument that completely new traditions could not have been developed in the course of the first century.[25]

This problem can be illustrated with a mock analogy. Imagine in your golden years you are accused of murdering a child many decades ago and put on trial for it. The prosecution claims you murdered a little girl in the middle of a public wedding in front of thousands of guests. But as evidence all they present is a religious tract written by 'John' which lays out a narrative in which the wedding guests watch you kill her. *Who is this John?* The prosecution confesses they don't know. *When did he write this narrative?* Again, unknown. Probably thirty or forty years after the crime, maybe even sixty. *Who told John this story?* Again, no one knows. He doesn't say. *So why should this even be admissible as evidence?* Because the narrative is filled with accurate historical details and reads like an eyewitness account. *Is it an eyewitness account?* Well, no, John is repeating a story told to him. *Told to him by an eyewitness?* Well . . . we really have no way of knowing how many people the story passed through before it came to John and he wrote it down. Although he does claim an eyewitness told him some of the details. *Who is that witness?* He doesn't say. *I see. So how can we even believe the story is in any way true if it comes from unknown sources through an unknown number of intermediaries?* Because there is no way the eyewitnesses to the crime, all those people at the wedding, would have allowed John to lie or make anything up, even after thirty to sixty years, so there is no way the account can be fabricated.

If that isn't obviously an absurd argument to you, then you didn't understand what has just been said and you need to read that paragraph again

the extensive and excellent analysis of an important case study by Theodore Weeden in 'Kenneth Bailey's Theory of Oral Tradition: A Theory Contested by its Evidence', *Journal for the Study of the Historical Jesus* 7 (January 2009), pp. 3-43. See also Paul Foster, 'Memory, Orality, and the Fourth Gospel: Three Dead-Ends in Historical Jesus Research', *Journal for the Study of the Historical Jesus* 10 (July 2012), pp. 191-227. By contrast, all recent attempts to argue for a reliable oral tradition behind the Gospels are mired in naivete and *possibiliter* fallacies (on such fallacies see Carrier, *Proving History*, pp. 26-29).

25. On all these points see Carrier, *Proving History*, pp. 121-206 (especially p. 179); H.W. Shin, *Textual Criticism and the Synoptic Problem in Historical Jesus Research: The Search for Valid Criteria* (Dudley, MA: Peeters, 2004), p. 144; and the entire issue of the *Journal for the Study of the Historical Jesus* 6 (2008).

until you do. Because seen in this more neutral context, that last argument *is monumentally absurd.* As any judge or lawyer in this country will tell you, the evidential value of 'John's' account is exactly nil, and the value of the 'eyewitness check' defense of his account's reliability is *less* than nil. So why would we suddenly do a complete reversal on this point as soon as it's a story about Jesus? There is really no sane answer to that question. In this hypothetical trial, your obvious defense would be that the prosecution can't even prove the allegedly murdered girl *ever even existed* (much less that you killed her, even if anyone did). That entails far more than a reasonable doubt. The prosecution's inability to offer any evidence even for the girl's *existence* other than 'John's' book about her murder would get you acquitted faster than any jury could even sit to deliberate. Historians cannot behave differently.[26]

The objection that 'someone would have said something', however, is actually an appeal to the role of evidence in changing our conclusion for Jesus compared to other Rank–Raglan heroes, and therefore it cannot affect our prior probability anyway. If that is a problem at all, if it makes any difference at all, then it will do so when we estimate the consequent probabilities of the surviving evidence on either the theory that Jesus existed or that he did not. It does not affect the *prior*, which is the probability *before* we take evidence like that into account. And that is what subsequent chapters will do. So this also cannot be an objection to the prior probability arrived at here. Hence I will revisit it where it belongs, in Chapter 8 (§12).

8. *Conclusion*

Therefore, the prior probability [or P(h|b)] that Jesus was historical can be no more than 1 in 3 or 33% (which translates into prior 'odds' against *h* of 2 to 1). That does *not* mean the probability that Jesus was historical is 33%. For we still have to look at all the evidence pertaining to the various hypotheses for how Jesus became a member of both the Rank–Raglan hero class *and* the set of all other celestial savior deities. And when we do, we could find that the evidence is so improbable, unless Jesus really existed, that even a prior probability as low as 1 in 16, or 6.25% (which entails prior odds against *h* of 15 to 1), would be more than overcome.

For example, even if Caesar Augustus had a Rank–Raglan score of 20, we *also* have a vast array of evidence supporting his existence, each piece of which is highly improbable unless there really was a Caesar Augustus, and all of it *combined* would be even more improbable. So if ¬*h* is any

26. See my even closer analogy to the same conclusion (the imaginary case of 'Hero Savior of Vietnam') in Richard Carrier, *Why I Am Not a Christian: Four Conclusive Reasons to Reject the Faith* (Richmond, CA: Philosophy Press, 2011), pp. 48-52.

variation of 'Caesar Augustus did not really exist', then the actual evidence we have of his existence would entail a P(e|¬h.b), the consequent probability of the evidence, hundreds if not thousands or millions of times *less* than 6%, yet with a corresponding P(e|h.b) very nearly equal to 1. Such a combination would produce a P(¬h|e.b), the probability that Caesar Augustus didn't exist, of very well near zero. So we would still be fully justified believing in his historicity—even with a prior probability of it of only 6%.

That's why we need to look at the evidence for the existence of Jesus. Is it as strong as the evidence for the existence of Caesar Augustus? And even if not that strong (and we already know it isn't, as I discussed in Chapter 2, §2), is it still strong enough to make historicity more probable than ahistoricity, no matter what Rank–Raglan score Jesus has? To that question we now turn.

7

Primary Sources

> The surviving evidence does not provide an unproblematic entry into the historical Jesus of Nazareth and to his role in the process of the formation of Christian beginnings.[1]

1. *What Counts as Evidence?*

When examining the evidence for a claim about ancient history, what that means in practice is the relevant *primary source material.* That would be the evidence, which survives for us to see it, that's earliest in the chain of causation. This chapter will discuss what the relevant primary source material is for the historicity of Jesus, what we know about that evidence, and how we will break that evidence down in coming chapters.

For something to count as 'relevant primary evidence', it must meet two criteria: it must be plausibly capable of being causally connected with the facts (persons, properties or events) whose existence is in question, and it must be relevantly independent of all other primary evidence.[2] An example of failing to meet the first condition would be a book written by a psychic who claims to have supernaturally viewed the past. That doesn't count as evidence, because it is not plausible that what they saw (or claim to have seen) is *actually* causally connected in any relevant way to what happened.[3] By contrast, a medieval manuscript of Lucian's account of his interactions with Proteus Peregrinus (in Lucian's *Death of Peregrinus*) is evidence of what happened to Peregrinus, because more than plausibly it is causally

1. Helmut Koester, 'The Historical Jesus and the Historical Situation of the Quest: An Epilogue', in *Studying the Historical Jesus: Evaluation of the State of Current Research* (ed. Bruce Chilton and Craig Evans; New York: Brill, 1994), pp. 535-45 (541).

2. For the mathematical definition of 'plausibility' see Carrier, *Proving History*, pp. 83, 101-102.

3. In Bayesian terms, the consequent probabilities for this item of 'evidence' are the same on any plausible hypothesis, and therefore this 'evidence' has no effect on the probability of any of those hypotheses being true.

connected to that: the best explanation (or at the very least a definitely *plausible* explanation) of the manuscript's existence is that it sits at the end of a chain of causally connected copies of an original book written by Lucian (either literally, in his own hand, or by a scribe at his dictation and correction), which in turn was causally connected to what happened to Peregrinus by the fact that Lucian actually saw what happened to Peregrinus. Or so Lucian claims, of course—but even if that claim is false, the text *could* still be causally connected to what happened by another chain of causation of several intermediaries passing information on, at the start of which is some witness who actually did see it. If not, then of course the account is bogus, and is no longer evidence of what happened to Peregrinus—unless its content (or even mere existence) still entails something about that (for instance, if Peregrinus more likely didn't exist if Lucian fabricated such an account of him, in which case the evidence is in that respect causally connected to the fact of Peregrinus *not* existing).[4]

Disputes over the validity of evidence thus often focus on how securely that evidence is actually causally connected to what is being claimed about the past (such as that some person existed, or some event occurred). In the most basic terms, a historical claim (such as that 'Peregrinus existed and burned himself alive to prove a point') is ultimately a hypothesis about how that evidence came about (that evidence being, in this case, Lucian's book; but there can sometimes be a lot of other evidence besides: see examples in Chapter 2, §2). I discussed all of this already in *Proving History,* so I won't revisit the logic of historical argument any further here, except to reiterate the general conclusion that what we want to know is how likely it is that we would have a given piece of evidence (like the text of Lucian's *Death of Peregrinus*) if *h* is true (the hypothesis we are testing), and how likely it is that we would have that same evidence if *h* is false (and some other hypothesis is true instead, which means any one of all other hypotheses exclusive of ours).

So for the first criterion. But meeting the second criterion is just as important: evidence must be independent. If someone wrote something about Peregrinus for which their sole source of information was Lucian's *Death of Peregrinus*, then only the latter counts as evidence. A fact or quotation taken from that book can be evidence of that *book's* existence (or of its content at a particular point in time), but it is not evidence of what happened to Peregri-

4. As, e.g., by supporting an argument from silence (Carrier, *Proving History*, pp. 117-19) or making Peregrinus's existence more absurd (Carrier, *Proving History*, pp. 114-17). On the causal logic of evidence in historical reasoning generally, see Carrier, *Proving History*, pp. 45-49, 51-57, 229-31, and 'causal reasoning', p. 334; on proving non-existence: pp. 204-205 (see also Chapters 1 through 3 in the present volume).

nus, as long as we have the earlier (which is in our case the *primary*) source, which is the text of Lucian's book. In Bayesian terms, the probability of having information taken from a book if that book's content is unknowingly false (and no other sources consulted) is the same as the probability if the content is true. Therefore, having the secondary source can have no effect on the epistemic probability that the claim in question is true. Having a copy of someone's letter, for example, does not make the original letter any more likely to be genuine or its contents any more likely to be true. Being *dependent* evidence, the copy is useless, and should simply be ignored (unless it contains or entails unique information, but then only that unique information is evidence of something; e.g. that a copy was made).

Unfortunately this conclusion still follows even if we merely cannot *establish* that a source is independent. For example, if someone after Lucian, whom we know likely had access to Lucian's book (whether they used it or not), says things about Peregrinus that are things Lucian already said about him, then that later source still can no longer count as relevant evidence for Peregrinus (though it does count as evidence of a more widespread knowledge of the *story* of Peregrinus, but that's not the same thing). Of course it's *possible* this later author had a source independent of Lucian; but 'possibly, therefore probably' is a fallacy.[5] Accordingly, we can make nothing of it—such evidence is no more likely to exist on a claim's being true than its being false (since the information is just as likely to come from Lucian as from anywhere else, whether the claim is true or false), and therefore can make no mathematical difference to the probability that the claim is true. Our only relevant evidence in that case would just be Lucian's book.

This is significant because almost all the evidence 'for Jesus' cannot be established as independent of earlier evidence we already have (such as the canonical Gospels). Therefore almost all evidence 'for Jesus' must be discarded. Likewise all evidence that is not plausibly connected to the actual truth of the matter (such as 'feeling in your heart' that Jesus existed). When all that evidence is properly excluded, we are left with very little. And that is a problem, one we will revisit as we proceed through the following chapters. But first we must identify and describe what little evidence is left.

2. *Breaking Down the Evidence*

For any claim about antiquity the evidence we might have can come in many forms—original documents, tombstones, coins, excavated buildings (or indeed anything physically recovered from the past, from dolls to doorknobs), astronomical or geographical facts, graffiti on an ancient wall; in

5. Carrier, *Proving History*, pp. 26-29.

short, all kinds of things. However, in the case of Jesus, there is no directly relevant archaeological evidence.[6] And no indirect evidence is relevant to

6. Many claims to the contrary exist but all are unfounded: The Shroud of Turin, e.g., is a medieval fake: Walter McCrone, *Judgment Day for the Shroud of Turin* (Amherst, NY: Prometheus Books, rev. edn, 1999); Harry Gove, *Relic, Icon or Hoax? Carbon Dating the Turin Shroud* (Philadelphia, PA: Institute of Physics,1996); Joe Nickell, *Inquest on the Shroud of Turin: Latest Scientific Findings* (Amherst, NY: Prometheus Books, 1998). See also Steven Schafersman's 'Skeptical Shroud of Turin Website' (http://freeinquiry.com/skeptic/shroud); and the Skeptic's Dictionary entry on the 'Shroud of Turin' (http://www.skepdic.com/shroud.html).

Likewise the so-called James ossuary (which supposedly once contained the brother of Jesus Christ) is inconclusive as evidence for any particular Jesus (its inscription fails to mention that he is the brother of the Jesus regarded as the Messiah, as opposed to some other Jesus), and is also probably a fake (or rather, part of the inscription on it is): Ryan Byrne and Bernadette McNary-Zak (eds.), *Resurrecting the Brother of Jesus: The James Ossuary Controversy and the Quest for Religious Relics* (Chapel Hill, NC: University of North Carolina Press, 2009). See also the Wikipedia page on the 'James Ossuary' (http://en.wikipedia.org/wiki/James_Ossuary).

By the same reasoning the Talpiot Tomb almost certainly has no connection to Jesus Christ (nor do any of the other tombs alleged to have been 'the' tomb of Jesus): Stephen Pfann and James Tabor, 'Forum: The Talpiot "Jesus' Family Tomb"', *Near Eastern Archaeology* 69 (September–December 2006), pp. 116-37; Charles Quarles, *Buried Hope or Risen Savior: The Search for the Jesus Tomb* (Nashville, TN: B & H Academic, 2008); Don Sausa, *The Jesus Tomb: Is It Fact or Fiction? Scholars Chime In* (Fort Myers, FL: Vision Press, 2007). See also the Wikipedia page on 'The Lost Tomb of Jesus' (http://en.wikipedia.org/wiki/The_Lost_Tomb_of_Jesus). The claim that the name cluster there is too improbable otherwise is refuted by none of those claims taking into account the fact that there were more than a dozen and as many as twenty bodies in that same tomb, greatly increasing the frequency of chance name combinations. For example, another startling chance combination of Jesus-related names had already been found elsewhere in the nineteenth century: Carl Kraeling, 'Christian Burial Urns?', *Biblical Archaeologist* 9 (February 1946), pp. 16-20. Jesus' family can't have been buried in two places at once. These kinds of finds are statistically inevitable and therefore meaningless. See the discussions of this point in Pfann and Tabor, 'Forum'; with Randall Ingermanson, 'Discussion of: Statistical Analysis of an Archaeological Find', *Annals of Applied Statistics* 2 (2008), pp. 84-90.

Similarly, coins and inscriptions claimed to provide evidence for Jesus actually contain no such information: Richard Carrier, 'Pseudohistory in Jerry Vardaman's Magic Coins: The Nonsense of Micrographic Letters', *Skeptical Inquirer* 26 (March–April 2002), pp. 39-41, 61; and Richard Carrier, 'More on Vardaman's Microletters', *Skeptical Inquirer* 26 (July–August 2002), pp. 60-61, both reproduced in Richard Carrier, *Hitler Homer Bible Christ: The Historical Papers of Richard Carrier 1995–2013* (Richmond, CA: Philosophy Press, 2014), pp. 155-56.

And so on. I needn't tour through all the forgeries and dubious claims in this category, like fragments of the true cross and all that rubbish: see Joe Nickell, *Relics of the Christ* (Lexington, KY: University Press of Kentucky, 2007).

determining historicity.[7] Nor will I address 'negative archaeology', that is, claims that archaeological evidence is missing, since none of that has any relevant effect on the probability of *minimal* historicity (as defined in Chapter 2).[8] There is only one kind of evidence left: texts (books, letters, etc.), which are reconstructed (by modern scholars) from a variety of manuscripts (which are copies of copies of copies of even earlier originals now lost).

I will consider only texts that are known to have been written (or *probably* written) before 120 CE (or that record information from an identifiable source before that date), as after that time we can't reasonably expect there to have been any surviving witnesses to the original decade of the cult's

7. For example, the fact that we have archaeological evidence that Pontius Pilate existed (and we do) makes no significant difference to the probability of either hypothesis, since myth can incorporate real historical facts as easily as histories do (using real people, places and customs, because narrative context and background were common in fiction of the time, and a common feature of faith literature: see Elements 44 and 45; and could be got from reference books, histories and common knowledge: see Carrier, *Proving History*, p. 176). Only an extreme *non*-confirmation could have made a difference (see following note). That does mean the probability of historicity would have been greatly reduced by not having *any* ancillary evidence (or by having contrary evidence, e.g., proof that Pilate was a fictional person), and it is therefore greatly increased by *having* that evidence, but only relative to historicity *without* that evidence, which is of no interest to us. Since we shall assume as a given that ancillary evidence exists, we needn't survey it (since its effect on the consequent probabilities will be the same no matter what that evidence is).

8. For example, arguments like 'Nazareth or Capernaum didn't exist in the time of Jesus, therefore Jesus didn't exist' are fallacious (with respect to minimal historicity) even if their premises are true; and their premises can rarely be proven anyway. As to the fallacy: on a hypothesis of myth, all locations were necessarily invented for Jesus (whether using actually existing locations or not), which can be just as likely on a (minimal) theory of historicity (i.e., on which most of Jesus' story is still just as mythical); ergo, even if Nazareth didn't exist (or in fact even if it did), this is just as likely if Jesus existed as if he didn't, or near enough as to make no notable difference (this argument only ceases to be fallacious if the 'invented' elements are too extensive to explain as a product of mythic development over a historical person, which for Jesus is not the case: see Chapter 6). As to the premises, see 'Capernaum', in *The Archaeological Encyclopedia of the Holy Land* (ed. Avraham Negev and Shimon Gibson; New York: Continuum, rev. and updated edn, 2001), pp. 111-14; likewise in the same volume, 'Nazareth', pp. 362-63, along with Carrier, *Proving History*, pp. 142-45, and the debate in *Bulletin of the Anglo-Israel Archaeological Society* 26 (2008), pp. 95-135, which was initiated by René Salm over the contents of Stephen Pfann, Ross Voss and Yehudah Rapuano, 'Surveys and Excavations at the Nazareth Village Farm (1997-2002): Final Report', *Bulletin of the Anglo-Israel Archaeological Society* 25 (2007), pp. 19-79. The results are similar for every other 'negative' claim (except perhaps claims regarding geographical error in Mark, but those are vague enough that I shall set them aside: see Chapter 10, §5).

creation (in the 30s CE), due to the limits of life expectancy (Element 22); and also because after that time the quantity of bogus literature about Jesus and early Christianity exploded to an immense scale, making the task of sorting truth from fiction effectively impossible (Element 44). It should be noted that this fact entails that the origin of Christianity is historically in a different class from other more mundane historical questions: other events simply did not generate nearly the same explosion of forgery and redaction; in fact, few events generated much of any, and therefore the survival and detection of accurate information is more frequently possible on other questions of history, but radically less so for the question we are here to examine.

The remaining relevant texts can be divided into two general categories: things written by Christians and things not written by Christians. In the latter category we have almost nothing. We do have some such material, but most of it cannot be established as independent of things we already have that were written by Christians (like the canonical Gospels), and therefore almost all of it must be excluded as irrelevant. What little we have any plausible reason still to consider will be examined in the next chapter. There we will also examine what little we have of 'independent' and 'causally relevant' Christian texts that are not already in the NT. Again, most Christian literature is irrelevant, either not being demonstrably independent (e.g. statements based on the Gospels) or not being plausibly connected to anything actually true about Jesus (e.g. the Infancy Gospels). But all the evidence in these categories that *is* relevant, whether Christian or non-Christian, is generally the latest primary evidence we have, chronologically speaking. I will therefore address it first (in the next chapter), and work back in time to the earliest surviving evidence.

That leaves the NT. Whether any Christian documents that we presently have date earlier than or even to the same period as the documents in the NT is a vexed question that has never been answered with certainty. And not being able to date a document is often the death knell for establishing relevance. Because if we can't even prove something was written in the first century, then we often can't prove its independence or its causal link to any actual facts of the matter. 'Speculating' earlier dates does not get around this problem, because only a speculative conclusion can be reached with a speculative premise. Since there is no Christian document pertaining to Jesus that we can confidently date earlier than the NT, any such evidence will be examined, if at all relevant, in the next chapter along with all other 'extrabiblical' evidence.

As for the NT itself, it can be divided into five categories: authentic letters, inauthentic letters, uncertain letters, the Gospels and Acts. I distinguish Acts from the Gospels because Acts, unlike the Gospels, is a history of the spread of Christianity *after* the death of Jesus, and thus could have different sources than the Gospels and covers a different subject of inquiry.

It also comes later than the earliest of the Gospels we have, and thus is also among the latest evidence we have. I therefore will treat it second (Chapter 9), after the extrabiblical evidence (Chapter 8). Then I will treat the four canonical Gospels (Chapter 10). And finally the Epistles (Chapter 11), the authentic ones being the earliest, the nearest to the origins of Christianity of any evidence we have. The inauthentic letters date later, in some cases much later. Likewise the book of Revelation. The uncertain letters can't be reliably placed in time at all. But any of these worth a look will nevertheless be treated in that chapter.

There is a great deal wrong with how a 'consensus' has been reached on the dates and authorship of all these Christian materials, and the conclusions usually cited as established tend to be far more questionable than most scholars let on. Nevertheless, as I found the task of trying to sort this out impossible, I will mostly rely on the majority consensus for no other reason than that I haven't anything better to work with. I projected it would take a minimum of seven years of full-time research to adequately examine and analyze all the evidence and arguments regarding the dating and authorship of these materials, and that with no actual prospect of any clear resolution for any of it, since it is not simply a given that we actually know the answers to any debated question.[9] I think there is a lot of work here that needs to be properly redone in NT studies, and I'm not alone in thinking that.[10] That caveat aside, this is what we 'know'.

3. *The Epistles*

The current consensus in regard to the canonical Epistles is best summarized in Bart Ehrman's *Forged*.[11] Seven letters are commonly agreed to be

9. See my lament (and calculation) in Richard Carrier, 'Ignatian Vexation', *Richard Carrier Blogs* (October 1, 2008) at http://richardcarrier.blogspot.com/2008/09/ignatian-vexation.html.

10. One of the things that needs to happen is a system for organizing and cataloguing the state of fact-claims in the field and what has been written on each specific one better than the haphazard, incomplete, low utility databases presently in play: see, e.g., Frank Zindler, 'Prolegomenon to a Science of Christian Origins', in *Sources of the Jesus Tradition: Separating History from Myth* (ed. R. Joseph Hoffmann; Amherst, NY: Prometheus, 2010), pp. 140-56 (excepting 143-49, much of whose content I disagree with). For another, more extensive argument on how NT studies should reform itself, see Burton Mack, *The Christian Myth: Origins, Logic, and Legacy* (New York: Continuum, 2001).

11. Bart Ehrman, *Forged* (New York: HarperOne, 2011). See also Bart Ehrman, *Forgery and Counterforgery: The Use of Literary Deceit in Early Christian Polemics* (New York: Oxford University Press, 2014); and the relevant chapters in *The New Interpreter's Bible: New Testament Survey* (Nashville, TN: Abingdon Press, 2006). I

authentically written by the apostle Paul in or around the 50s CE.[12] Those are 1 and 2 Corinthians, Galatians, Romans, Philippians, 1 Thessalonians and Philemon. With the possible exception of Philemon (which has no relevant content for our purposes),[13] I think that assessment is probably correct—although we know that even these seven letters have been meddled with.[14] The remaining letters do indeed deviate too greatly from Pauline

shall rely on these for all that follows, except where noted. See also L. Michael White, *From Jesus to Christianity* (San Francisco, CA: HarperSanFrancisco, 2004), pp. 169-214, 261-90, 314-23.

12. This dating is perhaps too gullibly based on Acts; but Paul certainly wrote before the Jewish War, which began in 66, and probably before the Neronian persecution of 64 (if such there was), as neither are ever mentioned in his letters; and he wrote well after Aretas assumed control of Damascus (which he mentions in 2 Cor. 11.32), which was between the years 37 and 40; and most (if not all) of his literary activity came fourteen to seventeen years after his conversion (Gal. 1.15-18; 2.1; possibly also 2 Cor. 12.2); all of which argues for his letters being written in the 50s. Gerd Lüdemann, *Paul, the Founder of Christianity* (Amherst, NY: Prometheus Books, 2002), details why we should trust a chronology derived only from Paul's letters and not from Acts.

13. There is a plausible case to be made that Philemon is a forgery, based in part on the fact that it looks a lot like a letter written by Pliny the Younger almost a century later (*Letters* 9.21): Robert Price, *The Pre-Nicene New Testament: Fifty-Four Formative Texts* (Salt Lake City, UT: Signature Books, 2006), pp. 467-69 (however, Price's assumption, in note c on p. 469, that a self-referencing inscription is telltale of forgery, is refuted by the fact that I have seen such things in actual letters recovered from the sands of Egypt, but even with that argument removed, a case for forgery remains, even if not a conclusive one). However that may be, Philemon contains no data relevant to the historicity of Jesus, so it can be disregarded anyway.

14. Examples of 'meddling' with the authentic Paulines are the many textual variants, interpolations and rearranged passage sequences (e.g. in Romans 16). Philippians is the poster child for the latter: see Philip Sellew, '"Laodiceans" and the Philippians Fragments Hypothesis', *Harvard Theological Review* 87 (January 1994), pp. 17-28. I discuss the two most well-known interpolations (1 Thess. 2.14-16 and 1 Cor. 14.34-35) in Richard Carrier, 'Pauline Interpolations', *Richard Carrier Blogs* (June 1, 2011) at http://richardcarrier.blogspot.com/2011/06/pauline-interpolations.html. For more: William Walker, *Interpolations in the Pauline Letters* (London: Sheffield Academic Press, 2001); Rainer Reuter, 'Introduction to Synoptic Work on the New Testament Epistles', *Journal of Higher Criticism* 9.2 (Fall 2002), pp. 246-58; and E. Randolph Richards, *Paul and First-Century Letter Writing: Secretaries, Composition, and Collection* (Downers Grove, IL: InterVarsity Press, 2004), pp. 99-121. The Gospels, Acts, and other Epistles have been subject to all the same phenomena. See Bart Ehrman, Daniel Wallace and Robert Stewart, *The Reliability of the New Testament* (Minneapolis, MN: Fortress Press, 2011); Bart Ehrman, *The Orthodox Corruption of Scripture: The Effect of Early Christological Controversies on the Text of the New Testament* (New York: Oxford University Press, 1993); Bruce Metzger, *The Text of the New Testament: Its Transmission, Corruption, and Restoration* (New York: Oxford University Press, 3rd edn, 1992).

style to be by his hand or even his dictation.[15] That would mean 2 Thessalonians, Ephesians and Colossians are forgeries (although they could include pastiches or edits or redactions of Pauline letters, and are close enough in outlook and content to be of the Pauline 'school', perhaps from the latter half of the first century), and 1 and 2 Timothy and Titus are even more certainly forgeries (definitely not from a Pauline 'school', and of significantly later date).[16] As forgeries, none of those letters can provide any evidence *for* the historicity of Jesus, because any evidence in them is then by definition 'made up'. They could even have been forged to promote that historicity, or, by superficially following the Gospels, simply taken it for granted.[17] They *might* provide evidence *against* historicity, however, since if such they do, it cannot have been by design or presumption, but would have to reflect real evidence known to their authors, who would surely not *invent* evidence against historicity. (But if anyone wishes to argue otherwise in any particular case, they are welcome to try.)

Of the other Epistles, some are of uncertain authorship (1, 2 and 3 John, Jude, James, and Hebrews) and therefore of uncertain date and reliability. They could have been composed anywhere between the 30s to 130s CE (or in some cases even later), and they could have been written by anyone of those names (none of the authors identify themselves as the apostles of the same names, or as relatives of Jesus, or anyone else in particular; and Hebrews

15. Richards, in *Paul and First-Century Letter Writing*, attempts to argue against this consensus (while in the process usefully surveying all the evidence in the matter), but his premises are ultimately implausible (e.g. Paul did in fact use various co-authors for all his letters [Rom. 16.22; 1 Cor. 1.1; 2 Cor. 1.1; Phil. 1.1; Phlm. 1; Gal. 1.1-2; 1 Thess. 1.1], yet all of his authentic letters maintain a consistent style; thus the fact of his employing co-authors would not explain the huge deviations in the other letters, whereas there are better explanations of them as the product of later redactional activity—see following note).

16. Note that Ephesians is widely regarded as a redaction of Colossians and some of the other letters: James Hering, *The Colossian and Ephesian Haustafeln in Theological Context: An Analysis of their Origins, Relationship, and Message* (New York: Peter Lang, 2007); with Price, *Pre-Nicene New Testament*, pp. 439-53. 2 Thessalonians is likewise regarded as a redaction of 1 Thessalonians, and 2 Peter and Jude as each in a different way a redaction of 1 Peter: Reuter, 'Introduction to Synoptic Work'. But in every case these are still redactions made by someone later than Paul: Thomas Brodie, Dennis MacDonald and Stanley Porter, *The Intertextuality of the Epistles: Explorations of Theory and Practice* (Sheffield: Sheffield Phoenix Press, 2006). Several scholars have also argued that 1 and 2 Timothy (and possibly Titus) were forged by the author or redactor of Luke–Acts: see Price, *Pre-Nicene New Testament*, pp. 497-98.

17. So keen to deceive were the forgers of 2 Thessalonians, by the way, that they even have Paul in it denounce forged letters! (2 Thess. 2.2-3; 3.17, probably meaning in fact the *authentic* letter, 1 Thessalonians). This illustrates the importance Christians placed on convincing readers that their forgeries were genuine.

is anonymous). The preponderance of evidence suggests the Johannines (1, 2 and 3 John, none of which actually says they were written by anyone named John) are late (perhaps early second century), whereas the others could be earlier, but we have no definite proof of that. We just don't know. The best case to be made is that Hebrews was written in or near Paul's lifetime (see Chapter 11, §5). As such, apart from Hebrews perhaps, these letters cannot provide evidence *for* historicity (because in such a capacity they cannot be established as either reliable—and thus causally connected to the facts—or as independent of other sources already 'promoting' historicity, like the Gospels), but they could provide evidence against it (if such they do), for the same reasons as the forged letters (as noted above).

Finally, 1 and 2 Peter are regarded as forgeries. 2 Peter most definitely was not written by the same author as 1 Peter (they are far too divergent stylistically), and therefore we can certainly place 2 Peter with all the other forgeries (in fact, its author certainly knew the Gospels and was therefore not writing independently of them), so we must therefore draw the same conclusions regarding its value as evidence.[18] However, 1 Peter could be authentic, and if so it should be included with the authentic Pauline letters, because it would be of roughly the same date, and by the very man who may have founded the entire Christian religion (having received the first revelation of Jesus Christ that started it all, if we're to trust 1 Cor. 15.5). Few scholars would agree with this position, but I personally believe it has more merit than is supposed. For the only reason given to assume it's a forgery is that Peter was an illiterate fisherman, but that is information only the Gospels produce, and they have every reason to invent or exaggerate the humble origins of the cult's founder (so as to make their appeal to the masses and their subsequent brilliance look all the more miraculous), whereas based on every precedent in history, prior probability heavily favors any religious leader and founder of the period being educated (whatever stories he then told his congregations later).

Analogously, Muhammad is often claimed to have been illiterate, and so his production of the Qur'an 'must be' miraculous; yet as the son of one of the wealthiest mercantile families in Arabia, he could not plausibly have been illiterate or even uneducated. The same trend may be evident in the treatment of Peter, especially if the Gospel authors wanted to reify the 'least shall be first' doctrine of the gospel by embodying it in the apostles themselves.[19] It's otherwise quite unlikely that the highly educated Paul would defer to the authority of an illiterate Peter (Galatians 1–2) or never

18. See, e.g., Jerome Neyrey, 'The Apologetic Use of the Transfiguration in 2 Peter 1.16-21', *Catholic Biblical Quarterly* 42 (October 1980), pp. 504-19.

19. See Carrier, *Not the Impossible Faith*, pp. 312-15; and Carrier, 'Spiritual Body', in *Empty Tomb* (ed. Price and Lowder), pp. 163-65.

mention the disparity in their educations (and thus, their knowledge of the scriptures) in his disputes over who should be in charge. Accordingly, I think assuming Peter was actually 'an illiterate fisherman' requires considerable gullibility. Nevertheless, I have by no means proven the contrary. So I will treat this item of evidence (the epistle of 1 Peter) as uncertain.

There are also letters from Jesus in the NT, included within the book of Revelation, which purports to record an extensive hallucination of the celestial Jesus by an unknown person named John, who composed this book like an extended epistle to various churches of his time. Accordingly, I shall treat Revelation as an epistle. Its date and authorship are still debated, as well as whether it has gone through several redactions. But the version we have most likely dates from the early 90s CE and is by some unknown author named John, and is almost certainly an elaborate fiction.[20] With such a late date, we cannot establish its independence from the Gospels. So it has little evidential value.

4. *The Gospels*

The 'usual' consensus on the four canonical Gospels is that Mark was written around 70, Matthew around 80, Luke around 90, and John around 100.[21] Those are all arbitrary ballpark figures, which don't really have much basis in fact. Of course, fundamentalists want all those dates to be earlier, while many well-informed experts are certain they are later, and I find the arguments of the latter more persuasive, if inconclusive. As to authorship, none of the Gospels was written by the person they were named after, or in fact by any known person. We know they were not written by the disciples of Jesus or anyone who knew Jesus. The titles of the Gospels conspicuously assign them as 'according to' the names given (Mark, Matthew, Luke and

20. Revelation 17.10-11 describes a sequence of eight emperors that most suitably fits Domitian as the eighth of them, and the whole of Revelation reads like a veiled commentary on his reign; as such the 80s or early 90s are its most likely date. See Adela Yarbro Collins, *Crisis and Catharsis: The Power of the Apocalypse* (Philadelphia, PA: Westminster Press, 1984); and now Elaine Pagels, *Revelations: Visions, Prophecy, and Politics in the Book of Revelation* (New York: Viking, 2012). Irenaeus, *Against Heresies* 5.30.3, corroborates this conclusion.

21. For a summary of the consensus on the Gospels see Bart Ehrman, *Jesus, Interrupted: Revealing the Hidden Contradictions in the Bible (and Why We Don't Know about Them)* (New York: HarperOne, 2009), pp. 102-12; and White, *From Jesus to Christianity*, pp. 231-314; and again the relevant chapters of the *New Interpreter's Bible: New Testament Survey*. But for a possible new direction in identifying dates and authors for this evidence (Gospels and Epistles) see David Trobisch, *The First Edition of the New Testament* (Oxford: Oxford University Press, 2000); and David Trobisch, 'Who Published the Christian Bible?', *CSER Review* 2.1 (2007), pp. 29-32.

John), which designation in Greek was not used to name the *author* of a work, but its source, the person from whom the information was received or learned, as in 'according to [the tradition of] Mark'.[22] And none of the Gospels says who these people are (nowhere is the titular Matthew or John ever called a disciple, e.g., or identified in any way). I have used and will continue to use these names *as if* they were the authors, merely for convenience's sake. Although it must also be noted that all of the Gospels have undergone redactional activity after their original composition, so really they've been meddled with by multiple authors.[23]

Mark was certainly written after 70 (the year the Jerusalem temple was destroyed), but how long after is an open question (some attempts have been made to argue it was written earlier, but on grounds far too speculative to consider here).[24] We really have no evidence that Mark was written

22. Ben Witherington, *The Gospel of Mark: A Socio-Rhetorical Commentary* (Grand Rapids, MI: William B. Eerdmans, 2001), pp. 65-66.

23. In addition to the general sources cited in a previous note, and the examples in Ehrman, *Jesus, Interrupted*, see also Wayne Kannaday, *Apologetic Discourse and the Scribal Tradition: Evidence of the Influence of Apologetic Interests on the Text of the Canonical Gospels* (Atlanta, GA: Society of Biblical Literature, 2004); and C.S.C. Williams, *Alterations to the Text of the Synoptic Gospels and Acts* (Oxford: Basil Blackwell, 1951). The most infamous example is the long ending of Mark, which was added later, after all the other Gospels had been written: see Richard Carrier, 'Mark 16:9-20 as Forgery or Fabrication', *Errancy Wiki* (2009) at http://www.errancywiki.com/index.php?title=Legends2. The Gospel of John was likewise reorganized and expanded by someone subsequent to the original author (see this section; and Chapter 10, §7). We also have parallel redactions of Luke–Acts (to be mentioned shortly).

24. Some scholars do still try to argue earlier dates for Mark, but only by rejecting a lot of evidence, such as how pervasively Mark assumes the Jewish War has passed and that God has abandoned the temple cult (these facts do not just feature in Mark 13: see, e.g., Chapter 10, §4). Mark also includes an apologetic for the failure of the apocalypse to have come yet, which entails he wrote many decades after Jesus predicted the end was nigh (Mk 13.28-37; see Carrier, *Proving History*, pp. 148-49), which can't be any earlier than the 60s. The fact that Mark has Jesus say several 'wars' had to pass first entails Mark knew the Jewish War had not only passed, but hadn't brought about the apocalypse, and therefore he had to have his Jesus explain this (Mk 13.7-8). Likewise, Paul knows nothing of the stories in Mark (see Chapter 11), so Mark can hardly have been circulating before the 60s. Even Hebrews and *1 Clement* are unaware of the content of Mark (see Chapter 11, §5, and Chapter 8, §5), and insofar as we know those books were written after Paul died, that leaves almost no room for Mark to have been composed before the War. Much discussion hovers around Mark's Jesus claiming a pagan shrine would be erected where the Jewish temple once stood, and though (as far as we know) that did not come to pass (until the Bar Kockhba revolt: see note on the *Epistle of Barnabas* in Chapter 8, §6), Mark still had to know the temple was destroyed to have such an expectation in the first place (and post-war rumors that Rome would do this would not be an improbability; it is, after all, what Rome eventually did). Because

any earlier than 100, in fact, so it's simply presumption really that puts his Gospel in the first century. I suspect Mark was written in the 70s or 80s, but only because its author seems to have the Jewish War still in mind as a relatively recent event, but that's a largely subjective judgment. Nevertheless, I will leave it at that until someone proves otherwise. Nothing is known of the author. Late tradition claims he was Peter's secretary, but there is no reason to trust that information, and it seems most unlikely. Mark is advocating against Torah-observant Christianity (see Chapter 10, §5) and thus would have been Peter's opponent, not representative.

There is no evidence really that Matthew was written in the 80s. He certainly wrote after Mark (as everyone knows he copies Mark, often verbatim, and is in fact polemically redacting Mark, as I'll show in Chapter 10). But it is by no means a given that he would only redact Mark near to when Mark was written; and we don't know when Mark was written anyway. Likewise, any assumption that Jewish Christianity faded after the 80s has no basis in evidence either. That sect's existence continues to be attested for centuries (see §1 of the next chapter), and though it certainly declined in size and influence in the second century, that is no help in dating Matthew. I will conclude that Matthew was written in the 80s or 90s simply to err on the side of the earliest likely period, and for no other reason.[25] Nothing is known of the author. We

Mark assumes this desecration would follow the Jewish War (Mk 13.7-8) and the preaching of the gospel worldwide (Mk 13.10), so he cannot be referring to the threat of Caligula in the 40s (which came to nothing, and was far too early for the gospel to already have been preached to all nations, much less for several wars of 'nation against nation' to have passed, much less such wars as Jesus would have to apologize for as not ending the world). Since the event of Mk 13.14 (which predicts the desecrating shrine) was to begin a phase of worldwide doom (Mk 13.15-20) accompanied by false messiahs (Mk 13.21-22), concluding with the end of the world (Mk 13.24-27), Mark was not retrofitting recent history into the prophecy of Jesus in Mk 13.14; rather, he is conceiving a future apocalyptic sequence of events—but one that presupposes the Jewish temple no longer stood. Mark is thus writing after. For the best attempt to argue otherwise (and in the process citing and discussing the whole gamut of scholarship on dating Mark) see James Crossley, *The Date of Mark's Gospel: Insight from the Law in Earliest Christianity* (New York: T. & T. Clark International, 2004). In addition to the refutation this note already provides, Crossley's argument from Aramaic is multiply flawed (see Chapter 10, §4, and the scholarship challenging Casey, on whom Crossley partly relies, in a note for Element 41).

25. For the best (but still occasionally flawed) analysis of the evidence for dating Matthew, see David Sim, *The Gospel of Matthew and Christian Judaism: The History and Social Setting of the Matthean Community* (Edinburgh: T. & T. Clark, 1998), pp. 31-40, 257-87. Sim argues there for dating Matthew between 70 and 100, with 85-95 most likely; but he has since argued a date in the early second century is more likely than he once thought: David Sim, 'Reconstructing the Social and Religious Milieu of Matthew: Methods, Sources, and Possible Results', in *Matthew, James, and Didache:*

know 'Matthew' was not an eyewitness, because he copies Mark verbatim and just modifies and adds to him (and much of what he adds is ridiculous and literarily crafted, not eyewitness material, as I'll show in Chapter 10), which is not the behavior of a witness, but of a late literary redactor.

Luke also wrote after Mark (as Luke also copied from Mark), and I am increasingly convinced that in fact Luke is also a redaction of Matthew and therefore postdates Matthew (see Chapter 10, §6). The evidence that Luke used the *Jewish Antiquities* of Josephus for some of his material is also convincingly strong, and that would place this Gospel after 93 CE.[26] Many experts have argued for Luke–Acts postdating 115 CE.[27] I will conclude that most likely Luke wrote between the 90s and 130s, and then arbitrarily side with the earlier of those dates. Nothing is known of the author. Late tradition claims he was a doctor and Paul's companion, but there is no reason to

Three Related Documents in their Jewish and Christian Settings (ed. Huub van de Sandt and Jürgen Zangenberg; Atlanta, GA: Society of Biblical Literature, 2008), pp. 13-32 (15-19). One could argue that Matthew was written before the 90s because Matthew is repeatedly echoed in the book of Revelation, which we know was written around then (see end of §3), but all those correspondences might be explained the other way around, by Matthew knowing and echoing Revelation. On those correspondences see the list in Dennis MacDonald, *Two Shipwrecked Gospels: The Logoi of Jesus and Papias's Exposition of Logia about the Lord* (Atlanta, GA: Society of Biblical Literature, 2012), p. 555 n. 2. For another survey of positions on dating Matthew and the arguments for and against, see W.D. Davies and Dale Allison, *A Critical and Exegetical Commentary on the Gospel according to Saint Matthew*, vol. I (Edinburgh: T. & T. Clark, 1988), pp. 127-38.

26. Richard Pervo, *Dating Acts: Between the Evangelists and the Apologists* (Santa Rosa, CA: Polebridge, 2006); Barbara Shellard, *New Light on Luke: Its Purpose, Sources, and Literary Context* (New York: Sheffield Academic, 2002), pp. 31-34; Steve Mason, 'Josephus and Luke–Acts', *Josephus and the New Testament* (Peabody, MA: Hendrickson Publishers, 1992), pp. 185-229; Gregory Sterling, *Historiography and Self-Definition: Josephos, Luke–Acts and Apologetic Historiography* (Leiden: Brill, 1992); Heinz Schreckenberg, 'Flavius Josephus und die lukanischen Schriften', in *Wort in der Zeit: Neutestamentliche Studien* (ed. Karl Rengstorf and Wilfrid Haubeck; Leiden: Brill, 1980), pp. 179-209; Max Krenkel, *Josephus und Lucas: Der schriftstellerische Einfluss des jüdischen Geschichtschreibers auf den Christlichen* (Leipzig: H. Haessel, 1894).

27. For example, Joseph Tyson, *Marcion and Luke–Acts: A Defining Struggle* (Columbia, SC: University of South Carolina Press, 2006); and Joseph Tyson, 'Why Dates Matter: The Case of the Acts of the Apostles', in *Finding the Historical Jesus: Rules of Evidence* (ed. Bernard Brandon Scott; Santa Rosa, CA: Polebridge, 2008), pp. 59-70; Richard Pervo, *Dating Acts,* and Richard Pervo, *Acts: A Commentary* (Minneapolis, MN: Fortress Press, 2009), pp. 5-7; Trobisch, 'Who Published the Christian Bible?'; and now MacDonald, *Two Shipwrecked Gospels*, pp. 43-67. See also Carrier, *Not the Impossible Faith*, pp. 174-76; and Price, *Pre-Nicene New Testament*, pp. 481-99.

trust that information, and it seems most unlikely. Luke explicitly says he is not an eyewitness and doesn't appear to know anyone who was.[28] And certainly if he had Paul as an authority he would have trumpeted those credentials in his preface. The scattered 'we' passages in Acts are sometimes offered as evidence the author was Paul's companion, but there are other, more plausible explanations for those abrupt changes of narrative pose.[29] There is also evidence that Luke–Acts has undergone editing over time, and even now there are two different versions of them (only one of which was canonized).[30]

John wrote after Luke—as almost everyone agrees, but as I will demonstrate in Chapter 10, John is almost certainly a polemical redaction of Luke (just as Matthew is of Mark; only John employs a freer, less verbatim style), making John the last of all.[31] External evidence placing the Gospel of John's appearance in history is also the scarcest. It could have been written as late

28. Carrier, *Not the Impossible Faith*, pp. 178-82.

29. See note in Chapter 9 (§1).

30. For example, Thomas Brodie, 'Re-Opening the Quest for Proto-Luke: The Systematic Use of Judges 6–12 in Luke 16:1–18:8', *Journal of Higher Criticism* 2 (Spring 1995), pp. 68-101; W.A. Strange, *The Problem of the Text of Acts* (New York: Cambridge University Press, 1992); and Pervo, *Acts*. See §5 of this chapter.

31. That John is responding to Luke is actually a growing consensus in Johannine studies; likewise that John has been multiply redacted, such that our version is not the one originally written. On both points see Herman Waetjen, *The Gospel of the Beloved Disciple: A Work in Two Editions* (New York: T. & T. Clark, 2005); C.K. Barrett, *The Gospel according to St. John* (Philadelphia, PA: Westminster Press, 2nd edn, 1978), pp. 15-26; F.L. Cribbs, 'St. Luke and the Johannine Tradition', *Journal of Biblical Literature* 90 (1971), pp. 422-50, expanded in 'A Study of the Contacts That Exist between St. Luke and St. John', in *Society of Biblical Literature 1973 Seminar Papers* (ed. George MacRae; Cambridge, MA: Society of Biblical Literature, 1973), II, pp. 1-93; C.H. Dodd, *Historical Tradition in the Fourth Gospel* (Cambridge: Cambridge University Press, 1963); P. Parker, 'Luke and the Fourth Evangelist', *New Testament Studies* 9 (1963), pp. 317-36; John Bailey, *The Traditions Common to the Gospels of Luke and John* (Leiden: E.J. Brill, 1963); and Raymond Brown, *An Introduction to the Gospel of John* (New York: Doubleday, rev. edn, 2003); and Raymond Brown, *The Gospel according to John* (Garden City, NY: Doubleday, 1966–1970). These studies are reinforced by Manfred Lang, *Johannes und die Synoptiker: Eine redaktionsgeschichtliche Analyse von Joh 18–20 vor dem markinischen und lukanischen Hintergrund* (Göttingen: Vandenhoeck & Ruprecht, 1999); G. van Belle, 'Lukan Style in the Fourth Gospel', in *Luke and his Readers* (ed. R. Bieringer, G. van Belle and J. Verheyden; Dudley, MA: Peeters, 2005), pp. 351-72; and Andrew Gregory, 'The Third Gospel? The Relationship of John and Luke Reconsidered', in *Challenging Perspectives on the Gospel of John* (ed. John Lierman; Tübingen: Mohr Siebeck, 2006), pp. 109-34 (although Gregory argues the reverse thesis, he nevertheless summarizes the scholarship arguing the authors of John knew the Gospel of Luke; likewise Shellard, *New Light on Luke*, pp. 200-88; and Thomas Brodie, *The Birthing of the New Testament: The Intertextual Development of*

as the 140s (some argue even later) or as early as the 100s (provided Luke was written in the 90s). I will arbitrarily side with the earlier of those dates. John was redacted multiple times and thus had multiple authors.[32] Nothing is known of them. John's authors (plural) claim to have used a written source composed by an anonymous eyewitness (21.20-25), but that witness does not exist in any prior Gospel, yet is conspicuously inserted into John's redaction of their narratives (e.g. compare Jn 20.2 with Lk. 24.12) and so is almost certainly a fabrication (as I show in Chapter 10, §7).

Finally, you will often see cited as a source for early Christianity a document called 'Q', for *Quelle*, which is German for 'source'. But this actually doesn't exist. It is a hypothetical document, whose contents, redactional history and even nature (whether written or oral) are endlessly debated in the scholarship. There are serious methodological flaws in the defenses made of the existence and contents of Q, and it looks far more likely to me that what we call 'Q' was nothing more than additions made to Mark by Matthew, which were then redacted into Luke.[33] I see no merit in assuming otherwise without very good evidence, and the evidence presented even by staunch

the New Testament Writings [Sheffield: Sheffield Phoenix Press, 2004], pp. 267-70). See also Chapter 10 (§7).

32. I'll discuss some of the evidence for this in Chapter 10, but this is already the consensus of Johannine experts; in addition to the scholarship cited in the previous note, see White, *From Jesus to Christianity*, pp. 305-14; and Mark Strauss, *Four Portraits, One Jesus: An Introduction to Jesus and the Gospels* (Grand Rapids, MI: Zondervan, 2007), pp. 334-35.

33. The best case yet made for there being no Q source at all is in Mark Goodacre, *The Case against Q: Studies in Markan Priority and the Synoptic Problem* (Harrisburg, PA: Trinity Press International, 2002). See also Mark Goodacre, *The Synoptic Problem: A Way through the Maze* (London: Sheffield Academic Press, 2001); Mark Goodacre, *Thomas and the Gospels: The Case for Thomas's Familiarity with the Synoptics* (Grand Rapids, MI: Eerdmans, 2012), and his supplementary Website http://www.markgoodacre.org/Q, as well as Mark Goodacre and Nicholas Perrin (eds.), *Questioning Q: A Multidimensional Critique* (Downers Grove, IL: InterVarsity Press, 2004). His conclusion is well corroborated by Shellard, *New Light on Luke*, pp. 58-84; Michael Goulder, 'Is Q a Juggernaut?', *Journal of Biblical Literature* 115 (1996), pp. 667-81' and Michal Goulder, *Luke: A New Paradigm* (2 vols.; Sheffield: JSOT, 1989); Allan MacNicol (ed.), *Beyond the Q Impasse: Luke's Use of Matthew: A Demonstration by the Research Team of the International Institute for the Renewal of Gospel Studies* (Valley Forge, PA: Trinity Press International, 1996); John Drury, *Tradition and Design in Luke's Gospel: A Study in Early Christian Historiography* (London: Darton, Longman & Todd, 1976), pp. 120-73; N. Turner, 'The Minor Verbal Agreements of Mt. and Lk. against Mk', *Studia Evangelica* 1 (1959), pp. 223-34; and most famously A.M. Farrer, 'On Dispensing with Q', in *Studies in the Gospels: Essays in Memory of R.H. Lightfoot* (ed. D.E. Nineham; Oxford: Basil Blackwell, 1955), pp. 55-88 (even the last of these remains required reading for anyone still enamored with Q). See also Stanley Porter, *The Criteria for Authenticity in Historical-Jesus Research: Previous*

advocates of Q cannot honestly be described as even 'good'. Whereas the evidence for Luke using Matthew *is* very good (see Chapter 10, §6).[34]

The best case for anything like Q proposed so far is Dennis MacDonald's theory that there was a whole lost Gospel, which was also used as a source by Mark, but his reconstruction of it is highly speculative; and even if such a text existed he concedes it was mostly if not wholly fictional (essentially just a rewrite of Deuteronomy with Jesus in place of Moses).[35] And in any event, even if Q existed in the traditional sense, it was clearly just another Gospel no different in character from the Gospels we have (complete with narratives and conversations, such as narratives about John the Baptist and Jesus' interactions with the centurion of Capernaum), and not just a list of sayings as Q is sometimes described; and since we don't have it (and thus don't know all of what it said or even the whole context of what we might infer it did say) we can draw no usable conclusions about its date or reliability. Accordingly, when I treat the Gospels (the only *actual* evidence we have), I will only regard as reliable *what is in the Gospels*. I am thereby dismissing all other 'hypothetical' sources as well (such as the so-called Signs Gospel or the speculated sources behind the unique material in Matthew, and so on) as being mere speculation, and therefore not *evidence*.

5. *Acts*

Acts is essentially the 'sequel' to the Gospel of Luke, covering the origins and early development of 'the church' (as Luke wanted to represent it) from the 30s up to around the year 60. There is considerable debate (still) as to

Discussion and New Proposals (Sheffield: Sheffield Academic Press, 2000), pp. 87-88; and Brodie, *Birthing of the New Testament*, pp. 260-67.

34. For the best attempt to rehabilitate the Q hypothesis in the face of this overwhelming evidence against it see John Kloppenborg, 'On Dispensing with Q?: Goodacre on the Relation of Luke to Matthew', *New Testament Studies* 49 (2003), pp. 210-36. His case is wholly unpersuasive, ignoring all the positive evidence of definite borrowing (only some of which I survey in Chapter 10, §6), and then arguing solely from what he insists Luke 'should' have done, relying on arbitrary 'psychic' knowledge of the methods and intentions of Luke in using and adapting Matthew, which is no more reliable than any alternative set of assumptions about Luke's designs, and there are more such alternatives that dispense with Q than require it. And yet Kloppenborg concedes that Q's existence is only 'at least as plausible' as its absence (236) and that defenders of Q are far too confident in their assertions (214-18). In other words, even Kloppenborg admits we don't really know there was a Q.

35. MacDonald, *Two Shipwrecked Gospels*, esp. pp. 69-89. Against using his thesis to argue for historicity see my discussion in Richard Carrier, 'Historicity News: Notable Books', *Richard Carrier Blogs* (October 17, 2012) at http://freethoughtblogs.com/carrier/archives/2669.

whether the same author wrote both or, even if he did, whether many decades separate their composition. But the overall consensus (and my own opinion) is that the same author wrote both around the same time, but that they might have undergone subsequent editing by later redactors (as many experts agree they have). We have two versions of Luke–Acts, for example, and one is 10 to 20 percent longer than the other. The 'canon' contains the shorter text. But both are equally ancient, and scholars cannot agree which is the original.[36] Even the shorter text could be a redaction of some earlier version we no longer have. Still, I will accept a date for Acts in the 90s (because it certainly was written after the Gospel of Luke), merely for convenience, still recognizing that it could date several decades later than that (just as Luke's Gospel could).

6. *Extrabiblical Evidence*

For everything in this category, on matters of dating and authorship I will follow Van Voorst (who collects and analyzes all the relevant extrabiblical evidence in one place), except where I state otherwise.[37]

There is a variety of largely undatable Christian literature, such as the *Didache* (*Didachē*) or *1 Clement,* that could have come anywhere from the mid-first to late second century. For example, *1 Clement,* a letter to the Corinthian church by Clement of Rome in (supposedly) the generation after Paul, is traditionally dated to around the year 95, but in fact we have no secure reason to trust that it was actually written then, or even by Clement of Rome. It's just 'assumed'. The year 95 puts this securely later than the Paulines and (by any usual estimates) the earlier Gospels. And this is the earliest extrabiblical Christian document we have (among those for which we can assign dates at all).

However, I must say I find this traditional date implausible.[38] Apart from later tradition, there is no evidence in the letter that would suggest it was

36. A translation of the longer (non-canonical) version of Acts is available in Price, *Pre-Nicene New Testament*, pp. 563-634 (but alas, not the longer version of Luke). For a discussion of the two versions of Acts and their textual history see Strange, *Problem of the Text of Acts.*

37. Robert Van Voorst, *Jesus Outside the New Testament* (Grand Rapids, MI: William B. Eerdmans, 2000). See also Gerd Theissen and Annette Merz, *The Historical Jesus: A Comprehensive Guide* (trans. John Bowden; Minneapolis, MN: Fortress Press, 1998), pp. 17-124; Craig Evans, 'Jesus in Non-Christian Sources', in *Studying the Historical Jesus* (ed. Chilton and Evans), pp. 443-78; and David Wenham (ed.), *Gospel Perspectives: Studies of History and Tradition in the Four Gospels*, vol. V. *The Jesus Tradition outside the Gospels* (Sheffield: JSOT Press, 1984).

38. I'm not alone; see White, *From Jesus to Christianity*, pp. 335-40 (he doesn't entertain an earlier date—instead putting it between 100 and 120 CE—but he does not

written in or anywhere near the year 95. Instead, the letter says Peter's and Paul's deaths were among those 'happening most recently' (*tous eggista genomenous, 1 Clem.* 5.1), being of Clement's 'own generation' (*tēs geneas hēmōn*), and that some of the elders who were deposed had been appointed by the very apostles themselves (which would mean in this case, by Paul: *1 Clem.* 44.1-5). That would sooner suggest it was written in the 60s. There is no evidence in the letter to contradict that conclusion.[39] Clement refers to 'sudden and repeated misfortunes and setbacks' (*tas aiphnidious kai epallēlous . . . sumphoras kai periptōseis*) in the church at Rome that have delayed his writing to them (*1 Clem.* 1.1). But that is so vague it can refer to any period, particularly as we don't know what happened in the churches from the 60s to the 90s (Element 22)—and are not well informed as to what really happened even in the 90s or for many decades after that. More telling is the fact that Clement shows no knowledge of any extant Gospel (not even when he certainly would have mentioned any that existed, e.g. in 43.1 or 45; see §5 of the next chapter), which would also mean he wrote before the 70s, unless the Gospels were written *very much later* than the consensus now assumes (in §4). He is also completely unaware of the fact that the temple at Jerusalem was destroyed and the liturgical rites are no longer performed there (*1 Clement* 40–41), or even that the Jews were or had ever been at war with Rome (which would have been a model example of the consequences of disobedience that would be hard for Clement not to make use of, not least in his chap. 51), both of which in my estimation should definitely place this letter before the year 70.

Possibly by the 'recent' series of setbacks and calamities Clement is referring hyperbolically to internal dissensions such as those at Corinth, perhaps in conjunction with other ordinary problems, such as the natural deaths of important church leaders, sporadic persecutions, financial losses, famine. Given the fact that his phrasing means *several* unexpected setbacks,

consider the arguments I present here).

39. It is sometimes claimed that when Clement calls the Corinthian church 'ancient' this must mean he is writing a very long time after its founding, but the term *archaios* frequently just means venerable, early-begun, or original: for instance, in Acts 21.16, Mnason, who accompanied an embassy, is called an *archaios mathētēs*, an 'early disciple', which doesn't even imply he was old (much less 'ancient'), just that he was with the movement from very early on (and even insofar as he *was* old, the Corinthian church was in the same sense 'old' by the 60s, even some of its first elders having already died: *1 Clem.* 44.2, 4). Likewise, Clement sent to the Corinthians an embassy of elderly Christians who had lived 'blamelessly among us' since their youth (*neotēs*), a term that meant the period after childhood up to the age of thirty, but he does not say they were converted to Christianity in their youth, only that they were known personally to members of the church at Rome since their youth and in all that time had lived morally upright lives. This is fully consistent with a time period of the 60s.

and not a singular catastrophic burning of the city followed by a purge of nearly the whole church (an event so enormous it would surely warrant more comment from him than this), the author does not likely mean Nero's persecution in 64. In fact, Clement does not exhibit any awareness of that event (e.g. in his survey of Christian martyrs, in *1 Clement* 5–6, those supposedly burned by Nero in Clement's own city don't get any mention). Nor does he likely mean any great persecution under Domitian, since there is actually no evidence of there having been one, outside late Christian legends, which took a documented persecution of Jews and later rewrote it as a persecution of Christians, which ensures the latter is a fabrication.[40] For all that, this letter looks like it was written in the early 60s (or else its author wants us to believe it was), a few years after the deaths of Peter and Paul. Nevertheless, I will not rely on this conclusion, but I will treat it as if it were written *either* in the early 60s (as I think is most probable) *or* in the mid 90s (as is traditional and most generally assumed).

Since this is well the earliest datable Christian text outside the NT, our conclusion regarding all other extrabiblical Christian texts must be the same: since they can't be established as early, they can't be established as independent, and few of them can be established as tracing back to any early-first-century sources. None of them contains anything either different from what's found in the NT or that's believable even if different (e.g. the Infancy Gospels or the *Acts of Peter* or the bizarrely improbable sayings attributed to Jesus in the *Gospel of Thomas*). One can speculate that some of it did, but that's insufficient to build an argument from, because all qualifiers in an argument's premises commute to its conclusion; in other words, 'speculation in, speculation out'.

Which means none of this can argue for historicity, precisely because none of it can be established as both independent and reliable, and without

40. The claim that Clement was bishop of Rome between 93 and 96 and wrote this letter during the reign of Domitian comes only from Hegesippus a century later, whom we shall see is not a reliable source (in Chapter 8, §8; see Eusebius, *History of the Church* 3.16-20; notice how Eusebius has no sources to cite anywhere near the time of Clement). That the Domitianic persecution is fabricated, compare Eusebius, *History of the Church* 3.19 with the original story as preserved in Cassius Dio, *Roman History* 67.14 and Suetonius, *Domitian* 10 (both of whom knew very well what Christians were, yet neither of whom mention Christians being involved in this event at all: see Carrier, *Not the Impossible Faith*, pp. 156-57). Christians were fond of rewriting history to place Christians in stories they were not previously in; see the example of the 'rain miracle' of Marcus Aurelius, in which a story about pagan magic with no Christians in it was quickly transformed into a story about a whole Christian legion, completely replacing the original pagan sorcerer in the story (Carrier, *Sense and Goodness*, pp. 228-31; with, now, Péter Kovács, *Marcus Aurelius' Rain Miracle and the Marcomannic Wars* [Leiden: Brill, 2009]).

confirming both, the mathematical effect on the probability of historicity is zero—unless one of those items contains evidence *against* historicity, as in the case of the Epistles (as I explained in §3). Accordingly, I will select only a few key examples to examine in the next chapter (*1 Clement*, Ignatius and Papias, as being possibly early; and Hegesippus, as being possibly informative), and I will discuss some additional problems with assigning dates and authors to these sources there. Everything else dates later than the year 120, long after any eyewitnesses would have died (Element 22).[41]

Of *non*-Christian extrabiblical evidence there is very little that can be established as independent and reliable. In fact, in the next chapter I will conclude that none can. But the 'usual' view is that some can. This includes one very late source, the Babylonian Talmud, completed in the fifth century (the early Middle Ages), which I will consider only because it says things very different from what the NT does and therefore would appear to be independent of the NT—unless the things it says are polemical inventions created *in response* to the NT (or some other Gospels outside the canon). In fact, a common conclusion scholars reach is that because it is so late, its contents don't in fact trace back to any actual first-century source at all;

41. So, e.g., I rule out Aristides and Quadratus: even though both are said to have written their quoted texts in 124 CE (Eusebius, *History of the Church* 4.3; neither of their original texts survives), making them among the earliest surviving extrabiblical Christian authors, that still falls outside my cut-off date, and modern scholars dispute that date anyway (all recent scholarship on Aristides or Quadratus argues that the texts attributed to them may well date decades later). Since we have no way to authenticate their texts, quotes, sources or dates, we cannot use them as evidence. Moreover, although both appear to argue for a historical Jesus, the surviving quotations we have from them lack any apparent sources for their claims beyond the Gospels (and perhaps Acts). I also rule out the *Gospel of Thomas,* which claims to relate sayings that Jesus secretly told 'Didymus Judas Thomas', since I suspect that's a fictional character invented by the authors of the Gospel of John, which would mean *Gospel of Thomas* post-dates even John; and even if not, for all we actually know, the contents of *Gospel of Thomas* derive from Matthew, Mark and Luke (with additions thereto), possibly through oral or other intermediaries: Mark Goodacre, *Thomas and the Gospels: The Case for Thomas's Familiarity with the Synoptics* (Grand Rapids, MI: W.B. Eerdmans, 2012); Klyne Snodgrass, 'The Gospel of Thomas: A Secondary Gospel', *Second Century* 7 (1989–1990), pp. 19-38; Raymond Brown, 'The Gospel of Thomas and St. John's Gospel', *New Testament Studies* 9 (1963), pp. 155-77; Price, *Pre-Nicene New Testament*, pp. 969-88. It therefore cannot be established as independent. This does mean I disagree with Gregory Riley, *Resurrection Reconsidered: Thomas and John in Controversy* (Minneapolis, MN: Fortress Press, 1995), pp. 2-5: some of the *ideas* in *Gospel of Thomas* may predate John (to which John may be responding), but I think it's more likely *Gospel of Thomas* itself is a response to John, not the other way around. That John was redacted several times (see previous note) complicates such relative dating anyway.

although, as I will show, that would make its contents very hard to explain. I suspect it reflects (and responds to) a first-century non-canonical Gospel (as I will explain in the next chapter). Its relevance, either way, is limited but not lacking.

All other non-Christian extrabiblical sources do not say anything substantially different from known Christian literature, and therefore (being also late) cannot be established as independent. And some of it doesn't even exist (contrary to it often being cited as if it does). Accordingly, I will include only the earliest examples. These begin with the *Jewish Antiquities* of Josephus, completed in or shortly after 93 CE, the extant text of which contains two references to Jesus. Next is a letter of Pliny the Younger written around 112 CE about his interrogation of some local Christians in what is now northern Turkey. Then a passage in the *Annals* of Tacitus (about the Neronian persecution at Rome in the year 64), completed around 116 CE. Then a passage in the *Lives of the Caesars* of Suetonius, completed around 119 CE, about a certain 'Chrestus' instigating a riot in Rome, whom some take to mean Christ. And finally an alleged reference in the *Histories* of Thallus, which is undatable with any certainty but probably comes from the late second century (as I will discuss in §11 of the next chapter). Every other author is much too late to be relevant—Celsus, Lucian and Mara bar Serapion, e.g., all wrote in the 150s or later, and no other non-Christian text mentioning Jesus predates them.[42]

That's it. That's all there is.

7. *The Problem of Compromised Evidence*

Everyone agrees all the Christian documents so far mentioned have been selected, forged, meddled with or edited. In fact the NT underwent a considerable amount of editing, interpolation and revising over the course of its first two centuries, and not merely as a result of transcription and scribal error, but often with specific dogmatic intent.[43] Extra-biblical literature often underwent even more of the same, with quite blatant forgery and revision not uncommon (as we'll see in the case of Ignatius in the next chapter, §6;

42. Van Voorst, *Jesus Outside the New Testament*, pp. 56-57 (for Mara), pp. 58-59 (for Lucian), p. 64 (for Celsus); attempts to date Mara bar Serapion to the first century depend on fallacious reasoning, which simply doesn't survive scrutiny in the face of the analysis in Van Voorst. See Earl Doherty, *Jesus: Neither God nor Man (The Case for a Mythical Jesus)* (Ottawa: Age of Reason, 2009), pp. 652-56. I am also excluding Dio Cassius, *Roman History* 67.14, about the persecution of some converts to Judaism under Domitian (in the 90s), not only because it's late (early third century) but also because it mentions neither Jesus nor Christians and was only presumed to be about Christians in later Christian legend (see earlier note).

43. See earlier notes for examples and references.

we saw it already in the Christian 'redacting' of the *Ascension of Isaiah* in Chapter 3, §1, and of Christian 'fabrication' generally in Element 44). This is not something to sweep under the rug. It makes a real difference in how we estimate probabilities. Unlike most other questions in history, the evidence for Jesus is among the most compromised bodies of evidence in the whole of ancient history. It cannot be said that this has no effect on its reliability.

This does not entail or require any particular 'conspiracy theory', however. Of course, the fact of it is so firmly in evidence it cannot be disputed (only its degree); so even if a conspiracy theory were required, it would be more than amply established by the evidence we have. But it isn't needed, because all that one does need is a sect of fanatical believers who (a) have a common dogma to promote (e.g. that Jesus really lived and really said and did certain things conducive to the doctrines they wanted to promote), as we know the 'orthodox' sect did, and (b) have no qualms against destroying evidence (or just not mentioning or preserving it), forging evidence and doctoring evidence, as we again know the 'orthodox' sect did (i.e. these are not mere hypotheses, but established facts in our background knowledge).[44] Any such community will organically produce the same effect as a conspiracy, without ever having to conspire to do anything. They do not require any top–down instructions or orders to follow, nor any collusion. If each independently did what made sense to him, each on his own initiative, the effect on the evidence that survives for us now will have been the same.

For example, no one 'colluded' to forge an ending to Mark. It was not an order issued from the pope or some cabal of archbishops. Someone just did it.[45] It then so agreed with what everyone wanted to be there that they increasingly preserved it at the expense of other versions of Mark. In this case, the evidence of this survived for us to detect it. But this will not have been the case for everything. In actual fact, most corruptions and forgeries occur early in a text's history, when it is far easier to eclipse earlier drafts (there being fewer copies of them, less widely distributed) and avoid detection (as the more time passes, the more suspicious a remarkable new discovery becomes); and yet that is precisely the period of a text's development that we know the least about (because we have few to no manuscripts or fragments to judge from). From the interpolations we have detected, for example, projecting the *same* rate of meddling back into the period for which we have no manuscripts with which to detect such things (roughly 50–150 CE), I calculate there must be at least twenty significant interpola-

44. Besides the scholarship referenced in previous notes, see again Element 44.

45. Quite possibly they 'appended' a paragraph from a commentary (not itself intended as a forgery), passing it off as being by the hand of Mark (and thus 'manufacturing' a forgery): see my analysis in Carrier, 'Mark 16:9-20 as Forgery or Fabrication'.

tions in the text of the NT *that we will have no way of detecting* (except when we are lucky enough that internal evidence gives us a clue). And again, the actual rate would not then have been the same as in subsequent centuries, but substantially *higher*. So twenty is a definite undercount.[46] The same goes for deletions, harmonizations, alterations and destroyed or suppressed documents.

That some text has been forged, or interpolated, or altered by Christians even outside the canon is a caveat I encounter in scholarly analysis of document after document, to the point that it becomes frustrating; and it would be alarming in any other field. And yet, it's so common to this field that it is now simply taken for granted and thus often shrugged off. Already the fact that half the letters in the NT are recognized forgeries warns us against ever implicitly trusting any of the evidence we have. The fact that we can see the same and worse across the whole early history of Christian literature and textual tradition only reinforces that conclusion. And that *must* effect our estimates of probability.

Nevertheless, throughout this book I shall assume that any passage in the NT is *not* an interpolation, unless I cite or present a specific argument for it, or there is already unanimous agreement among experts (and thus no argument need be made). For example, there are many arguments for interpolations in Paul's letter to the Romans, including 1.3-4 (which is often cited in support of historicity) and 16.25-27 (which is often cited in support of mythicism). I do not find those arguments entirely convincing. But neither do I find them wholly without merit. Yet I shall assume these passages are authentic, because no conclusive case can be made otherwise.[47]

46. See my debate with J.P. Holding: Richard Carrier and J.P. Holding, 'The Text of the New Testament: Do We Have What They Had?', at the Amador Christian Center in Plymouth, California, on April 9, 2011 (for video see Richard Carrier, 'Debates & Interviews', *Richard Carrier Blogs* [February 24, 2012] at http://freethoughtblogs.com/carrier/archives/389; and for my accompanying slideshow: http://www.richardcarrier.info/NTReliabilitySlideshow.pdf). On the whole problem of detecting interpolations in the Epistles see Winsome Munro, 'Interpolation in the Epistles: Weighing Probability', *New Testament Studies* 36 (1990), pp. 431-43; and William Walker, 'The Burden of Proof in Identifying Interpolations in Pauline Letters', *New Testament Studies* 33 (1987), pp. 610-18; and William Walker, 'Text-Critical Evidence for Interpolation in the Letters of Paul', *Catholic Biblical Quarterly* 50 (1988), pp. 622-31, which are all required reading on the subject.

47. See Robert Jewett, *Romans: A Commentary* (Minneapolis, MN: Fortress Press, 2007), pp. 4-18, 99-108, 997-1011. Jewett surveys claims that these two passages are not only interpolations but have both undergone multiple redactions as well (Jewett himself concludes in favor of Paul editing the first and a later redactor inserting the second). That seems needlessly complicated and overly speculative to me. In each case, concluding an interpolation has occurred depends on several improbable assumptions, e.g.: (a) that Romans is a unified letter (when in fact it is probably a mashup of several:

8. *The Role of Consequent Probabilities*

The way evidence affects the probability of a hypothesis is by comparing the consequent probabilities of that evidence on every viable hypothesis. If an item of evidence (its existence, its content) is more likely on one hypothesis than on another, then it increases the probability of the former hypothesis against the latter. But that *alone* does not render the supported hypothesis the more probable. First, all evidence must be considered (because even if a single item of evidence supports a hypothesis, the remaining evidence might still support an alternative more). Second, even after all evidence is considered, any prior probability against a hypothesis must be overcome. These points I have already explained in *Proving History*. Here all that we need remember are the questions we have to ask of each piece of evidence:

1. How likely is it that we would have this evidence if our hypothesis is true? (Is this evidence expected? How expected?)
2. How likely is it that the evidence would look like it does if our hypothesis is true? (Instead of looking differently; having a different content, for example.)
3. Conversely, how likely is it that we would have this evidence if the *other* hypothesis is true? (Again, is this evidence expected? How expected?)
4. And how likely is it that the evidence would look like it does if that other hypothesis is true? (Instead of looking differently; having a different content, for example.)

And when asking these questions, the 'evidence' includes not just what we have, but also what we *don't* have.[48] Does the evidence—what we have and what we don't, what it says and what it doesn't—make more sense on one hypothesis than the other? How much more? That's the question. And the

see note in Chapter 11, §2); (b) that these two passages are not inherited or stylized creedal statements like the Philippians hymn (when in fact they probably are); and (c) that Rom. 16.25-27 says God has abandoned the Jews and only sent his salvation to the Gentiles (when in fact it says no such thing). That last assumption Jewett bases on the fact that it says the gospel has been made known 'to all the nations' without mention of the Jews, but the exact same thing is said in Mt. 24.14; 25.32; and 28.19, which by no stretch of the imagination can be saying what Jewett imagines. In Rom. 16.26 likewise the phrase does not imply exclusion of the Jews, but furtherance of such scriptural promises as Ps. 82.8; Gen. 26.4; Isa. 52.10; and Jer. 3.17. It is indeed repeated in Rom. 1.5, necessitating an assumption of double interpolation. That it agrees with the overall point of Romans 15 confirms that Paul is saying God meant the gospel to be universal (and thus *inclusive of the Gentiles*), which some Jewish Christians were questioning; he does not thereby imply the Jews were being excluded.

48. On the logic and importance of an argument from silence in history see Carrier, *Proving History*, pp. 117-19.

answer, in conjunction with the prior probability (in this case developed in Chapter 6), determines which hypothesis is more likely true.

The two hypotheses we are comparing are (a) that Jesus was minimally historical (Chapter 2) and (b) that Jesus was originally a cosmic being known only by revelation who was later set in history through the production of allegorical myths that were later taken or intended literally (Chapter 3). The former shall be our h, while the latter is effectively $\neg h$. When estimating probabilities, I shall use the method of arguing *a fortiori*: in each case I will settle on the probability that is the furthest in favor of h that I can reasonably believe it to be, just as I did when determining the prior (in Chapter 6). I will also run the numbers for what I think the actual probabilities are more likely to be, but the conclusion of this book will argue mainly from the other result, because ultimately I do not believe any reasonable person will be able to disagree with it. I will explain and complete the equation in Chapter 12.

9. *Conclusion*

In truth, the only evidence that Jesus *really* existed as a historical person, as opposed to merely being *believed* to have existed by the dawn of the second century, lies in the contents of the NT. There is no other source, document or artifact that *independently* corroborates the historical reality of Jesus. In most cases this is obvious, but in some it is disputed, and those cases I will take up in the next chapter. The remaining chapters deal with the NT.

Independent or not, *all* extrabiblical mentions of Jesus come later than 90 CE, by which time a belief that Jesus was historical will already have arisen. Even the contents of the NT did not begin to be written until twenty or so years after Jesus is supposed to have lived, and most of it was written half a century or more after, some of it nearly as much as a century after. And all of it was written by fanatical believers, not neutral observers, while all the evidence we have from neutral parties was dependent on these fanatical Christians as their source. The NT itself was assembled in the middle of the second century, by obvious devout historicists, who thus selected (and in some cases even modified) the contents of the NT specifically to support their agenda.[49]

We do *not* have any first-century documents from *other* sects of Christianity, and no second-century collections arranged by them either. Thus, for example, if Paul wrote a letter that more clearly identified Jesus as solely

49. Harry Gamble, 'Canonical Formation of the New Testament', in *Dictionary of New Testament Background* (ed. Craig Evans and Stanley Porter; Downers Grove, IL: InterVarsity Press, 2000), pp. 183-95; Bruce Metzger, *The Canon of the New Testament: Its Origin, Development, and Significance* (New York: Oxford University Press, 1987); Lee Martin McDonald and James Sanders (eds.), *The Canon Debate* (Peabody, MA: Hendrickson Publishers, 2002); Trobisch, *First Edition of the New Testament.*

a cosmic being, we cannot expect to have it—because the sect that chose which letters of his to preserve dogmatically rejected that view (as we shall see in the next chapter), and therefore would not have preserved any such letters, but only those that could be interpreted to favor *their* view, rather than what the *earliest* Christians may have really believed. It is therefore more than a little significant that we know of several letters by Paul that have not been preserved—begging the question why.[50] What did they say? I shall have more to say about this in Chapters 11 and 12.

Therefore, though the whole range of extrabiblical evidence constitutes our fourth category, and the first we shall examine, we shall find (in the next chapter) that it argues very little in favor of historicity and even somewhat against, leaving our primary focus on the probability that the NT would contain the text it does if *h* is true (and Jesus did exist) and the probability that it would contain that text if *h* is *not* true (and Jesus *didn't* really exist). Yet, as we've seen, this evidence is enormously compromised by a legacy of selective preservation, doctoring, interpolation, and forgery, is worryingly late for our needs (all of it dating decades to half a century after the fact, or later), and almost all of it is useless (because we can't establish its independence from earlier material that we have, or its reliability even if independent). These facts must be taken into account when estimating probabilities.

No argument can follow from the premise that any disciple or eyewitness wrote the Gospels or Epistles, for example. If by an 'eyewitness' record we mean a record actually written by an eyewitness, we simply have no eyewitness record of Jesus ever existing, much less of anything that Jesus said or did. That alone proves nothing, of course, because it's as true of countless other historical persons. But *they* do not have an initially low probability of existing, whereas Jesus does (see Chapter 6), being, unlike most everyone else, a worshiped savior and celestial demigod already in our earliest evidence. The evidence for Jesus, therefore, has to be substantially *better* than usual to overcome that low prior. In fact, we'll find it is generally *worse*, being more likely to exist in the state it does if Jesus *didn't* exist than if he did. But that has yet to be demonstrated. So to that we now turn.

50. 1 Corinthians 5.9, 11 (referring to the *original* 'first' letter to the Corinthians; *our* first Corinthians is actually the second, which in fact assumes the reader has already read the first one, now missing). Colossians 4.16 also refers to a letter 'from Laodicea' that the author of Colossians wants read in the churches; we don't have that letter (although one was later forged in its place). Fragments of these lost letters *might* survive 'inside' the letters we have, insofar as any of them are edited pastiches of choice parts of several letters combined into new, effectively fictional letters: see Reuter, 'Introduction to Synoptic Work'. But fragments do not entail a whole, and we cannot know what Paul wrote that was *not* preserved by this process (and we know some parts are missing: see, e.g., Chapter 11, §10). There were also letters written *to* Paul, which he is responding to (1 Cor. 7.1), yet those were not preserved either.

8

Extrabiblical Evidence

1. *Jesus When?*

Jesus was born around the time of either Herod the Great's death (4 BCE) or the Roman annexation of Judea (6 CE), then preached in Galilee and was crucified under Pontius Pilate (26–36 CE) during the reign of Emperor Tiberius (14–37 CE). Right? Well, we're not really sure. Because Christians weren't really sure. Some Christians believed Jesus died during the reign of Emperor Claudius (41–54 CE). Others believed he was executed by a Herod, not Pilate. And still others were certain he was born and died in the reign of King Alexander Jannaeus (103–76 BCE). That's right. Some Christians believed Jesus had lived and died a hundred years earlier than our Gospels claim.

In the late fourth century the Christian scholar Epiphanius compiled an extensive dossier on all the 'heresies' he knew of, calling it the *Panarion*, 'Medicine Chest'. One of these 'heresies' he covers is that of the 'Nazorians', who were still practicing Jews; as Epiphanius says, these 'Nazorians confess that Christ Jesus is the Son of God, but all their customs are in accordance with the Law'.[1] This would mean a sect that descended directly from the *original* Christian sect founded by Peter, John and James (the 'pillars' of Galatians 2), before Paul's innovation eliminated Torah observance (Element 20). These Nazorians were still Torah observant, and still called themselves by their original name (Acts 24.5; Jerome, *Letters* 112.13), the name they held before the sects we are more familiar with came to be called Christians (Acts 11.26).[2]

Epiphanius then says a curious thing: *these* Christians say Jesus had lived and died in the time of Alexander Jannaeus. This is what he says they preach:

1. See Epiphanius, *Panarion* 29.

2. In Epiphanius and Acts the word is identical: the *Nazōraioi* (Acts 24.5), which in English corresponds to 'Nazorian', by analogy with *Athēnaioi*, 'Athenian' (see discussion in Chapter 10, §3).

> The priesthood in the holy church is [actually] David's throne and kingly seat, for the Lord joined together and gave to his holy church both the kingly and the high-priestly dignity, transferring to it the never-failing throne of David. For David's throne endured in line of succession until the time of Christ himself, rulers from Judah not failing until he came 'to whom the things kept in reserve belonged, and he was the expectation of the nations'. With the advent of the Christ the rulers in line of succession from Judah, reigning until the time of the Christ himself, ceased. For the line fell away and stopped from the time when he was born in Bethlehem of Judea under Alexander, who was of priestly and royal race. From Alexander onward this office ceased—from the days of Alexander and Salina, who is also called Alexandra, to the days of Herod the king and Augustus the Roman emperor.[3]

The Babylonian Talmud not only confirms this, but its Jewish authors appear to have known no other form of Christianity. This means the Jews east of the Roman Empire (where this Talmud was compiled, assembled from the third to fifth centuries) were reacting to this Nazorian Christianity. As one passage declares, 'when King Jannaeus was killing our rabbis, R. Jesus ben Periah and Jesus [the Nazarene] escaped to Alexandria, Egypt; and when peace was restored', they returned (echoes here of Matthew's nativity account, in this case told of Jesus rather than his parents), and this Jesus, who is explicitly identified as 'Jesus the Nazarene', was condemned for immorality, sorcery and worshiping idols, and eventually executed because he 'practiced magic and led Israel astray'.[4]

3. Epiphanius, *Panarion* 29.3.

4. Babylonian Talmud, *Sanhedrin* 107b; *Soṭah* 47a; Jerusalem Talmud, *Ḥagigah* 2.2 (cf. Jerusalem Talmud, *Sanhedrin* 23c; the latter includes only part of this story and omits the name of Jesus, but such deletions of Jesus' name are typical in surviving manuscripts of the Talmud). See Robert Van Voorst, *Jesus Outside the New Testament: An Introduction to the Ancient Evidence* (Grand Rapids, MI: William B. Eerdmans, 2000), pp. 104-22 (111-12), although note that his data is inaccurate: more references exist in the Talmud than he collects, and many of the passages he cites actually have had references to Jesus expunged from them by Christian scribes. When we look at more reliable manuscripts, 'Jesus of Nazareth' is repeatedly and explicitly identified as 'Jesus ben Pantera' and 'Jesus ben Stada', leaving no such doubts as Van Voorst voices about their equivalence. See Craig Evans, 'Jesus in Non-Christian Sources', in *Studying the Historical Jesus: Evaluation of the State of Current Research* (ed. Bruce Chilton and Craig Evans; New York: Brill, 1994), pp. 443-78; Graham Twelftree, 'Jesus in Jewish Traditions', in *Gospel Perspectives: Studies of History and Tradition in the Four Gospels*, Vol. V. *The Jesus Tradition outside the Gospels* (ed. David Wenham; Sheffield: JSOT Press, 1984), pp. 289-341 (310-41); Peter Schäfer, *Jesus in the Talmud* (Princeton, NJ: Princeton University Press, 2007), cf. esp. pp. 131-44; and the Wikipedia entry for 'Jesus in the Talmud' (http://en.wikipedia.org/wiki/Jesus_in_the_Talmud), which is becoming a valuable point of reference.

Elsewhere we learn that this 'Jesus' who 'practiced magic and led Israel astray' was stoned and crucified 'on the day before the Passover' (in some manuscripts of the Talmud, it even says 'on a Sabbath eve', in both respects corresponding to the timeline in the Gospel of John, which actually agrees with Jewish law; the other Gospels depict an impossible event: an execution on a high holy day).[5] This Jesus was also known as 'Ben Stada', meaning 'Son of the Unfaithful', a woman named Mary, who committed adultery with her lover Pandera (most likely that means Panthera, 'Panther', a popular nickname for Roman soldiers, as this was the Jewish polemic as reported in the second century) and thus gave birth to Ben Stada, who was thus also known as 'Ben Pandera', which may be a pun on *ben Parthenos*, 'Son of the Virgin', a pun that was already part of Jewish anti-Christian polemic in the second century (based on the legend of a Roman soldier named Panther being the real father of Jesus), as confirmed by Celsus and Origen—and therefore Ben Stada is indeed our Jesus.[6] Although in the Talmudic account he is tried and executed in Lydda, not Jerusalem.

Van Voorst insists 'Ben Stada' is not our Jesus, but none of his arguments are valid.[7] The stoned were always crucified ('hanged') under Jewish law; thus there are not two different executions being described.[8] Nor does the account of Jesus' stoning (the one Van Voorst agrees is about Jesus) say he was *not* stoned in Lydda or not tried before the Beth Din (Jewish court). So there is no contradiction between these accounts, as Van Voorst claims. And the fact that these accounts contradict the canonical Gospels is precisely the point. Even the passages Van Voorst agrees *are* about Jesus contradict the Gospels we have, so he doesn't even obey his own logic. But

5. That it was illegal even for Romans to perform executions on Jewish holy days in Judea at that time: Carrier, 'Burial of Jesus', in *Empty Tomb* (ed. Price and Lowder), p. 373-75, 377-78, 382-85 (with Mishnah, *Sanhedrin* 4.1k-l and 5.5a). See also Carrier, *Proving History*, pp. 139-41, 154, and 317 n. 68. That some manuscripts of the Talmud include 'on the Sabbath eve' see Schäfer, *Jesus in the Talmud*, pp. 131-44, which also shows they also included the phrase 'Jesus the Nazarene' in many of the passages Van Voorst presents as lacking it, because it was later deleted by Christian scribes from the manuscripts Van Voorst derives his texts from.

6. Babylonian Talmud, *Shabbat* 104b (Tosefta, *Shabbat* 11.15); Babylonian Talmud, *Sanhedrin* 43a, 64a and 67 (Tosefta, *Sanhedrin* 7.16; 10.11); Babylonian Talmud, *Giṭṭin* 56b-57a. Other passages are collected in Van Voorst and Schäfer etc. (see previous note). On Origen and Celsus on the ben Panthera polemic see Origen, *Against Celsus* 1.32.

7. Van Voorst, *Jesus Outside the New Testament*, p. 116; he almost immediately contradicts himself and says (without explanation) that the passages about Ben Stada *are* about Jesus (p. 120). I can only assume he changed his mind and didn't edit the text to reflect which position he held at the time of publication. A confusing error indeed. In any event, his first opinion is wrong.

8. Carrier, 'Burial of Jesus', in *Empty Tomb* (ed. Price and Lowder), pp. 375-79.

the point is that here we have knowledge of a completely different gospel tradition placing Jesus the Nazarene, apostate, 'son of the virgin Mary', under Alexander Jannaeus, with a different crucifixion account, occurring in a different location.

That Ben Stada is Jesus the Nazarene is further entailed by the fact that he is explicitly called Ben Pandera, and described as the son of Mary who cheated on her husband with Pandera, facts that are explicitly part of known Jewish polemic about Jesus and make no sense in any other way. That he was also executed 'on the day before Passover' (indeed, 'on the Sabbath eve') and condemned for sorcery and leading Israelites astray (which latter crime was allegedly confirmed, at least in Jewish polemic, by spies, possibly those called 'false witnesses' in our Gospels) only confirms the conclusion that this is the same person. Van Voorst sees a contradiction between the one Talmudic account of there being witnesses for the prosecution and the other Talmudic account claiming no witnesses could be found for his defense, but it should be obvious that that entails no contradiction.

Not that it matters. What is said about Ben Stada could be ignored entirely. The apostate 'Jesus' under Jannaeus is still explicitly identified as 'Jesus the Nazarene' and as being stoned and crucified 'on the day before the Passover' (on 'a Sabbath eve' even) for 'practicing magic and leading Israel astray'. So we clearly see that the Jews who compiled the Babylonian Talmud only knew of a Jesus executed under Jannaeus, not any Jesus executed under Pilate.[9] And Epiphanius confirms that some Torah-observant Christians, from the original sect of Christianity, actually did preach that. So there was some sort of Gospel circulating in the East, from a more conservative and faithful descendant of the original Christian sect, that narrated a Jesus born of the virgin Mary (as the Jewish polemic in the Talmud entails these Christians were claiming) in Bethlehem (according to

9. This also became the tradition used in the Middle Ages to construct the polemical anti-Christian tract, the sefer *Toledot Yeshu* (cf. 2.1, 31-32). Note that Schäfer, *Jesus in the Talmud* (e.g. pp. 122-29) thinks the Talmudic accounts derive from the canonical Gospels (the Gospel of John especially), but he has no good evidence for this—he just tries to force the evidence there is to fit that hypothesis. The most pertinent example is his speculation that the Jannaeus-period tale was not originally about Jesus (pp. 36-39), but he has no actual evidence of that, and it is illogical: there is no way medieval Jews would produce the contradiction of placing Jesus under the Jewish king Jannaeus if they knew he had been crucified by Pilate during the Roman occupation a hundred years later; and there is simply no evidence they had any knowledge of Pilate or Roman involvement at all. Schäfer's thesis is therefore untenable. Moreover, Epiphanius confirms the Jews did not invent the association of Jesus with the period of Jannaeus: Christians in the very region were already preaching that.

the Christians themselves who adopted this version of events) and executed under Jannaeus for working miracles and 'leading people astray'.[10]

How can the descendants of the original sect of Christians have come to believe Jesus lived and died a hundred years before our Gospels say he did? It is nearly impossible to imagine how such a doctrine could have developed. Unless there was no historical Jesus. Then he could be placed in history wherever each sect desired. In other words, if originally Jesus was not placed in history, then when he *was* placed in history—after the sects had split, ideologically and geographically—each sect could place him differently, developing their own myths in accord with their own needs and creativity. That would then influence neighboring sects and daughter sects connected with them, but if this was done twice, in separate regions, once inside the Roman Empire and once outside, those could have become the seeds of two different traditions spreading and developing independently of each other.

Even in the West there was not an established date or narrative for Jesus. Already, of course, no one could agree on when Jesus was born, Matthew placing his birth under Herod the Great; Luke, under Quirinius, more than ten years later.[11] And they also couldn't agree in what year he was killed, John placing the event the day before the Passover of either 30 or 33 CE;

10. In making these observations I am not endorsing any particular theory that has been built on them by other scholars (who have also noted these same facts, but then developed elaborate theories from them). I shall rely solely on the singular facts here stated and established from primary sources, nothing more. But if anyone wants to pursue the many strange theories developed out of these facts, such speculations began as early as the work of theosophist G.R.S. Mead in his *Did Jesus Live 100 B.C.? An Enquiry into the Talmud Jesus Stories, the Toldoth Jeschu, and Some Curious Statements of Epiphanius* (London: Theosophical Publishing Society, 1903); after that, Hugh Schonfield, *According to the Hebrews: A New Translation of the Jewish Life of Jesus (the Toldoth Jeshu), with an Inquiry into the Nature of its Sources and Special Relationship to the Lost Gospel according to the Hebrews* (London: Duckworth, 1937); more recently, Alvar Ellegård, *Jesus: One Hundred Years before Christ* (Woodstock, NY: Overlook, 1999); and Michael Wise, *The First Messiah: Investigating the Savior before Christ* (New York: HarperSanFrancisco, 1999); as well as Frank Zindler, *The Jesus the Jews Never Knew: Sepher Toldoth Yeshu and the Quest of the Historical Jesus in Jewish Sources* (Cranford, NJ: American Atheist Press, 2003); and John Marco Allegro, *The Dead Sea Scrolls and the Christian Myth* (Buffalo, NY: Prometheus Books, 1984), which he summarizes in 'Jesus and Qumran: The Dead Sea Scrolls', in *Jesus in Myth and History* (ed. R. Joseph Hoffmann and Gerald Larue; Buffalo, NY: Prometheus, 1986), pp. 89-96.

11. See my summary of these facts (and attempts to deny them by Christian apologists) in Richard Carrier, 'Luke vs. Matthew on the Year of Christ's Birth', *Hitler Homer Bible Christ: The Historical Papers of Richard Carrier 1995–2013* (Richmond, CA: Philosophy Press, 2014), pp. 213-30.

the Synoptics, during the Passover of 27 or 34 CE.[12] But those kinds of confusions or distortions would not be too surprising even for a historical man, about whom such confusions or distortions could arise. A bit more surprising is the fact that they couldn't agree on who executed Jesus: the Romans, at the command of Pontius Pilate (as the canonical Gospels claim), or the Jews, at the command of King Herod Antipas (as the *Gospel of Peter* claims, e.g., 1.2; 6.3; and all of 1.1–7.1; and as some hints even in canonical sources could be taken to suggest, e.g., Acts 5.30 in combination with Gal. 3.13 and the interpolation in 1 Thess. 2.15-16). Curiously, Luke alone inserts this Herod into the story (by adapting a story originally told about Pilate in Mark: Mk 15.15-20 becoming Lk. 23.11). A Herod is not in any way involved in Jesus' trial or death in any other Gospel account (see Mark 14–15; Matthew 26–27; and John 18–19). But in the *Gospel of Peter* not only is he as involved as Luke imagines, but *he* is the one who executes Jesus, *not* Pilate. And yet this Gospel was popular in the East, before our familiar canon came to replace it.[13]

Also surprising is the fact noted earlier, that many early Christians thought Jesus died in the reign of Emperor Claudius rather than Emperor Tiberius (between whom reigned Caligula from 37 to 41; Claudius reigned 41 to 54). They mistakenly thought Pontius Pilate was governing Judea at the same time (even though he had been deposed by Tiberius in 36), but they were sure it was in the 40s that Jesus was killed, not the 30s, and their reasons are telling. Irenaeus says that it was in accordance with prophecy that 'King' Herod and 'Caesar's' man Pilate would do this:

> For Herod the king of the Jews and Pontius Pilate, the governor of Claudius Caesar, came together and condemned him to be crucified. For Herod feared, as though [Jesus really] were to be an earthly king, lest he should be expelled by him from the kingdom. But Pilate was constrained by Herod and the Jews that were with him against his will to deliver him to death, [for they threatened him, asking] if he should not rather do this, than act contrary to Caesar by letting go a man who was called a king.[14]

12. Jack Finegan, *Handbook of Biblical Chronology: Principles of Time Reckoning in the Ancient World and Problems of Chronology in the Bible* (Peabody, MA: Hendrickson Publishers, rev. edn, 1998; orig. edn, Princeton, NJ: Princeton University Press, 1964), pp. 359-65 (§ 615-24).

13. Serapion (Bishop of Antioch) discovered the *Gospel of Peter* was a principal text used in some Eastern churches, but when he finally read it, he deemed it heretical and had the text banned, sometime near the end of the second century, according to Eusebius, *History of the Church* 6.12.

14. Irenaeus, *Demonstration of the Apostolic Preaching* 74 (citing Ps. 2.1-2; which is cited to similar effect in Acts 4.25-27).

Notably this does not correspond to any known Gospel. In the canonicals, Herod does not threaten Pilate with this argument (although 'the Jews' in general do, but only in Jn 19.12); and Herod never expresses any such fear (although Herod *the Great* did, forty years earlier: Mt. 2.1-19), and never condemns Jesus to be crucified at all, much less 'together' with Pilate, as if in the same court (though something similar occurs in the *Gospel of Peter*). Thus, even such an orthodoxist as Irenaeus could not agree on the narrative.

More importantly, Irenaeus was doing 'scriptural math' here, not history. His reasoning was that Jesus had to have been nearly fifty when he died (because Jn 8.57 said so), and yet was around thirty in the year 29 CE (because Lk. 3.1-2 and 3.23 said so), so he 'had' to have died in the 40s CE, and therefore in the reign of Claudius.[15] But this is precisely the kind of methodology that generates myths and legends. If similar calculations determined that scripture declared the Christ had to have died in the time of Pilate (as we know they easily could: Element 7), then that is where myth would place him. Matching that math differently to the facts would produce a different period to place him in (as we saw the original authors of Daniel intended, and there were yet other ways the same calculations could be run).

But the problem of 'where to put him' in history, which was just as easily answered for every other euhemerized demigod in antiquity (Element 45), could also be solved by the obvious logic of placing him at the imagined founding of the city or institution that worships him. That is why the mythical Romulus was placed in history 'at the founding of Rome'. Jesus, then, would most naturally fit into history 'at the founding of the Church'. From the letters of Paul we know that that was most likely the late 30s CE.[16] Paul's new sect was certainly launched then; but so was the original Torah-observant sect not long before, if that is indeed when the first 'revelations' of Jesus occurred (which is what 1 Cor. 15.3-8 claims; Peter, i.e., Cephas, being the first revelator, contemporary with Paul: 1 Cor. 1.12; 3.22; 9.5; Gal. 1.18; 2.9-14), and indeed those revelations might themselves have been inspired by calculations from Daniel, producing an exuberant expectation that something new would be revealed about this mysterious dying Christ 'any time now'. In that scenario, the revelations came first; the euhemerizing myth later.

Why another offshoot of the original Christian sect decided to place him instead a hundred years earlier we cannot so easily deduce, because we don't have their Gospels and Epistles, and thus we can't reconstruct their logic the way we can for the sect whose texts we do have. All we know is

15. Irenaeus, *Against All Heresies* 2.22.5-6.

16. See note in Chapter 7 (§3).

that they did, indeed, place him a hundred years earlier. Epiphanius may be providing us a clue, however, since in his account their 'scriptural math' appears to have been based on the assumption that somehow scripture ordained that the messiah would come when the last king died who could claim descent from David (see Chapter 11, §9, for a likely scriptural basis). They had concluded that that was Alexander Jannaeus, therefore Jesus 'had' to have appeared then (either actually, or allegorically for the purposes of their exoteric myth). They might also have been deriving the date from Daniel (Element 7), employing a different scheme than Christians in the West did. Either would reflect a similar mindset to Irenaeus. And a similar disinterest in actual facts.

Of course, if Jesus actually lived in the 30s, then that would also explain why our Gospels place him there. But it would not explain why another branch of Christianity, which stayed closer to its original teachings, placed him a hundred years before that. The hypothesis that Jesus didn't exist, however, can explain both facts, and with more ease. As a general rule, it must surely be more common for a mythical man to be placed in different historical periods than for this to happen to a historical man, for whom there would only be one core tradition originating from his own time, well known to his worshipers and tradents. I have no data on the relative frequency of this phenomenon (How many people do we know to have been set in different historical periods? How many of them never existed to begin with? What would those numbers then be in a hypothetical infinite repetition of history?).[17] But it must surely beg all credulity to believe that this happens to historical persons exactly as often as non-historical ones—even for the simple reason that it is so much easier to do this to non-historical persons. As I noted before, if there is no actual set of historical events anchoring that person to reality, then they can easily be inserted into history wherever any given mythographer wants. This must surely be harder to do for a man already solidly linked to his actual historical context, and widely known to be so among all who worship him.

In mathematical terms, this would mean the ratio must be greater than 2 to 1—in other words, being placed in different historical periods must happen to mythical persons twice as often as it happens to historical persons. In fact, more than twice, surely. But I am committed to erring as far against the mythicist hypothesis as is reasonably possible, so I will assume this ratio to be 2 to 1.[18] That means the consequent probability of this fact (of

17. On building hypothetical reference classes like this see Carrier, *Proving History*, pp. 257-65 (example on pp. 272-75).

18. For example, if this happens to one in a million historical persons, I'm saying we'll find it happens to at least two in a million mythical persons, for consequent probabilities of 0.000001 and 0.000002, respectively (which gives an odds ratio of 2/1

Jesus being placed in both the 30s CE and the 70s BCE) on the hypothesis of myth is twice the consequent probability of this same fact on the hypothesis of historicity, and so we can treat the consequent probability on historicity as 0.5 and the consequent probability on myth as 1. In fact, to argue even more *a fortiori*, I'll allow (even against all reason) that there could be as much as an 80% probability that this would happen to a historical Jesus (which makes the odds 4 to 5), even though I think that's absurd. Either way, this fact is evidence against the historicity of Jesus. Not *conclusive* evidence. But it counts against, by at least as much as just stated.

2. *The Socrates Analogy*

To understand the rest of this chapter, it will help to grasp the analogy of Socrates. He is comparable to Jesus in being a famous sage whose influence was profound and everlasting (he is the father of what we now mean by Philosophy, in essentially the same way Jesus is of Christianity) without having written anything himself, his influence being entirely through his 'disciples', who each developed communities that then fragmented and modified his teachings into many competing sects.

And yet Socrates' existence is not in any doubt, nor plausibly doubtable. Why? Because very much *unlike* Jesus, we know the names of over a dozen eyewitnesses who wrote books about Socrates; in some cases we even know the titles of these books, and a number of paraphrases and quotations from them survive in other sources. And in two of those cases, the books even survive: we have the many works of Plato and Xenophon, each

in favor of myth). We can reduce those consequents to 1 and 0.5 by canceling out the coefficient of contingency (Carrier, *Proving History*, pp. 215-19, and 'coefficient of contingency', p. 334): if $n = 0.000002$, then P(e|historical) = $0.5n$ and P(e|¬historical) = $1n$; n then cancels out in any full BT equation, leaving P(e|historical) = 0.5 and P(e|¬historical) = 1. This does not mean the probability that e on h is literally 50% (as if every other historical person were placed in different periods of history), or that the probability that e on $\neg h$ is literally 100% (as if *every* mythical person were placed in different periods of history), rather this is simply their relative probabilities, after a mathematical reduction. No matter what the consequent probabilities actually are (i.e. no matter how many historical or mythical persons this actually happens to), they will always reduce to 0.5 and 1, *if* it happens twice as often to mythical persons as historical. Therefore, if that ratio is a warranted belief, then we don't need to know the actual frequencies. Because whatever they are, they will always reduce to that same ratio. Another way to think of it is that being placed in different periods of history is the sort of thing we expect of a mythical person more than of a historical one (see Carrier, *Proving History*, pp. 77-81, 214-28), such that if we cancel out the common contingency between them, it is then 100% expected on $\neg h$ but only 50% expected on h (or, as will soon be suggested, 100% and 80%, respectively, if arguing *a fortiori*).

of whom was an eyewitness and disciple to Socrates, who each recorded his teachings and reported stories and other information about him. We have nothing at all like this for Jesus. Even more unlike Jesus, we also have an eyewitness account of Socrates from a relatively *unfriendly* source as well: *The Clouds* of Aristophanes is a comic play specifically written to poke fun at Socrates and his teachings and disciples, written by an eyewitness contemporary to both; Socrates even sat in the audience of its first production![19] What we knew of Jesus would be vastly more credible and quantifiable if we had anything even remotely like this for him. Yet we have none of the above: we have no eyewitness records *at all*, much less from neutral or hostile parties; we don't even know of any written eyewitness accounts ever having existed (much less dozens upon dozens of them), and we certainly don't have anything like identifiable quotations from them or their titles and authors.

So why do we have so much better a historical record of what Socrates said and did, than we have for Jesus? It is not as if the first century was 'underrepresented' by writers interested in Judean affairs (see the next section). The unusually high rate of survival of texts from classical Athens is a product of medieval selection, not of any discernible difference in volume of literature produced. And yet if *Socrates* had immediately become worshiped as the resurrected Son of God, and his every pronouncement the founding principles of a great Church, which went on centuries later to survive as the only institution with means and interest in preserving

19. See Luis Navia, *Socrates: A Life Examined* (Amherst, NY: Prometheus, 2007), pp. 29-31. We have other contemporaries attesting his historical existence in Athens (e.g. Aristotle: Navia, *Socrates,* pp. 139-58) who knew and cite his personal acquaintances; and we know the names of at least sixteen pupils of Socrates who wrote books about him. Principal examples: Aeschines Socraticus, Ameipsias, Antisthenes, Aristippus of Cyrene, Cebes of Thebes [not the author, however, of the extant Socratic dialog forged in his name], Chaerephon, Crito, Euclides, Teleclides, Simmias, Simon the Cobbler [whose shoe shop we've even excavated], Polycrates and Phaedon—see entries for each in the *Oxford Classical Dictionary* (ed. Simon Hornblower and Antony Spawforth; Oxford: Oxford University Press, 1995). Historians also quickly took notice of Socrates and wrote about him (e.g. 'Idomeneus (2)', *Oxford Classical Dictionary*, p. 746, wrote *On the Followers of Socrates* about a century after Socrates' death). Even now the surviving attestations and quotations of Socrates and his witnesses fill four volumes: Gabriele Giannantoni, *Socratis et socraticorum reliquiae* (4 vols.; Naples: Bibliopolis, 1990). See also Luis Navia and Ellen Katz, *Socrates: An Annotated Bibliography* (New York: Garland, 1988); Thomas Brickhouse and Nicholas Smith, *The Trial and Execution of Socrates: Sources and Controversies* (Oxford: Oxford University Press, 2002); Debra Nails, *The People of Plato: A Prosopography of Plato and Other Socratics* (Indianapolis, IN: Hackett, 2002); and Sara Ahbel-Rappe and Rachana Kamtekar (eds.), *A Companion to Socrates* (Oxford: Blackwell, 2006). Jesus scholars could only dream of having this much information about Jesus.

materials into the future, we would surely have nearly *everything* written about him—which would consist of many hundreds of volumes of material: dialogues, discourses, biographies and memoirs from eyewitnesses, as well as numerous organizational documents such as wills and deeds and letters among his disciples (which even the illiterate could produce, through recourse to hired scribes, who were ubiquitously available specifically to serve such a market; in fact, even in the case of Jesus we can hardly assume no such scribes became disciples or followers soon enough after the mission began to put themselves precisely to such use).

A viable theory of historicity for Jesus must therefore instead resemble a theory of historicity for Apollonius of Tyana or Musonius Rufus or Judas the Galilean (to list a few very famous men who escaped the expected record in more or less the same degree Jesus did). And yet unlike for them, that theory cannot involve the claim that records of Jesus existed but weren't preserved out of disinterest, since such records were exactly the sorts of things the many first-century churches *would* preserve, and most such records would certainly still have existed to be preserved by the time of the assembly of Origen's library (at the very least), and many would still be around, through continual copying, even in the fourth century or beyond, when the Church had increasingly vast resources at its command—situations that never obtained for Apollonius or Musonius or Judas (or even Socrates). So where are all these texts and documents for Jesus?

There are really only two options available to the historicist that have any plausibility: (1) that Jesus was not at all famous but in fact so insignificant and uninfluential that he inspired almost no following whatever and was completely unnoticed by any literate person of the age (until—and except—Paul, though even he didn't know Jesus, and showed next to no interest in his actual teachings and story: see Chapter 11); or (2) massive quantities of documents were deliberately destroyed or allowed to rot away unnoticed and unread (somehow no Christian of the second century having any access to them or showing any interest in them). Neither is a particularly attractive hypothesis. A conspiracy to suppress vast quantities of information is perhaps least attractive of all; yet the alternative must be that Jesus was an uninfluential, unimpressive, unknown rabbi whom no one of any note noticed, and who made no significant impression on any literate person who ever saw or met him, and attracted no literate person into his circle of disciples or admirers—a person of such *actual* insignificance as not to resemble in the least the Jesus portrayed in the Gospels. An unsavory conclusion indeed. Yet, what else can we suppose?

On the other hand, this vastly peculiar absence of documents is readily explicable if there was no historical Jesus about whom any such documents would be written, but instead only a small mystery cult targeting primarily illiterate converts and aiming to keep the bulk of its teachings secret (and thus 'off the books' as it were), from whom later churches diverged so greatly in aims and ideology that they had no desire to preserve more than a minuscule selection of the original documents (a mere handful of letters) from the movement's earliest missions, then forged a great many more to suit their needs instead (Elements 11 to 14, and 44).

Or we could resort in either case to noting again the great disruption in the church's transmission of authority and information in the middle of the first century (Element 22), and posit a third option for the historicist: (3) that *this* great disruption resulted in the loss of nearly all the documents there may have been. But that requires granting that so awesome a destruction and loss of records really did occur, and was really that incredibly pervasive, even spanning three continents and dozens of cities. Which I suspect scholars will find even more unsavory than options (1) and (2). All of these options—whether (1), (2), or (3), or the denial of historicity—have consequences that must be accepted and not ignored. You have to pick one; because if you don't like the consequences of it, you can only avoid them by picking another. And that is going to pin you down, hemmed in on all sides by undesirable consequences.

The most desperate and implausible move is (4) to explain the absence of such writing among the disciples and apostles of Jesus as an apocalyptic disinterest in creating a written record (on which I'll have more to say in Chapter 11). Because if we grant such a disinterest, then we cannot explain the letters of Paul (which not only in their very existence refute such disinterest, but whose contents betray on every page the continuing need for writing things down and transmitting and preserving them in physical rather than oral form), which likewise leaves us unable to plausibly explain why only Paul wrote letters. No other missionary for the whole first three decades of the cult's spread ever wrote any letter to anywhere or anyone? What about the letters we know that churches wrote to Paul? (1 Cor. 7.1)

We would then also have to dispense with the idea that there was any effort to preserve the story of Jesus *orally*, either. For any interest in the latter would entail an interest in the former. If preserving his sayings and narratives accurately was at all valued by anyone, they would have been recorded in writing early and often, so that missionaries would have aids to memory (and church leaders a means to control doctrine, a key need evinced throughout the letters of Paul: Element 21) as well as a means of leaving communities and congregations with accurate information to rely upon and meditate on after their departure (since, as Paul's letters attest, the apostles were not always present among every active congregation, yet disputes and questions constantly arose). These needs would be just as pressing in the face of a looming apocalypse—as again, Paul's letters attest (as well as simple common sense). In other words, historicists cannot claim the Christians strove to accurately preserve information, while simultaneously claiming that they saw no need to accurately preserve information. It can only be one or the other.

Thus, there are only a few possibilities with any respectable chance of being true. Either all the evidence of the first decades of Christianity was actively (and very successfully) suppressed, or it was uncontrollably (and very thoroughly) lost despite every desire to preserve it, or Christianity was so small, insignificant and pervasively illiterate that such evidence never existed (and Paul was a lone educated freak in a sea of illiterate country hicks spinning yarns far and wide). You may choose the one you prefer. But you must then accept the actual consequences of that being true. First among them is the fact that we simply cannot claim to know the story and teachings of Jesus even the minutest fraction as reliably or well as we do those of Socrates—and yet even for Socrates every expert concurs that we do not know his story and teachings with superlative reliability. Plato's dialogues, for example, are universally regarded as predominately a fiction promoting the views of *Plato* rather than Socrates; indeed Plato himself entitles those dialogues a *Peirastikos*, 'Fiction'. If such is the state of our knowledge of Socrates, our knowledge of Jesus must be regarded a thousand times less.

3. *Missing Evidence*

The obvious, and usually cited, writers on first-century Judean affairs are Nicolaus of Damascus (d. c. 10 CE), official court historian of Herod the Great (although of course all he could have attested to are any famous events relating to the birth of Jesus, which pretty much everyone already agrees aren't historical) and Justus of Tiberias, King Agrippa's personal secretary (the same Agrippa of Acts 25–26, before whom we're told Paul goes on trial and procures an appeal to Nero in Rome), and commander of armies in the Jewish War of 66–70, who then wrote a history of that war, including the century of Judean affairs leading up to it. He was a primary source for Josephus's own account of that war (and thus is the most likely source for his accounts of messiahs in this period: Element 4), yet we know from a later Christian reader that he never mentioned Jesus or Christianity.[20] We do not have the works of Nicolaus or Justus, but we have the works of Josephus, who used them as sources, and we can safely conclude that if either author had mentioned anything about Christ, Christians or Christianity, later Christian authors would have preserved at least mention of it, if at the very least to rebut it or make note of their attestation to Jesus or early Christians or Christianity. And these would not have been the only writers

20. Photius, *Library* 33. On Justus see Josephus, *Life* 9, 12, 17, 35, 37, 54, 65, 70, 74, etc.

covering Judean affairs at the time. They are just the ones we happen to have mention of, because Josephus employed them.

There were numerous other writers we know about from that same century who could plausibly have mentioned Christianity and its claims—and such texts or mentions, we would normally expect, would surely have been preserved by later Christians, even if only to rebut or correct them.[21] Philo is the most obvious example, a prolific Jewish author who wrote in Alexandria, Egypt, at the very time Christianity was taking root there. My bookshelf copy of his complete works in English extends to nine hundred pages of multi-columned small type, which isn't even complete (many of his works were not preserved), and though what we have is mostly theology and exegesis, he commented a lot on Jewish sects and Jerusalem and Judean interests. Philo made pilgrimages to Jerusalem and knew about Palestinian affairs and wrote about the Herods and Pontius Pilate.[22] And Christians must have begun evangelizing the Jewish community in Alexandria almost immediately: it was the single largest population center, with a large and diverse Jewish community, almost directly adjacent to Judea, along a well-established trade route well traveled by Jewish pilgrims. So it's not as if Philo would not have heard of their claims even if he had never left Egypt; and yet we know he did, having traveled to Judea and Rome. Moreover, Philo just happens to be the one Jew of the period whose work Christians bothered to preserve. He would not have been alone.

There was also all manner of *other* first-century Jewish literature and apocrypha—most not preserved, or not discussing the first century, but there surely had to have been Jewish writing about Christians or early Judea, even if we no longer know of it. It cannot be claimed Jews were uninterested in writing about their own places and times. And it's outright contradictory to suppose Jews showed such sustained, even international interest in suppressing Christianity from its very beginning (if we trust Acts at all on this point), and were its first principal targets for evangelization in Judea and all across the diaspora (as again Acts claims, depicting Christians preaching in its synagogues everywhere), yet never saw occasion to ever once write anything about it (contrary to what we're told in Acts 9.1-2, where Paul is said to have had, and to have sent, letters from the Jewish elite explaining why Christians were outlaws). And yet, we have not one surviving citation. We must conclude Christians actively avoided preserving any of it, not even rebuttals of it, not even so much as a mention of it.

21. The following survey relies on the corresponding entries for each author in the *Oxford Classical Dictionary* (ed. Hornblower and Spawforth; 3rd edn).

22. See, e.g., Philo, *Embassy to Gaius* and *Against Flaccus*, and *On Providence* 2.64 (Eusebius, *Preparation for the Gospel* 8.14.64).

We know of countless pagan writers who might have written something on all this, too. Marcus Velleius Paterculus sketched a history of the Romans from their mythic past up to the year 29 (of which parts survive) and King Juba of Mauretania did the same up to around the year 20 (none of which survives), although these weren't as likely to mention anything pertinent as Marcus Servilius Nonianus (2 BCE to 59 CE), who we know wrote a dedicated history of the first century up to at least the year 41. We also know Pamphila of Epidaurus wrote thirty-three volumes of *Historical Notes* up to her own time (c. 60 CE). We know Aufidius Bassus (d. c. 60 CE), then a much-admired writer, wrote a history up to at least the year 31; and Pliny the Elder (d. 79 CE) had written a monumental thirty-one-volume history continuing where Bassus left off, hence from around the year 31 to at least beyond Nero's reign (so, roughly an entire volume for each year), which could hardly have omitted mention of Christians (such as their supposedly rather public persecution under Nero in 64; see Element 22) unless they were truly insignificant (and thus not even prominently known as the victims of Nero in 64); which in turn means he would surely have made note of Christian beliefs, or any 'famous' or 'amazing' claims surrounding Jesus (if there really were any). And yet we can be fairly certain Pliny did not mention Christians at all (see §10).

We also know that Cluvius Rufus, ex-consul and Nero's personal herald in the mid-first century, having served in the Senate since the 30s, wrote a detailed history of events during the reign of Nero, beginning with the reign of Caligula in the year 37, and continuing past Nero up to the reign of Otho in the year 69. This surely would have discussed Nero's persecution of Christians in 64, which would have required a digression on Jesus and Christianity, which in turn would likely touch on the relevant details of the appellate case of Paul before Nero in 62 (if that even happened) and what was claimed in that case, and how it degenerated into the execution of scores if not hundreds of Christians just a couple years later for the crime of burning the city of Rome, surely the single most famous event of that or any adjacent year (see my following discussion of the *Testimonium Taciteum*, §9).

There were also the memoirs of Julia Agrippina (Nero's mother, Caligula's sister, and Claudius's wife), which Tacitus employed as a source. She was assassinated by Nero in 59, too early to report on events of 64, but her work must have covered events up to at least 54 (Nero's accession). She was born in 15, and her close position to Caligula and Claudius makes it reasonable to expect she might have mentioned Christianity if it were at all significant (e.g. if the Chrestus event under Claudius really did have anything to do with Christ: see §11). We know Petronius wrote in 66 CE (just before his own death) a treatise against Nero's entire reign, which could not have failed to ignore the fire and persecution of 64 and any necessary digressions on the Christian story that that would have required. We know Fabius Rusticus wrote a history during Nero's reign that covered events up to his own time, which may have gotten as far as his death or at least the persecution, and at any rate covered events under Augustus and Tiberius (and Claudius) and thus would very likely have noticed Christianity if it was notable at all.

If *any* of these authors I've surveyed up to this point had mentioned *any* of these things, it's hard to believe that no Christian would ever know of it, neither quoting nor citing it, not even to rebut anything it may have said that was unfavorable to them; and equally hard to believe that no pagan critic of Christianity ever noticed it either, nor made any use of it, not even to answer it or attack it if it was at all favorable to Christians, or to use it against them if it wasn't. To the contrary, we should expect Christians or their critics to have made notice of anything these authors said about Christ or Christianity, whether to use it or to rebut it. So did none of these authors even notice Christianity at all? Or was everyone in antiquity, Christians and their critics alike, wholly disinterested in what they said about it? It has to be one or the other. Take your pick.

We know emperors Vespasian and Titus published commentaries on their government service, including their prosecution of the Jewish War (these being among the sources, again, that Josephus used). So if Christians ever significantly came up in their invasion and conquest of Judea, or in their government of Rome, they would have mentioned it, too. We know Seneca the Elder wrote a *History of Rome* that covered events from the first century BCE to around 40 CE. Then Seneca the Younger wrote a treatise *On Superstition* sometime between 40 and 62 CE that lambasted every known cult at Rome, even the most trivial or obscure—including the Jews—but never mentioned Christians, an omission Augustine later struggled to explain.[23] And that despite the fact that this Seneca was the brother of the same Gallio whom Christians are brought on trial before in Greece according to Acts 18.12-17 (he was the governor of that province in the early 50s). (Likewise, the Jewish historian Josephus was the personal friend of the same Agrippa before whom Christians went on trial according to Acts 25–26.)

Works in later centuries are relevant as well, for they could have cited or quoted sources from the first century (but as we know, none did—or at least none that we have do). We know that just after the dawn of the second century, for example, Pliny the Younger's friend Pompeius Saturninus

23. Augustine, *City of God* 6.10-11 (Seneca 'also found fault' with the Jews but 'the Christians, however . . . he did not dare to mention, either for praise or blame, lest, if he praised them, he should do so against the ancient custom of his country, or, perhaps, if he should blame them, he should do so against his own will', each a rather lame excuse for his silence).

wrote histories that Pliny highly regarded, which likely covered the first century. And in the middle of the second century was Aulus Claudius Charax, author of a universal history, still known and read into Byzantine times (but no longer extant). Since he had an infamous penchant for digressions on the fabulous, we should expect him to have mentioned Jesus or Christianity (and thus, perhaps, quoting or referencing earlier sources on them), but if he did, no Christian ever noticed, not even in the whole of the Byzantine era when his works were widely read by Christians for centuries. And we know in the third century Marius Maximus wrote biographies of all the emperors in the second century, in which he notoriously included extensive quotations of official documents; so in a century that saw several imperial engagements with Christianity, it is astonishing he never had occasion to mention or digress on the origins or treatment of Christianity.

Also in the third century we know Publius Herrennius Dexippus wrote a history of the world from mythical times to his own day, and Gaius Asinius Quadratus wrote a history of Rome from its founding in the eighth century BCE also up to the third century CE (he also wrote a *History of Parthia*, which could have covered notable events in Edessa or Damascus). The only thing comparable that survives is the sweeping *History of Rome* by Dio Cassius, who likewise covered the history of the whole Roman Empire from the city's founding to his own time (the early third century CE). His material for the years Jesus lived includes discussion of Judean affairs, but no Jesus or Christians or Christianity. Granted, those sections are sometimes either abridged or fragmentary, but a complete abridgment was made by Christians (who thus would have preserved, even if to alter or correct, any notable information about Jesus or Christianity),[24] and his history meticulously proceeds year by year. So its silence is certainly significant (even more so considering what Christians may have deleted from it: see below).

Of perhaps lesser significance but still illustrative of the kind of literature being produced in the first century (of which we now have only a small fraction) is Valerius Maximus, whose *Memorable Deeds and Sayings* (which we have), written around the year 32, compiles records of memorable deeds and sayings, usually of Romans, sometimes of foreigners, to show how Romans were more impressive. Anything amazing about Jesus being popularized at the time could have been entered as a memorable deed or saying, even if he tried to one-up it with a Roman story. It's unlikely he would have known of any, but how many other authors in the first and

24. For example, in his epitome, Xiphilinus pauses to complain about the fact that Dio doesn't mention Christians being responsible for the 'rain miracle' of Marcus Aurelius and rectifies this oversight by inserting the Christian version of the legend as known to Xiphilinus, then resuming his abridgment: see Dio Cassius, *Roman History* 71.9 (see note on dating Clement of Rome in Chapter 7, §6).

second century were compiling similar collections of amazing stories? We know Phlegon did, in the mid-second century, and he even mentions Jesus (or so we're told) although his information was apparently vague and confused.[25] But there were a lot of collections of amazing stories then, including a whole genre of literature called *paradoxography*. The several we know about date all the way from the third century BCE (e.g. Callimachus, Philostephanus, Antigonus of Caristus, Archelaus of Egypt, Myrsilus of Methyma) to the second and third centuries CE (e.g. Phlegon, Isigonus, Aelian), including many early forged collections (e.g. from Aristotle, Theopompus, Ephorus), all of which would have been only a small fraction of those written, including many satires of the same genre (e.g. by Lucian).[26] Tales of Jesus evidently didn't find their way into any first-century productions of this genre. Nor did they appear in any of the *florilegia* of the first two centuries, collections of random commentaries and stories about life, religion and philosophy in the empire, extant examples of which include (from the late first and early second century) the *Moralia* of Plutarch, and (from the second century) the *Attic Nights* of Aulus Gellius and the *Florida* of Apuleius, and (from the early third century) the *Dinnersages* of Athenaeus. Again, these would have been but a fraction of the genre.

Nor does any mention survive from any first-century collection of letters. For example, we have all of Seneca's *Moral Epistles*, written in the early 60s, and his collection wouldn't have been the only one made. This represents what was in fact a commonplace literary publishing activity; it just happens to be the only one from the first century that medieval Christians chose to preserve (just as Cicero's many volumes of letters is the only collection preserved from the previous century, yet was certainly not the only one published from that period either). Nor is there any mention in any of what would have been countless volumes of published speeches from the era. For example, we have the collected speeches of Maximus of Tyre (the same Tyre Jesus supposedly visited: Mk 3.8; 7.24-31) from the mid-second century, but he was certainly not the only literate orator in Tyre even then, much less for all preceding centuries; it's just that his happens to be the only collection from Tyre that medieval Christians chose to preserve. There would have been many published orators there in the first century. Likewise in *every* major metropolis—for Tyre was not the only city with a

25. Origen, *Against Celsus* 2.14 (Phlegon did *not* connect Jesus with an eclipse and earthquake, however: Origen, *Against Celsus* 2.33 and 2.59; see my discussion of Thallus in §11; nor did he relate a resurrection appearance: Origen, *Against Celsus* 2.59, continues with a quotation from Celsus, not Phlegon, citing Phlegon only for the eclipse and earthquake).

26. See 'paradoxographers' in the *Oxford Classical Dictionary* (ed. Hornblower and Spawforth), p. 1112 (as well as entries for each author named).

literary elite publishing books on diverse topics every year. The quantity of literature produced in antiquity was *vast*, far beyond the minuscule fraction that we now have. And speeches on popular topics were among the genres frequently published, as well as histories and paradoxographies and epistolaries and florilegia (not to forget also poetry, encyclopedias, medical and technical literature, and so on).

Satire was also a huge and popular genre at the time. Lucian, for example, mocked or satirized several religions (including Christianity), and though he wrote in the late second century, there would have been many satirists like him in the preceding century, even earlier than Juvenal, who in the early second century satirized numerous religious and philosophical targets, but never found cause to mention Christians (unless he did so in a section now deleted: see below). In the first century we have the fragmentary remains of the *Satyricon* of Petronius, which mocks several religions in its narrative, even poking fun at crucifixion, but never finds occasion to mention Christ, Christians or Christianity. In fact none of the early pagan religious novels mentions Christians, despite involving adventures across the whole empire with frequent encounters with religious cults.[27] But satires were even more common. Aulus Persius Flaccus was a Roman satirist under Nero, from whom nothing survives, but it's possible he would have found opportunities for satire of, if not Christians, then Nero's treatment of them. Lucillius also wrote satirical poems under Nero, including lampoons of religious practices, and once on how Nero burned a robber alive in an amphitheater, so again he might have had opportunity to lampoon Christians or Nero's treatment of them. Turnus was likewise a late-first-century satirist who could have lampooned Christians if ever he noticed any. And again, these are just among the authors we know about.

For any single one of these authors I've named in this whole survey, there is surely some probability that they just happened not to mention either Christ, Christians or Christianity (though in some cases, as I've noted, that probability might be low). But the probability that *none* of them would is quite low. For example, if the probability of any *one* of them mentioning Christ, Christians or Christianity is a mere 1 in 20, then the probability that

27. See Bryan Reardon (ed.), *Collected Ancient Greek Novels* (Berkeley, CA: University of California Press, 1989); and Susan Stephens and John Winkler, *Ancient Greek Novels: The Fragments* (Princeton, NJ: Princeton University Press, 1995); with Niklas Holzberg, *The Ancient Novel: An Introduction* (New York: Routledge, 1995); Gareth Schmeling, *The Novel in the Ancient World* (Leiden: Brill, 1996); and Tim Whitmarsh (ed.), *The Cambridge Companion to the Greek and Roman Novel* (Cambridge: Cambridge University Press, 2008).

none of them would do so is less than 1 in 3.[28] Yet these are only the authors we *know* about. In fact, not even that: these are only the authors who just happen to have received entries in the *Oxford Classical Dictionary*, which certainly does not catalogue more than a small fraction of all the authors we have surviving evidence of. And the number of actual authors and books written in that period is at least an order of magnitude (if not *many* orders of magnitude) greater than the number we have any surviving reference to, and the latter will already be several times the number of authors I just enumerated. So the probability that *none* of what must have been at least two hundred relevant first-century writers would mention anything, if each had only a 1 in 20 chance of doing so, is nearly 30,000 to 1 against.[29] Pretty long odds.

Of course, it could be claimed that there were indeed many such mentions but none were preserved. And that may even be true (in the case of Jewish and Neronian literature, it almost has to be true). It's certainly true for countless other people, fads and events in the Roman Empire. But none of those people, fads or events had a massive Church devoted to preserving records of its resurrected God, which then became almost solely responsible for preserving all literature whatever. This is why we have a hundred times more faith literature from Christians about Christianity (even just from the first to fourth centuries) than we do from any other faith group of the period. Only Judaism comes anywhere near a (very) distant second, and that only because Christians also avidly preserved a lot of Judaica, and because apart from Christianity, Judaism is the only religious community

28. P(no mention in any) = 0.95^{20} (for twenty authors) and 0.95^{30} (for thirty authors) = 0.358 and 0.215 = 36% and 22%, respectively.

29. P(no mention in any) = 0.95^{200} (for two hundred authors) = 0.000035 $\approx$ 1 in 28,500. Two hundred is only my estimated count of first-century authors writing books that have a relevant possibility of mentioning Christ, Christians or Christianity (i.e. with an odds of a mention equal to 1 in 20), based on the list I just enumerated and how much of an undercount it must be of comparable works written in the same period. By contrast, the actual number of *authors* in the first century would have been in the thousands. For example, if in the Roman Empire there were a hundred major cities with a literary elite (and there were at least that many, as will be evidenced throughout Richard Carrier, *Science Education in the Early Roman Empire* [in review]; the number of cities in which Christians had established congregations by the year 100 has likewise been estimated at seventy, which was by no means all the major cities in the empire; cf. Carrier, *Not the Impossible Faith*, pp. 420-25) and only ten authors published in each city every ten years (an enormous undercount, being only one book each year per city), then for any given century there would be 10,000 published authors in that century, producing an average of some 100,000 titles. And again, even that may be an enormous undercount. It's often not appreciated how much literature we have lost from the ancient world.

to continuously survive from the Roman Empire to the present.[30] Many Christian scholars such as Origen and Eusebius were particularly keen on referencing or quoting authors who attested to Jesus or Christianity, or rebutting unsavory things said about either. Mentions of Jesus in first-century pagan or Jewish literature would therefore have had the highest probability of preservation of anything written in the whole of antiquity—either outright (as, e.g., some have suggested that the works of Tacitus and Josephus were preserved by medieval Christians simply because they contained references to Jesus) or in quotation, paraphrase or rebuttal. Even then, of course, not everything would be certain to survive; maybe even a lot of it would still have been lost. But it seems very unusual that absolutely *nothing* survived.

A clue to this strange silence lies in the treatment of the few critical writings about Christians we do know about: every single one of them was destroyed. The only reason we know anything about them is that in each case Christian authors either refer to them or wrote a rebuttal (and later Christians liked those rebuttals so well that they kept them). But these critiques cannot possibly have been the only ones written, and are unlikely to have been the earliest ones written. And in any event, they were not preserved; they were replaced instead with Christian propaganda. These known cases include an extensive treatise by the Epicurean philosopher Celsus (a friend of Lucian's) in the mid-second century (his attack on Christianity was jokingly entitled *The True Logos*), inspiring Origen's extensive rebuttal.[31] Around the same time, Fronto, the teacher, friend and correspondent of Emperor Marcus Aurelius, wrote something like a 'Discourse against the Christians' (we're unsure of its exact title), which inspired the Christian Minucius Felix to write the propagandistic *Octavius* in response. A century later Hierocles wrote *The Lover of Truth*, summarizing several critical treatises on Christianity up to his time, including a chapter comparing Jesus to Apollonius of Tyana using the then-recent publication of the *Life of Apollonius* by Philostratus. Notably this one chapter is the only part that Eusebius bothers to attack in his *Treatise against Hierocles* (which in turn is pretty much the only reason we know Hierocles' book existed). Eusebius even says he ignored the rest of Hierocles' book as being deriva-

30. Even papyrological finds are hugely skewed by this fact, as papyri pertaining to Christianity or Judaism are worth a great deal more on the black market and thus are far more likely to surface or gain any attention. Just contrast the money, time and resources that have been devoted to the Nag Hammadi and Qumran caches, of Christian and Jewish texts respectively, with that devoted to recovering the pagan library at Herculaneum, which after two hundred years still remains almost entirely unexcavated.

31. On this Celsus see Carrier, *Not the Impossible Faith*, p. 120 n. 7.

tive of 'previous' Christian critics. Whom, of course, excepting Celsus and Fronto, we know next to nothing about.

Later in the third century the Neoplatonist Porphyry wrote his own fifteen-volume treatise *Against the Christians*, which again does not survive, except for diverse scattered quotations in later Christian authors. A century after that Emperor Julian (the last pagan emperor, himself taking the throne only after a long line of Christian emperors) wrote *Against the Galileans*, his own critique of the religion that had transformed the empire he inherited. Once again, this does not survive; all we have are portions of Cyril of Alexandria's treatise *Against Julian*. Eunapius then wrote in the year 414 a *History against the Christians* (perhaps not literally named that, but it was regarded as such by later Christians), an extensive critique of Christian 'versions' of historical events from 270 to 404 CE. This, too, does not survive; his otherwise inoffensive *Lives of the Sophists* was preserved instead. The only reason we know of his anti-Christian work is that before it faded into oblivion, many later historians, including Christians, employed it as a source.

Again, these are just the ones we know about. Which would be a fraction of what there was. All of it was tossed out or destroyed. Instead, we get to read only what medieval Christians wanted us to read. Another example of this phenomenon is that of the 'mysterious lacuna'. Several texts that were preserved have sections removed. Sections whose disappearance seems convenient for Christians. Now, a lot of ancient literature, indeed arguably most, has missing material. This is typically a result of carelessness and accident, multiplied by time. But in some cases the precision and location of what was lost is a bit more peculiar than chance accident would suggest.

For example, the Christian scholar Hippolytus in the early third century wrote his *Refutation of All Heresies* in ten volumes. At the end of the first of them he says he will next explain the secret doctrines of the several mystery religions (which would have included the Passion Narratives of the different savior gods, including miraculous births, deaths and resurrections, and their sacred meals and baptisms: see Elements 11-14 and 31) and what they teach about the things in outer space (which would have included such material as in Elements 34-38), and then he would describe the teachings of the astrologers. But the second and third volumes are missing. The text skips directly to volume 4, which begins his discourse on astrology. This does not look like an accident. Some Christian or Christians decided to destroy those two volumes—for some reason fearing their contents. The resulting loss in our knowledge of the mystery religions is beyond considerable.

Another strange loss concerns the annual festival of Romulus in which his death and resurrection were reenacted in public passion plays (see Chapter 4, §1). That festival was held on the 7th of July. At the beginning of the first century Ovid wrote an elaborate poem, the *Fasti*, describing all the festivals throughout the year at Rome and what went on in them and why. This only survives in its first half, covering January to June, the remaining months are lost. It seems strange that the text cuts off precisely before the month in which a passion play is described that was the most similar to that of Jesus Christ. The fact that we have other descriptions of this festival (albeit none as complete as Ovid's would have been) does mean there was no organized conspiracy to doctor the record (except when it came to controlling faith literature, for which we have clear evidence of Christians actively eliminating disapproved Gospels, for example), but this along with all the other cases (above and below) indicates a common trend among individual Christians to act as gatekeepers of information, suppressing what they didn't like. Which collectively destroyed a lot of information.

Another example along similar lines is a mysterious gap in the text of Plutarch's *Moralia*, a huge multivolume library of treatises on diverse subjects. In one of these, the *Tabletalk*, Plutarch is discussing the equivalence of Yahweh and Dionysus, and linking Jewish theology to the mystery religions, when suddenly the text is cut off. We have no idea how much is missing, although the surviving table of contents shows there were several sections remaining on other subjects besides this one. If an accident, this seems like a very convenient one.

A similar mysterious gap is found in the *Annals* of Tacitus. The text of the *Annals* survives in only two manuscript traditions, one containing the first half, the other the second half, with a section in between missing—and thus its loss is explicable. But there is *another* gap in the text that is harder to explain: two whole years from the middle of 29 CE to the middle of 31. That the cut is so precise and covers precisely those two years is too improbable to posit as a chance coincidence. The year 30 was regarded by many early Christians as the year of Christ's ministry and crucifixion (see Element 7). Robert Drews analyzed all the gaps in the *Annals* and concluded that this one has no more plausible explanation than that Christians excised those two years out of embarrassment at its omission of any mention of Jesus or associated events (like the world darkness reported in the Synoptic Gospels).[32] Tacitus digresses on Christianity in his coverage of the year 64, in such a way that guarantees he made no mention of it earlier (if the passage there is authentic: see §10)—although Tacitus surely must have discussed other events under Pontius Pilate. So we can be certain Christians weren't trying to hide anything embarrassing said *about* Jesus. But the embarrassment of *saying nothing* was evidently enough to motivate their targeted destruction of the corresponding text.

32. Robert Drews, 'The Lacuna in Tacitus' *Annales* Book Five in the Light of Christian Traditions', *American Journal of Ancient History* 9 (1984), pp. 112-22.

A similar mysterious gap exists in the *Roman History* of Cassius Dio: all the years from 6 to 2 BCE are gone. There is evidence from remarks elsewhere that Dio discussed Herod's death in this period.[33] A Christian would have expected Dio to discuss the slaughter of the innocents and the miraculous star and other amazing events surrounding the birth of Jesus, and Dio's silence on all of these might have been just as embarrassing as the silence of Tacitus. That this loss might be no accident is suggested by the fact that it is quite thorough—even subsequent epitomes exclude it—combined with the coincidence of date: the gap beginning exactly two years before Herod's death, in accordance with Mt. 2.16, and ending two years after it for good measure (there being at the time some uncertainty among Christians as to when exactly Herod died). What about Dio's treatment of the year 30? Yes, something is mysteriously missing around there, too. In the middle of volume 58, covering the years 29 to 37 CE, we have a reference to an event (in 58.17.2) that was evidently described in a section that had to have been deleted somewhere between 57.17.8 (the year 15) and 58.7.2 (the year 30). Might it have been a section also mentioning Judean affairs, whose silence was again considered too embarrassing to retain?

Another strange loss are certain volumes of Philo of Alexandria. Despite Christians having saved vast quantities of the writings of Philo, the ones that would most have occasion to mention Jesus or Judean affairs under Pontius Pilate are missing or mangled. According to Eusebius, Philo wrote *five* books about his embassy to Caligula (after the year 36) and the events precipitating it, only *two* of which survive.[34] What happened to the other three? We know they covered three other subjects, each a major persecution of Jews under Tiberius: one volume on Pilate (in Judea), another on Sejanus (at Rome), the ones we have (on Flaccus in Egypt; then one on Caligula), and a final volume showing what happened to Caligula after all this.[35] All of these may have embarrassingly omitted mention of any Christians at Rome (such as was claimed in the apocryphal but popular *Acts of Pilate*)

33. Peter Michael Swan, *The Augustan Succession: An Historical Commentary on Cassius Dio's Roman History Books 55–56 (9 B.C.–A.D. 14)* (Oxford: Oxford University Press, 2004), pp. 36-38, 188.

34. These being the books now separately titled *Against Flaccus* and *Embassy to Gaius* (Eusebius, *History of the Church* 2.5.1).

35. Philo, *Against Flaccus* 1, assumes that the preceding volume discussed Sejanus's persecution of the Jews in Rome; Philo, *Embassy to Gaius* 8, assumes that the troubles under Tiberius had all just been covered (so that now, the troubles under his successor Caligula would be), and *Embassy to Gaius* 373 says the next volume would be an account of Caligula's repentance and death. Eusebius, *History of the Church* 2.5.7, then says another treated Pilate (which would have been under Tiberius). Thus, the five volumes were either (1) Pilate, (2) Sejanus, (3) Flaccus, (4) Caligula, (5) Conclusion; or (1) Sejanus, (2) Flaccus, (3) Pilate, (4) Caligula, (5) Conclusion.

or in Jerusalem or Alexandria. But the most important volume would have been the one on Pilate's persecution of the Jews in Judea. Christians would surely expect *that* volume to mention Pilate's execution of Jesus in some respect; but as it probably did not, again its silence would have been as embarrassing as all the others surveyed so far.[36]

It's also curious that treatises against popular religion were not preserved, even though they would have been invaluable to Christian opposition to paganism and heresy. We have the rather brief *On Superstition* by Plutarch, but not the detailed *On Superstition* by Seneca (mentioned earlier) or that of Porphyry. There is also a strange lacuna in Juvenal's rant against superstition in his *Satires* 6.511, where scholars can't make sense of the sentence and the subject-transition here, and conclude there is an extended deletion, right where he passes onto the subject of attacking popular religions. The surviving text jumps into the middle of a discussion of the cults of Cybele and Isis and eventually the Jews. What material was deleted? Why? Once again our desire to know more about the religious context of Christianity appears thwarted by an editor with something to hide.

We can add to these the complete 'excision' of the history of first-century Judea by Justus of Tiberias and the interpolation that 'corrected' the silence of Josephus (the *Testimonium Flavianum*: §9), as well as all the losses we *don't* know about but which must have occurred (as surveyed previously). That leaves us with a string of evidence of historicizing Christians seeking to alter the record to hide the embarrassing absence of Jesus in secular history. Any one of these examples might just be a coincidence. But all of them? That seems unlikely. Again, this doesn't demonstrate any organized conspiracy, but there seems to have been a zeitgeist motivating many Christian scholars and scribes, independently of one another, to remove embarrassingly silent sections of secular histories, or to remove embarrassingly silent histories altogether (by simply not preserving them).

There are many other mysterious gaps in ancient literature, which I won't bother listing as they are not as ominous, but there is no telling what was in them, or conspicuously *not* in them, that may have motivated Christians to remove them, or that would have changed our conclusions about the origin and nature of early Christianity and its religious environment if we still had them.[37]

36. See Gregory Sterling, 'Philo of Alexandria', in *The Historical Jesus in Context* (ed. Amy-Jill Levine, Dale Allison, Jr, and John Dominic Crossan; Princeton, NJ: Princeton University Press, 2006), pp. 296-308 (298).

37. On this more general problem (which is caused even by the extent of *accidental* losses), see Carrier, 'Spiritual Body', in *Empty Tomb* (ed. Price and Lowder), pp. 180-82.

4. *Missing Christian Evidence*

However you choose to deal with the peculiar silence of secular, pagan and Jewish literature throughout the first and most of the second century (I surveyed your options in §2), we at least have the few things that Christians *did* choose to preserve. And that starts with their own literature. Yet even there the selection is strange: among the dateable, nothing at all from Christianity's entire first sixty years *except* what later became canonized as the NT—and that represents what can only have been a fraction of what existed, even just counting only the letters that must have been written across all those decades (see, again, Element 22). After that the first thing we get is a single, very long letter from Clement of Rome written to the church in Corinth, supposedly in or near the year 95, or in any event, after the deaths of Peter and Paul. Then, supposedly, a collection of letters from Ignatius to various churches in what is now Turkey, traditionally dated around 110 (but, as we'll see, more probably dating decades later). And nothing else until after the year 120 (see previous chapter), almost a century after the religion began. It's hard to imagine how a church can thrive across three continents for almost a hundred years and produce almost no letters or literature.

Of all the second-century Christian writings we know about, the most helpful might have been the 'histories' of the church written sometime between 120 and 180 by Papias and Hegesippus. We otherwise know of no historical treatments of early Christianity except Acts and writings *after* the second century, which are so rife with legend and dogma as to be useless for our purposes (see previous chapter; we shall soon see that Papias and Hegesippus were actually very much worse in this regard: see §§7 and 8). I will therefore discuss what we know about those books after treating *1 Clement* and the Ignatian epistles. Because Hegesippus and Papias evidently represent the 'best' historical research that Christians were bothering with in that century.

But we can't proceed without also noting what we *don't* have. Again, we should have the hundreds of letters that must have been written in the first century, possibly dozens by Paul alone. Yet we have only seven of his, though we know there were more; although the seven we have might actually be pasted together excerpts of more than seven letters, there still is a lot missing.[38] When it comes to other first-century authors, we have either no letters or only a handful at most. Yet we should have letters from numerous apostles, and letters communicating between churches, in great quantity, from every decade beginning with Paul. As to why we don't, there are no verifiable explanations to be had (as noted in §2). It can be presumed only that they were destroyed or tossed aside without mention or explanation.

38. See, e.g., Chapter 7 (§3).

It cannot be presumed that none were written. That would defy all common sense and all probability. For example, are we to think *only* Paul ever wrote doctrinal letters for the whole first three decades of the cult? That after Paul's many letters (of which we now have only a fraction), no one ever once wrote another doctrinal letter for over thirty more years? Then suddenly, out of the blue, after all that time, Clement decided to write just one really long letter, and that's it? These are all extreme improbabilities.

We could also have church records and family records. To argue that family documents were not preserved because Jesus' family died out, or lost their files, or no one else considered such records important until a century or more later (when they might have long since been tossed into the trash), is entirely plausible *only if you assume* that no one at first thought Jesus was the Son of God and Savior and therefore the most important historical person ever to walk the earth. But if you start with the assumption that people did think this from the start (and the letters of Paul certainly must indicate this if Jesus existed), then it becomes harder to explain the lack of interest in keeping his family records. It's not *impossible* that they would still all be abandoned or ignored, but that's not exactly what we would *expect* to happen, is it?

Families of the time could receive census and tax receipts from the government, documenting their family relations, births, property, place of residence, and taxes paid, among other things. They would have deeds for any properties they owned; they would have written copies of any contracts they entered into; they would have documents pertaining to any trials they were involved in (civil or criminal); they would have copies of any letters they received (which they surely would have received if they were at all involved in the church administration and mission after Jesus' death). It's hard to imagine these would be of no interest at all.[39] Likewise *church* records: homeowners who offered their buildings for services and meetings would *have* to have kept around all deeds and contracts and tax receipts related to them (that was the purpose of having such documents in the first place, to guarantee legal title and prove to the government that all taxes had been properly paid). What happened to all those?

39. See, e.g., J.R. Alexander, 'Graeco-Roman Papyrus Documents from Egypt', *Athena Review* 2 (1999), available at www.athenapub.com/egypap1.html. For more detail see Charles Hedrick, *Ancient History: Monuments and Documents* (Oxford: Blackwell, 2006), pp. 89-107; Hannah Cotton, Walter Cockle and Fergus Millar, 'The Papyrology of the Roman Near East: A Survey', *Journal of Roman Studies* 95 (1995), pp. 214-35; Rafael Taubenschlag, *The Law of Greco-Roman Egypt in the Light of the Papyri, 332 B.C.–640 A.D.* (Warsaw: Państwowe Wydawnictwo Naukowe 1955); E.G. Turner (ed.), *Greek Papyri: An Introduction* (New York: Oxford University Press, 2nd edn, 1980), pp. 74-96, 127-53; Roger Bagnall, *Reading Papyri, Writing Ancient History* (New York: Routledge, 1995); etc.

Perhaps Christians changed homes and locations so often, perhaps persecution or apostasy created so much confusion, that no one could keep track of any church's location or legal or business affairs for hundreds of years. Perhaps we can imagine no one was interested in them, that these things were just considered too boring or obsolete. Perhaps conflicts among the churches led to getting rid of records that might have proved embarrassing to this or that faction. Perhaps they expected they'd all be burned up in the apocalypse anyway. Or whatever. Explain it all away as you wish. *We still don't have them.* Yet they certainly would have existed. What was in them? We have to accept the fact that we really don't know.

But that still leaves the vast deletion of what must have been dozens if not hundreds of doctrinal letters in the first century, including several penned by Paul himself. That Christians preserved seven of his letters (or seven mishmashes of them) *proves* that they had the means and an interest in preserving letters—it therefore also proves they had the means and an interest in *suppressing* letters: all the letters that they chose not to preserve. Compared to Socrates, who inspired a vast quantity of literary activity immediately upon his death (in fact already during his life), Jesus inspired none (or none that we have any knowledge of), and once literary activity definitely did begin (evidenced by the letters of Paul), later Christians discarded *almost all of it.*

This *can* be explained on a theory of historicity, but only by adding *ad hoc* elements to it ('additional' add-ons to the theory that explain why all this evidence did not accumulate for the Church to preserve to us, as we would normally expect); and any explanation you accept has consequences you must also accept. No theory of historicity that does not address this can be credible; likewise the loss or absence of pagan and Jewish discussions of Christianity (entirely from the first century, and almost entirely from the second). But as this is also true for mythicism, I will regard minimal historicity to be as capable of predicting this state of affairs as well as minimal mythicism, and therefore this silence does not affect the probability of either. But others might find that decision far too generous to historicity.

5. *Clement of Rome*

Tradition has it that thirty or forty years after the letters of Paul, twenty years after the Gospel of Mark, maybe ten years after the Gospel of Matthew, perhaps around the very time Luke–Acts was being composed, Clement of Rome (supposedly then bishop of Rome, or at any rate the highest ranking man of that church at the time; in fact the letter never gives his rank or name) decided to write a massive letter (of well over ten thousand words) to the church at Corinth to resolve a troubling sedition there, in which younger men deposed their elders and took over (we're not told why).

Clement asks that things be put back the way they were, in an elaborate letter about humility and submission and patience and obedience. Further letters and homilies were later forged in this Clement's name, but here we are only concerned with what presumably is his only surviving authentic letter, supposedly written around 95 CE (but possibly written as early as the 60s, as argued in §6 of the previous chapter).

What does this letter tell us about the historical Jesus? Nothing. It never once places Jesus in history or ever tells any stories about him, never uses his stories as an example for anything (despite the letter being a long series of arguments by example), nor ever quotes anything Jesus says in the Gospels. Apart from his death, it never mentions any event in his life, any fact about his life, or anything narrated in the Gospels. And this despite the fact that this letter is supposed to end a major rebellion in the church (for which citing the example of Jesus would be of inestimable value) and is almost as long as *both* of Paul's letters to the Corinthians combined (and each of those is quite a long letter in itself), over ten thousand words or so. How can this be? Can you imagine a church official writing such a massive admonition to a backsliding church without ever mentioning anything about Jesus? (Other than that he is a dying-and-rising godman in outer space whose revealed teachings they all follow?)

What we find instead is this: Clement praises the Corinthians, telling them, 'you were satisfied with the things Christ provided you and carefully held to his words, taking them to heart, and his sufferings were before your eyes' (2.1, *ta pathēmata autou ēn pro ophthalmōn humōn*). Which means 'witnessing' the suffering of Christ was something one could do metaphorically, inwardly, in the imagination (since obviously none of *these* Corinthians can possibly have been physically present at the crucifixion, much less all of them, and especially not the younger ones he is specifically writing to). Thus, he says, 'let us gaze intently upon the blood of Christ' (7.4), with obviously the same meaning; he likewise says that through faith in Christ we can behold all manner of amazing things, including the 'heights of heaven', even the face of Jesus himself (36.2). Obviously, then, this 'Christ's' words could have come by similar means: inwardly, by revelation (as we know they could: see Elements 16 and 19); and the possibility of this is all but admitted in *1 Clem.* 8.1 and 59.1.[40]

Clement reports that Paul was recently killed (in 'their' generation: 5.2, 7) at the hands of state officials ('by those in charge', *epi tōn hēgoumenōn*) at the 'end of the western world' (*epi to terma tēs duseōs*), which means Spain (Rome was not the 'terminus' of where the 'sun sets'; that was universally recognized as the Spanish coast). The fact that this contradicts all

40. And perhaps elsewhere. See the analysis of Earl Doherty, *Jesus: Neither God nor Man (The Case for a Mythical Jesus)* (Ottawa: Age of Reason, 2009), pp. 462-64.

later legend (which has Paul executed by Nero in Rome) suggests, first, that that was indeed only a later legend and, second, that Paul did in fact die in Spain—as otherwise there would be no reason for Clement to make this up, unless Clement invented that fate by merely conjecturing that that is where Paul is last heard to have been. According to Paul himself, he was to venture on to Spain after he stopped at Rome (Rom. 15.24-28; notably, Paul clearly was not going to Rome in chains when he wrote that—contrary to the narrative in Acts—but was simply planning to go there on his own and only stop by 'briefly' on his way to Spain). But if Clement is doing *that*, then no knowledge existed as to Paul's actual fate—not even the bishop of Rome himself knew. Either way, Paul's martyrdom at Rome is proved to be a myth (that tale either not existing yet, or it being known at Clement's time that in fact Paul was martyred in Spain).[41]

Clement does not say why Paul was killed, only that it was a result of some sort of envy and its resulting betrayal. He mentions Peter having been martyred for the same reason, but not where or when. He then mentions other recent Christian martyrs in general (naming no one in particular). Notably absent is any mention of James having been martyred—despite that supposedly happening around the same time as Peter and Paul, and despite his supposedly being the very brother of Jesus (and in later legend a major leader of the church). In fact, Clement does not appear to have any knowledge of Jesus having had brothers.

Clement does say Jesus was a 'gift' of Jacob (i.e. Israel) 'according to the flesh' (32.2), suffered a passion (2.1; as all savior gods did: Elements 11 and 31), that his blood was poured out as a sacrifice (7.4; 21.6; 49.6), and that he was resurrected (24.1). But these things would be just as true on minimal mythicism (see Chapter 3; and for Jesus being a Jew, Chapter 11, §9). He also says 'the Holy Spirit' tells us that Christ 'did not come in the pomp of pride or arrogance . . . but in a lowly condition' (16.2), but as evidence all he cites is Isaiah 53. Not any actual story about or witness to Jesus. Clement thus doesn't appear to have any 'evidence' that Christ came humbly, except that the OT said so (16.17) and that the Holy Spirit told them so (either directly, as in 8.1, or through the scriptures, as in 45.2). Likewise, when Clement wants to cite numerous 'sayings' of their 'Lord'

41. The so-called Muratorian Canon (a fragment discussing the books in the NT, variously dated to the late second or even the fourth century) curiously says, 'The Acts of all the Apostles . . . evidently relates the death of Peter and also Paul's departure from the city as he was proceeding to Spain' (§§ 23-25), which could suggest there is a missing chapter to our copy of Acts (which otherwise never mentions either of those things), but more likely this remark confuses the Acts of the Apostles with the *Acts of Peter and Paul* (late-second-century forgeries that do relate those things). These were evidently unknown to the author of *1 Clement*.

and 'master' in support of a point (such as that God will save the penitent: *1 Clement* 8; or that God will raise the dead: *1 Clement* 24–26; or that we must not succumb to pride and hypocrisy: *1 Clement* 30), he quotes the OT (and that extensively), not Jesus, and gives examples (of repentance, forgiveness, resurrection) only from the OT, never from the Gospels (or any tradition they supposedly record). And when Clement says the Lord adorned himself with good works and rejoiced (33.7), he is not referring to Jesus, but to God the Creator: *He* is the one rejoicing, and the 'good works' he is rejoicing at are the whole of creation (see 33.2, then 33.7, then review the material in between: 33.3-6).[42]

The only time Clement 'quotes' Jesus himself, he either simply quotes the OT or he says something that fits no Gospel narrative we have. For example, Clement once quotes commandments not matching any Gospel—and even though in that one instance each commandment on his list is expanded into more elaborate teachings, parables and stories in the Gospels, Clement appears to be unaware of any of those (13.2). Instead, he only knows of 'the words Jesus spoke' as being a quick series of declarations of reciprocity more akin to an updated book of proverbs, and he says *these* are the words we are to obey (13.3). It would appear there may have been only a collection of very brief sayings attributed to Jesus (all of which could have been learned by revelation), which the Gospels then expanded into narratives and discourses. Because the latter are all unknown to Clement (one of the reasons I suspect *1 Clement* was written in the 60s and not the 90s: see Chapter 7, §6).

Similarly, at another point Clement says to the Corinthians (while clearly assuming they know what he is referring to):

> Remember the words of our Lord Jesus, for he said, 'Woe to that man! It would have been good for him not to be born, rather than cause one of my chosen to stumble. Better for him to have a millstone cast about his neck and be drowned in the sea than to have corrupted one of my chosen' (*1 Clem.* 46.7-8).

42. *1 Clement* 33 as a whole appears to paraphrase elements of Proverbs 8, in which Wisdom is the one rejoicing at creation, which might incline one to suspect Clement is here attributing to Jesus this speech in Proverbs 8, but on that interpretation it is still creation itself Jesus was rejoicing at, as declared in Proverbs 8.38, not any historical event in his life—which would make this a reference to Jesus as a preexistent divine being (in fact, it would make him the Wisdom of God, the one speaking in Proverbs 8, as if in accordance with a literal reading of 1 Cor. 1.24), which would argue *against* the historicity of Jesus. I think the full language of *1 Clem.* 33.2-7 is clear in referring to 'the creator and master of all', i.e. God, not Jesus. But anyone who turns away from that interpretation falls on the horns of the only other remaining: that Clement is saying Jesus was a preexistent being who helped God create the world and rejoiced at what he'd done. There is no evidence for historicity here.

This is clearly represented here as a quotation of one unified saying, yet in the Gospels it is two completely unrelated ones: one part spoken during Jesus' ministry, in the presence of a group of children, about people tempting his followers to sin ('Whoever causes one of these little ones who believe in me to sin, it would be better for him if a great millstone were hung round his neck and he were thrown into the sea', Mk 9.42, echoed in Lk. 17.1-2 and expanded in Mt. 18.3-7), another part spoken about Judas at the Last Supper ('Woe to that man, by whom the Son of Man is betrayed! It would have been good for that man not to be born', Mk 14.18-21 and Mt. 26.23-25, abbreviated in Lk. 22.22-23). Clement clearly does not know of the Judas story, and the phrase 'Woe to that man! It would have been good for him not to be born' was evidently never originally anything Jesus said about Judas, but a generic statement about those who lead the Lord's 'children' to sin, meaning Christians (Jesus' 'chosen ones': see Mt. 18.3-7 and Element 13). Which means Jesus almost certainly never said this—because it reflects the concept of a church community, of 'believers' in Jesus that did not exist until after he had died. Which makes this a good candidate for a post-mortem revelation (Element 16), or once again some pre-Christian scripture that Clement is quoting but we no longer have (Element 9).

Apart from perhaps those two instances, for Clement the words of Jesus always come from scripture. When Clement says, 'Christ himself calls to us through the Holy Spirit', and then quotes 'Christ' at length, what we find in fact is simply a quotation of the Psalms (*1 Clem.* 22.1-8, which matches Pss 34.11-17, 19; and 32.10). Thus Clement assumes that Jesus 'speaks' to us through the scriptures (hence again Element 16). Clement didn't even have to say this. He simply assumes that a quotation of scripture can be described as a quotation of 'Christ' without explanation or citation—the fact that the Corinthians don't need this to be explained to them entails this was routinely understood within the churches of the time: that Jesus speaks *through scripture*, rather than human tradition. Likewise, when Clement says Jesus is their 'high priest' (36.1; see also 58.2; 61.3; 64.1) he quotes or paraphrases either Hebrews or some lost scripture that was also used in Hebrews, which (like Hebrews) declared Jesus to be their high priest, appointed to a higher office than all the angels (compare *1 Clem.* 36.2 with Heb. 1.3-4), securely identifying him as a celestial being.[43]

Which leads us to wonder if in fact the list of reciprocity proverbs he quoted earlier (in *1 Clem.* 13.2-3) is a quotation of a lost scripture (see Ele-

43. Clement and Hebrews could be paraphrasing or loosely quoting each other (which means Hebrews either pre-dates *1 Clement* or vice versa), but it's also possible some lost scripture is being consulted by both. There are also parallels between Clement and Ephesians (compare *1 Clem.* 46.6 with Eph. 4.4-6), which could stem from any of the same three options.

ment 9, and of course Element 8) and not even a *revealed* saying of Jesus, much less actually spoken by a historical Jesus. For example, in 23.3-4 and 46.2 Clement quotes from what he explicitly calls 'scripture' passages that do not exist in any known scripture. Thus, clearly he was using scriptures we now no longer have, lost scriptures which all Christians regarded as the word of God, in fact even the word of Christ, through the Holy Spirit (per 8.1). So might not the reciprocity proverbs (of 13.2-3) come from this same lost scripture, a different passage of which is being quoted in 23.3-4? And likewise the millstone woe (of 46.7-8)?

Either way, the 'commandments' of Christ (49.1) appear to come by revelation or scriptures; Clement mentions no other source—except through apostles as proxies for both. Thus, where Clement says the apostles learned 'through our Lord Jesus Christ' that they must establish offices and rules of succession in the church (44.1), even though most scholars would doubt that that is true (it's a concern most scholars regard as having arisen later), nevertheless Clement seems to imagine the apostles learning this from Jesus, through scripture (42.5; 43.1-6). He again never mentions any other source on this point (e.g. despite making an extensive scriptural defense of it, Clement never quotes any words of Jesus, which surely would have been more important to his argument). We might imagine the apostles were warned by revelation, and then sought and found the scriptural support they needed. But either way there is no evidence here of a Jesus having taught them this while ever alive and walking among them.

When Clement says that 'concerning His Son the Lord said, "Thou art my Son, today have I begotten Thee"', he quotes only the Psalms; he doesn't mention this also being said by God at Jesus' baptism or any other event (36.5, echoed in 59.2, 3, 4; cf. Mt. 3.16-17). When he says God promised that Jesus would sit at his right hand (36.5), Clement doesn't seem to know that Jesus also said this (Mk 14.62) or that a witness saw Jesus seated there (Acts 7.55). When he says that everyone should accept their place and serve one another and not try to be exalted (37-38), he doesn't think to tell the story about how Jesus admonished James and John on that very same point (Mk 10.35-45). It's the same all throughout the letter. He never tells *any* story about Jesus, not from the Gospels nor from any tradition that came to be recorded in the Gospels nor from any tradition not in the Gospels. As far as Clement appears to be concerned, there simply are no stories about Jesus.

Clement cannot even adduce any story of Jesus' humility and submission to include among his examples admonishing the Corinthians to be humble and submissive (*1 Clement* 14–15); he can only assure them that the OT *says* Jesus was humble and submissive (*1 Clement* 16). When he wants to prove that all things are obedient to God, not a single instance of Jesus exorcising demons or doing miracles is mentioned as evidence (*1 Clement*

27), nor any of Jesus' sayings in the Gospels that made the same point. When he needs examples of men of honor being killed by unjust authorities, the crucifixion of Jesus doesn't make the list, nor the beheading of John the Baptist, nor the stoning of Stephen (*1 Clement* 45–46). Likewise in his list of 'betrayals' born of envy in chaps. 4 to 6 (beginning with Cain and Abel), in which Judas's betrayal of Jesus would naturally belong (through envy of money: Mk 14.10-11; and as the vehicle for the envy of the Pharisees: Mk 15.10), the Judas example, the very best example he could have, is conspicuously not mentioned. Instead, when he says he will move from 'ancient' examples to those more recent (5.1), he skips immediately to the deaths of Peter and Paul. In fact, of all the dozens of stories Clement summarizes as examples for Christians to follow, all come from the OT, none from any Gospel or anything in the life of Jesus (not just in *1 Clement* 4–5, but also 9–12, 15–18, etc.).

When Clement does get to telling the story of Jesus, this is all he has to relate:

> The apostles received the gospel for us from the Lord Jesus Christ; and Jesus Christ was sent from God. And so Christ is from God, and the apostles from Christ. Each occurred in an orderly way from the will of God. And so having received their orders and being fully reassured by the resurrection of our Lord Jesus Christ and persuaded in the word of God, with the full assurance of the holy spirit, they went out spreading the good news that the kingdom of God was at hand (*1 Clem.* 42.1-4).

This account of what happened looks a lot more like the mythicist thesis, in which Jesus came to the apostles by revelation and convinced them of his death and resurrection, proving it by appeal to the scriptures and through gifts of the holy spirit. There is no mention here of Jesus being born, preaching a ministry in Galilee, teaching the gospel to thousands (as opposed to only the apostles having received it), performing miracles or signs that proved who he was, being executed by Pilate or any detail at all that would connect Jesus to a historical narrative. Instead, Jesus is sent directly from God only to the apostles. And the apostles are the only ones who could tell us about it.

If we had no other sources on Christianity but *1 Clement*, we would conclude that Jesus was some sort of divine emissary in heaven, a supreme archangel, who communicated to the apostles through visions and secret messages in various holy scriptures (some of which we no longer have but that the early Christians regarded as inspired), and who underwent some sort of ordeal of incarnation, death and resurrection like other mythical demigods. It would never occur to us that he was a human man who conducted a ministry, performed great deeds among the people, and was railroaded in a Jewish trial and eventually crucified by Pontius Pilate. The fact that this lengthy document fully agrees with the expectations of minimal mythicism, but looks very strange on any version of historicity, *makes this evidence for the former and against the latter.*

The fact that the content of this letter is in many ways unexpected on historicity, even minimal historicity, entails it cannot have a consequent probability on *h* anywhere near 100%. But the fact that on minimal mythicism this is exactly the kind of letter we would expect to be written in the first century entails that its consequent probability on mythicism *is* 100% (or near enough). By contrast, I cannot believe there is even a 50% chance minimal historicity would cause a letter like this to be produced (of such great length, filled with so many opportunities to reference the facts of Jesus' life but never doing so, and with scripture and revelation the only mentioned sources for Jesus' deeds and sayings), which means as evidence, the content of *1 Clement* is at least twice as likely on mythicism as on historicism. This makes another factor of 2 to 1 in favor of myth (which, as before, can be represented as a consequent probability of 50% for *h* and 100% for ¬*h*). But again, to argue *a fortiori*, I'll say there is as much as an 80% probability that the letter of *1 Clement* would look like this if Jesus existed (which makes the odds 4 to 5), even though I think that's absurd.

6. *Ignatius of Antioch*

Tradition has it that in the reign of Trajan (98–117 CE) a prominent churchman, Ignatius of Antioch, was arrested by the Romans and taken to Caesar, over a long circuitous route from the Middle East to Rome, in which his Roman jailers (implausibly) allowed him to meet with other illegal Christian church congregations and write and exchange letters with yet more illegal Christian churches across the region as he went, all without arresting or disbanding any of them on the way.

Those letters survive. If tradition were correct about how they were produced, then this would be the next earliest datable Christian writing after *1 Clement* (outside the NT).[44] However, almost every single element of this

44. The *Epistle of Barnabas* (which assumes the historicity of Jesus) could conceivably date around this same time, but it has not been any more precisely dated than 70–130 CE, and in my opinion it surely dates to the period 130–132 CE. Barnabas 16.4 says the Jewish temple 'was pulled down by their enemies and now the very servants of their enemies shall build it up' again, which can only refer to Hadrian's construction of a pagan temple over its ruins (dedicated to Jupiter, Father of the Gods, a frequently assumed parallel to Yahweh), since otherwise at no time were pagans ever 'rebuilding the Jewish temple'. Hadrian actually started planning this shortly before the Bar Kokhba revolt in 132 (and in fact this plan was said to have caused that revolt: Cassius Dio, *Roman History* 69.12), and then he built it as planned after the revolt was put down in 135 CE. Barnabas seems to know of the plan but not its completion or the rebellion in between, so he was most likely writing between 130 and 132. What few

tradition has been challenged by modern scholars, many of whom do not believe Ignatius wrote these letters, or that they were written so early, or even in the circumstances assumed.[45] There are also several forged Ignatian letters, fabricated by someone who also rewrote the authentic ones by inserting a large number of interpolations into them, but that version of the Ignatians (combining the expanded and forged letters) is universally rejected as inauthentic. Here we are only concerned with the 'authentic' Ignatian letters, and those only in their shorter, more authentic versions.

Whether these letters were written by a man named 'Ignatius' or whether they were written around 110 CE or 160 CE or anywhere in between, even whether they describe an actual captivity or a metaphorical one, won't matter for our present purposes, so I will leave those questions aside. For the sake of arguing *a fortiori*, let's just assume the traditional account of them is correct.[46] Whether that's the case or not, they still have three features pertinent to determining how they affect the consequent probability of

things *Barnabas* says about Jesus are rarely specific and never sourced anyway—its content thus can't be ascertained as having any source independent of the Gospels or Christian tradition influenced by the Gospels. It could reflect an early example of historicist theology, but as such it is no less expected on myth as on historicity and thus makes no difference to their consequents.

45. See Timothy D. Barnes, 'The Date of Ignatius', *Expository Times* 120 (2008), pp. 119-30; Roger Parvus, *A New Look at the Letters of Ignatius of Antioch and Other Apellean Writings* (New York: iUniverse, 2008); L. Michael White, *From Jesus to Christianity* (San Francisco, CA: HarperSan Francisco, 2004), p. 346 (with n. 50 on p. 480). These (and other scholars they cite) date the 'middle recension' of the Ignatian letters to the 140s or 160s CE (everyone agrees the 'longer recension' dates to the fourth century and that the 'shorter recension' of a few of them, which we have in Syriac translation, is an abbreviation of the middle recension, despite some scholars once having argued those were the original versions). Even most other scholars now agree the original Ignatian letters could have been written anytime between 105 and 140 CE: see survey in Richard Pervo, *The Making of Paul: Constructions of the Apostle in Early Christianity* (Minneapolis, MN: Fortress Press, 2010), pp. 134-35 (esp. p. 329 nn. 130 and 135). Pervo himself dates them at the end of that range; entertaining similar thoughts (and citing additional scholarship on the subject): David Sim, 'Reconstructing the Social and Religious Milieu of Matthew: Methods, Sources, and Possible Results', in *Matthew, James, and Didache: Three Related Documents in their Jewish and Christian Settings* (ed. Huub van de Sandt and Jürgen Zangenberg; Atlanta, GA: Society of Biblical Literature, 2008), pp. 13-32 (17-18).

46. I do not include here the letter of Polycarp to the Philippians, which would more likely date to the mid-to-later second century, yet came to be included as a preface to the Ignatian letters. This letter doesn't in fact mention Ignatius or his letters until the penultimate section (§ 13), which many scholars believe to be an interpolation (and even if authentic, it only attests to some form of the letters existing and being revered a generation or two 'later'). There is also a supposed Ignatian letter to Polycarp, but it contains no information pertaining to the historical Jesus.

myth or historicity: (1) their author is very definitely, and very adamantly, a historicist; (2) their author is desperate to defend that fact against certain unnamed Christians who were apparently denying elements of it; and (3) these letters contain one key passage that looks more like it originated in a gospel about a cosmic Jesus than an earthly one, which a modern historicist will have to explain.

That a Christian writer of 110 CE would be a convinced historicist presents no challenge to minimal mythicism, since that theory entails such Christians certainly existed by then, already having had their own historicist Gospels for decades. And nothing in the letters of Ignatius can be shown to be independent of the Gospels, or to have any other source but the Gospels, except material that agrees as much (or more) with myth as historicity. What is peculiar is not that Ignatius is convinced of the historicity of Jesus, but that he is very concerned to insist upon this fact, against fellow Christians who were apparently denying some form of it. The existence of Christians denying the historicity of Jesus would be more expected on myth than historicity.[47] Of course, such Christians would have believed there really was a Jesus, but that he was only a cosmic actor, and not someone who conducted a ministry in Galilee or died on earth at the hands of Romans or Jews (see Chapter 3).

However, it is not certain that Ignatius is contending with such Christians. Ignatius insists that his fellow Christians 'stop their ears' from hearing alternative forms of the Christian gospel, such that:

> . . . when anyone speaks to you without the Jesus Christ who was descended from David, who was from Mary, who really was born, and ate and drank, and really was persecuted under Pontius Pilate, and really was crucified and died, as seen by those in heaven and on earth and under the earth. He was also truly raised from the dead.[48]

Because, he says, if these 'godless unbelievers' say that Jesus only 'seemed' to suffer, then Ignatius is living a lie, and dying for nothing.[49] (Note that this fallacy is his only argument in defense of the historicity of Jesus—he

47. In technical terms, the existence of mythicist Christians in the early second century is not guaranteed—those ideas could well have died out by then. It is only *more likely* that there would be such Christians if Jesus never existed than if he did. Because it is less likely Christians would later start to deny the reality of a Jesus who did exist. But conversely, less likely does not mean impossible: that some Christians would later start to deny the reality of a Jesus who did exist is *also* not guaranteed—that development could well have occurred, too. It's just *less likely* that a historical Jesus would spawn faithful deniers of his historicity than that a nonhistorical Jesus would. Thus the existence of such Christians is evidence for myth, but not thereby a proof of it.

48. Ignatius, *To the Trallians* 9. See also Ignatius, *To the Magnesians* 11, 18 and 20.

49. Ignatius, *To the Trallians* 10.

does not actually cite any evidence or source anywhere in his letters.) This appears to be an attack on Docetists, a diverse group of Christians who argued that Jesus never really became a man but only sent an illusion, and that it was this illusory body that was crucified (or at least, this is how their opponents represented their view, as we don't actually have any writings from the Docetists of this early period). But the word for 'seeming' (*dokeō*) can also mean 'was thought or imagined or pretended'. If these Christians were teaching that these things were allegories for what was really a cosmic drama (or that these things were only experienced in allegorical visions, as in the book of Revelation), then Ignatius's remarks would apply just as well. For example, if these things were presented in revelations that some might doubt (for example, if Paul saw Jesus 'taking bread and wine' in a vision and not in real life, as appears to be the case in 1 Cor. 11.23-26: see Chapter 11, §7), this could have been what the earliest Docetists were *really* claiming.

Whatever these other Christians were saying, Ignatius says against them that *real* Christians are:

> . . . fully persuaded when it comes to our Lord: that he really was descended from David 'according to the flesh', and the Son of God according to the will and power of God; that he really was born of a virgin, and baptized by John, in order that 'all righteousness might be fulfilled' by him; and that he really was nailed up under Pontius Pilate and Herod the Tetrarch on our behalf, in the flesh.[50]

In other words, he goes on to say, Jesus 'really suffered' and raised himself from the dead, and it is only 'certain unbelievers who maintain that he only "seemed" to suffer', just as 'they themselves only "seem" to be' Christians, and will thus not get their bodies back in the resurrection.[51]

It is this last point that reveals the reason Ignatius is so desperate to deny the Docetist thesis:

> For I know that even after his resurrection [Jesus] was in flesh, and I believe that he is so now. When, for instance, he came to those who were with Peter, he said to them, 'Lay hold, handle me, and see that I am not a bodiless demon'. And immediately they touched him, and believed, being convinced both by his flesh and by the spirit. And this is why they thought nothing of dying, and were found to be above death. After his resurrection he even ate and drank with them, as one of flesh, although spiritually he was united to the Father.[52]

50. Ignatius, *To the Smyrnaeans* 1.

51. Ignatius, *To the Smyrnaeans* 2 (see also §§ 4 and 5; and Ignatius, *To the Magnesians* 9).

52. Ignatius, *To the Smyrnaeans* 3.

Ignatius cannot abide the view (even though it appears to have been original to earliest Christianity) that our bodies of flesh will be discarded and replaced with entirely new bodies of cosmically superior material.[53] Willingness to die, and thus the glory of martyrdom, only makes sense to him if we will live again in the flesh (this thinking is evident as well in his letter to the Ephesians, as we saw). Thus Docetism, if true, would destroy everything Ignatius *needed* to be true.

Ignatius is therefore not rejecting Docetism because he knows of any evidence that argues against it. Apart from 'the prophets' his only source of information appears to be some Gospel or Gospels (possibly Matthew and Luke, or some other Gospel based on them that we don't have). Instead, he is rejecting Docetism simply and only because it has consequences he doesn't like. But this would have been equally true of the gospel of a cosmic Jesus, in which Jesus assumes a body of flesh in outer space and then discards it, rising again into a superior divine body, a gospel that would also be known only by revelation, and thus more easily doubted whether it was genuine.

Consequently, the very reason Ignatius has to hold onto his anti-Docetist mythology would have been as good a reason to invent that mythology in the first place. And that would have required relocating Jesus to earth and having him born and live and eat and drink and be touched by the first apostles (this development had other advantages as well, as I'll explore in §12). Historicity or not, this mythology had certainly been developed before Ignatius's time (complete with the fabricated story of Jesus appearing after his death and letting the disciples handle his body and dining with them to prove he is real, facts surely Paul would have made note of in 1 Corinthians 15 had any such story then existed, yet not even Matthew or Mark knew of it).[54] He is therefore not an independent source. He is simply relying on the Gospels for his information, and the most unreliable ones at that.

Unfortunately we cannot tell what manner of Docetists the Ignatians are attacking, whether a revelatory Docetism (teaching the events of Jesus' life were seen only in visions) or a historicist Docetism (teaching the events of Jesus' life were witnessed in the normal way, but were nevertheless illusions).[55] And that there would be *historicist* Docetists in the early

53. See 1 Corinthians 15 and 2 Corinthians 5, especially in light of my more extensive analysis in Carrier, 'Spiritual Body', in *Empty Tomb* (ed. Price and Lowder), and Carrier, *Not the Impossible Faith*, pp. 109-12. This two-body view of resurrection is also evident in the *Ascension of Isaiah*.

54. On this last point see my full analysis in Carrier, 'Spiritual Body', in *Empty Tomb* (ed. Price and Lowder), pp. 115-39.

55. An argument for revelatory Docetists is developed in Doherty, *Jesus: Neither God nor Man*, pp. 295-304.

second century is no more probable or improbable on historicity than on myth, given that this is in a period well after the Gospels had started circulating and Christians had begun to believe in a historical, earthly Jesus. Indeed, if *1 Clement* dates from the 60s and not the 90s, then we have no evidence that *any* Christian by the year 100 actually knew whether Jesus really existed or not, apart from what the Gospels claimed, which by then had been around for a whole generation. Once Jesus had been euhemerized or mythologized, a natural theological transformation of that mythology, like historicist Docetism, is not unexpected, whether Jesus ever really existed or not. At most, these letters demonstrate that there were by then no known sources of information about Jesus except the Gospels (whether ours or some others related to them), which confirms the futility of relying on any Christian writings after this period—even as early as 110 or 115 CE, if these letters really were written so early (though I doubt they were). So this information has no effect on the consequent probabilities.

But there is another peculiarity in Ignatius, one thing that doesn't fit. While scholars have had a hard time determining if he was really aware of or relying on any specific Gospel that we have (as opposed to some other based on them), there is one passage where Ignatius clearly references a narrative in a Gospel that he revered as an authoritative source, yet it is certainly not any Gospel we know. This is what he tells us:

> Now the virginity of Mary was hidden from the Prince of this World, as was also her offspring, and the death of the Lord; three mysteries of renown, which were wrought in silence by God. How, then, was he manifested to the world? A star shone forth in heaven above all the other stars, the light of which was inexpressible, while its novelty struck men with astonishment. And all the rest of the stars, with the sun and moon, formed a chorus to this star, and its light was exceedingly great above them all. And there was agitation felt as to whence this new spectacle came, so unlike everything else above. Hence every kind of magic was destroyed, and every bond of wickedness disappeared, ignorance was removed, and the old kingdom abolished, when God appeared in human form for the renewal of eternal life.[56]

Note that this is very definitely *not* a reference to the Gospel of Matthew. Ignatius does not appear to know Matthew's story about a nativity star. He

56. Ignatius, *To the Ephesians* 19. Note that 'appeared in human form' uses *phaneroumenos*, 'become visible', which means 'was seen' (in some way or other), and *anthrōpinōs*, 'humanly', an adverb, not a noun or adjective, which thus describes the verb, hence 'was humanly seen' or 'was seen humanly'. The meaning is either 'appeared to be a man' or 'appeared in a way perceptible to men'. Perhaps Ignatius meant 'in a human body', since he himself was so certain Jesus had such a body even after his resurrection. Or perhaps his source meant the alternative, and Ignatius was being deliberately ambiguous. It's not clear.

makes no reference to magi, nor any star rising in the east and settling over the manger, no Herod, no Bethlehem. And in Matthew the star is but a sign, not the Savior himself. Instead, Ignatius knows some very different story: one in which a star illuminates the whole of heaven, brighter even than the sun, astonishing men the world over, and in which this star was the manifestation of Jesus himself, and not a mere sign of his birth or birthplace.

In fact, this star is not said to accompany his birth. To the contrary, Ignatius appears to be saying this is how Jesus manifested to the world: not as a Galilean preacher but as a bright light in heaven. And at that moment all the powers of darkness were defeated and a new kingdom begun, feats traditionally accomplished by the *death* and *resurrection*, and not the *birth* of Jesus (see Elements 18 and 37). This 'Gospel' that Ignatius is describing has the very birth and death of Jesus being hidden from the world and revealed only in the bright light demonstrating his triumph (which could only be at his resurrection), and *that* was the event that granted men eternal life. Such a spectacle could hardly have been kept 'hidden' from the Prince of This World; it therefore must have followed and not preceded the death of Jesus. Also in this mysterious Gospel not only the virginity of Mary but even the identity of Jesus was also kept from both public and demonic knowledge until after his death—a fact that doesn't even fit the narrative of Mark, much less the other Gospels we know.

In the mythicist thesis, it was originally believed the Prince of This World killed Jesus not knowing who he was (1 Cor. 2.8), because everything about him was kept hidden (1 Cor. 2.7), and only revealed spiritually, by revelation to his elect (1 Cor. 2.10). Here that story has become transformed into a myth in which the revelation is accomplished by an incredible celestial event witnessed by the whole world—a claim obviously completely fabricated (illustrating how easy it then was to believe completely fabricated claims of wildly public facts). Notably, Paul's encounter with the risen Christ had been so described: Acts says Jesus appeared to him as 'a light from heaven brighter than the sun' (Acts 26.13).[57] And the Jewish theology of God's firstborn son (the preexistent Logos named Jesus: see Element 40) also pictured him as a supreme star that shines with a light brighter than the sun; though perceptible only to the eye of the mind, it was nevertheless 'surpassingly beautiful' and 'far more brilliant and splendid' than the sun or any other star in the universe, so overwhelmingly bright in fact that it would 'bewilder the eyes' of anyone so fortunate as to see it.[58]

Remember, too, the *Ascension of Isaiah* (Chapter 3, §1): there, in its earlier recension, Jesus will descend to the orbit below the moon, take on a

57. See also Lk. 1.78-79 (in light of the Septuagint text of Zech. 3.9); 1 Pet. 2.9; Heb. 1.3; Jn 1.4-5; etc.

58. Philo, *On the Creation* 31 (cf. §§ 30 and 71).

body of flesh, and be killed by the Prince of This World and his demonic minions 'without knowing who he is', because that fact is kept 'hidden from the heavens'. But when he rises from the dead and reveals who he really is, he shall be seen to have a 'glory surpassing that of all' and 'with the voice of Heaven' God will 'summon the angels and their lights'. Then who Jesus is will be manifest, and he will be victorious over the Prince of This World and his demonic minions. The Ignatian gospel sounds very similar: the birth and death of Jesus is kept hidden, then he is revealed with the most glorious light, and all the 'lights' of the heavens in chorus with it, at which he overpowers the forces of darkness.

Irenaeus also knew of such a narrative. He reports that even orthodox Christians were reading Psalm 24 as referring to Christ's hidden descent, unknown to the 'powers' in the 'firmament', and then his glorious ascent, after his resurrection, through the various 'gates' of heaven (odd details also found in the *Ascension of Isaiah*), which was seen and witnessed by all the creatures of the lower heavens.[59] Justin Martyr also appears to have known the same narrative.[60] Something similar might lie behind 1 Tim. 3.16, where Jesus is said to have been only 'seen by angels' and *then* people on earth were told about him. But just as the *Ascension of Isaiah* was doctored by inserting a standard historicist gospel narrative in the middle of it, we can presume the Gospel that Ignatius, Irenaeus and Justin were using had similarly been modified to tack-in the details involving Pontius Pilate, Herod the Tetrarch, and John the Baptist and other such elements. But like the *Ascension of Isaiah*, this clearly did not completely hide the fact that the original narrative was in accord with the earlier redaction of the *Ascension of Isaiah*, in which Jesus never dwells on earth, but is born and dies secretly in heaven, and then reveals himself *after* his resurrection, as a brilliant light surpassing all. This timing is also in accord with 1 Cor. 15.3-8, where again Jesus seems only to 'appear' to anyone *after* his resurrection (see Chapter 11, §2).

There are certainly other ways one could try to explain this strange Ignatian gospel narrative. But it must be admitted that it is at least *somewhat* more likely that we would see this here if the gospel he was using did indeed begin as a tale of a cosmic Jesus (just like the earlier redaction of the *Ascension of Isaiah*), and was converted into an earthly Jesus later on, if awkwardly. Because on any other explanation, its content makes no sense. That this strange cosmic gospel would be invented afterward (and Igna-

59. Irenaeus, *Demonstration of the Apostolic Preaching* 84. See discussion in Jonathan Knight, *Disciples of the Beloved One: The Christology, Social Setting and Theological Context of the Ascension of Isaiah* (Sheffield: Sheffield Academic Press, 1996), pp. 163-66.

60. Justin Martyr, *Dialogue with Trypho* 36.

tius still regard it as authoritative) is, by comparison, somewhat less likely. Thus this one passage affords some support for the mythicist thesis, which makes its content a bit more likely than minimal historicity does.[61] This odd detail therefore provides some small support to myth.

For Ignatius to cite stories about the manifestation of Jesus that match the mythicist thesis and not the historicist one is at least *somewhat* less probable on *h* than on ¬*h*. For ¬*h* it is 100% expected that such narratives existed, although not that any evidence of them would survive for us to see them now (since the low probability of their survival has no significant effect on whether ¬*h* is true).[62] To be honest, the very existence of such narratives at all is improbable on *h*, but not at all improbable on ¬*h*. So we should combine this fact now with the similar facts attested in the *Ascension of Isaiah* (surveyed in Chapter 3, §1), which also has (even clearer) traces of an earlier, similar narrative of a cosmic Jesus suffering a cosmic death. Neither is expected to exist on *h*; but on ¬*h*, there is nothing unexpected about either. Here I will be very generous and say the odds are 4 to 5 that we would still have both (the curious cosmic Jesus material in Ignatius, and the curious cosmic Jesus material in the *Ascension of Isaiah*; and their corroboration in Irenaeus and Justin) if *h* were true rather than ¬*h*, which can be translated into a 100% chance on ¬*h* and an 80% chance on *h*. Though I personally believe these odds are closer to 1 in 2, as I think there could hardly be more than a 50% chance both these clues would exist if Jesus did.

7. *Papias of Hierapolis*

According to Irenaeus (who most likely wrote between 180 and 200 CE), Papias of Hierapolis was a companion of Polycarp, and wrote when he was an old man.[63] According to Eusebius, Polycarp died in the 160s CE at the age

61. And any attempt to make minimal historicity more complex (so as to better explain the strange content of this passage) will reduce its relative prior probability, thus making no effective difference in the effect this evidence has on its posterior probability—unless the required additions to the theory can be shown to be (very probably) true if Jesus existed, independently of their ability to explain this one text. See Carrier, *Proving History*, pp. 80-81.

62. On the contingency of evidence survival and its effect on consequent probabilities see Carrier, *Proving History*, pp. 220-26.

63. For these and following details see Irenaeus, *Against All Heresies* 5.33.4; and Eusebius, *History of the Church* 3.39.1-2 and 4.14-15. The passage in Irenaeus survives only in Latin translation and in Greek quotation in Eusebius, but in both it is stated that he 'bore witness in writing as an old man' (*vetus homo per scripturam testimonium perhibet* / *archaios anēr eggreaphōs epimarturei*). This is sometimes translated as 'a man of old', i.e. of a long time ago, but that is the least likely intended meaning here:

of eighty-six, having been a Christian all his life. If we assume this is all true, then Polycarp would have been an elder in the church since the 130s, and Papias himself would have been an 'old man' sometime between then and the 160s. Thus his one known book, *Explanations of the Stories of the Lord* (in five volumes), is usually (and most plausibly) dated between 130 and 150 CE.[64]

We do not have that book. We only have various brief quotations from and descriptions of it (mainly in Irenaeus and Eusebius), in which Papias himself says he lived when none of the original apostles still did, but contemporary with some men who claimed to have known them—a claim that was not necessarily true; from the quotations we have, we can tell Papias was a very gullible fellow, so much so that even Eusebius called him 'a man of very little intelligence'.[65] Papias also said he rejected what books said and instead relied only on hearsay, because he considered that to be more reliable.[66] He was thus clearly the least reliable sort of source we could possibly want. Yet apart from the author of Acts, Papias is the earliest 'historian' of early Christianity we have, writing a hundred years after the religion began.

As expected, the things he tells us are ridiculous. For instance, one excerpt we have (from the fourth volume of Papias's book, as quoted by Apollinaris of Laodicea in the fourth century) tells us this story about Judas:

> His body bloated to such an extent that, even where a wagon passes with ease, he was not able to pass. No, not even his bloated head by itself could do so. His eyelids, for example, swelled to such dimensions, they say, that neither could he himself see the light at all, nor could his eyes be detected even by a physician's instrument, so deep had they sunk below

(1) Irenaeus would just say he wrote long ago, not that he was an 'old man', a phrase that more readily indicates the man himself was old, not his writings; and (2) a friend of Polycarp's would more likely be a contemporary of Polycarp, and thus have lived a generation before Irenaeus, as Polycarp did (hardly ancient times).

64. Eusebius, *History of the Church* 3.39.1: *Logiōn kuriakōn exēgēseōs*, lit. 'Exegesis of the Lordly Logia'. Some scholars really want Papias to have written earlier, perhaps in the reign of Trajan (c. 110–115 CE), but if that were so (as we shall see) this would make his testimony worse for historicity, as it would mean that the loss of knowledge about Jesus, and the growth of absurd fictions about him, was even earlier and more rapid, and that even at that early date no one knew any correct information about the Gospels or how they came to be written. Nevertheless, for the best attempt to date Papias to around 110 CE, see Dennis MacDonald, *Two Shipwrecked Gospels: The Logoi of Jesus and Papias's Exposition of Logia about the Lord* (Atlanta, GA: Society of Biblical Literature, 2012).

65. Eusebius, *History of the Church* 3.39.13.

66. Eusebius, *History of the Church* 3.39.3-4.

> the surface. His genitals, too, grew bigger and more disgusting than all that is horrid, and, to his shame, out of them oozed pus and worms from all throughout his body whenever he relieved himself. After suffering an agony of pain and punishment, he finally went, as they say, to his own place. And owing to the stench the ground has been deserted and uninhabited until now. In fact, even to the present day no one can pass that place without holding one's nose, so abundant was the discharge from his body and so far over the ground did it spread.[67]

Papias also said Jesus promised us vast clusters of gigantic grapes, and other nonsense. Clearly the legends and fabricated sayings had gotten out of hand by the time Papias wrote, and he just believed whatever he chanced to hear. This is illustrative of the state of Christian knowledge about Jesus by mid-second century—and the state of Christian fabrications about Jesus.

Does Papias come anywhere near to telling us anything useful? Not really. He says Mark was Peter's secretary and faithfully recorded his teachings (producing the Gospel according to Mark), but that can't be true because Peter was a Torah-observant Christian, and Mark's Gospel advocates against that and in favor of Pauline Christianity (that Paul and Peter were at odds on this point is clear throughout Galatians 2; see Element 20). Mark's Gospel also evinces possibly a poor understanding of the geography of Palestine (e.g. Mk 7.31 has Jesus simultaneously traveling north and south), which also makes no sense if he was faithfully recording the teachings of Peter.[68] That Mark composed his Gospel in Greek also makes less sense on that account, as Peter would more likely have preached in Hebrew or Aramaic and expected his Gospel to be recorded likewise (unless Peter preached only to Greek-speaking diaspora Jews, but even then his Gospel would not need to explain basic Jewish legal principles to its readers, e.g., Mk 7.3-4). Papias then says Matthew was composed in Hebrew and then translated various times into Greek, but that also can't be true, because Matthew copies extensively from Mark's Greek, frequently verbatim, and thus can't possibly have composed in Hebrew.[69] It's clear that Papias had

67. Quotation of Papias in Apollinaris of Laodicea, *Comments on Matthew* 136 (regarding Mt. 27.5). Most of this translation is from Bruce Metzger, *The Canon of the New Testament: Its Origin, Development, and Significance* (Oxford: Clarendon Press, 1987), p. 53 n. 23, but he omitted some material, which I restored, translating it myself from the original Greek.

68. On the (often poor or confused) geographical knowledge of the four Gospels, and the attempted (and sometimes failed) 'fixes' of Mark by Matthew, see C.C. McCown, 'Gospel Geography: Fiction, Fact, and Truth', *Journal of Biblical Literature* 60 (March 1941), pp. 1-25, although much research since has revised his results.

69. And if Matthew employed a Q source for the remaining material shared with Luke (see Chapter 7, §4), he also copied *that* verbatim in Greek (because Luke then also copied from Q, and often shows identical wording, so Q itself, or the version they

no idea what he was talking about, and had no reliable sources of information about the first century of Christianity. Correct information about that century of the church had evidently become completely lost by his time. It therefore can't likely have survived after his time, either. Which means everything claimed about that period after this point is most likely fabricated.

It is also curious that these five volumes of Papias were not preserved by medieval Christians. Such an early and extensive collection of contemporary lore about Jesus and the Gospels and apostles as this should have been cherished. What else must it have said to so offend medieval Christians that they threw the whole thing away? We'll never really know. What we can say is that from what we do know, nothing in Papias supports the historicity of Jesus. It confirms only that in the second century many Christians were assuming the historicity of Jesus, and were relying on written Gospels for that, and felt at liberty to invent any stories about him that suited them, while some were even claiming to have known someone who knew Jesus, to lend authority to whatever they invented about him.[70] This is fully expected on the Jesus myth theory, and perhaps no less expected on historicity. So Papias has no effect on the consequent probability of either.

8. *Hegesippus*

Near the end of the second century (c. 180 CE) the Christian scholar Hegesippus wrote a five-volume *Memoirs* that discussed various legends about the early churches and apostles (including the first succession lists of bishops), making this the third closest thing to a history of Christianity that existed up to then (the second being the *Explanations* of Papias, which we discussed above, and the first being the book of Acts, which we shall dis-

employed, must have been in Greek). That's moot, of course, if there was no Q and Luke just copied Matthew's Greek.

70. That these claims were false should be obvious (because we just saw the stories they were telling are unbelievable); in the same fashion, some were also claiming to have known those who had been the very people resurrected by Jesus (just as some Jews claimed to be descendants of those resurrected in Ezek. 37.1-14, even while other, more reasonable Jews, insisted that that story was just an allegory and never really happened: Babylonian Talmud, *Sanhedrin* 92b; cf. also 90b). Philip of Side reports that Papias had said, 'those resurrected by Christ from the dead lived until Hadrian', which was also claimed by Quadratus (so possibly Philip has confused them), according to Eusebius, *History of the Church* 4.3; on Philip's report, see James Kleist, *The Didache, The Epistle of Barnabas, The Epistles and The Martyrdom of St. Polycarp, The Fragments of Papias, The Epistle to Diognetus* (Westminster, MD: Newman Press, 1948), pp. 122-23.

cuss in the next chapter).[71] Once again, we do not have this book. We only have scattered references to and quotations from it. Again, why was such a valuable work not preserved? We may never know.

This work is so very late, and written in a period of such rampant fabrication and hearsay (see Element 44), that it cannot have any claim to reliability on the matter of first-century Christianity. Nevertheless, I discuss it because (a) it is the last known attempt at collecting historical data about first-century Christianity that we know of from the second century, (b) it discusses the fate of 'James the brother of Jesus', and (c) it is representative of all the Christian 'historical' literature we have any fragment of from the second century, and thus our conclusions regarding it can be understood as applicable to all.

The most important passages to survive from Hegesippus involve tales about the family of Jesus. But they are so obviously fictional we can place no value in them as history. Of these, the following story about James is the most extensive we have, and it reads just like any of several examples of fabricated 'Acts' (such as we have telling wild tales about Peter and John):

> Hegesippus, who lived immediately after the apostles, gives the most accurate account in the fifth book of his *Memoirs*. He writes as follows:
>
> James, the brother of the Lord, succeeded to the government of the Church in conjunction with the apostles. He has been called the Just by all from the time of our Savior to the present day; for there were many that bore the name of James. He was holy from his mother's womb; and he drank no wine nor strong drink, nor did he eat flesh. No razor came upon his head; he did not anoint himself with oil, and he did not use the bath. He alone was permitted to enter into the holy place; for he wore not woolen but linen garments. And he was in the habit of entering alone into the temple, and was frequently found upon his knees begging forgiveness for the people, so that his knees became hard like those of a camel, in consequence of his constantly bending them in his worship of God, and asking forgiveness for the people. Because of his exceeding great justice he was called the Just, and Oblias, which signifies in Greek, 'Bulwark of the People' [*actually, no such word exists in Greek—ed.*], and Justice, in accordance with what the prophets declare concerning him.
>
> Now some persons belonging to the seven [Jewish] sects existing among the people, which have been before described by me in these *Memoirs*, asked James: 'What is the door of Jesus?' And he replied that He was the Savior. In consequence of this answer, some believed

71. '[Hegesippus] records in five books the true tradition of apostolic doctrine', Eusebius, *History of the Church* 4.8, which passage, plus 4.11 and 4.21-22, are all we really have to date the man by, their content indicating that Hegesippus may have been alive in 130 CE (when Hadrian deified Antinous) but wrote after 174 (that being the year of the last datable event mentioned in the 'memoirs' of Hegesippus).

that Jesus is the Christ. But the sects before mentioned did not believe, either in a resurrection or in the coming of one to requite every man according to his works; but those who did believe, believed because of James. So, when many even of the ruling class believed, there was a commotion among the Jews, and scribes, and Pharisees, who said: 'A little more, and we shall have all the people looking for Jesus as the Christ'.

They came, therefore, in a body to James, and said: 'We entreat you, restrain the people: for they are gone astray in their opinions about Jesus, as if he were the Christ. We entreat you to persuade all who have come here for the day of the Passover, concerning Jesus. For we all listen to you; since we, as well as all the people, bear you testimony that you are just, and show partiality to none. Therefore, persuade the people not to entertain erroneous opinions concerning Jesus: for all the people, and we also, listen to you. Take your stand, then, upon the summit of the temple, that from that elevated spot you may be clearly seen, and your words may be plainly audible to all the people. For, in order to attend the Passover, all the tribes have congregated here, and some of the Gentiles also.'

The aforesaid scribes and Pharisees accordingly set James on the summit of the temple, and cried aloud to him, and said: 'O just one, whom we are all bound to obey, forasmuch as the people are in error, and follow Jesus the crucified, do tell us what is the door of Jesus the crucified'. And he answered with a loud voice: 'Why ask me concerning Jesus the Son of Man? He Himself sits in heaven, at the right hand of the Great Power, and shall come on the clouds of heaven.'

And, when many were fully convinced by these words, and offered praise for the testimony of James, and said, 'Hosanna to the son of David', then again the Pharisees and scribes said to one another, 'We have not done well in procuring this testimony to Jesus. But let us go up and throw him down, that they may be afraid, and not believe him.' And they cried aloud, and said: 'Oh! Oh! The just man himself is in error.' Thus they fulfilled the Scripture written in Isaiah: 'Let us away with the just man, because he is troublesome to us: therefore shall they eat the fruit of their doings'. So they went up and threw down the just man, and said to one another: 'Let us stone James the Just'. And they began to stone him: for he was not killed by the fall; but he turned, and kneeled down, and said: 'I beseech Thee, Lord God our Father, forgive them; for they know not what they do'.

And, while they were thus stoning him to death, one of the priests, the sons of Rechab, the son of Rechabim, to whom testimony is born by Jeremiah the prophet, began to cry aloud, saying: 'Stop! What are you doing!? The just man is praying for us.' But one among them, one of the fullers, took the staff with which he was accustomed to wring out the garments he dyed, and hurled it at the head of the just man.

And so he suffered martyrdom; and they buried him on the spot, and the pillar erected to his memory still remains, close by the temple. This

> man was a true witness to both Jews and Greeks that Jesus is the Christ. And immediately Vespasian besieged them.[72]

The historical and narrative implausibilities in this tale are so numerous we can be certain the story is in every respect a fabrication. The description of James is transparently mythical; the notion that 'he alone' was allowed into the temple's inner sanctum is obvious nonsense; that the Jewish authorities would have a Christian evangelist stand at the pinnacle of the temple to *dissuade* the crowds from adopting his teachings is obvious myth; and that James could survive a fall from there is impossible; in fact, the behavior of almost everyone in the whole narrative is not at all realistic (a major hallmark of fiction); the execution of James as described is in no way legal (and would thus have been murder under Jewish law); and a burial not only inside the city walls but beside the very temple itself is not only a guaranteed falsehood, it betrays the complete ignorance of the narrative's author of even the most basic facts of Jerusalem law and culture. In short, nothing in this story can possibly be true.

But what is notable is that nowhere in the story itself is this James ever said to be the brother of Jesus. Hegesippus describes him as such when introducing the narrative, but the assumption that this story, about a certain James the Just, is a story about James the brother of Jesus, appears to be an assumption introduced by Hegesippus. It is not supported by anything in the story. Indeed, this James is described as if he were a priest (doing service in the temple and even entering the Holy of Holies), not a carpenter or fisherman from distant Galilee. There is also no reference to a historical Jesus in this narrative. Jesus is called 'the crucified', but Jesus was celestially crucified on minimal mythicism, so that does not distinguish this narrative as historicist. To the contrary, nowhere is any reference made to witnesses or reports of Jesus having performed deeds or delivering teachings while on earth, or having even been on earth. Instead, James speaks only of a Jesus in outer space, who would descend to earth *in the future*. And the story assumes that no one thought Jesus was the Christ until James (not Jesus, nor anyone else) began preaching that he was. And this led to people *looking for* Jesus and *following* him—obviously that cannot mean following the living Jesus (who in this narrative was not then on earth), but the celestial Jesus declared by James.

The controversy at the heart of this narrative also centers around the bizarre question, 'What is the door of Jesus?' The answer to which was that 'he is the Savior' (the name 'Jesus' of course meaning 'savior'), implying that confessing Jesus is the Christ is the doorway to eternal life. The theo-

72. Eusebius, *History of the Church* 2.23.4-18. Translation adapted from *NPNF*², I, 207-208.

logical point may have had something to do with Jesus being the celestial high priest, who controlled access to the doors of heaven (which even some pre-Christian Jews might already have believed: Element 40). For example, Ignatius says Jesus 'is the door of the Father, by which enter' the holy and faithful into heaven, and that he had this power because he was given the secrets of God and controlled the Holy of Holies—which must mean that of the celestial temple, there being no other when Ignatius wrote.[73]

The material about James in Hegesippus confirms our conclusion from Papias, that true historical information about the early church no longer existed and had been replaced with absurd fabrications like this, which were believed without any doubt or question by such authors as this. But this narrative also joins the early redaction of the *Ascension of Isaiah* and the Star Narrative of Ignatius in further support of the hypothesis that there had been a sect of Christians who did not believe in a Galilean Jesus but only a cosmically crucified one, and that these Christians had their own tales and narratives, which other Christians could borrow and adapt to their own purposes. From such a sect we can expect this tale to lack any reference to a historical Jesus, most especially any reference to this James being his brother, despite it going on a great deal about his qualifications as a witness in being superlatively pious and just—conspicuously omitting from that list of qualifications his family connection and eyewitness status. These appear to have been unknown to the story's original author.

Such a complete absence of the historical Jesus in this James narrative could perhaps be explained away as just a happenstance omission, assuming that the author who made it all up just didn't think or see the need of including any such detail, or perhaps already having included it in sections not quoted by Hegesippus. But such an omission also fits minimal mythicism even more perfectly. Whereas the historicist's explanation requires positing something that is less than 100% certain to be the case, the mythicist's explanation does not require positing anything (beyond minimal mythicism itself, and established background knowledge, including Elements 21-22 and 44). This means this narrative in Hegesippus supports mythicism over historicity, at least slightly. I will be as generous to historicity as I can and posit a 90% chance a historicist author could compose the narrative as we have it, against a 100% chance that a mythicist could, for 9/10 odds. Although I believe 4 in 5 is closer to the truth (meaning an 80% chance a historicist author could compose the narrative like this).

Hegesippus recorded at least one other apocryphal tale about the family of Jesus, which can confirm neither historicity nor myth: the story that the grandchildren of his brother Jude (whom only 'some said' had been the

73. Ignatius, *Philadelphians* 9. Other references to Jesus being 'the door' or 'the gate' can be found in Jn 10.6-19 and *1 Clement* 48 (based on Ps. 117.19-20).

brother of Jesus) were hauled into the court of Domitian (in the 80s or 90s CE), because Domitian was afraid of the Second Coming of Christ (historically, a wholly implausible motive) and had commanded that all Davidic heirs be slain (even though the very notion that anyone thought there would be Davidic heirs to slay by then is not believable).[74] This story contains a number of implausibilities and does not look like anything we would credit as true. It also looks like it wasn't originally a story about Christians, but messianic Jews. In the core of the tale itself, no Jesus is ever mentioned, and the 'Judeans' hauled into court are never said to be anything but Jews expecting a messiah to come at the end of the world. This had apparently been converted into a story about Domitian persecuting, and then ending the persecution, of Christians. But from other sources we know only of Domitian persecuting Jews, and only those in his own household.[75]

Whatever the case may be, Hegesippus tips his hand when we learn from Eusebius that he told all these narratives in order to 'prove' that there had been no heresy before the reign of Trajan, because up until then the family of Jesus and his disciples had everywhere ensured a faithful adherence to the 'virgin' gospel, and only after they had passed away did false sects arise.[76] Such a fantasy is not only certainly false (the Epistles of Paul already attest to numerous schisms, including his own, and there had surely been countless further splits all through the first century), it is also an obvious motive for inventing tales of family and eyewitnesses to Jesus.[77] And from the details we find in the stories he told, we can tell they are unbelievable. Nor is any source given for them. So no reliable support for historicity can be had here. The probability of there being such tales is the same on either theory.

74. Eusebius, *History of the Church* 3.19-20 (Eusebius wrote in the early fourth century). Vespasian is supposed to have slain all the Davidic heirs already (3.12), which is almost as implausible; 3.11 also mentions the family of Jesus, with details that might derive from Hegesippus, such as that the Gospel figure of Clopas was the brother of the Joseph who was the father of Jesus; nothing is said of how Hegesippus would have known this—probably it is just an interpretation of Jn 19.25, which itself is probably fabricated. It's possible, as well, that the entire succession narrative Eusebius surveys came from Hegesippus, indeed much of it could be the latter's own invention (cf., e.g., Eusebius, *History of the Church* 3.32), the same way rabbinical authors invented haggadah for the various persons named in the OT; here, Hegesippus was composing haggadah for the persons named in the Gospels.

75. Suetonius, *Domitian* 10; and Dio Cassius, *Roman History* 67.14 (both authors certainly knew the difference between Christians and Jews). It was only later Christian legend that converted this event into a persecution of Christians. See Carrier, *Not the Impossible Faith*, p. 154.

76. Eusebius, *History of the Church* 3.32.

77. Confirming the Noll thesis (see §12).

9. *Josephus and the Testimonia Flaviana*

There are two passages in the *Jewish Antiquities* (or *Ant.*) of Josephus, originally published shortly after 93 CE, that (in the present text we have) mention Jesus Christ as a historical person.[78] However, both are almost certainly interpolations made by Christian scribes.[79] In fact Josephus never mentioned Jesus Christ or Christians. We can therefore exclude these passages from our evidence. This is a somewhat controversial conclusion, so I will summarize the very reasonable basis for it.

The first passage in question is called the *Testimonium Flavianum* (TF). It now reads as follows:

> And there was about this time Jesus, a wise man, if we really must call him a man, for he was a doer of incredible deeds, a teacher of men who receive the truth gladly, and he won over many Jews, and also many of the Greeks. This man was the Christ. And when, on the accusation of the leading men among us, Pilate had condemned him to a cross, those who had first loved him did not cease to. For he appeared to them on the third day, alive again, the divine prophets having spoken these and countless other marvels about him. And even until now the tribe of the Christians, so named from this man, has not failed.[80]

Of course, even at a glance anyone can see this would be an absurd paragraph from the hand of a devout Jew and sophisticated author who otherwise writes far more elegant prose, and usually responsibly explains to his readers anything strange. This passage is self-evidently a fawning and gullible Christian fabrication, in fact demonstrably derived from the Emmaus narrative in the Gospel of Luke, inserted into the text at a point where it does not even make any narrative sense, apart from being in a survey of the crimes of Pontius Pilate that contributed (in the long run) to inciting

78. The year the *Antiquities* was published can be inferred from remarks in *Ant.* 20.267.

79. I demonstrate this conclusively in Richard Carrier, 'Origen, Eusebius, and the Accidental Interpolation in Josephus, *Jewish Antiquities* 20.200', *Journal of Early Christian Studies* 20.4 (Winter 2012), pp. 489-54. For another extensive critical discussion see Doherty, *Jesus: Neither God nor Man*, pp. 533-86. For a crucial and extensive survey of scholarship examining these passages see James Carleton Paget, 'Some Observations on Josephus and Christianity', *Journal of Theological Studies* 52.2 (October 2001), pp. 539-624 (most of which treats the longer passage; pp. 546-54 treats the shorter passage); with Alice Whealey, *Josephus on Jesus: The Testimonium Flavianum Controversy from Late Antiquity to Modern Times* (New York: P. Lang, 2003); Van Voorst, *Jesus Outside the New Testament*, pp. 81-104; and Theissen and Merz, *The Historical Jesus*, pp. 64-74.

80. Josephus, *Ant.* 18.63-64.

the Jews to war.[81] There is no plausible way the above narrative fits that context: the Christians are not being connected with the war in any such way, and the Jewish elite are not outraged by the execution of Jesus but in fact endorse it.

Historians have tried to rescue this passage by 'rewriting' it, removing everything that Josephus would surely never say, and then claiming he surely said what's left and Christians just changed it up. But this is such an extraordinarily improbable thesis it must be rejected outright. For example, Josephus must have mentioned 'Christ' because he presumes it when he explains the name 'Christian' in the last line, but there is no plausible way Josephus would say this (or even 'he was believed to be the Christ', as some later quotations have it) without explaining to his intended Gentile

81. This paragraph is so heavily indebted to the Gospel of Luke we can be certain that that is its source: G.J. Goldberg, 'The Coincidences of the Testimonium of Josephus and the Emmaus Narrative of Luke', *Journal for the Study of the Pseudepigrapha* 13 (1995), pp. 59-77. Goldberg demonstrates nineteen unique correspondences between Luke's Emmaus account and the Testimonium Flavianum, all nineteen in exactly the same order (with some order and word variations only *within* each item). There are some narrative differences (which are expected due to the contexts being different and as a result of common kinds of authorial embellishment), and there is a twentieth correspondence out of order (identifying Jesus as 'the Christ'). But otherwise, the coincidences here are very improbable on any other hypothesis than dependence. Goldberg also shows that the Testimonium contains vocabulary and phrasing that is particularly Christian (indeed, Lukan) and un-Josephan. He concludes that this means either a Christian wrote it or Josephus slavishly copied a Christian source, and the latter is wholly implausible (Josephus would treat such a source more critically, creatively and informedly). Supporting the un-Josephan character of the language and phrasing of this paragraph is Ken Olson, 'Eusebius and the Testimonium Flavianum', *Catholic Biblical Quarterly* 61.2 (April 1999), pp. 305-22; whose conclusions are only tempered a bit by Paget, 'Some Observations', pp. 572-78; and Alice Whealey, 'Josephus, Eusebius of Caesarea, and the Testimonium Flavianum', in *Josephus und das Neue Testament: wechselseitige Wahrnehmungen* (ed. Christfried Böttrich and Jens Herzer; Tübingen: Mohr Siebeck, 2007), pp. 73-116. Although I remain undecided, Olson has made an increasingly strong case that Eusebius is the forger of the TF, and even famed Josephus expert Louis Feldman agrees that's plausible: see Ken Olson, 'A Eusebian Reading of the Testimonium Flavianum', in *Eusebius of Caesarea: Tradition and Innovations* (ed. Aaron Johnson and Jeremy Schott; Cambridge, MA: Harvard University Press, 2013), pp. 97-114; and Louis Feldman, 'On the Authenticity of the Testimonium Flavianum Attributed to Josephus', in *New Perspectives on Jewish Christian Relations* (ed. Elisheva Carlebach and Jacob Schechter; Leiden: Brill, 2012), pp. 14-30. In fact, the most common arguments for its authenticity are actually among the best arguments for Eusebian forgery: see Ken Olson, 'The Testimonium Flavianum, Eusebius, and Consensus', *Historical Jesus Research* (August 13, 2013) at http://historicaljesusresearch.blogspot.com/2013/08/the-testimonium-flavianum-eusebius-and.html.

readers what a 'Christ' was and what it meant for Jesus to have been one, and thus why Josephus is mentioning it or how Jesus even came to acquire the moniker.[82] So we can strike those two sentences. Josephus cannot have written them. He also would not have written such fawningly unintelligible things as 'if we really must call him a man' or 'doer of incredible deeds' or 'teacher . . . of the truth' without explaining to his Gentile readers what he meant—or giving examples, as Josephus normally would. So those sentences must be struck. He cannot have written them. Nor would Josephus say things like 'he won over' many Jews and Greeks, without explaining exactly *to what* he won them over—and thus what defined someone as a Christian, what doctrines they held. Josephus does this for every other sect he discusses (such as the Sadducees, Pharisees, Essenes, and, under the rubric of 'the fourth philosophy', the Zealots). So he certainly would do so here, the more so as his remarks would be unfathomable to most of his readers without that explanation. So we can strike that sentence. He cannot have written it.

Nor would Josephus give his readers a mysteriously truncated summary of what can only mean the Gospel story of 'leading men' accusing Jesus and getting him executed—without explaining what any of that meant. What leading men? What accusations? Why? Why did Pilate accede to them? Was Jesus guilty? Why did Pilate conclude he was? Why didn't the Jews execute Jesus themselves? And if he was such a wonderful, truth-telling, miracle-working wise man whom many loved, how did he end up being convicted of a capital crime? The failure to explain these things makes the paragraph intolerably maddening to any reader, and would have been likewise to Josephus. He could not possibly have written this. So that sentence must go.

Likewise why does Josephus mention Jesus 'appearing' on 'the third day', which is a Christian credal statement that Josephus would not possibly employ without explaining why, or what he thought this meant—did Jesus escape his execution? Was he therefore a fugitive on the run? What happened to him after this? Or did he appear in a dream or as a phantom? Or was he resurrected from the dead, a concept Josephus explains several times elsewhere in his work, so surely he would make a point of it here, if this is what he meant (or thought his source meant). So he cannot have written this, either. And surely it is absurd to think Josephus *agreed* (much less would just so casually say) that Jesus fulfilled biblical prophecy—at all, much less in these specific details (as well as 'countless others'), as this passage says. So he certainly did not write that sentence, either. That leaves us with only one sentence left over: 'and there was about this time Jesus, a

82. That the *Antiquities* was written specifically for a Gentile audience: Josephus, *Ant.* 1.pr.5-10.

wise man'. After which no story follows. We can conclude Josephus didn't write this, either. He discusses several men named Jesus throughout his works, so he would certainly either identify this one (as we'll see, e.g., he identifies another Jesus as 'the son of Damneus'), or explain why he is suddenly interrupting his narrative to talk about this one. Otherwise this transition is simply too abrupt and bizarre for Josephus.

All these improbable sentences stack up to an enormous improbability that Josephus wrote any of this. And that's just from examining its content alone.[83] The paragraph is simply unsalvageable. Nor should anyone desire to salvage it. It is obviously much too brief and much too obviously a simplistic Christian production based on the Gospel of Luke. Moreover, no other author had ever heard of this passage until Eusebius in the fourth century—not even Origen, who otherwise cites and quotes Josephus several times, so surely Origin would have mentioned this passage had it existed in his copy of the *Antiquities*. The probability of his silence is very low otherwise, and that probability reduces even further when we consider the silence of every other Christian and pagan author, even if (and even collectively) their silence is not as improbable as Origen's.[84]

Considering just Origen alone, there are several passages where it's almost certain he would have remarked upon this paragraph, even quoted it, had he known of it. For example, in his treatise *Against Celsus* Origen is tasked with proving there was any near-contemporary attestation to the affairs of Jesus.[85] Yet all he can present in said proof are passages in Josephus attesting John the Baptist and (supposedly) James (see below).[86] Likewise, at many other turns in his contest with Celsus, Origen would surely have had irresistible use of the fact that this same Josephus attested to the ministry of Jesus, declared him wise (and thus did not think him a charlatan, as Celsus persistently argues), corroborated his resurrection on the third day (a fact Celsus insists only Christians affirm), and confirmed that he fulfilled prophecy (a major point Origen struggles to establish, and for which the agreement of a Jew would have been priceless).

All attempts to explain away Origen's silence require adopting one or more *ad hoc* hypotheses for which there is no evidence, such as that Josephus had written something wildly different, which the TF then replaced; or are illogical—for instance, even if an original TF had treated Christians negatively, that would even more have demanded a response, not less so, as

83. On this general point see Paget, 'Some Observations', pp. 581-603 and 606-19.

84. That no writer before Eusebius references it, Origen most conspicuously: Paget, 'Some Observations', pp. 555-65; and Whealey, *Josephus on Jesus*, pp. 6-18.

85. This is the very task he sets forth in Origen, *Against Celsus* 1.42, in response to the several challenges made by Celsus as noted in *Against Celsus* 1.37-41.

86. Origen, *Against Celsus* 1.47.

the last thing Origen could allow is Celsus (or any other critic) citing Josephus, the very source whose authority Origen praises, against him, without a preemptive apologetic. So the silence of Origen is simply very improbable unless there was no TF at all. The silence of all the rest of Christian and anti-Christian literature only adds to that improbability. And the obvious improbability of the content of every single sentence (as just surveyed) adds even more. So we are already looking at an extremely low probability that this passage, or anything even remotely like it, existed in the original *Antiquities*.

And yet there are two more reasons that are even more decisive, sinking this probability well toward impossibility: (1) since the very next paragraph begins 'about the same time also another terrible thing threw the Jews into disorder' (*Ant.* 18.65), Josephus clearly had just ended with the sedition resulting in a public massacre (described in *Ant.* 18.60-62), leaving no logical place for the unrelated digression on Jesus and the Christians (in *Ant.* 18.63-64)—the *original* text obviously went directly from the massacre to the following scandal, with no digression in between; and (2) the fact that his very next story, also about a religious controversy (involving Judaism and Isis cult), is told at great and elaborate length (in *Ant.* 18.65-80, a narrative eight times longer than the TF, and yet on a much more trivial affair). The latter demonstrates that Josephus would have written a great deal more about the Jesus affair if he had written anything about it at all, whereas a forger would have been limited by what may have then been the remaining space available on a standard scroll for volume 18 (or by the space available in the margin, if that is where the passage began its life), hence explaining its bizarre brevity, in comparison with the preceding and following narratives, and in light of its astonishing content, which normally, as I've noted, would require several explanations and digressions which are curiously absent. I believe these two facts alone combine to argue conclusively that there cannot have been here any reference to Jesus in the original *Antiquities*, even one differently worded than we now have. When combined with the preceding considerations, the overall probability of any other conclusion approaches zero.

It is sometimes claimed that we have an Arabic version of this passage that comes from an earlier manuscript of Josephus than is quoted by Eusebius, and its content is closer to what a Jewish author might write, and therefore this 'confirms' Josephus wrote something close to the TF after all. However, it has since been proved that this Arabic quotation is of a Syriac quotation of a manuscript of Eusebius, and thus represents a text that does not precede Eusebius *but derives from him*.[87] Its content was simply altered

87. See Paget, 'Some Observations', pp. 554-624 (and pp. 568-71 for further reasons to reject the conclusion); Olson, 'Eusebius and the Testimonium Flavianum', pp. 319-

in transmission to sound more plausibly Jewish. But it most definitely does not come from Josephus.[88] There is therefore no basis whatever for believing any mention of Jesus Christ occurred at this point in the *Antiquities*.

That leaves one other passage in Josephus, where it is said, 'The brother of Jesus (who was called Christ), the name for whom was James, and some others' were tried and stoned by the high priest Ananus for unspecified crimes and in defiance of proper criminal procedure.[89] Obviously, if Jesus Christ had a brother, then Jesus Christ existed. So Josephus is here said to confirm the historicity of Jesus, by knowing details about his family. However, I have elsewhere demonstrated that the phrase 'who was called Christ' is an accidental interpolation and was never written by Josephus.[90] It entered the manuscripts of Josephus sometime in the late third century.

22; and most importantly, Alice Whealey, 'The Testimonium Flavianum in Syriac and Arabic', *New Testament Studies* 54 (2008), pp. 573-90.

88. The scholar who demonstrated this (Alice Whealey) has tried to argue that it nevertheless represents an original version of *Eusebius*'s quote of the TF and thus, in turn, represents the actual wording of Josephus—e.g. reading 'he was believed to be the Christ' rather than 'he was the Christ', thus sounding more like something a devout Jew might say (even though Josephus would then be compelled to explain what a 'Christ' was, yet doesn't). However, Whealey's theory requires the extraordinarily improbable assumption that all subsequent manuscripts of the *Antiquities* were emended to agree with the corruption (to 'he was the Christ', because all extant manuscripts now so read), and likewise *all manuscripts of Eusebius*, in all the places where he repeats this quote (because he repeats it several times, not just once). That all extant manuscripts of the *Antiquities* would so perfectly agree with a later corruption that somehow simultaneously occurred in all the works and manuscripts of Eusebius (which corruption by Whealey's argument must have occurred after the fourth century) is simply too improbable to be plausible. More likely some early copy of Eusebius's *History* alone was 'improved' by a scribe thinking to restore a more plausible quotation from a Jew (thus producing, e.g., 'he was believed to be the Christ'), and it is quotations of *this* that we see in Whealey's cited examples. Because it is inherently less likely that all manuscript traditions of all the works of Eusebius and all manuscript traditions of Josephus were conspiratorially emended the same way than that only one manuscript tradition of a single work of Eusebius was emended the other way and thus (as one would then expect) only occasionally evidenced in quotation (which, as Whealey shows, is what we observe). Her argument for authenticity is therefore to be rejected. Add to that the fact that even the altered TF that Wheeley defends is wholly implausible from Josephus (as I show from my survey of its content here), the total silence of all other authors (especially Origen) before Eusebius, and the two facts of its position in the text (that it interrupts the text as we have it, and is far too short to be a plausible insertion from Josephus), and there is simply no credible case to be made in defense of the TF whatever. It simply wasn't there, and we need to give up trying to rescue it.

89. Josephus, *Ant.* 20.200.

90. In Carrier, 'Origen, Eusebius, and the Accidental Interpolation'.

We know this because Origen never quotes this passage, even where scholars claim he does. In fact Origen shows no knowledge of this passage as we have it, or the story it relates, or where it was located in the works of Josephus; whereas Eusebius is the first to actually quote the passage we have in the present text of Josephus. *He* is thus the first to have known of it. Where Origen is now claimed to be citing this passage, he can be shown to have confused a story written by the Christian hagiographer Hegesippus (whom we just examined in §8) as being in Josephus. At that time, the original text of Josephus probably read either 'the brother of Jesus, the name for whom was James, and some others' or 'the brother of Jesus the son of Damneus, the name for whom was James, and some others', either way only later *accidentally* incorporating a Christian marginal or interlinear note (by insertion or replacement, to correct what a later copyist mistook as an error), thereby eclipsing the original meaning of the passage, which was that Ananus was punished for the offense of extralegally executing the brother of 'Jesus ben Damneus' by being removed from office and replaced by that same Jesus ben Damneus (as the narrative goes on to relate).

There are six arguments for this conclusion, which together establish such an extremely low probability that any Christ was originally mentioned here that we can dismiss this evidence as of no value to determining the historicity of Jesus.[91]

First, 'who was called Christ' is exactly the kind of thing a scholar or scribe would add as an interlinear note here—to remind him and future readers that (or so the annotator believed) the Jesus here mentioned is Jesus Christ, as we would do today with an informative footnote or marginal note. Indeed these kinds of marginal 'passage identifiers' are common in extant manuscripts. For example, one manuscript of Tacitus has similar comments in the margins identifying the passage mentioning Christ there, for the benefit of Christian readers skimming the text for passages of interest. And in this case, the idiom and vocabulary of 'who was called Christ' is a well-established Christian idiom (derived from the Gospels), commonly used by Origen, yet wholly alien to Josephus (who never otherwise uses the word 'Christ').[92] In fact the complete phrase 'Jesus, who was

91. Evidence and scholarship on all these points is provided in Carrier, 'Origen, Eusebius'.

92. The same idiom appears not only in Mt. 1.16, but also in Mt. 27.17 and 27.22; Jn 4.25; in the *Clementine Homilies* 18.4.5 and Justin Martyr, *Apology* 1.30.1 (as well as *Dialogue with Trypho* 32.1, although there perhaps derogatorily). The phrase is frequently quoted from the Gospels throughout Origen's works (e.g. *Against Celsus* pr.2.12; *Commentaries on the Gospel of John* 1.5.29; 1.21.126; 13.26; *Series of Commentaries on the Gospel of Matthew* 255; *Scholia on Matthew* 17.308) and is used in a related fashion in Origen, *Homilies (on Jeremiah)* 16.10 and *Against Celsus* 4.28. And of course in every case where Origen paraphrases Hegesippus and

called Christ' is (apart from a necessary change of case) identical to that of Mt. 1.16 (which happens to be a passage about Jesus' family), which is thus a phrase Josephus would not be as likely to use as a Christian annotator would. Though such a phrase would not be impossible for Josephus to construct on his own, such a coincidence is less probable than if it originated from a Christian hand.

Second, the words and structure chosen here are indeed the ones that would commonly be used in an interlinear note, essentially just a participial clause—remarkable brevity for something that would sooner otherwise spark a digression or cross-reference, had Josephus actually written those words. Obviously there would almost certainly be a reference to the TF, if it existed (perhaps even identifying the book in which it appeared, so readers would know what scroll to pick up to find out or remind themselves who or what this 'Christ' is and why he's being mentioned, or at the very least mentioning that he had previously discussed this person), especially since the reference is so obscure. The more so as the extant TF does not mention Jesus having a brother, nor explains why his brother would be a target of prosecution, much less defense by other leading Jews; indeed it mentions no persecution of Christians at all but instead emphasizes their unimpeded thriving 'to this day'. Thus, there would be much to explain here even if the TF had existed. For example, in this very same narrative about James, Josephus refers back to his previous discussion of the Sadducees when he mentions *them*, and explains why mentioning them is relevant to his present story.[93] Yet surely 'Christ' would rate at least the same treatment, being the more obscure (as Sadducees were already mentioned several times previously, even in the very same book: e.g. *Ant.* 18.16), and an explanation or cross-reference to the TF would be even more natural (e.g. 'the one called Christ whom I mentioned before')—after all, for the Sadducees he gave us both a reference *and* an explanation of relevance; likewise when he mentions Judas the Galilean in *Ant.* 20.102, we get an 'as I mentioned before' and an explanation besides.

Or if there was no TF (and as we just saw, surely there wasn't), certainly we'd find here an explanation of why this Jesus was called 'Christ', what that word even meant (at the very least explaining its connection to Christians and James's being one, if that is even what is meant—since James is not said to be a Christian here, or in the TF, thus the text as we have it here requires an assumption only a Christian would make, further arguing against this being from the hand of Josephus), and why Josephus thought it

mistakenly attributes the material to Josephus: Origen, *Against Celsus* 1.47 and 2.13; and *Commentary on Matthew* 10.17. By contrast, of course, Josephus never elsewhere uses it.

93. Josephus, *Ant.* 20.199 (probably referring to *Ant.* 13.293-98).

important to mention either, since the passage as written leaves no stated reason for either Jesus or his moniker Christ even to be mentioned at all—and any inferences to such a reason *would only occur to a Christian*, not to Josephus or his intended readers, who would not know anything about the obscurities of Jewish laws or religion, which is why he always explains such things when they come up elsewhere.[94] In short, such omissions here are far more probable if 'called Christ' is an accidental interpolation, than if they are the words of Josephus.

Third, the story as we have it makes no sense as being the execution of Christians, not only because no such basis for the executions is mentioned, but also because many influential Jews are outraged by the execution of this James and his men and seek the punishment *of Ananus* (and the Jewish and Roman authorities fully concur and duly punish him), which makes little sense if he was executing members of the hated (if not actually illegal) sect of Christians. Indeed, writing for a Roman audience in the era of Domitian, Josephus would be describing an inexplicable course of events, where the execution of Christians was considered a legal matter of course, not an act warranting outrage and dismissal from office.[95] In fact we get no sense from the way the story is told that there was *any* popular animosity toward this James and his affiliates. To the contrary, all the animosity in the story is against their killers. Regardless of what Josephus himself may have thought about Christians, it's more likely he would feel a need to explain this strange course of events to his Roman audience than simply gloss over it—whereas if this *wasn't* a passage about Christians, then its content is not improbable at all.

Fourth, apart from the execution being a stoning (the most common form of execution employed by the Jews, and therefore not at all peculiar to or indicative of Christian victims), this story does not agree with any other account of the death of James 'the brother' of Christ. It therefore is not likely to actually be an account of the death of James the brother of Christ.

94. Josephus otherwise never uses the word 'Christ' (even where it appears in the TF it is widely regarded as an interpolation even by scholars who accept the authenticity of the TF: Van Voorst, *Jesus*, pp. 91-92; and as explained in an earlier note, I find Whealey's attempt to defend it implausible). That Josephus often refers readers to his previous discussions of obscure persons and subjects: Paget, 'Some Observations', pp. 553-54. These and other considerations against this passage are further discussed in Olson, 'Eusebius', pp. 314-19.

95. See the comparable course of events, and elite reaction to it, in Pliny the Younger, *Epistles* 10.96-97; and of course Tacitus's remarks about popular sentiment in *Annals* 15.44 (if you accept that passage as authentic), and the representation of elite Jewish reaction to Christianity in Acts (if we are to trust its account at all).

It certainly was not known to be such by any Christian who composed those later accounts of that legendary figure's death (as we saw in §8).

Fifth, the book of Acts shows no knowledge of this event. And it is nigh impossible for a Christian of the time to know less than Josephus about the fate of 'James the brother of Jesus Christ' (particularly a Christian claiming to have researched the history of his church: Lk. 1.1-4). In fact Luke makes a point of always depicting the Romans protecting or rescuing Christians from the excesses of Jewish persecution or other dire fates (e.g. Gallio: Acts 18.12-23; Lysias and Festus: Acts 23–24; Roman guards: Acts 16.19-40; 27.42-44), and of depicting some among the Jewish elite as being less negatively disposed toward Christians (Gamaliel: Acts 5.34-42; even Herod Agrippa: Acts 25–26). In its present form, *Ant.* 20.200 has all of this. Indeed it hands Luke a rhetorical coup: Romans (and Herod Agrippa himself) *punishing* Jews for persecuting Christians. There is no possible way Luke would have passed up an opportunity to include this in his account. The only explanation for why he didn't that has any probability is that this event never happened—yet it is wholly improbable that Josephus would fabricate it. In fact, as Luke appears to have used Josephus as a source (Chapter 7, §4), Luke could not have found any story about James 'the brother of Christ' in Josephus. Therefore, it wasn't there.

Sixth, and most conclusively, Origen has no knowledge of this passage, despite being intimately familiar with Josephus and citing him often. We can therefore be certain Origen's copy did not contain a reference to Christ, here or anywhere. This has commonly been denied, but in ignorance: where scholars claim Origen is quoting this passage, he is demonstrably not. Meanwhile all other arguments against an interpolation occurring here are only against *deliberate* interpolation, but that is not what happened; the interpolation of 'called Christ' was more likely an accident. So we already have five arguments for, and none against, with a great weight of improbability ruling this passage out of consideration. But this sixth argument settles it: all passages where it is claimed Origen is attesting to Josephus's mention of Christ as the brother of James actually paraphrase a completely different story found only in Hegesippus, a story that is a patent Christian hagiography and thus cannot have originated with Josephus. Origen was simply misattributing it to him.

In each case Origen quotes *nothing* from Josephus, except the words 'the brother of Jesus who was called Christ', but that's just the combination of two phrases, 'the brother of Jesus' and 'who was called Christ', the former entirely common (and thus not distinctive of Josephus or Christianity) and the latter the accidental interpolation that did not originate with Josephus (for all the reasons already surveyed), but is instead (as I already noted) a well-established Christian idiom, commonly used by Origen. By contrast,

Josephus never otherwise uses the word 'Christ', and if he ever did, he would have explained what it meant and why he was using it. That he didn't entails he didn't write those words here. That Origen kept claiming he was paraphrasing Josephus, when instead he was actually paraphrasing Hegesippus, was simply a product of an error of memory, which Origen is known for; in fact Hegesippus and Josephus were known to be confused by others, too, so it was evidently an easy mistake to make.[96]

In summary, there is no evidence Josephus ever mentioned Jesus Christ. There is therefore no evidence here to consider.

10. *Pliny and Tacitus*

We can see Josephus is a wash. That leaves only two other authors who wrote before 120 CE that *actually* mention Jesus (or at least, Christ): Pliny the Younger and Tacitus.[97] These authors are particularly significant because they were not only contemporaries but best friends, who frequently corresponded and exchanged information for writing their histories, and were governing adjacent provinces at the very time Pliny first discovered what Christians preached.[98] Pliny tells us that he had no idea what Christians were or believed until he interrogated some of them and discovered it was some sort of base superstition involving the worship of a certain 'Christ' who was something like a God (*quasi deo*), but he gives no further details

96. A good example of Origen making errors of memory is very much like this one: he confused something he had read in the *Protevangelium of James* (specifically *Prot. Jas.* §23) as having been in Josephus, and thus incorrectly cites Josephus as his source; see Paget, 'Some Observations', pp. 550-51; and Whealey, *Josephus on Jesus*, p. 18. The authors Josephus and Hegesippus were also confused in some later manuscripts (thus it is an established error other readers of the time made), and some scholars have already suspected that this is what happened here: Paget, 'Some Observations', pp. 550-51 n. 43.

97. Pliny, *Letters* 10.96; and Tacitus, *Annals* 15.44. See, e.g., Van Voorst, *Jesus Outside the New Testament*, pp. 23-29 and 39-53; Theissen and Merz, *Historical Jesus*, pp. 79-83; and R.T. France, *The Evidence for Jesus* (Downers Grove, IL: InterVarsity Press, 1986), pp. 21-23 and 42-43; Howard Clark Kee, *Jesus in History: An Approach to the Study of the Gospels* (New York: Harcourt Brace Jovanovich, 2nd edn, 1970), pp. 45-47; and also Bradley Peper and Mark DelCogliano, 'The Pliny and Trajan Correspondence', in *The Historical Jesus in Context* (ed. Levine, Allison and Crossan), pp. 366-71. For extensive critical discussion see also Doherty, *Jesus: Neither God nor Man*, pp. 587-630 and 637-42.

98. On their being best friends, see evidence summarized in Richard Carrier, *Hitler Homer Bible Christ: The Historical Papers of Richard Carrier 1995–2013* (Amherst, NY: Prometheus, 2014), p. 372 n. 6.

about him (not even the name 'Jesus'), and says nothing pertinent to establishing historicity.[99]

At best, we might assume these Christians repeated to Pliny material from the Gospels (at least some of those had been in circulation by then), but as such this is not independent evidence and therefore useless. Pliny's procedure involved no independent fact-checking, and from his behavior and attitude, we can conclude his effort would have been typical, and thus Tacitus is unlikely to have done any better. Pliny had been governor of Bithynia (now northern Turkey) for over a year already before even learning there were any Christians in his province, and before that he held the post of consul (the highest possible office in the entire Roman Empire, short of actually being emperor). He had also been a lawyer in Roman courts for several decades, then served in Rome as praetor (the ancient equivalent of both chief of police and attorney general), and then served as one of Trajan's top legal advisors for several years before he was appointed to govern Bithynia. And yet, he tells us, he had never attended a trial of Christians and knew nothing of what they believed or what crimes they were guilty of. This confirms that his father, Pliny *the Elder*, never discussed Christians in his account of the Neronian fire—despite having been an eyewitness to those events and devoting an entire volume to that year (though his account is now lost). For if he had, his devoted admirer, nephew and adopted son Pliny the Younger would surely have read it and thus would *not* have known 'nothing' about Christians as he reports in his letter to Trajan.

We can therefore assume Tacitus would have been no better or otherwise informed when he wrote that Nero scapegoated the Christians for burning down the heart of Rome in 64 CE. The present text of Tacitus reads:

> Nero found culprits and inflicted the most exquisite tortures on those hated for their abominations, whom the people called Chrestians [*sic*]. Christ, the author of this name, was executed by the procurator Pontius Pilate in the reign of Tiberius, and the most mischievous superstition, checked for the moment, again broke out not only in Judea, the source of

99. For my complete analysis of this passage see Carrier, *Not the Impossible Faith*, pp. 418-22; see also Knight, *Disciples of the Beloved One*, pp. 34-36 and 209-12. Note that Pliny's hesitant phrase 'as if to a God' (*quasi deo*) could reflect his response to the exoteric myth (if his Christian informants were simply repeating the Gospels to him, in which Jesus is allegorically presented as a historical man) or the esoteric one (Jesus then being confusingly explained to him as a celestial archangel or demigod whom they pray to, but not exactly equal to 'God'). It could also be a textual corruption, as there is some external evidence that Pliny may have originally written *Christo et Deo*, 'to Christ and God', or *Christo ut Deo*, 'to Christ as God'. See Doherty, *Jesus: Neither God nor Man*, p. 640.

> this evil, but even in Rome, where all things hideous or shameful flow in from every part of the world and become popular.
>
> Accordingly, arrests were first made of those who confessed; then, upon their information, an immense multitude was convicted, not so much for the crime of burning the city as because of the hatred of mankind. Mockery of every sort was added to their death. . . . [*Tacitus here describes their torments.*] Hence, even for criminals who deserved the most extreme punishments, there arose a feeling of compassion; for it no longer appeared that they were being destroyed for the public good, but rather to glut the cruelty of one man.

They key line here is 'Christ, the author of this name, was executed by the procurator Pontius Pilate in the reign of Tiberius'. This is the first-ever reference to a historical Jesus outside the NT, dating to around 116 CE (very near our cut-off date for usable evidence).[100]

If the passage is authentic. I elsewhere demonstrate (following the arguments of scholars before me who have argued the same) that this line is probably an interpolation, and that Tacitus in fact originally described not the Christians being scapegoated for the fire, but followers of the Jewish instigator Chrestus first suppressed under Claudius (as reported by Suetonius: see §11). The line about Christ being executed by Pilate was added sometime after the mid-fourth century. Before then, no one, Christian or non-Christian, ever heard of this persecution event under Nero, or of any reference to Christians in Tacitus; this event is not mentioned even when second-century Christians told stories of Nero persecuting Christians![101] However, we need not rely on that conclusion for the present analysis, and to demonstrate that I will simply assume for the sake of argument that this passage is entirely authentic as received.

If we instead assume the passage has *not* been tampered with, then where would Tacitus have learned of this? Not likely from government records. His report contains no distinctive information that one would expect from such a source, and Tacitus would not have wasted countless hours of his life hunting through obscure archives just to verify a single embarrassing anecdote the Christians themselves were already admitting to. Moreover, it is very unlikely any such records would have survived in Rome for Tacitus to consult, the capitol's libraries having burned to the ground at least twice in the interim, once under Nero, and again under Titus.[102]

100. On dating the text: in Tacitus, *Annals* 2.61 and 4.4-5, references are made to Trajan's annexation of Parthian territories in 116 CE but not their loss a year or two later.

101. See Richard Carrier, 'The Prospect of a Christian Interpolation in Tacitus, *Annals* 15.44', *Vigiliae christianae* 68 (2014), pp. 1-20.

102. The fire of 64 CE is of course being recorded by Tacitus himself (and Cassius Dio, *Roman History* 62.16-18; also Pliny the Elder, *Natural History* 17.1.5, who was

It's also unlikely Tacitus learned of this from earlier historians of Nero (such as Pliny the Elder, as discussed in §3), since had they written about Christians we would probably know of this, from their histories having been preserved (precisely because they mentioned Christ) or quoted (by Christians or their critics). Likewise, that Christians appear to have had no knowledge of the Neronian persecution having any connection whatever with the burning of Rome further entails no earlier historian is likely to have made such a connection either (as otherwise such pervasive ignorance even by the Christians themselves is nearly inexplicable). If Tacitus really made such a connection, he was apparently the first, and possibly by mistake (conflating some other persecution of Christians, or even a Christian legend about a persecution that never really happened, with the burning of Rome; for as we shall see, Suetonius had no knowledge of such a connection, either).

But we know Tacitus asked Pliny for information to include in his historical books. Thus the fact that Pliny discovered what Christians preached in 110 CE, right when Tacitus was governing an adjoining province and writing his histories, and just a few years before Tacitus completed his *Annals* before 117 CE, suggests the most likely chain of information was Christians telling Pliny about the Gospels, then Pliny telling Tacitus, and Tacitus then reporting (what would be to him) the most embarrassing details in his *Annals*. That would explain why his information matches what was already reported in the Gospels by that time and gives no further detail. At the very least, this cannot be ruled out. Accordingly, we cannot verify that the information in Tacitus comes from any source independent of the Gospels. And non-independent evidence carries zero weight.

So either Tacitus never mentioned Christ or his mention of Christ cannot be shown to be independent testimony. Either way, his information has no effect on the probability of myth or historicity. And neither does the information recorded by Pliny.

living in Rome at the time); the fire of 80 CE is reported in Suetonius, *Titus* 8.3 (and Domitian was tasked with rebuilding the libraries: Suetonius, *Domitian* 20). Officially published records that we know Tacitus relied upon, like the acts of the Senate, would have survived in libraries elsewhere in the empire, but those would not mention an obscure execution in Judea. However, we must dismiss the argument that Tacitus can't have been citing government records because he gets the office of Pilate wrong, mis-identifying him as a procurator when in fact he was a prefect, because Pilate was *both* a procurator *and* a prefect (as most equestrian governors were), and Tacitus had particular rhetorical reasons to prefer mentioning the procuratorial office in a passage like this (it was more embarrassing, and more appalling, to be executed by a mere business manager). See Carrier, *Hitler Homer Bible Christ,* pp. 103-40.

Indeed, even if we blow past all probability and imagine that somehow Tacitus is paraphrasing or adapting a story from an earlier historian of Nero, Christians could already have been preaching the *exoteric* myth (some form of proto-Mark, for example) in 64, as an allegory (an extended parable) whose real meaning (it's *esoteric* meaning, that of a cosmic event) would be explained only to initiates (see Elements 13 and 14). Thus even a mention of Christ being crucified by Pilate at that date, if such a detail was only learned from Christians, would not strongly confirm historicity. And even if Christians hadn't yet gelled this exoteric myth by then, their claims that Jesus was celestially crucified by the 'rulers of this world' *during* the reign of Pilate could easily be misunderstood by a half-interested Roman audience as crucified *by* Pilate. Thus, even the 'cosmic crucifixion' of minimal mythicism could so easily be misreported in a historicist fashion that our inability to rule that possibility out further complicates third-hand evidence such as this.

And that only compounds the fact that, as I've shown, Tacitus almost certainly had no such Neronian-era source, was most likely just reporting information relayed to him from Pliny (who in turn learned it from second-century Christian informants), or taking his information directly from Christians himself. If he originally even mentioned Christians at all. This passage therefore has zero effect on the probability of either history or myth.

11. *Suetonius and Thallus*

Two other authors used as 'evidence' for a historical Jesus provide no evidence for a historical Jesus. The first of these is Suetonius; the second, Thallus.[103]

As for Thallus, I have already demonstrated elsewhere that he never mentioned Jesus.[104] The passage in the third book of the otherwise-lost *Histories* of Thallus, which was referenced by Julius Africanus (in another lost work, quoted by the medieval chronologer George Syncellus), almost cer-

103. See, e.g., Van Voorst, *Jesus Outside the New Testament*, pp. 20-23 and 29-39; Theissen and Merz, *The Historical Jesus*, pp. 83-85; Dale Allison, Jr, 'Thallus on the Crucifixion', in *The Historical Jesus in Context* (ed. Levine, Allison and Crossan), pp. 405-406; and France, *Evidence for Jesus*, pp. 24 and 40-42; Kee, *Jesus in History*, pp. 45-48. For extensive critical discussion see also Doherty, *Jesus: Neither God nor Man*, pp. 616-18, 630-36 and 643-52.

104. Richard Carrier, 'Thallus and the Darkness at Christ's Death', *Journal of Greco-Roman Christianity and Judaism* 8 (2011–2012), pp. 185-91. For an alternative argument that Thallus never mentioned Jesus: Jobjorn Boman, 'Comments on Carrier: Is Thallus Actually Quoted by Eusebius?', *Liber Annuus* 62 (2012), pp. 319-25.

tainly said nothing more than that for the year 32 CE, 'the sun was eclipsed; Bithynia was struck by an earthquake; and in the city of Nicaea many buildings fell', with no mention even of Judea, much less Jesus. For we can reliably deduce that we have this direct quotation of Thallus in several surviving fragments of Eusebius.[105] Which means when Africanus connected this entry in Thallus to Jesus, *he* was making that assumption, not Thallus.

As for Suetonius, there are only two relevant passages. The first is a reference to Jewish rioters, not Christians: Suetonius says of the emperor Claudius that 'since the Jews constantly made disturbances at the instigation of Chrestus, he expelled them from Rome'.[106] We have reason to doubt Suetonius has his story straight, since such an expulsion of all Jews from Rome would have been a near impossibility. There would have been tens of thousands of Jews in Rome at that time, complete with extensive real estate, synagogues, businesses, as well as countless Jewish slaves in both private and public hands that would have been indispensable to the urban economy, not to mention an enormous challenge to locate and drive out. In fact, we learn from Cassius Dio that

> As for the Jews, who had again increased so greatly that by reason of their multitude it would have been hard without raising a tumult to bar them from the city, Claudius did not drive them out, but ordered them, while continuing their traditional mode of life, not to hold meetings.

. . . which is a far more plausible report.[107] It's still possible some select Jews were expelled, as Suetonius does not actually say *all* Jews were

105. This same evidence indicates that Thallus wrote after Phlegon (whose work is usually dated between 120 and 140 CE), as the line Eusebius apparently quoted from Thallus appears to be an abbreviation of Phlegon (whose entry on the same events Eusebius explicitly quotes, and it too makes no mention of Judea or Jesus), because Thallus gives the exact same information in the exact same order, only with much less detail.

106. Suetonius, *Claudius* 25.4.

107. Dio Cassius, *Roman History* 60.6.6. The fifth-century Orosius, in *A History against the Pagans* 7.6.15-16, claims Josephus reported this expulsion, but there is no mention of this in Josephus's extant works (Orosius is probably confusing this with an expulsion incident under Tiberius, which *is* mentioned by Josephus); see Leonard Rutgers, 'Roman Policy towards the Jews: Expulsions from the City of Rome during the First Century C.E.', *Classical Antiquity* 13.1 (April 1994), pp. 56-74. Orosius also reads Christus instead of Chrestus in his quotation of Suetonius, and thus assumes he was speaking of Christianity. One might still ask why Josephus omits not only any mention of Claudius's edict against the Jews over the Chrestus affair or the riots that inspired it but also any mention of the burning of Rome or of any Jewish faction (whether Christians or Chrestians) being involved in it, despite the fact that Josephus was in Rome at the time, as a close acquaintance of Nero's wife (see Paget, 'Some

expelled, but only that *Jews* were. But a total expulsion cannot really be believed.[108]

Neither Suetonius nor Dio have any knowledge of this decree (or the riot inspiring it) being in any way connected to Christians. In fact not even Acts (cf. 18.2) shows any awareness of this expulsion being connected to Christians, yet the author of Acts would certainly have made use of the fact that the Jews were making trouble for Christians in Rome and were duly punished for it by the emperor, so we can be fairly certain no such thing occurred (and thus no such rhetorical coup was available to the author of Acts). Suetonius clearly wrote that the riots were instigated by Chrestus himself (*impulsore Chresto* means 'because of the *impulsor* Chrestus', an *impulsor* being the person who instigates something, not the reason for instigating it), and so it cannot plausibly be argued that this meant *Jesus*, who was neither alive nor in Rome at any time under Claudius.[109] Acts 28.17-30 likewise depicts Jews at Rome knowing little about Christianity beyond distant rumors, which hardly makes sense if the whole Jewish population of Rome had rioted over it just a decade before. Paul's entire letter to the Romans likewise exhibits no knowledge of such a thing.

Moreover, if the *second* passage in Suetonius has been soundly transmitted (see below), Suetonius knew the difference between Christians and Jews, and would have commented on the fact had Christians (much less Christ) been in any way the cause of these riots. Many scholars nevertheless try to press this evidence in that direction, but it's simply not able to bear any weight. Even supposing Suetonius is wildly wrong about Jesus being in Rome under Claudius and starting a riot there, that would entail his information was so hopelessly confused he cannot be attesting to any reliable evidence concerning the historicity of Jesus. Suetonius could just as easily have confused a report that Christ *as a revelatory archangel* 'instigated' the riots. Or if 'a belief in' or 'a preaching of' Christ had done so (even if

Observations', pp. 606-607). These omissions are probably deliberate: Josephus generally aimed to suppress any discussion of Jewish messianism, to downplay or diminish Jewish complicity in major incidents, and to paint Claudius as uniformly favorable to the Jews. So I think these events would have ruined his preferred storyline.

108. Acts 18.2 is alone in saying 'all the Jews' were expelled, but its reliability on this point is doubtful: see Richard Pervo, *Acts: A Commentary* (Minneapolis, MN: Fortress Press, 2009), pp. 446-47.

109. The use of 'Chresto' to mean 'Christo', though a linguistic possibility, is nevertheless not a necessary conjecture, Chrestus being a common name at the time (likewise we need not posit a textual corruption). See Stephen Benko, 'The Edict of Claudius of A.D. 49 and the Instigator Chrestus', *Theologische Zeitschrift* 25 (1969), pp. 407-408; and Dixon Slingerland, 'Chrestus: Christus?', in *New Perspectives on Ancient Judaism*, Vol. IV: *The Literature of Early Rabbinic Judaism* (ed. A.J. Avery-Peck; Lanham, MD: University Press of America, 1989), pp. 133-44.

Gospel-based), this, too, would be entirely compatible with minimal mythicism and therefore not a confirmation of historicity.[110]

The second passage in Suetonius is simply a casual and uninformative remark that during the reign of Nero 'punishments were inflicted on the Christians, a class of men given to a new and mischievous superstition'.[111] Which tells us nothing pertinent to the historicity of Jesus. It's even possible this sentence originally read *Chrestians* (later 'corrected' in transmission), and thus referred to the Jewish rioters whom, as we saw, Suetonius reported had begun to make trouble under Claudius (the same possibility we discussed for Tacitus). It's also possible that this line was an accidental interpolation of a marginal note summarizing the passage in Tacitus, although arguments made to that effect are not as strong as they sound.[112] But neither debate is relevant to our present purpose. Even as is, the probability that there were Christians for Nero to persecute is the same on either historicity or myth, making this evidence of no use to us.

12. *Missing Evidence: Contra Myth*

That ends our survey of all the relevant evidence outside the NT. As you can see, it is not only dismal, but overall it actually counts against historicity. One final objection that might be attempted is that surely someone would have gainsaid the invention of a historical Jesus. But who? Do we have writings from them? We cannot make an argument from the silence of documents we don't have or from the silence of persons we can't identify.[113]

Since Christianity, like all mystery religions, would likely have employed exoteric myths to conceal secret esoteric doctrines from outsiders (Elements 13 and 14), and there is a significant decades-long gap in the

110. For the suggestion that Christ *as a deity* (and not an actually present historical actor) inspired these riots see Édouard Will's review of Helga Botermann's *Das Judenedikt des Kaisers Claudius: Römischer Staat und Christiani im 1. Jahrhundert*, in *Gnomon* 71 (1999), pp. 610-16.

111. Suetonius, *Nero* 16.2.

112. Stephen Dando-Collins, *The Great Fire of Rome: The Fall of the Emperor Nero and his City* (Cambridge, MA: Da Capo Press, 2010), p. 6. To which one might add that the language of the line as we have it is also not in Suetonian style and reflects a Latin idiom that arose after the time of Suetonius, according to K.R. Bradley, 'Suetonius, *Nero* 16.2: "*afflicti suppliciis Christiani*"', *Classical Review* 22.1 (March 1972), pp. 9-10; and although Bradley argues that this means the text was corrupted by emendation and should be restored to align with the paraphrase of Orosius and the known style of Suetonius, that is not the only available explanation of the same evidence.

113. For what is required to make a valid argument from silence, see Carrier, *Proving History*, pp. 117-19.

early history of the cult where we cannot determine who survived or controlled the course of doctrine by the time the exoteric myths represented in the Gospels began circulating (Element 22), we cannot know what anyone was saying about them, how they were first being used, or who would be in a position to know they weren't really true (or even if they would say so if they knew). Indeed, nothing was preserved from this period even from sects we *know* disagreed with the communities that produced the Epistles and Gospels that we have. Yet we know there were many such sectarian schisms (Element 21). Since nothing they wrote or said was preserved, we have no way to know what those sectarian opponents gainsaid, or what arguments they deployed to gainsay it, because we don't have any of their critiques of what later became the 'orthodox' sect. Indeed, we almost never have writings gainsaying mythical people when they are historicized (see, again, the examples of Moses, King Arthur, and Ned Ludd in Chapter 1, §4).

And yet we do have hints that some sectarian Christians were indeed gainsaying the new historicist reliance on the exoteric myths as actual histories. A hint of the existence of doubters of Jesus' historicity appears in the character of the Jewish opponent created by Justin Martyr in his fictional *Dialogue with Trypho* in the mid-second century:

> But the Christ, if he has indeed been born, and exists anywhere, is unknown, and doesn't even yet know himself, and has no power until Elijah comes to anoint him, and make him appear to all. But you, on the basis of groundless hearsay, invent a Christ for yourselves, and for his sake you are now irresponsibly doomed.[114]

This could simply reflect a natural second-century Jewish criticism, not too unlike that found in the pagan critic Celsus of the same period, who argued (in his now-lost anti-Christian treatise that Origen critiques in *Against Celsus*) that the Gospels were the only evidence of historicity the Christians had, and yet were at best groundless hearsay. Celsus argues from the unproven assumption that they embellish a real story, while Justin's Trypho takes it one step further and suggests they might have been wholly fabricated.

Notably, Justin's reply to this suggestion is simply that 'we have not believed empty fables [*kenois mythois*], or stories without any proof [*anapodeiktois logois*], but stories filled with the Spirit of God, and bursting with power, and flourishing with grace', which merely gainsays the charge

114. Justin Martyr, *Dialogue with Trypho* 8.4. On which see the important remarks of Doherty, *Jesus: Neither God nor Man*, pp. 696-98.

without any proof offered. Indeed, the dialogue depicts Justin threatening to leave in a huff, rather than actually presenting any evidence that Trypho was in any way wrong; they change the subject instead.[115] More importantly, this looks very much like the response given *to fellow Christians* (of some opposing sect) in 2 Peter 1–2. This is a second-century forgery, passed off as written by the apostle Peter, an example of how readily Christians fabricated not only their own history but the documents attesting it (see, again, Element 44).[116] There we see an attack upon certain fellow Christians who were actually teaching that the story of Jesus was (as Justin also denies) a 'cleverly devised myth' [*sesophismenois mythois*] and who were thereby creating a 'destructive heresy'. Similar hints can be found in other forged Epistles (e.g. 1 Tim. 1.3-4; 4.6-7; 2 Tim. 4.3-4; 1 Jn 1.1-3; 4.1-3; 2 Jn 7-11; etc.). In 2 Peter we also see a related anxiety over the strange celestial Jesus found in Paul's letters—to the extent that now only the properly 'informed' were authorized to interpret them (2 Pet. 3.15-17).

Obviously the forgers of 2 Peter would have to *represent* these Christians as introducing a novel heresy. But in reality, these may have been Christians still connected to the original mysteries who knew the exoteric myths were only cleverly constructed allegories. The fact that this is all we ever hear of them demonstrates that we cannot expect to have heard more—for here, clearly, 2 Peter is attacking some Christian heresy we know nothing else about and have no documents from. Instead, we get a forged 'eyewitness testimony' cleverly designed to refute the claim that the Gospel was a myth—refuting it, that is, *with a fabricated historical report.* This letter is therefore a decisive proof-of-concept for the entire transition from the original Christian mysteries to a historicizing sect fabricating its own historical testimonies to 'prove' its claims.

The *Ascension of Isaiah* is another example of this: we can tell the original redaction had Jesus die in outer space (it therefore was composed by a Christian sect who clearly adopted what I am calling minimal mythicism), but later, some historicizing Christians inserted a section that had Jesus incongruously die on earth at the hands of Pilate in a summary of their own

115. Justin Martyr, *Dialogue with Trypho* 9.1. Note that the only reason Justin offers here is the affective fallacy: the Gospels are so moving and inspiring, they 'must' be true. I extensively demonstrate the defective epistemology of early Christians such as Justin, which indicates they were simply incapable of actually testing or investigating their own claims for any real truth value, in Carrier, *Not the Impossible Faith*, pp. 385-406. Likewise, that fact-checking their own claims was largely impossible anyway, and that Christians showed no evident interest in even trying: Carrier, *Not the Impossible Faith*, pp. 161-218 and 329-68.

116. See Bart Ehrman, *Forged* (San Francisco, CA: HarperOne, 2011), pp. 43-78.

fabricated Gospel (see Chapter 3, §1). This appears to be what typically happened to the evidence. It was erased, doctored or rewritten to support a historicist party line against a mythicist one (see, again, Element 44; as well as Chapter 7, §7).

That this would inevitably happen, and that the eventually successful sects would typically be the ones who started treating the exoteric myths as historical fact, has been logically demonstrated by Kurt Noll.[117] Using the development of false claims of the historicity of certain figures and tradents in early Islam, Noll shows that this is a common trend in the presence of intense sectarian competition over control of resources and ideology. An earthly Jesus known in the flesh would be a more effective tool for marketing a dogma than a revelatory cosmic Jesus would be. Therefore as churches competed for authority, there would have been an inevitable pressure to invent an earthly Jesus known in the flesh. The cult thus moved away from revelation as primary toward placing mythical 'traditions' as primary, which does indeed appear to be what happened (see Chapter 10, §8, and Chapter 11, §2).

As Noll concludes:

> [T]he data betray a clear evolutionary process from the proclamation of the so-called Jerusalem pillars, through the teachings of Paul, and ultimately into several competing varieties of post-Pauline Christianity. Earlier Christian doctrinal modes went extinct as later ones evolved. The doctrinal mode favoured by the Jerusalem pillars was extinct by the late first century. Although Paul's doctrinal mode was able to survive, it could do so only by evolving significantly new traits, including a conceptualization of a 'historical' Jesus guaranteed by allegedly eyewitness testimonies. This newly invented 'historical' Jesus effectively replaced Paul as the authority behind Paul's doctrinal mode.[118]

In short, it is more rhetorically effective to claim Jesus was a historical person and that your doctrine can be traced back to him through a line of living witnesses and tradents than to admit that everything known about Jesus came by revelation, which entails further revelations by upstarts and challengers could carry the same value and thus could undermine the

117. Kurt Noll, 'Investigating Earliest Christianity without Jesus', in *'Is This Not the Carpenter?' The Question of the Historicity of the Figure of Jesus* (ed. Thomas Thompson and Thomas Verenna; Sheffield: Equinox, 2012), pp. 233-66. Additional functions for the historicizing of myth are explored in Thomas Hatina, 'From History to Myth and Back Again: The Historicizing Function of Scripture in Matthew 2', in *Biblical Interpretation in Early Christian Gospels, Vol. 2: Gospel of Matthew* (ed. Thomas Hatina; London: T. & T. Clark, 2008), pp. 98-118. See also my discussion of the examples of King Arthur and Ned Ludd, and Daniel and Moses, in Chapter 1 (§4).

118. Noll, 'Investigating', pp. 265-66.

power of any growing church elite or the cohesion of any social mission. If Jesus was known only by revelation, one could preach *anything*, and claim it was revealed. But if one claimed to be the keeper of a verified historical tradition stemming from a real historical Jesus, one could argue against any 'new' revelation that 'that is not what Jesus said', because we have documents from 'men who were there and heard him' and we have men who claim to have 'known' men who knew those men, and thus guarded the tradition (hence Lk. 1.1-4 and Jn 21.24).

That this was indeed a later evolutionary development in the rhetorical battles among Christian sects is proved by Galatians 1, where Paul not only makes exactly the opposite argument (that human traditions were worthless and only direct revelations from the risen Jesus held any authority), but clearly feels compelled by his fellow Christians to say that (see Chapter 11, §2). It was evidently so commonly held at the time that human traditions were worthless and only direct revelations of value that Paul had to go out of his way to deny relying on human traditions and insist he had received his information by direct revelation instead. His audience in Galatia would accept no other argument from him, and were evidently alarmed by some accusations that Paul had (gasp!) relied on oral tradition, forcing Paul to remind them that he would do no such thing, and certainly never did; that in fact he relied only on direct revelations of the risen Jesus, the only source they evidently respected. But by the time 2 Peter was written, at least one major sect had completely reversed course on that point and was warring against any continued use of direct revelation by insisting upon verifiable human tradition. A human tradition it freely fabricated—as that letter itself is an example of. We have already seen Origen admitting that this tactic had utility in mobilizing the obedience of the vast majority of 'simpletons' in the Christian movement who (he claimed) were not sophisticated enough to grasp allegory but needed to rest their faith on literal truths (see Element 14).

So there evidently *was* 'gainsaying' after all. We just weren't allowed to hear much about it. Hence the objection that we would have more evidence of it does not have merit. Clearly the probability of that is too low to credit; it was all erased or destroyed or left to crumble into dust. This objection is also already refuted *in principle*: inordinately public events are fabricated in the Gospels (such as a darkness covering the whole world for three hours; a wandering star that troubled the entire population of Jerusalem; a mass of resurrected saints invading the city; the triumphal entry of Jesus; a city-wide earthquake shattering the very rocks; a very public, necessarily violent, large-scale vandalizing and clearing of the temple square; multiple miraculous feedings of thousands of people; the mass murder of two thousand pigs, and a whole town of babies and toddlers), which are obviously false, yet we have no extant document from anyone gainsaying any of it ('Hey, I was there, and I didn't see that!').[119] Therefore, evidently, we cannot expect there to be any.

In fact Jesus was said to have been famous all across not just Judea but the whole province of Syria (Mt. 4.24; 9.26, 31; Lk. 4.14). Yet we have no surviving record of anyone from those regions challenging this. Remarks like this create a logical conundrum for the historicist. For it is much easier to invent a man than to invent a *famous* man, yet Jesus is depicted as incredibly famous in the Gospels. But if he were so famous, then the silence of other writers and historians about him, indeed the lack of any literature about him being generated by any of the thousands of contemporaries impressed or intrigued by his fame (see the survey again in §2), is all but impossible. That is, extremely improbable. The consequent probability of this pervasive and thorough silence on the hypothesis that Jesus actually was that famous (much less that any of the incredibly famous events associated with him in the Gospels actually occurred—and I gave only a select list of examples) is *extremely small*.

So if the historicist wishes to maintain Jesus was really that famous, then historicity is *refuted* by the complete silence of all other literate persons of that age and region and of all who wrote about that region or about any famous persons and events like those. The consequent probability of *that* evidence (of silence) is so small that it guarantees historicity will also have a very small posterior probability, and must therefore be rejected as improbable. Just as for the darkening of the sun, as I have demonstrated before: we can be sure that never happened, because if it did, *someone* would have mentioned it (other than just the Synoptic Gospels).[120] It cannot be argued that 'someone would have gainsaid it', since that argument requires demonstrating someone existed who knew the truth, and knew the Gospels, and cared enough to even bother gainsaying the wild claims in the fawning hagiographical texts of an obscure religious cult, and did

119. See discussion of this point in Carrier, *Proving History*, pp. 41-45 (with 'eyewitness check', p. 336). On Matthew's massively embellished empty-tomb narrative, see Carrier, 'Why the Resurrection Is Unbelievable' in *Christian Delusion* (ed. Loftus), pp. 294-96. Three-hour eclipse of the sun: Mk 15.33; Mt. 27.45; Lk. 23.44-45. Wandering star disturbing all Jerusalem: Mt. 2.3. Mass of resurrected saints invading the city: Mt. 27.52-53. Devastating earthquake: Mt. 27.51. Triumphal entry of Jesus: Mk 11.8-11; Mt. 21.8-11; Lk. 19.35-40; Jn 12.12-19. Clearing the temple: Mk 11.15-18; Mt. 21.12-13; Lk. 19.45-47; Jn 2.13-16. Miraculous feeding of thousands of people: Mk 6.31-44; 8.1-9; Mt. 14.13-21; 15.32-39; Lk. 9.10-17; Jn 6.5-15. Mass murder of two thousand pigs: Mk 5.13-14 (cf. Lk. 8.33-37; Mt. 8.32-34). Mass murder of a whole town of babies and toddlers: Mt. 2.16.

120. Again, in Carrier, *Proving History*, pp. 41-45.

so in writing, and that this writing would have been preserved (by medieval Christians, remember) for us to know of it now. We can identify no such person, and have no reason to expect the survival of any such record. Indeed, we know there surely must have been people who would gainsay the Gospels even with lies, yet none of *their* texts were preserved either, not even in quotation or rebuttal. The first we hear of *anyone* taking *any* notice of Christianity and taking any trouble to gainsay its claims is Celsus, who wrote in the latter half of the second century, well over a hundred years after the fact, half a century (then a whole lifetime) after any Gospels began circulating. And we know about that only because we have the rebuttal of Origen. The actual critique itself was not even preserved.

Since no earlier responses to Christianity from any eyewitness critics have been preserved, not even in quotation, nor even by a mere mention, the probability that we would hear of an eyewitness gainsaying anything in the Gospels is effectively zero.[121] We don't even have the Gospels saying that the very Gospels they are contradicting had it wrong; they just rewrite the story, hoping no one would notice. For example, John doesn't say the other Gospels were mistaken in placing Jesus' clearing of the temple at the end of his ministry rather than the beginning (much less cite any witness gainsaying it), he just rewrites the story so that it occurs at the beginning of his ministry and not the end.

Therefore we must reject the argument that 'we would have witnesses gainsaying it'. Obviously, we wouldn't. From all the considerations above, the probability of *that* is extremely low. We have no direct witnesses at all, gainsaying or not. It's already uncertain whether many would even have been alive by the time the exoteric myths gained anything like wide circulation (Element 22), especially if the myth began as an in-house secret symbolically representing a private revealed religion (Elements 13 and 14). But regardless, we have no texts or quotations of anyone 'present at the time' who says anything whatever about the 'incredibly famous events' declared in the Gospels,

121. The one instance of Matthew claiming the Jews were spreading tales that the Christians stole the body of Jesus cites no source, no text, no name of anyone telling such a story (much less that they were present at the time, rather than from a later generation making up a skeptical explanation for what the Christians were by then claiming), and appears in an elaboration of the story in Mark that is certainly a fabrication and therefore never happened: see Carrier, 'Plausibility of Theft', in *Empty Tomb* (ed. Price and Lowder), pp. 359 and 363, with Carrier, *Proving History*, pp. 199-204. In fact, as Mark shows no awareness at all that any such accusation of theft was being made, that accusation (if it even was made) appears to have been a response to Mark's invention of a missing body and not to anything being claimed during the previous forty years of Christian evangelizing across three continents: Carrier, *Proving History*, p. 128.

pro *or* con. We therefore cannot argue from what they would have said. Without them (or any references at all to them), we just don't know.

The converse argument prevails: such famous events would have been broadly attested (and Christians would surely have gleefully preserved such attestations); yet they are not attested at all. So the historicist must accept that the reports of Jesus' incredible fame and all the incredibly famous things he was uniquely involved with are fabrications, legendary developments mapped onto what can only have been in actual fact a very obscure, barely known figure, who did nothing that won any attention among the literary elite. Hence *minimal historicity*, as explained in Chapter 2, is the only viable hypothesis. But that entails accepting massive legendary development had occurred, as I already explained in Chapter 6 (§7). Which entails we cannot argue that no one could invent a historical existence for Jesus. Since it is necessarily harder to get away with inventing a man's great and extraordinary fame than to invent a mere man. And the Gospels clearly succeeded in inventing a man's great and extraordinary fame (whether Jesus existed or not). So there would have been no obstacle whatever to their inventing the man altogether.

Getting away with inventing an actual man's extraordinary fame without being gainsaid is indeed no harder than getting away with wholly inventing an extraordinarily famous man without being gainsaid. Because inventing an obscure man is easy and thus getting away with that would be not at all improbable; but to then embellish his story into incredible fame requires no more luck or effort than embellishing the story of an actual man into incredible fame. The two outcomes are equally likely to succeed. This means the consequent probability of 'inventing an actual man's extraordinary fame without being gainsaid' on h (minimal historicity) is essentially the same as 'inventing an extraordinarily famous man without being gainsaid' on $\neg h$ (minimal myth). Since these two probabilities are essentially identical, they cancel out, and thus add nothing to the argument for historicity (or against).

13. *Weighing the Evidence*

When it came to the pervasive silence in other external documents (Christian *and* non-Christian), and the lack of many otherwise expected documents, I assigned no effect either way (although sterner skeptics might think that far too generous to minimal historicity). Conversely, as I just explained, no argument from silence can argue against minimal mythicism, either. But the peculiar existence of two separate traditions about when Jesus lived (placing him a century apart) leaves us with a factor of 2 to 1 against historicity (or 50% against 100%), or at least 4 to 5 (80% against 100%). I also found the same for the content of *1 Clement*. I also found that the content of Ignatius and the *Ascension of Isaiah* was slightly more likely on mythicism than on historicity (by a factor of 4 to 5 at least, which is the same as saying there's an 80% chance we'd have material like that on historicity if it had a 100% chance on myth; or at worst 1 in 2, which corresponds to 50% against 100%); and likewise, albeit less so, for the content of Hegesippus (by a factor of at least 9 to 10, for a 90% chance that that's what we'd find on historicity when there's a 100% chance of it on myth; although I think 4 in 5, or 80% against 100%, is closer to the truth).[122] Everything else was found to be no more likely on historicity than on myth and is therefore useless.

These estimates and the total odds they form are represented on the following table (measuring the odds of the evidence on h, minimal historicity, against $\neg h$, minimal mythicism), which you can use to input your own estimated odds and run your own calculations:

	best	*worst*
Twin traditions	4/5	1/2
Documentary silence	1/1	
1 Clement	4/5	1/2
Ignatius and *Ascension of Isaiah*	4/5	1/2
Papias	1/1	
Hegesippus	9/10	4/5
Josephus	1/1	
Pliny	1/1	
Tacitus	1/1	
Suetonius	1/1	
Thallus	1/1	
Lack of gainsaying witnesses	1/1	
For total odds of	576/1250	4/40
	288/625	1/10
	≈ 1/2.2	1/10
	= 0.4608	0.1000
	≈ 46%	10%

122. Note, again, that these estimates discount random evidence-loss. That is, when I say there is a '100% chance we'd have' something on mythicism, I mean, 'if it chanced to survive at all', not that it certainly would have survived. The probability of its survival might be extremely low; but not the probability of its having existed, or something sufficiently like it; and it is the latter probabilities we are concerned with. On the validity of discounting the probability of survival (because all coefficients of contingency cancel out) see Carrier, *Proving History*, pp. 219-24. On the validity of using the probability of having something sufficiently like x, as opposed to the probability of having exactly x, see Carrier, *Proving History*, pp. 77-79, 214-28.

The probabilities here estimated assume that nothing about the extrabiblical evidence is unexpected on minimal mythicism. So the consequent probability of all this extrabiblical evidence on $\neg h$ (minimal mythicism) can be treated as 100% across the board, whereas the probability of the same evidence looking this way on h (minimal historicity) is 46% at best, and 10% at worst.[123] Either way, as a whole, the extrabiblical evidence argues against a historical Jesus. It's simply hard to explain all its oddities on minimal historicity, but not hard at all on minimal mythicism.

123. Mathematically, if we reduce the consequent probability on $\neg h$ below 100%, we must reduce the consequent probability on h as well, since the ratios tabulated are the ratios between the consequent on h and the consequent on $\neg h$ (regardless of what those probabilities are).

9

The Evidence of Acts

1. *Acts as Historical Fiction*

The book of Acts has been all but discredited as a work of apologetic historical fiction.[1] Nevertheless, its author (traditionally Luke, the author of the Gospel: see Chapter 7, §4) may have derived some of its material or ideas from earlier traditions, written or oral. But the latter would still be extremely unreliable (note, for example, the condition of oral tradition under Papias, as discussed in Chapter 8, §7) and wholly unverifiable (and not only because teasing out what Luke inherited from what Luke chose to compose therefrom is all but impossible for us now). Thus, our best hope is to posit some written sources, even though their reliability would be almost as hard to verify, especially, again, as we don't have them, so we cannot distinguish what they actually said from what Luke added, left out, or changed.

1. See Richard Pervo, *The Mystery of Acts* (Santa Rosa, CA: Polebridge, 2008); and Richard Pervo, *Acts: A Commentary* (Minneapolis, MN: Fortress Press, 2009), for the most thorough accounting of this fact (see especially the latter, pp. 17-18), with substantial support in Thomas Brodie, *The Birthing of the New Testament: The Intertextual Development of the New Testament Writings* (Sheffield: Sheffield Phoenix, 2004), esp. pp. 377-445 (on Acts specifically); Dennis MacDonald, *Does the New Testament Imitate Homer? Four Cases from the Acts of the Apostles* (New Haven, CT: Yale University Press, 2003); and John Dominic Crossan, *The Power of Parable: How Fiction by Jesus Became Fiction about Jesus* (New York: HarperOne, 2012), pp. 196-217. See also Clare Rothschild, *Luke–Acts and the Rhetoric of History: An Investigation of Early Christian Historiography* (Tübingen: Mohr Siebeck, 2004); Loveday Alexander, 'Fact, Fiction and the Genre of Acts', *New Testament Studies* 44 (1998), pp. 380-99; and P.E. Satterthwaite, 'Acts against the Background of Classical Rhetoric', in *The Book of Acts in its Ancient Literary Setting* (ed. Bruce Winter and Andrew Clarke; Grand Rapids, MI: William B. Eerdmans, 1993), pp. 337-80. There are conservatives who protest, but not with logically valid arguments.

But that project has not gone well. Really only one underlying *historical* source has been confirmed with any probability, and that's Josephus,[2] who said nothing about Christ or Christianity (see Chapter 8, §9). Luke simply used him for background material. All the other sources we can discern in Luke are *literary*, not historical. Those include what may have been a now-lost hagiographical fabrication, essentially a rewrite of the Elijah–Elisha narrative in the OT Kings literature, but now casting Jesus and Paul in the principal roles. That is not what we would call a historical account—its sources are not eyewitnesses or historical memory, but the OT (as a literary model) and the imagination of the author reworking it. Thomas Brodie argues that this evident reworking of the Kings narrative starts in the Gospel of Luke and continues to Acts 15, indicating either that Luke wove this literary construct into his story or used an underlying source text, a previous Gospel, that covered both the acts of Jesus and the acts of apostles in one book. So Luke took either this source text or his own literary idea (or perhaps an early draft) and inserted more stories, thereby expanding it into two books, using material from Mark, Matthew, and perhaps other now-lost Gospels (see discussion in Chapter 10, §6), as well as some of the Epistles of Paul, and then continued the story from Acts 15 to 28 (which portion may have its own similar source-text or may be Luke's own invention).[3]

The remaining sources we can discern are not hypothetical, because we actually have them. For example, Dennis MacDonald has shown that Luke also reworked tales from Homer, casting them with new characters and giving them new outcomes as it suited him. For example:

> The shipwrecks of Odysseus and Paul share nautical images and vocabulary, the appearance of a goddess or angel assuring safety, the riding of planks, the arrival of the hero on an island among hospitable strangers, the mistaking of the hero as a god, and the sending of him on his way [in a new ship].[4]

2. That Luke used Josephus as a source to fill his account with various items of historical color, see note in Chapter 7 (§4). That similar details also appear in his account of apostolic travels *outside* Judea suggests Luke may have used other historians (of those regions) to color those accounts as well (those historians were simply not preserved for us to detect their influence now).

3. If Luke did not use a source text (a 'Kings Gospel') for the material equating Jesus and Paul to Elijah and Elisha, then Luke obviously had to have invented that material himself. That Luke knew and used (mainly to subvert) the Pauline Epistles see Dennis MacDonald, *Two Shipwrecked Gospels: The Logoi of Jesus and Papias's Exposition of Logia about the Lord* (Atlanta, GA: Society of Biblical Literature, 2012), pp. 50-52; and Richard Pervo, *Dating Acts: Between the Evangelists and the Apologists* (Santa Rosa, CA: Polebridge Press, 2006).

4. Dennis MacDonald, 'The Shipwrecks of Odysseus and Paul', *New Testament Studies* 45 (1999), pp. 88-107 (88); with Vernon Robbins, 'The "We" Passages in Acts

Paul himself says he was shipwrecked three times, and at least once spent a day and a night adrift (2 Cor. 11.25). Luke may have been inspired by this remark to invent a story about it, borrowing ideas from other famous shipwreck narratives (including those in Jonah, the *Odyssey* and the *Aeneid*). Acts rewrites Homer several other times. Paul's resurrection of the fallen Eutychus is based on the fallen Elpenor.[5] The visions of Cornelius and Peter are constructed from a similar narrative about Agamemnon.[6] Paul's farewell at Miletus is constructed from Hector's farewell to Andromache.[7] The lottery of Matthias is constructed from the lottery of Ajax.[8] Peter's escape from prison is constructed from Priam's escape from Achilles.[9] And so on.

The author of Acts used many other literary sources as well. For example, the prison breaks in Acts share themes with the famously miraculous prison breaks in the *Bacchae* of Euripides.[10] But the source Acts employs the most is the Septuagint. For example, while MacDonald shows the overall structure of the Peter and Cornelius episode is based on a story in Homer, Randel Helms has shown that other elements are borrowed from the book of Ezekiel, merging both models into one: both Peter and Ezekiel see the heavens open (Acts 10.11; Ezek. 1.1); both are commanded to eat something

and Ancient Sea Voyages', *Papers of the Chicago Society of Biblical Research* 20 (1975), pp. 5-18; and Henry Cadbury, '"We" and "I" Passages in Luke–Acts', *New Testament Studies* 3 (1956–1957), pp. 128-32. It is sometimes argued that the 'we' passages (portions of Acts where the author inexplicably switches from third person to first person plural and back again, without ever explaining why, or who 'we' are) indicate an actual source. Some even argue these prove the author was an actual companion of Paul, but few scholars believe that's likely—it isn't what the author himself ever says, yet it was standard practice of the time to say so, if that is what the author meant to be understood. But fabricating a fictional narrative using 'I' or 'we' is already evident in the pre-Christian book of *Jubilees,* a made-up rewrite of OT history adapted from Genesis, passed off as a revelation given directly to Moses, even though it was actually composed around the second or first century BCE So the motif has an established precedent in historical fiction. A more famous model for writing fiction in the first person is the *Odyssey* of Homer, and notably (as MacDonald demonstrates) the 'we' sections in Acts all center on sea travel.

5. Dennis MacDonald, *The Homeric Epics and the Gospel of Mark* (New Haven, CT: Yale University Press, 2000), pp. 9-14.

6. MacDonald, *Does the New Testament Imitate Homer?*, pp. 44-65 (with pp. 19-43).

7. MacDonald, *Does the New Testament Imitate Homer?*, pp. 74-102 (with pp. 69-73).

8. MacDonald, *Does the New Testament Imitate Homer?*, pp. 107-19 (with pp. 105-106).

9. MacDonald, *Does the New Testament Imitate Homer?*, pp. 137-45 (with pp. 123-36).

10. Euripides, *Bacchae* 440-49 (miraculous unlocking of chains), and 585-94 (escape due to an earthquake). Compare Acts 12.6-7 and 16.26.

in their vision (Acts 10.13; Ezek. 2.9); both *twice* respond to God, 'By no means, Lord! (using the exact same Greek phrase, *mēdamōs Kurie*: Acts 10.14 and 11.8; Ezek. 4.14 and 20.49); both are asked to eat unclean food, and both protest that they have never eaten anything unclean before (Acts 10.14; Ezek. 4.14).[11] Obviously the author of Acts is not recording historical memory here. He's assembling a story using literary structure and motifs from sources that have little or nothing to do with what actually happened to Peter or Paul. And he is doing this all to sell a particular (historically fabricated) account of how early Christianity abandoned the requirement of Torah observance, one that made it seem approved even by Peter all along, complete with the confirming approval of divine revelation—when in fact we know from Paul (in Gal. 2) that Paul was for a long time its only advocate and was merely tolerated by Torah observers like Peter, often contentiously. In just the same way, Acts 15.7-11 'pretty much puts Paul's speech from Gal. 2.14-21 into Peter's mouth', the exact opposite of what Paul tells us actually happened.[12]

Every other story in Acts is like this: a fictional creation, woven from prior materials unrelated to any actual Christian history, to sell a particular point Luke wanted to make. *Maybe* there was *some* authentic source material behind *some* of what appears in Acts, *somewhere*. But how can we find it? From beginning to end Acts looks like a literary creation, not a real history. It was written to sell a specific idea of how the church began and evolved.[13] It is clear 'the author of Acts wanted to stress the continuity of Judaism and Christianity, Paul's close relation to the other apostles, and the unity of the first believers' and thus had to 'subvert' the Epistles of Paul, especially Galatians.[14] For example, we know Paul 'was unknown by face to the churches of Judea' until many years after his conversion (as he explains in Gal. 1.22-23), and after his conversion he went away to Arabia before returning to Damascus, and he didn't go to Jerusalem for at least three years (as he explains in Gal. 1.15-18); whereas Acts 7–9 has him known to and interacting with the Jerusalem church continuously from the beginning, even before his conversion, and instead of going to Arabia immediately after his conversion, in Acts he goes immediately to Damas-

11. See Randel Helms, *Gospel Fictions* (Amherst, NY: Prometheus, 1988), p. 21.

12. Robert Price, *The Pre-Nicene New Testament: Fifty-Four Formative Texts* (Salt Lake City, UT: Signature, 2006), p. 841.

13. For a survey of Luke's methods as a historian compared to his contemporaries: Carrier, *Not the Impossible Faith*, pp. 173-87.

14. Joseph Tyson, 'Why Dates Matter: The Case of the Acts of the Apostles', in *Finding the Historical Jesus: Rules of Evidence* (ed. Bernard Brandon Scott; Santa Rosa, CA: Polebridge, 2008), pp. 59-70 (67).

cus and then back to Jerusalem just a few weeks later, and never spends a moment in Arabia. And yet we have the truth from Paul himself.

Clearly the author of Acts was not writing actual history but revisionist history. Which we call pseudohistory. He simply made things up, with little real care for historical accuracy or fact. Besides what we've already seen, the most obvious example of this is Luke expanding Jesus' post-resurrection stay on earth to an incredible forty days of hanging out with his disciples and more than a hundred other believers in secret the whole while, teaching them daily—even more, apparently, than he could think to teach them while alive—and then flying up into outer space to the accompaniment of angels (Acts 1.3-12). This is myth, not history.

Burton Mack gives another example of how Luke's version of the history of early Christianity in Acts is wholly unrealistic: 'Luke says that the standard sermon was preached to the Jews on the day of Pentecost and often thereafter, whereupon hundreds converted and the world became the church's parish overnight', but this is 'a story that does not make sense as history by any standard'. Not only in respect to its absurdly hyperbolic growth, but even just in the context of how people would really behave.[15] As Mack puts it:

> No Jew worth his salt would have converted when being told that he was guilty of killing the messiah. No Greek would have been persuaded by the dismal logic of the argumentation of the sermons. The scene would not have made sense as history to anyone during the first century with first-hand knowledge of Christians, Jews, and the date of the temple in Jerusalem. So what do we have on our hands? An imaginary reconstruction in the interest of aggrandizing an amalgam view of Christianity early in the second century. Luke did this by painting over the messy history of conflictual movements throughout the first century and in his own time. He cleverly depicted Peter and Paul as preachers of an identical gospel. . . . That is mythmaking in the genre of epic. There is not the slightest reason to take it seriously as history.[16]

In short, the narrative we have in Acts is so unrealistic, it cannot have been based on anything that actually happened. It's what Luke wishes to have happened, maybe what he wants people to believe happened; but it's certainly not what happened, even in outline. And as for this instance, so for all others in Acts.

15. On the rate of Christian expansion and growth almost certainly being nothing like what is depicted in Acts, see Carrier, *Not the Impossible Faith*, pp. 407-48.

16. Burton Mack, 'Many Movements, Many Myths: Redescribing the Attractions of Early Christianities. Toward a Conversation with Rodney Stark', *Religious Studies Review* 25.2 (April 1999), pp. 132-36 (134).

This conclusion should not surprise us, since all other Acts literature written by Christians was wholly fabricated as well. The *Acts of Peter,* the *Acts of Paul,* the *Acts of Andrew,* the *Acts of John* and the *Acts of Thomas* all look substantially like the Acts of the Apostles in the NT, yet are obviously not based on any kind of history. They are literary creations, telling stories the authors wanted, using known legendary characters (the various apostles after which they are named, plus in each its own cast of characters, some historical, some mythical, some invented to the purpose). There is really no reason we should privilege the Acts in the NT as somehow more historical or more reliable than any of these others, which were all written within decades of each other. Indeed for this very reason we should have presumed Acts to be fiction all along, albeit historical fiction, just like the Maccabean literature before it and other purported works of religious history (see, again, Element 44). Prior probability favors no other conclusion.

The literary coincidences in Acts are also too numerous to be believable history, and reflect the deliberate intentions of the author to create a narrative that served his purpose. For example, as Robert Price observes:

> Peter and Paul are paralleled, each raising someone from the dead (Acts 9.36-40; 20.9-12), each healing a paralytic (3.1-8; 14.8-10), each healing by extraordinary, magical means (5.15; 19.11-12), each besting a sorcerer (8.18-23; 13.6-11), each miraculously escaping prison (12.6-10; 16.25-26).

Similarly, just as Peter is sent by God to save Cornelius when Cornelius sends for him after a vision (Acts 10), Paul is sent by God to save the Macedonians 'when a certain Macedonian man' sends for him in a vision (Acts 6.9-10).[17] Luke makes Paul's story parallel Christ's as well: 'both undertake peripatetic preaching journeys, culminating in a last long journey to Jerusalem, where each is arrested in connection with a disturbance in the temple', then 'each is acquitted by a Herodian monarch, as well as by Roman procurators'.[18] Both are also plotted against by the Jews, and both are innocent of the charges brought against them. Both are interrogated by 'the chief priests and the whole Sanhedrin' (Acts 22.30; Lk. 22.66; cf. Mk 14.55; 15.1), and both know their death is foreordained and make predictions about what will happen afterward, shortly before their end (Lk. 21.5-28; Acts 20.22-38; cf. also 21.4).

But Paul does almost everything bigger than Jesus: his journeys encompass a much larger region of the world (practically the whole northeastern Mediterranean); he travels on and around a much larger sea (the Mediterranean rather than the Sea of Galilee); and though, like Jesus, on one of these journeys at sea he faces the peril of a storm yet is saved by faith,

17. Price, *Pre-Nicene New Testament*, p. 484.
18. Price, *Pre-Nicene New Testament*, p. 483.

Paul's occasion of peril actually results in the destruction of a ship. Likewise, Paul's trial spans years instead of a single night, and unlike Jesus, veritable armies plot to assassinate Paul, and actual armies come to rescue him (Acts 23.20-24). While Jesus stirs up violence against himself by reading scripture in one synagogue (Lk. 4.16-30), Paul stirs up violence against himself by reading scripture in *two* synagogues (Acts 13.14-52 and 17.1-5).[19] However, whereas Christ's story ends with his gruesome death (which had a grand salvific purpose, which could not be claimed for Paul's ultimate death, and which to end well had to be followed by a once-and-final resurrection, something that could also not be claimed for Paul), Paul's story ends on a conspicuously opposite note: 'and he abode two whole years in his own hired dwelling, and received all that went to him, preaching the kingdom of God, and teaching the things concerning the Lord Jesus Christ with all boldness, none forbidding him', something even *Jesus* could not accomplish when *he* was in Roman custody (Acts 28.30-31). Thus Paul outdoes Jesus even in that.

Paul and Jesus also both die and rise again from the dead, yet unlike Jesus, Paul actually stomps right back into the city unmolested and continues to publicly preach throughout the land, winning many more disciples for Jesus (Acts 14.19-21 and thereafter). In contrast, Jesus wins no new disciples after his resurrection and doesn't even try. And all this occurs immediately after Paul, also just like Jesus, is hailed as a god (Lk. 22.70)—and yet again Paul outdoes Jesus by humbly denying the claim (Acts 14.11-18). And in the end Paul, unlike Jesus, is sent to meet the emperor of Rome, something even Jesus did not accomplish. In other words, by Luke's account, Paul was vastly more famous and successful than Jesus.

The extent of the parallels drawn between Peter and Paul, and between Paul and Jesus, are altogether improbable as history. Likewise, the account of Paul's conversion in Acts 9.1-20 is simply a rewrite of the Emmaus narrative in Lk. 24.13-35 (which, as we'll see in Chapter 10, §6, is obviously mythical): (1) Both stories feature a journey on a road from Jerusalem to another city (Emmaus: Lk. 24.13; Damascus: Acts 9.1-3); (2) both stories feature a revelation of Christ; (3) in Luke the revelation came as 'they drew near (*eggizein*)' the city where 'they were going (*poreuein*)' (Lk. 24.28), while in Acts the revelation came as Paul 'drew near (*eggizein*)' the city where 'he was going (*poreuein*)' (Acts 9.3); (4) in both stories Jesus appears and rebukes the unbeliever and instructs him, and as a result they become believers and go on to preach their newfound faith; (5) in both stories there are at least three men on the road together and yet only one of them is

19. The parallels among these three synagogue incidents are even more numerous and obviously intentional: see Crossan, *Power of Parable*, pp. 205-207.

named (Paul [as Saul] in Acts; Cleopas in Lk. 24.18);[20] (6) in both stories 'the chief priests' of Jerusalem are the named enemies of the church (Lk. 24.20; Acts 9.1, 14); (7) in Luke God says Jesus had to suffer (Lk. 24.26), while in Acts God says Paul had to suffer (Acts 9.16); (8) both stories feature blindness (Paul is blinded by the divine light of his vision in Acts 9.8; Cleopas and his companion's eyes are blocked from seeing that their fellow traveler is Jesus in Lk. 24.16); (9) both stories end with this blindness being lifted (Acts 9.17-18; Lk. 24.31); (10) in Luke the visitation occurs on the third day (Lk. 24.21), in Acts the visitation is followed by a blindness of three days (Acts 9.9); and (11) in Luke the blindness ends after a meal commences (Lk. 24.30-31), while in Acts a meal commences after the blindness ends (Acts 9.18-19).

The author of Acts also uses features of the John the Baptist narrative to construct Paul's conversion story: (1) the names of John (the Baptist) and Ananias (who restores Paul's sight) mean the same thing in Aramaic (John = *iō-annēs* = *yahu-ḥanan* = 'Yahweh Is Gracious'; Ananias = *anan-ias* = *ḥanan-yahu* = 'Gracious Is Yahweh'); (2) John says 'prepare the way [*hodos*] of the Lord, make his paths straight [*euthus*]' (Lk. 3.4), and so Paul takes shelter on Straight Street (*euthus*: Acts 9.11) after attempting to destroy 'the way' (*hodos*: Acts 9.2), but instead sees the Lord *in* the way (*hodos*: Acts 9.27) and takes up the cause of preaching the way; (3) and finally, the initial order of events is almost exactly reversed: God speaks to Paul in a vision from heaven (Acts 9.3-8), then Paul prays (Acts 9.11), and is baptized (Acts 9.18), then goes on to teach the gospel (Acts 9.20); Jesus is baptized, *then* prays, *then* God speaks to him in a vision from heaven (Lk. 3.21-22), and then (in this case just like Paul) goes on to teach the gospel (Lk. 3.23).

Luke has also taken elements from the book of Tobit. When Paul is healed after his blinding vision, by Ananias acting on God's orders, we're told 'immediately [the blindness] fell from his eyes like scales [*lepides*], and he saw again and rose and was baptized' (Acts 9.18). In Tob. 3.17, the angel Rafael is told by God to 'scale away' (*lepisai*, the verb of *lepides*) Tobias's blindness. Literally the text in Tobit says, 'to scale away the whiteness', as Tobias's eyes had become clouded with white (Tob. 2.10), so here scaling away the whiteness makes sense, whereas there is no intelligible reason why Paul's blindness should be described as like scales, except as an allusion to the tale in Tobit, which also involves a story of traveling on a road with a divine being in disguise (in this case an angel), on a mission that would result in saving lives. And just as Paul is given letters from the high priest authorizing him to arrest Christians in Damascus (Acts 9.1-2),

20. Though in Luke the third man on the journey is Jesus walking along in disguise (Lk. 24.15) he never tells anyone his name; whereas in Acts Jesus appears as a light from heaven, but Paul is accompanied by at least two unnamed men (Acts 9.7).

Tobias was given a letter from his father authorizing him to claim a deposit of money—also, like Paul, in a foreign city (Tob. 5.1-3). More tellingly, the angel accompanying Tobias poses as 'the son of Ananias' (Tob. 5.12), and provides the means to cure the blindness of Tobias, just as in Acts the analogous divine being (the Lord Christ) provides the means to cure the blindness of Paul through a man named Ananias (Acts 9.10-17). Other descriptive elements of Paul's encounter on the road also derive, more loosely and creatively, from Ezekiel and Daniel.[21]

For this to be history, one has to posit all these agreements and parallels are historical coincidences, which is far less probable than that they are inventions, intelligently designed to reflect each other. And when you remove them all, you have no real story left to call authentic. Any one or two or even three of these parallels or coincidental details *could* be historical (at a stretch), but not all of them together. Maybe there is some historical core to either or both tales that has been dressed up with all these fabricated symbols and coincidences and tall tales, but we have no way of knowing what that core might be, or even if there is one. Therefore these stories cannot be relied upon as evidence of any historical fact, beyond the vaguest of generalizations, such as that Jesus may have originally appeared as a divine heavenly light, or that Christians may have believed God could visit them in the guise of an ordinary stranger; but such conclusions are neither certain nor helpful to the present purpose.

The same kind of analysis repeatedly destroys every narrative in Acts. I've presented only a few examples.[22] But even in general, Acts shares too many features with popular adventure novels of the same period to warrant trusting it as a genuine history: (1) they all promote a particular god or religion; (2) they are all travel narratives; (3) they all involve miraculous or amazing events; (4) they all include encounters with fabulous or exotic peoples (e.g. 'bull-sacrificing pagans of Lycaonia in Acts 14.8-19, superstitious natives of Malta in 28.1-6, and philosophical Athenian dilettantes in chapter 17', as well as fanatical pagan silversmiths of Ephesus in 19.23-41, and so on); (5) they often incorporate a theme of chaste couples separated and then reunited (a token nod to this element exists in Paul's chaste interaction with Lydia in Acts 16.13-40 and his many women followers, named and unnamed); (6) they feature exciting narratives of captivities and escapes (as in Acts 12, 16, 21 and 26); and (7) they often include themes of persecu-

21. Ezek. 1.26–2.3. Alan Segal, 'Conversion and Messianism: Outline for a New Approach', in *The Messiah: Developments in Earliest Judaism and Christianity* (ed. James Charlesworth; Minneapolis, MN: Fortress Press, 1992), pp. 296-340 (331-35). Similarly, Dan. 10.2-21.

22. For many more, see the scholarship cited in earlier notes (esp. n. 1). For example, Pervo, *Mystery of Acts*, pp. 55-91, 101-40.

tion, (8) scenes involving excited crowds (who become a character in the story, as in Ephesus and Jerusalem, in Acts 18–19 and Acts 6–7 and 21–22), (9) and divine rescues from danger; and (10) divine revelations are always integral to the plot (through oracles, dreams and visions, *all* of which feature in Acts).[23] In fact, Acts looks far more like a novel than any historical monograph of the period.[24] If Acts looks exactly like an ancient novel (and it does), are we really going to chalk this up to coincidence?

2. *What Happened to the Body?*

So the canonical Acts is not really to be trusted any more than any of the other apocryphal Acts that Christians produced. But let's at least suppose that its author started with some sort of bare outline of what happened in the early years of the spread of Christianity, and maybe even some actual historical sources, or semi-historical sources (perhaps something with a historical core embellished with legends and tall tales), even if he didn't use them very much. At the very least, let's assume such materials and information were *known to him*, even if he didn't use them at all, surely even then, he would take them into account and be inspired by their content when constructing his own story of what happened.

Whether we grant such assumptions or not, Luke obviously constructed tales affirming the historicity of Jesus, as well as the physical resurrection of his corpse, which left behind a conspicuously empty tomb, got touched by the disciples, slept and dined with them during a secret forty-day closed-door conference and then flew off into outer space before their very eyes (Luke 24 and Acts 1). This is all obviously nonsense.[25] Notably, no witnesses are claimed for any of this but fanatical followers. No one else is reported to have verified any of it. Instead, the public history of the Christian mission begins only in Acts 2, which depicts the first time Christians *publicly* announced their gospel.

But something very strange happens at that point. In Acts' history of the movement, from the moment the flock first goes public, in the very city of Jerusalem itself, at no point in the story (anywhere in all subsequent 27 chapters spanning three decades of history) do either the Romans

23. Price, *Pre-Nicene New Testament*, pp. 492-93.

24. See the table in Pervo, *Mystery of Acts*, pp. 168-70, where he enumerates ten different respects in which Acts is notably unlike ancient historiography (yet all ten are commonly encountered in ancient fiction).

25. I've more than adequately demonstrated this in Carrier, 'Why the Resurrection Is Unbelievable' in *Christian Delusion* (ed. Loftus); Carrier, 'Christianity's Success Was Not Incredible', in *End of Christianity* (ed. Loftus); Carrier, 'Spiritual Body', in *Empty Tomb* (ed. Price and Lowder); and Carrier, *Not the Impossible Faith*.

or the Jews ever show any knowledge of there being a missing body. Nor do they ever take any action to investigate what could only be to them a crime of tomb robbery and desecration of the dead (both severe death penalty offenses), or worse.[26] The Gospel of Matthew even claims the Jewish authorities accused the Christians of such crimes before Pilate himself (Mt. 27.62-66; 28.4, 11-15). Although that is certainly fiction (as I have argued elsewhere, external and internal evidence confirms Matthew's story is a poetic and apologetic fabrication), it does reflect *what could not fail to have happened*—if any body had actually gone missing.[27]

Since Christians were supposedly capitalizing on this fact (i.e. a missing body as evidence of a risen Jesus), they would be the first suspects—or at least the second, if (as the Gospels claim) Joseph of Arimathea was really the last person known to have had custody of the body (Mk 15.43-46; Mt. 27.57-60; Lk. 23.51-56; Jn 19.38-42). In that case he would be the first man hauled in for questioning. Yet he vanishes completely from this (the earliest) history of the church, as if no one knew anything about him—or he didn't exist at all. Yet unless he was found and confessed to getting rid of the body, the Christians would be next in the dock. And yet, though Christians would certainly be *suspects* in a capital crime of grave robbery, and though Acts records case after case of them being interrogated at trial before both Jews and Romans on other offenses (e.g. Acts 4, 5, 6–7, 18.12-17, 23, 24, 25, 26, etc.), never once in this entire history of the church are they suspected of or questioned about grave robbery. It's as if there was no missing body to investigate; no empty tomb known to the authorities. Which means the Christians can't really have been pointing to one. If they had, they would have been questioned about it (and possibly convicted for it, innocent or not). Yet Acts shows there were no disputes at all regarding what happened to the body, not even false accusations of theft, or even questions or expressions of amazement.

The Romans would have had an even more urgent worry than body-snatching: the Christians were supposedly preaching that Jesus (even if with supernatural aid) had escaped his execution, was seen rallying his followers, and then disappeared. Pilate and the Sanhedrin would not likely believe claims of his resurrection or ascension (and there is no evidence they did), but if the tomb *was* empty and Christ's followers *were* reporting that he had continued preaching to them and was still at large, Pilate would

26. On the ancient crime of graverobbing see the sources and scholarship surveyed in Richard Carrier, 'The Nazareth Inscription', *Hitler Homer Bible Christ*, pp. 315-26.

27. On Matthew's invention of the guarded tomb and associated accusations of theft: Carrier, 'Plausibility of Theft', in *Empty Tomb* (ed. Price and Lowder), pp. 358-64; with Carrier, *Proving History*, pp. 128 and 199-204.

be compelled to haul every Christian in and interrogate every possible witness in a massive manhunt for what could only be in his mind an escaped convict (not only guilty of treason against Rome for claiming to be God and king, as all the Gospels allege [Mk 15.26; Mt. 27.37; Lk. 23.38; Jn 19.19-22] but now also guilty of escaping justice). And the Sanhedrin would feel the equally compelling need to finish what they had evidently failed to accomplish the first time: finding and killing Jesus.

Yet none of this happens. No one asks where Jesus is hiding or who aided him. No one is at all concerned that there may be an escaped convict, pretender to the throne, thwarter of Roman law and judgment, dire threat to Jewish authority, alive and well somewhere, and still giving orders to his followers. Why would no one care that the Christians were claiming they took him in, hid him from the authorities and fed him after his escape from justice (especially according to Acts 1), unless in fact they weren't claiming any such thing? This is enough to confirm Acts' account of events is a fabrication, and a rather unrealistic one at that.

Thus, either Acts deliberately suppresses the truth about what happened to the body and what was really being argued, said and done about it (which eliminates Acts as being of any historical value), or there was no missing body and no one was claiming there was. The fact that Acts fails to mention any debate or investigation or discussion about any tomb being empty or any body being missing (it never even occurs as an argument or a defense in any of the trials or debates that Acts records, for instance), or likewise about an executed convict being reported alive and well, would agree with the theory that the original Christians were in fact preaching that Jesus rose in an entirely new body, not the old one he discarded and left behind in the grave. As Paul wrote, the body that dies 'is not the body that is to come', but rather the buried body is left to be destroyed, while a superior 'replacement' body is already stored up in heaven awaiting us (1 Cor. 15.35-50; 2 Cor. 5.1-4).[28]

So Acts' account could perhaps be rescued on minimal historicity: a real historical Jesus could still have been in his grave (which would not really have been a private grave owned by Joseph but the graveyard owned by the court for the burial of convicted criminals), and Acts' source materials could *for that reason* lack any mention of inquests or disputes over the

28. For a thorough defense of this theory, with extensive citation of primary evidence and scholarship in agreement, see Carrier, 'Spiritual Body', in *Empty Tomb* (ed. Price and Lowder), with its associated FAQ: http://www.richardcarrier.info/SpiritualFAQ.html. Note that even Peter's street sermon in Acts 2, which references David's tomb, fails to make any appeal to the actual emptiness of Jesus' tomb, nor does anyone present affirm its emptiness or challenge it. It simply doesn't even come up. See Carrier, *Not the Impossible Faith*, pp. 343-46.

missing body, because there wasn't one.[29] (Of course, these omissions could instead be because the author of Acts, in fabricating his story, simply didn't think about having the authorities or even the evangelists behave realistically.)

That could well be why those claims are dismissed as mere madness (Acts 26.24), involving no possible criminal charge of any kind under Roman law (as we're told was repeatedly said: Acts 18.12-17; 23.26-35). Otherwise, the crime of either robbing graves or aiding and abetting an escaped felon and royal pretender would certainly have been obvious grounds for an inquest or trial. Yet neither occurs. Thus, if Acts records any truth about the history of the first church, its narrative all but entails there was no empty tomb, the body of Jesus was not missing, and that the earliest Christians, including Paul, were instead preaching a resurrection by transfer to a new body, now in heaven, a fact known only by private revelations and interpretations of scripture. Which would be dismissed by Roman and Jewish authorities alike as nothing but vain superstition at best, idle madness at worst.

So, evidentially, this detail is a wash. Both historicists and mythicists can adduce equally plausible explanations of it (though only by assuming the first Christians were not preaching an empty tomb). But there is something even stranger missing from Acts.

3. *The Mysterious Vanishing Acts*

The second peculiar thing about Acts is how thoroughly all the people associated with a historical Jesus (as opposed to a cosmic, 'revealed' Jesus) disappear from the historical record entirely. This a historicist cannot plausibly explain. Not only do Pontius Pilate and Joseph of Arimathea immediately vanish from Christian history (Pilate alone gets mentioned only as the crucifier of Jesus and only in speeches by Christians echoing Luke's Gospel), as do Simon of Cyrene and his sons (Mk 15.21; Lk. 23.26), and Martha (Lk. 10.38-42; Jn 11.1-12.2), and her brother Lazarus (Jn 11–12), and Nicodemus (Jn 3.1-9; 7.50; 19.39), and Mary Magdalene (from Acts 2 on, none of these people is ever mentioned, or ever does or says anything, nor is their departure or lack of involvement ever noted or explained), but so does the entire family of Jesus.

Even though Jesus' mother, Mary, and his brothers are explicitly said to have joined the church congregation in Acts 1.14, as soon as Christianity becomes public news they immediately vanish from history—completely. As does Jesus' father, Joseph, though his omission in Acts 1.14 could be

29. That Jesus would ultimately have been interred in a public grave managed by the Sanhedrin and not a private tomb: Carrier, 'Burial of Jesus', in *Empty Tomb* (ed. Price and Lowder).

taken to imply he had died (although it is at least a bit strange that that fact never gets mentioned anywhere); likewise, we might explain away the disappearance of his sisters (which he is supposed to have had: Mk 6.3; Mt. 13.56) by supposing their insignificance. But his mother and brothers?

The disappearance of some characters can readily be accepted by a historicist as being a consequence of their never having existed. Joseph of Arimathea, for example, could readily be dispensed with without impugning the historicity of Jesus. The absence of major characters introduced by John (Lazarus and Nicodemus, who already don't appear in any prior Gospel, much less Acts) can be explained away even more readily as inventions of John—their importance and connection with Jesus is so prominent in his Gospel that their absence even in prior Gospels is already sufficiently inexplicable (and there is other evidence of their non-existence even more decisive, likewise for other named characters, as I show in Chapter 10, §7). But Pilate's absence cannot be explained in that way. Certainly, if Pilate never had anything to do with the death of Jesus, his absence from Acts' sources for the early Jerusalem church is easily explained; somewhat less so otherwise. So this disappearing act agrees fully with minimal mythicism; but is at least *slightly* unexpected on minimal historicity.

It's the complete disappearance of Jesus' family that is really hard to explain on minimal historicity. After the report of her being with the congregation in Acts 1.14, mother Mary is never mentioned again. She never says or does anything, is never spoken to or heard of again, and nothing ever happens to her. We aren't even told when or why or where she lived or died. She literally disappears from history—as if she never existed. Though Acts 1.14 also says Jesus' brothers were present just weeks before the Pentecost announcement recorded in Acts 2, all of his brothers then disappear. They are never mentioned again. According to Acts, they had no role at all to play in the history of the church, and are never heard from. No one even seems to be aware they exist. This includes, most conspicuously, his brother James, who is supposed to have been one of the most important leaders of the movement, one of three pillars on which the new church was founded—if that is what we are to understand Gal. 1.19; 2.9 or 12 to mean, or 1 Cor. 15.7, as many scholars insist or suppose (I will discuss whether that is what Paul actually meant in Chapter 11, §10). Later legend certainly had Jesus' brother James lead the church in precisely the time covered by Acts. So why is he not in it?

The entirety of Luke–Acts mentions only two men by the name of James, yet identifies neither as the brother of Jesus. To the contrary, it specifically distinguishes both of them from his brothers (Acts 1.13-14). One of them is indeed one of the three pillars named by Paul (Peter, James and John: Gal. 2.9, in light of Mk 3.16-17; 5.37; 9.2; 14.33; Lk. 5.10; 8.51; 9.28; etc.; see Chapter 11, §3), who was clearly *not* the brother of Jesus (as all the Gospels agree), but the brother of the other pillar, John. Acts says this James was beheaded by Herod Agrippa (12.1-2). The only other James in Luke–Acts is James the son of Alphaeus (Lk. 6.15; Acts 1.13), who must therefore be the James still around after the first one is killed (Acts 12.17; 15.13; 21.18), although Acts has so egregiously toyed with the chronology (contradicting the firsthand accounts of Paul in almost every particular) that we might guess Luke has accidentally transposed a story actually about James the Pillar to a later period, forgetting he had killed him off earlier. After all, Luke does not otherwise explain why this second James is suddenly and consistently treated as the leader of the church in Jerusalem, which James *the Pillar* is known to have been. Later Christian legend (first attested only late in the second century, a whole lifetime or two after Acts was written) replaced this James ben Alphaeus with James 'the brother of the Lord', but Luke clearly has no knowledge of this connection (nor, we must conclude, did any sources he may have had). Nor do any of the other Gospels show any awareness that any brothers of Jesus ever had a role in the church at all, much less as a leader. Mark had already suggested *none* of Jesus' family entered the church, as he has Jesus essentially disown them.[30]

So after the first chapter of Acts, the moment Christianity's history becomes public record, it suddenly appears as if Jesus had no family whatever. That is certainly more likely if there was no Jesus in the first place. For if Jesus didn't exist, then our author's genuine historical sources, insofar as he had any, would only have begun with the origin of the church under Peter (as represented from Acts 2 on), and these sources would never mention any of the family of Jesus (or Pontius Pilate, or anyone who buried Jesus, or carried his cross), because no such people existed. Or else they had nothing to do with a historical Jesus. Minimal historicity, by contrast, cannot as easily explain this.

One might shoot from the hip and argue that Luke had some motive for erasing the family of Jesus from the history of the church, but that is refuted by the fact that he didn't: he includes them in the original congregation (Acts 1.14); it is also rendered intrinsically improbable by the fact that if later legend were true, and James the brother of Jesus was a major leader and key figure in the early church, erasing him from the history of the early church should have been impossible (any Christian aware of the legends would want to know how Luke could erase so important a figure from his account and still be trusted as a historian). It also has no plausible motive. If Luke wanted to downplay the role of Jesus' family in favor of Peter and Paul, for example, he would far sooner invent accounts of them explicitly doing so; he would not simply forget they existed. Just compare how Luke

30. Mk 3.31-34 (repeated in Mt. 12.46-50 and Lk. 8.19-21; echoed less directly in Jn 7.5 and 19.26-27). See Chapter 10 (§4).

rewrote the entire history of Paul's interaction with Peter and the Jerusalem church in Galatians 1–2: that's what he does with historical facts he doesn't like. He doesn't just delete people. He makes them say and do the things he wants (indeed, needs).[31]

I must conclude that the history of the early church as recounted in Acts looks very much unlike what we would expect on minimal historicity. Contortions are required to get what we have to fit (such as assuming *ad hoc* that in fact Jesus had no family, or that strange motives were available to erase them from history completely, motives that would not sooner motivate a rewrite of what they said and did or what happened to them). Even the point about there being no missing body (the narrative simply makes no sense on the supposition that there was one; but makes perfect sense on the supposition that there wasn't, which agrees with there being no Jesus to bury) and the disappearance of Pilate (as if he would be wholly unconcerned that a man he executed was reported to have escaped) are exactly what we expect on minimal mythicism, but not exactly what we expect on minimal historicity. But there at least we can retreat to combining minimal historicity with an early resurrection doctrine that did not require a missing body. Though I think that is much less *ad hoc* (since a strong, independent case can be made that that is probably in fact what the original Christian resurrection doctrine was), it is not 100% guaranteed.

Or we can retreat to supposing Acts is almost complete fiction, and thus all of its strange omissions are just the result of Luke being an insufficiently imaginative writer. On that theory, having inherited no material about the early church other than perhaps the letters of Paul, Luke had no knowledge of Jesus' family, and so didn't think to include them in his tale. Likewise everything else that makes no historical sense. This entails a dilemma: one must either reject Acts entirely as evidence (being so wholly fabricated that it cannot be trusted as reliably attesting to anything), or one must accept that its omissions are improbable on minimal historicity but exactly to be expected on minimal myth. This does not mean impossible, just improbable. So we must assign some probability less than 100%. This is true even if Luke is wholly fabricating, since even then it is not 100% likely he would forget these things. Those omissions are unlikely even in fiction, requiring an explanation, which requires a supposition not in evidence, which lowers the probability of any explanation we muster.

My most generous estimate would be a 4 in 5 chance (roughly an 80% chance) that Luke would write Acts 2–28 as we have it, *if* he used or was aware of any kind of genuine sources for the early history of Christianity.

31. The argument in James Tabor, *The Jesus Dynasty* (London: HarperElement, 2006), pp. 247-54, that Luke is deliberately erasing Jesus' brothers (and mother) is for all these reasons wholly untenable.

Which is the same as saying there is only a 20% chance he would have included material about the brothers of Jesus or any of the other missing people in his life (and thus an 80% chance he wouldn't). Yet I think an 80% chance Luke would completely omit Jesus' family from the whole public history of the church, as well as other things we should otherwise expect to be there, is being absurdly generous.[32] My more realistic estimate of this probability would be 2 in 5 (or a 40% chance he'd leave all this stuff out; hence a 60% chance that he would have said *something* about these missing people and events). If, however, Luke neither used *nor knew* any real stories or sources, but just made it all up (or adapted sources that did), and given that he himself was clearly a historicist (or certainly was selling that dogma with these books, whatever he personally may have believed), then there is no longer any logical connection between these bizarre omissions and any actual absences in the history of the church. But even then these omissions would not have 1 to 1 odds, as if they were equally mysterious on h or $\neg h$, because they would still be at least a little weird, requiring a supposition (not in evidence) that Luke was not a sufficiently imaginative writer to realize what he was leaving out.

I think it's improbable that Luke had *no* lore to work from, no information about the earliest missions or the family of Jesus. Regardless of whether he used any of it or not, it's surely more likely that at least a basic outline of what happened was known to him. I think there had to be by his time tales about the role and fate of Jesus' family (especially Mary and James, or even Jude), if such people existed; and likewise what happened in Jerusalem the first time it was announced that an executed convict had risen from the dead. So was Luke writing in total ignorance or from a starting point of at least some knowledge? I'll assume the latter (on what to do if you disagree, see §7).

4. *The 'Trial Transcripts' of Paul*

Another curious thing about Acts is that when the trials of Paul are examined (rather than his sermons elsewhere or the speeches of others), the historical Jesus himself mysteriously disappears. Surely this is at least somewhat less likely on h than on $\neg h$, since on the latter hypothesis we

32. Note that anyone who attempts to bypass this estimate by claiming Jesus had no brothers (or none ever connected with the church) must also agree that Paul could never have referred to brothers of Jesus holding prominent positions in the church in that case, which means you then cannot cite his doing so as evidence for historicity (see Chapter 11, §10). As long as you can accept that consequence, then you can change the estimate here from 2/3 to 1/1 (since the non-mention of non-existent brothers is always 100% likely, and thus would be so on h as well as $\neg h$).

can expect that in any actual trials Paul was in, only a cosmic, 'revealed' Jesus was attacked, defended and debated (and that appears to be what Acts reports to have happened), whereas on the former hypothesis many issues and facts pertaining to the actual deeds and sayings and fate of the historical Jesus would come up as pertinent or even essential.

Again, what we make of this strange omission depends on whether the author of Acts is making it all up, in ignorance of what actually happened, or whether he is adapting, reworking or rewriting some earlier source that portrayed what happened at those trials. That source need not be historical. It could itself be a complete fabrication, perhaps itself an earlier Acts of Paul, telling tall tales of how he stood up to the authorities in legal contexts and won, but still written by people more in the know (whether the actors themselves, or those who knew them), and thus building on assumptions held at the time about what *would* occur in such trials or what would make sense to them given what the first Christians such as Paul actually believed. For example, if this proposed source-text were written by a companion of Paul who had no conception of a historical Jesus recently executed by Pontius Pilate (because that exoteric myth hadn't been invented yet), then even his made-up accounts of the trials would reflect that.

One argument for this being the case is the remarkable disparity between these trial accounts, and speeches and sermons that take place elsewhere. If Luke were simply fabricating the whole thing, these accounts should be consistent: the actors would say the same things when asked to pronounce and defend the gospel, regardless of where they were. But strangely, they are not. Everywhere else, the speeches and sermons in Acts are conspicuously historicist; but when Paul is on trial, where in fact historicist details are even more relevant and would even more certainly come up, they are suddenly completely absent. That is very strange; which means, very improbable. The best explanation of this oddity is that Paul's trial accounts were not wholesale Lukan fabrications but came from a different source than the speeches and sermons Luke added in elsewhere—a source that did not know about a historical Jesus.

In Acts, Paul faces two trials: one brief encounter in Greece and an extended period of hearings in Judea. The first occurs before Gallio, then the Roman governor of Greece, on a charge of 'persuading men to worship god contrary to the law' (Acts 18.13). But Gallio dismisses the case. His bench decision reads:

> If there were any wrongdoing or violent crime here, then it would be reasonable to pay attention to you. But if this concerns questions about words and names and your own laws, then see to the matter yourselves. I'm not interested in being a judge of these matters (Acts 18.14-15).

This is all too vague to be of any help, since nothing about Jesus even comes up. It's the next series of hearings in Judea that are more conspicuous.

This is the story of it as told in Acts: after Paul inadvertently causes a riot throughout the whole of Jerusalem (21.17-31), the Roman garrison commander, Claudius Lysias, intervenes (21.31-39), calms things down, and lets Paul give a public speech essentially summarizing his story up to that point (21.39–22.21), which for some unexplained reason outrages the crowd and they start rioting again, calling for his death (22.22-23), at which Lysias takes him back into custody and retreats to interrogate him to find out what is going on, when he discovers Paul is a Roman citizen (22.24-30, a detail Paul himself never mentions in his letters. In fact, in 2 Cor. 11.25 he says he was caned three times, which contradicts Luke's depiction of Paul as touting his citizenship to avoid a beating).[33] In Paul's speech to the people during this episode, he makes no mention of a historical Jesus, only a Lord known by revelation (22.6-15, 17-18). Indeed, Paul has *another* revelatory encounter with Jesus shortly thereafter (23.11).

Lysias then brings Paul to a meeting of the Jewish elite to find out why the riot occurred. At this inquest, the Pharisees present concluded, 'we find nothing wrong in this man; maybe a spirit spoke to him, or an angel' (Acts 23.9), but then they get into a fight with their Sadducee peers over religious differences, and a riot breaks out again. So Lysias takes Paul out of there (23.10). Lysias then learns a small army of Jews was forming a plot to assassinate Paul on his next day in court, at which he immediately ships Paul off to the Roman governor under massive guard—nearly a hundred horsemen and two hundred infantry (23.12-24). To explain this extraordinary action, Lysias wrote an official letter to the governor explaining the disposition of Paul's case, and that letter reads as follows:

> Claudius Lysias, to Felix, the most excellent governor, greetings. This man was seized by the Jews and they were about to kill him. And so I set out with an army and took him out of there, having learned he is a Roman. Since I wanted to know what they accused him of, I brought him into their court, where I found he was accused regarding questions of their law, but there was nothing in the charge worthy of death or prison. When a secret plot against the man was revealed to me, I sent him to you

33. Roman citizens were immune to being caned without a trial (and even after a trial had the right to appeal all the way to the imperial court at Rome), and although one could be illegally caned or choose to accept caning rather than appeal, Acts 22.25-30 shows Paul readily resorting to an appeal (and in general, Pliny the Younger didn't even wait for citizen Christians to appeal, he just immediately exempted them from local punishment and shipped them off to Rome for trial: Pliny the Younger, *Letters* 10.96.4). On the legalities: Brian Rapske, *The Book of Acts and Paul in Roman Custody* (Grand Rapids, MI: William B. Eerdmans, 1994), pp. 47-56.

> at once and ordered his accusers to charge him before you. Farewell (Acts 23.26-30).

This cannot be an authentic document as presented, since it lacks features a real one would necessarily have, such as Paul's full Roman name and indeed the full names of Claudius and Felix, and the date, for example. But whether a fabrication or a literary abbreviation of a real letter, it still conspicuously lacks any mention of a historical Jesus. Yet the fact that Paul was advocating the worship of an executed convict would certainly have been pertinent information for Lysias to mention to Felix. The more so if that convict was believed escaped and still at large and giving orders to his co-conspirators. Even just the fact that Paul's case was connected to the execution of an accused insurrectionist and pretender to the throne could not fail to be essential information here, considering that Paul was advocating the *worship* of that pretender to the throne, which would surely put Paul under suspicion of being an insurrectionist or a traitor. Instead, the letter says his case only had to do with obscure matters of *Jewish religion*, and involved no violation of Roman law.

Paul is then brought under that massive guard to Felix (Acts 23.31-35). His accusers are then brought in and allowed to plead their case (24.1-9). They accuse him of fomenting insurrection and defiling the temple (neither of which, of course, Paul was guilty of, nor did they have any evidence to back up those charges). Yet again, no mention is made of his worshiping a convicted felon who was executed on suspicion of declaring himself king—yet surely, in reality, his accusers would have made a great deal of hay out that. Paul is then allowed to respond (24.10-21). He also makes no mention of Jesus, only that they have no evidence to convict him on, and that he is only really being accused because he agrees with the Pharisees that there will be a resurrection of the dead. Felix ends the inquiry, makes no judgment and keeps Paul locked up for two years, for no explicable reason (and somewhat against the law protecting the rights of Roman citizens). During this illegal imprisonment, Felix has Paul over for dinner on occasion, where Paul scares him with talk about future apocalyptic judgment (24.22-27), but still never a word about a historical Jesus. Even though he tells them all about 'the faith in Jesus Christ' (24.24), we're not told what that means.

A new governor moves in, named Festus, and the Jews try to get *him* to ship Paul back to Jerusalem, but instead he holds an inquiry (Acts 24.27–25.12), at which nothing changes (the same vague charges are advanced, which Paul simply denies), except that Paul appeals to be sent before Caesar, and his request is granted. While Paul awaits departure, Festus is joined by King Herod Agrippa, and they bring Paul in to discuss his case for some unexplained reason (25.13-27.1), and Paul is eventually shipped off to

Rome. It is here that we finally hear more details about the case. Festus tells Agrippa that Paul's accusers 'brought no charges of crimes as I suspected, but only certain questions against him having to do with their religion, and concerning a certain Jesus, who was dead, whom Paul affirmed to be alive' (25.18-19), which means he didn't even know who this 'Jesus' person was—an impossibility if he had been executed by Pontius Pilate some years before, as surely Festus would have learned by now. Indeed, it looks like the dispute over whether Jesus was dead or alive is only understood here to be an obscure question of Jewish theology.

At this point, Paul finally gets to say his piece, providing us with a lengthy speech spanning twenty-two verses (Acts 26.1-23). Yet at no point does he ever refer to a historical Jesus. We hear only of a cosmic, revelatory Jesus. No mention is made of Jesus having a ministry, or having appointed disciples, or of having been executed (on charges false or true), or having proved himself divine by miracles or teachings or anything at all. This is very much unlike Paul's speech to the synagogue in Antioch (Acts 13.23-41), which goes into explicit details of the gospel account of who Jesus was and what happened to him. But here, in his trial speech (of comparable length), Jesus is known only through a 'heavenly vision' (26.13-19). The only mention Paul makes of the death and resurrection of Jesus is to say that 'Moses and the prophets said it was going to happen', not that anyone had actually seen it happen nor that there was any real evidence it did, much less that Pontius Pilate played a role in it and Roman records would confirm it (26.22-23). In fact the only source Paul cites for it is scripture. Paul preached only what 'the prophets and Moses said would happen, whether the Christ would suffer, whether from a resurrection from the dead he would be the first to proclaim light to [God's] people and to the Gentiles' (26.23). Revelations and scripture—his only sources, his only offered evidence.

It thus makes sense why Festus would answer, 'You've gone mad, Paul! Your abundant learning has driven you mad!' (26.24). Since the only thing Paul says he was accused of preaching is what he learned from scripture and from voices in the sky, the only rebuttal Festus *could* offer is that Paul had gone off his rocker. Paul assures him he hasn't, and says to Agrippa that, as a Jew, 'he knows about these things', because none of the facts Paul relates 'are hidden from him, since this has not been done in a corner' (Acts 26.26). What 'things' does Paul mean? That Paul has long been a devoted Pharisee (26.4-5); that he was being accused of merely hoping for the fulfillment of scripture (26.6), even though all Jews share that same hope (26.7), which is the hope that God would raise the dead (26.8); that Paul persecuted Christians (26.9-11), but then saw a blinding celestial vision from God (26.12-18), and he obeyed this vision and preached its message, which was simply 'to repent and turn to God and do works worthy of repentance', which he preached all over, and eventually to the Gentiles (26.19-20); and that the Jews seized Paul for preaching this message (26.21), and now he's on trial, 'saying nothing but what both the prophets and Moses said was going to happen' (26.22). Not a single reference to a historical Jesus. Every single fact here could be true without there having been a historical Jesus. As the Pharisees had already said of Paul at the first court inquest starting this whole series of hearings, 'maybe a spirit spoke to him, or an angel' (Acts 23.9). Indeed. In this whole account, from Acts 23 to Acts 26, that's all Paul appears to know about.

Even as fiction, the historical deeds and fate of Jesus would be crucial rhetorical material for both the prosecution and defense in all of Paul's trials. They should have been arguing over the facts of Jesus' ministry, teachings, miracles, the facts of his death and the fate of his body, the charges against him and the significance of his conviction, and whether he was still alive and at large, and what he was instructing his spiritual soldiers to do. That Luke wouldn't even think of this when inventing these narratives is hard to explain, especially since when he provides us with speeches elsewhere, not just from Peter but even from Paul (as in his Antioch synagogue speech), he gives us something of what we expect. Whereas here, all of those details have mysteriously vanished, despite this being collectively the longest and most detailed series of trial hearings related in Acts. I have to conclude it's at least *somewhat* more likely that Luke is reworking some narrative he received, a lost Acts of Paul, in which there was no Jesus executed by Pilate, but a cosmically dying-and-rising Christ known only through revelation and scripture.

Still, this does not leave me with a strong certainty. Possibly Luke wholly fabricated Paul's trials like everything else, and it just by coincidence didn't occur to him to put the same things in them that he did in most other speeches in Acts (even Paul's). Or maybe those things were in his sources for those episodes and he cut them for space, not realizing the coincidental effect his decision would produce. And so on. Whether any of those scenarios is plausible or probable I don't know. But I can imagine enough of them to say I would not rest an argument on this strange elision of the historical Jesus from the trials of Paul. I will say the probability of it, if historicity is true, is at best 9 in 10 (which means I'll allow a 90% probability that Luke would write the Pauline trial accounts in the way he did, even if Jesus existed), or at worst 1 in 2 (for a 50% probability he would do this). If, of course, he was using sources (and thus these elisions can reflect omissions in those sources). If not, then the odds might be nearer 1 in 1, because again, that would be almost as mysterious a thing to do on either historicity or myth.

5. *Stephen's Trial Speech*

I've already noted Burton Mack's observation that the sermons used to persuade Jews to become Christians all throughout Acts are simply not believable history.[34] In general we know the standard practice in antiquity, even for the soberest of historians, was to fabricate the speeches of historical actors, based on what the historian was sure they 'must' have said (see Element 44). They were rarely likely to have sources for the content of speeches anyway, and even when they had them, they were rarely likely to use them if they didn't agree with the story the author wanted to tell. And we can often tell this is what has happened.

Consider, for example, the longest speech in all of Acts, that of Stephen, delivered to the Sanhedrin immediately before he is executed by stoning (Acts 6.9–8.2), in the presence of Paul and with his approval (then called Saul: Acts 7.58; 8.1). There are historical inaccuracies in this account as we have it (Mishnah law required that a capital sentence be voted on the day after the trial, so the judges could think on it before taking a life, whereas Acts has the court stone him instantly, without even a vote), but that could be explained as a truncation of what really happened or as part of the original fiction Luke may be using as his source.[35] Similarly, Stephen's speech draws on the Septuagint (a popular Greek translation of the OT, perhaps an odd thing to do for a supposed native of Palestine in a Jerusalem courtroom, where summarizing the Hebrew original would be more expected), complete with errors only present in the Septuagint, but that could be a reflection of either its author's method of composing the fiction or Stephen's.[36]

Those elements don't concern us that much. But the overall content does. Stephen's speech is also unique in Acts in many other respects, for its

34. See also my survey in Carrier, *Not the Impossible Faith*, pp. 332-51. Although I am there rebutting Christian apologetics by adopting *a fortiori* their own system of assumptions (such as that Acts is mostly telling the truth), from an objective point of view the behavior of converts and evangelists surveyed there is simply far too unrealistic to have any historical plausibility.

35. On the one-day delay required of capital sentences: Mishnah, *Sanhedrin* 5.5.

36. On the 'mistakes' Stephen makes in recounting the OT see Rex Koivisto, 'Stephen's Speech: A Theology of Errors?', *Grace Theological Journal* 8 (1987), pp. 101-14. Though Koivisto is (absurdly) attempting to defend the inerrancy of Acts, he nevertheless thoroughly surveys the problems with the text. For a more secular treatment of the same problem: G.E. Sterling, '"Opening the Scriptures": The Legitimation of the Jewish Diaspora and the Early Christian Mission', in *Jesus and the Heritage of Israel: Luke's Narrative Claim upon Israel's Legacy* (ed. D.P. Moessner; Harrisburg, PA: Trinity Press International, 1999), pp. 199-225.

content, its construction, its length and its being assigned to an otherwise insignificant speaker. Stephen is only suddenly and inexplicably introduced in Acts 6.5, so as to immediately become the first Christian executed for the faith, a strange course of events given that Peter and John were twice tried for the exact same crimes and repeatedly acquitted, suggesting a huge narrative inconsistency that might again reflect Luke's employment of different sources (one treating the story of Paul; another, Peter and John), or else his remarkable ineptitude as an author.

Stephen himself is likely a fictional creation, a stock character representing a generic martyr. His name, *stephanos,* meaning 'crown', evokes the standard epithet for a faithful Christian and martyr: Rev. 2.10 encourages all Christians, 'Be faithful unto death, and I will give thee the crown of life [*stephanos tēs zōēs*]', and Jas 1.12 says all who remain faithful in the face of temptation will 'receive the crown of life [*stephanos tēs zōēs*]'. Also, 1 Pet. 5.4 says that when Jesus appears to the faithful, 'you shall receive the crown of glory [*stephanos tēs doxēs*] that never fades away', and 2 Tim. 4.8 says martyrs 'who love the appearing of Jesus' will receive 'the crown of righteousness' [*stephanos tēs dikaiosunēs*]—and notably Jesus 'appears' to Stephen immediately before he dies for the faith. Hebrews 2.7-8 likewise says Jesus was 'crowned with glory and honor' for his martyrdom, and the death of Stephen is indeed modeled on the death of Jesus: like Jesus, Stephen forgives his killers just before his death (Acts 7.60; Lk. 23.34); and just before they die, both Stephen and Jesus declare aloud that they give their spirit to God (Acts 7.59; Lk. 23.46); both deliver their last words 'with a great cry', *phōnē megalē* (Acts 7.60; Lk. 23.46); both have their garments taken and given away (Acts 7.58; Lk. 23.24); and just as Jesus says in his trial that his *accusers* will see 'the son of man sitting at the right hand of the power of God' (Lk. 22.69), Stephen says in his trial that *he* indeed sees 'the son of man sitting at the right hand of God' (Acts 7.55-56), yet his accusers don't (presumably because it is not yet the apocalypse).

Luke has also borrowed elements from Mark. Like Jesus, Stephen is accused by false witnesses that his enemies drum up against him (adapting Mk 14.55-59 to construct Acts 6.11-14), and the false accusations are also the same: Stephen is accused of claiming that 'this Jesus the Nazarene' was going to destroy the temple and change the laws, the same thing Jesus was charged with (in Mark). Notably, even though we know Luke used Mark as a source in constructing his Gospel, he omitted both of these details in his account of the arrest and trial of Jesus; he uses them, instead, only here. Yet we know he knew of them. So we can be certain Luke made a conscious choice to use those details, originally said of Jesus, in the account of Stephen instead. Which is a clear sign of fabricating the story. There is also a curious parallel between the unnamed young man [*neaniskos*] who has his garment torn away and flees naked at Jesus' arrest (Mk 14.51-52) and the *named* young man [*neanias*], Saul (i.e. Paul), who is *given* the garment torn from *Stephen* at his execution (Acts 7.58).

So when Luke inserts into Stephen's speech a brief reference to the historicity of Jesus (the Jews 'betrayed and murdered' Jesus just like their fathers murdered the prophets who foretold his coming: Acts 7.52-53), this could obviously be Luke importing his own narrative assumptions—particularly as he does not have Stephen provide any further detail nor have the Sanhedrin argue the point with him. Or it could have been a charge of mere cosmic responsibility, since Stephen in fact says, 'now you have become his betrayers and murderers *because* you received the law as an ordinance from angels and you did not keep it', implying it was their disobedience that compelled Christ's death (and not their actually killing him). Either way, Luke just assumes there would be no argument (which is historically implausible) and no reason for Stephen to be any more specific—even though he has Stephen speak over 1,200 words, consuming five pages of Greek, needlessly summarizing, at tedious length, the whole biblical history of the Jews . . . surely the miracles, ministry, trial and fate of Jesus were far more important facts to mention in his defense (Acts 7.2-53). As thus an evident fiction constructed by Luke, Stephen's speech is of no use in supporting historicity.

6. *The Possibility of 'Aramaic' Sources*

This is also why we cannot make any headway arguing that Luke had source material for the speeches in Acts 'because' a greater preponderance of so-called Semitisms are found in them than in the narrative sections—which is to say, idioms, grammar and vocabulary more distinctive of the Greek spoken by Hellenized Jews (like Luke himself may have been) or translated from Hebrew or Aramaic.[37] On the one hand, this information is of little use, since it cannot be determined which is occurring (are the Semitisms just how Luke writes in his own dialect or do they reflect his use of a source?), nor does either make the historicity of the speeches any more likely (since fictional speeches can be composed just as easily in Aramaic as in Greek. And even supposing these Semitisms indicate the use of a source, we cannot determine whether that source was in Aramaic, for example, or was simply an original composition by another author in a Semitized Greek, which could again be

37. See, e.g., the survey of D.F Payne, 'Semitisms in the Books of Acts', in *Apostolic History and the Gospel: Biblical and Historical Essays Presented to F.F. Bruce* (ed. W. Ward Gasque and Ralph P. Martin; Exeter: Paternoster Press, 1970), pp. 134-50.

just as fictional).[38] On the other hand, Semitisms can also be an effect of a greater reliance on the Septuagint (a text already written in a highly Semitized Greek) when composing speeches, where more extensive and more frequent allusions to and quotations of scripture are expected, even if the speeches are entirely composed by the same author writing the narrative sections.

For example, the very first speech in Acts, in which Peter implausibly persuades thousands of Jews to become Christians in a single day (Acts 2.41), is sometimes offered as a good example of the concept of being in a more Semitized Greek than the surrounding narrative, and yet in it Peter quotes not the Hebrew Bible or an Aramaic Targum but the Greek Septuagint, verbatim. The most crucial part of his speech turns on his interpretation of Pss. 16.9-10 in Acts 2.26-31, but instead of quoting the Hebrew original, he gives a verbatim quote of the Septuagint (Ps. 16.10 is word-for-word identical between Acts and the Septuagint, and Ps. 16.9 is also identical in every word, with only a few insignificant changes of order). In reality, Peter would hardly attempt to persuade Jews in Jerusalem by haranguing them in Greek, much less succeed at it; and he certainly wouldn't have persuaded many of them by appealing to a Greek translation of the Bible rather than the original Hebrew text. No, this is *Luke's* construction of the speech. Luke is using the Septuagint to build the quotes in Peter's argument. That destroys any hope of recovering what Peter might have originally said, even if Luke somehow had some source for it.

Finally, as D.F. Payne says:

> Luke's indebtedness to the [Septuagint] was profound, but it was by no means his only influence. Other Old Testament textual traditions were known to him; Semitic idioms common in the contemporary church . . . [also] affected his diction; and there is no good reason to doubt that he had access to traditions or documents couched in, or translated from, a Semitic language. . . . However, such Semitic elements in Luke's writing must not be pressed to support conclusions which they will not bear. [Hedley] Sparks emphasizes, after analysis of his specimen passages, that Lucanisms surround the Semitisms. [Max] Wilcox too, on the basis of his more full analysis, asserts that his survey shows that 'in almost every case the material in which they ["hard-core" Semitisms] are embedded has a strongly Lucan stamp'.[39]

In other words, even where Semitisms appear in greater abundance, those sections also show unmistakable evidence of distinctly Lukan style. Which means Luke has completely reworked any sources he may have used, delet-

38. On the logical inadequacy of 'arguments from semitisms' in general see Carrier, *Proving History*, pp. 185-86.

39. Payne, 'Semitisms in the Books of Acts', p. 145-46.

ing, changing and adding to them as he pleased. We therefore cannot know what any sources he may have used actually said. For all we know Luke may have taken a mythicist speech collection (such as I just argued for Paul's trial speeches) and added historicist flourishes to it. Since we have abundantly demonstrated that Acts was literarily crafted and much of its content freely invented by Luke, and Luke was certainly interested in promoting historicity, Acts' reliability for demonstrating the historicity of Jesus is essentially non-existent.

7. *Weighing the Evidence*

Luke's wanton fabrications, including his use of Josephus to make his story seem more historically informed, and his complete rewrite of history to reverse the facts reported directly by Paul, and his overt attempts to make his books look like histories (e.g. adding such embellishments as Lk. 1.1-4; 2.1-2; and 3.1-2), pretty much establish that he is not honestly reporting the facts as he knows them. He is trying to create facts and sell them as the truth. This makes it impossible for us to know if Luke was a historicist himself, or merely trying to sell a historicist creed.

But either way, we cannot use Acts as evidence for historicity. For anything in it will have been *designed* to convince us of historicity, with no assurance of any real basis in fact, and abundant reason to doubt there is any. But a text specifically fabricated to convince us of historicity, such as this, *can* give us evidence of myth, if material in it doesn't make sense otherwise. The evidence in that case has slipped through—against what Luke obviously would have wanted, but due most likely to his not being able to think of everything, as most authors don't. After all, as the ubiquity of implausible novels and film scripts today well enough attests, even the smartest of people don't consistently compose realistic narratives or realize the holes in the plots they've contrived.

If Acts is a wholesale fabrication, however, written in total ignorance of what may have actually happened, then Acts might afford no evidence for either historicity or myth. Its historical value either way could then be simply nil. So its effect on the probability of historicity depends on whether we conclude Acts was composed in total ignorance of what may have actually happened or with some awareness of what actually happened during the first years and decades of Christianity, and thus has been at least partly influenced by that information. As I argued after discussing the trial transcripts (§§4 and 5) and the vanishing acts (§3), I think it's unlikely the author of Acts had *no* information. His having some better explains the oddities I document. I will therefore assume he did (that the probability of this approaches 100%, close enough not to have to consider the alternative mathematically). But you may have a different view, believing it more likely that Acts was written in total ignorance, in which case you have a harder mathematical task ahead of you.[40]

Setting that aside, tabulating my previous estimates (so you can substitute your own) we get the following ratios between the consequent probability that Acts would look like it does if minimal historicity is true, and the consequent probability that Acts would look like it does if minimal historicity is false:

	best	*worst*
Vanishing family *et al.*	4/5	2/5
Omissions in Paul's trials	9/10	1/2
Remainder of Acts	1/1	1/1
Totals	36 / 50	2 / 10
	8 / 25	1 / 5
	1 / 1.39	1 / 5
	0.7200	0.2000
	72%	20%

Conversely, nothing in Acts is unexpected on minimal mythicism, as on that account anything historicizing in it is a mythical invention of Luke's (and we've proved Luke was doing that a lot), while the omissions and vanishing acts would be the inevitable result of there being no historical Jesus. So the same consequent probabilities on $\neg h$ can be treated as all 100% across the board.[41] That leaves the probability of Acts looking this way on h equal to 72% at best, and 20% at worst. The content of Acts is therefore evidence against the historicity of Jesus.

40. If we designate the evidence of Acts as e_a, then the basic equation for the effect of Acts on our results is $P(e_a|h.b) = [P(knowledge) \times P(e_a|knowledge)] + [P(ignorance) \times P(e_a|ignorance)]$, where P(knowledge) is your estimate of the probability that Luke had *some* sources or information ultimately dating back to the time in question; and P(ignorance) is the converse of that (i.e. P(ignorance) = 1 - P(knowledge)). Then $P(e_a|ignorance) = 1$ (since in that event any oddities in Acts no longer have any causal connection to the truth) and $P(e_a|knowledge)$ is either the probability I assign to Acts or whatever your estimate of that is. For some of the problems you will face here, see discussion in Chapter 12 (§2).

41. And even if not (if instead we set this probability at *less* than 100%), it doesn't matter, since the ratio of the two probabilities will remain the same. See note in Chapter 8 (§13).

10

The Evidence of the Gospels

1. *How to Invent a Gospel*

Among the many texts recovered from the fourth-century stash of codices recovered from Nag Hammadi, Egypt, are two in particular: *Eugnostos the Blessed* and the *Wisdom of Jesus Christ*. The peculiar thing about these two texts is that they pull away the curtain and reveal a key pathway by which Jesus tradition was invented.

Eugnostos is a fake epistle written by what is almost certainly a fake person ('Eugnostos' means 'well knowing', an obviously fictional name), possibly composed before Christianity, as it contains no material distinctive of Christianity, but appears to outline an esoteric doctrine of Jewish theology concerning the firstborn celestial Son of God, called the Savior and Son of Man (see Elements 39 to 41). The *Wisdom of Jesus Christ* then takes direct quotations from this epistle and puts them on the lips of Jesus, and expands on them, to fabricate a post-resurrection narrative scene with dialogue between Jesus and his disciples. So here we see whole sayings of Jesus being invented by fabricating a historical conversation (a Gospel-style narrative), borrowing things said by Eugnostos and representing them as things said by Jesus in conversation with his disciples.[1] This could be how much of the canonical Gospels were composed: things said by other people, in other texts, being 'lifted' and adapted and placed on the lips of Jesus. Certainly these two texts prove this was being done. And we have no *a priori* reason to believe this isn't how it was always done.

We've already seen examples of the sayings of Jesus being lifted directly from the scriptures in *1 Clement* (see Chapter 8, §5). And knowing that 'the scriptures' included more books and variants than we have (Element 9), this raises the possibility that sayings of Jesus were lifted from *lost* scriptures, too. Sayings were also invented for Jesus from previous Christian writings. Of course, sayings for Jesus, and situations for him to say them in, could also have been simply invented by each Gospel author as he required,

1. See the side-by-side translations in *The Nag Hammadi Library in English* (ed. James Robinson; San Francisco, CA: Harper & Row, 3rd edn, 1988).

or by the author of whatever (now lost) Gospel they were redacting. This is how entire collections of sayings were invented for Daniel and Moses. So why not also for Jesus? Indeed the Mishnah (apart from lines attributed to subsequent rabbis) was supposed to be the accumulated teachings of Moses passed down orally (the 'Oral Torah'), but surely it is really just an accumulated collection of what other men said, not Moses; attributing it all to Moses was simply a way of bestowing authority.[2] We also know sayings for Jesus came from revelations, which could then have been placed on the lips of Jesus in a fabricated historical setting as if said by a historical man, rather than, as originally, an imagined spirit of Jesus communicating to an entranced apostle (whether hallucinating or pretending to be: Elements 15 and 16; see next chapter, §4).

If historical settings could be invented to make Jesus say what Eugnostos said, certainly historical settings could be invented to make Jesus say what he was believed to have said in revelations (such as to Paul or any other apostle), or was claimed to have said in revelations—as, for example, in the book of Revelation. We'll see in the next chapter that revelation and scripture appear to be the only source Paul knew for the sayings of Jesus. He shows no knowledge of them existing in any kind of historical narrative—except in one instance, the inauguration of the Eucharist, and that he explicitly says came to him by revelation! (See Element 16; and in the next chapter, §7.) Inventing historical narratives in which to place or adapt sayings was commonplace in ancient biography, even in general, but especially in faith literature (Element 44). That was actually the norm.

So the question is: Are the Gospels fictional constructs, like the *Wisdom of Jesus Christ* and Plutarch's *Life of Romulus*? In other words, are they just myths? Or are they some kind of historical records we can rely on to prove Jesus existed?

2. Deuteronomy is likewise wholly fiction, yet begins very similarly to the Gospel of Mark: 'these are the words Moses spoke unto all Israel beyond the Jordan in the wilderness' (Deut. 1.1). Dennis MacDonald has argued that the earliest (but now lost) Gospel on which all others are based is essentially a rewrite of Deuteronomy, only casting Jesus (the new 'savior') as Moses and revising its moral program: see Dennis MacDonald, *Two Shipwrecked Gospels: The Logoi of Jesus and Papias's Exposition of Logia about the Lord* (Atlanta, GA: Society of Biblical Literature, 2012). Note that Islam saw a similarly rapid invention of large bodies of sayings for Muhammad, in order to lend greater authority to what *others* in fact had said, and if that can happen to Muhammad, it could happen to Jesus: see Robert Price, 'The Abhorrent Void: The Rapid Attribution of Fictive Sayings and Stories to a Mythic Jesus', in *Sources of the Jesus Tradition: Separating History from Myth* (ed. R. Joseph Hoffmann; Amherst, NY: Prometheus Books, 2010), pp. 109-17; with Ram Swarup, *Understanding the Hadith: The Sacred Traditions of Islam* (Amherst, NY: Prometheus Books, 2002); and Muhammad Zubayr Siddiqi, *Hadith Literature: Its Origin, Development and Special Features* (ed. and rev. Abdal Hakim Murad; Cambridge: Islamic Texts Society, 2nd edn, 1993).

2. *What Is Myth?*

There has been frequent debate over the genre of the Gospels and whether they are fundamentally myth or history.[3] But myth is not really a literary 'genre' in the standard sense, since it crosses all genres of literary composition. Plutarch's biography of Romulus is entirely myth, for example, yet written in the genre of historical biography (see Chapter 4, §1, and Element 47). Most attempts at identifying the genre of the Gospels consist of comparing it to other literary forms, but this has only resulted in either unresolved disagreement or classifying the Gospels as a unique genre of their own, which unhelpfully eliminates the opportunity to interpret them (or assess their historical value) by comparison with documents of similar genre. Even classifying the Gospels as biographies is unhelpful, as demonstrated by the example of Plutarch's *Life of Romulus*: even if the Gospels perfectly corresponded with the genre of ancient historical biography, that in itself would not indicate whether they were in fact historical or mythical. For in fact, a great deal of ancient biography, even of real people, was constructed of myth and fiction.[4] Accordingly, our aim should not be identifying the 'genre' of the Gospels but the intent of their authors: whatever literary form they chose or created, were they writing myth or history?

3. This debate is partly surveyed in Paul Rhodes Eddy and Gregory Boyd, 'The Genre and Nature of the Canonical Gospels', in *The Jesus Legend: A Case for the Historical Reliability of the Synoptic Jesus Tradition* (Grand Rapids, MI: Baker Academic, 2007), pp. 309-61. Prominent examples of diverse views on the matter (not all of them plausible) include Charles Talbert, *What Is a Gospel? The Genre of the Canonical Gospels* (Philadelphia, PA: Fortress Press, 1977); David Aune, *The New Testament in its Literary Environment* (Philadelphia, PA: Westminster Press, 1987), pp. 17-76; Richard Burridge, *What Are the Gospels? A Comparison with Graeco-Roman Biography* (New York: Cambridge University Press, 1992); Lawrence Wills, *The Quest of the Historical Gospel: Mark, John, and the Origins of the Gospel Genre* (New York: Routledge, 1997); Michael E. Vines, *The Problem of Markan Genre: The Gospel of Mark and the Jewish Novel* (Leiden: Brill, 2002); Thomas Thompson, *The Messiah Myth: The Near Eastern Roots of Jesus and David* (New York: Basic Books, 2005); and Richard Bauckham, *Jesus and the Eyewitnesses: The Gospels as Eyewitness Testimony* (Grand Rapids, MI: William B. Eerdmans, 2006). See also (as particularly relevant to the present discussion) Meredith Kline, 'The Old Testament Origins of the Gospel Genre', *Westminster Theological Journal* 38 (1975), pp. 1-27; Mary Ann Tolbert, *Sowing the Gospel: Mark's World in Literary-Historical Perspective* (Philadelphia, PA: Fortress Press, 1989), pp. 48-79; and Evan Fales, 'Taming the Tehom: The Sign of Jonah in Matthew', in *Empty Tomb* (ed. Price and Lowder), pp. 307-48 (esp. pp. 307-19).

4. See discussion and scholarship cited in Element 44. That the genres of 'history' and 'biography' had become fully merged with mythmaking by the time the Gospels were written is also demonstrated by Charles Talbert, 'Biographies of Philosophers and Rulers as Instruments of Religious Propaganda in Mediterranean Antiquity', *Aufstieg und Niedergang der römischen Welt II* 16 (1978), pp. 1619-51.

There are countless definitions of myth employed in a variety of fields, and debate persists as to what exactly myth is.[5] But such debates need not be resolved here. If someone claims the Gospels are 'myth' they can define myth any way they please, so long as they demonstrate the Gospels conform to that definition, and then remain consistent with that definition when drawing conclusions. The major trend in the study of myth today is reflected and well surveyed by Radcliffe Edmonds in his own summary of myth scholarship and its main conclusions.[6] In that school of thought, myth consists of factually untrue stories that are historically improbable but symbolically meaningful. Myths in that sense operate according to three basic rules:

(1) A mythic story is a seemingly straightforward account of something that happened, yet its content and structure are carefully arranged to convey a deeper meaning than the superficial narrative might suggest. (2) This is accomplished using symbols familiar to the audience (keywords, ironies, allusions, double entendres, etc., relying on a known database of cultural, literary, religious, grammatical and other facts). And (3) what an author of a myth changes is often the point of the myth. For example, if the story is highly allusive to another myth, yet reverses or radically alters certain elements of that myth, the allusions indicate what myth to compare the changes to, and the changes indicate how the author's message is meant to differ from the message of the earlier myth.

In the words of Radcliffe Edmonds:

> Not only can an exploration of the various ways in which authors use a common set of elements uncover the different agendas of these authors and provide a deeper understanding of the individual texts, but it can also shed light on the ways in which myth was used . . . as a device for communication, a mode of speaking in which they could convey meaning densely through the manipulation of mythic motifs and patterns that each had its own resonance for the audience.[7]

Very often this communicated message involved plans for reforming society, or proposing and defending models for how society or the world should function (or do function). To this end, myths communicate the values and universal truths embraced by the author, which the author desires his audience to embrace in turn.

5. See, e.g., Bruce Lincoln, *Theorizing Myth: Narrative, Ideology, and Scholarship* (Chicago: University of Chicago Press, 1999).

6. Radcliffe Edmonds, *Myths of the Underworld Journey: Plato, Aristophanes, and the 'Orphic' Gold Tablets* (Cambridge: Cambridge University Press, 2004), pp. 1-13. For a more extensive treatise on Edmonds-style understanding of myth see William Doty, *Mythography: The Study of Myths and Rituals* (Tuscaloosa, AL: University of Alabama Press, 2nd edn, 2000); and Walter Burkert, *Structure and History in Greek Mythology and Ritual* (Berkeley, CA: University of California Press, 1979).

7. Edmonds, *Myths*, p. 4.

As Edmonds puts it:

> The Greek poetic and mythic tradition provides the *models of* and *models for* the society, models which are given authoritative status as a description of the way the cosmos is constituted and of the proper modes of behavior within it . . . [and] their elements are symbols that enunciate a model with a general application. However, each myth, each telling of a traditional tale, presents a different variation of the model; as the teller shapes the narrative according to his perceptions of the cultural models . . . [so] the symbolic elements within the tradition are manipulated by the teller . . . [and] this symbolic system provides a language by which the myth-teller may communicate with his audience . . . [and] as a result, every myth is shaped by its context and the motivations of its narrator.[8]

If the Gospels are 'myth' in this sense, then we have a ready explanation for the considerable contradictions and changes in the Jesus-story across the four canonical Gospels (and other Gospels beyond), to which modern apologists respond with increasingly implausible *ad hoc* harmonizations, while historians respond with attempts to develop criteria to isolate the historical truth behind the conflicting accounts (a method that has consistently been found invalid).[9]

But if the Gospels are myth, then both efforts are futile, as both assume the intent of the authors is to record (if perhaps embellish) a collection of historical facts reported to them. If instead the intent of the authors is to construct symbolic myths about Jesus, then we have no reason to expect any of their content to be historical. Some of it may be, but since distinguishing fact from fiction would not have been of primary interest to the Gospels' authors, we will have little hope of finding clues to such distinctions in the texts themselves. We can work with external corroboratory evidence to isolate the factual elements (an ideal example being the archaeological and literary confirmation of the existence of Pontius Pilate). So confirming the Gospels are myth would not in itself entail, for example, the conclusion that Jesus did not exist. But it would greatly alter and limit our ability to know the historical truth about Jesus, and would fundamentally change our focus in studying the content of the Gospels—from an interest in extracting history from that content, to an interest in ascertaining its mytho-symbolic meaning and intent (see Chapter 12, §3).

This is often easier to see outside the field of biblical studies, where blinding bias runs less rampant. In the *Iliad*, for example, Homer depicts a boxing match between two young men named Epeius and Euryalus. Epeius boasts of being undefeatable, in typical Homeric fashion, and then over-

8. Edmonds, *Myths*, p. 6. Edmonds further shows that myth is independent of genre, as it can appear in any and every literary genre imaginable: Edmonds, *Myths*, p. 7.

9. As I demonstrate in Carrier, *Proving History*, pp. 11-16 and 121-206.

whelmingly defeats his opponent. Centuries later, in the *Aeneid*, Virgil mimicked this boxing match. But Virgil replaces Epeius and Euryalus with the Roman heroes Dares and Entellus and changes its geographical location, its historical date and even its outcome.[10] Nevertheless, there are enough intentional similarities to confirm that updating Homer's tale was Virgil's intent, and the changes Virgil made (apart from the trivia of when, where and who) become more meaningful when this emulation is recognized. In Virgil's account, instead of the boxers being two young men, Entellus is an old man who laments his lost youth. Then the Homeric plot is reversed: young Dares, the powerful braggart, does not win as his counterpart does in Homer. Instead, the old man, Entellus, although taking a fall just like his Homeric counterpart Euryalus, returns with a fury and overwhelmingly defeats his foe, who is described the same way Homer had described the defeated Euryalus: carried by his comrades and spitting out blood. Unlike the Homeric story, in Virgil's account Entellus was driven to return to the fight by a sense of shame and valor, which were moral values emphasized in Roman culture. Virgil's story also reverses the Homeric glorification of youth and denigration of the elderly, again to reflect the more 'modern' values of Virgil's time.[11] The following diagram maps the parallels:

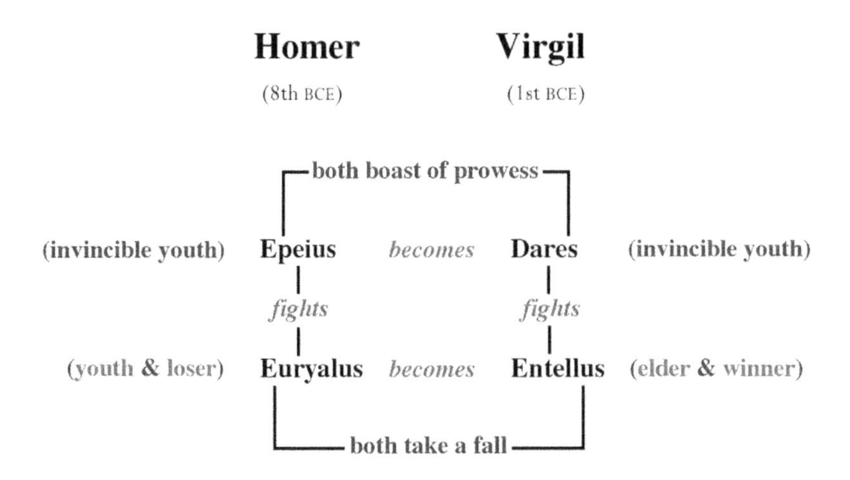

Figure 1. From Homer to Virgil

10. *Iliad* 23.624-99; and *Aeneid* 5.387-484.

11. On this latter point see Thomas Falkner, *The Poetics of Old Age in Greek Epic, Lyric, and Tragedy* (Norman: OK: University of Oklahoma Press, 1995); see, e.g., *Iliad* 23.624-50.

Thus, Virgil has told the same story as Homer, but he has recast the characters into a different historical setting and changed the plot in order to reflect and communicate how Roman values differ from Homeric values.

This was a common practice: how you changed a myth was a way of communicating how your message differed from the earlier myth. Thus, when we find parallels in a later myth with an earlier myth, the way those two myths *differ* from each other is often the author's reason for borrowing from the earlier myth in the first place. What the new author leaves out, what he adds, what he changes is all the point of the story, and is what we need to look at in order to understand what the author is saying. Virgil was certainly not saying that Homer got the historical context wrong, that the boxing match really took place at a different time and place between different people. Nor was Virgil saying that Homer incorrectly reported the historical outcome of the boxing match. It's doubtful either Homer or Virgil believed this boxing match actually happened, even though they both place the match in history and record it in a straightforward narrative that looks no different from any poetic record of witness testimony.

Instead, Virgil is retelling this event in order to symbolically communicate his different values. What matters to him is not whether this boxing match occurred. What matters to him are the underlying values and message the story conveys. We thus don't gain any understanding if we try to harmonize these contradictory tales or to ascertain what actual historical event inspired them (even if any did). We gain understanding only by recognizing the parallels and changes intended by Virgil, and the significance of the resulting symbolism of the story's structure and content.[12] What the story *means* is all we can study, and all we should study, not whether it actually happened. Only rarely are we able to do more.

It is therefore crucially important to determine whether the Gospels are myth. This cannot be achieved by identifying their genre, because myth exists in all genres. It can be achieved only by confirming whether they contain narratives that conform more to the definition of myth than of history. Are the central narratives of the Gospels historically improbable but symbolically meaningful? Is this meaning concealed by a superficially 'historical' narrative that is highly allusive to other myths, texts or concepts that increase both the *interpretability* and *likelihood* of the content of that narrative, more than a supposition of history would? And is this evident in both the parallels to and the conspicuous deviations from those targets

12. Virgil's *Aeneid* is full of such transvaluations of Homer, rewriting Homeric narratives with Roman characters and values; e.g. 'Virgil imitated the death of Hector [in Homer's *Iliad*] when composing his account of the death of Turnus', Dennis MacDonald, 'Imitations of Greek Epic in the Gospels', in *Historical Jesus in Context* (ed. Levine, Allison and Crossan), pp. 372-84 (380); see pp. 375-80.

of allusion? In short, is the content of those narratives more likely on the theory that they are myth or on the theory that they are history?

Characteristics of myth are (1) strong and meaningful emulation of prior myths (or even of real events); (2) the presence of historical improbabilities (which are not limited to 'miracles' but can include natural events that are very improbable, like amazing coincidences or unrealistic behavior); and (3) the absence of external corroboration of key (rather than peripheral) elements (because a myth can incorporate real people and places, but the central character or event will still be fictional). No one of these criteria is sufficient to identify a narrative as mythical. But the presence of all three is conclusive. And the presence of one or two can also be sufficient, when sufficiently telling.[13]

We must avoid 'parallelomania', of course, the error of finding patterns everywhere by relaxing what counts as a parallel or finding parallels that have no identifiable reason to be present. Avoiding that requires focusing only on features that, altogether, are very improbable on any other explanation. Thus, chance correlations can be distinguished from genuine signatures of mytho-symbolic composition. This does mean we might have to set aside correlations that might be mytho-symbolic but cannot be proven to be. But that does not mean concluding they are *not* mytho-symbolic, only that we cannot be certain they are. Meanwhile, in many cases we *can* be reasonably certain. And if we find enough of those in a single text, this supports the conclusion that the remainder are as well, according to the principle of contamination, which Stephen Law has formally articulated for 'miracle' content.[14] His argument can be fully extended to *all* improbabilities, including emulative features of a story that are improbable coincidences if posited as history but not improbable as an authorial creation.[15]

In Bayesian terms, and with respect to the Gospels, what we are looking for in each pericope (each internally complete narrative unit within a Gospel) are features that are improbable as history but probable as myth. More precisely, that means features that have a lower consequent probability on h ('history') than they have on $\neg h$ ('myth'), not in respect to Jesus being a myth but just in respect to the pericope itself being a myth. If we start with no assumptions and thus assign a prior probability of 0.5 for h in this sense (and thus also for $\neg h$, i.e., assuming both are equally probable at the

13. For the logic underlying this, see Carrier, *Proving History*, pp. 114-17 (for emulation as a signature: 192-204; for improbable events as a signature: 177-79; and for when missing corroboration can be a signature: 117-19).

14. Stephen Law, 'Evidence, Miracles, and the Existence of Jesus', *Faith and Philosophy* 28 (April 2011), pp. 129-51, available at http://stephenlaw.blogspot.com/2012/04/published-in-faith-and-philosophy-2011.html.

15. Carrier, *Proving History*, pp. 195-204.

outset), and count the whole content of a pericope as *e*, and then find that $P(e|h) < P(e|\neg h)$, the result will be that $P(h|e)$ will be less than 0.5, and that means the prior, the $P(h)$, that we use to examine the *next* pericope will be less than 0.5. If we find that $P(e|h) < P(e|\neg h)$ for that pericope, too, then $P(h)$ falls even further. And so on. If for any pericope $P(e|h) = P(e|\neg h)$, it then has no effect. But if $P(e|h) > P(e|\neg h)$ for any pericope, then that can start to restore credibility by raising $P(h|e)$ for that pericope and thus raising the $P(h)$ for the next or remaining pericopes. However, if that never happens, or rarely happens, or happens only too weakly, then the cumulative effect of the other pericopes will be a substantially reduced prior probability that *any* pericope is historical rather than mythical. In short, if there are many clear instances of mythmaking in a Gospel, and no clear instances of the contrary, then the remainder of that Gospel must be assumed to be (more probably than not) mythical, even if we can't prove it in any of those remaining cases.

The effect of this on historicity will not be to establish that Jesus didn't exist but to eliminate evidence for his existence. That technically does mean it raises the probability of the ahistoricity of Jesus, but only by the amount that that probability *would have been lowered* by the Gospels being historical accounts of him. The net effect is simply the removal of the Gospels as evidence (as Burton Mack has already argued we should do).[16] We already know, as a general rule, that completely fictional accounts can be written about historical persons *and* seemingly straightforward historical accounts can be written about non-historical persons. So which it is (whether the Gospels are fictions about a historical person, or fictions about a nonhistorical person) will have to depend on what the remaining evidence indicates (that of the Epistles, to be examined in the next chapter, or that of the other evidence, examined in Chapters 8 and 9).

There is one important exception to this point: the Rank–Raglan data, which was used to construct our prior probability (in Chapter 6), because it can be correlated with enough examples to derive an actual probability that such data would accumulate for a real man. But we have already employed that evidence in our calculation (and only if we didn't would we introduce it here: see Chapter 6 and the end of §2 in Chapter 12). Thus, the mythic character of the Gospels overall *will* affect our estimate of historicity. But only as much as it already has.

16. See Burton Mack, *The Christian Myth: Origins, Logic, and Legacy* (New York: Continuum, 2001), who also argues we need a better theory of the origin of Christianity, one that takes the role of mythmaking in early Christianity seriously (and I agree). Mack also extensively discusses what the term 'myth' means and what its functions were, much in line with what I have argued here.

3. *Examining the Gospels*

Several scholars have confirmed that by the standards of myth I just spelled out, the Gospels are primarily and pervasively mythical.[17] In the words of Marcus Borg, we have to admit '(1) that much of the language of the Gospels is metaphorical; (2) that what matters is the more-than-literal meaning and (3) that the more-than-literal meaning does not depend upon the historical factuality of the language'.[18] That makes the Gospels allegorical myth, not remembered history (see Element 14). I will here extract and summarize the best examples illustrating this, and show how the end result must be a dismissal of the Gospels as evidence for historicity. But first I must address several other aspects of the Gospels that reinforce this point.

Elsewhere I have already demonstrated that they lack all substantive (as opposed to superficial) markers of being researched histories, even by the lax standards of antiquity.[19] At no point do the Gospels name their sources or discuss their relative merits or why they are relying on them; at no point do the Gospels exhibit any historiographical consciousness (such as discussing methods, or the possibility of information being incorrect, or the existence of non-polemical alternative accounts); they don't even express amazement at anything they report, no matter how incredible it is (unlike a more rational historian); and they never explain why they changed what their sources said, nor do they even acknowledge the fact that they did (as when, e.g., Luke or Matthew alters what they derive from Mark). And unlike many other ancient authors, they do not explain who they are or why they are qualified to relate the accounts they do. Only one Gospel, Luke, employs even the superficial trappings of actual history writing, such as explaining what his purpose in writing is and attempting to date events. But as we already saw (in Chapter 9) that appears to be a ruse.

17. Besides the others I shall cite as I go, the best examples, which are required reading on this subject, are, in order from introductory to advanced: (1) John Dominic Crossan, *The Power of Parable: How Fiction by Jesus Became Fiction about Jesus* (New York: HarperOne, 2012); (2) Randel Helms, *Gospel Fictions* (Amherst, NY: Prometheus Books, 1988); (3) Dennis MacDonald, *The Homeric Epics and the Gospel of Mark* (New Haven, CT: Yale University Press, 2000); (4) Thomas Thompson, *The Messiah Myth: The Near Eastern Roots of Jesus and David* (New York: Basic Books, 2005); and (5) Thomas Brodie, *The Birthing of the New Testament: The Intertextual Development of the New Testament Writings* (Sheffield: Sheffield Phoenix Press, 2004).

18. Marcus Borg, *Jesus: Uncovering the Life, Teachings, and Relevance of a Religious Revolutionary* (San Francisco, CA: HarperSanFrancisco, 2006), p. 52.

19. See Carrier, *Not the Impossible Faith*, pp. 161-218; and Carrier, *Sense and Goodness*, pp. 246-47.

As we shall see through the rest of this chapter, the Gospels also cannot be classified as eyewitness testimony or even the collection of it.[20] They do not read as such, and they do not identify themselves as such. Even John, who alone cites what we shall see is a fabricated unnamed witness, claims to have been using something that witness *wrote*, in other words a prior Gospel, perhaps the Gospel our John is redacting; but more likely, as with Luke, this is again just a ruse (see §7). Instead, the Gospels look like the edifying but fictional biographies composed for many other heroes and sages (see Element 44). As David Gowler observes, they appear to be an assembled network of vignettes (*pericopes* in the language of biblical studies) that were already identified in ancient schools as *chreiai*, a standard rhetorical device that was extensively taught to all students of literary Greek (and as the authors of the Gospels wrote in literary Greek, we know they attended those schools).

Students were actually taught to invent narratives about famous and legendary persons, and to build a symbolic or moral message out of general rules or proverbs.[21] As Gowler explains, 'the composition of the stories in the Synoptic Gospels is very similar to such exercises as the expansion and elaboration of *chreiai* found in other ancient literature and delineated in ancient rhetorical handbooks', in which authors 'were free to vary the wording, details, and dynamics of *chreiai* according to their ideological and rhetorical interests', and in fact they 'were taught and encouraged' to make both minor and major changes even to traditional stories in order to make whatever point they desired.[22] Schools also taught the method of emulating

20. Christian apologist Richard Bauckham, in *Jesus and the Eyewitnesses*, attempts to argue otherwise, but there are far too many implausibilities in his case, combined with an over-reliance on the *possibiliter* fallacy (Carrier, *Proving History*, pp. 26-29). See the various critiques in the *Journal for the Study of the Historical Jesus* 6 (2008); and the critical review of Dean Bechard (of the Pontifical Biblical Institute in Rome) in *Biblica* 90 (2009), pp. 126-29; and the argument of Thomas Brodie, *Beyond the Quest for the Historical Jesus: A Memoir of a Discovery* (Sheffield: Sheffield Phoenix Press, 2012), pp. 115-36. The present chapter's evidence of extensive literary artifice is alone sufficient to refute his case (see also Chapter 6, §7); a conclusion only reinforced by the extensive evidence of precedent (see Elements 44 to 48). Likewise, Christian apologists Paul Eddy and Gregory Boyd, in *The Jesus Legend: A Case for the Historical Reliability of the Synoptic Jesus Tradition* (Grand Rapids, MI: Baker, 2007), also attempt to argue as Bauckham does, but their case is even more mired in implausibilities, contradictions and undemonstrated assertions, as illustrated by Ken Olson in his review of their book for the online *Review of Biblical Literature* (December 20, 2008) at http://www.bookreviews.org/pdf/6281_6762.pdf; and by Robert Price in his extended critique in 'Jesus: Myth and Method', in *Christian Delusion* (ed. Loftus), pp. 273-90.

21. David Gowler, 'The *Chreia*', in *The Historical Jesus in Context* (ed. Levine, Allison, and Crossan), pp. 132-48.

22. Gowler, 'The *Chreia*', pp. 132, 134.

old stories by rewriting them into new ones with new characters and outcomes—in other words, what we saw Virgil had done to Homer was a standard method of composing stories taught in all schools of the day.[23] Which means ancient schools taught their students how to construct symbolically meaningful historical fiction, by both innovating and emulating other fiction. And as I'll show, this is what we see happening in the Gospels.

So the Gospels are simply not historical records, even when they try to pass themselves off as such (like other fictional literature often did: see Element 44). To the contrary, they are literary constructs through and through, intelligently designed by their authors to communicate what they wanted, not simply what they were told. In fact it will become quite clear that the Gospels operate through extended parables, not recollections of memory, direct or transmitted. Insofar as they incorporate any materials passed on to them, their sources could have been prior scriptures and texts (like the use of *Eugnostos* in writing the *Wisdom of Jesus Christ* or the use of the Psalms to derive sayings for Jesus in *1 Clement*) or revelations (like those reported by Paul) or the inventions of prior Gospel authors (like, as we shall see, John's use of Luke, Luke's use of Matthew, and Matthew's use of Mark).[24]

It's also known that much of the Gospels consists of rewrites of pre-Christian Jewish tales (and sometimes pagan), from scripture and beyond, such

23. Tim Whitmarsh, *Greek Literature and the Roman Empire: The Politics of Imitation* (New York: Oxford University Press, 2001); Raffaella Cribiore, *Gymnastics of the Mind: Greek Education in Hellenistic and Roman Egypt* (Princeton, NJ: Princeton University Press, 2001); MacDonald, *Homeric Epics*, pp. 4-6; and Dennis MacDonald, *Christianizing Homer: The Odyssey, Plato, and the Acts of Andrew* (New York: Oxford University Press, 1994). There is a good survey of the evidence and scholarship on this aspect of ancient education and composition in Brodie, *Birthing of the New Testament*, pp. 2-79.

24. I am rejecting outright all apologetic arguments, such as that of Mark Strauss, who claims 'it pushes the limits of credulity to argue that the same early Christians who taught the greatest ethical system in the world, passionately proclaimed the truth of their message, and suffered and died for their faith were at the same time dishonest schemers and propagators of a great fraud' (Mark Strauss, *Four Portraits, One Jesus: An Introduction to Jesus and the Gospels* [Grand Rapids, MI: Zondervan, 2007], p. 388), as that ignores the reality of the whole of Christian literature which is awash with such fraud (even in the NT itself), and likewise all faith literature generally (see Element 44), and all the obvious evidence of invention and fabrication in the Gospels, and also unjustifiably presumes the Gospels were written by martyrs (he cannot possibly know this; see Chapter 7, §4), and that martyrs don't have even more incentive to lie to promote the moral system they are dying for (when in fact the risks they undertake highly incentivize lying to ensure their victory: see Carrier, *Not the Impossible Faith*, pp. 219-36 and 281-85; and Carrier, 'Why the Resurrection Is Unbelievable', in *Christian Delusion* [ed. Loftus], p. 29; and lying through allegory was widely accepted see Element 14). Strauss is therefore simply substituting propaganda for reality.

as the way Matthew borrows from stories about Moses and then expands on that to turn Jesus into a full-blown Rank–Raglan hero (see Element 48; and Chapter 6), or borrows from Daniel to rewrite the empty-tomb narrative of Mark, or (as we shall see) how Mark created the crucifixion narrative out of Psalm 22, or invented the notion that the disciples were fisherman in order to make Jesus into the new Odysseus with his clueless sailors.[25] We already saw how nearly the whole core Gospel narrative can be derived from scripture (Element 17), and that's not even including the many scriptures we no longer have and which could thus have contained even more inspiration than we know about (see Element 9, and examples in *1 Clement* discussed in Chapter 8, §5). In fact, we'll see that creating the Gospel narratives by rewriting both pagan and Jewish 'scripture' was the norm, not the exception. Parables and sayings in the Gospels also resemble those in Jewish rabbinical legends, often in style and sometimes even in content, and those legends also contain dubious narratives similarly constructed to communicate the moral of a story, not to preserve any real historical memory.[26] Often influences from either Jewish or pagan moral traditions can be detected or suspected (see Elements 32 and 33).

All of this is generally admitted by most scholars, who nevertheless are usually certain these literary constructs are built around some sort of historical core or the barest seeds of real transmitted memories. All they have to do, they assume, is develop the tools needed to extract those historical needles from the rhetorical haystacks of the Gospels. But none of the tools they have developed work. Every expert who has published a direct examination of them has concluded that they are invalid and incapable of doing what is claimed.[27]

25. For Matthew's use of Daniel: Carrier, *Proving History*, pp. 199-204; and Carrier, 'Why the Resurrection Is Unbelievable', in *Christian Delusion* (ed. Loftus), pp. 294-95. For Mark's use of the Psalms: Carrier, *Proving History*, pp. 131-34; and Carrier, 'Spiritual Body', in *Empty Tomb* (ed. Price and Lowder), pp. 158-61. For many more examples, peruse the works listed in the earlier general note; e.g. on the invention of the idea of the disciples being fishermen, see MacDonald, *Homeric Epics*.

26. Gary Porton, 'The Parable in the Hebrew Bible and Rabbinic Literature', in *The Historical Jesus in Context* (ed. Levine, Allison and Crossan), pp. 206-21; and in the same volume, Herbert Basser, 'Gospel and Talmud', pp. 285-95; Peter Flint, 'Jesus and the Dead Sea Scrolls', pp. 110-31; and Craig Evans, 'The Recently Published Dead Sea Scrolls and the Historical Jesus', in *Studying the Historical Jesus: Evaluation of the State of Current Research* (ed. Bruce Chilton and Craig Evans; New York: E.J. Brill, 1994), pp. 559-61; and Craig Evans, 'Jesus and the Dead Sea Scrolls from Qumran Cave 4', in *Eschatology, Messianism, and the Dead Sea Scrolls* (ed. Craig Evans and Peter Flint; Grand Rapids, MI: William B. Eerdmans, 1997), pp. 91-100.

27. See Carrier, *Proving History*, pp. 11-16.

This includes the ever-popular Criterion of Embarrassment, which I and others have demonstrated is simply incapable of extracting reliable history from the Gospels.[28] I have already refuted all such arguments elsewhere (such as for the historicity of the crucifixion of Jesus, his origin at Nazareth, his baptism by John, his betrayal by Judas, and so on).[29] Those arguments are invalid. That alone does not make these facts unhistorical; it only makes it impossible for us to know whether they are historical. In other words, historical confidence in those claims is unfounded, by any methods so far used. Although in some cases the evidence *does* tend to suggest non-historicity. For example, the rhetorical, literary and theological utility of a baptism by John argues slightly in favor of its invention; while the accumulated evidence suggests 'Nazareth' as the town Jesus originated from was a late eponymous inference from what was originally the completely unrelated *title* of 'Nazorian', having something to do with what Jesus was or represented, not where he was from.[30]

The latter should already be obvious from the fact that Christians were originally called Nazorians (Acts 24.5), and the originating sect of Christianity, which remained Torah-observant, continued to be so-named for centuries (see Chapter 8, §1). Yet Christians neither came from nor were based at Nazareth. So the word clearly meant something else.[31] And this is explicitly admitted in later Christian sources.[32] In fact, that the messianic fable had to be set in Galilee was already established in scripture (Isa. 9.1-7); and scripture likewise insisted the messiah had be a 'Nazorian' (Mt. 2.23, obviously reading some scripture or variant we no longer have: see Element 9).[33] These facts obviously inspired the selection for Jesus' home

28. See Carrier, *Proving History*, pp. 124-69.

29. In Carrier, *Proving History*, pp. 121-92.

30. Baptism: Carrier, *Proving History*, pp. 145-48; Nazareth: Carrier, *Proving History*, pp. 142-45. Whether Nazareth actually existed (I am convinced it did, though some have their doubts) is irrelevant to this conclusion.

31. For Christians to call themselves Nazarenes because their founder was from Nazareth would make no more sense than Platonists calling themselves Athenians because their founder was from Athens. It's even worse than that, really, because they were not calling themselves (or even Jesus) Nazarenes, but Nazorians, which is analogous to Platonists calling themselves Athonians (see note below); or even more analogously (and thus even more inexplicably), Athonenes.

32. Cited in Carrier, *Proving History*, pp. 142-45.

33. Contrary to the usual claim that Matthew must have made this up, there is no way Matthew would invent a scriptural reference. It would defeat the purpose to cite a scripture that didn't exist in order to prove Jesus fulfilled scripture—even in general, much less to a well-informed Jewish readership, as Matthew's readership was intended to be. Moreover, even if he wanted to invent a scripture, he would not invent *this*: because the 'scripture' he 'quotes' here does not in fact fit the name of the town of Nazareth (see following note); if Matthew were inventing, he would invent a correctly

a town in Galilee with the nearest-sounding name, 'Nazareth'. That this is what happened is supported by the fact that those two words (*Nazōraios* and *Nazareth*) are not at all related, yet Matthew reports that scripture said Jesus would be a Nazorian, and Acts says the Christians were called Nazorians, and Epiphanius confirms a Torah-observant Christian sect did exist in Palestine called the Nazorians, and Jesus is frequently called a Nazorian in the Gospels (in John and Matthew, he is *only* so called). So the scripture and the name came first; the Gospel narrators then forced a fit, as best they could, with otherwise unrelated background facts (like a town with a near-enough-sounding name).[34]

matching word. Note that Lk. 24.19 might be based on this very passage in Matthew, and if so, Luke (or a subsequent scribe) changed the spelling (see following note).

34. In addition to everything else I adduce in Carrier, *Proving History*, pp. 142-45, that supports this conclusion, *Nazōraios* (Mt. 2.23; Acts 24.5) simply has no grammatical connection to *Nazara*, *Nazaret* or *Nazareth*, and does not in fact form the word 'Nazarene'. *Nazōraios* would instead form in English 'Nazorian'; and if it referred to a town of origin at all (and there is no particular reason to believe it originally did), it would indicate an inhabitant of *Nazōrai* ('Nazors'), by analogy to 'Athenian' (*Athēnaios*), meaning 'from Athens' (*Athēnai*). 'Nazors' is not 'Nazareth', or indeed any known town. It should be clear that *Nazōr-* and *Nazar-* are completely different roots; and *-eth* and *-ai* are completely different terminations. The original meaning was probably not a town of origin but an attribute or label (a name with a secret meaning, as I show in *Proving History* some Christians in fact believed). This lack of connection between the terms is actually an argument for the historicity of Nazareth (at least when the Gospels were written), as there is no other explanation why *Nazōraios* would generate an assignment to *Nazareth* other than that there was an actual Nazareth and that sounded close enough (otherwise, if the evangelists were *inventing* the town, they would have named it *Nazōrai*). Conversely, this also argues that Jesus did not come from Nazareth, as otherwise there is no good explanation why he was called a Nazorian (Mt. 26.71; Lk. 18.37; Jn 18.5-7 and 19.19) and his followers Nazorians, other than that this was a term originally unconnected with Nazareth and therefore *preceded* the assignment of that town to Jesus (it's not as if Matthew, e.g., *needed* to find scriptural confirmation that he originated in Nazareth; Mark didn't, and neither did Luke or John). Otherwise Jesus would have been called a *Nazaretos* ('Nazarethan') or a *Nazaranos* ('Nazaran'). Mark created the loosely similar word, *Nazarēnos,* for this purpose, unless that was a later scribal modification. And we have reason to believe it was, because Mk 10.47 originally agreed with the other Gospels in saying *Nazōraios* (e.g. in Codex Sinaiticus); Mk 14.67 may have (e.g. Codex Koridethi and Codex Sangallensis 48); as might Mk 16.6 (e.g. Codex Sangallensis 48 and Codex Regius); and there is significant confusion in the mss. as to the spelling in Mk 1.24, as also in those other three verses, leaving all cases accounted for—for Mk 1.24 alone Swanson identifies no less than five different variant spellings; cf. Reuben Swanson, *New Testament Greek Manuscripts: Variant Readings Arranged in Horizontal Lines against Codex Vaticanus: Mark* (Sheffield: Sheffield Academic Press, 1995), p. 15. Matthew knows no other spelling than *Nazōraios* (and he was using Mark as a source). John also knows no other spelling than *Nazōraios*. Luke uses *Nazarēnos* only twice, only one of which is a lift from

We similarly must reject attempts to argue that a given statement is historical because it appears to derive from an Aramaic source. Aramaic was spoken by millions continually for centuries across a broad geographical area (far beyond just Palestine), and therefore even if an Aramaic source could be demonstrated, that tells us nothing about its authenticity or date or place of origin. Stories can be fabricated in Aramaic, and revelations can be delivered and reported in Aramaic (and later inserted into an invented narrative) by anyone in the first century as easily as in any other language. Actually demonstrating an Aramaic source (as opposed to Semitic Greek, or the use of the Septuagint or an Aramaic targum of the OT to draw material from) is a lot harder than is pretended anyway. But the fact that even succeeding at it accomplishes nothing is sufficient reason to abandon hope that historicity can be recovered that way.[35]

With all that said, we must now look at the evidence for pervasive literary artifice in the canonical Gospels, beginning with the one that all the others employed as their primary model.

4. *The Mythology of Mark*

A good example of how Mark is creating fiction about Jesus can be seen in the appearance of a previously unmentioned insurrectionist named Barabbas in his crucifixion narrative. As Mark tells the tale:

> At the feast, Pilate used to release to them one prisoner of their choice. And there was one called Barabbas, chained up with those who'd engaged in rebellion, who in the insurrection had committed murder. The mob went up and began to ask him to do what he usually did for them. And Pilate answered them, saying, 'Do you want me to release to you the King of the Jews?' For he realized the chief priests had seized [Jesus] out of jealousy. But the chief priests stirred up the mob, so he would release Barabbas to them instead. And Pilate again answered and said to them,

Mark (Lk. 4.34, redacting Mk 1.24), the other introduced in a story unique to Luke (Lk. 24.19), but elsewhere, in another lift from Mark, he uses *Nazōraios* (Lk. 18.37, redacting Mk 10.47), and this spelling can't have come from Matthew, who does not use the word at all in his redaction of the same story (in Mt. 20.29-34). It therefore must have come from Mark, which argues that Mark originally wrote *Nazōraios*. Notably, in Luke's one lift from Mark that reads *Nazarēnos*, the manuscripts again don't agree on the spelling (some seven variants are known, including spellings similar to *Nazōraios*); and in his one unique use, a great many mss. in fact read *Nazōraios*. See Reuben Swanson, *New Testament Greek Manuscripts: Variant Readings Arranged in Horizontal Lines against Codex Vaticanus: Luke* (Sheffield: Sheffield Academic Press, 1995), pp. 73, 317 and 411. It would appear that *Nazarēnos* was a later scribal invention and might never have been in the Gospels of Mark or Luke originally.

35. Carrier, *Proving History*, pp. 185-86.

> 'So what should I do about the one you call the King of the Jews?' And they cried out again, 'Crucify him!' And Pilate said, 'What evil has he done?' But they cried out more, 'Crucify him!' And Pilate, wishing to satisfy the mob, released to them Barabbas, and sent Jesus to be whipped and crucified (Mk 15.6-15).

This is surely myth, not fact. No Roman magistrate (least of all the infamously ruthless Pilate), would let a murderous rebel go free, and no such Roman ceremony is attested as ever having existed; nor is it at all plausible.[36] But the ceremony so obviously emulates the Jewish ritual at Yom Kippur of the scapegoat and atonement, *in a story that is actually about*

36. Raymond Brown, *The Death of the Messiah from Gethsemane to the Grave: A Commentary on the Passion Narratives in the Four Gospels* (New York: Doubleday, 1994), I, pp. 814-20 (§ 34.C); and Robert Merritt, 'Jesus Barabbas and the Paschal Pardon', *Journal of Biblical Literature* 104 (1985), pp. 57-68. Merritt finds a similar religious tradition in ancient Babylonian, Assyrian and Hittite royal cult, involving a ceremony in which the king would be symbolically 'punished' in place of a pardoned prisoner, the king 'taking upon himself' the sins of the released prisoner, while the latter is set free, symbolically freeing the land from sin (see also Element 43); but in this ceremony the king would select the prisoner (and thus would obviously not select a murderous insurrectionist) and would only conduct the ritual as a religious ceremony in his role as sovereign (representing the whole land in his person), presenting no realistic analogy to what Pilate does (and certainly no such religious ceremony existed in Roman government). Merritt thinks Mark may have invented his ritual using this archaic ceremony as a model. Merritt also finds that a general release of prisoners would sometimes occur during the Greek festival of Dionysus Eleuthereus ('The Liberated', so-named for his own miraculous escape from prison) and some other similar Greek and Roman festivals, but this was only a temporary parole, and extended not to one but to all prisoners who were sufficiently pure and posted bond to guarantee their return—it therefore did not include murderers or traitors or anyone convicted of high crimes, and 'the release was merely a parole for the duration of the festival and not an amnesty, with bond required to be furnished on behalf of a released prisoner' (p. 63), thus bearing no analogy at all to what Mark describes. Mark's invention instead more clearly borrows and transvalues the 'widespread knowledge of the choice given to the crowd at Roman gladiatorial games, the choice to determine whether a wounded gladiator would be killed or allowed to live' (p. 68), and is thus a literary invention that doubles as a social commentary on Jewish behavior and Roman culture. Unlike the Synoptics, which tend to claim (following Mark) that the custom was Roman, Jn 18.38-40 claims the custom was Jewish, but there is no evidence of that, either. Attempts to claim Mishnah, *Pesaḥim* 8.6b refers to such a custom mistake what is there said; that law refers to *anyone* who is in prison during the time the Passover sacrifice is slaughtered but is expected to be released in time to eat of it, and therefore needs someone on the outside to conduct the sacrifice on their behalf (8.6a and 8.6d). There is no reference here to anyone being pardoned or any kind of custom peculiar to Passover; it simply covers anyone who was already granted acquittal or parole but not yet released in time to perform the ritual.

atonement, that its status as allegorical myth is clear.[37] We already saw that Jesus' death was understood by the earliest Christians to have merged the sacrifices of Passover and Yom Kippur (Element 18). Here, Mark has cleverly merged the sacrifices of Passover and Yom Kippur by having Jesus be a Yom Kippur sacrifice performed during Passover.

Barabbas, in reality a very unusual name, means 'Son of the Father' in Aramaic, and we know Jesus was deliberately styled the 'Son of the Father' himself.[38] So we have two sons of the father; one is released into the wild mob containing the sins of Israel (murder and rebellion), while the other is sacrificed so his blood may atone for the sins of Israel—the one who is released bears those sins literally; the other, figuratively.[39] This is the Yom Kippur ceremony of Leviticus 16 and Mishnah tractate *Yoma*: two 'identical' goats were chosen each year, and one was released into the wild containing the sins of Israel (which was eventually killed by being pushed over a cliff), while the other's blood was shed to atone for those sins.[40] Hebrews already says Jesus' death was the ultimate Yom Kippur atonement sacrifice, and this concept was central to the earliest Christian teaching we have any record of (see Elements 10, 18 and 28). Mark is thus telling us, with his own parable, to reject the sins of the Jews (especially violence and rebellion) and embrace instead the eternal salvation of atonement offered in Christ.

37. By contrast, Brown, *Death of the Messiah*, pp. 811-14 (§ 34.B), completely overlooks the Levitical connection and therefore his judgment in favor of the historicity of Barabbas is uninformed.

38. William John Lyons, 'The Hermeneutics of Fictional Black and Factual Red: The Markan Simon of Cyrene and the Quest for the Historical Jesus', *Journal for the Study of the Historical Jesus* 4 (June 2006), pp. 139-54 (149-50 for the translation of 'Barabbas').

39. That Jesus was imagined to have borne our sins only figuratively, not literally, should be obvious even from its basis in Isaiah 53 (where the servant who 'bears our sins' and thus dies to atone for them is in fact innocent, and thus is not *literally* containing our sins: 53.9 vs. 53.11; that this passage inspired Christian teaching on the point, see Elements 5 and 6). Likewise in earliest Christian writing: 1 Pet. 2.24 and Heb. 9.28 say Jesus 'carried away' our sins (*anapherō*; compare the use of this same verb in Mk 9.2/Mt. 17.1), not 'bore' them in the sense of actually embodying them (as in being a sinner, as Barabbas was; or having the world's sins magically cast into his body, which is the fate of the scapegoat). 1 Pet. 2.22-23 and 1 Jn 3.5 both make this theological point clear. Similarly, 2 Cor. 5.21, which says 'him who knew no sin' (thus, in distinct contrast to Barabbas) 'God made [equal to] sin' (not 'made him sin' in the sense of sinning, nor 'made him bear sins' in the sense of Barabbas or the goat sent to the Devil, but rather, made him a stand-in for sin, so that killing *him* was ritually equivalent to killing *sin*). See A.H. Wratislaw, 'The Scapegoat—Barabbas', *Expository Times* 3 (1891/1892), pp. 400-403.

40. That the goats had to be in some sense identical: Mishnah, *Yoma* 6.1b.

Had this story appeared in any other book, we would readily identify it as myth and not historical fact. As fact it's hopelessly implausible. As myth it makes perfect sense. Because the name of Barabbas is improbably convenient, and the ceremony depicted is very improbable as history, but lines up improbably well with the Yom Kippur ritual of atoning for Israel's sins, which we know Mark understands Jesus to be doing here—yet another improbable coincidence.[41] In Bayesian terms, with all these factors considered, the consequent probability on 'Mark is recording what happened at the crucifixion' is extremely low, while the consequent probability on 'Mark invented this as an allegory for the gospel' is extremely high. Given any plausible prior probability (especially an initial prior of 50/50), this difference in consequents entails a very high probability that Mark composed this as an allegory for the entire gospel.[42] We should conclude then that he did. This story is fiction.

Adding weight to this conclusion is manuscript evidence that the story either acquired or originally had the name 'Jesus Barabbas'. Thus we really had, most improbably of all, two men named 'Jesus Son of the Father',

41. I am not the first to notice this. It was already extensively argued by Wratislaw, in 'The Scapegoat—Barabbas', over a hundred years ago, and more recently by Daniel Stökl ben Ezra, *The Impact of Yom Kippur on Early Christianity: The Day of Atonement from Second Temple Judaism to the Fifth Century* (Tübingen: Mohr Siebeck, 2003), pp. 165-73; Jennifer K. Berenson Maclean, 'Barabbas, the Scapegoat Ritual, and the Development of the Passion Narrative', *Harvard Theological Review* 100 (July 2007), pp. 309-34, and many others (from William Arthur Heidel, in *The Day of Yahweh: A Study of Sacred Days and Ritual Forms in the Ancient Near East* [New York: Century, 1929], p. 298, to Nicole Wilkinson Duran, in *The Power of Disorder: Ritual Elements in Mark's Passion Narrative* [London: T. & T. Clark, 2008], pp. 85-87).

42. The hypothesis 'Mark is recording what happened' is meant generically here: it must be devoid of *a priori* assumptions about what historically happened; if instead we define this hypothesis as literally 'exactly this happened', then the evidence is more or less 100% expected, but then it's the prior probability that is very small (since *that* hypothesis requires assuming *a priori* a number of unlikely coincidences, against all our background knowledge of how history actually works). The mathematical outcome is the same (because the improbabilities just transfer from one term to the other in the same equation). See Carrier, *Proving History*, pp. 79-80, 239-42. This is similar to the example in Carrier, *Proving History*, p. 133, where P(HAPPENED|e) does not mean happened *exactly as described* but that the author is recording whatever happened—the hypothesis making no assumptions about what it was that happened. This amounts to saying the hypothesis is that the author is generally honest and reliable: the probability that an honest and reliable documenter of history would report this sort of story is low, because the story's collection of improbabilities and convenient coincidences is incongruous with what we know to usually come from honest and reliable recorders of history.

exactly the same name.[43] The odds of that being history are very small indeed; but the odds of it if it was an intentional fiction are effectively 100%. In the early third century, Origen not only attests to there being Greek manuscripts of Matthew that read that way, he himself makes the connection between Barabbas and the scapegoat at Yom Kippur, saying of the Barabbas narrative in the Gospels:

> You see! You have here the goat who is released alive into the wilderness, bearing in himself the sins of the people who were shouting and saying 'Crucify! Crucify!' *He* is therefore the goat released alive into the wilderness, while the other [i.e. Jesus] is the goat dedicated to God as a sacrifice to atone for those sins, making of himself a true atonement for those who believe.[44]

Origen also sees Barabbas as symbolic of Israel's sin, since Barabbas 'is figuratively the Devil', and Israel has adulterously chosen him as her husband instead of her true groom, Jesus.[45] His reasoning is that in the Yom

43. In Mt. 27.16-17: see Merritt, 'Jesus Barabbas', p. 57; Reuben Swanson, *New Testament Greek Manuscripts: Variant Readings Arranged in Horizontal Lines against Codex Vaticanus: Matthew* (Sheffield: Sheffield Academic Press, 1995), pp. 279-80; also in several Armenian, Georgic and Syriac manuscripts, demonstrating that even in Greek the variant existed as early as the fourth century (we have it attested in several later Greek manuscripts as well), and Origen reports that he saw it in Greek manuscripts of the early third century. In these manuscripts Barabbas is named 'Jesus Barabbas' *twice* (in two distinct verses: 27.16 and 27.17), which cannot be accidental; therefore either a scribe deliberately changed his name to Jesus Barabbas in both verses (indicating the *scribe* understood the mythic symbolism and intended to make it even more clear) or that is what Matthew originally wrote. The latter is the more probable hypothesis (see following note). Matthew often improves on Mark in this way, though the copy of Mark that Matthew derived his text from may also have said 'Jesus Barabbas', since the evident tendency to delete them from Matthew could also have purged them from Mark. But even if Matthew added them, that entails *Matthew* understood the mythic symbolism (and thus intended to make it even more clear), since there would be no other reason to add them (either by Matthew or later scribes).

44. Origen, *Homily on Leviticus* 10.2.2. That manuscripts included it is mentioned in Origen, *Commentary on Matthew* 121, where he also gives the reason why the name 'Jesus' was then being removed from manuscripts: it was considered inappropriate to associate the name 'Jesus' with a sinner. And indeed, the name 'Jesus' is conspicuously absent from the Gospels (apart from *the* Jesus), despite that being one of the most common names of the time (even in Acts only one other person is ever even *mentioned* as having the name: Elymas the Sorcerer's father was supposedly named 'Jesus', according to Acts 13.6-8; and that is probably a literary invention).

45. Origen, *Commentary on Matthew* 19 (on Jesus as the husband of the church, the heiress of the former Israel, see Element 48). Philo of Alexandria, in *On Plantation* 61, had likewise said the scapegoat represents the fate of those who honor the world (they fall to their deaths like it does), and the atonement goat represents the fate of those who honor god instead (possibly alluding to martyrdom); likewise in Philo,

Kippur ceremony, the scapegoat either represented or was delivered to the Devil (more specifically Azazel, either Satan himself or one of Satan's angels).[46] Thus, to choose him was to throw in your lot with the Devil rather than the Lord.

The Christian book of *Barnabas* discerns another aspect of Mark's allegory:

> [The Torah says to] take two goats of goodly aspect, and similar to each other, and offer them. And let the priest take one as a burnt-offering for sins. And what should they do with the other? 'Accursed', says He, 'is the one'. Note how the type of Jesus now comes out. 'And all of you spit upon it, and pierce it, and encircle its head with scarlet wool, and thus let it be driven into the wilderness'. . . . What does this mean? Heed what is said, 'one upon the altar, and the other accursed'. And why is the one that is accursed crowned? Because they shall see Him then in that day having a scarlet robe about his body down to his feet; and they shall say, 'Is not this He whom we once despised, and pierced, and mocked, and crucified? Truly this is He who then declared Himself to be the Son of God. For how like is He to Him!' With a view to this, the goats had to be of goodly aspect, and similar, that, when they see Him then coming, they may be amazed by the likeness of the goat. Behold, then, the type of Jesus who was to suffer (*Barnabas* 7.6-10).

Observe how in Mark's story Jesus is treated by the Jews exactly like the scapegoat: scorned and beaten and spat upon and dressed in scarlet and crowned and pierced, yet Barabbas is the *actual* scapegoat, whom the Jews *embrace* instead of abuse. So the Jews have not correctly discerned who the actual scapegoat is and who the actual sin offering is. Mark has thus created an allegory for Jewish blindness to what Jesus represents, the Jews choosing instead their sins over their salvation—Jesus Barabbas, instead of Jesus Christ.

This was notably also a choice between two kinds of messiahs: a doomed one of military revolution (Barabbas is a murderous revolutionary) and one of spiritual victory whose death eliminated the need for military revolution (see Elements 23 to 28). As Stökl ben Ezra explains, 'Jesus of Nazareth is the Messiah as God wants him to be, while Jesus Barabbas is the Messiah as the people want him to be', and by not letting the choice fall to a lottery (and thus to God), 'the people usurp the role of God on Yom Kippur in choosing between the two'.[47] Thus, as a literary allegory, Mark's composition is near brilliant, conveying everything he wants to say about the gospel

Who Is the Heir of Things Divine 179, the atonement goat represents the virtuous, while the scapegoat represents those who abandon virtue. Mark was thus working with established typology.

46. Azazel: Stökl ben Ezra, *Impact of Yom Kippur*, pp. 85-101.

47. Stökl ben Ezra, *Impact of Yom Kippur*, pp. 170-71.

and its acceptance and rejection. But there is nothing of history here. None of this actually happened.

In fact, the entire crucifixion scene is a fabrication, a patchwork assembled from verses in the Psalms, in order to depict Jesus as a standard Jewish mytho-type of 'the just man afflicted and put to death by evildoers, but vindicated and raised up by God'.[48] Numerous Psalms were mined for this purpose, but especially Psalm 22:

Mark 15.24: 'They part his garments among them, casting lots upon them'.	**Psalm 22.18:** 'They part my garments among them, and cast lots upon them'.
Mark 15.29-31: 'And those who passed by blasphemed him, shaking their heads and saying, ". . . Save yourself. . ." and mocked him, saying "He who saved others cannot save himself!"'	**Psalm 22.7-8:** 'All those who see me mock me and give me lip, shaking their head, saying "He expected the lord to protect him, so let the lord save him if he likes"'.
Mark 15.34: 'My God, my God, why have you forsaken me?'	**Psalm 22.1:** 'My God, my God, why have you forsaken me?'

Table 1. From Psalms 22 to Mark 15

Even the whole concept of a crucifixion of God's chosen one arranged and witnessed by Jews comes from Ps. 22.16, where 'the synagogue of the wicked has surrounded me and pierced my hands and feet'. Other texts Mark used to construct his crucifixion narrative include Psalm 69, Amos 8.9, and elements of Zechariah 9–14, Isaiah 53, and Wisdom 2.[49] This is myth, not memory. Many scholars agree.

Notably, even the Aramaic that Mark provides when he reports Jesus' cry on the cross, which Mark translates into Greek similar to that of the Septuagint, appears to derive from a targum of the Psalms.[50] The targums (in the Hebrew plural, *targumim*) were Aramaic translations of the Hebrew Bible as then known, and many were in circulation, so the ones we have

48. Carrier, *Proving History*, pp. 131-33, with p. 315 n. 43.

49. See G.K. Beale and D.A. Carson (eds.), *Commentary on the New Testament Use of the Old Testament* (Grand Rapids, MI: Baker Academic, 2007), pp. 235-37; and Darrell Bock, 'The Function of Scripture in Mark 15.1-39', in *Biblical interpretation in Early Christian Gospels. Vol. 1. The Gospel of Mark* (ed. Thomas R. Hatina; New York: T. & T. Clark, 2006), pp. 8-17. Notably, while Mark borrows the last words of Jesus from Ps. 22.1, Luke changed the last words of Jesus by borrowing from Ps. 30.5 instead (which in the LXX is identical to what Jesus says in Lk. 23.46 but for the tense of the verb and its address to 'father').

50. Roger Aus, *Barabbas and Esther and Other Studies in the Judaic Illumination of Earliest Christianity* (Atlanta, GA: Scholars Press, 1992), p. 12.

today do not necessarily reflect the exact targum used by Mark, which may have contained all manner of variant readings now unknown to us that influenced him (see again Element 9). Targums were very loose and creative translations, often more like interpretations, paraphrasing and rephrasing the OT, often updating the original passages with new theology or simply rewriting scripture.[51]

That Mark relied on a targum is not only evidenced in his lifting and adaptation of an Aramaic phrase here (obviously from the Psalms) but in several other places. For example, Mark appears to have relied on an extant targum of Isa. 6.9-10. The original Hebrew there reads, 'Go, and tell this people, "Indeed you hear, but do not understand; and indeed you see, but do not perceive"', because, the text says, their ears and eyes must be blocked, 'lest they see with their eyes, and hear with their ears, and understand with their heart, and turn again, and be healed'. An extant targum of this replaces 'healed' with 'forgiven', which happens to match exactly Jesus' saying in Mk 4.11-12, 'And he said unto them, ". . . all things are done in parables, so that seeing they may see, and not perceive, and hearing they may hear, and not understand, lest they turn again, and be forgiven."' Apart from the fact that this saying of Jesus has apparently been redacted out of Isaiah (and thus is being read out of scripture and thus no longer requires Jesus to have said it: see again Elements 16 and 17), it seems here that Mark has drawn this saying not from the Hebrew or the Septuagint text but from an Aramaic targum.[52] It is for this reason that finding evidence of an underlying Aramaic in Mark's text cannot entail it originates from Jesus or even early-first-century Palestine. Because it could originate from a targum (or Aramaic-speaking Gentiles or apostles, or lost scriptures in Aramaic, and so on: see the end of §3 above; and Chapter 9, §6).

Another example is that an extant targum of Zech. 14.21 changes the original Hebrew from 'in that day there shall never again be Canaanites in the house of Jehovah of hosts' to 'in that day there shall never again be traders in the house of Jehovah of hosts', which thus becomes an obvious inspiration for the clearing of the temple in Mk 11.15-17.[53] The conversion

51. See Bruce Chilton, 'Targum, Jesus, and the Gospels', in *Historical Jesus in Context* (ed. Levine, Allison and Crossan), pp. 238-55.

52. For this and other examples see Chilton, 'Targum' (for this one: pp. 245-46).

53. Henk Jan de Jonge, 'The Cleansing of the Temple in Mark 11:15 and Zechariah 14:21', in *The Book of Zechariah and its Influence* (ed. Christopher Tuckett; Burlington, VT: Ashgate, 2003), pp. 87-100. For other examples of Mark adapting material from Zechariah to construct his narrative about Jesus see Mark Black, 'The Messianic Use of Zechariah 9–14 in Matthew, Mark and the Pre-Markan Tradition', in *Scripture and Traditions: Essays on Early Judaism and Christianity in Honor of Carl R. Holladay* (ed. Patrick Gray and Gail R. O'Day; Boston: Brill, 2008), pp. 97-114; and Carrier, *Proving History,* p. 155 (with p. 318 nn. 70-71).

of ‘Canaanite’ to ‘trader’ was a known trend, happening in other verses even in Greek, and thus Mark might here have been relying on a lost Greek translation instead, or making the conversion on his own. But the fact that we find it in a targum makes that a more likely origin for Mark’s interpretation. Thus, when in an obviously fictional story about Jesus resurrecting a girl (Mk 5.41) Mark repeats the magical words of Jesus in Aramaic (*talitha koum*) and then translates them into Greek (‘Girl, rise!’) we can rightly wonder if he adapted those words from a targum, just as he did with Psalm 22. Certainly, Jesus never actually spoke those words, since the story is entirely a fiction.

That tale in fact is a rewrite of another mythical story, told of Elisha in 2 Kgs 4.17-37, which illustrates another way Mark fabricated material.[54] In that story, a woman of Shunem (meaning ‘double resting place’ in Hebrew, where Elisha would often take his rest—2 Kgs 4.8-11—coincidental names being a common marker of mythmaking) seeks out the miracle-working Elisha and begs him to resurrect her son. She goes looking for Elisha outdoors and falls at his feet, begging his help, then someone checks on the boy and confirms he is dead; but Elisha is not deterred and goes into her house himself and works his magic, by word and touch, resurrecting the boy. In Mark’s version (Mk 5.22-43), the same things happen: Jairus comes looking for Jesus outdoors and falls at his feet and begs his help; someone then comes to confirm his daughter is dead, but Jesus is not deterred and goes himself into the petitioner’s house and works his magic, by word and touch, resurrecting the girl. Several elements have been conspicuously reversed in Mark’s version, producing even more telltale coincidences: instead of a woman begging for her son, a man comes begging for his daughter; and while in the OT an *unnamed* woman comes from a *named* town that means ‘rest’, in Mark a *named* man comes from an *unnamed* town, and the man’s name (Jairus) means ‘awaken’ (*yair*, ‘to bring light, enlighten, awaken’ in the Hebrew).

In his conclusion Mark even borrows from the Greek version of this Elisha tale: the clause *exestēsan euthus ekstasei megalē*, ‘immediately they were amazed with great amazement’ at what Jesus had done (Mk 5.42) is an allusion to *exestēsas hēmin pasan tēn ekstasin tautēn*, ‘you have been amazed with all this amazement for us’ (2 Kgs 4.13), which is how the woman had earlier reacted to having Elisha as a guest, and for which he blessed her with a miraculous conception—of the very son he would later

54. See Helms, *Gospel Fictions*, pp. 65-67. For a detailed analysis of how Mark employs the Elijah–Elisha narrative in the Kings literature as source material for constructing stories about Jesus throughout his Gospel see Adam Winn, *Mark and the Elijah–Elisha Narrative: Considering the Practice of Greco-Roman Imitation in the Search for Markan Source Material* (Eugene, OR: Pickwick Publications, 2010).

resurrect. Thus Mark accomplishes another literary reversal, reversing the placement of this reaction (of double amazement) from the child's miraculous conception to the child's miraculous *resurrection*, and from what earns the miraculous reward to what follows it.

Mark also frames this story around another, in which, as Jesus is walking with the man who is begging his help and is about to hear confirmation of his daughter's death, a woman who has been endlessly menstruating for twelve years touches Jesus' cloak and is healed, and he does not know who touched him, but blesses the woman when she confesses (Mk 5.25-34). The girl he then goes to resurrect is said to be twelve years old (Mk 5.42), not only the same number of years as the woman was endlessly menstruating but also the age at which menstruation traditionally began. Jesus is also explicitly asked to touch the girl (Mk 5.23) and does (Mk 5.41), while in between the woman seeks to touch Jesus (5.28) and does (5.27), and by this means both are 'saved' (5.23, 28, 34) by 'faith' (5.34, 36) in spite of 'fear' (5.33, 36), and both the girl and the woman are called 'daughter' (5.23, 34), even though there is no apparent reason for Jesus to call the woman this. The integration of these tales obviously had some symbolic importance to Mark, even if we cannot discern it now. But whatever its meaning, this is all clearly myth, not history. Such coincidences do not commonly occur in real life. But in myth they are routine. Nor would such details be relevant to a remembered story; but they would be relevant to a myth, even if only esoterically (see Elements 13 and 14). And the story of a woman being healed of a bizarre malady and Jesus just 'mystically' knowing that had happened is not remotely realistic. Nor is a resurrection of a dead girl by a single touch and command.

Another clue that Mark is writing historical fiction is the way he structures his narrative to suit literary aims rather than historical ones. The ceaseless incomprehension of the disciples, for example, is wholly unrealistic. No real human beings would ever be that dense or take so long to understand what Jesus was saying and doing, or learn nothing in between episodes (as if they never spoke to one another except in the few brief exchanges Mark depicts). In reality a single hour's conversation with Jesus would have resolved all questions. This literary fiction of the dense lackeys is adapted either from Homer's similarly unrealistic depiction of the fickleness and incomprehension of Odysseus's crew or from Exodus's equally unrealistic depiction of the fickleness and incomprehension of the Jews—most likely both (as I suggested before). In each case such 'group stupidity' only makes sense as a deliberate literary device; in Mark's case, to illustrate something he wanted to say about the gospel—and possibly about the pre-Pauline sect Mark was dissenting from, which was associated with the first apostles, most especially Peter, James and John (see Galatians 1–2 with Mk 9.2 and Element 20).

Mark develops this theme in multiple ways, among which is ring composition, a common literary device of the time, both in myth (e.g. Homer) and history (e.g. Suetonius).[55] When ring composition requires the invention of narrative material to make the structure work, especially when it is implausible and unrealistic material that has an obvious pedagogical purpose, we are far more likely looking at myth than history. Mark's use of ring composition throughout his chaps. 4 through 8 has already been demonstrated by Norman Petersen.[56] In this central part of his narrative (which revolves around his travel by sea, which I'll call the Sea Narrative) Mark carefully constructed nested cycles of themes specifically to convey an underlying message about faith and the ability (or inability) to understand the gospel.

This Sea Narrative's structure is consistently artificial:

Cycle 1:	Phase 1 (4.1-34)	Jesus with crowds by sea [*preaching from a boat*]	
	Phase 2 (4.35-41)	eventful crossing of sea	
	Phase 3 (5.1-20)	landing with healings / exorcisms	
	Interval 1:	Step 1 (5.21-43)	first stop [*after an uneventful boating*]
		Step 2 (6.1-6)	second stop
		Step 3 (6.6-29)	going around
Cycle 2:	Phase 1 (6.30-44)	Jesus with crowds by sea [*with an uneventful boating*]	
	Phase 2 (6.45-52)	eventful crossing of sea	
	Phase 3 (6.53-55)	landing with healings / exorcisms	
	Interval 2:	Step 1 (6.56–7.23)	going around
		Step 2 (7.24-30)	first stop
		Step 3 (7.31-37)	second stop

55. See Mary Douglas, *Thinking in Circles: An Essay on Ring Composition* (New Haven, CT: Yale University Press, 2007); and T.D. Benedikston, 'Structure and Fate in Suetonius' *Life of Galba*', *Classical Journal* 92 (1997), pp. 167-73. That Suetonius employed ring composition all throughout his imperial lives has been demonstrated by Matthew Ferguson, *Thematic Rings and Structure in Suetonius' De Vita Caesarum* (MA thesis, University of Arizona, 2012), available at http://www.richardcarrier.info/FergusonSuetonius.pdf.

56. Norman Petersen, 'The Composition of Mark 4:1-8:26', *Harvard Theological Review* 73 (January–April 1980), pp. 185-217.

Cycle 3:	Phase 1 (8.1-12)	Jesus with crowds by sea [*with an uneventful boating*]
	Phase 2 (8.13-21)	eventful crossing of sea
	Phase 3 (8.22-26)	landing with healings / exorcisms

Table 2. Structure of the Sea Narrative in Mark

Thus, as Petersen notes, the Sea Narrative of Mark 4 through 8 is 'comprised of three triadically composed intervals, the central one of which is surrounded by triadically composed intervals, each of which contains one triadically composite minimal unit'.[57] Indeed, as Petersen explains, the structure is even more brilliantly crafted than that.

Each Phase 1 (in all three cycles) takes place during the day and 'depicts Jesus' actions with crowds on one side of the sea'.[58] Each Phase 2 occurs on the evening of that same day (only in Cycle 3 is this not stated, though it is implied by what would be a long sea crossing) and 'depicts actions between Jesus and the twelve in the boat while in transit across the sea'. And each Phase 3 'represents Jesus' healing [or exorcising] of people who either come to him or are brought to him following his debarkation on the other side of the sea'. Other healings or exorcisms are then interspersed among the Intervals (that follow each Phase 3).

Each Cycle occupies one day, so the whole sequence represents three days and ends with a resolution on the third day—all of which concludes by transitioning into a debate about who Jesus really is and a declaration of what the gospel really is (Mk 8.27–9.1, the first time in all this time that we hear Jesus speak on any of this). Prior to this cyclical triad Jesus had also journeyed *to* the sea and taught *by* the sea three times (Mk 1.16; 2.13; 3.7) without embarking on a boat, but now he embarks on a boat (Mk 4.1; cf. 3.9) and makes six journeys by boat, three eventful ones (each part of a three-phase cycle repeated three times) and three uneventful ones that make a looser pattern (Mk 5.21; 6.32; 8.10).

Between the three eventful sea journey cycles are two intervals where Jesus notably travels inland *away* from the sea of Galilee and *back* again, and these two journeys also share a triadic pattern: three land journeys in chiastic arrangement. First from the shore to the house of Jairus (Mk 5.22), then from the house of Jairus to the hometown of Jesus (Mk 6.1), and then from the hometown of Jesus to circulating around the towns (Mk 6.6), completing Interval 1; and then the sequence is reversed: circulating around the towns (Mk 6.56), then stopping at Tyre (Mk 7.24), then back

57. Petersen, 'Composition of Mark', p. 200.
58. Petersen, 'Composition of Mark', p. 196.

to the shore (Mk 7.31), completing Interval 2. The arrangement is ABC : CBA (stop on the way from the shore, another inland stop, circulating; then circulating, another inland stop, stop on the way to the shore).

In both intervals the *first* stop is always at a house, and in each case involves women and children. And each *circulating* phase involves both the disciples (in the first case sent on their own ministries; in the second case attacked for ignoring purity laws) and the authorities (in the first case Herod reacting to Jesus, and murdering John; in the second case the Pharisees reacting to the disciples and subverting God's law with human law). The *second* stop in each Interval is also an inversion of the other: in the first case, in his hometown (a metaphor for Israel) 'those hearing him' are 'astonished' and don't believe in him (a metaphor for the Jews rejecting the gospel), while in the second case in a foreign country (the Greek Decapolis, among the Gentiles) he miraculously makes a man 'hear' and the people are 'astonished' in quite the opposite sense, saying he does everything well and publishing his fame far and wide. The two reactions are clearly meant to be contrasted: in both there appears the exact phrase *exeplēssonto legontes*, 'they were amazed, saying' something in each case the opposite of the other. Indeed in the second case, when Jesus is abroad, where the locals accept his miracles, they are 'even more amazed', thus emphasizing a contrast between positive amazement and negative amazement.

Every unit of this narrative has the same literary purpose, a message about faith and the gospel, playing the incomprehension of the disciples (and rejection of Jesus by neighbors and kin) against the ready faith of outsiders (Gentile foreigners and Jews who are not his neighbors or kin) even though they don't understand. The cyclic triad even begins and ends on the theme of 'seeing, hearing, understanding' (compare Mk 4.12 with 8.17-21), and continually contrasts human expectations (e.g. Herod thinking Jesus is John resurrected; the Pharisees preferring human laws to God's laws; his kin expecting one thing, foreigners another) with the true realities offered by the gospel (the spiritual kingdom of a spiritual messiah who has a greater incomprehensible plan of salvation than anyone seems able to comprehend).

When you look at what Mark has to do to force the narrative to fit this elegant structure so perfectly, and the central role of unbelievable events or behaviors in nearly every one of his scenes, it is no longer possible to believe Mark is recording memory or even re-crafting historical lore. He is inventing all of this, each scene his own parable, usually with Jesus cast as the central character, illustrating symbolically something the reader needs to understand about the gospel. This is an artful literary creation, start to finish.

This becomes all the clearer when we see how Mark has layered another pattern within this one. Within the above triadic ring structure he has interwoven two matching sequences of five miracles each, interspersed with parables and preaching and generic references to miracles (i.e. other miracles mentioned but not narrated).[59] In fact, all the *narrated* miracles in Mark's Sea Narrative correlate into a carefully crafted sequential structure as follows:

First Sequence	*Second Sequence*
Mastery of the Waters Stilling of the Storm (4.35-41)	*Mastery of the Waters* Jesus Walks on the Sea (6.45-51)
Exorcism of a Gentile Man The Gerasene Demoniac (5.1-20)	*Exorcism of a Gentile Woman* The Syrophoenician Woman (7.24-30)
Curing an Older Woman The Woman with a Hemorrhage (5.25-34)	*Curing a Deaf Man with Spit* The Deaf-Mute (7.32-37)
Curing a Younger Woman Jairus' Daughter (5.21-23, 35-43)	*Miraculous Feeding* Feeding of the 4,000 (8.1-10)
Miraculous Feeding Feeding of the 5,000 (6.34-44, 53)	*Curing a Blind Man with Spit* The Blind Man of Bethsaida (8.22-26)

Table 3. The 2 x 5 Miracle Sequence in Mark

Many miracle narratives of Jewish holy men, including Moses, exhibit a sequence of five miracles, and the sequence that Mark twice repeats has evident correlations with the wilderness narrative of Moses (Exod. 13–17).[60] The assembly of these two pairs of five miracles (which combined make ten: a decalogue) is clearly Mark's intention.

The Moses sequence begins with a 'mastery of the waters' in his parting of the Red Sea (Exod. 13–15), in which he simultaneously commands the waters, and treads upon them (crossing the sea). Then the second miracle, which alludes to the power of God to heal, occurs after the Jews have wandered in the wilderness and are perishing from thirst, when on the 'third day' Moses calls a magical tree to appear that makes a bitter pool

59. For the following, I'm adopting some of the analysis (but not all of the conclusions) of Paul Achtemeier in 'Toward the Isolation of Pre-Markan Miracle Catenae', *Journal of Biblical Literature* 89 (September 1970), pp. 265-91; and Paul Achtemeier, 'The Origin and Function of the Pre-Marcan Miracle Catenae', *Journal of Biblical Literature* 91 (June 1972), pp. 198-221.

60. Achtemeier, 'Origin and Function', pp. 204-205.

drinkable, at which he says if they obey God's commandments God will inflict no diseases on them, 'for I am Jehovah who heals you' (Exod. 15.22-27). Moses' third miracle in this narrative is a 'miraculous feeding', when Moses calls manna down from heaven (Exod. 16). Then the Jews run out of water again, so for his fourth miracle Moses strikes water from a rock (Exod. 17.1-7). In this tale the Jews are worried Moses will kill them with thirst (17.3), and the moral of the story is that, despite their fear and doubt, Moses (thanks to God) will save them. And the fifth and final miracle of Moses in this narrative occurs when he raises his staff to ensure the victory of the armies of Joshua against the Amalekites (Exod. 17.8-16), a tribe in southern Canaan.[61] But he grew tired so they put a stone under him to sit upon and two others held up his arms.[62] This miracle symbolizes power over the violent forces of evil.

These five miracles are echoed in the miracles of Jesus. Like Moses, Jesus begins each sequence of five miracles with a sea miracle (a rather conspicuous coincidence), in which he proves his dominance over the waters of chaos. Like Moses, Jesus treads on them and commands them—and in the same order: Moses parts the sea, then crosses; so in sequence one, Mark has Jesus calm the sea, then in sequence two, Mark has Jesus walk on it. From there the order of miracles does not match Exodus, but conceptual parallels remain. Jesus heals the sick (for which we are given two full narratives each, conspicuously the same number in each sequence, and in one sequence both are women, while in the other, both are men), corresponding to the second miracle of Moses, in which the faithful are assured power over diseases. Jesus also exorcises demons (for which we are given one full narrative each, also conspicuously the same number in each sequence, and in one sequence a woman, in the other a man, this time reversed), cor-

61. Num. 13.29; 14.25, 43-45 (cf. also Num. 24.20).

62. I have to wonder if this was taken to be a prediction of Peter 'the rock' and the other two 'pillars', James and John, propping up the church, forming a cross. That Moses was lifting his staff, and not just his hand, is clear from Exod. 17.9; evidently he was raising it horizontally, with both hands, requiring one man to hold up each arm. But before those men came to his aid, Moses would have been forming the figure of a cross (his body erect with his hands stretched across a wooden cross beam); similarly, the miracle of the bitter waters is accomplished by God revealing a 'tree', but the word used in the Septuagint is *xulon*, more typically meaning a piece of finished lumber; the same word is used to describe the cross of Jesus (see Chapter 4, §3). Christians may have imagined foreshadowing in all this and seen in both scenes a symbolism predicting some salvific role for a wooden cross. Although note that in earliest Christian art, Jesus was also typically depicted as performing his miracles with a wand (as might Moses also have been imagined): see Thomas Mathews, *The Clash of Gods: A Reinterpretation of Early Christian Art* (Princeton, NJ: Princeton University Press, 1993).

responding to the fifth miracle of Moses, which exhibits power over the forces of evil (except demons in this case rather than soldiers). And near the end of each sequence we get a miraculous feeding, echoing Moses' power to call mana from heaven (and thus miraculously provide sustenance for his flock, his third miracle in Exodus). Like Moses, Jesus' miraculous feedings take place in the wilderness, involve 'gathering up' the food, everyone is fed, and they end up with more than they start with (compare Exod. 16.4-5 with Mk 6.43; 8.8; and 8.19-20).[63]

Finally, Moses performs two water miracles that end the people's thirst: the tree revealed by God (making bitter water drinkable again, his second miracle), and the flow of water struck from a rock (his fourth miracle). Mark has split these up, so that each inspires *two* miracle narratives for Jesus, but in different sequences, thus keeping the total miracle narratives in each sequence at five—yet another conspicuous coincidence, evincing considerable artifice. In the first sequence Mark draws on the water-from-a-rock episode, which carried the theme of faith overcoming fear and thus obtaining salvation. Hence, the episodes of Jairus's daughter and the woman with a hemorrhage have the same theme of faith overcoming fear to achieve salvation from suffering or death. The woman also flowed with blood, while the rock flowed with water. And in the Jairus narrative Jesus takes only his top three apostles with him into the bed chamber (the pillars Peter, James and John: Mk 5.37), just as Moses is told to take only three elders with him to strike the rock (Exod. 17.5). The Exodus narrative likewise has the Jews perishing and worried about dying (17.3), thus Mark produces parallel narratives about a woman *perishing* (besides the obvious

63. Both of Jesus' miraculous feeding narratives also emulate a similar story told of Elisha (in 2 Kgs 4.43-44): 'There is in all three stories the initial assessment of how much food is available, the prophetic command to divide it among a hopelessly large number, the skeptical objection, puzzled obedience, and the astonishing climax in which not only all are fed, but they had leftovers as well', Robert Price, *The Christ–Myth Theory and its Problems* (Cranford, NJ: American Atheist Press, 2011), pp. 93-94. Mark also employed a Homeric framework for working in these biblical features (see earlier notes on the work of MacDonald), and both of Mark's feeding tales ultimately allegorize the Eucharist: see the analysis of Achtemeier, 'Toward the Isolation'; and Achtemeier, 'Origin and Function', pp. 206-207, 212-21 (e.g. they are linked to the Eucharist with similar vocabulary: taking, blessing, breaking and giving, all in the same order; cf. Mk 6.41; 8.6; and 14.22). Another reason Mark duplicates the feeding narratives is so that he can have one among Jews on the western side of the lake (6.35-43) and one among Gentiles on the eastern side of the lake (8.1-9) to teach that the Jews and Gentiles should receive the same communion (8.14-17). That the boat in Mark (and everything that happens in and with it, including its journeys) is a metaphor for the church: Marcus Borg, *Reading the Bible Again for the First Time: Taking the Bible Seriously but Not Literally* (San Francisco, CA: HarperSanFrancisco, 2001), pp. 206-209.

fact that she was slowly bleeding to death, that her condition was worsening is explicitly stated: Mk 5.26) and a girl who *died*.

In Mark's second sequence he draws on the magical tree episode. Which explains the otherwise very odd detail that the blind man of Bethsaida (8.22-26) sees trees at first instead of men (Mk 8.24), just as Moses did; and to cure the deaf mute, Jesus looks to heaven and cries out, just as Moses must cry out to God in heaven, who shows him the magical tree. (I must wonder if a lost tradition held that the tree was revealed from the heavens and thus Moses was looking up at it.) In both cases, while Moses must put the tree *into* the water to drink it, Jesus must put spit *onto* the afflicted to open their eyes, ears or tongue. The magical tree episode also concludes with the declaration, 'if you will diligently *hear* the *voice* of the Lord your God, and will do what is pleasing in his *sight*, and will *give ear* to his commandments' then God will heal you (Exod. 15.26), in each case supplying inspiration for Jesus to heal eyes, ears and tongue (to restore the mute's 'voice').

Thus, Mark shows he has consciously created these double narrative sequences. He is not 'accidentally' duplicating them (as many scholars assume). He probably does not have sources for them, either. Because of the way he distributes allusions to the underlying miracles of Moses (probably signifying some mystical teaching not given in the text), he is clearly conscious of what he is doing in doubling the sequence of five, even in deciding what miracles they should be, and thus clearly has every motive to fabricate every single one of these stories, just as we have it, in order to fit his scheme of allusions. For example, he knew he was going to have two healing miracles in the first sequence echo the water-from-the-rock miracle, and two healing miracles in the second sequence echo the magical tree miracle, and thereby still maintain five miracles in each sequence. His reversals of gender are likewise organized, showing knowledge of both sequences mirroring each other. Mark does this again for the fifth miracle (placed second in each sequence for Jesus), which echoes Moses' power over the forces of evil (the Amalekites). Here Mark divides different allusions between the two sequences: in the first sequence, the demons are equated with soldiers (they are named 'Legion'), thus reminding us of the Amalekite soldiers; and in the second sequence, the one cured is a Canaanite (a woman of Syria and Phoenicia), thus reminding us of the Amalekites themselves (who lived in Canaan). The extent of literary artifice here evinces considerable genius. This is what myth looks like.

What about the rest of Mark? It likewise shows elegant structure along similar lines, but more varied, to suit Mark's purposes. The entire Gospel of Mark has this overall structure:

The Discipling Narrative (chaps. 1–3)
The Sea Narrative (chaps. 4.1–8.26)

The Road Narrative (chaps. 8.27-10)
The Passover Narrative (chaps. 11–16)

And while there is elegant internal structure in the Sea Narrative, there is a similar chiastic or 'ring' structure surrounding it, as the Road Narrative recapitulates the Discipling Narrative in reverse. And each of those narratives contains a consistent internal theme found nowhere else in the Gospel—just as the Sea Narrative uniquely centers around sea journeys, the Discipling Narrative uniquely centers around Jesus' ever-increasing fame (again, thrice: 1.21-34, 39-45; 3.7-12) and discipling (again, thrice: 1.14-20; 2.13-22; 3.13-19), while the Road Narrative uniquely centers around a common metaphor of 'the road' as 'the way', meaning the gospel.[64] The metaphor is repeatedly cued by this double entendre (in this narrative's very first and last verses, 8.27 and 10.52; and again in 9.33-34; 10.17, 32; and 10.46, making two pairs of three: three mentions on the road to Jerusalem, and three mentions before that), a device conspicuously never used in any of the other narratives. Mark then folds into this 'road narrative' a triad of three predictions of his death (8.31-32; 9.31; 10.33-34), thrice not understood by his disciples, who instead seek to exalt themselves (8.32; 9.33-34; 10.35-41), and thrice Jesus corrects them (8.33–9.1; 9.35-37; 10.42-45), thus thrice teaching the reader a key aspect of discipleship and the gospel. It is no accident that this sequence is sandwiched between two instances of Jesus making the blind see (8.22-26 and 10.46-52).[65]

To grasp the artificial nature of all this, note that in all of Jesus' ministry throughout chaps. 1 through 3 never once does Jesus actually teach the gospel (he never mentions the gospel or what it is, or tells any parables about it), even though the whole narrative begins by having Jesus declare 'repent and believe in the gospel!' (Mk 1.15), an odd demand when you never explain what that is. In the Sea Narrative Jesus starts telling parables about the gospel (even beginning with an explanation of the whole concept of parable as a way of concealing the true meaning behind fictitious stories: Mk 4.9-12), but never mentions anything resembling its *kerygma* (that Jesus had to die to atone for everyone's sins and that this would procure eternal life for those who believe—in other words, the actual *gospel*). Only in the Road Narrative does Jesus start expounding the actual gospel, all in preparation for its actual enactment in the following Passover Narrative. This makes no sense as history. It only makes sense as artificial suspense-driven literature, and in particular as a slow-building teaching tool that

64. See Mk 1.3; 12.14; 'the way', *hodos*, also means 'road', and thus is here a double entendre; that this word could be used to mean Christianity, see Acts 16.17; 18.25-26; 19.9, 23; 24.14, 22.

65. See the analysis in Crossan, *Power of Parable*, pp. 162-68.

would operate in a single sitting (or series of them) as you went through the Gospel story as Mark crafts it.

While they wrap around the Sea Narrative, the Discipling and Road Narratives mirror *each other*, in a series of coincidences that once again betray the literary invention:

A peripheral ministry begins (1.14-34)
B people looking for Jesus to be healed (1.35-38)
(but Jesus says he needs to teach more people)
C Jesus ventures out ('throughout all Galilee', 1.39-45)
D Jesus stops at Capernaum (2.1-12)
(explains he can forgive sins)
E problems and controversies (2.13–3.12)
F an important gathering on a mountain (3.13-19)
G Jesus is accused of being in league with Baalzebul (3.20-35)
(and preaches those who reject Jesus are damned)
— **The Sea Narrative** (chaps. 4–8)
G Jesus accuses Peter of being in league with Satan (8.27–9.1)
(and preaches those who blaspheme Holy Spirit are damned)
F an important gathering on a mountain (9.2-13)
E problems and controversies (9.14-32)
D Jesus stops at Capernaum (9.33-50)
(explains dangers of sin)
C Jesus ventures out (expands his ministry *beyond* Galilee, 10.1-16)
B people looking to Jesus for boons (10.17-45)
(but Jesus teaches them the error of their ways)
A peripheral ministry ends (10.46-52)

Jesus' ministry has two phases, the central (in Jerusalem) and the peripheral (outside Jerusalem), as was typical in the myths and legends of counter-cultural sages (see Element 46). His central ministry corresponds to Mark's Passover Narrative. But his peripheral ministry consumes the prior three narratives, and begins (1.14-28) with the first preaching about the importance of faith in one's salvation ('have faith in the gospel', 1.15), the first insistence that people keep quiet about Jesus' identity ('be quiet', 1.25), and the first men called to follow him (1.16-20), and then ends with the *last* preaching about the importance of faith in one's salvation ('your faith has made you whole', 10.52), the *last* insistence that people keep quiet about Jesus' identity ('many rebuked him, to keep him quiet', 10.48, which Jesus now does not enforce—since he is about to go public in chap. 11), and the *last* man called to follow him (Bartimaeus, 10.49-52).

You might notice that I omitted from the Discipling Narrative Jesus' baptism (1.1-11) and temptation (1.12-13). These do not line up with the Road

Narrative in any fashion; instead, the mirroring of the Discipling Narrative in the Road Narrative begins and ends where Jesus' ministry begins and ends (before he enters Jerusalem). But as was common in literary artifice, Mark's introduction lines up with his *conclusion*, again in such a fashion as to betray the extent of his literary invention. Indeed, the beginning of Mark's Gospel matches the end, only in reverse, and in such a manner as to be a very peculiar way to end a Gospel, exposing the fact that he has forced the literary symbolism:

Behold, I **send** my **messenger** into your presence, who shall prepare your way. The **voice** of one calling out in the wilderness, 'Make ready the **way** of the Lord. Make his **paths** straight.' . . . And there went out to him all the country of Judaea, and all the people of Jerusalem (Mk 1.2-3, 5).	'**Go, tell** his disciples and Peter, "He **goes before you** into Galilee; there you'll see him, as he told you."' And they went out, and fled from the tomb; for trembling and astonishment had come upon them: and they said **nothing to any one**; for they were afraid (Mk 16.7-8).
So: *John (a **man**) delivers the **message** **fearlessly** and **loudly** to **everyone**, preparing the **path** of the Lord.*	So: *The **women** fail to deliver the **message** they are given, and so do not prepare the **path** of the Lord, because of **fear**, and instead are **silent** and tell **no one**.*
Jesus comes from Galilee . . . (Mk 1.9) *. . . then enters the wilderness to battle Satan* (Mk 1.12-13).	*Jesus goes to Galilee . . .* (Mk 16.7) *. . . after having left the wilderness* [the land of the dead] *having defeated Satan.*

Table 4. Reversal of Mark 1 in Mark 16

Mark's ending is also a reversal of expectation on a wider scale: Mark has Jesus repeatedly tell people to be silent, but then they talk (e.g. Mk 1.43-45), while his ending reverses this: the women are told to talk, but then they are silent.[66] Mark's literary fondness for triads is also reflected again in his invention of three women who appear three times, touching each of the three days of Jesus' death and resurrection (at his death, at his burial, and at his resurrection), and every time they appear, they 'behold' something (using the same exact verb: *theōreō*).[67] These named women, notably, never appear elsewhere

66. As noted by Bart Ehrman in *Misquoting Jesus: The Story Behind Who Changed the Bible and Why* (San Francisco, CA: HarperSanFrancisco, 2005), p. 68. The women are also told to go back to Galilee, which to the reader can be understood as an instruction to go back to the beginning of the Gospel (where Jesus begins in Galilee: Mk 1.9; then begins his ministry in Galilee: Mk 1.14).

67. Mk 15.40, 15.47, 16.4 (that his burial ended with the start of the second day is implied by 15.42, which says evening had come); only in their second appearance (Mk

in Mark's Gospel; they only suddenly appear here, without explanation. And so on. Several peculiarities of Mark's conclusion are thereby explained as a literary device. I have already shown elsewhere how nearly every element of Mark's empty-tomb narrative has scriptural or allegorical functions that make its content far more probable as myth than history.[68]

The baptism narrative also matches the crucifixion narrative. This makes literary sense, because theologically baptism was understood as a symbolic death-and-resurrection—it was how Christians came to be crucified with Christ (e.g. Rom. 6.3-4). In Mark the parallels are numerous and conspicuous enough to be improbable as anything but literary design:

John cries with a [loud] voice (*phōnē boōntos*, Mk 1.3).	Jesus cries with a loud voice (*eboēsen . . . phōnē megalē*, Mk 15.34).
An allusion is made to Elijah (Mk 1.6; cf. 2 Kgs 1.8).	An allusion is made to Elijah (Mk 15.34-36).
The heavens are torn (*schizō*, Mk 1.10).	The temple curtain is torn (*schizō*, Mk 15.38), symbol of the barrier between earth and heaven.
Holy Spirit descends upon Jesus (*to pneuma . . . katabainon eis auton*, 'the pneuma . . . descended upon him', Mk 1.10).	Holy Spirit departs from Jesus (*exepneusen*, 'he exhaled the pneuma', Mk 15.37).
God calls Jesus his son (Mk 1.11).	The centurion (a Roman official) calls Jesus God's son (Mk 15.39).

Table 5. Reversal of Mark 1 in Mark 15

15.47) are all three not named (Salome is conspicuously not mentioned at the burial; her absence is not explained). But the fact that they had never been introduced before and only appear as a literary device to witness the death, burial and resurrection, and otherwise fit a multiply triadic structure, makes them more likely a literary fiction (I make a more extensive case for this conclusion in Carrier, *Not the Impossible Faith*, pp. 312-21).

68. Drawing on both Jewish scripture and pagan equivalents: Carrier, 'Spiritual Body', in *Empty Tomb* (ed. Price and Lowder), pp. 156-65; and Carrier, *Not the Impossible Faith*, pp. 312-21; with Element 47 and MacDonald, *Homeric Epics*, pp. 154-68.

In fact the centurion says God's claim is now 'true' because of the witness of the Holy Spirit ('when the centurion *saw* how he exhaled the *spirit*, he said, "*Truly* this man was the *Son of God*."'), just as at his baptism Jesus 'saw' the Holy Spirit descend and heard God's own voice declare the very same thing. There is a larger parallel as well, not only in that baptism symbolizes death (and thus in both scenes the curtain of heaven is torn *after* Jesus passes through the threshold of death), but also in that John's baptism remits sins (1.4-5), and so does Jesus' death.[69]

So it would seem the entire Gospel of Mark is a fabrication from chap. 1 to chap. 10, and we've already seen several examples of the fabricatory nature of chaps. 15 and 16 (e.g. the crucifixion and Barabbas and empty tomb narratives). What about the rest of the Passover Narrative, chaps. 11 to 14? This is also a product of design, modeling Jewish Passover ritual and lore. According to the Torah the Passover lamb had to be singled out and set aside on the tenth day of the month (Exod. 12.3) and then is slain at twilight on the fourteenth day (Exod. 12.6), when 'the whole congregation of Israel must slay it together'. And then the lamb is eaten when Passover begins on the fifteenth of the month (Jewish days begin at sundown, so this means the lamb is slain just before sunset and eaten just after).

This is essentially what happens to Jesus. On the tenth of the month he is singled out and set aside—by his triumphal entry into Jerusalem (Mark 11).[70] Which narrative Mark literarily constructs from a number of scriptural source texts, demonstrating he had no need of historical sources.[71]

69. On the various ways that Mark's baptism narrative deliberately parallels his death narrative, the scholarship is summarized and expanded in David Ulansey, 'The Heavenly Veil Torn: Mark's Cosmic "Inclusio"', *Journal of Biblical Literature* 110 (Spring 1991), pp. 123-25. Ulansey also notes that Josephus says the *outer* veil of the temple was an enormous tapestry eighty feet high on which was depicted the heavens (Josephus, *Jewish War* 5.212-14), thus anyone witnessing it tearing would indeed be seeing the 'heavens' torn. Ulansey also assumes the centurion at the crucifixion could be imagined as seeing this veil from Golgotha, but that might be doubtful (although perhaps Mark did not know that; and in any case, his actually seeing it is not narratively required).

70. That the triumphal entry occurs on the tenth day is evident from the arrangement of Mark's narrative: the tenth day is his arrival in Jerusalem, after which he visits the temple but then leaves, returning to Bethany (Mk 11.1-11); the eleventh day begins (Mk 11.12-25) when Jesus reenters Jerusalem and cleanses the temple; the twelfth day follows with another visit to Jerusalem (Mk 11.27–13.37), where he preaches all day; then on the thirteenth day he is back at Bethany, where we are told it is just two days away from the Passover (14.1-3), which was to be the fifteenth; and on the fourteenth day Jesus instructs his disciples to prepare for the Passover (14.12). So counting back, the triumphal entry is the tenth, precisely when the Passover lamb is chosen.

71. For the many scriptural inspirations and allusions Mark employed in constructing this narrative see Deborah Krause, 'The One Who Comes Unbinding

Then on the fifteenth of the month Jesus is symbolically eaten in place of the Passover lamb (at the Last Supper, he declares the food and drink there to be his body and blood; ordinarily, they would at that time be eating the Passover lamb: Mk 14.16-17, 14.22-24).[72] He is killed the next afternoon. Although the Gospel of John would later change things around so that Jesus is killed at exactly the same time as the Passover lamb (having Jesus executed on the 14th rather than the 15th), this mars the parallel of the Last Supper as a symbolic Passover consumption of the Lord.[73] Mark preferred the latter symbolism, and instead preserved the former symbolism by having Jesus die at exactly the same *time* as the Passover lambs were slaughtered (albeit the day before him): at the ninth hour.[74]

the Blessing of Judah: Mark 11.1-10 as a Midrash on Genesis 49.11, Zechariah 9.9, and Psalm 118.25-26', in *Early Christian Interpretation of the Scriptures of Israel: Investigations and Proposals* (ed. Craig Evans and James Sanders; Sheffield: Sheffield Academic Press, 1997), pp. 141-53 (e.g. 'Mark 11.1-10 presents a complex web of organically related Scripture traditions', p. 147).

72. The Greek also conceals a clue to this symbolic death: in Mk 14.14 Jesus instructs his disciples to ask, 'Where is my *kataluma*, where I shall eat the Passover with my disciples?' The noun *kataluma* comes from the verb *kataluō,* which means dissolve, disintegrate, destroy, kill; but that noun form just happened to acquire instead the meaning of a place where one 'breaks up' a journey (like an inn or lodge). But the pun is still there. Mark uses the verb in three places: in every one (13.2; 14.58; 15.29) referring to the destruction of the temple, which we know for Mark was a metaphor for Jesus' body (with the use of the same verb and building metaphor by Paul in 2 Cor. 5.1: see Carrier, *Proving History*, p. 190). Mark thus has Jesus say, in effect, that he will be destroyed (broken up) in that room at Passover, just as the Passover lamb would be.

73. The Last Supper, as the model for the Christian Eucharist ritual, *had* to represent the consumption of the sacrificed Christ in place of the Passover lamb (Element 18), but also had to precede his actual death, since in the earliest esoteric tradition Christ was delivered to the powers (and thus killed) *after* he symbolically inaugurated the 'Lord's Supper' (1 Cor. 11.23-26; cf. 11.20, although this was only known by revelation: 1 Cor. 11.23; it thus never actually happened; see Element 16 and Chapter 11, §7). Mark is thus trying to preserve the original esoteric order, while still making his exoteric myth fit as well as he can.

74. At that time of year, the ninth hour (Mk 15.33-34) corresponded to our 3 P.M.; that this is when the Passover lambs were slaughtered is reported in Josephus, *Jewish War* 6.423. It's possible this was a coincidence resulting from Mark's fondness for triads, however, since Mark narrates that Jesus is hung on the cross exactly three hours after sunrise (Mk 15.25), and exactly three hours later darkness covers the earth (Mk 15.33), and exactly three hours after that Jesus dies (Mk 15.34). At that time of year the sun would then go down exactly three hours after that; so Jesus is hung exactly three hours after sunrise and dies exactly three hours before sundown (and his burial is completed by sundown, completing the last three-hour period: Mk 15.42). Possibly Mark was aware of the poetry of this triadic coincidence, which the hour of slaughter allowed him to exploit.

Mark has thus deliberately arranged his narrative to symbolically represent Jesus as the Passover lamb. And as we saw, he also used the Barabbas narrative to symbolically represent Jesus as also the goat of Yom Kippur (and we know Jesus was always imagined to have been both: Element 18). But he was also known as the 'firstfruits' of the general resurrection (1 Cor. 15.20-23), and the Torah commands that the Day of Firstfruits take place the day after the first Sabbath following the Passover (Lev. 23.5, 10-11). In other words, on a Sunday. Thus Mark has Jesus rise from the dead on Sunday, the firstftuits of the resurrected, symbolically on the very Day of Firstfruits itself. So the whole choice of what day (and even year) in which to have Jesus crucified is decided by literary symbolism, not historical plausibility.[75] Indeed, since executions would not be performed on holy days, Mark's narrative has no historical credibility. Likewise trials for capital crimes had to be conducted over the course of two days and could not be conducted on or even interrupted by a Sabbath or holy day, nor ever conducted at night. So in reality had Jesus been arrested during Passover he would have been held over in jail until Sunday, and could only have been convicted on Monday at the earliest.[76] So as history, Mark's narrative makes zero sense. But as symbolic myth, every oddity is explained, and indeed expected.[77]

75. A specific calendar date can align only with a specific day of the week in a specific year, so in order to have Jesus rise on the third day after his death, counting inclusively as they did, while also rising on the Day of Firstfruits, it follows that even what year Jesus was crucified is a literary choice, and not decided by reference to any historical fact (beyond the presumed fact that it was some year during which Pontius Pilate governed Judea, although see again Chapter 8, §1). That John felt free to change the date (and thus the year), again for symbolic reasons, only goes to prove further how irrelevant historical facts were to constructing the Gospel narratives.

76. On these facts see Carrier, 'Burial of Jesus', in *Empty Tomb* (ed. Price and Lowder), pp. 371-79, with Mishnah, *Sanhedrin* 4.1k and 5.5a; trials for capital crimes could be held only during the day: *Sanhedriun* 4.1j (in explicit contrast with property cases, which must begin during the day but can end at night). There is no plausible reason why these procedures would have been violated for Jesus, as even Mark was aware that such gross violation of the laws of the land and of God would cause a riot in the city (Mk 14.1-2), whereas it would have been no trouble at all to simply jail Jesus, incommunicado, until the holy day had passed and the city was emptied of pilgrims. That would obviously be what any sensible leadership would have done.

77. There were several other reasons Mark had to choose Sunday as the day of resurrection: Sunday was also traditionally the first day of creation (since God rested on the seventh day of creation, making that the Sabbath, hence Saturday; so creation began on a Sunday, the first day of the week: Gen. 1.5 and 2.2), and Jesus was also imagined as inaugurating a new creation (e.g. 2 Cor. 5.17), and thus logically *had* to rise on a Sunday; and the fact that scripture also said he had to rise on the third day (1 Cor. 15.4) required the date of his execution to be Friday. Mark also saw this in the

In fact, the overall structure of the Passover Narrative is centered on this Passover symbolism. Chapter 11, as we just saw, corresponds to the singling out of the Passover lamb; chap. 14 to the Passover itself (it narrates its preparation and commencement); chap. 15 then symbolically narrates the slaughter of the Passover lamb (merging it literarily with the sacrifice of Yom Kippur), and chap. 16 symbolizes the rescue from death that the Passover represents. On the original Passover, the angel of death 'passes over' those who are protected by the lamb's blood and kills the 'firstborn sons' of those who are not; in Mark, *the* firstborn son (Jesus) is rescued from death (as evidenced by his empty tomb), and his blood protects those who share in it. The symbolism is thus complete—except for chaps. 12 and 13. How do they fit the Passover theme?

Chapter 13 is devoted to explaining how Christian missionaries will suffer for a time, but the end will come, which is the new Exodus for the elect: a period of wandering and distress, ending in salvation, as they are saved from death, after their trials and tribulations, while everyone else is damned. They are then told to keep watch for the coming of the messiah. These themes are also echoed in the Passover seder, where watch is also kept for the messiah (or his herald, Elijah) and where the story of salvation (the original Exodus) is retold, including the tribulations the Jews endured. Such a discussion and instruction would be a common way to conclude a Passover seder.

It is thus fitting that chap. 12 symbolically represents the *previous* conversational phase of the seder, as noted by Calum Carmichael.[78] Carmichael shows how the entire narrative arc of Mark 12 mimics the Passover haggadah, the discourse acted out during a Passover seder. This is yet another example of how Mark's narrative has been created to serve a

Psalms: as we've seen, he saw the crucifixion in Psalm 22, and then the sojourn among the dead in Psalm 23, and then the resurrection 'on the first day of the week', that is, Sunday, in Psalm 24 (which in the Septuagint is sung 'on the first day of the week', a line essentially quoted by Mark in 16.2, using the same distinctive idiom in the Greek). See Carrier, 'Spiritual Body', in *Empty Tomb* (ed. Price and Lowder), pp. 158-61. See also *Barnabas* 15, which explicitly links Sunday with the new-creation theology as well as spiritual circumcision (which took place on the eighth day, which *Barnabas* notes corresponds to the 'second' first day in a seven-day week); and Justin Martyr, *Dialogue with Trypho* 85 and 97-106 (where he explicitly says Psalm 22 predicts the messiah's crucifixion and Psalm 24 his resurrection; the latter is also corroborated by Irenaeus in *Demonstration of the Apostolic Preaching* 84 and Justin Martyr, *Dialogue with Trypho* 36).

78. Calum Carmichael, 'The Passover Haggadah', in *Historical Jesus in Context* (ed. Levine, Allison and Crossan), pp. 343-56.

mytho-symbolic purpose, which almost certainly does not 'coincidentally' represent an actual history.[79] As Carmichael explains:

> Mark 12 recounts together four incidents involving questions. This series evokes the section of the *Haggadah* wherein three types of sons ask their own question and a fourth son, unable to engage his curiosity, has it aroused for him: a wise son asks about all the detailed rules of Passover; a wicked son asks in such a way as to exclude himself from the Jewish community; a son of plain piety inquires about essentials; and a son unable to ask is initiated into learning what Scripture says about the Exodus story.[80]

The 'wicked son' in particular asks a question that risks excluding him from the deliverance from bondage and death offered by God in the Exodus, in parallel to the similar Christian concern now arising from their new Exodus, that of the Apocalypse, which was likewise a rescue from bondage and death for the new elect (the new Israel), the believers in Christ.[81] Thus the analogy to Mark becomes clear:

In Mark, questioners first ask Jesus about a tricky legal requirement concerning the payment of taxes (Mk 12.13-17, like the first question in the seder, a query about technicalities). Next, questioners inquire in such a way as to mock the notion of resurrection and thereby (according to tradition [e.g. Mishnah, *Sanhedrin* 10]) cut themselves off from the community (Mk 12.18-27, like the second question in the seder, a wicked query that threatens exclusion). Then, a questioner asks about fundamental requirements of the moral life (Mk 12.28-34, like the third question in the seder, a query about essentials). Finally, Jesus himself, in response to his audience's 'not daring to ask him any question' (Mk 12.34), poses a problem about conflicting scriptural verses (Mk 12.35-37, so like the fourth 'question' in the seder, those unable to ask are answered anyway).[82]

Jesus then follows with teachings about priestly wealth and hypocrisy (Mk 12.38-44), before getting into the 'be vigilant for the messiah' narrative of chap. 13. In parallel with that closing sentiment, Jesus had *preceded* this Passover haggadah with a parable about corruption in the temple cult and God's coming wrath (Mk 12.1-12).[83] So it is no coincidence that the

79. For this purpose it does not matter whether the seder traditions later developed were post-temple. The coincidences of the features to follow demonstrates that *those* elements at least preceded the Jewish war (as otherwise those coincidences are hard to explain).

80. Carmichael, 'Passover Haggadah', p. 345.

81. Carmichael, 'Passover Haggadah', p. 347.

82. Carmichael, 'Passover Haggadah', p. 345.

83. That this parable is a veiled attack on the corruption of the temple priesthood: Chilton, 'Targum, Jesus, and the Gospels', in *Historical Jesus in Context* (ed. Levine,

vanity and destruction of the temple likewise opens the apocalypse discourse in chap. 13, just as it had opened the Passover haggadah of chap. 12. So in chap. 12 this produces another simple ring structure:

A Corruption of the temple priesthood
B Passover Haggadah
A Corruption of the temple priesthood

It is obviously by literary artifice that the middle section of chap. 12 exactly matches up with the ritual haggadah of the Passover seder, which had been replaced with a fundamental ritual of the Christian mystery (the Eucharist), about salvation from slavery and death (Exodus/Passover), and explicitly linked to whether we will be resurrected or not—and here, as expected, it is specifically *resurrection* that is the theme of exclusion (those who mock it will be excluded, while those who pursue the truth, through recognition and union with Christ, are saved). Mark 12.10-11 even recites Ps. 118.22-23, a psalm that was also recited as part of the Passover haggadah, in which God 'becomes our salvation' (118.21) and God's 'right hand is exalted' (118.16), and it is declared that we 'shall not die, but live' (118.17) and gain entry into the land of the righteous (118.18-20).

So the entire narrative of Mark is a fictional, symbolic construct, from beginning to end. He adapted many other literary motifs and techniques to flesh it out, of course. Some we've seen here. Others we've noted before—for example, Mark borrows a framework from the Socratic-Aesopic mythotype (Element 46) and many elements from traditional pagan heroic translation fables (Element 47); and he has already co-opted more than half the features of the Rank–Raglan hero-type (counting fourteen hits out of twenty-two; or fifteen, if Jesus' metaphorical marriage to the heiress of his predecessor is counted, per Mk 2.18-22; the remaining features might already have been part of the core Jesus mythology and Mark simply omitted them—unless those features were added by Matthew: see Element 48).

Indeed, even how Mark decides to construct the sequence of the Passover narrative appears to be based on the tale of another Jesus: Jesus ben Ananias, the 'Jesus of Jerusalem', an insane prophet active in the 60s CE who is then killed in the siege of Jerusalem (roughly in the year 70).[84] His story is told by Josephus in the *Jewish War*, and unless Josephus invented him, his narrative must have been famous, famous enough for Josephus to know of it, and thus famous enough for Mark to know of it, too, and make use of it to model the tale of his own Jesus. Or if Josephus invented the

Allison and Crossan), p. 247.

84. According to Josephus his arrest and trial take place between 62 and 64 CE, as that was the term of office of Lucceius Albinus, the prefect overseeing his trial.

tale, then Mark evidently used Josephus as a source.[85] Because the parallels are too numerous to be at all probable as a coincidence.[86] Some Mark does derive from elsewhere (or matches from elsewhere to a double purpose), but the overall scheme of the story in Josephus matches Mark too closely to believe that Mark just came up with the exact same scheme independently. And since it's not believable that Josephus invented a new story using Mark, we must conclude Mark invented his story using Josephus—or the same tale known to Josephus.

It would appear this story inspired the general outline of Mark's entire Passover Narrative. There are at least twenty significant parallels (and one reversal):

1	Both are named Jesus.	
2	Both come to Jerusalem during a major religious festival.	Mk 14.2 = *JW* 6.301
3	Both entered the temple area to rant against the temple.	Mk 11.15-17 = *JW* 6.301
4	During which both quote the same chapter of Jeremiah.	Jer. 7.11 in Mk; Jer. 7.34 in *JW*
5	Both then preach daily in the temple.	Mk 14.49 = *JW* 6.306
6	Both declared 'woe' unto Judea or the Jews.	Mk 13.17 = *JW* 6.304, 306, 309
7	Both predict the temple will be destroyed.	Mk 13.2 = *JW* 6.300, 309
8	Both are for this reason arrested by the Jews.	Mk 14.43 = *JW* 6.302
9	Both are accused of speaking against the temple.	Mk 14.58 = *JW* 6.302
10	Neither makes any defense of himself against the charges.	Mk 14.60 = *JW* 6.302
11	Both are beaten by the Jews.	Mk 14.65 = *JW* 6.302

85. The *Jewish War* of Josephus was written between 74 and 79 CE, as it was written after Masada was destroyed in 74, and was dedicated to Vespasian, who died in 79.

86. Theodore Weeden, 'Two Jesuses, Jesus of Jerusalem and Jesus of Nazareth: Provocative Parallels and Imaginative Imitation', *Forum* N.S. 6.2 (Fall 2003), pp. 137-341; Craig Evans, 'Jesus in Non-Christian Sources', in *Studying the Historical Jesus* (ed. Chilton and Evans), pp. 443-78 (475-77).

12	Then both are taken to the Roman governor.	Pilate in Mk 15.1 = Albinus in *JW* 6.302
13	Both are interrogated by the Roman governor.	Mk 15.2-4 = *JW* 6.305
14	During which both are asked to identify themselves.	Mk 15.2 = *JW* 6.305
15	And yet again neither says anything in his defense.	Mk 15.3-5 = *JW* 6.305
16	Both are then beaten by the Romans.	Mk 15.15 = *JW* 6.304
17	In both cases the Roman governor decides he should release him.	
18	. . . but doesn't (Mark); . . . but does (*JW*).	Mk 15.6-15 vs. *JW* 6.305
19	Both are finally killed by the Romans (in Mark, by execution; in the *JW*, by artillery).	Mk 15.34 = *JW* 6.308-309
20	Both utter a lament for themselves immediately before they die.	Mk 15.34 = *JW* 6.309
21	Both die with a loud cry.	Mk 15.37 = *JW* 6.309

Table 6. Parallels of Jesus 'Christ' with Jesus ben Ananias

Given that Mark is essentially a Christian response to the Jewish War and the destruction of the Jewish temple, it is more than a little significant that he chose *this* Jesus to model his own Jesus after. This also tells us, yet again, how much Mark is making everything up. (It also confirms that Mark wrote after the Jewish War.)

There was also, of course, a Jewish mythotype that Mark adapted to construct his Passion Narrative, as noted by George Nickelsburg.[87] In Jewish myths and legends, 'tales about a wise [or righteous] man [or woman] who, as the object of a conspiracy or plot, is persecuted, consigned to death, rescued, vindicated, and exalted to high position in the royal court' were commonplace, as were wisdom tales that feature a righteous man 'who is put to death but exalted in the heavenly courtroom where he confronts his enemies as their judge'. And what is shared across both genres is 'the

87. George Nickelsburg, 'The Genre and Function of the Markan Passion Narrative', *Harvard Theological Review* 73 (January–April 1980), pp. 153-84.

rescue and vindication of a persecuted innocent person'.[88] Nickelsburg analyzes the Markan Passion Narrative and finds it is just another rewrite of this same mytheme.[89]

The shared plot structure is: introduction (of the characters and situation), provocation (of the authorities by some act of or for the hero), conspiracy (in which the authorities look for the right moment or means to dispose of the hero), interwoven with a subplot of decision (the hero must choose between obeying God or the authorities), trust (the decision to obey God is described in terms of trusting God's will) often voiced in a prayer (for deliverance), and obedience (to God and the hero's fate, usually death); and many versions of this tale accomplish these elements with a trial at court. Formal accusations are brought against the hero (usually false or distorted); s/he faces a trial (or the equivalent), is condemned; attempts are made to save him or her (as in Mark's case, Pilate attempts to let Jesus go), but these fail, so s/he undergoes an ordeal, and is then rescued, vindicated, and exalted. These stories also usually narrate the different reactions of those witnessing the key events, and often involve the hero being invested with royal power. God is then praised, the hero's new status acclaimed, and the persecutors punished (by the hero or at his or her decision or on his or her behalf).

Although 'these stories have emplotted a common theme in a highly consistent series and sequence of narrative components, each story has its own particular inner consistency and storyline that runs through its major elements and differentiates it from other stories in the genre'.[90] They also often contain allusions or links to God's suffering righteous servant in the OT (including Isaiah 53; hence, note again Elements 5 through 7).[91] Mark's Passion Narrative follows this generic storyline thoroughly.[92] For example, in the scene at Gethsemene, Jesus chooses to trust and obey God and prays for deliverance, while the whole preceding Gospel builds the theme of provocation (e.g. Mk 3.6; 11.18; 14.1).[93]

Nickelsburg imagines the clearing of the temple as the final provocation (Mk 11.18). Of course, that scene is hardly believable: the temple grounds were enormous, occupying many acres (the temple as a whole occupied nearly forty acres, and a large portion of that, at least ten acres, was devoted to public space), extensively populated (there would have been *hundreds* of merchants and moneychangers there), and heavily guarded by an armed

88. Nickelsburg, 'Genre', p. 156.
89. Nickelsburg, 'Genre', pp. 157-62.
90. Nickelsburg, 'Genre', p. 162.
91. Nickelsburg, 'Genre', p. 163.
92. Nickelsburg, 'Genre', pp. 164-66.
93. Nickelsburg, 'Genre', p. 171.

force deployed to prevent just this sort of thing.[94] They would have killed Jesus on the spot. So the story is obviously fiction even on that point alone. But its literary artistry leads us to the same conclusion.[95] When Jesus clears the temple he quotes Jer. 7.11 (in Mk 11.17), whose own narrative bears too many coincidental parallels to be accidental: Jeremiah and Jesus both enter the temple (Jer. 7.1-2; Mk 11.15), make the same accusation against the corruption of the temple cult (Jeremiah quoting a revelation from the Lord, Jesus quoting Jeremiah), and predict the destruction of the temple (Jer. 7.12-14; Mk 14.57-58; 15.29).

Though that is said to be a false accusation in Mark, given Mk 13.1-2, where Jesus does indeed predict the temple's destruction (and earlier, albeit more elusively, in 11.12-21), and given the 'Jeremiah' context that Jesus himself alludes to, what is false about the accusation is not the predicted destruction but that Jesus would do the destroying. Mark is thus exhibiting knowledge that the Romans would destroy it in 70 CE. Hence, again, Mark is writing after that year, and composing a fictional story to suit—a hindsight already confirmed by Mark's knowledge of the temple's destruction elsewhere (Mark 13; e.g. 13.2). Thus Mark may still have meant that Jesus really did say what his accusers report but did not mean it literally—and it is by taking it literally that their accusations become false, a theme of incomprehension among his enemies, mistaking the figurative for the literal, that Mark repeats throughout his Gospel. Mark's reference to 'false witnesses' (*pseudomarturoi*) would then be an allusion to the 'false prophets' (*pseudoprophētai*) who similarly accused Jeremiah at trial (Jer. 26.7-11; in the Septuagint, 33.7-11).[96] Although *their* accusation was true: Jeremiah *had* predicted the temple's destruction. And it is for this 'crime' that Jeremiah stands trial, just as Jesus does (Mk 14.57-58 and 15.29), and though Jeremiah is acquitted (Jer. 26; LXX: 33), he says God will spare the city and sanctuary if the Jews repent of their crimes (Jer. 26.13), but they don't, and of course the temple (the first temple) is destroyed by a foreign army. The parallel this draws with the fate of the second temple, similarly

94. Besides Acts 4.1 and 1 Chronicles 26, see Josephus, *Antiquities of the Jews* 15.403-409, and the analysis of Robert Miller, 'The (A)Historicity of Jesus' Temple Demonstration: A Test Case in Methodology', in *Society of Biblical Literature 1991 Seminar Papers: One Hundred Twenty-Seventh Annual Meeting* (ed. Eugene Lovering; Atlanta, GA: Scholars Press, 1991), pp. 235-52.

95. Nickelsburg, 'Genre', p. 166.

96. Nickelsburg, 'Genre', p. 179, argues that what was false is their claim to have *heard* the prediction, when Jesus in fact had only said it in private to his disciples; although one could wonder why then Judas, a disciple, was not brought as a witness, it's always possible Mark didn't think of that when composing his fiction (as I've said before, many a novelist and screenwriter has made a similar mistake).

destroyed by a foreign army, and in Christian imagination because the Jews failed to repent of their crimes, is Mark's obvious intention.

As I noted earlier, the cleansing of the temple as a fictional scene has its primary inspiration from a targum of Zech. 14.21, where it is said 'in that day there shall never again be traders in the house of Jehovah of hosts', in combination with the whole intended theme of the Passover Narrative in Mark, which is against the corruption of the temple priesthood, most particularly in respect to money, as we see not only in Mk 11.15-18 but yet again in the beginning and ending of Mark 12 (which sandwich Mark's emulation of the Passover haggadah, as we just saw). And all of this connects with the temple's eventual destruction as promised in Mark 13, creating a consistent through-line across chaps. 11, 12 and 13. And the crimes and corruption of the priesthood that would necessitate carrying out that promise are then narratively illustrated in chaps. 14 and 15 (where Jesus, unlike Jeremiah, is not acquitted but unjustly killed), ending with the vindication of Jesus in chap. 16.

In the Passover Narrative the trial sequence and the Barabbas story and the clearing of the temple aren't the only elements that have no historical plausibility (but have obvious symbolic meaning, and thus make perfect sense as fiction). The Passover Narrative also contains one of the most peculiar (and obviously fictional) episodes in Mark's entire Gospel: the withering of the fig tree. As history it makes no sense at all, not only because it defies the laws of physics, but also because Jesus' behavior would be wholly illogical had such a thing actually happened—for he curses a fig tree because it isn't bearing figs for him to eat . . . even though it wasn't the season for figs! (Mk 11.12-14). The fig tree promptly withers to death before nightfall (Mk 11.19-22). Obviously this story is completely made up. But why write such a bizarre story? To illustrate a point. In other words, this is a parable about Jesus and the Gospel, a bit of fiction Mark has composed to communicate something he wants to say, using Jesus as its central character. As here, so everywhere else in his Gospel: Mark is writing parables about Jesus as a mythical character; he is not recording anyone's memories of a historical man.

The meaning of the fig tree episode is most plausibly explained by R.G. Hamerton-Kelly, who shows that it is really a parable that structurally symbolizes the Christian rejection of the whole system of temple sacrifice (see again Element 28).[97] 'The key to understanding' the strange fig tree story, Hamerton-Kelly explains, is that 'the attack on the traders is placed *within*

97. R.G. Hamerton-Kelly, 'Sacred Violence and the Messiah: The Markan Passion Narrative as a Redefinition of Messianology', in *The Messiah: Developments in Earliest Judaism and Christianity* (ed. James Charlesworth; Minneapolis, MN: Fortress Press, 1992), pp. 461-93 (467-71).

the account of the attack on the fig tree'. In other words, the beginning and end of the fig tree story is wrapped around (and contains within its center) the clearing of the temple. We saw Mark do this before, when he took the tale of the raising of Jairus's twelve-year-old daughter and wrapped *that* around a symbolically related story of the woman who had bled for twelve years. The purpose of this structure (called intercalation) is to communicate that the one story illuminates the meaning of the other. Mark uses this device repeatedly.[98] In this case, 'the tree is a symbol of the sacrificial system whose time is now passed', hence 'it was not the season for figs' any more (Mk 11.13); therefore 'may no one eat fruit of you again' (Mk 11.14). Which finally, and perfectly, explains this strange story.

So the fig tree and its fate are a metaphor for the temple and its fate, and the need to 'feed the religiously hungry'. Jesus' attack on the fig tree in fact deliberately parallels and thus explains Jesus' attack on the temple. As Hamerton-Kelly explains:

> [T]here is no question of a 'cleansing' of the Temple, as if the presence of holy trade somehow polluted it; such a judgment is a parochialism and an anachronism, arising out of the Protestant delicacy about the association of money with religion, and a far cry from an ancient Temple devoted to animal slaughter, in which the exchange of money was perhaps the least offensive thing to a modern Protestant sensibility. No, the attack on the traders was a prophetic symbolic act advocating and foretelling the destruction of the sacrificial system.[99]

The mere role of money and trade was not the problem (that was necessitated by God's law); the corruption—and inevitable corruptibility—of that system was the problem (hence Elements 25 to 27, with Element 43).[100]

98. See David Neville, *Mark's Gospel—Prior or Posterior? A Reappraisal of the Phenomenon of Order* (New York: Sheffield Academic Press, 2002), pp. 258-66; Francis Gerald Downing, 'Markan Intercalation in Cultural Context', in *Doing Things with Words in the First Christian Century* (Sheffield: Sheffield Academic Press, 2000), pp. 118-32; T. Shepherd, 'The Narrative Function of Markan Intercalation', *New Testament Studies* 41 (1995), pp. 522-40; G. Van Oyen, 'Intercalation and Irony in the Gospel of Mark', in *The Four Gospels 1992: Festschrift Frans Neirynck*, Vol. II (ed. Frans van Segbroeck; Leuven: Leuven University Press, 1992), pp. 943-74; J.R. Edwards, 'Markan Sandwiches: The Significance of Interpolations in Markan Narratives', *Novum Testamentum* 31 (1989), pp. 193-216.

99. Hamerton-Kelly, 'Sacred Violence and the Messiah', p. 469.

100. See Victor Eppstein, 'The Historicity of the Gospel Account of the Cleansing of the Temple', *Zeitschrift für neutestamentliche Wissenschaft und die Kunde der älteren Kirche* 55 (1964), pp. 42-58. He argues that historicity may be suggested by the fact that Jesus visits the temple the day before and only on his second visit clears it, but as we've seen, Mark did that simply to insert an additional day in his narrative, so that Jesus' triumphal entry would occur on the tenth of Nisan.

The conclusion is that 'the sacrificial system is to be replaced by faith and prayer, founded on the renunciation of vengeance', thus also explaining the strange unexplained transition from the fate of the fig tree to Jesus' discourse on the power of faith and prayer (Mk 11.17, 22-25). That meant 'if faith and prayer are to replace the sacrificial mechanism, vengeance must be renounced' so that 'to renounce vengeance and to break with the mechanism of sacrifice is the same thing'. That's why Jesus explains that one must forgive others in order to receive forgiveness from God, all in order for your prayers to be answered (Mk 11.25). Forgiveness was normally achieved by the temple sacrifice system. But Jesus has done away with the temple cult from its very roots; hence the fig tree was withered from its very roots (Mk 11.20). But to replace that system, a greater sacrifice was needed. Hence anyone who wanted to get rid of the corrupt temple system had to imagine something like a messianic death, as that was the only thing that could logically achieve it (thus Elements 23 to 28, and 43). No actual messiah needed to die for a theologian to come to this conclusion. Thus, a historical Jesus was not necessary. A cosmic Jesus could be imagined for the job just as easily. (And that's what Heb. 9 appears to do; see Chapter 11, §5.) In that case, Mark just fabricated a mythic narrative about an *earthly* Jesus as a vehicle for conveying his system of parables about Christianity and what it represents. And that is the sort of thing that regularly happened to cosmic gods, who were also 'brought down to earth' in allegorical fiction like this (see Elements 14 and 45).

Hamerton-Kelly goes on to show that the whole of Mark 11–16 contains an escalating system of symbols and teachings about replacing the temple cult with a new cult comprised of the faithful, without central authority or location, eliminating the corrupting role of money or worldly authority. And while Mark is inventing narratives to fit his symbolic structure and to communicate abstract messages about the gospel, he often ignores historical plausibility, not only inventing narratives that center around blatant defiances of the laws of physics (walking on water, withering trees), but making his characters behave in completely implausible ways, such as having the disciples act completely surprised at the second miraculous feeding, as if some time-traveling *Men in Black* had erased their memory of the first one; or having Jesus curse a fig tree for failing to bear fruit out of season.

Scholars have long been aware of this. For example, Mark describes Jesus on two separate occasions calling to fishermen—complete strangers—who just leave their jobs on the spot and follow him as disciples, with no persuasion or explanation. This does not exactly defy any law of physics. But it does defy every human probability. As Robert Funk says,

> [These] scenes in Mark, repeated almost word-for-word in Matthew, make sense only in retrospect, in the context of a movement now already some years old. From that distance, it was plausible for some storyteller

> to relate how the [four men] decided on the spur of the moment to leave their jobs and become itinerant followers of Jesus. [These] are thus not actual scenes but the product of an imagination informed by the subsequent course of events . . . [*and perhaps*] stylized from constant repetition.[101]

Many more examples could be produced, but you get the picture. Again and again we see the same indicators—such as miracles and improbabilities, literary constructs, symbolic narratives, artificial structures, rewrites of biblical tales, emulations of mythic plots—in every scene of Mark's Gospel. This is what myth looks like, not history.

Dennis MacDonald has famously shown how Mark created his fiction by fusing Homeric parallels with biblical ones. Just as Virgil updated Homer by recasting the time and place and all the characters to suit Roman mythology, and then changed key things to communicate how Roman values were superior to Greek, Mark updated Homer by recasting the time and place and all the characters to suit Jewish and (newly minted) Christian mythology, and to fit the Roman history and political reality the Christians now lived in, and then changed key things (often by drawing on the Septuagint) to communicate how *Christian* values were superior to Jewish, Greek and Roman values. Jesus is not only the new (and better) Moses and Elijah and Elisha, he is also the new (and better) Odysseus and Romulus (see Chapter 4, §1, and Element 47), and the new Socrates and Aesop (Element 46). The point of inventing this kind of narrative is the same as inventing or reworking the legend of King Arthur or Ned Ludd (see Chapter 1, §4), or indeed Moses or Daniel, whose narratives are equally fictional, yet also represented as histories.

As MacDonald explains:

> Mark and Luke wrote not to convert their readers but to provide the burgeoning Christian movement a literary narrative to shape its identity, much as classical Greek poetry—Homeric epic above all—had shaped Greek culture, including religion. In this respect, Mark and Luke–Acts are similar to the *Aeneid*, which was composed about a century earlier. In this Latin epic, Vergil transformed Homeric epic and other literature into a lavish and powerful mythology that profoundly shaped Roman politics, society, and culture.[102]

These narratives created models to follow, and stories to use to symbolize and communicate ideals (and criticize the competing ideals in Jewish and Greco-Roman society). They were a way to explain and understand the

101. Robert Funk, 'Do the Gospels Contain Eyewitness Reports?' in *Finding the Historical Jesus: Rules of Evidence* (ed. Bernard Brandon Scott; Santa Rosa, CA: Polebridge, 2008), pp. 31-39 (32).

102. MacDonald, 'Imitations of Greek Epic', pp. 374-75.

gospel through parables. Thus was created a myth around which churches could seek a common unity. As such, each of the Gospels we have is in direct competition with the others, each author disagreeing with his predecessors and rewriting the narrative to communicate what *he* thought those unifying values should be.

What became the subsequently victorious Church simply chose those Gospels it thought could most optimally accomplish two ends simultaneously: be most easily reconciled with a particular common set of core values, while drawing into their circuit of control the widest network of established Christian communities, as by then every church community had taken sides by adopting or preferring one Gospel or other. The second of these aims gave them a strategic advantage in their competition with other Christian sectarian movements: more members, more resources, more influence, and more geographic supremacy (thus explaining why their Church, and hence their canon, eventually won). But that advantage could only be bought at a cost: a set of Gospels rife with contradictions and conflicting values. Had they cast their net too widely, the canon would have been too inconsistent to create a unity movement at all; but if cast too narrowly, they would have unified too few communities to gain any advantage. The canon they chose no doubt represented the best strategic compromise possible. The resulting contradictions and conflicts could then be resolved with rhetoric, handwaving and creative exegesis. And that is exactly what we see happened.

But it is the construction process we are interested in here, not the selection process, which came after. In constructing his Gospel, the first we know to have been written, Mark merged Homeric with biblical mythology to create something new, a mythical syncretism, centered around his cult's savior god, the Lord Jesus Christ, and his revelatory message, the 'gospel' of Peter and (more specifically) Paul.[103] We observed already how Mark created the crucifixion narrative from the Jewish Bible, for example; that he also honed it by drawing in features from the epics of Homer is what Dennis MacDonald has shown, noting that 'virtually all of Mark 15.22-46 seems to have been generated from biblical texts and *Iliad* 22 and 24' and thus 'need not have known a coherent oral narrative of Jesus' death', just as we saw Clement of Rome seems not have known one (Chapter 8, §5), and yet 'one can trace all stories in the NT concerning Jesus' demise to Mark's literary creativity'.[104] Even John's account is a close redaction of Mark's, and not substantially independent of it (see §7). So there clearly

103. See my definition of godhood in Chapter 4 (§3), and discussion of syncretism in Element 11 and Elements 30 to 33. On the innovations to the gospel introduced by Paul, which are reflected in Mark, see Element 20.

104. MacDonald, 'Imitations of Greek Epic', p. 380.

was no historical memory of Jesus' death—beyond that it happened and involved some sort of humbling, suffering and crucifixion, the only details we find in Paul (see next chapter). And as for this, so for nearly every story in Mark, which combines OT with Homeric source materials to create a new mythology.[105]

Often Mark finds agreements between the Bible and Homer and thus uses details to double effect, simultaneously evoking both. For example, MacDonald sees Jesus' refusal of an offer of wine on his death-march (Mk 15.23) as an imitation of Homer's narrative of Hector's death, who also refused an offer of wine. But this was also a fulfillment of Jesus' own 'Nazirite' promise not to drink the fourth seder cup (the Cup of Redemption) until the end of days (Mk 14.25).[106] Mark likely intended both allusions, specifically to exploit the overlap of double meaning. Indeed he may have been inspired to invent the one by the discovery of the other. Likewise for the rending of the temple curtain, which also has a parallel in Homer but at the same time communicates the Jewish soteriological message that the barrier between heaven and earth is now broken, and as a result the temple is no longer the barrier between men and God.[107] Similarly, Joseph of

105. For how the *Iliad* and *Odyssey* influenced Mark's crucifixion narrative, see MacDonald, *Homeric Epics*, pp. 184-85, 154-61, 135-47 and 40-45; Mark's sea narratives: pp. 55-62, 148-53, 174-75 and 177; the Gerasene demoniac narrative: pp. 63-74 and 175-76; the death of John the Baptist: pp. 77-82 and 176; the miraculous feedings: pp. 83-90 and 176-78; the transfiguration: pp. 91-96 and 178-79; healings of the blind: pp. 97-101; the triumphal entry: pp. 102-10 and 179-80; the clearing of the temple: pp. 33-38 and 180-81; the apocalyptic discourse: pp. 181-82; the anointing: pp. 111-19 and 181; the Last Supper and Gethsemane narratives: pp. 124-34, 182-84; the argument over James and John: pp. 24-32; the procuring of the Passover room: pp. 120-23; the betrayal of Judas: pp. 38-40; the messianic secret: pp. 44-54; and for how it influenced Mark's first chapter, the baptism and inauguration of Jesus' ministry: pp. 173-74; and Mark's last chapter, the empty tomb narrative: pp. 74-76, 162-68 and 185-87; for additional examples and discussion: pp. 15-19, 188-90. Notably, Matthew and Luke often eliminate the Homeric features and allusions when they copy Mark: pp. 187-88. Among all these, not every case is as certain as MacDonald claims (in some cases mere coincidence can be as likely an explanation of the noted parallels), and many cases may simply reflect adaptive coloring (the core narrative is not Homeric but has simply been tweaked using Homeric allusions and motifs), but in several cases the emulation is well established (where 'coincidence' is far too improbable an explanation) and extends to the very root and purpose of the story (and thus is far more likely a story Mark wholly invented than anything he inherited from prior myths and legends of Jesus), and this happens in enough places in Mark to firmly establish that such a method of invention and composition was a pervasive trend for Mark.

106. See MacDonald, 'Imitations of Greek Epic', p. 381; and Carmichael, 'Passover Haggadah', p. 343.

107. MacDonald, 'Imitations of Greek Epic', p. 382.

Arimathea is not just a fictive recreation of Priam, who in Homer seeks the body of Hector (as MacDonald shows), but also a type of Joseph the Patriarch, who in Gen. 50.4-6 asks Pharaoh for permission to bury Jacob (i.e. Israel), and lays him in the cave-tomb Jacob had hewn, just like the tomb in which the parallel Joseph lays Jesus. Thus, Mark derived the burier's name as 'Joseph'. The rest of his description comes from Mark's use of Homer and his own symbolic imagination.[108]

MacDonald also thinks the centurion's declaration, 'Truly, this man was the son of God!' is a sarcastic gloat ('Oh really, *this* man was God's son!?') rather than an expression of awed belief—because it parallels a passage in Homer, where Achilles similarly mocks the alleged deity of the expired Hector. That might make more narrative sense, since otherwise the centurion's declaration is oddly unmotivated (although Matthew and Luke create a motivation for him: contrast Mt. 27.54 or Lk. 23.47 with Mk 15.39). But that would mean that even though the centurion doesn't believe what he is saying, he is nevertheless the only one who said it (rather than any of the Jews), and thereby *ironically* recognized Christ's deific status (being blind to its reality), which matches Mark's consistent theme of witnesses failing to comprehend what is really going on (noted earlier), and would then echo

108. In Mark all we ever hear of this Joseph is that he was *iōsēph apo arimathaias euschēmōn bouleutēs hos kai autos hēn prosdechomenos tēn basileian tou theou*, 'Joseph from Arimathea, a prominent council-member, who was himself also awaiting [or accepting or receiving] the kingdom of God', even though it is never explained why he gets involved in the story or what became of him (later Gospels try to make sense of this by adding minor details: see Mt. 27.57; Lk. 23.50-51; Jn 19.38). He exists only as a literary device, instantly produced on the stage when he is needed, without explanation or introduction, and then instantly removed when his role is done, just as inexplicably, never to be heard of again (not even in Acts: see Chapter 9, §3). His name likely has a symbolic meaning. Besides the fact that *euschēmōn bouleutēs* ('a prominent council-member') is a pun (it also means 'one who makes good decisions'), Arimathaia is probably an invented word, meaning 'Best Doctrine Town' (*ari-* being a standard Greek prefix for 'best', *math-* being the root of 'teaching', 'doctrine', and 'disciple' [e.g. *mathē, mathēsis, mathēma, mathētēs*], and *-aia* being a standard suffix of place). No such town is known to have existed. Although close alternatives have been suggested (e.g. that Mark means one of the many biblical cities named *Ramah* ['Hightop'], the most famous of which also had the more elaborate name *Ramathaimzophim* ['Watchers' Peaks'], which in 1 Sam. 1.1 is spelled in the Septuagint *Armathaimsipha*, which with the *sipha* removed is only a couple of letters away from Aramathaia), the coincidence of Mark's exact spelling with an apposite Greek meaning is more telling (Joseph comes from the place of the 'best doctrine' and thus makes 'good decisions' and receives the Kingdom of God by honoring Jesus with the legally required burial). For a summary of the various perspectives on this Joseph's historicity, see William John Lyons, 'On the Life and Death of Joseph of Arimathea', *Journal for the Study of the Historical Jesus* 2 (January 2004), pp. 29-53 (although see his updated remarks in Lyons, 'Hermeneutics').

the *matching* irony of Pilate earlier accidentally (and thus, again, ironically) declaring Christ the King of the Jews ('Pilate asked him, "Are you the King of the Jews?" And Jesus answering him said, "You said it"', Mk 15.2).

Another double parallel is how Mark patterns the disciples after the Jews in the Exodus, who are likewise implausibly fickle and stupid, never understanding anything even after repeatedly witnessing Moses perform incredible miracles (just like the disciples with Jesus), but also after the crew of Odysseus, who are likewise fickle and stupid. Which explains the strangely excessive role of sea travel and sailors (the leading disciples are all fishermen and a large chunk of the story occurs at sea), which gives Mark endless opportunities to build deliberate allusions to themes developed in the *Odyssey*.[109] MacDonald isn't the only one to notice how implausible it is that Jesus' story would extensively feature sea voyages and sailors, in a landlocked territory.[110] This would mean, of course, that the actual pillars (the Peter, James and John known to Paul, the same three Mark consistently casts as Jesus' top three disciples) were never really fishermen. And indeed I believe that is most likely a literary invention of Mark's, which he found especially convenient for grounding his literary device of *literal* fishermen becoming *figurative* 'fishers of men' (Mk 1.17). Which casts doubt on the assumption that they were ever really uneducated or illiterate (as Acts 4.13 dubiously claims; see Chapter 7, §3, and Chapter 11, §3).

This in turn casts doubt on the historicity of Jesus' status as a carpenter. Odysseus was also famously a carpenter, having built his own marital bed (a fact that plays a key role in the plot) and the doorways of his palace, and even building his own boat to escape Calypso's island.[111] Of course, even if Jesus himself were historical and actually a carpenter (Mk 6.3) or a carpenter's son (Mt. 13.55), that would not entail he was uneducated or illiterate, either. Lucian of Samosata, one of the most educated literary wits of the second century, was the son of a stonemason (and trained as one himself). In fact, all rabbis of Jesus' day were expected to learn and practice a manual trade as well as complete a literate education, and all the Gospels identify Jesus as a rabbi.[112] But Jesus' occupation is likely a fiction.

109. Examples appear throughout MacDonald, *Homeric Epics* (but see especially pp. 15-23, 55-62 and 187).

110. See Edmund Leach, 'Fishing for Men on the Edge of the Wilderness', in *The Literary Guide to the Bible* (ed. Robert Alter and Frank Kermode; Cambridge, MA: Harvard University Press, 1987), pp. 579-99.

111. Homer, *Odyssey* 23.178 (with 23.189) and 5.234-56 (see also 17.266-68 and 22.126-28, 155-56, and 257-58; and 23.190-201). Odysseus is thus called 'the builder [*tektōn*]' in 17.340-41 and 21.42-43.

112. Carrier, *Not the Impossible Faith*, pp. 55-60 and 324-28. That Jesus was a rabbi: Mk 10.51; 11.21; 14.45; Mt. 26.25, 49; Jn 1.38, 49; 3.2; 4.31; 6.25; 9.2; 11.8; 20.16. Luke translates the Hebrew for 'rabbi' into Greek equivalents: Lk. 5.5; 7.40; 8.24,

A *tektōn* would be any craftsman, not necessarily a carpenter. One normally had to distinguish a *tektōn* of wood from a *tektōn* of stone (as in 2 Sam. 5.11 [LXX]); or of brass (as in 1 Kgs 7.14 [LXX]); or of iron (as in 1 Sam. 13.19 [LXX]). But generically God could be figured as a *tektōn*, being the craftsman of the universe. And being God's agent of creation (as Paul declares in 1 Cor. 8.6; see Elements 10 and 40), Jesus would also have been figured as such (as in Mark); and if not him, then certainly his father (as in Matthew). The *tektones* were also the ones who 'oversee the house of Jehovah' (2 Kgs 22.5-6; having built and continuing to maintain the temple). In both roles, God and Christ were the 'builder of better houses', as Paul explains in 2 Cor. 5.1 ('we know that if the earthly house of our tabernacle be dissolved, we have a building from God, a house not made with hands, eternal, in the heavens'), which belies the hidden meaning behind Mk 14.58 ('we heard him say, "I will destroy this temple that is made with hands, and in three days I will build another made without hands"'), which is clearly an allegory for resurrection.[113]

Likewise, God was the 'builder [*technitēs*] and designer [*dēmiourgos*]' of the perfect celestial city we all await (Heb. 11.10; 11.16; 12.22; 13.14). So it is probably no accident that Mark retained the Pauline 'God as builder' resurrection metaphor, and at the same time calls Jesus 'a builder', meaning he will fashion for himself a superior resurrected body (the actual meaning of Mk 14.58). And that would likewise be a metaphor for the church (the terrestrial body of Christ: Element 18) with which indeed he would in three days' time replace the Jewish temple (as we've seen to be the whole underlying message of Mark's Gospel). Thus when Jesus is identified as a carpenter in Mark (the only time it ever comes up; he otherwise is never so called, and never works any trade), an allusion is even made to its fictive meaning: 'Where did he get these things? What wisdom has been given him? What mighty works *are wrought by his hands*? Is this not the *craftsman* . . . ?' (Mk 6.2-3).

Jesus being called a craftsman is thus a device by which Mark can illustrate again the incomprehension of the Jews, missing the point that Jesus is the *true* craftsman, which they ought to have realized once they see 'mighty works are wrought by his hands'. Just as in his crucifixion narrative Mark has the Jews treat him like the scapegoat, not comprehending that they have the wrong man, so also they derogatorily call him a craftsman without

45, 49; 9.33, 38, 49; 10.25; 11.45; 12.13; 17.13; 18.18; 19.39; 20.21, 28, 39; 21.7; 22.11. Accordingly, Luke assumes Jesus could read the Torah scroll (Lk. 4.16, even stating that he did this regularly), and the author of the *Pericope adulturae* assumed Jesus could write (Jn 8.6-8).

113. See Element 18, Carrier, *Proving History*, p. 190; and Carrier, 'Spiritual Body', in *Empty Tomb* (ed. Price and Lowder), pp. 139-47.

realizing he is in fact *the* craftsman. Thus, the only time Mark ever calls Jesus a carpenter is in a literary context where he has an obvious reason to completely invent that detail for the sake of his desired irony. Once we see all of this, Jesus *actually* being a craftsman becomes a somewhat unlikely coincidence. But it's not at all improbable as a literary myth—one quite possibly invented by Mark, who is the first to ever mention it.

So here again, we have a double inspiration: the Homeric origin of a hero who is a *tektōn* to be used as a Jewish-minded literary-theological device. Mark's use of Homer afforded many similar parallel patterns merging Jewish and Greek mythology to produce a new Christian mythology. For example, Mark's strange theme of the 'messianic secret' (which Jesus always insists upon, even though almost no one ever complies) makes no sense as history, or really even as theology or apologetic, yet makes perfect sense as reflecting the theme of Odysseus in disguise among the suitors in his palace who were maliciously courting his wife. Like Jesus, Odysseus endeavors, even when occasionally recognized, to maintain that disguise until he can get his revenge on those suitors (the sinners who would usurp his place to slake their greed) who have inhabited his house—analogous to the priests and Pharisees inhabiting the temple (God's house), who are likewise corrupt sinners mired in hypocrisy and greed, and likewise courting the same woman: the church.

This connects with the entire 'wedding' theme in Christianity (see Element 48), in which Jesus is the groom and the church his bride (the New Israel), the heiress to the preceding world order (the Old Israel). Which parallels a similar wedding theme in the *Odyssey*, where the suitors are hoping to become Penelope's new husband; but her true husband, Odysseus, returns like a thief in the night to strike them down, all the while moving among them and conversing with them, yet they do not know who he is. He appears as a lowly vagabond and storyteller (just like Jesus does in Mark), but all the while he is the very king himself. With Jesus the analog of Odysseus, the Jewish elite become the analog of the suitors, confirming a consistent message of Mark's Gospel: like the suitors, the Jewish elite are greedy, conniving, immoral and undeserving—and will soon be destroyed by God and replaced by the true king, whom they do not know, even though he is standing before them.

In many ways like this (many in fact even more specific and telling than these), we can see that 'once the evangelist linked the sufferings of Jesus to those of Odysseus, he found in the epic[s of Homer] a reservoir of landscapes, characterizations, type-scenes, and plot devices useful for crafting his narrative'.[114] Mark's Gospel's main function is to illustrate what the

114. MacDonald, *Homeric Epics*, p. 19.

gospel means and to provide a system of models for Christian life (particularly missionary life) and for use in teaching its social ideals and theology. In many scenes in Mark's Gospel, for example, Jesus is made to say and do things that symbolize how Christians, especially Christian missionaries, are to behave or think. He gives us a model of what baptism means (adoption by God, and symbolic death and rebirth); a model of how to face martyrdom (the trial and crucifixion); a model of how to react to family pressure (one must follow Jesus and leave any stubborn family behind and adopt instead one's new kin group: Mk 3.31-35); models of healing and exorcism; even models of what not to do (such as doubt or fear or the military messianism of Barabbas, or the internecine betrayal of a Judas—or any putting of self before the group, the message of Mk 10.35-45).

As I concluded in *Proving History*, 'that Jesus had enemies who slandered him, that Jesus went to parties with sinners to save them, that Jesus' family rejected him', are all stories that reflect the realities of Christian missionaries and the situations they face, so Mark is crafting these stories to model how they are to deal with them. Thus:

> The experiences of Christians themselves in their battles, trials, and evangelizations were being mapped onto Jesus as a model to follow and commiserate with. . . . For example, Jesus being called crazy aligns too well with the fact that Christians themselves faced this charge—so how apposite to depict their Lord as being unjustly accused of the same, and then supplying him with clever speeches refuting it. . . . Christians similarly faced conflict from their families, which statistically must have involved on occasion the same charge of insanity or demonic possession from them; so depicting their Lord as trading his family in for a new one in result (Mark 3.21-35, and that in the very same scene), is again too convenient [to be real].[115]

Mark even *tells* us (on the sly) that he is writing parables, so that those who follow the exoteric meaning will not understand and thus not be saved—only those who follow the *esoteric* meaning (the symbolic meaning) will get the *real* meaning and be on the road to salvation (Mk 4.9-12; see again Element 14). So Mark even invented a story about Jesus that provides us with a model for how to read Mark's Gospel. Of course, to serve this function, his text becomes considerably more powerful and effective if it is also taken *literally* (as I've suggested before, but will soon explain further), although it's clear Mark had not yet realized that. He was still using the literal word to *conceal* his real meaning, not to persuade people of it.

I've given enough examples to demonstrate Mark has no interest in historical facts or sources, that he is simply inventing his stories to suit his aims; the other scholarship I have cited here (including my own) pro-

115. Carrier, *Proving History*, p. 156.

vides many examples more. But before I move on to discuss the subsequent redactions of Mark (the remaining canonical Gospels), I should address one general objection with a few specific examples. Often an argument is made that some item or other in Mark can't have any other explanation for why it's there other than that it *happened*, and somehow the tradition of it had reached Mark. These arguments tend to be illogical as well as ill-informed, as I have already demonstrated elsewhere.[116] But though I treated all the principal examples there, others remain.

In some cases, of course, the evidence actually ends up proving the contrary (e.g. it's very unlikely Nazareth is really where Jesus was from: see again §3). But in other cases, though we can infer Mark's literary purpose, we cannot prove it. Such cases afford no evidence either for or against their content's historicity, since that content is just as likely either way. And in the end, every item in Mark's Gospel falls in one of those two categories: either it's more likely a fiction than a historical tradition; or it's just as likely either way. In sum, Mark's Gospel leaves us with no evidence for the historicity of Jesus. But it also does not count as evidence *against* the historicity of Jesus, since some of its content could yet be historical—we just can't prove it—and even if none of it is, it's still possible to write a completely fictional story about a genuinely historical man. (Although one does struggle to explain why anyone had to, if that man is supposed to have inspired a dozen men to launch an international religion; but I already explored the curious absence of the kind of documentation such a new religion is expected to generate in Chapter 8, §§2 and 3.)

A prominent example of a case in this latter category (of undecidable historicity) is a curious detail Mark provides: naming the sons of Simon of Cyrene. This is most bizarre, since Mark states no reason at all for doing so. Why do we need to know this information? Why does Mark think it's important? And why is this the only instance in his whole Gospel where Mark names the sons of *anyone* Jesus encounters? (One wonders why none of his disciples had sons worth mentioning.) Mark does not even say these sons became Christians (and one would expect him to if that was the point) or were his sources for the account (as again, one would expect him to say so). So as history, this detail is just inexplicably weird. For these and other reasons (such as the historical implausibility of Romans pressing into service random bystanders like this) many scholars conclude the appearance of Simon of Cyrene is fictional.[117]

116. See Carrier, *Proving History*, pp. 123-69.

117. The competing views and arguments on this question are surveyed in Lyons, 'Hermeneutics', pp. 139-54. It is sometimes argued that a tomb recovered in Judea in which is buried an Alexander, son of Simon of Cyrene, is the tomb of this Simon's son and thus corroborates his historicity. For example, Tom Powers, 'Treasures in the

By contrast, we can easily explain this whole verse as an esoteric allegory. We know Mark was fond of using 'reversals of expectation' in his construction of narrative, to embody the gospel message, which was all about reversing expectations (e.g. 'the least shall be first').[118] Mark makes a point of mentioning that Jesus had told Simon Peter he had to 'take up his cross and follow' Jesus. After rebuking Peter for objecting to Jesus' plan of effecting a sacrificial death,

> [Jesus] rebuked Peter, and said, 'Get behind me, Satan! For you have your mind not on the things of God, but the things of men.' And he called to him the multitude with his disciples, and said to them, 'If any man would come after me, let him deny himself, and *take up his cross, and follow me*' (Mk 8.33-34).

Storeroom: Family Tomb of Simon of Cyrene', *Biblical Archaeology Review* 29 (July/August 2003), pp. 46-51, 59; and Tom Powers, 'Simon of Cyrene Tomb Connection', *Artifax* (Autumn 2000), pp. 1, 4-6. But alas there is actually no mention of Cyrene in that tomb (nor any Rufus), there is only the name Alexander ben Simon (in Greek). Even in Judea these were common names. More than 1 in 10 were named Simon and more than 1 in 109 were named Alexander, which means there were more than 1 in 1090 Alexander ben Simons buried in Judea. Even if only 100,000 Jews were ever interred in ossuaries in Judea, a gross undercount, then almost a hundred Alexander ben Simons would be found there if we could recover every ossuary there was. Even an origin in Cyrene would not make a significant difference. Acts already reports there were so many Cyrenaean Jews in Judea that they even had their own synagogues in Jerusalem, and many Judean pilgrims and Christians were from Cyrene (Acts 2.10; 6.9; 11.20; 13.1; and even if fictions, Luke is most likely basing these details on historical facts). If we imagine only a thousand or so Cyrenaeans were ever buried in Judea, we still can expect at least one Alexander ben Simon of Cyrene to be found there by chance alone, especially given that Alexander was a much more common name among Greek-speaking diaspora Jews and thus the frequency of Alexander ben Simons among that subgroup would have been even higher. But this Greek-speaking 'Alexander ben Simon' we recovered need not hail from Cyrene anyway; he could have come from anywhere in the Hellenistic diaspora. Note, also, that even if there was a real Simon of Cyrene who had the sons Alexander and Rufus in the Christian church at the time, that would still not entail Mark's story of him is in any way true; after all, Mark just as readily fictionalizes tales about the otherwise-historical Peter and Pilate.

118. I give several examples of this feature in Mark in Carrier, 'Spiritual Body', in *Empty Tomb* (ed. Price and Lowder), pp. 163-65; but this aspect of Mark's composition has been noted and demonstrated before: Jerry Camery-Hoggatt, *Irony in Mark's Gospel: Text and Subtext* (New York: Cambridge University Press, 1992); Paul Danove, *The End of Mark's Story: A Methodological Study* (New York: Brill, 1993); Adela Yarbro Collins, 'The Empty Tomb in the Gospel according to Mark', in *Hermes and Athena: Biblical Exegesis and Philosophical Theology* (ed. Eleonore Stump and Thomas Flint; Notre Dame, IN: University of Notre Dame Press, 1993), pp. 107-40; Deborah Krause, 'The One Who Comes Unbinding'; etc.

This is thus what Peter is instructed to do. But our expectations are reversed: instead of Simon Peter 'taking up his cross and following Jesus', Simon *the Cyrenaean* does (Mk 15.21).[119] This is a complete stranger, never mentioned before nor ever again. He appears in just this single verse. Meanwhile, Simon *Peter* not only abandons Jesus but denies him.[120]

This makes sense of why Mark invented a second Simon to stand in for Simon Peter, being not only a stranger (to contrast with Peter being Jesus' number-one disciple) but also a foreigner (from the distant land of Cyrene, a province on the other side of Egypt and thus not even bordering Palestine), a perfect representation of 'the least shall be first'. Contrary to expectation, it is, of all people one could imagine, *Simon of Cyrene* who is the first to take up his cross and follow. A powerful message indeed. But Mark does not merely say this. He says, 'They pressed into service a certain fellow passing by, Simon the Cyrenaean, who was coming from the countryside, the father of Alexander and Rufus, to carry his cross'. Who are Alexander and Rufus? And why is Simon specifically a *Cyrenaean*?

There was a large Jewish presence in Cyrene, and to come from beyond Egypt (the realm of slavery and death) had symbolic overtones. But I suspect the more likely reason was that, according to Strabo, in those days 'the most famous Cyrenaeans' were the Cyrenaics, a sect of hedonistic philosophers known as avowed atheists and the one sect most wholly attached to the physical world and its pleasures (rejecting all spiritual doctrines).[121] The sect had long since died out (or so we suppose), having been replaced by the more attractive and agnostic materialism of Epicurus, but the sect remained legendary, such that Strabo (who lived and wrote when Jesus would have been growing up) could say that even then 'the most famous Cyrenaeans' were still the leading philosophers of the Cyrenaics. This was a perfect choice to symbolize the exact opposite of the gospel: the complete rejection of all spiritual realities and the complete immersion in the materialistic pleasures and wisdom of men. Moreover, as Mark would have known, the Cyrenaean Jews had recently attempted a violent rebellion (shortly after the war in Judea) and were put down by the might of Rome.[122] Cyrene was thus

119. Jesus had given his first disciple the name Peter as of Mk 3.16, but before that he is referred to only as Simon.

120. On which see Carrier, *Proving History*, p. 157.

121. Strabo, *Geography* 17.3.22; Diogenes Laertius, *Lives of Eminent Philosophers* 2.65-104.

122. Josephus, *Life* 76.424-25. The revolt was led by a certain Jonathan, who gathered two thousand men to fight, which happens to be the number of the demonic 'Legion' drowned by Jesus (Mk 5.13). It has alternatively been suggested that the Gerasene swine represent Christ's eventual destruction of the Romans (suggesting he will drive the legions into the sea), owing to the fact that at the conclusion of the Jewish War, the Tenth Legion (*Legio X Fretensis*) was garrisoned in Jerusalem and tasked

a perfect allegory for two things Mark rejected: it had most famously given birth to *both* the basest worldly philosophy *and* the doomed path of war.

Paul wrote that 'they that are of Christ Jesus have crucified the flesh with the passions and the lusts thereof' (Gal. 5.24) by placing it 'on the cross of our Lord Jesus Christ, through which the world hath been crucified unto me, and I unto the world' (Gal. 6.14). Though Simon is not said to have been crucified, his carrying of the cross symbolizes everything that was on the cross when *Jesus* is killed on it: attachment to the world, and to the 'flesh with the passions and the lusts thereof'. He does so in two respects: as an allegory for everything the Cyrenaic school stood for (materialism, attachment to worldly lusts, and the philosophies of men, generally derided by Christians as demonic and ungodly, e.g., 1 Cor. 1.20; 2.5, 13; Rom. 1.20-25; Col. 2.8; Jas 3.15) and as an allegory for everything Barabbas also stood for (the use of violence and rebellion, as the Cyrenaean Jews were then most recently known for), two different ways to choose attachment to worldly ways and things over spiritual ones. What Mark may have symbolically intended, then, is that by extended contact with Simon the Cyrenaean, the cross of Jesus symbolically absorbed these things (which this Simon represents) and were then crucified with Jesus.

The sons of Simon corroborate this analysis: as then these are the *sons* of worldly wisdom and the way of military conquest. Thus, what *they* represent are what the idea of 'Cyrene' gave birth to. The names are thus significant. I suspect they are meant to refer to the most famous men of all time who held those names: Alexander the Great and Musonius Rufus. Alexander the Great was the world's most famous deified conquerer, the paragon of military victory and of the use of violence to effect power, the ideal any militaristic messiah would want to emulate. Musonius Rufus was the world's most famous pacifist, a philosopher of greatest renown, second only to Socrates—according to the Christian scholar Origen, for example, popular sentiment held that the very best men in history were two in num-

with ensuring the city was never rebuilt (Josephus, *Jewish War* 7.17), and that legion's emblem is known to have been a boar (see, e.g., http://en.wikipedia.org/wiki/Legio_X_Fretensis). However, a legion's standard complement was six thousand men, and that was not counting auxiliaries (cavalry, archers, slingers and light infantry), who were also assigned at Jerusalem. I think Mark's choice of number (far too low to be an actual legion) has to reflect his intended symbolism and match themes he consistently echoes elsewhere in his Gospel; and the best fit is the fate of Jonathan, who represents the way of violent rebellion, which Mark criticizes repeatedly (e.g. in the Barabbas narrative; even the Judas narrative criticizes Jewish resort to military force: Mk 14.43-49), and whose own attempt to replace the 'legions' counted a mere two thousand men, the same number of pigs drowned.

ber: Socrates and Rufus.[123] Rufus was also a contemporary of Mark and a Roman, making him a perfect contrast to the long-dead Alexander, a Greek (really, a Macedonian, but by then the distinction had been all but forgotten), thus representing the origin of the present world order (Alexander's conquest being the first to subject the second temple to foreign domination) and its end (Mark's own day, the temple having just recently been destroyed) and at the same time representing the entire gamut of foreign interference in Judea (Greek and Roman, military and philosophical).

Musonius Rufus was a Stoic philosopher who taught many things very similar to Jesus, representing the closest Mark could imagine 'worldly wisdom' came to arriving at the gospel by reason rather than revelation.[124] Rufus preached charity, pacifism and forgiving one's enemies, and declared that 'evil consists in injustice and cruelty and indifference to a neighbor's trouble, while virtue is brotherly love and goodness and justice and beneficence and concern for the welfare of one's neighbor'.[125] Rufus was also famously a close friend of Emperor Vespasian (the latest greatest military conquerer known to Mark) who had just recently destroyed Jerusalem and its temple (through the agency of *his* son Titus). And Rufus was recently renowned for risking his own death trying to stop the civil war of 69 CE by preaching a doctrine of peace to the armies that were about to meet on the battlefield.[126] They were not persuaded. For Mark this would have illustrated the failure of the 'way of human reason' that Rufus advocated.[127] For Mark (as for Paul), the gospel was superior, empowered by the Holy Spirit.

123. Origen, *Against Celsus* 3.66. This sentiment is confirmed by Pliny the Younger, *Letters* 3.11; Philostratus, *Life of Apollonius of Tyana* 4.46; Dio of Prusa, *Orations* 31.122; Julian, *Letter to the High Priest Theodorus* 16; and Julian, *Letter to Themistius* 20-22; etc.

124. See Richard Carrier, 'On Musonius Rufus: A Brief Essay', *The Secular Web* (1999) at http://www.infidels.org/library/modern/richard_carrier/musonius.html, which summarizes on this point the evidence documented in Cora Lutz, *Musonius Rufus: The Roman Socrates* (New Haven, CT: Yale University Press, 1942), as well as Cynthia King, *Musonius Rufus: Lectures and Sayings* (Charleston, SC: Createspace, 2011); and M.P. Charlesworth, *Five Men: Character Studies from the Roman Empire* (Cambridge, MA: Harvard University Press, 1936).

125. Musonius Rufus, *Discourses* 10, 14, 19 (quote: 14.29-33).

126. Tacitus, *Histories* 3.81; Cassius Dio, *Roman History* 65.18-19.

127. For Musonius, 'the primary concern of philosophy is the care of the soul in order that the qualities of prudence, temperence, justice, and courage may be perfected in it. This education should begin in infancy and continue throughout life, for every member of human society,' and his educational program included logic and debating skills, for the express purpose of building the ability to reason through ethical decisions competently (Lutz, *Musonius*, p. 27). This contrasted with the Christian insistence on faith (and trust in authority and the Holy Spirit), not reason, as the only path to moral competence.

Rufus can also be linked to the destruction of the temple, a favorite theme for Mark. He failed to persuade Vespasian to choose peace over war, and Vespasian brought about the destruction of the temple in Jerusalem the following year. Coincidentally, the war Rufus failed to stop also destroyed the corresponding temple in Rome, the temple of Jupiter Capitolinus, supreme God of the Roman Empire, which was felled in a battle between Vitellius and Vespasian's *other* son, Domitian. So Vespasian's two sons destroyed two temples, the Jewish and the Roman, in nearly the same year (the Roman temple fell in December of 69, the Jewish temple in July of 70).[128] As Mark would see it, philosophy cannot stop the wrath of God and cannot save us from destruction.

An even more telling link can be made between Alexander the Great and the Jewish temple, in a story that exactly reverses that of Musonius Rufus. According to a popular Jewish legend, when Alexander reached Judea in his conquest, the Samaritans sent a delegation to try and convince him to destroy the Jerusalem temple, but he refused; which is in contrast to Rufus, who similarly goes out to try and convince a conquerer on his march to end his wars—but Vespasian refuses, and the temple is destroyed after all (and at long last). In one account of the Alexander tale, the high priest of the temple, a featured hero of the story, is even named Simon.[129] But in both accounts, the high priest goes out to meet Alexander on his approach and Alexander recognizes him from visions he had been receiving from God and thus favors the Jews over the Samaritans and is thus dissuaded from destroying the temple. Revelation and trusting in God are thus contrasted with rational argumentation: Alexander, the warrior, exhibited the one, and chose peace; Rufus, the pacifist, exhibited the other, and failed to avert destruction. Another way the stories mirror each other as opposites is that Alexander is the petitioned conquerer, while Rufus was the one petitioning the conqueror.

128. Philostratus, *Life of Apollonius* 5.30; Suetonius, *Life of Domitian* 1; Tacitus, *Histories* 3.71-72 and 4.53 (Tacitus declares, 'this was the most lamentable and appalling disaster in the whole history of the Roman commonwealth'). See Josephus, *Jewish War* 6.93-168 for the end of the Jewish temple.

129. We have two versions of the tale, one from Josephus, in which the high priest at the time is Jaddus, and one in the Talmud, in which the high priest is Simon. See Erich Gruen, 'Fact and Fiction: Jewish Legends in a Hellenistic Context', in *Hellenistic Constructs: Essays in Culture, History, and Historiography* (ed. Paul Cartledge, Peter Garnsey and Erich Gruen; Berkeley, CA: University of California Press, 1997), pp. 72-88 (78-79); James VanderKam, *From Joshua to Caiaphas: High Priests after the Exile* (Minneapolis, MN: Fortress Press, 2004), pp. 63-85 and 137-57; and Thomas Verenna, *Of Men and Muses: Essays on History, Literature, and Religion* (Raleigh, NC: Lulu, 2009), pp. 102-12. The two principal accounts are in the Talmud, *b. Yoma* 69a, and in Josephus, *Antiquities of the Jews* 11.325-47.

We can easily imagine how readily Mark would find this pairing attractive, being so rich with esoteric exegesis exactly in line with Mark's gospel message. The way of Cyrene (attachment to the world) gave birth to the two ways of the world (military might and man-made philosophy), which end in destruction—unless we submit to God. Those worldly ways were just what Christ had destroyed along with his own flesh, replacing them with the gospel of faith in God's newly revealed plan of salvation (Rom. 16.25-26). The many motifs the pairing could evoke for him are illustrated here:

Simon of Cyrene (gives birth to . . .)	
Alexander (the Great)	Rufus (Musonius)
world's most famous conquerer	world's most famous pacifist
prime example of seeking immortality through military glory	prime example of seeking immortality through philosophy
petitioned on the battlefield to destroy the Jewish temple	petitions on the battlefield to stop war (and thus the destroying of temples)
trusts in God and chooses peace	trusts in reason and fails to bring peace
temple is spared	*temple is destroyed*
both war (Alexander) and human reason (Rufus) are the way of ruin; only faith in God and revelation bring salvation	

Table 7. Allegorical Hypothesis for Simon of Cyrene

Obviously it cannot be proved this is what Mark intended in naming this Simon and his sons, and he certainly would have expected these points to be revealed only in secret, through the private illumination of his parable (in accordance with Mk 4.10-12). But we have no more evidence for this than we have for the names deriving from an authentic historical tradition. Mark gives no indication that that is why these names are here; he gives no indication at all of why they are here. Symbolic intent is thus as likely a reason (even if not the one I suspect).

It may seem strange to include such a complex hidden message with so sparse a remark, but it's obvious the Gospel authors often did this. As we saw before, there is surely some esoteric meaning to the 'twelve years of bleeding' and the 'twelve years of age' in the Jairus narrative. And there was certainly some now-lost meaning to the miraculous catch of precisely

153 fish in Jn 21.7-12 (as I'll discuss in §7), or the number of loaves and baskets in Mk 8.19-21. As the reader is not told what these things mean, clearly they had a secret meaning never written down but only communicated to initiates of sufficient rank (and probably eventually forgotten over time). We saw a similar rich depth of meaning in Mark's juxtaposition of elements in the Barabbas narrative, and in the deep structure with which he patterned his entire Gospel.

Christian and Jewish theologians routinely understood casual references to names and groups of names in scripture to indicate deep complex meaning. And as I noted before, if they could *read* texts that way, they surely would have *written* texts that way (see Element 14). For example, Origen finds three men mentioned together in a single line in Gen. 26.26 and says they symbolize philosophy: Abimelech represents logic, and his two subordinates, Ahuzzath and Phicol, represent the other two branches of philosophy, which depend on and derive from logic: Ahuzzath symbolizes natural philosophy, and Phicol moral philosophy. And he comes to this conclusion from an esoteric exegesis of their names. If Origen could think the author of Genesis intended this under inspiration of the Holy Spirit, Mark could think the Holy Spirit had inspired him to do likewise with the names of Simon and his sons (or other name triads, like the three women attending the tomb, as I noted earlier, whose names also have plausible allegorical meaning).[130] The feeling of awe he would feel at the neat parallels and reversals produced by linking his Simon with the triad of Cyrene and Alexander the Great and Musonius Rufus could easily be mistaken as inspired (see Elements 15 and 16).

So I consider this passage undecidable: it's just as likely on minimal mythicism and on minimal historicity, as the arguments for and against each balance each other out, leaving us with no certainty which may be in this case—apart from what prior probability we bring to it, but this piece of evidence would not alter that prior and therefore this passage can be disregarded. I think it is more than clear that even if we started with no assumptions about Mark, and then analyzed one pericope after another, in each case updating our prior probability (a procedure I lay out on p. 168 of *Proving History*), we would end up with a low prior probability that anything in it is historical, and a high prior probability that *all* of it has some esoteric allegorical or symbolical purpose. Such a low prior would then only be overcome by strong external corroborating evidence (such as we have for the existence, at least, of Peter and Pilate), in the absence of which, for any detail in Mark, we should assume a symbolical meaning is always more likely. The net result is that Mark provides us no evidence either for or against historicity. We simply

130. Origen, *Homilies on Genesis* 14.3. For the three women in Mark as an allegorical name triad: Carrier, *Not the Impossible Faith*, pp. 315-16.

cannot identify anything in it as a historical fact about Jesus—even if there are such facts in Mark, we simply have no means to identify them. We therefore must rely only on evidence for Jesus *external* to Mark.

The same could be said for any other curious passage or detail in Mark. For example, Mk 14.3-9 has the very odd story of the woman who spontaneously and for no historically intelligible reason anoints Jesus with precious oil from a priceless jar, which evokes an exchange between Jesus and his disciples that obviously has its entire origin solely within Mark's literary imagination. It is clearly another parable. Yet he concludes all this by having Jesus declare, 'Wheresoever the gospel shall be preached throughout the whole cosmos, what this woman has done will also be spoken of as a memorial of her' (Mk 14.9). Yet Mark doesn't even name her. So how is *she* being remembered? Her deed alone is getting the memorial.

There is obviously some symbolic meaning to this. Mark does not really mean this *actually* happened and that is why he is including it ('because Jesus said to!'). The event is historically implausible in every way: no random nameless stranger would have anointed Jesus for burial (Mk 14.8) days before his death (a death no one, according to Mark, was even expecting). And they certainly would not be carrying around an $18,000 pot of oil, much less smash it over someone's head to make an allegorical point—indeed, it is often overlooked that the woman does not just pour the oil but even breaks its delicate stone container, a wholly pointless and wasteful thing to do (Mk 14.3).[131] Jesus' excuse for wasting so much money (that he needed to be anointed for burial) is also not plausible, not only because he wasn't dead yet (only a corpse could be 'anointed for burial'), but also because such a rare oil would not be needed for that, nor would the jar it came in have to be broken.

Mark simply doesn't explain why this was done with an alabaster jar, why it was 'pure nard oil' that had to be used, why this woman isn't given a name yet is supposed to be eternally remembered, why Jesus didn't get the point that even for the purpose of his anointing such great waste was unnecessary, or how this woman got the idea of doing this, or who she was that could afford to waste essentially $18,000 on a pointless gesture. And, of course, she is never mentioned again, nor was ever mentioned before.

131. Minimum wage in antiquity was around three obols per day (which was then about one denarius or half a Greek drachma); minimum wage in the United States is over $60 per day. Therefore 300 denarii = 300 x $60 = $18,000. Oil of nard (a mountain flower) was indeed extraordinarily rare and expensive in antiquity; the container (carved from alabaster: Mk 14.3) would also not have been cheap and would have had considerable resale value even when emptied. It is unclear if the valuation at 300 denarii (Mk 14.5) was only for the oil or for the oil and its container together, since both were destroyed.

She is a literary device, not a person with a history. We might no longer know Mark's point in inventing all this, but invent it he did. Just as he (or someone before him) invented the betrayal by Judas, the baptism by John, the origin at Nazareth, and so much else.[132]

Even the names of Jesus' family members are a likely fabrication. Mythical heroes often had mythical families, and memorizing their genealogies and the names of their kin relations was a standard practice in ancient schools of the time.[133] Evidently people expected mythic heroes to have families. This was just as true in Jewish legends. The patriarch Joseph, a mythical person, also had a father, mother and numerous brothers, all named. Obviously they weren't any more historical than he was. The names of the brothers of Jesus (Simon, Joseph, Jacob and Judas) are all among the most common of male names at the time. In fact, Simon was the most common Jewish name of all (roughly 1 in every 10 Jewish men were so named), and the other three names (plus Jesus) are all the most common names among those also found in the OT: Joseph was the second most common name (at 1 in every 12 men); Judas the fourth (at 1 in every 16 men); Jesus the sixth (at 1 in every 26 men); and Jacob (i.e. James) the eleventh (at 1 in every 65 men).[134] And the latter were

132. That someone (if not Mark himself) could have invented the story that Jesus was crucified by Romans: Carrier, *Proving History*, pp. 139-41; and likewise the story that Jesus was baptized by John: Carrier, *Proving History*, pp. 145-48; and stories of Jesus' professed or supposed ignorance: Carrier, *Proving History*, pp. 148-51; and Jesus' birth in Nazareth: see discussion here in conjunction with Carrier, *Proving History*, pp. 142-45; and likewise the story that Jesus was betrayed by Judas, 'one of the twelve': Carrier, *Proving History*, pp. 151-55 (with pp. 317-19 nn. 67-72: I there had said I'd say more on this point here, but what I say there is sufficient; others agree: see, e.g., Hamerton-Kelly, 'Sacred Violence and the Messiah', pp. 483-85; and John Shelby Spong, *The Sins of Scripture: Exposing the Bible's Texts of Hate to Reveal the God of Love* [San Francisco, CA: HarperSanFrancisco, 2005], pp. 199-204; note also there was apparently no betrayal by Judas in the *Gospel of Peter: Gos. Pet.* 14.59).

133. See, e.g., Edmonds, *Myths*, p. 77 n. 138; Alan Cameron, *Greek Mythography in the Roman World* (New York: Oxford University Press, 2004), p. 172; Timothy Gantz, *Early Greek Myth: A Guide to Literary and Artistic Sources* (Baltimore, MD: Johns Hopkins University Press, 1996), I, pp. xxv-xliii, and II, pp. 803-21; Timothy Wiseman, *The Myths of Rome* (Exeter: University of Exeter Press, 2004), p. 140. Genealogies and families were also developed for Osiris and other gods in his mythic cycle: Plutarch, *On Isis and Osiris* 38.366c.

134. Bauckham, *Jesus and the Eyewitnesses*, p. 85. In Mark the names are given only once, in 6.3, where most mss. say 'James [= Jacob], and Joses [= Joseph], and Judas [= Judah], and Simon', while some mss. have 'Joseph' in place of 'Joses', in agreement with the parallel passage in Mt. 13.55, but Joses is just a shortened form of Joseph (like 'Rick' for 'Richard'). Some mss. of Matthew have 'John' in place of 'Joseph' (an evident error) while others have 'John and Joses' (which would make Jesus' family consist of *every* popular Jewish name starting with 'J'). Mark does not mention the name of Jesus' father, and one might wonder if in fact the name was present in Mk 6.3

all symbolically significant names: evoking the Jacob who became Israel, Joseph his most famous son, the Jesus (i.e, Joshua) who conquered Israel, and Judas the founder of Judah (Judea).

If someone were to rattle off five random names to just sound like a typical family (like we used to do with the phrase 'every Tom, Dick and Harry'), and one that was especially evocative of Jewish biblical heritage, it would look exactly like this list: the most common of all names (Simon, our 'John Doe') and the most common names of the time that were evocative of the OT (Jacob, Joseph, Jesus and Judah). In other words, this looks exactly like a made-up list. Moreover, the family of Jesus does not exist in Mark except as props for making literary points (and we already saw the family of Jesus does not exist in Acts, either: see Chapter 9, §3). They enter unexplained, and vanish unexplained, and never do anything relevant to the history of the church. Indeed, contrary to common assumption, in Mark the mother of Jesus does not show even at the cross—it is only the Gospel of John that inserts her there. Otherwise, all the Synoptics fail to identify *any* of the Mary's at the end of their story as actually the mother of Jesus.[135] (The two Mary's at the end of Mark's Gospel appear only in a highly stylized triadic function that has the hallmarks of literary invention anyway, as earlier noted.)

Just like his mother, Jesus' brothers appear only twice, and each time they are effectively impotent characters in a parable. The first time they are mentioned, neither they nor his mother are even named:

> And there come his mother and his brothers; and, standing outside, they sent to him, calling him. And a multitude was sitting about him; and they said to him, 'Behold, your mother and your brothers outside are looking for you'. And he answered them, and said, 'Who is my mother and my brothers?' And looking around on them that sat around him, he said, 'Behold, my mother and my brothers! For whosoever shall do the will of God, the same is my brother, and sister, and mother' (Mk 3.31-35).

Here Mark has introduced Jesus' family for only one purpose: to give him occasion to make a statement about the creation of a fictive kinship among Christians that shall replace biological kinship (Element 12; a feature of all mystery religions: Element 11). They are therefore just props for the story. Note, especially, that this scene shows no knowledge that any of Jesus' brothers would later join the church. Mark has no idea of this James taking command of the church after Peter, or this Jude playing a major role either. To the contrary, Mark has Jesus effectively renounce his family and declare only those who follow him his brethren—thereby deliberately reversing the

but dropped in transmission; in any event, the 'dying messiah' could be expected to have a father named Joseph, according to the Talmud, *b. Sukkah* 52a (see Element 5).

135. Mk 15.40, 47 and 16.1; Mt. 27.56, 61 and 28.1; Lk. 24.10; vs. Jn 19.25-27.

story of Moses' family (also duly named) coming to see *him*, another example of a fictional family visiting a fictional hero in a narrative treated as historical, all just to make a symbolic point.[136] Mark's story is no less fictional.

Jesus' brothers' second appearance is just as fictional as the first one:

> And he went out from there; and he came into his own country; and his disciples followed him. And when the sabbath had come, he began to teach in the synagogue: and many hearing him were astonished, saying, 'Where did he get these things? What wisdom was given to this man? What mighty works have been wrought by his hands? Is this not the carpenter, the son of Mary, and brother of James, and Joses, and Judas, and Simon? Are not his sisters here with us?' And they were offended by him. And Jesus said to them, 'A prophet is not without honor, except in his own country, and among his own kin, and in his own house'. And he could do no mighty work there, except that he laid his hands upon a few sick folk, and healed them. And he marveled because of their unbelief. So he went around the villages teaching [instead] (Mk 6.1-6).

Once again his brothers are serving only a literary function here. They aren't even actually in this story (they are not present; others are merely naming them). Christian missionaries would have faced the very problem this parable addresses: people rejecting their authority and their miracle-working because they used to just be ordinary folk known to the community, whereas when missionaries visited new towns they did not have to overcome that kind of skepticism. Mark has invented a story whereby this same thing happens to Jesus, giving missionaries a story to tell to explain away not only occasions of failure ('even Jesus could not heal those with insufficient faith') but also their rejection by family members and friends ('even Jesus faced that kind of rejection'). A generic list of names is thus just what one would expect Mark to provide here.[137]

136. On how this narrative in Mark reverses an otherwise-similar story of a family visit told of Moses in Exodus 18 (particularly when compared with the version in the LXX) see Price, *Christ-Myth Theory*, pp. 76-77. Unlike Price, though, I see no attack on dynasticism here; to the contrary, Mark seems unaware (here and throughout his Gospel) that the family of Jesus was ever even involved in the church. Mark is simply reversing the ideal of family represented in Exodus (through a tale told of Moses' treatment of his family) in order to promote the new Christian ideal as having supplanted it (through a tale told of Jesus' treatment of his family).

137. Even 'Mary' was then the most common woman's name (and thus like our 'Jane Doe'); between 1 in 4 and 1 in 5 women had it: Bauckham, *Jesus and the Eyewitnesses*, p. 89. Although her name probably predates Mark (since Mary is Jesus' mother's name in the separate Babylonian tradition: see Chapter 8, §1), and there was symbolic utility in the name (it therefore need not have been chosen merely because it was generic): see Carrier, *Not the Impossible Faith*, pp. 312-16; and Joan Taylor, *Jewish Women Philosophers of First-Century Alexandria: Philo's 'Therapeutae' Reconsidered* (Oxford: Oxford University Press, 2003), 322-40. As Taylor documents, in

This parable also provides a deeper symbolic meaning: Jesus' kin are here analogs for the Jews and Judea as a whole (his own 'country and kin'), which rejected the gospel, requiring him (and thus, analogously, his missionaries) to go elsewhere and preach the gospel. This is therefore a tale illustrating Jewish unbelief generally, and providing an etiological myth for why Christians evangelized abroad. The commonness of the names (Simon the most common of all) *and* their biblical significance (Joseph, Jacob *and* Judah) only reinforce this symbolism of Jesus' own kin and country rejecting the gospel. This narrative also reminds us (no doubt deliberately) of the earlier one, in which Jesus rejects even his kin for his cultic brethren instead (where he also mentions 'sisters' as well as brothers, just as here). So we cannot establish that the family of Jesus is historical, either. In Mark it could just as easily be fiction.

Obviously I can continue with example after example, exhausting every scene in Mark, proving it either is more likely fiction than history, or as likely as not.[138] There is no good case to be made that any scene in Mark reflects a historical Jesus. Because most scenes clearly do not, and even if any do, we cannot discern which, or what in them is historical.

5. *The Mythology of Matthew*

That Matthew is essentially a redaction of Mark is almost universally agreed. He borrows extensively from Mark (nearly the whole narrative), and frequently duplicates his material verbatim. Matthew then added a ridiculous Nativity Narrative (which no reasonable historian should regard as

Jewish legend 'Miriam's Well' was the rock that gave birth to the flow of water after Moses struck it with his staff (noted earlier). Paul equated Jesus with that rock (1 Cor. 10.1-4). But if Jesus were equated with the water that flowed from it, the rock would then become his mother. Thus 'Mary's well' would have been Jesus' mother in Paul's conceptual scheme. Note that in legend, 'Miriam's Well' not only traveled with the Jews, but finally settled in the Sea of Galilee, where it could 'effect magical cures for those who were able to get to it' (Taylor, *Jewish Women*, pp. 335-36). Philo equated that rock with the celestial being named Wisdom (*Life of Moses* 1.181-86, 188-90, 210-11, 255-57; *On Flight and Finding* 183-87), which was then considered the feminine dimension of God (Taylor, *Jewish Women*, p. 336; e.g. 'Miriam is thus associated with an everlasting well which will never dry up', a legend ripe to be paralleled with the mothering of Jesus). Note that 'Miriam's Well' also had symbolic parallels to 'Jacob's Well', and Mark symbolically equated the empty tomb of Jesus with the latter (Carrier, 'Spiritual Body', in *Empty Tomb* [ed. Price and Lowder], pp. 161, 163); thus his birth and his death were in Mark associated with life-giving wells.

138. For example, see Dale Miller and Patricia Miller, *The Gospel of Mark as Midrash on Earlier Jewish and New Testament Literature* (Lewiston, NY: E. Mellen Press, 1990).

anything but fiction) and a brief but vague resurrection-appearance narrative (to fix what he may have regarded as the unsatisfying ending of Mark), which most historians also doubt is historical, and then revised the material in between, often altering or expanding on the stories Mark invented, occasionally inventing new ones and adding large sections attributing new teachings to Jesus.[139]

The traditional view is that this added material (at least where it also appears in Luke–Acts) Matthew derived from another lost Gospel or source, commonly designated Q. But that theory does not have as much to commend it as is claimed (see Chapter 7, §4 and §6 below), and should honestly be regarded as too speculative to generate reliable hypotheses. Of course, even if this theory were in some sense correct, *that* source could be fabricated every bit as much as Mark and Matthew were. So its existence does not support historicity any more than the existence of Mark does. And as we saw, Mark does not support historicity at all; although neither does the content of Mark argue *against* historicity—it just has no determinate value in that regard. Neither does Matthew. Neither would Q.

The material Matthew adds (or draws from some other Gospel) could be wholly fabricated (by Matthew or the author of his source Gospel), or could be newly invented historical contexts into which were set what were originally mystically revealed sayings or teachings (such as pronounced by the celestial Jesus to the first apostles) or the borrowing of material once written by or about someone else and attributed to Jesus (as in the Eugnostos case we saw earlier).[140] His sources in any such case would then be moot. And since we've already seen this is how Mark composed his Gospel, and

139. It has been suggested that Matthew actually derived his nativity and appearance narratives from the lost cover leaf of Mark (which in codex form would have contained the first and last pages of his Gospel). However, the fact that Mark as we have it perfectly mirrors its beginning with its ending (as noted in the previous section) argues against this, as it would be a remarkable coincidence if the lost material corresponded so perfectly at both ends to a Markan *inclusio*. But possibly there were earlier nativity and appearance narratives that Mark has excluded and that Matthew embellishes. In any case, to explore the possibility of a lost beginning and ending of Mark see N. Clayton Croy, *The Mutilation of Mark's Gospel* (Nashville, TN: Abingdon, 2003); C.H. Roberts, 'The Codex', *Proceedings of the British Academy* 40 (1954), pp. 168-204 (190); and C.H. Roberts, 'The Ancient Book and the Ending of St. Mark', *Journal of Theological Studies* 40 (1939), pp. 253-57. See also James McGrath, *The Burial of Jesus: History and Faith* (Charleston, SC: BookSurge, 2008), pp. 111-12; supporting which is the curious agreement between *Gos. Pet.* 14.50-60 and John 21, which might indicate an original ending of Mark (redacted in Lk. 5).

140. For example, Clare Rothschild, *Baptist Traditions and Q* (Tübingen: Mohr Siebeck, 2005) argues that a lot of the material attributed to Jesus in 'Q' (including core elements of the nativity) actually originated in documents about John the Baptist and were simply transferred to Jesus by Matthew, just as happened to Eugnostus in the

Matthew simply copies Mark's Gospel and tweaks it and adds to it, we have no good reason to trust he has any more reliable source material than Mark. That Matthew clearly and routinely and even egregiously fabricates narratives (such as his nativity, or his absurd redaction of Mark's empty-tomb narrative) only further raises the prior probability that that is just what he did everywhere else in his Gospel.[141] We have no particular reason to believe otherwise.

It is generally agreed that Matthew rewrote Mark not only to fix and improve on it but also to reverse its too-Gentile-friendly argument. Unlike Mark, which favors a brand of Christianity developed by Paul (in which Torah observance was optional), the author of Matthew comes from a community of Torah-observant Christians and is keen to have Jesus insist that we continue to make all converts remain or become practicing Jews (complete with circumcision and obedience to dietary and other laws, only minus the temple cult rituals).[142] Many of Matthew's rewrites reflect this specific need to rewrite Mark. But that Matthew had to do this by *rewriting*

Wisdom of Jesus Christ (see §1). That thesis might be neither probable nor disprovable; but it would have to be ruled out before it could be dismissed.

141. That Matthew's redaction of the empty-tomb narrative is fiction I have demonstrated elsewhere (see Carrier, 'Why the Resurrection Is Unbelievable', in *Christian Delusion* [ed. Loftus], pp. 293-96, and *Proving History*, pp. 199-204, with Carrier, 'Plausibility of Theft' in *Empty Tomb* [ed. Price and Lowder], pp. 358-68; to which should be added the fact that Mt. 27.51-53 derives the additions of an earthquake and risen hoard of holy men in part from the Septuagint text of Zech. 14.5, 'when you flee from the earthquake . . . Jehovah my God shall come, and all the holy ones with him'). That the nativity is fiction is evident enough from how clearly it conforms to the Rank–Raglan hero type (Element 48); it is clearly based extensively on the expanded Nativity Narrative of Moses in the first-century *Biblical Antiquities* (see D.J. Harrington, 'Pseudo-Philo', in *Dictionary of New Testament Background* [ed. Craig Evans and Stanley Porter; Downers Grove, IL: InterVarsity Press, 2000]: 864-68, cf. p. 866; the section treating Moses is *Bib. Ant.* 9); see also Charles Talbert, 'Miraculous Conceptions and Births in Mediterranean Antiquity', in *Historical Jesus in Context* (ed. Levine, Allison and Crossan), pp. 79-86; Calum Carmichael, 'The Passover *Haggadah*', in *Historical Jesus in Context* (ed. Levine, Allison and Crossan), pp. 343-56 (344-45), and in the same volume, George Nickelsburg, '*First* and *Second Enoch*: A Cry against Oppression and the Promise of Deliverance', in *Historical Jesus in Context* (ed. Levine, Allison and Crossan), pp. 87-109 (92-93). Its incorporation of a genealogy does not lend any more credence to it: genealogies of mythic heroes were a mainstay of ancient mythography (see earlier note); and the NT even reports that many genealogies were being invented for Jesus and that all should be rejected as fabrications (1 Tim. 1.4 and Tit. 3.9); e.g. the *Biblical Antiquities* added several genealogies for biblical heroes like Sampson that are similarly bogus (Harrington, 'Pseudo-Philo', p. 866).

142. See David Sim, *The Gospel of Matthew and Christian Judaism: The History and Social Setting of the Matthean Community* (Edinburgh: T. & T. Clark, 1998), e.g., pp. 123-39.

Mark (rather than simply producing his own Gospel) proves that Matthew had no actual independent sources from which to argue his position. He thus had to fabricate what he needed—but not by composing his own text, but instead simply constructing a better Mark. *Maybe* for that purpose he had some prior documents to work from, but since we don't have those, we cannot know if he did, or how Matthew has transformed them. As we shall see (in §6), Luke clearly knew and employed Matthew along with Mark as his primary sources, so separating what came from Matthew and what came from 'Q' can only be an exercise in speculation (as is even the existence of Q).

Matthew often 'improves' Mark by supposedly fixing Mark's omissions or mistakes in geography, scripture or Jewish lore and law.[143] But sometimes Matthew's 'fixes' even make the story more ridiculous. For example, in the story of Jesus riding triumphantly into Jerusalem, Mark has him sit on a young donkey that he had his disciples fetch for him (Mk 11.1-10). Matthew changes the story so the disciples instead fetch *two* donkeys, not only the young donkey of Mark but also his mother, then Jesus rides into Jerusalem on *both donkeys at the same time* (a logistical impossibility: Mt. 21.1-9).[144] Why? Because Matthew wanted the story to better match a 'literal' reading of the OT prophecy that had originally inspired the detail in Mark; indeed, Matthew also 'improves' on Mark by actually quoting the scripture that Mark clearly also used as his source material but didn't actually mention: Zech. 9.9, 'Behold! Your king is coming to you! He is righteous and brings salvation. He is meek, and riding on a donkey *[and] on a baby donkey*'.[145]

As Marcus Borg observes, these 'changes indicate a human author at work who felt free to modify the story he received'. And so we have to ask, 'are the two animals in Matthew's story history remembered? Obviously not. Clearly, the second animal is there not because Matthew had better historical information on the basis of which to correct Mark', but because Matthew wanted to make the connection to Zechariah explicit and more literal, hence 'it is an instance of prophecy historicized—that is, a passage from the Hebrew Bible regarded as prophecy is generating details in the

143. See, e.g., Chapter 8 (§7).

144. See the analysis of Marcus Borg, 'The Historical Study of Jesus and Christian Origins', in *Jesus at 2000* (ed. Marcus Borg; Boulder, CO: Westview Press, 1997), pp. 121-48. Note that (as Borg observes) a child donkey would not even stand at the same height or run at the same pace as its mother, so the picture Matthew paints of Jesus straddling both is quite absurd.

145. The Septuagint text reads *epi hupozugion kai pōlon neon*, lit. 'on an ass and a new foal' (meaning a very young baby donkey); the original Hebrew reads 'on an ass, on a young male ass, the child of a [female] ass', which was probably originally a poetic idiom for just 'young male donkey', but if taken literally would seem to say 'on a donkey and a baby donkey', and that is how Matthew took it.

gospel narrative' that are then 'reported as an event in the gospel', which 'is not only a characteristic of Matthew but also a factor shaping the development of the gospel tradition and the New Testament as a whole'.[146] But that means the whole Gospel could be 'prophecy historicized', not 'history remembered'. It's already clear Matthew does not care about getting the historical facts right. He does not compare sources or investigate what happened. He just makes up what he wants or feels is needed.

Matthew also completely destroys Mark's own beautiful literary structure by moving things around (e.g. the Sabbath controversies are bumped from Mk 2.23–3.6 into Matthew 12), and adding or subtracting details, and packing in long sections of new teaching, such as the Sermon on the Mount (Matthew 5–7) and the Olive Mount parables (Matthew 24–25). But Matthew recycles the pieces of Mark to create large-scale structure of his own, as discovered and demonstrated by Dale Allison and others.[147] For example, after Matthew introduces Jesus' ministry, he adds a five-fold division of sections by repeating five times the complete phrase 'and it happened when Jesus had finished' (*kai egeneto hote etelesen ho Iēsous*: 7.28-29; 11.1; 13.53; 19.1; and 26.1).[148] Each phrase ends an extended insertion of discourse that Matthew has added to the teachings in Mark (though in some cases incorporating and transforming Markan teachings).

As Matthew's aim was to greatly expand the teachings in Mark and make them more strict and more firmly Jewish, his overall structure reflects this intent, using those five repeated catch-phrases to alternate between narrative and discourse:

1-4 Narrative (INTRODUCTION: of birth, baptism and ministry)
5-7 Discourse ('Jesus' demands upon Israel')
ending with the key phrase at 7.28-29
8-9 Narrative ('Jesus' deeds' within and for Israel)
10 Discourse (teaching the disciples how to do the same)
ending with the key phrase at 11.1

146. Borg, 'Historical Study', p. 135.

147. Dale Allison, *Studies in Matthew: Interpretation Past and Present* (Grand Rapids, MI: Baker Academic, 2005), pp. 135-56. For surveys of other structural studies on Matthew (which include many more examples than I shall discuss) see Marianne Meye Thompson, 'The Structure of Matthew: An Examination of Two Approaches', *Studia biblica et theologica* 12 (1982), pp. 195-238; and David Bauer, *The Structure of Matthew's Gospel: A Study in Literary Design* (Sheffield: Almond Press, 1988).

148. In addition to Allison (previous note) see also the analysis in Craig Evans, '"The Book of the Genesis of Jesus Christ": The Purpose of Matthew in Light of the Incipit', in *Biblical Interpretation in Early Christian Gospels, Vol. 2: Gospel of Matthew* (ed. Thomas Hatina; London: T. & T. Clark, 2008), pp. 61-72.

11-12 Narrative ('Israel's negative response')
13 Discourse ('explanation of Israel's negative response')
ending with the key phrase at 13.53
14-17 Narrative ('founding of the church')
18 Discourse ('teaching for the church')
ending with the key phrase at 19.1
19-22 Narrative (entering Judea and ending in Jerusalem)
23-25 Discourse (on 'the future judgment and salvation')
ending with the key phrase at 26.1
26-28 Narrative (CONCLUSION: betrayal, crucifixion, resurrection)

There are shorter teachings interspersed in the narrative sections, but unlike Mark, Matthew inserts these five special 'long discourse' sections (called the five 'Great Discourses') in this overall structure.[149]

But like Mark, Matthew has also crafted his Gospel into a large chiastic superstructure:[150]

A Genealogy (summary of past times: 1.1-17)
B Mary [1], an angel arrives, and the birth of Jesus (1.18-25)
C Gifts of wealth at birth (magi), attempt to thwart birth (Herod) (2.1-12)
D Flight to Egypt, woe to the children, Jeremiah laments destruction of the first temple (2.13-21)
E Judea avoided (2.22-23)
F Baptism of Jesus (3.1–8.23)
G Crossing the sea [twice] (8.24–11.1)
H John's ministry (11.2-19)
I Rejection of Jesus (11.20-24)
J Secrets revealed through Jesus (11.25-30)
K Attack of Pharisees (12.1-13)
L Pharisees determine to kill God's Servant (12.14-21)
K Condemnation of Pharisees (12.22-45)
J Secrets revealed through Jesus (13.1-52)
I Rejection of Jesus (13.53-58)

149. Quotations are from Allison, *Studies in Matthew*, pp. 141-42; Allison groups chap. 23 with the narrative unit of chaps. 19–22, but I think it goes with the discourse unit of chaps. 24–25, and thus my table reflects that assumption. Apart from that, the order is Allison's. For Allison's alternative placement of chap. 23 he refers to the analysis in Meye Thompson, 'The Structure of Matthew'.

150. This structural outline (and the subunits to follow) is adapted and expanded from James Jordan, 'Toward a Chiastic Understanding of the Gospel according to Matthew', *Biblical Horizons Newsletter* 94 and 95 (April and May, 1997).

H John's death (14.1-12)
G Crossing the sea [twice] (14.13–16.12)
F Transfiguration of Jesus (16.13–18.35)
E Judea entered (19.1–20.34)
D March to Jerusalem, woe to the children (24.19), Jesus predicts destruction of the second temple (21.1–27.56; cf. 23–25)
C Gift of wealth at death (Joseph of Arimathea), attempt to thwart resurrection (Sanhedrin and the guards) (27.57-66)
B Mary [2], an angel arrives, and the resurrection of Jesus (28.1-15)
A Commission (summary of future times: 28.16-20)

Within this overall structure are several sub-structures that certify the larger one. For example, the F segments (the baptism of Jesus, paired with the transfiguration of Jesus) parallel each other in a common structure:

<table>
<tr><th>Baptism Ministry</th><th>Transfiguration Ministry</th></tr>
<tr><td>Preliminary setting: John's witness (3.1-12)</td><td>Preliminary setting: Peter's witness (16.13-28)</td></tr>
<tr><td>Revelation of the Son (3.13-17)</td><td>Revelation of the Son (17.1-8; with a reference back to John: 17.9-13)</td></tr>
<tr><td>Satan resisted (4.1-11)</td><td>Satan cast out (17.14-23)</td></tr>
<tr><td>Removal to Capernaum (4.12-16)</td><td>Removal to Capernaum (17.24-27)</td></tr>
<tr><td>Recruiting of disciples (4.17-22) and beginning of ministry (4.23-25)</td><td rowspan="4">Sermon on discipleship, faith, recruiting, and forgiveness (18)</td></tr>
<tr><td>Sermon on the Mount (5.1–8.1, in part about forgiveness)</td></tr>
<tr><td>Faith and worship produce healing (8.2-17)</td></tr>
<tr><td>What disciples must give up (8.18-23)</td></tr>
</table>

Table 8. Baptism Narrative Paralleled in Transfiguration Narrative

Matthew has also recrafted the crucifixion narrative specifically to be more elegantly chiastic than Mark's version:

A Passover and crucifixion (26.1-2)
B Priests plot (26.3-5)
C Jesus anointed for burial (26.6-13)
D Preparations: Judas enlisted (26.14-16); Passover prepared (26.17-19)
E Judas exposed (26.20-25)
F Lord's Supper [a mock death] inaugurated (26.26-28)
G Nazirite vow made (26.29)
H Removal to Olivet (26.30)
I Abandonment (26.31-35)
J Jesus asks God not to be released (26.36-46)
K Judas betrays Jesus (26.47-56)
L Trial before Sanhedrin (26.57-68)
M Denial of Peter (26.69-75)
L Sanhedrin delivers Jesus to Pilate (27.1-2)
K Judas hangs himself (27.3-10)
J Pilate does not release Jesus (27.11-26)
I Mockery (27.27-31)
H Removal to Golgotha (27.32-33)
G Nazirite vow fulfilled (27.34)
F Crucifixion (27.35-44) and death (27.45-50)
E Temple exposed (27.51)
D Results: Jesus' lordship confirmed (27.52-54); the least are faithful (27.55-56)
C Jesus buried (27.57-61)
B Priests plot (27.62-66)
A Passover and resurrection (28.1-10)

It was necessary for Christ's sacrifice that he be completely abandoned by men (so his humbling would be thorough: Phil. 2.7-8), and so Peter's denial is essential to the story. Accordingly, Matthew makes it the centerpiece of his Passover chiasmus.

Of course much of this could be 'explained away' as Matthew just creatively rearranging 'facts' to fit his literary design. Although even that entails accepting that Matthew doesn't really care all that much about the facts—getting history straight is not his concern; creating an elegantly symbolic literary structure is. But it is very unlikely that history worked out so well to begin with, generating all the right 'facts' that Matthew could arrange in this way. He certainly had to invent some things to get it all to fit. And a lot, of course, he got from Mark, and we already saw how the status of those details as 'facts' is already in question, since many of them (if not all of them) were invented by Mark to suit *his* aims. Thus, Matthew could take invented details from Mark, and add invented details of his own, to produce a completely invented Gospel narrative, whose literary design has completely eclipsed any interest in historical truth.

For example, Matthew adds the otherwise pointless and inexplicable detail at the beginning that 'they shall call his name Immanuel, which means, "God is with us"' (Mt. 1.23), even though that never happens (Jesus is not named Immanuel and never so called anywhere in the ensuing story). This weird detail only makes sense because Matthew concludes his story by having Jesus declare, 'I am with you' (28.20). Matthew has thus consciously invented material to parallel the end with the beginning and thereby communicate a fundamental concept of the Christian gospel. But as we've seen, this is just a small piece of a large and complex structure organizing Matthew's entire Gospel.

None of this can really have been orally transmitted. This kind of detailed and intricate structure (just like Mark's) can only really be crafted, preserved and understood using a written text. Yet Matthew and Mark rearranged everything to create their own unique texts. This means there was no transmitted structure or order; these authors are inventing it. And since they are also freely inventing details to suit their structures, why should we believe they are not freely inventing *all* of it? Even if some of it comes from elsewhere, what elements are those? We cannot tell. And even if we could tell, what reason have we to believe that *that* wasn't invented too—by earlier authors? None, really. Maybe some of it goes back to the original revelations from the Lord received by apostles such as Paul or Peter. But even if that's the case, those are still not from a historical Jesus, but a dreamed or hallucinated Jesus. The complex and deliberate structures of Mark and Matthew show that there was no *narrative* into which these sayings were placed, because they each freely created one of their own, and inserted and rearranged sayings in different ways to suit their own aims (as we'll see Luke did, too). As we saw in *1 Clement* (in Chapter 8, §5) and will see in Paul (in the next chapter), it would seem that for a long time there *were* no narratives associated with Jesus (other than what the apostles hallucinated, or pretended to—or what they reconstructed from ancient scriptures). So there is no case to be made that any of the sayings of Jesus that might go back to the beginning of the cult *don't* come from revelations rather than a Galilean ministry. Because the Galilean ministry was clearly a Gospel add-on (originated by Mark, to pair his Palestinian adventure with a 'sea' of sufficient size to use as his preferred metaphor).

The same goes for the 'deeds'. The miracle stories and other events all have obvious symbolic and mythical roles to play in Matthew's story, just as in Mark's. There is no reason to believe any of those things happened, either. In every case, if it's not already an implausible event used to illustrate a literary and theological point (like, as we saw earlier, the clearing of the temple), it could easily just be a model for missionaries to follow or cite in their ongoing work (like the healings and exorcisms). In fact, most of the sections Matthew adds or changes deal with missionary activity and how to run the church or how to live in it, and thus reflect interests that would have primarily arisen and been worked out *after* Jesus had died, and thus are most likely later creations and not original to Jesus.

Even the narrative sections have allegorical functions in the same direction. For example, in the fourth narrative unit, Dale Allison observes:

> That the ecclesia is indeed the most important subject of [Matthew 14–17] appears not only from the ever-increasing focus upon the disciples as opposed to the crowds but also from Peter's being the rock upon which the church is built, because it is precisely in this section that Peter comes to the fore. Among the insertions into the Markan material are these four passages:
>
> 14.28-33 Peter walks on the water
> 15.15 Peter asks a question
> 16.13-20 Jesus blesses Peter
> 17.24-27 Peter asks a question and answers a question
>
> Peter's emerging preeminence [thus] correlates with the emergence of the church.
>
> Matthew 18, the next major discourse, confirms this. The chapter addresses issues specific to the ecclesia, to the Christian community. How often should one forgive a brother (18.21-22)? What is the procedure for excommunicating someone (18.15-20)? These and other ecclesiastical questions merit attention precisely at this point because Jesus has just established his church.[151]

It is clear that Matthew has integrated all this *into* Mark's narrative; Mark seems unaware of any of it. It thus would appear to reflect needs and interests subsequent to Mark or developed during his generation in a community separate from his. Which means none of these things happened, and Jesus never said any of it.

Illustrating every point made so far is the Sermon on the Mount, which is a well-crafted literary work that cannot have come from some illiterate Galilean. In fact, we know it originated in Greek, not Hebrew or Aramaic, because it relies on the Septuagint text of the Bible for all its features and allusions. It relies extensively on the Greek text of Deuteronomy and Leviticus especially, and in key places on other texts.[152] For example, the section

151. Allison, *Studies in Matthew*, p. 140.

152. Thomas Brodie, 'An Alternative Q/Logia Hypothesis: Deuteronomy-Based, Qumranlike, Verifiable', in *The Sayings Source Q and the Historical Jesus* (ed. A. Lindemann; Leuven: Leuven University Press, 2001), pp. 729-43.

on turning the other cheek and other aspects of legal pacifism (Mt. 5.38-42) has been redacted from the Greek text of Isa. 50.6-9.[153] These are not the words of Jesus. This famous sermon as a whole also has a complex literary structure that can only have come from a *writer*, not an everyday speaker. And again, it reflects needs and interests that would have arisen *after* the apostles began preaching the faith and organizing communities and struggling to keep them in the fold. So it's unlikely to come from Jesus.

Once again, Allison has thoroughly demonstrated many of these points.[154] In particular, he reveals its extensive and brilliant use of triadic structure:

A. **Introduction** (crowds ascend the mountain: 4.23-5.1)
B. The Nine **(3 x 3)** Blessings (5.3-12)
C. Summary Statement (*salt and light:* 5.13-16)
[D. The Three Pillars Begun]
[1] How to Obey the Torah (5.17-48)
General Principles (5.17-20)
[a] 1. Murder (5.21-26)
2. Adultery (5.27-30)
3. Divorce (5.31-32)
[b] 1. Oaths (5.33-37)
2. Vengeance (5.38-42)
3. Loving Your Enemies (6.43-48)
[2] How to Pay Cult to God (6.1-18)
General Principle (6.1)
1. Almsgiving (6.2-4)
2. Prayer (6.5-15)
[1] Not as the Hypocrites or the Gentiles (6.5-8)
[*central focus*] **[2]** The Lord's Prayer (6.9-13) [*everything thus centers on this*]
1. Introduction and Address (6.9a-b)
[*exact center*] **2.** Three **(3)** 'Thou' Petitions (6.9c-10) [*God is thus at the center*]
3. Three **(3)** 'We' Petitions (6.11-13)
[3] On Forgiveness (6.14-15)
3. Fasting (6.16-18)
[3] How to Deal with Society (6.19-7.12)
[a] General Principles (*store up treasure in heaven:* 6.19-21)
1. Eye Parable (6.22-23)
2. Value Parable (*God before mammon:* 6.24)
3. Encouragement (6.25-34)
[b] General Principles (*do not judge:* 7.1-2)

153. Allison, *Studies in Matthew*, pp. 219-22.

154. Allison, *Studies in Matthew*, pp. 173-216, along with Dale Allison, 'The Structure of the Sermon on the Mount', *Journal of Biblical Literature* 106 (1987), pp. 423-45; and Dale Allison, 'Q's New Exodus and the Historical Jesus', in *The Sayings Source Q* (ed. Lindemann), pp. 395-428.

1. Eye Parable (7.3-5)
2. Value Parable (*pearls before swine:* 7.6)
3. Encouragement (7.7-11)
[D. The Three Pillars Concluded]
C. Summary Statement (*the Golden Rule:* 7.12)
B. The Three **(3)** Warnings (7.13-27)
A. **Conclusion** (crowds descend the mountain: 7.28-8.1)

This is simply far too elegant, too intricately organized, and too obviously literary to be a casual speech. It is, from beginning to end, a *written* product, carefully thought out and painstakingly arranged. It's far more likely that Matthew wrote this himself than that he just extracted it from some other text—a text for some reason no one bothered to preserve.

Allison also shows that this Sermon on the Mount fits neatly within known rabbinical debates over how Jews could still fulfill the Torah after the destruction of the temple cult; the general consensus among the rabbis was that good deeds now fulfill that role (especially acts of love and mercy). That is essentially also what the Sermon on the Mount says.[155] Its solution is even more complete, by creating a new kind of worship (in simple, humble almsgiving, prayer, forgiveness and fasting). As Allison points out:

> Simeon the Just, a rabbi of the Maccabean period . . . is purported to have declared: 'Upon three things the world standeth: upon Torah, upon Temple service and upon *gemilut hasidim*' ([Mishnah] *Abot* 1.2). The two words left untranslated are usually rendered, 'deeds of loving-kindness'. . . . [So] Simeon declares that three things matter most: the law, the cult, and social or religious acts of benevolence. Now . . . the parallel with the Sermon on the Mount is remarkable. Matthew 5–7 addresses three fundamental issues, the law, the cult, and social behavior; that is, it addresses the three things upon which, according to Simeon the Just, the world stands, and it addresses them in precisely the same order. [Thus it seems Matthew] arranged his discourse so as to create a Christian interpretation of the three classical pillars.[156]

Notably, it does this by simply assuming the temple cult doesn't exist. At no point does Jesus in this very long speech explain what to do about the temple sacrifice code in Leviticus or Deuteronomy, for example—even to reject it or avoid it or that it isn't needed. To the contrary, the speech simply assumes that's no longer an issue. In other words, it assumes the temple cult has already been destroyed. Which means this speech was written after 70 CE. It does not come from Jesus.

155. Allison, 'Structure of the Sermon', pp. 442-45.
156. Allison, 'Structure of the Sermon', p. 443.

In addition to all that, Matthew adds details that make Jesus more into a new Moses.[157] Scholars have long known, for example, that Matthew's Nativity Narrative is a rewrite of the nativity of Moses (drawing not only on Exodus but on its first-century expansion in the anonymous *Biblical Antiquities*), and that Matthew has Jesus deliver his new commandments on a mountain (in the Sermon on the Mount) to emulate Moses delivering the commandments of God from Mount Sinai. And in Matthew, Jesus' Great Commission from a mountain is designed to echo in several respects Moses' Great Commission before he ascended a mountain to die (Deut. 31–34).[158] And the five Great Discourses (delivered by Jesus) are obviously meant to replace the five books of the Pentateuch (which were believed to be written by Moses).[159]

There are many instances like this of Matthew's literary-historical revisionism. For example, Matthew expands Jesus' forty-day sojourn in the wilderness and temptation by the Devil (an event already in Mark evoking the forty years of temptation in the wilderness of Moses and the Jews) into an elaborate parable in which Jesus undergoes the exact same temptations as the Jews—but, unlike them, Jesus conveniently passes every test with flying colors, thus reversing the bad mojo their previous failure had cursed the Jews with. Accordingly:

> Israel was in the wilderness for forty years [Dt. 8.2]; Jesus is there for forty days [Mt. 4.2]. Israel was tempted by hunger and fed upon manna [Ex. 16.2-8]; the hungry Jesus [Mt. 4.2] is tempted to turn stones into bread [Mt. 4.3-4]. Israel was tempted to put God to the test [Ex. 17.1-3]; the same thing happens to Jesus [Mt. 4.6-7]. And just as Israel was lured into idolatry [Ex. 32], so the devil confronts Jesus with the same temptation to worship something other than Israel's God [Satan himself: Mt. 4.8-10].[160]

157. Extensively discussed in Dale Allison, *The New Moses: A Matthean Typology* (Minneapolis, MN: Fortress Press, 1993). See also Paul Hughes, 'Moses' Birth Story: A Biblical Matrix for Prophetic Messianism', in *Eschatology, Messianism, and the Dead Sea Scrolls* (ed. Craig Evans and Peter Flint; Grand Rapids, MI: William B. Eerdmans, 1997), pp. 10-22.

158. See Kenton Sparks, 'Gospel as Conquest: Mosaic Typology in Matt 28:16-20', *Catholic Biblical Quarterly* 68 (2006), pp. 651-63.

159. This does not mean each discourse corresponds to a specific book in the Torah. Many have tried to force such interpretations, but it is clear no one-to-one correspondence was intended. These five new discourses are simply the new Torah, reinterpreting the old.

160. Allison, 'Q's New Exodus', pp. 395-96 (see also 404). Matthew also has Jesus become more like Moses here by having Jesus 'fast for forty days and forty nights' (Mt. 4.2) just as Moses did on Mount Sinai (Exod. 34.28).

Matthew has thus invented a narrative, and put words in Jesus' mouth, all to create a literarily symbolic episode, involving an obviously fictional event, out of what began as a brief line, also invented by Mark.[161] This is not history. This is mythmaking.

There is in fact no way to discern what if anything Matthew has added to Mark has any historical basis, or even a source (and its having a source would still in no way establish that it's historical; after all, Mark is one of Matthew's sources, and Mark's tales are not historical). The same conclusion must therefore follow for Matthew that we reached for Mark: nothing in it is any less likely on myth than on historicity. It therefore has no evidential value. The burden is therefore on anyone who would insist there is anything in Matthew that is any more authentic than what's in Mark. As it is, I deem Matthew to be just as fictional, showing a wanton readiness to fabricate, and no signs of any interest in historical truth or any ability to discern it, or any indication he has employed any sources more reliable than Mark. Matthew's value for determining historicity is therefore nil. Even if any historical facts about Jesus are in it, we have no way to identify them.

6. *The Mythology of Luke*

Luke is the first Gospel to overtly represent itself as history. Matthew comes close by suggesting that the things he says happened fulfilled scripture, but that could still have lent itself to an allegorical reading. Luke, however, writes like a historian, adding superficial historical details as local color and attempting to date some events and even including an albeit-vague preface explaining what he is doing by writing. Luke also creates a resurrection narrative that is engineered to answer skeptics of Matthew's account, a tactic that 'requires' his story to be true. Although on this count we know it is a fabrication. No prior Gospel, nor Paul, had ever heard of the peculiar and convenient details that suddenly make their first appearance in Luke, such as that Peter double-checked the women's claim that the tomb was empty and handled the burial shroud (Lk. 24.11-12), or that Jesus showed the disciples his wounds and made sure the disciples touched him and fed him food to prove he wasn't a ghost (Lk. 24.36-43), or that the

161. That Mark (or his lost source) invented the temptation (Mk 1.13) is obvious from how it has Jesus reverse the role of the Jews in the Exodus before beginning his own spiritual conquest of the Holy Land: while they wander forty years in the wilderness before crossing the Jordan to enter the Holy Land, Jesus departs the Holy Land to cross the Jordan and spend forty days in that same wilderness; and as the Jews there endured trials and receive miraculous aid, so does Jesus. Another indication is the fact that devils and angels don't exist, much less tempt and minister to people in deserts. That happens only in myths.

resurrected Jesus actually hung out and partied with dozens of his followers for over a month before flying up into the clouds of heaven (Acts 1.2-9).[162]

So we know Luke is making a lot of things up in order to deliberately sell a fake history, for purposes of winning an argument against doubters (both within and without Christianity, as his opponents included, for example, Christians with very different ideas about the nature of the resurrection). This already warns us not to trust anything he has added to the story found in Mark and Matthew: we should assume it is, like those, a convenient fabrication invented for some purpose, unless we can find sufficient evidence to believe otherwise. In accord with this conclusion, despite his pretense at being a historian, preface and all, Luke's methods are demonstrably nonhistorical: he is not doing research, weighing facts, checking them against independent sources, and writing down what he thinks most likely happened. He is simply producing an expanded and redacted literary hybrid of a couple of previous religious novels (Matthew and Mark), each itself even more obviously constructed according to literary conventions rather than historiographical (as I've shown in the preceding sections of this chapter). Unlike other historians of even his own era, Luke never names his sources or explains why we are to trust them (or why *he* did), or how he chose what to include or exclude. In fact, Luke does not even declare any critical method at all, but rather insists he slavishly followed what was handed on to him—yet another claim we know to be a lie (since we have two of his sources and can confirm he freely altered them to suit his own agenda).[163]

As I mentioned in Chapter 7 (§4) the more popular view is that Luke did not redact Matthew but in fact used a (hypothetical) source in common with Matthew, now called Q. It is time for this theory to be discarded. It has no merit. It is no longer reasonably deniable that Luke knew and used Matthew as a source directly, and if he did that, there is no basis left for supposing there was any other source involved. The evidence for Luke's extensive reliance on (and purposeful redaction of) Matthew is documented in the works of Goodacre, Goulder and MacDonald.[164] It should already have been clear that Luke deliberately transformed Matthew's Nativity and Pas-

162. That these are all fabrications is obvious from the fact that Paul would have known and made use of them were they known claims of his time (see Carrier, 'Spiritual Body', in *Empty Tomb* [ed. Price and Lowder], pp. 120-26, 135, 190-93), and Mark and Matthew would likewise have known of them and could hardly have failed to mention any of them.

163. I thoroughly discuss the meaning of Luke's preface and compare him to other historians of his own time in how he constructs and argues for his version of events in Carrier, *Not the Impossible Faith*, pp. 161-218.

164. See relevant notes in Chapter 7, §4.

sion Narratives and Matthew's account of Judas's suicide, sometimes even repeating Matthew's Greek verbatim or borrowing heavily from it.

For example, Mk 14.65a reads, 'and some began to spit on him, and to cover his face, and to buffet him, and to say to him, "Prophesy!"', which Mt. 26.67-68 expanded to 'then did they spit in his face and buffet him: and some smote him with the palms of their hands, **saying, "Prophesy** unto us, Christ! **Who is he that struck thee?"'** Luke 22.63-64 essentially combines Mark with Matthew, repeating the concluding text of Matthew verbatim: 'and the men that held Jesus mocked him, and beat him; and they blindfolded him, and asked him, **saying, "Prophesy! Who is he that struck thee?"'** Except for dropping 'unto us, Christ' to economize the passage, the Greek of Luke here is identical to that of Matthew (*legontes, Prophēteuson [hēmin Christe]! Tis estin ho paisas se?*). Luke then combines this with Mark's detail that they covered his eyes, which Matthew omitted (or rather altered, having them spit 'in his face' rather than cover 'his face'). Luke thus combined Mark with Matthew, recast mostly but not entirely in his own words, to make what he deemed to be a better passage.[165] That Luke knows the details Matthew added, and even borrows his exact words, is sufficient proof that Luke knew and used Matthew. Note that on no theory of Q is this element of the Passion Narrative a part of Q, so this cannot be explained by appealing to Q. Luke is using Matthew. And if here, so everywhere. There is simply no need of an imaginary Q.

There are likewise many places where Matthew redacts a passage in Mark, and Luke follows the Greek of Matthew rather than Mark, showing that Luke knew Matthew and occasionally preferred Matthew's version to Mark's original.[166] Another example: Luke redacts Matthew's Sermon on the Mount, conspicuously 'reversing' it into a Sermon on a Plain. How do we know Luke is redacting Matthew? Because both speeches are followed by the otherwise-unrelated narrative of Jesus healing the centurion's son in Capernaum. The latter occurs in Mt. 8.5-13, the Sermon having ended at 8.1 (only a brief healing of a leper lies in between). Luke 6.17-49 redacts that Sermon, and then immediately in Lk. 7.1-10 the centurion's servant is healed in Capernaum, the story in many respects identical, even down to specific words and phrases (such as revising the centurion's 'son' into the centurion's 'boy', which some translators render as 'servant', but in context this is obviously just a different way of saying 'son'). Likewise, Mt. 4.23–5.1 precedes the Sermon with a general account of Jesus healing many, and Lk. 6.17-19 does the same thing. These parallels are very improbable unless Luke was following and redacting Matthew's narrative—unless Q was an

165. MacDonald, *Two Shipwrecked Gospels*, pp. 76-87.

166. See, e.g., R.T. Simpson, 'The Major Agreements of Matthew and Luke against Mark', *New Testament Studies* 12 (1965–1966), pp. 283-84.

actual complete narrative Gospel with the same exact sequence of events, written in Greek. But as we've already seen, there is no need of that over-complicated hypothesis, and plenty of evidence against it.

That Luke redacted Matthew does not mean he always simply copied or paraphrased him. He creatively redacts Matthew, and often deliberately reverses his themes, as when Luke converts the Sermon on the Mount into a Sermon on a Plain. More conspicuously, when Luke rewrites Matthew's Nativity Narrative, he conspicuously reverses almost all of it's key elements: whereas Matthew depicts Jesus' family as essentially outlaws, fleeing Bethlehem and Herod's rule and cowering abroad for over a decade, Luke describes Jesus' family as *obeying* the law and *going to* Bethlehem in accordance with their emperor's command (Lk. 2.1-4); and while Matthew has Herod searching to kill the baby Jesus, Luke has Jesus being presented in the Jerusalem temple to repeated public pronouncements of his messianic status (by the prophets Anna and Simeon), an event that would not have escaped Herod's supposedly murderous eye (or memory), nor that of his agents and informants; and then Luke has Jesus' family living dutifully in their home at Nazareth the whole while (the period when Matthew has them hiding in Egypt), bringing Jesus back to Jerusalem for the Passover every single year without fail, in full compliance with Levitical law (Lk. 2.41).

Luke thus deliberately changed the reason Jesus was 'born in Bethlehem' but 'came from Nazareth', an aim first attempted in Matthew. It's an unlikely coincidence that Luke would attempt the same harmonization, unless he knew Matthew had started this Bethlehem tradition. There are many other unlikely coincidences—for example, in the way angels send essentially the same messages to Joseph and Mary in both accounts, and the fact that both accounts involve an annunciation, a virgin birth, and a genealogy (displaced in Luke but still there; displacement of elements like this being a common procedure in Luke). Even the annunciations, for example, are too similar to be chance coincidence: both Matthew and Luke have an angel report that Mary will conceive and bear a son, they shall name him Jesus, and he shall be something great—the same three-part announcement, in the same order, with the middle phrase identically the same (*kai kaleseis to onoma autou iēsoun,* 'and you will call his name Jesus'), Luke having copied Matthew at that point verbatim (compare Mt. 1.21 with Lk. 1.31-32). His changes (such as that the angel reports to Mary rather than Joseph, or phrasing the same things in different words, or expanding what the angel says) do not disguise the fact that Luke is clearly redacting Matthew. He is not coming up with these things independently of him.

Many of the differences are also just as improbable if they weren't intentional. For Luke, the family of Jesus is always obedient to religious and secular law and is never in danger and never hiding in a foreign country.[167] Similarly, Luke erased the involvement of foreigners (the Persian 'magi') and replaced them with (evidently Jewish) shepherds, and replaced Matthew's magical star (informing the magi) with an angelic light from heaven (informing the shepherds: Lk. 2.8-18). Luke clearly did not approve of Matthew's version of events, and thus changed them all around to 'fix' the story as Luke preferred.[168] There are many other respects in which it is clear Luke is borrowing ideas and material from Matthew, and deliberately changing others, in effect to 'correct' or 'fix' Matthew, as many scholars have shown.[169] In much the same way Luke borrowed and deliberately changed Matthew's tale of the death of Judas (inserting it into Acts 1.16-20), and replaced Matthew's genealogy with Luke's own. Luke cannot have been getting these things from Q, which did not include nativities, genealogies, or Judas's suicide. Luke must have been redacting Matthew, even if freely (as redactions often were—it is fallacious to assume a redaction must be literal or verbatim or line-by-line).

Many scholars have argued that Luke aimed to unify the two major divided factions of Christianity, the Gentile and Torah-observant sects, and his account (across Luke and Acts) revises history to tell a tale of continuous harmony between them, while simultaneously portraying Jesus and Christianity as a valid, devout, law-abiding philosophical sect respected by the Romans and opposed only by a faction of the hard-lined Jewish elite (see again Chapter 9). Luke is thus in effect a 'rebuttal' to Matthew, just as Matthew was an attempted 'rebuttal' to Mark. Mark promoted Gentile Christianity; Matthew promoted Torah-observant Christianity; Luke promotes a harmonious church, one that is a good and faithful evolution of Judaism into what is essentially (but carefully never said to be) the Gentile church.[170]

167. That this role of obedience to the law explains many of the changes Luke made to Matthew's nativity story, as well as many other elements throughout Luke–Acts, is well argued by Robert Smith, 'Caesar's Decree (Luke 2.1-2): Puzzle or Key?', *Currents in Theology and Mission* 7 (December 1980), pp. 343-51.

168. His changes then created a historical contradiction between the Gospels: Luke's story entails Jesus was born in 6 CE; Matthew's entails Jesus was born before 4 BCE. See my summary in Richard Carrier, 'Luke vs. Matthew on the Year of Christ's Birth', *Hitler Homer Bible Christ*, pp. 213-30.

169. P.J. Thompson, 'The Infancy Gospels of St. Matthew and St. Luke Compared', *Studia evanglica* 1 (1959), pp. 217-22; Michael Goulder, *Luke: A New Paradigm*, Vol. I (Sheffield: JSOT, 1989), pp. 205-69.

170. See the examples and analysis in Robert Price, *The Pre-Nicene New Testament: Fifty-Four Formative Texts* (Salt Lake City, UT: Signature Books, 2006), pp. 481-99;

So Luke not only borrows and redacts extensively from Matthew and Mark, who we've seen are not exactly reliable sources of history, but he also makes changes and additions that conveniently suit his own purposes and that were conspicuously unknown to Matthew or Mark, suggesting that his aims were also more literary than historically reliable. Indeed, Luke's additions are often not plausible and look self-evidently like embellishments of the kind one would expect for a work like this—pretending at being history but reinforcing the author's rhetorical aims by creating better stories, better models or better evidence in support of them. Luke's evident use of Josephus (noted in Chapter 7, §4) only reinforces this conclusion; likewise his use of Homer as a model for some of his stories.[171] But clinching it is how much of the material that Luke adds to Mark and Matthew is demonstrably fabricated by essentially rewriting the Elijah–Elisha narrative in 1 and 2 Kings, just as we saw Mark had done (in §4), casting Jesus in the central role and updating the details to fit the conditions of Roman Palestine.[172]

This last point has been extensively demonstrated by Thomas Brodie (as I noted in Chapter 9). The parallels are sometimes direct and sometimes inversions (where Luke takes what is in the Kings narrative and reverses it or key elements of it) and are too numerous and distinct to be chance coincidence. Luke (or his source for this material, if he did not invent it himself) is thus creating a literary myth by reworking the OT, not by recording historical facts passed down to him by witnesses. Examples include:

and Gregory Sterling, *Historiography and Self-Definition: Josephos, Luke–Acts, and Apologetic Historiography* (New York: E.J. Brill, 1992).

171. For example, Dennis MacDonald, *Does the New Testament Imitate Homer? Four Cases from the Acts of the Apostles* (New Haven, CT: Yale University Press, 2003); and Dennis MacDonald, 'The Ending of Luke and the Ending of the *Odyssey*', in *For a Later Generation: The Transformation of Tradition in Israel, Early Judaism, and Early Christianity* (ed. Randal Argall, Beverly Bow and Rodney Werline; Harrisburg, PA: Trinity Press International, 2000), pp. 161-68.

172. Extensively demonstrated in Thomas Brodie, *Proto-Luke: The Oldest Gospel Account: A Christ-Centered Synthesis of Old Testament History Modeled Especially on the Elijah–Elisha Narrative: Introduction, Text, and Old Testament Model* (Limerick, Ireland: Dominican Biblical Institute, 2006), and summarized and updated in Brodie, *Beyond the Quest*, pp. 51-76; and Brodie, *Birthing of the New Testament*, pp. 146-88, 282-446. But he is not the only one to have noticed and argued this: see Raymond Brown, 'Jesus and Elijah', *Perspective* 12 (1971), pp. 85-104; and Craig Evans, 'Luke's Use of the Elijah/Elisha Narratives and the Ethic of Election', *Journal of Biblical Literature* 106 (1987), pp. 75-83.

Lk. 1.5-17 reverses 1 Kgs 16.29–17.1.[173]
Lk. 7.1-10 transforms 1 Kgs 17.1-6.[174]
Lk. 7.11-17 transforms 1 Kgs 17.17-24.[175]
Lk. 7.18-25 transforms 1 Kgs 22.[176]
Lk. 7.36-50 plays on 2 Kgs 4.1-37.[177]
Lk. 8.1-3 plays on 1 Kgs 18.[178]
Lk. 9.51-56 transforms 2 Kgs 1.1–2.6.[179]
Lk. 9.57-62 transforms 1 Kgs 19.[180]
Lk. 10.1-20 transforms 2 Kgs 2.16-3.27.[181]
Lk. 22–24 adapts elements from 2 Kgs 2.7-15.[182]

To illustrate what I mean, I'll focus on two examples from this list which typify the rest.

In Lk. 7.11-17 we learn of a new story not found in Matthew or Mark, the healing of the Widow's Son at Nain. This story is already intrinsically dubious. The elements of drama and the miraculous in it are typical of fictions, not realities, and this kind of story was a trope at the time—essentially the same tale is told of the medical doctor Asclepiades by Apuleius a few decades later, and similar tales were referenced by Pliny the Elder before Luke even put pen to paper.[183] It has the air of an urban legend, a standard tale retold a dozen times of different people in different places, but always coincidentally the same improbable story that we conveniently never hear of from an eyewitness. But what further demonstrates this particular version of the tale is a fiction is that it is just a rewrite of the same legend told of Elijah in the first book of Kings. Here are the parallels, all of which Luke literarily modifies, merges, or improves in various ways:

173. Brodie, *Birthing of the New Testament*, pp. 284-89.
174. Brodie, *Birthing of the New Testament*, pp. 291-301.
175. Brodie, *Birthing of the New Testament*, pp. 302-11.
176. Brodie, *Birthing of the New Testament*, pp. 312-24.
177. Brodie, *Birthing of the New Testament*, pp. 325-38.
178. Brodie, *Birthing of the New Testament*, pp. 339-45.
179. Brodie, *Birthing of the New Testament*, pp. 347-58.
180. Brodie, *Birthing of the New Testament*, pp. 359-64.
181. Brodie, *Birthing of the New Testament*, pp. 365-76.
182. Brodie, *Birthing of the New Testament*, pp. 377-82.
183. Apuleius, *Florida* 19; Pliny the Elder, *Natural History* 7.176-179 and 26.15. See also Philostratus, *Life of Apollonius of Tyana* 4.45; Aulus Cornelius Celsus, *On Medicine* 2.6.15; Diogenes Laertius, *Lives of Eminent Philosophers* 8.67-8.

1 Kings 17.10 and 17.17-24	Luke 7.6 and 7.11-17
It happened after this . . . (17.17)	It happened afterwards . . . (7.11)
At the gate of Sarepta, Elijah meets a widow (17.10).	At the gate of Nain, Jesus meets a widow (7.11-12).
Another widow's son was dead (17.17).	This widow's son was dead (7.12).
That widow expresses a sense of her unworthiness on account of sin (17.18).	A centurion (whose 'boy' Jesus had just saved from death) had just expressed a sense of his unworthiness on account of sin (7.6).
Elijah compassionately bears her son up the stairs and asks 'the Lord' why he was allowed to die (17.13-14).	'The Lord' feels compassion for her and touches her son's bier, and the bearers stand still (7.13-14).
Elijah prays to the Lord for the son's return to life (17.21).	'The Lord' commands the boy to rise (7.14).
The boy comes to life and cries out (17.22).	'And he who was dead sat up and began to speak' (7.15).
'And he gave him to his mother', *kai edōken auton tē mētri autou* (17.23). The widow recognizes Elijah is a man of God and that 'the word' he speaks is the truth (17.24).	'And he gave him to his mother', *kai edōken auton tē mētri autou* (17.15). The people recognize Jesus as a great prophet of God and 'the word' of this truth spreads everywhere (7.16-17).

Table 9. Brodie Thesis for Luke 7 Adapting 1 Kings 17

The giveaway is Luke's use of the exact same clause, verbatim, as the Septuagint text of the Elijah story, 'and he gave him to his mother', every word identical and in identical order. This fact, combined with all the other obvious parallels, indicates that literary borrowing has occurred. The links are simply too improbable otherwise.

Even some of the differences are too coincidental to be probable as anything but a deliberate transformation of the emulated tale. There are many respects, in fact, in which Luke sees himself as 'improving' on the original story. For example, Thomas Brodie observes that with several of the changes Luke makes 'there is a fundamental change' in the message the story conveys:

> Whereas in the Old Testament text the sense of sinfulness leads to a kind of despair, to an idea that (the man of) God is a bothersome visitor who comes to punish with death, in the New Testament text the sense

> of unworthiness is combined with a profound faith—with an immense reverence for the [Lord] . . . [and] also with a clear conviction that despite one's unworthiness the [Lord] comes to heal, to save from the encroachment of death. In other words, the Old Testament picture of God visiting the sin of a mother on her child is replaced by the New Testament image of the life-giving [Lord] as looking not on one's unworthiness but on one's faith.[184]

Likewise, while the OT version suggests 'that the Lord is the author of evil, the one who brings harm to the widow (1 Kgs 17.20)', the NT version suggests God is the one who comforts and heals instead (Lk. 7.7).[185] And so on.[186]

In the case of Lk. 9.51-56 emulating 2 Kgs 1.1–2.6 there are even more direct verbatim and near-verbatim lifts of Greek from the Septuagint as well as numerous parallels and deliberate changes and reversals. And both accounts have the same five-part structure: a plan of death and assumption into heaven (2 Kgs 1.1-6; 1.15-17; and 2.1; Lk. 9.51), a sending of messengers (2 Kgs 1.2; Lk. 9.52), the messengers being turned back (2 Kgs 1.3-6; Lk. 9.53), mention of calling down fire from heaven upon those who rejected them (2 Kgs 1.7-14; Lk. 9.54-55), then journeying from one place to another (2 Kgs 2.2-6; Lk. 9.56). Luke is thus expanding on Matthew and Mark by adding made-up stories rewritten from the OT. As Brodie explains:

> Such similarities are striking, particularly when they occur in essentially the same order. What is doubly striking, however, is that three of the five sections [the first, second, and fourth] contain elements that are unique in the entire (Greek) Bible. Nowhere else save in these passages does one find a picture of *someone setting off for assumption*, a combining of 'and *he sent messengers*' with [the Greek word] *poreuomai*, and an image of *calling down fire from heaven*. In addition to these unique similarities are other significant similarities of detail, some of them intriguing.
>
> The differences are great. In comparison with Luke, the Old Testament text is long and repetitive. Furthermore, it involves not just one main character but two: King Ahaziah and Elijah. And it sets the image of departing for assumption not at the beginning of the death-related episode, but after its conclusion. However, though the differences are indeed great, they are not jumbled or incoherent, at odds with one another and with all known literary procedures. On the contrary, they correspond to steady patterns of adaptation such as modernization, abbreviation, fusion, and emulation—patterns which are common both in general imi-

184. Brodie, *Birthing of the New Testament*, pp. 302-304; table adapted from p. 302.

185. Brodie, *Birthing of the New Testament*, p. 304.

186. Brodie's analysis goes on to highlight the obvious rationale behind the many changes Luke makes, but the differences are partly the point (they are made on purpose) and partly just a common effect of creativity (a talented author does not slavishly duplicate but transforms and varies a literary tale).

> tation and in other instances where Luke imitates the Old Testament. Since these differences may be explained through the procedures of imitation, they may not be invoked to prove that imitation was not used.[187]

Not only did Luke lift story ideas from the Kings narratives. He also emulated several other OT books.[188] Luke's nativity story for John the Baptist is in part based on the nativity of Samson told in the *Biblical Antiquities*, an anonymous first-century elaboration on the Bible.[189] Mary's song (now often called the Magnificat) in Lk. 1.46-55 is based on Hannah's song in 1 Sam. 2.1-10.[190] Even the names he selects have rather convenient literary meanings: Elizabeth means 'God's promise', and Zechariah means 'God has remembered'. Thus, it is rather conspicuous that Mary's song of praise references both God's remembering and promising ('He has helped his servant Israel, in *remembrance* of his mercy, according to the *promise* he made to our ancestors', Lk. 1.54-55). Which is the fabrication? The song, or the names of John's parents? Probably both.

Luke's literary structure is more *ad hoc* than Matthew's or Mark's, because he is attempting to interweave so many components. Many scholars have found evidence of literary structures in Luke that are occasionally interrupted with additional material, suggesting what may be the haphazard expansion of sources (or an earlier version of Luke's text) that were even more obviously fictional.[191] For example, Brodie has identified a conspicuous structure in the material borrowing from the Elijah–Elisha narrative, making an eight-part diptych, which could be proof that Luke

187. Brodie, *Birthing of the New Testament*, pp. 357-58 (summarizing his complete analysis on pp. 251-58). On the Bayesian confirmation that Brodie's reasoning is correct, see Carrier, *Proving History*, pp. 192-204.

188. For many examples of possible OT sources for material in Luke–Acts see the footnotes throughout Price, *Pre-Nicene New Testament*, pp. 499-562 (some of the suggested links here are more speculative, but others are more definite). More importantly see Brodie, *Birthing of the New Testament*, pp. 448-537; and Thomas Brodie, 'Re-Opening the Quest for Proto-Luke: The Systematic Use of Judges 6–12 in Luke 16:1–18:8', *Journal of Higher Criticism* 2 (Spring 1995), pp. 68-101. Other examples include the fact that Luke portrays Jesus as the new temple by echoing elements of the birth of the temple in 1 Chronicles 21–22 in elements of the birth of Jesus in Lk. 2.1-20 (including the role of an imperial decree).

189. See D.J. Harrington, 'Pseudo-Philo', in *Dictionary of New Testament Background* (ed. Craig Evans and Stanley Porter; Downers Grove, IL: InterVarsity Press, 2000), pp. 864-68 (866). The Samson story is told in *Bib. Ant.* 42.

190. John Court (ed.), *New Testament Writers and the Old Testament: An Introduction* (London: SPCK, 2002), pp. 21-22.

191. See Craig Blomberg, 'Midrash, Chiasmus, and the Outline of Luke's Central Section', in *Gospel Perspectives* (ed. R.T. France and David Wenham; Sheffield: JSOT Press, 1983), III, pp. 217-61; Barbara Shellard, *New Light on Luke: Its Purpose, Sources, and Literary Context* (New York: Sheffield Academic, 2002), pp. 85-147.

used a source, a previous Gospel unrelated to the others that was fabricated to make Jesus into the new Elijah.[192] For example, the first section of eight consists of Jesus' infancy narrative, which has the two-part (diptych) structure of 'annunciations—births'. Yet even that structure is composed of further diptychs: John's birth is foretold (Lk. 1.5-25), then John is born (Lk. 1.57-80); Jesus' birth is foretold (Lk. 1.26-38), then Jesus is born (Lk. 2.1-14). Then another diptych of 'visits' is formed with numerous parallel elements: Mary is visited by an angel, then journeys to Judah, meeting Elizabeth, an old woman who breaks into prophecy (Lk. 1.39-56; cf. 1.7), and then circumcises and names her own child (John) on the eighth day after his birth (Lk. 1.57-59), a sequence repeated again when shepherds are visited by an angel and visit Mary, then Mary journeys to Jerusalem, meeting Anna, an old woman who breaks into prophecy (Lk. 2.15-52), and Mary circumcises and names her own child (Jesus) on the eighth day after his birth. Each of the three diptychs is increasingly more complex than the last, but all fit within the overarching diptych of 'annunciation, birth' (ending with circumcision), but doubled (one sequence for John, one for Jesus, with the third diptych establishing the theme of Jesus' supremacy to John). Throughout, the continuous theme is obedience to the law. Similar structures track all of Luke's lifts from the Kings narratives, such that if one extracted those from the rest of Luke–Acts one has a very elegant and consistent repeating diptych structure. Brodie argues that that would be unlikely unless these tales originally existed together, and Luke only broke them apart to intersperse them into his narrative.[193]

192. This thesis is elaborately argued, with intriguing tables and analysis, in Thomas Brodie, *Proto-Luke: The First Edition of Luke–Acts: A Christ-Centered Synthesis of Septuagintal Historiography Modeled Especially on the Elijah–Elisha Narrative and Matthew's Logia: A Foundational Arrangement of Gospel Sayings Deuteronomy-Based, Qumranlike (an Alternative to Q)* (Limerick, Ireland: Dominican Biblical Centre, 2002), pp. 5-7; and Brodie, *Proto-Luke: The Oldest Gospel Account*, pp. 146-65. That either Luke or a previous redaction of Luke appears to have also modeled its narrative in sequential agreement with Deuteronomy in order to create, in effect, a 'Christian Deuteronomy', see Brodie, *Birthing*; MacDonald, *Two Shipwrecked Gospels*; and C.F. Evans, 'The Central Section of St. Luke's Gospel', in *Studies in the Gospels: Essays in Memory of R.H. Lightfoot* (ed. D.E. Nineham; Oxford: Basil Blackwell, 1955), pp. 37-53.

193. Luke often creates dispersed diptychs (see Chapter 9, §1, for example), so that might have simply been the way he composed. I am thus not here affirming Brodie's theory is correct, only that it is worth examining; although even if *incorrect*, his same evidence confirms Luke's compositional style as one of creating paired events even if not adjacent to each other. Which is evidence of fiction either way. Note that this same observation applies to all other studies (per earlier note) that find structure in Luke but are then uncertain because it is interrupted: interrupting structure appears to be particularly Lukan, which means either the structure comes from better-organized

But even if we accede to that hypothesis, it then only confirms the same point: that Luke is not writing history, but myth. He or his sources are simply making everything up. His tales are told for their meaning and rhetorical effect, not because they were researched or came from witnesses. I'll close with one more example of this, the Emmaus narrative of Luke 24, a resurrection-appearance tale found in no other Gospel and thus distinctive of Luke's style of invention. Here Luke tells the story of a man named Cleopas (along with an unnamed friend) who journeys by road from Jerusalem to nearby Emmaus, after they learn the corpse of Jesus has vanished. On the way, the resurrected Jesus appears to them (albeit in disguise) and explains the secrets of the kingdom (which happens to be a spiritual kingdom, not a physical one), then vanishes, and Cleopas recognizes who he was and goes on to proclaim what he was told. Conveniently, the name Cleopas means 'tell all', in other words, 'proclaim'.[194] The story thus has several telltale markers of myth: a name invented or selected for its meaning to the tale rather than any historical truth; an absurdly ahistorical narrative (never heard of from any earlier source) of a disguised divine visitor; an unrealistic conversation with a complete stranger; a miraculous vanishing; and an all-too-convenient rhetorical purpose for all of it. This is the Vanishing Hitchhiker legend—ancient Roman style.[195]

mythic texts that Luke has added to, or Luke constructed his own organization and then edited-in more material. Fiction, either way. That Luke appears to have been multiply redacted may have significance here (see note in Chapter 7, §4); like John (see §7), our text of Luke may have undergone numerous editorial stages.

194. *Kleopas* is occasionally claimed to be a contraction of *Kleopatros* (which means 'renowned father'), but there is no need of that hypothesis when the apposite meaning is clear: the deliberate combination of *kleo* (glory, fame, report) and *pas* (all, everything). There are few precedents for such a name, as a contraction or otherwise. It thus appears to be Luke's invention. In extant literature, *Kleopas* as a name is mentioned only later by the second-century grammarian Aelius Herodianus (*Definitions* 64); but he does not identify it as a contraction of *Kleopatros*, and he doesn't identify anyone as actually having that name (sometimes hypothetical examples appear in Aelius). Aelius says that 'every phrase deriving from the syllable *kle* is written with a bare epsilon, e.g., *kleos*, as in *doxa* [i.e. glory/opinion/reputation], and *kletzō*, in speaking, as in *doxazō* [i.e. to extol], and the following proper names derive from the same word: *Kleon*, *Kleonikos*, *Kleopatros*, and *Kleopas*'. Thus, we should infer that *Kleōn*, from *Kleo* + *os*, means Glorious, Reputable, Extolled; *Kleonikos*, from *Kleo* + *nikos*, means Famous Victory; *Kleopatros* = *Kleo* + *patros*, means Renowned Father; and so *Kleopas*, from *Kleo* + *pas* = All Glorious, Everywhere Famed, Proclaiming All.

195. The 'vanishing hitchhiker' is a commonly replicated ghost story found in many forms across several centuries: for a good summary see the Wikipedia entry for 'Vanishing hitchhiker' (http://en.wikipedia.org/wiki/Vanishing_hitchhiker) and for scholarly analysis see Jan Harold Brunvand, *The Vanishing Hitchhiker: American Urban Legends and their Meanings* (New York: Norton, 1981). For an analogous oft-

As it happens, the founding myth of Rome, then famously known everywhere and celebrated in annual passion plays, is almost the exact same story: a man named Proculus (archaic Latin for 'Proclaimer' or 'He Who Proclaims', thus not only again a fictional name designed for the story but essentially the same name as Cleopas) journeys by road from nearby Alba Longa to Rome, after the Roman people learn the corpse of Romulus has vanished; and on the way, the resurrected Romulus appears to him (*not* in disguise but this time in glorious form) and explains the secrets of the kingdom (literally: how to conquer and rule the world), then ascends into heaven (as Luke eventually has Jesus do as well), and Proculus recognizes who he was and goes on to proclaim what he was told. I've already demonstrated the extent to which the Gospels have borrowed this Romulan resurrection tale for Jesus (see Chapter 4, §1, and Element 47). Mark had already fashioned his passion account in light of it, and Matthew embellished it even more in accord. So it is not unexpected that Luke would take the same model further.

And indeed he has. Not only in the ways I have already pointed out in previous chapters but also here, in the tale of Cleopas on the road to Emmaus. If we accept the identification of Luke's intended Emmaus as the Ammaus mentioned by Josephus as a town nearby Jerusalem, then in both Luke's narrative and the Romulan tale the Proclaimers are journeying *from* a city on a mountain *to* a city in a valley, roughly the same direction (east to west, like the sun), and roughly the same distance (seven to twelve miles).[196]

replicated ghost story (the revenant lover), which illustrates the general features of such legends (such as the presence of details designed to make the story sound authentic; you simply cannot claim the Emmaus story 'rings true' until you notice how all ghost legends do), see William Hansen, *Phlegon of Tralles' Book of Marvels* (Exeter, UK: University of Exeter Press, 1996), pp. 68-85 (where he shows the story was later recast in early modern Ireland, complete with all the same details aimed at authenticity, only altered to sound authentic to its new setting, thus illustrating how legends actually get composed).

196. Josephus, *Jewish War* 7.217, which says soldiers were stationed in the 'region' (*chōrion*) called *Ammaous,* thirty stadiums from Jerusalem (roughly three and a half miles); Luke says the town was sixty stadiums distant (roughly seven miles: Luke 24.13), although some manuscripts add *hekaton*, giving a result of 160 stadiums (roughly eighteen miles, e.g., in Codex Sinaiticus); cf. Swanson, *New Testament Greek Manuscripts . . . Luke*, p. 409. It seems more likely, but not certain, that the *hekaton* was accidentally dropped than that it was added; in fact it could have been removed deliberately, since a 60-stadium distance could be crossed twice in a day (as Luke's story requires) while a 160-stadium distance could not—in fact that would take nearly three days in all—so a scribe who realized the story was impossible may have removed the 100 stadiums to restore its plausibility. An original reading of 160 stadiums would be almost exactly the actual distance from Jerusalem to Nicopolis, later identified as Emmaus (and even later known as Imwas), although some scholars

But the changes are the point. While Proculus receives his gospel on the road *to* Rome, Cleopas receives his gospel on the road *from* Jerusalem: so while the old story suggests 'all roads lead to Rome', the new story suggests all roads lead *from* Jerusalem. While Romulus appears in awesome glory, befitting the awesome glory of Rome's dominion and the very visible empire he promises, Jesus appears in disguise, hidden, just as the kingdom he promises is hidden, and which, like Jesus, becomes visible (and thus knowable) only in the communion of believers. Luke has thus transvalued the Romans' founding myth: unlike the Romans, *their* resurrected hero promises a *hidden* spiritual kingdom originating from Jerusalem on high. And just as the glorious visage of Romulus is what confirmed to Proculus that what he said was true, so it is the powerful *word* of the gospel that confirms to Cleopas that what *Jesus* said was true. Luke thus rewrites the story to communicate how Christian values differ from mainstream Roman values.[197] This is a classic hallmark of mythmaking (as we saw in the example from Homer and Virgil in §2).

Evidence that Luke fabricated the Emmaus narrative also lies not only in how thoroughly it is written in Lucan style (its vocabulary and syn-

argue this may have been why the *hekaton* was added. Whatever its distance, Luke may have intended it to be the same Ammaus mentioned as situated in Judea in 1 Macc. 3.39-40 (although Luke might not have written Emmaus at all, as I'll soon discuss). On identifying the location of Emmaus see Hershel Shanks, 'Emmaus: Where Christ Appeared', *Biblical Archaeology Review* 38 (March/April 2008), pp. 41-51, 80; E.H. Scheffler, 'Emmaus—A Historical Perspective', *Neotestamentica* 23 (1989), pp. 251-67; J.H. Landau, 'Two Inscribed Tombstones', *Atiqot* 11 (1976), pp. 89-91; Joachim Wanke, *Die Emmauserzählung: Eine redaktionsgeschichtliche Untersuchung zu Lk 24, 13-35* (Leipzig: St.-Benno-Verlag, 1973); F. Spadafora, 'Emmaus: Critica testuale e archeologia', *Rivista biblica italiana* 1 (October–December 1953), pp. 255-68. See also Steve Reece, 'Seven Stades to Emmaus', *New Testament Studies* 48 (January 2002), pp. 262-66, for even more obscure variant readings in this passage.

197. For more on the Romulus parallels and reversals in the Emmaus narrative see Arnold Ehrhardt, 'The Disciples of Emmaus', *New Testament Studies* 10 (January 1964), pp. 182-201 (194-95); and Francis Gerald Downing, 'A Rival to Romulus', in *Doing Things with Words*, pp. 133-51. An intriguing thesis has also been advanced that Luke has further crafted this narrative to reverse the Garden of Eden story (Adam and Eve, whose eating shared food inaugurates death and sin, is corrected by Cleopas and his companion, whose eating shared food signals an end to death and sin—Jesus replacing the Serpent and thus setting right what the Serpent had set wrong): see Jean Magné, 'The Emmaus Disciples and Adam and Eve in Paradise', in *From Christianity to Gnosis and from Gnosis to Christianity: An Itinerary through the Texts to and from the Tree of Paradise* (Atlanta, GA: Scholars Press, 1993), pp. 41-51. This thesis is bolstered by N.T. Wright, *The Resurrection of the Son of God* (Minneapolis, MN: Fortress Press, 2003), pp. 652; and Frédéric Manns, 'Quelques variantes du Codex Bezae de Luc 24', *Liber annuus* 55 (2005), pp. 131-39.

tax is entirely his) but also in how well it is crafted to echo Luke's opening chapters (Luke 1–2), which means Luke must have created it for that purpose.[198] N.T. Wright identifies parallels throughout, but most strongly in the concluding tale of Lk. 2.40-50 (echoed throughout Lk. 24.13-33), where we have 'another Passover, another Jerusalem visit' and another 'couple beginning their journey away from Jerusalem', either discovering or mistakenly believing 'that Jesus was not with them'. Both couples are distraught at having lost Jesus, and both quickly return to Jerusalem when the pivotal plot point is discovered (when Cleopas and his companion discover Jesus is present; or when Mary and Joseph discover Jesus is absent). Mary and Joseph find Jesus 'after three days' (Lk. 2.46), and so do Cleopas and his companion (Lk. 24.21). In both accounts Jesus asks what they are doing ('why are you looking for me?' / 'what are you talking about?'), and explains scripture to those present, and says 'it is necessary' for him to have done what he did ('it's necessary [*dei*] for me to be among the things of my father' / 'it's necessary [*dei*] for the messiah to suffer these things').[199] Both stories also feature the theme of people not understanding what has happened, and both feature a disappearance of Jesus. And both, despite being far too remarkable for any previous Gospel to omit, suddenly appear for the first time in Luke. It's obvious he invented them both, deliberately in imitation of each other.

Notably in accord with this, at Lk. 24.13, the often-intriguing Codex Bezae has this whole event occur not at Emmaus (spelled Ammaous in other treatises of the period) but at Oulammaous.[200] This is a name that appears uniquely in the Septuagint narrative of Jacob (Israel) searching for a wife (Gen. 28.19), immediately after which he meets and marries Rachel (Gen. 29), who would give birth to the last two tribes of Israel (Joseph and Benjamin). Oulammaous is there identified as the original name of the village of Luz, which Jacob here renames Bethel ('God's House', even translated as such, *oikos theou*, in the Septuagint), which is metaphorically also where Jesus is 'found' after 'three days' in the matching couple-on-a-road-from-Jerusalem story in Luke, that being the most obvious meaning of his cryptic remark at Lk. 2.49, and considering where he was (2.46)—and so most Bibles today indeed translate him as saying he had to be in his father's 'house'. Oulammaous is the more difficult reading here (being

198. Lucan style: Scheffler, 'Emmaus', pp. 257-58. Emulation of Luke 1–2: N.T. Wright, *Resurrection*, pp. 649-51.

199. Wright, *Resurrection*, p. 649.

200. I owe this observation to Sylvie Chabert d'Hyères (see http://codexbezae.perso.sfr.fr/comm/oulam_en.html), although it has also been noted and discussed in Manns, 'Quelques variantes du Codex Bezae de Luc 24', who in turn cites several other scholars who have analyzed this variant and its significance.

otherwise so strange) and cannot have been accidental—since the name is uniquely found in the Septuagint, and in a story with meaningful parallels, and thus can only have arrived in this Lucan verse deliberately.[201] It is therefore arguably the original.[202]

The significance of this allusion to Gen. 28.19 is that this is the account of Jacob's ladder (Gen. 28.10-22), which links all this to the epiphany of the shepherds in Luke, where also a hoard of angels descend and ascend (Lk. 2.8-15); it is also where Jacob blesses the stone he slept on, declaring 'this stone, which I have set up for a pillar, shall be God's House' (Gen. 28.22, hence the name Bethel). Bethel is also where Jacob is (again) renamed Israel and promised he'd father an eternal kingdom (thus beginning the first vision of Israel as a nation).[203] It is also where 'Israel' was traveling from when Rachel died in labor bearing Benjamin, completing the last of the twelve tribes of Israel—just outside Bethlehem, exactly where Jesus would be born (Gen. 35; Jacob had first met Rachel on *his* way from Bethel, and she later dies on *her* way from Bethel). And from Jerusalem, Bethel happens to be on the road to Galilee.[204] Since Luke (24.13, 29, 33) assumes it is possible to get there in a day (and back again by midnight), this would then have to be the very same town where Jesus' parents stopped and returned to find the missing Jesus (Lk. 2.44-45), further linking these two stories (beyond all the other parallels I noted earlier). So Jesus' parents stop at 'God's House' and return to find Jesus in God's House; and both couples

201. The reading of *Oulammaous* in the Septuagint is attested in Justin Martyr, *Dialogue with Trypho* 58.13 and corroborated in Eusebius, *Onomasticon* 40.21; modern editions of the Septuagint read *Oulammlouz*, an evident corruption or variant. Codex Alexandrinus reads *Oulammaus*.

202. It is common in textual criticism to conclude that the *lectio difficilior* ('the more difficult reading') is more likely original, since accidents are unlikely to produce it and there are fewer motives to make such a change deliberately. Scribes not understanding it must have assumed the '*Oul-*' was a corruption and dropped it to leave *Ammaous* (a far-better-known town, in both Josephus and 1 Maccabees), which then was modified or corrupted into *Emmaous*. Note that in Codex Bezae (which dates c. 400 CE), the parallel Latin text reads *Ulammaus*, so the reading of *Oulammaous* in the Greek was even acknowledged by the translator.

203. There are two contradictory stories of how, when and where Jacob was renamed Israel: Gen. 32.28 (where he famously wrestles an angel) and here, Gen. 35.10; the two verses are almost identically worded, yet attached to completely different stories that show no awareness of each other.

204. If *Oulammaous* was the original reading, then the shared direction of travel with the Romulus narrative is north, not west (the road to Rome runs northwest from Alba Longa, so either could have been intended), since Bethel is north of Jerusalem. The distance from Jerusalem to Bethel was believed at the time to be 96 stadiums (12 Roman miles according to Eusebius), which is roughly in between the variant Lucan readings of 60 and 160 stadiums.

'find' Jesus in 'God's House' (Mary and Joseph in the Jerusalem temple, where the old Israel ends; and Cleopas and his companion in Bethel, where the old Israel began). This does not seem a likely coincidence. Someone understood the connections between Luke 24 and Luke 2 and made them even more elegant and complete by renaming the town. The original author is the most likely candidate for such an achievement.

Whether we grant the variant reading of Codex Bezae or not, it's still clear Luke created his Emmaus narrative to echo (and in a sense 'complete') his previous 'lost boy' narrative. That Luke was fond of this story-model is also evident from the fact that he reuses it in Acts to create the meeting between Philip and the Ethiopian eunuch (Acts 8.26-40), which also occurs on a road journey 'from Jerusalem' to another town, also features an overt mention of an ignorance of scripture and a question ('Do you understand what you are reading?' matches 'What are you discussing?') and a consequent explanation of the gospel from scripture, a request for the 'interpreter' to stay longer, a featured 'sacrament' (in this case, baptism; in the Emmaus narrative, it's the Lord's Supper), an apostolic 'opening' (Cleopas's eyes are 'opened' to see the truth; Philip's mouth is 'opened' to reveal the truth), and the sudden disappearance of the 'interpreter' (in this case Philip, who inexplicably vanishes in the midst of the sacrament being performed, just as Jesus does in the Emmaus tale).[205] This is another unbelievable yarn, yet it obviously deliberately adapts the same storyline as the Emmaus tale. Both are fictions.

I mentioned the additional evidence of the variant reading of Oulammaous here because it has another significance, which is to illustrate the general point (applicable to all the Gospels) that we often cannot trust modern reconstructions of the original text of the Gospels (especially Luke–Acts, as noted in Chapter 7, §4; and John, as we'll see shortly). They are always to some extent hypothetical; the Gospels could easily have said different things in their original composition, and scholars admit as much for many specific verses already. We just saw it's likely Codex Bezae preserves the original text of Luke here, and that this story was probably said to have taken place not at Emmaus but in fact Oulammaus—in other words, Bethel.

This same Codex Bezae may preserve *other* original readings, as it contains several variants like this that reflect a clearer consciousness of literary structure in Luke's stories—which is, again, a phenomenon more

205. See I.H. Marshall, *The Gospel of Luke: A Commentary on the Greek Text* (Exeter: Paternoster, 1978), p. 890. Note also that in the scripture quoted (Isa. 53.7) the Lord does not 'open his mouth' (*anoigei to stoma autou*) but then Philip the apostle 'opens his mouth' (*anoixas . . . to stoma autou*), Acts 8.32 vs. 8.35; similarly in the Emmaus narrative Cleopas's eyes are 'opened' (*dianoigō*), and then he realizes Jesus had 'opened' the scriptures to him (*dianoigō*), Lk. 24.31 vs. 24.32.

likely to come from the original author than a later copyist.[206] For example, its text makes Peter's escape from prison in Acts more clearly echo God's departing from the Jerusalem temple.[207] The same is then accomplished by Bezae's Luke making the stone blocking Jesus' tomb require 'twenty men' to open, just as Josephus had said of the door to the Jerusalem temple—which he says opened of its own accord one midnight to signal God's departure from Jerusalem—an allusion that turns Jesus' departing the tomb into a symbol of God's thereby departing the old Jewish regime.[208] The wording is even similar: Josephus says 'barely twenty men' could close it (*molis hup' anthrōpōn eikosi*); Luke says it was 'hard for twenty' to roll it (*mogis eikosi* [sc. *anthrōpois*]). This also accords with the evidence that Luke mined Josephus for details to include in his Gospel (noted in Chapter 7, §4), which further argues that this reading was original, as otherwise we must suppose a later scribe knew to *continue* adding details from Josephus, a less likely hypothesis.

Whatever we make of these facts, I have surveyed several examples even from the most widely accepted text demonstrating that Luke is inventing his story, from beginning to end, and not using reliable sources or trying to get at the truth. Even what sources he uses are just previous myths: Mark and Matthew and, at best, other fictional Gospels now lost, with local color added from historians like Josephus who didn't write about Jesus or Christians at all (see Chapter 8, §9). We already verified this conclusion in Chapter 9, demonstrating his extensive fabrication of Acts, so we should not be surprised to find his Gospel similarly compromised. So once again, there is in fact no way to discern what if anything that Luke has added to Mark and Matthew has any historical basis or even a source. And its having a source would still not establish that it's historical; after all, his primary sources, Mark and Matthew, are not demonstrably historical, so why would any of his other, unknown sources be? All his added 'historical color' comes from Josephus and (probably) other now-lost historians, from whom Luke derives nothing about Jesus; and many of his additions (like changes to the nativity or embellishments of the resurrection narrative) are historically implausible and rhetorically all too convenient—some

206. Obviously this won't always be the case. Many variant readings in Codex Bezae are obviously later revisions or corruptions; e.g. it occasionally harmonizes Luke with Matthew by inserting verses from the latter into the former (the most egregious example being half the genealogy).

207. Jenny Heimerdinger, 'The Seven Steps of Codex Bezae: A Prophetic Interpretation of Acts 12', in *Codex Bezae: Studies from the Lunel Colloquium, June 1994* (ed. D.C. Parker and C.B. Amphoux; Leiden: Brill, 1996), pp. 303-10.

208. See Swanson, *New Testament Greek Manuscripts . . . Luke*, p. 404 (Lk. 23.53) and compare Josephus, *Jewish War* 6.292-93.

even come from rewriting the Elijah–Elisha narrative in 1 and 2 Kings. As history, all this entails an improbable plethora of coincidences; but as historical fiction, it's exactly what we'd expect.

The same conclusion must therefore follow for Luke that we reached for Mark and Matthew: nothing in it is any less likely on myth than on historicity. It therefore has no evidential value. The burden is therefore on anyone who would insist there is anything in Luke that is any more authentic than what's in Mark or Matthew. As it is, I deem Luke to be just as fictional, showing a wanton readiness to fabricate, and there are no signs of any genuine interest in historical truth or any real ability to discern it, or any indication he has employed any relevant sources more reliable than Matthew or Mark. Luke's value for determining historicity is therefore nil. Even if any historical facts about Jesus are in it, we have no way to identify them.

7. *The Mythology of John*

John is a free redaction of the previous Gospels. Some maintain he is independent of them, but there is no evidence of that. To the contrary, the evidence is abundant that John knew all three previous Gospels and used them as sources. He simply redacted them more freely, rewriting everything in his own words, which was the more common way ancient writers used sources. In the words of L. Michael White:

> [John's many changes to the Synoptics] may well have been made intentionally and with full awareness of the Synoptic tradition. Several features of the Johannine narrative seem to reflect such an awareness and use of the Synoptic tradition, including direct verbal similarities with distinctive linguistic formulations or narrative elements in Mark and Luke, respectively.[209]

In fact I would say this evidence is adequately conclusive (and that Matthew was also known to John, albeit less used).

For example, John copies Mark's pairing of the feeding of 'five thousand' and Jesus' walking on the water (John 6 thus derives from Mk 6.31-52), in the exact same sequence. Yet as we saw earlier (in §4), this pairing and sequence was a product of Markan literary structure. It also involves absurd events that obviously never really happened. Accordingly, the only likely reason John would connect these same events in the same order is that he is borrowing the whole sequence from Mark. This is also the only likely explanation for why they share so many precise details in common, such as that 'five thousand' were fed (Jn 6.10; Mk 6.44), that exactly 'twelve baskets' of crumbs remained (Jn 6.13; Mk 6.43), that Jesus started with

209. White, *From Jesus to Christianity*, p. 309.

exactly ‘five loaves and two fishes’ (Jn 6.9; Mk 6.41), and that feeding the crowd would otherwise have cost ‘two hundred denarii’ (Jn 6.7; Mk 6.37).[210] John likewise borrows the literary structure of Mark’s narrative of Peter’s denial of Christ (compare Jn 18.15-27 with Mk 14.53-72); and the notion that Jesus once cured a blind man with spit (Jn 9.6 redacts Mk 8.23) but had to back that up with additional magic to get the spell to work (Jn 9.7 re-imagining Mk 8.24-25). And so on.

There are many similar matches between John and material in Luke and Matthew as well.[211] Luke especially. Both John and Luke, and they alone, insert the same new character into the story: Martha, the sister of Mary (Lk. 10.38-42; Jn 11.1–12.2). Both alone have Jesus produce a miraculously vast catch of fish (Lk. 5.1-11; Jn 21.1-4). Both alone claim there was a second Judas among the twelve disciples (Lk. 6.16; Jn 14.22). Both alone claim Judas Iscariot was possessed by Satan (Lk. 22.3; Jn 13.16-27). Both alone report that it was the *right* ear of the high priest’s slave that the disciples chopped off (Lk. 22.50; Jn 18.10). Both alone have Pilate *thrice* declare Jesus innocent (Lk. 23.4, 16, 23; Jn 18.38 and 19.4, 6). Both alone say Jesus was buried ‘where no man had yet been laid’ (Lk. 23.53; Jn 19.41). Both alone have *two* angels seen at his tomb (Lk. 24.4; Jn 20.12). Both alone have the risen Jesus visit the disciples in Jerusalem (not Galilee) and in a room (not outdoors) and show his wounds and share a meal with them (Lk. 24.33-43; Jn 20.18-29; 21.12-13).[212] And so on. John changes and expands many of the things he gets from Luke, but the num-

210. See John Dominic Crossan, ‘Empty Tomb and Absent Lord’, in *The Passion in Mark: Studies on Mark 14–16* (ed. Werner Kelber; Philadelphia, PA: Fortress Press, 1976), pp. 135-52 (esp. 139-44).

211. Despite frequent protestations and a few dissenting opinions, it is now pretty well agreed among experts on John that he knew and redacted both Mark and Luke, and most likely Matthew as well. In addition to the following note, see the additional bibliography in MacDonald, *Two Shipwrecked Gospels*, p. 48 n. 11, and the analysis in Crossan, *Power of Parable*, pp. 218-42, and Louis Ruprecht, *This Tragic Gospel: How John Corrupted the Heart of Christianity* (San Francisco, CA: Jossey-Bass, 2008). For an example of John’s use of Matthew, note that John’s adaptation of the raising of the centurion’s boy (Jn 4.46-53, redacting Mt. 8.5-13, which was also redacted in Lk. 7.1-10) copies two elements from Matthew’s version: the official approaches Jesus directly, rather than through intermediaries, and the word ‘son’ is used instead of ‘boy’ (see Keith Pearce, ‘The Lucan Origins of the Raising of Lazarus’, *Expository Times* 96 [1985], pp. 359-61).

212. See also Carrier, ‘Spiritual Body’, in *Empty Tomb* (ed. Price and Lowder), pp. 191-93 (with notes on pp. 230-31); John Loftus, *Why I Became an Atheist: A Former Preacher Rejects Christianity* (Amherst, NY: Prometheus Books, 2008), pp. 329-32; Price, *Pre-Nicene New Testament*, pp. 665-718. And for scholarship confirming the same see note in Chapter 7 (§4).

ber of coincidences is too great to conclude John isn't simply using Luke as a source, however creatively.

Once we concede John is not independent of the other Gospels but in fact freely using them as sources, we can see that he (or they, as this Gospel appears to have had multiple authors and to have been redacted multiple times) aimed to rebut a theme common to them all: that 'no sign shall be given' that Jesus is the messiah (Mk 8.11-12). Mark had clearly written when no miracles had yet been imagined for Jesus (thus he had to explain this); as Paul says, no signs were given to the Jews that Jesus was the Christ (1 Cor. 1.22-24; see Chapter 12, §4). Hence even when Mark invents miracles to put in his story as allegories, he makes sure no one other than the disciples ever either notices or talks about them or understands them. Even the witnesses of the empty tomb never tell anyone about it (Mk 16.8).

Matthew had already expanded and corrected this by having Jesus say instead that 'an evil and adulterous generation seeks a sign' and therefore 'there shall no sign be given *except* the sign of Jonah' (Mt. 12.39 and 16.4), meaning the resurrection of Jesus. Matthew thus slightly retreats from Mark by allowing one sign—and accordingly, unlike Mark, Matthew actually narrates a resurrected Jesus and makes sure that in his story the Jews 'know' about it (the purpose of Mt. 28.11-15). This was not the case before. Matthew is inventing new evidence. The same point was then reinforced by Luke's repetition of Matthew's expanded revision of Mark (Lk. 11.29) *and* by his invention of the parable of Lazarus (Lk. 16.19-31) and the public announcement to the Jews (Acts 2).

John 'refutes' this entire sentiment by littering his Gospel with explicitly identified 'signs' and by reversing Luke's parable of Lazarus with an actual tale of Lazarus (Jn 11–12), as I'll soon demonstrate. Indeed, John's Jesus fills his ministry with 'signs' that 'manifested his glory', and it is for *this* reason 'his disciples believed in him' (Jn 2.11), a notion not found in the previous Gospels. When Jesus is asked for a sign (Jn 2.17-18), he does not declare, as the other Gospels do, that no sign will be given or that only an evil generation would ask for one; rather, he simply says (albeit cryptically) that his resurrection will be a sign. This is essentially what Matthew and Luke had Jesus say (using a different cryptic metaphor), 'correcting' Mark (who did not even allow the resurrection of Jesus to be a sign; for Mark it only accomplishes Jesus' defeat of death); but John conspicuously does *not* say this will be the *only* sign. To the contrary, he immediately tells us, 'having seen the signs he did, many believed in his name' (Jn 2.23), and 'a great multitude followed him because they beheld the signs he did' (Jn 6.2), and when people 'see the sign he did', they declare him a true prophet (Jn 6.14), and we're told 'no one can do these signs that you do, unless God be with him' (Jn 3.2), and Jesus says, 'you will in no way believe unless you see signs and wonders' and although this is a rebuke, he nevertheless dutifully performs a miracle to provide them one (Jn 4.48-54).

These signs are explicitly said to be the evidence that Jesus is the Christ (Jn 7.31; 9.16; 10.41-42), and the Jewish elite lament the fact that 'he has done many signs' (11.47) and that the people are believing in him because he does these signs (12.18), and we're told that those who didn't believe did so specifically *in spite of* all the signs he did (12.37). And though John narrates (and sometimes numbers) seven or eight especially significant 'signs' (all but one, the turning of water into wine at Cana, are inspired by the previous Gospels: 2.1-11; 4.46-54; 5.1-9; 6.1-14, 15-25; 9.1-8; 11.1-45), he alludes to many others, and says there were even more than he recorded (20.30), and that the ones he did record, he did so for the express purpose of convincing people to believe in Jesus ('but these [signs] were written down, so that you will believe that Jesus is the Christ, the Son of God, and that in believing you may have life in his name', 20.31). And yet, those who believe without seeing signs (like, e.g., John's readers) are said to be the *more* blessed and have an even greater and more admirable faith (20.29).

This obsessive focus on 'signs' (in other words, 'proof') is unique to John and characterizes a lot of what he has done to change up the story, including inventing the most absurd resurrection narrative of all: the Doubting Thomas episode (Jn 20.24-29). The authors of John are thus very keen to create 'proof' and to insist it is this 'evidence' that justifies belief, a concern not thus voiced in the earlier Gospels. This is why John alone invents an eyewitness 'source' (albeit seemingly unnamed, and never heard of before) and claims he has his information from him (Jn 19.35 and 21.24; more on this later), and obsessively talks about who and what bears witness of Jesus—and I mean *obsessive*. John talks about providing evidence ('bearing witness') over thirty-one times, half of those littering three extended discourses on the subject.[213] There is nothing like this in any of the previous Gospels. The authors of John were clearly maniacal on the subject and eager to beat that dead horse to a pulp, thereby 'improving' on the previous Gospels who didn't do this but even badmouthed the whole idea. This also makes John the most ruthlessly propagandistic, and thus the most thoroughly untrustworthy, of all the canonical Gospels.

This is already evident from the rest of the Gospel's content. John's Gospel contains long, implausible, never-before-imagined speeches of Jesus (and yet, no Sermon on the Mount, or indeed hardly any moral instruction of any sort), and entirely new characters and events also never heard of

213. Jn 1.7, 8, 15, 19, 32, 34; 2.25; 3.11; 10.25; 12.17; 15.26-27; 18.37; 19.35; 21.24; and three long discourses: 3.26-33 (five times); 5.31-39 (seven times); 8.13-18 (four times).

before (Nicodemus, Lazarus, Cana). John also changes everything around, such as moving Jesus' clearing of the temple to the beginning rather than the end of his ministry, expanding his ministry from one to three years (with multiple trips to Judea and Jerusalem rather than only one), and moving the date (and thus even the year) of Jesus' execution to make Jesus' death correspond exactly with the slaughter of the Passover lambs (as I noted earlier). John has thus run wild with authorial gluttony, freely changing everything and inventing whatever he wants. By modern standards, John is lying.[214]

A major problem with evaluating what John has done is that we don't have what he originally wrote. We know someone later reorganized the Gospel, putting scenes out of order and adding or subtracting in the process (though we can rarely know what). That the Gospel has been meddled with is already evident from the fact that it has two endings, each of which seemingly ignorant of the other: Jn 20.30-31 and 21.24-25, each concluding different appearance narratives (Jn 21.1 being a hastily added line attempting to stitch them together), a phenomenon that also plagued the Gospel of Mark (which had at least five different known endings).[215] And of course everyone knows that the story of the adulteress (Jn 7.53–8.11, which gave us the famous line, 'let he who is without sin cast the first stone') was added by a later editor. But there is even more evidence the whole document has been corrupted, with material inserted (and possibly deleted) and sections moved around, often sloppily.

214. Though I shall demonstrate this to be the case, recent attempts by Christian apologists to rehabilitate the Gospel of John as of any historical use are already adequately rebutted by James Crossley, 'Can John's Gospel Really Be Used to Reconstruct a Life of Jesus? An Assessment of Recent Trends and a Defence of a Traditional View', in *'Is This Not the Carpenter?' The Question of the Historicity of the Figure of Jesus* (ed. Thomas Thompson and Thomas Verenna; Sheffield: Equinox, 2012), pp. 163-84. See also Maurice Casey, *Is John's Gospel True?* (London: Routledge, 1996).

215. Besides the three endings for Mark sometimes noted in modern Bibles (a conclusion at 16.8, a shorter ending that adds one more verse and a longer ending that adds twenty), there are at least two other known endings (one incorporating an ascension narrative into the empty-tomb narrative and one adding a whole new speech from Jesus in the so-called longer ending). See Richard Carrier, 'Mark 16:9-20 as Forgery or Fabrication', *Hitler Homer Bible Christ*, pp. 231-312 (236-42). As for John, there is Jn 20.19-31 and John 21, and there are arguments for and against either as interpolation and the other as original, complicated by the fact that the redactor who added either may have also added other material throughout the Gospel (e.g. if Jn 20.19-31 is an interpolation, so might 11.16 be). Both 'endings' are redacted from Luke: John 21 redacts Lk. 5.4-10, which is not there a resurrection appearance, and Lk. 24.42; while Jn 20.19-31 redacts Lk. 24.33-48.

For example, in John 5 Jesus goes to Judea (Jerusalem in fact: 5.1) yet in John 6 he is not in Judea (6.1, 24, 59); instead, (in John 5) Jesus is in Jerusalem and then immediately (in Jn 6.1) he 'went off to the other side of the sea of Galilee', but the sea of Galilee is nowhere near Jerusalem, nor even in Judea—clearly, in the original text preceding that verse, Jesus had been in Galilee somewhere on the opposite shore of its sea and not in Jerusalem. The order of events has thus become jumbled. Similarly we're told Jesus is in Jerusalem (2.13, 23) and then that he entered Judea (3.22), but if he was in Jerusalem he was already in Judea. Evidently some mention of his return to Galilee has been moved or (more likely) deleted. Likewise, at one point Jesus concludes a speech by saying to his disciples, 'Arise, let us go from here' (Jn 14.31), but instead of doing that, for no intelligible reason he gives another long rambling speech (spanning three whole chapters: Jn 15–17), and only after that do they depart (Jn 18.1). The last line of chap. 14 and the first line of chap. 18 clearly followed each other in the original text; which means someone inserted this vast speech in between. An even more glaring example is when we're helpfully told that a certain Mary 'was that Mary who anointed the Lord with ointment, and wiped his feet with her hair, whose brother Lazarus was sick' (Jn 11.2), yet that event hadn't happened yet (12.2-3); evidently, originally, the resurrection of Lazarus *followed* the anointing by Mary, but someone reordered the sections and added a new back-reference (12.1) but forgot to delete the original back-reference, or at least to rewrite it so that it looked forward to a future event rather than a past one.[216] Because of all this, and other evidence besides, experts on John's Gospel generally agree it had multiple authors and went through multiple redactions before coming to its present form.[217]

216. See also later note for another example of John's chapters being out of sequence. On these and other examples of disorder in John and what to make of it see Price, *Pre-Nicene*, pp. 666-67; Thomas Cottam, *The Fourth Gospel Rearranged* (London: Epworth Press, 1952); and Dwight Moody Smith, *The Composition and Order of the Fourth Gospel: Bultmann's Literary Theory, with the Greek Text as Rearranged by R.C. Bultmann* (New Haven, CT: Yale University Press, 1965), although these latter reconstructions go too far by assuming John originally matched the Synoptics in sequencing.

217. See note in Chapter 7 (§4). The so-called Egerton Gospel (one of the earliest papyrus fragments of any Christian Gospel we have) may be a piece of an earlier version of John (into which our John has inserted material and moved content around), since it definitely has lines found in John but in a different order and mixed with different material: see Helmut Koester, 'Apocryphal and Canonical Gospels', *Harvard Theological Review* 73 (January–April 1980), pp. 105-30 (see pp. 119-23); and Kurt Ehrland, 'Papyrus Egerton 2: "Missing Link" zwischen synoptischer und johanneischer Tradition', *New Testament Studies* 42 (January 1996), pp. 12-34.

Nevertheless, some evidence of John's original literary artifice has survived this hacking up and reordering and altering of his text. One of the best examples is the brilliantly framed sequence where Jesus travels from Cana to Cana, an adventure (and city) nowhere else mentioned in the other Gospels, although it incorporates one story from them, which John has completely rewritten. This role of Cana is John's invention (as I'll show later), a literary construct meant to illustrate different degrees of faith and what one must do to achieve them. The Gospel begins with a multi-day sequence that has become garbled: John is preaching about the coming Jesus (Jn 1.15-28) and then 'the next day' (1.29) Jesus just suddenly appears, John identifies him, and Jesus begins recruiting disciples and preaching about who he is, and then 'the next day' (1.35) we hear more of the same, and then 'the next day' (1.43) Jesus decides to go to Galilee (evidently, unlike the other Gospels, in John Jesus recruits his principal disciples near the Jordan river in Judea or Perea, not in Galilee or by its sea), so four days have passed and the next day should be the fifth day. Yet now we are told that 'on the third day there was a marriage in Cana of Galilee' that Jesus attended (we're not told why, or who is getting married . . . I suspect those elements may have been deleted). So something might be out of order. But visible structure begins at this point.

The sequence now starts with this miracle at Cana 'on the third day' and ends with another miracle at Cana on *another* third day. That Jesus' second visit to Cana occurs on the third day is discernible from the text: he spends 'two days' with the Samaritans (Jn 4.40, the number of days Jesus would later reside in the land of the dead; he even dies at the very hour that he meets the first Samaritan, at the 'sixth hour', 4.6 deliberately echoing 19.14, thus making his descent into Samaria and return a metaphor for his death and resurrection) and then 'after the two days' (4.43) he went to Galilee, and to Cana in particular, which means it is once again 'the third day' when he arrives at Cana. And so we're told 'he came therefore *again* unto Cana of Galilee, where he made the water wine' (4.46) and performs there 'the second sign that Jesus did' (4.54), the previous miracle at Cana having been the first sign (2.11), thus even reminding us how and where this sequence of events began.

The allusion to Jesus' resurrection 'on the third' day is obvious. It thus frames the whole sequence and is metaphorically represented in his journey through Samaria (on his way from Jerusalem to Cana). But it is most obvious in Jn 2.19, where Jesus' resurrection 'in three days' is made explicit, albeit through a metaphor, which of course is not understood by the Jews. . . . John's readers are thus being warned not to make that same mistake (and miss John's metaphors). That the sequence begins with turning water into wine—a miracle unique to John's Gospel, which is echoed in the fact that water *and blood* run from Jesus' wound at his crucifixion (Jn

2.6-10), another miracle unique to John's Gospel (19.34)—and then ends with a 'resurrection' of a son (Jn 4.47-53, the boy is 'about to die' and yet 'lives' at the word of Jesus) only reinforces the metaphor. The centerpiece of what goes on in between is the speech of John the Baptist explaining it: Jesus is both the bridegroom (3.29), thus echoing the 'wedding' at Cana, and the savior (3.36), thus echoing the subsequent act of 'saving' a child (the official's son). John also says people should believe on Jesus' word alone (3.32-34).

The overall structure of what happens in between this 'sandwich' of appearances at Cana is in fact superbly elegant:

<table>
<tr><td>Traditional context

[features a woman as a mother]</td><td>Jn 2.1-12 — A wedding completed at Cana.
Featuring a mother and her son.
A miracle is requested and fulfilled.
Complete faith in a traditional Jewish context.
Story ends at Capernaum (2.12).</td></tr>
<tr><td rowspan="3">I. Traditional context

[ends with a man]</td><td>A. Jn 2.13-22 — Clearing of the temple.
A miracle is requested and not fulfilled (2.18).
Jesus' words are thrown back at him (2.19 = 2.20).
A question is thus voiced as disbelief (2.20).
A metaphor [of resurrection] is misunderstood (2.19-22)
The temple Jews have no faith.</td></tr>
<tr><td>B. Jn 3.1-21 — Nicodemus the Pharisee.
Jesus is believed because of his miracles (3.1-2).
Jesus' words are thrown back at him (3.3 = 3.4).
A question is thus voiced as doubt (3.4).
A metaphor [of rebirth] is misunderstood (3.3-4).
A 'teacher of the Jews' (3.10) has partial faith.</td></tr>
<tr><td>C. Jn 3.22-36 — John the Baptist.
Jesus is believed because of his word (3.27-34).
Jesus' words are explained; Jesus is the savior (3.35-36).
John has complete faith.</td></tr>
</table>

II. Marginal context *[begins with a woman]*	A. Jn 4.1-15 — The Samaritan woman at Jacob's Well (cf. 4.5-6). A **miracle** is **requested** and **not** fulfilled (4.15). Jesus' words are thrown back at him (4.10, 13-14 = 4.11-12, 15). A **question** is thus voiced as **disbelief** (4.11-12; 4.15 is sarcasm). A **metaphor** [of living water] is misunderstood. The woman has **no** faith.
	B. Jn 4.16-38 — The Samaritan woman reconsiders. Jesus is believed because of his **miracle** (4.16-19). Jesus' words are thrown back at him (4.16 = 4.17). A question is then voiced as **doubt** (4.29). A **metaphor** [of a spiritual messiah] is misunderstood (4.21-25). The Samaritan woman has **partial** faith.
	C. Jn 4.39-42 — The Samaritans of Sychar (cf. 4.5). Jesus is believed because of his **word** (e.g. 4.41). Jesus' words are understood; Jesus is the savior (4.42). The Samaritans have **complete** faith.
Marginal context *[features a man as a father]*	Jn 4.43-53 — A funeral averted at Cana. Featuring a **father** and his **son**. A miracle is **requested** and fulfilled. **Complete** faith in a **marginal** Jewish context. Story **began** at Capernaum (4.46).

Table 10. Structure of the Cana-to-Cana Sequence in John

The parallels are far too numerous and neat to be accidental. They are clearly composed in awareness of each other—even beyond the deliberate connections outlined in the table above. For example, unit II.C presupposes knowledge of what was said in unit I.C, since nothing is said in II.C about what Jesus tells the Samaritans that convinces them—we're simply to understand it is essentially what the Baptist says in I.C, their structural parallel.

John has invented all of this material to make a point, and has designed it all to fit his desired pattern of parables and metaphors: two miracles that parallel and invert each other happening at Cana, and in between two sequences of three conversational narratives, the first of those triads paralleling the second in its development of examples from having no faith, to having partial faith, to having complete faith. We also see the one triad in a traditionally Jewish context, and then the second triad repeating all the same themes in a more marginal context, and alternating the roles of men and women (as we saw Mark once did, in §4).[218]

The two framing events also share structure: each involves an announced 'problem' (running out of wine; an official's son is ill), a 'request' (Jesus is asked to fix the problem), a 'sharp rebuke' (Jesus says something snarky to the one making the request), a 'reaction' (the requester puts complete faith in Jesus), and its 'consequence' (the deed is done: what they believed he could do, he does). The first occurs in a traditionally Jewish context (a Jewish wedding); the second in a marginal one: the 'official', a *basilikos*, was neither surely Jewish nor surely Gentile; being from the court of the Herods, he would have had a dubious status among conservative Jews (as possibly 'not really Jewish', even if he really was). In between we see a similar contrast: Jesus first interacts with traditional Jews, and then Samaritans—who actually were Jews (being a divergent sect of Judaism), but not considered as such by 'traditional' Jews (a marginal status similar to Mormons among Catholics and Protestants today).[219] Thus, John repeats the same literary

218. For an extensive analysis of the structure of these scenes and the intervening sequence (from which I have adapted and expanded my table of parallels and the shared five-fold structure of the two incidents at Cana) see Francis Moloney, 'From Cana to Cana (John 2.1–4.54) and the Fourth Evangelist's Concept of Correct (and Incorrect) Faith', *Salesianum* 40 (October–December 1978), pp. 817-43. Moloney believes that the inserted remarks at 2.23-25 and 4.30-38 (where a metaphor of spiritual food is misunderstood by the disciples) are also part of the structure (Moloney, 'From Cana to Cana', p. 841), but they are too dissimilar and not logically integrated with the surrounding material. John 2.23-25 are about Jesus knowing the minds of men and judging them, a subject that is not any part of the narrative at this point, which is entirely about believing or not believing in Jesus; the transition from 2.22 to 2.23 is thus nonsensical. The transition from 4.38 to 4.39 is likewise illogically abrupt, and the question posed at 4.33 makes no sense in light of the fact that they are supposed to have seen Jesus having just met someone; a clumsy solution to this problem is 4.27, which is a strange addition and otherwise serves no narrative purpose other than to try and fix the problem created by inserting the following conversation. Accordingly, I think it's clear that both 2.23-25 and 4.30-38 are out of place and thus later insertions. Nevertheless, if you disagree, then Moloney shows how they still fit into the structure.

219. Moloney (previous note) believes this is a 'non-Jewish' context and that the sequence treats in balance both Jewish and non-Jewish contexts, but since Samaritans were marginal Jews, and since John deliberately changed the 'centurion' to a 'basilicus' (the long-distance healing of an official's son in Capernaum is obviously a redaction of the long-distance healing of the centurion's son at Capernaum in Matthew 8 and Luke

elements in both traditional and marginal contexts: first, a traditional context (a wedding) followed by another traditional context (temple Jews and John the Baptist), followed by a marginal context (Samaria) that is followed by another marginal context (helping a Herodian official).

Thus, we see elegant literary invention in John just as we saw in the earlier Gospels. Almost certainly the whole Gospel once had a complete and elegant structure throughout, just as we saw Mark and Matthew did. It has simply been lost by later editors reorganizing the text.[220] As also for the other Gospels, John likewise employs the device of inventing his stories by creatively, and meaningfully, rewriting stories (or adapting story ideas) from the OT. The first miracle at Cana, John's only 'new' miracle for Jesus (every other has precedents in the other Gospels), is a perfect example of this.[221] It reifies the Word of God in the book of Exodus, where Aaron 'did the signs in the sight of the people, and the people believed' (Exod. 4.30-31), the basic model for John's entire Gospel. And here in particular, God had told Moses he will give him three signs to perform, such that if they don't believe after the first two signs, they will believe after the last (Exod. 4.1-9). That last miracle God explains to him thus:

> If they will not believe even after these two signs, nor listen to you, then you shall take some of the water from the river, and pour it on the dry ground, and the water that you took out of the river shall become blood upon the ground (Exod. 4.9).

So the last miracle Moses was to perform was to turn water into blood (in other words, water into wine). John has Jesus perform this as his *first* miracle, thus starting where Moses left off, and turning the last into the first.

At the crucifixion, of course, Jesus spews water and blood from his body (Jn 19.34), thus ending his ministry with a reminder of the miracle he started it with, a fact Jesus even alludes to in Jn 2.4, which contains two references to John's crucifixion scene: Jesus references the hour of his death (which like the bridegroom theme is also evoked again in this sequence at 4.6) and the fact that he would no longer be his mother's son (Jn 19.26-27), another addition unique to John (just as is a wound spewing water and blood), proving that John had this in mind and rewrote the crucifixion scene to match his scene at Cana. Indeed the one scene is an antitype of the

7), he clearly avoided a Gentile context and created *another marginal context instead*. Thus, John is paralleling traditional and marginal contexts, not Jewish and Gentile (though the implication may be that Gentiles are likewise a marginal group who can likewise come to faith and salvation).

220. For an attempt to extract its original structure see Ernst Lohmeyer, 'The Structure and Organization of the Fourth Gospel', *Journal of Higher Criticism* 5 (Spring 1998), pp. 113-38.

221. The following analysis summarizes that of Helms, *Gospel Fictions*, pp. 85-88.

other: at Cana his mother gives a command to Jesus, but at the cross Jesus gives a command to his mother; at Cana his mother says to do whatever he says, and at the cross Jesus says what to do; at Cana his mother asks Jesus to give them wine from water, and at the cross he gives them blood with water; at Cana Jesus asks what he has to do with her, and at the cross he says he has nothing to do with her (transferring her kinship); at Cana he says his hour is not yet come, and at the cross it has come. He even repeats the very same Exodus theme: the miracle of the water and blood at the cross occurred 'so that you may believe' (Jn 19.35), exactly as God told Moses would happen. In just the same fashion, from the water miracle at Cana 'the disciples believed in him' (Jn 2.11), therefore so should you.

John is thus simply duplicating the last miracle of Moses. He needed to develop other themes, such as a wedding, to evoke the metaphor of Christ as the bridegroom that he would introduce in this overall sequence (Jn 3.29), a mother-and-son scene to reverse the father-and-son scene he was to conclude with, some way to introduce his desired number symbolism (the number and volume of the pots had some significance now lost to us: Jn 2.6), and to make the features of this tale line up with the one he would close with and to create the message about faith that the whole sequence was designed for, and so on. The result was this fanciful tale. But he also got several of the ideas for it from a similar tale of miraculous provisions told of Elijah in 1 Kgs 17.8-24. There we are also told of a woman and her son—though who in this case are starving to death and expect soon to die (1 Kgs 17.12); and indeed her son approaches death from illness and Elijah must heal him (1 Kgs 17.24), just as Jesus would then save a *man's* son from deadly illness for his *second* miracle at Cana.

As Randel Helms explains:

> One of the most puzzling aspects of this first miracle in the Fourth Gospel is Jesus' rudeness to his mother: 'Woman, what have I to do with you?' [*Ti emoi kai soi, gunai*]. . . . [This] statement is here not a historical report but an antitype of Elijah: for the woman [*gunē*] in need of food says to the prophet, 'What have I to do with you?' [*Ti emoi kai soi*] [1 Kgs 17.18 in the Septuagint] In both stories the prophet instructs those in need of sustenance to take empty pitchers (*hydria* [in the Septuagint text of the Elijah story. 1 Kgs 17.12, 14, 16], *hydriai* [in Jn 2.6]) and remove from them the needed provision, which miraculously appears.[222]

222. Helms, *Gospel Fictions*, p. 86. Note also that when Aaron performs the water-to-blood miracle for the Egyptians, water in 'stone pots' is also transformed (Exod. 7.19); the pots in John's miracle are also made of stone (Jn 2.6). We know later Jewish lore also held that when Moses struck the rock in the wilderness (which rock the Christians equated with Jesus: 1 Cor. 10.4), blood came out at the first blow, and water at the second (*Midrash Tehillim* 105.12; *Shemoth Rabbah* 122; Targum Pseudo-Jonathan, Exod. 17 and Num. 20), but I could not confirm that this belief existed in early

From this, and the healing of her son (the very same two miracles John frames his whole Cana-to-Cana sequence with), the woman concludes Elijah truly is 'a man of God' (1 Kgs 17.24). That both stories copy the exact same unusual phrase ('What have I to do with you?' = *Ti emoi kai soi*), have the same equipment (*hudria* / *hudriai*) and involve essentially the same feat (miraculously appearing sustenance) is a sufficient clue to what John has done.[223] This is a literary construct. It is not history. And it is clear John is well aware of that fact, since he carefully links this miracle with his revised account of the crucifixion and carefully integrates it into his overall Cana-to-Cana structure. Thus, we can know John does not *really* care

Christian times (though that does not mean it didn't). An extensive case has also been made that John's wedding at Cana is modeled after a wedding in Esther 1: Roger Aus, 'The Wedding Feast at Cana (John 2.1-11), and Ahasuerus' Wedding Feast in Judaic Traditions on Esther 1', in *Water into Wine and the Beheading of John the Baptist: Early Jewish-Christian Interpretation of Esther 1 in John 2:1-11 and Mark 6:17-29* (Atlanta, GA: Scholars Press, 1988), pp. 1-37. The parallels are intriguing but inconclusive (it thus remains a possibility, perhaps true but unprovable). Aus also discusses the pagan parallels (of Dionysian pots miraculously producing wine, a frequently performed miracle in ancient temples), pp. 34-37.

223. Why Cana? We can only speculate. No previous Gospel mentions anything ever happening there, whereas John deliberately frames a whole literary sequence with two incredible events there, so the selection of Cana is clearly an invention of John. There was a Cana (Josephus camped there: *Life* 86), but its selection by John was probably mytho-symbolic. The tale of the Syrophoenician woman in Mk 7.25-30 had become the tale of the Canaanite woman (*Kananaia*, nearly the same word that would be used of someone 'from Cana') in Mt. 15.22-28. This was a tale of the faith of a foreign woman earning God's grace (and in which a demon is cast out of the woman's daughter as she requested), which has certain parallels with the Cana-to-Cana sequence in John (which is also about faith earning a reward, and adapts the foreign-woman theme into the encounter with the Samaritan woman; note that John deletes *all* exorcism scenes from Jesus' story). John may have chosen to frame the Samaritan encounter with events at Cana to create a parallel between the beginning, end, *and* middle (the latter to remind us of the woman 'from Cana' in Matthew and its parallel message). Another possibility are certain parallels with Joseph's feats of dream interpretation in Genesis 40, where Joseph interprets the dreams of a 'master of wine' (*archioinochos*) and a 'master breadmaker' (*archisitopoios*), just as John's story features a 'master of the feast' (*architriklinos*), which combines both roles—both stories involve an actual feast where something eventful happens 'on the third day'. In the OT tale Joseph explains to the breadmaster that 'the three baskets' of bread in his dream represent 'three days' (*ta tria kana treis hēmerai:* Gen. 40.18) after which he would be crucified (40.19), while the other of the two men (the winemaster who dreams of creating wine from three vines) will be saved. The word used here for 'baskets' in the Septuagint is *kana* (the plural of *kaneon*), the exact same spelling of the town of Cana (in John: *Kana*).

about history. He is weaving tales—*and passing them off* as history (19.35; 20.31; 21.24).

A key demonstration of this is John's invention of an eyewitness: the seemingly unnamed 'Beloved Disciple' (Jn 21.24; also: 19.35; cf. 19.25-27; and 20.2-8). That he is an invention should already be evident from the fact that he is inserted into the story told by the previous Gospels, which never heard of him. No male disciples are at the cross in any other Gospel (much less told, by Jesus as he hangs on the very cross, to take Jesus' mother in), nor does anyone else run to inspect the tomb (other than Simon Peter in Luke, and even that is a fabrication, since in Mark and Matthew no disciples are even in Jerusalem at the time), nor is anyone resting (a most remarkable thing!) on Jesus' breast at the Last Supper.[224] John has clearly 'inserted' this figure into these stories he inherited from the Synoptics, and then claimed this new character as his 'source' who saw all these things (Jn 21.24). In plain terms, that's simply a lie.

Confirmation of this fact lies in a detail often overlooked: that in fact the Beloved Disciple is *not* unnamed. As Floyd Filson had already famously argued over half a century ago, and as have many others since, it should be obvious that the author of John 'had taken sufficient pains to make clear' that the Beloved Disciple was Lazarus.[225] Only one character in his Gospel

224. Peter running with the Beloved to see the burial cloths in the now-empty tomb (Jn 20.2-8) is most likely adapted from Luke (and this inspired John's use of burial-cloth symbolism here and in his account of the raising of Lazarus). Almost all manuscripts of Luke have Peter running to see the empty tomb and finding the burial cloths within (the *othonia*, Lk. 24.12, as repeated in Jn 20.6-7), and I believe this was indeed in Luke's original, as Luke is the first Gospel to imagine the disciples are present in Jerusalem for the women to report to (in Mark and Matthew the disciples are in Galilee and never receive the women's report), and Lk. 24.12 omits mention of a second disciple (and many other details in John, like the presence of the *soudarion*, the face napkin) and thus is not likely a harmonization with John (the more so as reference to 24.12 is found in 24.24, and a double redaction is unlikely). In fact John repeats several elements from Luke: that there were two angels instead of one (Jn 20.11-12), which only women saw; that Mary reported the empty tomb to the disciples (and wasn't believed); that Jesus appeared in disguise and was only recognized in a special moment (Jn 20.14-18); that the first to recognize the risen Jesus went to report it to the disciples, who were gathered together in a room in Jerusalem; and (if we accept Lk. 24.12), Peter's running to the tomb and finding burial cloths within.

225. Floyd Filson, 'Who Was the Beloved Disciple?', *Journal of Biblical Literature* 68 (June 1949), pp. 83-88 (84); the same conclusion is defended by Pearce, 'The Lucan Origins of the Raising of Lazarus' and many others. For a survey of other scholars arguing the same conclusion (that Lazarus is the Beloved Disciple) see James Charlesworth, *The Beloved Disciple: Whose Witness Validates the Gospel of John?* (Valley Forge, PA: Trinity Press International, 1995), pp. 185-92. Charlesworth himself argues against them, but his arguments are far more feeble, gullible and fallacious—as

is described repeatedly as 'the one whom Jesus loved', and that's Lazarus (Jn 11.3, 5, 36); and right after Lazarus is introduced (and described as Jesus' beloved), he is reclining with Jesus at supper the next day (12.1-2, 9-11). So when we hear that 'the one whom Jesus loved' is reclining with Jesus at the Last Supper as well (13.23-25), the allusion should be obvious. Likewise every other appearance of 'the one whom Jesus loved' (at the crucifixion: 19.26-27, 35; at the empty tomb: 20.2-8; and at the resurrection: 21.7, 20).[226]

This conclusion is only confirmed by the fact that in Jn 21.21-24 we're told the notion had spread that the Beloved Disciple would never die—and there is no reason why such speculation would surround that one disciple unless he was Lazarus, who alone in John's Gospel had undergone resurrection, provoking the question whether he could die a second time.[227] We're also told the Beloved Disciple was the first to see the burial cloths Jesus had cast off in his now-empty tomb—and Lazarus had been wrapped in burial cloths also cast off at *his* resurrection. And so it is he who is the first to believe Jesus had risen (Jn 20.8).[228] In both accounts the peculiar detail of the deathly veil is mentioned (the *soudarion*, a napkin covering the face of the dead), and in both accounts this is distinguished from the burial wrappings, and in both accounts we find references to being bound or unbound by these (as a metaphor for being bound by or freed from death), and in both accounts we're given a vivid picture of these burial wrappings and their disposition.[229]

you can judge for yourself: see the paragraph spanning pp. 187-88, and pp. 288-92. His 'seventh' argument on p. 290 is an absolute howler, and representative of the kind of mindset we're dealing with here: Lazarus can't be the Beloved Disciple because Lazarus could not possibly run faster than Peter (in Jn 20.3-5), since he had recently been resurrected from the dead . . . and we all know people recently miraculously resurrected from the dead are too feeble to outrun anyone (oh no, not even in fiction!). Charlesworth's case for 'Thomas' being meant (the thesis of his whole book) is similarly far weaker than any case that can be made for Lazarus.

226. Lazarus may have been explicitly declared a disciple in a passage since deleted from the original John, but even if not, the Beloved is clearly Lazarus, now discipled.

227. Since John has clearly invented the Lazarus and Beloved storylines, this question about whether he could die again is either an invention of the author to make a point about people raised by Jesus in general (such as in the earlier Gospels), or a later redaction answering a question that had arisen in response to an earlier edition of John (or an anticipation of such).

228. Lazarus also rose from a tomb (Jn 11.38), the only resurrection account in the Gospels in which that was the case, other than the resurrection of Jesus; and although whereas Lazarus was expected to stink of death (Jn 11.39), Jesus was extensively perfumed (Jn 19.39-40).

229. For Jesus we're told 'the linen cloths [*othonia*]' were in the tomb and 'the napkin [*soudarion*] that was upon his head, which was not lying with the linen cloths,

So the Beloved Disciple is Lazarus, who alone is said to be 'the one whom Jesus loved', the one who thereafter reclined with Jesus at meals, whom people thought might have been freed from death forever, and who first recognized Jesus had risen from the dead when he recognized the burial cloths cast off, a fate he and Jesus shared. But this exposes the grand lie of John's Gospel. Because this Lazarus never existed. He therefore cannot have witnessed anything, much less have been John's 'source' for anything. And it is not as if John didn't know this and was just gullibly repeating what he'd read in some earlier now-lost Gospel. For John is clearly the one who invented him.

This is already clear from the fact that no one had ever heard of this Lazarus before (he is completely unknown to Mark, Matthew and Luke), or his incredible resurrection (the most incredible resurrection tale of all told in the Gospels), which are definite signs of fabrication. Indeed, John's invention is even more exposed as a lie by the importance he assigns to this novel event: so famous and integral to the plot is this raising of Lazarus in John's account that according to John the Jews plotted to kill Jesus *because* of the raising of Lazarus, which was converting so many to Jesus (Jn 11.53).[230] This was originally the first occasion their plotting was mentioned in John, since it says it was '*from that day on* that they plotted to kill him', not before; so earlier references in John to this Jewish plotting are now out of their original order.[231] But the point of note here is that this is *not*

but rolled up in one place' (Jn 20.6-7); for Lazarus we're told he walked out of the tomb 'bound hand and foot with grave-clothes [*keiriai*], and his face was bound about with a napkin [*soudarion*]', and Jesus told those present to 'loose him and let him go' (Jn 11.44), verbs that evoke freeing from slavery or prison, just as 'bound' (*dedemenos*) evokes slavery or imprisonment: thus at Jesus' command Lazarus is freed from the bondage of death. Jesus, meanwhile, would free himself.

230. They also plotted to kill Lazarus, presumably to silence his testimony (Jn 12.9-11), even though, we're told, 'it was not lawful' for them 'to put any man to death' (Jn 18.31), a remark that may have been intended to illustrate the crime of the Jews in killing Jesus, rather than to explain why they asked Pilate to do it for them (since killing through an agent would not be any more lawful in God's eyes; and it is not clear that the Jews actually lacked the authority to execute their own).

231. In Jn 5.18 we're told it's because Jesus healed a man on the Sabbath (which in fact was never a crime under Jewish law). But actually it says there that the Jews plotted 'the more' to kill him because of this miracle, indicating that they had started plotting *earlier* (and thus for some other reason), yet this is the first time we hear of it. Evidently this section is out of order and originally followed one of the other references to the Jews plotting to kill Jesus. Then we get references to the Jews plotting to kill Jesus for no stated reason in Jn 7.1, 19-21, 25. Jesus here says he had performed only a 'single' miracle—we're not told which one—but he must mean just one before that particular audience, as many miracles had occurred in this Gospel by now (as is even stated in 7.3, 31), and the one miracle here must mean his miraculous display of knowledge (7.14-

a reason known to any prior Gospel. Yet surely if the raising of Lazarus was so famous and so effective at winning over believers that it was the very reason the Jews arranged to kill Jesus, those prior Gospels cannot possibly have *not known* of it. It is thus more than evident that John has invented this story and completely rewritten history to suit his own peculiar emphasis on 'signs' having proved Jesus was the messiah.

The final proof of this is the fact that John has invented this Lazarus tale to reverse and thus 'refute' Luke's parable of Lazarus.[232] The reification of imaginary people into real people is a major marker of mythmaking. And here we have just that. There is in fact only one other mention of any Lazarus in the Gospels: the *fictional* Lazarus in a parable told by Jesus in Lk. 16.19-31 (both facts are astonishing given that Lazarus was the third most common male Jewish name). Luke is the first to have Jesus tell that parable, and it has key similarities to Greek and Egyptian parables, folk-tales and rhetorical exercises in Greek schools of the era (both in its content and message).[233] It was almost certainly Luke's invention.[234]

16). Then in Jn 8.37-40 Jesus says to the Jews themselves that they were plotting to kill him, but not why (other than in the esoteric sense that they didn't believe his gospel). But Jn 11.53 says that *Lazarus* is the reason, 'so from that day forth they took counsel that they might put him to death', clearly having no idea that the Jews had been plotting this for several chapters and Jesus knew it and was even throwing it back in their faces. The author of 11.53 clearly meant this was when the Jews *began* to plot to kill Jesus. This therefore originally preceded the other references to their plotting. John is out of order. The most likely order was chap. 11, chaps. 7 and 8, then chap. 5, not necessarily contiguously.

232. See Pearce, 'The Lucan Origins of the Raising of Lazarus'. Many other scholars over the years have concurred with Pearce; a surprisingly good study is a senior thesis at the University of Massachusetts (Amherst) by Keith Yoder, *From Luke to John: Lazarus, Mary and Martha in the Fourth Gospel* (2011), available at http://www.umass.edu/wsp/project/senior/FromLukeToJohn.pdf. Yoder cites and summarizes past scholarship on the point and shows many deliberate parallels between John 11–12 (containing the associated stories of the anointing by Mary and the raising of Lazarus) and Luke's corresponding stories also of the sisters Mary and Martha in Luke 10 and the parable of Lazarus in Luke 16, showing they are all interrelated, and that in both cases John has borrowed from (and by his changes 'responded' to) Luke.

233. See K. Grobel, '". . . Whose Name Was Neves"', *New Testament Studies* 10 (1963–1964), pp. 373-82; Ronald Hock, 'Lazarus and Micyllus: Greco-Roman Backgrounds to Luke 16:19-31', *Journal of Biblical Literature* 106 (1987), pp. 447-63; Thomas Brodie, 'Re-Opening the Quest for Proto-Luke: The Systematic Use of Judges 6–12 in Luke 16:1–18:8', *Journal of Higher Criticism* 2.1 (Spring 1995), pp. 68-101; and Tim Brookins, 'Dispute with Stoicism in the Parable of the Rich Man and Lazarus', *Journal of Greco-Roman Christianity and Judaism* 8 (2011–2012), pp. 34-50.

234. The parable could also have been a commonplace in Jewish folklore (as its parallels were in pagan folklore). Lazarus happens to be the name of Abraham's steward (Gen. 15.2, probably the same man in Gen. 24.2; Lazarus is a common Greek form of

But be that as it may, the telling point is that in this parable, a rich man ends up burning in hell and sees up in heaven a dead beggar he once knew named Lazarus, resting on the 'bosom of Abraham', so he begs Abraham to let Lazarus rise from the dead and warn his still-living brothers to avoid his own hellish fate. The parable ends with Abraham refusing, because 'if they will not listen to Moses and the prophets, neither will they be persuaded if someone rises from the dead' (Lk. 16.31). Key to this parable is that this fictional Lazarus does *not* rise from the dead, and that even if he did, it would convince no one, and therefore it *won't* be done. This is thus another expanded exercise in making the repeated point that Jesus will not perform signs because they will not persuade anyone (as I surveyed earlier).

Notice what happens in John: he reverses the message of Luke's parable, by having Jesus *actually raise this Lazarus from the dead*, which actually *convinces* many people to turn and be saved, the very thing Luke's Jesus said wouldn't work. In fact, just as the rejected request in Luke's parable imagined Lazarus going to people and convincing them, John's Lazarus is then cited as a witness to the crucifixion, empty tomb and resurrection of Jesus, and is so cited *specifically to convince people*—again what Luke's Jesus said wouldn't work. John has thus reified a fictional character and integrated him into his version of the story in order to argue against that particular message in Luke, even to the point of claiming this fictional Lazarus is the eyewitness John is using as a source.[235] In addition to the evidence already just adduced that Lazarus is the Beloved, we can now see that the idea of the Beloved's reclining 'on Jesus' bosom' (Jn 13.23) references the fact that the Lazarus of Luke's parable was reclining 'on Abraham's bosom' (Lk. 16.22-23), thus John clearly meant them to be one and the same.[236]

Lazarus has thus been pulled out of Luke's fiction into John's history, and there does what Luke's parable said would be no use: he goes around

the Jewish name Eleazar), originally the only male heir born to his household, which possibly originated the notion that in the afterlife this Lazarus rested in Abraham's bosom. His poverty in John might thus be an embellishment from the fact that God had disinherited him (Gen. 15.4).

235. Fabricating sources like this was a commonplace in ancient mythography: an entire chapter is dedicated to the subject ('Bogus Citations') in Alan Cameron, *Greek Mythography in the Roman World* (New York: Oxford University Press, 2004), pp. 124-63. Cameron documents many other commonplace features of ancient mythmaking, including such devices as adding vivid details to a narrative (just as John also does, as, e.g., in his account of the empty tomb). See Carrier, *Proving History*, pp. 182-83.

236. Thus reversing Luke's parable again: Abraham was asked but refused to raise Lazarus and send him as a sign; yet when Jesus was asked, he did what Abraham refused. Jesus is thus now sitting in the place of Abraham, deciding who rises from the dead.

telling everyone (i.e. the reader) that all this is true, 'in order that you may be saved' (20.31; 21.24), the very thing the rich man had asked Abraham to raise Lazarus for. John isn't even coy about it. He has Jesus declare to God at the raising of Lazarus that this is all done 'because of the multitude that stands around', so that 'they may believe that you did send me' (Jn 11.42), a rather artless giveaway. Even the act itself of reifying the parable is a refutation of Luke: John is thereby saying this is no parable, oh no, *this really happened.* This is reason enough to dismiss John's Gospel as a complete fabrication, of no historical value in discerning the historicity of Jesus.[237]

Another example of reifying a parable and 'correcting' its message like this is seen in John's version of the miraculous catch, an idea he adapts from Luke (5.4-11), who told it as a story of converting Simon Peter to discipleship, whereas John revises it into a post-resurrection narrative (Jn 21.3-11).[238] Luke had already created this story by reifying a parable in Mt. 13.47-50, where Jesus says 'the kingdom of heaven is like a net cast into the sea, which gathered every kind, and when full, they drew it to shore and sat down, and gathered the good into vessels and threw away the bad'. Luke makes this happen for real, with obvious symbolism: they could not catch any fish until they followed the word of the Lord (5.5-6); the load became too much to bear (their nets breaking and boats sinking from the weight), prompting Peter to conclude he must be a sinner (5.7-9); but Jesus tells him not to fear, because this signifies he will become a fisher of men (5.10). Thus Luke creatively expanded the simple story of the calling of Simon in Mk 1.16-18 (repeated in Mt. 4.18-20), turning it into an absurd tale with symbolic meaning, and he did this by reifying the parable of the net in Matthew, combining it with Mark's story of the calling of Simon Peter. Classic mythmaking.

The author of John 21 then took this story from Luke and improved on it. For example, he made sure to mention that the net did *not* break after all (Jn 21.11)—thus, with effort, no souls will be lost (whereas Luke's reification of the parable implies the nets *were breaking*, and thus souls were being lost:

237. Lazarus isn't the only character John invents. He also invented Nicodemus (whose name means 'Victory for the People'), who, like the Beloved Lazarus, is inserted into stories he nowhere appeared in before (like the burial of Jesus: Jn 19.38-42). This new character, a member of the Jewish elite (a Pharisee, a Jewish studies professor, and a top ranking government official: Jn 3.1, 10), who somehow no one had ever heard of before, defies the Jewish elite by standing up for the people (Jn 7.31-52) and joining them in following Jesus (Jn 7.50). See Carrier, *Not the Impossible Faith*, pp. 68-70, 194-95.

238. Robert Grant, '"One Hundred Fifty-Three Large Fish" (John 21.11)', *Harvard Theological Review* 42 (October 1949), pp. 273-75; and Edmund Leach, 'Fishing for Men on the Edge of the Wilderness', in *The Literary Guide to the Bible* (ed. Robert Alter and Frank Kermode; Cambridge, MA: Harvard University Press, 1987), pp. 579-99.

Lk. 5.6). The number of fish counted may then have been meant to reinforce this. Jerome believed the number '153' symbolized the totality of species of fish then known (more in fact were known, but possibly this was a common folk belief of the time), so the point of the story is that all would be saved—or at least, an elect would be saved *from all nations* (a nation being the proper analog to a species here).[239]

We already know John was fond of number symbolism—many instances of curious numbers appear in his narrative, from the number and size of the pots at Cana (2.6) to the number of years it took to build the Jerusalem temple (2.20) to the number of stadium lengths the disciples had rowed before Jesus walked on the water (6.19), and much else besides. A famous example is that of the paralyzed man cured at Bethesda, who had been paralyzed for 'thirty-eight years' (5.5), and thus was beginning the thirty-ninth year of his infirmity when he was cured and 'took up his bed and walked' (5.9), at which the Jews rebuked him because 'it is not lawful for you to pick up your bed' on the Sabbath (5.10). As it happens, 'picking up your bed and moving it' on the Sabbath is the thirty-ninth prohibition of labors in the Mishnah, the last of the 'forty less one' prohibited acts ('he who transports an object from one domain to another').[240] So here we have a man who was accused of violating the thirty-ninth Sabbath prohibition, violating it in his thirty-ninth year of illness. This is myth, not history. However much John colors his account with historical trivia about old Jerusalem, he is still just making all this up.[241]

8. *Weighing the Evidence*

The Gospels generally afford us no evidence whatever for discerning a historical Jesus. Because of their extensive use of fabrication and literary invention and their placing of other goals far ahead of what we regard as 'historical truth', we cannot know if anything in them has any historical

239. Leach, 'Fishing for Men', p. 595; see also Grant, 'One Hundred Fifty-Three Large Fish'. Other theories of what the number meant were proposed by ancient Christian exegetes (surveyed by Grant) and modern mythicists (such as that it has some connection with Pythagorean mysticism), but Jerome's is the simplest and makes the most interpretive sense of the number's placement in the text.

240. Mishnah, *Shabbat* 7.2 (lines L and M).

241. On various other difficulties with this passage see David Wieand, 'John V.2 and the Pool of Bethesda', *New Testament Studies* 12 (1965–1966), pp. 392-404. Among the other artifices in this tale are the covert fact that Jesus himself is the Sheep Gate (Jn 10.7 thus explains Jn 5.2) and the more overt fact that the whole story creatively redacts (and changes the message of) a well-known Synoptic pericope (Mk 2.1-12, which became Mt. 9.1-8 and Acts 9.33-34) by combining it with another Johannine reification of a Lucan parable (Lk. 11.46).

basis—except what we can verify externally, which for Jesus is next to nothing. They are simply myths about Jesus and the gospel. They are not seriously researched biographies or historical accounts—and are certainly not eyewitness testimonies or even collected hearsay. Their literary art and structure are simply too sophisticated for that. This is equally expected on both minimal historicity and minimal mythicism, however, and therefore (apart from what we've already accounted for in determing the prior probability in Chapter 6) the Gospels have no effect on the probability that Jesus existed, neither to raise or lower it.[242]

A more ardent skeptic could disagree. Here I am arguing *a fortiori*, and as such granting historicity its best shot. But some will still ask why the Gospels appear out of nowhere forty to eighty years after the fact, as fully structured literary myths, rather than there first being more mundane reports, memoirs and accounts, closer to the events concerned, only later evolving into increasingly grandiose myths. Like the example of Haile Selassie in Chapter 2 (in §1): we have abundant mundane records of the man, and then later appear the sacred myths. Why is this not the case for Jesus? On background evidence we can perhaps expect the why of it is that the Church had no motive to preserve any of that earlier stuff; I have already discussed that possibility well enough in Chapter 8 (in §§3, 4 and 12). The matter logically belongs there; although a related matter is why there aren't such details even in the Epistles (as we'll see in the next chapter). Here we are concerned only with the content of the Gospels by themselves. And as such, even as completely fabricated myths, they could be such for a historical man or a cosmic one. From the material examined here, I see neither as inherently more likely. We have to look elsewhere for evidence.

A more ardent *apologist* might disagree in the other direction, and ask how it is the cosmic myths became earthly myths. Isn't a historical Jesus in fact *more mundane*, and thus a shift in an *unexpected* direction? More mundane, yes; but unexpected, no. That very trend to euhemerize (and thus make more mundane the tales of cosmic gods) was actually typical (Element 45). Indeed, to serve their obvious function as models for missionary life, values and teaching, not only must Jesus' story be transformed to resemble the earthly experience of missionaries (by having him interact with the world and society they live in), but a Gospel's text also becomes considerably more powerful and effective if it is also taken *literally*. As I've said before (Chapter 8, §12). Because it's harder to believe you should follow a fictional model, whereas if you believe Jesus *really* did and said these things, then you have a much stronger impetus to be awed by that and strive to follow his example.

242. This represents the mathematical result of the 'excess of improbabilities' defining the principle of contamination in Stephen Law, 'Evidence, Miracles' (as such improbabilities need not be confined to the miraculous, as discussed in §2).

Such historicizing also gave church hierarchies more control over doctrine and a rhetorical advantage over competitors, and thus it is more likely to be an observed feature of the eventually prevailing sect. As noted in Chapter 8 (§12), this gave church hierarchies more control over doctrine because they could then claim to have it from an unbroken line of tradents, in a set of documents and claims they themselves controlled, so no one could bypass their authority by continuing to receive updated revelations from Jesus or his angels. Paul was already trying to battle this problem in Gal. 1.8-10; the Montanist sect would represent the last vestige of that Pauline model of establishing authority, and that was stamped out by more successful sects, who (to win such debates) invented a canon and a tradition history, which once established could not as easily be changed—and so those in power got to pick their successors from then on, the ultimate dream of every oligarchy.

We already saw that this was a routine trend all across ancient religion (see Element 44). The result is that the later Gospels (Luke and John) began explicitly selling themselves as historical truth (even while they continued composing in the same fictional-symbolic way, evidently in a nod to the 'more enlightened' Christians, as well as in a bid to market to everyone the ideas those stories symbolized, this time in a package more ardently sold as 'historically true'), while the other Gospels (Mark and Matthew) also began to be sold as such, even if they did not so obviously sell themselves that way at first. Possibly higher ranking insiders were let in on the truth, but the majority could not be, for fear they 'couldn't handle it' and thus would reject the gospel and not be saved. This elitist disdain for the lower ranks of the membership is reflected in later Christian literature, where we saw that this doctrine of double-meaning (one, the symbolic and allegorical, for the elite; and the other, the literal, for the *hoi polloi*) had certainly become standard in the church by the end of the second century (which necessitated keeping the purely esoteric meaning as far from public knowledge as reasonably possible). There is no reason to believe this two-tiered system of knowledge did not already exist from the very beginning. In fact, Paul attests to such a system already existing in his churches, and it appears to have existed even before he arrived. (On all of this, see again Element 13.)

As I noted earlier, this should have consequences to future research on the Gospels. We need to shift entirely to asking the question 'What is the author attempting to say or accomplish with this story, or with his revision of this story?' and not 'Did that actually happen?' Because the latter simply wasn't a concern of these authors. Even if they were concerned to convince people it happened, they were not themselves concerned if it actually did. They had a different agenda, and are crafting the myths they need to sell it. The Gospels were produced by faith communities for preaching, teaching and propaganda, and not as disinterested or even *interested* biographical inquiry. There is no indication in them of a quest to determine what Jesus *really* said or did. There is no discussion of sources or of reasons to prefer one claim to another or of attempts to interpret contradictory data or even any mention of the *existence* of real alternative accounts (even though we know they knew of them—because they all covertly used them as source material). Each author just makes Jesus say or do whatever they want. They change the story as suits them and neglect to mention they did so. They craft literary artifices and symbolic narratives routinely. They frequently rewrite classical and biblical stories and just insert Jesus into them. If willing to do all that (and plainly they were), the authors of the Gospels clearly had no interest in any *actual* historical data. And if they had no interest in that (and plainly they didn't), they didn't need a historical Jesus. Even if there had been one, he was wholly irrelevant to their aims and designs. These are thus not historians. They are mythographers; novelists; propagandists. They are deliberately inventing what they present in their texts. And they are doing it *for a reason* (even if we can't always discern what that is). The Gospels simply must be approached as such. We have to stop thinking we can use them as historical sources.

The consequence of this to the present query is simple: from the survey in this chapter it's clear that if we went from pericope to pericope assessing the likelihood of it being true (rather than invented to communicate a desired point or to fit a pre-planned narrative structure), each time updating our prior probability that *anything* in the Gospels can be considered reliable evidence for a historical Jesus, then that probability would consistently go down (or level off somewhere low), but never rise.[243] In fact I have not found a single pericope in these Gospels that is more likely true than false. These Gospels are therefore no different than the dozens of other Gospels that weren't selected for the canon (as discussed in Element 44). They are all just made-up stories.

To change this conclusion, historicists need to find a way to prove that *something* about the historical Jesus in the Gospels is probably true (not *possibly* true, but *probably* true). They have often attempted this, but so far only with completely invalid methods (as I have already thoroughly documented in Chapter 5 of *Proving History*). I see no prospect of any valid method ever succeeding at that task. But only time will tell. For now, my conclusion is that we can ascertain nothing in the Gospels that can usefully verify the historicity of Jesus. But neither do they prove he didn't exist. As evidence, they simply make no difference to that equation.

243. On how one would apply this method of iteration using Bayes's Theorem, see 'iteration, method of', in Carrier, *Proving History*, p. 337.

11

The Evidence of the Epistles

1. *The Passion of Pliny the Elder*

Pliny the Younger wrote a lot about his uncle and adoptive father, Pliny the Elder.[1] And the younger Pliny's good friend Tacitus was fascinated by his uncle's heroic death. So he wrote Pliny a letter asking him to tell him all he knew about the circumstances of the elder Pliny's death and how he bore it and how he acted in his final days. Tacitus wanted to include something on it in the history he was writing, but it's obvious he really just wanted to hear about this remarkable and heroic story. Who wouldn't? Human curiosity is universal, and something like this could not just be let aside as of no interest. The circumstances of his death, after all, were 'so memorable that it is likely to make his name live forever'.[2] Much like Jesus, according to some.

Glad to answer Tacitus, the younger Pliny wrote him a letter containing an extensive eyewitness account of all he saw and knew about his father's death, in around 1,500 words.[3] For comparison, Paul's letter to the Galatians, one of his shortest, contains around 3,000 words; Romans, nearly

1. For example: Pliny, *Letters* 3.5, 5.8, 6.16, 6.20.

2. Pliny, *Letters* 6.16.2. We've met these Plinys before (see Chapter 8, §§3 and 10). We have abundant direct and indirect textual, eyewitness and archaeological evidence of Pliny the Elder's life and influence and know far more about him than Jesus, likewise Pliny the Younger (both making a good example of the kind of evidence we *could* have had for Jesus had he been as famous or influential). This evidence is discussed even in Wikipedia ('Pliny the Elder' at http://en.wikipedia.org/wiki/Pliny_the_Elder) and Livius ('Pliny the Younger [1]' at http://www.livius.org/pi-pm/pliny/pliny_y.htm). For more formal confirmation see 'Pliny (1) the Elder' and 'Pliny (2) the Younger' in the *Oxford Classical Dictionary* (ed. Simon Hornblower and Antony Spawforth; Oxford: Oxford University Press, 3rd edn, 1995), pp. 1197-98.

3. Pliny, *Letters* 6.16. This letter is, by the way, a good example of what an honest, straightforward historical account looks like, in contrast to the farcical literary artifices of the Gospels (as shown in the previous chapter). That is not to say that nothing in Pliny's account can be questioned, but rather that Pliny is doing precisely what the authors of the Gospels were not—to the extent that we know we can trust most of what Pliny says, but none of what the Gospels do. In Bayesian terms, Pliny's letter contains

10,000 (although either or both may be a pastiche of what had previously been several shorter letters).[4] Overall we have around 20,000 words from Paul. But in Pliny's mere 1,500 words we learn that his father died from respiratory failure after breathing the ashfall of Mount Vesuvius in his attempt to investigate the disaster and rescue survivors as commander of the Roman naval fleet stationed nearby. Pliny relates as much detail as he was witness to and those present informed him of.[5] Pliny's response peaked Tacitus's curiosity and questions even more, and he wrote again, asking what the younger Pliny himself did in the days immediately following that tragedy. Pliny again obliged him with an account of that in a following letter.[6] As Pliny says, 'the letter which you asked me to write on my uncle's death has made you eager to hear about the terrors and also the hazards I had to face' afterward.[7]

This is the kind of exchange of letters we should expect to have from the earliest Christians. Not necessarily in every respect, but surely something like it. Curiosity, the burning desire to know, to have firsthand accounts, to have specific questions answered and desires for knowledge satisfied, would dominate every congregation under Paul and beyond, most especially in respect to the Son of God and Savior of the Universe whose deeds and speeches and death were (for them) the most important in all of history. The same burning desires exhibited by Tacitus and eagerly satisfied

attributes that place it within a completely different reference class from the Gospels, one in which the prior probability of honesty and reliability is far greater.

4. For example, there is evidence that Romans was originally at least three separate letters, one of which was actually a church manual, which was split up and merged with an unrelated letter on a similar subject, and then a third letter was tacked onto the end (chap. 16, originally a stand-alone letter of introduction for Phoebe, per Rom. 16.1, which itself has become corrupted: many mss. show that Rom. 16.25-27 was originally part of another letter, and indeed it more logically belongs after Rom. 14.23, while Rom. 16.17-20 is even more clearly out of place and has probably likewise been displaced from that other letter, although we do not have clues as to its original location), all more or less edited to make the resulting 'Frankenstein's monster' look like a single continuous letter: Junji Kinoshita, 'Romans: Two Writings Combined: A New Interpretation of the Body of Romans', *Novum Testamentum* 7 (October 1965), pp. 258-77. Many scholars suspect the letters to the Corinthians, Galatians, Philippians and Thessalonians are likewise mishmashes of what were originally multiple letters (and not necessarily to the same destinations), and that some letters are redactions of others: see Rainer Reuter, 'Introduction to Synoptic Work on the New Testament Epistles', *Journal of Higher Criticism* 9.2 (Fall 2002), pp. 246-58; Philip Sellew, '"Laodiceans" and the Philippians Fragments Hypothesis', *Harvard Theological Review* 87 (January 1994), pp. 17-28; etc. For some evidence that this is the case for 1 Corinthians, see §10.

5. Pliny, *Letters* 6.16.22.

6. Pliny, *Letters* 6.20.

7. Pliny, *Letters* 6.20.1.

by Pliny would have been multiplied a hundredfold in the two decades of Paul's mission, given the number of Christians and distant churches there were by then, spanning three continents. For not even one person to have ever exhibited this interest in writing nor for any to have so satisfied it is bizarre. Saying this all went on in person is simply insufficient to answer the point: if everything was being resolved in person, Paul would never have written a single letter; nor would his congregations have so often written him letters requesting he write to satisfy their questions—which for some reason always concerned only doctrine and rules of conduct, never the far more interesting subject of how the Son of God lived and died. On the other matters Paul was compelled to write tens of thousands of words. If he had to write so much on those issues, how is it possible no one ever asked for or wrote even one word on the more obvious and burning issues of the facts of Jesus' life and death?

This oddity is all the greater given that there were countless moral and doctrinal disputes arising in these congregations (the very reason Paul wrote such long and detailed letters), which must necessarily have rested on many questions that the actual facts of Jesus' words, life and death would have addressed, answered or pertained to. Such facts would thus necessarily become points of query, debate and contention. Which in turn would have involved eyewitnesses weighing in, either directly (writing letters themselves), indirectly (by dictating letters through hired scribes, which were abundantly available for just that purpose; there were surely even scribes within Christian congregations willing to volunteer), or by proxy (communicating with educated leaders like Paul, who would then relay what they learned). I've made this point already (as in Chapter 8, §4). But it bears repeating here because it proves by contrast how very bizarre the letters of Paul actually are.

It is crucial to understand the methodological logic from here forward—not only when we think about what's just been said but even more so when we go through the remaining sections of this chapter. Because, although the following applies to *every* piece of evidence examined in this book, and beyond, here biases are the most pernicious. If you approach the text with gut reactions of what you think Paul (or any other author) probably meant, you are not thinking in a logically sound way. Those estimates of probability are in fact measures of the strength of your bias toward one conclusion over another, and *not* the probability of those biases being correct. Hence those probabilities, those estimates, those gut feelings are precisely what you should discard. This is why we need Bayesian reasoning, to prevent us from simply enshrining our biases as the truth (on this point, my book *Proving History* is essential reading). You would have to justify those biases at the stage of determining the prior probability (Chapter 6). Otherwise, you cannot abide by them at all.

The logically correct way to reason from evidence to a conclusion is to assume that a hypothesis is true (for the sake of argument—in other words, wholly regardless of whether you already think the hypothesis is probable or not, you must assume it is not only probable *but in fact true*), and *then* ask how likely the particular piece of evidence you are looking at would be *in that case*. You must do this for both competing hypotheses (thus generating *two* estimates of probability, not one). Thus, you must assume minimal historicity is true (*then* estimate how likely the passage you are looking at would be what Paul would write, for example) but you must also assume minimal mythicism is true (and then estimate how likely the passage you are looking at would be what Paul would write in *that* case). The difference in those probabilities is the weight of the evidence (toward whichever hypothesis entails the higher of those probabilities). If there is no difference, then the passage argues for neither hypothesis (it is equally likely on either one).

The reason I make a point of this is that the most common, and wholly erroneous, way scholars look at arguments like the following is to simply assume, *a priori*, that a particular interpretation is unlikely. But that is simply a measure of the strength of your bias. It is not a measure of any logically valid effect of that evidence on your conclusion. The question you should ask here is not 'Is that likely what Paul would have meant by that?' but rather, 'If Paul was in fact a mythicist, *is that likely what he would write*?' (and then 'If Paul was in fact a historicist, is that likely what he would write?', for the comparative probability). You will find time and again the answer to the first question is 'yes, almost certainly'. Which means that that passage cannot argue for historicity even if Paul was a historicist, and even if historicity happened to be true. Because if a passage is already effectively 100% what we expect on mythicism, its likelihood on historicity cannot be any significantly higher (since 100% is as high as any probability can be), and thus the difference in those two probabilities will favor neither hypothesis, even at best (i.e. even if the passage is also 100% what we expect on historicity). And if that passage or chapter or letter is not what we expect on historicity but looks a little weird in that case, then that probability has to be less than 100% (even if only a little), and that means the evidence argues *against* historicity (even if only a little). So even if, for example, a passage is 90% expected on history (and thus very probable in that case), if that same passage is 100% expected on myth, then that evidence argues *for myth* (because the probability of historicity must then be multiplied by 9/10ths on that evidence, a small reduction but a reduction all the same). I'll say more about that in the next chapter.

This is often hard for historians to grasp, because they typically have not studied logic and don't usually know the logical basis for any of their modes of reasoning and thus have all too often simply enshrined *ad hoc* estimates of their bias-strength as arguments for a conclusion, which is not logical. The 'consensus' in history in fact is often based on that faulty logic, which is why history as a field has a deep and abiding methodological problem, and 'consensus' is not an intrinsically reliable guide to what's true in history (see Chapter 1 of *Proving History* for how bad this has become in the study of Jesus, though the problem is not unique to that topic). I am not the first to point this out. It was extensively documented by David Hackett Fischer in *Historians' Fallacies: Toward a Logic of Historical Thought* (New York: Harper & Row, 1970).

So when we approach interpretations of the Epistles of Paul (as with any evidence at all) we must look at each passage *with the assumption that mythicism is true* (something historians of Jesus have typically never done), and *then* estimate how likely it would be that the passage would look like that. And *then* look at that same passage with the assumption that historicity is true and do the same. The latter probability may even be high. But is it as high as the probability on mythicism? (Or higher?) That's the only question that logically matters. Because what we want is the difference in those two probabilities. Though biases can still affect these estimates, we are at least not simply using our biases as our premises but actually attempting to reason out which theory the evidence fits better, and taking *both* theories seriously when we do. With that understood, we can proceed.

3. *The Peculiar Indifference of Paul and his Christians*

As a psychologist once put it (about Paul's letter to fellow congregants in Rome, whom he had not yet met and thus can't have shared his own stories with):

> Imagine for a moment that one of your friends writes you a twenty-page letter passionately wanting to share her excitement about a new teacher. This letter has only one topic, your friend's new teacher. [But] at the end of her letter, you still do not know one thing about her teacher. Yet, Paul presents the central figure of his theology this way. . . . It [seems] impossible to imagine how Paul could avoid telling one story or parable of—or fail to note one physical trait or personal quality of—Jesus.[8]

Indeed, Paul mentions 'Jesus' or 'Christ' in his seven authentic letters at least 280 times—and that doesn't count other references to him as only 'the Lord' or 'Son of God'. Altogether, Paul found over three hundred occasions to mention Jesus (by some name or title), and on at least half of those occasions he tells us some particular fact or other about this Jesus. But (as

8. Billy Wheaton and Joy Fuller, *Hooks and Ladders: A Journey on a Bridge to Nowhere with American Evangelical Christians* (Bloomington, IN: iUniverse, 2009), p. 31.

we'll see) not one of those facts connects Jesus with an earthly life (without adding suppositions not in the text). His crucifixion is mentioned over fifteen times; and his resurrection, over thirty times. But never any details. So those could have occurred in outer space (as explained in Chapter 3). We hear very little else.[9]

In fact, as we'll see in this chapter, the *only* Jesus Paul shows any knowledge of is a celestial being, not an earthly man. Paul's Jesus is only ever in the heavens. Never once is his baptism mentioned, or his ministry, or his trial, or any of his miracles, or any historical details about what he was like, what he did, or suffered, or where he was from, or where he had been, or what people he knew. No memories from those who knew him are ever reported. Paul never mentions Galilee or Nazareth, or Pilate or Mary or Joseph, or any miracles Jesus did or any miraculous powers he is supposed to have displayed . . . or anything about the life of Jesus *not* in the Gospels. Paul never references any event in Jesus' life as an example to follow (beyond the abstractions of love, endurance and submissiveness), and never places anything Jesus said in any earthly historical context whatever. So far as these letters tell us, no Christian ever asked Paul about these things, either. Nor did any of these things ever become relevant in any dispute Paul had with anyone. Not one of his opponents, so far as Paul mentions, ever referenced a fact about Jesus' life in support of their arguments. And no one ever doubted anything claimed about Jesus and asked for witnesses to confirm it or explain it or give more details. The interest Tacitus showed in Pliny's father is never exhibited by any of them, nor is Pliny's eagerness to talk about his father ever exhibited by Paul in *his* eagerness to talk *about Jesus*—and yet Paul talks obsessively and repeatedly about Jesus.

That's all simply *bizarre*. And bizarre means unexpected, which means infrequent, which means improbable. Accordingly, historicists have to explain why in Paul's letters there are no disputes about what Jesus said or did, and why no specific example from his life is ever referred to as a model, not even to encourage or teach anything or to resolve any disputes, and why the only sources Paul ever refers to for anything he claims to know about Jesus are *private revelations* and *hidden messages in scripture* (Element 16), and why Paul appears not to know of there being any other sources than these (like, e.g., *people who knew Jesus*). Whatever explanation historicists devise for these curiosities has to be *demonstrably true*, and not something

9. After completing this book I received notice of a handy Webpage listing all the alleged instances of Paul referencing a historical Jesus, assembled by Dave Mack, 'What Did Paul Know about the Life and Teachings of Jesus?' *bibleLAD* (May 17, 2013) at http://biblelad.wordpress.com/category/historical-jesus-2. I already addressed them all in this chapter, but felt it worthwhile to include this link for its utility. I will cite scholarly articles on the same point in coming notes.

they just make up to explain away the evidence. Because such 'making up of excuses' would risk the fallacy of gerrymandering, which necessarily lowers your theory's prior probability since you have to assume facts that aren't in evidence and that aren't made probable by any evidence there is.[10]

All this is evident in such passages as Gal. 1.11-16, where Paul says he received the gospel only by revelation, and in Rom. 15.25-26, where scripture and revelation are the only sources of information about Jesus that Paul mentions Christians having. In Rom. 15.3-4 Paul even appears to say that we have to learn things about Jesus by discovering them in scripture; Paul apparently knew nothing about any community of witnesses to consult for such things (he even appears to deny any such sources existed in 1 Cor. 4.6, beyond revelators such as himself). Combining both observations, in 1 Cor. 15.1-9 Paul says the gospel that was revealed to him (as he says in Gal. 1; see §4) was known only by revelation and scripture. Stranger still, that gospel lacked any reference to Jesus having a ministry or ever preaching the gospel, or performing great deeds, or having parents who were Davidic heirs, or being chosen by God at his baptism. All Paul tells us is this:

> For I delivered to you first of all that which also I received: that *according to the scriptures* Christ died for our sins, and that he was buried, and that *according to the scriptures* he has been raised on the third day, and that he appeared to Cephas, and then to 'the twelve' and then he appeared [to hundreds of brethren all at once] and then he appeared to James, and then to all the apostles, and last of all to me as well, as if to an aborted fetus—because I am the least of the apostles, who is not fit to be called an apostle, because I persecuted the Assembly of God.[11]

Note what is missing here. We're told Christ's death and resurrection are known from the scriptures; but he was only *seen* after that. There is no ref-

10. See Carrier, *Proving History*, pp. 80-81, 104-105, 277-80. On the often-invisible reliance on such *ad hoc* assumptions to 'read into' Paul things that aren't there, see my commentary on one example in Richard Carrier, 'The Goodacre Debate', *Richard Carrier Blogs* (December 20, 2012) at http://freethoughtblogs.com/carrier/archives/2839.

11. 1 Cor. 15.3-9. I believe this passage has become multiply corrupted, deliberately and accidentally, and that it originally may have referenced only Cephas and Paul and 'all the brethren at the Pentecost' (not 'five hundred brethren', the word *pentakosiois* being just a few letters away from *pentēkostēs*, 'Pentecost', meaning the very event fictionalized by Luke in Acts 2). I think the verbal and narrative similarities are too numerous to be a coincidence (see Carrier, 'Spiritual Body', in *Empty Tomb* [ed. Price and Lowder], pp. 192-93). Indeed, this would connect with Paul's claim in the same chapter that Christ's resurrection was the 'firstfruits' (1 Cor. 15.20), which actually references the Pentecost. For an even more extreme view, see Robert Price, 'Apocryphal Apparitions: 1 Cor. 15.3-11 as a Post-Pauline Interpolation', in *Empty Tomb* (ed. Price and Lowder), pp. 69-104. However, to avoid needlessly controversial premises here, I will simply assume the passage as we have it is what Paul wrote.

erence here to 'Cephas' or 'the twelve' (or any of the others) seeing Jesus *before* his death, or having traveled with him, or having sat at his feet, or having been personally chosen by him. In other words, according to Paul's gospel, Jesus had no ministry and was personally unknown to anyone until he appeared to an elect number *after* his resurrection. This is confirmed in Phil. 2.5-11, where again Jesus has no ministry: all he does is descend from heaven, submit to death and reascend (discussed in §4).

This accords with what we found in *1 Clement* (as I demonstrated in Chapter 8, §5), where not only is scripture and private revelation again the only way anyone appears to have known about Jesus, but where Clement actually quotes scripture as the words of Jesus, and only cites scripture as his evidence that certain things happened to Jesus, and says it is only through the apostles that Jesus transmitted the gospel (thus effectively denying Jesus had any public ministry). Thus, exactly as Paul (or one of his successors) says, the gospel was only ever learned from 'revelation' and the 'writings of the prophets' (Rom. 16.25-26).[12] Not from any public ministry. And thus not from any (actual) historical Jesus. Thus, we see the same in Gal. 1.11-12 (where revelation is his only source) and 1 Cor. 15.3-8 (where scripture and revelation are the only sources he or anyone else has).

Even in 1 Cor. 11.23-25 Paul references revelation as his only source (as I'll explain in §7), precisely where we should expect human testimony to be his only possible source; and in Rom. 15.3-4 Paul all but admits to there being no actual stories about Jesus, that to learn things about him we have to turn to the scriptures (or again, revelations). This is what these letters simply say, when taken by themselves (and this is corroborated by other letters from the Pauline school: e.g. Eph. 3.3-12 and Col. 1.24-29). It therefore requires no other added suppositions. This is therefore the simplest hypothesis for why Paul never showed any interest in the historical Jesus, nor did any of his congregations, nor did any of his opponents. Because there was no historical Jesus. There was only a revealed being. Which was not anything one could dispute—except by claiming to have contrary revelations (hence Gal. 1.6-9).

Apologetic attempts to dodge this bullet always involve suppositions, which are either not in evidence or implausible. Like, for example, the excuse that the earliest Christians, including even Paul and his opponents in the church, simply weren't interested in anything Jesus said or did in his life. There is no evidence of that. To the contrary, the letters are full of interest in Jesus' death and what it accomplished and what words he revealed to his apostles. And a disinterest in everything else goes against all precedents in history and human nature. It should also be pointed out that if no Chris-

12. On who wrote this verse see Chapter 7 (§7).

tians were interested in any details of Jesus' life, then they cannot have transmitted any details of his life, either. The Gospels are therefore confirmed as fictions. For as I already remarked (in Chapters 6, §7, and 8, §4), you cannot claim the Christians were simultaneously keen to accurately preserve memories of Jesus *and* completely uninterested in any memories of Jesus. So the notion that 'they didn't care about any of that' is simply a non-starter. Only the desperately illogical would cling to such a thesis.

Another common excuse is to say that Paul's letters were just 'occasional', addressing only the specific issues that came up, and were not thorough treatises on what Jesus said and did. The premise here is certainly correct. The conclusion is not. Why weren't any facts about the life or deeds or teachings or trial or execution of Jesus ever *themselves* an 'occasion' of query or example or proof or dispute? Why were such things never relevant to any doctrine or question or dispute in the church that Paul spent thousands of words addressing? It's not that the letters we have suggest Paul was asked or tasked with discussing or mentioning such things and he failed to answer. Rather, it's that, so far as we can tell, no letters sent to him ever asked or tasked him with discussing or mentioning such things. No event in Jesus' life, no details of Jesus' life, ever had any relevance to any of the occasional issues he addressed, and no one ever used such events or details in any argument Paul ever had to confront. No one was even curious about such things. *That* is what is extremely improbable. Simply saying the letters were only 'occasional' does not make that fact any more likely.

Indeed, we're not just faced with the extremely high expectation that at least *something* along those lines would come up or be relevant or asked about or debated. It's also improbable that even casual or incidental mentions of historical facts about Jesus would never arise, not once in twenty thousand words. Like Paul's happenstance mention of baptizing for the dead (1 Cor. 15.29) or the fear of what angels might do if Christian women don't cover their hair in church (1 Cor. 11.9-10) or the fact that Christians will one day judge the angels (1 Cor. 6.3). Paul lets slip countless incidental details like these about Christian practice and belief, not because he was required to but simply because that sort of thing can't really be avoided. You would actually have to try very hard not to ever mention anything in twenty thousand words beyond the bare few facts you need to communicate. That these kinds of incidental details about Jesus never appear, yet incidental details about many other things do, is again simply improbable. Unless there were no incidental details about Jesus.[13]

13. Many historians fail to grasp the mathematical point here. They will explain away any single instance of something not being mentioned and then conclude that that explains why none are, not aware of the fact that the latter is less probable. For example, suppose for any given chapter of Paul's letters there was only a 1 in 20 (a mere 5%)

Sure, there must have been a lot of details about the *celestial* Jesus and his ordeal in outer space (as, e.g., we know from Ignatius that the early Christians had a complex angelology: see Chapter 8, §6), but those were esoteric aspects of cult belief and doctrine, part of the Christian mysteries, and thus would often be secrets (Element 13; which the same example in Ignatius illustrates), or obviously not applicable to earthly affairs (and in these letters Paul generally only deals with earthly affairs). But public facts about the biography, ministry, feats, trial and execution of Jesus could not have been secrets. Nor would most of Jesus' teachings have been. Nor could public disputes about what he actually said or did not have arisen (when disputes about everything else did), nor could such disputes arise and not ever appeal to who was present to see and report them. Nor could it be that *nothing* in Jesus' life was relevant to the earthly affairs of Paul's Christian congregations. Or, again, that no one was curious to know them, or eager to reference or employ them in their arguments and communications. We simply never hear Paul say, 'from James I learned that Jesus, who was his brother in life, had said/done *x*', or answer, 'Peter says he was there when Jesus said *x*, so why is your teaching at odds with *x*?', or argue 'my revelations of Jesus are as good as those other apostles having known the man personally', or anything comparable. These are simply not arguments anywhere found in these Epistles, nor anything like them. And this was in a time when eyewitnesses were supposedly still living, abundant and running the church. That's weird.

Many scholars have said much the same. In Gerd Lüdemann's study of these letters he concluded:

> Not once does Paul refer to Jesus as a teacher, to his words as teaching, or to [any] Christians as disciples. In this regard it is of the greatest significance that when Paul cites 'sayings of Jesus', they are never so designated; rather, without a single exception, he attributes such sayings to 'the Lord'. . . . Paul thought that a person named Jesus had lived and that he now sat at the right hand of God in heaven. Yet he shows only a passing

chance that he would mention or describe *some* definitely historical fact about Jesus. There are over sixty chapters in Paul's letters. Even if such a mention in any one of those chapters is that improbable (1 in 20), that there would be no mention in *any* of them is even more improbable: P(none) = $1 - (0.05)^{60} = 0.046$ (rounded), in other words, *less* than 5%. Which means there is a more than 95% chance we would have at least one such mention. So the fact that we have *none* is bizarre. And that's assuming every chapter had only a 5% chance of mentioning *something* of the intended sort, which is surely unrealistically *low*. Many chapters would have benefitted hugely from such a mention or could hardly have been written without referencing such a thing, and if Jesus existed, many chapters would have been specifically *about* his ministry or people's recollections of him, either to use them as examples or premises or to debate or dispute or defend them (or answer someone's curiosity about them).

> acquaintance with traditions related to his life and nowhere an independent acquaintance with them. In short, Paul cannot be considered a reliable witness to either the teachings, the life, *or the historical existence* of Jesus.[14]

Indeed, despite Jesus being so central to Paul's every argument, 'it seems strange indeed that the Epistles so seldom make reference to [Jesus'] life and teachings'.[15] Lüdemann likewise finds modern excuses for this implausible:

> The argument that [Paul] could assume his readers' familiarity with these [facts] because he had already passed them on in his missionary preaching [and therefore never had to mention them] is not convincing. He could and does presume some familiarity with the Greek translation of the Scripture, the Septuagint, which was mediated to his converts either by himself or earlier by the local Jewish community. For this reason *he repeatedly and specifically cites it* in the course of his ethical teaching. Moreover, when Paul himself summarizes the content of his missionary preaching in Corinth (1 Cor. 2.1-2; 15.3-5), there is no hint that a narration of Jesus' earthly life or a report of his earthly teachings was an essential part of it. . . . In the letter to the Romans, which *cannot* presuppose the apostle's missionary preaching and in which he attempts to summarize its main points, we find not a single direct citation of Jesus' teaching. One must record with some surprise the fact that Jesus' teachings seem to play a less vital role in Paul's religious and ethical instruction than does the Old Testament.[16]

Lüdemann is not convinced Jesus didn't exist, but he finds the Epistles can be of no help in proving he did, and expresses his surprise at this. But if it's surprising, it's improbable. Because that's what 'surprising' means. In contrast, minimal mythicism maintains the Jesus 'Paul believed had lived as a man' only lived so in outer space; thus on that theory Paul's not mentioning any fact of his earthly life is *not* surprising. It is therefore more probable.

Margaret Barker likewise expresses her perplexity at Paul's letters: 'at the centre of [Paul's] preaching there is not the teacher from Galilee but the Redeemer from heaven. Why?' Indeed, she argues, from his letters one would have to conclude that 'the Jesus who was only a teacher from Gali-

14. Gerd Lüdemann, 'Paul as a Witness to the Historical Jesus', *Sources of the Jesus Tradition: Separating History from Myth* (Amherst, NY: Prometheus Books, 2010), pp. 196-212 (211-12; emphasis added).

15. Lüdemann, 'Paul', p. 200.

16. Lüdemann, 'Paul', p. 211 (emphases added). See also Wells's additional argument and evidence in support of Lüdemann's point, summarized in Robert Price, *The Christ-Myth Theory and its Problems* (Cranford, NJ: American Atheist Press, 2011), pp. 356-59; see also Earl Doherty, *Jesus: Neither God nor Man (The Case for a Mythical Jesus)* (Ottawa: Age of Reason, 2009), pp. 25-82.

lee disappeared from the tradition at a very early date, so early that one wonders whether it was ever there at all'.[17] Nikolaus Walter more or less concurs, concluding that 'we can detect no hint that Paul knew of the narrative tradition about Jesus', which anyone ought to agree is 'surprising'.[18] Even Helmut Koester admits, 'it is generally agreed that Paul's letters do not permit any conclusions about the life of Jesus'.[19] Kurt Noll goes further, concluding that the evidence in Paul's letters demonstrates that no fully formed Jesus traditions, of either sayings or narratives, existed in Paul's day, and that all such traditions therefore post-date his generation.[20]

Scholars are thus starting to rethink the sequence of events. Nikolaus Walter has concluded that many of the teachings attributed to Jesus in the Gospels were in fact fabricated *out of the sayings of Paul*, and that there simply wasn't any collection of teachings from Jesus beyond occasional revelations.[21] James Dunn confesses that this 'would seem an odd conclusion to be forced to' given what appears in the Gospels, but once we agree the Gospels are fiction, it does not look so odd after all, and even Dunn admits the letters are peculiar on any other assumption—so Dunn himself had to resort to the implausible hypothesis that Paul was everywhere simply *implying* Jesus as his authority.[22] But that notion is exploded by the fact that Paul makes no such assumptions when citing *scripture* as his authority (so, as Lüdemann argued, why would he treat Jesus differently?), and in fact Paul frequently identifies Jesus ('the Lord') as his authority, and even takes care to distinguish between commands he received from his revealed Lord

17. Margaret Barker, 'The Secret Tradition', *Journal of Higher Criticism* 2 (Spring 1995), pp. 31-67 (58).

18. Nikolaus Walter, 'Paul and the Early Christian Jesus-Tradition', in *Paul and Jesus: Collected Essays* (ed. A.J.M. Wedderburn; Sheffield: Sheffield Academic Press, 1989), pp. 51-80 (60).

19. Helmut Koester, 'The Historical Jesus and the Historical Situation of the Quest: An Epilogue', in *Studying the Historical Jesus: Evaluation of the State of Current Research* (ed. Bruce Chilton and Craig Evans; Leiden: Brill, 1994), pp. 535-45 (540).

20. Kurt Noll, 'Investigating Earliest Christianity without Jesus', in *'Is This Not the Carpenter?' The Question of the Historicity of the Figure of Jesus* (ed. Thomas Thompson and Thomas Verenna; Sheffield: Equinox, 2012), pp. 233-66.

21. Nikolaus Walter, 'Paul'. His conclusion has been corroborated by Jens Schröter, 'Jesus and the Canon: The Early Jesus Traditions in the Context of the Origins of the New Testament Canon', in *Performing the Gospel: Orality, Memory and Mark: Essays Dedicated to Werner Kelber* (ed. R.A. Horsley, J.A. Draper and J.M. Foley; Minneapolis, MN: Fortress Press, 2006), pp. 104-22, 222-28. Their results are supported by the related conclusions of Frans Neirynck, 'Paul and the Sayings of Jesus', in *Collected Essays, 1982–1991: Evangelica, Gospel Studies* (ed. F. van Segbroeck; Leuven: Leuven University Press, 1991), pp. 511-68.

22. James Dunn, 'Jesus Tradition in Paul', in *Studying the Historical Jesus* (ed. Chilton and Evans), pp. 155-78 (173).

and his own opinions (e.g. 1 Cor. 7.25 vs. 14.37 or 9.8 vs. 9.14).[23] We have to face the fact of it. There simply *is* no source known to Paul, for him or anyone, but scripture and revelations from his celestial Jesus. And that all but rules out a historical Jesus.

Mogens Müller attempts to save Jesus from this conclusion by admitting there is nothing in Paul's letters that confirms that Jesus recently existed but that 'we need, however, a broader understanding of the predicate "historical" as used in connection with the person of Jesus', such that:

> 'historical' should not be employed simply in connection with attempts to reconstruct details in the life and teaching of Jesus, treating him solely as a figure of the past. The predicate 'historical' should be allowed also to include his impact as it has been conveyed to us through the meanings attached to his life. . . .[24]

But in that sense of 'historical', the mythic Christ—the Christ whom Paul would have said really did exist, living and dying and rising *in outer space*—would also be a 'historical' Jesus. The term then becomes meaningless—unless Müller wants to argue that Paul was right, there *really is* a Jesus Christ living in outer space. But that's a question for theology, not history. Either way, the effects of this 'Lord's' revelations, and how he was understood from reading scripture, would then be the cause of all the 'effects' on Paul and his ideas that Müller then catalogues. Those effects therefore cannot distinguish between minimal historicity and minimal mythicism. Müller's study is therefore impotent. Indeed, the fact that Müller had to resort to this tactic, that he was forced to concede Paul never talks about a historical Jesus in the 'other' sense, ought to be admitted as strange, and is itself confirmation that the mythicist thesis makes this evidence more likely. Accordingly, Thomas Verenna followed Müller's study with a contrary one finding that Paul's letters more readily indicate that Paul had no knowledge of an earthly historical Jesus, but only a celestial one.[25] These letters therefore are evidence for minimal mythicism.

Other scholars are in denial over this. And in their efforts to deny it, they resort to fallacious and self-refuting notions. Robert Van Voorst provides a typical example when he says 'we should not expect to find exact

23. For a complete list and discussion of Paul's only direct citations of 'the Lord' see Dale Allison, 'The Pauline Epistles and the Synoptic Gospels: The Pattern of the Parallels', *New Testament Studies* 28 (1982), pp. 1-32. See also Price, *Christ-Myth Theory*, pp. 359-60.

24. Mogens Müller, 'Paul: The Oldest Witness to the Historical Jesus', in *'Is This Not the Carpenter?'* (ed. Thompson and Verenna), pp. 117-30 (120-121).

25. Thomas Verenna, 'Born under the Law: Intertextuality and the Question of the Historicity of the Figure of Jesus in Paul's Epistles', in *'Is This Not the Carpenter?'* (ed. Thompson and Verenna), pp. 131-59.

historical references in early Christian literature, which was not written for primarily historical purposes'.[26] This attempt to deny the conclusion is twice fallacious. Because, in the first place, 'exact historical references' are not the only thing missing. The silence extends even to *inexact* historical references—in fact, all historical references of any kind, beyond details so vague they are *just as expected* on minimal mythicism and thus unable to demonstrate minimal historicity. And in the second place, the general rule Van Voorst is presuming (that if early documents about a person were not written for primarily historical purposes, then we should not expect to find in those documents any historical details about that person) is not even remotely defensible, and in fact is generally false. Letters about persons almost always contain historical references to them. In fact, our expectation should be exactly the opposite in exactly this case: when the person in question is believed by the letter writer (and his intended readers) to have been God's Incarnate Son, the Savior of the Universe, the most important being ever to walk the earth, whose every utterance is the Word of God and every act evidence of his mission and teachings and qualifications as divine and the ultimate example for all doctrine and conduct, when every letter about him is primarily on conveying knowledge or resolving disputes about who he was and what his true teachings were, it is simply impossible to avoid ever once mentioning any details about that man's life and character. Such a writer could not fail to call upon or have to debate things Jesus actually said and did or that were said and done to him.

In short, it is simply not conceivable that the historical Jesus never said or did anything, nor was anything ever said or done to him, that was relevant to resolving any dispute or supporting any teaching raised in these letters, or to satisfying anyone's curiosity, or even just to be mentioned in passing. Even if the author wanted to avoid mentioning every single thing Jesus did say or do and every single thing said or done to him, because it all—all of it, every last bit of it—contradicted what they were teaching, then their audience (and especially their opponents) would be asking them and challenging them with exactly that fact, so *even then* they would be compelled to respond, and thus compelled to mention such things anyway.

Quite simply, the more you write about a man, the more the probability rises that at some point you'll mention in passing at least some such details about him (things he said, did, heard, suffered; matters regarding his friends and relations, his origins and travels; people's memories of him, including any reports being spread by his enemies; and so on). To avoid ever mentioning even *one* such detail in over twenty thousand words becomes increasingly improbable, until that probability starts to become small to the point

26. Robert Van Voorst, *Jesus Outside the New Testament: An Introduction to the Ancient Evidence* (Grand Rapids, MI: William B. Eerdmans, 2000), p. 15.

of peculiarity.[27] We simply must concede: the silence of these letters is *very improbable*. To insist it is nevertheless 'possible' is irrelevant: you still have to face the fact of its improbability, and that improbability must always factor into your equation.[28]

Thus it becomes very significant (as Lüdemann pointed out) that Paul never once mentions anyone being Jesus' 'disciple' (he never uses that word at all; not even 'the twelve' in 1 Cor. 15.5 are said to be 'the twelve disciples'). Paul only knows of 'apostles', who, like him, received revelations of the Lord (1 Cor. 9.1; Gal. 1.1; etc.) and confirmed their status by proving God had bestowed on them miraculous powers (2 Cor. 12.12). So when Paul ranks the members of the church in order of authority, he says, 'God has set some in the church, *first* apostles, *secondly* prophets, *thirdly* teachers, *then* those with powers [most likely exorcists], *then* charismatic healers, *then* aides, administrators, and speakers in tongues' (1 Cor. 12.28). Disciples don't make the list. They don't exist. Instead, first in rank are simply all the 'apostles' like Paul. A special category of those who knew Jesus in life and were personally selected by him then, or were his family, is entirely absent. And these apostles include people we never hear about elsewhere, such as Apollos (1 Cor. 3.4-5) or possibly Andronicus and Junias (or Junia, Rom. 16.7).

Paul never even says the three pillars (the Cephas, James and John of Gal. 2.9) were Jesus' followers in life or were specially appointed by him. Only in the Gospels does that legend appear (Cephas then being Peter).[29] And

27. See earlier note on the mathematical point.

28. To do otherwise is to commit the logical fallacy of *possibiliter ergo probabiliter*, and thus violate a basic axiom of sound historical reasoning: see Carrier, *Proving History*, pp. 26-29.

29. Cephas means 'rock' in Aramaic, and Peter means 'rock' in Greek. The former appears unique (it is not a known name in Aramaic, therefore is a distinct appellation); and though the latter is not (Peter was a known name in Greek), the Gospels claim Jesus renamed Simon 'Rock' (hence 'Peter'), and obviously that would not have occurred in Greek (even by revelation), so Peter would actually have been thus renamed Cephas. So it is reasonably assumed the Cephas that Paul frequently refers to is the Peter of the Gospels and Acts (and most later legend). The fact that Paul names the top three 'pillars' Cephas, James and John, and the Gospels identify the top three disciples as Peter, James and John (see §10), supports that conclusion. Like Pontius Pilate or Caiaphas, these top three disciples in the Gospels would have been based on real people (the very ones Paul knew as the Pillars), but just as fictionalized there as Pilate and Caiaphas were. Whether Peter was really originally Simon and renamed Rock by Jesus cannot be certain (the mere fact is only mentioned in Mk 3.16, then becomes a story in Mt. 16.15-19), but even if based on a real event, it could have happened by revelation (perhaps in Peter's first vision of Jesus). Certainly Cephas cannot have been his birth name, so at the very least, he renamed himself (possibly all the Pillars had symbolic names befitting allegorical 'pillars' holding up the 'truth', as I suggested in the previous chapter, in §4; the main

1 Cor. 15.3-8 also fails to mention any such relationship—which is even more bizarre. There, they are only appointed (so far as we can tell) by being blessed with visions of the *risen* Lord. That is Paul's point in including himself in that list—he simply assumes his calling as an apostle (as in Gal. 1 and 1 Cor. 9.1) was the same as theirs. So we have to ask, why would Peter—or James or John for that matter—accept Paul into the apostolate at all if he hadn't been chosen by Jesus in life and struggled with him in life? How could his claim to be an apostle carry any weight whatever? Why did visions of the Lord take precedence over actually having had the man himself appoint you in person? This, too, is improbable—not impossible, but definitely improbable. Unless that's the only way *anyone* was appointed: by revelation. Then Peter would have a harder time kicking Paul to the curb. For then any challenge to Paul's claim would be just as usable to challenge Peter's.

This fact exposes the weakness of another common apologetic argument, that Paul deliberately avoided talking about eyewitness testimony because he wouldn't call attention to the fact that he himself wasn't one. This does not explain why his 'not being one' did not cause his rejection by Peter and the pillars. It does not explain why they ended up treating him as their equal, an apostle just like them. Moreover, this excuse, that Paul is trying to hide his status as a non-witness, simply doesn't make logical sense. As someone once phrased this objection to me (about why Paul never discusses anyone knowing Jesus), 'it's not surprising he doesn't relate details about their relationship to the historical Jesus, especially if that was already common knowledge to his readers. Why would he put a finger on his own weakness?' Because if it *was* his weakness, he would *have* to. We need to put ourselves in the shoes of the actual Christian congregations he was writing to. Paul is not writing to persuade *us*, some random foreigners two thousand years later. He's writing to persuade actual contemporaries—from whom he could *not* hide so decisive a weakness. So if it was a weakness, he would constantly have to address it, head on. Because it would constantly be thrown

pillar would then be the rock, which is supported by James, i.e. Jacob, 'the one who holds', otherwise known as Israel, and John, 'the grace of God', so that the church would be built on a rock and held up by Israel and God's grace). Paul refers only once to a 'Peter' (Gal. 2.7-8), and debate exists as to whether this is a scribal insertion or if Paul meant Cephas or is referring to a different person (even ancient Christian scholars were confused on this point). I suspect Paul did write this and meant a different person, someone well known at the time, another apostle like Paul and Apollos (and for whom 'Peter' was simply by coincidence his actual birth name), but it's impossible to know for sure. For summaries of evidence and scholarship on all of the above see Bart Ehrman, 'Cephas and Peter', *Journal of Biblical Literature* 109 (Autumn 1990), pp. 463-74; Dale Allison, Jr, 'Peter and Cephas: One and the Same', *Journal of Biblical Literature* 111 (Autumn 1992), pp. 489-95; and most importantly Markus Bockmuehl, 'Simon Peter's Names in Jewish Sources', *Journal of Jewish Studies* 55 (Spring 2004), pp. 58-80.

in his face, and constantly used against him, becoming a constant hurdle he would have to overcome. Yet there is no sign in his letters that it was. This is therefore just another made-up excuse, for which we have no evidence, and ample evidence to the contrary.

For example, 1 Cor. 11.23-26 and 15.3-8 focus prominently on the witness of Paul and his peers. There is no indication he was shy about this at all. In fact, Paul's whole argument of Galatians 1–2 is that human testimony was evidently distrusted by the Galatians, to the point that Paul had to deny he ever relied on it, and had to insist instead that he had all his information by direct revelation, and that he didn't even talk to anyone else in the church for years (he is even forced to swear to this). He clearly had to argue this way to persuade the Galatians his gospel was legitimate. So the Galatians only trusted direct revelation. That makes no sense on anything but minimal mythicism. How could Paul make this argument if there was a historical Jesus and therefore eyewitness companions and a family of Jesus still living and active in the church whose authority could never be trumped in such a way and whose direct testimony would surely be paramount to deciding all doctrinal authority within the church? The Galatians could not possibly have wanted Paul to prove anything but that he had his information from the eyewitnesses whose authority would then be paramount. Only if there were no such witnesses would *revelation* be the defining feature of apostolic authority, and only then would Paul have to defend his relying on nothing but that, as only then would the Galatians accept only that—rejecting human testimony instead as illegitimate (as apparently they were). Otherwise Paul would have to insist here *that he learned the gospel from the first witnesses* and then swear they can confirm to the Galatians that he had stuck to what they told him. But that's not what he argues.

It's a curious question. How can what Jesus said and did in life not be relevant to anything in Galatians 1–2? How can Paul never talk about it, when his opponents would be talking about it all the time? They would have been making arguments against Paul, or posing questions and challenges to him, by citing testimony from and about the historical Jesus, which Paul would have been compelled to answer, or at least address. There would be no plausible way Paul could expect to win any argument by *never* even addressing his opponents' evidence or even acknowledging it existed. His opponents would then win every argument and every congregation. Paul may as well be writing to himself for all the good it would do. Yet that is not what we see happening in these letters. The 'anxiety' Paul is supposed to have had over his not being an eyewitness never appears. It's a modern fiction.

This is evident, for example, in the passages where Paul uses the phrase 'super-apostles', *huper lian apostoloi*, literally 'apostles beyond exceedingly', which some who make this argument cite as evidence of his anxiety over not being an eyewitness like them. But in fact Paul never says this phrase relates to their having known Jesus. To the contrary, he says it relates to their being much better speakers than him (2 Cor. 11.1-7 and 12.7-13, which in context I suspect indicates that the famous 'thorn in his side' he complains of was a stutter or speech impediment). Remember that 'apostle' means 'messenger', so being a 'super great messenger' has a more obvious meaning in the Greek: they were better at it than he was. Paul *might* have also been concerned about the fact that they were apostles *first* (as that could have been a problem for him even if Jesus didn't exist), but he never says that, and he doesn't mean that when he calls the others 'apostles super exceedingly'. He means they are spectacularly good at selling the gospel, while he is but a poor speaker and less impressive in person. So when he asserts that he's as good as them, he refers to his ability to receive 'revelations of the Lord' as they did (2 Cor. 12.1-7) and perform miracles (2 Cor. 12.12) and demonstrate spiritual knowledge (*gnōsis*: 2 Cor. 11.6). His only failing compared to them, Paul says, is simply not being a good speaker (2 Cor. 11.6; likewise implied in 1 Cor. 2.3-4). Conspicuously absent, again, is any argument that his revelations ought to be reckoned as good as their knowing the man personally. To the contrary, he always assumes his access to Jesus was identical to theirs (1 Cor. 9.1 and 15.5-8) and that it was the most *anyone* could claim (Gal. 1.11-24).[30]

Supporting this conclusion is the fact that Paul speaks of people preaching 'another Jesus' than the one he preached, and that this involved receiving a 'different' spirit and thus a 'different' gospel (2 Cor. 11.4; see also Gal. 1.6-9). Paul would not likely speak of 'other' Jesuses like this if Jesus were a historical man. For then there would obviously be only the one Jesus, and the only gospel the one he taught, so Paul would have to say his opponents were saying false things *about* Jesus, or *misrepresenting* Jesus, or getting what Jesus said *wrong* (and, of course, Paul would have to constantly respond to the same claims against him from his opponents). But Paul never once talks like that, or as if anyone did. Yet that's how one would have to talk about a tradition based on the friends and witnesses of an actual man. But if Jesus was only a revealed deity, then it would certainly be more likely that we'd hear about different revealed deities named Jesus appearing to different people, or false spirits claiming to be Jesus, teaching different gospels, such that for Paul only one of these Jesuses was the real one, even if angels themselves said otherwise (Gal. 1.8). Because Paul had a direct line to his Jesus, and no one could honestly claim anything better.

30. In 1 Cor. 15.8-10 Paul refers to himself being 'the least' of the apostles, but in an entirely different sense: there he is referring to the fact that he didn't *deserve* to be chosen by God to be an apostle because he persecuted God's church. See parallel remarks in Gal. 1.13-16 and 1.22-24, where Paul's having been a persecutor was not being counted against him as an apostolic authority, but in fact in his favor.

Accordingly, the usual excuses simply do not hold water—they go against the evidence of the Epistles themselves, and against all our background knowledge regarding how people behave. If historicity is to survive as the more probable hypothesis, some new theory must be conjured, which not only admits and explains the bizarre silence of the Epistles but does so in accord with proven facts of comparable cases and human nature, thus either (a) having strong support in established background knowledge rather than careening violently against everything we know, or (b) in a way that can be strongly and independently confirmed from evidence in the Epistles themselves; or ideally, both. As I have never seen such an argument, despite surveying a century of trying by many scholars in the field, I have to conclude the evidence of the Epistles, on all we presently know, is simply improbable on *h* (minimal historicity), but almost exactly what we expect on $\neg h$ (minimal mythicism).

That leaves one remaining argument against this conclusion: the claim that the Epistles are not in fact silent about the historical Jesus, that in fact there are 'implicit' references in them that establish his historicity. The rest of this chapter will be devoted to answering that.

3. *Epistles from the Pillars?*

As I explained in Chapter 7, we cannot count as evidence any forgeries or demonstrable interpolations among the Epistles. Fabricated evidence of historicity is not evidence of historicity. Although if forgeries or the other Epistles let slip evidence of nonhistoricity, that can be telling. And a few examples of that can be found.

The epistles of James and 1 Peter are *also* oddly silent about a historical Jesus—an oddity later rectified by the forgery of a second letter from Peter (see Chapter 8, §12), and perhaps by the forgery of the Epistles of John (since 1 Jn 1.1-3 seems to serve a similar purpose as 2 Pet. 1.16–2.1, indeed it even appears to protest too much). Thus were produced letters from all three of the pillars, and indeed these letters were arranged in the NT in the same unusual order as Paul names them in Gal. 2.9 (placing Peter not first or last but between the brothers James and John), and the number of letters from each counts up to three (one from James, two from Peter, three from John), an obvious contrivance. Following them is the Epistle of Jude (literally, Judas), which also makes no reference to the historical Jesus—not even to claim the author was his brother, despite introducing himself (in Jude 1) as the brother of James. Notably Jude concurs with *1 Clement* (see Chapter 8, §5) in suggesting that the words of Jesus only came to be communicated to the world *through the apostles* (Jude 17), making no mention of disciples or of Jesus having preached to the public.

The Epistle of James makes no mention of its author being the brother of Jesus, either. Instead, Jas 5.11 imagines that *all* Christians have 'seen' Jesus die (just like Clement did) and implies Jesus has never been on earth before—he will only one day come (Jas 5.7-8); James does not say Jesus is 'returning' or coming a second time (such a specific notion is never found in the letters of Paul, either; on something close in Hebrews, see §5). It thus appears that as far as this author knew, Jesus hadn't yet been on earth at all. This James also says things that *later* appear on the lips of Jesus in the Gospels, yet were clearly not the words of Jesus when James wrote them.[31] So the sequence of events is again reversed: sayings came to be invented for Jesus by adapting sayings from common lore, lost scriptures and even the apostles themselves (real or fictional). James was also written by someone defending a Torah-observant sect of Christianity (the original sect before Paul's innovation: see Element 20)—exactly as Paul implies James the Pillar had done (Gal. 2.9-12). This letter might thus be an authentic letter from the original, actual James (who was not the brother of Jesus, but of the other pillar, John: see, e.g., Mk 5.37, and the discussion in §10). That this letter looks more in agreement with minimal mythicism than minimal historicity is therefore noteworthy.

1 Peter looks similarly curious.[32] We know this was written by a different author than 2 Peter (their style is too divergent). Could it have been written by the actual Peter himself? We cannot know for sure.[33] But it's notewor-

31. For example, Jas 1.12 and 5.12. See also James Tabor, *The Jesus Dynasty* (New York: Simon & Schuster, 2006), pp. 273-77. Tabor, of course, implausibly assumes James lifted these things from Jesus (even though there is no evidence of that and it's contrary to logic to think he would pass off the words of Jesus as his own and not even mention the authority behind them), and also argues this James is Jesus' brother (even though James conspicuously does not say this in his letter's introduction, where surely he would mention it), thus exemplifying the unreasonable lengths scholars will go to in order to fabricate entire pet histories for a non-existent Jesus (a point I already made from the example of Chilton in Chapter 2, §2).

32. This might originally have been two letters, the first ending at 4.11 and the second picking up at 4.12 in mid-letter (its original introduction having been deleted). Also, 1 Pet. 5.12 says he 'wrote in only a few words' (*di' oligōn egrapsa*), which he sent in the care of Silvanus (who is not mentioned in the introduction at 1 Pet. 1.1). Such a remark would not describe the whole letter as we have it (which is much longer than average letters in antiquity and thus in no sense 'a few words'), but would be explicable if it referred to the much shorter letter of 4.12–5.20, which is indeed oddly brief enough to apologize for (even if a few verses are now missing). Notably, we have no reference to Peter in this second letter, so it's possible that it was not originally a letter of Peter's and only came to be attached to Peter's epistle (of 1.1–4.11) because it sounded a similar theme.

33. Arguments to the contrary are not well founded (see Chapter 7, §3), but neither is there any way to confirm its authenticity at present.

thy again that knowledge of a historical Jesus is conspicuously absent in 1 Peter. The author only describes himself as an 'apostle', not a disciple (1 Pet. 1.1, which 2 Pet. 1.1 emulates). 1 Peter 1.10-12 describes the actual process by which facts about Jesus were discovered: scripture (vv. 10-11) and revelation to the apostles (v. 12). Jesus having ministered to the public and been known to anyone in person is again conspicuously absent here. This is practically minimal mythicism in a nutshell. Nor is Jesus ever quoted in this letter, not even to back anything it argues, even though it contains an extended summary of moral advice (instead, Peter's knowledge comes only from scripture: e.g. 1 Pet. 2.6-8, which he frequently cites to back what he says: e.g., 1 Pet. 3.8-12, where Jesus' teachings on the Golden Rule and turning the other cheek are directly on point yet strangely not mentioned—we get instead just a quotation from the Psalms). Nor is any event in Jesus' life brought up as an example or encouragement—other than the mere fact of his suffering death and that only in vague terms.

For example, this letter mentions Jesus having shed his blood as ransom for all (1 Pet. 1.18-19) and being resurrected by God (1.21), but those are facts already expected on minimal mythicism. In contrast, it mentions Jesus as having appeared only in a 'manifestation' (*phaneroō*), hence by revelation (1.20), rather than as a man born and lived or chosen from among men, which is not a remark we expect on minimal historicity. This letter also says Jesus will actually *visit* us only in the *future*, as if he had not done so before (2.12). It then says Jesus 'suffered' and his enduring that suffering is an example we are to follow when persecuted (2.21, concluding the argument of 2.13-20; also 4.13), and that part of what he endured was being abused without speaking or fighting back (2.23) and being crucified (2.24), but it also cites no authority for these facts but scripture. In fact, all Peter does here is quote and paraphrase material in Isaiah 53—directly quoting Isa. 53.9 in 2.22 and then paraphrasing Isa. 53.7 in 2.23, and Isa. 53.4 and 53.11 in 22.4, and Isa. 53.6 in 2.25. Thus even the part about Jesus not speaking or fighting back is a lift from Isaiah. There is no mention here of anyone having seen Jesus do any of this, or how Peter knows he did, or who the Lord's abusers were. Rather, it appears this information had simply been learned from scripture (hence Element 17). There evidently was no actual witness to quote other than Isaiah. Equally strange is the fact that when Peter insists all earthly authorities are 'sent by [God] for the punishment of evildoers' and thus are always to be obeyed (1 Pet. 2.13-14), he seems to have no idea that it's these same earthly authorities who killed Jesus—who, in Peter's view, could hardly have been an evildoer.

We're likewise told that Jesus preached to infernal spirits (1 Pet. 3.19-20) after being resurrected (3.18-19, 21), but curiously we're never told that he preached to men on earth before that. All we hear about is a celestial Jesus who suffers and dies in some sense 'in the flesh' (3.18; 4.1), descends to preach to imprisoned spirits (3.19-20), including spirits of the dead (4.6), and then ascends back to heaven once he is put in charge of the universe (3.22).[34] This is all in agreement with minimal mythicism, and in fact sounds a lot like the *Ascension of Isaiah* and the Ignatian mini-gospel (see Chapter 8, §7). So when at last Peter tells us he was a 'witness of the sufferings of Christ' (1 Pet. 5.1), possibly in what was originally a separate letter (possibly not even by Peter),[35] we must either convict the Gospels of lying (as in their accounts Peter is not present at the crucifixion) or conclude he means by revelation, the very way Paul saw Jesus offering the bread and cup (in 1 Cor. 11.23-25), or the way James said *all* Christians saw Jesus suffer (Jas 5.11). I think the latter is more likely regardless, and at worst is no less likely. For as we saw, Peter could only quote and paraphrase Isaiah for details of Christ's suffering rather than recalling what he witnessed (as we'd otherwise expect—even his vision must therefore have been vague on such details).

The content of even these Epistles therefore is less probable on h than on $\neg h$. So these also count as evidence for minimal mythicism and against historicity. They were simply co-opted by the historicizing sect because they said nothing overtly contrary to their aims, and thus could be 'interpreted' as being in agreement with them, even though we can see this agreement is strained and requires arbitrary, dogmatic assumptions to maintain. In all honesty, I cannot fathom the content of James, Jude and 1 Peter being even 60% likely on h (while it's not at all unexpected on $\neg h$). However, arguing *a fortiori*, I shall say it cannot reasonably be more than 80% likely.

Meanwhile, I shall not count here the fact that some of the forged epistles in the NT show a reaction against 'mythical' Jesuses as evidence for either theory, since that evidence is consistent with both. But it does refute the claim that we should have some such evidence yet don't—because we do, in fact even more than we might have expected (I discussed this evidence in Chapter 8, §12).

4. *The Earliest Gospels*

A few times in Paul's letters (and in the Pauline letters composed in his name afterward) we are given actual statements of the gospel 'kerygma', the core doctrine that defined what Christians believed (Element 10). It is

34. The actual process of descending and ascending is, however, not explicit here. We're only told Jesus 'went' to preach to imprisoned spirits after his death. So the location of these spirits in relation to where Jesus started and ended up may be debatable. But background knowledge (Elements 34-38) and evidence in Paul (Phil. 2.6-11; cf. Element 10) make some kind of descent and ascent most probable.

35. See earlier note on the fragmented nature of 1 Peter.

sometimes claimed that these demonstrate belief in a historical Jesus. However, it's obvious they do not, and indeed they make much less sense on the supposition that a historical Jesus is what these gospels refer to.

The most commonly cited in this respect is 1 Cor. 15.1-8, which I already discussed (in §2). This only says Christians believed Jesus died (sacrificially for their sins), was buried, and rose again, and then (and, it would seem, *only* then) appeared to select church leaders. No mention of his birth, ancestry, ministry, miracles, teachings, promises, appointing of disciples or anything else we encounter in the Gospels. This looks exactly like minimal mythicism (especially given such background facts as Elements 37 and 38). Indeed, as a statement of a belief about a historical man, the things it omits are very strange. The fact that he is mentioned as appearing only after he died (as if his ministry and deeds in life were wholly unremarkable and not at all relevant to his status or gospel) is especially strange. This gospel thus provides no evidence for historicity; in fact, it supports mythicism. Because its content is quite unexpected on the former but not at all on the latter. And unexpected is just another way of saying improbable.

Next most commonly cited is the introduction to Paul's letter to the Romans:

> [T]he gospel of God, which he announced in advance through his prophets in the holy scriptures, concerns his Son, who was born from the sperm of David according to the flesh, who was appointed to be the Son of God in power according to the spirit of holiness by resurrection from the dead, in other words Jesus Christ our Lord, through whom we received grace and apostleship, into obedience of faith among all the nations, for the sake of his name, and among whom you, too, are called to be Jesus Christ's (Rom. 1.1-6).

The specific peculiarity of Paul saying Jesus was 'born from the sperm of David' I will address later (in §9); the rest is no less peculiar than the gospel recited in 1 Corinthians 15.[36] The only source cited for knowledge of these facts is scripture, and the only facts constituting Christian belief here are that Jesus is now Lord because he was given a human body formed of

36. Some scholars over the years have argued that this is an interpolation, but I do not find their arguments convincing. I find this passage compatible with Philippians 2, and its non-Pauline language (which consists of a single unique use of 'holy scriptures', a phrase Paul never otherwise uses) can be due to this being a hymn-like recitation not originally of his composition (just like Phil. 2.4-11). Its unusual length for a Pauline introduction can be due to the fact that this is a letter about the basics of the gospel, which he thus could have chosen to emphasize by reciting it in his introduction. This introduction also echoes Rom. 16.25-26, even its unusual wording and concepts, so it's possible both come from a Pauline redactor; it would thus still reflect thoughts and ideas from Paul's school of thought (see Chapter 7, §7).

Davidic seed and then appointed to supreme heavenly authority at his resurrection (which presupposes his death).

This is all compatible with minimal mythicism. Not a single detail is more likely on minimal historicity. Indeed, Paul here says it is through Jesus that he and all other apostles were appointed, which again implies only by revelation, as no distinction is made between those Jesus appointed when he was alive and those who saw him only after he died. And again, no mention is made of Jesus' ministry, miracles or teachings. And though now we hear something of his birth, all we get is a generic theological statement, that he was 'made [*genomenos*] from the sperm of David'. We're not told how anyone knew that, or who his parents were, or where he was born, or anything else that would make this a definite statement of earthly existence in human history (and not, e.g., just a doctrine of heavenly incarnation). Whether we can make any more out of that I'll query later (in §9), but overall we don't have any definite evidence supporting historicity over mythicism here. This gospel still looks weird for a historical Jesus—as if anything Jesus said or did as a historical man was wholly irrelevant to Christian belief. All that mattered was how he was created and what God did for him after he died. That sounds more like mythicism than historicity. Though it's compatible with both, at this early stage it's strange to see his ministry and deeds in life already wholly elided as irrelevant.

The next version of the gospel Paul gives us is the most detailed we get from him—and yet the most clearly in accord with the mythicist thesis:

> Have this mind [of humble love] in you, which was also in Christ Jesus, who, existing in the form of God, did not decide to seize equality with God, but emptied himself, taking the form of a slave, being made in the likeness of men, and being discovered as a man in outward form, he humbled himself, becoming obedient to the point of death, a death of a cross. For this [act] God also highly exalted him, and granted him the name that is above all names, so that in the name of Jesus every knee should bend, of those in heaven and those on earth and those under the earth, and that every tongue should confess that Jesus Christ is Lord, for the glory of God the Father[37] (Phil. 2.5-11).

Here we have important parallels with the prefatory gospel in Romans: the key role of the 'name of Jesus' (Rom. 1.5), Jesus being exalted into celestial power at his resurrection (Rom. 1.4), and Jesus being 'made' [*genomenos*] into a man (Rom. 1.3) so he could die. Whereas his resurrection is declared and his death is presupposed in the Romans gospel, here his death is declared and his resurrection presupposed. But otherwise this appears to be more or less an expansion of the same gospel in Romans.

37. Modern editions all concur in reading *en Christō Iēsou* in Phil. 2.5, using a Hebraicized dative for *Iēsous*.

First, we're told Jesus was a preexistent being, the Form of God. We know from Philo there was already a Jewish tradition of a preexistent being named Jesus who was the Form of God (Element 40). It cannot be claimed Philo came up with this notion on his own, since that would entail a wildly improbable coincidence. So we surely are looking at a derivation from an earlier Divine Logos doctrine. Then we're told this Jesus did not try to seize power from God in heaven (as by some accounts Satan had once done, resulting in his fall to the lower realms), but instead divested himself of all his power and higher being, enslaving himself (either to God's plan or the world of flesh) by 'being made' [*genomenos*] in the 'likeness' of men (not literally becoming a man, but assuming a human body, and thus wearing human 'flesh'). Then we're told he was 'discovered' in that form, and apparently in result was thought to be a man (*schēma* being the outward form, the appearance of a thing).

The latter point is most curious. To say Jesus was 'found' that way entails someone did the finding, and mistook him for a man (*heuretheis* meaning 'being found, discovered'). Who would that be? In the original *Ascension of Isaiah*, it was Satan and his demons who found him in that form—and then killed him, not knowing who he really was (see Chapter 3, §1). This gospel says Jesus is dutifully obedient to God's plan, to the point of being killed on a 'cross' (a *stauros*, literally an 'upright stick', not necessarily a cross *per se*: see discussion in Chapter 4, §3). And for this obedience God rewarded him by assigning him the most powerful of all names (it seems as though that means the name 'Jesus' itself: Phil. 2.10), with the result that this Jesus then became God's appointed 'Lord' over all things in the universe (in, above and below the earth). The notion evidently being that Zechariah 6 was thought by Christians to describe the event of his naming, after his resurrection (Elements 6 and 40), before which he may have had some *other* name.[38]

38. His previous name being Melchizedek, perhaps (Elements 5 and 42). Some scholars argue that the name he was assigned that is 'above all names' is 'Lord' (Phil. 2.11), but that seems to disagree with what is stated (2.10) and the fact that many beings had the title of Lord (celestial: 1 Cor. 8.5; and human: Eph. 6.5). Jesus could be called the 'Lord of Lords' (1 Tim. 6.15; Rev. 17.14), but that is not said here. However, many men were called Jesus, too (and Paul seems to imagine there were other celestial beings so named as well: 2 Cor. 11.4). Possibly what Paul means is that by assigning the name 'Lord' to Jesus the name 'Jesus' acquired special power (Phil. 2.10). But that is not obvious from the text. Either way, because 'Jesus' can be in the genitive or dative case in 2.10, an ambiguity remains as to *which* name was above all names (the name 'Jesus' itself or some other name Jesus was given), or whether that name was already above all names or whether God merely declared that that name would now be above all names. If

Key things to notice here are that again no mention is made of Jesus having a ministry, teaching anything or performing any miracles. To the contrary, having 'emptied' himself of all he was and 'humbling' himself completely to the status of a 'slave' imply he would have had no supernatural powers at all. Likewise, no mention is made of his being born to the virgin Mary or killed by Pontius Pilate (or even the Jews or Romans)—even though these had become essential components of the gospel creed by the time of Ignatius (see Chapter 8, §6; which raises the question of *why* they later became essential components of the creed).[39] Nor do we find here any other details placing these generic events on earth or in human history. This hymn's use of the word for 'born' is also metaphysically vague: *genomenos* is used twice, once for his being 'formed' into the likeness of men, and once for his 'becoming' obedient, without distinguishing one from the other. So is this a human birth or a celestial incarnation? We cannot tell from the wording (see later discussion in §9).

These facts all accord with minimal mythicism. Whereas on minimal historicity, they are odd. So odd, in fact, that some scholars have had to insist this entire passage must be an interpolation, that Paul can't possibly have said this. But there is no evidence it's an interpolation. No manuscripts omit it; no significant variants exist for it (beyond variant spellings of a few words, which is common); it also does not contradict anything else Paul says in this or any other letter, and it does not interrupt the flow of thought in Philippians 2—it even matches the thought of the surrounding argument, emphasizing the theme of Christ's self-humbling and obedience as an example the Christian is exhorted to follow.[40] I must conclude that this passage is authentic. I must further conclude that its content is improbable on h, but not at all improbable on $\neg h$. It is therefore evidence against historicity, not for it.

the text was meant to say he was given the name Jesus after his resurrection, that might signal an evolution of the doctrine reported by Philo (Element 42).

39. Indeed, I find that suspicious already. Why did it matter so much what the name was of the officer who executed Jesus? Why was it important that 'crucified *by Pontius Pilate*' become a requirement of Christian confession (as most creeds from the second century onward declare)? It seems as though there were other creeds whereby that was not the case, wherein Jesus was crucified *by someone else*, and therefore to exclude them from inclusion converts had to specify which crucifixion myth they were aligning themselves with (hence see Chapter 8, §1). This would make far more sense on minimal mythicism than minimal historicity. But, alas, we can't be certain that was the reason. So I have mentioned it only in a note.

40. For a full analysis see Ralph Martin, *A Hymn of Christ: Philippians 2:5-11 in Recent Interpretation and in the Setting of Early Christian Worship* (Downers Grove, IL: InterVarsity Press, 1997).

Paul claimed these things came to him by revelation, another thing we expect on mythicism but not quite so much on historicity. Because Paul consistently employs the same phrases to reference his gospel revelations. For example:

> For I would have you know, brethren, the **gospel** which was **preached** by me is not according to a man. For I did not **receive** it from a man, nor was I taught it, but it came through a revelation of Jesus Christ (Gal. 1.11-12).
>
> For I **received** from the Lord just what I **delivered** to you . . . (1 Cor. 11.23).
>
> And I would have you know, brethren, the **gospel** I **preached** to you . . . I **delivered** to you first of all what I **received**, that according to the scriptures Christ died for our sins . . . (1 Cor. 15.1, 3).

Nevertheless, it could be argued that Paul must have *really* gotten this information from human tradition. Based on their style, all the 'earliest gospels' we've surveyed are arguably pre-Pauline and thus in reality most likely learned the usual way (and not by revelation), which opened Paul to attack among the Galatians as a possible fraud (i.e. not a 'real' apostle). This is why he had to at least *pretend* Jesus gave him this gospel material directly (or that Jesus had thus reaffirmed it to him, even if the precisely worded creeds he picked up were from members of the church). Because to be an apostle, you had to have been sent by the Lord himself (1 Cor. 9.1). It was necessary, therefore, to have learned the gospel that way.

Paul might not have had to lie about this. He may have actually had this material repeated back to him in his hallucinations of Jesus, and thus was not pretending, even though in reality his brain had learned that material from human sources, such as the Christians he had previously persecuted (1 Cor. 15.8-9; Gal. 1.13-14 and 1.23-24). But it's also possible Paul's 'gospel' summaries *are* Pauline originals and not in his usual style because they derived from conversations with his alter-ego (the hallucinated Jesus) in Hebrew, or were carefully formulated to look like he didn't invent them. It's only the list of appearances in 1 Cor. 15.5-8 that certainly must derive from human informants (because we can reasonably assume Paul was not psychic so as to magically know who saw Jesus), but that does not mean this is what Paul was claiming in 1 Cor. 15.1-2. To the contrary, by using the exact same formula there as in Gal. 1.11-12, Paul is claiming he got even this material from revelation. Thus, he was either lying or really did hallucinate Jesus telling him that—after having already heard it elsewhere. Or else the list of appearances was not a part of the gospel but only the proof of Jesus having taught it. In which case, Paul means by 'what he received' only 1 Cor. 15.3-4. The subsequent list then only argues that it had indeed been received (by the apostles, of whom he was the last: 15.5-8). It does not appear to have been received by any of the apostles in any other way. And

Christians who received it from the apostles could not themselves be called apostles.

When we look at the other Epistles in Paul's name that most closely share his thoughts and ideas, we find another summary of the gospel: Col. 1.12-20. Here we get something a bit more grandiose, but with more of the esoteric backstory revealed:

> [Give] thanks to the Father, who made us fit to be part of the inheritance of those holy in the light, he who delivered us from the authority of the darkness and transferred [us] to the kingdom of the Son of His love, in whom we have [our] redemption, the forgiveness of [our] sins, he who is the Image of the unseen God, the firstborn of all creation. For in him were all things created, in the heavens and on earth, things seen and unseen, whether thrones or dominions or principalities or authorities, all things have been created through him, and for him. And he is before all things, and in him all things are held together. He is also the head of the body, the church, and he is the beginning, the firstborn from the dead, so that he would have preeminence in all things. He was pleased that in him should all the fulness dwell and through him all things should be fully reconciled with himself, having made peace [with them] through the blood of his cross—whether things upon the earth, or things in the heavens (Col. 1.12-20).

And *that*, we're told, is 'the mystery that has been hidden for ages and generations, but now has been manifested to his holy ones', the ones 'to whom God wished to make known what the riches are of the glory of this mystery among the Gentiles', that being the realization of 'Christ in you, the hope of glory' (Col. 1.26-27).

Notice that despite the elaborate description here of who Jesus Christ is and what he did and why it matters, at no point is his being born and living on earth mentioned, or his having a ministry, or performing miracles, or choosing disciples, or being executed by Pontius Pilate, or anything at all that would place him in earth's history—we're not told who put him on the cross, for example, or where.[41] But what we do see here is corroboration of the Philippians gospel: Jesus was a preexistent being, in fact the firstborn of all creation (thus again clearly identifying him with a known celestial figure in early Judaism: Elements 39 and 40); and also the firstborn from

41. Another letter from the Pauline school quotes and interprets a passage from Ps. 68.18 as attesting to the ascent and descent of Jesus (Eph. 4.8-14), but its account is too vague to pin down exactly what is meant cosmically, and it is not presented as a summary of the gospel, just a part of what they believed. That passage does assume that the descent of Jesus required scriptural evidence (Eph. 4.9) and thus was not witnessed by anyone, but that does not entail minimal mythicism. Although I do believe the author of Ephesians had no knowledge of a historical Jesus, that can only be inferred, not proved, and it is a forgery anyway.

the dead ('so that he would be first in everything'); he was also the 'image of God'. These are three facts that match Pauline thought—that Jesus was a preexistent being, in fact God's agent of creation (1 Cor. 8.6; see Element 10), and that Jesus was 'the firstborn from the dead' (Rom. 8.29 and 1 Cor. 15.20), and that he was the 'image of God' (2 Cor. 4.4). So it is very much in accord with the gospel known to Paul. Yet here this celestial being is the one who submitted to death (Col. 1.18, 20) and has now been assigned all of God's power and authority (Col. 1.19) because his blood sacrifice has somehow magically effected harmony in the universe (Col. 1.20). This sure sounds like a celestial demigod working a celestial deed.[42] There is nothing here that sounds like a historical man who recently lived and died on earth.

Thus, every time Paul or his closest successors describe anything like a complete gospel 'kerygma' we see no clear evidence of a historical Jesus, but a consistently celestial being doing magical things in a supernatural realm, whose deeds and teachings in life (if any there were) are completely absent and somehow of no relevance to Christian belief.[43] What are the odds of that? It's simply *strange*. And strange means unusual, which means infrequent, which means *improbable*. This evidence therefore has a significantly lower consequent probability on h compared to $\neg h$. And we must add to all this the evidence of Hebrews.

5. *The Gospel in Hebrews*

Things only get worse for historicity when we look at the most elaborate early gospel of all: that recounted in the book of Hebrews. The author of this text is not named, and though some claimed it was Paul, that's unlikely (stylistically for sure), although it may have been composed by a contemporary or successor of Paul (as I suspect is the case for *1 Clement*: see Chapter 8, §5; where I also mention evidence that *1 Clement* might even have used Hebrews as a source). In Heb. 13.13 the author claims to be a companion of Timothy, which could be the same Timothy Paul traveled with; the author also implies at least some of his readers were evangelized by the original

42. Likewise in Col. 2.15, where we're told Jesus 'cast off the principalities and authorities and made a public example of them, freely triumphing over them', which sooner ties the immediately preceding claim of Col. 2.14 (that Jesus 'nailed [our sin] to the cross') to a cosmic event, not an earthly one (see discussion of this passage in Element 37). Jesus is here being freed from the power of corruption and death, not freed from the Romans and Jews. Jesus is also the one driving the nails here, which we must suppose is metaphorical.

43. Even the gospel declared in 1 Timothy is odd: though the author of 1 Timothy may have been a historicist (as suggested, e.g., by 1 Tim. 6.13; although see note below), the gospel he summarizes (in 1 Tim. 3.16) looks pre-historicist in origin (see discussion in Chapter 8, §6).

apostles, and long enough ago that they should be teachers themselves by now (2.3; 5.12); and in 10.32-34 the author appears to refer to their initial persecution in the time of Paul years before (which Paul himself references in Gal. 1.13)—if these remarks are not fabrications, they would place this letter as early as the late 40s or as late as the early 60s.[44]

Many scholars instead want to date Hebrews after the canonical Gospels, but that faces two serious objections: Hebrews shows no knowledge of those Gospels (it never references any of their unique content and never quotes from them, and what it does argue often seems to be in ignorance of what they say); and Hebrews assumes without explanation that the Jewish temple cult is still operating—that the temple hasn't been destroyed by the Romans and the rites there outlawed. Both facts should date Hebrews before 70 CE and therefore before all the canonical Gospels. That would make it in a sense the earliest Christian 'Gospel', since it is mostly an elaborate treatise on the gospel and why it should be believed (it just isn't a narrative of Jesus or a collection of his sayings, so it's not analogous to other Gospels only in structure and genre).

The first fact is strong enough (if written later, Hebrews should reflect knowledge of the Gospels), but the second fact is the most telling. The overall argument of this letter is that Jewish Christians should not backslide now, because Judaism can no longer guarantee their salvation (this letter does not advocate Torah-observant Christianity: e.g. Heb. 13.9).[45] That the temple cult no longer existed (and God did nothing to save the Jews from destruction, not even as a nation, but neither to save his temple and the cult being paid to him there) would have been so extremely effective and important an argument in this context that for the author never once to use it is all but impossible—unless Hebrews was written before the year 70, before even the year 66 (when the Jewish War started, since that fact alone could hardly escape mention). For example (and this is just one example among many), in Heb. 10.1-4 it is clearly assumed the temple sacrifices are still being performed: because the author makes an argument against their effectiveness, yet the obvious argument—that they aren't even being performed any more and therefore can't be effective even if ever they were—doesn't occur to him. He even asks as a rhetorical question if the effects of

44. That a certain Timothy was Paul's close friend and companion and frequent co-worker: Rom. 16.21; 1 Cor. 4.17; 16.10; 2 Cor. 1.1, 19; Phil. 1; 2.19; 1 Thess. 1.1; 3.2, 6; Phlm. 1.1. That he was nevertheless not an apostle is implied in 2 Cor. 1.1.

45. See also Heb. 2.1; 3.12-14; 5.12; 10.25; 12.12, etc. Hence the 'Hebrews' to which the letter is addressed—whether the author added that title or it was added by later editors as a descriptor—were clearly both Christian believers and also Jews or former Jews (or possibly also prospective converts to Judaism), as both facts are assumed throughout the letter.

these sacrifices lasted longer than a year, 'would they not have ceased to be offered [by now]?' (10.2). It's undeniably clear the author has no idea here that they *had* ceased. We must conclude, then, that they had not. I find this so decisive a point that maintaining a later date for Hebrews is simply not tenable. I know of no logically valid argument for that. I therefore side with those scholars who accept it as early.[46]

Whatever its date, this letter is almost entirely about Jesus, yet seems wholly unaware of his having been any kind of earthly man. I suspect this epistle represents, at least in its core elements (indeed if not in its entirety), what the gospel of Jesus was that Paul was preaching and what that gospel was before the Gospels mythically euhemerized Jesus into an earthly man. But whether that's the case or not, Hebrews certainly appears to imagine a solely cosmic Jesus. The simplest explanation for this fact is that this letter preserves the gospel in its earlier form, rather than it being a later (and thus radical) departure from the stories and sayings tradition found in the Gospels. Those stories and sayings are completely absent here, and would seem to be unknown to this author. Surely if the author of Hebrews were radically departing from established or widespread tradition he would be compelled to argue against it and to argue for his own claims and interpretations in place of them—he would thus be compelled to explain why he is rejecting nearly everything those Gospels say about Jesus. That he doesn't suggests he is writing before they (and their stories and sayings tradition) even existed or were known. And either way, the historicist is still faced with the very difficult task of explaining why the historical Jesus has completely disappeared in Hebrews.

The gospel repeatedly emphasized throughout the book of Hebrews is that 'Jesus the Son of God is the great high priest who has passed through the heavens' (Heb. 4.14; see also 6.19-20, in reference to the account in Heb. 5; etc.). You might notice that that sounds exactly like the celestial high priest named Jesus in early Jewish theology (Element 40) undertaking the very task described for the celestial Jesus in the *Ascension of Isaiah* (Chapter 3, §1). We saw that in the earliest discernible redaction of the latter, the Jesus who passes through the heavens dies in outer space, in the

46. For a summary of the issues and scholarship see 'Hebrews, Epistle to the', in *Oxford Dictionary of the Christian Church* (ed. F.L. Cross and E.A. Livingstone; Oxford: Oxford University Press, 3rd edn, 1997), pp. 742-43; and James Thompson, 'Hebrews, Epistle to the', in *Eerdmans Dictionary of the Bible* (ed. David Noel Freedman; Grand Rapids, MI: William B. Eerdmans, 2000), pp. 568-70. See also Hugh Anderson, 'The Jewish Antecedents of the Christology in Hebrews', in *The Messiah: Developments in Earliest Judaism and Christianity* (ed. James Charlesworth; Minneapolis, MN: Fortress Press, 1992), pp. 512-35.

sublunar heaven, not on earth. This also appears to be what the author of Hebrews believes:

> The sum of what we've said is this: we have such a High Priest, who is set on the right hand of the throne of His Majesty in the heavens, a minister of the sanctuary and of the true tabernacle that the Lord set up, not man. For every high priest is ordained to offer gifts and sacrifices, therefore it is necessary that this One have something to offer, too. For if He were on earth, He would not be a priest, since there are already priests who offer gifts according to the law, and who only give service to the copy and shadow of heavenly things [*because Moses was instructed to make on earth copies of the things he saw in heaven*] (Heb. 8.1-5).

This certainly seems to say Jesus died in outer space.[47] Because here we're told that Jesus not only performed his sacrifice in the celestial temple (as in Heb. 9, as we'll see in a moment), but that he *had* to do so. Otherwise the magic of it wouldn't have worked. We're also told that Jesus wasn't ever on earth—instead, he could only have been God's *celestial* high priest (so as to perform the ultimate sacrifice) if he *wasn't* on earth. Because 'if he were on earth, he would not be a priest', since earth already has its priests—but Jesus needs to be a priest, in order to mediate the new covenant (Heb. 8.6). We're also told here the same thing Isaiah was told in the *Ascension*: that everything on earth has a duplicate version of it in the heavens (hence Element 38). The implication is that Jesus' blood must have been spilled on the heavenly duplicate of God's altar—not on earth, where there already are priests making blood sacrifices, which are less effective than celestial ones. Yet Jesus, being perfect, was the most powerful sacrifice of all (Heb. 7.27-28).

But we needn't rely on just implication here. Because the author of Hebrews goes on to say exactly that when he essentially elaborates the Philippians gospel into a full-blown explanation of what Jesus did and why:

> Christ, **arriving as a High Priest** of the good things to come, through a greater and more perfect temple, **the one not made with hands** (that is to say, not of [human] construction), and neither through the blood of goats and calves, but through his own blood, he entered into the holy place once and for all, finding eternal redemption. For if the blood of goats and

47. This also entails that the high priests on earth are the earthly copies of Jesus, who is the celestial high priest, the 'realized' Platonic form of all human high priests; that is, the perfect and eternal high priest of which all earthly priests are but poor and mortal imitations (the *actual* Platonic form would be a thought in the mind of God; see Element 38). After Christ's resurrection, his copy on earth became the Christian church (1 Cor. 12.27; Col. 1.18, 24), which was also a copy of the celestial temple (Element 18), because the temple is the body and Christ (as its high priest) is the spirit inhabiting it. Believers, being the parts of Christ's body, are similarly imagined as being the new temple priesthood in 1 Pet. 2.5 and 2.9 (tending their body as the temple).

bulls, and sprinkling the ashes of a heifer, made holy again those who were defiled, cleansing their flesh, how much more should the blood of Christ (who through the eternal Spirit offered himself without blemish unto God) cleanse your conscience from dead works to serve the living God!

And it is for this reason that [Christ] is the mediator of a new testament, so that by a death having taken place for the redemption of the transgressions that were under the first testament, they that have been called may [now] receive the promise of the eternal inheritance. For where a testament is, it must follow on the death of him that made it. For a testament is only valid upon death; it doesn't go into effect when he that made it still lives. For this reason even the first testament was not enacted without blood . . . [*since Moses inaugurated the old testament with a blood sacrifice*].

Pretty much, according to the law, all things are cleansed with blood and without bloodshed no forgiveness occurs. And so **it was necessary** that the **copies** of the things in the heavens should be cleansed with these, but **the heavenly things themselves** with *better* sacrifices than these. For Christ did not go into the holy place made with hands, the antitype of the true one, but into heaven itself, now to appear before the face of God on our behalf. Nor does he need to present himself time and again, like the high priest does who goes into the holy place year by year with the blood of another. Otherwise [Christ] must have suffered repeatedly since the foundation of the world. But *now*, once and for all, at the end of the ages, he has **appeared** to put away sin by sacrificing himself.

And insofar as men are appointed to die only once, and after that comes judgment, so Christ also, having been offered once to bear the sins of many, **shall appear a second time**, without sin, to those who eagerly wait for him, for salvation. For the law, containing only a shadow of the good things to come and not the actual image of them, can never perfect those who would draw near with the same sacrifices year by year, which they offer continually. Otherwise wouldn't they have ceased to be offered? Because then worshippers, having been cleansed once and for all, would have no more sins on their conscience. But in these [sacrifices] there is a remembrance of sins year by year. For it is impossible that the blood of bulls and goats should take away sins [for good].

For this reason, when **coming into the world, [Christ] says**, 'Sacrifice and offering you did not desire . . .' [*here beginning a lengthy quotation of Ps. 40.6-8*]. [And so] he put an end to the first, so he could establish the second. By this testament we have been made holy through the offering of **the body of Jesus Christ** once and for all. Indeed every priest stands day by day ministering and offering the same sacrifices time and again, which can never take away sins. But he, when he offered one sacrifice for sins for all time, sat down on the right hand of God. Thereafter waiting, until his enemies are put down to be a footstool under his feet. For by one offering he has perfected forever those who are made holy.

And the Holy Spirit also bears witness to us, for **after that he said** . . . [*here quoting Jer. 31.33-34*]. For where the pardoning of sins be, there is no more offering for sin [required] (Heb. 9.11–10.18).

Here we see unveiled the entire logic of the Christian gospel: the temple sacrifices were insufficient for salvation and had to be done away with (Element 28), but to do that a more perfect sacrifice had to be conceived, one with eternal magical power (rather than one that lasts only a year) and one that can cleanse sins to their celestial core, and not just the earthly veneer of them (Element 18). Logic then entails that this sacrifice has to be of a divine body, not an earthly one—and has to be performed in the divine temple, not the earthly one. And the author here says that is exactly what Jesus did, that that was his whole purpose. That is the sum of the gospel.

Jesus is here being declared the superior replacement for Moses. So we should ask whether Jesus is just as mythical as Moses. Evidence for that conclusion can be found all throughout this elaboration on the gospel, which again says nothing about Jesus being crucified by Pontius Pilate, or conducting a ministry, or performing miracles, or teaching anything. Instead, when this author quotes Jesus ('he says . . .', Heb. 10.5; and 'after that he said . . .', Heb. 10.15), he simply quotes the scriptures. He thus evinces no instances of a historical Jesus having said anything. Apparently, the only way the author of Hebrews knows to learn the words of Jesus on this subject is by finding them in scripture. For the author actually believes these are the words of Jesus, and not an interpretation of the words of Jeremiah or the Psalmist. Because he says these are the words of Jesus, which were transmitted through the Holy Spirit to the authors of those texts, and that therefore this is how Jesus speaks to us. Just as we saw in *1 Clement* (Chapter 8, §5). The fact that nowhere in Hebrews, in all its thirteen chapters, do any historical words of Jesus appear, yet Jesus is often 'quoted' by quoting scripture, is not only evidence the Gospels had not been written yet but that there was no historical Jesus to quote. (Revelations may have been quotable, and the author of Hebrews does seem aware of this, but never quotes them directly—their content was evidently such that he never had occasion to, or was not permitted to, as in 2 Cor. 12.3-5.)

Further evidence lies in the fact that Jesus in this gospel sprinkles his blood on objects in outer space, not on earth. Though he does not die in the celestial temple, he nevertheless must carry his blood there. And only once he does (and thus, only after his ascension) is the new covenant established and the sins of the elect forgiven. Which means that feat had *not* been accomplished on the cross. More importantly, this author sees no need to explain how a man crucified by the Romans could do any of this. It seems to be taken for granted that Jesus performs his sacrifice in the heavens, in parallel to the priests who perform theirs on earth. Sacrifices performed on earth are feeble; only a sacrifice in heaven has lasting power. The logic of this fits that of the earlier redaction of the *Ascension of Isaiah*. It doesn't fit the historicizing narratives in the Gospels. Indeed, as Paul says we are baptized into Christ's death and buried with him (Rom. 6.3-4), we might infer he meant *that* is the earthly copy of the perfect death and burial of Jesus, which to be perfect had to be in heaven, where the author of Hebrews says all such superior antitypes are.

Despite all of that, it is sometimes claimed that here at least the author admits Jesus appeared on earth. But that is actually, and quite conspicuously, *not* said here. There is no mention of any of this occurring on earth. The author says that to perform his sacrifice Jesus 'once and for all, at the end of the ages, **appeared** [*phaneroō*] in order to put away sin by sacrificing himself' (Heb. 9.26), the verb here being a common term for divine revelations and manifestations (it actually means 'make known, make clear, reveal'). Then he 'shall appear [*optanomai*] a second time' (9.28), this time a verb of more concrete seeing—so we will observe his next arrival with our eyes. This is exactly in accord with minimal mythicism, whereby Jesus 'appeared' the first time in revelations to communicate that he had just performed this sacrifice (1 Cor. 15.3-8), and then will 'appear' a second time, more concretely in the very air above us, at the end of the world (1 Thess. 4.16-17). Likewise that Jesus had a 'body' to sacrifice, from which could pour 'blood', is exactly what minimal mythicism entails: he assumed a body of flesh in the sublunar firmament so that it could be killed, then returned to the upper heavens from whence he came. Exactly as the *Ascension of Isaiah* describes Jesus did, and just like what many believed happened to Osiris (Elements 14 and 31).

Later on the author of Hebrews mentions an additional detail about where Jesus died:

> For the bodies of those beasts whose blood is brought into the holy place by the high priest [as an offering] for sin are then burned outside the camp. For this reason Jesus also suffered outside the gate, in order to make the people holy through his own blood. Therefore, let us go out to him, outside the camp, bearing the same reproach he did. For we do not have a lasting city here, but we seek after a city to come (Heb. 13.11-14).

From the context the argument here is metaphorical, 'leaving the camp' meaning departing Judaism and the temple cult. The two cities are metaphors for the two worlds: the present world of flesh is where they have no city, while their future life in the heavens is the city they look for (see Heb. 11.16 and 12.22; Paul said much the same in Phil. 3.20—and Gal. 4.25-26, on which see §9).

But for the latter metaphor to work, the author cannot mean Jesus was crucified outside the gates of Jerusalem. That is in *this* world, where we have no city, and is certainly not where we must go to meet Jesus now. Clearly, for us to 'go out to him, outside the camp' means outside this world, into heaven (spiritually for now, literally only later: as explained in Rom. 8). But this also operates as a double metaphor: it also means going outside the protections of Jewish cult practice, and thus leaving Judaism, for which they must 'bear reproach' as Jesus did when he was abused and killed. This must refer to the fact that Jesus ended that old covenant with his sacrifice, and that he did so 'outside the gate' of heaven. As the *Ascension of Isaiah* explains (Chapter 3, §1), Jesus had to pass through the many gates of heaven to reach the firmament and be killed by Satan and his demons.[48] He thus had to sacrifice himself 'outside the gate' of the heavenly temple and carry his blood back into it to effect the new covenant (as we saw explained in Heb. 9). There is therefore no clear evidence for historicity here.

The silence throughout Hebrews, coupled with many examples of exactly what we'd expect on minimal mythicism, makes the evidence of Hebrews at least somewhat less probable on minimal historicity. It therefore also counts as evidence in favor of minimal myth. Indeed, it practically evinces and describes the first stage of it: a cosmic sacrifice of a cosmic 'high priest' (a preexistent being already known in Jewish theology: Element 40). Notably, as well, there is no evident embarrassment at any of what is being described here. The author is completely confident that this sacrificial system makes obvious and elegant sense and requires no defense, indeed the logic of it *is* its only defense (that, and finding secret messages from Jesus saying so in scripture). This author sees no need to justify, argue or explain how an executed convict could be this perfect celestial sacrifice. It's simply not an issue. Nor is any issue raised of how he came to be this celestial high priest. There is no discussion of his birth or life or sayings or deeds. There is no response here to the very Jewish polemic that would have been threatening to cause the backsliding this author is arguing to prevent—*other* than to defend its theological logic. Which means there was no historical narrative to defend, just a theology.

This is all clear enough. But to bring my point home, I shall go through Hebrews from start to finish to illustrate how the whole of it corroborates the points just made, starting with Hebrews 1 and 2, which repeat essentially the gospel of Philippians, with elaborations and scriptural citations as proof. Here the first Christians learned of Jesus the same way the prophets of old did: by revelation, God speaking to them through his Son (1.1). This

48. In fact, the account of these gates in *Ascension of Isaiah* happens to match the model of the Jerusalem temple: only the three lower heavens and the firmament have gates, corresponding to the inner and outer sanctum of the temple (the gates down to the third and second heaven, respectively), the outer gate of the temple itself (the gate down to the first heaven), and the gate of the city as a whole (the gate into the firmament); thus the upper heavens (in which is no lawlessness or decay) corresponds as one unit to Jerusalem; and the sublunar realm corresponds to everything outside the walls of Jerusalem (such that what is 'in the city' is all that is holy, and what is without is all that is base and corrupt).

Son was a preexistent being, God's agent of creation, and was later (after his resurrection) appointed his right-hand man, being put in charge of the whole universe (1.2-3); this Son is the 'image' of God, a supremely radiant being, in the same supernatural sense claimed in 2 Cor. 4.4 and Col. 1.15 (1.3); who is now, since his sacrifice, sitting at God's right hand and holding the world together (1.3); a supreme being (equivalent to an archangel) with a name greater than any other name (1.4). There is no nativity, no ministry, no mention of Jesus having lived on earth. Hidden messages in scripture are regarded as revealing what God had said to Jesus at his incarnation (1.5-13) or about him (2.5-8); and yet again at no point is any historical saying quoted (not even from John the Baptist, who is entirely absent from this gospel).

This last point is most telling. For verse after verse we are told what God said to Jesus at his entry into the lower world, one of which (Heb. 1.5) the Gospel authors later used as what God had said to Jesus at his baptism (e.g. Mk 1.11) or transfiguration (e.g. Mk 9.7; likewise 2 Pet. 1.17) or resurrection (Acts 13.32-35, though there admitted to be known only from scripture), but which here is more ambiguously said to have been declared at his entry into the world. The word 'birth' is not here used. Rather, we're told this happened when God 'led the firstborn into the inhabited place' (Heb. 1.6), a rather oblique way to say 'born', but not such an oblique way to say 'supernaturally sent down into the world of flesh and clothed in a new body'. The author of Hebrews later seems to assume that these things were actually said at his death and resurrection, not his birth (e.g. in Heb. 5). But either way, we are here given extended speeches from God about Jesus, which, we're told, God 'spoke' at whichever event. Obviously this is not history being recorded here. This is a myth. (As many scholars agree.)

So when immediately after this we are told to 'pay even more attention to the things we heard' so we won't drift away from them (Heb. 2.1), 'what we heard' means these readings and interpretations of scripture, as just stated. Not any kind of historical report or testimony. No such thing is found or referred to here. Much of this information (perhaps regarding what scriptures to read and how to interpret them) was delivered by 'angels' (2.2), while the rest of it was directly revealed to the apostles by Jesus (2.3), who was confirmed as God's chosen by the fact that the apostles could then perform miracles (2.4). Notably, no mention is made of *Jesus* being confirmed by the fact that *he* could perform miracles. In fact there is no knowledge here of Jesus ever performing miracles. God communicates the gospel 'through the Lord' (2.3), and his words are only confirmed to later converts by 'those who heard' him, not by those who saw him or met him or heard about him. Instead, those 'first hearers' then had 'God bearing witness with them' with 'signs and wonders and various powers and gifts of the Holy Spirit according to his will' (2.4), a reference to Paul's point that Christians receive gifts given according to God's will (as in Heb. 6.4-6), and apostles prove themselves with such powers.[49] The apostles could thus prove they heard Jesus by doing miracles. This makes sense if the existence of Jesus was only known privately to those apostles, such that they had to prove he appeared to them. Other interpretations are possible, but not entailed. So far, this all looks just like what we'd expect to hear if minimal mythicism were true.

On account of all this, we're told, they now 'look at Jesus who was assigned to a rank a little below angels by his suffering of death crowned by glory and honor' (Heb. 2.9). The author probably does not mean 'look at' literally, of course, but that they 'look at' him in their thoughts and hopes (they 'consider him' in such terms, a frequent sense of the verb *blepō*; but the same metaphor is evident even in the more concrete imagery of Heb. 12.2). But what this author does mean literally is that God made Jesus into a 'lower rank' [*elattoō*, 'diminish; lessen; reduce in rank or influence'] than an 'angel' so he could suffer death—but only 'a little lower' than angels, a possible hint that he descended only to the sublunar firmament and not all the way to earth.

We're then told that this makes theological sense because Jesus had to share the experience of death to partake of all things and thus have dominion over all things in order to save us, too, from death (2.10). The author then 'quotes' Jesus declaring Christians his brothers, but again what he 'quotes' is just scripture (2.11-13). We're then told that we could have shared in his inheritance as his brothers only if he shared our death with us: 'since children share flesh and blood, he also shared these in the same way', so that he would gain power over death, 'that is, the Devil' (2.14-15), and therefore be able to buy us out of our own enslavement to death. He likewise, by assuming a body of flesh, could experience temptation to sin, and so help those who experience the same (2.16-18; 4.15). Thus, we have a theory of incarnation that neither mentions nor requires any sojourn on earth, any birth or childhood, or anything to do with a ministry or what we would deem the life of a historical man. He simply had to assume a body of flesh and blood to be tempted (Phil. 2.6), resemble a human (Phil. 2.7) and die (Phil. 2.8), and for that feat he gained supreme supernatural power (Phil. 2.9). This could all be accomplished in accord with minimal mythicism. There is therefore no evidence for historicity here, either.

The notion that Jesus had to 'become like his brothers in all respects' (Heb. 2.17) is sometimes adduced as evidence a historical Jesus is meant, but this does not follow, nor is it all that plausible. This phrase is very strangely worded if a regular man is meant, who was born to human parents

49. See, e.g., 1 Cor. 12.8-10 and 12.28-31; 2 Cor. 12.12; Rom. 15.18-19. See also Justin Martyr, *Dialogue with Trypho* 30.

and grew up and toured the country as a man (and as a celibate preacher and miracle worker besides). You do not normally describe this as a supernatural preexistent being 'becoming like' [*homoioō*] a human. And 'in all respects' translates the phrase *kata panta*, 'according to everything', in other words, everything that matters to being someone's 'brother', a fact known only from scripture. Thus, to make the scripture true, Jesus had to be sufficiently 'like us' in all the respects that would establish us as his brothers. Therefore (at least this theologian is inferring) he 'must' [*opheilō*] have put on a body of flesh so he could be tempted and suffer and die like us. Here Jesus is not being 'born' as one of us but simply 'becoming sufficiently like' us. And it appears we know this happened only because it's theologically required by scripture and logic.[50] A cosmic supernatural event of donning a human body fits this way of speaking well enough, and arguably better.

This likewise explains why they imagined that their calling to join this new religion (their *homologia*, 'agreed-upon creed') came 'from heaven' and not from an earthly ministry (Heb. 3.1). After that we again get quotations of scripture and still not a single quotation from a historical Jesus. Likewise all the remaining chapters in Hebrews. Instead, we see this author argue that 'every high priest taken from among men is appointed on behalf of men' in order to offer continual sacrifices for sins (5.1), including his own (5.2-3), all of which would entail Jesus did not come from among men. As this author has already said, he came from God's celestial host. And just as these human high priests do not 'take the honor [of being a high priest] for themselves' but wait to be called by God (5.4), so also Jesus 'did not glorify *himself* so as to become a high priest', but waited to be called by God (5.5-6), which (evidently) we know only because scripture says so. Jesus himself, once again, is not quoted on this, but we get instead the scripturally constructed myth of God's speech at Jesus' incarnation (as recounted in Heb. 1). The fact that Jesus is being regarded here not as a human high priest but as only *analogous* to one suggests further that Jesus did not live among men.

We're then told that:

50. Likewise, many Bibles translate Heb. 2.16 as saying, 'assuredly he does not give help to angels but he gives help to the sperm of Abraham', but *epilambanō* normally only means 'help' with the dative, and 'angels' and 'sperm' are in the genitive here; as such it means 'grab, lay hold of, obtain', hence rescue. The author is thus saying Jesus is not redeeming or rescuing *angels*, but Jews, although as this author accepts Gentile Christians he cannot mean that literally but only figuratively: 'sperm of Abraham' is thus being used here as a Jewish-friendly idiom for 'men', since we can all be the sperm of Abraham (as Gal. 4 patiently explains). Note that it does not say here that Jesus was born to a Jewish family but that he assumed a body of flesh to save Jewish families (and Gentiles who have spiritually joined the Jewish family, per Rom. 2.29).

> In the days of his flesh, [Jesus] offered prayers and supplications to him who was able to save him from death, with loud cries and tears, and he was heard because of his piety. Although he was a Son, he learned obedience from what he suffered, and was perfected (Heb. 5.8-9).

This is often taken as evidence of knowledge of the story of Gethsemane (e.g. Mk 14.32-42), where Jesus prays and cries and begs God to release him from the planned sacrifice. However, here Jesus is praying for his *resurrection*, not to be excused. Because here we're told his prayer is *answered*, unlike the Gospel account at Gethsemane, where Jesus' request that he be excused is denied. This is most likely yet another scripturally derived inference about what happened to Jesus in outer space (when Satan and his demons abused and killed him), or a revelation of such an event, like Paul's vision of Jesus inaugurating the Eucharist (see §7).

Either way, this is no more likely on historicity than on mythicism. All the possible details that could have secured this as an earthly event witnessed in human history, rather than a cosmic event learned mystically, are absent. It therefore argues for neither hypothesis, except insofar as it is weird to get nothing here more specifically terrestrial, which argues for myth. After all, though the author of Hebrews says he has *a lot* to say about Jesus (5.11-12), not one of those things places Jesus in earth history. None are stories about his ministry, about the occasions of his deeds and sayings, or why any of these lofty theological conclusions were reached about an ordinary executed convict. In contrast, this author feels free to discuss what he believes are the historical details of the Melchizedek that he is comparing Jesus to (in Heb. 7; see Element 42), making it all the stranger that he never once does the same for Jesus. Instead, this author believes Melchizedek had 'no father, no mother, no ancestry' and was never born and never died, but was 'made just like the Son of God' (7.3), here using the word *aphomoioō*, an emphatic form of *homoioō*, the same word we saw used to say Jesus had been 'made like' men (in Heb. 2.17). So they *both* had no father, no mother, no ancestry (in the usual sense). This again sounds like a description of a cosmic Jesus, not an earthly one.

At this point we hear that Jesus became a high priest in the manner of this supernatural Melchizedek and not in the manner of the original human high priest Aaron (Heb. 7.11) because it was necessary that the priesthood be transferred from the one order to the other (7.12). And this is again all learned from scripture (7.17). But here we get a piece of information that some cite as evidence of historicity: this transfer entailed the demotion of the priestly tribe of Levi, 'for the one about whom these things are said belongs to another tribe, from which no one has officiated at the altar' (7.13), because 'it was made clear before that the Lord has arisen from Judah' (7.14), which fact is 'more abundantly clear' when we acknowledge that 'another priest is raised up after the likeness of Melchizedek, who was not born according to the law of a carnal commandment but according to the power of an eternal life' (7.15-16), as scripture says Jesus was (7.17). Jesus was thus not actually born; and we know he was spawned from the blood of Judah only because scripture and logic say he must have been.

Here it is sometimes claimed that the author is saying Jesus had parents from the tribe of Judah and therefore was a historical man. But what this author is actually saying is that it was 'foretold' [*prodēlos*] that the Christ would be of the tribe of Judah (being 'of the sperm of David', as it is put in Romans: see §4 above and §9 below), and a change of order *theologically* required a transfer of the priesthood from one tribe to another, and the scriptures said such a transfer had occurred. The author therefore is not working from historical information, but scripture and logic. This is therefore just another reference to the Christ being formed 'of the sperm of David' as scripture required.[51] He is thus explaining how a Davidic messiah can be a celestial high priest. Whether this entails historicity or not therefore depends on whether such a belief (that a celestial Christ donned a body formed from the sperm of David) is any less probable on minimal mythicism, which question I shall examine later (in §9).

In contrast to obscurely ambiguous and indirect remarks like this, when we expect more concrete references to Jesus' life story and eyewitness testament to it, we get none (just as we get no quotations from Jesus, ever, except as derived from scripture). For example, Hebrews 11 is an extended discussion of how we need to have faith (that Jesus will give us eternal life: 10.39) without evidence, just as others have had faith in God's promises without evidence—and numerous examples are summarized from the OT.[52] Curiously absent here are any examples of faith from the life of Jesus, from Jesus himself, or from his disciples, or the women who purportedly followed him even to the very end, or any of the many people the Gospels claim Jesus had praised for their great faith when he healed them or their loved ones (see Chapter 10).

How could that be? Why is the only evidence to be found instead in the ancient scriptures? This is especially peculiar given that when the author of Hebrews concludes by saying, 'therefore, having so great a cloud of witnesses lying around us, let us put aside every burden' and trust it will all

51. Because David was of the tribe of Judah (1 Chron. 2.15) and no other kings would reign but those of Judah (1 Kgs 12.20); and, as Paul said scripture tells us, the messiah had to be Davidic (Rom. 15.12, quoting Isa. 11.10). Many other scriptural passages affirmed the same (e.g. Gen. 49.10 and 2 Sam. 7.4-17), including those no longer in the canon but regarded as scripture by the earliest Christians (e.g. *Pss. Sol.* 17.21: see Element 9). For a survey see Joel Marcus, *Mark 1–16: A New Translation with Introduction and Commentary* (New York: Doubleday, 2000), pp. 119-20.

52. See my analysis in Carrier, *Not the Impossible Faith*, pp. 236-40.

work out (12.1), he means the examples he just surveyed. None of which are testimonies to the life, teachings or deeds of Jesus or anyone he encountered. Instead, by 'witnesses' this author means the long-dead people whose stories are told in the scriptures. This is very odd. Unless there were no 'witnesses' to the life of Jesus who could reassure them that their trust in Jesus is well placed. They simply had to trust scripture. This looks like minimal mythicism.

Here we at least do see Christians exhorted to endure the unbelief of those around them just as Jesus does, since he also 'has endured from sinners such gainsaying against him' (Heb. 12.3), but this appears to refer to the present, not the past (as has always been the case, sinners are still abusing Jesus with their doubts, and he bears it well, and so should we), unless it is a veiled reference to the abuse Jesus endured from his killers, which on minimal mythicism would be Satan and his demons, who did not know who he was at the time. Had this verse said anything like 'he endured so much abuse from Roman soldiers' or 'so much hatred from the Jewish mob' then we would have evidence for historicity, but alas we get nothing like that here. In a similar fashion, when we're told Jesus 'thought little of the shame' of 'enduring the cross' (12.2), we again aren't hearing anything not already expected on minimal mythicism. So that's inconclusive, but we still have the very strange absence of evidence and witnesses cited in Hebrews 11 as previously noted.

The same peculiarity plagues Hebrews 12, where an elaborate example is derived from the Jews who were not persuaded by the many signs Moses did among them. So we expect now to hear about the many signs Jesus did among them. Instead we get the opposite: 'if they did not escape when they rejected the one who warned them on earth, even less shall we [escape] who turn away from the one [who warned] from heaven' (Heb. 12.25), meaning in both cases God the Father (whose voice 'shook the earth' in those days but now in scripture promises to shake the earth in the future: 12.26-28). The implication is that Moses lived, taught and gave signs among them on earth (and God's voice was actually heard on earth, to the point of shaking it), but the Jews didn't listen and were killed; whereas Jesus did not live, teach or give signs among them on earth, all we get is God's voice in scripture. In other words, there was evidently nothing Jesus did that was equivalent to shaking the earth or transmitting God's voice; nothing analogous to Moses. That is almost a plain declaration of minimal mythicism. Indeed, the word on which the parallel turns here, *chrēmatizō*, actually means more than 'to warn'. In fact it means regularly transacting business, 'having dealings' with someone, in other words giving speeches and performing deeds and negotiating contracts. It thus encompasses the whole public biography of Moses. This passage therefore implies Jesus didn't have one of those—none at all, by which to build a stronger analogy with Moses. We just have to trust scripture instead. *They* had Moses and God's voice. *We* only have God's voice (now communicated 'from heaven'). Jesus is very conspicuously missing from history at this point.

All of these features of the text of Hebrews that I have surveyed so far are not *impossible* on historicity, even as a whole. But they *are* less probable. If Hebrews was written by someone who knew only of a cosmically suffering and dying Christ, then its content is essentially exactly what we'd expect. Yet it is certainly not 'exactly' what we'd expect on historicity. In fact, especially as a whole, it's very much unexpected. Some passages can be interpreted as veiled references to either a historical *or* a cosmic Jesus, although even those are often oddly ambiguous if a historical Jesus were meant (but not if a cosmic one were meant), and thus even those passages are somewhat unexpected, especially when we notice how consistently this is the case. Meanwhile several passages are downright bizarre on the assumption of historicity, yet readily expected on myth.

So, yes, it's still 'possible' that these are all veiled references to a historical Jesus and historical events. But it's *less probable* that they are than that they are more overt references to a cosmic Jesus known only through scripture and revelation. And *that* is a fact we must enter into our equation. The peculiar absence of any clear reference to any facts about a historical Jesus, any quotations of him, any stories about him that can definitely be placed on earth, throughout all thirteen chapters of this extended letter or homily about Jesus is again bizarre. Yes, it's still 'possible' that the author just never felt the need to relate any such information, not even once, not even where it is expected and would even greatly improve his argument. But this is still *improbable*. And that's the essential point we cannot sweep beneath the rug. Hebrews is simply strange. Unless Jesus didn't exist.

We saw the same was true of the other 'gospels' found in Paul's letters and in the pseudo-Pauline letter to the Colossians. Putting this all together, I do not believe the probability that *all* of these gospels would look like that can be anything higher than 40%, relative to nearly 100% on mythicism—which would far more likely produce texts like this, among those that would survive the 'filter' of later Christian document selection. We might expect more explicitly mythicist texts to have been *produced*, but we have no reason to believe they would have been preserved (see Chapter 8, §12). Accounting for that, these 'gospels' are exactly what we'd expect to survive for us to see them now, if mythicism were true. And already I think 40% is being generous to historicity. But arguing *a fortiori*, I shall say it cannot reasonably be more than 60% likely.

6. *Things Jesus Said*

So it is for all the gospels declared in the Epistles worth considering. What about occasions when the sayings of Jesus appear in the Epistles? It's often claimed Paul attests to a historical Jesus because he quotes or cites some sayings of Jesus, though never quite anything we find in the Gospels (proving there was no accurate or controlled tradition even then, and thus there could not have been one later for the Gospels to draw upon: see Chapters 6, 7 and 10).

But this evidence is often ginned up and abused. Ginned up are occasions where Paul says something that sounds like the Gospel Jesus, even though Paul shows no awareness at all that he is quoting or paraphrasing Jesus. These are just the words of Paul. They were *later* redacted and attributed to Jesus. As already noted, no other account makes any human sense (see §2). And in any case, the converse can't be proved.[53] Thus such passages cannot be used as evidence of a historical Jesus. Abused are occasions where Paul says he has a commandment 'from the Lord' to apply to a situation, which he carefully distinguishes from his own opinions—thus demonstrating considerable reverence for making clear when he is speaking for the Lord and when he is speaking for himself (further refuting the notion that he would ever quote or paraphrase the Lord without attribution).[54] To cite such passages as evidence of historicity is to abuse the evidence beyond what it's capable of proving. For we know Paul routinely received messages from Jesus by revelation (Element 16). He therefore did not need a historical Jesus to learn commandments from.

That this adequately explains all such evidence is supported by the fact that never once does Paul place any such saying in a historical context, nor does he ever say who told it to him (e.g. he never says anything like 'Peter told me Jesus said . . .'). The only source he ever cites is the Lord himself. Which means revelation, not tradition. Indeed Paul never refers to any tradition coming to him from any other source but revelation (and the scriptures). He never uses the word 'disciple' and never says anyone handed anything down to him. To the contrary, again, the words he uses for received and transmitted doctrine are the same exact words he uses for direct revela-

53. For some examples see David Sim, *The Gospel of Matthew and Christian Judaism: The History and Social Setting of the Matthean Community* (Edinburgh: T. & T. Clark, 1998), p. 264; and the various examples collected throughout Lüdemann, 'Paul'; Müller, 'Paul'; Walter, 'Paul'; Neirynck, 'Paul'; Verenna, 'Born under the Law'; and Dunn, 'Jesus Tradition in Paul'.

54. For example, 1 Cor. 7.10-11 (compare 7.12 and 7.25); 9.13-14; 14.37; 1 Thess. 4.15-18. For scholarship see previous note.

tion (see below; and again Elements 16 and 17). So even the 'traditions' he mentions in 1 Cor. 11.2 ('hold to the traditions just as I delivered them to you') may simply be the revelations he passed on to his congregations (which 'passing on' did *not* make them apostles, as it was human transmission, not revelation). For as we saw earlier, in Gal. 1.11-24 (as we shall see) he felt compelled to repeatedly and emphatically deny relying on any oral tradition. Because evidently his congregations would not trust him unless he was teaching what was directly revealed to him. Consequently, Paul never refers to Jesus having had a ministry before he died or having provided any body of teachings to those who sat before him or anything of that kind. And Paul's congregations evidently hadn't heard of any such things, either.

Indeed, Paul essentially says Jesus never taught on earth. In Rom. 10.14-17 he says no Jews ever heard him teach, and that the only way anyone could ever have heard the words of Jesus is through an apostle like himself. As Paul says there of the Jews (among everyone else):

> How then shall they call on him in whom they have not believed? And how shall they believe in him *whom they have not heard*? And how shall they hear *without a preacher*? And how shall they preach, *except [a preacher] be sent*?

Referring to the apostles [those 'sent', *apostalōsin*]. It is only 'their' words whom the Jews heard (Rom. 10.18). Paul is assuming here (and assuming everyone reading this would agree) that it is *only* through apostles anything Jesus said or did can be learned. The Jews 'have not heard' him because no preacher was sent to tell them about him, and therefore apostles were needed to do so, and sent for that purpose, and *they* are the ones the Jews heard (but nevertheless resisted: Rom. 10.16). But that means Jesus had no ministry among the Jews (because they 'have not heard' him, and could not have but for the apostles' preaching).

This is even clearer than the parallel passage in *1 Clement* 42 (see Chapter 8, §5), where it seems that only the apostles received any communications from the Lord, and thus only they could relay what they heard to the public. Likewise in Rom. 16.25-26, 'the preaching of Jesus Christ' is known only by 'revelation' and 'scripture' (and not any historical ministry). We get a peak at this process in 2 Corinthians 12, where Paul says God sent him a scourge 'to keep me from becoming conceited because of the greatness of the revelations' he frequently received, and he begged Jesus to remove it, three times even, 'but [the Lord] said to me, "My grace is sufficient for you, for my power is made perfect in weakness"' (vv. 7-10). So Paul is having (or claiming) entire hallucinatory conversations with Jesus, which generated actual 'sayings of Jesus'. For we see one such saying generated here. And this is certainly not a historical Jesus.

More ridiculous versions of this kind of thing can be found in the book of Revelation, where we find the dead Jesus dictating whole letters from heaven (Rev. 1–3)—so Jesus was still 'teaching' and delivering sayings almost half a century after even Paul was dead. This was almost certainly a fabrication. But it passes itself off as authentic ('the spirit of prophecy is the testimony of Jesus', Rev. 19.10), which means this was the sort of pathway to knowing the sayings of Jesus that Christians understood and respected. Yet no historical Jesus was needed to generate sayings this way. Rather, one could just pretend to have heard Jesus in revelations (Element 44) or actually think one had (Element 15). Sayings of Jesus could likewise come from scripture (as we saw, Hebrews and *1 Clement* quote 'Jesus' and yet in fact are just quoting scripture; Paul almost implies as much himself in Rom. 15.2-4), or from an author's expedient imagination (as most likely in Revelation, and certainly many times in the Gospels: see Chapter 10), or by simply adapting what someone else said into something Jesus said (as noted earlier, in §2; and witnessed in Chapter 10), which could include things adapted from lost scriptures (Element 9) or Jewish or pagan sages (Elements 30 to 33).

That this is what happened is evidenced by the fact that even some of the most famous teachings of Jesus appear not to have come from him. His famous teaching on paying taxes ('Render under Caesar what is Caesar's', Mk 12.14-17) is completely unknown to Paul when he exhorts his fellow Christians (including Jewish Christians) in Rome to pay taxes (Rom. 13.6-7), and this is generally believed to be Paul's last letter, dating to the end of the 50s, which can only mean no teaching from Jesus on this point existed then for him to cite (as by then he surely would have known such a thing if it were a tradition that could be known to Mark twenty years later). Thus, we see that *Paul's* teachings about taxes became reformulated into a pithy scene in Jesus' life, a scene that is for all we know the free literary invention of Mark. There are many more examples like this, for instance in 1 Corinthians 5 Paul extensively argues the Corinthians should condemn and expel the fornicators in their midst and abandon them to the Devil, yet somehow Paul knows nothing of Jesus having said that those who even look on women with lust would be better off cutting out their eyes than burning in hell, and that *actual fornicators* would be better off chopping off their hands (Mt. 5.27-30; indeed, even their testicles: Mt. 19.12). So it would seem more likely again that Paul's more prosaic idea of abandoning fornicators to the Devil became Jesus' more colorful teaching about abandoning fornicators to Hell—and not the other way around.

The most surprising example of this pertains to the Golden Rule, considered so characteristic of Jesus. Paul teaches the concept of turning the other cheek and loving your neighbor many times, in Rom. 12.14-21; Gal. 5.14-15;

1 Thess. 5.15; and Rom. 13.9-10. Indeed in that last passage he even declares outright to 'love your neighbor as yourself'. Yet not once does Paul show any knowledge that Jesus had said this, or said anything at all relevant to the topic. He never quotes Jesus or reminds them that Jesus commanded these things or appeals to any of Jesus' sayings or parables on the subject. Instead, Paul's only known source is Lev. 19.18 (the actual origin of the Golden Rule). Everything else is just Paul's own thoughts and wishes. Thus, all of Jesus' famous teaching about turning the other cheek and loving your neighbor appears not to have existed yet. Which means we can't establish it ever came from a historical Jesus. It was just as likely invented by the Gospel authors, most likely to capture what were in fact the teachings of Paul or other apostles by cleverly constructing sayings and scenes and attributing them to Jesus.

Confirming this is the fact that nothing the Gospels claim Jesus said on this subject was known to the author of *1 Clement,* either. When Clement does quote Jesus on the matter of how to treat others, he quotes a completely different saying that conveys a concept of reciprocity, with a sequence of lines (unknown to the Gospels) all communicating the same principle in different forms: that 'as you treat others, *so shall you be treated*' (*1 Clem.* 13.2-3), a notably different sentiment than Jesus is made to voice in the Gospels (the closest analog is Mt. 7.2, which is still quite different from the Golden Rule). This more pragmatic version of the ethic that Clement learned may have been extracted from a lost scripture (as I discuss in Chapter 8, §5), and thus could have been 'discovered' after Paul wrote to the Romans. But even if it was known to Paul, he had no need of it, since he already cites one of the scriptures as his authority, one that his Jewish-leaning audience in Rome would be more certain to accept: Leviticus.

By contrast, the scripture that may have contained the passage Clement cites on the Lord's sayings on reciprocity could have been sufficiently unorthodox that it would not be recognized as scripture by all Christians, perhaps especially Jewish Christians, and thus would have been less persuasive to a more conservative audience than a citation of Leviticus. But in any event, citing scripture is citing scripture. Once you've done that, you don't need to do it again. So even if Paul knew the Clementine saying, he must have known it as a passage in scripture, something not in the canon now. He clearly can't have known it as something declared by Jesus directly, as surely then he would have referenced it, as the most powerful argument a Christian could possibly adduce to persuade his peers: the very words of their Lord Jesus Christ. And again the saying attributed to Jesus in *1 Clement* consists only of a series of simple commandments, each of which, I noted before, gets expanded into more elaborate teachings, parables and stories in the Gospels. That is how sayings and stories were invented for Jesus: a brief revelatory or scriptural passage gets 'interpreted' into the Gospels by an author formulating a story depicting Jesus saying more about it.

Another evidence for this conclusion is the fact that the most typical mode of teaching attributed to Jesus in the Gospels (at least the Synoptics) is the parable. Yet parables seem completely unknown to Paul. He never once cites one or uses one. There evidently were no parables from Jesus at that time. Those must have been later fabrications, most likely by the authors of the Gospels themselves. For surely the parables of Jesus would have been the main vehicle for teaching morals and doctrine in the church, even for Paul (who after at least fourteen years could not possibly still be ignorant of them). They certainly would have been the best known and most persuasive arguments and examples to teach with, coming from the very Son of God himself, and being, we're to suppose, so beautiful and moving. How could Paul so thoroughly neglect them? Most likely, because they hadn't been invented yet.

However, that almost everything Jesus says in the Gospels is nonhistorical is not the same as Jesus *himself* being nonhistorical. If we are to honestly test *minimal* historicity, we must concede it's entirely possible Jesus was historical but didn't teach very much at all, or much of any subsequent use. Thus, the 'silence' in Paul regarding the historical sayings of Jesus is indeterminate. It is, at best, equally likely on either h or $\neg h$.[55] Although I admit that's over-generous. Since it is still hard to explain how Jesus could have been so rapidly worshiped as a demigod if he hardly ever taught anything worth repeating.[56]

7. *The Eucharist*

Transitioning from sayings to deeds, we have the middle case of what Paul says about the origin of the Eucharist ritual, which could be the lone excep-

55. Note that this is only true for *minimal* historicity; historians who insist Jesus said many important things relevant to Christian life and teaching or that would inspire Christian dispute, inquiry or curiosity are *reducing* the likelihood of Jesus' existence, because then their theory will have a much harder time explaining the silence in Paul's letters—in fact, the more things of this nature a historian posits Jesus said, the lower the probability of Paul's silence about them (and thus the lower the probability that a Jesus existed who said those things). As I am only testing minimal historicity, I won't query more elaborate alternative theories here. They are even less likely than minimal historicity.

56. Which creates a Catch-22 for historicists: claiming Jesus said many inspiring things makes the letters of Paul improbable (see previous note), and thus reduces historicity's consequent probability, while claiming Jesus said few inspiring things makes the origin of Christianity improbable (because then that worship of Jesus so quickly arose is improbable), which thus reduces historicity's consequent probability. Either way, the probability should go down. I am thus being extremely generous to historicity by overlooking this conundrum.

tion to the last point made. This is both an event that supposedly happened and a 'saying' Paul learned 'from the Lord' about it. It appears not to be derived from witnesses or oral tradition but from Paul's hallucinated conversations with Jesus (or so Paul claimed).[57] Paul says (using again the same language of receiving and communicating revelations he employs in Galatians):

> For I received from the Lord that which I also delivered to you, that the Lord Jesus in the night in which he was delivered up took bread, and having given thanks, he broke it and said, 'This is my body, which is for your sake. Do this in remembrance of me.' Likewise also the cup after the eating, saying, 'This cup is the new testament in my blood. Do this, as often as you drink, in remembrance of me.' For as often as you eat this bread, and drink the cup, you proclaim the Lord's death until he comes (1 Cor. 11.23-26).

There are strong verbal similarities with the scene in the Gospels (whose accounts all derive from Mk 14.22-25), indicating dependence on this passage in Paul. But note how Mark alters Paul's account. Where Paul only knows of Jesus taking these objects and requesting those hearing repeat the ritual to establish communion with him, Mark turns it into a narrative scene with guests present: 'as *they* were eating, Jesus took bread, and blessed and broke it, and gave it to *them*', and so on (Mk 14.22). Gone also is the instruction to 'do this in remembrance of me', and inserted are repeated references to people (the disciples) being present and eating and drinking with Jesus.[58]

If we see this for what it is—Mark having turned Paul's ritual instruction *from* Jesus into a story *about* Jesus—we can no longer presume that Paul is talking about an actual historical event.[59] The more so as he says he was told this directly by Jesus, not by anyone who was present at the meal. It probably resembled the experience reported of Peter in Acts 10.9-17, where another dinner scene is hallucinated, with words also being spoken by the celestial being conducting it. Hence in Paul's case, he refers to no one else being present but Jesus. And Paul tells us he had been preaching the gospel and founding churches for three whole years before he ever spoke to anyone who could have been there (Gal. 1.15-20), and he couldn't possibly have

57. See discussion in Verenna, 'Born under the Law', pp. 155-57.

58. The 'remembrance' line (essentially verbatim) is restored only much later in Luke's elaboration of Mark (Lk. 22.14-20). That it is absent from Matthew confirms it was never in Mark's account, which Matthew essentially duplicates (Mt. 25.26-29). We know Luke had access to and used Paul's letters (see Chapter 9, §1).

59. So also Paul Achtemeier, 'The Origin and Function of the Pre-Marcan Miracle Catenae', *Journal of Biblical Literature* 91 (June 1972), pp. 198-221 (see pp. 213-18). Likewise Lüdemann, 'Paul', pp. 202-203, and Walter, 'Paul', pp. 62-63.

been doing that without teaching the Eucharist ritual. He therefore must have received this revelation then, or claimed to have (Gal. 1.11-12).

This 'revelation' of course may have been based on things he learned from the Christians he had been persecuting outside Judea (Paul never persecuted Christians in Judea, as he was completely unknown there, except by reputation, until fourteen years after his conversion: Gal. 1.21–2.1), but it's clear he could only claim to have known it by revelation to be counted an apostle (as I already noted). Otherwise he would have properly cited this as the common tradition handed down by the first apostles, as the Corinthians would then expect him to, as that would then be the only way for him to affirm and verify its authenticity—and yet, instead, he validates it by declaring it a direct communication from Jesus. Evidently, that's how all the other apostles were claiming to know it, thus Paul had to as well, lest he be exposed as not really an apostle. Which means all the other apostles could have been claiming to have it by revelation as well. Though alternatives are possible, nothing here confirms them.

In the narrative Paul relates, Jesus appears to be speaking to the future Christian community: his body is 'for your sake' (meaning all Christians, not just those who would be present if he were just speaking to his dinner guests), and 'you' (plural) are to always repeat the ritual he describes (which obviously cannot mean just those present at the dinner, but all future believers). Paul also says nothing about this event being a dinner.[60] Jesus simply takes up bread and a cup and gives instructions on how to use them to achieve communion.[61] That an actual historical Jesus would have done any of this is also doubtful: that would entail he fully planned his death, and fully understood it to be a supernatural atoning sacrifice, and fully expected a lasting church tradition to be established afterward, based on a strange form of allegorical cannibalism, that would continue until he returned at the end of days. That is a right big stack of implausibilities.

60. In 1 Cor. 11.25 Paul says Jesus said the same thing of the cup as of the bread 'after the eating' (*meta to deipnēsai*), which most Bibles translate as 'after supper', but the word is not *deipnon* ('supper, meal') but the past (aorist) infinitive of the verb *deipneō* ('to eat, dine') following the neuter definite article (*to*), which more ambiguously means 'after the eating', which can mean after Jesus ate, or after the Christian eats as Jesus instructed. Conspicuously absent is any more overt form like 'after *they* ate'. Note that only subsequent performances of the ritual are called the 'the Lord's Supper' (*kuriakon deipnon*) in Paul (1 Cor. 11.20, not referring to when Jesus taught the ritual, but to ongoing performances of it by Christians).

61. That taking bread and a cup like this was a common form of communion ritual securing salvation see Randall Chesnutt, '*Joseph and Aseneth*: Food as an Identity Marker', in *Historical Jesus in Context* (ed. Levine, Allison and Crossan), pp. 357-65 (cf. *Joseph and Aseneth* 8.5-9 and 15.1-4). And Paul is explicit about this being the Eucharist's function: 1 Cor. 10.16-20. See also Elements 11 and 31.

Note also that Paul says we do this to proclaim his death until he comes, not until he 'returns', thus evincing no idea that Jesus had already come (to convey this instruction in a room in Jerusalem, for example); and we do it not to proclaim that Jesus is coming, but to proclaim *that he had died.* One does not have to perform a ritual to proclaim someone has died whom everyone knows had died. But if his death was only mystically known, one *would* have to proclaim their belief in that death in order to partake of its riches (the atonement it procured and the resurrection it promised). Thus, Paul's Eucharist does not look like a historicist's account of a Last Supper but a celestial vision of an instruction from their Lord, directed to future generations and not to present dinner guests.

This leaves us to ask what Paul means by saying Jesus told him he had said these things 'in the night in which he was delivered up'. Translations often render this as 'in the night in which he was betrayed', but in fact the word *paradidōmi* means simply 'hand over, deliver', which is too ambiguous to assume that what underlies it is the implausible Judas narrative found in the Gospels.[62] It most likely means when he was handed over to be killed (when he was 'offered up'), as Paul says elsewhere ('he was delivered up', Rom. 4.24-25; 'God delivered him up', Rom. 8.32; 'he delivered himself up', Gal. 2.20; all the same word).[63] On minimal mythicism this would be when he was handed over to Satan, in the same way Job had been (using the same word in the Septuagint text of Job 2.6), and just as Paul says of a Christian congregant 'delivered up' to Satan (in 1 Cor. 5.5, again the same word), and of all Christians who are 'delivered up to death' (in 2 Cor. 4.11). Paul never mentions anything about Jesus having been betrayed (and if 1 Cor. 15.5 has not been altered, Paul had no knowledge of a disciple betraying Jesus).[64] Instead, he always uses this word to refer to Jesus being offered up by God, or offering himself up, for us. The notion most likely

62. See Carrier, *Proving History*, pp. 151-55. Mark's euhemerization would logically transfer Jesus' demonic enemies to earthly ones, leading to the allegory of internecine betrayal in the Judas narrative (where the whole world conspires to kill him: Romans, Jews and 'Christians'). On which see also Carrier, *Proving History*, pp. 317-19 nn. 69-72.

63. Although one can wonder if Paul means *when the Lord delivered this information to Paul*, hence 'in the night in which [this] was communicated [to me]'. For the word 'delivered' is identical here to that used in the same sentence for 'I delivered to you' what the Lord had said. Similarly in Dan. 7.13, Daniel's revelations of a messiah figure whom we know some Christians associated with Jesus (the Son of Man: Element 41) are said to have come 'in visions during the night'. Daniel often received his revelations 'during the night' (Dan. 2.19; 7.2, 7).

64. That this passage rules out the Judas narrative in the time of Paul: Carrier, *Proving History*, pp. 151-52.

derives from Isa. 53.12, which in the Septuagint uses exactly the same word of the very servant offered up to atone for everyone's sins (see Element 5).

On that reading, Jesus in effect cast a ritual spell that would permit those who repeated it to share in what would then happen to him: passing through death, and thence to resurrection. He then 'revealed' this to an elect (the apostles, eventually Paul among them), so they and those they taught could enact the spell themselves and thereby commune with him and share in his defeat of death.[65] As we saw, such communion rituals, having essentially the same purpose, were already a staple feature of mystery cults of the time (Elements 11 and 31). This was simply the Christian version, adapted with some creative Jewish ideology. That the original casting of this 'spell' happened during a specific past night conforms to minimal mythicism, on which this celestial sacrifice *was* believed to have taken place at a specific recent time, with all attending events along with it (ritual, abuse, burial).

The specific idea that it occurred at night probably derived from scripture, like many other facts Paul and the authors of *1 Clement* and Hebrews discovered about Jesus. There could be connections with Psalm 119, where God's 'servant' will remember God and his laws 'in the night' (119.49-56) as the wicked abuse him, and the 'cords of the wicked have been wrapped' around him at 'midnight' (119.61-62), as they have 'overthrown him wrongfully' (119.78) in their pride (but for which they will be put to shame), along with other telling concepts befitting a Christian pesher on the night Jesus is delivered up (e.g. 119.80-84, 87-89, etc.), including a reference to his being buried by his lawless enemies (119.85) and his praying to God to save him (e.g. 119.145-50, a possible inspiration for Heb. 5.8-9). Indeed much of this Psalm sounds like the prayer of God's servant about to be executed unjustly by evil men. Taking it as a hidden message about Jesus would thus 'teach' a Christian that this all happened at night.

However, the fact that Paul understood Jesus to be merging in himself both the Yom Kippur goat and the Passover lamb (Element 18), leads us

65. Christians are uncomfortable seeing this as blood magic, but all sacraments and sacrificial atonement rituals are a form of magic only semantically disguised (see Carrier, 'Christianity's Success Was Not Incredible', in *End of Christianity* [ed. Loftus], pp. 72-73). Attempts to distinguish 'magic' from 'religion' are apologetical anachronisms (even in antiquity). One man's religion is always another man's magic (as anyone familiar with old Protestant polemics against Catholicism will well know). See Robert Shanafelt, 'Magic, Miracle, and Marvels in Anthropology', *Ethnos* 69 (September 2004), pp. 317-40, in light of Rabbi G.W. Dennis, *The Encyclopedia of Jewish Myth, Magic, and Mysticism* (Woodbury, MN: Llewellyn, 2007); David Frankfurter, *Religion in Roman Egypt: Assimilation and Resistance* (Princeton, NJ: Princeton University Press, 1998); and Miranda Aldhouse-Green and Stephen Aldhouse-Green, *The Quest for the Shaman: Shape-Shifters, Sorcerers and Spirit-Healers of Ancient Europe* (London: Thames & Hudson, 2005).

to more readily see this Eucharist ritual as a new Passover, symbolically reenacting what the original Passover had done: the salvation of those who properly ritualized the use of flesh and blood at the Lord's instruction.[66] Exodus 12.7-14 shares many features with Paul's Eucharist account: the element of it all occurring 'in the night' (vv. 8, 12, using the same phrase in the Septuagint, *en tē nukti*, that Paul employs), a ritual of 'remembrance' securing the performer's salvation (vv. 13-14), the role of blood and flesh (including the staining of a cross with blood, an ancient door lintel forming a double cross), the breaking of bread, and the death of the firstborn—only Jesus reverses this last element: instead of the ritual saving its performers from the death of *their* firstborn, the death of *God's* firstborn saves its performers from their own death. Jesus is thus imagined here as creating a new Passover ritual to replace the old one, which accomplishes for Christians what the Passover ritual accomplished for the Jews.

So either Jesus really did that (which seems most unlikely) or this was a lie (his disciples claiming he really did that) or it was learned by revelation (Elements 15 and 16), inspired by creatively reading scripture (Elements 8 and 9). We cannot decide among these options from the evidence available in Paul. I find it too easily explained on minimal mythicism (revelation makes better sense of its oddities in Paul and its divergence from Mark and its intrinsic historical implausibility), and too unusual and sparsely detailed on minimal historicity (leaving us no definite evidence it didn't derive from

66. This is well enough demonstrated in Calum Carmichael, 'The Passover *Haggadah*', in *The Historical Jesus in Context* (ed. Levine, Allison and Crossan), pp. 343-56. I shall draw from and expand on his analysis. But he adds other observations worthy of note, such as that early Jewish tradition held that the messiah would arrive at Passover (p. 344), which would thus create the assumption that Jesus' messianic act occurred then; that Paul calls this 'Eucharist' cup the 'Cup of Blessing' (1 Cor. 10.16), which was the name of the third of four cups drunk at a Passover seder (the fourth, the Cup of Redemption, Christians would drink with Jesus in the future world: pp. 343-44, 354; cf. Mk 14.25); and that the Passover seder invoked the salvation of the participant (p. 353), the very same thing the Christians were doing. For the Eucharist as a 'transformation' of the traditional Passover, see also Gillian Feeley-Harnik, *The Lord's Table: Eucharist and Passover in Early Christianity* (Philadelphia, PA: University of Pennsylvania Press, 1981). And for the Eucharist also possibly incorporating old Jewish temple rituals see Margaret Barker, *The Great High Priest: The Temple Roots of Christian Liturgy* (New York: T. & T. Clark, 2003), pp. 56-72; and Margaret Barker, 'The Temple Roots of the Christian Liturgy', in *Christian Origins: Worship, Belief and Society* (ed. Kieran O'Mahony; Sheffield: Sheffield Academic Press, 2003), pp. 29-51. Notably Melchizedek also performed a ritual of bread and wine for Abram in Gen. 14.18 (which may have occurred 'in the night', if the events of 14.15 and 14.17 were imagined, or even stated in a variant or targum, as occurring in close proximity), and Jesus was linked with this Melchizedek (Element 42).

revelations), producing at best a 50/50 fit either way. It thus argues for neither historicity nor mythicism.

8. *Things Jesus Did*

We just covered the question of whether Jesus actually broke bread at a historical Last Supper and found the question unresolvable from Paul's letters alone. What about other things Jesus did or had done to him? Does Paul mention anything else like that? Not much. In Chapter 3 we addressed the bare facts of Jesus having suffered and died and been buried and resurrected, which are all expected beliefs on minimal mythicism—as on that theory, these events all occurred in outer space (in the original Christian belief). Jesus would have been buried in a grave or tomb somewhere above the clouds, just as Adam was (Element 38). He would likewise have been abused and crucified there, by Satan and his sky demons (Element 37), just as the earliest discernible redaction of the *Ascension of Isaiah* imagined.[67]

Of these, it's most obvious that the *resurrection* occurred only in secret. In 1 Cor. 15.3-8 the risen Jesus appears only to believers, evidently in private, and only on scattered, isolated occasions.[68] The sole exception Paul mentions is himself, having been an enemy of the church who 'saw Jesus' (1 Cor. 9.1), the only such person Paul seems to know; yet he says he saw Jesus in a revelation (Gal. 1) and thereupon became a believer. There is therefore no public appearance of Jesus known to Paul. Indeed, only once does Paul clearly say Jesus ever appeared to more than one person at the same time (1 Cor. 15.6), but even then it was still *post mortem*, and only to believers (and in an unspecified manner). All of which indicates hallucination, actual or pretended (see Element 15). Paul never mentions Jesus having been seen by anyone before that, much less in person. Again, his only cited sources for the crucifixion and burial are 'the scriptures' (1 Cor. 15.3-4). We therefore have no indication there was any more evidence for *those* events than for the resurrection. Indeed, we should sooner conclude that there was decidedly less. On a plain reading, that's what Paul seems to be saying.

67. The original 'revealed' death and burial *could* have been imagined as occurring on earth and still be (from our perspective) mythical, if, e.g., the passion sequence was 'revealed' to have occurred somewhere like the Garden of Eden, a place no one knew the actual location of and thus where no ordinary witnesses could have been available (of course, the earliest Christians thought even the Garden of Eden was in outer space: 2 Cor. 12.2-4; see Element 38).

68. I believe this passage has been multiply corrupted and originally said something a bit different from the present text (see earlier note), but to argue *a fortiori*, I shall operate on the assumption otherwise.

Indeed, the 'cross' of Jesus (as in Gal. 6.14; 1 Cor. 1.17; and Phil. 3.18) sounds like a cosmically potent object, and not just some everyday pole or crossbeam manufactured by the Romans and used repeatedly for the executing of countless others besides Jesus. In fact, the one time Paul says anything about who killed Jesus (apart from one passage many scholars agree is an interpolation, which I shall discuss next), it looks more like he means the demons of the air than any earthly human authority. Paul writes:

> We speak a wisdom among the mature [*i.e. the fully initiated: see Element 13*], a wisdom not of this age, nor of the rulers of this age [*archontōn tou aiōnos toutou*], who are being abolished, but we speak God's wisdom, in a mystery, that has been hidden, which God foreordained before the ages [*aiōnōn*] for our glory, which none of the rulers of this age [*archontōn tou aiōnos toutou*] had known. For if they had known it, they would not have crucified the Lord of Glory. But as it is written, 'Things which eye saw not, and ear heard not, and which entered not into the heart of a man, those things God prepared for those who love him'. For God revealed them to us through the Spirit . . . (1 Cor. 2.6-10).

Here we are told that all these things were hidden and revealed only to the elect. No one saw or heard them transpire. That means God's *plan*, not necessarily that Jesus had died. But what is key here is that the 'hidden things' Paul is talking about are the fact that Christ's death rescued us from the wages of sin and thus secured us eternal life. In other words, that Jesus had thereby 'atoned for our sins' (1 Cor. 15.3). Paul is saying that if 'the rulers of this age' had known that that would be the effect of his death, they would not have killed him.

This cannot mean the Jewish elite, or the Romans, or any human authority. None of them would have been dissuaded by knowing such a fact; indeed they would either have gladly gone through with it (to save all mankind) or not cared one whit (if they didn't really believe it would have such an effect). There is only one order of beings who was invested in preventing such a result: Satan and his demons, those who reveled in maintaining death and corruption in the human world, the only beings uniformly set against God's plan. It is not plausible to suggest that Paul really meant the Jews wanted to prevent our salvation and deliberately thwart God's plan. Such an anti-Semitic notion is not found anywhere in Paul's letters. Moreover, Paul does not say 'the Jews', but the 'rulers of this age', as a collective whole. This cannot mean just Pontius Pilate and the Sanhedrin. This is *everyone* in power: *they* killed Jesus, and did so only because they were kept from knowing their doing so would save the human race. This entails a whole world order whereby if any of 'the rulers of this age' had known what would happen, they would have told their peers and stopped the crucifixion, to prevent its supernatural effect. This does not describe any human world order. This describes the Satanic world order, the realm of demons and fallen angelic powers.

Thus, when Paul says 'the rulers of this age' (*archontōn tou aiōnos toutou*) were the ones kept in the dark and who in result crucified Jesus, he is using *archōn* in its then-common supernatural sense: the demonic powers (Element 37).[69] Paul almost never uses this word of earthly authorities, and never so uses it in conjunction with the cosmic vocabulary of *aeons*. And here he certainly cannot be using it in a human sense, as the motives he is imputing to these archons then make no sense. Rather, this exactly describes what we saw in the earlier redaction of the *Ascension of Isaiah*: Satan and his demons kill Jesus only because his identity was kept hidden from them, so they wouldn't know what his death would accomplish (see Chapter 3, §1; with Chapter 8, §6). And they would have known had Jesus not disguised himself, because a self-sacrifice of the high priest of God's celestial temple would have had effects as obvious to them as to the author of Hebrews (see §5). The same could not be said of Pontius Pilate or the Jewish Sanhedrin, who did not possess the requisite supernatural knowledge. And even if we imagined they did (if God had revealed it to them, for example), why would they then stop the crucifixion? Obviously they would see its value and recognize it as what the supreme God of all peoples wanted; and if they didn't, they would have no reason not to kill Jesus anyway.

It is usually assumed that what Paul means here is that had the authorities known Jesus was the *messiah* they would have bowed down to him rather than killed him, although that would not make sense to the Romans (who would try all the more to kill a Jewish messiah). It also ignores the fact that in earliest Christian understanding the messiah's death is precisely how God effects our salvation. This is clear not only in Hebrews 8–9 but also throughout the letters of Paul, as he most elaborately explains in Romans 5–6. That is, again, the 'hidden mystery' Paul is talking about, the very 'stumbling block' that trips up the Jews and seems 'foolish' to the Gentiles (1 Cor. 1.23; on which see Chapter 12, §4). Which means if the Jews had known this, they would not have bowed down to Jesus *rather* than kill him; they would have done both. Only if they wanted to *prevent* the salvation of mankind would they have refrained from carrying out the sacrifice God commanded. And that kind of cosmic vindictiveness is not the sort of thing Paul ever attributes to the Jews—or the Romans. To the contrary, Paul's view of earthly authority is that it always does God's will (Romans 13), not that it is genocidally warring against it. It also makes no sense for God to hide his plan of salvation from his own chosen people; whereas it *does*

69. See Verenna, 'Born under the Law', pp. 145-50; and Doherty, *Jesus: Neither God nor Man*, pp. 104-109.

make sense that he had to hide it from Satan and his minions by communicating it to his chosen people in code (Element 8).

It therefore makes more sense to conclude that it is the archons of the sky that Paul is saying God wanted to thwart by keeping all of this hidden, so *they* would kill Jesus, not knowing it would *secure their destruction*. For Paul says these archons are 'being abolished' (*katargoumenōn*, a present passive participle). This does not plausibly refer to the Jewish or Roman elite (who were still fully in power, and could still be as saved as anyone by joining Christ). It most plausibly means that those sharing in the sacrifice of Jesus now had power over the demons, to exorcise them and escape their clutches—thereby escaping the power of death. Because it is by his death that Jesus had triumphed over those dark celestial powers (just as Col. 2.15 would later say). The early Christian scholar Origen agreed: he could only understand Paul here to be saying that *unseen* powers of darkness were being abolished, not any earthly authorities, and that these demonic powers were the ones who plotted against and crucified Jesus.[70]

Someone still mired in dogma and tradition might not be ready to see this. They can still say (as perhaps Origen meant) that this is all just a veiled way of referring to Pilate and the Sanhedrin, or some such thing, that Paul is somehow imagining a world conspiracy of the Roman Empire and the Jews to thwart God's plan, and thus all the oddities just noted can be explained away with a battery of *ad hoc* excuses. So a historicist reading of this passage can be shoehorned in. But what cannot reasonably be denied is how well the mythicist reading of this passage fits without any shoehorning at all. It then matches exactly what is said in the early redaction of the *Ascension of Isaiah*. And nothing at all is then odd about it. Nothing needs to be explained away. The probability that Paul would write this passage if mythicism were true is therefore surely higher than the probability that he would write it if historicity were true. On the latter we would sooner expect something far less vague and far less bizarrely damning of the Romans and Jews as the enemies of God (and indeed of all humankind), and something far more plausible about how they would have acted had they 'known the truth'. Whereas on the former theory, this is pretty much exactly what we'd expect Paul to write. On the one reading, we need excuses for everything; on the other, we need none.

Diehards will then appeal to another passage as their prize counter-example, where indeed Paul appears to say *the Jews* specifically (no mention of Romans) are the ones who killed Jesus, and then got their just desserts for it: 1 Thess. 2.15-16.[71] But this has long been recognized as an interpolation. It

70. Origen, *Commentary on 1 Corinthians*, fragment 9.14-25.

71. The opposite is said in 1 Tim. 6.13, which declares that Jesus 'testified the good confession before Pontius Pilate', thus claiming (supposedly) that the Romans killed

was not anything Paul wrote. This is not something mythicists cooked up *ad hoc*; many well-respected historicist scholars agree, and their case has been made in major peer-reviewed journals. I find their case decisive.[72] Contrary to what this passage states, Paul never blames the Jews for the death of Jesus elsewhere; Paul never talks about God's wrath as having come, but as coming only at the future judgment (e.g. Rom. 2.5; 3.5-6; 4.15); and Paul teaches the Jews will be saved, not destroyed (e.g. Rom. 11.25-28). Most importantly, Paul was almost certainly dead by the time the 'wrath had come upon [the Jews of Judea] to the uttermost', a statement that can only refer to the destruction of the Jewish nation and temple in 70 CE. So obviously Paul can't have said any such thing.

Attempts to defend this passage's authenticity are wholly untenable. They require us to believe too many improbable things. The present text reads (emphasis added):

> For you, brethren, became imitators of the churches of God **which are in Judaea** in Jesus Christ, for you also suffered the same things **from *your own* countrymen** as they did **from the Jews** who both killed the Lord Jesus and the prophets, and drove us out, and pleased not God, and are contrary to all men, forbidding us to speak to the Gentiles that they may be saved, to fill up their sins for evermore—but the wrath has come upon them to the uttermost (1 Thess. 2.14-15).

Paul is writing to pagan converts (1 Thess. 1.9) being persecuted *by pagans*, not by Jews (this is what he means in 2.14). So why would he suddenly break into a tirade against 'the Jews' here? This makes no sense in context and violates the entire thread of his argument, that the Thessalonians are to be commended for having withstood a pagan persecution, just as the Judean churches had withstood a Jewish one (or even a Judean one). Everything after "as they did from the Jews" is therefore illogical in context.

Even reading 'Jews' as 'Judeans' here does not work, not only because the difference is not relevant here (e.g. when Paul elsewhere says the Jews

him (and that, contrary to the Gospels, Jesus preached the gospel to Pilate). Although the Greek here could be read as saying only that Jesus 'testified to the good news *in the time of* Pontius Pilate'. However, 1 Timothy is a late forgery, and therefore useless as evidence—so what it may have meant here doesn't matter.

72. See Birger Pearson, '1 Thessalonians 2.13-16: A Deutero-Pauline Interpolation', *Harvard Theological Review* 64 (1971), pp. 79-94; G.E. Okeke, '1 Thessalonians 2.13-16: The Fate of the Unbelieving Jews', *New Testament Studies* 27 (1981), pp. 127-36; and Earl Richard, *First and Second Thessalonians* (Collegeville, MN: Liturgical Press, 1995), pp. 123-27. See also my summary and additional analysis in Richard Carrier, 'Pauline Interpolations', *Hitler Homer Bible Christ*, pp. 203-11; and the analysis of Neil Godfrey, 'Taking Eddy & Boyd Seriously (3)', *Vridar* (January 5, 2010), at http://vridar.wordpress.com/2010/01/05/taking-eddy-boyd-seriously-3; and the arguments in Doherty, *Jesus: Neither God nor Man*, pp. 657-59.

will be saved, as a generic category, and thus *not* damned, he necessarily must mean Judeans as well), but also because many Christian churches were *comprised* of Judeans (Gal. 1:22) for decades (1:18; 2:1), and thus were not driven out (indeed, Paul was able to come and go freely), and Paul never elsewhere mentions the Judean churches having been destroyed or purged (not even in Romans, where it could hardly escape mention, since the fact of it would be the first question on his audience's mind that he had to explain). Paul also makes no mention of Judeans preventing his preaching to the Gentiles, even when he was *in* Judea preaching to Gentiles. This is clear in Galatians 2, where it is Jewish *Christians*, and them only, who were wagging their fingers at this; there is no mention of the Jews generally attacking him, forbidding him or driving him out for it (indeed not even the Jewish Christians did that), or of these being problems he had to confront (to the contrary, his only obstacle there is the disapprobation of a certain faction *of Christians*).

But most damning is the fact that these suspect verses say God's wrath has come upon the Jews 'to the uttermost' (*eis telos*, literally 'to the end, with finality'). This cannot be twisted into meaning the exact opposite of what it actually says. For one thing, it unmistakably refers to something that affected the Jews *in Judea* ('For you became imitators of the churches of God which are *in Judaea* . . . for you also suffered the same things of your own countrymen as *they* did of the Jews who' killed Jesus and the prophets *in Judea*, and 'drove us out' *of Judea*, etc.). So claiming this refers to an earlier expulsion of Jews from Rome, for example, is a complete non-starter. That was a purely temporary and isolated event (and thus not by any stretch of the imagination 'final'), and hardly anything one would call the wrath of God (as if the worst God could do to display his 'wrath' is force some Jews living in pagan Rome to go back to the Holy Land), and only affected Jews in Rome, *not the Jews in Judea*—so how could God's wrath have been visited on the Jews *of Judea* by punishing Jews *in Rome*? The only thing a 'final judgment' on 'the Jews' in 'Judea' can possibly have been is the end of Judea itself (as a province) and the end of the Jewish cult (in the destruction of the temple), widely recognized by Christians thereafter as God's final abandonment of the Jews. No other event makes any sense. And Paul was dead by then. So even on that point alone we can be certain this is an interpolation.

This is only further confirmed by how unusual this passage is. Not in any of Paul's 20,000 or so words, and dozens of discussions of the Jews, is there anything like it. Paul blaming the Jews for the death of Jesus is simply unprecedented. Paul also never talks about the Jews as if he wasn't one of them (see Gal. 2.15; 1 Cor. 9.20; Rom. 9.1-5; 11.1; Phil. 3.4-5). Paul even himself says he was one of the 'Jews' persecuting the church (1:13-14, 23) that he would here be saying God has damned, which makes no sense. Paul likewise acknowledged Jews, *even Jews in Judea*, as members of his own church, so he wouldn't damn them as a group like this, and never does (see Gal. 1.22-24; 1 Cor. 1.24; 12.13; 2 Cor. 11.12; Rom. 9.24; 10.12). Instead, Paul says things like, 'Did God cast off his people? God forbid! For I also am a Jew, of the seed of Abraham, of the tribe of Benjamin' (Rom. 11.1), and 'Are they Hebrews? So am I. Are they Israelites? So am I. Are they the seed of Abraham? So am I' (2 Cor. 11.22). That Paul actually taught the Jews would be saved, not damned, is repeatedly clear (e.g. Rom. 11.25-28; likewise Rom. 2.5; 3.5-6; 4.15; even 1 Thess. 1.10). This again must necessarily include the Jews of Judea (and hence 'Judeans'), even Jews who persecuted Christians—because Paul himself did, and he surely can't be damning himself here, thus redemption was possible even for that, and Paul makes this clear in the other verses cited as well. 1 Thessalonians 2.15-16 is therefore simply not anything Paul would write. It can only be what a later anti-Semitic Christian inserted.[73]

Just as Jesus' death cannot be placed on earth using anything Paul actually wrote, neither can his 'suffering', which likewise would have occurred at the hands of the same demons who killed him; nor his humbleness or love, which were likewise displayed by his obedience to God's plan in the heavens, allowing himself to suffer abuse and be killed there; nor his having

73. In Bayesian terms, the consequent probability of *interpolation* is so much higher than *authenticity* that it would far overwhelm *any* prior probability based on the known frequency of interpolation. For example, any sound analysis will find the known rate of interpolation in the NT is higher than 1 in 1000 verses per century (counting both interpolated passages and verses with interpolated text within them), and we have at least one whole century of no manuscripts to check by, so *at least* 1 in 1000 verses in the NT are or contain interpolations undetectable in extant manuscripts (there are nearly 8,000 verses in the NT, so this means at least eight interpolations in the NT will not be detected in extant manuscripts). But the probability that Paul would write vv. 15-16 on known background evidence is easily millions to one against. In the main text I identified five unlikely features, one of which is extremely unlikely (which I'd estimate can't be any more likely than 1 in 10,000), and the others very unlikely (no more likely than 1 in 10 apiece, for total odds against of 1 in 10,000), which combined makes the ratio of consequent probabilities 1 in 100,000,000 (one in a hundred million). When this is weighed against a prior of 1 in 1000 against interpolation, the odds that Paul wrote this come out to be less than 1 in 100,000 (odds of authenticity = 1000/1 x 1/100,000,000 = 1/100,000). Even if the five counts against it have a probability of 1 in 100 (for the least likely) and 1 in 4 (for the remaining four, for 1 in 256 odds), making a ratio of consequents equal to 1 in 25,600 against a prior of 1 in 1000, that leaves us with odds of less than 1 in 25, or about a 4% chance the passage is authentic (odds of authenticity = 1000/1 x 1/25,600 = 1/25.6). And those latter numbers are surely unrealistic. See Carrier, *Proving History*, 'Bayes's Theorem, odds form', p. 333.

been a man, since as we saw in the Philippians gospel (in §4), in order to die Jesus had to be clothed in a human body, which the *Ascension of Isaiah* originally placed in outer space. So when Paul says we ought to imitate Christ's endurance of abuse (e.g. 1 Cor. 11.1 and 1 Thess. 1.6), we have nothing that anchors this to an earthly event.

Hence also Paul's references to Jesus being a man. According to Paul's logic, sin entered the world through one man, Adam; therefore sin had to be removed from the world through another man, Jesus Christ—and as sin entered through the one man's disobedience, it had to be removed through the other man's obedience (Rom. 5.12-21). This all conforms to minimal mythicism and therefore is no more likely to have been said on minimal historicity.[74] Indeed, Paul qualifies this logic elsewhere, saying (in Phil. 2.7) that Christ was not actually a man, but came 'in the *likeness* of men' (*homoiōmati anthrōpōn*) and was found 'in a form *like* a man' (*schēmati euretheis hōs anthrōpos*) and (in Rom. 8.3) that he was only sent 'in the *likeness* of sinful flesh' (*en homoiōmati sarkos hamartias*). This is a doctrine of a preexistent being assuming a human body, but not being fully transformed into a man, just looking like one, having a flesh-and-blood body to abuse and kill.[75] This fits minimal mythicism exactly.

Christ's 'obedience' (and his 'love' for us) is similarly represented in Paul not by a biography full of examples but by this single instance of allowing himself to be clothed in a body, abused and killed (Rom. 5.19; Phil. 2.6-8; likewise Rom. 15.3 and Gal. 2.20). This is also what is referred to when Paul says, 'you know the grace of our Lord Jesus Christ: though he was rich, yet for you he became poor, so that through his poverty you might become rich' (2 Cor. 8.9). Obviously Paul is not saying Jesus was a wealthy man and gave all his money and property away (any more than he is saying that Christians now would all get rich). Rather, he is referring to the fact

74. Because on minimal mythicism Jesus was also a man (he was incarnated as one, wearing the flesh of a human being), it's just that he became a man in heaven, just as in some Jewish theology Adam did (in *2 Enoch* and the *Revelation of Moses*, e.g.; see Element 38), and indeed even apart from that, Philo also spoke of the cosmic Jesus as not only a man, but a man in parallel to Adam, just as Paul here does (Element 39).

75. Hence when Paul says Jesus 'knew no sin' but 'was made into sin' for our sake (2 Cor. 5.21), this refers to Jesus' preexistent status as a sinless celestial being, God then making him take the place of sin in order to kill it along with his body (as in Col. 2.14); Paul is thus not referring to biographical evidence that Jesus never sinned. Some likewise claim Paul says God 'displayed publicly' Jesus' death, following the NASB translation of Rom. 3.25, but as most other translations show, that is a mistranslation. The word is 'planned, proposed, put forward' (*protithēmi*), not 'displayed publicly'. Similarly Gal. 3.1, where the NASB has Paul saying, 'you foolish Galatians, who has bewitched you, before whose eyes Jesus Christ was publicly portrayed as crucified?' The verb here is *prographō*, 'forewritten', not 'portrayed' (as I'll discuss later in this section).

that Jesus was a supreme being; yet rather than claim that power, he lowered himself, temporarily divesting himself of all his potency (his supernatural riches), exactly as Phil. 2.6-8 says.

On the other hand, when Paul begs the Corinthians 'by the mildness and kindness of Christ' not to force him to be mean to them, he is referring to Christ's *current* gentleness as a judge, in parallel to what Paul is implying he will be, too, when he arrives personally (2 Cor. 10.1-2). The words he uses are *prautēs* and *epieikeia*, which mean 'mildness, gentleness' and 'reasonableness, fairness', respectively; their antonyms are *hagriotēs*, 'savageness, cruelty', and *anepieikeia*, 'being unreasonable, unfair'. In the context of 2 Corinthians 10 Paul is therefore referring not to any past event in Jesus' life but to Jesus' present character as a kind and fair judge at the right hand of God (as opposed to being a savage, cruel, unreasonable and unfair one).[76] Likewise when Paul says we 'always carry about in the body the dying of Jesus, so that the life of Jesus may show in our body, too' (2 Cor. 4.10-11) he means Jesus' *current* life (as resurrected savior), not some biographical life he once lived. Paul is saying that by dying to the world, we display to the world the living spirit of Christ in us.[77]

In the same way, when Paul says, 'although we have known Christ according to the flesh, now we no longer know him that way' (2 Cor. 5.16), he is not excusing the fact that he did not know Jesus personally as the other apostles did, because he is referring not to himself but to *all* Christians, including the Corinthians he is writing to (as the context indicates: 2 Cor. 5.1-15). This is therefore a reference to our living no longer 'according to the flesh' but according to the spirit (Romans 8). So it is not Christ's fleshly existence Paul is referring to here (because even on historicity the Corinthians can't possibly have known Christ that way), but *our* fleshly existence, and our choice to live 'in' the flesh or out of it—and the fact that Christians begin in it, and ascend out of it. Thus, we *all* know Christ when we are in the flesh, but then we evolve beyond that. As Paul says in the very next line (2 Cor. 5.17).

Sometimes it's claimed Paul referred to Jesus having had a ministry among the Jews when he said, 'Christ has been made a deacon of circumcision for the sake of God's honesty, in order to confirm [his] promises to the patriarchs' (Rom. 15.8). But all Paul is saying here is that Jesus had

76. Notably, Plutarch says exactly the same thing of Pericles, using the same two words conjoined, in *Pericles* 39, when explaining that Pericles never used his power unjustly to carry out personal vendettas or desires. The same pair of terms conjoined appears a dozen or so times in Greek literature in a similar sense, so it was evidently a common idiom.

77. Rom. 8.2-10. See Carrier, 'Spiritual Body', in *Empty Tomb* (ed. Price and Lowder), pp. 149-50.

to be given a Jewish body (formed from the sperm of David: see §9) and appear first to Jews (Element 20) to fulfill scripture. That does not entail an earthly ministry. The word 'deacon' (*diakonos*), which is sometimes translated 'minister', as in preacher, actually means 'servant, attendant', someone who does another's will. As such it can mean someone's messenger or a temple attendant. But it does not refer to 'having a ministry' in the sense historicists require. It means (in this context) doing God's will. It can mean doing God's will by relaying God's will, and as such it can refer to 'having a ministry' in an *indirect* sense, but as such it would equally apply to revealing God's will from heaven. This passage is therefore, once again, ambiguous. It cannot be confidently anchored to an earthly event. To the contrary, as we saw in Rom. 10.14-17, Paul appears to say Jesus had no historical ministry of the kind historicists want.

The same goes for everything else in Paul's letters. Paul mentions there having been a group called 'the twelve' (1 Cor. 15.5), but he does not call them disciples or say anything about them having been chosen by Jesus before his death.[78] Paul likewise says God put 'in Zion a stone of stumbling' although anyone who trusts in it will not be ashamed (Rom. 9.33); but he is quoting scripture here (not citing a historical fact), and the context is the Torah and the gospel (Rom. 9.30-32), not Jesus.[79] Thus Paul does not mean Jesus was crucified 'in Zion' as some sort of geographical fact. Even if Paul believed he had been (as could be the case on minimal historicity), that is not what Paul is talking about here. The subject is not Jesus at all, but the old Torah law that Jews were still trying to obey, yet could never succeed at (Rom. 9.30–10.6). They are thus stumbling over the gospel's concept that faith succeeds where works fail (9.32), as God intended (9.33); but it was still Paul's hope that the Jews would be saved (Rom. 10.1).[80] It is thus the *gospel* that originated 'in Zion'. And even that is not geography but ethnography: he simply means it originated within Judaism.

More importantly, just like we saw in 1 Pet. 2.13-14 (in §3), in Romans 13 Paul appears to have no knowledge of the fact that Jesus was unjustly executed by earthly authorities. For here Paul insists repeatedly that all earthly authorities are chosen by God and only serve justice. 'Those in

78. See Carrier, *Proving History*, pp. 151-55. And on whether we should even trust this verse see earlier note.

79. The scripture he quotes is a conflation of Isa. 8.14 with Isa. 28.16. Most likely Paul's copy of Isaiah had a variant reading for the latter, which had been contaminated by the former (or vice versa).

80. One might read Paul here as saying it was the Torah law they were stumbling on, but the whole line he quotes from scripture implies he means the gospel (in which Christians trust), by analogy to 1 Cor. 1.23 and Gal. 5.11 (and 1 Pet. 2.7-8). See Hans Conzelmann, *1 Corinthians: A Commentary on the First Epistle to the Corinthians* (Philadelphia, PA: Fortress Press, 1975), pp. 612-14.

power (*archontes*) are not a terror to good work but to evil' (Rom. 13.3), as they only visit God's wrath on the unjust (13.4). This seems an impossible thing to say for someone who believed Pilate and the Sanhedrin had conspired to kill Jesus without honest cause. Such a notion could not have existed in Paul's time. Otherwise the Christians he is writing to would have balked. If the authorities only wield the sword against the evil and unjust (13.3-5), then Christ must have been evil and unjust. As the latter is impossible, yet Paul asserts the former, it cannot have been believed at the time that Jesus was killed by any earthly authorities. This passage in Romans is therefore improbable on minimal historicity, but exactly what we could expect on minimal mythicism.

Similarly, in Gal. 3.1, where Paul says, 'Oh you foolish Galatians! Who has bewitched you, before whose eyes Jesus Christ was foretold as crucified?', he is referring to scripture (*proegraphē*, 'written beforehand', hence 'foretold') and the fact that they had seen the relevant passages with their own eyes. He is chastising the Galatians for forgetting that Jesus was crucified and that this canceled the old Torah law (2.17-21). Paul conspicuously doesn't say, 'there were eyewitnesses to his death, some are still alive today, so why would you doubt it?' or 'everyone knows, by report told far and wide, that Pilate crucified Jesus and confirmed he had died on the cross' or 'the Roman and Jewish authorities both testify that they crucified Christ and took him down from the cross dead' or any of countless other things like that. No, the only evidence Paul has to offer the Galatians is that *scripture* said Christ was crucified. That is the only evidence anyone's *eyes* had seen. At most we might think he means the supernatural effects of this death were known from scripture, but that is not what he says: he says the messiah's *crucifixion* was known from scripture. So here again, at best we do not find any support for minimal historicity—and at worst, we find the opposite.

And that's it. That's all Paul ever says about Jesus' deeds in life that could possibly have any link to a historical man. Paul says he was incarnated, suffered, crucified, died, and buried, and spoke about a ritual meal on the night that happened; and that he is humble, fair and loving. All of which can be true of a cosmically incarnated Jesus. As far as Paul seems to care, there were no miracles, no ministry, no trial, no names or dates or places or any details at all of anyone or anyplace involved, and quite simply nothing anyone witnessed before his death. That's all very odd. Which means very improbable. Unless, of course, minimal mythicism is true. Then it makes perfect sense.

Perhaps we needn't trouble ourselves over the complete absence of earthly deeds in Paul's conception of Jesus, since on minimal historicity, it's *possible* Jesus actually did nothing Paul would have any occasion to note. We've otherwise already examined the problem of the weird absence of any debate or curiosity even over the historical details surrounding the *death* of

Jesus, or his character, or (we might now add) where his body now lay or had lain (and whether it is or should be venerated or was of any interest to anyone to visit), or how an earthly man (much less an executed convict) could be the celestial being Paul expects Christians to emulate and worship. On that last point alone, Jesus' deeds seem an impossible thing to leave out of account. How could who exactly killed him be inconsequential? How could Paul write thousands of words never once having to combat the polemics or apologetics of the Jewish elite who were supposedly blamed for killing the messiah and zealously campaigning against the Christian heresy? How could *none* of Jesus's earthly deeds, nor any of the particulars of them, ever be used as arguments or examples, or questioned? We can excuse the absence of any one or two such things, perhaps—but all of them?

The probability that *none* would come up, in any manner clearly locating them in earth history, is certainly not '100%', as if we *expected* every specific historical fact about Jesus to be completely ignored by Paul and all his congregations and opponents—indeed, as if we expected this with such certainty that it would be *surprising* if he mentioned even one! No, it's quite the other way around. The probability of this *must* be less than 100%. Whereas this silence is essentially 100% expected on mythicism. Once again, we might expect more references to have been made to the events of Jesus' life transpiring in outer space, but we also expect such references to have been lost or expunged (as explained in Chapter 8, §12), so *their* absence is not unexpected. If Paul ever wrote a letter on such things, that is precisely the letter we should expect not to have survived. And we know Paul wrote letters that curiously have not survived.[81]

So here we do have a balance in favor of mythicism. It's remotely possible Jesus never said anything that was ever deemed relevant or interesting. But it's not possible that he never *did* anything that was ever deemed relevant or interesting. And even if you think that's possible, it can't be possible that he *neither* did *nor* said anything relevant or interesting. Though several vague references in Paul could go back to historical facts (both as to sayings and events in his life), in not one case can we prove this is any more likely than the alternative (and in some, it looks more the other way around). I do not believe this is even 50% likely, as if there were really a 50/50 chance Paul would never be asked or forced or have occasion to clearly identify any historical fact about Jesus' life, experiences and deeds, or how or why Jesus generated such a fanatical following that he was practically deified upon his death. But arguing *a fortiori*, I shall say it can't possibly be any more than 75% likely.[82] Whereas this is all 100% expected on minimal mythicism.

81. See Chapter 7 (§§3 and 7).

82. Note that, as with the sayings (mentioned in a previous note), these estimates are for *minimal* historicity; historians who insist Jesus did many important things relevant to

9. *Women and Sperm*

There are only two remaining pieces of evidence that historicists cling to as 'evidence' Paul and his Christians knew of a historical Jesus: some vague references to his parentage, and mentions of there being 'brothers of the Lord'. I shall begin with the matter of parentage, on which there are two pertinent verses in Paul, one could be related to Jesus' father; the other, to his mother.

Jesus' father is never named or even mentioned by Paul; nor is his hometown or genealogy or anything else distinctive of an actual man. As noted before, in Rom. 1.3 Paul says Jesus was 'made from the sperm of David, according to the flesh', in contradistinction to Jesus being 'declared the Son of God in power, according to the spirit', in the one case referencing his incarnation (cf. Phil. 2.5), in the other his resurrection (cf. Phil. 2.9). Likewise, Heb. 7.11-17 says scripture 'foretold' that the Christ would 'arise' (*anatellō*) from the tribe Judah, and Rom. 15.12 says scripture foretold that the Christ would be a 'root of Jesse' (the father who sired King David). The same is implied in Rom. 9.5 and 15.8. These all hinge then on what it means to be 'made from the sperm of David, according to the flesh', since these all reference that same fact. An allegorical meaning is possible.[83] But so is a literal one—even on minimal mythicism.

Philippians 2.6-11 portrays this fact as an act of divine construction, not human procreation (as noted in §4): Jesus 'took' human form, was 'made' to look like a man and then 'found' to be resembling one (see also Heb. 2.17). No mention of birth, childhood or parents. In Rom. 1.3 (just as in Gal. 4.4) Paul uses the word *genomenos* (from *ginomai*), meaning 'to happen, become'. Paul never uses that word of a human birth, despite using it hundreds of times (typically to mean 'being' or 'becoming'); rather, his

Christian life and teaching or that would inspire Christian dispute, inquiry, fanaticism or curiosity are *reducing* the likelihood of Jesus' existence, because then their theory will have a much harder time explaining the silence in Paul's letters—in fact, the more things of this nature a historian posits Jesus did (or had done to him), the lower the probability of this silence (and thus the lower the probability a Jesus existed who did those things). As I am only testing minimal historicity, I won't query more elaborate alternative theories here. They are even less likely than minimal historicity. Yet explaining how Jesus could be virtually deified without having said or done anything worth Paul ever talking about is certainly not an easy task, so my estimates are still being absurdly generous.

83. See Verenna, 'Born under the Law', pp. 152-55; and Doherty, *Jesus: Neither God nor Man*, pp. 167-72. For example, in Gal. 3.26–4.29 every Christian comes from 'the sperm of Abraham' by spiritual adoption; Jesus could have been understood to come from 'the sperm of David' in a similar way. Paul even uses the same phrase in his discussion of allegorical heritage here (*kata sarka*, 'according to the flesh', Gal. 4.23, 29) that he uses of Jesus in Rom. 1.3.

preferred word for being born is *gennaō*.[84] Notably, in 1 Cor. 15.45, Paul says Adam 'was made', using the same word as he uses for Jesus; yet this is obviously not a reference to being born but to being constructed directly by God. If so for Adam, then so it could be for Jesus (whom Paul equated with Adam in that same verse). Likewise in 1 Cor. 15.37 Paul uses the same word of our future resurrection body, which of course is not born from a parent but directly manufactured by God (and already waiting for us in heaven: 2 Cor. 5.1-5). Thus, Paul could be saying the same of Jesus' incarnation.

Scripture said the prophet Nathan was instructed by God to tell King David (here following the Septuagint translation, although the Hebrew does not substantially differ):

> When your days are done, and you sleep with your fathers, I will raise up your sperm after you, which shall come from your belly, and I will establish his kingdom. He will build for me a house in my name, and I will establish his throne forever. I will be his father, and he will be my son (2 Samuel 7.12-14a).

If this passage were read like a pesher (Element 8), one could easily conclude that God was saying he extracted semen from David and held it in reserve until the time he would make good this promise of David's progeny sitting on an *eternal* throne. For otherwise God's promise was broken: the throne of David's progeny was *not* eternal (Element 23). Moreover, the original poetic intent was certainly to speak of an unending royal line (and not just biologically, but politically: it is the *throne* that would be eternal, yet history proves it was not); yet God can be read to say here that he would raise up a *single son* for David who will rule eternally, rather than a royal line, and that 'his' will be the kingdom God establishes, and 'he' will build God's house (the Christian church: Element 18), and thus *he* will be the one to sit upon a throne forever—and this man will be the Son of God. In other words, Jesus Christ (the same kind of inference Paul makes in Gal. 3.13–4.29, where he infers Jesus is also the 'seed of Abraham' also spoken of in scripture).

It would not be unimaginable that God could maintain a cosmic sperm bank. After all, God's power was absolute; and all sorts of things could be stored up in heaven (Element 38), even our own future bodies (2 Cor. 5.1-5). Later Jewish legend imagined demons running their own cosmic sperm bank, even stealing David's sperm for it, to beget his enemies with, so surely God could be imagined doing the same.[85] When the prophecy of

84. See Rom. 9.11 and Gal. 4.23, 29 (yet notably not 4.4). Likewise Heb. 11.23.

85. In later Jewish legend, the demoness Igrath was believed to collect semen from sleeping men, and once did so from David himself, using his sperm to beget rival kings: G.W. Dennis, *Encyclopedia of Jewish Myth, Magic, and Mysticism* (Woodbury, MN: Llewellyn, 2007), p. 126.

Nathan is read in conjunction with subsequent history, this would be the most plausible way to rescue God's prophecy: God could not have been speaking of David's hereditary line (as no one ever established or sat on an eternal throne), so he must have been speaking of a special son who will be born of David's sperm *in the future*, using the sperm God took up 'from his belly' when David still lived. For the prophecy does not say God will set up an eternal throne for the one born of sperm from a *subsequent heir's* belly, but of sperm from *David's own* belly.

The notion of a cosmic sperm bank is so easily read out of this scripture, and is all but required by the outcome of subsequent history, that it is not an improbable assumption. And since scripture *required* the messiah to be Davidic, anyone who started with the cosmic doctrine inherent in minimal mythicism would have *had* to imagine something of this kind. That Jesus would be made 'from the sperm of David' is therefore all but entailed by minimal mythicism.

Paul also never names Jesus' mother, and only mentions Jesus having a mother in a strangely vague passage, in a chapter where Paul otherwise speaks of mothers being allegorical; he says nothing about Jesus' mother otherwise.[86] The passage in question reads:

> If you are Christ's, then you [like him] are the sperm of Abraham, heirs according to **the promise**. And I say that as long as the heir is a child, he's no different from a slave. Even though he is lord of all, he is under guardians and stewards until [the day] the father has foreordained. And so we, too, were enslaved **under the elements** of the universe when we were children. But when the fullness of time came, God sent his son, made **from a woman**, made **under the law**, in order to rescue those **under the law**, in order that we might receive adoption as sons. And because you are sons, God has sent the spirit of his Son into our hearts, crying 'Abba, father!' As a result, you are no longer a slave, but a son; and if a son, then also an heir by God. . . . [*So, Paul asks, why are you returning to the* ***elements*** *that had enslaved you, whom you know aren't really gods? Remember how things were when we met? Why re-subject yourself to the Torah law all over again?*]
>
> For it is written, that Abraham had two sons, one **from a slave woman** and one **from a free woman**—but the one from the slave woman was born **according to the flesh**, and the one from the free woman by **the promise**. Which things are said allegorically, for these [women] are the two testaments, the first being the one from Mount Sinai, which gives birth to slavery. That's Hagar—Hagar meaning Mount Sinai in Arabia, which

86. See Verenna, 'Born under the Law', pp. 150-52 (although Verenna mistakenly concludes that Paul means Jesus' mother in Gal. 4.4 is the heavenly Jerusalem; in fact that would be Jesus' mother *after* his death—while at his incarnation Jesus is born to the *other* mother of us all, the mother of slavery, as Paul goes on to explain). For a different approach: Doherty, *Jesus: Neither God nor Man*, pp. 197-212.

corresponds to Jerusalem now, for she is enslaved with her children. But the Jerusalem above is free, and *she* is *our* mother . . . [*as scripture says*].
So now, [my] brothers, we are the children of **the promise**, like Isaac [*the son of the free woman, i.e., Sarah*]. But as in those days the one born **according to the flesh** [*i.e. Ishmael*] persecuted the one according to the spirit [*i.e. Isaac*], so it is now. But what does the scripture say? Cast out the slave girl and her son, for the son of the slave girl will not be heir with the son of the free woman [= *Genesis 21.10*]. Accordingly, [my] brothers, we are not children of the slave woman, but of the free one. For freedom did Christ set us free [*so don't go back to being a slave to the elements.*] (Gal. 3.29–4.7 and 4.22–5.1).

It's clear that Paul is speaking from beginning to end about being born to allegorical women, not literal ones. The theme throughout is that Christians are heirs of 'the promise' (to Abraham), and as such have been born to the allegorical Sarah, the free woman, which is the 'Jerusalem above', meaning the heavenly city of God. Jesus was momentarily born to the allegorical Hagar, the slave woman, which is the Torah law (the *old* testament), which holds sway in the earthly Jerusalem, so that he could kill off that law with his own death, making it possible for us to be born of the free woman at last. This is what Paul means when he says Jesus was made 'under the law' and 'from a woman'; he means Hagar, representing the old law; but we now (like Jesus now) have a new mother: God's heavenly kingdom.[87]

87. Philo similarly allegorizes Sarah and Hagar in *On Mating with the Preliminary Studies* 6–7, concluding that Sarah (whom he says was a perpetual virgin) symbolically gave birth to 'wisdom', so if we pursue wisdom, we 'receive a share of her seed' (*spermata*), thereby also using 'sperm' allegorically. See also *On the Change of Names* 23(130)–28(152) on Isaac being virginally conceived by God (Isaac was Christ's sacrificial parallel: Element 18; Philo even calls him here the Son of God); and see *On Drunkenness* 8(30-31) on all things (including celestial angels) having God as their father and Wisdom as their mother. Wisdom (Sophia) was often imagined to be God's bride (e.g. Prov. 8.22-36; Wisdom 7.25; etc.). Accordingly, the 'woman' of Gal. 4.4 has been interpreted as meaning Wisdom by Margaret Barker in *The Great High Priest*, pp. 229-61. But as I'm about to explain, I do not believe that fits the context (any more than an actual human woman does). Nor do I think the Holy Spirit is meant, even though many later Christians did in fact believe Jesus' mother Mary was the Holy Spirit (complete with magical powers): Origen, *Commentary on John* 2.12 (quoting the now-lost *Gospel according to the Hebrews*) and *Homily on Jeremiah* 15.4; see also Jerome, *Commentary on Isaiah* 9.9; similarly in Cyril of Jerusalem's *Discourse on Mary*, as translated in E.A. Wallis Budge, *Miscellaneous Coptic Texts in the Dialect of Upper Egypt* (New York: AMS Press, 1977 [1915]), p. 637. Mary already appears as a divine being in the canonical book of Revelation: see the analysis of G.H. Dix, 'The Heavenly Wisdom and the Divine Logos in Jewish Apocalyptic: A Study of the Vision of the Woman and the Man-Child in Revelation XII 1-5, 13-17', *Journal of Theological Studies* 26 (1925), pp. 1-12; likewise Barker, 'The Temple Roots of the Christian Liturgy', p. 45 (see following

That this chapter constitutes a single continuous argument is clear from the fact that it begins speaking about the same themes it ends with: our previous slavery to the Torah law, our being children of the promise made to Abraham (and thus born from Abraham, allegorically), and our being now the children of Abraham's free wife (again, allegorically) and thus the 'heirs' of that original promise (and so no longer enslaved to the OT law). This is how Paul starts the chapter and ends it, and everything in between leads logically from the one to the other. In the process Paul parallels *our* being 'under' (*hupo*) the sway of the elemental spirits with *Jesus* being put 'under' (*hupo*) the sway of the law, so we *all* could be rescued from being 'under' (*hupo*) the sway of that law, and thus of the elemental spirits. That's why, Paul says, God 'sent' his son (thus, a preexistent being) and 'made' him (again, *genomenos*) 'from' [*ek*] a woman just as we are born 'from' [*ek*] a woman—either the slave woman or the free, but either way, not a literal woman. And as for us, so for Jesus (and vice versa).[88]

It's obvious to me that by 'born of a woman, born under the law' Paul means no more than that Jesus was, by being incarnated, placed under the sway of the old covenant, so that he could die to it (and rise free, as shall we). So the 'woman' here is simply the old covenant, not an actual person. Paul does not mean a biological birth to Mary or any other Jewess. Indeed, that would make little sense here. Other than to reflect his upcoming allegorical point, why would Paul mention Jesus having a mother here at all? What purpose does that fact serve in his argument? It cannot be that this made Jesus a Jew, as in antiquity that fact would have been established by patrimony or circumcision (Exod. 12.48), not the identity of his mother (except in mixed marriages, which cannot have been the circumstance of Jesus—much less what Paul had in mind, as if he was implying Jesus did not have a Jewish father).[89] As we have seen, Paul already says (even in this very argument: Gal. 3.16) that Jesus is of the seed of Abraham and David. If all he wanted to establish was that Jesus was a Jew, that would have sufficed. Indeed, Paul cannot be citing Jesus' birth 'to a woman' to establish he was a Jew, for he does not even specify that this woman was Jewish—she is simply 'a woman'. That isn't even specific enough to certainly mean a

note). Whether Paul believed any such thing of Jesus cannot be discerned from Galatians 4, but neither can it be ruled out (since he is not there concerned with Jesus' actual mother).

88. Paul alludes to a similar allegory in Rom. 9.6-8 and 4.13-16, where all Christians are again the 'seed' of Abraham, regardless of biology; and in Gal. 3.13-18, this is implied to transpire through becoming the brothers of Christ (who, by being the 'seed' of David, was thus the 'seed' of Abraham that God had promised eternal rule).

89. Shaye Cohen, *The Beginnings of Jewishness: Boundaries, Varieties, Uncertainties* (Berkeley, CA: University of California Press, 1999), pp. 305-306.

human woman—gods, angels, spirits and demons could also be women, and give birth.[90]

Even if we just assume he means a human, that is already a rather odd thing to say of a historical man—aren't all men born to a woman? What woman does Paul mean? Why mention her? And why mention her only in such an abstract way—as simply a generic 'woman'? The only plausible answer is the answer Paul himself gives us in the completion of his argument: he is talking about allegorical women. Hence the generic term 'a woman', and hence the paralleled concepts of being born enslaved to the law and being born free, and hence the whole point of even mentioning this detail about Jesus here in the first place. The assumption that he means Jesus had a human mother simply doesn't make sense of the text as we have it.

So Paul's reference to Jesus being 'made' (*genomenos*) of the 'seed' (*sperma*) of David and being 'made' (*genomenos*) from a woman are essentially expected on minimal mythicism and thus do not argue against it. In fact, that Christians were aware of the distinction between Paul saying 'made' rather than 'born' is proved by orthodox attempts to change what he said from one to the other.[91] And in fact we know many Christians did conceive of these things celestially. Irenaeus documents this extensively in his first book *Against All Heresies*, where we learn of celestial 'seeds' impregnating

90. In Jewish legend the fallen angel Mahalath (aka Malkat) was not only a woman (in later legend one of the four demon queens) but she bore a daughter, the demoness Igrath (on whom see previous note), also a woman, who had command of a legion of fallen angels: *b. Pesaḥim* 112b (see Dennis, *Encyclopedia of Jewish Myth*, pp. 126, 211); Shida, another demoness, bore a son (also a demon): *b. Pesaḥim* 111b; etc. The existence of women among the angels is attested as early as Zech. 5.9 (even if not explicitly angels, they are certainly winged celestial beings); and that angels could mate and bear offspring not only is attested in Gen. 6.4, but it was the entire basis of Jewish demonology (see scholarship cited for Element 37). That 'Wisdom' (Sophia) was also conceived as a female celestial being, who was regarded as a mother capable of giving birth to a son (and even if usually meant metaphorically, it would not be a leap to conclude it could happen literally), is evident in Proverbs 9 and Sir. 15.2-3 (see Barker, 'The Temple Roots of the Christian Liturgy', p. 45). Psalm 110, which compares God's immortal messianic agent with Melchizedek (Element 42), might also be read as saying he will be born from the womb of Mishchar ('Dawn'), which could be interpreted as a celestial being (angel of the dawn; although the intended meaning was surely otherwise, e.g., the LXX translates, 'born from the womb before dawn'). And so on. Thus it is notable that many later Christians did indeed imagine Jesus' mother to have been a celestial being (as we know from Irenaeus). But in Galatians 4 (as we shall see) such a notion is not required (although it could have been understood).

91. In both of these passages (Rom. 1.3 and Gal. 4.4) later attempts were made to change the wording so Jesus would be 'born' rather than 'made' from sperm and a woman: Bart Ehrman, *The Orthodox Corruption of Scripture* (New York: Oxford University Press, 1993), p. 239.

the celestial 'wombs' of celestial 'women' (e.g. 1.1.1; 1.5.6; 1.8.4), and of Jesus being fully understood as having been born to a 'woman' of exactly that sort (e.g. 1.30.1-3). Irenaeus also documents how these Christians saw the Gospels as allegories and not histories. Irenaeus himself assumes the Gospels are histories, of course, but it does not look like they did.

How many other Christian sects had thought the same? How many of their ideas date back to the beginning? We have no way to be sure the answer is none (Element 22). All the sects Irenaeus speaks of are as late and evolved as the 'orthodoxy' Irenaeus was defending against them, and thus all as divergent from original Christianity (Chapter 4, §3). But they may have retained kernels of the original faith that Irenaeus's sect had abandoned or suppressed. So the question is which kernels are the more original, and which the later inventions? We cannot answer this from the armchair as Irenaeus did, and certainly not with his specious apologetical methods and biases. Instead, if we start with minimal mythicism, we can easily predict the original kernel to most likely have been that Jesus was indeed made from a celestial sperm that God snatched from David, by which God could fulfill his promise to David against the appearance of history having broken it. That this fits what we read in Paul therefore leaves us with no evidence that Paul definitely meant anything else. As for Jesus having a mother, Paul never says any such thing—he only speaks of women allegorically in that context.

Minimal mythicism practically entails that the celestial Christ would be understood to have been formed from the 'sperm of David', even literally (God having saved some for the purpose, then using it as the seed from which he formed Jesus' body of flesh, just as he had done Adam's). I do not deem this to be absolutely certain. Yet I could have deduced it even without knowing any Christian literature, simply by combining minimal mythicism with a reading of the scriptures and the established background facts of previous history. And that I could do that entails it has a very high probability on minimal mythicism. It is very much expected. So my personal judgment is that its probability is as near to 100% as makes all odds. At the very least, the probability that Paul would only ever speak of Jesus' parents so obliquely and theologically on minimal historicity is no greater than the probability that he would imagine Jesus was incarnated from Davidic sperm on minimal mythicism, making this a wash. But arguing *a fortiori*, I shall set the latter probability at 50%, against a 100% probability on minimal historicity. Thus, although I do not believe this counts as evidence for historicity at all, I am willing to allow that it might, in those proportions. In other words, although I doubt it, these vague passages might be twice as likely on historicity.

The same follows for Paul's saying that Jesus was 'made from a woman, made under the law'. I showed how even in context that reads as an allegorical statement, not a literal one. And I am personally certain that's how Paul meant it. So I believe it has a 100% probability on minimal mythicism, given that such allegories are completely expected (Element 14), and given the context of the whole chapter in which he says it (and the preceding chapter as well, where Paul repeatedly talks about the law as a cosmic force and not a biological inheritance, and about assuming identities allegorically and not literally). But since all this is not yet commonly accepted (I am looking at the text *without* the presuppositions of historicity that all previous scholars have done), I will argue *a fortiori* by saying it has only a 50% chance of being what we'd expect given those facts. And for comparison I'll assume that this bizarre and inexplicable way of talking about Jesus' mother is 100% expected on minimal historicity—even though it isn't. So again, although I doubt it, this passage might also be twice as likely on historicity.

I will thus tabulate these two features (the references to Jesus being 'made from the seed of David' and 'made from a woman') separately.

10. *Brothers of the Lord*

The last evidence historicists appeal to (and in my opinion the only actual evidence they have) is that twice Paul mentions 'brothers of the Lord', once as a generic group (1 Cor. 9.5) and once naming a specific person as belonging to it: James (Gal. 1.19). The first of these appears where Paul argues as follows:

> Am I not free? Am I not an apostle? Have I not seen Jesus our Lord? Are you not my work in the Lord? If I am not an apostle to others, at least I am to you. For you are my seal of apostleship in the Lord. My defense to those who are putting me on trial is this: Do we not have the right to eat and drink? Do we not have the right to take along with us a sister as a wife, as also the other apostles and the brothers of the Lord and Cephas do? Or is it only Barnabas and I who have no right to give up working for our keep? (1 Cor. 9.1-6).

Note that this passage is out of place: the argument that Paul is answering has been lost (whatever charge he says he is defending himself against in 9.3). It would have been explained in the preceding verses, but in fact in the present letter, those verses are on a different and largely unrelated controversy (1 Cor. 8.1-13), and then the subject abruptly and inexplicably changes. Like other epistles, 1 Corinthians seems to be a mishmash of several letters, this being an example of where two were mashed together, and here the preceding part of whatever letter this came from was left out (a curious fact in itself).

Nevertheless, from what Paul goes on to say we can tell he was accused of being a lazy moocher (or threatening to be), not earning his keep but just lying about and eating the Corinthians out of house and home. And

Barnabas, too, apparently; and evidently a wife in their company (most likely the wife of Barnabas, as Paul elsewhere implies he did not marry: 1 Cor. 7.7-8). Paul seems to think every traveling minister was allowed to take his wife with him, to be fed by the community along with him, at least if she was a believer (a 'sister' of the Lord). Paul's defense is that every other traveling minister was allowed to do this—that is, to do no other work but minister to the congregation, and in return be fed at the congregation's expense. He goes on to cite scripture and commandments from Jesus (which on minimal mythicism he would have received by revelation) and other arguments in defense of the principle, but his first argument is to cite the fact that Paul and Barnabas are being singled out unfairly, that since everyone else got to do it, so should they.[92]

It's important to note this context. Because Paul is not talking about the right to be married or have wives. He is only talking about the right to *bring one with him* when he travels and to expect the community to feed her and not expect her or him to work (beyond whatever church business they are traveling for). He is therefore only talking about Christians who are traveling on church business, which would have included not just apostles (those who received revelations of the Lord—the primary qualification he opens with—and thus who were sent *by the Lord himself* to minister) but Christians of other ranks and duties (those sent by human authorities to deliver letters or conduct inter-church business).

Thus, when Paul says 'the other apostles and the brothers of the Lord and Cephas' get to take wives with them on church business without having to work for their keep, he is not singling out the family of Jesus as some sort of specially privileged group never elsewhere mentioned by Paul—not even when he lists the ranks of people in the church (in 1 Cor. 12.28), where surely he would have mentioned it if the family of Jesus was being given special privileges and authority. Rather, Paul is talking about all other Christians, who were all 'brothers of the Lord' (Element 12).[93] This is evi-

92. Strangely, despite extensively defending his right to material support (in 1 Cor. 9.3-11, 13-14), Paul also insists he never availed himself of this right (in 1 Cor. 9.12, 15, 18), although that leaves unclear why he didn't think that was a sufficient defense in itself (wouldn't the fact that he never did it be sufficient response to someone accusing him of doing it?), thus he must have availed himself of it on some occasion, or asserted he could if he wanted to, or recently insisted he receive the privilege on a future visit, requiring him to defend his right to do so here. Since we are missing the first part of the argument (containing the actual charge Paul is defending himself against) we cannot know exactly what it was.

93. This is even made clear in one manuscript (designated K, from the ninth century) which omits the definite article before 'brothers', making the sentence read 'the other apostles and brothers' as one unit, and not 'the other apostles and the brothers' as two units. Conversely, another manuscript (designated 1874, from the tenth century) shows

dent from the fact that Paul is unaware of any need here to distinguish biological from adoptive brothers. Since all baptized Christians were the brothers of the Lord, and all Christians knew this, Paul would need to be more specific when using this phrase of actual biological kin. Indeed, such a distinction would probably have become standard practice (such as by saying 'brothers of the Lord in the flesh'). Moreover, since other Christians besides apostles must have been in the position Paul has in mind (of traveling on church business and thus in need of being fed), we should expect him to have included them in his examples. Yet they are conspicuously absent if we assume he is talking only about Jesus' kin.

It must be noted as well that Paul does not say here (or anywhere) 'brothers of Jesus', but 'brothers of the Lord', which can only be a cultic title. One does not become the brother of 'the Lord' until the person in question is hailed 'the Lord', thus the phrase 'brother of the Lord' is a creation of Christian ideology. Yes, one might have earned that cultic title by actually being the brother of Jesus. But as ample evidence shows, one would also have earned it by simply being a baptized Christian. Indeed, Paul seems quite certain that one could not have any special privilege from biological relation, because apart from what tasks God had assigned you to perform in the church (1 Cor. 12.28), all Christians are equals—as Paul says in Gal. 3.26-29, where he even specifically argues that we are all equally related as sons of the same family.

Of course, it's possible (though not in evidence) that the use of the phrase 'brothers of the Lord' was being policed in such a fashion that it was only ever used of Jesus' actual kin. And thus, even though every Christian was in fact a brother of the Lord and all knew it, they were forbidden to refer to themselves with that specific sequence of words—instead they could only call themselves 'brother', and the fact that it was 'of the Lord' would then be understood but never written or spoken in that exact way.[94] In such a

someone tried changing it the other way around by actually inserting the names of Jesus' brothers, lifted from the Gospels, into the next verse (1 Cor. 9.6). See Reuben Swanson, *New Testament Greek Manuscripts: Variant Readings Arranged in Horizontal Lines against Codex Vaticanus: 1 Corinthians* (Sheffield. Sheffield Academic Press, 2003), p. 125.

94. Some have claimed that Paul uses the phrase 'brother in Christ' to mean Christian, and therefore 'brother of the Lord' was reserved for actual kin, but this is false. Paul never uses the phrase 'brother in Christ'. Paul often speaks of 'those in Christ' (and on single occasions 'saints in Christ', Phil. 4.21; 'man in Christ', 2 Cor. 12.2; 'babes in Christ', 1 Cor. 3.1; and 'churches in Christ', 1 Thess. 2.14) but that does not play on the fact of their adoption as sons of God but on their communion with Christ and thus their all sharing the same body (Rom. 12.5). Otherwise Paul routinely calls Christians 'brothers', and the only sense in which they were brothers is that they were, like Jesus, the sons of God (by adoption: Rom. 1.4; with Element 12) and thus were all the brothers

case, Paul could use that phrase without further qualification and always be understood to mean Jesus' actual kin. But this presumes an unlikely fact not in evidence (this unusual policing of terminology within church communications), and any theory that requires us to resort to such a thing is less probable than a theory that does not.[95] Whereas without that implausible assumption, 'brother of the Lord' would mean any baptized Christian whatever (again: Element 12).

Moreover, it is just as likely such policing of the phrase occurred in the *other* direction, and that only Christians who had obtained the highest stage of initiation were allowed to be referred to with the complete phrase 'brother of the Lord'. This would match what Clement of Alexandria reports, that Christians achieving the highest stage of initiation were alone fully heirs, and thus *fully* the sons of God (and so just as fully the brothers of *the* son of God: see Element 13). Since this is just as likely (or just as unlikely), even the possibility that the phrase 'brother of the Lord' was policed to mean only biological kin is then washed out by the equal possibility it was policed to mean only apostles of supreme rank. As either is as likely on prior considerations, neither prevails. And still more likely than both is that 'brothers of the Lord' is simply what Christians commonly called themselves before they acquired the name 'Christian' (an appellation Paul shows no knowledge of). The use of the complete phrase would then not be necessary other than occasionally for emphasis, hence Paul repeatedly speaks of Christians being simply 'the brethren', because everyone understood that was shorthand for 'brethren of the Lord'.

This makes 'brother of the Lord meant Christian' the simplest hypothesis (it requires the fewest *ad hoc* assumptions). Furthermore, that it would mean that is actually in evidence (we know all Christians in Paul's time deemed themselves brothers of the Lord in cultic fact), whereas that it meant something else is not. Not one time in all of Paul's letters does he ever say or even imply that this phrase means only *biological* brothers—or apostles of supreme rank, for that matter, unless that's implied by the sequence in 1 Cor. 9.5, if that sequence is supposed to indicate ascending rank: apostles, supreme apostles, and supremest apostle (i.e. Cephas). There being apostles

of God's first son, the Lord. Paul links both concepts in 1 Cor. 15.31, but still does not use the phrase 'brothers in Christ' even there. Only in the Pseudo-Pauline text of Col. 1.2 do we find the phrase 'to the holy and faithful brothers in Christ', but that was not written by Paul (indeed, that clause in and of itself is conspicuously un-Pauline). The NIV translation of Phil. 1.14 reads 'because of my chains most of the *brothers in the Lord* have been encouraged to speak' more boldly, but this is in error; the NASB correctly translates this clause as 'most of the brethren, *trusting in the Lord* because of my imprisonment', speak more boldly. Although either is technically possible, the context supports the latter (as does Paul's practice everywhere else).

95. See 'gerrymandering' in Carrier, *Proving History*, p. 336.

of higher rank could also be implied by 'the twelve' (in 1 Cor. 15.5) or 'the pillars' (in Gal. 2.9). Could these higher ranked apostles be the biological brothers of Jesus? One would sooner think that the higher ranked apostles would be the disciples (a group once again notably completely absent here—more evidence Paul knew of no such group), or (as just noted) the pillars or the twelve (which were in no account the family of Jesus).

In fact, there is no evidence anywhere (even outside of Paul) that the brothers of Jesus were deemed as a collective whole to be the highest ranking apostles. So that cannot be what Paul means here. Nor can he mean ascending ranks at all. He can only mean that all the other apostles, even regular Christians, and even Cephas himself, get this privilege and so should Paul. Because Paul's argument requires that the Corinthians would agree Paul has the same rights as all three examples Paul names, which entails Paul *cannot* mean these examples to be ascending in rank—otherwise he could easily be rebutted by pointing out to him that he doesn't get the privileges of ranks he has not attained. So Paul can only be assuming *none* of these groups outrank him (and furthermore, for his argument to work, he can only be assuming *that the Corinthians would agree*). Because Paul's argument is that he should have the *same* rights as they do. And since he says 'the other apostles', he is including himself in that rank, so he cannot mean he has the same rights as 'the brothers of the Lord and Cephas' unless 'the brothers of the Lord and Cephas' were consistently understood to have no more rights than apostles.

Therefore, Paul must mean by 'brothers of the Lord' here simply Christians—and in particular, Christians *below* apostolic rank. That finally makes the point of his argument clear: if even regular Christians were being given this privilege (of being supported by the communities they traveled to on church business), then surely *Paul* should be, being an actual *apostle*. He is thus arguing *a fortiori*. Likewise, by mentioning Cephas, Paul clearly assumes the Corinthians understood Cephas (i.e. Peter) and himself to be equals and deserving of equal rights. Paul assumes this elsewhere, too (1 Cor. 1.12 and 3.22). Probably Cephas was known to frequently travel with his wife (more so than other apostles Paul might have named). In any case, what is required for Paul's argument is that Cephas and Paul were of equal rank, and thus whatever Cephas got, the Corinthians would be forced to agree Paul should get. Otherwise Paul could not use Cephas to make this argument. And the same entails that Paul cannot mean the biological brothers of Jesus: for how could Paul expect the Corinthians to assume he was the equal of even the Lord's own family? Unless the Corinthians would already have agreed that their being his family gained them no special privileges—but then, if that were the case, why would Paul single them out as an example?

Thus, Paul's argument here would make no sense if he was talking about the family of Jesus. But it makes perfect sense if he was talking about Christians as a whole, and especially Christians of lower rank than himself. Against this conclusion historicists can refer only to evidence outside the Epistles, but that does not support them. The Gospels, as we saw, do conceive brothers for Jesus (and even name them), but then essentially declare that Jesus renounced them (see Chapter 10, §4). The authors of the Gospels show no knowledge of these brothers even having been *believers*, much less apostles; even less, privileged ones. Except Luke, who alone imagines them in the first congregation (in Acts 1), but then shows no knowledge of them ever doing anything, much less being apostles; even less, apostles of special status. For none of them appear anywhere in Acts' record of the church's public history (see Chapter 9, §3). That they don't exist in the earliest recorded history of the church argues for the conclusion that they didn't exist altogether. It certainly does not argue for the opposite conclusion, that they were a recognized privileged group in church leadership. No brothers of Jesus are found anywhere else in the NT, either; not even letters with their names on them claim such (see §3). And when it comes to evidence outside the NT, we already saw how ridiculous and unreliable it all is on exactly this point (see Chapter 8).

So Paul is surely just referring to non-apostolic Christians in 1 Cor. 9.5, and not to the family of Jesus. What about his one other reference to this category? To the Galatians Paul explains:

> When it was the good pleasure of the God who separated me from my mother's womb, and called me through his grace, to reveal his Son in me, that I might preach him among the Gentiles, I did not confer with flesh and blood right away, nor did I go to Jerusalem to those that were apostles before me, but I went to Arabia and again I returned to Damascus. Then after three years I went to Jerusalem, to consult with Cephas, and I stayed with him for fifteen days, but I did not see any other of the apostles, except James the brother of the Lord. And look, these things I'm writing to you, by God, I'm not lying! Then I went into the regions of Syria and Cilicia. And I was still unknown by face to the congregations of Judea that were in Christ (Gal. 1.15-22).

Here I believe this is another fictive kinship title, not a reference to James literally being the brother of Christ.[96] We've already seen how Paul can use the phrase 'brother of the Lord' to mean Christian, since all Christians were brothers of the Lord, and why Paul would have needed to be more specific if he meant 'brother of the Lord' by birth and not adoption. So here he may

96. So also Verenna, 'Born under the Law', pp. 157-59; and Doherty, *Jesus: Neither God nor Man*, pp. 60-63.

be simply saying the same thing, that James was a fellow brother in Christ. Indeed, Paul goes on to say that this James (unless he means a different one) was one of the three pillars of highest repute in the church, 'James and Cephas and John' (Gal. 2.9). The Gospels imagine these three as disciples, not the family of Jesus. In fact, the Gospels uniformly report that this James and John were the brothers of each other, not of Jesus.[97] Might Paul have only known them as such, too?

Certainly in Gal. 1.19 Paul meant either James the Pillar or another James. And if he meant James the Pillar, then he did not mean he was literally the brother of Jesus—as that James appears to have been the brother of John, not Jesus. So to maintain that Paul means this James was the literal brother of Jesus, you have to conclude that Paul meant a different James in 1.19 than the one he mentions soon afterward (in Gal. 2.9 and 2.12). But that means whichever James he is speaking of in 1.19 might not have been an apostle at all. And that means Paul may be using 'brother of the Lord' yet *again* to distinguish apostles from other Christians, and not to identify the family of Jesus.

The context of Paul's remark is again key. Paul is arguing that he received all he knows about the Christian mysteries from direct revelation (Gal. 1.6-12), that he didn't 'steal' any of it by hearing other apostles teaching it and then passing himself off as an apostle who had heard it from the Lord himself (see earlier discussion in §2). Thus it was crucial to argue that Paul had not even met any apostles until long after he had been preaching the gospel and initiating converts. That's why he insists not any Christian at all in Judea had ever met him (1.22-23) and that he only ever met one apostle (Cephas, i.e., Peter) or two (if he means James was an apostle), and even that was only after three years of conducting his own ministry in Arabia and Damascus (1.17-18), then spending just two weeks in Jerusalem, then meeting no one else there for another fourteen years (2.1).

Whether Paul is actually lying about any of this is not relevant to what Paul wants the Galatians to think and thus what Paul means to say here. And what he means to say is that no one in Judea ever met him. He swears to this most emphatically (Gal. 1.20). He admits there were only two exceptions, Peter and James, and only for a brief time (and that years after he saw the Lord personally). But in saying so, why didn't Paul just say 'of them that were apostles before me [1.17] I met none except Peter and James

97. Mk 5.37; 9.2; 14.33; Mt. 17.1; Lk. 5.10; 8.51; 9.28; Acts 12.2. Paul himself mentions a James in only two places: here in Paul's defense to the Gal. (1.19; 2.9; 2.12) and in 1 Cor. 15.7 (although that verse may be an interpolation: see earlier note). The latter does not indicate the brother of Jesus is meant, yet neither would one expect that James to be the Pillar, either, as James the Pillar would have been among 'the twelve' in 1 Cor. 15.5.

[1.18-19]'? Why does he construct the convoluted sentence 'I consulted with Peter, but another of the apostles I did not see, except James'? As L. Paul Trudinger puts it, 'this would certainly be an odd way for Paul to say that he saw only two apostles, Peter and James'.[98] To say that, a far simpler sentence would do. So why the complex sentence instead? Paul could perhaps mean that he *consulted* with Peter (*historeō*) but only *saw* James (*eidō*)—that is, he didn't discuss anything with James. But if that were his point, he would make sure to emphasize it, since that would be essential to his argument. Yet he doesn't. In fact, if he is saying that he saw *none* of the other apostles, that would entail he was claiming he did not *consult* with any, either.

So it's just as likely, if not more so, that Paul means he met only the apostle Peter and only one other Judean Christian, a certain 'brother James'. By calling him a brother of the Lord instead of an apostle, Paul is thus distinguishing this James from any apostles of the same name—just as we saw he used 'brothers of the Lord' to distinguish regular Christians from apostles in 1 Cor. 9.5. Indeed, this would explain his rare use of the complete phrase in only those two places: he otherwise uses the truncated 'brother' of his fellow Christians; yet every time he specifically distinguishes apostles from non-apostolic Christians he uses the *full* title for a member of the Christian congregation, 'brother *of the Lord*'. This would be especially necessary to distinguish in such contexts 'brothers of the apostles' (which would include kin who were not believers) from 'brothers of the Lord', which also explains why he doesn't truncate the phrase in precisely those two places.

You might see how that would be important to Paul's argument in 1 Cor. 9.5, where indeed he takes similar care in specifying that only *believing* wives have the right in question; he therefore must distinguish (so as to exclude) unbelieving *brothers* for the same reason. If the James in Gal. 1.19 could likewise be mistaken for an unbelieving brother of Peter (especially by readers who did not know what brothers Peter may have had), Paul would need to be equally specific there, and thus again use the complete phrase.[99] And if that's the case, then Paul would in effect be saying, 'I didn't

98. L. Paul Trudinger, '[*Heteron de tōn apostolōn ouk eidon, ei mē iakōbon*]: A Note on Galatians I 19', *Novum Testamentum* 17 (July 1975), pp. 200-202 (200).

99. Some claim Paul's use of the definite article ('*the* brother of the Lord') is significant, but that is not the case. For example, 1 Cor. 16.12 ('Apollos the brother'); Phil. 2.25 ('Epaphroditus the brother'); Rom. 14.10 ('the brother of you'); 1 Thess. 4.6 ('the brother of one [of us]'); 1 Cor. 8.13 ('the brother of me'); 2 Cor. 2.13 ('Titus the brother of me'); 1 Thess. 3.2 ('Timothy the brother of us'), etc. Likewise, some claim Paul would say 'James our brother' to designate his status as a Christian, but Paul never uses a personalizing pronoun of anyone not his personal friend (see 1 Cor. 1.1; 2 Cor. 1.1; 2.13; 8.22-23; Rom. 16.1; 1 Thess. 3.2; Phil. 2.25; Phlm. 1, 2, 20; rhetorical intimacy: 1 Cor. 8.13), and if this is the same James as in Gal. 2.9 and 2.12, Paul was

meet another of the apostles, unless you count brother James [who joined us but was not an apostle]'. Many biblical scholars have concluded the same: that Paul meant this James was not an apostle (whether or not he was the actual brother of Jesus).[100]

In fact, the Greek here is quite strange, unless Paul actually meant 'other *than* the apostles I saw only James', meaning quite specifically that this James was not an apostle. Ordinarily, to say you saw 'no other apostle' you would write *heteron ton apostolon ouk* (compare Rom. 7.23; 13.9; etc.) or *oudena heteron tōn apostolōn* (as Paul usually does: e.g. 1 Cor. 1.14; 2.8; 9.15; etc.) or things similar. But here Paul instead chose the unusual (and for Paul, unprecedented) construction *heteron tōn apostolōn*. Without *oudeis*, the word *heteron* plus the genitive in this fashion more often means 'other *than*', rather than 'another *of*'.[101] Paul would then be simply classifying a meeting with 'Cephas' as a meeting with 'the apostles' (as anticipated in 1.17), and then making sure he named *all* the Christians he met on that occasion (Cephas and James) in anticipation of his claim that no one in Judea had ever seen him (1.22). The latter claim would be a lie if he had met *any* Christian, even one who was not an apostle, during his visit to Cephas (in 1.18). So Paul *has* to name all the Christians he met on that occasion. And, lying or not, that number needed to be low for his argument to hold. Accordingly, Paul says there was only one other: brother James.

The fact that Paul needs to say he met no Christians at all (and not just apostles) in Gal. 1.18 in order to sustain his claim in 1.22 that no one else in Judea had seen him means that we should *expect* Paul to have named any non-apostolic Christians he met in Gal. 1.18-19. And lo and behold, that's what he appears to do: he insists he met no one else but a certain 'brother James'. We should conclude then that Paul is doing the same thing here that he did in 1 Cor. 9.5, using 'brother of the Lord' as an appellation for Christians, every time he wants to distinguish Christians generally from 'apostles' specifically. Otherwise, as I pointed out before, Paul would need

anything but James's personal friend—and even if he was, he certainly would not want to remind the Galatians of that fact in an argument insisting on how little he knew these people.

100. See Trudinger, '[*Heteron*]', p. 200 n. 3; and Hans Dieter Betz, *Galatians: A Commentary on Paul's Letter to the Churches in Galatia* (Minneapolis, MN: Fortress Press, 1979), p. 78.

101. This is argued in Trudinger, '[*Heteron*]'. I find the only rebuttal to Trudinger's argument inconclusively weak: George Howard, 'Was James an Apostle? A Reflection on a New Proposal for Gal. I 19', *Novum Testamentum* 19 (January 1977), pp. 63-64. Howard's first argument is refuted by the fact that both the apostles and James *are* of the same class (they are all Christians, which is precisely Paul's point), and his second argument is refuted by relying on a premise of pure speculation that actually expects Paul to have written an even *more* convoluted sentence than he did.

to make clear that he meant a biological brother of the Lord and not an adoptive brother of the Lord like any other Christian. That he made no such distinction here all but entails he intended none.[102] We should conclude the same.

One way to look at these two passages would be to ask what would we think if we only had Paul's (authentic) letters? If that was all the evidence we had for Christianity, would we conclude that Paul was describing with the title 'brother of the Lord' a biological relation or a cultic relation? The evidence in Paul's letters alone strongly supports the existence of the cultic relation, while providing no evidence for anyone having a biological relation to the Lord. Thus, you'll find the biological interpretation is always based on evidence *outside* Paul's letters. Which we have surveyed in previous chapters and found wholly unreliable. I have to conclude that there simply is no evidence in these two passages supporting historicity. They are fully explicable without it and do not make up for the gaping silence even in these passages, much less the vast and strange silence throughout the rest of Paul's letters—and *all* first-century Christian literature, in none of which do brothers of Jesus get mentioned in any historically credible way.[103]

So the question at hand is how likely it is that Paul would use the phrase 'brothers of the Lord' on the two occasions he does (in Gal. 1.19 and 1 Cor. 9.5), in their given context (as just analyzed), and given our background knowledge that all Christians would be known as brothers of the Lord (Element 12), and whether that probability is any different for minimal historicity (h) than it is for minimal mythicism ($\neg h$). My own conclusion is that there is at best no difference in probability and at worst a difference favoring myth—since on historicity we should expect far more frequent and far less ambiguous discussion of the family of Jesus, especially if (as these passages would then entail) they were playing a major leadership role in the church at the time. I find the silence of Paul everywhere else, and his extreme ambiguity in these two passages, less likely on historicity. So my most skeptical estimate is that this is just what we'd expect on mythicism (for Paul to occasionally, and in contexts most demanding it, refer to other

102. Some may note that indeed Origen, in *Against Celsus* 1.47, denies that Paul meant this James in Gal. 1.19 was the actual brother of Jesus, claiming instead that it was a title of honor. But Origen does not say how he knows this, so I consider that information of little use.

103. Another possibility, of course, is that 'the brother of the Lord' in Gal. 1.19 is a scribal interpolation, intended to create a reference to Jesus' brother where once there was none. But that is very unlikely. It would have a prior probability of perhaps 1 in 1000 (see earlier note). Nevertheless, one could adopt this assumption *ad hoc*, thereby reducing the prior probability of mythicism by a factor of a thousand, and yet still come to a result that mythicism is more likely—if you adopt my less *a fortiori* estimates of the consequent probabilities elsewhere. See Chapter 12.

Christians as 'brothers of the Lord') but somewhat not what we'd expect on historicity (which would sooner lead to our hearing much more about these people), at a ratio of 2 to 1 (equivalent to it being 100% likely on $\neg h$ and only 50% likely on h).

However, I must argue *a fortiori*, and to that end I shall say it's reasonably possible these probabilities go the other way around. In other words, that Paul would speak like this on those two occasions could be only 50% expected on mythicism but exactly what we expect on historicity (or 50% expected on historicity but only 25% expected on myth, etc.). In other words, I actually think this evidence is twice as likely on mythicism, but, though I doubt it, I'll allow that it might be twice as likely on historicity. I certainly cannot reasonably believe these passages (including their internal ambiguity and surrounding silence) are any *more* expected than that on h than on $\neg h$.

11. *Weighing the Evidence*

When Shirley Jackson Case responded in the early twentieth century to scholars then advocating the Jesus myth theory he summarized his own take on the Pauline Epistles.[104] He claims they are not lacking references to a historical Jesus but in fact: (1) they refer to his 'human ancestry and family connections' (but as we saw, only in ways entirely strange, highly theological or oddly nonspecific, and in no case clearly referring to an *actual* ancestry or family); (2) and to his 'association with disciples' (but as we saw, Paul in fact never mentions disciples; such personages as Peter he knows only as apostles like himself, and he only mentions Jesus 'associating' with anyone *after* his death); (3) and to his 'righteous life' (but as we saw, in fact Paul only ever mentions a single righteous *act*, nothing more, and credits Jesus as being a sinless being, as any cosmic archangel would be); (4) and to the fact that he 'lived in worldly poverty' (but as we saw, Paul doesn't mention 'worldly' poverty but only a vague lowering and loss of status, which in the Philippians gospel is wholly cosmic); (5) and they refer to his 'self-sacrificing service' (which even celestial beings could provide); (6) and to his 'heavenly exaltation as a reward for obedience' (ditto); (7) and to the 'circumstances of his death' (but none placing that death on earth); (8) and include 'numerous references to his crucifixion' (which was not necessarily terrestrial); (9) as well as to an 'awakening of faith through his appearances' (yet only in revelations); (10) and also include such things

104. Shirley Jackson Case, *The Historicity of Jesus: A Criticism of the Contention That Jesus Never Lived; A Statement of the Evidence for his Existence; An Estimate of his Relation to Christianity* (Chicago: University of Chicago Press, 2nd edn, 1928), pp. 126 and 193-95.

as references to his future coming (none of which mention his having been on earth before—e.g. not once does Paul say Jesus will 'return'), his present significance (which a cosmic being can also have), and his teachings (which as we saw even Paul seems to believe came only by revelation or scripture).

In short, none of the 'evidence' Case could adduce requires Jesus to have lived on earth. Such an existence is conspicuously absent from all of Paul's authentic letters. That is simply strange. Case can avoid that conclusion only by imagining all kinds of things are in Paul's letters that in fact are not there. Case insists Paul thought Jesus was as 'historical' as Adam (though of course we know Adam is mythical), but Paul thought God and angels and Satan and his demons were 'historical', too, so this has no bearing on where Paul thought Jesus had lived or died. Case says Paul shows Christians 'remembered' Jesus' Last Supper, but as we saw, that's not what Paul says: he learned of this event (Paul never calls it a 'last' supper or in fact even a supper) directly by revelation, not anyone's memory (Paul never refers to anyone else being there or anyone 'recollecting' it, other than himself). Case likewise says Paul calls upon Christians to imitate Jesus' earthly career, but Paul never mentions an earthly career. He only calls for imitating Christ in his loving subservience and self-sacrifice, all represented by just a single event (his submission to death), which need not have been performed on earth.

Overall, it's the mythicists who were right, and not Case. They argued that (1) some passages in Paul's letters are exactly what we would expect on their theory but not as expected if Jesus actually existed; that (2) the scant few passages in the Epistles that might refer to a historical Jesus are not only vague or problematic but also no less expected on the mythicist hypothesis; and that (3) the absence of more, clearer and more detailed references to a historical Jesus is strange and unexpected on any sound understanding of history and human nature. The excuses made up to explain away these facts are (1) not intrinsically probable and (2) not confirmed in any evidence (they are literally just 'made up').

Yes, we lack a smoking gun, such as an Epistle wherein Paul explicitly says Jesus was known to exist only by revelation, but we fully expect no such evidence to have survived for us to see it: the victorious sect did not preserve such things and even actively suppressed them (see Chapters 6, §7; 7, §7; and 8, §12; and Elements 20-22 and 44). Paul may well have said such things in the letters we know he wrote but that we do not have or in unpreserved parts of the letters that survive inside the present canon. Many other letters must have existed, written by many apostles in his generation (see Chapter 8, §4). Yet we conspicuously don't have even a mention of them, much less their contents. That is profoundly suspicious. But more importantly, this fact rules out the argument that we 'should' have more evidence supporting minimal mythicism. To the contrary, that a historicist sect won out and was so avid at altering and fabricating documents as well as throwing out or destroying them entails we are lucky even to have the evidence we do.[105]

Romans 16.25-26 outright says the 'gospel' and 'preaching' of Jesus Christ was discovered by revelation and finding secrets hidden in scripture. We should conclude that's indeed exactly what happened. We should not try to import into this or any other passage in Paul things invented by the authors of the Gospels decades later. But everything is a matter of probabilities. The estimates just surveyed are represented on the following table (measuring the odds of the evidence in the Epistles on *h*, minimal historicity, against ¬*h*, minimal mythicism), which you can use to input your own estimated odds and run your own calculations:

	best	*worst*
Other canonical Epistles	4/5	3/5
'Gospels' in Paul, Hebrews, Colossians	3/5	2/5
Things Jesus said	1/1	1/1
The Eucharist (1 Cor. 11.23-26)	1/1	1/1
Things Jesus did	3/4	1/2
Made from sperm	2/1	1/1
Made from a woman	2/1	1/1
Brothers of the Lord:	2/1	1/2

Totals		288 / 100	6 / 100
	=	72 / 25	3 / 50
	≈	2.88 / 1	1 / 16.67
	≈	[*0.3472*]	0.06
	≈	100%	6%
		vs.	
		34.7%	

In other words, when arguing *a fortiori*, if we assume the evidence in the Epistles is exactly 100% expected on *h* (minimal historicity), then the probability of that same evidence on ¬*h* (minimal mythicism) is just over 34%. Even if we granted that the Epistles are altogether strange on *h* (as in fact they are, even if many scholars still can't see it), and thus assigned them a lower probability of being that way (reflecting the fact that they are *not* exactly what we expect), when arguing *a fortiori* the *ratio* would still be the same. So on this account the evidence of the Epistles, as strange as it is, is

105. On the mathematical logic of 'historical filters' like this, see the example of 'Pilate's records' in Carrier, *Proving History*, pp. 219-24.

still more likely on h than on $\neg h$, by just over 3 to 1 (and thus about three times more likely if Jesus existed, than if he didn't).

But I think that's being far too generous to historicity. Given my own estimates (which are closer to what I think the odds actually are), the evidence of the Epistles is exactly 100% expected on *minimal mythicism*, and has a probability of only 6% on minimal historicity. Or again, whatever the percentages, I think the evidence of the Epistles is at least sixteen times *less* likely on historicity. Because they are simply so very strange on minimal historicity but not at all strange on minimal mythicism. In fact, these are pretty much exactly the kind of letters we should expect to now have from Paul (and the other authors as well) if minimal mythicism is true. Not so on historicity. Nevertheless, the *a fortiori* estimates are intended to be as generous to the biases of historicity defenders as I can reasonably be, to the point of outright Devil's advocacy. And yet, even on so generous estimates, the historicity of Jesus is still not defensible, as we shall see in our concluding calculation.

12

Conclusion

1. *The Final Calculation*

Bayes's Theorem entails a concluding probability (the probability that Jesus existed) from estimating three other probabilities: (1) the prior probability that Jesus existed; (2) the probability of the evidence if Jesus did exist; and (3) the probability of that same evidence if Jesus didn't exist. If our estimates of those three probabilities are as far in favor of historicity as we can reasonably believe them to be, then our conclusion will be as far in favor of historicity as we can reasonably believe it to be. But of course, stretching the limits of what is reasonable this way only gives us an upper limit on the probability that Jesus existed (given what we know so far). In reality that probability will likely be much lower.

Thus, I have made two estimates in every case, one *a fortiori* (the most favorable to historicity as I can reasonably be), and the other realistic (closer to what I honestly think those probabilities actually are). That gives us an upper and a lower bound.[1] However, the probability that Jesus existed could be even lower still, since my most critical estimates are also perhaps higher than they should be. So I shall call the lower bound I calculate the *a fortiori* lower bound: although I know the actual probability could be even lower, I believe it is *at least* as low as that. Whereas my upper bound is already as high as it could possibly be.

The first of the three required estimates, identified as P(h), the prior probability that Jesus existed, I established in Chapter 6. The probability of the evidence on *h* (historicity) and ¬*h* (non-historicity), identified as P(e|h) and P(e|¬h) respectively, I established in Chapters 8 through 11, generating a separate estimate for each category of evidence: the extrabiblical evidence (EXTRA), canonical Acts (ACTS), the canonical Gospels (GOSPELS), and the canonical Epistles (EPISTLES). These must all be combined here by multiplication into one estimate: P(e|h) = P (EXTRA|h) x P (ACTS|h) x P (GOSPELS|h) x

1. On this method of arguing *a fortiori* see Carrier, *Proving History*, pp. 85-88 (and '*a fortiori*, method of' on p. 333); on the concept of upper and lower bounds see Carrier, *Proving History*, pp. 87-88 (and 'margin of error' on p. 337 and 'confidence level' on p. 334).

P (EPISTLES|h). That leaves the third required number, P(e|¬h). That I calculated in Chapters 8 through 11 to be simply 1. Because all the evidence is effectively 100%, what we could expect if Jesus didn't exist and minimal mythicism, as defined in Chapter 3, is true (all other possibilities of non-historicity being ruled out there).[2] Except in Chapter 11, where, when arguing *a fortiori*, I allowed the Epistles to be evidence in favor of historicity, and thus set P(e|h) = 1 instead, and estimated P(e|¬h) to be near 1 in 3.

This can be tabulated as follows (so here you can substitute your own findings). The individual 'consequent probabilities' (probabilities of the evidence) have already been built from separate tables of subdivisions in each category of evidence in previous chapters:

PRIOR PROBABILITIES

	a fortiori (upper bound)		*a judicantiori* (lower bound)	
	ODDS	PROBABILITY	ODDS	PROBABILITY
P(h)	1 / 2	33% (1/3)	1 / 15	6.25% (1/16)
which entails . . .				
P(¬h)	2 / 1	67% (2/3)	15 / 1	93.75% (15/16)

CONSEQUENT PROBABILITY ON MINIMAL HISTORICITY (*h*)

	a fortiori (upper bound)		*a judicantiori* (lower bound)	
	ODDS	PROBABILITY	ODDS	PROBABILITY
P(e|h) =				
P (EXTRA|h)	288 / 625	46.08%	1 / 10	10%
x				
P (ACTS|h)	18 / 25	72%	1 / 5	20%
x				
P (GOSPELS|h)	1 / 1	100%	1 / 1	100%
x				
P (EPISTLES|h)	72 / 25	100%	3 / 50	6%
P(e/h) / P(e|¬h) = 373248 / 390625			3 / 2500	
P(e|h) =		33.1776%		00.12%

2. In reality we could assign lower estimates to P(e|¬h) in every case (to reflect how much the evidence might not be *exactly* what we'd expect if minimal mythicism were true), but we would then have to lower every corresponding value for P(e|h) according to the ratios determined in Chapters 8, 9 and 11 (since the evidence is never 'exactly' what we expect on historicity, either). See note at the end of Chapter 8, §1; and n. 10 in this chapter.

CONSEQUENT PROBABILITY ON MINIMAL MYTHICISM (¬*h*)

	a fortiori (upper bound)		*a judicantiori* (lower bound)	
	ODDS	PROBABILITY	ODDS	PROBABILITY
P(e|¬h) =				
P (EXTRA|¬h)	625 / 288	100%	10 / 1	100%
x				
P (ACTS|¬h)	25 / 18	100%	5 / 1	100%
x				
P (GOSPELS|¬h)	1 / 1	100%	1 / 1	100%
x				
P (EPISTLES|¬h)	25 / 72	34.7222 . . .%	50 / 3	100%
P(e/h) / P(e|¬h) =	390625 / 373248		2500 / 3	
P(e|¬h) =		34.7222 . . .%		100%

We can thus calculate our concluding probability (known as the posterior probability) using the odds form of Bayes's Theorem or the standard long form.[3] The odds form is:

$$\frac{P(h|e.b)}{P(\sim h|e.b)} = \frac{P(h|b)}{P(\sim h|b)} \times \frac{P(e|h.b)}{P(e|\sim h.b)}$$

Figure 2. Bayes's Theorem, Odds Form

Which can be expressed as:

[ODDS ON *H*] = [PRIOR ODDS] x [CONSEQUENT ODDS]

Which we can complete using the above tables as follows (using the *a fortiori* estimates):

3. See Carrier, *Proving History*, pp. 284-85. The odds form is much simpler to use, but more confusing if you want to convert its result into a probability. The standard form is much scarier, but directly calculates the probability. However, using decimal fractions is also problematic because rounding off many numbers in a multiplication introduces deviations and thus generates small differences in the result depending on where and how you rounded, so it is best to multiply with standard fractions, and then reduce the final result to a decimal probability.

$$
\begin{aligned}
[\text{BEST ODDS ON } H] &= [\ 1 / 2\ ] \times [\ 373248 / 390625\ ] \\
&= 373248 / 781250 \\
&\approx 1 / 2.0931123542524 \text{ [odds]} \\
&\approx .3232989576422 \text{ [probability]} \\
&\approx 32\%
\end{aligned}
$$

The final step here (of converting the odds into a probability) is the only one that won't be obvious to someone unfamiliar with converting odds to probabilities. In this particular case, you can follow a simple rule: when the odds are $1 / x$, just add 1 to x and complete the division. So, when we round everything off to the second decimal place, 1 / 2.09 becomes 1 / 3.09, which is 0.3236, or a tad over 32%, which is how the above result is derived.[4] As verification, note that the same result will also come from using the standard equation.[5] So even on the most outrageously generous estimates possible, there is barely a 1 in 3 chance Jesus existed. Which means, he probably didn't.

And yet that is using the absurdly generous estimates concluding every chapter, and especially the last chapter on the Epistles, the only place I could claim to find *any* credible evidence for a historical Jesus. So 1 in 3 is only the maximum possible probability Jesus existed, meaning we can say with confidence that the probability Jesus existed is in fact *less* than 1 in 3. Indeed, I conclude it's far less than that. Using the above tables again, but this time plugging in the *a judicantiori* estimates (the 'more judicious' estimates):

4. The reason 1/2.09 'odds on' historicity entails a roughly 32% chance of historicity (and not a 48% chance as one might expect from dividing 2.09 into 1) is that 1/2.09 is the 'odds on' h, and the 'odds' in this sense are in respect to total probability, because the probability of h and the probability of $\neg h$ must sum to 1. Logically their sum can never be more or less than 1, since the probability that 'either h or $\neg h$' is true is always exactly 100%, since h and $\neg h$ exhaust all possibilities (see Chapter 3, §3), and you can't have a probability higher than 100%. The term '1/2.09' in this equation's conclusion is thus saying $\neg h$ occupies 2.09 times more of the total probability-space as h does (i.e. that it is 2.09 times as probable). The only way for $P(h|e) + P(\neg h|e) = 1$ and for $\neg h$ to be 2.09 times as probable as h is if the probability of h is (about) 32% and the probability of $\neg h$ is (about) 68%. Then, 0.32 + 0.68 = 1 and 0.68 is (about) 2.09 times as large as 0.32 (and exactly so, if you do the math without rounding off any of the decimals, since we're actually talking about 0.6767010423578 being 2.0931123542524 times as large as 0.3232989576422). This can be confusing since we often misuse the word 'odds' as if it were an exact synonym of 'chances' or 'probability' (I've often done so myself).

5. For those who want to see what that looks like: the standard formula is $P(h|e.b) = [P(h|b) \times P(e|h.b)] / [[P(h|b) \times P(e|h.b)] + [P(\neg h|b) \times P(e|\neg h.b)]]$; therefore, using the percentages instead of the odds from the same tables, and rounding all decimals to the sixth place: $P(h|e.b) = [0.333333 \times 0.331776] / [[0.333333 \times 0.331776] + [0.666667 \times 0.347222]] = 0.110592 / [0.110592 + 0.231481] = 0.110592 / 0.342073 = 0.323299$ or 32%.

$$
\begin{aligned}
[\text{Worst Odds on } H] &= [\ 1 / 15\ ] \times [\ 3 / 2500\ ] \\
&= 3 / 37500 \\
&= 1 / 12500 \text{ [odds]} \\
&\approx 0.00008 \text{ [probability]} \\
&\approx 0.008\%
\end{aligned}
$$

In other words, in my estimation the odds Jesus existed are less than 1 in 12,000.[6] Which to a historian is for all practical purposes a probability of zero. For comparison, your lifetime probability of being struck by lightning is around 1 in 10,000. That Jesus existed is even less likely than that. Consequently, I am reasonably certain there was no historical Jesus. Nevertheless, as my estimates might be too critical (even though I don't believe they are), I'm willing to entertain the possibility that the probability is better than that. But to account for that possibility, when I entertain the most generous estimates possible, I find I cannot by any stretch of the imagination believe the probability Jesus existed is better than 1 in 3.

You can redo the math with your own estimates, of course. But you can also add new evidence in. With the odds form this is especially easy: you can just multiply additional odds ratios into the same equation if you want to introduce new evidence that I haven't considered. The equation would then look like this:

$$
[\text{Odds on } H] = [\text{Prior Odds}] \times [\text{Consequent Odds}] \times \mathbf{[New\ Consequent\ Odds]}
$$

The 'new consequent odds' here will be the odds ratio for anything you want to add in (and you can do this multiple times, as long as each piece of evidence is independent of all others considered). For example, if you find another piece of evidence (one I haven't already considered and estimated odds on), and you believe it's three times more likely on historicity than on myth, then the value for this 'new consequent odds' would be 3/1. Just multiply that in and you get your result. Like so (if we start with our original *a fortiori* result):

$$
\begin{aligned}
[\text{Best Odds on } H] &= [\ 1 / 2\ ] \times [\ 373248 / 390625\ ] \times [\ 3 / 1\ ] \\
&= [\ 373248 / 781250\ ] \times [\ 3 / 1\ ] \\
&= 1119744 / 781250 \\
&\approx 1.433272 / 1
\end{aligned}
$$

6. Using the standard formula (see previous note): $P(h|e.b) = [0.0625 \times 0.0012] / [[0.0625 \times 0.0012] + [0.9375 \times 0.9988]] = 0.000075 / [0.000075 + 0.936375] = 0.000075 / 0.93645 = 0.000080$ or 0.008%.

The odds have now flipped the other way around and favor h over $\neg h$. The simplest way to convert that into a probability is to first determine the probability of $\neg h$ by inverting the odds back to 1/1.433272 and following the same rule described earlier, which gets us $P(\neg h|e) \approx 1/2.433272 \approx 0.410969 \approx 41\%$. Then $P(h|e)$ will simply be the converse of that. So: $P(h|e) = 1 - P(\neg h|e) \approx 100\% - 41\% \approx 59\%$. Thus, finding such an item of evidence would make Jesus almost 60% likely to exist. Although that would *still* mean there was a very good chance he didn't (better than 40% in fact; that's almost 50/50)—so you would still have to reserve some doubt even then.

But we didn't find any evidence like that (beyond what we already considered and put in). Moreover, that only follows if we start with the *a fortiori* estimates, which only gets us the upper bound, the *highest* that probability could be. Even with this imaginary new evidence for historicity the lower bound would only change to:

$$\begin{aligned}[\text{WORST ODDS ON } H] &= [\,1 / 15\,] \times [\,3 / 2500\,] \times [\,3 / 1\,] \\ &= [\,3 / 37500\,] \times [\,3 / 1\,] \\ &= 9 / 37500 \\ &\approx 1 / 4166.6667\end{aligned}$$

Which means even with that hypothetical evidence added in we would still end up with a lower bound on the probability Jesus existed of about 1 in 4,000. Since you could be in as much error trusting the *a fortiori* estimates as I can be in trusting my more critical estimates, you must honestly admit the probability Jesus existed may still be near zero, for the same reason I must presently admit it may be as much as 1 in 3 (on the *actual* evidence we have). So this new hypothetical evidence would only update the probability Jesus existed to somewhere between roughly 1/40% of 1% and 60%. You could not be certain where in that range it fell. And so you should still be skeptical of Jesus' existence. Even with such new evidence as that.[7]

And again, we don't have that evidence. Instead, with the evidence we have, the probability Jesus existed is somewhere between 1 in 12,500 and 1 in 3. In other words, less than 33% and most likely nearer to zero. We should conclude that Jesus probably did not exist.

2. *On Trying to Avoid the Conclusion*

I suspect those so invested in the traditional and dogmatic views and interpretations, and those so terrified of going against 'the consensus', that they simply cannot countenance all that I've argued (no matter how soundly I've

7. See my discussion of this conundrum in Carrier, *Proving History*, pp. 87-88.

argued it) won't be willing to concede this conclusion, even if God Himself descended from heaven and told them it was correct. Their careers, reputations or religious faith may rest too firmly on their past assumptions, making them impervious to change. But I can't believe this will describe all experts, especially of the next generation, which won't have become invested yet in any status quo (although their seniors could threaten to 'punish' them if they entertain such ideas, thereby maintaining historicity by argument *ad baculum*).

Nevertheless, it is legitimate to ask how any of this can be gainsaid. A theory is not defensible if we cannot explain what would refute it. To do that, you must find different probabilities, and not just claim them, but make a sound case for why we should adopt them. Accordingly, that is where the argument must now proceed. Is even my *a fortiori* estimate of historicity's prior probability wrong? Let's see you prove it. I am not certain you can't. I am only certain you can't dismiss my estimate with one of your own without a sound argument. I want to see that sound argument. Are any of my *a fortiori* estimates of the consequent probabilities wrong? Let's see you prove it. Once again, I am not certain you can't. I am only certain you can't do it without a sound argument. So again, I want to see that argument. But beware: if you do not know how to detect logical fallacies, you will not know how to detect them even in your own arguments. You may be surprised to discover how many you rely on.

For the prior probability, the question becomes one of what 'reference class' Jesus belongs to and what we do with that information. I've already surveyed the options on this point here (in Chapter 6) and in general elsewhere.[8] I do not see much room to move on this point. Right from the start Jesus simply looks a lot more like a mythical man than a historical one. And were he not the figure of a major world religion—if we were studying the Attis or Zalmoxis or Romulus cult instead—we would have treated Jesus that way from the start, knowing full well we need more than normal evidence to take him back out of the class of mythical persons and back into that of historical ones. Jesus can no longer be treated as just any person claimed to have existed. He's not. From the Epistles alone, but even more from the Gospels, we can tell that Jesus was, from the earliest recorded point in Christian history, a rapidly mythicized cosmic savior lord. That remains a fact even if he was a historical man. Yet that fact takes him out of the category of ordinary men. Jesus is simply not like Pontius Pilate.

That leaves the evidence, which can in principle turn the tide of any low prior (as I showed for Caesar in Chapter 6, §8). I divided the consequent probabilities of the evidence for Jesus into four general categories (Epistles,

8. See Carrier, *Proving History*, pp. 229-65.

Gospels, Acts, and Everything Else), each of which in turn can be broken down into any sub-units you prefer (as long as they don't relevantly overlap in content, otherwise you'll be counting the same evidence twice in your estimates of probability). I have only chosen the units that seemed reasonable to me, in Chapters 8 (Everything Else), 9 (Acts), and 11 (Epistles). One can tease out units from among the Gospels, too; I simply didn't because I found nothing of use there (in Chapter 10). But in each of these categories the questions become: How do you explain the oddities I've surveyed? How much do you have to arbitrarily 'suppose' in order to do that? How likely are those suppositions to be true? You have to honestly answer these questions. Especially that last one. Because if you can't argue for a probability, you can't claim to argue it's probable.

Likewise if you think there is evidence I've overlooked, evidence that argues for historicity: you need to present it and argue for why that evidence is more likely on h than on $\neg h$ (in the way those alternatives have been defined, in Chapters 2 and 3). And not just more likely, but so much more likely that it overcomes all the other factors against it—even on estimates *as far against* historicity as you can reasonably admit possible: because you, too, are obligated to measure the extent to which your own estimates could be disputed or in error. You cannot enshrine your own opinions as the truth. If I have to admit the probability Jesus existed could be as high as 1 in 3, you have to admit the probability could be as low as . . . well, how low? You have to honestly answer that question.

I already showed earlier how to introduce new evidence into the equation. And how to re-do the math after changing the estimates that I've already made should also be clear. For example, I considered (but dismissed) the possibility that Acts is such complete fiction that it has absolutely no basis in any facts whatever, and thus despite its oddness perhaps can't argue either for *or* against historicity because it could not even in principle contain clues either way (see Chapter 9). If we instead decide to adopt that extreme assumption, then the ratio of consequent probabilities for Acts becomes simply 1/1. This changes the total consequent probability on h from 0.331776 to 0.4608 (by altering the estimate of 72% for Acts back to simply 100%), and changes the odds ratio from 373248/390625 to 20736/15625.[9] The odds Jesus existed then become 1/2 x 20736/15625 = 20736/31250 = 1/1.507. The probability of historicity would then be no greater than 1/2.507 ≈ 40%. This is essentially what we would have ended up with if Acts didn't have any evidence against historicity—if for example it contained fictions about the family of Jesus and their affairs in the early church (assuming they lacked anything we could verify as true), or had a

9. Because 288/625 x 1/1 x 1/1 x 72/25 = 20736/15625.

plot that actually made historical sense (given the fact that it was claimed that Jesus escaped the clutches of Rome).

But in fact Acts contains very strange oddities on the assumption that Luke was making the whole thing up. The notion that Luke would not put the family of Jesus, or a plausible historical plot, or plainly historicizing trial speeches into his fabrication is simply not that likely. Such strange omissions really make sense only if Luke was altering and embellishing some actual outline of the early church's first trials and internal struggles. Only then might he not realize that his outline lacked any mention of the family of Jesus having anything to do with the church, that the trial speeches lacked any mention of a historical Jesus, and that the plot made no sense unless Jesus was only known as a revealed being even to the Jewish and Roman elite. Certainly, we must admit that these oddities are not what we'd expect from such a text. They cannot therefore have a 100% probability. My estimates reflect that fact. So must yours. Quite simply, the strange content of Acts must have *some* probability below 100%.

And yet even if we adopted such an extreme tactic of claiming (against all common sense) that Acts is exactly as we should expect it on historicity, we still don't find that Jesus' existence is likely. It's not even 50/50 on that account. And that again would only be the upper bound, the highest *possible* probability that he existed, not the actual probability he did. So that tactic cannot rescue historicity. One might try instead to argue that Acts includes things that are improbable unless Jesus existed—such as the fact (as many Christian apologists argue) that the street sermons in it contain evidence of drawing on Aramaic sources and are 'therefore' authentic and datable to the time of Christ and so cannot be assuming a historical Jesus unless there had been one. But I already explained why that argument fails, both on its premises and its logic (Chapter 9, §6). That means you would have to find some way around the problems I identified. I don't see one. But maybe I missed something. If I did, someone has to point out what that is, and redo the math. Until then, my conclusion represents our current state of knowledge. You will find that in all of the last five chapters (7 through 10) I have similarly addressed (directly or indirectly) almost every conceivable argument one might adduce like this. What I've said in each case must be dealt with. It cannot be ignored.

So, likewise, any other attempt at changing the odds by adducing evidence I overlooked. For each case, you have to ask yourself, 'How likely would that be if h were true?', and 'How likely would that be if $\neg h$ were true?' The ratio between your two answers is what you plug into the equation. For example, if you think a piece of evidence is 100% likely on h but only 80% likely on $\neg h$, then the ratio is 100/80, which is simply 5/4. Multiply that in. The strange content of Acts will again serve as an example. If you had never seen or heard of Acts, if it was a newly discovered text written near the end of the first century and you were about to be the first one to ever read it, then before you cracked it open, what probability would you *honestly* say there was that it would never mention any brothers of Jesus having anything to do with the first three decades of the church, even though the book expends twenty-five chapters on no other subject than what happened in the first three decades of the early church? I seriously doubt you would say '100%', as if you would be totally confident it would absolutely not mention a single thing about the brothers of Jesus in any part of its public history, that it would fail to depict them doing a single thing in the early church or having any notable role in it or any interaction with it. Surely you don't *honestly* believe that. Therefore, the probability you assign *has* to be less than 100%.

So think about it, and be honest. Before cracking that book open, what probability would you assign? How likely would the strange features I outlined in Chapter 9 be? *That's* the probability of those features of Acts on h. Which is why I found that probability to be lower than 100%. On the other hand, since $\neg h$ already entails there were no brothers to mention (and likewise all the other missing things), their not being mentioned is 100% expected. Even the historicizing details are fully expected, since we know Luke freely makes stuff up to support what he wants his readers to believe, and from his Gospel we know he assumes, or wants his readers to assume, Jesus existed.[10] You can now form your odds ratio. I came up with 2 in 5 (40% in ratio to 100%), which I doubled to 4 in 5 (80% in ratio to 100%) to argue *a fortiori*. Can you *honestly* produce a more favorable result? To the contrary, I dare say your honest estimates might even be *lower* than mine. Acts, considered honestly and objectively, is just bizarre on the assumptions of historicity.[11]

10. Note that this would obviously assume the canceling-out of a coefficient of contingency (Carrier, *Proving History*, pp. 77-79, 215-19), given that multiple outcomes are compatible with $\neg h$. Thus, that the absence of Jesus' family after Acts 1 is 100% expected on $\neg h$ does not entail their presence would have been 0% expected on $\neg h$, since fabricated histories are still compatible with $\neg h$ (and given b, e.g., Element 44, they are not even unexpected). It's just that the coefficient of contingency (c = the probability that Luke would fabricate a history for Jesus' family *whether they existed or not*) cancels out in any equation, and thus can be disregarded. So to be strictly literal, on $\neg h$ the absence of Jesus' family after Acts 1 is expected to a probability of 100% x (100% - c), and is therefore not 100% *per se*. But likewise the probability that his family would be absent after Acts 1 on *historicity*, i.e., h, is (on my *a fortiori* estimate) 72% x (100% - c), so the (100% - c) cancels out, leaving us with just 100% against 72% (as explained in *Proving History*, pp. 215-19).

11. Note that even the extreme tactic of concluding *all* the evidence has no value (making a ratio of consequents across the board of just 1/1) *except* the Epistles, and then using the *a fortiori* estimate of consequents for their content *still* does not get a result

The same points apply even at the stage of prior probability. If we began instead with straight up even odds, and stuck only with *a fortiori* estimates from there on out, the probability Jesus existed would only be about 49%. In other words, pretty much even money. We simply could not say whether he existed or not. You may as well flip a coin. And yet that would still be cheating. For if we did that, then we would have to move the Rank–Raglan data back into the evidence of the Gospels. Which means we would end up having to reduce the final odds by 2 to 1 all over again. Because evidence can't be ignored—a point I already demonstrated in Chapter 6. As I showed there, the evidence of the fourteen known members of the Rank–Raglan hero class is that a historical man is *at least* two times less likely to become a member of it than a mythical man (unless there have been more mythical men in history than historical men, which is obviously not at all likely). Since the Gospels show Jesus *did* become a member of it, the odds that that would have happened on historicity (rather than on mythicism) are 2 to 1 against. So my estimate of 1/1 for the Gospels would then have to become 1/2. Which means we will have simply swapped the original 1/2 for this 1/1 in the equation, producing no net difference in the outcome. The original *a fortiori* sequence of **1/2** x [288/625 x 18/25 x **1/1** x 72/25] simply becomes **1/1** x [288/625 x 18/25 x **1/2** x 72/25], which produces exactly the same conclusion: nearly a 1 in 3 chance Jesus existed. No more.

3. *What We Should Conclude*

There is only about a 0% to 33% chance Jesus existed. Furthermore, given my analysis in Chapter 3, this means the probability that *minimal mythicism* is true is about 67% to 100% (and most likely nearer the high end of that range).

What does that mean for Jesus studies? It means all later tales of a historical Jesus and his family need to be seen as legendary, mythical and propagandistic inventions, and studied for their literary and rhetorical purpose and not for their specific historical content. But more importantly, it means we need to re-examine the earliest evidence from a completely different perspective. That means the authentic letters of Paul, but also other Epistles close to him in thought, such as Colossians, Ephesians, Hebrews, 1 Peter,

of high confidence: you then only end up with less than a 60% chance Jesus existed. Such an extreme tactic is not reasonable (it is not plausible that the evidence surveyed in Chapters 8 and 9 does not lend *any* support to minimal myth, as if all of it were perfectly expected on minimal historicity), but even were it resorted to, a 60% chance Jesus existed is not that high, as it entails a 40% chance he didn't, odds high enough to still make Jesus' existence reasonably uncertain.

and *1 Clement*; and perhaps other literature as well, such as the *Didache*. We need to reconsider all the evidence now from a new perspective. We need to see it in light of what the present study has shown to be the most likely account of the origin and early development of the Christian religion, which now fits the theory of minimal mythicism (as outlined in Chapter 3), in the context of the background knowledge (all forty-eight elements) surveyed in Chapters 4 and 5.

In summary: Before the 20s, the Jesus that Christians would later worship was known by some Jews as a celestial being, God's agent of creation (Elements 40-42). Sometime between the 20s and 40s a small fringe sect of Jews, probably at the time led by a man named (or subsequently renamed) Cephas, came to believe that this Jesus figure had undergone a salvific incarnation, death and resurrection in outer space, thus negating the cultic role of the Jerusalem temple, freeing them from it politically, spiritually and physically, which was a very convenient thing to conceive at the time (Elements 1-7, 10, 18, 23-29, 43). They also came to believe that through this act their salvation had been secured through the defeat of the demonic world order, so long as they shared in that sacrifice metaphysically through baptism and ritual communion, a concept already adopted by many similar cults of the time (Elements 11-12, 18, 31, 37).

This sect, like many others of the same period (Element 2), had been looking for 'hidden' messages from God in the OT (Elements 8-9) in order to learn how and when God would solve their present woes (Elements 3-7, 23-29). And also like many Jews, this sect was under syncretistic influences from diverse Jewish sects and the most popular and culturally diffused aspects of Greco-Roman religion and philosophy (Elements 30-39). Its members were also highly prone to having (or claiming to have) 'visions' (what we now would call dreams or hallucinations), and with a combination of such visions and their searching for creative reinterpretations of scripture that spoke to their present troubles they convinced themselves that this celestial self-sacrifice occurred and was part of God's plan and had now been 'revealed' from heaven to a select few (Elements 15-17). We cannot know now whether the idea was discovered in scripture first, inspiring visions to corroborate or elaborate it, or whether it was creatively arrived at in visions first, inspiring the apostles to then find corroboration and elaboration in scripture. It could have been both, each a catalyst for the other.

This cult began as a Torah-observant Jewish sect that abandoned their reliance on Levitical temple cult, and was likely preaching the imminent end of the world, in accordance with the scriptures, signs and revelations of the celestial Jesus. In the 30s or 40s an active enemy of the cult, named Paul, had (or claimed to have) his own revelation from this Jesus and became an apostle spreading rather than attacking the faith. Over the next twenty years he converts many, preaches widely, and writes a body of letters. During this time the original sect driven by Cephas fragmented. There are many church schisms, and many alternative versions of the original gospel arise, including the version inaugurated by Paul, which abandoned Torah observance and more avidly sought the conversion of pagans, seeking to unify Jew and Gentile in a common community (Elements 19-21).

Between the 30s and 70s some Christian congregations gradually mythicize the story of their celestial Jesus Lord, just as other mystery cults had done for their gods, eventually representing him rhetorically and symbolically in overtly historical narratives, during which time much of the more esoteric truth of the matter is reserved in secret for upper levels of initiation (Elements 11-14, 44-48). Right in the middle of this process the Jewish War of 66–70 destroyed the original church in Jerusalem, leaving us with no evidence that any of the original apostles lived beyond it. Before that, persecutions from Jewish authorities and famines throughout the empire (and, if it really happened, the Neronian persecution of 64, which would have devastated the church in Rome) further exacerbated the effect, which was to leave a thirty-year dark age in the history of the church (from the 60s to the 90s), a whole generation in which we have no idea what happened or who was in charge (Element 22). In fact this ecclesial dark age probably spans fifty years (from the 60s to 110s), if *1 Clement* was written in the 60s and not the 90s (see Chapter 8, §5), as then we have no record of anything going on until either Ignatius or Papias, both of whom could have written well later than the 110s (Chapter 8, §§6 and 7).

It's during this dark age that the canonical Gospels most likely came to be written, by persons unknown (Chapter 7, §4), and at least one Christian sect started to believe the myths they contain were real, and thus began to believe (or for convenience claim) that Jesus was a real person, and then preached and embellished this view. Because having a historical founder represented in controlled documents was a significant advantage (Chapter 8, §12; and Chapter 1, §4), this 'historicizing' sect gradually gained political and social superiority, declared itself 'orthodox' while condemning all others as 'heretics' (Chapter 4, §3), and preserved only texts that agreed with its view, and forged and altered countless texts in support. As a result, almost all evidence of the original Christian sects and what they believed has been lost or doctored out of the record; even evidence of what happened during the latter half of the first century to transition from Paul's Christianity to second-century 'orthodoxy' is completely lost and now almost wholly inaccessible to us (Elements 21-22 and 44).

No element of the theory I just outlined is *ad hoc*. The letters of Paul corroborate the hypothesis that Christianity began with visions (real or claimed) and novel interpretations of scripture, and this is not a fringe proposal but is actually a view shared by many experts. The idea of a 'celestial savior' is corroborated by documents such as the *Ascension of Isaiah* and has precedents in theologies like the continual death-and-resurrection of Osiris, and is found even in the Dead Sea Scrolls. Euhemerization of god-men by placing them in historical contexts was commonplace in antiquity. That ancient texts could have symbolic and allegorical content is well established in classics and religious studies, has ample support in the sociology of religion and was common practice in ancient mystery cults and Judaism. Christianity did possess the central features of ancient mystery cults. And the fact that such 'mysteries' were kept secret and revealed only to initiates, who were then sworn to secrecy, is a well-known fact of ancient religion. Everything else is an undeniable fact: the Epistles *do* reveal the constant vexation of novel dogmas; the devastating events of the 60s *did* occur; the history of the church *is* completely silent from then until the mid-90s or later; a historicist sect *did* later gain supreme power and *did* decide which texts to preserve, and it *did* doctor and meddle with numerous manuscripts and even produced wholesale forgeries to that same end—and not as a result of any organized conspiracy, but simply from independent scribes and authors widely sharing similar assumptions and motives.

The only element of the basic myth theory that is even incredible (at least at first look) is the idea that a transition from a secret cosmic savior to a public historical one happened within two generations, and without a clear record of it occurring. But the unusual circumstances of a major disruption in the church opened the door to rapid developments in its dogmas, and the complete silence of the record in the following period blocks any attempt to argue 'from silence' that there was no transition from myth to legend. That this development did not get recorded is because *nothing* got recorded.

When we consider the prospect of newly evangelized Christians, handed a euhemerized Gospel, but not yet initiated into the full secret, and then being set loose to spread their unfinished beliefs and founding their own churches and developing their own speculations, the idea that a myth could be mistaken as and transformed into 'history' in just a few generations is not so implausible as it may seem, particularly given that the geographical distances involved were large, lifespans then were short, and legends often grow with distance in both time and space. There may even have been a 'transitional' state of the cult in which the historical narratives were seen as playing out what was simultaneously occurring in the heavens (so one could believe both narratives were true), or in which certain sect leaders chose to downplay or reinterpret the secret doctrines and sell the public ones as the truth instead (as Origen seems to have thought was a good idea).

Any number of possibilities present themselves; without any data from that period, we cannot know which happened. Hence I already dealt with this objection more than adequately in Chapters 6 (§7), 7 (§7), and 8 (§§4 and 12). For comparison, even if we granted historicity, then we do not know how some sects transitioned to a cosmically born Jesus in the Christianities Irenaeus attacks as heresies (Chapter 11, §9) or a cosmically killed Jesus in the *Ascension of Isaiah* (Chapter 3, §1), or to a Jesus who lived and died a hundred years earlier (Chapter 8, §1). Thus, our ignorance in the matter of how the cult transitioned is not solved by positing historicity. Either way, we're equally in the dark on how these changes happened.

4. *The Last Desperate Objection*

Hence, I believe our conclusion should be in favor of minimal mythicism. Jesus began life as a celestial being whose suffering, death and resurrection was known only through revelations (real or pretended) and secret messages in scripture, and who only later became a mythically historicized person as a model to follow and hang new dogmas upon.

That leaves the last and most common objection to this conclusion: that 'the Jews' would never conceive of a dying messiah (Element 3), much less a dying messiah who would become a celestial Lord, the conduit through whom one worshiped God. Of course, in its most naive formulation, this objection is self-refuting. If Jews would never conceive of it, Christianity would never have happened—because Christianity obviously began within sectarian Judaism (Elements 1, 20 and 33). So the very existence of Christianity itself refutes the objection. It is only further refuted by the fact that it relies on a hidden assumption, that the Jews were monolithic in their thinking about theology and religion, which is false: Judaism was remarkably diverse and innovative in exactly this period (Element 2), and all manner of ideas were being tried to resolve the existential dilemma the Jews as a conquered people were in (Element 23). So we cannot claim the Jews 'could not' have done this. Because they did.

Cornered by these facts, objectors will concede that some Jews evidently *were* able to conceive of such a thing, but then insist that some compelling event must have precipitated so wild a break with Jewish thinking, and only the crucifixion of an actual historical man could have done such a thing. But that's a non sequitur. If early-first-century Jews could conceive of a dying messiah becoming a celestial Lord (and clearly they could), they could conceive of this being true of a celestial man as easily as a historical one. In other words, these objectors admit that some Jews could conceive of a historically crucified man becoming celestial Lord. But if the Jews could do that, they could conceive of a *celestially* crucified man becoming celestial Lord. Which negates this objection from the start.

We already saw that this very idea (or ideas sufficiently like it) had become increasingly popular in the Roman Empire; in fact it was already diffusing into every other foreign culture under its umbrella, from the Syrian to the Persian to the Egyptian (Element 31). So we should actually have expected Jewish culture to find a way to integrate the same idea; after all, every other national culture was doing so. And this is where we have to look at the possibilities in light of what we now know. Had I been born in the year 1 and was asked as a young educated man what a Jewish mystery religion would look like, based on what I knew of the common features of mystery cult and the strongest features of Judaism, I could have described Christianity to you in almost every relevant particular—before it was even invented. It would involve the worship of a mythical-yet-historicized personal savior, a son of god, who suffered a death and resurrection, by which he obtained salvation for those who communed with his spirit, thereby becoming a fictive brotherhood, through baptism and the sharing of sacred meals. How likely is it that I could predict that if that wasn't in fact how it came to pass? Influence is the only credible explanation. To propose it was a coincidence is absurd.

Objectors will then resort to the going myth that the Jews never syncretized their religion with others. But we know that is false (Elements 30 and 32). In fact, earliest Christianity is demonstrably just like all those other mystery religions in precisely the ways they were *all* like each other (Elements 11 and 12). That, again, cannot be a coincidence. The fact that all those mystery religions involved a suffering (and often dying-and-rising) intermediary demigod as their lord and savior (Element 31), just like Christianity, points clearly to the direction of causation. It's simply not possible that the Jews independently just thought up exactly the same idea, somehow not aware that that idea was everywhere around them already.

It's even false that the theological concepts behind this adaptation were foreign to Judaism to begin with. The exaltation of martyrs and the role of human sacrifice achieving salvation for the living was already as Jewish as it was pagan (Element 43), and the Jews had already been toying with the idea of dying messiahs (Elements 5 and 6), and one of their own scriptures could easily be read as predicting this would happen in the early first century, signaling the imminent end of the world (Element 7), just as the earliest Christians were claiming (e.g. 1 Cor. 15.23-24 and 1 Thess. 4.13-18), and as many other Jews were expecting (Element 4).

Furthermore, the Jews were already acknowledging the problems the temple cult was posing for them. The idea of a special divine sacrifice eliminating the need of that temple cult would certainly have been attractive to at least some of them (Elements 23 to 28). It surely cannot be a coincidence that the whole idea of Jesus was conveniently constructed to serve exactly that role (Elements 10 and 18). Anthropology even confirms how common exactly this kind of syncretistic revolutionary movement is in exactly the circumstances Judaism was then in (Element 29). *This* was the most likely 'impetus' that drove the innovative ideas behind Christianity—not some historical man who just happened to get himself killed. Because if you think about it, *that* makes far less sense.

That the whole Christian gospel could be read out of scripture, and indeed without much effort (Element 17), in conjunction with the fact that in the century leading up to Christianity many Jews were scrambling to find secret messages in scripture (Element 8), should already be enough to lead us to expect that one of those groups 'discovered' in that effort to find hidden meanings in scripture something to satisfy their pressing need to deal with the Roman occupation and the impenetrable corruption of the Jewish temple elite *without* the futile option of military revolt (again, Elements 23 to 28). The celestial Jesus doctrine does exactly that, so superbly well that once again we cannot imagine this is a coincidence. The fact that 'scripture' then meant a larger body of documents than we now have access to, and variant readings in documents we have that we no longer know about (Element 9), only makes this even more likely.

That Christianity began as a visionary cult prone to hallucinating fantastical things (Elements 15 and 16) makes it all more likely still—because it eliminates the need of a historical man to die. A charismatic leader could simply hallucinate a dying savior in the sky. And the fact that all mystery religions composed exoteric (public) myths to conceal their esoteric (secret) cosmological doctrines (Element 14), and Christianity had secret doctrines from its earliest recorded time (Element 13), best explains the sequence of evidence in the record: no historical Jesus in the earliest documents and gospels (those in the Pauline and quasi-Pauline Epistles, as shown in Chapter 11), then suddenly wildly mythological literary constructs of Jesus in the Gospels (Chapter 10), with no corroborating evidence outside these sacred documents (Chapter 8), and even some evidence of a progression from myth to history (Chapters 8 and 9). In fact, Paul does not seem to have known of any evidence of Jesus other than by revelation and scripture (Element 19, with Chapter 11). Jesus was then rapidly built up into a standard but otherwise Jewish version of a Rank–Raglan hero (Element 48). Yet no known Rank–Raglan heroes have ever been historical (Chapter 6, §3), which only further pushes us to the obvious conclusion.

And that's it. There simply is no other evidence to go by (Chapter 7). Indeed, we can already tell from Hebrews 8–9; Rom. 16.25-26; and 1 Cor. 15.3-5 that Christianity *as a religion* originated with visions (and the finding of hidden messages in scripture) of God's celestial high priest (the celestial Jesus, God's image or Logos, a supernatural being recognized by at least some Jews of the time: Element 40). From Philippians 2 and other passages (Element 10; and Chapter 11, §4) we can tell that in earliest documented Christian belief, Jesus began as what conservative Jews would have called an archangel (angels often being hailed as 'lords' like Jesus), descending to assume the body of a man, possibly no further than sublunar space (as was the case for Osiris: Element 37; and for the Jesus found in the earlier redaction of the *Ascension of Isaiah*: Chapter 3, §1), where he was mocked and killed and buried by Satan and his sky demons, and thereby gained power over them, and was raised from the dead to be appointed God's right-hand man, celestial Lord of the universe, with dominion now even over Satan and his demonic host, even over Death itself.

This accords with all we know about the cosmological beliefs of many Jews of the time, including the multi-layered nature of the heavens (Element 34), the existence of intercessory beings traveling among them (Element 36; known as 'angels' and 'archangels' in Jewish vocabulary but by other terms in pagan vocabulary: see Chapter 4, §3), and the status of the vast sublunar realm as the realm of death and the dead (Element 35), in which resided countless hosts of dark supernatural beings (Element 37) and a plethora of distant objects such as castles and gardens (Element 38).[12] It accords, too, with ideas of a celestial 'Adam' (Element 39), a celestial 'son of man' (Element 41), a celestial 'high priest' (Element 42), and, again, a celestial 'Jesus' known as the 'Logos' (Element 40), all of which Jesus had been associated with by mid-first century (only the early explicit designation of him as 'the Logos' cannot be confirmed, although it can be inferred).

And though the evidence shows that Christianity most probably began this way, it also shows it evolved into a historicizing sect, and that that sect won out, and then destroyed or altered or let vanish almost all documents supporting its opponents, and then preserved only documents it agreed with, even inventing and editing documents as it needed for that purpose (Element 21), which was actually the normal practice for all religions of that period, *especially* those (like Judaism and many pagan cults) that originated with mythical people (Elements 44 and 45). And we cannot observe this transition in the case of Christianity, because no documents or knowledge survives from the period in which it occurred (Element 22). The Gospels were simply constructed to euhemerize Jesus, as all mythical demigods had been (Element 45), modeling him after other historical and mythical counter-cultural heroes (Element 46), and then ultimately integrating him into the ubiquitous Rank–Raglan hero-type (Element 48), and matching an equally popular model of celestially translated heroes (Element 47), all appropriately Judaized.

Even though this all makes sense, fits all the evidence (better even than any alternative, with a minimum of *ad hoc* suppositions), and accords well with all our background knowledge, the objectors often still won't see reason. As the counter-argument was once described to me, Paul says 'we proclaim Christ crucified: for Jews a stumbling block, for Gentiles foolishness'

12. In outer space; for the possibility of a terrestrial myth, see note in Chapter 11 (§8).

(1 Cor. 1.23), so there can't be any way Jews themselves would think up a stumbling block on purpose; it therefore must be an accident, and that means a historical Jesus who got himself accidentally killed, which his followers then tried to spin into some grand notion. But this reasoning is multiply fallacious—even apart from everything I just surveyed, and even apart from the fact that Paul qualifies his statement almost immediately: it was not a stumbling block to *some* Jews nor foolish to *some* pagans. Therefore this very same passage in Paul immediately proves this framing of the argument to be a fallacy of false generalization, unjustifiably leaping from 'most Jews' to 'all Jews'. To some, 'both Jews and Greeks', Christ's death was not a stumbling block at all but 'the power of God', nor was it foolish, but rather 'the wisdom of God' (1 Cor. 1.24).

Even apart from that, to imagine Christianity happened because 'a historical Jesus got himself accidentally killed, which his followers then tried to spin into some grand notion' predicts an entirely different body of evidence than we have. Paul's Epistles, for example, would look very different than they do, and contain many different disputes and claims. This hypothesis therefore has a very low consequent probability. Indeed, if that really had been the sequence of events, we would not have gotten the Christianity we find in Paul's letters even in outline. Jesus would instead have simply been proclaimed a martyr exalted or resurrected by God, not a celestial Lord and God's intermediary. It's that additional leap that is confusing, not the dying part (nor the rising part: resurrections abound in the Jewish scriptures, hence note that it is not the 'resurrection' of Jesus that Paul says was the stumbling block). Jews did not stumble over the idea of exalted martyrs; they manufactured them by the dozens (indeed even their own scriptures exalted them, for 'precious in the sight of Jehovah is the death of his holy ones', Ps. 116.15; Wis. 5 even offers a model example of a generic martyr being resurrected and exalted). They had even invented and embraced a dying messiah in their own scriptures (Dan. 9.26—even if not *the* messiah, certainly *a* messiah: see Chapter 4, §3) and never had any evident trouble imagining their future messiah would be killed (as we see Talmudic Jews fully embraced the idea: Element 5).

It's worth emphasizing here that we have *absolutely no evidence* that any ancient Jews (much less *all* of them) considered the idea of exalting a slain messiah to be blasphemous or illegal or even inconceivable—that's a modern myth. To the contrary, the evidence we do have (from the Talmud, for example) shows they had no trouble conceiving and allowing such a thing (Element 5). Nor would such a notion be foolish to pagans, who had their own dying saviors, historical (Element 43) and mythical (Element 31). So the only thing Paul could mean the Jews were stumbling over was the notion that a *celestial being* could be crucified—as that would indeed seem strange, and would indeed be met with requests for evidence ('How do you know *that* happened?').

And that is in fact the context of Paul's remark: in the immediately preceding sentence Paul had said the problem he's talking about was that the 'Jews ask for signs, and the Greeks seek after wisdom' (1 Cor. 1.22), but the Christian gospel met neither standard (that is the meaning of v. 23, which is referring to v. 22 and then qualified in v. 24). It certainly seems as if he means they had no evidence to present that Christ was crucified (because they could produce no sufficient 'signs' that proved what they preached was true), and to Greek philosophers the notion of it sounded silly, as it did not follow from reason or empirical evidence, but rather derived from dubious private revelations and a crazy toying with the ancient equivalent of Bible codes, neither being a 'method of knowing' accepted by the pagan elite. If anything, this passage all but proves minimal mythicism. Because it's almost inconceivable on minimal historicity. A martyred savior was never a stumbling block to Jews nor foolish to pagans (Element 43). Nor did it require signs or mystical evidence.

But even apart from all *that* (which is really quite enough to debunk this objection), the entire logical form of the argument is invalid. The general rule that 'only a real event would inspire people to preach a scandalous doctrine promoting that event' is demonstrably false. I here present a demonstration of this by showing that in other cases the rule fails:

Attis Cult	Jesus Cult
Attis was preached castrated. ⬇	Jesus was preached crucified. ⬇
'Attis castrated' was a stumbling block for many (Augustine, *City of God* 6.10-11). ⬇	'Jesus crucified' was a stumbling block for many (1 Cor. 1.22-24). ⬇
Therefore, Attis was an actual historical man castrated.	Therefore, Jesus was an actual historical man crucified.

Table 11. Competing Embarrassment: Attis Cult versus Jesus Cult

Clearly if the rule so easily fails, it cannot be assumed to apply. There simply is no relevant difference between Attis cult and Jesus cult sufficient to sustain this kind of objection. Attis was not castrated—in fact there never was any such person. Yet if a non-existent Attis could be preached castrated, so could a non-existent Jesus be preached crucified. In actual fact the entire mode of 'arguing from embarrassment' like this is simply not sound, as I have already thoroughly demonstrated.[13] It just doesn't work here.

Other objections are easily dispatched. For example, it will sometimes be asserted that even though the Gospels and Acts are obviously literary constructs, with deliberate structure and invented details serving the purpose of communicating abstract ideas about the gospel and missionary life, and not aiming at determining or even recording historical facts (all of which was proven in Chapters 9 and 10), there could still be historical facts behind them. The authors may have simply taken real stories and organized them into these elegant literary constructs, adding, deleting or changing what they needed to 'sculpt' them into what they wanted. But this doesn't get us to any valid argument. 'Possibly, therefore probably' is a fallacy.[14] What's possible is irrelevant. What you have to prove is that any story in the Gospels (even if stripped down to its core) is *probably* true, not that it 'possibly' is. And there is simply no valid argument to be made that any are. Some *might* be, sure. But that gets us nowhere. The Gospels, therefore, must be discarded as evidence.

The same fallacy destroys any parallel argument made for the Epistles, such as that all the oddities in them 'might' disguise historical facts about Jesus in any of the veiled quotations or theological references we surveyed (or any others even less clear), and that we 'could' explain the Epistles on an assumption of minimal historicity—*if* we adopt a number of convenient unproven and improbable assumptions about how they came to look very much unlike what we would usually expect if that were the case. Here, again, 'possibly, therefore probably' is a fallacy. No valid argument is to be made here. You have to prove that any of these references *probably* derives from a historical Jesus, not that it possibly does. And here things are worse, since the historicist explanation of the Epistles' content is improbable—certainly significantly less probable than the mythicist explanation, which requires fewer unproven assumptions (in fact, almost none really, beyond the hypothesis itself and what it entails in light of established background knowledge). Yes, 'improbable' does not mean *impossible*. But it still does mean improbable. Only by arguing *a fortiori* was I able to come to anything near a different conclusion, and even then it was not enough.

After that, objections become increasingly more specious and fallacious, and should not even have to be addressed. There is simply no way to recover an argument to historicity from the extrabiblical evidence, for example—as I already explained in Chapter 8.

13. Carrier, *Proving History*, pp. 124-69.
14. Carrier, *Proving History*, pp. 25-29.

5. *What Now?*

From here things can go one of three ways:

1. Minimal mythicism *is* more likely how Christianity began. If that's true, we can prove it. If we can prove it, it will eventually become the broadest consensus of all but Christian apologists (who obviously will reject evidence and reason when in conflict with their faith).
2. Minimal mythicism is *not* more likely how Christianity began. If that's true, we can prove it. If we can prove it, what we will then have proved will become the broadest consensus. We will then have *some* facts about a historical Jesus we can assert as confidently known.
3. It's not possible on present evidence to know whether minimal mythicism is more likely how Christianity began. If that's true, we can prove it. If we can prove it, mythicists and historicists will both have to concede the point. Historicists will have to accept mythicism as a viable theory, and mythicists will have to accept some historical Jesus scenarios may be viable, too. We just won't have the data we need in order to know which it is.

Accordingly, I intend this book not to end but to begin a debate about this, regarding both its methods and its conclusions. Hence, if readers object even to employing Bayes's Theorem in this case (or in any), then I ask them to propose alternative models for structuring the debate. If, instead, readers accept my Bayesian approach, but object to my method of assigning prior probabilities, then I ask them to argue for an alternative method of assigning prior probabilities (e.g. if my choice of reference class is faulty, then I ask you to argue why it is, and to argue for an alternative). On the other hand, if readers accept my method of assigning prior probabilities, but object to my estimates of consequent probability, then I ask them to argue for alternative consequent probabilities—not just assert some, but actually argue for them. Because the mythicist case hinges on the claim that these things cannot reasonably be done. It is time that claim was *properly* put to the test. And finally, of course, if readers object to my categories and subcategories of evidence or believe there are others that should be included or distinguished, then I ask them to argue the case.

I know many devout Christian scholars will balk and claim to find all manner of bogus or irrelevant or insignificant holes or flaws in my arguments, but they would do that anyway. Witness what many Christian scholars come up with just to reject evolution, or to defend the literal miraculous resurrection of Jesus (which they claim they can do even with the terrible and paltry evidence we have). Consequently, I don't care anymore what

Christian apologists think. They are not rational people. I only want to know what rational scholars think. I want to see a helpful critique of this book by objective, qualified experts who could live with the conclusion that Jesus didn't exist, but just don't think the case can be made, or made well enough to credit. And what I want from my critics is not useless hole punching but an alternative proposal: if my method is invalid, then what method is the correct one for resolving questions of historicity? And if you know of none, how can you justify any claim to historicity for *any* person, if you don't even know how such a claim can be justified or falsified at all? Also correct any facts I get wrong, point out what I missed, and if my method then produces a different conclusion when those emendations are included, we will have progress.[15] Even if the conclusion is the same, it will nevertheless have been improved.

But it is the method I want my fellow historians to correct, replace or perfect above all else. We can't simply rely on intuition or gut instinct when deciding what really did happen or who really did exist, since that simply leans on unexamined assumptions and relies on impressions and instincts that are often not reliable guides to the truth. We need to make explicit why we believe what we do rather than something else, and we need this as much in history as in any other field. And by the method I have deployed here, I have confirmed our intuitions in the study of Jesus are wrong. He did not exist. I have made my case. To all objective and qualified scholars, I appeal to you all as a community: the ball is now in your court.

15. On how this process of back-and-forth can eventually produce progress toward a more secure consensus see Carrier, *Proving History*, pp. 88-93, 208-14.

Bibliography (Modern Scholarship)

Abegg, Martin, 'Messianic Hope and 4Q285: A Reassessment', *Journal of Biblical Literature* 113 (1994), pp. 81-91.

Achtemeier, Paul, 'The Origin and Function of the Pre-Marcan Miracle Catenae', *Journal of Biblical Literature* 91 (1972), pp. 198-221.

— 'Toward the Isolation of Pre-Markan Miracle Catenae', *Journal of Biblical Literature* 89 (1970), pp. 265-91.

Ahbel-Rappe, Sara, and Rachana Kamtekar (eds.), *A Companion to Socrates* (Oxford: Blackwell, 2006).

Albertson, Fred, 'An Isiac Model for the Raising of Lazarus in Early Christian Art', *Jahrbuch für Antike und Christentum* 38 (1995), pp. 123-32.

Aldhouse-Green, Miranda, and Stephen Aldhouse-Green, *The Quest for the Shaman: Shape-Shifters, Sorcerers and Spirit-Healers of Ancient Europe* (London: Thames & Hudson, 2005).

Alexander, J.R., 'Graeco-Roman Papyrus Documents from Egypt', *Athena Review* 2 (1999) at www.athenapub.com/egypap1.html.

Alexander, Loveday, 'Fact, Fiction and the Genre of Acts', *New Testament Studies* 44 (1998), pp. 380-99.

Allegro, John Marco, *The Dead Sea Scrolls and the Christian Myth* (Buffalo, NY: Prometheus Books, 1984).

— 'Jesus and Qumran: The Dead Sea Scrolls', in *Jesus in Myth and History* (ed. R. Joseph Hoffmann and Gerald Larue; Buffalo, NY: Prometheus, 1986), pp. 89-96.

Allison, Dale, 'The Historians' Jesus and the Church', in *Seeking the Identity of Jesus: A Pilgrimage* (ed. Beverly Roberts Gaventa and Richard Hays; Grand Rapids, MI: William B. Eerdmans, 2008), pp. 79-95.

— *The New Moses: A Matthean Typology* (Minneapolis, MN: Fortress Press, 1993).

— 'The Pauline Epistles and the Synoptic Gospels: The Pattern of the Parallels', *New Testament Studies* 28 (1982), pp. 1-32.

— 'Peter and Cephas: One and the Same', *Journal of Biblical Literature* 111 (1992), pp. 489-95.

— 'Q's New Exodus and the Historical Jesus', in *The Sayings Source Q and the Historical Jesus* (ed. A. Lindemann; Leuven: University Press, 2001), pp. 395-428.

— 'The Structure of the Sermon on the Mount', *Journal of Biblical Literature* 106 (1987), pp. 423-45.

— *Studies in Matthew: Interpretation Past and Present* (Grand Rapids, MI: Baker Academic, 2005).

— 'Thallus on the Crucifixion', in *The Historical Jesus in Context* (ed. Amy-Jill Levine, Dale Allison, Jr, and John Dominic Crossan; Princeton, NJ: Princeton University Press, 2006), pp. 405-406.

Alvarez, Jaime, *Romanising Oriental Gods: Myth, Salvation and Ethics in the Cults of Cybele, Isis and Mithras* (Leiden: Brill, 2008).

Anderson, Hugh, 'The Jewish Antecedents of the Christology in Hebrews', in *The Messiah: Developments in Earliest Judaism and Christianity* (ed. James Charlesworth; Minneapolis, MN: Fortress Press, 1992), pp. 512-35.

Anderson, R.T., 'Samaritan Literature', in *Dictionary of New Testament Background* (ed. Craig Evans and Stanley Porter; Downers Grove, IL: InterVarsity Press, 2000), pp. 1052-56.

Angus, Samuel, *The Mystery-Religions and Christianity: A Study in the Religious Background of Early Christianity* (London: J. Murray, 1925).

Arbman, Ernst, *Ecstasy, or Religious Trance, in the Experience of the Ecstatics and from the Psychological Point of View* (3 vols.; Stockholm: Bokförlaget, 1963–70).

Arnal, William, *Jesus and the Village Scribes: Galilean Conflicts and the Setting of Q* (Minneapolis, MN: Fortress Press, 2001).

— *The Symbolic Jesus: Historical Scholarship, Judaism and the Construction of Contemporary Identity* (London: Equinox, 2005).

Arnold, Clinton, *Powers of Darkness: Principalities and Powers in Paul's Letters* (Downers Grove, IL: InterVarsity Press, 1992).

Arnold-Biucchi, Carmen, *Alexander's Coins and Alexander's Image* (Cambridge, MA: Harvard University Art Museums, 2006).

Ascough, Richard, 'Historical Approaches', in *Dictionary of Biblical Criticism and Interpretation* (ed. Stanley Porter; New York: Routledge, 2007), pp. 157-59.

Aslan, Reza, *Zealot: The Life and Times of Jesus of Nazareth* (New York: Random House, 2013).

Athanassiadi, Polymnia, and Michael Frede (eds.), *Pagan Monotheism in Late Antiquity* (New York: Oxford University Press, 1999).

Aune, David, 'Christian Prophecy and the Messianic Status of Jesus', in *The Messiah: Developments in Earliest Judaism and Christianity* (ed. James Charlesworth; Fortress Press, 1992), pp. 404-22.

— *The New Testament in its Literary Environment* (Philadelphia, PA: Westminster Press, 1987).

Aus, Roger, *Barabbas and Esther and Other Studies in the Judaic Illumination of Earliest Christianity* (Atlanta, GA: Scholars Press, 1992).

— 'The Wedding Feast at Cana (John 2.1-11), and Ahasuerus' Wedding Feast in Judaic Traditions on Esther 1', in *Water into Wine and the Beheading of John the Baptist: Early Jewish-Christian Interpretation of Esther 1 in John 2:1-11 and Mark 6:17-29* (Atlanta, GA: Scholars Press, 1988), pp. 1-37.

Avalos, Hector, *The End of Biblical Studies* (Amherst, NY: Prometheus Books, 2007).

Avery-Peck, Alan, 'The Galilean Charismatic and Rabbinic Piety: The Holy Man in the Talmudic Literature', in *The Historical Jesus in Context* (ed. Levine, Allison and Crossan), pp. 149-65.

Babinski, Edward, 'The Cosmology of the Bible', in *The Christian Delusion: Why Faith Fails* (ed. John Loftus; Amherst, NY: Prometheus Books, 2010), pp. 109-47.

Bagnall, Roger, *Reading Papyri, Writing Ancient History* (New York: Routledge, 1995).

Bailey, John, *The Traditions Common to the Gospels of Luke and John* (Leiden: E.J. Brill, 1963).

Barker, Margaret, *The Great Angel: A Study of Israel's Second God* (Louisville, KY: Westminster/John Knox Press, 1992).

— *The Great High Priest: The Temple Roots of Christian Liturgy* (New York: T. & T. Clark, 2003).

— *On Earth as It Is in Heaven: Temple Symbolism in the New Testament* (New York: T. & T. Clark, 1995).

— 'The Secret Tradition', *Journal of Higher Criticism* 2 (Spring 1995), pp. 31-67.

— 'The Temple Roots of the Christian Liturgy', in *Christian Origins: Worship, Belief and Society* (ed. Kieran O'Mahony; Sheffield: Sheffield Academic Press, 2003), pp. 29-51.

Barnes, Timothy, 'The Date of Ignatius', *Expository Times* 120 (2008), pp. 119-30.

Barnstone, Willis, *The Other Bible* (San Francisco, CA: HarperCollins, 1984).

Barrett, C.K., *The Gospel according to St. John* (Philadelphia, PA: Westminster Press, 2nd edn, 1978).

Basser, Herbert, 'Gospel and Talmud', in *The Historical Jesus in Context* (ed. Levine, Allison and Crossan), pp. 285-95.

Bauckham, Richard, *Jesus and the Eyewitnesses: The Gospels as Eyewitness Testimony* (Grand Rapids, MI: William B. Eerdmans, 2006).

Bauer, David, *The Structure of Matthew's Gospel: A Study in Literary Design* (Sheffield: Almond Press, 1988).

Baum, Paul Franklin, 'The Mediæval Legend of Judas Iscariot', *Proceedings of the Modern Language Association of America* 31 (1916), pp. 481-632.

Beale, G.K., and D.A. Carson (eds.), *Commentary on the New Testament Use of the Old Testament* (Grand Rapids, MI: Baker Academic, 2007).

Bechard, Dean, 'Review of Richard Bauckham, *Jesus and the Eyewitnesses*', *Biblica* 90 (2009), pp. 126-29.

Beck, Roger, *Beck on Mithraism* (Burlington, VT: Ashgate, 2004).

— *The Religion of the Mithras Cult in the Roman Empire: Mysteries of the Unconquered Sun* (New York: Oxford University Press, 2006).

Beilby, James, and Paul Rhodes Eddy (eds.), *The Historical Jesus: Five Views* (Downers Grove, IL: IVP Academic, 2009).

Bell, Vaughan, 'Ghost Stories: Visits from the Deceased', *Scientific American Online* (December 2, 2008) http://www.scientificamerican.com/article.cfm?id=ghost-stories-visits-from-the-deceased.

Belle, G. van, 'Lukan Style in the Fourth Gospel', in *Luke and his Readers* (ed. R. Bieringer, G. van Belle and J. Verheyden; Dudley, MA: Peeters, 2005), pp. 351-72.

Benedikston, T.D., 'Structure and Fate in Suetonius' *Life of Galba*', *Classical Journal* 92 (1997), pp. 167-73.

Benko, Stephen, 'The Edict of Claudius of A.D. 49 and the Instigator Chrestus', *Theologische Zeitschrift* 25 (1969), pp. 407-408.

Bentall, Richard, Gordon Claridge and Peter Slade, 'The Multi-Dimensional Nature of Schizotypal Traits: A Factor Analytic Study with Normal Subjects', *British Journal of Clinical Psychology* 28 (1989), pp. 363-75.

Bergsma, John Sietze, *The Jubilee from Leviticus to Qumran: A History of Interpretation* (Leiden: Brill, 2007).

Beskow, Per, 'Tertullian on Mithras', in *Studies in Mithraism: Papers Associated with the Mithraic Panel Organized on the Occasion of the XVIth Congress of the International Association for the History of Religions, Rome 1990* (ed. John Hinnells; Rome: L'Erma di Bretschneider, 1994), pp. 51-60.

Betz, Hans Dieter, *Galatians: A Commentary on Paul's Letter to the Churches in Galatia* (Minneapolis, MN: Fortress Press, 1979).
— *The 'Mithras Liturgy': Text, Translation, and Commentary* (Tübingen: Mohr Siebeck, 2003).
— 'Plutarch's Life of Numa: Some Observations on Graeco-Roman "Messianism"', in *Redemption and Resistance: The Messianic Hopes of Jews and Christians in Antiquity* (ed. Markus Bockmuehl and James Carleton Paget; New York: T. & T. Clark, 2007), pp. 44-62.
Binfield, Kevin (ed.), *Writings of the Luddites* (Baltimore, MD: Johns Hopkins University Press, 2004).
Black, Mark, 'The Messianic Use of Zechariah 9–14 in Matthew, Mark and the Pre-Markan Tradition', in *Scripture and Traditions: Essays on Early Judaism and Christianity in Honor of Carl R. Holladay* (ed. Patrick Gray and Gail R. O'Day; Boston: Brill, 2008), pp. 97-114.
— 'The Messianism of the Parables of Enoch: Their Date and Contribution to Christological Origins', in *The Messiah: Developments in Earliest Judaism and Christianity* (ed. James Charlesworth; Minneapolis, MN: Fortress Press, 1992), pp. 145-68.
Blackhirst, R., 'Barnabas and the Gospels: Was There an Early *Gospel of Barnabas*?', *Journal of Higher Criticism* 7 (Spring 2000), pp. 1-22.
Blenkinsopp, Joseph, *et al., The New Interpreter's Bible: Old Testament Survey* (Nashville, TN: Abingdon Press, 2006).
Blomberg, Craig, 'Midrash, Chiasmus, and the Outline of Luke's Central Section', in *Gospel Perspectives* (ed. R.T. France and David Wenham; Sheffield: JSOT Press, 1983), III, pp. 217-61.
Bock, Darrell, 'The Function of Scripture in Mark 15.1-39', in *Biblical interpretation in Early Christian Gospels, Vol. 1, The Gospel of Mark* (ed. Thomas R. Hatina; New York: T. & T. Clark, 2006), pp. 8-17.
— 'Is That All There Is? A Response to Lara Guglielmo's 11Q13, Malchî Sedek, Co-Reference, and Restoration of 2 18', *Henoch* 33 (2011), pp. 73-76.
Bockmuehl, Markus, 'Simon Peter's Names in Jewish Sources', *Journal of Jewish Studies* 55 (Spring 2004), pp. 58-80.
Bockmuehl, Markus, and James Carleton Paget (eds.), *Redemption and Resistance: The Messianic Hopes of Jews and Christians in Antiquity* (New York: T. & T. Clark, 2007).
Boman, Jobjorn, 'Comments on Carrier: Is Thallus Actually Quoted by Eusebius?', *Liber Annuus* 62 (2012), pp. 319-25.
Borg, Marcus, 'The Historical Study of Jesus and Christian Origins', in *Jesus at 2000* (ed. Marcus Borg; Boulder, CO: Westview Press, 1997), pp. 121-48.
— *Jesus: Uncovering the Life, Teachings, and Relevance of a Religious Revolutionary* (San Francisco, CA: HarperSanFrancisco, 2006).
— *Reading the Bible Again for the First Time: Taking the Bible Seriously but Not Literally* (San Francisco, CA: HarperSanFrancisco, 2001).
Bosworth, A.B., *From Arrian to Alexander: Studies in Historical Interpretation* (New York: Oxford University Press, 1988).
Boyarin, Daniel, *The Jewish Gospels: The Story of the Jewish Christ* (New York: The New Press, 2012).
Boyer, Pascal, *Religion Explained: The Evolutionary Origins of Religious Thought* (New York: Basic Books, 2001).

Bower, Bruce, 'Night of the Crusher: The Waking Nightmare of Sleep Paralysis Propels People into a Spirit World', *Science News* 168 (July 9, 2005), pp. 27-29.
— 'Visions for All', *Science News* 181 (April 7, 2012), pp. 22-25.
Bradley, K.R., 'Suetonius, *Nero* 16.2: "*afflicti suppliciis Christiani*"', *Classical Review* 22.1 (March 1972), pp. 9-10.
Brakke, David, *The Gnostics: Myth, Ritual, and Diversity in Early Christianity* (Cambridge, MA: Harvard University Press, 2010).
Brandon, S.G.F., *Jesus and the Zealots* (New York: Scribner, 1967).
— *The Saviour God: Comparative Studies in the Concept of Salvation* (Westport, CT: Greenwood Press, 1963).
Brant, Jo-Ann, Charles Hedrick and Chris Shea (eds.), *Ancient Fiction: The Matrix of Early Christian and Jewish Narrative* (Atlanta, GA: Society of Biblical Literature, 2005).
Brickhouse, Thomas, and Nicholas Smith, *The Trial and Execution of Socrates: Sources and Controversies* (Oxford: Oxford University Press, 2002).
Brisson, Luc, *How Philosophers Saved Myths: Allegorical Interpretation and Classical Mythology* (trans. Catherine Tihanyi; Chicago: University of Chicago Press, 2004).
Broadhead, Edwin, 'Reconfiguring Jesus: The Son of Man in Markan Perspective', in *Biblical Interpretation in Early Christian Gospels. Vol. 1, The Gospel of Mark* (ed. Thomas R. Hatina; New York: T. & T. Clark, 2006), pp. 18-30.
Brodie, Thomas, 'An Alternative Q/Logia Hypothesis: Deuteronomy-Based, Qumranlike, Verifiable', in *The Sayings Source Q and the Historical Jesus* (ed. A. Lindemann; Leuven: University Press, 2001), pp. 729-43.
— *Beyond the Quest for the Historical Jesus: A Memoir of a Discovery* (Sheffield: Sheffield Phoenix, 2012).
— *The Birthing of the New Testament: The Intertextual Development of the New Testament Writings* (Sheffield: Sheffield Phoenix Press, 2004).
— *Proto-Luke: The First Edition of Luke–Acts: A Christ-Centered Synthesis of Septuagintal Historiography Modeled Especially on the Elijah–Elisha Narrative and Matthew's Logia: A Foundational Arrangement of Gospel Sayings Deuteronomy-Based, Qumranlike (an Alternative to Q)* (Limerick, Ireland: Dominican Biblical Centre, 2002).
— *Proto-Luke: The Oldest Gospel Account: A Christ-Centered Synthesis of Old Testament History Modeled Especially on the Elijah–Elisha Narrative: Introduction, Text, and Old Testament Model* (Limerick, Ireland: Dominican Biblical Institute, 2006).
— 'Re-Opening the Quest for Proto-Luke: The Systematic Use of Judges 6–12 in Luke 16:1–18:8', *Journal of Higher Criticism* 2 (Spring 1995), pp. 68-101.
Brodie, Thomas, Dennis MacDonald and Stanley Porter, *The Intertextuality of the Epistles: Explorations of Theory and Practice* (Sheffield: Sheffield Phoenix Press, 2006).
Brookins, Tim, 'Dispute with Stoicism in the Parable of the Rich Man and Lazarus', *Journal of Greco-Roman Christianity and Judaism* 8 (2011–2012), pp. 34-50.
Brown, Peter, *Cult of the Saints: Its Rise and Function in Latin Christianity* (Chicago: University of Chicago Press, 1981).
Brown, Raymond, *The Birth of the Messiah: A Commentary on the Infancy Narratives in the Gospels of Matthew and Luke* (Garden City, NY: Doubleday, 1993).

— *The Death of the Messiah from Gethsemane to the Grave: A Commentary on the Passion Narratives in the Four Gospels* (2 vols.; New York: Doubleday, 1994).
— *The Gospel according to John* (Garden City, NY: Doubleday, 1966–1970).
— 'The Gospel of Thomas and St John's Gospel', *New Testament Studies* 9 (1963), pp. 155-77.
— *An Introduction to the Gospel of John* (New York: Doubleday, rev. edn, 2003).
— 'Jesus and Elijah', *Perspective* 12 (1971), pp. 85-104.
Bruce, F.F., 'The Book of Daniel and the Qumran Community', in *Neotestamentica et Semitica: Studies in Honour of Matthew Black* (ed. E. Earle Ellis and Max Wilcox; Edinburgh: T. & T. Clark, 1969), pp. 221-35.
Bruce, F.F., and E. Güting, *Ausserbiblische Zeugnisse über Jesus und das frühe Christentum: einschliesslich des apokryphen Judasevangeliums* (Basel: Brunnen Verlag, 2007).
Brunvand, Jan Harold, *The Vanishing Hitchhiker: American Urban Legends and their Meanings* (New York: Norton, 1981).
Buchanan, George Wesley, *Jewish Documents of Deliverance from the Fall of Jerusalem to the Death of Nahmanides* (Dillsboro, NC: Western North Carolina Press, 1978).
Buckman, Robert, *Can We Be Good without God? Biology, Behavior, and the Need to Believe* (Amherst, NY: Prometheus Books, 2002).
Budge, E.A. Wallis, *Miscellaneous Coptic texts in the Dialect of Upper Egypt* (New York: AMS Press, 1977 [orig. 1915]).
Budin, Stephanie Lynn, *The Myth of Sacred Prostitution in Antiquity* (New York: Cambridge University Press, 2008).
Burkitt, F. Crawford, *Jewish and Christian Apocalypses* (London: H. Milford, 1914).
Burkert, Walter, *Structure and History in Greek Mythology and Ritual* (Berkeley, CA: University of California Press, 1979).
Burridge, Kenelm, *Mambu: A Study of Melanesian Cargo Movements and their Ideological Background* (New York: Harper & Row, 1960).
Burridge, Richard, *What Are the Gospels? A Comparison with Graeco-Roman Biography* (New York: Cambridge University Press, 1992).
Byrne, Ryan, and Bernadette McNary-Zak (eds.), *Resurrecting the Brother of Jesus: The James Ossuary Controversy and the Quest for Religious Relics* (Chapel Hill, NC: University of North Carolina Press, 2009).
Cadbury, Henry, '"We" and "I" Passages in Luke–Acts', *New Testament Studies* 3 (1956–1957), pp. 128-32.
Callahan, Tim, *Bible Prophecy: Failure or Fulfillment?* (Altadena, CA: Millennium Press, 1997).
Cameron, Alan, *Greek Mythography in the Roman World* (New York: Oxford University Press, 2004).
Cameron, Averil (ed.), *History as Text: The Writing of Ancient History* (Chapel Hill, NC: University of North Carolina Press, 1990).
Camery-Hoggatt, Jerry, *Irony in Mark's Gospel: Text and Subtext* (New York: Cambridge University Press, 1992).
'Capernaum', in *The Archaeological Encyclopedia of the Holy Land* (ed. Avraham Negev and Shimon Gibson; New York: Continuum, rev. and updated edn, 2001), pp. 111-14.
Carmichael, Calum, 'The Passover Haggadah', in *The Historical Jesus in Context* (ed. Levine, Allison and Crossan), pp. 343-56.

Carr, Wesley, *Angels and Principalities: The Background, Meaning, and Development of the Pauline Phrase* hai archai kai hai exousiai (New York: Cambridge University Press, 1981).

Carrier, Richard, 'B.C.A.D.C.E.B.C.E.', *Richard Carrier Blogs* (January 16, 2012) at http://freethoughtblogs.com/carrier/archives/166.

— 'The Burial of Jesus in Light of Jewish Law', in *The Empty Tomb: Jesus beyond the Grave* (ed. Robert M. Price and Jeffery Lowder; Amherst, NY: Prometheus Books, 2005), pp. 369-92.

— 'Christianity's Success Was Not Incredible', in *The End of Christianity* (ed. John Loftus; Amherst, NY: Prometheus Books, 2011), pp. 53-74, 372-75.

— 'Christianity Was Not Responsible for Modern Science', in *The Christian Delusion: Why Faith Fails* (ed. John Loftus; Amherst, NY: Prometheus Books, 2010), pp. 396-419.

— 'Critical Review of Maurice Casey's Defense of the Historicity of Jesus', *Richard Carrier Blogs* (March 3, 2014) at http://freethoughtblogs.com/carrier/archives/4282.

— 'The Date of the Nativity in Luke', *The Secular Web* (6th edn, 2011) at http://www.infidels.org/library/modern/richard_carrier/quirinius.html.

— 'Did Jesus Exist? Earl Doherty and the Argument to Ahistoricity', *The Secular Web* (2002) at www.infidels.org/library/modern/richard_carrier/jesuspuzzle.html.

— 'Ehrman on Historicity Recap', *Richard Carrier Blogs* (July 24, 2012) at freethoughtblogs.com/carrier/archives/1794.

— *Empty Tomb FAQ* (n.d.) http://www.richardcarrier.info/SpiritualFAQ.html.

— 'Flash! Fox News Reports That Aliens May Have Built the Pyramids of Egypt!', *Skeptical Inquirer* 23 (September–October 1999), pp. 46-50.

— 'The Goodacre Debate', *Richard Carrier Blogs* (December 20, 2012) at http://freethoughtblogs.com/carrier/archives/2839.

— 'Herod the Procurator: Was Herod the Great a Roman Governor of Syria?' (2011) http://www.richardcarrier.info/HerodSyrianGovernor.pdf.

— 'Historicity News: Notable Books', *Richard Carrier Blogs* (October 17, 2012) at http://freethoughtblogs.com/carrier/archives/2669.

— *Hitler Homer Bible Christ: The Historical Papers of Richard Carrier 1995–2013* (Richmond, CA: Philosophy Press, 2014).

— "How Not to Argue for Historicity," in *Bart Ehrman and the Quest of the Historical Jesus of Nazareth: An Evaluation of Ehrman's* Did Jesus Exist? (ed. Frank Zindler and Robert M. Price; Cranford, NJ: American Atheist Press, 2013), pp. 15-62.

— 'Ignatian Vexation', *Richard Carrier Blogs* (October 1, 2008) at http://richardcarrier.blogspot.com/2008/09/ignatian-vexation.html.

— 'Luke vs. Matthew on the Year of Christ's Birth', in Carrier, *Hitler Homer Bible Christ,* pp. 213-30.

— 'Mark 16:9-20 as Forgery or Fabrication', in Carrier, *Hitler Homer Bible Christ,* pp. 231-312.

— 'More on Vardaman's Microletters', *Skeptical Inquirer* 26 (July–August 2002), pp. 60-61.

— 'The Nazareth Inscription', in Carrier, *Hitler Homer Bible Christ,* pp. 315-26.

— *Not the Impossible Faith: Why Christianity Didn't Need a Miracle to Succeed* (Raleigh, NC: Lulu.com, 2009).

— 'On Musonius Rufus: A Brief Essay', *The Secular Web* (1999) at http://www.infidels.org/library/modern/richard_carrier/musonius.html.

— 'On the Dual Office of Procurator and Prefect' (2012) http://www.richardcarrier.info/TheProvincialProcurator.pdf.

— 'Origen, Eusebius, and the Accidental Interpolation in Josephus, *Jewish Antiquities* 20.200', *Journal of Early Christian Studies* 20.4 (Winter 2012), pp. 489-54.

— 'Pauline Interpolations', in Carrier, *Hitler Homer Bible Christ*, pp. 203-11.

— 'The Plausibility of Theft', in *The Empty Tomb: Jesus beyond the Grave* (ed. Robert M. Price and Jeffery Lowder; Amherst, NY: Prometheus Books, 2005).

— 'The Prospect of a Christian Interpolation in Tacitus, *Annals* 15.44', *Vigiliae christianae* 68 (2014), pp. 1-20.

— *Proving History: Bayes's Theorem and the Quest for the Historical Jesus* (Amherst, NY: Prometheus Books, 2012).

— 'Pseudohistory in Jerry Vardaman's Magic Coins: The Nonsense of Micrographic Letters', *Skeptical Inquirer* 26 (March–April 2002), pp. 39-41, 61.

— *Sense and Goodness without God: A Defense of Metaphysical Naturalism* (Bloomington, IN: AuthorHouse, 2005).

— 'The Spiritual Body of Christ and the Legend of the Empty Tomb', in *The Empty Tomb: Jesus beyond the Grave* (ed. Robert M. Price and Jeffery Lowder; Amherst, NY: Prometheus Books, 2005), pp. 105-232.

— 'Stephen Davis Gets It Wrong' (2006) at http://www.richardcarrier.info/Carrier--ReplyToDavis.html.

— 'Thallus and the Darkness at Christ's Death', *Journal of Greco-Roman Christianity and Judaism* 8 (2011–2012), pp. 185-91.

— 'Why the Resurrection Is Unbelievable', in *The Christian Delusion: Why Faith Fails* (ed. John Loftus; Amherst, NY: Prometheus Books, 2010), pp. 291-315.

Why I Am Not a Christian: Four Conclusive Reasons to Reject the Faith (Richmond, CA: Philosophy Press, 2011).

Carrier, Richard, and J.P. Holding, 'The Text of the New Testament: Do We Have What They Had?', a debate at the Amador Christian Center in Plymouth, California, on April 9, 2011 [video: http://freethoughtblogs.com/carrier/archives/389; slides: http://www.richardcarrier.info/NTReliabilitySlideshow.pdf].

Carson, D.A., 'Pseudonymity and Pseudepigraphy', in *Dictionary of New Testament Background* (ed. Craig Evans and Stanley Porter; Downers Grove, IL: InterVarsity Press, 2000), pp. 857-64.

Case, Shirley Jackson, *The Historicity of Jesus: A Criticism of the Contention That Jesus Never Lived; A Statement of the Evidence for his Existence; An Estimate of his Relation to Christianity* (Chicago: University of Chicago Press, 2d edn, 1928).

Casey, Maurice, *Is John's Gospel True?* (London: Routledge, 1996).

— *Jesus: Evidence and Argument or Mythicist Myths?* (Edinburgh: T. & T. Clark, 2014).

— 'Son of Man', in *The Historical Jesus in Recent Research* (ed. James Dunn and Scot McKnight; Winona Lake, IN: Eisenbrauns, 2005), pp. 315-24.

Castillo, Richard, 'Trance, Functional Psychosis, and Culture', *Psychiatry* 66 (Spring 2003), pp. 9-21.

Chancey, Mark, *The Myth of a Gentile Galilee* (Cambridge: Cambridge University Press, 2002).

Charlesworth, James, *The Beloved Disciple: Whose Witness Validates the Gospel of John?* (Valley Forge, PA: Trinity Press International, 1995).

— (ed.), *The Bible and the Dead Sea Scrolls*. Vol. 3, *The Scrolls and Christian Origins* (Waco, TX: Baylor University Press, 2006).

— (ed.), *Jesus and the Dead Sea Scrolls* (New York: Doubleday, 1992).

— (ed.), *Jesus' Jewishness: Exploring the Place of Jesus within Early Judaism* (New York: Crossroad, 1991).

— (ed.), *The Messiah: Developments in Earliest Judaism and Christianity* (Minneapolis, MN: Fortress Press, 1992).

— (ed.), *The New Testament Apocrypha and Pseudepigrapha: A Guide to Publications with Excursuses on Apocalypses* (Chicago: American Theological Library Association, 1987).

— (ed.), *The Old Testament Pseudepigrapha* (2 vols.; Garden City, NY: Doubleday, 1983–1985).

Charlesworth, James, *et al.* (eds.), *Qumran-Messianism: Studies on the Messianic Expectations in the Dead Sea Scrolls* (Tübingen: Mohr Siebeck, 1998).

Charlesworth, James, and Petr Pokorný (eds.), *Jesus Research: An International Perspective* (Grand Rapids, MI: William B. Eerdmans, 2009).

Charlesworth, M.P., *Five Men: Character Studies from the Roman Empire* (Cambridge, MA: Harvard University Press, 1936).

Chazon, Esther, Michael Stone and Avital Pinnick (eds.), *Pseudepigraphic Perspectives: The Apocrypha and Pseudepigrapha in Light of the Dead Sea Scrolls* (Leiden: Brill, 1999).

Chesnut, Glenn, 'The Ruler and the Logos in Neopythagorean, Middle Platonic, and Late Stoic Political Philosophy', *Aufstieg und Niedergang der römischen Welt* II.16.2 (New York: W. de Gruyter, 1978), pp. 1310-32.

Chesnutt, Randall, '*Joseph and Aseneth*: Food as an Identity Marker', in *Historical Jesus in Context* (ed. Levine, Allison and Crossan), pp. 357-65.

Chester, Andrew, 'High Christology—Whence, When and Why?', *Early Christianity* 2 (2011), pp. 22-50.

Chilton, Bruce, 'Commenting on the Old Testament (with Particular Reference to the Pesharim, Philo and the Mekilta', in *It Is Written—Scripture Citing Scripture: Essays in Honour of Barnabas Lindars, SSF* (ed. Barnabas Lindars, D.A. Carson and H.G.M. Williamson; New York: Cambridge University Press, 1988), pp. 122-40.

— *The Glory of Israel: The Theology and Provenience of the Isaiah Targum* (Sheffield: JSOT Press, 1982).

— 'Historical Jesus', in *Dictionary of Biblical Criticism and Interpretation* (ed. Stanley Porter; New York: Routledge, 2007), pp. 159-62.

— *Rabbi Jesus* (New York: Doubleday, 2000)

— 'Targum, Jesus, and the Gospels', in *The Historical Jesus in Context* (ed. Levine, Allison and Crossan), pp. 238-55.

Chitwood, Ava, *Death by Philosophy: The Biographical Tradition in the Life and Death of the Archaic Philosophers Empedocles, Heraclitus, and Democritus* (Ann Arbor, MI: University of Michigan Press, 2004).

Cialdini, Robert, *Influence: The Psychology of Persuasion* (New York: William Morrow, 1993).

Claridge, Gordon, 'Schizotypy and Schizophrenia', in *Schizophrenia: The Major Issues* (ed. Paul Bebbington and Peter McGuffin; London: Heinemann Professional, 1988), pp. 187-200.

— (ed.), *Schizotypy: Implications for Illness and Health* (New York: Oxford University Press, 1997).

Claridge, Gordon, and Charles McCreery, 'A Study of Hallucination in Normal Subjects', *Personality and Individual Differences* 2 (November 1996), pp. 739-47.

Clauss, Manfred, *The Roman Cult of Mithras: The God and his Mysteries* (New York: Routledge, 2000).

Cohen, Shaye, *The Beginnings of Jewishness: Boundaries, Varieties, Uncertainties* (Berkeley, CA: University of California Press, 1999).

Cole, Susan Guettel, *Theoi Megaloi: The Cult of the Great Gods at Samothrace* (Leiden: Brill, 1984).

Collins, Adela Yarbro, *Crisis and Catharsis: The Power of the Apocalypse* (Philadelphia, PA: Westminster Press, 1984).

— 'The Empty Tomb in the Gospel according to Mark', in *Hermes and Athena: Biblical Exegesis and Philosophical Theology* (ed. Eleonore Stump and Thomas Flint; Notre Dame, IN: University of Notre Dame Press, 1993), pp. 107-40.

Collins, Adela Yarbro, and John Collins (eds.), *King and Messiah as Son of God: Divine, Human, and Angelic Messianic Figures in Biblical and Related Literature* (Grand Rapids, MI: Eerdmans, 2008).

Collins, John, *Daniel: A Commentary* (Minneapolis, MN: Fortress Press, 1993).

— 'The Expectation of the End in the Dead Sea Scrolls', in *Eschatology, Messianism, and the Dead Sea Scrolls* (ed. Craig Evans and Peter Flint; Grand Rapids, MI: William B. Eerdmans, 1997), pp. 74-90.

Collins, John, and Craig Evans (eds.), *Christian Beginnings and the Dead Sea Scrolls* (Grand Rapids, MI: Baker Academic, 2006).

Conzelmann, Hans, *1 Corinthians: A Commentary on the First Epistle to the Corinthians* (Philadelphia, PA: Fortress Press, 1975).

Cornwell, John, *The Hiding Places of God: A Personal Journey into the World of Religious Visions, Holy Objects, and Miracles* (New York: Warner Books, 1991).

Cosmopoulos, Michael (ed.), *Greek Mysteries: The Archaeology and Ritual of Ancient Greek Secret Cults* (New York: Routledge, 2003).

Costa, C.D.N., *Greek Fictional Letters* (New York: Oxford University Press, 2001).

Cottam, Thomas, *The Fourth Gospel Rearranged* (London: Epworth Press, 1952).

Cotton, Hannah, Walter Cockle and Fergus Millar, 'The Papyrology of the Roman Near East: A Survey', *Journal of Roman Studies* 95 (1995), pp. 214-35.

Court, John (ed.), *New Testament Writers and the Old Testament: An Introduction* (London: SPCK, 2002).

Courtney, Gary, *Et Tu, Judas? Then Fall Jesus!* (Lincoln, NE: iUniverse, 2nd edn, 2004).

Cribbs, F.L., 'St. Luke and the Johannine Tradition', *Journal of Biblical Literature* 90 (1971), pp. 422-50.

— 'A Study of the Contacts That Exist between St. Luke and St. John', in *Society of Biblical Literature 1973 Seminar Papers* (ed. George MacRae; Cambridge, MI: Society of Biblical Literature, 1973), II, pp. 1-93.

Cribiore, Raffaella, *Gymnastics of the Mind: Greek Education in Hellenistic and Roman Egypt* (Princeton, NJ: Princeton University Press, 2001).

Cross, F.L., and E.A. Livingstone (eds.), *Oxford Dictionary of the Christian Church* (Oxford: Oxford University Press, 3rd edn, 1997).

Crossan, John Dominic, 'Empty Tomb and Absent Lord', in *The Passion in Mark: Studies on Mark 14–16* (ed. Werner Kelber; Philadelphia, PA: Fortress Press, 1976), pp. 135-52.

— *The Power of Parable: How Fiction by Jesus became Fiction about Jesus* (New York: HarperOne, 2012).

Crossley, James, 'Against the Historical Plausibility of the Empty Tomb Story and the Bodily Resurrection of Jesus', *Journal for the Study of the Historical Jesus* 3 (June 2005), pp. 171-86.

— 'Can John's Gospel Really Be Used to Reconstruct a Life of Jesus? An Assessment of Recent Trends and a Defence of a Traditional View', in *"Is This Not the Carpenter?" The Question of the Historicity of the Figure of Jesus* (ed. Thomas Thompson and Thomas Verenna; Sheffield: Equinox, 2012), pp. 163-84.

— *The Date of Mark's Gospel: Insight from the Law in Earliest Christianity* (New York: T. & T. Clark International, 2004).

— *Why Christianity Happened: A Sociohistorical Account of Christian Origins (26–50 CE)* (Louisville, KY: Westminster John Knox Press, 2006).

Croy, N. Clayton, *The Mutilation of Mark's Gospel* (Nashville, TN: Abingdon Press, 2003).

Dando-Collins, Stephen, *The Great Fire of Rome: The Fall of the Emperor Nero and his City* (Cambridge: Da Capo Press, 2010).

Danove, Paul, *The End of Mark's Story: A Methodological Study* (New York: Brill, 1993).

D'Aquili, Eugene, and Andrew Newberg, *The Mystical Mind: Probing the Biology of Religious Experience* (Minneapolis, MN: Fortress Press, 1999).

— *Why God Won't Go Away: Brain Science and the Biology of Belief* (New York: Ballantine, 2001).

Davies, W.D., 'The Jewish Sources of Matthew's Messianism', in *The Messiah: Developments in Earliest Judaism and Christianity* (ed. James Charlesworth; Minneapolis, MN: Fortress Press, 1992), pp. 494-511.

Davies, W.D., and Dale Allison, *A Critical and Exegetical Commentary on the Gospel according to Saint Matthew*. Vol. I (Edinburgh: T. & T. Clark, 1988).

Day, S., and E. Peters, 'The Incidence of Schizotypy in New Religious Movements', *Personality and Individual Differences* 27 (July 1999), pp. 55-67.

Dennis, Rabbi G.W., *The Encyclopedia of Jewish Myth, Magic, and Mysticism* (Woodbury, MN: Llewellyn, 2007).

Depuydt, Leo, 'The Time of Death of Alexander the Great: 11 June 323 BC, ca. 4:00-5:00 PM', *Die Welt des Orients* 28 (1997), pp. 117-35.

Desmond, William, *Cynics* (Berkeley, CA: University of California Press, 2008).

— *The Greek Praise of Poverty: Origins of Ancient Cynicism* (Notre Dame, IN: University of Notre Dame Press, 2006).

Derrett, J. Duncan M., 'Financial Aspects of the Resurrection', in *The Empty Tomb: Jesus beyond the Grave* (ed. Robert M. Price and Jeffery Lowder; Amherst, NY: Prometheus Books, 2005), pp. 393-409.

Dever, William, *What Did the Biblical Writers Know, and When Did They Know It? What Archaeology Can Tell Us about the Reality of Ancient Israel* (Grand Rapids, MI: William B. Eerdmans, 2001).

Dix, G.H., 'The Heavenly Wisdom and the Divine Logos in Jewish Apocalyptic: A Study of the Vision of the Woman and the Man-Child in Revelation XII 1-5, 13-17', *Journal of Theological Studies* 26 (1925), pp. 1-12.

Dodds, E.R., *The Greeks and the Irrational* (Berkeley, CA: University of California Press, 1951).

Dodd, C.H., *Historical Tradition in the Fourth Gospel* (Cambridge: Cambridge University Press, 1963).

Doherty, Earl, *Jesus: Neither God nor Man (The Case for a Mythical Jesus)* (Ottawa: Age of Reason, 2009).

— *The Jesus Puzzle: Did Christianity Begin with a Mythical Christ?* (Ottawa: Canadian Humanist Press, 2000).

Donalson, Malcolm Drew, *The Cult of Isis in the Roman Empire: Isis Invicta* (Lewiston, NY: E. Mellen Press, 2003).

Doran, Robert, 'Narratives of Noble Death', in *The Historical Jesus in Context* (ed. Levine, Allison and Crossan), pp. 385-99.

Doty, William, *Mythography: The Study of Myths and Rituals* (Tuscaloosa, AL: University of Alabama Press, 2nd edn, 2000).

Douglas, Mary, *Thinking in Circles: An Essay on Ring Composition* (New Haven, CT: Yale University Press, 2007).

Downing, Francis Gerald, *Cynics and Christian Origins* (Edinburgh: T. & T. Clark, 1992).

— *Cynics, Paul and the Pauline Churches* (London: Routledge, 1998).

— 'Markan Intercalation in Cultural Context', in *Doing Things with Words in the First Christian Century* (Sheffield: Sheffield Academic Press, 2000), pp. 118-32.

— 'A Rival to Romulus', in *Doing Things with Words in the First Christian Century* (Sheffield: Sheffield Academic Press, 2000), pp. 133-51.

Drews, Robert, 'The Lacuna in Tacitus' *Annales* Book Five in the Light of Christian Traditions', *American Journal of Ancient History* 9 (1984), pp. 112-22.

Droge, A.J., 'Jesus and Ned Lud[d]: What's in a Name?', *CAESAR: A Journal for the Critical Study of Religion and Human Values* 3 (2009), pp. 23-25.

— '"The Lying Pen of the Scribes": Of Holy Books and Pious Frauds', *Method and Theory in the Study of Religion* 15 (2003), pp. 117-47.

Drury, John, *Tradition and Design in Luke's Gospel: A Study in Early Christian Historiography* (London: Darton, Longman & Todd, 1976).

Dunn, James, 'Jesus Tradition in Paul', in *Studying the Historical Jesus: Evaluation of the State of Current Research* (ed. Bruce Chilton and Craig Evans; Leiden: Brill, 1994), pp. 155-78.

Dunn, James, *et al.*, Responses to Richard Bauckham's *Jesus and the Eyewitnesses*, *Journal for the Study of the Historical Jesus* 6 (2008), pp. 85-253.

Duran, Nicole Wilkinson, *The Power of Disorder: Ritual Elements in Mark's Passion Narrative* (London: T. & T. Clark, 2008).

Eddy, Paul, and Gregory Boyd, *The Jesus Legend: A Case for the Historical Reliability of the Synoptic Jesus Tradition* (Grand Rapids, MI: Baker Academic, 2007).

Edmonds III, Radcliffe, *Myths of the Underworld Journey: Plato, Aristophanes, and the 'Orphic' Gold Tablets* (Cambridge: Cambridge University Press, 2004).

Edwards, J.R., 'Markan Sandwiches: The Significance of Interpolations in Markan Narratives', *Novum Testamentum* 31 (1989), pp. 193-216.

Ehrhardt, Arnold, 'The Disciples of Emmaus', *New Testament Studies* 10 (January 1964), pp. 182-201.

Ehrland, Kurt, 'Papyrus Egerton 2: "Missing Link" zwischen synoptischer und johanneischer Tradition', *New Testament Studies* 42 (January 1996), pp. 12-34.

Ehrman, Bart, 'Cephas and Peter', *Journal of Biblical Literature* 109 (1990), pp. 463-74.

— *Did Jesus Exist? The Historical Argument for Jesus of Nazareth* (San Francisco, CA: HarperOne, 2012).

— *Forged: Writing in the Name of God—Why the Bible's Authors Are Not Who We Think They Are* (New York: HarperOne, 2011).

— *Forgery and Counterforgery: The Use of Literary Deceit in Early Christian Polemics* (New York: Oxford University Press, 2014).

— *Jesus: Apocalyptic Prophet of the New Millennium* (New York: Oxford University Press, 1999).

— *Jesus, Interrupted: Revealing the Hidden Contradictions in the Bible (and Why We Don't Know about Them)* (New York: HarperOne, 2009).

— *Lost Christianities: The Battles for Scripture and the Faiths We Never Knew* (New York: Oxford University Press, 2005).

— *Lost Scriptures: Books That Did Not Make It into the New Testament* (New York: Oxford University Press, 2003).

— *Misquoting Jesus: The Story Behind Who Changed the Bible and Why* (San Francisco, CA: HarperSanFrancisco, 2005).

— *The Orthodox Corruption of Scripture: The Effect of Early Christological Controversies on the Text of the New Testament* (New York: Oxford University Press, 1993).

— *Peter, Paul, and Mary Magdalene: The Followers of Jesus in History and Legend* (New York: Oxford University Press, 2006).

Ehrman, Bart, Daniel Wallace and Robert Stewart, *The Reliability of the New Testament* (Minneapolis, MN: Fortress Press, 2011).

Eliade, Mircea, *Zalmoxis the Vanishing God: Comparative Studies in the Religions and Folklore of Dacia and Eastern Europe* (Chicago: University of Chicago Press, 1972).

Elias, Julius, *Plato's Defense of Poetry* (Albany, NY: State University of New York Press, 1984).

Elledge, C.D., *The Bible and the Dead Sea Scrolls* (Atlanta, GA: Society of Biblical Literature, 2005).

Ellegård, Alvar, *Jesus: One Hundred Years before Christ* (Woodstock, NY: Overlook, 1999)

Ellens, J. Harold, 'The Dead Sea Scrolls and the Son of Man: An Assessment of 11Q13', *Henoch* 33 (2011), pp. 77-87.

Ellspermann, Gerard, *The Attitude of the Early Christian Latin Writers toward Pagan Literature and Learning* (Washington, DC: Catholic University of America Press, 1949).

Engberg-Pedersen, Troels, *Cosmology and Self in the Apostle Paul: The Material Spirit* (Oxford: Oxford University Press, 2010).

— 'Paul's Body: A Response to Barclay and Levison', *Journal for the Study of the New Testament* 33 (June 2011), pp. 433-43 [with pp. 406-32].

Eppstein, Victor, 'The Historicity of the Gospel Account of the Cleansing of the Temple', *Zeitschrift für neutestamentliche Wissenschaft und die Kunde der älteren Kirche* 55 (1964), pp. 42-58.

Evans, Craig, '"The Book of the Genesis of Jesus Christ": The Purpose of Matthew in Light of the Incipit', in *Biblical Interpretation in Early Christian Gospels, Vol. 2: Gospel of Matthew* (ed. Thomas Hatina; London: T. & T. Clark, 2008), pp. 61-72.
— (ed.), *The Interpretation of Scripture in Early Judaism and Christianity: Studies in Language and Tradition* (Sheffield: Sheffield Academic Press, 2000).
— 'Jesus and the Dead Sea Scrolls from Qumran Cave 4', in *Eschatology, Messianism, and the Dead Sea Scrolls* (ed. Craig Evans and Peter Flint; Grand Rapids, MI: William B. Eerdmans, 1997), pp. 91-100.
— 'Jesus in Non-Christian Sources', in *Studying the Historical Jesus: Evaluation of the State of Current Research* (ed. Bruce Chilton and Craig Evans; Leiden: Brill, 1994), pp. 443-78.
— 'Josephus on John the Baptist and Other Jewish Prophets of Deliverance', in *The Historical Jesus in Context* (ed. Levine, Allison and Crossan), pp. 55-63.
— 'Luke's Use of the Elijah/Elisha Narratives and the Ethic of Election', *Journal of Biblical Literature* 106 (1987), pp. 75-83.
— 'Messianism', in *Dictionary of New Testament Background* (ed. Craig Evans and Stanley Porter; Downers Grove, IL: InterVarsity Press, 2000), pp. 698-707.
— (ed.), *From Prophecy to Testament: The Function of the Old Testament in the New* (Peabody, MA: Hendrickson Publishers, 2004).
— 'The Recently Published Dead Sea Scrolls and the Historical Jesus', in *Studying the Historical Jesus: Evaluation of the State of Current Research* (ed. Bruce Chilton and Craig Evans; Leiden: Brill, 1994), pp. 547-65.
— 'Zechariah in the Markan Passion Narrative', in *Biblical Interpretation in Early Christian Gospels. Vol. 1, The Gospel of Mark* (ed. Thomas R. Hatina; New York: T. & T. Clark, 2006), pp. 64-80.
Evans, Craig, and Peter Flint (eds.), *Eschatology, Messianism, and the Dead Sea Scrolls* (Grand Rapids, MI: William B. Eerdmans, 1997).
Evans, Craig, and James Sanders (eds.), *Early Christian Interpretation of the Scriptures of Israel: Investigations and Proposals* (Sheffield: Sheffield Academic Press, 1997).
Evans, C.F., 'The Central Section of St. Luke's Gospel', in *Studies in the Gospels: Essays in Memory of R. H. Lightfoot* (ed. D.E. Nineham; Oxford: Basil Blackwell, 1955), pp. 37-53.
Fairweather, Janet, 'Fiction in the Biographies of Ancient Writers', *Ancient Society* 5 (1974), pp. 231-75.
— 'Traditional Narrative, Inference, and Truth in the Lives of the Greek Poets', *Papers of the Liverpool Latin Seminar* 4 (1983), pp. 315-69.
Fales, Evan, 'Can Science Explain Mysticism?', *Religious Studies* 35 (1999), pp. 213-27.
— 'The Road to Damascus', *Faith and Philosophy* 22 (2005), pp. 442-59.
— 'Scientific Explanations of Mystical Experiences, Part I: The Case of St. Teresa', *Religious Studies* 32 (1996), pp. 143-63.
— 'Scientific Explanations of Mystical Experiences, Part II: The Challenge to Theism', *Religious Studies* 32 (1996), pp. 297-313.
— 'Taming the Tehom: The Sign of Jonah in Matthew', in *The Empty Tomb: Jesus Beyond the Grave* (ed. Robert M. Price and Jeffery Lowder; Amherst, NY: Prometheus Books, 2005), pp. 307-48.
Falk, Harvey, *Jesus the Pharisee* (New York: Paulist Press, 1985).

Falkner, Thomas, *The Poetics of Old Age in Greek Epic, Lyric, and Tragedy* (Norman, OK: University of Oklahoma Press, 1995).

Fantuzzi, Marco, and Richard Hunter, *Tradition and Innovation in Hellenistic Poetry* (New York: Cambridge University Press, 2004).

Farrer, A.M., 'On Dispensing with Q', in *Studies in the Gospels: Essays in Memory of R.H. Lightfoot* (ed. D.E. Nineham; Oxford: Basil Blackwell, 1955), pp. 55-88.

Feder, Yitzhaq, *Blood Expiation in Hittite and Biblical Ritual: Origins, Context, and Meaning* (Atlanta, GA: Society of Biblical Literature, 2011).

Fee, Gordon, *The First Epistle to the Corinthians* (Grand Rapids, MI: William B. Eerdmans, 1987).

Feeley-Harnik, Gillian, *The Lord's Table: Eucharist and Passover in Early Christianity* (Philadelphia, PA: University of Pennsylvania Press, 1981).

Feldman, Louis, 'On the Authenticity of the Testimonium Flavianum Attributed to Josephus', in *New Perspectives on Jewish Christian Relations* (ed. Elisheva Carlebach and Jacob Schechter; Leiden: Brill, 2012), pp. 14-30.

— *Judaism and Hellenism Reconsidered* (Leiden: Brill, 2006).

Ferguson, Matthew, 'Ten Reasons to Reject the Apologetic 10/42 Source Slogan', *AdversusApologetica* (October 14, 2012) http://adversusapologetica.wordpress.com/2012/10/14/ten-reasons-to-reject-the-apologetic-1042-source-slogan.

— *Thematic Rings and Structure in Suetonius' De Vita Caesarum* (MA thesis, Department of Classics, University of Arizona, 2012), available at http://www.richardcarrier.info/FergusonSuetonius.pdf.

Festinger, Leon, Henry Riecken and Stanley Schachter, *When Prophecy Fails: A Social and Psychological Study of a Modern Group That Predicted the Destruction of the World* (Minneapolis, MN: University of Minnesota Press, 1956).

Figge, Horst, 'Spirit Possession and Healing Cult among the Brasilian Umbanda', *Psychotherapy and Psychosomatics* 25 (1975), pp. 246-50.

Filson, Floyd, 'Who Was the Beloved Disciple?', *Journal of Biblical Literature* 68 (June 1949), pp. 83-88.

Fine, Steven, *Art and Judaism in the Greco-Roman World: Toward a New Jewish Archaeology* (Cambridge: Cambridge University Press, 2005).

Finegan, Jack, *Handbook of Biblical Chronology: Principles of Time Reckoning in the Ancient World and Problems of Chronology in the Bible* (Peabody, MA: Hendrickson Publishers, rev. edn, 1998 [orig. edn, Princeton, NJ: Princeton University Press, 1964]).

Finkelstein, Israel, and Neil Silberman, *The Bible Unearthed: Archaeology's New Vision of Ancient Israel and the Origin of its Sacred Texts* (New York: Free Press, 2001).

Finkelstein, Israel, and Amihai Mazar, *The Quest for the Historical Israel: Debating Archaeology and the History of Early Israel* (Atlanta, GA: Society of Biblical Literature, 2007).

Finlan, Stephen, *The Apostle Paul and the Pauline Tradition* (Collegeville, MN: Liturgical Press, 2008), pp. 26-28.

Finsterbusch, Karin, 'The First-Born between Sacrifice and Redemption in the Hebrew Bible', in *Human Sacrifice in Jewish and Christian Tradition* (ed. Karin Finsterbusch, Armin Lange and K.F. Diethard Römheld; Leiden: Brill, 2007), pp. 87-108.

Fitzmyer, Joseph, 'Crucifixion in Ancient Palestine, Qumran Literature, and the New Testament', *Catholic Biblical Quarterly* 40 (1978), pp. 493-513.

— *The Dead Sea Scrolls and Christian Origins* (Grand Rapids, MI: William B. Eerdmans, 2000).

— 'Further Light on Melchizedek from Qumran Cave 11', in *Essays on the Semitic Background of the New Testament* (London: Geoffrey Chapman, 1971), pp. 245-67.

Fletcher-Louis, Crispin, 'Jesus as the High Priestly Messiah: Part 1', *Journal for the Study of the Historical Jesus* 4 (2006), pp. 155-75.

— 'Jesus as the High Priestly Messiah: Part 2', *Journal for the Study of the Historical Jesus* 5 (2007), pp. 157-79.

Flint, Peter, 'The Daniel Tradition at Qumran', in *Eschatology, Messianism, and the Dead Sea Scrolls* (ed. Craig Evans and Peter Flint; Grand Rapids, MI: William B. Eerdmans, 1997), pp. 41-60.

— 'Jesus and the Dead Sea Scrolls', in *The Historical Jesus in Context* (ed. Levine, Allison and Crossan), pp. 110-31.

Flusser, D., 'Paganism in Palestine', in *The Jewish People in the First Century*. Vol. II (ed. Shemuel Safrai and Menahem Stern; Assen: Van Gorcum, 1974-76), pp. 1065-1100.

Fornara, Charles, *The Nature of History in Ancient Greece and Rome* (Berkeley, CA: University of California Press, 1983).

Forsythe, Gary, *A Critical History of Early Rome* (Berkeley, CA: University of California Press, 2005).

Foster, Benjamin, 'Descent of Ishtar to the Netherworld', in *Before the Muses: An Anthology of Akkadian Literature* (Bethesda, MD: CDL Press, 3rd edn, 2005), pp. 498-505.

Foster, Paul, 'Memory, Orality, and the Fourth Gospel: Three Dead-Ends in Historical Jesus Research', *Journal for the Study of the Historical Jesus* 10 (July 2012), pp. 191-227.

Fox, Robin Lane, *Pagans and Christians* (New York: Alfred A. Knopf, 1987).

Frankfurter, David, *Religion in Roman Egypt: Assimilation and Resistance* (Princeton, NJ: Princeton University Press, 1998).

France, R.T., *The Evidence for Jesus* (Downers Grove, IL: InterVarsity Press, 1986).

Francis, James, *Subversive Virtue: Asceticism and Authority in the Second-Century Pagan World* (University Park, PA: Pennsylvania State University Press, 1995).

Freedman, David Noel (ed.), *Eerdmans Dictionary of the Bible* (Grand Rapids, MI: William B. Eerdmans, 2000).

Freyne, Sean, 'The Herodian Period', in *Redemption and Resistance: The Messianic Hopes of Jews and Christians in Antiquity* (ed. Markus Bockmuehl and James Carleton Paget; New York: T. & T. Clark, 2007), pp. 29-43.

Frymer-Kensky, Tikva, 'The Tribulations of Marduk: The So-Called "Marduk Ordeal Text"', *Journal of the American Oriental Society* 103 (January–March 1983), pp. 131-41.

Funk, Robert, 'Do the Gospels Contain Eyewitness Reports?', in *Finding the Historical Jesus: Rules of Evidence* (ed. Bernard Brandon Scott; Santa Rosa, CA: Polebridge, 2008), pp. 31-39.

Gager, John, 'The Gospels and Jesus: Some Doubts about Method', *Journal of Religion* 54 (July 1974), pp. 264-66.

Galanter, Marc, 'Cults and Charismatic Group Psychology', in *Religion and the Clinical Practice of Psychology* (ed. Edward Shafranske; Washington, DC: American Psychological Association, 1996), pp. 269-96.
— *Cults: Faith, Healing, and Coercion* (New York: Oxford University Press, 1989).
Gamble, Harry, *Books and Readers in the Early Church: A History of Early Christian Texts* (New Haven, CT: Yale University Press, 1995).
— 'Canonical Formation of the New Testament', in *Dictionary of New Testament Background* (ed. Craig Evans and Stanley Porter; Downers Grove, IL: InterVarsity Press, 2000), pp. 183-95.
Gantz, Timothy, *Early Greek Myth: A Guide to Literary and Artistic Sources* (Baltimore, MD: Johns Hopkins University Press, 1996).
Gasparro, Giulia Sfameni, *Soteriology and Mystic Aspects in the Cult of Cybele and Attis* (Leiden: Brill, 1985).
Gempf, Conrad, 'Public Speaking and Published Accounts', in *The Book of Acts in its First Century Setting: I: Ancient Literary Setting* (ed. Bruce Winter and Andrew D. Clarke; Grand Rapids, MI: William B. Eerdmans, 1993), pp. 259-303.
Gentili, Bruno, and Giovanni Cerri, *History and Biography in Ancient Thought* (Amsterdam: J.C. Gieben, 1988).
Gericke, Jaco, 'Can God Exist if Yahweh Doesn't?', in *The End of Christianity* (ed. John Loftus; Amherst, NY: Prometheus Books, 2011), pp. 131-54.
Giannantoni, Gabriele, *Socratis et Socraticorum reliquiae* (4 vols.; Naples, Italy: Bibliopolis, 1990).
Gieschen, Charles, *Angelomorphic Christology: Antecedents and Early Evidence* (Boston: Brill, 1998).
— 'The Different Functions of a Similar Melchizedek Tradition in 2 Enoch and the Epistle to the Hebrews', in *Early Christian Interpretation of the Scriptures of Israel: Investigations and Proposals* (ed. Craig Evans and James Sanders; Sheffield: Sheffield Academic Press, 1997), pp. 364-79 (378-79).
Giovannoli, Joseph, *The Biology of Belief: How our Biology Biases our Beliefs and Perceptions* (Rosetta Press, 2000).
Girard, René, *Violence and the Sacred* (trans. Patrick Gregory; Baltimore, MD: Johns Hopkins University Press, 1977).
Godfrey, Neil, 'Taking Eddy & Boyd Seriously (3)', *Vridar* (January 5, 2010) at http://vridar.wordpress.com/2010/01/05/taking-eddy-boyd-seriously-3.
Godwin, Joscelyn, *Mystery Religions in the Ancient World* (New York: Harper & Row, 1981).
Goff, Matthew, 'Gilgamesh the Giant: The Qumran *Book of Giants*' Appropriation of Gilgamesh Motifs', *Dead Sea Discoveries* 16.2 (2009), pp. 221-53.
Goguel, Maurice, *Jesus the Nazarene: Myth or History?* (New York: D. Appleton, 1926).
Goldberg, G.J., 'The Coincidences of the Testimonium of Josephus and the Emmaus Narrative of Luke', *Journal for the Study of the Pseudepigrapha* 13 (1995), pp. 59-77.
Gooch, Paul, *Reflections on Jesus and Socrates: Word and Silence* (New Haven, CT: Yale University Press, 1996).
Goodacre, Mark, *The Case against Q: Studies in Markan Priority and the Synoptic Problem* (Harrisburg, PA: Trinity Press International, 2002).
— *The Synoptic Problem: A Way through the Maze* (London: Sheffield Academic Press, 2001).

— *Thomas and the Gospels: The Case for Thomas's Familiarity with the Synoptics* (Grand Rapids, MI: William B. Eerdmans, 2012).
Goodacre, Mark, and Nicholas Perrin (eds.), *Questioning Q: A Multidimensional Critique* (Downers Grove, IL: InterVarsity Press, 2004).
Goodenough, Erwin, 'The Political Philosophy of Hellenistic Kingship', *Yale Classical Studies* 1 (1928), pp. 55-102.
Goodman, Felecitas, *Speaking in Tongues: A Cross-Cultural Study in Glossolalia* (Chicago: University of Chicago Press, 1972).
Goodman, Felicitas, Jeanette Henney and Esther Pressel, *Trance, Healing, and Hallucination* (New York: Wiley, 1974).
Goodman, Martin, 'Messianism and Politics in the Land of Israel, 66–135 C.E.', in *Redemption and Resistance: The Messianic Hopes of Jews and Christians in Antiquity* (ed. Markus Bockmuehl and James Carleton Paget; New York: T. & T. Clark, 2007), pp. 149-57.
Gordon, Richard, *Image and Value in the Graeco-Roman World: Studies in Mithraism and Religious Art* (Brookfield, VT: Ashgate, 1996).
Goulder, Michael, 'The Baseless Fabric of a Vision', in *Resurrection Reconsidered* (ed. Gavin D'Costa; Oxford: Oneworld Publications, 1996), pp. 48-61.
— 'The Explanatory Power of Conversion Visions', in *Jesus' Resurrection: Fact or Figment: A Debate between William Lane Craig and Gerd Lüdemann* (ed. Paul Copan and Ronald Tacelli; Downers Grove, IL: InterVarsity Press, 2000), pp. 86-103.
— 'Is Q a Juggernaut?', *Journal of Biblical Literature* 115 (1996), pp. 667-81.
— *Luke: A New Paradigm* (2 vols.; Sheffield: JSOT, 1989).
Gove, Harry, *Relic, Icon or Hoax? Carbon Dating the Turin Shroud* (Philadelphia, PA: Institute of Physics,1996).
Gowler, David, 'The *Chreia*', in *The Historical Jesus in Context* (ed. Levine, Allison and Crossan), pp. 132-48.
Grant, Michael, *Greek and Roman Historians: Information and Misinformation* (New York: Routledge, 1995).
Grant, Robert, '"One Hundred Fifty-Three Large Fish" (John 21.11)', *Harvard Theological Review* 42 (October 1949), pp. 273-75.
Gray, Rebecca, *Prophetic Figures in Late Second Temple Jewish Palestine: The Evidence from Josephus* (New York: Oxford University Press, 1993).
Graziosi, Barbara, *Inventing Homer: The Early Reception of Epic* (New York: Cambridge University Press, 2002).
Green, C., and C. McCreery, *Apparitions* (London: Hamish Hamilton, 1975).
Green, Peter, *Alexander to Actium: The Historical Evolution of the Hellenistic Age* (Berkeley, CA: University of California Press, 1990).
Greenfield, Jonas, 'The Languages of Palestine, 200 B.C.E. 200 C.E.', in *Al Kanfei Yonah: Collected Studies of Jonas C. Greenfield on Semitic Philology*, Vol. I (ed. Shalom Paul, Michael Stone and Avital Pinnick; Leiden: Brill, 2001), pp. 376-87.
Gregory, Andrew, 'The Third Gospel? The Relationship of John and Luke Reconsidered', in *Challenging Perspectives on the Gospel of John* (ed. John Lierman; Tübingen: Mohr Siebeck, 2006), pp. 109-34.
Griffiths, J. Gwyn, *The Isis-Book: Metamorphoses, Book XI* (Leiden: Brill, 1975).
— *Plutarch's De Iside et Osiride* (Cardiff: University of Wales Press, 1970).

Grobel, K., '"... Whose Name Was Neves"', *New Testament Studies* 10 (1963–1964), pp. 373-82.

Gruen, Erich, *Diaspora: Jews amidst Greeks and Romans* (Cambridge, MA: Harvard University Press, 2002).

— 'Fact and Fiction: Jewish Legends in a Hellenistic Context', in *Hellenistic Constructs: Essays in Culture, History, and Historiography* (ed. Paul Cartledge, Peter Garnsey and Erich Gruen; Berkeley, CA: University of California Press, 1997), pp. 72-88.

— *Heritage and Hellenism: The Reinvention of Jewish Tradition* (Berkeley, CA: University of California Press, 1998).

Guglielmo, Lara, '11Q13, Malchî Sedek, Co-Reference, and Restoration of 2 18', *Henoch* 33 (2011), pp. 61-72.

Gutmann, Joseph, *Ancient Synagogues* (Chico, CA: Scholars Press, 1981).

Haar, Stephen, *Simon Magus: The First Gnostic?* (New York: Walter de Gruyter, 2003).

Habermas, Gary, and Mike Licona, *The Case for the Resurrection of Jesus* (Grand Rapids, MI: Kregel Publications, 2004).

Hagner, Donald, *The Jewish Reclamation of Jesus: An Analysis and Critique of Modern Jewish Study of Jesus* (Grand Rapids, MI: Academie Books, 1984).

Hahn, Thomas, 'Judas: The Medieval Oedipus', *Comparative Literature* 32 (Summer 1980), pp. 225-37.

Hallquist, Chris, *UFOs, Ghosts, and a Rising God: Debunking the Resurrection of Jesus* (Cincinnati, OH: Reasonable Press, 2008).

Hällström, Gunnar, *Fides simpliciorum according to Origen of Alexandria* (Helsinki: Societas Scientiarum Fennica, 1984).

Halperin, D.J., 'Crucifixion, the Nahum Pesher and the Rabbinic Penalty of Crucifixion', *Journal of Jewish Studies* 32 (1981), pp. 32-46.

Hamerton-Kelly, R.G., 'Sacred Violence and the Messiah: The Markan Passion Narrative as a Redefinition of Messianology', in *The Messiah: Developments in Earliest Judaism and Christianity* (ed. James Charlesworth; Minneapolis, MN: Fortress Press, 1992), pp. 461-93.

Hankins, James, 'Socrates in the Italian Renaissance', in *A Companion to Socrates* (ed. Sara Ahbel-Rappe and Rachana Kamtekar; Oxford: Blackwell, 2006), pp. 337-52.

Hansen, William, *Phlegon of Tralles' Book of Marvels* (Exeter, UK: University of Exeter Press, 1996).

Hanson, John, 'Dreams and Visions in the Graeco-Roman World and Early Christianity', *Aufstieg und Niedergang der römischen Welt* II 23 (New York: W. de Gruyter, 1980), pp. 1395-1427.

Hard, Robin, and H.J. Rose, *The Routledge Handbook of Greek Mythology* (New York: Routledge, 2004).

Harrington, D.J., 'Pseudo-Philo', in *Dictionary of New Testament Background* (ed. Craig Evans and Stanley Porter; Downers Grove, IL: InterVarsity Press, 2000), pp. 864-68.

Harris, William, *Dreams and Experience in Classical Antiquity* (Cambridge, MA: Harvard University Press, 2009).

Harrison, Thomas, *Divinity and History: The Religion of Herodotus* (New York: Clarendon Press, 2000).

Hartman, Lars, *'Into the Name of the Lord Jesus': Baptism in the Early Church* (Edinburgh: T. & T. Clark, 1997).

Hatina, Thomas, 'From History to Myth and Back Again: The Historicizing Function of Scripture in Matthew 2', in *Biblical Interpretation in Early Christian Gospels, Vol. 2. Gospel of Matthew* (ed. Thomas Hatina; London: T. & T. Clark, 2008), pp. 98-118.

'Hebrews, Epistle to the', in *Oxford Dictionary of the Christian Church* (ed. F.L. Cross and E.A. Livingstone; Oxford: Oxford University Press, 3rd edn, 1997), pp. 742-43.

Heckel, Waldemar, and Lawrence Tritle, *Alexander the Great: A New History* (Malden, MA: Wiley-Blackwell, 2009).

Hedrick, Charles, *Ancient History: Monuments and Documents* (Oxford: Blackwell, 2006).

— 'The 34 Gospels: Diversity and Division among the Earliest Christians', *Bible Review* 18 (June 2002), pp. 20-31, 46-47.

Heidel, William Arthur, *The Day of Yahweh: A Study of Sacred Days and Ritual Forms in the Ancient Near East* (New York: The Century Co., 1929).

Heilbrun, Alfred, 'Hallucinations', in *Symptoms of Schizophrenia* (ed. Charles Costello; New York: John Wiley & Sons, 1993), pp. 56-91.

Heimerdinger, Jenny, 'The Seven Steps of Codex Bezae: A Prophetic Interpretation of Acts 12', in *Codex Bezae: Studies from the Lunel Colloquium, June 1994* (ed. D.C. Parker and C.B. Amphoux; Leiden: Brill, 1996), pp. 303-10.

Heisserer, A.J., *Alexander the Great and the Greeks: The Epigraphic Evidence* (Norman, OK: University of Oklahoma Press, 1980).

Helms, Randel, *Gospel Fictions* (Amherst, NY: Prometheus Books, 1988).

Hemer, Colin, 'Ancient Historiography', *The Book of Acts in the Setting of Hellenistic History* (Tübingen: J.C.B. Mohr, 1989).

Hengel, Martin, 'The Effective History of Isaiah 53 in the Pre-Christian Period', in *The Suffering Servant: Isaiah 53 in Jewish and Christian Sources* (ed. Bernd Janowski and Peter Stuhlmacher; Grand Rapids, MI: William B. Eerdmans, 2004), pp. 75-146.

— *Judaism and Hellenism: Studies in their Encounter in Palestine during the Early Hellenistic Period* (Philadelphia, PA: Fortress Press, 1974).

Henze, Matthias (ed.), *Hazon Gabriel: New Readings of the Gabriel Revelation* (Atlanta, GA: Society of Biblical Literature, 2011).

Hering, James, *The Colossian and Ephesian Haustafeln in Theological Context: An Analysis of their Origins, Relationship, and Message* (New York: Peter Lang, 2007).

Heyob, Sharon Kelly, *The Cult of Isis among Women in the Graeco-Roman World* (Leiden: Brill, 1975).

Hock, Ronald, 'Lazarus and Micyllus: Greco-Roman Backgrounds to Luke 16:19-31', *Journal of Biblical Literature* 106 (1987), pp. 447-63.

Hoek, Annewies van den, 'Allegorical Interpretation', in *Dictionary of Biblical Criticism and Interpretation* (ed. Stanley Porter; New York: Routledge, 2007), pp. 9-12.

Holden, Katharine, and Christopher French, 'Alien Abduction Experiences: Some Cues from Neuropsychology and Neuropsychiatry', *Cognitive Neuropsychiatry* 7 (2002), pp. 163-78.

Holladay, Carl, *Fragments from Hellenistic Jewish Authors. Volume IV. Orphica* (Atlanta, GA: Scholars Press, 1996).

Holt, Frank, *Alexander the Great and Bactria: The Formation of a Greek Frontier in Central Asia* (Leiden: Brill, 1988).

Holzberg, Niklas, *The Ancient Novel: An Introduction* (New York: Routledge, 1995).

Horbury, William, 'The Cult of Christ and the Cult of the Saints', *New Testament Studies* 44 (1998), pp. 444-69.

Horgan, John, *Rational Mysticism: Dispatches from the Border between Science and Spirituality* (Boston: Houghton Mifflin, 2003).

Hornblower, Simon, and Antony Spawforth (eds.), *Oxford Classical Dictionary* (Oxford: Oxford University Press, 3rd edn, 1995).

Horsley, Richard, *The Liberation of Christmas: The Infancy Narratives in Social Context* (New York: Crossroad, 1989).

— '"Messianic" Figures and Movements in First-Century Palestine', in *The Messiah* (ed. Charlesworth), pp. 276-95.

Hovenden, Gerald, *Speaking in Tongues: The New Testament Evidence in Context* (London: Sheffield Academic, 2002).

Howard, George, 'Was James an Apostle? A Reflection on a New Proposal for Gal. I 19', *Novum Testamentum* 19 (January 1977), pp. 63-64.

Howard-Johnston, James, and Paul Antony Hayward (eds.), *The Cult of Saints in Late Antiquity and the Middle Ages: Essays on the Contribution of Peter Brown* (New York: Oxford University Press, 1999).

Hughes, Paul, 'Moses' Birth Story: A Biblical Matrix for Prophetic Messianism', in *Eschatology, Messianism, and the Dead Sea Scrolls* (ed. Craig Evans and Peter Flint; Grand Rapids, MI: William B. Eerdmans, 1997), pp. 10-22.

Hultgren, Stephen, 'The Origin of Paul's Doctrine of the Two Adams in 1 Corinthians 15.45-49', *Journal for the Study of the New Testament* 25 (2003), pp. 343-70.

Hunt, Stephen, 'Anthropology and Interpretation', in *Dictionary of Biblical Criticism and Interpretation* (ed. Stanley Porter; New York: Routledge, 2007), pp. 12-14.

— 'Socio-Scientific Approaches', in *Dictionary of Biblical Criticism and Interpretation* (ed. Stanley Porter; New York: Routledge, 2007), pp. 337-40.

Hurst, L.D., 'Did Qumran Expect Two Messiahs?', *Bulletin for Biblical Research* 9 (1999), pp. 157-80.

Hurtado, Larry, 'Monotheism, Principal Angels, and Christology', in *The Oxford Handbook of the Dead Sea Scrolls* (ed. Timothy Lim and John Collins; Oxford: Oxford University Press, 2010), pp. 546-64.

— *One God, One Lord: Early Christian Devotion and Ancient Jewish Monotheism* (Philadelphia: Fortress Press, 1988).

Hurtado, Larry, and Paul Owen (eds.), *Who Is This Son of Man? The Latest Scholarship on a Puzzling Expression of the Historical Jesus* (New York: T. & T. Clark, 2011).

Ingermanson, Randall, 'Discussion of: Statistical Analysis of an Archaeological Find', *Annals of Applied Statistics* 2 (2008), pp. 84-90.

Jackson, Mike, and K.W.M. Fulford, 'Spiritual Experience and Psychopathology', *Philosophy, Psychiatry, and Psychology* 4 (1997), pp. 41-65; 66-90.

James, Francis, and Miriam Hill (eds.), *Joy to the World: Two Thousand Years of Christmas* (Portland, OR: Four Courts, 2000).

James, William, *The Varieties of Religious Experience: A Study in Human Nature* (London: Longmans, Green, 1902).

Jarvie, I.C., *The Revolution in Anthropology* (London: Routledge & K. Paul, 1964).

Jassen, Alex, *Mediating the Divine: Prophecy and Revelation in the Dead Sea Scrolls and Second Temple Judaism* (Leiden: Brill, 2007).

Jensen, Robin Margaret, *Understanding Early Christian Art* (New York: Routledge, 2000).

Jewett, Robert, *Romans: A Commentary* (Minneapolis, MN: Fortress Press, 2007), pp. 566-69.

Johns, L.C., *et al.*, 'Prevalence and Correlates of Self-Reported Psychotic Symptoms in the British Population', *British Journal of Psychiatry* 185 (2004), pp. 298-305.

Johnson, Fred, *The Anatomy of Hallucinations* (Chicago: Nelson-Hall, 1978).

Johnson, Sara Raup, *Historical Fictions and Hellenistic Jewish Identity: Third Maccabees in its Cultural Context* (Berkeley, CA: University of California Press, 2004).

Jonge, Henk Jan de, 'The Cleansing of the Temple in Mark 11:15 and Zechariah 14:21', in *The Book of Zechariah and its Influence* (ed. Christopher Tuckett; Burlington, VT: Ashgate, 2003), pp. 87-100.

Jordan, James, 'Toward a Chiastic Understanding of the Gospel according to Matthew', *Biblical Horizons Newsletter* 94 and 95 (April and May, 1997).

Judge, E.A., 'The Reaction against Classical Education in the New Testament', *Journal of Christian Education* 77 (1983), pp. 7-14.

Kanavou, Nikoletta, 'Personal Names in the *Vita Aesopi* (*Vita G* or *Perriana*)', *Classical Quarterly* 56 (May 2006), pp. 208-19.

Kannaday, Wayne, *Apologetic Discourse and the Scribal Tradition: Evidence of the Influence of Apologetic Interests on the Text of the Canonical Gospels* (Atlanta, GA: Society of Biblical Literature, 2004).

Kasser, Rodolphe, *et al.*, *The Gospel of Judas: From Codex Tchacos* (Washington, DC: National Geographic, 2006).

Kazen, Thomas, 'The Coming of the Son of Man Revisited', *Journal for the Study of the Historical Jesus* 5 (June 2007), pp. 155-74.

Kee, Howard Clark, *Jesus in History: An Approach to the Study of the Gospels* (New York: Harcourt Brace Jovanovich, 2nd edn, 1970).

Keel, Othmar, and Christoph Uehlinger, *Gods, Goddesses, and Images of God in Ancient Israel* (trans. Allan Mahnke; Minneapolis, MN: Fortress Press, 1996).

Keith, Chris, and Anthony LeDonne (eds.), *Jesus, History and the Demise of Authenticity* (New York: T. & T. Clark, 2012).

Kennedy, Harry Angus Alexander, *St. Paul and the Mystery-Religions* (London: Hodder & Stoughton, 1913).

Kent, Jack, *The Psychological Origins of the Resurrection Myth* (London: Open Gate, 1999).

Kim, Jintae, 'The Concept of Atonement in Early Rabbinic Thought and the New Testament Writings', *Journal of Greco-Roman Christianity and Judaism* 2 (2001-2005), pp. 117-45.

— 'The Concept of Atonement in the Fourth Servant Song in the LXX', *Journal of Greco-Roman Christianity and Judaism* 8 (2011-2012), pp. 21-33.

— 'Targum Isaiah 53 and the New Testament Concept of Atonement', *Journal of Greco-Roman Christianity and Judaism* 5 (2008), pp. 81-98.

King, Cynthia Ann Kent, *Musonius Rufus: Lectures and Sayings* (Charleston, SC: Createspace, 2011).

Kingsley, Peter, *Ancient Philosophy, Mystery, and Magic: Empedocles and Pythagorean Tradition* (New York: Oxford University Press, 1995), pp. 264-69.

Kinoshita, Junji, 'Romans: Two Writings Combined: A New Interpretation of the Body of Romans', *Novum Testamentum* 7 (October 1965), pp. 258-77.

Kirsch, Jonathan, *A History of the End of the World* (San Francisco, CA: Harper, 2006).

Klass, Philip J., *The Real Roswell Crashed Saucer Coverup* (Amherst, NY: Prometheus Books, 1997).

Klawans, Jonathan, 'Moral and Ritual Purity', in *The Historical Jesus in Context* (ed. Levine, Allison and Crossan), pp. 266-84.

Kleist, James, *The Didache, The Epistle of Barnabas, The Epistles and The Martyrdom of St. Polycarp, The Fragments of Papias, The Epistle to Diognetus* (Westminster, MD: Newman Press, 1948).

Kline, Meredith, 'The Old Testament Origins of the Gospel Genre', *Westminster Theological Journal* 38 (1975), pp. 1-27.

Kloppenborg, John, 'Associations in the Ancient World', in *Historical Jesus in Context* (ed. Levine, Allison and Crossan), pp. 323-38.

— 'On Dispensing with Q?: Goodacre on the Relation of Luke to Matthew', *New Testament Studies* 49 (2003), pp. 210-36.

Knight, Jonathan, *The Ascension of Isaiah* (Sheffield: Sheffield Academic Press, 1995).

— *Disciples of the Beloved One: The Christology, Social Setting and Theological Context of the Ascension of Isaiah* (Sheffield: Sheffield Academic Press, 1996).

Koester, Helmut, 'Apocryphal and Canonical Gospels', *Harvard Theological Review* 73 (January–April 1980), pp. 105-30.

— 'The Historical Jesus and the Historical Situation of the Quest: An Epilogue', in *Studying the Historical Jesus: Evaluation of the State of Current Research* (ed. Bruce Chilton and Craig Evans; Leiden: Brill, 1994), pp. 535-45.

Koivisto, Rex, 'Stephen's Speech: A Theology of Errors?', *Grace Theological Journal* 8 (1987), pp. 101-14.

Komarnitsky, Kris, *Doubting Jesus' Resurrection: What Happened in the Black Box?* (Drapper, UT: Stone Arrow Books, 2nd edn, 2014).

Kooten, George H. van, *Cosmic Christology in Paul and the Pauline School: Colossians and Ephesians in the Context of Graeco-Roman Cosmology, with a New Synopsis of the Greek Texts* (Tübingen: Mohr Siebeck, 2003).

Kovacs, David, 'And Baby Makes Three: Aegeus' Wife as Mother-to-Be of Theseus in Euripides' Medea', *Classical Philology* 103 (July 2008), pp. 298-304.

Kraeling, Carl, 'Christian Burial Urns?', *Biblical Archaeologist* 9 (February 1946), pp. 16-20.

Kramer, Samuel Noah, *History Begins at Sumer: Thirty-Nine Firsts in Man's Recorded History* (Philadelphia, PA: University of Pennsylvania Press, 3rd rev. edn, 1981).

Krause, Deborah, 'The One Who Comes Unbinding the Blessing of Judah: Mark 11.1-10 as a Midrash on Genesis 49.11, Zechariah 9.9, and Psalm 118.25-26', in *Early Christian Interpretation of the Scriptures of Israel: Investigations and Proposals* (ed. Craig Evans and James Sanders; Sheffield: Sheffield Academic Press, 1997), pp. 141-53.

Krenkel, Max, *Josephus und Lucas: Der schriftstellerische Einfluss des jüdischen Geschichtschreibers auf den Christlichen* (Leipzig: H. Haessel, 1894).

Kurke, Leslie, 'Aesop and the Contestation of Delphic Authority', in *The Cultures within Ancient Greek Culture: Contact, Conflict, Collaboration* (ed. Carol Dougherty and Leslie Kurke; New York: Cambridge University Press, 2003), pp. 77-100.

Kydd, Ronald, *Charismatic Gifts in the Early Church* (Peabody, MA: Hendrickson Publishers, 1984).
Lacocque, André, *The Book of Daniel* (Atlanta, GA: John Knox Press, 1979).
Lamberton, Robert, *Homer the Theologian: Neoplatonist Allegorical Reading and the Growth of the Epic Tradition* (Berkeley, CA: University of California Press, 1986).
Lancellotti, Maria Grazia, *Attis, between Myth and History: King, Priest, and God* (Leiden: Brill, 2002).
Landau, J.H., 'Two Inscribed Tombstones', *Atiqot* 11 (1976), pp. 89-91.
Lang, Manfred, *Johannes und die Synoptiker: eine redaktionsgeschichtliche Analyse von Joh 18–20 vor dem markinischen und lukanischen Hintergrund* (Göttingen: Vandenhoeck & Ruprecht, 1999).
Lapham, F., *Introduction to the New Testament Apocrypha* (London: T. & T. Clark International, 2003).
Lapin, Kenneth, 'Picturing Socrates', in *A Companion to Socrates* (ed. Sara Ahbel-Rappe and Rachana Kamtekar; Oxford: Blackwell, 2006), pp. 110-55.
Lapinkivi, Pirjo, *The Neo-Assyrian Myth of Ištar's Descent and Resurrection* (Helsinki: Neo-Assyrian Text Corpus Project, 2010).
Law, Stephen, 'Evidence, Miracles, and the Existence of Jesus', *Faith and Philosophy* 28 (April 2011), pp. 129-51; http://stephenlaw.blogspot.com/2012/04/published-in-faith-and-philosophy-2011.html.
Lawrence, Peter, *Road Belong Cargo: A Study of the Cargo Movement in the Southern Madang District, New Guinea* (Manchester: Manchester University Press, 1964).
Lawson, R.P., *Origen: The Song of Songs, Commentary and Homilies* (Ancient Christian Writings, 26; London: Longmans, Green, 1957).
Leach, Edmund, 'Fishing for Men on the Edge of the Wilderness', in *The Literary Guide to the Bible* (ed. Robert Alter and Frank Kermode; Cambridge, MA: Harvard University Press, 1987), pp. 579-99.
Lease, Gary, 'Mithraism and Christianity: Borrowings and Transformations', *Aufstieg und Niedergang der römischen Welt* II.23.2 (New York: W. de Gruyter, 1980), pp. 1306-32.
Lefkowitz, Mary, 'Biographical Mythology', in *Antike Mythen: Medien, Transformationen und Konstruktionen* (ed. Ueli Dill; New York: Walter de Gruyter, 2009), pp. 516-31.
— *The Lives of the Greek Poets* (Baltimore, MD: Johns Hopkins University Press, 1981).
Le Rider, Georges, *Alexander the Great: Coinage, Finances, and Policy* (Philadelphia, PA: American Philosophical Society, 2007).
Levenson, Jon, *The Death and Resurrection of the Beloved Son: The Transformation of Child Sacrifice in Judaism and Christianity* (New Haven, CT: Yale University Press, 1993).
Levine, Amy-Jill, Dale Allison, Jr, and John Dominic Crossan (eds.), *The Historical Jesus in Context* (Princeton, NJ: Princeton University Press, 2006).
Levine, Amy-Jill, and Marc Zvi Brettler (eds.), *The Jewish Annotated New Testament* (Oxford: Oxford University Press, 2011).
Lewis, I.M., *Ecstatic Religion: A Study of Shamanism and Spirit Possession* (New York: Routledge, 1989).

Lincoln, Andrew, 'The "Philosophy" Opposed in the Letter [to the Colossians]', in *The New Interpreter's Bible: New Testament Survey* (ed. Fred Craddock; Nashville, TN: Abingdon Press, 2005), pp. 242-47.

Lincoln, Bruce, *Theorizing Myth: Narrative, Ideology, and Scholarship* (Chicago: University of Chicago Press, 1999).

Littlewood, Roland, 'From Elsewhere: Prophetic Visions and Dreams among the People of the Earth', *Dreaming* 14 (June–September 2004), pp. 94-106.

Loftus, John, 'At Best Jesus Was a Failed Apocalyptic Prophet', in *The Christian Delusion: Why Faith Fails* (ed. John Loftus; Amherst, NY: Prometheus Books, 2010), pp. 316-43.

— *Why I Became an Atheist: A Former Preacher Rejects Christianity* (Amherst, NY: Prometheus Books, 2008).

Lohmeyer, Ernst, 'The Structure and Organization of the Fourth Gospel', *Journal of Higher Criticism* 5 (Spring 1998), pp. 113-38.

Lorimer, W.L., 'Romans IX. 3-5', *New Testament Studies* 13 (1967), pp. 385-86.

Lüdemann, Gerd, 'Paul as a Witness to the Historical Jesus', *Sources of the Jesus Tradition: Separating History from Myth* (Amherst NY: Prometheus Books, 2010), pp. 196-212.

— *Paul, the Founder of Christianity* (Amherst, NY: Prometheus Books, 2002).

— *Untersuchungen zur simonianischen Gnosis* (Göttingen: Vandenhoeck & Ruprecht, 1975).

Luhrmann, Tanya, *When God Talks Back* (New York: Alfred A. Knopf, 2012).

Lutz, Cora, *Musonius Rufus: The Roman Socrates* (New Haven, CT: Yale University Press, 1947).

Lyons, William John, 'The Hermeneutics of Fictional Black and Factual Red: The Markan Simon of Cyrene and the Quest for the Historical Jesus', *Journal for the Study of the Historical Jesus* 4 (June 2006), pp. 139-54.

— 'On the Life and Death of Joseph of Arimathea', *Journal for the Study of the Historical Jesus* 2 (January 2004), pp. 29-53.

Maccoby, Hyam, *Jesus the Pharisee* (London: SCM Press, 2003).

MacDonald, Dennis, *Christianizing Homer: The Odyssey, Plato, and the Acts of Andrew* (New York: Oxford University Press, 1994).

— 'A Conjectural Emendation of 1 Cor 15.31-32: Or the Case of the Misplaced Lion Fight', *Harvard Theological Review* 73 (January–April 1980), pp. 265-76.

— *Does the New Testament Imitate Homer? Four Cases from the Acts of the Apostles* (New Haven, CT: Yale University Press, 2003).

— 'The Ending of Luke and the Ending of the *Odyssey*', in *For a Later Generation: The Transformation of Tradition in Israel, Early Judaism, and Early Christianity* (ed. Randal Argall, Beverly Bow and Rodney Werline; Harrisburg, PA: Trinity Press International, 2000), pp. 161-68.

— *The Homeric Epics and the Gospel of Mark* (New Haven, CT: Yale University Press, 2000).

— 'Imitations of Greek Epic in the Gospels', in *Historical Jesus in Context* (ed. Levine, Allison and Crossan), pp. 372-84.

— 'The Shipwrecks of Odysseus and Paul', *New Testament Studies* 45 (1999), pp. 88-107.

— *Two Shipwrecked Gospels: The Logoi of Jesus and Papias's Exposition of Logia about the Lord* (Atlanta, GA: Society of Biblical Literature, 2012).

MacGregor, G.H.C., 'Principalities and Powers: The Cosmic Background of Paul's Thought', *New Testament Studies* 1 (1954), pp. 17-28.
Mack, Burton, 'The Christ and Jewish Wisdom', in *The Messiah* (ed. Charlesworth), pp. 192-221.
— *The Christian Myth: Origins, Logic, and Legacy* (New York: Continuum, 2006).
— 'Many Movements, Many Myths: Redescribing the Attractions of Early Christianities. Toward a Conversation with Rodney Stark', *Religious Studies Review* 25.2 (April 1999), pp. 132-36.
Mack, Dave, 'What Did Paul Know about the Life and Teachings of Jesus?', *bibleLAD* (May 17, 2013) at http://biblelad.wordpress.com/category/historical-jesus-2.
Maclean, Jennifer K. Berenson, 'Barabbas, the Scapegoat Ritual, and the Development of the Passion Narrative', *Harvard Theological Review* 100 (July 2007), pp. 309-34.
MacNicol, Allan (ed.), *Beyond the Q Impasse: Luke's Use of Matthew: A Demonstration by the Research Team of the International Institute for the Renewal of Gospel Studies* (Valley Forge, PA: Trinity Press International, 1996).
Magné, Jean, 'The Emmaus Disciples and Adam and Eve in Paradise', in *From Christianity to Gnosis and from Gnosis to Christianity: An Itinerary through the Texts to and from the Tree of Paradise* (Atlanta, GA: Scholars Press, 1993), pp. 41-51.
Malina, Bruce, *The New Jerusalem in the Revelation of John: The City as Symbol of Life with God* (Collegeville, MN: Liturgical Press, 2000).
— *The New Testament World: Insights from Cultural Anthropology* (Atlanta, GA: John Knox Press, 3rd edn, 2001).
— *The Social Gospel of Jesus: The Kingdom of God in Mediterranean Perspective* (New York: Routledge, 2000).
Malina, Bruce, and John Pilch, *Social Science Commentary on the Book of Revelation* (Minneapolis, MN: Fortress Press, 2000).
Manns, Frédéric, 'Quelques variantes du Codex Bezae de Luc 24', *Liber Annuus* 55 (2005), pp. 131-39.
Marcus, Ivan, *The Jewish Life Cycle: Rites of Passage from Biblical to Modern Times* (Seattle, WA: University of Washington Press, 2004).
Marcus, Joel, *Mark 1–16: A New Translation with Introduction and Commentary* (New York: Doubleday, 2000).
Marincola, John, *Authority and Tradition in Ancient Historiography* (New York: Cambridge University Press, 1997).
Marks, Susan, *Finding Betty Crocker: The Secret Life of America's First Lady of Food* (New York: Simon & Schuster, 2005).
Marrou, Hénri, *A History of Education in Antiquity* (New York: Sheed & Ward, 3rd edn, 1956).
Marshall, I.H., *The Gospel of Luke: A Commentary on the Greek Text* (Exeter: Paternoster, 1978).
Martin, Dale Basil, 'When Did Angels Become Demons?', *Journal of Biblical Literature* 129 (2010), pp. 657-77.
Martin, Ralph, *A Hymn of Christ: Philippians 2:5-11 in Recent Interpretation and in the Setting of Early Christian Worship* (Downers Grove, IL: InterVarsity Press, 1997).
Martínez, Florentino García, and Eibert Tigchelaar (eds.), *Qumranica Minora*, Vol. II (Boston: Brill, 2007).

Mason, Steve, 'Josephus and Luke–Acts', *Josephus and the New Testament* (Peabody, MA: Hendrickson Publishers, 1992), pp. 185-229.

Mathews, Thomas, *The Clash of Gods: A Reinterpretation of Early Christian Art* (Princeton, NJ: Princeton University Press, 1993).

Mavromatis, A., *Hypnagogia: The Unique State of Consciousness between Wakefulness and Sleep* (London: Routledge, 1987).

Mayor, Adrienne, *The Poison King: The Life and Legend of Mithradates, Rome's Deadliest Enemy* (Princeton, NJ: Princeton University Press, 2010).

McCormick, Matt, 'The Salem Witch Trials and the Evidence for the Resurrection', in *The End of Christianity* (ed. John Loftus; Amherst, NY: Prometheus Books, 2011), pp. 195-218.

McCown, C.C., 'Gospel Geography: Fiction, Fact, and Truth', *Journal of Biblical Literature* 60 (March 1941), pp. 1-25.

McCreery, Charles, and Gordon Claridge, 'Healthy Schizotypy: The Case of Out-of-the-Body Experiences', *Personality and Individual Differences* 32 (January 5, 2002), pp. 141-54.

McCrone, Walter, *Judgment Day for the Shroud of Turin* (Amherst, NY: Prometheus Books, rev. edn, 1999).

McDonald, Lee Martin, and James Sanders (eds.), *The Canon Debate* (Peabody, MA: Hendrickson Publishers, 2002).

McDonough, Sean, *Christ as Creator: Origins of a New Testament Doctrine* (New York: Oxford University Press, 2009).

McGinn, Bernard, *et al.*, *The Continuum History of Apocalypticism* (New York: Continuum, 2003).

McGrath, James, *The Burial of Jesus: History and Faith* (Charleston, SC: BookSurge, 2008).

McNamara, Jo Ann, and John Halborg, *Sainted Women of the Dark Ages* (Durham, NC: Duke University Press, 1992).

Mead, G.R.S., *Did Jesus Live 100 B.C.? An Enquiry into the Talmud Jesus Stories, the Toldoth Jeschu, and Some Curious Statements of Epiphanius* (London: Theosophical Publishing Society, 1903).

Meggitt, Justin, 'Popular Mythology in the Early Empire and the Multiplicity of Jesus Traditions', in *Sources of the Jesus Tradition: Separating History from Myth* (ed. R. Joseph Hoffmann; Amherst, NY: Prometheus, 2010), pp. 55-80.

Meier, John, *A Marginal Jew: Rethinking the Historical Jesus* (4 vols.; New York: Doubleday, 1991–2009).

Mendels, D., 'Pseudo-Philo's *Biblical Antiquities*, the "Fourth Philosophy", and the Political Messianism of the First Century C.E.', in *The Messiah* (ed. Charlesworth), pp. 261-75.

Mercer, Samuel, *The Pyramid Texts* (Longmans, Green, 1952).

Merkelbach, Reinhold, *Isis Regina, Zeus Sarapis: die griechisch-ägyptische Religion nach den Quellen dargestellt* (Stuttgart: B.G. Teubner, 1995).

Merritt, Robert, 'Jesus Barabbas and the Paschal Pardon', *Journal of Biblical Literature* 104 (1985), pp. 57-68.

Mettinger, Tryggve, 'The Dying and Rising God: The Peregrinations of a Mytheme', in *Ethnicity in Ancient Mesopotamia* (ed. W.H. van Soldt; Leiden: Nederlands Instituut voor het Nabije Oosten, 2005), pp. 198-210.

— *The Riddle of Resurrection: "Dying and Rising Gods" in the Ancient Near East* (Stockholm: Almqvist & Wiksell International, 2001).

Metzenthin, Christian, *Jesaja-Auslegung in Qumran* (Zurich: TVZ, 2010).
Metzger, Bruce, *The Canon of the New Testament: Its Origin, Development, and Significance* (New York: Oxford University Press, 1987).
— 'Considerations of the Methodology in the Study of the Mystery Religions and Early Christianity', *Harvard Theological Review* 48 (January 1955), pp. 1-20.
— *The Gnostic Discoveries: The Impact of the Nag Hammadi Library* (San Francisco, CA: HarperSanFrancisco, 2005).
— 'Literary Forgeries and Canonical Pseudepigrapha', in *New Testament Studies: Philological, Versional, and Patristic* (Leiden: Brill, 1980), pp. 1-22.
— 'The Punctuation of Rom. 9:5', in *Christ and the Spirit in the New Testament* (ed. B. Lindars and S. Smalley; Cambridge: Cambridge University Press, 1973), pp. 95-112.
— *The Text of the New Testament: Its Transmission, Corruption, and Restoration* (New York: Oxford University Press, 3rd edn, 1992).
Meyer, Marvin (ed.), *The Ancient Mysteries: A Sourcebook of Sacred Texts* (Philadelphia, PA: University of Pennsylvania Press, 1987).
— 'The Mithras Liturgy', in *The Historical Jesus in Context* (ed. Levine, Allison and Crossan), pp. 179-92.
Milik, Józef T. (ed.), *The Books of Enoch: Aramaic Fragments of Qumran Cave 4* (Oxford: Clarendon Press, 1976).
Miller, Dale, and Patricia Miller, *The Gospel of Mark as Midrash on Earlier Jewish and New Testament Literature* (Lewiston, NY: E. Mellen Press, 1990).
Miller, Richard C., 'Mark's Empty Tomb and Other Translation Fables in Classical Antiquity', *Journal of Biblical Literature* 129 (2010), pp. 759-76.
Miller, Robert, 'The (A)Historicity of Jesus' Temple Demonstration: A Test Case in Methodology', in *Society of Biblical Literature 1991 Seminar Papers: One Hundred Twenty-Seventh Annual Meeting* (ed. Eugene Lovering; Atlanta, GA: Scholars Press, 1991), pp. 235-52.
Mills, Watson, *Speaking in Tongues: A Guide to Research on Glossolalia* (Grand Rapids, MI: William B. Eerdmans, 1986).
Mojsov, Bojana, *Osiris: Death and Afterlife of a God* (Oxford: Blackwell, 2005).
Moloney, Francis, 'From Cana to Cana (Jn 2.1–4.54) and the Fourth Evangelist's Concept of Correct (and Incorrect) Faith', *Salesianum* 40 (October–December 1978), pp. 817-43.
Moo, Douglas, *The Epistle to the Romans* (Grand Rapids, MI: William B. Eerdmans, 1996).
Moreira-Almeida, Alexander, Francisco Lotufo Neto and Bruce Greyson, 'Dissociative and Psychotic Experiences in Brazilian Spiritist Mediums', *Psychotherapy and Psychosomatics* 76 (2007), pp. 57-58.
Morgan, Kathryn, *Myth and Philosophy from the Presocratics to Plato* (New York: Cambridge University Press, 2000).
Moss, Candida, *The Myth of Persecution: How Early Christians Invented a Story of Martyrdom* (New York: HarperOne, 2013).
Moyise, Steve (ed.), *The Old Testament in the New Testament* (Sheffield: Sheffield Academic Press, 2000).
Müller, Mogens, *The Expression 'Son of Man' and the Development of Christology: A History of Interpretation* (Oakville, CT: Equinox, 2008).

— 'Paul: The Oldest Witness to the Historical Jesus', in *'Is This Not the Carpenter?' The Question of the Historicity of the Figure of Jesus* (ed. Thomas Thompson and Thomas Verenna; Sheffield: Equinox 2012), pp. 117-30.

Munro, Winsome, 'Interpolation in the Epistles: Weighing Probability', *New Testament Studies* 36 (1990), pp. 431-43.

Murphy, Frederick, *Pseudo-Philo: Rewriting the Bible* (New York: Oxford University Press, 1993).

Mussies, G., 'Greek in Palestine and the Diaspora', in *The Jewish People in the First Century*, Vol. II (ed. Shemuel Safrai and Menahem Stern; Assen: Van Gorcum, 1974-76), pp. 1040-64.

Nails, Debra, *The People of Plato: A Prosopography of Plato and Other Socratics* (Indianapolis, IN: Hackett, 2002).

Navia, Luis, *Socrates: A Life Examined* (Amherst, NY: Prometheus Books, 2007).

Navia, Luis, and Ellen Katz, *Socrates: An Annotated Bibliography* (New York: Garland, 1988).

Nawotka, Krzysztof, *Alexander the Great* (Newcastle upon Tyne: Cambridge Scholars, 2010).

Neusner, Jacob, *Messiah in Context: Israel's History and Destiny in Formative Judaism* (Philadelphia, PA: Fortress Press, 1984).

Neusner, Jacob, *et al.* (eds.), *Judaisms and their Messiahs at the Turn of the Christian Era* (New York: Cambridge University Press, 1987).

Neville, David, *Mark's Gospel—Prior or Posterior? A Reappraisal of the Phenomenon of Order* (New York: Sheffield Academic Press, 2002).

Neyrey, Jerome, 'The Apologetic Use of the Transfiguration in 2 Peter 1.16-21', *Catholic Biblical Quarterly* 42 (1980), pp. 504-19.

Neirynck, Frans, 'Paul and the Sayings of Jesus', in *Collected Essays, 1982–1991: Evangelica, Gospel Studies* (ed. F. van Segbroeck; Leuven: Leuven University Press, 1991), pp. 511-68.

Newell, Ronald R., 'The Forms and Historical Value of Josephus' Suicide Accounts', in *Josephus, the Bible, and History* (ed. Louis Feldman and Gohei Hata; Leiden: Brill, 1989), pp. 278-94.

Nickell, Joe, *Inquest on the Shroud of Turin: Latest Scientific Findings* (Amherst, NY: Prometheus Books, 1998).

— *Relics of the Christ* (Lexington, KY: University Press of Kentucky, 2007).

Nickelsburg, George, 'The Experience of Demons (and Angels) in 1 Enoch, Jubilees, and the Book of Tobit', *PSCO Minutes* [Philadelphia Seminar on Christian Origins] (March 10, 1988) http://ccat.sas.upenn.edu/psco/year25/8803a.shtml.

— '*First* and *Second Enoch*: A Cry against Oppression and the Promise of Deliverance', in *The Historical Jesus in Context* (ed. Levine, Allison and Crossan), pp. 87-109.

— 'The Genre and Function of the Markan Passion Narrative', *Harvard Theological Review* 73 (January–April 1980), pp. 153-84.

Nilsson, Martin, *The Dionysiac Mysteries of the Hellenistic and Roman Age* (Lund: Gleerup, 1957).

Nock, A.D., *Conversion: The Old and the New in Religion from Alexander the Great to Augustine of Hippo* (Baltimore, MD: Johns Hopkins University Press, 1933).

Noll, Kurt, 'Investigating Earliest Christianity without Jesus', in *'Is This Not the Carpenter?' The Question of the Historicity of the Figure of Jesus* (ed. Thomas Thompson and Thomas Verenna; Sheffield: Equinox 2012), pp. 233-66.

Nordgaard, Stefan, 'Paul's Appropriation of Philo's Theory of "Two Men" in 1 Corinthians 15.45-49', *New Testament Studies* 57 (2011), pp. 348-65.

Novenson, Matthew, *Christ among the Messiahs: Christ Language in Paul and Messiah Language in Ancient Judaism* (Oxford: Oxford University Press, 2012).

Ober, W.B., 'Weighing the Heart against the Feather of Truth', *Bulletin of the New York Academy of Medicine* 55 (July–August 1979), pp. 636-51.

Ogden, Schubert (ed.), *New Testament and Mythology and Other Basic Writings by Rudolf Bultmann* (Philadelphia, PA: Fortress Press, 1984).

Ohayon, Maurice M., 'Prevalence of Hallucinations and their Pathological Associations in the General Population', *Psychiatry Research* 97 (December 27, 2000), pp. 153-64.

Okeke, G.E., '1 Thessalonians 2.13-16: The Fate of the Unbelieving Jews', *New Testament Studies* 27 (1981), pp. 127-36.

Olson, Ken, 'A Eusebian Reading of the Testimonium Flavianum', in *Eusebius of Caesarea: Tradition and Innovations* (ed. Aaron Johnson and Jeremy Schott: Cambridge, MA: Harvard University Press, 2013), pp. 97-114.

— 'Eusebius and the Testimonium Flavianum', *Catholic Biblical Quarterly* 61 (1999), pp. 305-22.

— 'Review of Paul Eddy and Gregory Boyd, *The Jesus Legend*', in *Review of Biblical Literature* (December 20, 2008) at http://www.bookreviews.org/pdf/6281_6762.pdf.

— 'The Testimonium Flavianum, Eusebius, and Consensus', *Historical Jesus Research* (August 13, 2013) at http://historicaljesusresearch.blogspot.com/2013/08/the-testimonium-flavianum-eusebius-and.html.

Otto, Susanne, 'The Composition of the Elijah–Elisha Stories and the Deuteronomistic History', *Journal for the Study of the Old Testament* 27 (June 2003), pp. 487-508.

Overman, J. Andrew, and Robert MacLennan (eds.), *Diaspora Jews and Judaism* (Atlanta, GA: Scholars Press, 1992).

Pagels, Elaine, *Revelations: Visions, Prophecy, and Politics in the Book of Revelation* (New York: Viking, 2012).

Paget, James Carleton, 'Some Observations on Josephus and Christianity', *Journal of Theological Studies* 52.2 (October 2001), pp. 539-624.

Pakkanen, Petra, *Interpreting Early Hellenistic Religion: A Study Based on the Mystery Cult of Demeter and the Cult of Isis* (Helsinki: Suomen Ateenan-Instituutin Saatio, 1996).

Parker, P., 'Luke and the Fourth Evangelist', *New Testament Studies* 9 (1963), pp. 317-36.

Parkin, T.G., *Demography and Roman Society* (Baltimore, MD: Johns Hopkins University Press, 1992).

Partridge, Christopher (ed.), *UFO Religions* (New York: Routledge, 2003).

Parvus, Roger, *A New Look at the Letters of Ignatius of Antioch and Other Apellean Writings* (New York: iUniverse, 2008).

Pastor, Jack, *Land and Economy in Ancient Palestine* (New York: Routledge, 1997).

Payne, D.F., 'Semitisms in the Books of Acts', in *Apostolic History and the Gospel: Biblical and Historical Essays Presented to F.F. Bruce* (ed. W. Ward Gasque and Ralph P. Martin; Exeter: Paternoster Press, 1970), pp. 134-50.

Pearce, Keith, 'The Lucan Origins of the Raising of Lazarus', *Expository Times* 96 (1985), pp. 359-61.

Pearson, Birger, '1 Thessalonians 2.13-16: A Deutero-Pauline Interpolation', *Harvard Theological Review* 64 (1971), pp. 79-94.

Peebles, Rose Jeffries, *The Legend of Longinus in Ecclesiastical Tradition and in English Literature, and its Connection with the Grail* (Baltimore, MD: J.H. Furst, 1911).

Peper, Bradley, and Mark DelCogliano, 'The Pliny and Trajan Correspondence', in *The Historical Jesus in Context* (ed. Levine, Allison and Crossan), pp. 366-71.

Pépin, Jean (ed.), *La tradition de l'allégorie de Philon d'Alexandrie à Dante: Études historiques* (Paris: Études Augustiniennes, 1987).

— *Mythe et allégorie: les origines grecques et les contestations judéo-chrétiennes* (Paris: Études Augustiniennes, 1976).

Perrin, Nicholas, *Thomas and Tatian: The Relationship between the Gospel of Thomas and the Diatessaron* (Leiden: Brill, 2002).

Perry, B.E., 'Demetrius of Phalerum and the Aesopic Fables', *Transactions and Proceedings of the American Philological Association* 93 (1962), pp. 287-346.

— *Studies in the Text History of the Life and Fables of Aesop* (Haverford, PA: American Philological Association, 1936).

Pervo, Richard, *Acts: A Commentary* (Minneapolis, MN: Fortress Press, 2009).

— *Dating Acts: Between the Evangelists and the Apologists* (Santa Rosa, CA: Polebridge, 2006).

— *The Making of Paul: Constructions of the Apostle in Early Christianity* (Minneapolis, MN: Fortress Press, 2010).

— *The Mystery of Acts* (Santa Rosa, CA: Polebridge, 2008).

Petersen, Norman, 'The Composition of Mark 4:1–8:26', *Harvard Theological Review* 73 (January–April 1980), pp. 185-217.

Petty, Richard, and John Cacioppo, *Attitudes and Persuasion: Classic and Contemporary Approaches* (Dubuque, IA: William C. Brown, 1981).

Pfann, Stephen, and James Tabor, 'Forum: The Talpiot "Jesus" Family Tomb', *Near Eastern Archaeology* 69 (September–December 2006), pp. 116-37.

Pfann, Stephen, Ross Voss and Yehudah Rapuano, 'Surveys and Excavations at the Nazareth Village Farm (1997–2002): Final Report', *Bulletin of the Anglo-Israel Archaeological Society* 25 (2007), pp. 19-79.

Pflock, Karl T., *Roswell: Inconvenient Facts and the Will to Believe* (Amherst, NY: Prometheus Books, 2001).

Porter, Stanley, *The Criteria for Authenticity in Historical-Jesus Research: Previous Discussion and New Proposals* (Sheffield: Sheffield Academic Press, 2000).

— (ed.), *Hearing the Old Testament in the New Testament* (Grand Rapids, MI: William B. Eerdmans, 2006).

— (ed.), *The Messiah in the Old and New Testaments* (Grand Rapids, MI: William B. Eerdmans, 2007).

Porton, Gary, 'The Parable in the Hebrew Bible and Rabbinic Literature', in *The Historical Jesus in Context* (ed. Levine, Allison and Crossan), pp. 206-21.

Posey, T.B., and M.E. Losch, 'Auditory Hallucinations of Hearing Voices in 375 Normal Subjects', *Imagination, Cognition and Personality* 3 (1983), pp. 99-113.

Powers, Tom, 'Simon of Cyrene Tomb Connection', *Artifax* (Autumn 2000), pp. 1, 4-6.

— 'Treasures in the Storeroom: Family Tomb of Simon of Cyrene', *Biblical Archaeology Review* 29 (July/August 2003), pp. 46-51, 59.

Price, R.G., *The Gospel of Mark as Reaction and Allegory* (n.p.: RationalEvolution.net, 2007).
—*Jesus: A Very Jewish Myth* (n.p.: RationalEvolution.net, 2007).
Price, Robert M., 'The Abhorrent Void: The Rapid Attribution of Fictive Sayings and Stories to a Mythic Jesus', in *Sources of the Jesus Tradition: Separating History from Myth* (ed. R. Joseph Hoffmann; Amherst, NY: Prometheus Books, 2010), pp. 109-17.
— 'Apocryphal Apparitions: 1 Corinthians 15.3-11 as a Post-Pauline Interpolation', in *The Empty Tomb: Jesus beyond the Grave* (ed. Robert M. Price and Jeffery Lowder; Amherst, NY: Prometheus Books, 2005), pp. 69-104.
— *The Case against the Case for Christ: A New Testament Scholar Refutes Lee Strobel* (Cranford, NJ: American Atheist Press, 2010).
— *The Christ-Myth Theory and its Problems* (Cranford, NJ: American Atheist Press, 2011).
— *Deconstructing Jesus* (Amherst, NY: Prometheus Books, 2000).
— *The Incredible Shrinking Son of Man* (Amherst, NY: Prometheus Books, 2003).
— 'Is There a Place for Historical Criticism?', *Religious Studies* 27 (1991), pp. 371-88.
— *Jesus Is Dead* (Cranford, NJ: American Atheist Press, 2007).
— 'Jesus: Myth and Method', in *The Christian Delusion: Why Faith Fails* (ed. John Loftus; Amherst, NY: Prometheus Books, 2010), pp. 273-90.
— *The Pre-Nicene New Testament: Fifty-Four Formative Texts* (Salt Lake City, UT: Signature Books, 2006).
Prince, Susan, 'Socrates, Antisthenes, and the Cynics', in *Companion to Socrates* (ed. Ahbel-Rappe and Kamtekar), pp. 75-92.
Quarles, Charles, *Buried Hope or Risen Savior: The Search for the Jesus Tomb* (Nashville, TN: B & H Academic, 2008).
Rahner, Hugo, *Greek Myths and Christian Mystery* (New York: Harper & Row, 1963).
Rapske, Brian, *The Book of Acts and Paul in Roman Custody* (Grand Rapids, MI: William B. Eerdmans, 1994).
Reardon, Bryan (ed.), *Collected Ancient Greek Novels* (Berkeley, CA: University of California Press, 1989).
Reece, Steve, 'Seven Stades to Emmaus', *New Testament Studies* 48 (January 2002), pp. 262-66.
Rees, W.D., 'The Hallucinations of Widowhood', *British Medical Journal* 4 (1971), pp. 37-41.
Reeves, John, *Trajectories in Near Eastern Apocalyptic: A Postrabbinic Jewish Apocalypse Reader* (Atlanta, GA: Society of Biblical Literature, 2005).
Reicke, Bo, 'The Law and This World according to Paul', *Journal of Biblical Literature* 70 (1951), pp. 259-76.
Reinmuth, Eckart, *Pseudo-Philo und Lukas: Studien zum Liber Antiquitatum Biblicarum und seiner Bedeutung für die Interpretation des lukanischen Doppelwerks* (Tübingen: Mohr, 1994).
Remsberg, John E., *The Christ: A Critical Review and Analysis of his Existence* (Amherst, NY: Prometheus Books, 1994 [orig., 1909]).
Reuter, Rainer, 'Introduction to Synoptic Work on the New Testament Epistles', *Journal of Higher Criticism* 9.2 (Fall 2002), pp. 246-58.
Richard, Earl, *First and Second Thessalonians* (Collegeville, MN: Liturgical Press, 1995), pp. 123-27.

Richards, E. Randolph, *Paul and First-Century Letter Writing: Secretaries, Composition, and Collection* (Downers Grove, IL: InterVarsity Press, 2004), pp. 99-121.
Richey, Matthew, 'The Use of Greek at Qumran: Manuscript and Epigraphic Evidence for a Marginalized Language', *Dead Sea Discoveries* 19 (2012), pp. 177-97.
Riley, Gregory, *Resurrection Reconsidered: Thomas and John in Controversy* (Minneapolis, MN: Fortress Press, 1995).
Robbins, Vernon, 'The "We" Passages in Acts and Ancient Sea Voyages', *Papers of the Chicago Society of Biblical Research* 20 (1975), pp. 5-18.
Roberts, C.H., 'The Ancient Book and the Ending of St. Mark', *Journal of Theological Studies* 40 (1939), pp. 253-57.
— 'The Codex', *Proceedings of the British Academy* 40 (1954), pp. 168-204.
Roberts, Diane, *The Myth of Aunt Jemima: Representations of Race and Region* (New York: Routledge, 1994).
Robinson, James, *The Nag Hammadi Library in English* (San Francisco, CA: Harper & Row, 3rd edn, 1988).
Roisman, Joseph (ed.), *Brill's Companion to Alexander the Great* (Leiden: Brill, 2003).
Roller, Lynn, *In Search of God the Mother: The Cult of Anatolian Cybele* (Berkeley, CA: University of California Press, 1999).
Rosenbaum, Stanley, *Understanding Biblical Israel: A Reexamination of the Origins of Monotheism* (Macon, GA: Mercer University Press, 2002).
Rosenmeyer, Patricia, *Ancient Epistolary Fictions: The Letter in Greek Literature* (New York: Cambridge University Press, 2001).
Ross, C.A., S. Joshi and R. Currie, 'Dissociative Experiences in the General Population', *American Journal of Psychiatry* 147 (1990), pp. 1547-52.
Rothschild, Clare, *Baptist Traditions and Q* (Tübingen: Mohr Siebeck, 2005).
— *Luke–Acts and the Rhetoric of History: An Investigation of Early Christian Historiography* (Tübingen: Mohr Siebeck, 2004).
Ruprecht, Louis, *This Tragic Gospel: How John Corrupted the Heart of Christianity* (San Francisco, CA: Jossey-Bass, 2008).
Rutgers, Leonard, 'Roman Policy towards the Jews: Expulsions from the City of Rome during the First Century C.E.', *Classical Antiquity* 13.1 (April 1994), pp. 56-74.
— (ed.), *What Athens Has to Do with Jerusalem: Essays on Classical, Jewish, and Early Christian Art and Archaeology in Honor of Gideon Foerster* (Leuven: Peeters, 2002).
Sacks, Oliver, *Hallucinations* (New York: Alfred A. Knopf, 2012).
Sæbø, Magne (ed.), *Hebrew Bible, Old Testament: The History of its Interpretation. Volume I: From the Beginnings to the Middle Ages (until 1300). Part 1: Antiquity* (Göttingen: Vandenhoeck & Ruprecht, 1996).
Safrai, Zeev, 'The Gentile Cities of Judea: Between the Hasmonean Occupation and the Roman Liberation', in *Studies in Historical Geography and Biblical Historiography* (ed. Zecharia Kallai, Gershon Galil and Moshe Weinfeld; Leiden: E.J. Brill, 2000), pp. 63-90.
Salm, René, 'A Response to "Surveys and Excavations at the Nazareth Village Farm (1997–2002): Final Report"' [with replies by Stephen Pfann, Yehudah Rapuano and Ken Dark], *Bulletin of the Anglo-Israel Archaeological Society* 26 (2008), pp. 95-135.
Salvesen, Alison, 'Messianism in Ancient Bible Translations in Greek and Latin', in *Redemption and Resistance: The Messianic Hopes of Jews and Christians in*

Antiquity (ed. Markus Bockmuehl and James Carleton Paget; New York: T. & T. Clark, 2007), pp. 245-61.

Samuelsson, Gunnar, *Crucifixion in Antiquity: An Inquiry into the Background of the New Testament Terminology of Crucifixion* (Tübingen: Mohr Siebeck, 2011).

Sanders, E.P., *The Historical Figure of Jesus* (London: Penguin Press, 1993).

— *Jesus and Judaism* (Philadelphia, PA: Fortress Press, 1985).

Sanders, J.A., 'Dissenting Deities and Philippians 2.1-11', *Journal of Biblical Literature* 88 (September 1969), pp. 279-90.

Satterthwaite, P.E., 'Acts against the Background of Classical Rhetoric', in *The Book of Acts in its Ancient Literary Setting* (ed. Bruce Winter and Andrew Clarke; Grand Rapids, MI: William B. Eerdmans, 1993), pp. 337-80.

Sausa, Don, *The Jesus Tomb: Is It Fact or Fiction? Scholars Chime In* (Fort Myers, FL: Vision Press, 2007).

Saylor, Dylan, 'Dirty Linen, Fabrication, and the Authorities of Livy and Augustus', *Transactions of the American Philological Association* 136 (Autumn 2006), pp. 329-88.

Schäfer, Peter, *Jesus in the Talmud* (Princeton, NJ: Princeton University Press, 2007), cf. esp. pp. 131-44.

Schaper, Joachim, *Eschatology in the Greek Psalter* (Tübingen: J.C.B. Mohr [Paul Siebeck], 1995).

Scheffler, E.H., 'Emmaus—A Historical Perspective', *Neotestamentica* 23 (1989), pp. 251-67.

Schiffman, Lawrence, and James VanderKam (eds.), *Encyclopedia of the Dead Sea Scrolls* (New York: Oxford University Press, 2000).

Schmeling, Gareth, *The Novel in the Ancient World* (Leiden: Brill, 1996).

Schneemelcher, Wilhelm, and R. McL. Wilson (eds.), *New Testament Apocrypha* (2 vols.; Louisville, KY: Westminster/John Knox Press, 1991).

Schonfield, Hugh, *According to the Hebrews: A New Translation of the Jewish Life of Jesus (the Toldoth Jeshu), with an Inquiry into the Nature of its Sources and Special Relationship to the Lost Gospel according to the Hebrews* (London: Duckworth, 1937).

Schor, Adam, 'Conversion by the Numbers: Benefits and Pitfalls of Quantitative Modeling in the Study of Early Christian Growth', *Journal of Religious History* 33 (December 2009), pp. 472-98.

Schreckenberg, Heinz, 'Flavius Josephus und die lukanischen Schriften', in *Wort in der Zeit: Neutestamentliche Studien* (ed. Karl Rengstorf and Wilfrid Haubeck; Leiden: Brill, 1980), pp. 179-209.

Schröter, Jens, 'Jesus and the Canon: The Early Jesus Traditions in the Context of the Origins of the New Testament Canon', in *Performing the Gospel: Orality, Memory and Mark: Essays Dedicated to Werner Kelber* (ed. R.A. Horsley, J.A. Draper and J.M. Foley; Minneapolis, MN: Fortress Press, 2006), pp. 104-22, 222-28.

Schweitzer, Albert, *The Quest of the Historical Jesus* (trans. John Bowden; London: SCM Press, 2000 [orig. 1913]).

Scott, James, 'Throne-Chariot Mysticism in Qumran and in Paul', in *Eschatology, Messianism, and the Dead Sea Scrolls* (ed. Craig Evans and Peter Flint: Grand Rapids, MI: William B. Eerdmans, 1997), pp. 101-19.

Seaford, Richard, 'Dionysiac Drama and the Dionysiac Mysteries', *Classical Quarterly* 31 (1981), pp. 252-75.

Segal, Alan, 'Conversion and Messianism: Outline for a New Approach', in *The Messiah* (ed. Charlesworth), pp. 296-340.

— 'Heavenly Ascent in Hellenistic Judaism, Early Christianity and their Environment', *Aufstieg und Niedergang der römischen Welt* II.23.2 (New York: W. de Gruyter, 1980), pp. 1333-94.

— *In Quest of the Hero* (Princeton, NJ: Princeton University Press, 1990).

— 'Jesus and First-Century Judaism', in *Jesus at 2000* (ed. Marcus Borg; Boulder, CO: Westview Press, 1997), pp. 55-72.

— 'Religiously-Interpreted States of Consciousness: Prophecy, Self-Consciousness, and Life after Death', in *Life after Death: A History of the Afterlife in the Religions of the West* (New York: Doubleday, 2004), pp. 322-50.

— 'Ruler of This World: Attitudes about Mediator Figures and the Importance of Sociology for Self-Definition', in *Jewish and Christian Self-Definition*, Vol. II, *Aspects of Judaism in the Graeco-Roman Period* (ed. E.P. Sanders; Philadelphia, PA: Fortress Press, 1981), pp. 245-68, 403-13.

— *Two Powers in Heaven: Early Rabbinic Reports about Christianity and Gnosticism* (Leiden: Brill, 1977).

Sellew, Philip, '"Laodiceans" and the Philippians Fragments Hypothesis', *Harvard Theological Review* 87 (January 1994), pp. 17-28.

Semenyna, Scott, and Rodney Schmalz, 'Glossolalia Meets Glosso-Psychology: Why Speaking in Tongues Persists in Charismatic Christian and Pentecostal Gatherings', *Skeptic* 17 (2012), pp. 40-43.

Shanafelt, Robert, 'Magic, Miracle, and Marvels in Anthropology', *Ethnos* 69 (September 2004), pp. 317-40.

Shanks, Hershel, 'Emmaus: Where Christ Appeared', *Biblical Archaeology Review* 38 (March/April 2008), pp. 41-51, 80.

— 'The "Pierced Messiah" Text—An Interpretation Evaporates', *Biblical Archaeology Review* 18 (July/August 1992), pp. 80-82.

Shellard, Barbara, *New Light on Luke: Its Purpose, Sources, and Literary Context* (New York: Sheffield Academic Press, 2002).

Shepherd, T., 'The Narrative Function of Markan Intercalation', *New Testament Studies* 41 (1995), pp. 522-40.

Sherif, Muzafer, and Carl Hovland, *Social Judgment: Assimilation and Contrast Effects in Communication and Attitude Change* (New Haven, CT: Yale University Press, 1961).

Shin, H.W., *Textual Criticism and the Synoptic Problem in Historical Jesus Research: The Search for Valid Criteria* (Dudley, MA: Peeters, 2004).

Shorter, Edward, *From Paralysis to Fatigue: A History of Psychosomatic Illness in the Modern Era* (New York: Maxwell Macmillan International, 1992).

Siddiqi, Muhammad Zubayr, *Hadith Literature: Its Origin, Development and Special Features* (ed. and rev. Abdal Hakim Murad; Cambridge: Islamic Texts Society, 2nd edn, 1993).

Sim, David, *The Gospel of Matthew and Christian Judaism: The History and Social Setting of the Matthean Community* (Edinburgh: T. & T. Clark, 1998).

— 'Reconstructing the Social and Religious Milieu of Matthew: Methods, Sources, and Possible Results', in *Matthew, James, and Didache: Three Related Documents in their Jewish and Christian Settings* (ed. Huub van de Sandt and Jürgen Zangenberg; Atlanta, GA: Society of Biblical Literature, 2008), pp. 13-32.

Simpson, R.T., 'The Major Agreements of Matthew and Luke against Mark', *New Testament Studies* 12 (1965–1966), pp. 283-84.

Skarsaune, Oskar, 'The Question of Old Testament Canon and Text in the Early Greek Church', in *Hebrew Bible, Old Testament: The History of its Interpretation. Volume I: From the Beginnings to the Middle Ages (until 1300). Part 1: Antiquity* (ed. Magne Sæbø; Göttingen: Vandenhoeck & Ruprecht, 1996), pp. 443-50.

Slade, Peter, and Richard Bentall, *Sensory Deception: A Scientific Analysis of Hallucination* (Baltimore, MD: Johns Hopkins University Press, 1988).

Slingerland, Dixon, 'Chrestus: Christus?', in *New Perspectives on Ancient Judaism, Vol. IV: The Literature of Early Rabbinic Judaism* (ed. A.J. Avery-Peck; Lanham, MD: University Press of America, 1989), pp. 133-44.

Smith, Dwight Moody, *The Composition and Order of the Fourth Gospel: Bultmann's Literary Theory, with the Greek Text as Rearranged by R.C. Bultmann* (New Haven, CT: Yale University Press, 1965).

Smith, Mark, *The Origins of Biblical Monotheism: Israel's Polytheistic Background and the Ugaritic Texts* (New York: Oxford University Press, 2001).

— *The Ugaritic Baal Cycle*, Vol. I (Leiden: E.J. Brill, 1994).

Smith, Mark, and W. Pitard, *The Ugaritic Baal Cycle*, Vol. II (Leiden: E.J. Brill, 2009).

Smith, Morton, 'Palestinian Judaism in the First Century', in *Israel: Its Role in Civilization* (ed. Moshe Davis; New York: Seminary Israel Institute of the Jewish Theological Seminary of America, 1956), pp. 67-81.

— *Palestinian Parties and Politics That Shaped the Old Testament* (New York: Columbia University Press, 1971).

Smith, Robert, 'Caesar's Decree (Luke 2.1-2): Puzzle or Key?', *Currents in Theology and Mission* 7 (December 1980), pp. 343-51.

Snodgrass, Klyne R., 'The Gospel of Thomas: A Secondary Gospel', in *The Historical Jesus: Critical Concepts in Religious Studies, Vol. IV: Lives of Jesus and Jesus outside the Bible* (ed. Craig Evans; New York: Routledge, 2004).

Spadafora, F., 'Emmaus: Critica Testuale e Archeologia', *Rivista Biblica Italiana* 1 (October–December 1953), pp. 255-68.

Spanosa, Nicholas, Cheryl Burgessa and Melissa Faith Burgessa, 'Past-Life Identities, UFO Abductions, and Satanic Ritual Abuse: The Social Construction of Memories', *International Journal of Clinical and Experimental Hypnosis* 42 (1994), pp. 433-46.

Sparks, Kenton, 'Gospel as Conquest: Mosaic Typology in Matt 28:16-20', *Catholic Biblical Quarterly* 68 (2006), pp. 651-63.

Spong, John Shelby, *The Sins of Scripture: Exposing the Bible's Texts of Hate to Reveal the God of Love* (San Francisco, CA: HarperSanFrancisco, 2005).

Staikos, Konstantinos, *The History of the Library in Western Civilization*, Vols. I and II (Athens: Kotinos Publications, 2004).

Standing, Edmund, 'Against Mythicism: A Case for the Plausibility of a Historical Jesus', *Think* 9 (Spring 2010), pp. 13-27.

Stem, Rex, 'The Exemplary Lessons of Livy's Romulus', *Transactions of the American Philological Association* 137.2 (Autumn 2007), pp. 435-71.

Stephens, Susan, and John Winkler, *Ancient Greek Novels: The Fragments* (Princeton, NJ: Princeton University Press, 1995).

Sterling, Gregory, *Historiography and Self-Definition: Josephos, Luke–Acts and Apologetic Historiography* (Leiden: Brill, 1992).

— '"Opening the Scriptures": The Legitimation of the Jewish Diaspora and the Early Christian Mission', in *Jesus and the Heritage of Israel: Luke's Narrative Claim upon Israel's Legacy* (ed. D.P. Moessner; Harrisburg, PA: Trinity Press International, 1999), pp. 199-225.

— 'Philo of Alexandria', in *The Historical Jesus in Context* (ed. Levine, Allison and Crossan), pp. 296-308.

Stern, Jacob, 'Heraclitus the Paradoxographer: *Peri Apistōn*, "On Unbelievable Tales"', *Transactions of the American Philological Association* 133 (Spring 2003), pp. 51-97.

Stökl ben Ezra, Daniel, *The Impact of Yom Kippur on Early Christianity: The Day of Atonement from Second Temple Judaism to the Fifth Century* (Tübingen: Mohr Siebeck, 2003).

Stone, J., *et al.*, 'Conversion Disorder: Current Problems and Potential Solutions for DSM-5', *Journal of Psychosomatic Research* 71 (2011), pp. 369-76.

Stone, Michael, 'The Fall of Satan and Adam's Penance: Three Notes on the "Books of Adam and Eve"', *Journal of Theological Studies* 44 (April 1993), pp. 143-56.

Strange, W.A., *The Problem of the Text of Acts* (New York: Cambridge University Press, 1992).

Strauss, Mark, *Four Portraits, One Jesus: An Introduction to Jesus and the Gospels* (Grand Rapids, MI: Zondervan, 2007).

Stroumsa, Guy, *Hidden Wisdom: Esoteric Traditions and the Roots of Christian Mysticism* (Leiden: Brill, 1996).

Struck, Peter, *Birth of the Symbol: Ancient Readers and the Limits of their Texts* (Princeton, NJ: Princeton University Press, 2004).

Stuckenbruck, Loren, *Angel Veneration and Christology* (Tübingen: J.C.B. Mohr, 1995).

Swan, Peter Michael, *The Augustan Succession: An Historical Commentary on Cassius Dio's Roman History Books 55–56 (9 B.C.–A.D. 14)* (Oxford: Oxford University Press, 2004), pp. 36-38, 188.

Swanson, Reuben, *New Testament Greek Manuscripts: Variant Readings Arranged in Horizontal Lines against Codex Vaticanus: 1 Corinthians* (Sheffield: Sheffield Academic Press, 2003).

— *New Testament Greek Manuscripts: Variant Readings Arranged in Horizontal Lines against Codex Vaticanus: Luke* (Sheffield: Sheffield Academic Press, 1995).

— *New Testament Greek Manuscripts: Variant Readings Arranged in Horizontal Lines against Codex Vaticanus: Mark* (Sheffield: Sheffield Academic Press, 1995).

— *New Testament Greek Manuscripts: Variant Readings Arranged in Horizontal Lines against Codex Vaticanus: Matthew* (Sheffield: Sheffield Academic Press, 1995).

Swarup, Ram, *Understanding the Hadith: The Sacred Traditions of Islam* (Amherst, NY: Prometheus Books, 2002).

Tabor, James, '4Q285: A Pierced or Piercing Messiah?—The Verdict Is Still Out', *Biblical Archaeology Review* 18 (November/December 1992), pp. 58-59.

— *The Jesus Dynasty: The Hidden History of Jesus, His Royal Family, and the Birth of Christianity* (London: HarperElement, 2006).

— *Things Unutterable: Paul's Ascent to Paradise in its Greco-Roman, Judaic, and Early Christian Contexts* (Lanham, MD: University Press of America, 1986).

Takacs, Sarolta, *Isis and Sarapis in the Roman World* (Leiden: Brill, 1995).

Talbert, Charles, 'Biographies of Philosophers and Rulers as Instruments of Religious Propaganda in Mediterranean Antiquity', *Aufstieg und Niedergang der römischen Welt II* 16 (1978), pp. 1619-51.

— 'Miraculous Conceptions and Births in Mediterranean Antiquity', in *The Historical Jesus in Context* (ed. Levine, Allison and Crossan), pp. 79-86.

— *What Is a Gospel? The Genre of the Canonical Gospels* (Philadelphia, PA: Fortress Press, 1977).

Tannehill, Robert, *et al., The New Interpreter's Bible: New Testament Survey* (Nashville, TN: Abingdon Press, 2006).

Taubenschlag, Rafael, *The Law of Greco-Roman Egypt in the Light of the Papyri, 332 B.C.–640 A.D.* (Warsaw: Państwowe Wydawnictwo Naukowe, 1955).

Taylor, Charles, *Varieties of Religion Today: William James Revisited* (Cambridge, MA: Harvard University Press, 2002).

Taylor, Joan, *The Immerser: John the Baptist within Second Temple Judaism* (Grand Rapids, MI: William B. Eerdmans, 1997).

— *Jewish Women Philosophers of First-Century Alexandria: Philo's "Therapeutae" Reconsidered* (New York: Oxford University Press, 2003).

Theissen, Gerd, and Annette Merz, *The Historical Jesus: A Comprehensive Guide* (Minneapolis, MN: Fortress Press, 1996).

Theissen, Gerd, and Dagmar Winter, *The Quest for the Plausible Jesus: The Question of Criteria* (Louisville, KY: John Knox Press, 2002).

Thompson, James, 'Hebrews, Epistle to the', in *Eerdmans Dictionary of the Bible* (ed. David Noel Freedman; Grand Rapids, MI: William B. Eerdmans, 2000), pp. 568-70.

Thompson, Marianne Meye, 'The Structure of Matthew: An Examination of Two Approaches', *Studia biblica et theologica* 12 (1982), pp. 195-238.

Thompson, P.J., 'The Infancy Gospels of St. Matthew and St. Luke Compared', *Studia evanglica* 1 (1959), pp. 217-22.

Thompson, Thomas, *Early History of the Israelite People: From the Written and Archaeological Sources* (New York: Brill, 1992).

— *The Historicity of the Patriarchal Narratives: The Quest for the Historical Abraham* (New York: W. de Gruyter, 1974).

— *The Messiah Myth: The Near Eastern Roots of Jesus and David* (New York: Basic Books, 2005).

— *The Mythic Past: Biblical Archaeology and the Myth of Israel* (New York: Basic Books, 1999).

Thorburn, Thomas James, *The Mythical Interpretation of the Gospels: Critical Studies in the Historic Narratives* (New York: Scribner, 1916).

Tolbert, Mary Ann, *Sowing the Gospel: Mark's World in Literary-Historical Perspective* (Philadelphia, PA: Fortress Press, 1989), pp. 48-79.

Too, Yun Lee (ed.), *Education in Greek and Roman Antiquity* (Boston: Brill, 2001).

Trafton, Joseph L., 'The Psalms of Solomon', in *The Historical Jesus in Context* (ed. Levine, Allison and Crossan), pp. 256-65.

Trigg, Joseph, 'Divine Deception and the Truthfulness of Scripture', in *Origen of Alexandria: His World and his Legacy* (ed. Charles Kannengiesser and William Peterson; Notre Dame, IN: University of Notre Dame Press, 1988), pp. 147-64.

Trobisch, David, *The First Edition of the New Testament* (Oxford: Oxford University Press, 2000).

— 'Who Published the Christian Bible?', *CSER Review* 2.1 (2007), pp. 29-30.

Trompf, G.W., *Cargo Cults and Millenarian Movements: Transoceanic Comparisons of New Religious Movements* (New York: Mouton de Gruyter, 1990).

Trudinger, L. Paul, '[*Heteron de tōn apostolōn ouk eidon, ei mē iakōbon*]: A Note on Galatians I 19', *Novum Testamentum* 17 (July 1975), pp. 200-202.

Tuckett, Christopher, 'Forty Other Gospels', in *The Written Gospel* (ed. Markus Bockmuehl and Donald Hagner; Cambridge: Cambridge University Press, 2005), pp. 238-53.

Turner, E.G. (ed.), *Greek Papyri: An Introduction* (New York: Oxford University Press, 2nd edn, 1980).

Turner, N., 'The Minor Verbal Agreements of Mt. and Lk. against Mk', *Studia evangelica* 1 (1959), pp. 223-34.

Twelftree, Graham, 'Jesus in Jewish Traditions', in *Gospel Perspectives: Studies of History and Tradition in the Four Gospels*, Vol. V: *The Jesus Tradition outside the Gospels* (ed. David Wenham; Sheffield: JSOT Press, 1984), pp. 289-341.

Tyson, Joseph, *Marcion and Luke–Acts: A Defining Struggle* (Columbia, SC: University of South Carolina Press, 2006).

— 'Why Dates Matter: The Case of the Acts of the Apostles', in *Finding the Historical Jesus: Rules of Evidence* (ed. Bernard Brandon Scott; Santa Rosa, CA: Polebridge, 2008), pp. 59-70.

Tzoref, Shani, 'Qumran Pesharim and the Pentateuch: Explicit Citation, Overt Typologies, and Implicit Interpretive Traditions', *Dead Sea Discoveries* 16 (2009), pp. 190-220.

Ulansey, David, 'The Heavenly Veil Torn: Mark's Cosmic "Inclusio"', *Journal of Biblical Literature* 110 (Spring 1991), pp. 123-25.

— *The Origins of the Mithraic Mysteries* (New York: Oxford University Press, 1989).

Vaage, L.E., 'Jewish Scripture, Q and the Historical Jesus: A Cynic Way with the Word?', in *The Sayings Source Q and the Historical Jesus* (ed. A. Lindemann; Leuven: University Press, 2001), pp. 479-95.

VanderKam, James, *From Joshua to Caiaphas: High Priests after the Exile* (Minneapolis, MN: Fortress Press, 2004).

— 'Righteous One, Messiah, Chosen One, and Son of Man in 1 Enoch 37–71', in *The Messiah: Developments in Earliest Judaism and Christianity* (ed. James Charlesworth; Minneapolis, MN: Fortress Press, 1992), pp. 169-91.

VanderSpek, Bert, 'The Astronomical Diaries as a Source for Achaemenid and Seleucid History', *Bibliotheca orientalis* 50 (1993), pp. 91-101.

— 'Darius III, Alexander the Great and Babylonian scholarship', *Achaemenid History*, Vol. XIII (Leiden: Nederlands Instituut voor het Nabije Oosten, 2003), pp. 289-346.

Van Oyen, G., 'Intercalation and Irony in the Gospel of Mark', in *The Four Gospels 1992: Festschrift Frans Neirynck*, Vol. II (ed. Frans van Segbroeck; Leuven: Leuven University Press, 1992), pp. 943-74.

Van Voorst, Robert, *Jesus outside the New Testament* (Grand Rapids, MI: William B. Eerdmans, 2000).

Verenna, Thomas, 'Born under the Law: Intertextuality and the Question of the Historicity of the Figure of Jesus in Paul's Epistles', in *'Is This Not the Carpenter?' The Question of the Historicity of the Figure of Jesus* (ed. Thomas Thompson and Thomas Verenna; Sheffield: Equinox, 2012), pp. 131-59.

— *Of Men and Muses: Essays on History, Literature, and Religion* (Raleigh, NC: Lulu, 2009).
Vermès, Géza, *The Complete Dead Sea Scrolls in English* (New York: Penguin Press, 7th edn, 2011).
— *Jesus in his Jewish Context* (Minneapolis, MN: Fortress Press, 2003).
— *Jesus the Jew* (London: Collins, 1973).
— *The Religion of Jesus the Jew* (Minneapolis, MN: Fortress Press, 1993).
Vernant, Jean-Pierre, 'Mortals and Immortals: The Body of the Divine', *Mortals and Immortals: Collected Essays* (Princeton, NJ: Princeton University Press, 1991), pp. 27-49.
Versnel, Hendrik Simon, 'Self-Sacrifice, Compensation and the Anonymous Gods', in *Le sacrifice dans l'antiquité* (ed. Jean Pierre Vernant, *et al.*: Geneva: Fondation Hardt, 1980), pp. 135-194.
— *Ter unus: Isis, Dionysos, Hermes: Three Studies in Henotheism* (Leiden: Brill, 1990).
— 'Two Types of Roman *devotio*', *Mnemosyne* 29 (1976), pp. 365-410.
Vines, Michael E., *The Problem of Markan Genre: The Gospel of Mark and the Jewish Novel* (Leiden: Brill, 2002).
Waetjen, Herman, *The Gospel of the Beloved Disciple: A Work in Two Editions* (New York: T. & T. Clark, 2005).
Wainwright, A.W., 'The Confession "Jesus is God" in the New Testament', *Scottish Journal of Theology* 10 (1957), pp. 278-82.
Walck, Leslie, *The Son of Man in the Parables of Enoch and in Matthew* (London: T. & T. Clark, 2011).
Walker, William, 'The Burden of Proof in Identifying Interpolations in Pauline Letters', *New Testament Studies* 33 (1987), pp. 610-18.
— *Interpolations in the Pauline Letters* (London: Sheffield Academic Press, 2001).
— 'Text-Critical Evidence for Interpolation in the Letters of Paul', *Catholic Biblical Quarterly* 50 (1988), pp. 622-31.
Wallbank, F.W., 'Speeches in Greek Historians', in *Selected Papers: Studies in Greek and Roman History and Historiography* (New York: Cambridge University Press, 1985), pp. 242-61.
Walter, Nikolaus, 'Paul and the Early Christian Jesus-Tradition', in *Paul and Jesus: Collected Essays* (ed. A.J.M. Wedderburn; Sheffield: Sheffield Academic Press, 1989), pp. 51-80.
Wanke, Joachim, *Die Emmauserzählung: Eine redaktionsgeschichtliche Untersuchung zu Lk 24, 13-35* (Leipzig: St.-Benno-Verlag, 1973).
Watson, David, 'The Life of Aesop and the Gospel of Mark: Two Ancient Approaches to Elite Values', *Journal of Biblical Literature* 129 (2010), pp. 699-716.
Watters, Ethan, *Crazy like Us: The Globalization of the American Psyche* (New York: Free Press, 2010).
Weeden, Theodore, 'Kenneth Bailey's Theory of Oral Tradition: A Theory Contested by its Evidence', *Journal for the Study of the Historical Jesus* 7 (January 2009), pp. 3-43.
— 'Two Jesuses, Jesus of Jerusalem and Jesus of Nazareth: Provocative Parallels and Imaginative Imitation', *Forum* N.S. 6.2 (Fall 2003), pp. 137-341.
Wells, G.A., and Morton Smith, 'The Historical Jesus' [an exchange], in *Jesus in History and Myth* (ed. R. Joseph Hoffmann and Gerald Larue; Buffalo, NY: Prometheus Books, 1986), pp. 25-54.

Wenham, David (ed.), *Gospel Perspectives: Studies of History and Tradition in the Four Gospels*, Vol. V: *The Jesus Tradition outside the Gospels* (Sheffield: JSOT Press, 1984).
West, M.L., *The Orphic Poems* (New York: Oxford University Press, 1983).
Whealey, Alice, 'Josephus, Eusebius of Caesarea, and the Testimonium Flavianum', in *Josephus und das Neue Testament: wechselseitige Wahrnehmungen* (ed. Christfried Böttrich and Jens Herzer; Tübingen: Mohr Siebeck, 2007), pp. 73-116.
— *Josephus on Jesus: The Testimonium Flavianum Controversy from Late Antiquity to Modern Times* (New York: P. Lang, 2003).
— 'The Testimonium Flavianum in Syriac and Arabic', *New Testament Studies* 54 (2008), pp. 573-90.
Wheaton, Billy, and Joy Fuller, *Hooks and Ladders: A Journey on a Bridge to Nowhere with American Evangelical Christians* (Bloomington, IN: iUniverse, 2009).
White, L. Michael, *From Jesus to Christianity* (San Francisco, CA: HarperSan Francisco, 2004).
Whitmarsh, Tim (ed.), *The Cambridge Companion to the Greek and Roman Novel* (Cambridge: Cambridge University Press, 2008).
— *Greek Literature and the Roman Empire: The Politics of Imitation* (New York: Oxford University Press, 2001).
Wieand, David, 'John V.2 and the Pool of Bethesda', *New Testament Studies* 12 (1965–1966), pp. 392-404.
Wiebe, Phillip, *Visions of Jesus: Direct Encounters from the New Testament to Today* (New York: Oxford University Press, 1997).
Wiechers, Anton, *Aesop in Delphi* (Meisenheim: A. Hain, 1961).
Wiens, Devon, 'Mystery Concepts in Primitive Christianity and in its Environment', *Aufstieg und Niedergang der römischen Welt* II.23.2 (New York: W. de Guyter, 1980), pp. 1248-84.
Wild, Robert, *Water in the Cultic Worship of Isis and Sarapis* (Leiden: Brill, 1981).
Will, Édouard, 'Review of Helga Botermann's *Das Judenedikt des Kaisers Claudius: Römischer Staat und Christiani im 1. Jahrhundert*', *Gnomon* 71 (1999), pp. 610-16.
Williams, C.S.C., *Alterations to the Text of the Synoptic Gospels and Acts* (Oxford: Basil Blackwell, 1951).
Williams, F.E., 'The Vailala Madness in Retrospect', in *Essays Presented to C.G. Seligman* (ed. E.E. Evans-Pritchard, *et al.*; London: Kegan Paul, Trench, Trubner, 1934), pp. 369-79.
Williams, Jarvis, *Maccabean Martyr Traditions in Paul's Theology of Atonement: Did Martyr Theology Shape Paul's Conception of Jesus's Death?* (Eugene, OR: Wipf & Stock, 2010).
Williams, Margaret, *The Jews among the Greeks and Romans: A Diasporan Sourcebook* (Baltimore, MD: Johns Hopkins University Press, 1998).
Williamson, H.G.M., and C.A. Evans, 'Samaritans', in *Dictionary of New Testament Background* (ed. Craig Evans and Stanley Porter; Downers Grove, IL: InterVarsity Press, 2000), pp. 1056-61.
Wills, Lawrence, 'The Aesop Tradition', in *The Historical Jesus in Context* (ed. Levine, Allison and Crossan), pp. 222-37.
— (ed.), *Ancient Jewish Novels: An Anthology* (New York: Oxford University Press, 2002).

— *The Quest of the Historical Gospel: Mark, John, and the Origins of the Gospel Genre* (New York: Routledge, 1997).

Wilson, Emily, *The Death of Socrates* (Cambridge, MA: Harvard University, 2007).

Wink, Walter, *Naming the Powers: The Language of Power in the New Testament* (Philadelphia, PA: Fortress Press, 1984).

Winn, Adam, *Mark and the Elijah–Elisha Narrative: Considering the Practice of Greco-Roman Imitation in the Search for Markan Source Material* (Eugene, OR: Pickwick Publications, 2010).

Wisc, Michael, *The First Messiah: Investigating the Savior before Christ* (New York: HarperSanFrancisco, 1999).

Wiseman, Timothy, *The Myths of Rome* (Exeter: University of Exeter Press, 2004).

Witherington, Ben, *The Gospel of Mark: A Socio-Rhetorical Commentary* (Grand Rapids, MI: William B. Eerdmans, 2001).

Wittkower, E.D., 'Spirit Possession in Haitian Vodun Ceremonies', *Acta psychotherapeutica et psychosomatica* 12 (1964), pp. 72-80.

Wood, Michael, *In Search of Myths and Heroes: Exploring Four Epic Legends of the World* (Berkeley, CA: University of California Press, 2005).

Worsley, Peter, *The Trumpet Shall Sound: A Study of "Cargo" Cults in Melanesia* (London: MacGibbon & Kee, 2nd edn, 1968).

Wratislaw, A.H., 'The Scapegoat—Barabbas', *Expository Times* 3 (1891/1892), pp. 400-403.

Wright, Archie, *The Origin of Evil Spirits: The Reception of Genesis 6:1-4 in Early Jewish Literature* (Tübingen: Mohr Siebeck, 2nd edn, 2013).

Wright, N.T., *The Resurrection of the Son of God* (Minneapolis, MN: Fortress Press, 2003).

Yoder, Keith, *From Luke to John: Lazarus, Mary and Martha in the Fourth Gospel* (Senior Thesis, University of Massachusetts [Amherst], 2011) at http://www.umass.edu/wsp/project/senior/FromLukeToJohn.pdf.

Zetterholm, Magnus (ed.), *The Messiah in Early Judaism and Christianity* (Minneapolis: Fortress Press, 2007).

Zimbardo, Philip, and Robert Vallone (eds.), *Persuasion, Coercion, Indoctrination and Mind Control* (Lexington, MA: Glenn Custom, 1983).

Zindler, Frank, *The Jesus the Jews Never Knew: Sepher Toldoth Yeshu and the Quest of the Historical Jesus in Jewish Sources* (Cranford, NJ : American Atheist Press, 2003).

— 'Prolegomenon to a Science of Christian Origins', in *Sources of the Jesus Tradition: Separating History from Myth* (ed. R. Joseph Hoffmann; Amherst, NY: Prometheus, 2010), pp. 140-56.

Zusne, Leonard, and Warren Jones, *Anomalistic Psychology: A Study of Extraordinary Phenomena of Behavior and Experience* (Hillsdale, NJ: Erlbaum Associates, 1982).

Scripture Index

Author Index

Subject Index

Numbers in bold indicate the most important discussion of a concept, such as where it is defined and explained.

CPSIA information can be obtained
at www.ICGtesting.com
Printed in the USA
LVHW080723070523
746321LV00004B/49